D1475520

CAMBRIDGE STUDIES
IN MEDIEVAL LIFE AND THOUGHT

Edited by G. G. COULTON, M.A.
Fellow of St John's College, Cambridge
and University Lecturer in English

*   ' . .

MEDIEVAL ENGLISH NUNNERIES

CAMBRIDGE UNIVERSITY PRESS
C. F. CLAY, Manager
LONDON : FETTER LANE, E.C. 4

NEW YORK : THE MACMILLAN CO.
BOMBAY
CALCUTTA } MACMILLAN AND CO., Ltd.
MADRAS
TORONTO : THE MACMILLAN CO.
OF CANADA, Ltd.
TOKYO : MARUZEN-KABUSHIKI-KAISHA

PLATE I

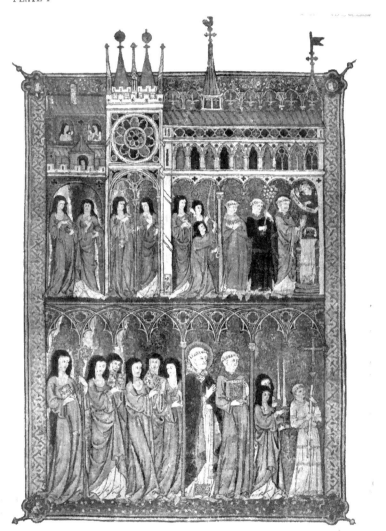

PAGE FROM *LA SAINTE ABBAYE*

(At the top of the picture a priest with two acolytes prepares the sacrament; behind them stand the abbess, holding her staff, her chaplain and the sacristan, who rings the bell; behind them a group of four nuns, including the cellaress with her keys. At the bottom is a procession of priest, acolytes and nuns in the quire.)

MEDIEVAL
ENGLISH NUNNERIES

c. 1275 to 1535

BY

EILEEN POWER

SOMETIME FELLOW AND LECTURER OF GIRTON COLLEGE
CAMBRIDGE

MADAME EGLENTYNE
(From the Ellesmere MS.)

CAMBRIDGE
AT THE UNIVERSITY PRESS
1922

TO

M. G. J.

PRINTED IN GREAT BRITAIN

GENERAL PREFACE

THERE is only too much truth in the frequent complaint
that history, as compared with the physical sciences, is
neglected by the modern public. But historians have the
remedy in their own hands; choosing problems of equal
importance to those of the scientist, and treating them with
equal accuracy, they will command equal attention. Those
who insist that the proportion of accurately ascertainable
facts is smaller in history, and therefore the room for speculation wider, do not thereby establish any essential distinction between truth-seeking in history and truth-seeking
in chemistry. The historian, whatever be his subject, is as
definitely bound as the chemist "to proclaim certainties as
certain, falsehoods as false, and uncertainties as dubious."
Those are the words, not of a modern scientist, but of the
seventeenth century monk, Jean Mabillon, they sum up his
literary profession of faith. Men will follow us in history as
implicitly as they follow the chemist, if only we will form
the chemist's habit of marking clearly where our facts end
and our inferences begin. Then the public, so far from dis-
couraging our speculations, will most heartily encourage
them; for the most positive man of science is always grateful
to anyone who, by putting forward a working theory, stimu-
lates further discussion.

The present series, therefore, appeals directly to that
craving for clearer facts which has been bred in these times
of storm and stress. No care can save us altogether from
error; but, for our own sake and the public's, we have elected
to adopt a safeguard dictated by ordinary business common-
sense. Whatever errors of fact are pointed out by reviewers
or correspondents shall be publicly corrected with the least
possible delay. After a year of publication, all copies shall
be provided with such an erratum-slip without waiting for

the chance of a second edition; and each fresh volume in this series shall contain a full list of the errata noted in its immediate predecessor. After the lapse of a year from the first publication of any volume, and at any time during the ensuing twelve months, any possessor of that volume who will send a stamped and addressed envelope to the Cambridge University Press, Fetter Lane, Fleet Street, London, E.C. 4, shall receive, in due course, a free copy of the *errata* in that volume. Thus, with the help of our critics, we may reasonably hope to put forward these monographs as roughly representing the most accurate information obtainable under present conditions. Our facts being thus secured, the reader will judge our inferences on their own merits; and something will have been done to dissipate that cloud of suspicion which hangs over too many important chapters in the social and religious history of the Middle Ages.

G. G. C.

October, 1922.

AUTHOR'S PREFACE

THE monastic ideal and the development of the monastic rule and orders have been studied in many admirable books. The purpose of the present work is not to describe and analyse once again that ideal, but to give a general picture of English nunnery life during a definite period, the three centuries before the Dissolution. It is derived entirely from pre-Reformation sources, and the tainted evidence of Henry VIII's commissioners has not been used; nor has the story of the suppression of the English nunneries been told. The nunneries dealt with are drawn from all the monastic orders, except the Gilbertine order, which has been omitted, both because it differed from others in containing double houses of men and women and because it has already been the subject of an excellent monograph by Miss Rose Graham.

It remains for me to record my deep gratitude to two scholars, in whose debt students of medieval monastic history must always lie, Mr G. G. Coulton and Mr A. Hamilton Thompson I owe more than I can say to their unfailing interest and readiness to discuss, to help and to criticise. To Mr Hamilton Thompson I am specially indebted for the loan of his transcripts and translations of Alnwick's Register, now in course of publication, for reading and criticising my manuscript and finally for undertaking the arduous work of reading my proofs. I gratefully acknowledge suggestions received at different times from Mr Hubert Hall, Miss Rose Graham and Canon Foster, and faithful criticism from my friend Miss M. G. Jones. I have also to thank Mr H. S. Bennett for kindly preparing the index, and Mr Sydney Cockerell, Director of the Fitzwilliam Museum, for assistance in the choice of illustrations.

EILEEN POWER.

GIRTON COLLEGE,
    CAMBRIDGE.
  September 1922

CONTENTS

CHAPTER IV. MONASTIC HOUSEWIVES

CHAPTER V. FINANCIAL DIFFICULTIES

CHAPTER VI. EDUCATION

o

CHAPTER VII. ROUTINE AND REACTION

CONTENTS

LIST OF PLATES

MAP

MEDIEVAL ENGLISH NUNNERIES

CHAPTER I

THE NOVICE

Then, fair virgin, hear my spell,
For I must your duty tell.
First a-mornings take your book,
The glass wherein yourself must look;
Your young thoughts so proud and jolly
Must be turn'd to motions holy;
For your busk, attires and toys,
Have your thoughts on heavenly joys:
And for all your follies past,
You must do penance, pray and fast.
You shall ring your sacring bell,
Keep your hours and tell your knell,
Rise at midnight to your matins,
Read your psalter, sing your Latins,
And when your blood shall kindle pleasure,
Scourge yourself in plenteous measure
You must read the morning mass,
You must creep unto the cross,
Put cold ashes on your head,
Have a hair cloth for your bed,
Bind your beads, and tell your needs,
Your holy Aves and your Creeds,
Holy maid, this must be done,
If you mean to live a nun

The Merry Devil of Edmonton.

THERE were in England during the later middle ages (c 1270–
1536) some 138 nunneries, excluding double houses of the Gilbertine order, which contained brothers as well as nuns. Of these
over one half belonged to the Benedictine order and about a
quarter (localised almost entirely in Lincolnshire and Yorkshire)
to the Cistercian order. The rest were distributed as follows: 17 to
the order of St Augustine and one (Minchin Buckland), which
belonged to the order of St John of Jerusalem and followed the
Austin rule, four to the Franciscan order, two to the Cluniac order,
two to the Premonstratensian order and one to the Dominican

order. There was also founded in the fifteenth century a very famous double house of the Brigittine order, Syon Abbey. Twenty-one of these houses had the status of abbeys; the rest were priories They were distributed all over the country, Surrey, Lancashire, Westmorland and Cornwall being the only counties without one, but they were more thickly spread over the eastern than over the western half of the island. They were most numerous in the North, East and East Midlands, to wit, in the dioceses of York, Lincoln (which was then very large and included Lincolnshire, Northamptonshire, Rutland, Bedfordshire, Huntingdonshire, Leicestershire, Buckinghamshire, Oxfordshire and part of Hertfordshire) and Norwich; there were 27 houses in the diocese of York, 31 in the diocese of Lincoln, ten in the diocese of Norwich and in London and its suburbs there were seven. On the other hand if nunneries were most plentiful in the North and East Midlands it was there that they were smallest and poorest. The wealthiest and most famous nunneries in England were all south of the Thames. Apart from the new foundation at Syon, which very soon became the largest and richest of all, the greatest houses were the old established abbeys of Wessex, Shaftesbury, Wilton, St Mary's Winchester, Romsey and Wherwell, which, together with Barking in Essex were all of Anglo-Saxon foundation; and Dartford in Kent, founded by Edward III. The only houses north of the Thames which approached these in importance were Godstow and Elstow Abbeys, in Oxfordshire and Bedfordshire respectively; the majority were small priories with small incomes

An analysis of the incomes and numerical size of English nunneries at the dissolution gives interesting and somewhat startling results Out of 106 houses for which information is available only seven had in 1535 a gross annual income of over £450 a year. The richest were Syon and Shaftesbury with £1943 and £1324 respectively; then came Barking with £862, Wilton with £674, Amesbury with £595, Romsey with £528 and Dartford with £488. Five others (St Helen's Bishopsgate, Haliwell and the Minories all in London, Elstow and Godstow) had from £300 to £400, nine others (Nuneaton, Clerkenwell, Malling, St Mary's Winchester, Tarrant Keynes, Canonsleigh, Campsey, Minchin Buckland and Lacock) had from £200 to £300. Twelve had between

£100 and £200 and no less than 73 houses had under £100, of which 39 actually had under £50; and it must be remembered that the net annual income, after the deduction of certain annual charges, was less still[1]. An analysis of the numerical size of nunneries presents more difficulties, for the number of nuns given sometimes differs in the reports referring to the same house and it is doubtful whether commissioners or receivers always set down the total number of nuns present at the visitation or dissolution of a house, while lists of pensions paid by the crown to ex-inmates after dissolution are still more incomplete as evidence. A rough analysis, however, leaves very much the same impression as an analysis of incomes[2] Out of 111 houses, for which some sort of numerical estimate is possible, only four have over thirty inmates, viz. Syon (51), Amesbury (33), Wilton (32) and Barking (30) Eight (Elstow, the Minories, Nuneaton, Denny, Romsey, Wherwell, Dartford and St Mary's Winchester) have from 20 to 30; thirty-six have from 10 to 20 and sixty-three have under 10. These statistics permit of certain large generalisations First, that the majority of English nunneries were small and poor Secondly, that, as has already been pointed out, the largest and richest houses were all in London and south of the Thames, only four houses north of that river had gross incomes of over £200 and only three could boast of more than 20 inmates. Thirdly, the nunneries during this period owned land and rents to the annual value of over £15,500 and contained perhaps between 1500 and 2000 nuns.

To understand the history of the English nunneries during the later middle ages it is necessary not only to understand the smallness and poverty of many of the houses and the high repute of others; it is necessary also to understand what manner of women took the veil in them. From what social classes were the nuns drawn, and for what reason did they enter religion? What

---

[1] Based on Professor Savine's analysis of the returns in the *Valor Ecclesiasticus* (Oxford Studies in Social and Legal History), I, 269–288.

[2] I have based this estimate partly on a list compiled by M. E. C. Walcott, *English Minsters*, vol II ("The English Student's Monasticon"), partly on one compiled by Miss H T. Jacka in an unpublished thesis on *The Dissolution of the English Nunneries*, the figures, if not always exactly correct, are approximately correct as far as the classification into groups, according to size, is concerned It must be remembered, however, that there were more nuns at the beginning than at the end of the period 1270–1536, the convents tended to diminish in size, especially those which were poor and small to begin with.

function did monasticism, so far as it concerned women, fulfil
in the life of medieval society?

It has been shown that the proportion of women who became
nuns was very small in comparison with the total female population. It has indeed been insufficiently recognised that the medieval nunneries were recruited almost entirely from among the
upper classes. They were essentially aristocratic institutions, the
refuge of the gently born. At Romsey Abbey a list of 91 sisters
at the election of an abbess in 1333 is full of well-known county
names[1]. The names of Bassett, Sackville, Covert, Hussey, Tawke
and Farnfold occur at Easebourne[2]; Lewknor, St John, Okehurst,
Michelgrove and Sidney at Rusper[3], the two small and poor
nunneries in Sussex The return of the subsidy in 1377 enumerates
the sisters of Minchin Barrow and, as their historian points out,
"among the family names of these ladies are some of the best
that the western counties could produce"[4]. The other Somerset
houses were equally aristocratic, and an examination of the roll
of prioresses for almost any medieval convent in any part of
England will give the same result, even in the smallest and
poorest nunneries, the inmates of which were reduced to begging
alms[5]. These ladies appear sometimes to have had the spirit of
their race, as they often had its manners and its tastes. For
21 years Isabel Stanley, Prioress of King's Mead, Derby, refused to
pay a rent due from her house to the Abbot of Burton, at last the
Abbot sent his bailiff to distrain for it and she spoke her mind in
good set terms. "Wenes these churles to overlede me," cried this
worthy daughter of a knightly family, "or sue the lawe agayne
me? They shall not be so hardy but they shall avye upon their
bodies and be nailed with arrows; for I am a gentlewoman,
comen of the greatest of Lancashire and Cheshire, and that they
shall know right well"[6]. A tacit recognition of the aristocratic

---

[1] These are discussed in Liveing, *Records of Romsey Abbey*, pp 112 *sqq*.

[2] *V.C H. Sussex*, II, p. 84.   [3] *Ib* II, p 63

[4] Hugo, *Medieval Nunneries of the County of Somerset, Minchin Barrow*,
p. 108.

[5] Well-known names occur, for instance, among the prioresses of the
poor convents of Ivinghoe, Ankerwyke and Little Marlow in Bucks. *V.C H
Bucks*, I, p 355

[6] Lysons, *Magna Britannia*, v, p 113. Compare the remark of a nun
of Wenningsen, near Hanover, who considered herself insulted when the
great reformer Busch addressed her not as "Klosterfrau" but as "Sister"
"You are not my brother, wherefore then call me sister? My brother is

character of the convents is to be found in the fact that bishops were often at pains to mention the good birth of the girls whom, in accordance with a general right, they nominated to certain houses on certain occasions. Thus Wykeham wrote to the Abbess of St Mary's Winchester, bidding her admit Joan Bleden, "quest de bone et honeste condition, come nous sumes enformes"[1]. More frequently still the candidates were described as "domicella" or "damoysele"[2] At least one instance is extant of a bishop ordering that all the nuns of a house were to be of noble condition[3].

The fact that the greater portion of the female population was unaffected by the existence of the outlet provided by conventual life for women's energies is a significant one. The reason for it—paradoxical as this may sound—lies in the very narrowness of the sphere to which women of gentle birth were confined. The disadvantage of rank is that so many honest occupations are not, in its eyes, honourable occupations. In the lowest ranks of society the poor labourer upon the land had no need to get rid of his daughter, if he could not find her a husband, nor would it have been to his interest to do so; for, working in the fields among his sons, or spinning and brewing with his wife at home, she could earn a supplementary if not a living wage. The tradesman or artisan in the town was in a similar position He recognised that the ideal course was to find a husband for his growing girl, but the alternative was in no sense that she should eat out her heart and his income during long years at home, and if he were too poor to provide her with a sufficient dower, he could and often did apprentice her to a trade. The number of industries which were carried on by women in the middle ages shows that for the burgess and lower classes there were other outlets besides marriage; and then, as now, domestic service provided for many. But the case of the well-born lady was different. The knight or the county gentleman could not apprentice his superfluous

clad in steel and you in a linen frock" (1455)   Quoted in Coulton, *Medieval Garner*, p 653

[1] *Wykeham's Register* (Hants Rec Soc), II, p 462   Cf *ib* II, p 61

[2] E g *Reg... of Rigaud de Asserio* (Hants Rec Soc), p 394; *Reg ... Stephani Gravesend* (Cant and York. Soc), p 200, *Wykeham's Register, loc cit.*

[3] Bishop Cobham of Worcester at Wroxall in 1323 (*V C H Warwick*, II, p 71). Cf the case of Usk in Monmouthshire, "in quo monasterio solum virgines de nobili prosapia procreate recipi consueverunt et solent" (*Chron. of Adam of Usk*, ed. E. M. Thompson, p 93).

daughters to a pursemaker or a weaver in the town; not from them were drawn the regrateresses in the market place and the harvest gatherers in the field, nor was it theirs to make the parti-coloured bed and shake the coverlet, worked with grapes and unicorns, in some rich vintner's house. There remained for him, if he did not wish or could not afford to keep them at home and for them, if they desired some scope for their young energies, only marriage or else a convent, where they might go with a smaller dower than a husband of their own rank would demand.

To say that the convents were the refuge of the gently born is not to say that there was no admixture of classes within them The term gentleman was becoming more comprehensive in the later middle ages. It included the upper class proper, the families of noble birth; and it included also the country gentry. The convents were probably at first recruited almost entirely from these two ranks of society, and a study of any collection of medieval wills shows how large a proportion of such families took advantage of this opening for women. A phrase will sometimes occur which shows that it was regarded as the natural and obvious alternative to marriage Sir John Daubriggecourt in 1415 left his daughter Margery 40 marks, "if she be wedded to a worldly husband, and if she be caused to receive the sacred veil of the order of holy nuns" ten pounds and twenty shillings rent[1], and Sir John le Blund in 1312 bequeathed an annuity to his daughter Ann, "till she marry or enter a religious house"[2]. The anxiety of the upper classes to secure a place for their children in nunneries sometimes even led to overcrowding. At Carrow the Prioress was forced to complain that "certain lords of England whom she was unable to resist because of their power" forced their daughters upon the priory as nuns, and in 1273 a papal bull forbade the reception of more inmates than the revenues would support[3]. Archbishop William Wickwane addressed a similar mandate to two Yorkshire houses, Wilberfoss and Nunkeeling, which public rumour had informed him to be overburdened with nuns and with secular boarders "at the instance of nobles"[4]; and in 1327 Bishop

[1] Gibbons, *Early Lincoln Wills*, p 117
[2] Sharpe, *Cal. of Wills enrolled in the Court of Husting*, I, p 236. Cf. ib I, p. 350 and *Testamenta Eboracensia* (Surtees Soc), I, pp 170, 354
[3] Dugdale, *Mon* IV, p 71
[4] *Reg of Archbishop William Wickwane* (Surtees Soc), p. 113.

Stratford wrote to Romsey Abbey that the house was notoriously burdened with ladies beyond the established number, and that he had heard that the nuns were being forced to receive more "damoyseles" as novices, which he forbade without special licence[1] A very strong personal connection must in time have been established between a nunnery and certain families from which, in each generation, it received a daughter or a niece and her dower. Such was the connection between Shouldham and the Beauchamps[2] and between Nunmonkton and the Fairfaxes[3]. A close link bound each nunnery to the family of its patron Thus we find a Clinton at Wroxall and a Darcy at Heynings; nor is it unlikely that these noble ladies sometimes expected privileges and homage more than the strict equality of convent life would allow, if it be permissible to generalise from the behaviour of Isabel Clinton[4] and from the fact that Margaret Darcy received a rather severe penance from Bishop Gynewell in 1351 and a special warning against going beyond the claustral precincts or speaking to strangers[5], while in 1393 there occurs the significant injunction by Bishop Bokyngham that no sister was to have a room to herself except Dame Margaret Darcy (doubtless the same woman now grown elderly and ailing) "on account of the nobility of her race"; an old lady of firm will and (despite his careful mention of extra pittances and of tolerating for a while) a somewhat sycophantic prelate[6].

[1] Liveing, *Records of Romsey Abbey*, p 98.

[2] William de Beauchamp, Earl of Warwick, mentions two daughters, nuns at Shouldham, in his will (1296) Sir Guy de Beauchamp mentions his little daughter Katherine, a nun there (1359) and his father Thomas de Beauchamp, Earl of Warwick, mentions the same Katherine and his own daughter Margaret, nuns there (1369). Katherine was still alive in 1400, when she is mentioned in the next Earl's will. *Testamenta Vetusta*, i, pp 52, 63, 79, 153

[3] See below, p 15.

[4] See below, pp 39–40

[5] "Et pur certayn cause nous auens enioynt a dame Margaret Darcy, vostre soer, qel ne passe les lieus de cloistre, cest assauoir de quoer, de cloistre, de ffraitour, dormitorie ou fermerie, tantque nous en aueroms autre ordeigne, et qele ne parle od nul estraunge gentz, et soit darreyn enstalle, et en chescun lieu qele ne porte anele, et qele die chescun iour un sautier et iune la quarte et la sexte ferie a payn et eu Ensement voilloms qe la dit dame Margaret se puisse confesser au confessour de vostre couent quant ele auera mester" *Linc Epis Reg. Memo Gynewell*, f 34*d*. It looks like the penance for immorality.

[6] "Item quod nulla monialis ibidem cameram teneat priuatam, sed quod omnes moniales sane in dormitorio et infirme in infirmaria iaceant

It is worthy of notice that Chaucer has drawn an unmistakable "lady" in his typical prioress. There is her delicate behaviour at meals.

> At mete wel ytaught was she with-alle;
> She leet no morsel from her lippes falle,
> Ne wette hir fingres in hir sauce depe
> Wel coude she carie a morsel, and wel kepe,
> That no drope ne fille upon hir brest.
> In curteisye was set ful muche hir lest.
> Hir over lippe wyped she so clene,
> That in hir coppe was no ferthing sene
> Of grece, whan she dronken hadde hir draughte
> Ful semely after hir mete she raughte[1].

This was the *ne plus ultra* of feudal table manners, Chaucer might have been writing one of those books of deportment for the guidance of aristocratic young women, which were so numerous in France So the *Clef d'Amors* counsels ladies who would win them lovers[2], and even so Robert de Blois depicts the perfect diner. Robert de Blois' ideal, the chivalrous, frivolous, sensuous ideal of "courtesy," which underlay the whole aristocratic conception of life and the attainment of which was the criterion of polite society, is the ideal of the Prioress also·

> "Gardez vous, Dames, bien acertes,"
> "Qu'au mengier soiez bien apertes,
> C'est une chose c'on moult prise
> Que là soit dame bien aprise
> Tel chose torne à vilonie
> Que toutes genz ne sevent mie,
> Se puet cil tost avoir mespris
> Qui n'est cortoisement apris[3]."

Later he warns against the greedy selection of the finest and largest titbit for oneself, on the ground that "n'est pas *cortoisie*."

atque cubant, preter dominam Margaretam Darcy, monialem prioratus antedicti, cui ob nobilitatem sui generis de camera sua quam tenet in privata, absque tamen alia liberata panis et ceruisie, extra casum infirmitatis manifeste, volumus ad tempus tollerare " *Linc. Epis Reg Memo Buckingham*, f. 397*d*.

[1] *Canterbury Tales* (ed Skeat), Prologue, ll 127 ff It is interesting to notice that the *Roman de la Rose*, of which Chaucer translated a fragment, contains some remarks upon this subject which are almost paraphrased in his description of Madame Eglentyne

[2] *La Clef d'Amors*. ., ed. Doutrepont (1890), v, 3227 ff

[3] Le Chastiement des Dames (Barbazon and Méon, *Fabliaux et Contes*, II, p 200)

The same consideration preoccupies Madame Eglentyne at her supper: "in *curteisye* was set ful muche hir lest " Good manners, elegant deportment, the polish of the court, all that we mean by nurture, these are her aim

> And sikerly she was of greet disport,
> And ful plesaunt, and amiable of port,
> And peyned her to countrefete chere
> Of court, and been estatlich of manere,
> And to be holden digne of reverence

Her pets are the pets of ladies in metrical romances and in illuminated borders, "smale houndes," delicately fed with "rosted flesh, or milk and wastel-bread " Her very beauty

> (Hir nose tretys, hir eyen greye as glas,
> Hir mouth ful smal, and ther-to soft and reed;
> But sikerly she hadde a fair forheed;
> It was almost a spanne brood, I trowe;
> For, hardily, she was nat undergrowe)

conforms to the courtly standard. Only the mention of her chanting of divine service (through the tretys nose) differentiates her from any other well-born lady of the day; and if Chaucer had not told us whom he was describing, we might never have known that she was a nun. It was in these ideals and traditions that most of the inmates of English convents were born and bred.

During the fourteenth and fifteenth centuries, however, another class rose into prominence and, perhaps because it was originally drawn to a great extent from the younger sons of the country gentry, found amalgamation with the gentry easy. The development of trade and the new openings for the employment of capital had brought about the rise of the English merchant class. Hitherto foreigners had financed the English crown, but during the first four years of the Hundred Years' War it became clear that English merchants were now rich and powerful enough to take their place; and the triumph of the native was complete when, in 1345, Edward III repudiated his debts to the Italian merchants and the Bardi and Peruzzi failed Henceforth the English merchants were supreme; on the one hand their trading ventures enriched them, on the other they made vast sums out of farming the customs and the war subsidies in return for loans of ready money, and out of all sorts of government contracts. The successful campaigns of Crécy and Poitiers were entirely financed by these English capitalists. Not only trade but industry swelled the ranks of the *nouveaux riches* and the clothiers of the fourteenth and fifteenth centuries grew rich and prospered Evidences of the wealth and importance of this middle class are to be found on all sides. The taxation of movables, which from 1334 became an important and in time the main source of national revenue, indicates the discovery on the part of the government that the wealth of the nation no longer lay in land, but in trade. The frequent sumptuary acts, the luxury of daily life, bear witness to the wealth of the *nouveaux riches*; and so also do their philanthropic enterprises, the beautiful churches which they built, the bridges which they repaired, the gifts which they gave to religious and to civic corporations. And it was in the fourteenth century that there began that steady fusion between the country gentry and the rich burgesses, which was accomplished before the end of the middle ages and which resulted in the formation of a solid and powerful middle class The political amalgamation of the two classes in the lower house of Parliament corresponded to a social amalgamation in the world outside. The country knights and squires saw in business a career for their younger sons, they saw in marriage with the daughters of the mercantile class a way to mend their fortunes, the city merchants, on the other hand, saw in such alliances a road to the attainment of that social prestige which went with land and blood, and were not loath to pay the price. "Merchants or new gentlemen I deem will proffer large," wrote Edmund Paston, concerning the marriage of one of his family. "Well I wot if ye depart to London ye shall have proffers large"[1].

This social amalgamation between the country gentry and the "new gentlemen," who had made their money in trade, was naturally reflected in the nunneries. The wills of London burgesses, which were enrolled in the Court of Husting, show that the daughters of these well-to-do citizens were in the habit of taking the veil. There is even more than one trace of the aristocratic view of religion as the sole alternative to marriage. Langland, enumerating the good deeds which will win pardon for

[1] See Mrs Green, *Town Life in the Fifteenth Century*, II, pp. 77–80

the merchant, bids him "marie maydens or maken hem nonnes"[1].
At Ludlow the gild of Palmers provided that.

If any good girl of the gild of marriageable age, cannot have the means
found by her father, either to go into a religious house or to marry,
whichever she wishes to do, friendly and right help shall be given
her out of our common chest, towards enabling her to do whichever
of the two she wishes[2].

Similarly at Berwick-on-Tweed the gild "ordained by the pleasure
of the burgesses" had a provision entitled, "Of the bringing up
of daughters of the gild," which ran: "If any brother die leaving
a daughter true and worthy and of good repute, but undowered,
the gild shall find her a dower, either on marriage or on going
into a religious house"[3]. So also John Syward, "stockfissh-
mongere" of London, whose will was proved at the Court of
Husting in 1349, left, "To Dionisia his daughter forty pounds
for her advancement, so that she either marry therewith or
become a religious at her election, within one year after his
decease"[4]; and William Wyght, of the same trade, bequeathed
"to each of his daughters Agnes, Margaret, Beatrix and Alice
fifty pounds sterling for their marriage or for entering a religious
house" (1393)[5]; while William Marowe in 1504 bequeathed to
"Elizabeth and Katherine his daughters forty pounds each, to
be paid at their marriage or profession"[6]. Sometimes, however,
the sound burgess sense prevailed, as when Walter Constantyn
endowed his wife with "the residue of his goods, so that she
assist Amicia, his niece,....towards her marriage or to some trade
befitting her position"[7].

The mixture of classes must have been more frequent in
convents which were situate in or near a large town, while the
country gentry had those lying in rural districts more or less

---

[1] Langland, *Vision of Piers the Plowman*, ed Skeat, passus A, VIII, l. 31.
[2] *English Gilds*, ed L. T Smith (E E T S), p 194
[3] *Ibid* p 340
[4] Sharpe, *op cit* I, p. 589
[5] Sharpe, *op. cit.* II, p 299 The Fishmongers, who, up to 1536, were
divided into the two companies of salt-fishmongers and stock-fishmongers,
were a powerful and important body, as the annals of the City of London in
the fourteenth century show, "these fishmongers" in the words of Stow
"having been jolly citizens and six mayors of their company in the space
of twenty-four years" Stow's *Survey of London* (ed Kingsford), I, p 214.
[6] Sharpe, *op cit* II, p 606
[7] Sharpe, *op cit* I, p. 594

to themselves. The nunnery of Carrow, for instance, was a favourite resort for girls of noble and of gentle birth, but it was also recruited from the daughters of prosperous Norwich citizens, among nuns with well-known county names there were also ladies such as Isabel Barbour, daughter of Thomas Welan, barber, and Joan his wife, Margery Folcard, daughter of John Folcard, alderman of Norwich, and Catherine Segryme, daughter of Ralph Segryme, another alderman, the latter attained the position of prioress at the end of the fifteenth century[1]. These citizens, wealthy and powerful men in days when Norwich was one of the most important towns in England, probably met on equal terms with the country gentlemen of Norfolk, and both sent their daughters with handsome downes to Carrow. The nunneries of London and of the surrounding district contained a similar mixture of classes, ranging from some of the noblest ladies in the land to the daughters of city magnates, men enriched by honourable trade or by the less honourable capitalistic ventures of the king's merchants The famous house of Minoresses without Aldgate illustrates the situation very clearly It was always a special favourite of royalty, and the storm bird, Isabella, mother of Edward III, is by some supposed to have died in the order. She was certainly its constant benefactress[2] as were Thomas of Woodstock, Duke of Gloucester and his wife, whose daughter Isabel was placed in the nunnery while only a child and eventually became its abbess[3]. Katherine, widow of John de Ingham, and Eleanor Lady Scrope were other aristocratic women who took the veil at the Minories[4]. But this noble connection did not prevent the house from containing Alice, sister of Richard Hale, fishmonger[5], Elizabeth, daughter of Thomas Padyngton, fishmonger[6], Marion, daughter of John Charteseye, baker[7], and Frideswida, daughter of John Reynewell, alderman of the City of London[8], girls drawn from the *élite* of the burgess class. An investigation of the wills enrolled in the Court of Husting shows the relative popularity

---

[1] Rye, *Carrow Abbey*, App IX, pp xvi, xvii, xviii
[2] See *Archaeologia*, xv (1806), pp 100–101, ib xxxv (1853), p 464
[3] *V C H London*, I, p 518   [4] *Ib.* pp 518–9
[5] Sharpe, *op cit* II, p 267 Two years previously (1396) John de Nevill had left legacies to his sister Eleanor and to his daughter Elizabeth, minoresses of St Clare, *Durham Wills and Inventories* (Surtees Soc), p 39
[6] Sharpe, *op. cit* II, p 589
[7] *Ib* II, p 331.   [8] *Ib.* II, p. 577

of different convents among the citizens of London. Between the years 1258 and the Dissolution, 52 wills contain references to one or more nuns related to the testators[1]. From these it appears that the most popular house was Clerkenwell in Middlesex, which is mentioned in nine wills[2]. Barking in Essex comes next with eight references[3], and St Helen's Bishopsgate with seven[4]; the house of Minoresses without Aldgate is five times mentioned[5], Haliwell[6] in London and Stratford-atte-Bowe[7] outside, having five and four references respectively, Kilburn in Middlesex three[8], Sopwell in Hertfordshire two[9], Malling[10] and Sheppey[11] in Kent two each Other convents are mentioned once only and in some cases a testator leaves legacies to nuns by name, without mentioning where they are professed. All these houses were in the diocese of London and either in or near the capital itself; they lay in the counties of Middlesex, Kent, Essex, Hertford and Bedford[12]. It was but rarely that city girls went as far afield as Denny in Cambridgeshire, where the famous fishmonger and mayor of London, John Philpott, had a daughter Thomasina.

Thus the nobles, the gentry and the superior rank of burgess —the upper and the upper-middle classes—sent their daughters to nunneries But nuns were drawn from no lower class; poor girls of the lowest rank—whether the daughters of artisans or of country labourers—seem never to have taken the veil. A certain degree of education was demanded in a nun before her admission and the poor man's daughter would have neither the money, the

---

[1] Not counting legacies left to various nunneries, without specific reference to a relative professed there

[2] Sharpe, *op cit* I, pp 107, 300, 313, 324, 408, 501, 585, 701 Philip le Taillour had three daughters here in 1292 (I, p 107), and William de Leyre had three daughters here in 1322 (I, p 300).

[3] *Ib* I, pp 222, 303, 569, 638, 688; II, pp 20, 76, 115

[4] *Ib.* I, pp 229, 303, 342, 400, 435, II, pp 47, 170. Ten nuns in all

[5] *Ib* II, pp 119, 267, 331, 577, 589

[6] *Ib.* I, pp 26, 126, 238, 349, 628 Ralph le Blund's three daughters and his sister-in-law were all nuns here in 1295 (I, p 126) and Thomas Romayn, alderman and pepperer, left bequests to two daughters and to their aunt in 1313 (*ib.* I, p. 288)

[7] *Ib* I, pp. 34, 111, 611; II, p 119

[8] *Ib.* II, pp. 167, 271, 274.

[9] *Ib.* II, pp. 474, 564.

[10] *Ib* I, pp 510, 638

[11] *Ib.* I, p 119, II, p. 306.

[12] There are two exceptions, Greenfield (Lincs) (*ib.* II, p. 327), and Amesbury (Wilts) (*ib.* II, p. 326), but the testators in these cases are not burgesses, but a knight and a clerk.

opportunity, nor the leisure to acquire it. The manorial fine paid by a villein when he wished to put his son to school and make a religious of him, had no counterpart in the case of girls[1]; the taking of the veil by a villein's daughter was apparently not contemplated. The chief barrier which shut out the poor from the nunneries was doubtless the dower which, in spite of the strict prohibition of the rule, was certainly required from a novice in almost every convent. The lay sisters of those nunneries which had lay sisters attached were probably drawn mainly from the lower class[2], but it must have been in the highest degree exceptional for a poor or low-born girl to become a nun

Medieval wills (our most trusty source of information for the *personnel* of the nunneries) make it possible to gauge the extent to which the upper and middle classes used the nunneries as receptacles for superfluous daughters. In these wills, in which the medieval paterfamilias laboriously catalogues his offspring and divides his wealth between them, it is easy to guess at the embarrassments of a father too well-blessed with female progeny. What was poor Simon the Chamberlain of the diocese of Worcester to do, with six strapping girls upon his hands and sons Robert and Henry to provide for too? Fortunately he had a generous patron in Sir Nicholas de Mitton and it was perhaps Sir Nicholas who provided the dowers, when two of them were packed off to Nuneaton; let us hope that Christiana, Cecilia, Matilda and Joan married themselves out of the legacies which he left them in his will, when he died in 1290[3]. William de Percehay, lord of Ryton, who made his will in 1344, had to provide for five sons and one is therefore not surprised to find that two of his three daughters were nuns[4]. It is the same with

---

[1] The corresponding fines for girls were *merchet* if they married off the manor and *leyrwite* if they dispensed with that ceremony The medieval lord, concerned above all with keeping up the supply of labour upon his manor, naturally held the narrow view of the functions of women, which has been expressed in our day by Kipling: "Now the reserve of a boy is tenfold deeper than the reserve of a maid, she having been made for one end only by blind Nature, but man for several" (*Stalky and Co* p 212)

[2] Henry de Causton, *mercator* of London, left a bequest to Johanna, a 'sister" at Ankerwyke, formerly servant to his father (1350) Sharpe, *op. cit.* i, p. 638.

[3] *Register of Bishop Godfrey Giffard* (Worc Hist Soc), ii, pp. 288–9

[4] *Testamenta Eboracensia* (Surtees Soc.), i, p 6.

the rich citizens of London and elsewhere; Sir Richard de la
Pole, of a great Hull merchant house (soon to be ennobled),
mentions in his will two sons and two daughters, one of whom
was a nun at Barking while the other received a legacy towards
her marriage[1], Hugh de Waltham, town clerk, mentions three
daughters, one at St Helen's[2]; John de Croydon, fishmonger,
leaves bequests to one son and four daughters, one at Clerkenwell[3]; William de Chayham kept Lucy, Agnes and Johanna with
him, but made Juliana a nun[4]. The will of Joan Lady Clinton
illustrates the proportion in which a large family of girls might
be divided between the convent and the world; in 1457 she left
certain sums of money to Margaret, Isabel and Cecily Francyes,
on condition that they should pay four pounds annually to their
sisters Joan and Elizabeth, nuns[5]. It was not infrequent for
several members of a family to enter the same convent, as the
lists of inmates given in visitation records, or in the reports of
Henry VIII's commissioners, as well as the evidence of the wills,
bear witness[6]. The case of Shouldham, already quoted, shows
that different generations of a family might be represented at
the same time in a convent[7], but it was perhaps not usual for
so many sisters to become nuns as in the Fairfax family; in
1393 their brother's will introduces us to Mary and Alice, nuns
of Sempringham, and Margaret and Eleanor, respectively prioress
and nun of Nunmonkton[8]. Margaret (of whom more anon) took
convent life easily; it is to be feared that she had all too little
vocation for it. Sometimes these family parties in a nunnery
led to quarrels; the sisters foregathered in cliques, or else they
continued in the cloister the domestic arguments of the hearth;
there was an amusing case of the kind at Swine in 1268[9], and
some years later (in 1318) an Archbishop of York had to forbid

[1] *Test. Ebor* I, p 9, dated 1345 Cf will of Roger de Moreton "civis et
mercerus Ebor " 1390; two of four daughters nuns at St Clement's, York
(*ib* I, p 133)
[2] Sharpe, *op. cit.* I, p. 400, dated 1335.   [3] *Ib.* I, p. 501, dated 1349.
[4] *Ib* I, p 503, dated 1348   [5] *Testamenta Vetusta*, I, p. 286.
[6] See above, p 7 There were two Welbys, two Lekes and two Pay-
nelles at Stixwould; *Alnwick's Visit* MS f 76. Other references might be
multiplied
[7] Cf also Sharpe, *op. cit.* I, p. 238, and *Reg of Bishop Ginsborough*
(Worc Hist Soc), p 51.
[8] *Testamenta Eboracensia* (Surtees Soc) I, pp 187 ff (will of Sir John
Fayrfax, rector of Prescot, 1393).   [9] See below, p 302.

the admission of more than two or three nuns of one family to Nunappleton, without special licence, for fear of discord[1]

Probably the real factor in determining the social class from which the convents were recruited, was not one of rank, but one of money. The practice of demanding dowries from those who wished to become nuns was strictly forbidden by the monastic rule and by canon law[2]. To spiritual minds any taint of commerce was repugnant, Christ asked no dowry with his bride The didactic and mystical writers of the period often draw a contrast between the earthly and the heavenly groom in this matter. The author of *Hali Meidenhad* in the thirteenth century, urging the convent life upon his spiritual daughter, sets against his picture of Christ's virgin-brides that of the well-born girl, married with disparagement through lack of dower:

What thinkest thou of the poor, that are indifferently dowered and ill-provided for, as almost all gentlewomen now are in the world, that have not wherewith to buy themselves a bridegroom of their own rank and give themselves into servitude to a man of low esteem, with all that they have? Wellaway! Jesu! what unworthy chaffer[3]

Thomas of Hales' mystical poem *A Luue Ron*, in the same century, also lays stress upon this point, half in ecstatic praise of the celibate ideal, half as a material inducement[4], and the same idea is repeated at the end of the next century in *Clene Maydenhod*:

> He asketh with the nouther lond ne leode,
> Gold ne selver ne precious stone.
> To such thinges hath he no neode,
> Al that is good is with hym one,
> Gif thou with him thi lyf wolt lede
> And graunte to ben his owne lemman[5].

In ecclesiastical language the same sentiment is expressed by the injunction of Archbishop Greenfield of York, who forbade the nuns of Arden to receive any one as a nun by compact, since that involved guilt of simony, but only to receive her "from promptings of love"[6].

[1] *V C H Yorks.* III, p 172   [2] On this subject see Coulton, *Monastic Schools in the Middle Ages* (Medieval Studies), pp 34–5
[3] *Hali Meidenhad*, ed. Cockayne (E E.T.S), p 8
[4] *Old English Miscellany*, ed Morris (E E T S, 1872), p. 96
[5] *Clene Maydenhod*, ed Furnivall (E E.T S), pp. 5–6.
[6] *V.C H. Yorks* III, p 113

This sentiment was, however, set aside in practice from early times, and a glance at any conventual register, such as the famous Register of Godstow Abbey, shows something like a regular system of dowries, dating certainly from the twelfth century. The Godstow Register contains 19 deeds, ranging between 1139 and 1278, by which grants are made to the nunnery on the entrance of a relative of the grantor, the usual phrase being that such and such a man gave such and such rent-charges, pasture-rights, lands or messuages, "with" his mother or sister or daughter "to be a nun "[1]. One very curious deed dated 1259, shows that the reception of a girl at Godstow was definitely a pecuniary matter. Ralph and Agnes Chondut sold to the nunnery a piece of land called Anfric,

for thys quite claime and reles, the seyd abbas and holy mynchons of Godstowe gafe to the seyde raph and Agnes hys wyfe liii⁰ marke, and made Katherine the sustur of the seyd Agnes (wyfe of the seyd raph) Mynchon in the monasteri of Godstow, with the costys of the hows,...and the seyd holy mynchons of Godstowe shold pay to the seyd raph and Agnes hys wyfe xxv marke of the forseyd liii marke in that day in whyche the foreseyd Katerine should be delyuerd to hem to be norysshed and to be mad mynchon in the same place and in the whyche the seyd penyes shold be payd,

and a second instalment at a place to be agreed upon when confirmation of the grant is obtained[2] That is to say the price of the land was £35. 6s. 8d. together with the cost of receiving

---

[1] *The English Register of Godstow Nunnery* (E E T S.), introduction, pp xxv–xxvi Cf *Cartulary of Buckland Priory* (Somerset Rec. Soc), introd. pp xxii–xxiii

[2] *Reg. of Godstow,* u s no 76, pp 78–9 See also an exceedingly interesting action of *quare impedit* brought by John Stonor (probably the Lord Chief Justice) against the Prioress of Marlow in 1339, probably merely to secure a record He had bought the advowsons of the two moieties of the church of Little Marlow and an acre of land with each and conveyed the whole to the Prioress, subject to the provision "that out of it the said Prioress and nuns shall find Joan and Cecily, sisters of the aforesaid John, and Katherine, daughter of the aforesaid John, nuns of the aforesaid place, 40s a year each during their lives, and also for the sustenance of all the nuns towards their kitchen half a mark of silver each year and for the vesture of the twenty nuns serving God there each year 10s of silver, to be divided equally between them " After the deaths of the Stonor ladies all the money is to go to the common funds of the house, with certain provisions *Year Books of Edward III, years* xii *and* xiii, ed. L. O Pike (Rolls Series, 1885), pp cxi–cxvii, 260–2 For the appropriation of these money downes to the use of the individual nuns, see below, Ch VIII, *passim*

Katherine, which was equivalent to a further sum of money, unfortunately not specified.

Any collection of wills provides ample evidence of this dowry system. Not only do they frequently contain legacies for the support of some particular nun during the term of her life, but bequests also occur for the specific purpose of paying for the admission of a girl to a nunnery, in exactly the same way as other girls are provided with downes for their marriage. The Countess of Warwick, in 1439, left a will directing "that Iane Newmarch have cc mark in gold, And I to bere all Costes as for her bryngynge yn-to seynt Katrens, or where-ever she woll be elles"[1] Even the clergy, who should have been the last to recognise a system so flagrantly contrary to canon law, followed the general custom, William Peke, rector of Scrivelsby, left one Isabella ten marks to make her a nun in the Gilbertine house of Catley[2] and Robert de Playce, rector of the church of Brompton, made the following bequest

Item I bequeath to the daughter of John de Playce my brother 100s. in silver, for an aid towards making her a nun in one of the houses of Wickham, Yedingham or Muncton, if her friends are willing to give her sufficient aid to accomplish this, but if, through lack of assistance from friends, she be not made a nun,

she was to have none of this bequest (1345)[3]. Sometimes, as has already been noted, the money is left alternatively to marry the girl or to make her a nun, which brings out very clearly the dower-like nature of such bequests[4]. The accounts of great folk

[1] Nicolas, *Testamenta Vetusta*, I, p. 118
[2] Gibbons, *Early Lincoln Wills*, p. 113
[3] *Testamenta Eboracensia*, I, p 11
[4] See above, p. 6. See also the interesting deed (1429–30) in which Richard Fairfax "scwyer," made arrangements for the entrance of his daughter "Elan," to Nunmonkton, always patronised by the Fairfaxes He left an annual rent of five marks in trust for her "yat my doghtir Elan be made nun in ye house of Nun Monkton, and yat my saydes feffis graunt a nanuel rent of fourty schilyngs...terme of ye lyffe of ye sayd Elan to ye tym be at sche be a nun " His feoffees were to pay nineteen marks "for ye makyng ye sayd Elan nun " And "if sche will be no nun" his wife and feoffees were to marry her at their discretion *V C H. Yorks* III, p 123 Cf an interesting case in which Matilda Toky, the orphan of a citizen of London, is allowed by the mayor and aldermen to become a nun of Kilburn in 1393, taking with her her share ($£38$ $5s$ $4\frac{1}{2}d$) of her father's estate, after which the prioress of the house comes in person to receive the money from the chamberlain of the city Riley, *Memorials of London*, p 535 The father's will is in Sharpe, *op. cit.* II, pp. 288–9; he had three sons and a daughter besides Matilda.

often tell the same tale. When Elizabeth Chaucy—probably a
relative of the poet Chaucer—became a nun at Barking Abbey
in 1381, John of Gaunt paid £51. 8s 2d in expenses and gifts
on the occasion of her admission[1], and the privy purse expenses
of Elizabeth of York contain the item, "Delivered to thabbesse
of Elnestowe by thands of John Duffyn for the costes and
charges of litle Anne Loveday at the making of her nonne
there £6. 13s. 4d."[2].

It is possible to determine the exact nature of these costs
and charges from an account of the expenses of the executors
of Elizabeth Sewardby, who died in 1468. This lady, the widow
of William Sewardby of Sewardby, had left a legacy of £6. 13s 4d.
to her namesake, little Elizabeth Sewardby, to be given her if
she should become a nun. The executors record certain payments
made to the Prioress of Nunmonkton during the period when
Elizabeth was a boarder there, before taking the vows, and then
follows a list of "expenses made for and concerning Elizabeth
Sewardby when she was made a nun at Monkton":

They say that they paid and gave to the Prioress and Convent of
Monkton, for a certain fee which the said Prioress and Convent
*claim by custom to have and are wont to have from each nun at her
entrance* £3 And in money paid for the habit of the said Elizabeth
Sewardby and for other attire of her body and for a fitting bed,
£3 13s. 6½d. And in expenditure made in connection with the aforesaid Prioress and Convent and with the friends of the aforesaid
Elizabeth coming together on the Sunday next after the feast of the
Nativity of the Blessed Virgin Mary A D 1460, £3 11s 4d In a
gratuity given to brother John Hamilton, preaching a sermon at the
aforesaid Monkton on the aforesaid Sunday, 2s And in a certain
remuneration given to Thomas Clerk of York for his wise counsel
concerning the recovery of the debts due to the said dame Elizabeth
Sewardby, deceased, 12d. Total £10. 7s. 10½d.[3]

---

[1] *V.C H Essex*, II, p 117
[2] Quoted in *V.C H. Beds.* I, p. 254.
[3] *Testamenta Eboracensia*, III, p 168 The sum left for entrance of Ellen
Fairfax to Nunmonkton was about the same, £10. 13s. 4d (16 marks).
Above, p. 18, note 4. There is an interesting note of the outfit provided for
an Austin nun of Lacock on her profession in 1395, attached to a page of
the cartulary of that house "Memorandum concerning the expenses of the
veiling of Joan, daughter of Nicholas Samborne, at Lacock, viz in the 19th
year of the reign of King Richard the second after the conquest. First paid
to the abbess for her fee 20s then to the convent 40s , to each nun 2s.
Item paid to John Bartelot for veils and linen cloth 102s " (this large sum
may include a supply for the whole house). "Item to a certain woman for
one veil 40d Item for one mantle 10s Item for one fur of shankes (a cheap

It will be noticed that Elizabeth took with her not only a lump sum of money, but also clothes and a bed, the cost of which more than doubled the dowry. Canon law specifically allowed the provision of a habit by friends, when the poverty of a house rendered this necessary; and it is clear from other sources that it was not unusual for a novice to be provided also with furniture. The inventory of the goods belonging to the priory of Minster in Sheppey, at the Dissolution, contains, under the heading of "the greate Chamber in the Dorter," a note of

stuff in the same chamber belonging to Dame Agnes Davye, *which she browghte with her*; a square sparver of payntyd clothe and iiij peces hangyng of the same, iij payre of shets, a cownterpoynt of corse verder and 1 square cofer of ashe, a cabord of waynscott carved, ij awndyrons, a payre of tonges and a fyer panne.

And under "Dame Agnes Browne's Chamber" is the entry:

Stuff given her by her frends:—A fetherbed, a bolster, ij pyllowys, a payre of blankatts, ij corse coverleds, iiij pare of shets good and badde, an olde tester and selar of paynted clothes and ij peces of hangyng to the same, a square cofer carvyd, with ij bad clothes upon the cofer, and in the wyndow a lytill cobard of waynscott carvyd and ij lytill chestes; a small goblet with a cover of sylver parcel gylt, a lytill maser with a bryme of sylver and gylt, a lytyll pece of sylver and a spone of sylver, ij lytyll latyn candellstyks, a fire panne and a pare of tonges, ij small aundyrons, iiij pewter dysshes, a porrenger, a pewter bason, ij skyllots, a lytill brasse pot, a cawdyron and a drynkyng pot of pewter

She had apparently been sent into the house with a complete equipment in furniture and implements[1].

fur made from the underpart of rabbit skin) for another mantle, 16s. Item for white cloth to line the first mantle, 16s. Item for white cloth for a tunic 10s. Item one fur for the aforesaid pilch 20s. Item for a maser (cup) 10s. Item for a silver spoon 2s. 6d. Item for blankets 6s. 8d. Item in canvas for a bed 2s. Item for the purchase of another mantle of worsted 20s. Item paid at the time of profession at one time 20s. Item for a new bed 20s. Item for other necessaries 20s... Item paid to the said Joan by the order of the abbess." The total (excluding the last item) is £17 6s. 2d. *Archaeol. Journ.* 1912, LXIX, p 117

[1] Mackenzie E. C. Walcott, *Inventories of ..the Benedictine Priory of St Mary and Sexburga in the Island of Shepey for Nuns* (1869) (reprinted from *Archaeologia Cantiana*, VII, pp 272–306). Compare the letter to Cromwell from Sir Thomas Willoughby, who asks that Elizabeth Rede, his sister-in-law, who had resigned the office of Abbess of Malling, may have suitable lodging within the monastery, "not only that but such plate as my father-in-law did deliver her to occupy in her chamber, that she may have it again." Wood, *Letters of Royal and Illustrious Ladies*, II, p 153

Throughout the middle ages a struggle went on between the Church, which forbade the exaction of dowries, and the convents which persisted in demanding them, sometimes in so flagrant a manner as to incur the charge of simony The earliest prohibition of dowries in English canon law occurred - at the Council of Westminster in 1175[1] and was repeated at the Council of London in 1200[2] and at the Council of Oxford in 1222[3]; this last had been anticipated by a decree of the fourth Lateran Council The history of the struggle to apply it is to be gathered from visitational records. Archbishop Walter Giffard, visiting Swine in 1268, finds that Alicia Brun and Alicia de Adeburn were simoniacally veiled[4], Bishop Norbury has to rebuke the Prioress of Chester for the simoniacal receipt of bribes to admit nuns[5]; Bishop Ralph of Shrewsbury has heard that the Prioress of Cannington received four women as sisters of that house for £20 each, falling into the pravity of simony[6]; William of Wykeham writes to the nuns of Romsey in 1387 that

in our said visitations it was discovered and declared that, on account of the reception of certain persons as nuns of your said monastery, several sums of money were received by the Abbess and Convent by way of covenant, reward and compact, not without stain of the pravity of simony and, if it were so, to the peril of your souls,

and he proceeds to forbid the exaction of a dowry "on pretext of any custom (*consuetudinis*) whatsoever, which is rather to be esteemed a corruption (*corruptela*)," a significant phrase, which shows that the practice was well established[7]. Bishop Bucking-

---

[1] "Nullus praelatus in recipiendo monacho, vel canonico, vel sanctimoniali pretium sumere vel exigere ab his, qui ad conversionem veniunt, aliqua pacti occasione praesumat. Si quis autem hoc fecerit anathema sit " Wilkins, *Concilia*, I, p 477.

[2] "Monachi etiam sub pretio non recipiantur in monasterio ...Si quis autem exactus pro sua receptione aliquid dederit, ad canonicos ordines non accedat " *Ib* p 508

[3] "Praeterea statuimus, praesenti concilio approbante, ut nullus de cetero pro receptione alicujus in religionis domum pecuniam vel quicquam aliud extorquere praesumat, adeo ut si pro paupertate domus ingrediens debeat vestire seipsum praetextu vestimentorum ultra justum pretium eorum ab eo nihil penitus recipiatur " *Ib* p. 591

[4] *Reg of Walter Giffard* (Surtees Soc), p 147

[5] *Reg. of Roger de Norbury* (Will. Salt Archaeol. Soc. Collections, 1), p. 259

[6] *Reg of Ralph of Shrewsbury* (Somerset Rec Soc), p 684

[7] *MS Register at New College*, f. 87d.

ham of Lincoln warns the nuns of Heynings against "the reception or extortion of money or of anything else by compact for
the reception of anyone into religion" (1392)[1], and Bishop
Flemyng enjoins at Elstow in 1422

> that hereafter fit persons be received as nuns; for whose reception or
> entrance let no money or aught else be demanded; but without any
> simoniacal bargain and covenant of any sum of money or other thing
> whatsoever, which were accustomed to be made by the crime of
> simony, let them henceforth be admitted to your religion purely,
> simply and for nothing[2].

But the most detailed information as to the prevalence of the
dowry-system is contained in the records of Bishop Alnwick's
visitations of religious houses in the diocese of Lincoln in 1440[3].
When the Bishop came to Heynings (which had already been
in trouble under Bokyngham) one of the nuns, Dame Agnes
Sutton, gave evidence to the effect that

> her friends came to the Prioress and covenanted that she should be
> received as a nun for twelve marks and the said money was paid down
> before she was admitted, and she says that no one is admitted before
> the sum agreed upon for her reception is paid.

She added that nothing was exacted save what was a free offering,
but from her previous words it is obvious that no nuns were
received at Heynings without a dowry. Similarly at Langley
Dame Cecily Folgeham said that her friends gave ten marks to
the house "when she was tonsured, but not by covenant." The
most interesting case of all was that of Nuncoton The Subprioress, Dame Ellen Frost, said "that it was the custom in
time past to take twenty pounds or less for the admission of
nuns, otherwise they would not be received." The Bishop proceeded to examine other members of the house; Dame Maud
Saltmershe confirmed what the Subprioress had said about the
price for the reception of nuns; two other ladies, who had been
in religion for fifteen and eight years respectively, deposed to
having paid twenty pounds on their entrance and Dame Alice
Skotte said that she did not know how much she had paid, but
that she thought it was twenty pounds. Clearly there was a
fixed entrance fee to this nunnery and it was impossible to become

[1] *Linc Epis Reg. Memo. Bokyngham,* f. 397d.
[2] *Linc Visit* I, p 49
[3] See *Linc. Visit.* II, and *Alnwick's Visit* MS., *passim.*

a nun without it; all pretence of free-will offerings had been dropped. When it is considered that this entrance fee was twenty pounds (i e about £200 of modern money) it is easy to see why poor girls belonging to the lower orders never found their way into convents; such a luxury was far beyond their means.

In each of these cases and at two other houses (St Michael's Stamford, and Legbourne) Alnwick entered a stern prohibition, on pain of excommunication, against the reception of anything except free gifts from the friends of a novice His injunction to Heynings may be quoted as typical of those made by medieval bishops on such occasions.

For as mykelle as we founde that many has been receyvede here afore into nunne and sustre in your sayde pryory by covenaunt and paccyons made be fore thair receyvyng of certeyn moneys to be payed to the howse, the whiche is dampnede by alle lawe, we charge yowe under the payn of the sentence of cursyng obove wrytene that fro hense forthe ye receyve none persons in to nunne ne sustre in your sayde pryore by no suche couenant, ne pactes or bargaines made before. Whan thai are receyvede and professede, if thaire frendes of thaire almesse wylle any gyfe to the place, we suffre wele, commende and conferme hit to be receyvede[1].

But the efforts at reform made by Alnwick and other visitors were never very successful; Nuncoton evidently continued to demand its entrance fee, for in 1531 the practice was once more forbidden by Bishop Longland[2]. Moreover it is easy to see that the distinction between the reception of what was willingly offered by friends (which was specifically permitted by the rule of St Benedict and by synods and visitors throughout the middle ages), and what was given by agreement as payment for the entry of a novice (which was always forbidden) might become a distinction without a difference, as it clearly was in the case of Heynings quoted above The Prioress of Gokewell, who declared to Alnwick that "they take nothing for the admission of nuns, save that which the friends of her who is to be created offer of their free-will and not by agreement"[3], may have acted in reality not very differently from her erring sisters of Heynings, Nuncoton and Langley. The temptation was in fact too great.

---

[1] *Linc Visit.* II, pp. 133, 134. See also the very sternly worded prohibition sent by Bishop Spofford of Hereford to Aconbury in 1438. *Reg. Thome Spofford* (Cantilupe Soc), pp 223-4.

[2] *Archaeologia*, XLVII, p. 57.   [3] *Linc. Visit* II, p. 117.

The clause of the Oxford decree, which permitted poor houses if necessary to receive a sum sufficient for the vesture of a new member and no more, broadened the way already opened by the permission of free-will offerings. The concluding words of Bishop Flemyng's prohibition of dowries at Elstow in 1422 show that this permission had been abused; "if they must be clothed at their own or their friends' expense, let nothing at all be in any sort exacted or required, beyond their garments or the just price of their garments"[1] Throughout the later middle ages an increase in the cost of living went side by side with a decrease in the monastic ideal of poverty, showing itself on the one hand in the constant breach of the rule against private property, on the other in the exaction of money with novices, until the dowry system (although never during the middle ages recognised by law) became in practice a matter of course.

Lest it should seem that everyone who had enough money could become a nun, it must, however, be added that the bishops took some pains that the persons who were received as novices should be suitable and pleasing to their sisters They seldom exercised their right of nomination without some assurance that their nominee was of honest life and station, "Mulierem honestam, ut credimus"[2], "bonae indolis, ut credimus, juvenculam"[3], "jeovene damoisele et de bone condicion, come nous sumez enformez"[4], "competeter ad hujusmodi officii debitum litterate"[5]. They were always ready to hear complaints if unsuitable persons had been admitted by the prioress; and they sometimes made special injunctions upon the matter. Bokyngham at Heynings in 1392 ordered "that they receive no one to the habit, nor even to profession, unless she be first found by diligent inquisition and approbation to be useful, teachable, capable, of legitimate age, discreet and honest"[6]. At Elstow Bishop Gray made a very comprehensive injunction:

Furthermore we enjoin and charge you the Abbess .that henceforward you admit no one to be a nun of the said monastery, unless

[1] *Linc Visit* I, p 49.
[2] *Reg Johannis Peckham* (Rolls Series), I, p 189
[3] *Ib* I, pp 40–1, 356
[4] *Wykeham's Reg.* II, pp 60–61 Cf *ib* p 462.
[5] *Reg Johannis de Pontissara*, pp. 240, 252
[6] *Linc Epis Reg Memo Bokyngham,* f 397d

with the express consent of the greater and sounder part of the same
convent; and no one in that case, unless she be taught in song and
reading and the other things requisite herein, or probably may be
easily instructed within short time, and be such that she shall be
able to bear the burdens of the quire (with) the rest that pertain to
religion[1].

Nevertheless, for all their precautions, some strange inmates
found their way into the medieval nunneries

The novice who entered a nunnery, to live there as a nun
for the rest of her natural life, might do so for very various
reasons   For those who entered young and of their own will,
religion was either a profession or a vocation   They might take
the veil because it offered an honourable career for superfluous
girls, who were unwilling or unable to marry; or they might take
it in a real spirit of devotion, with a real call to the religious
life. For other girls the nunnery might be a prison, into which
they were thrust, unwilling but often afraid to resist, by elders
who wished to be rid of them; and many nunneries contained
also another class of inmates, older women, often widows, who
had retired thither to end their days in peace   A career, a vocation, a prison, a refuge; to its different inmates the medieval
nunnery was all these things.

The nunnery as a career and as a vocation does not need
separate treatment. It has already been shown that in large
families it was a very usual custom to make one or more of the
daughters nuns   Indeed the youth of many of the girls who took
the veil is in itself proof that anything like a vocation, or even
a free choice, was seldom possible and was hardly anticipated,
even in theory   The age of profession was sixteen, but much
younger children were received as novices and prepared for the
veil; they could withdraw if they found the life distasteful, but
as a rule, being brought up from early childhood for this career,
they entered upon it as a matter of course; moreover the Church
was rather apt to regard the withdrawal of novices as apostasy.
Sir Guy de Beauchamp in his will (dated 1359) describes his
daughter Katherine as a nun of Shouldham and Dugdale notes
that Katherine, aged seven years, and Elizabeth, aged about one
year, were found to be daughters and heirs of the said Guy, who

---

[1] *Linc Visit* 1, p 53   Cf Flemyng's injunction in 1422, *ib*

died in the following year[1]. It might be supposed that this child
of seven was being brought up as a lay boarder in the convent,
but legacies left to Katherine "a nun at Shouldham" by her
grandfather and by her uncle, in 1369 and in 1400 respectively,
show that she had been thus vowed in infancy to a religious life[2].
One of the daughters of Thomas of Woodstock Duke of Gloucester,
was "in infancy placed in the monastery (of the Minoresses
without Aldgate) and clad in the monastic habit" and in 1401
the Pope gave her permission to leave it if she wished, but she
remained and became its abbess[3]. Bishops' registers constantly
give evidence of the presence of mere children in nunneries.
When Alnwick visited Ankerwyke in 1441, three of the younger
nuns complained that they lacked a teacher (*informatrix*) to teach
them "reading, song, or religious observance"; and at the end
of the visitation the Bishop noted that he had examined all
the nuns save three, whom he had omitted "on account of the
heedlessness of their age and the simplicity of their discretion,
since the eldest of them is not older than thirteen years"[4]. At
Studley in 1445 he found a girl who had been in religion for
two years and was then thirteen; she complained that one of
the maid-servants had slapped a fellow nun (doubtless also a
child) in church"[5] At Littlemore there was a certain Agnes
Marcham, who had entered at the age of thirteen, and had remained there unprofessed for thirteen years; she now refused to
take the full vows[6] Some of the nuns at Romsey in 1534 were
very young, two being fourteen and one fifteen[7]. Indeed the
reception of girls at a tender age was rather encouraged than
otherwise by the Church. Archbishop Greenfield gave a licence
to the Prioress of Hampole to receive Elena, daughter of the
late Reyner Spern, citizen of York, who was eight years old,
and (he added solemnly) "of good conversation and life"[8], and
Archbishop John le Romeyn described Margaret de la Batayle,
whom he sent to Sinningthwaite, as "*juvencula*"[9]. The great

---

[1] *Testamenta Vetusta*, I, pp 63–4   [2] See above, p 7, note 2
[3] *V C H London*, I, p 518   [4] *Linc Visit* II, p 5
[5] *Alnwick's Visit* MS f 26d   [6] *Linc Visit* II, p 217
[7] Liveing, *Records of Romsey Abbey*, p 248
[8] *V C H Yorks*, III, p 163. In 1312 the prioress of Hampole was rebuked for receiving a little girl (*puellulam*), not on account of her youth,
but because she had omitted to obtain the archbishop's licence *Ib.*
[9] *Reg of Archbishop John le Romeyn* (Surtees Soc), I, p. 66

Peckham went out of his way to make a specific defence of the practice in 1282, when the Prioress and Convent of Stratford sought to excuse themselves from veiling a little girl called Isabel Bret, by reason of her youth, "since on account of this minority she is the more able and capable to learn and receive those things which concern the discipline of your order"[1]

It is impossible to make the generalisation that even children professed at such an early age could have had no consciousness of a vocation for the religious life; the history of some of the women saints of the middle ages would be enough to disprove this[2]. The German monk Caesarius of Heisterbach, who is to be equalled as a gossip only by the less pious Salimbene, has some delightful stories of youthful enthusiasts in the *Dialogus Miraculorum*, which he wrote between 1220 and 1235 for the instruction of the novices in his own Cistercian house. One child, destined for a worldly match, protests daily that she will wed Christ only; and, when forced to wear rich garments, asserts "even if you turn me to gold you cannot make me change my mind," until her parents, worn out by her prayers, allow her to enter a nunnery where, although very young, she is soon made governess of the novices. Her sister, given to an earthly husband while yet a child, is widowed and, "*ipsa adhuc adolescentula*" enters the same house. Another girl, fired by their example, escapes to a nunnery in man's clothes; her sister, trying to follow, is caught by her parents and married, "but I hope," says the

---

[1] *Reg. Epis. Johannis Peckham* (Rolls Series), I, p. 356. Compare Caesarius of Heisterbach: "In the diocese of Trèves is a certain convent of nuns named Lutzerath, wherein by ancient custom no girl is received but at the age of seven years or less; which constitution hath grown up for the preservation of that simplicity of mind which maketh the whole body to shine" (*Dial. Mirac.* I, p 389, quoted in Coulton, *Medieval Garner*, p 255) The thirteenth century visitations of the diocese of Rouen by Eudes Rigaud make it clear that novices there were often very young, e g. at St-Saens in 1266 "una earum erat novicia et minima" (*Reg Visit Archiepiscopi Rothomagensis*, ed Bonnin, p. 566). The Archbishop ordered novices to be professed at the age of fourteen and not before (*ib* pp 51, 121, 207)

[2] For example the bégume Christina von Stommeln, who said of herself, "So far back as my memory can reach, from the earliest dawn of my childhood, whensoever I heard the lives and manners, the passion and the death of saints and especially of our Lord Christ and His glorious Mother, then in such hearing I was delighted to the very marrow" (quoted in Coulton, *op cit* p. 403). At the age of ten she contracted a mystic marriage with Christ, and at the age of thirteen she joined the bégumes at Cologne. Cf. St Catherine of Siena

appreciative Caesarius, "that God may not leave unrewarded so fervent a desire to enter religion"[1]. But the most charming tale of all is that of the conversion of Helswindis, Abbess of Burtscheid[2].

She, although the daughter of a powerful and wealthy man ..burned so from her earliest childhood with zeal to be converted (i e to become a nun), that she used often to say to her mother: "Mother, make me a nun." Now she was accustomed with her mother to ascend Mount St Saviour, whereon stood at that time the convent of the sisters of Burtscheid. One day she climbed secretly in through the kitchen window, went up to the dorter and putting on the habit of one of the maidens, entered the choir with the others When the Abbess told this to her mother, who wanted to go, she, thinking that it was a joke, replied "Call the child, we must go." Then the child came from within to the window, saying: "I am a nun; I will not go with thee " But the mother, fearing her husband, replied· "Only come with me now, and I will beg thy father to make thee a nun " And so she went forth It happened that the mother (who had held her peace) once more went up the mountain, leaving her daughter asleep. And when the latter rose and sought her mother in vain in the church, she suspected her to be at the convent, followed her alone, and, getting in by the same window, once more put on the habit When her mother besought her to come away she replied: "Thou shalt not deceive me again," repeating the promise that had been made to her. Then indeed her mother went home in great fear, and her father came up full of rage, together with her brothers, broke open the doors and carried off his screaming daughter, whom he committed to the care of relatives, that they might dissuade her. But she, being (as I believe) not yet nine years of age, answered them so wisely that they marvelled What more? The Bishop of Liège having excommunicated her father and those by whom she had been taken away, she was restored to the place and after a few years was elected Abbess there[3].

[1] Caesarius of Heisterbach, *Dialogus Miraculorum*, ed. Joseph Strange, I, pp 53–4

[2] This was Helswindis von Gimmenich, first abbess of Burtscheid after the transference thither of the nuns of St Saviour of Aachen c 1220–1222 See Quix, *Gesch der ehemaligen Reichs-Abtei Burtscheid* (Aachen 1834)

[3] Caesarius, *op cit* I, pp. 54–5 For another case of children in this convent see the charming story of Gertrude's purgatory, *ib* pp 344–5 There are fifteenth century English translations in the *Myroure of Oures Ladye* (E E T S), pp 46–7 and in *An Alphabet of Tales* (E E T S), p 249. A little girl of nine years old had died, and, after death, appeared in broad daylight in her own place in the choir, next to a child of her own age The latter was so terrified that she was noticed and on being questioned told the vision to the Abbess (from whom Caesarius professes to have had the story). The Abbess says to the child "Sister Margaret, ..if Sister Gertrude come to thee again, say to her· *Benedicite*, and if she reply to thee, *Dominus*, ask her whence she comes and what she seeks " On the following day (continues Caesarius) "she came again and since she replied *Dominus* when she was saluted, the

After these examples of infant zeal it is impossible to assert that even the extreme youth of many novices made a real vocation for religious life impossible. But there is no doubt that such a vocation was less probable, than in cases when a girl of more mature years entered a convent. And it is also certain that the tendency to regard monasticism as the natural career for superfluous girls and as the natural alternative to marriage, was capable of grave abuse. When medieval convents are compared unfavourably with those of the present day, and when the increasing laxity with which the rule was kept in the later middle ages is condemned, it has always to be remembered that the majority of girls in those days (unlike those of today) entered the nunneries as a career, without any particular spiritual qualification, because there was nothing else for them to do. Even in the fourteenth and fifteenth centuries monasticism produced saintly women and great mystics (especially in Germany), but it is remarkable that in England, although there must have been many good abbesses like Euphemia of Wherwell, there are no outstanding names. Monasticism was pre-eminently a respectable career.

It has been said that this tendency to regard monasticism as a career was capable of abuse; and there were not wanting men to abuse it and to use the nunnery as a "dumping ground" for unwanted and often unwilling girls, whom it was desirable to put out of the world, by a means as sure as death itself and without the risk attaching to murder. Kings themselves were wont thus to immure the wives and daughters of defeated rebels.

maiden added 'Good Sister Gertrude, why come you at such a time and what seek you with us?' Then she replied. 'I come here to make satisfaction. Because I willingly whispered with thee in the choir, speaking in half tones, therefore am I ordered to make satisfaction in that place where it befell me to sin. And unless thou beware of the same vice, dying thou shalt suffer the same penance' And when she had four times made satisfaction in the same way (by prostrating herself) she said to her sister. 'Now have I completed my satisfaction, henceforth thou shalt see me no more' And thus it was done For in the sight of her friend she proceeded towards the cemetery, passing over the wall by a miracle. Behold such was the purgatory of this virgin" It is a tender little tale, and kinder to childish sins than medieval moralists sometimes were; Saint Douceline beat a little girl of seven (one of her béguines) "so shrewdly that the blood ran down her ribs, saying meanwhile that she would sacrifice her to God" simply because she had looked at some men who were at work in the house (see Coulton, *op cit* p. 321).

Wencilian (Gwenllian) daughter of Llewelyn was sent to Sempringham as a child, after her father's death in 1283, and died a nun there in 1337, and the two daughters of Hugh Despenser the elder were forced to take the veil at the same convent after their father's fall[1]. The nunnery must often have served the purpose of lesser men, desirous of shaking off an encumbrance. The guilty wife of Sir Thomas Tuddenham, unhappily married for eight years and ruined by an intrigue with her father's servant, was sent to Crabhouse, where she lived for some forty years, and none thought kindly of her save—strangely enough— her husband's sister[2]. Sir Peter de Montfort, dying in 1367, left ten shillings to the lady Lora Astley, a nun at Pinley, called by Dugdale "his old concubine"[3]. Illegitimate children too were sometimes sent to convents. One remembers Langland's nunnery, where

Dame Iohanne was a bastard,
And dame Clarice a kni3tes dou3ter · ac a kokewolde was hire syre.

Nor were the clergy loath to embrace this opportunity of removing the fruit of a lapse from grace. Hugh de Tunstede, rector of Catton, left ten shillings and a bed to his daughter Joan, a nun of Wilberfoss[4], and at the time of the Dissolution there was a child of Wolsey himself at Shaftesbury[5]. It is

---

[1] *V C.H. Lincs* II, p. 184 But the usual custom was to place such women as lay boarders in the custody of a nunnery. See below, pp 419 ff.

[2] "Processus et sententia divortii inter Thomam Tudenham militem et Aliciam filiam quondam Johannis Woodhous armigeri, racione quia est monialis professa in prioratu de Crabhous et nunquam carnaliter cognita per maritum suum predictum durante matrimonio predicto, licet matrimonium predictum duravit et ut vir et uxor cohabitaverunt per spacium viij annorum Durante matrimonio unicus filius ab eadem suscitatus, non tamen per dictum Thomam maritum suum, sed per Ricardum Stapleton servientem patris ipsius Aliciae" (1437) Her husband's sister Margaret Bedingfield left her a legacy of 10 marks in 1474 *Norfolk Archaeology* (Norf and Norwich Arch Soc), XIII, pp 351–2.

[3] *Testamenta Vetusta*, I, p 74.

[4] *Testamenta Eboracensia*, I, p 18.

[5] See the letter from John Clusey to Cromwell in her favour "Rygthe honorable, after most humyll comendacyons, I lykewyce besuche you that the Contents of this my symple Letter may be secret; and that for as myche as I have grete cause to goo home I besuche your good Mastershipe to comand Mr Herytag to give attendans opon your Mastershipe for the knowlege off youre plesure in the seyd secrete mater, whiche ys this, My Lord Cardinall causyd me to put a yong gentyll homan to the Monystery and Nunry off Shafftysbyry, and there to be provessyd, and wold hur to be namyd my doythter, and the troythe ys shew was his dowythter, and now

significant that it was sometimes necessary to procure the papal dispensation of an abbess- or prioress-elect for illegitimacy, before she could hold office. The dispensation in 1472 of Joan Ward, a nun of Esholt, who afterwards became prioress, is interesting, for the Wards were patrons of the house and her presence illustrates one of the uses to which such patronage could be put[1]. The diocese of York affords other instances (they were common enough in the case of priests) of dispensation *"super defectu natalium"*, in 1474 one was granted to Cecily Conyers, a nun at Ellerton, "born of a married man and a single woman"[2] and in 1432 Alice Etton received one four days before her confirmation as Prioress of Sinningthwaite[3]. At St Mary's Neasham in 1437, the Bishop of Durham appointed Agnes Tudowe prioress and issued a mandate for her dispensation for illegitimacy and her installation on the same day[4].

Less defensible from the point of view of the house was the practice, which certainly existed, of placing in nunneries girls in some way deformed, or suffering from an incurable defect.

> Now earth to earth in convent walls,
> To earth in churchyard sod.
> I was not good enough for man,
> And so am given to God

by your Visitacyon she haythe commawynment to departe, and knowythe not whether Wherefore I humely besuche youre Mastershipe to dyrect your Letter to the Abbas there, that she may there contynu at hur full age to be professed Withoute dowyte she ys other xxiiij yere full, or shalbe at shuche tyme of the here as she was boren, which was abowyte Mydelmas. In this your doyng your Mastershipe shall do a very charitable ded, and also bynd hur and me to do you such servyce as lyzthe in owre lytell powers; as knowythe owre Lord God, whome I humely besuche prosperyusly and longe to preserve you. Your orator John Clusey " Ellis, *Original Letters*, Series I, II, pp 92–3. An injunction had been made that profession made under twenty-four years was invalid, and that novices or girls professed at an earlier age were to be dismissed

[1] *V C H Yorks* III, p 161

[2] *Test. Ebor.* III, p. 289, note. She was one of the Conyers of Hornby (Richmondshire) and is mentioned in the will of her brother Christopher Conyers, rector of Rudby in 1483.

[3] *V C H Yorks* III, p 177

[4] *V C H. Durham*, II, p 107 For another instance of dispensation and installation on the same day see *Reg. of Bishop Bronescombe of Exeter*, ed. Hingeston-Randolph, p 163 For other dispensations *super defectu natalium*, see *Cal of Papal Letters*, III, p 470 (cf *Cal of Petit* I, p. 367), V, p 549 and *Reg Johannis de Trillek Episcopi Herefordensis* (Cantilupe Soc), p. 404

It will be remembered that the practice roused the disapproba-
tion of Gargantua, whose abbey of Thélème contained only
beautiful and amiable persons.

Item, parcequ'en icelluy temps on ne mettoit en religion des femmes,
sinon celles qu'estoyent borgnes, boiteuses, bossues, laides, deffaictes,
folles, insensees, maleficiees et tarees,...("a propos, dist li moyne,
une femme qui n'est ny belle, ny bonne, a quoi vault elle?—A mettre
en religion, dist Gargantua.—Voyre, dist le moine, et a faire des
chemises."). .feut ordonne que la (i.e. à Thélème) ne seroyent receues,
sinon les belles, bien formees et bien naturees, et les beaux, bien
formez et bien naturez [1]

Occasionally the nuns seem to have resented or resisted these
attempts to foist the deformed and the half-witted upon them.
One of the reasons urged by the obstinate inmates of Stratford
against receiving little Isabel Bret was that she was deformed
in her person[2]. It was complained against the Prioress of Ankerwyke at Alnwick's visitation in 1441 that she made *ideotas* and
other unfit persons nuns[3]; and in 1514 the Prioress of Thetford
was similarly charged with intending shortly to receive illiterate
and deformed persons as nuns and especially one Dorothy
Sturges, a deaf and deformed gentlewoman. Her designs were
frustrated, but the nuns of Blackborough were less particular
and in 1532 Dorothy answered among her sisters that nothing
was in need of reform in that little house[4].

At the time of the Dissolution the Commissioners found that
one of the nuns of Langley was "in regard a fool"[5]; and a certain
Jane Gowring (the name of whose convent has not been preserved)
sent a petition to Cromwell, demanding whether two girls of
twelve and thirteen, the one deaf and dumb and the other an

---

[1] Rabelais, *Gargantua*, ch. LII
[2] *Reg. Epis. Johannis Peckham* (Rolls Ser.), I, p 367 Cf pp 191 ff.
below
[3] *Linc Visit* II, p 4 She was also charged with the introduction of
unsuitable persons as lay boarders, etc "Item priorissa introducit in
prioratum diuersos extraneos et ignotos, tam mares quam feminas et eos
sustentat communibus expensis domus et aliquas quasi ideotas et alias
inhabiles fecit moniales Negat articulum" But *ideota* probably simply
means unlearned here, and in the case of Agnes Hosey, below p 33 Compare the case at Bival in Normandy 1251 "Ibi est quedam filia burgensis
de Vallibus que stulta est" *Reg. Visit. Archiep Rothomag*, ed Bonnin, p. 111.
[4] *Visitations of the Diocese of Norwich* (Camden Soc), pp 91, 311
[5] Gasquet, *Henry VIII and the English Monasteries* (pop ed. 1899),
p. 293

idiot, should depart or not[1]. At Nuncoton in 1440 a nun informed Bishop Alnwick that two old nuns lay in the fermery and took their meals in the convent's cellar "and likewise the infirm, *the weak minded* (*imbecilles*) and they that are in their seynies do eat in the same cellar"[2] Complaints of the presence of idiots were fairly frequent. It is easy to understand the exasperation of Thetford over the case of Dorothy Sturges, when one finds Dame Katherine Mitford complaining at the same visitation that Elizabeth Haukeforth is "*aliquando lunatica*"[3]; but a few years later Agnes Hosey, described as "*ideota,*" gave testimony with her sisters at Easebourne and excited no adverse comment[4]. In an age when faith and superstition went hand in hand a mad nun might even bring glory to her house, the tale of Catherine, nun of Bungay, illustrates this. In 1319 an inquiry was held into the miracles said to have been performed at the tomb of the saintly Robert of Winchelsea, Archbishop of Canterbury, whose canonisation was ardently desired by the English; among these miracles was the following:

Sir Walter Botere, chaplain, having been sworn, says that the miracle happened thus, to wit that he saw a certain Catherine, who had been (so they say) a nun of Bungay, in the diocese of Norwich, mad (*furiosam*) and led to the tomb of the said father; and there she was cured of the said madness and so departed sane; and he says that there is public talk and report of this

Three other witnesses also swore to the tale[5]. Even cases of violent and dangerous madness seem at times to have occurred, judging from a note at Alnwick's visitation of Stainfield in 1440, in which it is said that all the nuns appeared separately before the Bishop, "with the exception of Alicia Benyntone, who is out of her mind and confined in chains"[6].

Lay and ecclesiastical opinion alike condemned another practice, which seems to have been fairly widespread in medieval England, that of forcing into convents children too young to realise their fate, or even girls old enough to resist, of whom

---

[1] Gairdner, *Letters and Papers, etc*, IX, no 1075
[2] *Alnwick's Visit* MS f 71d.
[3] *Visitations of the Diocese of Norwich*, p. 91.
[4] *Sussex Archaeol Coll* IX, p 26.
[5] Wilkins, *Concilia*, II, p. 487.
[6] *Alnwick's Visit.* MS. f 77.

unscrupulous relatives desired to be rid, generally in order to gain possession of their inheritance; for a nun, dead in the eyes of the law which governed the world, could claim no share in her father's estate[1]. It is true that influential people, who could succeed in proving that a nun was unwillingly professed, might obtain her release[2]; but many little heiresses and unwanted children must have remained for ever, without hope of escape, in the convents to which they had been hurried, for it is evident that the religious houses themselves did all they could to discourage the presentation of such petitions, or the escape of unwilling members The *chanson de nonne*, the song of the nun unwillingly professed, is a favourite theme in medieval popular poetry[3]; and dry documents show that it had its foundation in fact. It is possible to collect from various sources a remarkable series of legal documents which illustrate the practice of putting girls into nunneries, so as to secure their inheritance.

As early as 1197 there is a case at Ankerwyke, where a nun who had been fifteen years professed returned to the world and

[1] Hence the certificates sometimes required from bishops to testify whether or not a girl had actually been professed Such a certificate occurs in *Wykeham's Register* (II, p. 192), announcing that Joan, daughter of Stephen Asshewy, deceased, was not yet professed at St Mary's Winchester or at any other house The case of Isabel, daughter of Sir Philip de Coverle, is also interesting; she left the wretchedly poor house of Sewardsley to claim her share of her mother's inheritance, therewith to provide fit maintenance for herself among the nuns, but she was excluded from inheriting with her sisters on account of her religious profession (*V C H. Northants.* II, pp 125-6) Compare also the case of Joan, wife of Nicholas de Grene (1357-8); on a question of inheritance the King's court issued a writ of inquiry as to whether she had been professed at Nuneaton (*Reg of Bishop Roger de Norbury* (William Salt Archaeol. Soc. Collections, I), pp 285-7

[2] See e g the commission for the release of a novice preserved in the register of Ralph Baldock, Bishop of London (1310) "We have lately received the supplication of our beloved daughter in Christ, Cristina de Burgh, daughter of the noble Sir Robert Fitzwalter, to the effect that whereas she was delivered by her parents, while not yet of a marriageable age, into the order of St Augustine in the monastery of Haliwell of our diocese, and for some time wore the habit of a novice therein and still wears it, nevertheless there is no canonical reason why she should not freely return to the world at her own free will; and whereas we do condescend to licence her to return to the world, having diligently made inquiries in the aforesaid monastery for our information as to the truth of the aforesaid matters, etc etc "; the Bishop having no time to finish the inquiry himself commissions his official to carry it on and to release Cristina if the result is satisfactory. *Reg. Radulphi Baldock* (Cant and York Soc.), p. 129 But note that this girl is only a novice.

[3] See below, pp. 502-9, and Note H.

claimed a share of her father's property, on the ground that she
had been forced into the monastery by a guardian, who wished
to secure the whole inheritance. Her relatives energetically resisted a claim by which they would have been the losers and
appealed to the Pope. The runaway nun was excommunicated
and her case came into the Curia Regis, but the result has not
survived and it is impossible to say whether her story was true[1].
The case of Agnes, nun of Haverholme, illustrates at once the
reason for which an unwilling girl might be immured in a nunnery
and the obstacles which her order would place in the way of
escape. She enters history in a papal mandate of 1304, by which
three ecclesiastics are ordered to take proceedings in the case
of Agnes, whose father and stepmother (how familiar and like
a fairy tale it sounds) in order to deprive her of her heritage,
shut her up in the monastery of Haverholme. "The canons and
nuns of Sempringham (to which order Haverholme belonged) declare," continues the mandate, "that she took the habit out of
devotion, but refuse to confirm their assertion by oath"[2]. The
inference is irresistible. Another case, the memory of which is
preserved in a petition to Chancery, concerns Katherine and
Joan, the two daughters of Thomas Norfolk, whose widow Agnes
married a certain Richard Haldenby. Agnes was seised of certain
lands and tenements in Yorkshire to the value of £40 a year,
as the nearest friend of the two girls, whose share of their father's
estate the lands were   But her remarriage roused the wrath of
the Norfolk family and an uncle, John Norfolk, dispossessed her
of the land and took the children out of her guardianship, "with
great force of armed men against the peace of our lord the king,"
breaking open their doors and carrying away the deeds of their
possessions   Then, according to the petition of Agnes and her
second husband, "did he make the said Katherine a nun, when
she was under the age of nine years, at a place called Wallingwells, against her will, and the other daughter of the aforesaid
Thomas Norfolk he hath killed, as it is said." The mother begs
for an inquiry to be held[3].

But the most vivid of all these little tragedies of the cloister
are those concerned with Margaret de Prestewych and Clarice

---

[1] *V C.H. Bucks* I, p. 355.   [2] *Cal. of Papal Letters*, I, p 17.
[3] *P R O. Early Chanc. Proc.* 7/70.

Stil. The case of Margaret de Prestewych has been preserved in the register of Robert de Stretton, Bishop of Coventry and Lichfield; and it is satisfactory to know that one energetic girl at least succeeded in making good her protests and in escaping from her prison. In her eighth year or thereabouts, according to her own petition to the Pope, her friends compelled her against her will to enter the priory of the nuns of Seton, of the order of St Augustine, and take on her the habit of a novice. She remained there, as in a prison, for several years, always protesting that she had never made nor ever would willingly make any profession. And then, seeing that she must by profession be excluded from her inheritance, she feigned herself sick and took to her bed. But this did not prevent her being carried to the church at the instance of her rivals and blessed by a monk, in spite of her cries and protests that she would not remain in that priory or in any other order. On the first opportunity she went forth from the priory without leave and returned to the world, which in heart she had never left, and married Robert de Holand, publicly after banns, and had issue. The bishop, to whom the case had been referred by the Pope, found upon inquiry that these things were true, and in 1383 released her from the observance of her order[1].

Within a few years of this high spirited lady's escape the case of little Clarice Stil engaged the attention of the King's court. The dry-as-dust pages of the medieval law-books hide many jewels for whoever has patience to seek them, but none brighter than this story. It all arose out of a writ of wardship sued by one David Carmayngton or Scrvyngton against Walter Reynold, whom he declared to have unjustly deforced him of the wardship of the land and heir of Robert Stil, the heir being

---

[1] *Reg. of Bishop Robert de Stretton* (Will. Salt Archaeol. Soc. Collections, N.S. viii), pp. 149–50. With her case compare that of Jane Wadham, which came up after the Dissolution in 1541. She "after arriving at years of discretion was forced by the threats and machinations of malevolent persons to become a regular nun in the house of nuns at Romsey, but having both in public and in private always protested against this seclusion, she conceived herself free from regular observance and in that persuasion joined herself in matrimony with one John Foster, *per verba de presenti*, intending to have the marriage solemnised as soon as she was free from her religion." For the further vicissitudes of her married life, see Liveing, *Records of Romsey Abbey*, p. 255. Compare also the case of Margery of Hedsor who left Burnham in 1311. *V.C.H. Bucks.* i, p. 383.

Clarice. Walter, however, said that no action lay against him, because Clarice had entered into the order of St John of Jerusalem, of which the Prioress of Buckland was prioress, and had been professed in that order on the very day of the purchase of the writ. In answer David unfolded a strange story. He alleged that William Stil, the father of Robert, had married twice; by his first wife Constance he had one daughter Margaret, who was now the wife of Walter Reynold; by his second wife Joan he had two children, Robert and Clarice. William died seised of certain tenements which were inherited by Robert, who died without an heir of his body; whereupon (David alleged) Walter, by connivance with the Prioress of Buckland and in order to disinherit Clarice (in which case his own wife Margaret would be the next of kin), took Clarice after her brother's death and conveyed her to Buckland Priory, she being then eight years of age, and kept her there under guard. David's counsel gave a dramatic account of the proceeding:

Sir, we say that the same Walter by covinage to compel the said Clarice to be professed, took the said Clarice when she was between the ages of seven and eight years, to the house of nuns at Buckland, and in that place were two ladies, nuns, who were of his assent to cause the infant to be professed, and they told the child that if she passed the door the devil would carry her away.

It was furthermore pleaded that on the day of purchase of the writ, Clarice was within the age of twelve years and that she was still within that age, and that therefore she could not be considered professed by the law of the land. By this time one's sympathies are all on the side of David, and of terrified little Clarice, with whom the devil was to run away. Unfortunately the judges referred the matter to an ecclesiastical court and ordered a writ to be sent to the Bishop of Bath and Wells. The Bishop made his return

that the said Clarice on August 1st, 1383, of her own free will, was taken to the said Prioress of Buckland by Stephen Joseph, rector of the church of Northeleye, without any connivance on the part of the said Walter and the said Prioress, and she remained at the said priory for two years to see if the life would please her. Afterwards, on October 18th, 1385, she assumed the religious habit and made profession according to the manners and customs of the said house. And on the day when Clarice entered the house she was more than eight years old and on the day of purchase of the writ more than twelve years old, and at the present time is more than fourteen years old, and is well contented with the religious life

The Bishop also found that no guards had been placed over Clarice by Walter, or by the Prioress. So David lost his suit and was in mercy for a false claim; and he also lost, upon a technical point, another suit which he had brought against the Prioress of Buckland. Nevertheless one's sympathies remain obstinately on his side That touch about the devil assuredly never sprang even from the fertile brain of a lawyer[1].

The illegitimate, the deformed, the feeble-minded and the unwilling represent a not very pleasant side of the conventual system The nunneries contained other and less tragic inmates, who may be distinguished from the majority; for to them went in voluntary retirement a large number of widows[2]. If the nun unwillingly professed has always been a favourite theme in popular literature, so also has the broken-hearted wife or lover, Guinevere hiding her sorrows in the silent cloister.

Many of the widows who took the veil were, however, less romantic figures. Although their presence as secular boarders was discouraged, because it brought too much of the world

[1] *Year Book of 12 Richard II*, ed. G. F. Deiser (Ames Foundation, 1914), pp 71-7 Cf pp 150-3 It may be noticed that Marvell, in his poem "Upon Appleton House" (dedicated to the great Lord Fairfax), preserves the tradition of another of these cases In the time of Anna Langton, the last Prioress of Nunappleton, a certain Isabella Thwaites, who had been placed in her charge, fell in love with William Fairfax The Prioress, who wished her to become a nun, shut her up, but eventually Fairfax, having got the law upon his side, broke his way into the nunnery and released her and she married him in 1518 It was her sons who obtained the house on its dissolution (see Markham, *Life of the great Lord Fairfax*, pp. 3, 4)

For a somewhat similar case to that of Clarice Stil, see *Gentleman's Magazine*, vol 102, p 615 A widow Joan de Swainton married a widower Hugh de Tuthill She had four daughters by her first husband, and of these Hugh married two to his own two sons by his first wife, and placed the other two (they being under twelve years of age) in the nunnery of Kirklees, in order that his two sons might obtain through their wives the whole inheritance of the co-heiresses But the wardship of the girls belonged to a certain William de Notton, who prepared to dispute the arrangement, but was dissuaded by one of the young nuns.

[2] It was probably more common for widows to take a simple vow of chastity and to remain in the world But the will of Thomas de Kent, fishmonger, seems to show that it would be considered quite natural for a widow to take the veil, even in the burgess class, which possibly remarried more frequently than the nobles He left his wife a tenement for life, adding that should she wish to enter any religious house the same was to be sold and half the proceeds given for her maintenance (Sharpe, *op. cit.* I, p 124).

within cloister walls, those who desired to make regular profession were willingly received, the more so as they often brought a substantial dower with them. Thus when Margaret, Countess of Ulster, assumed the habit at Campsey in 1347, she took with her, by licence of the Crown, the issues of all her lands and rents in England for a year after her admission, and after that date 200 marks yearly were to be paid for her sustenance[1]. Such widows often enjoyed a respect consonant with their former position in society and not infrequently became heads of their houses. Katherine de Ingham and Eleanor Lady Scrope both entered the Minories in their widowhood and eventually became abbesses[2]. But it does not need much imagination, nor an unduly cynical temperament, to guess that this element of convent life must occasionally have been a disturbing one. The conventual atmosphere did not always succeed in killing the profaner passions of the soul; and the advent of an opinionated widow, ripe in the experience of all those things which her sisters had never known, with the aplomb of one who had long enjoyed an honoured position as wife and mother and lady of the manor, must at times have caused a flutter among the doves; such a situation, for instance, as Bishop Cobham found at Wroxall when he visited it in 1323[3]. Isabel Lady Clinton of Maxstoke, widow of the patron of the house, had retired thither and had evidently taken with her a not too modest opinion of her own importance. She found it impossible to forget that she was a Clinton and to realise that she, who had in time gone by given her easy patronage to the nuns and lodged with them when she would, was now a simple sister among them. Was she to submit to the rule of Prioress Agnes of Alesbury, she without whose goodwill Prioress Agnes had never been appointed? Was she to listen meekly to chiding in the dorter, and in the frater to bear with sulks? Impossible. How she comported herself we know not, but the bishop "found grave discord existing between the Prioress and dame Isabel Clinton, some of the sisters adhering to one and some to the other." Evidently a battle royal. The

---

[1] V C H. Suffolk, II, p. 113. Cf Testamenta Eboracensia, I, p 117.

[2] V C H. London, I, p 519 Cf Sybil de Felton, widow of Sir Thomas Morley, who became Abbess of Barking in 1393, at the age of thirty-four. V.C H. Essex, II, p 121

[3] V C H. Warwick, II, p. 71.

bishop, poor man, did his best. He enjoined peace and concord
among the inmates; the sisters were to treat the prioress with
reverence and obedience, those who had rebelled against her
were to desist and the prioress was to behave amicably to all
in frater, dorter, and elsewhere. And so my lord went his way.
He may have known the pertinacity of the late patroness, and
it was perhaps with resignation and without surprise that he
confirmed her election as prioress on the death of the harassed
Agnes.

The occasional cases in which wives left their husbands to
enter a convent were less likely to provoke discord Such women
as left husband and children to take the veil must have been
moved by a very strong vocation for religion, or else by excessive
weariness. Some may perhaps have found married life even such
an odious tale, "a licking of honey off thorns," as the misguided
realist who wrote *Hali Meidenhad* sought to depict it. In
any case, whether the mystical faith of a St Bridget drew her
thither, or whether matrimony had not seemed easy to her that
had tried it, the presence of a wedded wife was unlikely to provoke discord in the convent; the devout and the depressed are
quiet bedeswomen. It was necessary for a wife to obtain her
husband's permission before she could take the veil, since her
action entailed celibacy on his part also, during her lifetime
Sometimes a husband would endow his wife liberally on her
entry into the house which she had selected. There are two such
dowers in the Register of Godstow Nunnery. About 1165 William
de Seckworth gave the tithes of two mills and a grant of five
acres of meadow to the convent, "for the helth of hys sowle and
of hys chyldryn and of hys aunceters, with hys wyfe also, the
whyche he toke to kepe to the forseyd holy mynchons to serve
god"[1]; and a quarter of a century later Geoffrey Durant and
Molde his wife, "whan þe same Moole yelded herself to be a
mynchon to the same chirch," granted one mark of rent to be
paid annually by their son Peter, out of certain lands held by
him, "which were of the mariage of the said Moolde"[2]. Nor
did Walter Hauteyn, citizen of London, in his solicitude for his

---

[1] *English Register of Godstow Nunnery* (E E T S), p 43
[2] *Ib.* p 383 Confirmation of this deed of grant by Peter Durant, about
1200. *Ib* p 384.

son and three daughters, forget the mother who had left her
husband and children for the service of God; to Alice his wife,
a nun of St Sepulchre's Canterbury, he bequeathed in 1292 his
dwelling place and rents upon Cornhill for life, with remainder
to his heirs[1].

[1] Sharpe, *op. cit.* I, p 108

CHAPTER II

THE HEAD OF THE HOUSE

"My lady Prioresse, by your leve
So that I wiste I sholde you not greve,
I wolde demen that ye tellen sholde
A tale next, if so were that ye wolde.
Now wol ye vouche-sauf, my lady dere?"
"Gladly" quod she, and seyde as ye shal here.

CHAUCER

IT usually happened that the head of a nunnery was a woman of some social standing in her own right. All nuns were Christ's brides, but an earthly father in the neighbourhood, with broad acres and loose purse strings, was not to be despised. If a great lady retired to a nunnery she was very like to end as its head; Barking Abbey in Essex had a long line of well-born abbesses, including three queens and two princesses; and when Katherine de la Pole (the youngest daughter of that earl of Suffolk who was slain at Agincourt) is found holding the position of abbess at the tender age of twenty-two, it is an irresistible inference that her birth was a factor in the choice[1] The advantage in having a woman of local influence and rich connections as prioress is illustrated in the history of Crabhouse nunnery under Joan Wiggenhall[2]; how she worked and built "be the grace of

---

[1] *V C H Essex*, II, pp 120–2. Margaret Botetourt became Abbess of Polesworth in 1362, by episcopal dispensation, when under the age of twenty "This early promotion was not the only mark of favour which this prioress obtained. In 1390 the Pope granted her exemption from the jurisdiction of the Archbishop or Bishop of Lichfield " *V C.H. Warwick*, II, p. 63

[2] "I take it that Prioress Joan was an heiress, and, in fact, the last representative of the elder line of her family, and the nuns knew perfectly well what they were about when they chose a lady of birth and wealth, and highly connected to boot, to rule over them They certainly were not disappointed in any expectations they may have formed The new prioress set to work in earnest to make the nunnery into quite a new and imposing place and her friends and kinsfolk rallied round her nobly " Jessopp, *Ups and Downs of an Old Nunnery* in *Frivola*, pp 59–60

oure Lord God an be the helpe of Edmund Perys, Person of Watlington," her cousin; and how

whanne this good man beforeseyde was passid to God, oure Lord that is ful graciouse to alle his servauntis that have nede and that troste on hym, sente hem anothir goode frende hem to helpe and comforte in her nede, clepid Mayster Jon Wygenale, Doctoure of Canon and person of Oxborow, and Cosyn to the same Prioresse;

and how

in the xix yere of the same Prioresse, ffel a grete derth of corne, wherefore sche muste nedis have lefte werke with oute relevynge and helpe of sum goode creature, so, be the sternge of oure Lord, Mayster Jon Wygenale befor sayde sente us of his charite an 100 cowmbe malte and an 100 coumbe Barly and besyde this procurid us xx mark. And for the soule of my lord of Exetyr, of whos soule God of hys pyte he wil have mercy, we had of him xl pounte and v mark to the same werke, whiche drewe ccc mark, without mete and drinke And within these vij yere that the dortoure was in makynge the place at Lynne clepped Corner Bothe was at the gate downe and no profite came to the place many yeris beforne So that maystir Jon before seyde of hys gret charite lente the same prioresse good to make it up ageyne and procured hir xx mark of the sekatouris of Roger Chapeleyn[1].

The election of a superior was a complicated business, as may be gathered from the list of seventeen documents relating to the election of Alice de la Flagge as Prioress of Whiston in 1308, and enrolled in the *Sede Vacante* Register of Worcester diocese[2] Indeed there were so many formalties to be fulfilled

---

[1] *Reg of Crabhouse Nunnery,* ed Mary Bateson (*Norf Archaeology,* xi), pp 57–62 *passim*

[2] They are as follows: (1) *congé d'élire* by the Bishop-Elect as patron, (2) notification by the subprioress and nuns of the date appointed for the election, (3) formal warning by the subprioress that all who ought not to be present should leave the chapter house, (4) notification of the election of Alice de la Flagge, (5) declaration of Alice's assent, (6) letter from subprioress and convent to the Bishop-Elect praying him to confirm the election (7) letter from the Prior of Worcester to the same effect, to the Bishop-Elect, (8) the same to the commissary general, (9) commission from the Bishop-Elect to the Prior and to the commissary-general, empowering them to receive, examine and confirm the election, (10) instrument by the subprioress and convent appointing Richard de Bereburn, chaplain, their proctor to present the elect to the Bishop-Elect, (11) another appointing two of the nuns as proctors " to instruct and do things concerning the business of the election," (12) decree by the subprioress and convent, describing the method and result of the election and addressed to the Bishop-Elect, (13) acts concerning the election made before the Bishop's commissaries by Richard

that the nuns seem often to have found great difficulty in making a canonical election, and there are frequent notices in the episcopal registers that their election has been quashed by the Bishop on account of some technical fault; in such cases, however, the Bishop's action was merely formal and he almost always reappointed the candidate of their choice[1]. An election was, moreover, not only complicated but expensive; it began with a journey to the patron to ask for his *congé d'élire* and it ended with more journeys, to the patron and to the Bishop, to ask for confirmation, so that the cost of travel and the cost of paying a clerk to draw up the necessary documents were sometimes considerable; moreover a fee was payable to the Bishop's official for the installation of the new head. The account of Margaret Ratclyff, Prioress of Swaffham Bulbeck in 1482, contains notice of payments "to the official of the lord bishop, at the installation of the said prioress for his fee i. li." and to one Bridone "for the transcript of the decree of election of the prioress v. s."[2]. An account roll of St Michael's Stamford for the year 1375–6 illustrates the process in greater detail; under the heading of "expenses de nostre Elit" are the following items:

Paid for the hire of horses with expenses going to the abbot of Peterborough [the patron] to get licence to elect our choice 9½d. Paid for the hire of horses going to the bishop of Lincoln and to the abbot of Peterborough and for their expenses at our election 4s. 8½d. Paid for bread, ale and meat for our election on the election day 2s. 11½d.

de Bereburn, proctor, by the subprioress and by the two nuns, *instructrices*, examined on oath, (14) certificate by the Dean of the Christianity of Worcester that he had proclaimed the election, (15) confirmation of the election by the commissaries, (16) final declaration by the Prior of this confirmation and of the installation and benediction of the new prioress and of the injunction of obedience upon the nuns, and (17) a certificate by the commissaries of the Bishop-Elect that the business was completed. *Reg. Sede Vacante* (Worc. Hist. Soc.), pp. 111–4; the text in Nash, *Hist. and Antiquities of Worcestershire* (1781), I, pp. 212–6, which also contains many documents relating to the election of other prioresses of this house. There are frequent notices of elections in episcopal registers; for other very detailed accounts, see *Reg. of Bishop Grandisson of Exeter*, ed. Hingeston-Randolph, pt III, pp. 999–1002 (Canonsleigh) and *Reg. of Ralph of Shrewsbury* (Somerset Rec. Soc.) pp. 284–7 (Cannington). See also Eckenstein, *Woman under Monasticism*, pp. 367–8.

[1] See e.g. *V.C.H. Glouc.* II, p. 93; *Reg. of Bishop Grandisson*, pt II, p. 742; *V.C.H. Yorks.* III, pp. 114–5, 120, 124; Dugdale, *Mon.* IV, p. 636; *ib.* V, p. 207; *V.C.H. Durham*, II, p. 107.

[2] Dugdale, *Mon.* IV, p. 458.

PLATE II

ABBESS RECEIVING THE PASTORAL STAFF FROM A BISHOP

BENEDICTION OF AN ABBESS BY A BISHOP

Paid for a letter to the abbot of Peterborough for a licence to elect 3d.
Paid for the installation of our elect, 10s.[1] Total 18s. 8½d.[2]

The only necessary qualifications for the head of a house were
that she should be above the age of twenty-one[3], born in wedlock
and of good reputation; a special dispensation had to be obtained
for the election of a woman who was under.age or illegitimate.

As a rule the nuns possessed the right of free election, subject
to the *congé d'élire* of their patron and to the confirmation of
the bishop, and they secured without very much difficulty the
leader of their choice. Often enough it must have been clear,
especially in small communities, that one of the nuns was better
fitted to rule than her sisters, and, as at Whiston, they

unanimously, as if inspired by the Holy Spirit[4], chose dame Alice de
la Flagge, a woman of discreet life and morals, of lawful age, professed
in the nunnery, born in lawful matrimony, prudent in spiritual and
temporal matters, of whose election all approved, and afterwards,
solemnly singing Te Deum Laudamus, carried the said elect, weeping,
resisting as much as she could, and expostulating in a high voice,
to the church as is the custom, and immediately afterwards, brother
William de Grimeley, monk of Worcester, proclaimed the election
The said elect, after being very often asked, at length, after due
deliberation, being unwilling to resist the divine will, consented[5].

But Jocelin of Brakelond has taught us that a monastic election
was not always a foregone conclusion, that discussion waxed
hot and barbed words flew in the season of blood-letting "when
the cloistered monks were wont to reveal the secrets of their
hearts in turn and to discuss matters one with another," and
that "many men said many things and every man was fully
persuaded in his own mind" Nuns were not very different from
monks when it came to an election, and the chance survival of
a bishop's register and of another formal document among the

[1] Evidently this was the usual payment here, for, in the roll for 1392–3,
there is an item "Paye al officiale pour stalling de prioris xs." *P R O Mins
Accts* 1260/4
[2] *P R O. Mins Accts* 1260
[3] The Cistercians fixed the age at 30 Later the Council of Trent fixed
it at 40 including 8 years of profession.
[4] An election by acclamation was said to be conducted *via Spiritus
sancti* or *per inspirationem* For this and the methods of election *via
scrutinii* and *via compromissi*, see J. Wickham Legg, *On the Three Ways of
Canonical Election* (*Trans. St Paul's Eccles. Soc* III, 299–312).
[5] *Reg. Sede Vacante* (Worc Hist. Soc), p 114, and Nash, *op cit.* I, p. 214.

muniments of Lincoln, has preserved the record of an election comedy at Elstow Abbey, almost worthy to rank with Jocelin's inimitable account of the choice of Samson the subsacrist.

After the death of Abbess Agnes Gascoigne in July 1529, the nineteen nuns of Elstow, having received Henry VIII's *congé d'élire*, assembled in their chapter house on August 9th, to elect her successor. They chose Master John Rayn "*utriusque juris doctorem*," as director, Edward Watson, notary public as clerk, and the Prior of Caldwell and the rectors of Great Billing and Turvey as witnesses. Three novices and other lay persons having departed, the director and the other men explained the forms of election to the nuns in the vulgar tongue and they agreed to proceed by way of scrutiny. Matilda Sheldon, sub-prioress, Alice Boifeld, *precentrix*, and Anne Preston, *ostiaria* (doorkeeper) were chosen as scrutineers and withdrew into a corner of the chapter house, with the notary and witnesses There Matilda Sheldon and Anne Preston nominated Cecilia Starkey, *refectoraria*, while Alice Boifeld nominated Elizabeth Boifeld, sacrist, evidently a relative The three scrutineers then called upon the other nuns to give their votes; Anne Wake, the prioress, named Cecilia Starkey; Elizabeth Boifeld and Cecilia Starkey (each unable to vote for herself, but determined not to assist the other) voted for a third person, the subsacrist Helen Snawe; and Helen Snawe and all the other nuns, except two, gave their votes in favour of Elizabeth Boifeld Consternation reigned among the older nuns, prioress, subprioress, *refectoraria* and doorkeeper, when this result was announced. "Well," said the Prioress, "some of thies yong Nunnes be to blame," and on the director asking why, she replied: "For they wolde not shewe me so muche; for I asked diverse of them before this day to whome they wolde gyve their voices, but they wolde not shewe me" "What said they to you?" asked the director. "They said to me," replied the flustered and indignant prioress, "they wolde not tell to whome they wolde gyve their voices tyll the tyme of thellection, and then they wolde gyve their voices as God shulde put into their mynds, but this is by counsaill And yet yt wolde have beseemed them to have shewn as much to me as to the others." And then she and Dame Cecilia said, "What, shulde the yong nunnes gyve voices? Tushe, they shulde not gyve voices!"

Clearly the situation was the same which Jocelin of Brakelond had described over three centuries before: "The novices said of their elders that they were invalid old men and little capable of ruling an abbey." However the Prioress was obliged to admit that the younger nuns had voted in the last election and the subprioress thereupon, in the name of the scrutineers, announced the election of Dame Elizabeth Boifeld by the "more and sounder part of the convent" (poor Anne Wake!). But the Prioress and disappointed Dame Cecilia still showed fight; the votes must be referred to the Bishop of Lincoln. Further discussion; then Dame Cecilia gracefully gave way; she consented to the election of Dame Elizabeth Boifeld and would not proceed further in the matter. Master John Rayn published the election at the steps of the altar. Helen Snawe (whom after events showed to be a leading spirit in the affair) and Katherine Wingate were chosen as proctors, to seek confirmation from the Bishop, and Dame Elizabeth was taken to the altar (amid loud chanting of *Te Deum Laudamus* by the triumphant younger nuns) and her election announced. She, however, preserved that decorous semblance of unwillingness, or at least of indifference, which custom demanded from a successful candidate, even when she had been pulling strings for days, for when the proctors came to her at two o'clock "in a certain upper chamber called Marteyns, in our monastery" and asked her consent to her election, "she neither gave it nor refused." Away went the proctors, without so much as a wink to each other; let us leave our elect to meditate upon the will of God. At four p.m. they came to her "in a certain large garden, called the Pond Yard, within our monastery"; and at their repeated instances she gave her consent. "Wherefore we, the above-named nuns, pray the Lord Bishop to ratify and confirm our election of the said Elizabeth Boyfeld as our Abbess." Which the Lord Bishop did[1].

But this was by no means the end of the matter. A year later the whole nunnery was in an uproar[2]. The bishop, for reasons best known to himself, had removed the prioress Dame Anne Wake and had appointed Dame Helen Snawe in her place;

[1] From a document preserved at the Exchequer Gate, Lincoln.
[2] For the following account, see *Linc. Epis. Reg. Visit Longland*, ff. 22–25

perhaps Dame Anne had said "Tush" once too often under the new *régime*; perhaps she was getting too old for her work; or perhaps Abbess Elizabeth Boifeld had only commanded Dame Snawe's intrigues at a price, evidently the subsacrist was no less adroit than that other subsacrist of Bury St Edmund's At any rate Dame Anne Wake was put out of her office and Dame Helen Snawe ruled in her stead It might have been expected that this change would be welcomed by the nuns, considering how strong the Boifeld faction had been at the election of the Abbess. But no; during the year of triumph Helen Snawe had aroused the hearty dislike of her sisters; led by Dames Barbara Gray (who had voted against the Abbess at the last election) and Alice Bowlis they had strenuously opposed her substitution for the old Prioress; they had been impertinent to the Abbess of their own choice (indeed she was only a figure-head); they had written letters to their friends and refused to show them to her; and finally when the election of Dame Snawe was announced, they had risen in a body and left the chapter-house as a protest. This was intolerable, and the Bishop's vicar-general came down to examine the delinquents. Matilda Sheldon, the subprioress, admitted to having left the chapter, but denied that she had done so for the reason attributed and said that she did not know of the departure of the other nuns, until she saw them in the dorter Margaret Nicolson showed more spirit; she said that she went out "because she wold not consent that my lady Snawe shulde be priores," and that "ther was none that ded councell hir to goo" and that "my lady abbes did commaunde them to tary, that not withestandyng they went forthe"; and she gave the names of eight nuns who had followed the subprioress out. Dame Barbara Gray was next asked "yf she ded aske licence of my Lady Abbas to wryte letters to hir frends," and replied "that she ded aske licens to wryte to hir frends and my Lady Abbas sade, 'Yf ye showe me what ye wryte I am content,' and she saide agene, 'I have done my devoir to aske licence, and yf ye wyll nede see it I will wryte noo letters.'" Asked whether she had left the chapter house, this defiant young woman declared that "yf it were to do agene she wolde soo doo," and moreover "that she cannot fynde in hir hert to obbey my lady Snawe as priores, and that she wyll rather goo out of the house by

my lord's licence, or she wyll obbey hir...and that she wyll
never obbey hir as priores, for hir hert cannot serve hir." Asked
for her objection to Dame Snawe, she said that "she wyll shewe
noo cause at thys tyme wherfor she cannot love hir"; but after
a little pressure she declared with heat that "the priores maks
every faute a dedly syne"[1], treats all of them ill except her own
self and if she "doo take an oppynyon she wyll kepe itt," whether
it be right or wrong   Dame Margery Preston was next examined
and was evidently rather frightened at the result of her actions;
she said that she had left the chapter-house as a protest against
the deposition of the old prioress and not for any ill will that
she bore Dame Snawe, "and she sais," the record continues,
"that she ys well content to obbey my lady Snawe as priores.
And she desiers my lord to be a good lord to the olde priores,
because of her age." Ill-used Dame Cecilia Starkey, so unkindly
circumvented by Dame Snawe a year ago, next appeared before
the vicar-general and said "that she went forthe of the chapter
howse, but she sais she gave noo occasion to eny of hir susters
to goo forthe. And says she knewe not howe many of hir susters
went forthe whyle she come intoo the dorter, saynge that she
cannot fynde in hir hert nor wyll not accepte and take my lady
Snawe as priores" (an amusing comment on her vote in 1529).
Next came Dame Alice Foster, who admitted to having left the
chapter-house

and sais that they war commanded by the Abbes to tare styll. But
she and other went forth because the olde priores was put done [i.e.
down] wrongfully and my lady Snawe put in agenst ther wylle,
saynge that she wyll never agre to hir as long as she lyvys, she says
the sub-prioress went forthe of the chapiter howse fyrst and then she
and other folowyde;

and evidence in almost the same words was given by Dame
Anne Preston and by Dame Elizabeth Sinclere, the latter adding
that "she wyll take tholde priores as priores as longe as she levys
and no other, and she says yf my lord commaunde vs to take
my lady Snawe to be priores, she had lever goo forthe of the
howse to sum other place and wyll not tare ther." Dame Alice
Bowlis, another young rebel, asked

---

[1] Compare the complaint of one of the nuns at St Michael's Stamford in
1445, "Dicit quod priorissa est sibi nimis rigorosa in correccionibus, nam
pro leuibus punit eam rigorose" *Alnwick's Visit* MS f 96.

yf she ded aske lycence of the Abbes to wryte, she sais she ded aske
licens to wryte and my lady Abbes seyde "My lord hathe gevyn vs
soo strate commaundement that none shuld wryte no (letter) but ye
shewe it to me, what ye doo wryte"; and she sais she mayde aunswer
agene to thabbes, "It hathe not bene soo in tymis paste and I have
done my dewty. I wyll not wryte nowe at this tyme"; she admitted
that she left the chapter house, "but she says that nobody ded move
hyr to goo forthe; she says that she must neds nowe obbey the
priores at my lords commaundement, saynge that my lady Snawe ys
not mete for that offes, butt she wolde shewe noo cause wherfor."

Two other nuns declared with great boldness "That my lord ded
not commaunde vs to tak my lady Snawe as priores, but he
saide, 'Yf ye wyll not take hir as priores I wyll make hir priores'"
and that "they was wont to have the priores chosyn by the
Abbes and the convent, and not by my lord, after seynte Bennet's
rule," one of them remarking cryptically "that she wyll take
my lady Snawe as priores as other wyll doo" and not otherwise.
Meek little Dame Katherine Cornwallis was then interrogated
and said,

"that she was going forthe of the chapiter howse wt. other of hir
susters and then when she herde my lady abbes commaund them to
tary, she ded tary behynde, but she sais that she thynks that none
of the oder susters that went forthe ded here hyr, but only she" (kind
little Dame Katherine), "and she is sory that tholde priores ys put out
of hir offes. She says that my lady abbes ded tare styll and domina
Alicia Boyfelde, domina Snawe, domina Katherina Wyngate, domina
Dorothia Commaforthe, domina Elizabethe Repton, and domina
Elizabeth Stanysmore."

Finally the ill-used abbess made her complaint; she had bidden
saucy Dame Alice Bowlis and others to stand up at matins,
according to the custom of the house, "and went out of hir stall
to byde them soo doo, and lady Bowlis ded make hir awnswer
agene that, 'ye have mayde hir priores that mayde ye abbes!',
brekyng her silence ther." Evidently poor Elizabeth Boifeld
had not succeeded in living down the intrigues which had
preceded her election, and the convent suspected her of rewarding
a supporter at the expense of an old opponent.

Here was a pretty state of affairs in the home of buxomness
and peace. But the vicar-general acted firmly. Barbara Gray
and Alice Bowlis were given a penance for their disobedience; they were to keep silence; neither of them was to come
within "the howse calde the misericorde" (where meat was

allowed to be eaten), but they were always to have their meals in the frater; neither of them was to write any letters; and they were to take the lowest places of all among the sisters in "processions and in other placys." Finally all the nuns were enjoined to be obedient to the abbess and to the hated prioress. Their protests that they would never obey Dame Alice Snawe, while the old prioress lived, were all in vain; and when some ten years later the Reformation put an end to their dissensions by casting them all upon the world, Dame Elizabeth Boyvill (*sic*), "abbesse," received an annual pension of £50, Dame Helen Snawe, "prioresse," one of £4 and Dame Anne Wake, "prioresse quondam," one of 66s. 8d [1]

The turbulent diocese of York provides us with an even more striking picture of an election-quarrel In 1308, after a vacancy, the election of the Prioress of Keldholme lapsed to the Arch-bishop, who appointed Emma of York. But the nuns would have none of Emma. Six of them refused obedience to the new prioress and, six being probably at least half of the whole convent, Emma of York resigned. Not to be daunted the Archbishop returned to the charge; on August 5th he wrote to the Archdeacon of Cleveland stating that as he found no one in the house capable of ruling it he had appointed Joan de Pykering, a nun of Rose-dale, to be Prioress.

As a number of persons (named) had openly and publicly obstructed the appointment of the new prioress the Archdeacon was to proceed immediately to Keldholme and give her corporal possession and at the same time he was to admonish other dissentient nuns (named)

---

[1] Dugdale, *Mon* III, p. 415 For another instance of disturbances in a convent caused by the appointment of a Prioress (here the head of the house) by the Bishop contrary to the will of the nuns, see two letters written by the nuns of Stratford to Cromwell, about the same time that Longland was having such trouble at Elstow In one they ask his help "for the re-moving of our supposed prioress," explaining "Sir, since the time that we put up our supplication unto the king, we have been worse entreated than ever we were before, for meat, drink and threatening words; and as soon as we speak to have anything remedied she biddeth us to go to Cromwell and let him help us; and that the old lady, who is prioress in right, is like to die for lack of sustenance and good keeping, for she can get neither meat, drink nor money to help herself " In another letter they report "that the chancellor of my lord of London (the Bishop) hath been with us yesterday and that he sayeth the prioress shall continue and be prioress still, in spite of our teeth, and of their teeths that say nay to it, and that he commanded her to assault us and to punish us, that other may beware by us " Wood, *Letters of Royal and Illustrious Ladies*, I, nos. xxx and xxxi, pp. 68–70

that they and all others must accept Joan de Pyke333rng as prioress and reverently obey her.

It is clear in this case that the feuds of the convent had spread beyond its walls, for the Archbishop at the same time warned all lay folk to cease their opposition on pain of excommunication and shortly afterwards imposed a penance upon one of those who had interfered. But pandemonium still reigned at Keld-holme and he went down in person to interview the refractory nuns; the result of his visitation appears in a mandate issued to the official of Cleveland on September 3rd, stating that he had found four nuns, Isabella de Langetoft, Mary de Holm, Joan de Roseles and Anabilla de Lokton (all had been among the original objectors to Emma of York) incorrigible rebels. They were therefore to be packed off one after another, Isabella to Handale, Mary to Swine, Joan to Nunappleton and Anabilla to Wallingwells, there to perform their penances. In spite of this ruthless elimination of the discordant elements, the convent of Keldholme refused to submit. On February 1st following the Archbishop wrote severely to the subprioress and convent bidding them at once to direct a letter under their common seal to their patroness, declaring that they had unanimously elected Joan de Pyke333rng as prioress; on February 5th he issued a commission to correct the crimes and excesses revealed at his visitation, and on February 17th he directed the commissioners "to enquire whether Joan de Pickering" (luckless exile in the tents of Kedar) "desired for a good reason, of her own free will, to resign and if they found that she did to enjoin the subprioress and convent to proceed to the canonical election of a new prioress"; and on March 7th the triumphant convent elected Emma of Stapelton. At the same time the Archbishop ordered the transference of two other nuns to do penance at Esholt and at Nunkeeling, perhaps for their share in these disorders but more probably for immorality.

But this was not the end. Emma of York could not forget that she had once been prioress; Mary de Holm (who had either returned from or never gone to Swine) was a thoroughly bad character; and in 1315 the Archbishop

directed Richard del Clay, *custos* of the monastery, to proceed at once to Keldholme and to summon before him in the chapter Emma of

York and Mary de Holm, who like daughters of perdition were disobedient and rebels against the Prioress Having read the Archbishop's
letter in the mother tongue in the chapter, he was to admonish the
two nuns for the first, second and third times that they must humbly
obey the Prioress in all lawful and canonical injunctions They were
not to meddle with any internal or external business of the house in
any way, or to go outside of the enclosure of the monastery, or to
say anything against the Prioress, on pain of expulsion and of the
greater excommunication

At the end of the year, however, harassed Archbishop Greenfield went where the wicked cease from troubling; and the two
malcontents at Keldholme seized the opportunity to triumph.
Scarcely a couple of months after his death Emma of Stapelton
resigned, she said she was "oppressed by age," but since Emma
of York was at once elected and confirmed in her place, it is
probable that the rage, like Joan de Pickering's free will, was
something of a euphemism; her reason doubtless took a concrete
and menacing shape and wore a veil upon its undiminished head.
The last we hear of these very unsaintly ladies is in 1318, when
the new Archbishop enjoined a penance on Mary de Holm for
incontinence with a chaplain[1]. It is noticeable that this was
the second case of the kind which had occurred in the diocese
of York within fifteen years. At Swine in 1290 the appointment by Archbishop Romeyn of Josiana de Anlaby as Prioress
had been followed by similar disorders and he ordered an
inquiry to be held and the rebellious nuns to be sent to
Rosedale[2].

Much trouble might arise within a convent over the election
of its head, as these stories show. But sometimes external persons
interfered, great ladies used their influence and their wealth to

[1] *V.C H Yorks.* III, pp 167–9
[2] *Ib* III, p 180 and *Reg of John le Romeyn* (Surtees Soc), I, pp 213–4
Whether any nuns were sent to Rosedale does not appear, but shortly
afterwards two nuns, Elizabeth de Rue and Helewis Darains, were sent to
Nunburnholme and to Wykeham respectively; these punishments may not
have been connected with the election trouble *Reg Romeyn,* I, pp 177,
214 note, 225, compare p. 216 Josiana appears to have been twice Prioress,
she was confirmed in 1290 and finally resigned because of old age in 1320,
but Joan de Moubray is mentioned as Prioress in 1308 and she resigned in
1309   *V.C.H Yorks* III, p 181   There was discord over an election at
St Clement's, York, in 1316, one party in the convent electing Agnes de
Methelay, and the other Beatrice de Brandesby *Sede vacante,* the Dean
and Chapter appointed the former. *V.C.H. Yorks* III, p 129 See also a
case at Goring. *V C.H. Oxon.* II, p 103

secure the coveted post for a protégée of their own; and the protégée herself was not averse to oiling the palms of those in authority with good marks of silver; "blood-abbesses," Ensfrid of Cologne would have called them ("that is, foisted in by their kinsfolk") or "jester-abbesses" ("that is, such as had been thrust in by the power of great folks") or "simoniacs, who had crept in through money or through worldly services"[1]. In these cases there was likely to be more trouble still, for great ladies were not always careful of the character of a friend or relative whom they wished to settle comfortably as head of a convent. In 1528 the Abbess of Wilton died and Mr John Carey thought he would like the appointment for his sister Eleanor, one of the nuns. He was brother-in-law to lovely Anne Boleyn, and a word in her ear secured her warm support; the infatuated King wished to please Anne; and Wolsey, steering his bark in troubled waters, wished to please the King; so he promised that the lady should have the post, the election to which had been placed in his hands by the nuns. It seemed that all would go well with Dame Eleanor Carey, when Anne Boleyn pulled the strings; but trouble arose, and the action taken by the Cardinal and by the future oppressor of the monasteries is greatly to the credit of them both, for both had much to lose from Anne. "As touching the matter of Wilton" Henry wrote to her

My lord cardinal hath had the Nuns before him, and examined them, Mr. Bell being present; which hath certified me, that for a truth that she hath confessed herself, (which we would have had abbesse) to have had two children by two sundry priests; and furder, since, hath been kept by a servant of the Lord Broke, that was, and that not long ago; wherefore I would not for all the gold in the world clog your conscience nor mine to make her a ruler of a house, which is of so ungudly demeanor, nor I trust you would not that neither for brother nor sister I should so destain mine honor or conscience. And as touching the prioress [Isabel Jordan] or Dame Eleanor's eldest sister, though there is not any evident case proved against them, and that the prioress is so old that of many years she could not be as she was named [ill-famed]: yet notwithstanding to do you pleasure I have done that neither of them shall have it, but that some other good and well disposed woman shall have it, whereby the house shall be the better reformed (whereof I ensure you it had much need) and God much the better served[2].

[1] Translated from Caesarius of Heisterbach's *Dialogus Miraculorum* in Coulton, *A Medieval Garner*, pp. 251–2.   [2] Dugdale, *Mon.* II, p. 318.

Wolsey, however, gave the appointment to Isabel Jordan, who in spite of her having been the subject of some scandal in her youth, was favoured by the greater part of the convent as being "ancient, wise and discreet"; whereupon he brought down upon himself a severe rebuke from Henry, who had "both reported and promised to divers friends of Dame Elinor Carey that the Prioress should not have it"[1]. Without doubt pretty Mistress Anne was sulking down at Hever.

Not only did outside persons thus concern themselves in a conventual election; the nuns themselves were not always un-willing to bribe, where they desired advancement A series of letters written by Margaret Vernon to Cromwell, concerning the office of Prioress of St Helen's, Bishopsgate, throws a lurid light upon the methods which were sometimes employed:

"Sir," she wrote to her powerful friend in 1529, "Pleaseth it you to understand that there is a goldsmith in this town, named Lewys, and he sheweth me that Mr More hath made sure promise to parson Larke that the subprioress of St Helen's shall be prioress there afore Christ-mas-day. Sir, I most humbly beseech you to be so good master unto me, as to know my lord's grace's [the king's] pleasure in this case and that I may have a determined answer whereto I shall trust, that I may settle myself in quietness, the which I am far from at this hour. And farthermore if it might like you to make the offer to my said lord's grace of such a sum of money as we were at a point for, my friends thinketh that I should surely be at an end."

Soon afterwards she wrote again:

Sir, it is so that there is divers and many of my friends that hath written to me that I should make labour for the said house unto your mastership, showing you that the King's grace hath given it to master Harper, who saith that he is proffered for his favour two hundred marks of the King's saddler, for his sister; which proffer I will never make unto him, nor no friend for me shall, for the coming in after that fashion is neither godly nor worshipful And beside all this I must come by my lady Orell's favour, which is a woman I would least meddle with And thus I shall not only be burdened in conscience for payment of this great sum, but also entangled and in great cum-brance to satisfy the avidity of this gentlewoman And though I did, in my lord cardinal's days, proffer a hundred pounds for the said house, I beseech you consider for what purpose it was made. Your mastership knoweth right well that there was by my enemies so many high and slanderous words, and your mastership had made so great instant labour for me, that I shamed so much the fall thereof that

---

[1] See Brewer, *Reign of Henry VIII*, II, pp. 281–3.

I foresaw little what proffer was made; but now, I thank our Lord, that blast is ceased, and I have no such singular love unto it; for now I have two eyes to see in this matter clearly, the one is the eye of my soul, that I may come without burthen of conscience and by the right door, and, laying away all pomp and vanity of the world, looking warily upon the maintenance and supportation of the house, which I should take in charge, and cannot be performed, master Harper's pleasure and my lady Orell's accomplished. In consideration whereof I intend not willingly, nor no friend of mine shall not, trouble your mastership in this case.

In another letter she mentions a saying of Master Harper, that from the good report he has heard of her, he would rather admit her without a groat than others who offer money; but her conscientious scruples were not rewarded with St Helen's, though she almost immediately obtained an appointment as prioress at Little Marlow, and on the dissolution of that house among the lesser monasteries, received and held for a brief space the great Abbey of Malling[1]. It is true that these instances of simony and of the use of influence belong to the last degenerate years of the monasteries in England. But cases hardly less serious undoubtedly occurred at an early date The gross venality of the papal *curia*[2], even in the early thirteenth century, is not a very happy omen for the behaviour of private patrons; smaller folk than the Pope could summon a wretched abbot "Amice, ut offeras", nor was it only abbots who thus bought themselves into favour. The thirteenth century jurist Pierre Du Bois, whose enlightened plans for the better education of women included the suppression of the nunneries and the utilisation of their wealth to form schools or colleges for girls, mentioned the reception of nuns for money and rents, by means of compacts (i e. the dowry system) and the election of abbesses and prioresses by the same illicit bargains, as among the abuses practised in nunneries[3]

[1] See Wood, *op cit* II, nos xxi, xxii, pp 52–6 (See nos xxiii, xxiv, xxv, lxxiii and lxxiv for further letters from Margaret Vernon)

[2] See, for example, the account in the *St Albans Chronicles* (Rolls Series) of the great costs incurred by the Abbots of St Albans in seeking confirmation here A detailed account of expenses incurred at Rome for the confirmation of Abbot John IV in 1302 has been translated in Coulton, *Mediæval Garner*, p 517; the total was 2561 marks sterling, i e about £34,000 in modern money See also Froude's essay entitled "Annals of an English Abbey" in his *Short Studies on Great Subjects*, 3rd ser pp 1 *sqq*

[3] Pierre Du Bois, *De Recuperatione Terre Sancte*, ed. Ch -V Langlois (Paris, 1891), p 83.

Once having been installed, the head of a house held office
until she died, resigned or was deprived for incompetence or
for ill behaviour. Sometimes prioresses continued to hold office
until a very great age, as did Matilda de Flamstead, Prioress
of Sopwell, who died in 1430 aged eighty-one, having lived in
the rules of religion for over sixty years[1]. But the cases (quoted
below) of the prioresses of St Michael's Stamford and of Gracedieu prove that an aged and impotent head was bad for the
discipline of the house, and it appears that a prioress who was too
old or in too weak health to fulfil her arduous duties, was often
allowed to resign or was relieved of her office[2]. Sometimes an
ex-superior continued to live a communal life as an ordinary
nun, under her successor, but sometimes she was granted a
special room and a special allowance of food and attendance.
In some houses certain apartments were reserved for the occupation of a retired superior. Sir Thomas Willoughby, writing to
Cromwell on behalf of his sister-in-law, who had resigned her
office as Abbess of Malling, begs that she may

have your letter to my lady abbess of Malling (her successor), that
she at your contemplation will be so good to her as to appoint her
that room and lodging within the said monastery that she and other
of her predecessors that hath likewise resigned hath used to have,
and as she had herself a little space, or else some other meet and convenient lodging in the same house[3]

When Katherine Pilly, Prioress of Flixton, "who had laudably
ruled the house for eighteen years," resigned in 1432 because
of old age and blindness, the Bishop of Norwich made special
arrangements for her sustenance·

she was to have suitable rooms for herself and her maid; each week
she and the maid were to be provided with two white loaves, eight
loaves of "hool" bread and eight gallons of convent beer, with a daily
dish for both from the kitchen, the same as for two nuns in the refectory, and with two hundred faggots and a hundred logs and eight
pounds of candles a year. Cecilia Crayke, one of the nuns, was to

[1] Dugdale, *Mon.* III, p 363
[2] At the time of the suppression Joan Scott "late prioress" is placed
second in the list of nuns at Handâle and is described as "aet 90 and blynd "
V.C.H. Yorks III, p 166 At Esholt the ex-prioress was over 70 and is
described as "decrepita et non abilis ad equitandum, neque eundum "
Ib. p 162
[3] Wood, *op. cit* II, p. 153 See A H Thompson, *English Monasteries,*
p 123

read divine service to her daily and to sit with her at meals, having her portion from the refectory[1].

These aged ladies probably ended their days peacefully, withdrawn from the common life of the house. But sometimes a prioress resigned while still young enough to miss her erstwhile autocracy and to torment her unlucky successor. Then indeed the new head could do nothing right and feuds and factions tore the sisterhood. Such a case occurred at Nunkeeling early in the fourteenth century. Avice de la More resigned in 1316, and the Archbishop wrote to the nuns making the usual provision for her; she had "for a long period laudably and usefully superintended the house"; she was to have a chamber to herself and one of the nuns assigned to her by the Prioress as a companion; and daily she was to receive the portion of two nuns in bread, ale and victuals and her associate that of one nun; an end, one might suppose, of Avice de la More. But the Yorkshire nuns were quarrelsome ladies; and two years later the Archbishop addressed a severe letter to Avice, threatening to remove the provision made for her if she persisted in her "conspiracies, rebellions and disobedience to the prioress" and imposing a severe penance upon her. But seven penitential psalms with the litany upon Fridays, a discipline in chapter and fasting diet could not calm the temper of Avice de la More; she stirred up the nuns to rebellion and spread the tale of her grievances "to seculars and adversaries outside." There was some family feud perhaps between her relatives and the St Quintins to whose house the unhappy Prioress belonged; at any rate "clamorous

---

[1] *V.C.H. Suffolk*, II, p. 116. See also the provision made for Joyce Brome, ex-prioress of Wroxall. Dugdale, *Mon.* IV, p. 89 note. For the case of Isabel Spynys, prioress of Wilberfoss (1348), see *V.C.H. Yorks.* III, p. 126; and for an example of such an arrangement at a priory of monks see the very detailed ordinance for the living of John Assheby, ex-prior of Daventry, by Bishop Flemyng of Lincoln in 1420. *Linc. Visit.* I, pp. 39–42. It was not unusual to make provision in the form of corrodies such as these for other nuns, who were prevented by age and infirmity from taking part in the communal life of the convent. Isabel Warde of Moxby, "impotens et surda," held such a grant for life at the time of the dissolution (*V.C.H. Yorks.* III, p. 239) and Margaret de Shyrburn of Yedingham, who was ill of dropsy, had a secular girl to wait on her in 1314. *Ib.* p. 127 note. Compare the amusing case of Joan Heyronne of St Helen's, Bishopsgate (1385), who was ill of gout and not sympathised with by her sisters (*V.C.H. London*, I, p. 458), and see also cases at Romsey (1507), Liveing, *op. cit.* p. 230; Malling (1400), *Cal. of Pap. Letters*, V, p. 355; and St Mary's, Neasham, *V.C.H. Durham*, II, p. 107.

information" reached the Archbishop concerning the intrigues of certain of the nuns. Once more he wrote to Avice "with a bitter heart " She had broken her vow of obedience in arrogancy and elation of heart towards her prioress, "who was placed in charge of her soul and body and without whom she had no free will"; let her desist at once and study to live according to the rule; and a commission was sent to inquire into the misdeeds of the rebellious nuns of Keeling. But alas, the finding of that commission has long since powdered into dust and we hear no further news of Avice de la More[1].

The head of a house was an important person and enjoyed a considerable amount of freedom, in relation both to her convent and to the outside world. In relation to her convent her position laid her open to various temptations· she was, for instance, beset by three which must be faced by all who rule over communities. The first was the temptation to live with too great luxury and independence, escaping from the daily routine of communal life, to which her vows bound her. The second was the temptation to rule like an autocrat, instead of consulting her sisters. The third was the temptation to let human predilections have their way and to show favouritism. To begin with the first of these temptations, it is obvious that the fact that the superior nearly always had a separate room, or suite of rooms[2], and servants, and had the duty of entertaining important

---

[1] *V.C.H Yorks* III, pp 120–1 Compare an amusing and very similar disturbance at Flixton between 1514 and 1532 *Visit. of Dioc. Norwich,* ed. Jessopp (Camden Soc), pp 142–4, 185, 190, 261, 318

[2] The abbess's or prioress's chamber is constantly mentioned in the surveys of nunneries made at the time of the Dissolution, e g at Arthington, Wykeham, Basedale and Kirklees (*Yorks Archaeol Journ.* IX, pp 212 326, 327, 332); at Cheshunt (Cussans, *Hist of Herts, Hertford Hundred*, II, p 270), Sheppey (Mackenzie E C Walcott, *Inventories of St Mary's Hospital, Dover, etc* p 28), Kilburn (Dugdale, *Mon* III, p 424) See also the inventory of the goods of Langley in 1485 (Walcott, *Inventory of St Mary's Benedictine Nunnery at Langley* [Leic Architec Soc 1872], p 4) The last three contain interesting inventories of the furniture of the prioress's chamber At Sheppey it was hung with green "saye" and contained "a trussyng bed of waynscot with testar, sylar and cortens of red and yelow sarcenet", at Kilburn it was hung with "four peces of sey redde and grene, with a bordure of story," and contained "a standinge bedd with four posts of weynscott, a trundle bedd under the same a syller of yelowe and redde bokerame and three curteyns of the same work " At Langley also there were two beds in the prioress's chamber "hur owne bed " and "ye secunde bed in hur chambur." Clearly the prioress nearly always had a nun to sleep with her, and the evidence of visitations bears this out; see e g cases at Redlingfield,

guests, gave her much freedom within her house, especially if she were the head of one of the great abbeys. The Abbess of St Mary's Winchester, at the Dissolution, had her own house and a staff consisting of a cook, an undercook, a woman servant and a laundress, and she had also a gentlewoman to wait upon her, like any great lady in the world[1]. The Abbess of Barking had her gentlewoman, too, and her private kitchen; she dined in state with her nuns five times a year, and "the under celeresse must remember," says the *Charthe longynge to the Office of Celeresse,*

at eche principall fest, that my lady sytteth in the fraytour, that is to wyt five times in the yere, at eche tyme schall aske the clerke of the kychyn soper eggs for the covent, and that is Estir, Wytsontyd, the Assumption of our Lady, seynt Alburgh and Cristynmasse, at eche tyme to every lady two eggs, and eche double two egges, that is the priorisse, the celeresse and the kychener[2]

The stern reformer Peckham was forced to take in hand the conduct of the Abbesses of Barking, Wherwell and Romsey, who were abusing their independence of ordinary routine. The Abbess of Barking was forbidden to remain in her private room after sunset, at which hour all doors were to be locked and all strangers excluded, she might do so only very rarely, in order to entertain distinguished guests or to transact important business; and he ordered her to eat with the convent as often as possible, "especially on solemn days" (i.e. great feasts)[3]. The Abbess of Wherwell had apparently stinted her nuns in food and drink, but caused magnificent feasts to be prepared for her in her own room, and Peckham ordered that whenever there was a shortage of food in the convent, she was to dine with the nuns, and no meal was to be laid in her chamber for servants or strangers, but all visitors were to be entertained in the exterior guest-hall; if at such times she were in ill health, and unable to use the common diet, she might remain in her room, in the company of one or two of the nuns. At times when there was no lack of food in

1427 (*V C H Suffolk*, II, p 83), Littlemore, 1445 (*Linc Visit* II, p 217, "iacet de nocte in eodem lecto cum priorissa"), Flamstead, 1530 (*V C H Herts* IV, p 433). For the position of the prioress's chamber see plan of the nunnery buildings of St Radegund's, Cambridge (now Jesus College) (Gray, *Priory of St Radegund, Cambridge*, p 53).

[1] Dugdale, *Mon* II, p 458
[2] *Ib* I, pp. 443, 445
[3] *Reg. Epis. Johannis Peckham* (Rolls Series), I, p 84.

the convent and when she was entertaining guests in her own room, all potations were to cease and all servants and visitors to depart at the hour of compline[1] About the same time (1284) Peckham wrote two letters to the Abbess of Romsey, who had evidently been guilty of the same behaviour. She was not to keep "a number of" dogs or monkeys, or more than two maid servants, and she was not to fare splendidly in her own rooms while the nuns went short; his injunctions to her are couched in almost precisely the same language as those which he addressed to the Abbess of Wherwell[2].

According to the Benedictine rule the superior, when not entertaining guests, was permitted to invite the nuns in turn to dine with her in her own room, for their recreation, and notices of this custom sometimes occur in visitation reports, at Thicket (1309) the Prioress was enjoined to have them one by one when she dined in her room[3]; at Elstow (1421–2) the Abbess was to invite those nuns whom she knew to be specially in need of refreshment[4]; at Gracedieu (1440–1) the Prioress was ordered

that ye do the fraytour be keppede daylye...item that no mo of your susters entende up on yowe, save onely your chapeleyn, and otherwhile, as your rule wylle, ye calle to your refeccyone oon or two of your susters to thair recreacyone[5];

at Greenfield (1519) there was a complaint that the Prioress did not invite the nuns to her table in due order, and at Stainfield it was said that she frequently invited three young nuns to her table and showed partiality to them and she was ordered to invite all the senior sisters in order[6]. In Cistercian and Cluniac houses the superior was supposed to dine in the frater and to sleep in the dorter with the other nuns, and even in Benedictine houses it was considered desirable that she should do so. But the temptation to live a more private life was irresistible, and visitation records contain many complaints that the head of the house is lax in her attendance at dorter and frater and even in

[1] *Reg Epis Johannis Peckham*, II, pp 651–2.
[2] *Ib* II, pp. 659–60, 662–3 For another instance of a prioress faring better than her nuns, see Archbishop Lee's injunctions to Nunappleton in 1534: "That their be no difference betwene the breade and ale prepared for the prioresse and the bredde and ale provided for the covent, but that she and they eatt of oon breade, and drinke of oon drinke and of oon ale" *Yorks Archaeol Journ* XVI pp 443–4
[3] *V C H Yorks* III, p 214 [4] *Linc. Visit* I, p 50
[5] *Ib* II, p 124 [6] *V C H Lincs.* II, pp. 155, 131–2.

following the divine services in the choir[1]. Bishops frequently made injunctions like that given by Alnwick to the Prioress of Ankerwyke in 1441:

that nyghtly ye lygge in the dormytorye to ouersee your susters how thai are there gouernede after your rewle, and that often tyme ye come to matynes, messe and other houres .also that oftentymes ye come to the chapitere for to correcte the defautes of your susters . also that aftere your rewle ye kepe the fraytour but if resonable cause excuse yowe there fro[2]

Sometimes a minimum number of attendances was demanded. At St Michael's Stamford Alnwick ordered the old Prioress

that nyghtly ye lyg in the dormytorye emong your susters and that euery principale double fest and festes of xij or ix lessouns ye be at matynes, but if grete sekenes lette yowe, and that often tymes ye be at other howres and messes in the qwere, and also that ye be present in chapitres helpyng the supprioresse in correctyng and punisshyng of defautes[3].

It was further attempted to restrict the dangerous freedom of a superior's life, by ordering her always to have with her one of the nuns as a companion and as witness to her behaviour. So Peckham ordered the Abbess of Romsey to "elect a suitable companion for herself and to change her companions yearly, to the end that her honesty should be attested by many witnesses[4]'. Usually the nun whose duty it was to accompany the superior acted as her chaplain. It will be remembered that Chaucer says of his Prioress "another Nonne with hir hadde she, That was

[1] Sometimes, however, bishops licenced the head of a house to hear the service separately, e g in 1401 Wykeham licenced dame Lucy Everard, abbess of Romsey, to hear divine service in her oratory during one year, in the presence of one of her sisters and of her servants (familia) *Wykeham's Reg* (Hants Rec. Soc), II, p 538. Cf. similar licence to the prioress of Polsloe in 1388. *Reg. of Bishop Brantyngham of Exeter*, pt II, p 675

[2] *Linc Visit.* II, p. 8. The same injunction was sent to Stixwould *Alnwick's Visit.* MS f 75d.

[3] *Ib* f 83d. The next year when Alnwick came again this prioress announced that she did not lie in the dorter, nor keep frater, cloister and church on account of bodily weakness, she alleged that he had dispensed her from these observances, which he denied *Ib.* f. 39d Compare injunctions to Godstow, Gracedieu and Langley, *Linc Visit.* II, pp. 115, 125, 177 For other injunctions on these points, see *Alnwick's Visit.* MS f 78 (Nuncoton, 1440); *V.C.H. Yorks* III, pp 119 (Nunburnholme, 1318), 120 (Nunkeeling, 1314), 124 (Thicket, 1309), 188 (Arthington, 1318), 239 (Moxby, 1318).

[4] *Reg. Epis Johannis Peckham* (Rolls Series), II, p 662 Compare *V.C.H. Yorks* III, pp 113, 239 and *Alnwick's Visit.* MS. f 6

hir chapeleyne"[1], and episcopal registers contain frequent allusions to the office. William of Wykeham gave a comprehensive account of its purpose when he wrote to the Abbess of Romsey in 1387,

> since, according to the constitutions of the holy fathers, younger members must take a pattern from their rulers (*prelati*) and those prelates ought to have a number of witnesses to their own behaviour, we strictly order you (lady abbess) in virtue of obedience, that you annually commit the office of chaplain to one of your nuns...and thus the nuns themselves, who shall have been with you in the aforesaid office, shall (by means of laudable instruction) be the better enabled to excel in religion, while you will be able immediately to invoke their testimony to your innocence, if (which God forbid) any crime or scandal should be imputed to you by the malice of any person[2].

So at Easebourne in 1478 the Prioress was ordered

> that every week, beginning with the eldest ..she should select for herself in due course and in turns, one of her nuns as chaplain for divine services and to wait upon herself[3].

The Norwich visitations of Bishop Nykke afford further information; at Flixton discontented Dame Margaret Punder complained that the Prioress had no sister as chaplain, but slept alone as she pleased, in a chamber (*cubiculo*) outside the dorter, "without the continual testimony of her sisters," and the visitors enjoined

---

[1] Before it was realised that this office was often held by a woman in nunneries, scholars were much exercised to explain this passage in Chaucer's *Prologue*, though a search through Dugdale would have provided them with several instances. The office is still held in modern convents, and Dr Furnivall printed an interesting letter from a Benedictine nun, describing the duties attached to it. "It is in fact the nun who has special charge of attending on the Abbess and giving assistance when she needs it, either in writing when she (the Abbess) is busy, or in attending when sick, etc, but that which comes most often to claim her services is, on the twelve or fourteen great festivals," when the chaplain attends the Abbess in the choir and holds her crosier, while she reads the hymns, lesson, etc. *Anglia*, IV, pp 238–9. In the middle ages the chief stress was laid on the constant presence of a witness to the superior's mode of life, that it might be beyond suspicion. Miss Eckenstein has pointed out that in the allegory of the "Ghostly Abbey," by the béguine Mechthild of Magdeburg, in which the nuns are personified Virtues, Charity is Abbess and Meekness her Chaplain, and in the English version of the poem printed by Wynkyn de Worde (1500), Charity was Abbess and Mercy and Truth were to be her "chapeleyns" and to go about with her wherever she went. The Prioress (Wisdom) and the Sub-Prioress (Meekness) were also to have chaplains (Righteousness and Peace) because they were "most of worship." Eckenstein, *Woman under Monasticism*, pp 339, 377.

[2] *New College* MS, f. 88d

[3] *Sussex Archaeol Coll* IX, p. 15.

that henceforth she should have with her one sister in the office of chaplain for a witness, and especially when she slept outside the dorter[1]. At Blackborough one of the nuns complained that the Prioress had kept the same chaplain for three years[2] and at Redlingfield it was said that she never changed her chaplain[3]; the Abbess of Elstow in 1421-2[4] and the Prioress of Markyate in 1442[5] were ordered to change their chaplains every year, and this seems to have been the customary arrangement. The title of "chaplain" is sometimes found after the name of a nun in lists of the inmates of nunneries[6].

Besides the temptation to live too independent an existence the head of a house had also the temptation to abuse the considerable power given to her by the monastic rule. She was apt to govern autocratically, keeping the business of the house entirely in her own hands, instead of consulting her sisters (assembled in chapter) before making any important decision. There were constant complaints by the nuns that the Prioress kept the common seal in her own custody and performed all business without consulting them. Peckham's letter to the Abbess of Romsey illustrates the variety of matters which might thus be settled without any reference to the nuns; she had evidently been misusing her power, for he wrote sternly:

Know that thou art not mistress of the common goods, but rather the dispenser and mother of thy community, according to the meaning of the word abbess....We strictly command thee that thou study to transact all the more important business of the house with the convent. And by the more important business we intend those things which may entail notable expenditure in temporalities or in spiritualities, with which we wish to be included the provision of a steward; we order for the peace of the community, that H. de Chalfhunte, whom thou hast for long kept in the office of steward contrary to the will

---

[1] *Visit. of Dioc. of Norwich* (Camden Soc.), p. 190.

[2] *Ib.* p. 108.   [3] *Ib.* p. 138.

[4] *Linc. Visit.* I, p. 50. For other references to the abbess's nun-chaplain at Elstow, see *Archaeologia*, XLVII, p. 52 and Dugdale, *Mon.* III, p. 415.

[5] *Alnwick's Visit.* MS. f. 6. The Prioress was Denise Loweliche (see p. 458 below) and at the visitation Dame Margaret Loweliche *"cappellana priorisse"* (evidently a relative) said that she had held the office for the last eight years. Another nun said "that the Prioress ever holds and has held for seven years, one and the same nun as chaplain, without ever replacing her by another, and when she goes out she always has this young nun with her."

[6] E.g. at Campsey (1532) and Redlingfield (1526 and 1532). *Visit. of Dioc. of Norwich*, pp. 224, 291, 297. At Elstow (1539). Dugdale, *Mon.* III, p. 415. At Barking (still in receipt of pension in 1553). *Ib.* I, p. 438 note.

of the convent, no longer intermeddle in any way with this or with
any other bailiff's office (*bajulatu*) of the monastery Moreover we
make the same order concerning John le Frikiere. Let each of them,
having accounted for his office before Master Philip our official...look
out for an abode elsewhere Besides this thou shalt transact all minor
business of the church according to the rule with at least twelve of
the senior ladies. And because thou hast been wont to do much
according to the prompting of thine own will, we adjoin to thee three
coadjutresses of laudable testimony, to wit dames Margery de Ver-
dun, Philippa de Stokes and Johanna de Revedoune, without whose
counsel and attempt thou shalt not dare attempt anything pertaining
to the rule of the convent in temporalities or in spiritualities. And
whensoever thou shalt wittingly do the contrary in any important
matter, thou shalt know thyself to be on that account suspended from
the office of administration. And we mean by an important matter
the provision of bailiffs of the manors and internal obedientiaries,
the punishment of delinquents, all alienation of goods in gifts or
presents, or in any other ways, the sending forth of nuns and the
assignment of companions to those going forth, the beginning of
lawsuits and all manner of church business. And if it befall that any
of the aforesaid three be ill or absent, do thou receive in her stead
Dame Leticia de Montegomery or Dame Agnes de Lidyerd, having
called into consultation the others according to the number fixed
above And whenever thou shalt happen to fare forth upon the
business of the church, thou shalt always take with thee the aforesaid
three ladies, whom we have joined with thee as coadjutresses in the
rule of the monastery both within and without; and if ever thou goest
forth for recreation thou shalt always have with thee two, in such
wise that thou shalt in no manner concern thyself to pursue any
business without the three[1]

The danger of autocratic government to the convent is obvious; and it is significant that a really bad prioress is nearly
always charged with having failed to communicate with her
sisters in matters of business, turning all the revenues to any
use that she pleased Moreover the head of a house not only
sometimes failed to consult her convent; she constantly also
omitted to render an annual account of her expenditure, and by
far the most common complaint at visitations was the complaint
that the Prioress *non reddidit compotum*. At Bishop Nykke's
Norwich visitations the charge was made against the heads of
Flixton, Crabhouse, Blackborough and Redlingfield[2]. At Bishop

[1] *Litt. Johännis Peckham* (Rolls Series), II, pp. 658–9. Compare
injunctions to the Abbess of Chatteris in 1345. Dugdale, *Mon.* II, p. 619.
[2] *Visit of Dioc. of Norwich* (Camden Soc.), pp. 108, 109, 138–9, 143,
185, 190–1.

Alnwick's Lincoln visitations it was made against the heads of Ankerwyke, Catesby, Gracedieu, Harrold, Heynings, St Michael's Stamford, Stixwould, Studley; at Ankerwyke Dame Clemence Medforde had not accounted since her arrival at the house; at St Michael's Stamford the Prioress had held office for twelve years and had never done so; at Studley it was said that the last Prioress who ruled for 58 years never once rendered an account during the whole of that period, nor had the present Prioress yet done so, though she had been in office for a year[1]. Sometimes the delinquent gave some excuse to the Bishop; the Prioress of Catesby said she had no clerk to write the account[2], at Blackborough one of the nuns said that her object had been to avoid the expense of an auditor and another that she gave the convent a verbal report of the state of the house[3]. Sometimes she flatly refused, and the bishop's repeated injunctions on the subject seem to have been of little avail; the Prioress of Flixton had not rendered account since her installation *et dicit quod non vult reddere*; she was superseded, but six years later the same complaint was made against her successor and the visitors ordered the latter to amend her ways, *sub poena privationis, quia dixit se nolle talem reddere compotum*[4]. The bishops always inquired very carefully into the administration of the conventual income and possessions by the head of each house, and invented a variety of devices for controlling her actions[5].

There remains to be considered the third pitfall into which the head of a house was liable to fall. The wise Benedictine rule contained a special warning against favouritism, for indeed human nature cannot avoid preferences and it is the hardest task of a ruler to subdue personal predilections to perfect fairness The charge of favouritism is a fairly common one in medieval visitations. Alnwick met with an amusing case when he visited Gracedieu in 1440–1. The elder nuns complained the old prioress did not treat all equally; some of them she favoured and others she treated very rigorously; Dame Philippa Jecke even said that corrections were made so harshly and so fussily

---

[1] See *Linc. Visit* II, pp. 3, 48, 120, 130, 133; and *Alnwick's Visit.* MS. ff 83, 75d, 26d.
[2] *Linc. Visit.* II, p 49.
[3] *Visit. of Dioc. of Norwich*, p. 108.
[4] *Ib* pp. 143, 191.   [5] See below, p 216 ff.   ·

that all charity and all happiness had gone from the house. Moreover there were two young nuns whom she called her disciples and who were always with her; these nuns had many unsuitable conversations, so their sisters thought, with the Prioress' secular visitors, worse than this, they acted as spies upon the other nuns and told the Prioress about everything that was said and done in the convent, and then the Prioress scolded more severely than ever[1]; but her disciples could do no wrong. These nuns, indeed, were among the most voluble that Alnwick visited, and he must have remarked with a smile that the two disciples were the only ones who answered "Omnia bene"; but he did not intend to let them off without a rebuke.

"Agnes Poutrelle and Isabel Jurdane" runs the note in his Register, "who style themselves the Prioress's disciples, are thereby the cause of quarrel between her and her sisters, forasmuch as what they hear and see among the nuns they straightway retail to the prioress. They both appeared, and, the article having been laid to their charge, expressly deny it and all things that are contained therein; wherefore they cleared themselves without compurgators; howbeit, that they may not be held suspect hereafter touching these matters or offend herein, they both sware upon the holy gospels of God that henceforth they will discover to the prioress concerning their sisters nothing whereby cause of quarrel or incentive to hatred may be furnished among them, unless they be such matters as may tend to the damage of the prioress' body or honour"[2].

At two other houses there were complaints against the head; at Legbourne Dame Sibil Papelwyk said that the Prioress was not indifferent in making corrections, but treated some too hardly and others too favourably; and at Heynings Dame Alice Porter said that the Prioress was an accepter of persons in making corrections,

for those whom she loves she passes over lightly, and those whom she holds not in favour she harshly punishes...and she encourages her secular serving-women, whom she believes more than her sisters,

[1] Among "greuous defautes" enumerated in the "additions to the rules" of Syon Abbey (fifteenth century) is the following. "If any lye in a wayte, or in a spye, or els besyly and curyously serche what other sustres or brethren speke betwene themselfe, that they afterwardes may revele or schewe the saynge of the spekers to ther grete hurte"; others are, "if any sowe dyscorde amonge the sustres and brethren," and "if any be founde a preuy rowner or bakbyter" Aungier, *Hist. and Antiquities of Syon Monastery*, p. 257.
[2] *Linc. Visit.* II, pp. 121, 123.

in their words, to scold the same her sisters, and for this cause quarrels do spring up between her and her sisters[1]

In neither of these cases, however, was the charge corroborated by the evidence of the other nuns. Probably the two malcontents considered themselves to have a grievance against their ruler; at Legbourne Dame Sibil's complaint that the Prioress would not let her visit a dying parent gives a clue to her annoyance. Another charge sometimes made was that the Prioress gave more credence to the young nuns than to those who were older and wiser[2]. Injunctions that the head of a house was to show no favouritism were often made by visitors. One of Alnwick's injunctions may stand as representative:

Also we charge yow, prioress, vnder payn of contempte and vndere the peynes writen here benethe, that in your correccions ye be sad, sowbre and indifferent, not cruelle to some and to some fauoryng agayn your rule, but that ye procede and treet your susters moderly, the qualytee and the quantitee of the persons and defautes wythe owten accepcyone of any persone euenly considerede and weyed (Legbourne)[3].

So far the position of a superior has been considered solely from the point of view of internal government, of her power over the convent and of the peculiar temptations by which she was assailed. But the head of a house was an important person, not only in her own community, but also in the circumscribed little world without her gates; though here the degree of importance which she enjoyed naturally varied with the size and wealth of her house. In the middle ages fame and power were largely local matters; roads were bad and news moved slowly and a man might live no further away than the neighbouring town and be a foreigner The country gentry were not great travellers, occasionally they jaunted up to London, to court, or to parliament or to the law-courts, sometimes they followed the King and his lords to battles over sea or on the Scottish border; but for the most part they stayed at home and died in the bed wherein their mother bore them. The comfortable burgesses of the town travelled

---

[1] *Linc Visit* II, pp. 123, 185, 133.
[2] See e.g. *Visit of Dioc. of Norwich* (Camden Soc), pp 143, 290.
[3] *Linc Visit.* II, p 186 Compare *ib.* pp. 124, 135 (Gracedieu and Heynings); *Linc Epis Reg. Memo. Gynewell*, ff. 139–40 (Elstow, 1359); *Linc. Epis. Reg Memo Bokyngham*, ff. 343 (Elstow, 1387), 397 (Heynings, 1392), *V.C.H. Yorks*, III, pp. 117 (Moxby, 1252), 164 (Hampole, 1314).

still less; perhaps they betook themselves upon a pilgrimage, "clothed in a liveree of a solempne and greet fraternitee," and bearing a cook with them, lest they should lack the "chiknes with the marybones," the "poudre-marchant tart," the "galingale," the "mortreux," the "blankmanger" of their luxurious daily life; but they seldom had the Wife of Bath's acquaintance with strange streams. And the lesser folk—peasants and artisans—looked across the chequered expanse of the common fields at a horizon, which was in truth a barrier, an impassable line drawn round the edge of the world The fact that life was lived by the majority of men within such narrow limits gave a preeminent importance to the local magnate, and among the most local of local magnates (since a corporation never moved and never expired and never relaxed the grip of its dead fingers) must be reckoned the heads of the monastic houses Socially in all cases, and politically when their houses were large and rich, abbots and abbesses, priors and prioresses, ranked among the great folk of the country side. They enjoyed the same prestige as the lords of the neighbouring manors and some extra deference on account of their religion. It was natural that the Prioress of a nunnery should be "holden digne of reverence." The gentlemen whose estates adjoined her own sent their daughters to her as novices, or (if her house were poor and the Bishop not too strict) as school girls to receive their "nortelrye"; and they did not themselves scorn the discreet entertainment of her guest-chamber and a dinner of capons and wine and gossip at her hospitable board. The artisans and labourers on her land lived by her patronage. All along the muddy highroads the beggars coming to town passed word to each other that there stood a nunnery in the meadows, where they might have scraps left over from the convent meals and perhaps beer and a pair of shoes. The head of a house, indeed, was an important person from many points of view, as a neighbour, as a landlord and as a philanthropist.

The journeys which a prioress was sometimes obliged to take upon the business of the convent offered many occasions of social intercourse with her neighbours. It is, indeed, striking how great a freedom of movement was enjoyed by these cloistered women. There are constant references to journeys in account rolls. When Dame Christian Bassett, Prioress of St Mary de Pré, rode to

London for the suit against her predecessor in the Common
Pleas, she was accompanied on one occasion by her priest, a
woman and two men, on two other occasions she took four men;
and during the whole time that the suit dragged on, she was
continually riding about to take counsel with great men or with
lawyers and journeying to and fro between St Albans and London.
On another occasion the account notes a payment

in expenses for the prioresse and the steward with their servants and
for hors hyre and for the wages of them that wente to kepe the
courte wyth the prioresse atte Wynge atte two tymes xvjs vd,
whereof the stewards fee was that of vjs vujd; item paid to the
fermour of Wynge for his expenss ixd[1].

The accounts of St Michael's Stamford are full of items such as
"in the expenses of the Prioress on divers occasions going to the
Bishop, with hire of horses 3s." "in the expenses of the Prioress
going to Rockingham about our woods 1s 2½d ," "paid for the hire
of two horses for the prioress and her expenses going to Liddington
to the Bishop for a certificate 2s. 8d.," "paid for the expenses
of the Prioress at Burgh (i.e. Peterborough) for two days 5s. 8d.";
twice the Prioress went very far afield, as usual (it would appear)
on legal business, for in 1377–8 there is an entry, "Item for
the expenses of the Prioress and her companions at London for
a month and more, in all expenses £5. 13s. 4d." (a large sum, a
long distance and a lengthy stay), and in 1409–10 there is
another payment "to the Prioress for expenses in London 15s."[2]

In spite of repeated efforts to enforce stricter enclosure upon
nuns, it is evident that the head of the house rode about on the
business of the convent and overlooked its husbandry in person,
even where (as at St Michael's Stamford) there was a male prior
or *custos* charged with the ordering of its temporal affairs. The
general injunction that an abbess was never to leave her house
save "for the obvious utility of the monastery or for urgent

---

[1] Dugdale, *Mon* III, pp. 359–60. There are various other references to
"Wynge" (i e. Wing in Buckinghamshire) in the account, e g. "Item
receyvid of Richard Saie for the ferme of the personage of Wynge for a yere
and a half within the tyme of this accompte xlvuj*li*. Item. rec. of the same
Richard Saie as in party of payment of the same ferme for a quarter of a yere
x*s*," "item, paid to the bisshop of Lincolns officers for the licens of Wynge
for 1j yere xxijs vujd Item paid to the ffermour of Wynge for his goune for
1j yere xiijs iiijd." For the London lawsuit see below, p. 202.

[2] See *P.R.O. Mins. Accts* 1260, *passim*. The London references are in
1260/7 and 1260/17 respectively.

necessity"[1] was capable of a very wide interpretation, and it is clear from the evidence of visitations and accounts that it was interpreted to include a great deal of temporal business outside the walls If a house possessed a male *custos* the Prioress would have less occasion and less excuse for journeys, though for important affairs her presence was probably always necessary; Bishop Drokensford, appointing a *custos* to Minchin Barrow, warns the Prioress no longer "to intermeddle with rural business (*negociis campestribus*) and other secular affairs" but to leave these to the *custos* and to devote herself to the service of God and to the stricter enforcement of the rule[2]. But in houses where no such official existed the prioress doubtless undertook a certain amount of general estate management. One of Alnwick's orders to the Prioress of Legbourne in 1440 was "that ye bysylly ouersee your baylly, that your husbandry be sufficyently gouernede to the avayle of your house"[3]; and in the intervals of their long struggle to keep nuns within their cloisters, the Bishops seem to have recognised the necessity for some travel on the part of the heads of houses, and to have facilitated such travel by granting them dispensations to have divine service celebrated wherever they might be Thus in 1400 the Prioress of Haliwell obtained a licence to hear divine service in her oratory within her mansion of Camberwell, or elsewhere in the diocese, during the next two years[4], and in 1406 the Abbess of Tarrant Keynes was similarly allowed to have the service celebrated for herself and her household anywhere within the city and diocese of Salisbury[5].

It is significant that among the arguments used to oppose Henry VIII's injunction that monks and nuns should be strictly enclosed (which was, for the nuns, only a repetition of Pope Boniface's decree of three centuries earlier) was that of the

---

[1] Constitutions of the legate Ottobon in 1268. Wilkins, *Concilia*, II, p. 18.

[2] Hugo, *Medieval Nunneries of the County of Somerset*, Minchin Barrow, p. 81

[3] *Linc. Visit* II, p 187.

[4] *Wykeham's Reg.* (Hants Rec. Soc.), p. 500.

[5] *V C.H. Dorset*, II, p. 89. In 1374 the Abbess of Canonsleigh had licence to have divine service celebrated in her presence in the chapel of St Theobald in the parish of Burlescombe "dicto monasterio contigua," but her nuns were not to leave the claustral precincts on this pretext. *Reg. of Bishop Brantyngham*, ed. Hingeston-Randolph, pt I, p. 335.

difficulty of supervising the husbandry of a house, if its head
were confined to cloistral precincts

"Please it you to be advertised," wrote Cecily Bodenham, the last
Abbess of Wilton, to Cromwell in 1535, "that master doctor Leigh,
the King's grace's special visitor and your deputy in this behalf,
visiting of late my house, hath given injunction that not only all my
sisters, but I also, should continually keep and abide within the
precincts of my house which commandment I am right well content
with in regard of my own person, if your mastership shall think it so
expedient; but in consideration of the administration of mine office
and specially of this poor house which is in great debt and requireth
much reparation and also which without good husbandry is not like,
in long season, to come forward, and in consideration that the said
husbandry cannot be, by my poor judgment, so well by an other
overseen as by mine own person, it may please your mastership of
your goodness to license me, being associate with one or two of the
sad and discreet sisters of my house, to supervise abroad such things
as shall be for the profit and commodity of my house Which thing
though, peradventure, might be done by other, yet I ensure you that
none will do it so faithfully for my house's profit as mine own self
Assuring your mastership that it is not, nor shall be at any time
hereafter, my mind to lie forth of my monastery any night, except
by inevitable necessity I cannot then return home "[1].

It is, however, very plain that the journeys taken by abbesses
and prioresses were not always strictly concerned with the business of their convents, or at least they combined business most
adroitly with pleasure. These ladies were of good kin and they
took their place naturally in local society, when they left their
houses to oversee their husbandry, to interview a bishop or a
lawyer about their tithes, or quite openly to visit friends and
relatives They emerged to attend the funerals of great folk;
the Prioress of Carrow attended the funeral of John Paston in
1466[2], and Sir Thomas Cumberworth in his will (1451) left the
injunction:

I will that Ilke prior and priores that comes to my beryall at y^t day
hafe iiis iiij*d* and ilke chanon and Nune xij*d* ..and Ilke prior and
priores that comes to the xxx day (the month's-mind) hafe vjs viij*d*
and Ilke chanon or none that comes to the said xxx day haf xx*d*[3]

---

[1] Wood, *op. cit* II, pp 156–7. Even Ap Rice seems to have considered
Dr Legh's enforcement of enclosure as overstrict "for as many of these
houses stand by husbandry they must fall to decay if the heads are not
allowed to go out." Gairdner, *Letters and Papers, etc* IX, no. 139; cf preface,
p. 20   [2] Rye, *Carrow Abbey*, p 8.
    [3] *Linc Dioc. Documents*, ed A. Clark (E E T.S), pp 50, 53.

Sometimes they attended the deathbeds of relatives; among witnesses to the codicil to the will of Walter Skirlaw, Bishop of Durham, in 1404 was "religiosa femina Domina Johanna Priorissa de Swyna, soror dicti domini episcopi "[1]; and it was not unusual for an abbess or prioress to be made supervisor or executrix of a will[2]. Nor was the sad business of deathbeds the only share taken by these prioresses in public life. Clemence Medforde, Prioress of Ankerwyke, went to a wedding at Bromhale; and unfortunately a sheepfold, a dairy and a good timber granary chose that moment to catch fire and burn down, setting fire also to the smouldering indignation of her nuns; whence many recriminations when the Bishop came on his rounds[3] Stranger still at times were the matters for which their friends sought their good offices The aristocratic Isabel de Montfort, Prioress of Easebourne, was one of the ladies by whose oath Margaret de Camoys purged herself on a charge of adultery in 1295[4].

The fact that these ladies were drawn from the wealthy classes and constantly associated on terms of equality with their friends and relatives, sometimes led them to impart a most un-monastic luxury into their own lives. They came from the homes of lords like Sir John Arundel, who lost not only his life but "two and fiftie new sutes of apparell of cloth of gold or tissue,"

---

[1] *Test. Ebor* I, p 314

[2] For instance Margaret Fairfax of Nunmonkton was one of the *super-visores testamenti* of John Fairfax, rector of Prescot, in 1393 and of Thomas Fairfax of Walton in 1394. *Ib.* I, pp. 190, 204. The abbess of Syon was one of the three overseers of the will of Sir Richard Sutton, steward of her house in 1524. Aungier, *Hist. and Antiquities of Syon Mon.* p. 532. Emmota Fare-thorpe, Prioress of Wilberfoss, was executrix of John Appilby of Wilberfoss in 1438. *V.C.H. Yorks.* III, p. 126 note. Margaret Delaryver, Prioress of St Clement's York, was executrix of Elizabeth Medlay (probably a boarder there). *Ib* III, p 130 Joan Kay in 1525 left most of her property to her daughter the Prioress of Stixwould to found an obit there and made her executrix. *Linc. Wills,* ed. C W. Foster (Linc. Rec. Soc.), I, p 155 Sir John Beke, vicar of Aby, who left the greater part of his property to Greenfield for the same purpose, made the Prioress Isabel Smith executrix. *Ib* I, p 162. These offices were sometimes filled by nuns other than heads of houses, e g. the will of John Suthwell, rector of St Mary's South Kelsey, Lincs , was witnessed by his sister Margaret, a nun, in 1390 Gibbons, *Early Linc. Wills,* p. 76 Alice Conyers of Nunappleton was made coadjutress of the executors of Master John de Woodhouse in 1345 *Test. Ebor.* I, p. 15 For Carrow nuns (usually the prioress) as executors, supervisors and witnesses, see Rye, *Carrow Abbey,* pp. xv, xvi, xxii, xxiii, xxix.

[3] *Linc. Visit* II, p. 2.

[4] *V.C.H. Sussex,* II, p 84 See *Rot. Parl.* I, p. 147.

when he was drowned off the Irish coast; or Lord Berkeley who
travelled with a retinue of twelve knights, twenty-four esquires
"of noble family and descent" and a hundred and fifty men-at-
arms, in coats of white frieze lined with crimson and embroidered
with his badge, or else of country squires and franklins, like
the white-bearded gentleman of whom Chaucer says that

> To liven in delyt was ever his wone,
> For he was Epicurus owne sone,
>
> .   .   .   .   .   .
>
> Withoute bake mete was never his hous,
> Of fish and flesh, and that so plentevous
> It snewed in his hous of mete and drinke,
> Of alle deyntees that men coude thinke,

or else their fathers were wealthy merchants, living in great
mansions hung with arras and lighted with glass windows, rich
enough to provoke sumptuary laws and to entertain kings   It
is perhaps not surprising that abbesses and prioresses should
have found it hard to change the way of life, which they had
led before they took the veil and which they saw all around
them, when they rode about in the world. Carousings, gay
garments, pet animals, frivolous amusements, many guests,
superfluous servants and frequent escapes to the freedom of the
road, are found not only at the greater houses but even at those
which were small and poor. The diverting history of the flea and
the gout shows that the luxurious abbess was already a byword
early in the thirteenth century.

The tale runs as follows:

The lopp (flea) and the gout on a time spake together, and among
other talking either of them asked [the] other of their lodging and
how they were harboured and where, the night next before   And the
flea made a great plaint and said, "I was harboured in the bed of an
abbess, betwixt the white sheets upon a soft mattress and there
I trowed to have had good harbourage, for her flesh was fat and
tender, and thereof I trowed to have had my fill. And first, when
I began for to bite her, she began to cry and call on her maidens and
when they came, anon they lighted candles and sought me, but I hid
me till they were gone   And then I bit her again and she came again
and sought me with a light, so that I was fain to leap out of the bed;
and all this night I had no rest, but was chased and chevied ['charrid']
and scarce gat away with my life." Then answered the gout and said,
"I was harboured in a poor woman's house and anon as I pricked her
in her great toe she rose and wetted a great bowl full of clothes and

went with them unto the water and stood therein with me up to her knees, so that, what for cold and for holding in the water, I was near-hand slain " And then the flea said, "This night will we change our harbourage"; and so they did. And on the morn they met again and then the flea said unto the gout, "This night have I had good har-bourage, for the woman that was thine host yesternight was so weary and so irked, that I was sickerly harboured with her and ate of her blood as mickle as I would " And then answered the gout and said unto the flea· "Thou gavest me good counsel yestereven, for the abbess underneath a gay coverlet, and a soft sheet and a delicate, covered me and nourished me all night And as soon as I pricked her in her great toe, she wrapped me in furs, and if I hurt her never so ill she let me alone and laid me in the softest part of the bed and troubled me nothing. And therefore as long as she lives I will be harboured with her, for she makes mickle of me " And then said the flea, " I will be harboured with poor folk as long as I live, for there may I be in good rest and eat my full and nobody let [hinder] me "[1]

The Durham man, William of Stanton, who went down St Patrick's hole on September 20th, 1409, and was shown the souls in torment there, has much the same tale to tell. He witnessed the trial of a prioress, whose soul had come there for judgment, and

the fendis accusid hir and said that she come to religion for pompe and pride and for to have habundaunce of the worldes riches, and for ese of hir bodi and not for deuocion, mekenesse and lowenesse, as religious men and women owte to do; and the fendes said, "It is wel knowen to god and to al his angels of heven and to men dwellyng in that contree where she dwellid ynne, and all the fendes of hell, that she was more cosluer (sic) in puler [fur] weryng, as of girdelles of siluer and ouergilt and ringes on hir fingers, and siluer bokeles and ouergilt on hir shone, esy lieng in nyghtes as it were [a quene] or an emprise in the world, not daynyng hir for to arise to goddis servis[2]; and with all delicate metes and drinkes she was fedde ..and then the bisshop [her judge] enioyned hir to payne enduryng evermore til the day of dome "[3]

Our visitation documents show us many abbesses and prior-esses like the gout's hostess or the tormented lady in St Patrick's

[1] An Alphabet of Tales, ed. M. M Banks (E.E T.S., 1904), no. xv, pp. 13–14. I have modernised spelling This fifteenth century English version is ultimately derived from an exemplum by Jacques de Vitry, of which it is a close translation. Exempla e sermonibus vulgaribus J Vitria-censis, ed. T F. Crane, no. LIX, pp. 23–4.

[2] "Item Priorissa raro venit ad matutinas aut missas Domina Kater-ina Hoghe dicit quod quedam moniales sunt quodammodo sompnolentes, tarde veniendo ad matutinas et alias horas canonicas " Linc.Visit II, p 133.

[3] J. P. Krapp, The Legend of St Patrick's Purgatory, its later Literary History (1899), pp. 75–6.

Purgatory. In the matter of dress the accusations brought against Clemence Medforde, Prioress of Ankerwyke, in 1441, will suffice for an example:

> The Prioress wears golden rings exceeding costly with divers precious stones and also girdles silvered and gilded over and silken veils, and she carries her veil too high above her forehead, so that her forehead, being entirely uncovered, can be seen of all, and she wears furs of vair....Also she wears shifts of cloth of Reynes which costs sixteen pence the ell....Also she wears kirtles laced with silk and tiring pins of silver and silver gilt and has made all the nuns wear the like.... Also she wears above her veil a cap of estate furred with budge. Item she has round her neck a long cord of silk, hanging below her breast and on it a gold ring with one diamond.

She confessed all except the cloth of Rennes, which she totally denied, but pleaded that she wore fur caps "because of divers infirmities in the head." Alnwick made an injunction carefully particularising all these sins:

> And also that none of yow, the prioresse ne none of the couente, were no vayles of sylke ne no sylucre pynnes ne no gyrdles herneysed with syluere or golde, ne no mo rynges on your fyngres then oon, ye that be professed by a bysshope, ne that none of yow vse no lased kyrtels, but butoned or hole be fore, ne that ye vse no lases a bowte your nekkes wythe crucyfixes or rynges hangyng by thame, ne cappes of astate abowe your vayles...and that ye so atyre your hedes that your vayles come downe nyghe to your yene[1].

If anyone doubts the truth of Chaucer's portrait of a prioress, or its satirical intent, he has only to read that incomparable observer's words side by side with this injunction of Alnwick:

> But sikerly she hadde a fair forheed;
> It was almost a spanne brood, I trowe;
> For, hardily, she was nat undergrowe.
> Ful fetis was her cloke, as I was war.
> Of smale coral aboute hir arm she bar
> A peire of bedes, gauded al with grene;
> And ther-on heng a broche of gold ful shene,
> On which ther was first write a crowned A
> And after, *Amor vincit omnia.*

Margaret Fairfax of Nunmonkton (1397) and the lady (her name is unknown) who ruled Easebourne in 1441 are other

---

[1] *Linc. Visit.* II, pp. 3, 4, 5, 8. The Prioress of Brewood White Ladies in Shropshire was severely rebuked in the first part of the fourteenth century for *expensae voluptuariae*, dress and laxity of rule. *Reg. of Roger de Norbury* (Will. Salt Archaeol. Soc. Collections, I), p. 261.

examples of worldly prioresses; they clearly regarded themselves
as the great ladies they were by birth, and behaved like all the
other great ladies of the neighbourhood. Margaret Fairfax used
divers furs, including even the costly grey fur (gris)—the same
with which the sleeves of Chaucer's monk were "purfiled at the
hond"; she wore silken veils and "she frequently kept company
with John Munkton and invited him to feasts in her room...and
John Munkton (by whom the convent had for long been scandalised) frequently played at tables" (the fashionable game for
ladies, a kind of backgammon) "with the Prioress in her room
and served her with drink." No wonder she had to sell timber in
order to procure money[1]. The Prioress of Easebourne was even
more frivolous; the nuns complained that the house was in debt
to the amount of £40 and this principally owing to her costly
expenses:

because she frequently rides abroad and pretends that she does so
on the common business of the house, although it is not so, with a
train of attendants much too large, and tarries long abroad, and she
feasts sumptuously both when abroad and at home, and she is very
choice in her dress, so that the fur trimmings of her mantle are worth
a hundred shillings,

as great a scandal as Clemence Medforde's cloth of Rennes at
sixteen pence the ell. The Bishop took strong measures to deal
with this worldly lady; she was deposed from all administration
of the temporal goods of the priory, which administration was
committed to "Master Thomas Boleyn and John Lylis, Esquire,
until and so long as when the aforesaid house or priory shall be
freed from debt." It was also ordered

that the Prioress with all possible speed shall diminish her excessive
household and shall only retain, by the advice and with the assent
of the said John and Thomas, a household such as is merely necessary
and not more. Also that the Prioress shall convert the fur trimmings,
superfluous to her condition and very costly, to the discharge of the
debts of the house. Also that if eventually it shall seem expedient
to the said Masters Thomas and John at any time, that the Prioress
should ride in person for the common business of the house, on such
occasions she shall not make a lengthened stay abroad, nor shall she
in the interval incur expenses in any way costly beyond what is
needful, and thus when despatched to go abroad she must and ought
rightly to content herself with four horses only;

[1] Dugdale, *Mon.* IV, p. 194.

and those perhaps "bothe foul and lene," like the jade ridden
by the Nonnes Preeste when Chaucer met him on the Canterbury
road[1].

The charge of gadding about the country side, sometimes (as
in the Prioress of Easebourne's case) with a retinue which better
beseemed the worldly rank they had abjured, was one not infrequently made against the heads of nunneries[2]. The Prioress
of Stixwould was accused, in 1519, of spending the night too
often outside the cloister with her secular friends and the Bishop
ordered that in future she should sleep within the monastery,
but might keep a private house in the precincts, for her greater
refreshment and for receiving visitors[3]. The Prioress of Wroxall
was ordered to stay more at home in 1323[4], and in 1303 Bishop
Dalderby even found that the Prioress of Greenfield had been
absent from her house for two years[5]. Even more frequent was
the charge that abbesses and prioresses repaid too lavishly the
hospitality which they doubtless received at neighbouring manors
Many abbesses gave that "dyscrete enterteynement," which
Henry VIII's commissioners so much admired at Catesby[6]; but
others entertained too often and too well, in the opinion of their
nuns; moreover family affection sometimes led them to make
provision for their kinsfolk at the cost of the house. In 1441
one of the nuns of Legbourne deposed that many kinsmen of

[1] *Sussex Archaeol Coll* IX, pp. 7–9

[2] Compare the anecdote related by Caesarius of Heisterbach about
Ensfrid of Cologne. "One day he met the abbess of the holy Eleven Thousand Virgins, before her went her clerks, wrapped in mantles of grey fur
like the nuns; behind her went her ladies and maidservants, filling the air
with the sound of their unprofitable words; while the Dean was followed by
his poor folk who besought him for alms. Wherefore this righteous man,
burning with the zeal of discipline, cried aloud in the hearing of all: 'Oh,
lady Abbess, it would better adorn your religion, that ye, like me, should be
followed, not by buffoons, but by poor folk!' Whereat she was much
ashamed, not presuming to answer so worthy a man." Translated in Coulton,
A Medieval Garner, p. 251.

[3] *V.C.H Lincs.* II, p. 148   [4] *V C H Warwick*, II, p. 71.

[5] *V C H Lincs.* II, p. 155. Sometimes, however, the heads of houses
received episcopal dispensations to reside for a period outside their monasteries, for the sake of health. Joan Formage, Abbess of Shaftesbury, received one in 1368, allowing her to leave her abbey for a year and to reside
in her manors for air and recreation. *V.C.H. Dorset*, II, p. 78. Josiana de
Anlaby (the Prioress of Swine about whose election there had been so much
trouble) had licence in 1303 to absent herself on account of ill-health.
Dugdale, *Mon* V, p 493

[6] Dugdale, *Mon.* IV, p 638.

the prioress had frequent access to the house, though she did not know whether it was financially burdened by their visits; Alnwick ordered

that ye susteyn none of your kynne or allyaunce wythe the commune godes of the house, wythe owten the hole assent of the more hole parte of the couent, ne that ye suffre your saide kynne or allyaunce hafe suche accesse to your place, where thurghe the howse shall be chargeede[1]

A similar injunction had been made at Chatteris in 1345, where the abbess was warned not to bestow the convent rents and goods unlawfully upon any of her relatives[2]. The charge was, however, most common in later times, when discipline was in all ways relaxed. At Easebourne in 1478 one of the nuns complained "that kinsmen of the prioress very often and for weeks at a time frequent the priory and have many banquets of the best food, while the sisters have them of the worst"[3]. The neighbouring nunnery of Rusper was said in 1521 to be ruinous and "greatly burdened by reason of friends and kinsmen of the lady prioress who continually received hospitality there"[4], at Studley in 1520 there were complaints that the brother of the prioress and his wife stayed within the monastery, and ten years later it was ordered that no corrody should be given to the prioress' mother, until more was known of her way of life[5]. At Flixton in the same year one of the nuns asserted that the mother of the prioress had her food at the expense of the house, but whether she paid anything or not was unknown; it appears, however, that she was in charge of the dairy, so that she may have been boarded in return for her services. A characteristic instance is preserved in Bishop Longland's letter to the Prioress of Nuncoton in 1531, charging her

that frome hensforth ye do nomore burden ne chardge your house with suche a nombre of your kinnesfolks as ye haue in tymes past used   Your good mother it is meate ye haue aboute yow for your comforte and hirs bothe   And oon or ij moo of suche your saddest kynnes folke, whome ye shall thynk mooste conuenyent but passe not... And that ye give nemore soo lyberally the goods of your monastery as ye haue doon to your brother george thomson and your brodres children, with grasing of catell, occupying your lands,

---

[1] *Linc. Visit.* II, p. 187.   [2] Dugdale, *Mon* II, p. 619.
[3] *Sussex Archaeol. Coll.* IX, pp. 18–19.
[4] *Ib.* V, p. 256.   [5] *V.C H. Oxon.* II, p. 78.

making of Irneworke to pleugh, and carte, and other like of your stuff and in your forge[1].

Much information about the conduct of abbesses and prioresses may be obtained from a study of episcopal registers, and in particular of visitation documents. An analysis of Bishop Alnwick's visitations of the diocese of Lincoln (1436–49) gives interesting results. In all but four houses there were few or no complaints against the head Sometimes it was said that she failed to dine in the frater or to sleep in the dorter, sometimes that she was a poor financier, and in two cases the charge of favouritism was made, but the complaints at these sixteen houses were, on the whole, insignificant. The four remaining heads were unsatisfactory. The Prioress of St Michael's Stamford was so incompetent (owing to bodily weakness) that she took little part in the common life of the house and regularly stayed away from the choir, dined and slept by herself, though the Bishop refused to give her a dispensation to do so. The administration of the temporalities of the house was committed by Alnwick to two of the nuns, but when he came back two years later one of these had had a child and the other was unpopular on account of her autocratic behaviour. The moral condition of the house (one nun was in apostasy with a man in 1440, and in 1442 and 1445 two nuns were found to have borne children) must in part be set down to the lack of a competent head[2]. The Prioress of Gracedieu was also old and incompetent, her subprioress deposed that

by reason of old age and incapacity the prioress has renounced for herself all governance of matters temporal, nor does she take part in divine service, so that she is of no use; but if she makes any corrections, she makes them with words of chiding and abuse . She makes the secrets of their religious life common among the secular folk that sit at table with her. .and under her religious discipline almost altogether is at an end.

Other nuns gave similar evidence and all complained of her favouritism for two young nuns, whom she called her disciples Here, as at St Michael's Stamford, the autocratic behaviour of the nun who was in charge of the temporalities had aroused the resentment of her sisters and the whole convent was evidently seething with quarrels[3] The Prioress of Ankerwyke, Clemence

---

[1] *Archaeologia*, XLVIII, pp 56, 58.
[2] *Alnwick's Visit.* MS. ff. 83 and d, 39d, 96.
[3] *Linc. Visit.* II, pp. 120, 121.

Medforde, was equally unpopular with her nuns. The ringleader
against her was a certain Dame Margery Kirkby, who poured
out a flood of complaints when Alnwick came to the house.
The chief charge against her was that of financial mismanagement. She was obliged to admit that she received, paid
and administered everything without consulting the convent,
keeping the common seal in her own custody all the year round
and never rendering account. She was also said to have allowed
the sheepfold, dairy and granary to be burned down owing to
her carelessness, one result of which was that all the grain had
to stand in the church. She had alienated the plate and psalters
of the house, having lent three of the latter and pawned a
chalice; another chalice and a thurible had been broken up to
make a drinking cup, but, as she had been unable to pay the
sum demanded, the pieces remained in the hands of a monk,
who had undertaken to get the work done. She was charged
with having alienated timber in large quantities and with having
cut down trees at the wrong time of year, so that no new wood
grew again, but she denied this accusation. Another charge
made against her by Margery Kirkby, that of wearing jewels and
rich clothes, has already been described; she admitted it and
the fault was the more grave in that she omitted to provide
suitable clothes for the nuns, who went about in rags. It was
also complained that she behaved with undue severity to her
sisters, she made difficulties about giving them licence to see
their friends; and she had a most trying habit of coming late
to the services, and then making the nuns begin all over again.
It is obvious that she was greatly disliked by the convent, perhaps because she was a stranger in their midst, having been
imported from Bromhale to be Prioress, she evidently sought
relief from the black looks of her sisters by visiting her old home;
for she was away at a wedding in Bromhale when the farm
buildings caught fire, and one of the missing psalters had been
lent to the prioress of that place. Her *régime* at Ankerwyke
had been fraught with ill results to the convent, for no less
than six nuns had (without her knowledge, so she said) gone
into apostasy; perhaps to escape from her too rigorous sway.
Nevertheless one cannot help feeling that Margery Kirkby may
have been a difficult person to live with; the Prioress complained

that the nuns were often very easily moved against her and that Dame Margery had called her a thief to her face; and though it may have been conducive to economy that the triumphant accuser (elected by the convent) should share with the Prioress the custody of the common seal, it can hardly have been conducive to harmony[1]. At any rate poor luxury-loving Clemence died in the following year and Margery Kirkby ruled in her stead[2].

But the most serious misdemeanours of all were brought to light when Alnwick visited Catesby in 1442[3]. Here the bad example of the Prioress, Margaret Wavere, seems to have contaminated the nuns, for all of them were in constant communication with seculars and one of them had given birth to a child. The Prioress' complaint that she dared not punish this offender is easily intelligible in the light of her own evil life. The most serious charge against her was that she was unduly intimate with a priest named William Taylour, who constantly visited the nunnery and with whom she had been accustomed to go into the gardens in the village of Catesby; and one of the younger nuns had surprised the two *in flagrante delicto*. She was a woman of violent temper; two nuns deposed that when she was moved to anger against any of them she would tear off their veils and drag them about by the hair, calling them beggars and harlots[4], and this in the very choir of the church, if they committed any fault she scolded and upbraided them and would not cease before seculars or during divine service; "she is very cruel and severe to the nuns and loves them not," said one; "she is so harsh and impetuous that there is no pleasing her," sighed another; "she sows discord among the sisters," complained a third, "saying so-and-so said such-and-such a thing about thee, if the one to whom she speaks has transgressed." More serious still, from the visitor's point of view, were the threats by which she sought to prevent the nuns from revealing any-

---

[1] *Linc. Visit* II, pp. 2–4, 6.
[2] *Cal of Pat Rolls* (1441–6), p. 141.   [3] *Linc. Visit.* II, pp. 46–52.
[4] Compare the complaint of the sisters of the hospital of St James outside Canterbury in 1511, that the Prioress was a *diffamatrix* of the sisters and used to say publicly in the neighbourhood that they were incontinent *et publice meretrices*, to the great scandal of the house. The ages of the sisters were 84, 80, 50 and 36 respectively and the Prioress herself was 74. *Eng. Hist. Rev.* VI, p. 23.

thing at the visitation; two of them declared that she had beaten
and imprisoned those who gave evidence when Bishop Gray
came to the house, and sister Isabel Benet whispered that
the Prioress had boasted of having bribed the bishop's clerk
with a purse of money, to reveal everything that the nuns
had said on that occasion. Her practice of compelling the
nuns to perform manual labour was greatly resented—why
should they

> Swinken with hir handes and laboure
> As Austin bit? How shal the world be served?
> Lat Austin have his swink to him reserved.

It appeared, however, that they were anxious to

> studie and make hemselven wood
> Upon a book in cloistre alwey to poure,

or so they informed Alnwick. One Agnes Halewey complained
that, though she was young and wished to be instructed in her
religion and such matters, the Prioress set her to make beds
and to sew and spin; another sister declared that when guests
came the Prioress sent the young nuns to make up their beds,
which was "full of danger and a scandal to the house"[1]; another
deposed that the choir was not properly observed, because the
Prioress was wont to employ the younger nuns upon her own
business. There were also the usual charges of financial mismanagement and of wasting the goods of the convent; she had
let buildings fall to ruin for want of repair and two sheepfolds
had stood roofless for two whole years, so that the wood rotted
and the lambs died of the damp. Whereas thirteen years ago,
when she became prioress, the house was worth £60 a year, now
it was worth a bare £50 and was in debt, owing to the bad rule

---

[1] Compare Archbishop Bowet's injunction to the Prioress of Hampole
in 1411 that "Alice Lye, her nun who held the office of *hostilaria*, or anyone
who succeeded her in office, should henceforth be free from entering the
rooms of guests to lay beds, but that the porter should receive the bedclothes from the *hostilaria* at the lower gate, and when the guests had departed, should give them back to her at the same place." *V.C H. Yorks.*
III, p. 165 For the charge that the Prioress made the nuns work, compare
the case of Eleanor Prioress of Arden in 1396 (pp. 85–6 below) and the case
of the Prioress of Easebourne in 1441: "Also the Prioress compels her sisters
to work continually like hired workwomen (*ad modum mulieres conducti-
ciarum*) and they receive nothing whatever for their own use from their
work, but the prioress takes the whole profit (*totum percipit*)." *Sussex
Archaeol. Coll.* IX, p. 7.

of the Prioress and of William Taylour, and this in spite of the
fact that she had on her entry received from Joan Catesby a
sack and a half of wool and twelve marks, with which to pay
debts and make repairs. She had cut down woods. She had
pawned a sacramental cup and other silver pieces; the tablecloths "fit for a king" (*mappalia conueniencia pro seruiendo regi*),
and the set of a dozen silver spoons which she had found at
the priory, all had vanished away. She had not provided the
nuns with clothes and money for their food for three quarters
of the year, and she never rendered an account to them. Moreover all things in the house were ordered by her mother and by
a certain Joan Coleworthe, who kept the keys of all the offices;
and both the Prioress and her mother revealed the secrets of the
chapter to people in the village. Examined upon these separate
counts, the Prioress denied the majority of them; she said that
she had not been cruel to the nuns or laid violent hands upon
them, or called them liars and harlots or sowed discord among
them, that she had not set them to make beds or to do other
work; that she had never punished the nuns for giving evidence
at the last visitation or bribed the Bishop's clerk, that she had
never allowed her mother and Joan to rule everything, and that
she had never revealed the secrets of the chapter; on the contrary
those secrets were spread abroad by the secular visitors of the
nuns. She admitted her failure to render account, and gave as
a reason that she had no clerk to write it for her; she said that
she had pawned the cup with the consent of the convent, in
order to pay tithes, and that she had cut down trees for the use
of the house, partly with and partly without the consent of the
house; as to the ruinous buildings, she said that some had been
repaired and some not, and as to the outside debts she professed
herself ready to render an account. The most serious charge of
all, concerning William Taylour, she entirely denied. The Bishop
thereupon gave her the next day to purge herself with four of
her sisters for the things which she denied; but she was unable
to produce any compurgatresses[1] and Alnwick accordingly found
her guilty and obliged her to abjure all intercourse with Taylour
in the future.

It might be imagined that such a case as that of Margaret

[1] Compare the case of Denise Loweliche, p. 458 below.

Wavere was in the highest degree exceptional, likely to occur but once in a century. Unfortunately it appears to have occurred far more often. In the fifty years, between 1395 and 1445, Margaret Wavere can be matched, in different parts of the country, by no less than six other prioresses guilty of immorality and bad government; and it must be realised that this is probably an understatement, because so much evidence has been destroyed, or is as yet unexplored in episcopal registries. Of these cases two belong to the diocese of York, one (besides the case of Margaret Wavere) to the diocese of Lincoln, one to the diocese of Salisbury, one to the diocese of Winchester and one to the diocese of Norwich. Fully as bad a woman as Margaret Wavere was Eleanor, prioress of Arden, a little Yorkshire house which contained seven nuns, when it was visited by Master John de Suthwell in 1396 (during the vacancy of the see of York)[1] The nuns were unanimous and bitter in their complaints. The Prioress kept the convent seal in her possession, sometimes for a year at a time, and did everything according to her own will without consulting her sisters. She sold woods and trees and disposed of the money as she would, and all rents were similarly received and expended by her. When she assumed office the house was in good condition, owing some five marks only, but now it owed great sums to divers people, amounting to over £16 in the detailed list given by the nuns[2], and this in spite of the fact that she had received many alms and gifts during her year of office—£18. 13s. 4d. in all, indeed the two marks which had been given her by Henry Arden's executors that the convent might pray for his soul, had been concealed by her from the nuns, "to the deception of the said Henry's soul, as it appeared to them." She had pawned the goods of the house, at one time a piece of silver with a cover and a maser worth 40s., at another time a second maser and the Prioress' seal of office itself, for which she got 5s.; even the sacred vestments were not safe in her rapacious hands and a new suit was pawned, with the result

[1] *Test. Ebor.* I, pp 283–5 (summary in *V C H. Yorks* III, pp. 114–5)
[2] An analysis of receipts and expenditure by the Prioress during her term of office, given at the end of the *comperta*, stands thus.
In the first year: Receipts £22 7s. 6d.   Expenses £27. 6s. 8d.
In the second year. Receipts £25. 3s. 0d.   Expenses £40.
In the third year.   Receipts £26. 9s. 6d.   Expenses £27. 3s. 0d.

that it was soiled and worn and not yet consecrated. The walls
and roof of the church and dorter and the rest of the house were
in ruins; there were no waxen candles round the altar, no lights
for matins or for the other canonical hours, no Paschal candles;
when she first took office she found ten pairs of sheets of good
linen cloth (cloth of "lake" and "inglyschclath," to wit) and
now they were worn out and in all her time not one new pair
had been made; the nuns had only two sacred albs and one of
them had been turned to secular uses, viz. to "bultyng mele,"
and on several occasions had been found on the beds of laymen
in the stable. The allowances of bread and beer due to the nuns
were inadequately and unpunctually paid; sometimes she would
withdraw them altogether and the sisters would be reduced to
drinking water[1]. She was not even a good bargainer, for by her
negligence a bushel of corn was bought by an agreement for
11d, when it could have been had in the public market for 9d,
8d or 7d. Domineering she was, too, and sent three young nuns
out haymaking, so that they did not get back before nightfall
and divine service could not be said until then; and she provoked
secular boys and laymen to chatter in the cloister and church in
contempt of the nuns. There were graver charges against her in
connection with a certain married man, John Bever, with whom
she was wont to go abroad, resting in the same house by night;
and once they lay alone within the priory, in the Prioress' chamber
by night; and during the whole summer she slept alone in her
principal room outside the dorter and was much suspected on
account of John Bever   It will be noticed that this case presents
many points of similarity with that of Margaret Wavere, the
chief difference being that at Arden the Prioress alone seems
to have been in grave fault; she made no accusation against
her nuns, save that they talked in the choir and in the offices
and that the sacrist was negligent about ringing the bell for
divine service   Nor had they anything to say against each other.
The other Yorkshire case came to light in 1444, when Archbishop
Kemp stated that at his visitation of the Priory of Wykcham
very grave defaults and crimes had been detected against the

---

[1] The nuns of Swine made the same complaint in 1268. "Binis, tamen,
diebus in ebdomada aqua pro cervisia eisdem subministratur" *Reg. of
Walter Giffard* (Surtees Soc), p 148

Prioress, Isabella Westirdale, "who after she had been raised to that office had been guilty of incontinence with many men, both within and outside the monastery"; she was deprived and sent to do penance at Nunappleton.

After the case of Eleanor of Arden the next scandal concerning a prioress was discovered in 1404 at Bromhale in Berkshire. The nuns complained in that year to the Archbishop of Canterbury that the Prioress Juliana had for twenty years led an exceedingly dissolute life and of her own temerity and without their consent had usurped the rule of Prioress, in which position she had wasted, alienated, consumed and turned to her own nefarious uses the chalices, books, jewels, rents and other property of the house[1]. The next year an even more serious case occurred at Wintney in Hampshire, if the charges contained in a papal commission of 1405 were true[2] The Archdeacon of Taunton and a canon of Wells were empowered to visit the house:

the Pope having heard that Alice, who has been Prioress for about twenty years, has so dilapidated its goods, from which the Prioress for the time being is wont to administer to the nuns their food and clothing, that it is 200 marks in debt; that she specially cherishes two immodest nuns one of whom, her own (*suam*) sister, had apostatized and left the monastery and, remaining in the world, had had children, the other like the first in evil life and lewdness but not an apostate, and feeds and clothes them splendidly, whilst she feeds the other honest nuns meanly and for several years past has not provided them with clothing; that she has long kept and keeps Thomas Ferring, a secular priest, as companion at board and in bed (*in commensalem et sibi contubernalem*), who has long slept and still sleeps, contrary to the institutes of the order, within the monastery, beneath the dorter, in a certain chamber (*domo*), in which formerly no secular had ever been wont to sleep and in which the said priest and Alice meet together at will by day and night, to satisfy their lust (*pro explenda libidine*), on account of which and other enormous and scandalous crimes, which Alice has committed and still commits, there is grave and public scandal against her in those parts, to the great detriment of the monastery.

If these things were found to be true the commissioners were ordered to deprive the Prioress. In 1427 there occurred another very serious case of misconduct in a Prioress, which (as at Catesby) seems to have tainted the whole flock and is a still further illustration of the fact that a bad prioress often meant

---

[1] Dugdale, *Mon.* IV, p. 506 note.   [2] *Cal. of Papal Letters*, VI, p. 55.

an ill-conducted house. By her own admission Isabel Hermyte, Prioress of Redlingfield in Suffolk, had never been to confession nor observed Sundays and principal double feasts since the last visitation, two years before. She and Joan Tates, a novice, had not slept in the dorter with the other nuns, but in a private chamber She had laid violent hands on Agnes Brakle on St Luke's day; and she had been alone with Thomas Langeland, bailiff, in private and suspicious places, to wit in a small hall with closed windows " and sub heggerowes " Nor was the material condition of the house safer in her hands. There were only nine nuns instead of the statutory number of thirteen and only one chaplain instead of three; no annual account had been rendered, obits had been neglected, goods alienated and trees cut down without the knowledge and consent of the convent. Altogether she confessed that she was neither religious nor honest in conversation and the effect of her conduct upon her charges was only too apparent, for the novice Joan Tates confessed to incontinence and asserted that it had been provoked by the bad example of the Prioress. The result of this exposure was the voluntary resignation of the guilty woman, in order to save a scandal, and her banishment to the priory of Wix, the whole convent was ordered to fast on bread and beer on Fridays, and Joan Tates was to go in front of the solemn procession of the convent on the following Sunday, wearing no veil and clad in white flannel[1].

---

[1] *V.C.H. Suffolk*, II, pp. 83-4 The other cases may be noted more briefly. For the story of Denise Loweliche, Prioress of Markyate (Beds), see *Linc. Visit.* I, pp. 82-6, and below, pp. 458-9 Alice de Chilterne, Prioress of White Hall, Ilchester, was deprived for incontinence with the chaplain and for wasting the goods of the house to such an extent that the nuns were reduced to begging their bread (1323) Hugo, *Med Nunneries of Somerset, Whitehall in Ilchester*, pp. 78-9 and *Reg. John of Drokensford* (Somerset Rec Soc), pp. 227, 245, 259. In 1325 Joan de Barton, Prioress of Moxby, was deprived *super lapsu carnis* with the chaplain *V C.H Yorks* III, p 240. In 1495 Elizabeth Popelcy was deprived, two years after her confirmation as Prioress of Arthington, for having given birth to a child and for wasting the goods of the house *Ib.* p. 189. The case of Katherine Wells, Prioress of Littlemore, who put her nuns in the stocks and took the goods of the house to provide a dowry for her illegitimate daughter is noted below, Note F. See also the stories of Elizabeth Broke, Abbess of Romsey, and Agnes Tawke, Prioress of Easebourne. Liveing, *Rec Romsey Abbey*, pp 211-222 and *Sussex Archaeol. Coll.* IX, pp. 14-19. Joan Fletcher, Prioress of Basedale, resigned from fear of deposition in 1527 and then cast aside her habit and left the house. *Yorks Archaeol Journ.* XVI, pp. 431-2.

It is the darker side of convent life that these ancient scandals call up before our eyes. The system produced its saints as well as its sinners; we have only to remember the German nunnery of Helfta to be sure of that. The English nunneries of the later middle ages produced no great mystics, but there have come down to us word-pictures of at least two heads of houses worthy to rank with the best abbesses of any age; not women of genius, but good, competent housewives, careful in all things of the welfare of their nuns, practical as well as pious. The famous description of the Abbess Euphemia of Wherwell (1226–57) is too well-known to be quoted here in full[1]:

"It is most fitting," says her convent chartulary, "that we should always perpetuate the memory, in our special prayers and suffrages, of one who ever worked for the glory of God, and for the weal of both our souls and bodies. For she increased the number of the Lord's handmaids in this monastery from forty to eighty, to the exaltation of the worship of God. To her sisters, both in health and sickness, she administered the necessaries of life with piety, prudence, care and honesty. She also increased the sum allowed for garments by 12d. each. The example of her holy conversation and charity, in conjunction with her pious exhortations and regular discipline, caused each one to know how, in the words of the Apostle, to possess her vessel in sanctification and honour She also, with maternal piety and careful forethought, built, for the use of both sick and sound, a new and large farmery away from the main buildings and in conjunction with it a dorter and other necessary offices Beneath the farmery she constructed a watercourse, through which a stream flowed with sufficient force to carry off all refuse that might corrupt the air Moreover she built there a pláce set apart for the refreshment of the soul, namely a chapel of the Blessed Virgin, which was erected outside the cloister behind the farmery. With the chapel she enclosed a large place, which was adorned on the north side with pleasant vines and trees On the other side, by the river bank, she built offices for various uses, a space being left in the centre, where the nuns are able from time to time to enjoy the pure air. In these and in other numberless ways, the blessed mother Euphemia provided for the worship of God and the welfare of her sisters "

Nor was she less prudent in ruling secular business: "she also so conducted herself with regard to exterior affairs," says the admiring chronicler, "that she seemed to have the spirit of a

---

[1] It was translated by the Rev Dr Cox in *V C H. Hants*. II, pp. 132–3, from a chartulary of Wherwell Abbey compiled in the fourteenth century (*Brit. Mus. Egerton MS* 2104) and quoted by Gasquet, *English Monastic Life*, pp. 155–8.

man rather than of a woman." She levelled the court of the
abbey manor and built a new hall, and round the walled court
"she made gardens and vineyards and shrubberies in places
that were formerly useless and barren and which now became
both serviceable and pleasant"; she repaired the manor-houses
at Tufton and at Middleton; when the bell tower of the dorter
fell down, she built a new one "of commanding height and of
exquisite workmanship", and one of the last acts of her life was
to take down the unsteady old presbytery and to lay with her
own hands, "having invoked the grace of the Holy Spirit, with
prayers and tears," the foundation stone of a new building,
which she lived to see completed:

These and other innumerable works our good superior Euphemia
performed for the advantage of the house, but she was none the less
zealous in works of charity, gladly and freely exercising hospitality,
so that she and her daughters might find favour with One Whom Lot
and Abraham and others have pleased by the grace of hospitality.
Moreover, because she greatly loved to honour duly the House of
God and the place where His glory dwells, she adorned the church
with crosses, reliquaries, precious stones, vestments and books

Finally, she "who had devoted herself when amongst us to the
service of His house and the habitation of His glory, found the
due reward for her merits with our Lord Jesus Christ," and died
amid the blessings of her sisters.

Less famous is the name of another mighty builder, who
ruled, some two centuries later, the little Augustinian nunnery of
Crabhouse in Norfolk[1]. Joan Wiggenhall was (as has already
been pointed out) a lady of good family and had influential
friends; she was installed as Prioress in 1420, and began to
build at once In her first year she demolished a tumble-down
old barn and caused it to be remade; this cost £45. 9s. 6d.,
irrespective of the timber cut upon the estate and of the tiles
from the old barn, but the friends of the house helped and Sir
John Ingoldesthorpe gave £20 "to his dyinge," and the Archdeacon of Lincoln 10 marks. Cheered by this, the Prioress continued her operations; in her second year she persuaded the

---

[1] See the account in the *Reg. of Crabhouse Nunnery*, ed Mary Bateson
(*Norfolk Archaeology*, XI, pp. 59–63) Also a charming account of Crabhouse (founded largely on this register) in Jessopp, *Ups and Downs of an
Old Nunnery* (*Frivola*, 1896, pp. 28 ff.) The English portion of the register
was written some time after 1470.

Prior of Shouldham to co-operate with her in roofing the chancel of Wiggenhall St Peter's, towards which she paid 20 marks, and she also made the north end of her own chamber for 10 marks, and in her third year she walled the chancel of St Peter's and completed the south end of her chamber. Then she began the great work of her life, the church of the nunnery itself, and for three years this was the chief topic of conversation in all the villages round, and the favourite charity of all her neighbours:

"Also in the iiij yere of the same Jone Prioresse," runs the account in Crabhouse Register, "Ffor myschefe that was on the chyrche whiche myght not be reparid but if it were newe maid, with the counseyle of here frendys dide it take downe, trostynge to the helpe of oure Lorde and to the grete charite of goode cristen men and so with helpe of the persone before seyde (her cousin, Edmund Perys, the parson of Watlington) and other goode frendes as schal be shewyd aftyrward, be the steringe of oure Lorde and procuringe of the person forseyde sche wrowght there upon iij yere and more contynuali and made it, blessyd be God, whiche chirche cost cccc mark, whereof William Harald that lithe in the chapel of Our Lady payde for the ledynge of the chirch vij skore mark. And xl li. payede we for the roofe, the whiche xl li we hadde of Richard Steynour, Cytesen of Norwiche, and more hadde we nought of the good whiche he bequeathe us on his ded-bedde in the same Cyte, a worthly place clepyd Tom-londe whiche was with holde fro us be untrewe man his seketoures God for his mekyl mercy of the wronge make the ryghte."

The indignant complaint of the nuns, balked of their "worthly place clepyd Tomlonde," is very typical; there was always an executor in hell as the middle ages pictured it, and a popular proverb affirmed that "too secuturs and an overseere make thre theves"[1]. In this case, however, other friends were ready to make up for the deficiencies of those untrue men:

And the stallis with the reredose, the person beforeseyde payde fore xx pounde of his owne goode And xxvi mark for ij antiphoneres whiche liggen in the queer And xx li Jon Lawson gaf to the chirche. And xx mark we hadde for the soule of Jon Watson. And xx mark for the soule of Stevyn York to the werkys of the chirche and to other

---

[1] *Reliquiae Antiquae*, I, p. 314. See also a little further on in the Crab-house Register. "And xx mark we hadde of the gifte of Edmunde Peris persoun of Watlington before seyde sekatoure to the same Roger wiche was nought payed tyl xvj yere aftyr his day" Compare the complaint at Rusper in 1478: "Item dicit quod Johannes Wood erat executor domini Ricardi Hormer ..qui fuit a retro in solucione pensionis vs. per xxx annos priorisse et conventui de Rushper." But this may mean that the late Richard (a rector) had failed to pay. *Sussex Archaeol. Coll.* v, p. 255.

werkys doon before. And xxı mark of the gylde of the Trinite which Neybores helde in this same chirche The glasynge of the churche, the scripture maketh mencyon; onli God be worshipped and rewarde to all cristen soules

After the death of the good parson of Watlington, another cousin of the Prioress, Dr John Wiggenhall, came to her aid, and in her ninth year, she set to work once more upon the church, and she

arayed up the chirche and the quere, that is for to seye, set up the ymagis and pathed the chirche and the quere, and stolid it and made doris, which cost x pownde, the veyl of the chirche with the auter-clothis in sute cost xls [1]

During the building of the church the Prioress had not neglected other smaller works and a long chamber on the east side of the hall was built; but it was not until her tenth year, when the building and "arraying" of the church was finished, that she had time and money to do much; then she made some necessary repairs to the barn at St Peter's and built a new malt-house, which cost ten marks. In her twelfth year "for mischeef that was on the halle she toke it downe and made it agen"; but alas, on the Tuesday next after Hallowmas 1432, a fire broke

---

[1] With this account of the building of Crabhouse church it is interesting to compare the costs incurred in building the "newe church" of Syon Abbey in 1479–80. Two small schedules of accounts dealing with this work are preserved in the Public Record Office. The first is particularly interesting for its list of workmen employed: "Summa of the wages of Werkmen wirchyng as well opon and wyane the newe church of the monastery of Syun, as opon parte of the newe byldyng of the Brether Cloyster, chapitur-hous and library, that is to sey fr. the xth day of October in the xixth yere of the reigne of kyng E. the iiijth vnto the vijth day of October in the xxth yere of the reigne of the same kyng, as it is declared partelly in ij jurnalles of work thereof examyned It ffremasons ccxlv li xij s xj d. It. harde-hewers xxx li xj s. vij d ob. It Brekeleyers xvj li. xvj s ij d It chalk-hewers xlj s. iij d. It Carpenters and joynours xlvj s ix d It. Tawyers ix li. xvj s. iiij d. It. Smythes xliij li. xix s x d. It. Laborers xxxvj li xix s vij d It Paied to James Powle Brekeman for makyng of breks lxxvj li vij s. iiij d Summa to¹, cccclxvij li viij s. iij d. ob" (*P.R O. Mins Accts.* 1261/2). The other schedule gives further details "Expenses vpon our newe churche The makyng of the rof wᵗ tymber and cariage and workmanship ixᶜlxv li xviij s. iij d. qᵃ, lede castyng, jynyng, leyyng sawdir with diuers cariage vᶜxxxv li x s. x d Iron bought with cariage, weyng and whirvage lxxiij li. xvi s. x d. Ragstone, assheler ffreston with cariage, masons and labourers for the vantyng and ffurryng of the pilers and purvyaunes vnto the xxvij of man mˡmˡvᶜxlix li. xj s. j d ob Summa total for the church mˡmˡmˡmˡcxxxiij li xvij s ob. qᵃ. Expenses of the cloystor and dortour vnto the xxvij day of man vjᵉiijˣˣxvij li. ix s. x d. Summa to¹. mˡmˡmˡmˡviijᶜxxxiij li. vj s x d ob. qᵃ." (*Ib.* 1261/3)

out and burned down the new malt-house, and another malt-house with a solar above, full of malt. This misfortune (so common in the middle ages) only put new heart into Joan Wiggenhall:

thanne the same prioresse in here xiij yere with the grace of owre Lord God and with the helpe of mayster Johnne Wygenale beforseyd, and with helpe of good cristen men which us relevid made a malthouse with a Doffcote, that now ovyr the Kylne, whiche house is more than eyther of thoo that brent   And was in the werkynge fulli ij yere tyl her xiiij yere were passyd out, which cost l pounde   Also the same prioresse in her xv yere, sche repared the bakhous an inheyned [heightened] it and new lyngthde it, which cost x marc   And in the same yere she heyned the stepul and new rofyd it and leyde therupon a fodyr of led whiche led, freston, tymbur and werkmanshipe cost x pounde. Also in the same yere sche made the cloystir on the Northe syde and slattyd it, and the wal be the stepul, which cost viij li.

Then she began her greatest work, after the building of the church:

Also in the xvj yere of the occupacion of the same prioresse (1435) the dortoure that than was, as fer forthe as we knowe, the furste that was set up on the place, was at so grete mischeef and at the gate-downe [falling down], the Prioresse dredyinge perisschyng of her sistres whiche lay thereinne took it downe for drede of more harmys and no more was doon thereto that yere, but a mason he wande[1] with hise prentise, and in that same yere the same prioresse made the litil soler on the sowthe ende of here chaumber stondyng in to the paradise, and the wal stondinge on the weste syde of the halle, with the lityl chaumber stondynge on the southe syde, and the Myllehouse with alle the small houses dependynge there upon, the Carthouse, and the Torfehouse, and ij of stabulys and a Beerne stondynge at a tenauntry of oure on the Southe syde of Nycolas Martyn. Alle these werkys of this yere with the repare drewe iiij skore mark   In the xvij yere of the same Prioresse, be the help of God and of goode cristen men sche began the grounde of the same dortoure that now stondith, and wrought thereupon fulli vij yere betymes as God wolde sende hir good.

In the twenty-fourth year of her reign Joan Wiggenhall saw the last stone laid in its place and the last plank nailed. The future was hid from her happy eyes; she could not foresee the day, scarcely a century later, when the walls she had reared so carefully should stand empty and forlorn, and the molten lead of the roof should be sold by impious men. She must have said

---

[1] Mr Coulton suggests the reading 'a mason hewande,' i e a hard-hewer or rough hewer, as opposed to the better freemason.

with Solomon, as she looked upon her great church, "I have surely built thee an house to dwell in, a settled place for thee to abide in for ever"; and no flash of tragic prescience showed her the sheep feeding peacefully over the spot where its "heyned stepul" pointed to the sky. In 1451 she departed to the heaven she knew best, a house of many mansions; and her nuns, who for four and twenty years had lived a proud but uncomfortable life in clouds of sawdust and unending noise, buried her (one hopes) under a seemly brass in her church.

The mind preserves a pleasant picture of Euphemia of Wherwell and of Joan Wiggenhall, when Margaret Wavere, Eleanor of Arden, Isabel Hermyte and the rest are only dark memories, not willingly recalled. Which is as it should be. The typical prioress of the middle ages, however, was neither Euphemia nor Margaret. As one sees her, after wading through some hundred and fifty visitation reports or injunctions, she was a well-meaning lady, doing her best to make two ends of an inadequate income meet, but not always provident; ready for a round sum in hand to make leases, sell corrodies, cut down woods and to burden her successor as her predecessor had burdened her. She found it difficult to carry out the democratic ideal of convent life in consulting her sisters upon matters of business; she knew, like all rulers, the temptation to be an autocrat; it was so much quicker and easier to do things herself· "What, shulde the yong nunnes gyfe voices? Tushe, they shulde not gyfe voices!" So she kept the common seal and hardly ever rendered an account She found that her position gave her the opportunity to escape sometimes from that common life, which is so trying to the temper; and she did not always keep the dorter and the frater as she should She was rarely vicious, but nearly always worldly; she could not resist silks and furs, little dogs such as the ladies who came to stay in her guest-room cherished, and frequent visits to her friends. When she was a strong character the condition of her house bore witness, for good or evil, to her strength; when she was weak disorder was sure to follow. Very often she won a contented "omnia bene" from her nuns, when the Bishop came; at other times, she said that they were disobedient and they said that she was harsh, or impotent, or addicted to favourites. In the end it is to Chaucer

that we turn for her picture; as the Bishops found her, so he
saw her, aristocratic, tender-hearted, worldly, taking pains to
"countrefete chere of court," smiling "ful simple and coy" above
her well-pinched wimple; a lady of importance, attended by a
nun and three priests, spoken to with respect and reverence by
the not too mealy-mouthed host (no "by Corpus Dominus,"
or "cokkes bones," or "tel on a devel wey!" for her, but "cometh
neer my lady prioresse," and "my lady prioresse, by your leve");
clearly enjoying a night at the Tabard and some unseemly
stories on the road (though her own tale was exquisite and fitting
to her state). Religious? perhaps; but save for her singing the
divine service "entuned in her nose ful semely" and for her lovely
address to the Virgin, Chaucer can find but little to say on the
point:

> But for to speken of hir conscience
> She was so charitable and so pitous—

that she would weep over a mouse in a trap or a beaten puppy!
For charity and pity we must go to the poor Parson, not to friar
or monk or nun. A good ruler of her house? doubtless; but when
Chaucer met her the house was ruling itself somewhere at the
"shires ende." The world was full of fish out of water in the
fourteenth century, and, by séynt Loy, Madame Eglentyne (like
Dan Piers) held a certain famous text "nat worth an oistre."
So we take our leave of her—characteristically, on the road to
Canterbury.

CHAPTER III

WORLDLY GOODS

> Tomorrows shall be as yesterdays,
>   And so for ever! saints enough
>   Has Holy Church for priests to praise;
> But the chief of saints for workday stuff
>   Afield or at board is good Saint Use,
>   Withal his service is rank and rough;
> Nor hath he altar nor altar-dues,
>   Nor boy with bell, nor psalmodies,
>   Nor folk on benches, nor family pews
>   MAURICE HEWLETT, *The Song of the Plow.*

IN many ways the most valuable general account of monastic property at the close of the middle ages is to be found in the great *Valor Ecclesiasticus*, a survey of all the property of the church, compiled in 1535 for the assessment of the tenth lately appropriated by the King[1]. It is true that only 100 out of the 126 nunneries then in existence are described with any detail and that the amount of detail given varies very much for different localities. Nevertheless the record is of the highest importance, for in order to assess the tax the gross income of each house is given (often with the sources from which it is drawn,

---

[1] The *Valor Ecclesiasticus* was published in six volumes by the Record Commission (1810-34). It is the subject of a detailed study by Professor Alexander Savine, "English Monasteries on the Eve of the Suppression," in *Oxford Studies in Social and Legal History*, ed. Vinogradoff, vol I (1909). For this reason, and also because of their greater interest, I have preferred to base my study of nunnery finance on the account rolls of the nuns. The *Valor* as it affects nunneries has been largely drawn upon in an unpublished thesis by Miss H. T. Jacka, *The Dissolution of the English Nunneries, Thesis submitted for the Degree of M A in the University of London* (Dec. 1917). It is a pity that this useful little work is not published. I have been able to consult it and have made use (as will be seen from footnotes to this chapter) of the admirable chapter II on "The Property of the Nunneries", for my quotations from the *Valor* I have invariably used her analysis. Anyone wishing for an intensive study of the Dissolution from the point of view of monastic houses for women cannot do better than consult this thesis, which is far more detailed, exact and judicial in tone than any other modern account.

classified as temporalities and spiritualities) and the net income,
on which the tenth was assessed, is obtained by subtracting from
the gross income all the necessary charges upon the house,
payments of synodals and procurations, rents due to superior
lords, alms and obits which had to be maintained under the will
of benefactors, and the fees of the regular receivers, bailiffs,
auditors and stewards

Such a survey as the *Valor Ecclesiasticus*, though valuable,
could not by its nature give more than the most general indication of the main classes of receipts and expenditure of the
nunneries. The accounts kept by the nuns themselves, on the
other hand, are a mine of detailed information on these subjects.
Every convent was supposed to draw up an annual balance
sheet, to be read before the nuns assembled in chapter, and
though it was a constant source of complaint against the head
of a house that she failed to do so, nevertheless enough rolls
have survived to make it clear that the practice was common.
Indeed it would have been impossible to run a community for
long without keeping accounts. The finest set of these rolls which
has survived from a medieval nunnery is that of St Michael's
Stamford, in Northamptonshire[1]. There are twenty-four rolls,
beginning with one for the year 32-3 Edward I, and ranging
over the greater part of the fourteenth and fifteenth centuries.
A study of them enables the material life of the convent for two
centuries to be reconstructed and gives a vivid picture of its
difficulties, for though the nuns only once ended the year without
a deficit and a list of debts, yet the debts owed by various
creditors to them were often larger than those which they owed.

A very good series also exists for St Mary de Pré, near
St Albans, kept by the wardens 1341-57 and by the Prioress
1461-93[2], and there is in the Record Office a valuable little book
of accounts kept by the treasuresses of Gracedieu (Belton) during
the years 1414-18, which has been made familiar to many readers
by the use made of it by Cardinal Gasquet in *English Monastic*

---

[1] *P R O. Mins Accts.* 1260.
[2] The wardens accounts are in *P.R O. Mins Accts* 867/21-6 and the
prioress's accounts, *ib* 867/30, 32, 33-36 and *Hen. VII*, no 274 They are
briefly described in *V C H. Herts.* IV, pp 430-1 (notes 30, 31, 39). An
excellent prioress's account for 2-4 Hen. VII is printed by Dugdale, *Mon.* III,
pp. 358-61, the prioress being Christian Bassett.

Life[1]. Very full and interesting accounts have also survived from St Radegund's Cambridge (1449–51, 1481–2)[2], Catesby (1414–45)[3] and Swaffham Bulbeck (1483–4)[4]. These are all prioresses' or treasuresses' accounts of the total expenditure of the different houses; but there are in existence also a few obedientiaries' accounts, chambresses' accounts from St Michael's Stamford and Syon and cellaresses' accounts from Syon[5]. An analysis of these accounts shows, better than any other means of information, the various sources from which a medieval nunnery drew its income, and the chief classes of expenditure which it had to meet. It will therefore be illuminating to consider in turn the credit and debit side of a monastic balance sheet.

It is perhaps unnecessary to postulate that since monastic houses differed greatly in size and wealth, the sources of their income would differ accordingly. A very poor house might be dependent upon the rents and produce of one small manor, a large house sometimes had estates all over England: The entire income of Rothwell in Northamptonshire was derived from one appropriated rectory, valued in the *Valor* at £10. 10s. 4d. gross and at £5. 19s. 8d. net per annum[6] The Black Ladies of Brewood (Staffs.) had an income of £11. 1s 6d. derived from demesne in hand, rents and alms[7]. On the other hand Dartford in Kent held lands in Kent, Surrey, Norfolk, Suffolk, Wiltshire, Wales and London[8], the Minoresses without Aldgate held property in London, Hertfordshire, Kent, Berkshire, Staffordshire, Derbyshire, Bedfordshire, Buckinghamshire, Norfolk and the Isle of Wight[9] The splendid Abbey of Syon held land as far afield as Lancashire and Cornwall, scattered over twelve counties[10]. Similarly the proportionate income derived from house-rents and land-rents would differ with the geographical situation of the nunnery. London convents, for instance, would draw a large

---

[1] *P R O. Mins Accts* 1257/10 See Gasquet, *Eng Monastic Life*, pp. 158–176.

[2] A Gray, *Priory of St Radegund's, Cambridge*, pp 145–85

[3] Baker, *Hist. and Antiq of Northants* I, pp 278–83 Compare *P R O. Mins. Accts*. 1257/1 for a Catesby account roll for 11–14 Hen IV.

[4] Dugdale, *Mon* IV, pp 458–60 See also *P R O.* 1257/2 for Denney, 14 Hen IV–1 Hen V

[5] See Ch IV, *passim*.

[6] *Valor Eccles* IV, p. 302

[7] *Ib* III, p 103

[8] *Ib.* I, p 119

[9] *Ib* I, p 397

[10] *Ib.* I, p 424

income from streets of houses, whereas a house in the distant dales of Yorkshire would be dependent upon agriculture. At the time of the *Valor* twenty-two nunneries were holding urban tenements in fifteen towns, amounting in total value to £1076. 0s. 7d., but of this sum £969 11s. 10d. was held by the seven houses in London[1] With this proviso the conclusion may be laid down that the money derived from the possession of agricultural land, and in particular the rents paid by tenants in freehold, copyhold, customary and leasehold land, was the mainstay of the income paid into the hands of the treasuress

A word may perhaps be said as to the method by which the nuns administered their estates. Miss Jacka distinguishes two main types of administration, discernible in the *Valor*:

The London houses, except Syon and a number, chiefly, of the smaller nunneries scattered throughout the country, had a single staff of officials, steward, bailiff, auditor, receiver, their revenues were drawn from scattered rents and other profits rather than from entire manors There seem to have been about forty houses of this type in addition to the London houses The second group comprises the great country nunneries in the south of England, including Syon and a number of smaller houses whose revenues were reckoned under the headings of various manors each managed by its own bailiff ...The staff of Syon may be taken as an unusually complete and elaborate example of the usual system, whose principle appears worked out on a smaller scale, in the case of smaller nunneries. The nuns had in the first place what may be called a central staff, a steward at £3 6s 8d, a steward of the hospice at £23 15s 4d, a general receiver at £19 13s 4d and an auditor at £8 3s 4d Their lands in Middlesex were managed by their steward of Isleworth, Lord Wyndesore, whose fee was £3, a steward of courts at £1 and a bailiff at £2 13s. 4d, who had a separate fee of 13s. 4d. as bailiff of the chapel of the Angels at Brentford. Their extensive possessions in Sussex were managed by a receiver and a steward of courts for the whole county, whose fees were £3 and £2 respectively, by four stewards for various districts with fees from £1. 6s 8d. down to 13s. 4d. and by 13 bailiffs arranged under the stewards, of whom one received £2 3s. 4d and the rest from £1 to 6s 8d. Their one manor in Cambridgeshire was managed by a steward at 13s. 4d. and a bailiff at £1. With the central staff was reckoned a receiver for Somerset, Dorset and Devon, whose fee was £6 13s 4d, the ladies held no temporalities in Somerset, in Dorset they had a chief steward, £1. 6s. 8d, a steward of courts, 6s 8d, and a bailiff, 11s., and their large possessions in Devon were managed by two stewards (£2. 13s. 4d.), two stewards of courts (13s. 4d., 6s. 8d.), six

---

[1] Jacka, *op. cit.* f. 44.

bailiffs, with fees ranging from 4s. to £2 and an auditor, 3s. 4d. They
received £100 a year from unspecified holdings in Lancashire and had
there a steward of courts at £1. Their possessions in Lincolnshire
were mainly spiritual, but they employed a receiver, whose fee was
13s 4d In Gloucestershire they had large possessions The two chief
stewards of Cheltenham received each £3 6s 8d and the chief steward
of Minchinhampton £2. Two stewards of courts each received £1 6s 8d
and the two stewards at Slaughter £1   Three bailiffs received
£2 13s 4d., £2 and 13s 4d., with livery A bailiff and receiver of
profits arising from the sale of woods was paid £4 and the steward
of the abbot of Cirencester was paid 6s 8d. for holding the abbess'
view of frankpledge. In Wiltshire the nuns held a manor and a rectory
and paid £1 to a steward for both: they seem to have been leased.
In counties where all their possessions were spiritual they had no
local officials; in Somerset both the rectories they held were leased
and in Kent, although that is not stated, it is suggested by the round
sums which were received (£26 13s 4d., £10, £20) The leasing of
property for a fixed sum of course made the administration of it very
much simpler All the temporalities of the Minoresses without Aldgate
were leased and their staff consisted of a chief steward, Lord Wyndesore, whose fee was £2 13s 4d , a receiver at £4. 5s 10d and an
auditor at 13s. 4d [1]

A closer analysis of the chief sources of income of a medieval
nunnery, as they may be distinguished in the *Valor* and in
various account rolls, is now possible. They may be classified
as follows: *Temporalities*, comprising: (1) rents from lands and
houses, (2) perquisites of courts, fairs, mills, woods and other
manorial perquisites, (3) issues of the manor, i e. sale of farm
produce, (4) miscellaneous payments from boarders, gifts, etc.,
and *Spiritualities*, comprising (5) tithes from appropriated benefices, alms, mortuaries, etc. The distinction between temporalities
and spiritualities is a technical one and there was sometimes little
difference between the sources of the two kinds of income, but
the temporal revenues were usually larger[2].

(1) *Rents from lands and houses* A house which possessed
several manors besides its home farm would either lease them
to tenants ("farm out the manor" as it was called), or put in
bailiffs, who were responsible for working the estates and handing
over to the convent the profits of their agriculture, and who may
also have collected rents where no separate rent collector was

---

[1] Jacka, *op cit.* ff. 27, 29–30. The information about Syon and the
Minoresses is taken from *Valor Eccles.* i, p. 424 and i, p. 397 respectively
[2] See Jacka, *op. cit* f 25

employed. For besides the profits arising from the demesne land (of which some account will be given below), the convent derived a much more considerable income from the rents of all tenants (whatever the legal tenure by which they held) who held their land at a money rent. The number of such tenants was likely to increase by the commutation of customary services for money payments; since, except in the particular manor or manors wherein the produce of the demesne was reserved for the actual consumption of the community, it was to the interest of a convent to lease a great part of the demesne land to tenants at a money rent and so save itself the trouble of farming the land under a bailiff[1]. In addition to these rents from agricultural land an income was sometimes derived, as has already been pointed out, from the rent of tenements in towns.

In most account rolls a careful distinction was drawn between "rents of assize" and "farms" The former were the payments due from the tenants (whether freehold or customary) who held their holdings at a money rent; these rents were collected by

[1] If the demesne land were let out in farm the customary ploughing and other services of the villeins would no longer be needed and if only a portion of it were so farmed the number of villein services required would be proportionately less. This, as well as the increasing employment of hired labour on the demesne during the fourteenth and fifteenth centuries, accounts for the item "Sale of Works" which appears in the Romsey account for 1412 Liveing, *Records of Romsey Abbey*, p 194 From another point of view the number of rent-payers was increased by the fact that both free and unfree tenants could rent pieces of the demesne As to the farming of the demesne, note however the conclusion to which Miss Jacka comes from a study of the *Valor* and the Dissolution *Surveys* now in the Augmentation Office "The question 'to what extent did the nuns in 1535 farm their demesnes?' cannot be confidently answered on the evidence of any of the records before us. Apart from the fact that in many cases there is no statement at all, the word 'firma' or 'farm' is used so ambiguously that even where it occurs it is impossible to be certain that a lease existed . .There are, of course, unmistakeable cases in which the demesnes were farmed: Tarrant Keynes kept in hand the demesnes of 3 manors and farmed that of 7: Shaftesbury occupied the demesne of one manor and farmed that of 18 (*Valor Eccles.* I, pp 265, 276) But in none of the few cases in which the whole of the demesne is described as yielding a 'firma,' should we be justified, in view of the several uses of the word, in asserting that it had the definite character of a lease That is to say, whatever may be our suspicions, the evidence before us does not warrant the assertion that in a single case did the nuns farm the whole of their demesnes: and this conclusion is an unexpected and remarkable one, for we might well expect them to be among the first land holders who seized this method of simplifying their manorial economy." Jacka, *op. cit.* i. 47.

the different collectors of the nunnery or brought to the treasurers
by the tenants themselves. "Farms" were leases, i e payments
for land or houses which were held directly in demesne by the
nunnery, but instead of being worked by a bailiff, or occupied
by the household, were "farmed out" at an annual rent A
"farmer" might thus hold in farm an entire manor, and, for the
payment of an annual sum to the nuns, he would have the right
to the produce of the demesne and to the rents of rent-paying
tenants. He might be quite a small person and hold in farm
only a few acres of the demesne (in addition perhaps to an
ordinary tenant's holding on the manor) He might hold the
farm of a mill, or a stable, or a single house[1]. In any case he
paid a rent to the nuns and made what he could out of his "farm";
while they much preferred these regular payments to the trouble
of superintending the cultivation of distant lands, in an age when
communication was difficult and slow.

Nevertheless the rents were not always easy to collect, for
all the diligence of the bailiff and of the various rent-collectors[2].

[1] In the account roll of Dame Christian Bassett, Prioress of Delapré
(St Albans) for 2–4 Hen. VII, the "rente fermys" range between £7 from
Robert Pegge for the farm of the whole manor of Pray, to 2s received from
Richard Franklin "for the ferme of vj acres of londe in Bacheworth",
one John Shon pays 6s 8d. "for the ferme of certeyne londs in Bacheworth
and ij tenements in Seint Mighell strete with a lyme kylne", Richard
Ordeway pays 10s for rent farm of "an hous whin the Pray" and Robert
Pegge 8s. for rent farm of "an hous and a stable whin Praygate." Dugdale,
Mon. III, pp. 358–9. In this account her assize rents amount to £2. 11s. 2d
within the town of St Albans and her rents farm to £4 13s 2d ; while outside the town the rents of assize amount to £2. 5s 0d and the rents farm
to £11. 19s. 8d., while four items amounting to £1. 19s. 11d are doubtful,
but probably represent farms That is to say very nearly three quarters of
the lands and houses belonging to Delapré were farmed out, and if we except
payments from the town of St Albans, which were probably house-rents,
over four-fifths of its possessions were in farm Similarly in the account roll
of Margaret Ratclyff, Prioress of Swaffham, for 22 Ed. IV. the rents are
classified as *Redditus Assise* (£6 0s 4d in all), *Firma Terrae* (£13 0s. 3½d
in all) and *Firma Molendini*, the farm of a mill (£3 14s 4d) *Ib.* IV, p 459
[2] References to money paid in fees to rent-collectors, or in gratuities
to men who had brought rents up to the house often occur in account rolls,
e g in the Catesby roll for 1414–15, "Also in expenses of collecting rents
wheresoever to be collected ..xixs Also paid to divers receivers of rent
for the time vijs vijd " Baker, *Hist of Northants* I, p 280 In the
Delapré account of 2–4 Hen. IV, "Item paid to a man that brought money
from Cambryg for a rewarde vijd Item for divers men yᵗ brought in
their rent at dyvers tymes xxs ijd." Dugdale, *Mon* III, p. 359 In the
St Radegund's Cambridge account of 1449–51, "In the expenses of Thomas
Key (xvijd. ob) at Abyngton, Litlyngton, Whaddon, Crawden, Bumpsted

There are some illuminating entries in the accounts of St Radegund's Cambridge. In 1449–50 the indignant treasuress debits
herself with "one tenement in Walleslane lately held by John
Walsheman for 6s 8d. a year, the which John fled out of this
town within the first half of this year, leaving nought behind
him whereby he could be distrained save 7d., collected therefrom"; and in the following year she again debits herself "for
part of a tenement lately held by John Webster for 12s a year,
whence was collected only 7s for that the aforesaid John
Webster did flit [literally, *devolavit*] by night, leaving naught
behind him whereby he could be distrained" Yet these nuns
seem to have been indulgent landlords, in this year the treasuress
debits herself "for a tenement lately held by Richard Pyghtesley,
because it was too heavily charged before, 2s. 3d.,...and for
a portion of the rent owed by Stephen Brasyer on account of the
poverty and need of the said Stephen, by grace of the lady
Prioress this time only, 15d" and there are other instances of
lowered rents in these accounts[1]. Other account rolls sometimes
make mention of meals and small presents of money given to
tenants bringing in their rents

(2) *Various manorial perquisites and grants* Besides the rents
from land and houses the position of a religious community as
lord of a manor gave it the right to various other financial
payments. Of these the most important were the perquisites of
the manorial courts These varied very much according to the
extent and number of the liberties which had been granted to
any particular house To Syon, beloved of kings, vast liberties
had been granted (notably in 1447), so that the tenants upon its
estates were almost entirely exempt from royal justice The
abbess and convent had

view of frankpledge, leets, lawe-days and wapentakes for all people,
tenants resiant and other resiants aforesaid, in whatsoever places,
by the same abbess or her successors to be limited, where to them it
shall seem most expedient within the lordships, lands, rents, fees
and possessions aforesaid, to be holden by the steward or other officers.

and Cambridge for the business of the lady (prioress) and for levying rent.
and in the stipend of Thomas Key collecting rents in Cambridge and the
district this year xiiis. iiijd." Gray, *Priory of St Radegund, Cambridge*,
pp 173–4
    [1] Gray, *op cit* pp. 148, 164.

They had the assizes of bread and ale and wine and victuals and
weights and measures They had all the old traditional emolu-
ments of justice, which lords had striven to obtain since the days
before the conquest,

> soc, sac, infangentheof, outfangentheof, waif, estray, treasure-trove,
> wreck of the sea, deodands, chattels of felons and fugitives, of outlaws,
> of waive, of persons condemned, of felons of themselves [suicides],
> escapes of felons, year day waste and estrepement and all other
> commodities, forfeitures and profits whatsoever

They had the right to erect gallows, pillory and tumbrel for the
punishment of malefactors. They even had

> all issues and amercements, redemptions and forfeitures as well
> before our [the king's] heirs and successors, as before the chancellor,
> treasurer and barons of our exchequer, the justices and commissioners
> of us, our heirs or successors whomsoever, made, forfeited or adjudged
> ...of all the people...in the lordships, lands, tenements, fees and
> possessions aforesaid[1].

In the eyes of the middle ages justice had one outstanding
characteristic· it filled the pocket of whoever administered it.
"Justitia magnum emolumentum est," as the phrase went. All
the manifold perquisites of justice, whether administered in her
own or in the royal courts, went to the abbess of Syon if any
of her own tenants were concerned   It is no wonder that out
of a total income of £1944 11s. 5¼d the substantial sum of
£133. 0s. 6d. was derived from perquisites of courts[2]

Few houses possessed such wholesale exemption from royal
justice, but all possessed their manorial courts, at which tenants
paid their heriots in money or in kind as a death-duty to the lord,
or their fines on entering upon land, and at which justice was
done and offenders amerced (or fined as we should now call it).
Most houses possessed the right to hold the assize of bread and
ale and to fine alewives who overcharged or gave short measure
Some possessed the right to seize the chattels of fugitives, and
the abbess of Wherwell was once involved in a law suit over

---

[1] See for a translation of the whole charter, Aungier, *Hist of Syon*,
pp. 60–67 The original is given *ib* pp 411–8
[2] See the valuation of Syon Monastery, A D 1534, translated from the
Valor Ecclesiasticus, *ib*. pp 439–450 At Romsey in 1412 the perquisites
of courts brought in a total of £14 out of an annual income of £404 6s 0½d ,
made up of the rents and farms, sale of works, sale of farm produce and
perquisites of courts on six manors Liveing, *Records of Romsey Abbey*, p. 194.

this liberty, which she held in the hundred of Mestowe and
which was disputed by the crown officials. One Henry Harold
of Wherwell had killed his wife Isabel and fled to the church
of Wherwell and the Abbess had seized his chattels to the value
of £35 4s. 8d by the hands of her reeve[1]   A less usual privilege
was that of the Abbess of Marham, who possessed the right of
proving the wills of those who died within the precincts or
jurisdiction of the house[2]. The courts at which these liberties
were exercised were held by the steward of the nunnery, who
went from manor to manor to preside at their sittings, but
sometimes the head of the house herself would accompany
him. Christian Bassett, the energetic Prioress of Delapré (St
Albans), not content with journeying up to London for a lawsuit, went twice to preside at her court at Wing[3].

In rather a different class from grants of jurisdictional liberties
were special grants of free warren, felling of wood and fairs
Monasteries which possessed lands within the bounds of a royal
forest were not allowed to take game or to cut down wood there
without a special licence from the crown, but such grants to
exercise "free warren" (i.e. take game) and to fell wood were
often granted in perpetuity, as an act of piety by the king, or
for special purposes The Abbess of Syon had free warren in all
her possessions, and in 1489 it was recorded that the Abbess of
Barking had free chase within the bailiwick of Hainault to hunt
all beasts of the forest in season, except deer, and free chase
within the forest and without to hunt hares and rabbits and fox,
badger, cat and other vermin[4]. Grants of wood were more often
made on special occasions, thus in 1277 the keeper of the forest
of Essex was ordered to permit the Abbess of Barking and her
men to fell oak-trees and oak-trunks in her demesne woods
within the forest to the value of £40[5], while in 1299 the Abbess
of Wilton was given leave to fell sixty oaks in her own wood
within the bounds of the forest of Savernake, in order to rebuild

[1] *V.C.H. Hants* II, p 135
[2] *V.C.H. Norfolk*, II, p 370 So apparently had the Prioress of Carrow.
Rye, *Carrow Abbey*, p. 21.
[3] See p 70 above. Compare the Catesby roll for 1414–15. "And in the
expenses of the steward at the court this year and at other times vis. viiid."
Baker, *Hist and Antiq of Northants* I, p. 280.
[4] *V C H. Essex*, II, p 118.
[5] *Cal. of Close Rolls*, 1272–9, p. 392.

some of her houses, which had been burnt down[1]. The grant of
fairs and markets was even more common and more lucrative,
for the convent profited not only from the rents of booths and
from the entrance-tolls, but not infrequently from setting up
a stall of its own, for the sale of spices and other produce[2].
Henry III granted the nuns of Catesby a weekly market every
Monday within their manor of Catesby and a yearly fair for three
days in the same place; and almost any monastic chartulary will
provide other instances of such rights[3].

The majority of the special perquisites which have been described would originate in special grants from the Crown; but it
must be remembered that every manorial lord could count on
certain perquisites *ex officio*, for which no specific grant was required. For his manor provided him with more than agricultural
produce on the one hand and rents and farms on the other
Through the manor court he also received certain payments
due to him from all free and unfree tenants, in particular those
connected with the transfer of land, the heriot and the fines
already mentioned. From unfree tenants he could also claim
various other dues, the mark of their status, merchet, when
their daughters married off the estate, leyrwite, when they enjoyed themselves without the intermediary of that important
ceremony, a fine when they wished to send their sons to school

[1] *Cal of Close Rolls*, 1296–1302, p. 238
[2] In the account of the Prioress of Delapré already quoted occurs the
item "Receyvid for ij standyngs at Prayffayre at ij tymes vs " Dugdale,
Mon iii, p 359 The fair time was the feast of the Nativity of the B.V M.
(Sept. 8th) and the account for another year shows that over £1 was spent
on the convent and visitors at this time. The accounts for 1490–3 include
payments for making trestles and forms in connection with the fair.
V.C.H Herts iv, p 430 (note 31) and p 439 (note 39). The nuns of St Radegund's, Cambridge, were granted by Stephen a fair, which was afterwards
known as Garlick fair, and was held in their church-yard for two days on
August 14th and 15th They did not receive much from it; in 1449 the tolls
amounted only to 5s 2d.; moreover they had to give the toll collectors
6d. for a wage and they evidently made the occasion one for entertainment,
for they hired an extra cook for 3d. "to help in the kitchin at the fair time."
Gray, *Priory of St Radegund, Cambridge*, pp 49–50.
[3] The *Valor Eccles.* occasionally notes income derived from fairs
Tarrant Keynes had £2 from the fair at Woodburyhill, Shaftesbury had
£2 4s. 6d from Shaftesbury fair, Malling received £3. 6s. 8d. from Malling
market and fair and £3 from a market "cum terris et tenementis " at Newheth,
Blackborough had £1 from Blackborough fair and Elstow had £7. 12s. od.
from Elstow fair. *Valor Eccles* i, pp. 265, 276, 106; ii, p. 205, iii, p. 395,
iv, p. 188

and a number of other customary payments, exacted at the manor court and varying slightly from manor to manor. Moreover the tolls from the water- or wind-mill at which villeins had to grind their corn all went to swell the purse of the lord[1]. This is not the place for a detailed description of manorial rights, which can be studied in any text-book of economic history[2]; a word must, however, be said about the mortuary system, which did not a little to enrich the medieval church.

When a peasant died the lord of the manor had often the right to claim his best animal or garment as a mortuary or heriot, and by degrees there grew up a similar claim to his second best possession on the part of the parish priest.

"It was presumed," says Mr Coulton, "that the dead man must have failed to some extent in due payment of tithes during his lifetime and that a gift of his second best possession to the Church would therefore be most salutary to his soul"[3].

From these claims, partly manorial and partly ecclesiastical, religious houses benefited very greatly, and their accounts sometimes mention mortuary payments. The Prioress of Catesby in the year 1414–15 records how her live stock was enriched by one horse, one mare and two cows coming as heriots, while she received a payment of 20s. for two oxen coming as heriot of Richard Sheperd[4]. In the chartulary of Marham is recorded a mortuary list of sixteen people, who died within the jurisdiction of the house, and the mortuaries vary from a sorrel horse and a book to numerous gowns and mantles[5]. The system was

---

[1] The mill belonging to the home farm would be in the charge of a miller, who was one of the hired servants of the house and was paid a regular stipend Other mills would probably be farmed out. The nuns of Catesby had two mills, which brought them in 12s and 22s a year respectively, one, a windmill, was probably farmed, but the water-mill was in charge of Thomas Milner, at a wage of 20s and his servant, who was paid 2s 6d. The nuns also received tolls of grain in kind from the mill, a certain proportion of which was handed over to the miller for his household The mill does not seem to have paid very well, for a heavy list of "Costs of the Mill," amounting to 31s. 6d appears in the account, it includes the wages of the miller and his boy and payments to a carpenter for making the mill-wheel for seventeen days and in damming the mill-tail and buying shoes with nails for the mill horses Baker, op cit 1, pp. 279, 281 At Swaffham Bulbeck the "Firma Molendini" brought in £3 14s 4d Dugdale, Mon iv, p. 457 Malling Abbey had a fulling-mill Valor Eccles. i, p. 276.

[2] For instance in Hone, The Manor and Manorial Records (1906).

[3] Coulton, Med. Garn p 591

[4] Baker, op cit i, pp. 279, 282.   [5] V C.H. Norfolk, ii, p. 370.

obviously capable of great abuse, and Mr Coulton considers that it did much to precipitate the Reformation, for the unhappy peasant resented more and more bitterly the greed of the church, which chose his hour of sorrow to wrest from him the best of his poor possessions; it must have seemed hard to him that his horse or his ox should be driven away, if he could not buy it back, to the well-stocked farm of a community which was vowed to poverty, far harder than if his lord were a layman, as free as he was himself to accumulate possessions without soiling the soul When the parish priest followed the convent with a claim upon what was best, his despair must have grown deeper and his resentment more bitter. It was often difficult to collect these payments, just as it was often difficult to collect tithes, even when a priest was less loth to curse for them than Chaucer's poor parson Vicars were obliged to sue their wretched parishioners in the ecclesiastical courts, and monasteries were sometimes fain to commute such payments for an annual rent, collected by the tenants[1]. But the best ecclesiastics recognised that the system was somewhat out of keeping with Christian charity Caesarius of Heisterbach has a story of Ulrich, the good head of the monastery of Steinfeld, who one day

came to one of his granges, wherein, seeing a comely foal, he enquired of the [lay] brother whose it was or whence it came To whom the brother answered, "such and such a man, our good and faithful friend, left it to us at his death" "By pure devotion," asked the provost, "or by legal compulsion?" "It came through his death," answered the other, "for his wife, since he was one of our serfs, offered it as a heriot" Then the provost shook his head and piously answered: "Because he was a good man and our faithful friend, therefore hast thou despoiled his wife" Render therefore her horse to this forlorn woman; for it is robbery to seize or detain other men's goods, since the horse was not thine before [the man's death]"[2]

[1] For examples of mortuary law-suits, receipts and results, see Coulton, *Med Garn* pp 561–6 On the whole subject of mortuaries and the unpopularity which they entailed upon the church, see Coulton, *Medieval Studies*, no 8 ("Priests and People before the Reformation," pp 3–7)

[2] Translated in Coulton, *Med Garn*. p 323 Compare another of Caesarius' tales of the usurer who was taken by the devil through various places of torment· "There also he saw a certain honest knight lately dead, Elias von Rheineck, castellan of Horst, seated on a mad cow with his face towards her tail and his back to her horns, the beast rushed to and fro, goring his back every moment so that the blood rushed forth To whom the usurer said, 'Lord, why suffer ye this pain?' 'This cow,' replied the knight,

(3) *Issues of the manor.* Before passing on to sources of
income of a more specifically ecclesiastical character, some account must be given of the third great class of receipts which
came to a convent in its capacity of landowner, to wit the "issues
of the manor." Attached to almost every nunnery was its home
farm, which provided the nuns with the greater part of their
food[1]. A large nunnery would thus reserve for its own use several
manors and granges, but usually other manors in its possession
would be farmed by bailiffs, who sold the produce at market
and paid in the profits to the treasuress or to one of the obedientiaries; or else a manor would be leased to a tenant. The surplus
produce of the home farm, which could not be used by the nuns,
was also sold. The treasuress usually entered the receipts and
expenditure of the home farm in her household account and she
had to keep two sets of records, the one a careful account of all
the animals and agricultural produce on the farm, with details
as to the use made of them; and the other (under the heading
of "issues of the manor") a money record of the sums obtained
from sales of live stock, wool or grain. An analysis of the
produce of the home farm of Catesby (1414–5)[2] shows that the
chief crops grown were wheat and barley. Of these a certain
proportion was kept for seed to sow the new crops; almost all
the rest of the wheat was paid in food allowances to the servants
and 1 qr. 3 bushels in alms "to friars of the four orders and
other poor"; most of the barley was malted, except 6 qrs.
delivered to the swineherd to feed hogs; and what remained was
stored in the granaries of the convent. Oats and peas were also
grown and part of the crop used for seed, part for food-allowances
to the servants and oatmeal for the nuns. The Prioress also kept
a most meticulous account of the livestock on her farm. All
were numbered and classified, cart-horses, brood-mares, colts,
foals, oxen, bulls, cows, stirks (three-year old), two-year old,

'I tore mercilessly from a certain widow; wherefore I must now endure this
merciless punishment from the same beast.'" *Ib.* p. 214. Certainly the
medieval imagination had a genius for making the punishment fit the crime

[1] A nunnery in a large town would be far more dependent on buying
food Thus an account of the household expenses of St Helen's Bishopsgate,
in the sixteenth century shows that the nuns had to pay £22 for buying
corn and £60. 13s. 4d for meat and other foodstuffs. They were heavily
in debt, and their creditors included a brewer, a "cornman," two fishmongers
and a butcher. *V C H. London,* I, p 460   [2] Baker, *op cit* I, pp. 281–3

yearlings, calves, sheep, wethers, hogerells, lambs, hogs, boars, sows, hilts, hogsters and pigs. In each class it was carefully set down how many animals remained in stock at the end of the year and what had been done with the others. We know something of the consumption of meat by the nuns of Catesby and their servants in this year of grace 1414–5, when the old rule against the eating of meat was relaxed, and we see something of the cares of a medieval housewife in those days before root-crops were known, when the number of animals which could be kept alive during the winter was strictly limited by the amount of hay produced on the valuable meadow land. Only in summer could the convent have fresh meat; and on St Martin's day (Nov. 11) the business of killing and salting the rest of the stock for winter food began[1]. From good Dame Elizabeth Swynford's account it appears that five oxen, one stirk, thirty hogs and one boar were delivered to the larderer to be salted; in summer time, when the convent could enjoy fresh meat, five calves, fourteen sheep, ten hogs and twelve pigs were sent in to the kitchen; and twenty cows were divided between the larder and the kitchen, to provide salt and fresh beef There is unfortunately no record of the produce of the dairy, which supplied the convent with milk, cheese, eggs and occasional chickens.

But the home-farm served the purpose of providing money as well as food The hides of the oxen and the "wool pells" of the sheep, which had been killed for food or had fallen victim to that curse of medieval farming, the murrain, were by no means wasted. Five hides belonging to animals which had died of murrain were tanned and used for collars and other cart gear on the farm, but all the rest were sold, thirty-six of them in all. Most lucrative of all, however, was the sale of wool pells and wool, and Dame Elizabeth Swynford is very exact, eighteen wool pells, from sheep which the convent had eaten as mutton, sold before shearing for 35s. 10d , thirty-eight sold after shearing for 9s. 6d , thirty-six lamb skins for 1s.; and 6d. was received "for wynter lokes sold." Moreover the convent also sold one sack and eight weight of wool at £5. 4s. the sack, for a total of £6 16s.

---

[1] The convent bought 4½ qrs of salt for 25s for the operation this year Baker, *op cit* I, p. 280 Compare, for the operation at Gracedieu, Gasquet, *Eng Mon. Life,* p 174

Altogether the "issues of the manor" amounted to the substantial sum of £24. 8s 8d., chiefly derived from these sales of
wool and wool pells and from the sale of some timber for
£6. 13s. 4d [1] These details about wool are interesting, for it is
well known that the monastic houses of England, especially in
the northern counties, were great sheep farmers. Most accounts
mention this important source of revenue and in the series of
rolls kept by the treasuresses of St Michael's Stamford, it is
regularly entered under the heading "Fermes, dismes, leynes et
pensions," a somewhat miscellaneous classification [2]. In the thir-
teenth-century *Pratica della Mercatura* of Francesco Pergolotti
there is incorporated a list of monasteries which sell wool,
compiled for the use of Italian wool merchants and giving the
prices per sack of the different qualities of wool at each house.
The list contains a section specially devoted to nunneries, in
which twenty houses are mentioned, all but two of them in
Lincolnshire or Yorkshire [3]. Armed with this information the

---

[1] The account of the cellaress of Syon for the year 1536–7 gives very
full details of the income derived from the sale of hides and fells John
Lyrer, tanner, buys from her fifty-five ox-hides at 3s. 6d. each, and three
cow-hides, two steer-hides, one bull-hide, and one murrain ox-hide at 2s 4d
each, making a total of £10 8s. 10d The same John Lyrer buys 230 calf-
skins for £3. 16s. 8d. John Cockes, fellmonger, buys 287 "shorling felles,"
at 3s. the dozen, 190 "skynnes of wynter felles" at 6s. the dozen, 77
"skynnes somerfelles" at 8s. the dozen, for a total for £10. 18s 1d The
different qualities of wool were always carefully distinguished and priced
Myroure of Oure Ladye, ed Blunt, p xxix
[2] A few examples taken at random will suffice "By the sale of wool
4 marks 11s. 8d. From Gilbert of Chesterton for the wool *del aan ke est aveni*
100s " (32–3 Edw. I) *P R O. Mins Accts* 1260/1. "From the sale of 14 stone
of wool, price per stone 7s , 4l 18s." (48–9 Edw III) *Ib.* 1260/4 "Received
for one sack of 20 stone of wool sold last year, at 4s. per stone, 13 marks,
10s 8d Received for one sack of this years wool, at 4s. 6d per stone,
5l 17s 0d." (either 46–7 or 47–8 Edw. III) *Ib.* 1260/21 "From John of
the Pantry for 11½ stone of wool at 6s the stone, 69s." (1–2 Rich. II)
Ib. 1260/7. In 1412 Romsey Abbey derived £60 out of a total income of
£404 6s. 4½d. from the sale of wool Liveing, *op. cit.* p. 194.
[3] See, for this very interesting document, Cunningham, *Growth of English
Industry and Commerce* (1905 ed.), I, App D, pp 628–41 The nunneries
mentioned, with the amount of wool obtainable from each annually, are
Stainfield (from 12 sacks), Stixwould (from 15 sacks), Nuncoton (from
10 sacks), Hampole (from 6 sacks), St Leonard's Grimsby (from 2 sacks),
Heynings (from 2 sacks), Gokewell (from 4 sacks), Langley (from 5 sacks),
Arden (from 10 sacks), Keldholme (from 12 sacks), Rosedale (from 10 sacks),
St Clement's York (from 3 sacks), Swine (from 8 sacks), Marrick (from
8 sacks), Wykeham (from 4 sacks), Ankerwyke (from 4 sacks), Thicket
(from 4 sacks), Nunmonkton (number missing), Yedingham (do), Legbourne

Italians would journey from nunnery to nunnery and bargain with the nuns for their wool: the whole crop would sometimes be commissioned by them in advance, sold on the backs of the sheep. The English distrusted these dark smooth-spoken foreigners; many years later the author of the *Libel of English Policie* charged them with dishonest practices and complained of the freedom with which they were allowed to buy in England:

> In Cotteswold also they ride about,
> And all England, and buy withouten doubte
> What them list with freedome and franchise,
> More than we English may gitten many wise[1]

But it must have been a great day for the impoverished nuns of Yorkshire when slim Italian or stout Fleming came riding down the dales under a spring sun to bargain for their wool crop. What a bustling hither and thither there would be, and what a confabulation in the parlour between my lady Prioress and her steward and her chaplain and the stranger sitting opposite to them and speaking his reasons "ful solempnely." What a careful distinguishing of the best and the medium and the worst kind of wool, which the Italian calls *buona lana* and *mojano lana* and *locchi*. What a haggling over the price, which varies from nunnery to nunnery, but always allows the merchant to sell at a good profit in the markets of Flanders and Italy. What sighs of relief when the stranger trots off again, sitting high on his horse and taking with him a silken purse, or a blood-band or a pair of gloves in "courtesy" from the nuns. What blessings on the black-faced sheep, when the sorely-needed silver is locked up in the treasury chest and debts begin to look less terrible, leaking roofs less incurable, pittances less few and far between.

(4) *Miscellaneous payments*. A last source of temporal revenue consisted in the sums paid for board and lodging by visitors, regular boarders and schoolchildren. Though such visitors were frowned at by bishops as subversive of discipline, the nuns welcomed their contributions to the lean income of the convent,

---

from 3 sacks). A similar Flemish list mentions Hampole, Nuncoton, Stainfield and Gracedieu (33 lbs.) Varenbergh, *Hist des Relations Diplomatiques entre le Comté de Flandre et l'Angleterre au Moyen Âge* (Brussels, 1874), pp 214–7

[1] "The Libel of English Policie," in *Hakluyt's Voyages* (Everyman's Lib. edit.), I, p 186.

and in most nunnery accounts payments by boarders will be
found among other miscellaneous receipts.

(5) *Spiritualities.* In the revenues which have hitherto been
considered, the monastic rent-rolls differed in no way from those
of any lay owner of land The source of revenue now to be distinguished was more specifically ecclesiastical. All monasteries
derived a more or less large income from certain grants made
to them in their capacity as religious houses. Most important
of these was the appropriation of benefices to their use. When a
church was appropriated to a monastery, the monastery was
usually supposed to put in a vicar at a fixed stipend to serve
the parish, and the great tithes (which would otherwise have supported a rector) were taken by the corporation. Sometimes half
a church was so appropriated and half the tithes were taken.
The practice of appropriating churches was widespread; not only
the king and other lay patrons, but also the bishops used this
means of enriching religious bodies and the favourite petition
of an impecunious convent was for permission to appropriate
a church[1]. Over and over again the gift of the advowson of a
church to a monastery is followed by appropriation[2] The per-

---

[1] See, for instance, a petition from the nuns of Carrow asking to be
allowed to appropriate the church of Surlingham, of which they had the
advowson, "qar, tres dute seignour, lauoesoun ne les fait bien eynz de les
mettre en daunger de presentement en chescune voedaunce"; *P R.O Anct
Petit* 232/11587 It appears that the prioress had letters patent to appropriate
the church, probably in answer to this petition in 22 Edw. II; Rye, *Carrow
Abbey*, App. p. xxxvi It may be useful to give a few out of very many
references to the appropriation of a church to a nunnery on account of
poverty: Clifton to Lingbrook (*Reg. R de Swinfield*, p. 134), Wolferlow and
Bridge Sollers to Aconbury (*Reg A. de Orleton*, pp 176, 200), Rockbeare
to Canonsleigh (*Reg. Grandisson*, ii, p. 698), Compton and Upmardon to
Easebourne (*Bp. Rede's Reg* p 137), Itchen Stoke to Romsey (*Reg Sandale*,
p 269), Whenby to Moxby (*Reg Wickwane*, p 290), Horton to St Clement's
York (*Reg. Gray*, p. 107), Bishopthorpe to the same (*Reg. Giffard*, p 59),
Dallington to Flamstead (Dugdale, *Mon.* iv, p. 301), Quadring to Stainfield
(*V.C.H. Lincs* ii, p 131), Easton Neston to Sewardsley and Desborough
to Rothwell (*V C.H Northants* ii, p 137), Lidlington to Barking (*V.C H
Essex*, ii, p. 119), Bradford, Tisbury and Gillingham to Shaftesbury (*V.C H.
Dorset*, ii, p. 77).

[2] An analysis of the possessions of Carrow gives some good examples
of this. The churches of Earlham, Stow Bardolph, Surlingham, Swardeston,
East Winch and Wroxham were all appropriated soon after their advowsons
had been granted to the priory, which also possessed the advowsons of four
churches in Norwich, the moiety of another advowson, the moiety of a
rectory and various tithes or portions of tithes in different manors and
parishes Rye, *Carrow Abbey*, App x.

mission of the bishop of the diocese and of the pope was necessary for the transaction, but it seems rarely to have been refused; and it has been calculated that at least a third part of the tithes of the richest benefices in England were appropriated either in part or wholly to religious and secular bodies, such as colleges, military orders, lay hospitals, guilds, convents, even deans, cantors, treasurers and chancellors of cathedral bodies were also largely endowed with rectorial tithes[1].

The practice of appropriation became a very serious abuse, for not all monasteries were conscientious in performing their duties to the parishes from which they derived such a large income, and ignorant and underpaid vicars often enough left their sheep encumbered in the mire, or swelled with their misery and discontent the democratic revolution known by the too narrow name of the Peasants' Revolt[2]. Moreover there is no doubt that sometimes the monks and nuns neglected even the obvious duty of putting in a vicar, and the hungry sheep looked up and were not fed. The *Valor Ecclesiasticus* throws an interesting light on this subject. The nuns of Elstow Abbey held no less than eleven rectories, from which they derived £157. 6s. 8d., but they paid stipends to four vicars only, and the total of the four was £6. 6s. 8d.[3] The nuns of Westwood received £12.12s.10d from two rectories and paid to a deacon in one of them 11s. 4d.[4] The Minoresses without Aldgate held four rectories, from that of Potton (Beds.) they received £16 6s. 8d. and paid the vicar £2, from that of Kessingland, Suffolk, £9 and paid the vicar £2. 4s. 4d[5] Another very common practice which cannot have conduced to the welfare of the parishioners was that of farming out the proceeds of appropriated churches, just as manors were farmed out The farmer paid the nuns a lump sum annually and took the proceeds of the tithes The purpose of such an arrangement was convenience, since it saved the convent the trouble of collecting the revenues and tithes It was open to objection from all points of view; for on the one hand the

---

[1] Gasquet, *Eng Mon Life*, p. 194.

[2] For the abuses of appropriation, see Coulton, *Medieval Studies*, no. 8, pp. 6–8 For the part played by the lower clergy in the Peasants' Revolt, see Petit-Dutaillis, *Studies Supplementary to Stubbs' Constit Hist* II, pp. 270–1, and Kriehn, *Studies in the Sources of the Social Revolt in 1381* (*Amer. Hist Review*, 1901), VI, pp 480–4.

[3] *Valor Eccles* IV, p. 188.

[4] *Ib* III, p. 276.   [5] *Ib.* I, p. 897.

nuns might, and often did, make bad bargains, and on the other they were still less likely to care for the spiritual welfare of the unfortunate parishioners, whose souls were to all intents and purposes farmed out with their tithes; though the payment of a vicar was sometimes made by the nuns or stipulated for in the agreement with the farmer. The *Valor Ecclesiasticus* gives the total spiritual revenue of the 84 nunneries holding spiritualities as £2705. 17s. 5d. and of this sum spiritualities to the value of £1075. 0s. 6d., belonging to 33 houses were entered as being at farm[1].

Account rolls often throw a flood of light upon the income derived from appropriated churches. To the nuns of St Michael's Stamford had been assigned by various abbots of Peterborough the churches of St Martin, St Clement, All Souls, St Andrew and Thurlby, and in the reign of Henry II two pious ladies gave them the moieties of the church of Corby and chapel of Upton[2] Moreover in 1354, after the little nunnery of Wothorpe had been ruined by the Black Death, all its possessions were handed over to St Michael's and included the appropriation of the church of Wothorpe; the bishop stipulated that the proceeds of the priory with the rectory should be applied to the support of the infirmary and kitchen of St Michael's and that the nuns should keep a chaplain to serve the parish church of Wothorpe[3]. Corby and Thurlby were afterwards farmed out by the nuns[4] and in 1377–8 they brought in £19 and £20 respectively, while the nuns got £26. 0s 8d. from "the church of All Saints beyond the water," £1. 13s 4d. from the parson of Cottesmore and a pension of 6s. 8d. from the church of St Martin They paid the vicar of Wothorpe a stipend of £2 a year[5]. Over half their income was usually derived from "farms, tithes and pensions," i.e. from ecclesiastical sources of revenue

It was also very common to make grants of tithes out of

---

[1] Jacka, *op cit* f. 35 See the list of "Farms and Pensions" in the prioress of Catesby's accounts for 1414–5 Baker, *Hist. and Antiqs. of Northants* I, p 279.

[2] *V.C.H. Northants.* II, p. 98.   [3] Dugdale, *Mon.* IV, p. 268.

[4] This appears from the regular entry of the amount brought in by the farms of the two churches in the account rolls. In 1458 the nuns received formal permission from the bishop to lease out and dispose of the fruits and revenues of any of the appropriated churches. Madox, *Form. Anglic.* dxc

[5] *P.R.O. Mins. Accts.* 1260/7

piety to a monastery, even when a grant of the advowson of
the church was not made. A lord would make over to it the
tithes of wheat, or a portion of the tithes, in certain parishes,
or perhaps the tithes of his own demesne land. Sometimes the
rector of a parish would pay the monks or nuns an annual rent
in commutation of their tithes; sometimes he would dispute their
claim and the tedious altercation would drag on for years, ending
perhaps in the expense of a law-suit[1]. Besides advowsons and
tithes various other pensions and payments were bestowed upon
religious houses by benefactors, who would leave an annual
pension to a monastery as a charge upon a particular piece
of land, or church, or upon another monastery[2].

Another "spiritual" source of revenue consisted in alms and
gifts given to the nuns as a work of piety Sometimes a nunnery
possessed a famous relic, and the faithful who visited it showed
their devotion by leaving a gift at the shrine. The *Valor* sometimes gives very interesting information about these cherished
possessions, described under the unkind heading *Superstitio*. The
Yorkshire nuns possessed among them a great variety of relics,
some of them having the most incongruous virtues At Sinningthwaite was to be found the arm of St Margaret and the tunic of
St Bernard "believed to be good for women lying in"[3], at Arden
was an image of St Bride, to which women made offerings

---

[1] See for instance Norris' note (quoted by Rye) on the grant to Carrow
Priory of the tithes of all wheat growing in the parishes of Bergh and Apton,
which tithes "occasioned many disputes between the Rector and the Convent, till at length about the year 1237 it was agreed by the Prioress and
Convent and Thomas, the then Rector, that the Rector should pay to the
Convent 14 quarters of wheat in lieu of all their tithes there, which was
constantly paid, with some little allowance for defect of measure, until
29 Edw III, when there was a suit between Prioress and Rector about them.
What was the event of it I find not, but they soon after returned to the old
payment of 14 qrs , which continued until 21 Hen. VI, when the dispute was
revived and in a litigious way they continued above ten years, but I find they
afterwards returned again to the old agreement and kept to it, I believe, to
the dissolution of the Priory " Rye mentions a suit between the Rector
and Prioress in 1321. Similarly the nuns were involved in a tedious suit
(10 Edw I) about the tithes of the demesne of the manor of Barshall in
Riston, with the Rector of Riston. Rye, *Carrow Abbey*, App. pp. xxx,
xxxv
[2] See below, p 199, for the other side of the matter
[3] Similarly the nuns of Kingsmead, Derby, had part of the shirt of
St Thomas of Canterbury, and the nuns of Gracedieu had the girdle and part
of the tunic of St Francis, both of which were good for the same purpose.
V.C.H. Derby, II, p 43, Nichols, *Hist of Leic.* III, p 652

for cows that had strayed or were ill The nuns of Arthington
had a girdle of the Virgin and the nuns of St Clement's York
and Basedale both had some of her milk; at St Clement's
pilgrimages were made to the obscure but popular St Syth[1]. In
other parts of the country it was the same. St Edmund's altar in
the conventual church of Catesby was a place of pilgrimage, for he
had bequeathed his pall and a silver tablet to his sister Margaret
Rich, prioress there[2]; and in 1400 Boniface IX granted an indult
to the Abbess of Barking to have mass and the other divine
offices celebrated in an oratory called "Rodlofte" (rood-loft),
in which was preserved a cross to which many people resorted[3].
The nuns of St Michael's Stamford not infrequently record sums
received from a pardon held at one of their churches, and almost
every year they received sums of money in exchange for their
prayers for the souls of the dead. "Almes et aventures," souls
and chance payments, was a regular heading in their account
roll, and the name of the person for whose soul they were to
pray was entered opposite the money received. Miscellaneous
alms from the faithful were always a source of revenue, though
necessarily a fluctuating source[4].

Such were the chief sources from which a medieval nunnery
derived its income We must now consider the chief expenses
which the nuns had to meet out of that income. It has already
been shown that the total income of a nunnery was paid into
the hands of the treasuress or treasuresses, save when the office
of treasuress was filled by the head of the house, or when a male
custos was appointed by the bishop to undertake the business.
It has also been shown that the treasuress paid out certain
sums to the chief obedientiaries (notably to the cellaress), to
whose use certain sources of income were indeed sometimes

---

[1] *V C.H. Yorks.* III, pp. 115, 119, 130, 159, 178, 189.

[2] *V C H Northants.* II, p 122.

[3] *V C H. Essex,* II, p. 118

[4] See for instance the receipts of the nuns of St Michael's Stamford
from *Almes, Almoignes et Auenture* entered in their roll for 45–6 Edw. III
"From Sir John Weston for a soul, 13s. 4d. For the soul of Simon the
Taverner, 1s For the soul of Sir Robert de Thorp, £20 6s 7d. For the soul
of William Apethorp, 3s. 4d For the soul of Alice atte Halle, 3s. 4d. In
alms from William Ouneby, 6s 8d. In alms from Emma of Okham £5
Received from the pardon at the church 6s 8d For the pardon from
Lady Idayne and from Emma Okham £1" *P R O. Mins Accts.* 1260/3.
But this was an unusually good year.

earmarked, and that these obedientiaries kept their separate accounts The majority of nunnery accounts which have survived are, however, treasuresses' accounts; that is to say they represent the general balance sheet at the end of the year, including all the chief items of income and expenditure. The different houses adopt, as is natural, different methods of classifying their expenses[1]. The great abbey of Romsey classifies thus: (1) *The Convent*, including sums for clothing, for the kitchen expenses and for pittances, amounting in all to £105. 17s. 10d. (2) *The Abbess*, who kept her separate household in state; this includes provisions for herself and for her household and divers of their expenses, a sum of £8. 12s. in gifts, a sum in liveries for the household and spices for the guest-house and a sum in servants' wages, amounting to £108. 17s. in all. (3) *Divers outside expenses*, including repairs of houses belonging to the Romsey mills, a sum for legal pleas, another for annuities to the convent and to the king's clerks, who had stalls in the abbey, over £40 in royal taxes and £1. 14s. 8d. in procurations, amounting to £108 in all. (4) *Miscellaneous expenses* include £8. 19s. 4d in alms to the poor, £6. 13s 4d in wine for nobles visiting the abbess, a sum for mending broken crockery, a sum for shoeing the horses of the Abbess' household, and in horse-hire and expenses of men riding on her business, 14s. in oblations of the Abbess and her household and £10 in gift to Henry Bishop of Winchester on his return from the Holy Land. (5) *Repairs* and other expenses at six manors belonging to this wealthy house, amounting to

---

[1] The account rolls of St Michael's Stamford usually arrange expenses under the following headings: (1) rents, (2) petty expenses, (3) convent expenses, (4) cost of carts and ploughs, (5) repair of houses, (6) purchase of stock, (7) weeding corn and mowing hay, (8) threshing and winnowing, (9) harvest expenses, (10) hire of servants, (11) chaplains' fees. See *P R.O. Mins. Accts* 1260/*passim*. The active prioress of St Mary de Pré, Christian Bassett, classifies her payments as for (1) "comyns, pytances and partycions," (2) "yerely charges," (3) "wagys and flees," (4) "reparacions," (5) "divers expensis." Dugdale, *Mon* III, pp. 358–61. The prioress of Catesby (1414–5) classifies (1) rents, (2) petty expenses, (3) expenses of the houses (i e. repairs), (4) household expenses, (5) necessary expenses (miscellaneous), (6) expenses of carts, (7) purchase of livestock, (8) customary payments (to nuns, pittancers, farmers, cottagers, etc in clothing, details not given), (9) purchase of corn, (10) rewards (various small tips to nuns and servants), (11) tedding and making hay, harvest expenses, stubble, thrashing and winnowing corn, (12) costs of the mill, (13) servants' wages Baker, *Hist and Antiq. of Northants.* I, pp. 278–83

£77. 2s. 6½d. The total expenses of the abbey this year (1412) came to £431 18s. 8d., against a revenue of £404. 6s 1d., drawn from six manors and including rents, the commutation fees for villein services, the sale of wool, corn and other stores and the perquisites of the courts The deficit is characteristic of nun-neries[1].

An interesting picture of many sides of monastic life is given by a general analysis of the chief classes of expenditure usually mentioned in account rolls. They may be classified as follows: (1) internal expenses of the convent, (2) divers miscellaneous expenses connected with external business, (3) repairs, (4) the expenses of the home farm and (5) the wage-sheet.

(1) *The internal expenses of the convent* The details of this expenditure are sometimes not given very fully, because they were set forth at length in the accounts of the cellaress and chambress, but a certain amount of food and of household goods and clothes was bought directly by the treasuress and occasionally the office of cellaress and treasuress was doubled by the same nun, whose account gives more detail. Expenditure on clothing appears in one of two forms, either as dress-allowances paid annually to the nuns[2], or as payments for the purchase of linen and cloth and for the hiring of work-people to spin and weave and make up the clothes[3]. Expenditure on food is usually concerned with the purchase of fish and of spices, the only important foods which could not be produced by the home farm

Among other internal expenses are the costs of the guest-house and the alms, in money and in kind, which were given to the poor. Account rolls sometimes throw a side light on the fare provided for visitors· for instance the treasuress of St Radegund's, Cambridge, enters upon her roll in 1449–50 the following items under the heading *Providencia Hospicii*:

And paid to William Rogger, for beef, pork, mutton and veal bought for the guest house, by the hand of John Grauntyer, 24s 8d And for bread, beer, beef, pork, mutton, veal, sucking pigs, capons, chickens, eggs, butter and fresh and salt fish, bought from day to day for the guest house during the period of the account, as appears more fully set out in detail, in a paper book examined for this account,

---

[1] Liveing, *Records of Romsey Abbey*, pp 194–5.·
[2] See below, p 323   [3] See below, pp. 157–8.

£11. 7s. 4½d. And for one cow bought of Thomas Carrawey for the guest house vj s viij d. Total: £13 8s 8½d.[1]

In this year the total receipts were £77. 8s. 6½d. and the expenditure £72 6s. 4¾d., so that quite a large proportion of the nuns' income was spent on hospitality. On the other hand the food was no doubt partly consumed by these "divers noble persons," who paid the convent £8. 14s. 4d this year for their board and lodging. It is a great pity that the separate guest-house account book referred to has not survived. At St Michael's Stamford the roll for 15–16 Richard II contains a payment of 26s. 10d. "for the expenses of guests for the whole year," and 6s. 8d. "for wine for the guests throughout the year"[2]; this is a very small amount out of a total expenditure of £116. 15s. 4½d. and it seems likely that the greater part of the food used for guests was not accounted for apart from the convent food.

The expenditure of nuns on alms is interesting, since almsgiving to the poor was one of the functions enjoined upon them by their rule; and many houses held a part of their property on condition that they should distribute certain alms. Some information as to these compulsory alms, though not of course as to the voluntary almsgiving of the nuns, is given in the *Valor Ecclesiasticus*. A few entries may be taken at random. St Sepulchre's, Canterbury, paid 6s. 8d. for one quarter of wheat to be given for the soul of William Calwell, their founder, the Thursday next before Easter[3]. Dartford was allowed £5. 12s. 8d. for alms given twice a week to thirteen poor people[4]; Haliwell distributed 12s 8d. in alms to poor folk every Christmas day in memory of a Bishop of Lincoln[5]. Nuneaton was allowed "for certain quarters of corn given weekly to the poor and sick at the gate of the monastery at 12d. a week, by order of the foundress, £2. 12s. 0d.; for certain alms on Maundy Thursday in money, bread, wine, beer and eels by the foundation, to poor and sick within the monastery, £2. 5s. 4d.[6] Polesworth gave "on Maundy Thursday at the washing of the feet of poor persons, in drink and victuals, by the foundation £1. 6s 0d."[7] A chartulary

[1] Gray, *Priory of St Radegund, Cambridge*, p. 156.
[2] P.R.O *Mins. Accts.* 1260/10.
[3] *Valor Eccles.* I, p 84   [4] *Ib* I, p 119
[5] *Ib* I, p. 394.   [6] *Ib.* III, p 76
[7] *Ib.* III, p. 77.

of the great Abbey of Lacock, drawn up at the close of the thirteenth century, contains an interesting list of alms payable to the poor and pittances to the nuns themselves on certain feasts and anniversaries. It runs:

We ought to feed on All Souls' day as many poor as there are ladies, to each poor person a dry loaf and as a relish two herrings or a slice of cheese, and the convent the same day shall have two courses On the anniversary of the foundress (24 Aug 1261) 100 poor each shall have a wheaten loaf and two herrings, be it a flesh-day or not, and the convent shall have to eat simnels and wine and three courses and two at supper On the anniversary of her father (17 April 1196) each year thirteen poor shall be fed. On the anniversary of her husband thirteen poor shall be fed, and the convent shall have half a mark for a pittance On the anniversary of Sir Nicholas Hedinton they should distribute to the poor 8s. and 4d., or corn amounting to as much money, i.e. wheat, barley and beans, and the convent half a mark for a pittance The day of the burial of a lady of the convent 100 poor, to each a mite or a dry loaf....The day of the Last Supper, after the Maundy, they shall give to each poor person a loaf of the weight of the convent loaf, and of the dough of full bread, and half a gallon of beer and two herrings, and half a bushel of beans for soup[1]

Account rolls sometimes contain references to food or money distributed to the poor on the great almsgiving day of Maundy Thursday, or on special feast days. The nuns of St Michael's Stamford regularly bought herrings to be given to the poor on Ash Wednesday, Maundy Thursday, St Laurence's day, St Michael's day and St Andrew's day. The nuns of St Radegund's, Cambridge, in 1450–1 distributed 2s. 1d. among the poor on Maundy Thursday and gave 10d. "to certain poor persons lately labouring in the wars of the lord king"[2]. The Prioress of St Mary de Pré, St Albans, has an item "paid in expenses for straungers, pore men lasours, tennents and fermours for brede and ale and other vitaills xxxvjs viijd"[3]. It is interesting to note that nunneries are not infrequently found giving alms in money or kind to the mendicant friars The Prioress of Catesby gave away 1 qr. 3 bushels of wheat "to brethren of the four orders and other poor" in 1414–5[4]. The Oxford friary received from Godstow in memory of the soul of one Roger Whittell fourteen

---

[1] *Archaeol. Journ.* LXIX (1912), pp 120–1
[2] Gray, *op. cit* p. 172
[3] Dugdale, *Mon* III, p. 359. The heading under which this item comes is *Yerely Charges*.
[4] Baker, *Hist. and Antiq of Northants* I, p 281.

loaves every fortnight and 3s. 4d in money and one peck of
oatmeal and one of peas in Lent. The Friars Minor of Cambridge
were sometimes sent a pig by the Abbess of Denny[1]. It will be
seen in a later chapter that the poor Yorkshire nunneries of
St Clement's York and Moxby were considerably burdened by
the obligation to pay 14 loaves weekly to the friars of York[2]. In
general, however, it is difficult to form any just estimate as to
how much almsgiving was really done by the nuns. There is no
evidence as to whether they daily gave away to the poor, as
their rule demanded, the fragments left over from their own
meals; for such almsgiving would be entered neither in account
rolls nor in chartularies and surveys dealing with endowments
earmarked for charity

Another class of gifts which deserves some notice consists
of gratuities to friends, well-wishers or dependents of the house,
for benefits solicited or received. No one in the middle ages was
too dignified to receive a tip. The nuns of St Michael's, Stamford,
regularly give what they euphemistically term "gifts" or
"courtesies" to a large number of persons, ranging from their
own servants at Christmas to men of law, engaged in the various
suits in which they were involved. To the high and mighty they
present wine, or a capon, or money discreetly jingling in the
depths of a silken purse. To the lowly they present a plain un-
varnished tip. The nuns of St Radegund's, Cambridge, pay 12d.
"for a crane bought and given to the chancellor of the university
of Cambridge, for his good friendship in divers of my lady's
affairs in the interest of the convent"; and "the four waits of
the Mayor of Cambridge" receive a Christmas box of 2s 3d. "for
their services to the lady Prioress and convent." *Dono Data* is a
regular heading in their accounts, and in 1450–1 there is a long
list of small gifts to dependents, ranging from 1d to 10d, and
a sum of 2s. for linen garments bought for gifts at Christmas[3].
Similarly the cellaress of Syon in 1536–7 gave her servants at
Christmas a reward of 20s "with their aprons"[4]. Whether to
ensure that a lawsuit should go in favour of the convent, or
merely to reward faithful service or to celebrate a feast, such

[1] A. G Little, *Studies in English Franciscan History* (1917), pp. 25, 43.
[2] See below, p 199.
[3] Gray, *op. cit* pp. 156, 172.
[4] *Myroure of Oure Ladye*, ed. Blunt, introd. p. xxxi.

payments were well laid out and no careful housekeeper could afford to neglect them.

(2) *Divers expenses* include payments for various fines, amercements and legal expenses and also for the numerous journeys undertaken by the prioress or by their servants on convent business. The legal expenses which fell upon the nuns of St Michael's, Stamford, ranged from a big suit in London and various cases over disputed tithes at the court of the bishop of Lincoln, to divers small amercements, when the convent pigs "trespassed in Castle meadow"[1]. The payments for journeys often give a vivid picture of nuns inspecting their manors and visiting their bishop[2]. Under this heading is also included a payment for ink and parchment and for the fee of the clerk who wrote out the account

(3) *Repairs* were a very serious item in the balance sheet of every monastic house, and in spite of the amount of money, which account rolls show to have been spent upon them, visitation reports have much to say about crumbling walls and leaking roofs It was seldom that a year passed without several visits from the plumbers, the slaters and the thatchers, to the precincts of a nunnery; and once arrived they were not easy to dislodge. If perchance the nunnery buildings themselves stood firm, then the houses of the tenants would be falling about their ears; and once more the distracted treasuress must summon workmen. Usually the nuns purchased the materials used for repairs and hired the labour separately, and the workers were sometimes fed in the nunnery kitchen; for it was customary at this time to include board with the wages of many hired workmen.

The accounts of St Radegund's, Cambridge, in 1449–50 will serve as an example of the expenditure under this heading[3]. It was a heavy year, for the nuns were having two tenements built in "Nunneslane" adjoining their house, and the accounts give an interesting picture of the building of a little medieval house of clay and wattle, with stone foundations, whitewashed walls and thatched roof. First of all Henry Denesson, carpenter, a most important person, was hired to set up all the woodwork

---

[1] See below, p 202.   [2] See e.g above, p. 70.
[3] Gray, *op. cit.* pp. 153–5.

at a wage of 23s. 4d. for the whole piece of work; he had an
assistant John Cokke, who was paid 14d. for ten days' work;
Simon Maydewell was kept hard at work sawing timber for his
use for ten days at 14d. and over a cart load and a half of
"splentes" (small pieces of wood laid horizontally in a stud wall)
were purchased at a cost of 6s 2d Henry and John spent ten
days setting up the framework of the two cottages, but they
were not the only workers The "gruncill" (or beam laid along
the ground for the rest to stand on) had to be laid firmly on a
stone foundation, the walls had to be filled between the beams
with clay, strengthened with a mixture of reeds and sedge and
bound with hemp nailed firmly to the beams The account tells
us all about these operations:

and in hemp with nails bought for binding the walls 16d , and in stone
bought from Thomas Janes of Hynton to support the gruncill 6s. 8d ,
and in one measure of quicklime bought for the same work 3s , and
in six cartloads of clay bought of Richard Poket of Barnwell 18d ,
and in the hire of Geoffrey Sconyng and William Brann, to lay the
gruncill of the aforesaid tenements and to daub the walls thereof
(i.e to make them of clay), for the whole work 17s. 3d And in reeds
bought of John Bere, "reder," for the aforesaid tenements 2s. 4d ,
and in "1000 de les segh" (sedge) for the same work 5s. And in
22 bunches of wattles 22d., and in boards bought at the fair of St John
the Baptist to make the door and windows 2s 10d., and in 1000 nails
for the said work, together with 1000 more nails bought afterwards
2s. 8½d.

Finally the houses had to be roofed with a thatch of straw and
a fresh set of workmen were called in

and for the hire of John Scot, thatcher, hired to roof with straw the
two aforesaid tenements, for 12 days, taking 4d a day, at the board
of the Lady (Prioress) 4s. And for the hire of Thomas Clerk for 8½ days
and of Nicholaus Burnefygge for 10 days, carrying straw and serving
the said thatcher 3s 1d , and in the hire of Katherine Rolf for the
same work (women often acted as thatchers' assistants) for 12 days
at 1½d. a day, 18d.

And behold two very nice little cottages

But let not the ignorant suppose that this completed the
expenditure of the nuns on building and repairs Henry Denesson, the indispensable, soon had to be hired again to set up some
woodwork in a tenement in Precherch Street, and to build a
gable there. A kitchen had to be built next to these tenements,

and the business of hiring carpenters, daubers and thatchers was repeated; John Scot and John Cokke once more scaled the roofs. Then a house in Nun's Lane was burnt and sedge had to be bought to thatch it Then three labourers had to be hired for four days to mend the roofs of the hall, kitchen and other parts of the nunnery itself, taking 5d. a day and their board. Then the roofs of the frater and the granary began to leak and the same labourers had to be hired for four more days Then, just as the treasuress thought that she had got rid of the ubiquitous Henry Denesson for good, back he had to be called with a servant to help him, to set up the falling granary again. Then a lock had to be made for the guests' kitchen and for three other rooms in the nunnery; and when John Egate, tiler, and John Tommesson, tenants of the nuns, got wind that locks were being made, they must needs have some for their tenements. Then a defect in the church had to be repaired by John Corry and a cover made for the font. There was more purchase of reeds and sedge, boards and " 300 nails (12d.) and 100 nails (2d) bought at Stourbridge Fair" for 14d. Last came the inevitable plumber

And for a certain plumber hired to mend a gutter between the tenement wherein Walter Ferror dwells and a tenement of the Prior of Barnwell, with lead found by the said Prior, together with the mending of a defect in the church of St Radegund 14d. And in the hire of the aforesaid plumber to mend a lead pipe extending from the font to the copper in the brewhouse, together with the solder of the said plumber 8d.

In all the cost of repairs and buildings came to £8. 3s. 7d. out of a total expenditure of £72 6s. 4¾d.

(4) *Expenses of the home farm*. The home farm was an essential feature of manorial economy and particularly so when the lord of the manor was a community. The nuns expected to draw the greater part of their food from the farm; livestock, grain and dairy all had to be superintended. A student of these account rolls may see unrolled before him all the different operations of the year, the autumn ploughing and sowing, the spring ploughing and sowing, the hay crop mown in June and the strenuous labours of the harvest. He may, if he will, know how many sheep the shepherd led to pasture and how many oxen the oxherd drove home in the evening, for the inventory on the

back of an account roll enumerates minutely all the stock. There is something homely and familiar in lists such as the tale of cattle owned by the nuns of Sheppey at the Dissolution:

v contre oxen and iij western oxen fatt,...xviij leane contre oxen workers, xij leane contre sterys of ij or iij yere age, xxviij yeryngs, xxxviii kene and heifors . xxvi cattle of thys yere, an horse, j olde baye, a dunne, a whyte and an amblelyng grey, vj geldings and horse for the plow and harowe, with v mares, xliij hogges of dyvers sorts, in wethers and lammys cccc^{xxx},...and in beryng ewes vij^{o},... in twelvemonthyngs, ewes and wethers vi^{o}xxxv ..in lambys at this present daye v^{o}lx[1].

· How these lean country oxen, the "one old bay, a dun, a white and an ambling grey," bring the quiet English landscape before the reader's eyes. Time is as nothing; and the ploughman trudging over the brown furrows, the slow, warm beasts, breathing heavily in the darkness of their byre, are little changed from what they were five hundred years ago—save that our beasts to-day are larger and fatter, thanks to turnips and Mr Bakewell. Kingdoms rise and fall, but the seasons never alter, and the farm servant, conning these old accounts, would find nothing in them but the life he knew

> This is the year's round he must go
> To make and then to win the seed
> In winter to sow and in March to hoe
> Michaelmas plowing, Epiphany sheep;
> Come June there is the grass to mow,
> At Lammas all the vill must reap
> From dawn till dusk, from Easter till Lent
> Here are the laws that he must keep
> Out and home goes he, back-bent,
> Heavy, patient, slow as of old
> Father, granfer, ancestor went
> O'er Sussex weald and Yorkshire wold.
> O what see you from your gray hill?
> The sun is low, the air all gold,
> Warm lies the slumbrous land and still.
> I see the river with deep and shallow,
> I see the ford, I hear the mill;
> I see the cattle upon the fallow,
> And there the manor half in trees,
> And there the church and the acre hallow
> Where lie your dead in their feretories...

[1] Mackenzie Walcott, *Inventories of. Shepey*, pp 32-3.

I see the yews and the thatch between
The smoke that tells of cottage and hearth,
And all as it has ever been
From the beginning of this old earth[1].

The farm labourer to-day would well understand all these
items of expenditure, which the monastic treasuress laboriously
enters in her account. He would understand that heavy section
headed "Repair of Carts and Ploughs" He would understand
the purchases of grain for seed, or for the food of livestock,
of a cow here, a couple of oxen there, of whip-cord and horse-
collars, traces and sack-cloth and bran for a sick horse. Farm
expenses are always the same The items which throw light on
sheep-farming are very interesting, in view of the good income
which monastic houses in pastoral districts made by the sale
of their wool. The Prioress of Catesby's account for 1414–5
notes:

In expences about washing and shearing of sheep v s vj d. In ale
bought for caudles ij s. In pitchers viij d. In ale about the carriage
of peas to the sheepcote iv d ob In a tressel bought for new milk
viij d. In nails for a door there iv d ob. In thatching the sheepcote
viij d In amending walls about the sheepcote ix d ; .

and in her inventory of stock she accounts for

118 sheep received of stock, whereof there was delivered to the kitchen
after shearing by tally 14, in murrain before shearing 12, and there
remains 101; and for 5 wethers of stock and 2 purchased, whereof in
murrain before shearing 3, and there remains 4, and for 144 lambs
of issues of all ewes, whereof in murrain 23; and there remains 121[2].

The nuns of Gracedieu in the same spring had a flock of 103
ewes and 52 lambs; and there is mention in their accounts of
the sale of 30 stone of wool to a neighbour[2]; and the nuns of
Sheppey, as the inventory quoted above bears witness, had a
very large flock indeed

Some of the most interesting entries in the accounts are the
payments for extra labour at busy seasons, to weed corn, make
hay, shear sheep, thresh and winnow. The busiest season of all,

---

[1] Maurice Hewlett, *The Song of the Plow* (1916), pp 9–10.
[2] Baker, *Hist. and Antiq. of Northants.* I, p. 283. Compare the St Radegund's Cambridge accounts. "Et in butumine empto cum pycche hoc anno
pro bidentibus signandis et ungendis, ij s j d. Et in clatis emptis ad faldam,
iij s iij d. Et solutum pro remocione falde per diversas vices, iij d Et
in bidentibus hoc anno lavandis et tondendis ij s iij d " Gray, *op. cit.*
pp. 155, 171.

the climax of the farmer's year, was harvest time, and most
monastic accounts give it a separate heading. The nuns of St
Michael's, Stamford, year after year record the date "when we
began to reap" and the payments to reapers and cockers for
the first four or five weeks and to carters for the fortnight
afterwards. Extra workers, both men and women, came in
from among the cottagers of the manor and of neighbouring
manors; in some parts of the country migrant harvesters came,
as they do to-day, from distant uplands to help on the farms
of the rich cornland. To oversee them a special reap-reeve was
hired at a higher rate (the nuns of St Michael's paid him 13s. 8d.
in 1378), gloves were given to the reapers to protect them from
thistles[1], special tithers were hired to set aside the sheaves due
to the convent as tithes (the convent paid "to one tither of
Wothorpe," an appropriated church, "10s , and to two of our
tithers 13s. 4d ") The honest Tusser sets out the usage in jingling
rhyme:

Grant haruest lord more by a penie or twoo
    to call on his fellowes the better to doo:
Giue gloues to thy reapers, a larges to crie,
    and dailie to loiterers haue a good eie.
Reape wel, scatter not, gather cleane that is shorne,
    binde faste, shock apace, haue an eie to thy corne.
Lode safe, carrie home, follow time being faire,
    goue iust in the barne, it is out of despaire.
Tithe dulie and trulie, with hartie good will
    that God and his blessing may dwell with thee still:
Though Parson neglecteth his dutie for this,
    thank thou thy Lord God, and giue erie man his[2].

Usually the workers got their board during harvest and very
well they fared. The careful treasuresses of St Michael's get in
beef and mutton and fish for them, to say nothing of eggs and
bread and oatmeal and foaming jugs of beer. Porringers and
platters have to be laid in for them to feed from; and since they
work until the sun goes down, candles must be bought to light

---

[1] They are a regular item in the St Michael's, Stamford, accounts and
compare the accounts of St Radegund's, Cambridge· "And in viij pairs
of gloves bought for divers hired men at harvest as was needful xij d."
Gray, op. cit. pp 157, 172.
  [2] Tusser, Fiue Hundred Pointes of Good Husbandrie, ed. W. Payne and
S. J Herrtage (Eng Dialect. Soc. 1878), pp. 129–30

the board in the summer dusk. At the end of all, when the last sheaf was carried to the barn and the last gleaner had left the fields, the nuns entertained their harvesters to a mighty feast.

It was a time for hard work and for good fellowship. Says Tusser:

> In haruest time, haruest folke, seruants and all,
>   should make all togither good cheere in the hall:
> And fill out the black boule of bleith to their song,
>   and let them be merie all haruest time long
>
> Once ended thy haruest let none be begilde,
>   please such as did helpe thee, man, woman and childe.
> Thus dooing, with alway such helpe as they can,
>   those winnest the praise of the labouring man[1].

The final feast was associated with the custom of giving a goose to all who had not overturned a load in carrying during harvest, and the nuns of St Michael's always enter it in their accounts as "the expenses of the sickle goose" or harvest goose.

> For all this good feasting, yet art thou not loose
>   till ploughman thou giuest his haruest home goose
> Though goose go in stubble, I passe not for that,
>   let goose haue a goose, be she leane, be she fat[2]

An echo of old English gaiety sounds very pleasantly through these harvest expenses.

(5) *The wages sheet.* The last set of expenses which the monastic housewife entered upon her roll was the wages sheet of the household, the payments for the year, or for a shorter period, of all her male and female dependents, together with the cost of their livery and of their allowance of "mixture," when the convent gave them these. We saw in the last chapter that the nuns were the centre of a small community of farm and household servants, ranging from the reverend chaplains and dignified bailiff through all grades of standing and usefulness, down to the smallest kitchen-maid and the gardener's boy.

Such is the tale of the account rolls. It may be objected by some that this talk of tenement-building, and livestock, ploughshares and harvest-home has little to do with monastic life, since it is but the common routine of every manor. But this is the very reason for describing it. The nunneries of England

---

[1] Tusser, *op cit* p. 132.   [2] *Ib.* p. 181.

were firmly founded on the soil and the nuns were housewives and ladies of the manor, as were their sisters in the world This homely business was half their lives, they knew the kine in the byre and the corn in the granary, as well as the service-books upon their stalls. The sound of their singing went up to heaven mingled with the shout of the ploughmen in the field and the clatter of churns in the dairy. When a prioress' negligence lets the sheepfold fall into disrepair, so that the young lambs die of the damp, it is made a charge against her to the bishop, together with more spiritual crimes The routine of the farm goes on side by side with the routine of the chapel These account rolls give us the material basis for the complicated structure of monastic life. This is how nuns won their livelihood, this is how they spent it.

CHAPTER IV

MONASTIC HOUSEWIVES

Some respit to husbands the weather may send,
But huswiues affaires haue neuer an end

TUSSER, *Fiue Hundred Pointes of Good Husbandrie* (1573).

EVERY monastic house may be considered from two points of view, as a religious and as a social unit. From the religious point of view it is a house of prayer, its centre is the church, its *raison d'être* the daily round of offices From the social point of view it is a community of human beings, who require to be fed and clothed, it is often a landowner on a large scale; it maintains a more or less elaborate household of servants and dependents; it runs a home farm, it buys and sells and keeps accounts. The nun must perforce combine the functions of Martha and of Mary; she is no less a housewife than is the lady of the manor, her neighbour. The monastic routine of bed and board did not work without much careful organisation; and it is worth while to study the method by which this organisation was carried out.

The daily business of a monastery was in the hands of a number of officials, chosen from among the older and more experienced of the inmates and known as *obedientiaries*. These obedientiaries, as Mr C. T. Flower has pointed out in a useful article[1], fall into two classes: (1) executive officials, charged with the general government of a house, such as the abbess, prioress, subprioress and treasuress, and (2) nuns charged with particular functions, such as the chantress, sacrist, fratress, infirmaress,

---

[1] C. T. Flower, *Obedientiars' Accounts of Glastonbury and other Religious Houses* (St Paul's Ecclesiological Soc. vol VII, pt II (1912)), pp. 50–62. The nunnery accounts described include accounts of the Abbess of Elstow (22 Hen. VII), the Prioress of Delapré (4 and 9 Hen VII), the Cellaress of Barking, the Cellaress of Syon, the Sacrist of Syon and the Chambress of Syon On obedientiaries and their accounts in general, see the introduction to *Compotus Rolls of the Obedientiaries of St Swithun's Priory, Winchester*, ed G. W. Kitchin (Hants Rec Soc 1892).

mistress of the novices, chambress and cellaress. The number of obedientiaries differed with the size of the house. In large houses the work had naturally to be divided among a large number of officials and those whose offices were heaviest had assistants to help them. A list of the twenty-six nuns of Romsey in 1502, for instance, distinguishes besides the abbess, a prioress, subprioress, four chantresses, an almoness, cellaress, sacrist and four subsacrists, kitcheness, fratress, infirmaress and mistress of the school of novices[1]. But in a small house there was less need of differentiation, and though complaint is sometimes made of the doubling of offices (perhaps from jealousy or a desire to participate in the doubtful sweets of office), one nun must often have performed many functions It is common, for instance, to find the head of the house acting as treasuress, a practice which undoubtedly had its dangers

The following were the most important obedientiaries, whose duties are distinguished in the larger convents. (1) The *Treasuress*, or more often two treasuresses. Her duty was to receive all the money paid, from whatever source, to the house and to superintend disbursements; she had the general management of business and held the same position as a college bursar to-day. (2) The *Chantress* or *Precentrix* had the management of the church services, trained the novices in singing and usually looked after the library (3) The *Sacrist* had the care of the church fabric, with the plate, vestments and altar cloths and of the lighting of the whole house, for which she had to buy the wax and tallow and wicks and hire the candle-makers. (4) The *Fratress* had charge of the frater or refectory, kept the chairs and tables in repair, purchased the cloths and dishes, superintended the laying of meals and kept the lavatory clean (5) The *Almoness* had charge of the almsgiving. (6) The *Chambress* ordained everything to do with the wardrobe of the nuns; the *Additions to the Rules of Syon* thus describe her work:

The Chaumbress schal haue al the clothes in her warde, that perteyne to the bodyly araymente of sustres and brethern, nyghte and day, in ther celles and fermery, as wel of lynnen as of wollen; schapynge,

---

[1] Liveing, *Records of Romsey Abbey*, p 236 At St Mary's Winchester at the same date the 14 nuns included the abbess, prioress, subprioress, infirmaress, *precentrix* and three sub-chantresses, *scrutatrix*, *dogmatista* and librarian *V C H Hants.* II, p 124

sewynge, makyng, repayryng and kepyng them from wormes, schakyng them by the help of certayne sustres depute to her, that they be not deuoured and consumed of moughtes So that sche schal puruey for canuas for bedyng, fryses, blankettes, schetes, bolsters, pelowes, couerlites, cuschens, basens, stamens, rewle cotes, cowles, mantelles, wymples, veyles, crounes, pynnes, cappes, nyght kerchyfes, pylches, mantel furres, cuffes, gloues, hoses, schoes, botes, soles, sokkes, mugdors, gyrdelles, purses, knyues, laces, poyntes, nedelles, threde, waschɪng bolles and sope and for al suche other necessaryes after the dɪsposɪcɪon of the abbes, whiche in no wyse schal be ouer curyous, but playne and homly, wɪtheoute weuynge of any straunge colours of sylke, golde, or syluer, hauynge al thynge of honeste and profyte, and nothyng of vanyte, after the rewle, ther knyues un-poynted and purses beyng double of lynnen clothe and not of sylke[1].

(7) The *Cellaress* looked after the food of the house and the domestɪc servants, and usually superintended the management of the home farm It was her business to lay in all stores, obtaining some from the home farm and some by purchase ɪn the village market, or at periodical faɪrs. She had to order the meals, to engage and dismiss servants and to see to all repairs As one wrɪter very well says, her "manifold duties appear to have been a combination of those belonging to the offices of steward, butler and farmer's wife"[2]. The *Rules* of Syon again deserves quotation:

The Celeres schal puruey for mete and drynke for seke and hole, and for mete and drynke, clothe and wages, for seruantes of householde outwarde, and sche shall haue all the vessel and stuffe of housholde under her kepynge and rewle, kepynge ɪt klene, hole and honeste. So that whan sche receyueth newe, sche moste restore the olde to the abbes Ordenyng for alle necessaryes longynge to al houses of offices concernyng the bodyly fode of man, ɪn the bakhows, brewhows, kychen, buttry, pantry, celer, freytour, fermery, parlour and suche other, bothe outewarde and ɪnwarde, for straungers and dwellers, attendyng dɪligently that the napery and al other thynge ɪn her office be honest, profitable and plesaunte to al, after her power, as sche ɪs commaunded by her souereyne[3]

A very detaɪled set of ɪnstructɪons how to cater for a large abbey is to be found in a Barking document called the *Charthe longynge to the office of the Celeresse of the Monasterye of Barkinge*[4]. (8) The *Kɪtcheness* superintended the kitchen, under the direction

---

[1] Aungɪer, *Hɪst. of Syon Mon.* p. 392.
[2] *Myroure of Oure Ladye*, ed Blunt (E E T.S), ɪntrod. p. xxvɪɪɪ
[3] Aungier, *op. cɪt.* pp 392–3   [4] See below, Note A

of the cellaress. (9) The *Infirmaress* had charge of the sick in the infirmary; the author of the *Additions to the Rules* of Syon, a person of all too vivid imagination, charges her often to

chaunge ther beddes and clothes, geue them medycynes, ley to ther plastres and mynyster to them mete and drynke, fyre and water and al other necessaryes, nyghte and day, as nede requyrethe, after counsel of the phisicians,...not squames to wasche them, and wype them, nor auoyde them, not angry nor hasty, or unpacient thof one haue the vomet, another the fluxe, another the frensy, which nowe syngethe, now wel apayde, ffor ther be some sekenesses vexynge the seke so gretly and prouokynge them to ire, that the mater drawen up to the brayne alyenthe the mendes[1].

(10) The *Mistress of the Novices* acted as schoolmistress to the novices, teaching them all that they had to learn and super-intending their general behaviour.

Certain of these obedientiaries, more especially the cellaress, chambress and sacrist, had the control and expenditure of part of the convent's income, because their departments involved a certain number of purchases, indeed while the treasuress acted as bursar, the housekeeping of the convent was in the hands of the cellaress and chambress. Every well organised nunnery therefore divided up its revenues, allocating so much to the church, so much to clothing, so much to food, etc. Rules for the disposition of the income of a house were sometimes drawn up by a more than usually thrifty treasuress for the guidance of her successors, and kept in the register or chartulary of the nunnery. The Register of Crabhouse Priory contains one such document written (in the oddest French of Stratford-atte-Bowe) during the second half of the fourteenth century:

"The wise men of religion who have possessions," says this careful dame, "consider according to the amount of their goods how much they can spend each year and according to the sum of their income they ordain to divers necessities their portions in due measure And in order that when the time comes the convent should not fail to have what is necessary according to the sum of our goods, we have ordained their portions to divers necessary things. To wit, for bread and beer, all the produce of our lands and tenements in Tilney and all the produce of our half church of St Peter in Wiggenhall, and, if it be necessary, all the produce of our land in Gyldenegore For meat and fish and for herrings and for *feri* and *asser*[2] and for cloves is set

---

[1] Aungier, *op cit* p 395
[2] I have been unable to discover what is meant by *feri* and *asser*.

aside all the produce of our houses and rents in Lynn and in North Lynn and in Gaywood. For clothing and shoes all the produce of our meadow in Setchy, and the remnant of the land in Setchy and in West Winch is ordained for the purchase of salt For the prioress' chamber, for tablecloths and towels and *tabites*[1] in linen and saye, and for other things which are needed for guests and for the household, is set aside all the produce of our land and tenements in Thorpland and in Wallington. For the repair of our houses and of our church in Crabhouse and for sea dykes and marsh dykes and for the wages of our household and for other petty expenses is ordained all the produce of our lands, tenements and rents in Wiggenhall, with the exception of the pasture for our beasts and of our fuel Similarly the breeding of stock, and all the profits which may be drawn from our beasts in Tilney, in Wiggenhall and in Thorpland, and in all other places (saving the stock for our larder, and draught-beasts for carts and ploughs and saving four-and-twenty cows and a bull) are assigned and ordained for the repair of new houses and new dykes, to the common profit of the house[2]."

This practice of earmarking certain sources of income may be illustrated from almost any monastic chartulary, for it was common for benefactors to earmark donations of land and rent to certain special purposes, more especially for the clothing of the nuns, for the support of the infirmary, or for a special pittance from the kitchen[3] Similarly bishops appropriating churches to monastic houses sometimes set aside the proceeds for special purposes[4]. The result of the practice was that the obedientiaries of certain departments, more especially the cellaress, chambress and

[1] *Tabite* was a sort of *moiré* silk Probably carpets or tablecloths here
[2] *Register of Crabhouse Nunnery*, ed. M Bateson (Norfolk Archaeology, XI, 1892), pp. 38–9.
[3] See, for instance, the Godstow Register, charters nos 105, 139, 556 and 644 concern grants appropriated to clothing and nos. 52, 250, 536, 619 and 630 to the infirmary. No. 862 is a grant of five cartloads of alderwood yearly "to be take xv dayes after myghelmasse to drye their heryng " *Eng Reg. of Godstow Nunnery*, ed. A Clark (E E.T S 1905–11), pp. 102, etc. In the Crabhouse Register it is noted that a certain meadow is set aside so that "all the produce of the said meadow be forever granted for the vesture of the ten ladies who are oldest in religion of the whole house, so that each of the ten ladies receive yearly from the aforesaid meadow four shillings at the feast of St Margaret." *Op. cit* p. 37 When Wothorpe was merged in St Michael's, Stamford, the diocesan stipulated that the proceeds of the priory and rectory of Wothorpe should be applied to the support of the infirmary and kitchen of St Michael's. Dugdale, *Mon* IV, p. 268
[4] See, for instance, the payment of a yearly pension of five marks from the appropriated church of St Clement's for the clothing of the nuns of St Radegund's, Cambridge, and similar assignations of the income from appropriated churches at Studley, St Michael's Stamford, and Marrick. Gray, *Priory of St Radegund, Cambridge*, p 27

sacrist, had to keep careful accounts of their receipts and expenditure, which were submitted annually to the treasuress, when
she was making up her big account. Very few separate obedientiaries' accounts survive for nunneries, partly because the majority
were small and the treasuress not infrequently acted as cellaress
and did the general catering herself Cellaresses' accounts, however, survive for Syon and Barking, chambresses' accounts for
Syon and St Michael's Stamford (the latter merely recording the
payment to the nuns of their allowances) and sacrists' accounts
for Syon and Elstow[1]. In one column these accounts set out
the sources from which the office derives its income. This might
come to the obedientiary in one of two ways, either directly
from the churches, manors or rents appropriated to her, or by
the hands of the treasuress, who received and paid her the rents
due to her office, or if no revenues were appropriated to it,
allocated her a lump sum out of the general revenues of the
house. Thus at Syon the cellaress drew her income from the sale
of hides, oxhides and fleeces (from slaughtered animals and sheep
at the farm), the sale of wood, and the profits of a dairy farm
at Isleworth, while the chambress simply answered for a sum
of £10 paid to her by the treasuresses. In another column the
obedientiary would enter her expenditure. This might take two
forms According to the Benedictine rule and to the rule of
the newly founded and strict Brigittine house of Syon, all
clothes and food were provided for the nuns by the chambress
and cellaress; and accordingly their accounts contain a complete
picture of the communal housekeeping In the later middle
ages, however, it became the almost universal custom to pay the
nuns a money allowance instead of clothing, a practice which
deprived the office of chambress of nearly all its duties and
possibly accounts for the rarity of chambresses' account rolls. The
Syon chambress' account is an example of the first or regular
method; the St Michael's, Stamford, account of the second More
rarely the nuns received money allowances for a portion of their
food. The growth of this custom of paying money allowances

[1] See C T. Flower, *loc. cit.*, for an account of the Syon, Barking and
Elstow accounts, also Blunt, *Myroure of Oure Ladye*, introd pp xxvi–xxxi,
for Syon chambresses' and cellaresses' accounts (1536–7) and *P R O Mins.
Accts* 1261/4 for a Syon cellaress's account (1481–2) See *P R O Mins.
Accts* 1260/14 for a St Michael's Stamford chambress's account (1408–9).

will be described in a later chapter[1], here it will suffice to consider the housekeeping of a nunnery in which that business was
entirely in the hands of the chambress and cellaress

The accounts throw an interesting light on the provision of
clothes for a convent and its servants. An account of Dame
Bridget Belgrave, chambress of Syon (who had to look after
the brothers as well as the sisters of the house) has survived
for the year 1536-7 It shows her buying "russettes," "white
clothe," "kerseys," "gryce," "Holand cloth and other lynen
cloth," paying for the spinning of hemp and flax, for the weaving
of cloth, for the dressing of calves' skins and currying of leather,
and for 3000 "pynnes of dyuerse sortes " She pays wages to
"the yoman of the warderobe," "the grome," the skinner and
the 'shoemakers and she tips the "sealer" of leather in the
market place[2]. Treasuresses' accounts also often give interesting
information about the purchase and making up of various kinds
of material. At St Radegund's, Cambridge, the nuns were in
receipt of an annual dress allowance, but the house made many
purchases of stuff for the livery of its household and in 1449-50
the account records payments

to a certain woman hired to spin 21 lbs. of wool, 22d ; and to Alice
Pavyer hired for the same work, containing in the gross 36 lbs. of woollen
thread 6s.; and paid to Roger Rede of Hinton for warping certain
woollen thread 1½d ; and to the same hired to weave 77 ells of woollen
cloth for the livery of the servants 3s. 5d., and paid to the wife of
John Howdelowe for fulling the said cloth 3s 6d , and paid to a certain
shearman for shearing (i e finishing the surface of) the said cloth 14½d.

The next year the nuns make similar payments for cleaning,
spinning, weaving, warping, fulling and shearing wool (an interesting illustration of the subdivision of the cloth industry) and
disburse 9s. 9d. to William Judde of St Ives for dyeing and
making up this cloth into green and blue liveries for the servants
of the house[3].

The cellaresses' accounts, which show us how the nun-house-
keeper catered for the community, are even more interesting
than the chambresses' accounts The convent food was derived
from two main sources, from the home farm and from purchase.
The home farm was usually under the management of the

[1] See below, Ch viii   [2] Blunt, *op. cit.* pp. xxvi–xxviii
[3] Gray, *op. cit.* pp. 149, 165, 167.

cellaress and provided the house with the greater part of its
meat, bread, beer and vegetables, and with a certain amount of
dairy produce (butter, cheese, eggs, chickens). Anything which
the farm could not produce had to be bought, and in particular
three important articles of consumption, to wit the salt and
dried fish eaten during the winter and in Lent, the salt for the
great annual meat-salting on St Martin's day, and the spices and
similar condiments used so freely in medieval cooking and eaten
by convents more especially in Lent, to relieve the monotony
of their fasting fare The nuns of St Radegund's, Cambridge,
used to get most of their salt fish at Lynn, whence it was brought
up by river to Cambridge From the accounts of 1449–51 it
appears that the senior ladies made the occasion one for a
pleasant excursion. There is a jovial entry in 1450–1 concerning
the carnage by water from Lynn to Cambridge of one barrel[1]
and a half of white herrings, two cades[2] of red herrings, two
cades of smelts, one quarter of stockfish and one piece of timber
called "a Maste" out of which a ladder was to be made (2s. 4d.),
together with the fares and food of Dame Joan Lancaster, Dame
Margaret Metham, Thomas Key (the bailiff) and Elene Herward
of Lynn to Cambridge (2s. 8d). Another entry displays to us
Dame Joan Lancaster bargaining for the smelts and the stockfish at Lynn. Fish was usually bought from one John Ball of
Lynn, who seems to have been a general merchant of considerable
custom, for the nuns also purchased from him all the linen which
they needed for towels and tablecloths, and some trenchers.
Occasionally, also, however, they purchased some of their fish
at one or other of the fairs held in the district; in 1449–50 they
thus bought 8 warp[3] of ling and 6 warp of cod from one John
Antyll at Ely fair and 14 warp of ling from the same man at
Stourbridge fair, an interesting illustration of how tradesmen
travelled from fair to fair. At St John Baptist's fair in the same
year they bought a horse for 9s. 6d., 2 qrs. 5 bushels of salt,
some timber boards and three "pitcheforke staves." In the
following year they bought timber, pewter pots, a churn, 10 lbs
of soap and 3 lbs. of pepper at the famous fair of Stourbridge,

---

[1] A barrel contained ten great hundreds of six score each.
[2] A cade contained six great hundreds of six score each.
[3] A warp was a parcel of four dried fish.

and salt and timber at the fair of St John Baptist In 1481–2 they bought salt fish, salt, iron nails, paper, parchment and "other necessities" at the fairs of Stourbridge and of St Etheldreda the Virgin[1]

The fish-stores illustrate a side of medieval housekeeping, which is unfamiliar to-day. Fresh fish was eaten on fish-days whenever it could be got. Most monastic houses had fishing rights attached to their demesnes, or kept their own fish-pond or *stew*. The nuns of St Radegund's had fishing rights in a certain part of the Cam known as late as 1505 as "Nunneslake"[2]. But a great deal of dried and salted fish was also eaten. In their storehouse the nuns always kept a supply of the dried cod known as stockfish for their guest-house and for the frater during the winter It was kept in layers on canvas and was so dry that it had to be beaten before it could be used, it is supposed to have derived its name from the *stock* on which it was beaten, or, as Erasmus preferred to say, "because it nourisheth no more than a dried stock"[3] For Lent the chief articles of food were herrings and salt salmon, but the list of *salt store* purchased by the cellaress of Syon in 1536–7 shows a great variety of fish, to wit 200 dry lings, 700 dry haberden (salted cod), 100 "Iceland fish," 1 barrel of salt salmon, 1 barrel of [white] herring, 1 cade of red herring and 420 lbs. of "stub" eels[4] The chief food during Lent, besides bread and salt fish, was dried peas, which could be boiled or made into pottage. Thus Skelton complains of the monks of his day:

> Saltfysshe, stocfysshe, nor heryng,
> It is not for your werynge,
> Nor in holy Lenton season
> Ye wyll nethyr benes ne peason[5].

[1] Gray, *op cit.* See the accounts, pp. 145–79 *passim*   [2] *Ib* pp 10–11.
[3] *Catholicon Anglicum*, ed. S. J. Herrtage (E.E T S 1881), p 365
[4] Blunt, *op cit.* p xxx In 1481–2 their Lenten store included "saltfysshe," "stokfyssh," "white heryng," "rede haryng," "muddefissh," "lyng," "aburden," "Scarburgh fysshe," "salt samon," "salt elys," "oyle olyue" (34¾ gallons), a barrel of honey and figs At other times this year the cellaress purchased beans (1 qr. 4 bushels), green peas (7 bushels), "grey" (i e dried) peas (4 bushels), "harreos" (3 bushels), oatmeal (2 qrs 7 bushels), bread, wheat, malt, various animals for meat and to stock the farm, a kilderkin of good ale, 15 lbs. of almonds, 39 Essex cheeses, 111½ gallons of butter, white salt and bay salt, also firewood and coals. *P R O. Mins Accts* 1261/4
[5] *Poems of John Skelton*, ed W H Williams, pp. 107–8 (from "Colyn

In Lent also were eaten dried fruits, in particular almonds and raisins and figs, the latter being sometimes made into little pies called *risschewes*[1]. The nuns of Syon purchased olive oil and honey with their other Lenten stores. The list of condiments which they bought during the year, for ordinary cooking purposes, or for consumption as a relief to their palates in Lent, or as a pittance on high days and holidays, includes, in 1536–7, sugar (749¾ lb.), nutmegs (18 lb), almonds (500 lb), currants (4 lb.), ginger (6 lb.), isinglass (100 lb), pepper (6 lb.), cinnamon (1 lb), cloves (1 lb.), mace (1 lb.), saffron (2 lb), rice (3 qrs.), together with figs, raisins and prunes[2]. Surely the poor clown, whom Autolycus relieved so easily of his purse, was sent to stock a convent storehouse, not to furnish forth a sheep-shearing feast and the sister who sent him was a sister in Christ ·

Let me see, what am I to buy. .? Three pound of sugar; five pound of currants; rice,—what will this sister of mine do with rice?. .I must have saffron, to colour the warden pies; mace, dates,—none, that's out of my note; nutmegs seven; a race or two of ginger,—but that I may beg,—four pound of prunes and as many of raisins of the sun[3].

Lent fare was naturally not very pleasant, for all the mitigations of almonds and figs. At other times of the year the convent ate on fish-days fresh fish, when they could get it, otherwise dried or salt fish, and on meat-days either beef or some form of pig's flesh, eaten fresh as pork, cured and salted as bacon, or pickled as *sowce*[4]. Mutton was also eaten, though much more seldom, for the sheep in the middle ages was valued for its wool, rather than for its meat, and was indeed a scraggy little animal, until the discovery of winter crops and the experiments of Bakewell revolutionised stock-breeding and the English foodsupply in the eighteenth century. The nuns also had fowls on festive occasions, eggs, cheese and butter from the dairy and

Cloute," ll. 210–13) For the curious custom of eating dried peas on the fifth Sunday in Lent, called Passion or *Care* Sunday, see Brand, *Observations on Popular Antiquities* (1877 ed), pp 57 ff In the north of England peas boiled on Care Sunday were called *carlings*. Compare the St Mary de Pré (St Albans) accounts (2–4 Hen VII) "Item paid for ij busshell of pesyn departyd amongs the susters in Lente xvj d " Dugdale, *Mon.* III, p 359, and the Barking cellaress' *Charthe*, below, Note A.

[1] See below, p. 568.   [2] Blunt, *op. cit.* pp xxx–xxxi
[3] Shakespeare, *Winter's Tale*, IV, ii, 38 sqq.
[4] For *sowce*, see below, p. 565.

vegetables from the garden. The staple allowance of bread and
beer made on the premises was always provided by the convent,
even when the nuns had a money allowance to cater for themselves in other articles of food[1] Some idea of the menu of an
average house is given in the Syon rule:

For the sustres and brethren sche [the cellaress] shal euery day for
the more parte ordeyne for two maner of potages, or els at leste for
one gode and that is best of alle. If ther be two, that one be sewe
[broth] of flesche and fische, after [according to what] the day is; and
that other of wortes or herbes, or of any other thing that groweth in the
yerthe, holsom to the body, as whete, ryse, otemele, peson and suche
other Also sche schal ordeyne for two sundry metes, of flesche and
of fysche, one fresche, another powdred [salted], boyled, or rosted,
or other wyse dyghte, after her discrecion, and after the day, tyme
and nede requyreth, as the market and purse wylle stretche And
thys schal stonde for the prebende, which is a pounde of brede, welle
weyed, with a potel of ale and a messe of mete . .On fysche dayes sche
schal ordeyn for whyte metes, yf any may be hadde after the rewle,
be syde fysche metes, as it is before seyd. Also, ones a wyke at the
leste, sche schal ordeyn that the sustres and brethren be serued withe
newe brede, namely on water dayes, but neuer withe newe ale, nor
palled or ouer sowre, as moche as sche may. For supper sche schal
ordeyn for some lytel sowpyng, and for fysche and whyte mete, or for
any other thynge suffred by the rewle, lyghte of dygestyon equyua-
lente, and as gode to the bodyly helthe ..On water dayes sche schal
ordeyne for bonnes or newe brede, water grewel, albreys and for two
maner of froytes at leste yf it may be, that is to say, apples, peres
or nuttes, plummes, chiryes, benes, peson, or any suche other, and
thys in competent mesure, rosten or sothen, or other wyse dyghte
to the bodyly helthe, and sche must se that the water be sothen with
browne brede in maner of a tysan, or withe barley brede, for coldenes
and feblenes of nature, more thys dayes, than in dayes passed regnynge[2].

[1] The weekly allowance of beer to each member was supposed to be
seven gallons, four of the better sort and three weaker, but the amount
varied from house to house See *Linc. Visit.* ii, p 89 (note). The Syon nuns
had water on certain days, but doubtless as a mortification of the flesh,
for it was sometimes complained of as a hardship when nuns had to drink
water. ("Item they say that they do not get their corrody (i.e. weekly
allowance of bread and beer) at the due times, but it is sometimes omitted
for a fortnight and sometimes for a month, so that the nuns, by reason of
the non-payment of the corrody, drink water " *Test Ebor.* i, p 284) The
weekly allowance of bread was seven loaves. A note in the Register of
Shaftesbury Abbey (15th century) which then numbered about 50 nuns
and a large household, says: "Hit is to wytyng that me baketh and breweth
by the wike in the Abbey of Shaftesbury atte leste weye xxxvj quarters
whete and malt. And other while me baketh and breweth xlj quarters and
ij bz. whete and malte." Dugdale, *Mon.* ii, p. 473.

[2] Aungier, *op. cit.* pp. 393-4.

On certain special days the nuns received a pittance, or extra allowance of food, sometimes taking the shape of some special delicacy consecrated to the day. On Shrove Tuesday they often had the traditional pancakes, or fritters, called *crisps* at Barking[1] and *flawnes* at St Michael's, Stamford[2]. Maundy Thursday, otherwise called Shere Thursday (the Thursday before Easter) was the great almsgiving day of the year. On this day the kings and queens of England, as well as the greatest dignitaries of the church and of the nobility, were accustomed to give gowns, food and-money to the poor, who clustered round their gates in expectance of the event, and ceremonially to wash the feet of a certain number of poor men and women, to commemorate Christ's washing of His disciples' feet. Benefactors who left land to monastic houses for purposes of almsgiving often specified Maundy Thursday as the day on which the alms were to be distributed. It was customary also for monks and nuns to receive a pittance on this day; and welcome it must have been after the long Lenten fast. The nuns of Barking had baked eels, with rice and almonds and wine. The nuns of St Mary de Pré (St Albans) had "Maundy ale" and "Maundy money" given to them. The nuns of St Michael's, Stamford, had beer and wafers and spices[3]. There was always a feast on Christmas

[1] See below, p. 568

[2] They are diversely defined as pancakes, cheese cakes or custards, but they differed from our pancakes in being made in crusts. See the recipe in *Liber Cure Cocorum* for flawns made with cheese

Take new chese and grynde hyt fayre,
In morter with egges, without dysware;
Put powder therto of sugur, I say,
Coloure hit with safrone ful wele thou may,
Put hit in cofyns that ben fayre,
And bake hit forthe, I the pray.

Liber Cure Cocorum, ed. Morris (Phil. Soc. 1862), p 39. A fifteenth century cookery book gives this recipe for *Flathouns in lente*· "Take and draw a thrifty Milke of Almandes, temper with Sugre Water; than take hardid cofyns [pie-crusts] and pore thin comad [mixture] theron, blaunch Almaundis hol and caste theron Pouder Gyngere, Canelle, Sugre, Salt and Safroun, bake hem and serue forth." *Two Fifteenth Century Cookery Books*, ed. T. Austen (E E T S 1888), p 56

[3] For Maundy Thursday, see Brand, *op. cit* pp. 75–9. For the Barking Maundy see below, p 568, for the St Mary de Pré Maundy see Dugdale, *Mon.* III, p. 359, and for the St Michael's, Stamford, Maundy, see *P R O. Mins. Accts.* 1260 *passim*. The nuns of St Radegund's owned certain lands in Madingley which were held by the Prior of Barnwell on payment of a rent of 2s. 3d, called "Maundy silver." Gray, *op. cit* p 146. Maundy money is still distributed at Magdalen College, Oxford

day and on most of the great feasts of the church and the various feasts connected with the Virgin. There was a pittance on the dedication day of the convent and sometimes on other saints' days There were also pittances on the anniversaries of benefactors who had left money for this purpose to the convent, and sometimes also on profession-days, which were "the official birthdays of the nuns"[1]. In the monotonous round of convent life these little festivities formed a pleasant change and were looked forward to with ardour; in some of the larger houses a special obedientiary known as the *Pittancer* had charge over them.

Food is one of the housekeeper's cares; servants are another; and between them they must have wrinkled many a cellaress' brow, though the servant problem at least was a less complicated one in the middle ages than it is to-day The persons to whom regular yearly wages were paid by a convent fall into four classes: (1) the chaplains, (2) the administrative officials, steward, rent-collectors, bailiff, (3) the household staff and (4) the hinds and farm-servants.

---

[1] See below, p. 566, for the Barking pittances. The following extracts from one of the St Michael's, Stamford, accounts is typical of the rest: "Item paid for wassail 4d....paid to the convent on the Feast of St Michael and the dedication of the church 6s. Item paid for...on All Saints Day and St Martin's Day 3s. Item paid for a pittance of pork on two occasions 6d. Item paid for fowls at Christmas for the convent 5s 6d. Item paid for herrings on St Michael's Day for the poor 1s 8d Item paid for beer for the convent on Maundy Thursday (*Jour de Cene*) 10d. Item paid for bread and wafers on the same day 6d. Item paid for spices on the same day 3s. Item paid for herrings for the poor on the same day 1s. 8d Item given to the poor on the same day 1s. 9d. Item for holy bread on Good Friday 2d Item paid for *fflaunes* 2d. Item paid for herrings on St Laurence's Day 9d." *P.R O Mins Accts.* 1260/11. At this convent "holy bread" was always brought for Good Friday, "flaunes" (or sometimes eggs, saffron and spices to make them) for Rogationtide, beer and spices on Maundy Thursday, herrings on St Lawrence's Day, and various money pittances were paid to the nuns from time to time for the *misericord* of Corby and sometimes of Thurlby, the appropriated churches. On one occasion there is an entry "Paid to the convent for the misericord of Thurlby, to wit 28 fowls, 12 gallons of beer and mustard and a gift to the prioress 9s., paid to the convent for the misericord of Corby 9s , paid to the pittancer for a pittance from Thurlby throughout the year 14s. 4d " *Ib.* 1260/3. See an interesting list of pittances payable on forty different feasts throughout the year to the nuns of Lillechurch or Higham they are either extra portions of food or special sorts of food, e g. "crepis" on the Sunday before Ash Wednesday, "flauns" on Easter Day and 12d on St Radegund's Day. R. F Scott, *Notes from the Records of St John's Coll. Cambridge*, 1st series (from *The Eagle*, 1893, vol. XVII, no. 101, pp. 5–7).

(1) *The chaplains.* The account rolls of a nunnery of average size usually contain payments to more than one priest. The nuns had to pay the stipend of their own chaplain or mass-priest, of any chaplains or vicars whom they were bound to provide for appropriated churches, and sometimes of a confessor. The number of chaplains naturally varied with the size of the house and with the number of appropriated churches. Great houses such as Barking, Shaftesbury and Wilton had a body of resident chaplains attached to the nunnery church and paid the stipends of priests ministering to appropriated parishes. Poor and small nunneries, such as Rusper, paid the fee of one resident chaplain. It is worthy of note that certain important and old established abbeys in Wessex had canons' prebends attached to their churches. At each of the abbey churches of Shaftesbury, St Mary's Winchester, Wherwell and Wilton there were four prebendary canons, at Romsey there were two (one of whom was known as sacrist). Moreover at Malling in Kent there were two secular prebends, known as the prebends of *magna missa maioris altaris* and *alta missa*. These prebends were doubtless originally intended for the maintenance of resident chaplains, but as early as the thirteenth century the prebends were almost invariably held by non-residents and pluralists as sinecures, the reason being, as Mr Hamilton Thompson points out, "the rise in value of individual endowments and the consequent readiness of the Crown, as patron of the monasteries, to discover in them sources of income for clerks in high office." Thus these great abbeys also followed the usual custom of hiring chaplains to celebrate in their churches, though some of the wealthier prebends were taxed with stipendiary payments towards the cost of these[1]

The chaplain of a house usually resided on the premises, sometimes receiving his board from the nuns, occasionally inventories mention his lodgings, which were outside the nuns' cloister. Thus the Kilburn Dissolution inventory, after describing all the household offices, goes on to describe the three chambers for the chaplain and the hinds, the "confessor's chamber" and

---

[1] For these prebendal canonries see Mr Hamilton Thompson's article on "Double Monasteries and the Male Element in Nunneries," in *The Ministry of Women, A Report by a Committee appointed by his Grace the Lord Archbishop of Canterbury*, app VIII, pp 150 *sqq*

PLATE III

PAGE FROM *LA SAINTE ABBAYE*

(In the top left hand corner is a nun at confession; in the other corners are visions
appearing to a nun at prayer.)

the church[1]. At Sheppey the chamber over the gatehouse was called "the confessor's chamber" and was furnished forth with

a hangyng of rede clothe, a paynted square sparver of lynen, with iij corteyns of lynyn clothe, a good fetherbed, a good bolster, a pece of blanketts and a good counterpeynt of small verder, in the lowe bed a fetherbed, a bolster, a pece of blanketts olde, and an image coverled, a greate joynyd chayer of waynscot, an olde forme, and a cressar of iron for the chymneye[2]

The relations between the nuns and their priest were doubtless very friendly; he would be their guide, philosopher and friend, sometimes acting as *custos* of their temporal affairs and always ready with advice.

Madame Eglentyne, it will be remembered, took three priests with her upon her eventful pilgrimage to Canterbury, and one was the never-to-be-forgotten Sir John, whom she mounted worse than his inimitable skill as a *raconteur* deserved:

> Than spak our host, with rude speche and bold
> And seyde un-to the Nonnes Preest anon,
> "Com neer, thou preest, com hider thou sir John,
> Tel us swich thing as may our hertes glade,
> Be blythe, though thou ryde up-on a jade
> What though thyn hors be bothe foule and lene,
> If he wol serve thee, rekke not a bene,
> Look that thyn herte be mery evermo."
> "Yis, sir" quod he, "yis, host, so mote I go,
> But I be mery, y-wis I wol be blamed"—
> And right anon his tale he hath attamed,
> And thus he seyde unto us everichon,
> This swete preest, this goodly man, sir John[3].

Certainly the convent never went to sleep in a sermon which had the tale of Chauntecleer and Pertelote for its *exemplum*

Yet the nuns were not always happy in their priests. There is the case (not, it must be admitted, without its humour) of Sir Henry, the chaplain of Gracedieu in 1440–41. Sir Henry was an uncouth fellow, it seems, who was more at home in the

---

[1] Dugdale, *Mon.* III, p. 424.

[2] Walcott, M. E. C. *Inventories of.. the Priory of Minster in Shepey* (*Arch. Cant* 1869), p 30 This house paid stipends to three chaplains, one being "curat of the Paryshe churche", a "Vycar's chamber" is described among what are obviously outlying buildings. At Cheshunt the "Prestes Chamber" contained a feather bed, with sheets and coverlet and a "celer of blewe cloth," valued at 4s. 10d. Cussans, *Hist. of Herts. Hertford Hundred*, II, p 70

[3] Chaucer, *Cant Tales*, Prologue of the Nonne Prestes Tale, ll. 3998 ff.

stable than at the altar. He went out haymaking alone with
the cellaress, and in the evening brought her back behind him,
riding on the same lean jade. Furthermore "Sir Henry the
chaplain busies himself with unseemly tasks, cleansing the stables,
and goes to the altar without washing, staining his vestments.
He is without devotion and irreverent at the altar and is of ill
reputation at Loughborough and elsewhere where he has dwelt."
Poor Sir Henry,—

> See, whiche braunes hath this gentil Preest,
> So greet a nekke, and swich a large breest!
> He loketh as a sperhauk with his yen;
> Him nedeth nat his colour for to dyen
> With brasil, ne with greyn of Portingale.

The bishop swore him to "behave himself devoutly and reverently
henceforward at the altar in making his bow after and before
his masses"[1]

(2) *The administrative officials* These varied in number with
the size of the house and the extent of its possessions. The chief
administrative official was the *steward*, who is not, however,
found at all houses. Sometimes the office of steward was compli-
mentary and the fee attached was nominal. The *Valor Ecclesiasticus* shows that great men did not disdain the post; Andrew
Lord Windsor was steward of the Minoresses without Aldgate, of
Burnham and of Ankerwyke[2]. Henry Lord Daubeney was steward
of Shaftesbury[3], George Earl of Shrewsbury of Wilton[4], Henry
Marquess of Dorset of Nuneaton[5], Sir Thomas Wyatt of Malling[6],
Sir W. Percy of Hampole, Handale and Thicket[7], Lord Darcy
of Swine[8], the Earl of Derby of St Mary's Chester[9], and
Mr Thomas Cromwell himself of Syon and Catesby[10]. Some
houses, such as Wilton, had more than one steward, and Syon
maintained stewards as well as bailiffs in most of the counties
in which it had land. Some of these great men were obviously
not working officials; but many of the houses maintained
stewards at a good salary, who superintended their business affairs,
kept the courts of their manors, and were sometimes lodged

---

[1] *Linc. Visit* II, pp 120-1, 123.
[2] *Valor Eccles* I, p 397, IV, p. 220
[3] *Ib.* I, p 276.   [4] *Ib* II, p. 109
[5] *Ib.* III, p 76   [6] *Ib* I, p 106.
[7] *Ib* v, pp 43, 87, 94.   [8] *Ib* I, p 114
[9] *Ib.* v, p. 206.   [10] *Ib.* I, p. 424, IV, p. 339.

on the premises[1]. The larger houses also paid one or more receivers and rent-collectors and sometimes an auditor, but in the average house the most important administrative official was the bailiff.

While large landowners kept bailiffs at each of the different manors which they held, most nunneries employed a single bailiff, an invaluable factotum who performed a great variety of business for them, besides collecting rents from their tenants and superintending the home farm. Thomas Key, the bailiff of St Radegund's Cambridge, 1449–51, is an active person; he receives a stipend of 13s. 4d. per annum and an occasional gift from the nuns, he rides about collecting their rents in Cambridgeshire; he accompanies them to Lynn on the annual journey to buy the winter stock of salt fish, or sometimes goes alone; he can turn his hand to mending rakes and ladders (for which he gets 8d. for four days' work), or to making the barley mows at harvest time, taking 3d. a day for his pains; and indeed he is regularly hired to work during harvest, at a fee of 6s. 8d. and two bushels of malt[2]. Often the bailiff's wife was also employed by the nuns; the nuns of Sheppey paid their bailiff, his wife and his servant all substantial salaries[3]. Some nunneries had a lodging set apart for him in the convent buildings, outside the nuns' cloister[4].

Evidence often crops up from a variety of sources concerning the relations between the nuns and this important official That these might be very pleasant can well be imagined. Sometimes a bailiff of substance and standing will place his daughter in the nunnery which he serves[5]; sometimes when he dies he will remember it in his will[6] But all bailiffs were not good and faithful

[1] E.g. in the Sheppey inventory, after "the chamber over the Gate Howse called the Confessor's Chamber," comes "the Chamber next to that," "*the Steward's chamber*" (well furnished), "the next chamber to the same," "the chamber under the same," and "the Portar's Lodge," all evidently outside the cloister. Walcott, M. E. C. *op cit.* p. 31.

[2] Gray, *op cit.* pp 163, 167, 173 Cf pp. 156, 157, 158.

[3] Walcott, M. E C *op. cit* pp 30, 33

[4] E g Brewood (Black Ladies) See Dugdale, *Mon.* IV, p 500

[5] A Joan Key or Kay votes at the election of Joan Lancaster as prioress of St Radegund's in 1457 and is receiver-general, keeping the account in 1481–2 Gray, *op cit* pp. 38, 176

[6] See, for instance, an item in the accounts of St Radegund's Cambridge. "Paid in a pittance for the convent . at the month's mind of John Brown, lately bailiff there . in accordance with his last will." Gray, *op cit.* p. 151.

servants. Mr Hamilton Thompson considers that male stewards and bailiffs were often "responsible for the financial straits to which the nunneries of the fifteenth century were reduced, and...certainly did much to waste the goods of the monasteries, generally in their own interests"[1]. Such a man was Chaucer's Reeve, though he did not waste land, for the reason that one does not kill the goose that lays the golden eggs:

> His lordes sheep, his neet, his dayerye,
> His swyn, his hors, his stoor and his pultrye,
> Was hoolly in this reves governing,
> And by his covenaunt yaf the rekening...
> His woning was ful fair upon an heeth,
> With grene trees shadwed was his place.
> He coude bettre than his lord purchace
> Ful riche he was astored prively,
> His lord wel coude he plesen subtilly,
> To yeve and lene him of his owne good,
> And have a thank, and yet a cote and hood[2].

Several records of law-suits are extant, in which prioresses are obliged to sue their bailiffs in the court of King's Bench for an account of their periods of service[3], and visitation documents sometimes give a sorry picture of the convent bailiff. The bailiff of Godstow (1432) went about saying that there was no good woman in the nunnery[4]; the bailiff of Legbourne (1440) persuaded the prioress to sell him a corrody in the house and yet he "is not reckoned profitable to the house in that office, for several of his kinsfolk are serving folk in the house, who look out for

---

[1] *The Ministry of Women, loc. cit* pp. 162–3. So in 1492 it is complained at Carrow "quod mali servientes Priorissae fecerunt magnum dampnum in bonis prioratus" Jessopp, *Visit of Dioc. of Norwich*, p. 16.

[2] Chaucer, *Cant Tales*, Prologue, ll 597 ff

[3] See, for instance, the Prioress of Marrick *v* Simon Wayt, to give an account for the time when he was her bailiff in Fletham (1332), the Prioress of Molseby (Moxby) *v* Lawrence de Dysceford, chaplain, to give an account of the time when he was bailiff of Joan de Barton, late Prioress of Molseby at Molseby (1330)—an interesting case of a chaplain acting as bailiff for a small and poor house, Idonia, Prioress of Appleton *v*. John Boston of Leven for an account as bailiff and receiver in Holme (1413) *Notes on Relig. and Secular Houses of York*, ed W. P Baildon (Yorks Arch Soc 1895), I, pp. 127, 139, 161 Visitation injunctions sometimes regulate the presentation of accounts by bailiffs and receivers, e.g *Exeter Reg. Stapeldon*, p. 318, *V C.H. Beds.* I, p. 356.

[4] *Linc. Visit.* I, p 67.

themselves more than for the house "[1]; the bailiff of Redlingfield (1427) was the prioress's lover[2].

Romsey Abbey seems at various times to have been peculiarly unfortunate in its administrative officials. In 1284 Archbishop Peckham had to write to the abbess Agnes Walerand and bid her remove two stewards, whom she had appointed in defiance of the wishes of the convent and who were to give an account of their offices to his official[3] At the close of the fifteenth century, when the abbey was in a very disorderly state under Elizabeth Broke, there was serious trouble again. In 1492 this Abbess was found to have fallen under the influence of one Terbock, whom she had made steward She herself confessed that she owed him the huge sum of 80*l.* and the nuns declared that in part payment of it she had persuaded them to make over to him for three years a manor valued at 40*l.* and had given him a cross and many other things. His friends haunted her house, especially one John Write, who begged money from her for Terbock The nuns suspected him of dishonesty, asked that the rolls of account for the years of his stewardship might be seen and declared that the house was brought to ill-fame by him[4]. In 1501 Elizabeth Broke had fallen under the influence of another man, this time a priest called Master Bryce, but she died the next year. Her successor Joyce Rowse was equally unsatisfactory and equally unable to control her servants Bishop Foxe's vicar-general in 1507 enjoined that a nun should be sought out and corrected for having frequent access, suspiciously and beyond the proper time, to the house of the bailiff of the monastery, and others who went with her were to be warned and corrected too; moreover he summoned before him Thomas Langton, Christopher George and Thomas Leycrofte, bailiffs, and Nicholas Newman, *villicum agricultorem,*

---

[1] *Linc Visit* II, p 185 An illustration may be found in the Gracedieu rolls where on one occasion the nuns paid wages to the bailiff John de Northton, to his wife Joan, to his daughter Joan, to Philip de Northton (doubtless his son) and to Philip's wife Constance. *P.R O Mins. Accts.* 1257/10, ff 203–5

[2] *V.C H. Suffolk,* II, p. 84.

[3] *Reg. Epis J Peckham* (Rolls Ser), II, pp 658–9 Compare p 662 The injunction that the head of the house should not appoint stewards, bailiffs or receivers without the consent of the major part of the convent was a common one; cf *ib.* II, p. 652, Dugdale, *Mon.* II, p. 619.

[4] Liveing, *Records of Romsey Abbey,* pp. 218–22 *passim.*

and admonished them to behave better in their offices on pain of removal[1].

(3) The *household staff* naturally varied in size with the size of the nunnery. The Rule of St Benedict contemplated the performance of a great deal if not all of the necessary domestic and agricultural work of a community by the monks themselves. But this tradition had been largely discarded by the thirteenth century, and if the nuns of a small convent are found doing their own cooking and housework, it is by reason of their poverty and they not infrequently complain at the necessity. They were of gentle birth and ill accustomed to menial tasks. The weekly service in the kitchen would seem to have disappeared completely. The larger houses employed a male cook, sometimes assisted by a page, or by his wife, and supervised by the cellaress, or by the kitcheness, where this obedientiary was appointed. There were also a maltster, to make malt, and a brewer and baker, to prepare the weekly ration of bread and ale; sometimes these offices were performed by men, sometimes by women. There was a *deye* or dairy-woman, who milked the cows, looked after the poultry, and made the cheeses There was sometimes a *lavender* or laundress, and there were one or more women servants, to help with the housework and the brewing. The gate was kept by a male porter; and there was sometimes also a gardener In large houses there would be more than one servant for each of these offices; in small houses the few servants were men or maids of all work and extra assistance was hired when necessary for making malt or washing clothes In large houses it was not uncommon for each of the chief obedientiaries to have her own servant attached to her *checker* (office) and household, who prepared the meals for her mistress and for those nuns who formed her *familia* and messed with her. The head of the house nearly always had her private servant when its resources permitted her to do so, and sometimes when they did not.

(4) *The farm labourers* Finally every house which had attached to it a home farm had to pay a staff of farm labourers. These hinds, whose work was superintended by the bailiff and cellaress, always included one or two ploughmen, a cowherd and oxherd, a shepherd, probably a carter or two and some general

---

[1] Liveing, *op. cit* pp. 229–30, 232.

labourers. Again the number varied very considerably according to the size of the house and was commonly augmented by hiring extra labour at busy seasons. The farm was cultivated partly by the work of these hired servants, partly by the services owed by the villeins.

The nuns, with their domestic and farm servants, were the centre of a busy and sometimes large community, and a very good idea of their social function as employers may be gained from the lists of wage-earning servants to be found in account rolls or in Dissolution inventories. We may take in illustration the large and famous abbey of St Mary's, Winchester, and the little house of St Radegund's, Cambridge. St Mary's, Winchester, had let out the whole of its demesne in 1537, and the inventory drawn up by Henry VIII's commissioners therefore contains no list of farm labourers. The household consisted of the Abbess and twenty-six nuns, thirteen "poor sisters," twenty-six "chyldren of lordys knyghttes and gentylmen browght vp yn the sayd monastery," three corrodians and five chaplains, one of whom was confessor to the house, and twenty-nine officers and servants. The Abbess had her own household, consisting of a gentlewoman, a woman servant and a laundress, and the prioress, subprioress, sacrist and another of the senior nuns each had her private woman servant "yn her howse." There were also two laundresses for the convent. The male officers and servants were Thomas Legh, *generall Receyver* (who also held a corrody and had two little relatives at school in the convent), Thomas Tycheborne *clerke* (who likewise had two little girl relatives at school and a boy who will be mentioned), Lawrens Bakon, *Curtyar* (officer in charge of the secular buildings of the nunnery), George Sponder, *Cater* (caterer or manciple, who purchased the victuals for the community), William Lime, *Botyler*, Rychard Bulbery, *Coke*, John Clarke, *Vndercoke*, Richard Gefferey, *Baker*, May Wednall, *convent Coke*, John Wener, *vndercovent Coke*, John Hatmaker, *Bruer*, Wylliam Harrys, *Myller*, Wylliam Selwod, *porter*, Robert Clerke, *vnderporter*, William plattyng, *porter of Estgate*, John Corte and Hery Beale, *Churchemen*, Peter Tycheborne, *Chyld of the hygh aulter*, Rychard Harrold, *seruaunt to the receyver* and John Serle, *seruaunt to the Clerke*[1]

---

[1] *Essays on Chaucer*, 2nd Series, VII (Chaucer Soc), pp 191–4; also in Dugdale, *Mon* II, 456–7.

St Radegund's, Cambridge, in 1450 was a much smaller community, numbering about a dozen nuns. In the treasurers' accounts the wage-earning household is given as follows, together with the annual wages paid by the nuns The confessor of the house came from outside and was a certain friar named Robert Palmer, who received 6s. 8d. a year for his pains; they also paid a salary of 5l. a year to their mass-priest, John Herryson, 2s. 4d. to John Peresson, the chaplain celebrating (but only *per vices*, from time to time) at the appropriated church of St Andrew's, and 13s. 4d. to the "clerk" of that church, a permanent official. Thomas Key, the invaluable bailiff and rent-collector mentioned above, got the rather small salary of 13s 4d., but added to it by exactly half as much again during harvest. Richard Wester, baker and brewer to the house, received 26s 8d , John Cokke, maltster (and probably also cook, as his name suggests) received 13s. 4d. The women servants included one of those domestic treasures, who effectively run the happy household which possesses them, or which they possess. her name was Joan Grangyer and she is described as dairy-woman and purveyor or housekeeper to the Prioress, the nuns paid her 20s. in all, including 6s. 8d. for her livery and 2s 4d. as a special fee for catering for the Prioress Then there was Elianore Richemond, who seems to have been an assistant dairy-maid, for in the following year the nuns had replaced her by another woman, hired "for all manner of work in milking cows, making cheese and butter," etc.; her wages were 8s. 4d , including a "reward" or gift of 20d. The other women servants were Elizabeth Charterys, who received 3s 1d. for her linen and woollen clothes and her shoes, but no further wages, and Dionisia *yerdwomman*, who received 9s. and doubtless did the rough work. This completed the domestic household of the nuns. Their hinds included three ploughmen, John Everesdon (26s. 8d.), Robert Page (16s.) and John Slibre (13s 4d and 2s. 6d. for livery); the shepherd, John Wyllyamesson, who received 22s 8d. and 8d. for a pair of hose; the oxherd Robert Pykkell, who took 6s. 8d.; and Richard Porter, husbandman, who was hired to work from Trinity Sunday to Michaelmas for 13s 4d.[1]

It will thus be seen that the size of a convent household might vary considerably. The twenty-six nuns of St Mary's

[1] Gray, *op. cit.* p. 158, cf. p 174.

Winchester had gathered round themselves a large household of nine women servants, five male chaplains and twenty male officers and servants; but they boarded and educated twenty-six children, gave three corrodies and supported thirteen poor sisters (who may however have done some of the work of the house). The twelve nuns of St Radegund's lived more economically, with three male and four female servants and six hinds, besides the chaplains; but even their household seems a sufficiently large one The ten nuns of Wintney Priory employed two priests, a waiting maid for the prioress, nine other women servants and thirteen hinds[1]. It is notable that the maintenance of a larger household than the revenues of the house could support is not infrequently censured in injunctions as responsible for its financial straits. At Nuncoton in 1440 the Prioress said that the house employed more women servants than was necessary[2] and a century later Bishop Longland spoke very sternly against the same fault:

> that ye streight upon sight herof dymynishe the nombre of your seruants, as well men as women, which excessyve nombre that ye kepe of them bothe is oon of the grette causes of your miserable pouertye and that ye are nott hable to mayntene your housould nouther reparacons of the same, by reason whereof all falleth to ruyne and extreme decaye. And therefore to kepe noo moo thenne shalbe urged necessarye for your said house[3].

On the other hand many nunneries could by no means be charged with keeping up an excessive household. Rusper, which had leased all its demesnes, had only two women servants in its employ at the Dissolution[4], and nuns sometimes complained to their visitors that they were too poor to keep servants and had to do the work of the house themselves, to the detriment of their religious duties in the choir. At Ankerwyke one of the nuns deposed that

---

[1] V C.H. Hants. II, 151.
[2] Alnwick's Visit. MS. f. 71d. The Bishop forbade them to keep more than the necessary servants and made the same injunction at Legbourne. Linc. Visit. II, p 187
[3] Archaeologia, XLVII, pp. 57–8. Compare his injunction to Studley, ib pp. 54–5 In 1306 every useless servant who was a burden to the impoverished house of Arden was to be removed within a week. V.C.H. Yorks. III, p 113. In 1326 the custos of Minchin Barrow was told to remove the onerosa familia Reg John of Drokensford (Somerset Rec. Soc.), p 242.
[4] P.R.O. Suppression Papers, 833/39.

they had not serving folk in the brewhouse, bakehouse or kitchen from the last festival of the Nativity of St John the Baptist last year to the Michaelmas next following, in so much that this deponent, with the aid of other her sisters, prepared the beer and victuals and served the nuns with them in her own person

At Gracedieu there was no servant for the infirmary and the subcellaress had to sleep there and look after the sick, so that she could not come to matins. At Markyate and Harrold the nuns had no washerwoman, at the former house it was said "that the nuns have no woman to wash their clothes and to prepare their food, wherefore they are either obliged to be absent from divine service or else to think the whole time about getting these things ready"; at the latter a nun said "that they have no common washerwoman to wash the clothes of the nuns, save four times a year, and at other times the nuns are obliged to go to the bank of the public stream to wash their clothes"[1]. It was probably on account of the poverty of Sinningthwaite that Archbishop Lee ordered "the susters and the nonys there [that] they kepe no seculer women to serve them or doe any busynes for them, but yf sekenes or oder necessitie doe require"[2].

As to the relations between the servants and their mistresses both visitation reports and account rolls sometimes give meagre scraps of information, which only whet the appetite for more. The payment of the servants was partly in money, partly in board or in allowances of food, partly in livery; stock-inventories constantly make mention of allowances of wheat, peas, oats or oatmeal and maslin (a mixture of wheat and rye) paid to this or that servant, and account rolls as constantly mention a livery, a pair of hose, a pair of shoes, or the money equivalent of these things, as forming part of the wage. The more important agricultural servants had also sometimes the right to graze a

---

[1] *Linc. Visit.* II, pp 4, 121, 131; *Alnwick's Visit.* MS f. 6. At Ankerwyke Alnwick enjoined "that ye hafe an honeste woman seruaund in your kychyne, brewhowse and bakehowse, deyhowse and selere wythe an honeste damyselle wythe hire to saruf yowe and your sustres in thise saide offices, so that your saide sustres for occupacyone in any of the saide offices be ne letted fro diuine seruice." Compare the complaint of the nuns of Sheppey that they had no "covent servante" to wash their clothes and tend them when they were ill, unless they hired a woman from the village out of their own pockets. *E H.R* VI, pp 33–4. The provision of a laundress was ordered at Nunappleton in 1534 *Yorks. Arch. Journ* XVI, p 444.

[2] *Yorks. Arch Journ.* XVI, p. 443

cow, or a certain number of sheep on the convent's pastures. Some servants, however, received wages without board, others wages without livery. Account rolls seem to bear witness to pleasant relations; there is constant mention of small tips or presents to the servants and of dinners made to them on great occasions. This was Merry England, when the ploughman's feasts enlivened his hard work and comfortless existence, he must have his Shrovetide pancakes, his sheep-shearing feast, his "sickle goose" or harvest-home, and his Christmas dinner; and the household servants must as often as may be have a share in the convent pittance The very general custom of allowing the female servants to sleep in the dorter (against which bishops were continually having to make injunctions) must have made for free and easy and close relations between the nuns and the secular women who served them; and sometimes one of these would save up and buy herself a corrody in the house to end her days[1]. Occasionally these close relations led to difficulties; a trusted maid would gain undue influence over the prioress and the nuns would be jealous of her. Thus at Heynings in 1440 it was complained that the prioress "encourages her secular serving women, whom she believes more than her sisters in their words, to scold the same her sisters"[2] Sometimes also a servant would act as a go-between between the nuns and the outside world, smuggling in and out tokens and messages and sundry *billets doux*[3]

On the other hand there were sometimes difficulties of a different nature. The servants got out of hand, they brought discredit on the nuns by the indiscretions of their lives; they gossiped about their mistresses in the neighbourhood, or were quarrelsome and pert to their faces At Gracedieu in 1440–41 a nun complained "that a Frenchwoman of very unseemly conversation is their maltstress, also that the secular serving folk hold the nuns in despite, she prays that they may be restrained; and chiefly are they rebellious in their words against

---

[1] "Also she says that secular servingwomen do lie among the sisters in the dorter, and especially one who did buy a corrody there" (Heynings, 1440). *Linc. Visit.* ii, p. 133 The Abbess of Malling in 1324 was forbidden to give a corrody to her maid Wharton, *Anglia Sacra*, i, p. 364.

[2] *Linc. Visit.* ii, p. 133.

[3] See below, pp. 395, 396.

the kitchener"[1]; evidently the author of the *Ancren Riwle* spake
not utterly from his imagination when he bade his ladies "be
glad in your heart if ye suffer insolence from Slurry, the cook's
boy, who washeth dishes in the kitchen"[2]. At Markyate also the
servants had to be warned "that honestly and not sturdyly ne
rebukyngly thai hafe thaym in thaire langage to the sustres"[3]
and at Studley a maidservant had boxed the ears of a novice
of tender age[4] At Sheppey in 1511 it was said that "the men
servants of the prioress do not behave properly to the prioress,
but speak of the convent contemptuously and dishonestly, thus
ruining the convent"[5].

The peculiar difficulties suffered in this respect by an important house, which maintained a large body of servants, are
best illustrated, however, in the case of Romsey Abbey At this
house in 1302 Bishop John of Pontoise ordained

that a useless, superfluous, quarrelsome and incontinent servant and
one using insolent language to the ladies shall be removed within a
month, ..and especially John Chark, who has often spoken ill and
contumaciously in speaking to and answering the ladies, unless he
correct himself so that no more complaints be made to the bishop[6]

John Chark possibly learned to bridle his tongue, but the tone
among the Romsey servants was not good, for in 1311 Bishop
Henry Woodlock ordered that "no women servants shall remain unless of good conversation and honest; pregnant, incontinent, quarrelsome women and those answering the nuns
contumaciously, all superfluous and useless servants, [are] to be
removed within a month"[7]. In 1387 the difficulties were of
another order; writes William of Wykeham·

the secular women servants of the nuns are wont too often to come
into the frater, at times when the nuns are eating there, and into

---

[1] *Linc. Visit* II, p. 121 Alnwick notes "Amoueatur quedam francigena
manens in prioratu propter vite inhonestatem, nam omnes admittit vni-
formiter ad concubitus suos", and see his general injunction, *ib.* pp. 122, 125.

[2] *Ancren Riwle*, introd. Gasquet (King's Classics), p 287.

[3] *Alnwick's Visit* MS. f. 7.   [4] *Ib* f 26 d

[5] *E H R.* VI, p. 33   [6] Liveing, *op cit* p. 101.

[7] *Ib* p. 104 Compare Peckham's injunctions to Wherwell in 1284 "Et
si quis inveniatur, serviens masculus aut femina, qui amaris responsionibus
consueverit monialem aliquam vel aliquas molestare, nisi se monitione
praemissa sufficienter corrigat in futurum, illico expellatur" *Reg. Epist
J. Peckham*, II, p 654, also his injunctions to Barking and Holy Sepulchre,
Canterbury, *ib.* I, p 85; II, p 707 Also Thomas of Cantilupe's injunctions
to Lingbrook, c. 1277 *Reg Thome de Cantilupo*, p. 202.

the cloister while the nuns are engaged there in chapter meetings, contemplation, reading or praying, and there do make a noise and behave otherwise ill, in a way which beseems not the honesty of religion. And these secular women often keep up their chattering, carolling (*cantalenas*) and other light behaviour, until the middle of the night, and disturb the aforesaid nuns, so that they cannot properly perform the regular services. Wherefore we...command you that you henceforth permit not the aforesaid things, nor any other things which befit not the observances of your rule, to be done by the said servants or by others, and that you permit not these servants to serve you henceforth in the frater, and a servant or any other secular person who does the contrary shall be expelled from the monastery. Moreover we forbid on pain of the greater excommunication that any servants defamed for any offence be henceforth admitted to dwell among you, or having been admitted, be retained in your service, for from such grave scandals may arise concerning you and your house[1].

We have spoken hitherto about the regular hired servants of the house; but it must not be forgotten that nuns normally had a larger community dependent in part upon them. From time to time they were wont to hire such additional labour as they required, whether servants in husbandry taken on for the haymaking and harvest season, artificers hired to put up or repair buildings, workers in various branches of the cloth industry to make the liveries of the servants, itinerant candle-makers to prepare the winter dips, or a variety of casual workers hired at one time or another for specific purposes. The nuns of St Radegund's, Cambridge, entered in their accounts a large number of payments besides those to their regular servants. In moments of stress they were wont to fall back upon a paragon named Katherine Rolf. We first meet her in 1449–50 weeding the garden for four days, for the modest sum of $4\frac{1}{2}d$.; but soon afterwards behold her on the roof, aiding the thatchers to thatch two tenements, at $1\frac{1}{2}d$. a day for twelve days. In the next year she is more active still; first of all she is found helping the candle-makers to make up 14 lbs. of tallow candles for the guest-house. Then she combs and cleans a pound of wool for spinning. Then she appears in the granary helping the maltster to thresh and winnow grain. In the midst of these activities she turns an honest penny by selling fat chickens to the convent. The nuns also disburse small sums of money to the man who

---

[1] *New Coll.* MS. f. 87d.

cleanses the convent privies, to the *slawterman* for killing beasts
for the kitchen, to Richard Gardyner for beating stockfish, to
Thomas Osborne for making malt, to Thomas the Smith for
providing a variety of iron implements and *cart-clowtes*, for
shoeing the horses and for mending the ploughshares, and for
"blooding the horses on St Stephen's day" (Dec 26), to Thomas
Boltesham, *cowper*, for mending wooden utensils, to Thomas
Speed for helping in the kitchen on fair-day and to John Speed
for working in the garden Besides these they hire various day-
labourers to work in the fields during the sowing season, haymaking and harvest, or to lop trees round the convent and hew
up firewood, or to prune and tie up the vines (for there were
English vineyards in those days). Then there is a long list of
carpenters, builders, thatchers, and plumbers engaged in making
and repairing the buildings of the convent and its tenants.
Finally there are the various cloth workers, spinners, weaver,
fuller, shearman, dyer and tailor hired to make the servants'
clothes, concerning whom something has already been said[1]

Thus many persons came to depend upon a nunnery for part
of their livelihood, who were not the permanent servants of the
house, and this goes further than any imagined reverence for the
lives and calling of their inmates to explain the anxiety shown
in some places for the preservation of nunneries when the day of
dissolution came. The convents were not only inns and boarding-
houses for ladies of the upper class and occasionally schools for
their daughters, they were the great employers and consumers of
their districts, and though their places must sooner or later be
taken by other employers and consumers, yet at the moment many
a husbandman and artificer must have seen his livelihood about
to slip away from him. The nuns of Sheppey, in their distant
and lonely flats, clearly employed a whole village[2]. They could

---

[1] Gray. *op cit. passim*

[2] "*Names of the Servants now in Wages by the yere*. Mr Oglestone, taking
wages by the yere Mr White, taking 26 s 8 d by the yere and lyvere. John
Coks, butler, lyvere, xxvi s viij d, whereof to pay 1 quarter and lyvere.
Alyn Sowthe bayly, taking by yere for closure and hys servant 6 l 13 s 4 d
and two lyveryes Jhon Mustarde 20 s a kowes pasture and a lyvere.
William Rowet, carpentar, 40 s and lyvere. Richard Gyllys 26 s 8 d and
lyvere. The carter 33 s 4 d and no lyvere Thomas Thressher by yere
33 s 4 d and no lyvere. Robert Dawton by yere 33 s 4 d and no lyvere The
kowherd for kepyng of the kene and hoggys by yere 30 s and no lyvere.
Jhon Hartnar by yere 28 s and no lyvere Robard Welshe, brewer, by yere

not count on hiring carpenter and thatcher for piece-work when
they wanted them in that thinly populated spot, so they must
hire them all the year round. Twenty-six hinds and seven
women they had in all, working in their domestic offices or on
the wide demesne, most of which they farmed themselves, for
food was far to buy if they did not grow it. Three shepherds
kept their large flock, a cowherd drove their kine and hogs, a
horse-keeper looked to their 17 horses All the other men and
women were busy with the beasts and the crops in the field, or
with work in the brew house, the "bultyng howse," the bakehouse and the dairy. So also at the abbey of Polesworth, where
fifteen nuns employed in all thirty-eight persons, women servants,
yeomen about the household and hinds "In the towne of
Pollesworth," said the commissioners, who were gentlemen of
the district and not minded to lose the house.

ar 44 tenementes and never a plough but one, the resydue be artifycers,
laborers and vitellers, and lyve in effect by the said house ...And
the towne and nonnery standith in a harde soile and barren ground,
and to our estymacions, yf the nonnery be suppressed the towne
will shortely after falle to ruyne and dekaye, and the people therin,
to the nombre of six or seven score persones, are nott unlike to wander
and to seke their lyvyng as our Lorde Gode best knowith[1]

So also at St Mary's, Winchester, whose household we have
described:

the seid Monastery ..standith nigh the Middell of the Citye, of a
great and large Compasse, envyroned with many poore housholdes
20 s and no lyvere A thatcher 33 s 4 d, a hose cloth and no lyvere. William
Nycolls 20 s and no lyvere. Jhon Andrew 22 s 4 d and no lyverye Jhon
Putsawe 13 s 4 d and a shyrt redy made. George Myllar 21 s 8 d and no
lyverye. Robert Rychard, horse keper, 20 s and no liverye. Jhon Harryes,
Frencheman, 13 s 4 d, a shyrt and no lyverye Jhon Gyles the shepherd,
14 s, a payre of hoses, a payre of shoys and no lyverye Richard Gladwyn
for to make malte, 26 s 8 d by yere, he hath ben here 8 wekes, and no
lyverye Dorothe Sowthe, the baylyffe wyfe, owing for a yere's wages at
40 s by yere and no liverye Ales Barkar 13 s 4 d and lyvere Also Sykkers
13 s 4 d and lyverye. Gladwyn's wyfe 13 s 4 d and lyverye Ellyn at my ladyes
lyndyng. Emme Cawket 12 s and lyvere Rose Salmon 12 s, she hath been
here a month. Marget Lambard 13 s 4 d and lyvere. Sir Jhon Lorymer,
curat of the Parysche churche, 3 l 16 s 8 d and no lyvere. Sir Jhon Ingram,
chaplen, 3 l 3 s 3 d and no lyvere Jhon Gayton shepard 53 s 4 d and no
lyvere. Jhon Pelland 20 s and no lyverye. Jhon Marchant 13 s 4 d and
pasture for 40 shepe and no lyverye Jhon Helman 16 s and 10 shepes
pasture and no lyverye. Jhon Cannyng shepard by yere 20 s and no lyverye."
Walcott, E C M op. cit. pp. 33–4.

[1] *Letters relating to the Suppression of the Monasteries*, ed Thomas Wright
(Camden Soc. 1843), p 140

which haue theyr oonly lyuynge of the seid Monastery, And have no demaynes whereby they may make any prouysion, butt lyue oonly by theyr landes, making theyr prouysion in the markettes[1]

The old order changeth, yielding place to new, and a livelihood fulfils itself in many ways; yet many labouring folk as well as gentlemen must have felt like the commissioners at Polesworth and St Mary's, Winchester, when the busy monastic housewives were dispersed and the grain and cattle sold out of barn and byre. There is no-one so conservative as your bread-winner, and for the best of reasons.

[1] *Essays on Chaucer*, 2nd Series (Chaucer Soc.), p. 189

CHAPTER V

FINANCIAL DIFFICULTIES

Annual income twenty pounds, annual expenditure nineteen, nineteen, six; result, happiness. Annual income twenty pounds, annual expenditure twenty pounds, ought and six; result, misery

Mr Micawber.

In the history of the medieval nunneries of England there is nothing more striking than the constant financial straits to which they were reduced   Professor Savine's analysis of the *Valor Ecclesiasticus* has shown that in 1535 the nunneries were on an average only half as rich as the men's houses, while the average number of religious persons in them was larger[1]; and yet it is clear from the evidence of visitation documents that even the men's houses were continually in debt. It is therefore not to be wondered at that there was hardly a nunnery in England, which did not at one time or another complain of poverty. These financial difficulties had already begun before the end of the thirteenth century and they grew steadily worse until the moment of the Dissolution The worst sufferers of all were the nunneries of Yorkshire and the North, a prey to the inroads of the Scots, who time after time pillaged their lands and sometimes dispersed their inmates, Yorkshire was full of nunneries and almost all of them were miserably poor. But in other parts of the country, without any such special cause, the position was little better. When Bishop Alnwick visited the diocese of Lincoln in the first half of the fifteenth century, fourteen out of the twenty-five houses which he examined were in financial difficulties. Moreover not only is this true of small houses, inadequately endowed from their foundation and less likely to weather bad times, but the largest and richest houses frequently complained of insufficient means. It is easy to understand the distress of the poor nuns of Rothwell; their founder Richard, Earl of Gloucester,

---

[1] Savine, *English Monasteries on the Eve of the Dissolution* (Oxford Hist. Studies, ed. Vinogradoff, I, pp. 221–2). See also above, Ch. I, pp. 2–3.

had died before properly endowing the house, and the prioress and convent could expend for their food and clothing only four marks and the produce of four fields of land, in one of which the house was situated[1]. But it is less easy to account for the constant straits of the great Abbey of Shaftesbury, which had such vast endowments that a popular saying had arisen· "If the Abbot of Glastonbury could marry the Abbess of Shaftesbury, their heir would hold more land than the King of England"[2]. It is comprehensible that the small houses of Lincolnshire and the dangerously situated houses of Yorkshire should be in difficulties; but their complaints are not more piteous than those of Romsey, Godstow and Barking, richly endowed nunneries, to which the greatest ladies of the land did not disdain to retire

The poverty of the nunneries was manifested in many ways. One of these was the extreme prevalence of debt. On the occasion of Bishop Alnwick's visitations, to which reference has been made above, no less than eleven houses were found to be in debt[3]. At Ankerwyke the debts amounted to £40, at Langley to £50, at Stixwould to 80 marks, at Harrold to 20 marks, at Rothwell to 6 marks. Markyate was "indebted to divers creditors for a great sum" Heynings was in debt owing to costly repairs and to several bad harvests, and about the same time a petition from the nuns stated that they had "mortgaged for no short time their possessions and rents and thus remain irrecoverably pledged, have incurred various very heavy debts and are much depressed and brought to great and manifest poverty"[4]. In some cases the prioresses claimed to have reduced an initial debt; the Prioress of St Michael's, Stamford, said that on her installation twelve years previously the debts stood at £20 and that they were now only 20 marks; the Prioress of Gracedieu said that

---

[1] *Cal. of Papal Letters*, IV, p 436. In 1442 its numbers (which should have been fourteen) had sunk to seven and it was six marks in debt (*Alnwick's Visit* MS f 38) The clear annual value of the house in the *Valor Ecclesiasticus* was only £5. 19s 8½d. Compare the case of Heynings, whose founder, Sir John Darcy, had also died without completing its endowment. *Cal of Papal Letters*, V, p. 347

[2] Fuller, *Church History*, III, p 332. Its net income at the Dissolution was £1329 1s 3d. Compare *The Italian Relation of England* (Camden Soc), pp. 40–1

[3] *Linc Visit.* II, pp. 1, 49, 117, 119, 130, 133, 175, 184, *Alnwick's Visit.* MS. ff 6d, 38, 83

[4] *Cal of Papal Letters*, V, p. 347

she had reduced debts from £48 to £38, the Prioress of Legbourne
said that the debts were now only £14 instead of £63[1]. But from
the miserable poverty of some of these houses (for instance
Gokewell, where the income in rents was said to be £10 yearly
and Langley, where it was £20, less than half the amount of
the debts) it may be inferred that the struggle to repay creditors
out of an already insufficient income was a hopeless one; and
the effort to do so out of capital was often more disastrous still
Nothing is more striking than the lists of debts which figure in
the account rolls of medieval nunneries In thirteen out of
seventeen account rolls belonging to St Michael's Stamford[2] and
ranging between 1304 and 1410, the nuns end the year with a
deficit, and in fourteen cases there is a schedule of debts added
to the account. Sometimes the amount owed is small, but occasionally it is very large. In the first roll which has survived
(1304–5) the deficit on the account is some £5 odd; the debts
are entered as £23 1s 11d. on the present year (which were
apparently afterwards paid, because the items were marked
"vacat pour ceo ke le deners sount paye") and fifteen items
amounting to £52 3s 8d. and described as "nos auncienes
dettes estre cest aan", in fact the debts amount to considerably
more than the income entered in the roll[3]. Similarly in 1346–47
the debts amount to £51 odd and in 1376–77 to £53 odd, and in
other years to smaller sums. In some cases a list of debts due
to the convent is also entered in the account; but in only four
of these does the money owed to the house exceed the amount
owing by it; and "argent aprompté" or "money borrowed" is
a regular item in the credit account. Similarly the treasuresses'
accounts of Gracedieu end with long schedules of debts due by
the house[4]. Nor was it only the small houses which got into

---

[1] The Prioress of Ankerwyke also claimed to have reduced the debt from
300 marks to £40, but one of the nuns said that it had been only £30 on her
installation and that it had not been paid by the Prioress but from other
sources. *Linc. Visit* II, pp 1, 3.
[2] *P.R O Mins. Accts.* 1260 *passim*
[3] *P R O Mins Accts* 1260/1 It should, however, be noted that some
of the items which go to make up the total of the debts are sums of money
owing to members of the convent (e g the Prioress and Subprioress) by the
treasuresses, though the sums owing to outsiders are larger.
[4] *P R O. Mins Accts* 1257/10 ff 34 and 34d, 39d. Similarly the Prioress's
account of Delapré for 4 Henry VIII contains a long list of debts *St Paul's
Ecclesiological Soc.* VII (1912), p. 52 An analysis of Archbishop Eudes

debt. Tarrant Keynes was quite well off, but as early as 1292 the nuns asked the royal leave to sell forty oaks to pay their debts[1]. Godstow was rich, but in 1316 the King had to take it under his protection and appoint keepers to discharge its debts, "on account of its poverty and miserable state," and in 1335 the profits during vacancy were remitted to the convent by the King "because of its poverty and misfortunes"[2]. St Mary's, Winchester, was a famous house, but it also was in debt early in the fourteenth century[3]. It should be noticed that the last cases (and that of St Michael's Stamford, 1304–5) are anterior to the Black Death, to whose account it has been customary to lay all the financial misfortunes of the religious houses. It is undeniable that the Black Death completed the ruin of many of the smaller houses, and that matters grew steadily worse during the last half of the fourteenth and throughout the fifteenth century; but there is ample evidence that the finances of many religious houses, both of men and of women, had been in an unsatisfactory condition at an earlier date; and even the golden thirteenth century can show cases of heavy debt[4]

In the smaller houses the constant struggle with poverty must have entailed no little degree of discomfort and discouragement Sometimes the nuns seem actually to have lacked food and clothes, and it seems clear that in many cases the revenues of these convents were insufficient for their support and that they were dependent upon the charity of friends A typical case is that of Legbourne, where one of the nuns informed Bishop Alnwick (1440) that since the revenues of the house did not exceed £40 and since there were thirteen nuns and one novice, it was impossible for so many of them to have sufficient food and clothing from such inadequate rents, unless they re-

---

Rigaud's visitations of nunneries in the Diocese of Rouen gives even more startling information on this point, all but four of the fourteen houses show a list of debts growing heavier year by year and this was in the thirteenth century (1249–69). See *Reg Visit Archiep Rothomag.* ed Bonnin *passim.*

[1] *V.C H. Dorset,* II, p 88.   [2] *V C H Oxon.* II, p 73

[3] *Cal. of Papal Petit.* I, pp. 56, 122, 230

[4] For other cases of debt, in different centuries, see *V C.H. Yorks* III, pp. 124, 161, 163–4, 188, 239, 240, *Reg Walter Giffard* (Surtees Soc), p. 148, *V.C H. Oxon.* II, pp. 78, 104, *V C H Essex,* p. 122, *V.C.H Derby,* II, p. 43; *V C H Norfolk,* II, p 351; *V C H. Hants.* II, p 150; *V C H Bucks* I, p. 355, *Visit. of Diocese of Norwich* (Camden Soc.), pp. 108, 109; *Test. Ebor.* I, pp. 284–5, *Cal. of Papal Letters,* VI, p. 25, *Sussex Archaeol. Coll.* IX, p. 7.

ceived assistance from secular friends[1]. Fosse in 1341 was said
to be so slenderly endowed that the nuns had not enough to
live on without external aid[2]; and in 1440 Alnwick noted "all
the nuns complain ever of the poverty of the house and they
receive nothing from it save only food and drink"[3]. Of Buckland
it was stated that "its possessions cannot suffice for the sustenance of the said sisters with their household, for the emenda-
tion of their building, for their clothes and for their other
necessities without the help of friends and the offering of alms"[4].
Cokehill in 1336 was excused a tax because it was so inadequately
endowed that the nuns had not enough to live upon without
outside aid[5]. Davington in 1344 was in the same position;
although the nuns were reduced to half their former number,
they could not live upon their revenues without the charity
of friends[6]. Alnwick's visitations, indeed, show quite clearly that
in poor houses the nuns were often expected to provide either
clothes or (on certain days) food for themselves, out of the gift
of their friends[7]. At Sinningthwaite, in the diocese of York, the
position appears even more clearly; in 1319 it was declared that
the nuns who had no elders, relatives or friends, lacked the
necessary clothes and were therefore afflicted with cold, whereupon the Archbishop ordered them to have clothes provided
out of the means of the house[8]. The clause of the Council of
Oxford which permitted poor houses to receive a sum sufficient
for the vesture of a new member was evidently stretched to
include the perpetual provision of clothing by external friends,
and this is sometimes indicated in the wording of legacies. Thus
Roger de Noreton, citizen and mercer of York, left the following
bequest in 1390:

I bequeath to Isabel, my daughter, a nun of St Clement's, York, to
buy her black flannels (*pro flannelis suis nigris emendis*), according
to the arrangement of my wife Agnes and of my other executors, at
fitting times, according to her needs, four marks of silver[9].

[1] *Linc. Visit.* II, p 186.
[2] *V.C.H. Lincs* II, p. 157.   [3] *Linc Visit.* II, p 92
[4] *The Knights Hospitallers in England* (Camden Soc), p. 20.
[5] *V.C H Worcs* II, pp 157–8.   [6] Dugdale, *Mon.* IV. p 285
[7] See below, p. 340.   [8] *V C H. Yorks.* III, p. 177
[9] *Test. Ebor* I, p. 133. The account book of Gracedieu (1414–8) contains entries of money paid by William Roby "for the clothes of his relation
Dame Agnes Roby" and at another time by Margaret Roby for the same
purpose (6s. 8d.) Gasquet, *English Monastic Life*, p. 170.

Sir Thomas Cumberworth, dying in 1451, specifically directed that "ye blak Curteyne of lawne be cut in vailes and gyfyn to pore nones"[1].

The nuns were not always able to obtain adequate help from external friends in the matter of food and clothes; and evidence given at episcopal visitations shows that they sometimes went cold and hungry. Complaints are common that the allowance paid to the nuns (in defiance of canon law) for the provision of food and of garments had been reduced or withdrawn; and so also are complaints that the quality of beer provided by the convent was poor, though here the propensity of all communities to grumble at their food has to be taken into account[2]. But more specific information is often given; and though it is clear that financial mismanagement was often as much to blame as poverty, the sufferings of the nuns were not for that reason any less real. The Yorkshire nunnery of Swine is a case in point. It was never rich, but at Archbishop Giffard's visitation in 1268 the nuns complained that the maladministration of their fellow canons[3] had made their position intolerable. Although the means of the house, if discreetly managed, sufficed to maintain them, they nevertheless had nothing but bread and cheese and ale for meals and were even served with water instead of ale twice a week, while the canons and their friends were provided for "abundantly and sumptuously enough"; the nuns were moreover insufficiently provided with shoes and clothes; they had only one pair of shoes each year[4] and barely a tunic in every three and a cloak in every six years, unless they managed to beg more from relatives and secular friends[5] Fifty years later there was still scarcity at Swine, for the Prioress was ordered to see that the house was reasonably served with bread, ale and other necessities[6]. At Ankerwyke (1441) the frivolous and incompetent Prioress, Clemence Medforde, reduced her nuns to

---

[1] *Lincoln Diocese Documents* (E E T S), p 57

[2] It is amusing to notice the indignation of the nuns when their beer was not strong enough. See e g *Alnwick's Visit.* MS ff 71d, 72, *Visit of Dioc. of Norwich* (Camden Soc), p. 209, *Yorks. Archaeol. Journal*, XVI, p. 443.

[3] Dugdale, *Mon* v, pp 493–4

[4] When little Elizabeth Sewardby was boarding in Nunmonkton she had ten pairs in eighteen months! *Test Ebor* III, p 168.

[5] *Reg of Walter Giffard* (Surtees Soc.), pp. 147–8.

[6] *V C H. Yorks* III, p. 181

similar discomfort. Margery Kirkby, whose tongue nothing could stop, announced that "she furnishes not nor for three years' space has furnished fitting habits to the nuns, insomuch that the nuns go about in patched clothes The threadbareness of the nuns" added the bishop's clerk "was apparent to my lord. (*Patebat domino nuditas monialium*)" Three of the younger nuns also made complaints; Thomasine Talbot had no bedclothes "insomuch that she lies in the straw," Agnes Dychere "asks that sufficient provision be made to her in clothing for her bed and body, that she may be covered from the cold, and also in eatables, that she may have strength to undergo the burden of religious observance and divine service, for these hitherto had not been supplied to her"; and Margaret Smith also complained of insufficient bedclothes. Poor little sister Thomasine also remarked sadly that she had no kirtle provided for her use[1].

The history of Romsey shows that even the rich houses suffered from similar inconveniences. In 1284 Peckham speaks of a scarcity of food in the house and forbids the Abbess to fare sumptuously in her chamber, while the convent went short[2]; in 1311 it was ordered that the bread should be brought back to the weight, quantity and quality hitherto used[3]; and in 1387 William of Wykeham rather severely commanded the Abbess and officiaries to provide for the nuns bread, beer and other fit and proper victuals, according to ancient custom and to the means of the house[4]. Campsey was another flourishing house, but in 1532 a chorus of complaint greeted the ears of the visitor,

---

[1] *Linc Visit* II, pp. 4, 5 This lack of bedclothes for the younger nuns was partly due to the fact that the Prioress did not want them to sleep in the dorter, for Thomasine adds "and when my lord had commanded this deponent to lie in the dorter and this deponent asked bedclothes of the Prioress, she said chidingly to her 'Let him who gave you leave to lie in the dorter supply you with raiment.'" Mr Hamilton Thompson thinks that "probably sister Thomasine had previously been lodged separately with the other younger nuns and the Prioress and elders objected to the crowding of the dorter" But poverty was the main cause, for at a later visitation the Prioress stated that she was unable to supply the sisters with sufficient raiment for their habits "because of the poverty and insufficiency of the resources of the house" *Ib.* p. 7.

[2] The same injunction was sent to Wherwell. *Reg Epist Johannis Peckham* (Rolls Ser), II, pp 651, 659–60

[3] Liveing, *Records of Romsey Abbey*, p. 103.

[4] *New Coll.* MS f 86d

and (as in so many cases) the ills were all put down to the mismanagement of the Prioress, Ela Buttry. She was not too luxurious, but too stingy; Katherine Symon said that noble guests, coming to the priory, complained of the very great parsimony of the Prioress; Margaret Harmer said that the sisters were sometimes served with very unwholesome food; Isabel Norwich said that the friends of the nuns, coming to the house, were not properly provided for; Margaret Bacton said that dinner was late through the fault of the cook and that the meat was burnt to a cinder; Katherine Grome said that the beef and mutton with which the nuns were served were sometimes bad and unwholesome and that within the past month a sick ox, which would otherwise have died, had been killed for food, and that the Prioress was very sparing both in her own meals and in those with which she provided the nuns; and four other sisters gave evidence to the same effect[1]. One has the impression that the nuns were elderly and fussy, but there was evidently a basis for their unanimous complaint, and it is easy to imagine that food may sometimes have been very bad in convents which (unlike Campsey) were burdened with real poverty[2].

Another sign of the financial distress of the nunneries was the ruinous condition of their buildings. The remark written by a shivering monk in a set of nonsense verses may well stand as the plaint of half the nunneries of England:

> Haec abbathia ruit, hoc notum sit tibi, Christe,
> Intus et extra pluit, terribilis est locus iste.

("This abbey falleth in ruins, Christ mark this well! It raineth within and without; how fearful is this place!")[3]. Time after time

---

[1] *Visit. of the Diocese of Norwich* (Camden Soc), pp 290-2 Cf the complaint of the nuns of Studley in 1530 "They be oftentymes served with beffe and no moton upon Thursday at nyght and Sondays at nyght and be served oftentymes with new ale and not hulsome" *V C H Oxon* II, p 78.

[2] Other houses in the diocese of Norwich which complained of bad food were Flixton (1520) and Carrow (1492, 1514, 1526) Carrow was one of the most famous nunneries in England, but in 1492 one of the Bishop's *comperta* ran "That the present sisters are restricted to eight loaves, and this is very little for ten sisters, for the whole day Item there is often a lack of bread in the house, contrary to the good repute of the place." See *Visit. of the Diocese of Norwich*, pp. 16-17, 145, 185-6, 209

[3] *Reliquiae Antiquae*, I, p 291. Translated in Coulton, *A Mediaeval Garner*, p 597.

PLATE IV

pray for the Soule of Eel Buttry sutyme Pryores of Campelle on whose soule Jesu haue ... the xxviij day of Octobzum ...

Brass of Ela Buttry, the stingy Prioress of Campsey (†1546), in St Stephen's Church, Norwich. Stingy even in death, she has appropriated to her own use the brass of a 14th century laywoman.

visitations revealed houses badly in need of repair and roofs
letting in rain or even tumbling about the ears of the nuns;
time after time indulgences were granted to Christians who would
help the poor nuns to rebuild church or frater or infirmary. The
thatched roofs especially were continually needing repairs. It
will be remembered how the Abbess Euphemia of Wherwell
rebuilt the bell tower above the dorter,

which fell down through decay one night, about the hour of mattins,
when by an obvious miracle from heaven, though the nuns were in
the dorter, some in bed and some in prayer before their beds, all
escaped not only death but any bodily injury[1]

At Crabhouse in the time of Joan Wiggenhall

the dortour that than was, as fer forthe as we knowe, the furste that
was set up on the place, was at so grete mischeef and, at the gate-
downe, the Prioresse dredyinge perisschyng of her sistres whiche lay
thereinne took it doune for drede of more hermys,

and next year "sche began the grounde of the same dortoure
that now stondith and wrought thereupon fulli vij yere
betymes as God wolde sende hir good[2]." The Prioress of
Swine was ordered in 1318 to have the dorter covered
without delay, so that the nuns might quietly and in silence
enter it, without annoyance from storms, and to have the
roofs of the other buildings repaired as soon as might be[3]. At
St Radegund's Cambridge, in 1373, the Prioress was charged
with suffering the frater to remain unroofed, so that in rainy
weather the sisters were unable to take their meals there, to
which she replied that the nunnery was so burdened with debts,
subsidies and contributions, that she had so far been unable to
carry out repairs, but would do so as quickly as possible[4] At
Littlemore in 1445 the nuns did not sleep in the dorter for fear it
should fall[5]. At Romsey in 1502 the wicked Abbess Elizabeth
Broke had allowed the roofs of the chancel and dorter to become
defective, "so that if it happened to rain the nuns were unable

[1] V C H. Hants. II, p 135 The belfry of St Radegund's, Cambridge, fell
down and injured the church in 1277 Gray, Hist of the Priory of St Radegund, Cambridge, pp. 37–8, cf p 79 That of Esholt fell in 1445. V C H
Yorks. III, p 161.
[2] Reg. of Crabhouse Nunnery (Norfolk Archaeology, XI, 1892), pp 61,
62
[3] V C H Yorks. III, p 181. [4] Gray, op. cit. p. 32
[5] Linc. Visit. II, p. 217.

to remain either in the quire in time of divine service or in their beds and the funds that the abbess ought to have expended on these matters were being squandered on Master Bryce"; the fabric of the monastery in stone walls was also going to decay through her neglect, and so were various tenements belonging to the house in the town of Romsey[1] Over a hundred and twenty years before, William of Wykeham had found Romsey hardly less dilapidated, with its church, infirmary and nuns' rooms "full of many enormous and notable defects," and the buildings of the monastery itself and of its different manors in need of repair[2]. Of the unfortunate houses within the area of Scottish inroads, Arden, Thicket, Keldholme, Rosedale, Swine, Wykeham, Arthington and Moxby were all ruinous at the beginning of the fourteenth century; the monotonous list includes the church, frater and chapter house of Arden, the cloister of Rosedale, the bakehouse and brewhouse of Moxby, the dorter and frater of Arthington[3]

In the sixteenth century the distress was, as usual, at its worst At the visitation of the Chichester diocese by Bishop Sherburn in 1521 the cloister of Easebourne needed roofing and Rusper was "in magno decasu"; six years later Rusper was still "aliqualiter ruinosa"[4] At the Norwich visitations of Bishop Nykke the church of Blackborough was in ruins, and the roofs of cloister and frater at Flixton were defective, while at Crabhouse buildings were in need of repair and the roof of the Lady chapel was ruinous[5]; Joan Wiggenhall must have turned in her grave. Bishop Longland's visitations of the diocese of Lincoln show a similar state of affairs. In 1531 he commanded the

---

[1] *V C H Hants* II, pp 129–31 *passim* For another complaint that tenements and leasehold houses belonging to a priory were ruinous and like to fall down, through the negligence of the prioress and bailiff, see the case of Legbourne in 1440 *Linc Visit* II, p 185

[2] *New Coll* MS ff 87*d*–88 He ordered the Abbess to repair defects at once out of the common goods of the house Better still, he would seem to have assisted them from his own pocket to carry out the injunction, for by his will (1402) he remitted to them a debt of £40, for the repair of their church and cloister. Nicolas, *Testamenta Vetusta*, II, p. 708.

[3] *V C H. Yorks* III, pp 113, 124, 168, 174, 181, 183, 188, 240; Yedingham and Esholt (*ib* pp 128, 161) and St Mary, Neasham (*V C H Durham*, II, p 107) needed repair in the middle of the fifteenth century

[4] *Sussex Arch Coll* IX, p 23; V, pp 256, 258

[5] *Visitations of the Diocese of Norwich* (Camden Soc), pp 107–8, 109, 261, 311

Abbess of Elstow "that suche reparacons as be necessarye in and upon the buildinges within the said monasterye, and other houses, tenements and fearmes thereto belonging, be suffycyently doon and made within the space of oon yere," and the Prioress of Nuncoton, "that ye cause your firmary, your chirche and all other your houses that be in ruyne and dekaye within your monastery to be suffycyently repayred within this yere if itt possible may"; and reminded the nuns of Studley that they "muste bestowe lardge money upon suche reparacons as are to be doon upon your churche, quere, dortor and other places whiche ar in grete decaye"[1]. At Goring, also, the nuns all complained that the buildings were utterly out of repair, especially the choir, cloister and dorter[2].

The frequency of fires in the middle ages was probably often to blame for the ruin of buildings There were then no contrivances for extinguishing flames, and the thatched and wooden houses must have burned like stubble. Thus it was that "thorow the negligens of woman[3] with fyre brent up a good malt-house with a soler and alle her malt there" at Crabhouse,

---

[1] *Archaeologia*, XLVII, pp 52, 54, 59

[2] *V C H Lincs* II, p. 104 A few out of many other references to ruinous buildings may be given here. Easebourne (1411) *Bishop Rede's Reg* p. 137. Polsloe (1319). *Reg. of Bishop Stapeldon of Exeter*, p 318. Delapré (Northampton) (1303), Wothorpe (1292), Rothwell (fourteenth century), Catesby (1301, 1312). *V C H Northants* II, pp 101, 114, 138, 123 Rowney (1431) *V C H Herts* IV, pp 435–6. St Radegund's Cambridge Gray, *op cit* pp 36–8, 79. St Clare without Aldgate (1290) *Ely Epis. Records*, ed. Gibbons, p 415 St Mary's Winchester (1343–52). *Cal. of Pap. Pet* I, pp 56, 122, 230

[3] Perhaps in the same way that a fire broke out at Sempringham in the lifetime of St Gilbert. "A nun, bearing a light through the kitchen by night, fixed a part of a burnt candle to another she was going to burn, so that both were alight at once But when the part fixed on to the other was almost consumed, it fell on the floor, on which much straw was collected, ready for a fire The nun did not heed it, and believing that the fire would go out by itself, she went away and shut the door. But the flame, finding food, first devoured the straw lying close by, then the whole house with the adjacent offices and their contents, whence a great loss happened to the church " Quoted from MS. Cott *Cleop. B* I, f 77 by R. Graham, *St Gilbert of Sempringham and the Gilbertines*, p 135. It will be remembered that the author of the thirteenth century treatise, called "Seneschaucie," is most careful to declare that ploughmen, waggoners and cowherds must not carry fire into the byres, stables and cowhouse, either for light or to warm themselves, "unless the candle be in a lantern and this for great need and then it must be carried and watched by another than himself." *Walter of Henley's Husbandry*, ed E Lamond (1890), p 113

and Joan Wiggenhall had to repair it at a cost of five pounds[1]. There is a piteous appeal to Edward I from the nuns of Cheshunt, who had been impoverished by a fire and sought "help from the King of his special grace and for God's sake"; but "*Nihil fiat hac vice*," replied red tape[2]; an undated petition in the Record Office says that the house, church and goods of the nuns had twice been burned and their charters destroyed[3]. In 1299 the Abbess of Wilton received permission to fell fifty oaks in the forest of Savernake "in order to rebuild therewith certain houses in the abbey lately burnt by mischance"[4]. At Wykeham, in Edward III's reign, the priory church, cloisters and twenty-four other buildings were accidentally burned down and all the books, vestments and chalices of the nuns were destroyed[5]. Similarly the nuns of St Radegund's, Cambridge, lost their house and all their substance by fire at the beginning of the fourteenth century, and in 1376 their buildings were again said to have been burned, either they had never recovered from their first disaster or a second fire had broken out[6]. The nuns of St Leonard's, Grimsby, apparently lost their granaries in 1311, for they sought licence to beg on the ground that their houses and corn had been consumed by fire, and in 1459 they asked for a similar licence, because their buildings had been burnt, and their land inundated[7]. The convent of St Bartholomew's, Newcastle, gave misfortune by fire as one reason for wishing to appropriate the hospital or chapel of St Edmund the King in Gateshead[8].

Sometimes poverty, misfortune and mismanagement reduced the nuns to begging alms. About 1253 the convent of St Mary of Chester wrote to Queen Eleanor, begging her to confirm the election of a prioress "to our miserable convent amidst its multiplied desolations; for so greatly are we reduced that we are compelled every day to beg abroad our food, slight as it is"[9]. Similarly the starving nuns of Whitehall, Ilchester, were reduced to "begging miserably," after the *régime* of a wicked

---

[1] *Reg of Crabhouse Nunnery u.s.* p 61
[2] Dugdale, *Mon* IV, p. 328   See also *V C H Herts.* IV, p 426
[3] *V.C H. Herts. loc. cit*
[4] *Cal of Close Rolls*, 1296–1302, p. 238.
[5] *V C H Yorks* III, p 183   [6] Gray, *op cit* p 79
[7] *V C H. Lincs* II, p 179
[8] Dugdale, *Mon* IV, p 485.
[9] Wood, *Letters of Royal and Illustrious Ladies*, I, p. 35

prioress at the beginning of the fourteenth century[1] In 1308
the subprioress and convent of Whiston mentioned, in asking
for permission to elect Alice de la Flagge, that the smallness
of their possessions had compelled the nuns formerly to beg,
"to the scandal of womanhood and the discredit of religion"[2].
In 1351 Bishop Edyndon of Winchester "counted it a merciful
thing," to come to the assistance of the great Abbeys of Romsey
and St Mary's Winchester, "when overwhelmed with poverty,
and when in these days of increasing illdoing and social deteriora-
tion they were brought to the necessity of secret begging"[3] At
Cheshunt in 1367 the nuns declared that they often had to beg
in the highways[4]. At Rothwell in 1392 the extreme poverty of
the nuns compelled some of them "to incur the opprobrium
of mendicity and beg alms after the fashion of the mendicant
friars"[5]. In all these cases it is evident that objection was taken
to personal begging by the nuns, and it is clear that such a
practice, which took the nuns out into the streets and into
private houses, was likely to be subversive of discipline. The
custom of begging through a proctor was open to no such
objection, and it was common for bishops to give to the poorer
houses licences, allowing them to collect alms in this manner.
Early in the fifteenth century the nuns of Rowney in Hertfordshire petitioned the Chancellor for letters patent for a proctor to
go about the country and collect alms for them, and their request
was granted[6]. Many such licences to beg occur in episcopal
registers; Bishop Dalderby of Lincoln granted them to Little

[1] *Reg. of John of Drokensford* (Somerset Rec. Soc.), p. 227. Text in Hugo,
Medieval Nunneries of Somerset · Whitehall in Ilchester, p 78 But seven
years before they had been begging, according to the Bishop, by the compulsion of this expelled prioress, whose case was *sub judice*. *Reg.* p. 115
and Hugo, *loc cit*

[2] *Reg Sede Vacante* (Worc Rec Soc), pp 112–3.

[3] Liveing, *Records of Romsey Abbey*, p 145

[4] *V C H. Herts.* IV, p. 427   [5] *V.C.H. Northants* II, p. 137.

[6] *V C H. Herts.* IV, pp 434–5 The text of their petition is as follows:
"A tres reverend pier en dieu, mon treshonure seigneur le chaunceller
dengleterre, supphant voz pouers oratrices la prioresse et les noneyns de
Rowney en le countee de...qe come lour esglise et autres mesons sont en
poynt de cheyer a terre pur defaute de reparacion et ils nount dont lez re-
parailler, si noun dalmoigne de bones gens, qe plese a vostre treshonure
seignurie de vostre grace eux granter vn patent pur vn lour procuratour,
de aler en la paiis a coiller almoigns de bones gentz pur la sustenance et
releuacioun du dit pouere mesoun et en noun de charite." *P R O. Ancient
Petitions,* 302/15063.

Marlow (1300 and 1311)[1], St Leonard's Grimsby (1311)[2], and
Rothwell (1318)[3]; and St Michael's Stamford (1359) and Sewardsley (1366) received similar licences from his successors[4].
The distinction between begging by the nuns and begging by
a proctor is clearly drawn in the licence granted by Bishop
Dalderby to Rothwell. Addressing the clergy in the Archidiaconates of Northampton and Buckingham he writes:

Pitying, with paternal affection, the want of the poor nuns of Rothwell in our diocese, who are oppressed by such scarcity that they are
obliged to beg the necessities of life, we command and straitly enjoin
you, that when there shall come to you suitable and honest secular
proctors or messengers of the same nuns (not the nuns themselves,
that they may have no occasion for wandering thereby), to seek and
receive the alms of the faithful for their necessities, ye shall receive
them kindly and expound the cause of the said nuns to the people
in your churches, on Sundays, and feast days during the solemnisation
of mass, and promote the same by precept and by example once every
year for the next three years, delivering the whole of whatever shall
be collected to these proctors and messengers[5]

The Bishops sought to relieve necessitous convents by offering
particular inducements to the faithful to give alms, when they
were thus requested. Along with mending roads and bridges,
ransoming captives, dowering poor maidens, building churches
and endowing hospitals, the assistance of impecunious nunneries
was generally recognised as a work of Christian charity, and
indulgences were often offered to those who would aid a particular
house[6]. The same Bishop Dalderby, for instance, granted indulgences for the assistance of Cheshunt, Flamstead[7], Sewardsley,

---

[1] *V.C.H Bucks.* I, p 358.
[2] *V.C H Lincs.* II, p 179 Another licence in 1459
[3] *V.C H Northants* II, p. 137   [4] *Ib* pp. 100, 126.
[5] *Linc Epis Reg Memo Dalderby*, f 374 (*Pro monialibus de Rowell*)
It is surprising, however, that Peckham, in his constitution forbidding nuns
to be absent from their convents for longer than three, or at the most six,
days, adds. "We do not extend this ordinance to those nuns who are forced
to beg their necessities outside, while they are begging" Wilkins, *Concilia*,
II, p. 59 It is certain that the nuns did beg in their own persons When
Archbishop Eudes Rigaud visited St-Aubin in 1261 he ordered that the
younger nuns should not be sent out to beg (*pro questu*), and in 1263 two
of them were absent in France, seeking alms *Reg. Visit. Archiepiscopi
Rothomagensis*, ed Bonnin, pp 412, 471
[6] On this subject see an interesting article by C Wordsworth, "On some
Pardons or Indulgences preserved in Yorkshire 1412-1527" (*Yorks. Arch.
Journ* XVI, pp 369 ff).
[7] *V.C.H Herts* IV, pp 426, 432

Catesby, Delapré[1], Ivinghoe[2], Fosse[3], St James' outside Huntingdon and St Radegund's, Cambridge[4] Archbishop Kemp of York
granted an indulgence of a hundred days valid for two years
to all who should assist towards the repair of Arden (1440) and
of Esholt (1445), and Archbishop William Booth (1456) granted
an indulgence of forty days to penitents contributing to the
repair of Yedingham[5]; indeed it is probable that the money for
the much needed work of roofing a building could be collected
only by means of such special appeals The Popes also sometimes
granted indulgences; Boniface IX did so to penitents who on
the feasts of dedication visited and gave alms towards the con-
servation of the churches and priories of Wilberfoss, St Clement's,
York, and Handale[6]. The history of St Radegund's, Cambridge,
will serve to illustrate the method by which the Church thus
organised the work of poor-relief in the middle ages; and it will
be noticed that this nunnery was an object of care to Bishops
of other dioceses beside that of Ely[7]. In 1254 Walter de Suffield,
Bishop of Norwich, granted a relaxation of penance for twenty-
five days to persons contributing to the aid of the nuns; in 1268
Richard de Gravesend, Bishop of Lincoln, ordered collections to
be made in the churches of the Archidiaconates of Northampton
and Huntingdon on their behalf; in 1277 Roger de Skerning,
Bishop of Norwich, ordered collections to be made in his diocese
for the repair of the church, in 1313 the Official of the Archdeacon of Ely wrote to the parochial clergy of the diocese re-
commending the nuns to them as objects of charity, having
lost their house and goods by fire, and in the same year Bishop
Dalderby granted an indulgence on their behalf for this reason[8];
while in 1314 John de Ketene, Bishop of Ely, confirmed the
grants of indulgence made by his brother bishops to persons
contributing to their relief and to the rebuilding of the house
The next indulgence mentioned is one of forty days granted by

[1] V C H Northants II, pp 114, 123, 116
[2] V.C H Bucks. I, p. 353   [3] V.C H Lincs. II, p 157
[4] Linc. Epis. Reg Memo Dalderby, ff 96d, 244d
[5] V.C.H. Yorks III, pp 115, 128, 161
[6] Cal of Papal Letters, IV, p 393, V, p 373
[7] Except where otherwise stated the following references all occur in
Gray, op cit p 79 and are printed in full in R. Willis, Architectural Hist
of the Univ. of Cambridge, ed. J Willis Clark (1886), II, pp. 183–6
[8] Linc. Epis Reg Memo Dalderby, f 96d

Thomas Arundel, Bishop of Ely, in 1376, also on the occasion of a fire; in 1389 Bishop Fordham of Ely granted another forty days indulgence for the repair of the church and cloister and for the relief of the nuns[1], and in 1390 William Courtenay, Archbishop of Canterbury, made a similar grant, mentioning that the buildings had been ruined by violent storms; finally in 1457 Bishop Grey of Ely granted a forty days indulgence for the repair of the bell-tower and for the maintenance of books, vestments and other church ornaments[2] There is no need to suppose that St Radegund's was in any way a particularly favoured house; and such a list of grants shows that the Church fulfilled conscientiously the duty of organising poor-relief and that the objects for which indulgences were granted were not always as unworthy as has sometimes been supposed[3].

The financial straits to which the smaller convents were continually and the greater convents sometimes reduced grew out of a number of causes, and it is interesting to inquire what brought the nuns to debt or to begging and why they were so often in difficulties. A study of monastic documents makes it clear that a great deal of this poverty was in no sense the fault of the nuns. Apart from obvious cases of insufficient endowment, the medieval monasteries suffered from natural disasters, which were the lot of all men, and from certain exactions at the hands of men, which fell exclusively upon themselves. Of natural disasters the frequency of fires has already been mentioned. Another danger, from which houses situated in low lying land near a river or the sea were never free, was that of floods. The inundation of their lands was declared one of the reasons for appropriating the church of Bradford-on-Avon to Shaftesbury in 1343; and in 1380 the nuns were allowed to appropriate another church, in consideration of damage done to their lands by encroachments of the sea and losses of sheep and cattle[4]. In 1377 Barking suffered the devastation by flood of a large part of its possessions along the Thames and never recovered its former

---

[1] Gray, *op cit* p 36   [2] *Ib* pp 37–8
[3] A few other references may be given. Bishop Fordham of Ely for Rowney (1408) and Bishop Alcock of Ely for the Minories (1490) Gibbons, *Ely Epis. Records*, pp 406, 414 Bishop Sutton of Lincoln to Wothorpe (1292) *V C H Northants.* II, p 114
[4] *V C H Wilts* II, p 77

prosperity[1], and in 1394 Bishop Fordham of Ely granted an indulgence for the nuns of Ankerwyke, whose goods had been destroyed by floods[2]. In the north the lands of St Leonard's, Grimsby, were flooded in 1459[3], in 1445 the nuns of Esholt suffered heavy losses from the flooding of their lands near the river Aire, which had been cultivated at great cost and from which they derived their maintenance[4]; and in 1434 Archbishop Rotherham appealed for help for the nuns of Thicket, whose fields and pasturages had been inundated and who had suffered much loss by the death of their cattle[5]. Heavy storms are mentioned as contributing to the distress of Shaftesbury in 1365[6] and of St Radegund's, Cambridge, in 1390[7]. Moreover some houses suffered by their situation in barren and unproductive lands. Easebourne in 1411 complained of "the sterility of the lands, meadows and other property of the priory, which is situated in a solitary, waste and thorny place"[8]; Heynings put forward the same plea in 1401[9]; and Flamstead in 1380[10].

But far more terrible than fire and flood were those two other scourges, with which nature afflicted the men of the middle ages, famine and pestilence The Black Death of 1348–9 was only one among the pestilences of the fourteenth century; it had the result of "domesticating the bubonic plague upon the soil of England"; for more than three centuries afterwards it continued to break out at short intervals, first in one part of the country and then in another[11]. The epidemics of the fourteenth

[1] *V C H Essex*, II, p 119 References to this occur in 1380, 1382, 1384, 1392, 1402 and 1409
[2] Gibbons, *Ely Epis Records*, p 399
[3] *V C H Lincs* II, p 179 Cf Thetford. *V C H Norfolk*, II, p. 355
[4] *V C H Yorks* III, p 161   [5] *Ib* p 124
[6] *V C H Wilts* II, p 77 The reference is perhaps to the famous storm of St Maur's Day, 1362, which, together with the Black Death, is commemorated in a *graffito* in the church of Ashwell (Herts) and in a distich quoted by Adam Murimuth

> C ter erant mille, decies sex unus et ille
> Luce tua Maure, vehemens fuit impetus aurae.
> Ecce flat hoc anno, Maurus in orbe tonans.

[7] Gray, *op cit.* p 79
[8] *Bishop Rede's Reg* (Sussex Rec Soc), p 137.
[9] *Cal. of Papal Letters*, v, p 347
[10] Dugdale, *Mon* IV, p. 301
[11] The following account of medieval plagues and famines is taken mainly from Creighton, *Hist of Epidemics in Britain*, I, pp 202–7, 215–223 See also Denton, *England in the Fifteenth Century*, pp 91–105

century were so violent that in forty years the chroniclers count
up five great plagues, beginning with the Black Death, and
Langland, in a metaphor of terrible vividness, describes the
pestilence as "the rain that raineth where we rest should." The
Black Death was preceded by a famine pestilence in 1317-8,
when there was "a grievous mortalitie of people so that the
sicke might vnneath burie the dead " It was followed in 1361
by the Second Plague, which was especially fatal among the
upper classes and among the young The Third Plague in 1368-9
was probably primarily a famine sickness, mixed with plague
The Fourth Plague broke out in 1375; and the Fifth, in 1390-1
was so prolonged and so severe as to be considered comparable
with the Black Death itself. Moreover these are only the great
landmarks, and scattered between them were smaller outbreaks
of sickness, due to scarcity or to spoiled grain and fruit. The
pestilences continued in the fifteenth century (more than twenty-
one are recorded in the chronicles), but, except perhaps for the
great plague of 1439, they were seldom universal and came by
degrees to be confined to the towns, so that all who could used
to flee to the country when the summer heat brought out the
disease in crowded and insanitary streets. But if country convents escaped the worst disease, those situated in borough towns
ran a heavy risk.

Often enough these plagues were preceded and accompanied
by famines, sometimes local and sometimes general The English
famines had long been notorious and were enshrined in a popular
proverb: "Tres plagae tribus regionibus appropriari solent, An-
glorum fames, Gallorum ignis, Normannorum lepra"[1]. The three
greatest outbreaks took place in 1194-6, in 1257-9 and in
1315-6 (before the plague of 1318-9). The dearth which cul-
minated in the last of these famines had begun as early as 1289,
and the misery in 1315 was acute:

"The beastes and cattell also," says Stow, translating from Troke-
lowe, "by the corrupt grane whereof they fed, dyed, whereby it came
to passe that the eating of flesh was suspected of all men, for flesh of
beasts not corrupted was hard to finde Horse-flesh was counted
great delicates the poore stole fatte dogges to eate, some (as it was
sayde) compelled through famine, in hidden places did eate the flesh
of their owne children, and some stole others, which they devoured.

[1] Creighton, *op. cit.* I, p. 19.

Theeves that were in prisons did plucke in peeces those that were newly brought among them and greedily devoured them halfe alive."

There was another severe famine in 1322, and in 1325 a great drought, so that the cattle died for lack of water. Famine accompanied the pestilences of 1361, 1369, 1391 and 1439; and these are only the more outstanding instances. Here again, however, the fourteenth century was on the whole worse off than the fifteenth; almost every year was a year of scarcity and the average price of wheat during the period 1261 to 1400 was nearly six shillings (i e. nearly six pounds of modern money)[1]. Moreover the ravages of murrain among cattle and sheep were hardly intermittent from the end of the thirteenth to the middle of the fifteenth century[2]. The fatal years 1315–9 included not only a famine and a plague but also (1318–9) a murrain among the cattle, which was so bad that dogs and ravens, eating the dead bodies, were poisoned and died, and no man dared eat any beef. In the year of the Black Death also there was "a great plague of sheep in the realm, so that in one place there died in pasturage more than five thousand sheep and so rotted that neither beast nor bird would touch them"; and murrains accompanied the four other great plagues of the century. Indeed dearth, murrain and pestilence went hand in hand, in that unhappy time we call the "good old days."

These natural disasters could not but have an adverse effect upon the fortunes of the monastic houses; and many charters and petitions contain clauses which specifically attribute the distress of this or that nunnery to one of the three causes described above. During the famine years of 1314–5 Walter Reynolds, Archbishop of Canterbury, wrote to the Bishop of Winchester, urging him to take some steps for the relief of the nuns of Wintney, who were dispersing themselves in the world, because no proper provision was made for their food[3], and about the same time the convent of Clerkenwell addressed a petition to Queen Isabel, stating that they were "moet enpouerees par les durs annez" and begging her to procure for them the King's leave to accept certain lands and rents to the value of twenty

[1] Denton, *op cit.* p. 93
[2] *Ib.* p. 93 *sqq.*
[3] *V C.H. Hants* II, p. 150   He attributed their condition to negligence and bad administration

pounds[1]. In 1326 (after the great drought) the nuns of King's
Mead, Derby, begged the King to take them under his special
protection, granting the custody of the house to two *custodes*,
on the ground that, owing to the badness of past years and the
unusually heavy mortality among cattle their revenues were
reduced and they were unable to meet the claims made by
guests upon their hospitality[2] The ravages of the Black Death
were most severe of all and many houses never recovered from
it[3]. In the diocese of Lincoln the nunnery of Wothorpe lost all
its members save one, whom the Bishop made Prioress; and in
1354 it was annexed to St Michael's Stamford[4] Greenfield Priory,
when he visited it in 1350, "per tres menses stetit et stat
priorisse solacio destituta"[5]; and other houses in this large
diocese which lost their heads were Fosse, Markyate, Hinchinbrooke, Gracedieu, Rothwell, Delapré, Catesby, Sewardsley,
Littlemore and Godstow[6]. In the diocese of York the prioresses
of Arthington, Kirklees, Wallingwells and St Stephen's Foukeholm died; the latter house, like Wothorpe, failed to recover
and is never heard of again[7]. Other parts of the country suffered
in the same way. At Malling Abbey in Kent the Bishop made
two abbesses in succession, but both died and only four professed
nuns and four novices remained, to one of whom the Bishop
committed the custody of the temporalities and to another that
of the spiritualities, because there was no fit person to be made
Abbess[8]. At Henwood, in August 1349, there was no Prioress, "and
of the fifteen nuns who were lately there, three only remain"[9].

The death of the nuns themselves was, moreover, the least
disastrous effect of the pestilence, it left a legacy of neglected
lands, poverty and labour troubles which lasted for long after

---

[1] *P R O Ancient Correspondence*, XXXVI, no 201.
[2] *V C H Derby*, II, p 43   See below, p 200
[3] See P. G. Mode, *The Influence of the Black Death on the English
Monasteries* (Univ of Chicago, 1916), *passim*
[4] Dugdale, *Mon.* IV, p 268
[5] A Hamilton Thompson, *Registers of John Gynewell, Bishop of Lincoln
for the years* 1347-1350 (reprinted from *Archaeol Journ* LXVIII, pp 301–
360, 1912), p 328
[6] *Ib.* pp. 359–60
[7] A Hamilton Thompson, *The Pestilences of the Fourteenth Century in
the Diocese of York* (reprinted from *Archaeol Journ* LXXI, pp 97–154,
1914), pp. 121–2
[8] Wharton, *Anglia Sacra*, I, pp. 364, 375.
[9] *V C H Warwick* II, p. 65

a new generation of sisters had forgotten the fate of their predecessors. The value of Flixton dwindled after the Black Death
to half its former income, and the house was never prosperous
again[1]. In 1351 the nuns of Romsey petitioned for leave to
annex certain lands and advowsons and gave as one of the
reasons for their impoverishment "the diminution or loss of due
and appointed rents, because of the death of tenants, carried
off by the unheard of and unwonted pestilence"[2], and in 1352
the house of St Mary's Winchester made special mention, in petitioning for the appropriation of a church, of the reduction of its
rents and of the cattle plague[3]. The other great plagues of the
century aggravated the distress. St Mary's Winchester and
Shaftesbury mentioned the pestilence (of 1361) in petitions to
the King three years later[4]. Four of the sixteen nuns of Carrow
died in the year of the third pestilence (1369)[5], and in 1378, three
years after the fourth pestilence, the licence allowing Sewardsley
to appropriate the church of Easton Neston, recites that the value
of its lands had been so diminished by the pestilence that they
no longer sufficed to maintain the statutory numbers[6]. In 1381
(mentioned as a plague and famine year in some of the chronicles)
a bull of Urban IV, appropriating a church to Flamstead, after
recapitulating the slender endowments of the house, repeats the
complaint that

the servants of the said priory are for the most part dead, and its
houses and tenants and beasts are so destroyed that its lands and
possessions remain as it were sterile, waste and uncultivated, wherefore, unless the said Prioress and Convent be by some remedy succoured, they will be obliged to beg for the necessities of life from door
to door[7].

In 1395, four years after the "Fifth" pestilence and itself
a year of bad plague and famine, the nuns of Legbourne complained that their lands and tenements were uncultivated,
"on account of the dearth of cultivators and rarity of men,
arising out of unwonted pestilences and epidemics"[8]. The outbreak of 1405-7 was followed by a petition from Easebourne

---

1 *V C H Suffolk*, II, p 116   2 Liveing, *op cit* p. 146
3 *Cal of Papal Petitions*, I, p 230   4 *Cal. Pat Rolls*, 1364, pp. 21, 485.
5 Rye, *Carrow Abbey*, p. 37.   6 *V C.H. Northants*. II, p 126
7 Dugdale, *Mon.* IV, p. 301. Their petition had been presented in 1380.
V C H Herts. IV, p 433
8 *Cal. o Papal Letters*, IV, p 521

for licence to appropriate two churches, on the ground of
"epidemics, death of men and of servants," and because

the lands and tenements of the Prioress and Convent notoriously
suffer so great ruin that few tenants can be found willing to occupy
the lands in these days, and the said lands, ever falling into a worse
state, are so poor that they cannot supply the religious women with
sufficient support for themselves or for the repair of their ruinous
buildings[1]

The worst of these natural disasters was not the actual
damage done by each outbreak, but the fact that famine, murrain and pestilence followed upon pestilence, murrain and famine
with such rapidity, that the poorer houses had no chance of
recovery from the initial blow dealt them by the Black Death.
The nuns of Thetford, for instance, were excused from the
taxation of religious houses under Henry VI, on the ground that
their revenues in Norfolk and in Suffolk were much decreased
by the recent mortality and had so continued since 1349[2]. Even
the well-endowed houses found recovery difficult, and the history
of the great abbey of Shaftesbury illustrates the situation very
clearly. In 1365, shortly after the *pestis secunda*, the nuns received a grant of the custody of their temporalities on the next
voidance, and losses by pestilence were mentioned as one reason
for the decline in their fortunes. In 1380 their lands were flooded
and they suffered heavy losses in sheep and cattle. In 1382 (the
year of the fifth plague) they were obliged to petition once again
for help, representing that although their house was well-endowed,

toutes voies voz dites oratrices sont einsi arreriz a jour de huy, quoy
par les pestilences en queles lours tenantz sont trez toutz a poy
mortz, et par murryne de lour bestaille a grant nombre et value,
*nemye tant seulement a une place et a une foitz, einz a diverses foitz en
toutes leurs places,* quoy par autres grandes charges quelles lour convient a fine force de jour en autre porter et sustenir, q'eles ne purront,
sinoun qe a moelt grant peine, sanz lour endangerer al diverses bones
gentz lours Creditours, mesner l'an a bon fyn[3]

Again towards the middle of the fifteenth century Bishop
Ayscough sanctioned the appropriation of a church to the abbey,
which had pleaded its great impoverishment through pestilence,
failure of crops, want of labourers, and through the excessive

---

[1] *Bishop Rede's Reg* p 137.   [2] *V C H Norfolk*, II, p 335
[3] *Rot Parl* III, p 129 and Dugdale, *Mon* II, p. 485.

demands of such labourers as could be obtained[1]. If Shaftesbury found recovery so difficult, it may easily be imagined what was the effect of the natural disasters of the fourteenth century upon smaller and less wealthy houses.

The revenues of the nunneries, often scant to begin with and liable to constant diminution from the ravages of nature, were still more heavily burdened by a variety of exactions on the part of the authorities of Church and State. The procurations payable to the Bishop on his visitation fell heavily upon the smaller houses; hence such a notice as that which occurs in Bishop Nykke's Register under the year 1520: "Item the reverend father with his colleagues came down to the house of nuns that afternoon, and having seen the priory he dissolved his visitation there, on account of the poverty of the house"[2]. St Mary Magdalen's, Bristol, was on account of its poverty exempt from the payment of such procurations[3] and the Bishops doubtless often exercised their charity upon such occasions[4]. Papal exactions were even more oppressive; John of Pontoise, Bishop of Winchester, pleaded with the papal nuncio in 1285 that he would forbear to exact procurations from the poor nuns of Wintney, whom the Bishop himself excused from all charges in view of their deep poverty[5]; and in 1300 Bishop Swinfield of Hereford made a similar appeal to the commissary of the nuncio, and secured the remission of procurations due from the nuns of Lingbrook and the relaxation of the sentence of excommunication, which they had incurred through non-payment[6].

[1] V C H Dorset, II, p 77
[2] Visit of Diocese of Norwich (Camden Soc.), p. 155
[3] V C H Glouc. II, p. 93
[4] On other occasions, however, they were careful to take all their due Vide the great Bishop Grandisson's letter to the abbess and convent of Canonsleigh, announcing his forthcoming visitation and "mandantes quod in illum eventum de procuracione ea occasione nobis debita providere curetis in pecunia numerata" Reg of Bishop Grandisson, ed Hingeston-Randolph, pt II, p 767 At Davington in 1511 the Prioress deposed that "the house has to pay 20s to the Archbishop for board at the time of his visitation." E H R VI, p 28
[5] Reg. Johannis de Pontissara (Cant. and York Soc.), I, p 299
[6] Reg Rich de Swinfield (Cantilupe Soc), p 366 Other cases of excommunication are sometimes to be found in Bishops' Registers, e g in 1335 the Prioresses of Cokehill and Brewood were excommunicated for failure to pay the tenth, one owed 9½d. and the other 1s. 8½d —paltry sums for which to damn a poor nun's soul! Reg Thomas de Charlton (Cantilupe Soc), p 57.

The obligation to pay tithes also fell heavily upon the poorer houses, it was for this reason that Archbishop John le Romeyn appealed to the Prior of Newburgh in 1286 not to exact tithes from the food of animals in Nether Sutton, belonging to the poor nuns of Arden[1]; and in 1301 the Prior of Worcester desired his commissary to spare the poverty of the nuns of Westwood and not to exact tithes or any other things due to him from them or from their churches[2]. Added to ecclesiastical exactions were the taxes due to the Crown. In 1344 the nuns of Davington addressed a petition to Edward III, representing that, owing to their great poverty, they were unable to satisfy the King's public aids without depriving themselves of their necessary subsistence, a plea which was found to be true[3]. The frequency with which such petitions for exemption from the payment of taxes were made and granted, is in itself a proof that the burden of taxation was a real one, for the Crown would not have excused its dues, unless the need for such an act of charity had been great[4]; and it is obvious that the sheer impossibility of collecting the money from a poverty-stricken house must often have left little alternative. The houses that did contribute were not slow to complain. "The unwonted exactions and tallages with which their house and the whole of the English Church has been burdened" were pleaded by the nuns of Heynings as in part responsible for their poverty in 1401[5], similarly "the necessary and very costly exac-

---

[1] *Reg John le Romeyn* (Surtees Soc), I, p 159
[2] *Reg Sede Vacante* (Worc Hist. Soc), p 62 Cf remission of tithes by Bishop Dalderby to Greenfield, because of its poverty *V C H Lincs* II, p. 155 Some Cistercian houses held papal bulls exempting them from the payment of tithes, e g Sinningthwaite and Swine. Dugdale, *Mon* V, pp 463, 494
[3] Dugdale, *Mon* IV, p 288
[4] For a few out of many instances of remission of payment on account of poverty see Ivinghoe, Little Marlow, Burnham (*V C H Bucks* I, pp. 353, 358, 382); Cheshunt (*V.C H. Herts* IV, pp 426-7); Stixwould, Heynings, Greenfield, Fosse, St Leonard's Grimsby (*V C H. Lincs* II, pp 122, 147, 149, 155, 157, 179), Catesby (*V C H Northants* II, p 122), Ickleton, Swaffham, Chatteris, St Radegund's Cambridge (Dugdale, *Mon.* IV, p. 439); Malling (*Ib* III, p. 382), St Mary Magdalen's Bristol (*V C H Glouc* II, p 93); Minchin Barrow (Hugo, *op cit* p 108), Blackborough (*V C H Norfolk*, II, p 351), Arden (*V C H Yorks* III, p 113); Nunkeeling and Nunappleton (*Reg John le Romeyn*, I, pp 140, 234), Wintney (*V C H Hants* II, p 150)
[5] *Cal. of Papal Letters*, V, p 347 Compare the case of the hospital of St James of Canterbury which "grievoussement ad estez chargez pur diverse contribucions faitz au Roy entre les laiz, ou les biens. .ne sufficent mye ala sustinaunce de la Priouresse et les seoures." *Hist MSS Comm Report*, IX, p 87

tions of tenths and other taxes and unsupportable burdens"
occurs in a complaint by Romsey in 1351; and the Abbess and
Convent of St Mary's, Winchester, stated in 1468, that they
were so burdened with the repair of their buildings and with
the payment of imposts, that they could not fulfil the obligations of their order as to hospitality[1].

Nor was taxation for public purposes the only demand made
upon the religious houses Abbeys holding of the King in chief
had to perform many services appertaining to tenants in chief,
which seem oddly incongruous in the case of nunneries The Abbesses of Shaftesbury, St Mary's Winchester, Wilton and Barking,
were baronesses in their own right, the privilege of being summoned to parliament was omitted on account of their sex; but
the duty of sending a quota of knights and soldiers to serve the
King in his wars was regularly exacted[2]. In 1257 Agnes Ferrar,
Abbess of Shaftesbury, was summoned to Chester to attend
the expedition against Llewelyn ap Griffith, and her successor,
Juliana Bauceyn, was also summoned in 1277 to attack that
intrepid prince[3]. The Abbess of Romsey had to find a certain
number of men-at-arms with their armour for the custody of
the maritime land in the county of Southampton; she resisted
when an attempt was made to exact an archer as well and
successfully showed the King "that she has only two marks'
rent in Pudele Bardolveston in that county"[4]. Less lawful exactions were even more burdensome, and the nunneries suffered
with the rest of the nation under the demand for loans and the
burden of purveyance[5]. In December 1307 the Abbess of Barking,
in common with the heads of ten other religious houses, was
requested to lend the King

two carts and horses to be at Westminster early on the day of
St Stephen to carry vessels and equipments of the King's household
to Dover, the King having sent a great part of his carts and sumpter
horses to sea, so that he may find them ready when he arrives[6];

[1] *Cal of Pat Rolls*, 1467–77, pp. 138, 587.
[2] Dugdale, *Mon* II, p 472   Cf p 328
[3] *Ib.* p 473. Cf. *Parl Writs* (Rec Comm), II, div 3, 1424.
[4] *Cal of Close Rolls*, 1339–41, pp. 215, 217.
[5] On this subject see Rose Graham, *St Gilbert of Sempringham and the Gilbertines*, pp 90–2
[6] *Cal. of Close Rolls*, 1307–13, p 50. Compare the entry in the treasuresses' account of St Michael's, Stamford, for 1392–3. "Item done en curtasy
a le Balyf de Roy quant nostre carre fuist areste al seruice del roy viijd"
P R O Ministers' Accounts, 1260/10.

it is true that he engaged to pay out of his wardrobe the costs of the men leading the carts and of the horses going and returning, but meanwhile the Abbey lost their services, and carts and horses were very necessary on a manor; moreover it was common complaint that the tallies given by the King's servants for what they took were sometimes of no more value than the wood whereof they were made:

> I had catell, now have I none,
> They take my beasts and done them slon,
> And payen but a stick of tree

Similarly in June 1310 the King sent out a number of letters to the heads of religious houses, requesting the "loan" of various amounts of victuals for his Scottish expedition, and among the houses upon whom this call was made were the nunneries of Catesby, Elstow, St Mary's Winchester, Romsey, Wherwell, Barking, Nuneaton, Shaftesbury and Wilton[1].

The nunneries also suffered considerable pecuniary loss by the right possessed in certain cases by the patron of a house, to take the profits of its temporalities during voidance through the death or resignation of its superior, sometimes enjoying them himself and sometimes granting the custody of the house to someone else[2]. It is obvious that serious loss might be entailed upon the community, if the patron refrained for some time from granting his *congé d'élire*. It was for this reason that the Convent of Whiston wrote in 1308 to the Bishop-elect of Worcester, their patron, praying that "considering the smallness of the possessions of the nuns of Whiston, in his patronage, which compelled the nuns formerly to beg, and for the honour of religion and the frailness of the female sex" he would grant them licence to elect a new prioress and would confirm the same election; and the Prior of Worcester also addressed a letter to the commissary-general on their behalf[3]. The King exercised with great regularity his rights of patronage, and the direct pecuniary loss, sustained by a house in being deprived of the profits of its temporalities, seems to have been the least of the evils which

---

[1] *Cal of Close Rolls*, 1307–13, pp 262–6, *passim*

[2] For instance in 1275 the King granted the custody of Barking Abbey, void and in his hands, to his mother, Queen Eleanor *Cal. of Close Rolls*, 1272–9, p 210

[3] *Reg Sede Vacante* (Worc Rec Soc), pp 112–3 Compare the petition of St Mary's Chester to Queen Eleanor, p. 172 above

resulted, if the state of affairs described in the petition addressed
to the crown by the Abbess and Convent of Shaftesbury in 1382
was at all common. After a moving description of the straits
to which they were reduced[1], they begged that the King would,
on future occasions of voidance, allow the community to retain
the administration of the Abbey and of its temporalities, rendering
the value thereof to the King while the voidance lasted, so that
no escheator, sheriff or other officer should have power to meddle
with them:

understanding, most redoubtable lord, that by means of your grace in
this matter great relief and amendment, please God, shall come to your
same house, and no damage can ensue to you or to your heirs, nor to
any other, save only to your officers, who in such times of voidance
are wont to make great destructions and wastes and to take therefrom
great and divers profits to their own use, whence nothing cometh to
your use, as long as the said voidance endures, if only for a short time[2]

St Mary's, Winchester, also pleaded the royal administration of
its temporalities as one reason for its impoverishment, when
petitioning the Pope for leave to appropriate the church of
Froyle in 1343 and 1346[3].

Sometimes the abbeys found it cheaper to compound with
the King for a certain sum of money and thus to purchase the
right of administering their own temporalities, saving to the
King, as a rule, knights' fees, advowsons, escheats and sometimes wards and marriages. Romsey Abbey secured this privilege, after the escheator had already entered, in 1315, for a fine
of forty marks; but in 1333, when there was another voidance,
the convent had to agree to pay £40 for the first two months
and *pro rata* for such time as the voidance continued, saving to
the King knights' fees, advowsons and escheats[4] In 1340 the
royal escheator was ordered to let the Prioress and Convent of

---

[1] See above, p 182

[2] Dugdale, *Mon* II, p 485 and *Rot Parl.* III, p. 129 The petition was
granted, but the nuns seem to have shown themselves unworthy of the
royal clemency, for, after the death of Abbess Joan Furmage in 1394, the
King was forced to abrogate the grant, because by fraudulent means an
election had been obtained of an unfit person, who, with the object of
securing confirmation, had repaired with an excessive number of men to
places remote, to the waste and desolation of the convent *Cal of Pat. Rolls,*
1391–6, p 511.

[3] *Cal. of Papal Petitions,* I, pp 56–7

[4] *Cal. of Close Rolls* (1313–8), p 189 and *ib* (1333–7), pp. 70–1; cf.
ib. (1307–13), p 1 and *ib.* (1323–7), p 252 and *ib* (1349–54), p 29

Wherwell have the custody of their temporalities, in accordance
with a grant made some years previously, by which the house
was to render £230 for a year and *pro rata*[1]. In 1344 a similar
order was made in the case of Wilton, whose late Abbess (prudent
woman) had seized the opportunity to purchase the right for
£60 from the King, when he lay at Orwell before crossing the
sea[2]. Similarly, the next year, Shaftesbury received the custody
of its temporalities in consideration of a fine of £100, made with
the King by its Abbess, in the second year of his reign[3]. With
four great abbeys falling vacant in little over ten years, the
royal exchequer reaped a good harvest; and though the payment
of a lump sum was better than falling into the hands of the
escheator, and though the nuns would make haste to elect a new
abbess as soon as possible, a voidance was always a costly matter.

But perhaps the most serious tax upon the resources of the
nunneries was the right, possessed by some dignitaries (notably
the King and the Bishop of the diocese), to nominate to houses
in their patronage persons whom the nuns were obliged to receive
as members of their community or to support as corrodians,
pensioners or boarders. The right of nominating a nun might
be exercised upon a variety of occasions The Archbishop might
do so to certain houses in his province on the occasion of his consecration, and this right was energetically enforced by Peckham,
who nominated girls to Wherwell, Castle Hedingham, Burnham,
Stratford, Easebourne and Catesby[4] A Bishop possessed, in
some cases, a similar right on the occasion of his consecration
Rigaud d'Assier, Bishop of Winchester, sent nuns to Romsey,
St Mary's Winchester and Wherwell[5]; Ralph of Shrewsbury,
Bishop of Bath and Wells, nominated to Minchin Barrow and to
Cannington[6], Stephen Gravesend, Bishop of London, sent a girl

---

[1] *Cal of Close Rolls* (1339–41), p 377.

[2] *Ib* (1343–6), pp 407–8 Cf p. 418

[3] *Ib* (1343–6), p 599. The profits during vacancy were similarly remitted to Godstow in 1385 "because of its poverty and misfortunes"
(*V C H. Oxon.* II, p 73)

[4] *Reg Epist. Johannis Peckham* (Rolls Ser), I, pp 40–1, 56–7, 189–90,
356–7, 366–7, 577.

[5] *Reg of . Rigaud de Asserio* (Hants. Rec. Soc.), pp. 387, 388, 394–5
Compare nominations of John de Pontoise *Reg. Johannis de Pontissara*
(Cant and York. Soc), I, pp 240, 241, 252 and of William of Wykeham,
Wykeham's Reg (Hants Rec Soc), II, pp 60, 61

[6] *Reg of Ralph of Shrewsbury* (Somerset Rec Soc), pp. 26, 39, 146.

to Barking[1]; and the successive bishops of Salisbury exercised the prerogative of placing an inmate in Shaftesbury Abbey and of appointing one of the nuns to act as her instructor[2]. The existence of this right seems to have varied with different dioceses and its exaction with different bishops, if it is possible to judge from the absence of commendatory letters in some registers and their presence in others. The Bishop of a diocese also sometimes had the right of presenting a nun to a house when a new superior was created there. This was the case at Romsey, where nuns were thus nominated in 1307, 1333 and 1397[3], and at Romsey also there occurs one instance (the only one of the kind which search has yet yielded) of the nomination of a nun by the bishop, because of "a profession of ladies of that house which he had lately made" Bishop Stratford thus appointed Jonette de Stretford (perhaps a poor relative) "en regard de charite" in 1333, a month after having appointed Alice de Hampton by reason of the Abbess' creation[4].

The King possessed in houses under his patronage rights of nomination corresponding to those of the Bishop. That of presenting a nun on the occasion of his coronation was frequently exercised. Edward II sent ladies to Barking, Wherwell and St Mary's Winchester[5]; Barking received nuns from Richard II, Henry IV and Henry VI[6] and Shaftesbury from Richard II, Henry V and Henry VI[7]. He also possessed the right in certain abbeys of presenting a nun on the occasion of a voidance and there are many such letters of presentation enrolled upon the Close rolls; for instance Joan de la Roche was sent to Wilton in 1322[8], Katherine de Arderne to Romsey in 1333[9] and Agnes Turberville to Shaftesbury in 1345[10].

Sometimes similar rights to these were exercised by private persons, who held the patronage of a house or with whom it was connected by special ties; the family of le Rous of Imber, for

---

[1] Reg ..Stephani de Gravesend (Cant and York Soc), p 200.
[2] Dugdale, Mon II, p 473 and V.C H. Dorset, II, p. 75.
[3] Liveing, op cit pp 97–8 and Wykeham's Reg II, pp 461–2.
[4] Liveing, op. cit p 98
[5] Cal. of Close Rolls (1307–8), pp 48, 53, 134
[6] V C H Essex, II, p 117.   [7] V.C H Dorset, II, pp 76–7.
[8] Cal. of Close Rolls (1318–23), p 517 She was still unadmitted in 1327, when the order was repeated. Ib (1327–30), p 204.
[9] Ib. (1333–7), p 175.   [10] Ib (1343–6), p. 604.

example, had the right (resigned in 1313) of presenting two nuns, with a valet, to Romsey Abbey[1]. But the royal rights were always the most burdensome and, though such privileges as those described above, and the even more burdensome right to demand corrodies and pensions, normally affected only great abbeys such as Barking, Romsey, St Mary's Winchester, and Shaftesbury, the smaller houses (not under royal patronage) were not always exempt from sudden demands—witness the case of Polsloe below—and a wide range of nunneries was affected by archiepiscopal and episcopal rights. Moreover even the great houses, in spite of their large endowments, were crippled by the system, as may be gathered from their constant complaints of poverty and of overcrowding. The obligation to receive fresh inmates by nomination was especially burdensome when it was incurred on more than one occasion by the same house and coincided with other exactions. The case of Shaftesbury is noticeable in this connection, the King claimed the right to administer its temporalities during voidance, to nominate a nun on his own coronation and on the election of an Abbess, to demand a pension for one of the royal clerks on the latter occasion, and to send boarders or corrodians for maintenance; and the Bishop of Salisbury could nominate a nun on his own promotion to the see and could demand a benefice for one of his clerks on the election of an Abbess It is, of course, possible that all these prerogatives were not invariably exercised and that a new inmate was not sent to Shaftesbury every time a King was crowned, a Bishop consecrated or an Abbess elected; but it was exercised sufficiently often to be a strain upon the house

Even when the right of nomination was confined to one occasion, it seems to have been generally resented and frequently resisted. The reason for resistance lay in the fact that the house was forced to support another inmate without the hope of receiving the donation of land or rents, which medieval fathers gave to the convents in which their daughters took the veil, and as the dowry system became more and more common, the

---

[1] Liveing, *op cit* p 99, and in the Register of Bishop Norbury of Lichfield there is a certificate (dated 1358) of "having admitted, twenty years ago, *thirty* nuns at Nuneaton at the request of the patron, the E of Lancaster," Will Salt Arch Soc. Coll I, p 286 Perhaps there is a clerical error.

hardship of having to receive a nun for nothing would soon appear intolerable. In some cases a sturdy resistance against this "dumping" of nuns finds an echo in the bishops' Registers. Four houses out of the six to which Peckham nominated new inmates attempted a refusal, and the excuses which they offered are interesting. Two years after his consecration the nuns of Burnham were still refusing to receive his protégée, Matilda de Weston; they had begun by trying to question his right to nominate and he seems to have taken legal action against them, after which they pleaded poverty (resulting from an unsuccessful lawsuit) and also an obligation to receive no novice without the consent of Edmund Earl of Cornwall, son of their founder. The Archbishop directed a stern letter to them, rejecting both their excuses and announcing his intention of pursuing his right, but the end of the matter is not known[1]. An equally determined resistance was offered by the Prioress of Stratford, who had been ordered to receive Isabel Bret. In 1282 Peckham wrote to her for the third time, declaring that her excuses were frivolous, she had apparently objected that the girl was too young and that her house was too heavily burdened with nuns, lay sisters and debts for another inmate to be received, but the Archbishop declared the youth of the candidate to be rather a merit than a defect and pointed out that, so far from being a burden to their house, she would bring it honour, for by receiving her they would multiply distinguished friends and benefactors and would be able to rely on his own special protection in their affairs[2]. A further letter to the Bishop of London is interesting, because it mentions a third objection made by the recalcitrant nunnery.

"We have received your letter," writes Peckham, "in favour of the Prioress and Convent of Stratford, urgently begging us to moderate our purpose concerning a certain burden which is alleged to be threatening them from us, on account of the insupportable weight and the poverty of the house and the deformity of the person, whom we have presented to them for admission Concerning which we would have you know that already in the lifetime of your predecessor of good memory, we had ordered them to receive that same person and for two years we continued to believe that they would yield to our

---

[1] *Reg. Epist. Johannis Peckham* (Rolls Ser.), i, pp. 189–90.
[2] *Ib* i, pp. 356–7. The reference to "distinguished friends and benefactors" is interesting, because she was the daughter of Robert Bret, "*civis London*"

wishes in the matter, yet without burden to themselves, by the provision of the parents of the said little maid, especially seeing that
never yet have we been burdensome to any monastery making a
truthful plea of indigence. We believe that what they allege about
deformity would be an argument in favour of our proposal; would
that not only these women of Stratford, concerning whom so many
scandals abound, but also all who so immodestly expose themselves
to human conversation and company, were or at least appeared
notable for such deformity that they should tempt no one to crime!
We have moreover heard that the greater part of the convent would
willingly consent to the reception of the girl, were they not hindered
by the malice of the prioress; nevertheless, lest we should seem deaf
to your entreaties, we suspend the whole business until we come to
London, to ascertain how our purpose may be carried out without
notable damage to them[1]."

The Archbishop had his way however; for eleven years later the
will of Robert le Bret was enrolled in the Court of Husting and
contained a legacy of rents on Cornhill "to Isabella his daughter,
a nun of Stratford"[2]. Peckham also wrote in a tone of strained
patience to the nuns of Castle Hedingham, who had refused to
receive Agnes de Beauchamp, warning them that besides incurring severe punishment at his own hands, further obstinacy
would offend the Queen of England, at whose instance he had
undertaken the promotion of the said Agnes[3]. The Prioress of
Catesby was equally troublesome and as late as 1284 the Archbishop wrote reprimanding her for her inconstancy and feigned
excuses, because, after promising to receive the daughter of Sir
Robert de Caynes and after repeated requests on his part that
they should admit the girl, she and her nuns had written asking
to be allowed to admit another person in her stead[4]

Real poverty often nerved the nuns to such bold resistance.
In the Register of Bishop Grandisson of Exeter there is a letter
from Polsloe Priory, written in 1329 and addressed to Queen
Philippa, on the subject of a certain Johanete de Tourbevyle[5],

[1] *Op. cit.* I, pp 366–7. The assertion that the convent was required to
receive Isabel "without burden to themselves by the provision of the parents
of the said little maid" is interesting, partly because it suggests that the
royal and episcopal nominees were not always received at a loss, partly
because it looks suspiciously like a condonation of the dowry system by an
otherwise strict disciplinarian

[2] Sharpe, *Cal of Wills*, I, p. 111.

[3] *Op. cit* I, pp 56–7.   [4] *Ib.* II, p 704

[5] An Agnes Turberville was sent by the King to Shaftesbury in 1345
Cal of Close Rolls, 1343–6, p 604

whom she had requested the nuns to receive as a lay sister. Written in the French of their daily speech, with no attempt at formal phraseology, their naïve plea still rings with the agitation of the "poor and humble maids," torn between anxiety not to burden their impecunious house, and fear of offending the new-made Queen of England:

To their very honourable and very powerful and redoubtable lady, my lady Dame Philippa, by the grace of God queen of England, etc , her poor and humble maids, the nuns of Polsloe, in all that they may of reverence and honour, beseeching your sweet pity to have mercy on our great poverty. Our very noble dame, we have received your letters, by the which we understand that it is your will that we receive Johanete de Tourbevyle among us as sister of the house, to take the dress of a nun in secular habit Concerning the which matter, most debonair lady, take pity upon us, if it please you, for the love of God and of His mother. For certainly never did any queen demand such a thing before from our little house; though mayhap they be accustomed to do so from other houses, founded by the kings and holding of them in chief, but this do not we, wherefore it falls heavily upon us. And if it please your debonair highness to know our simple estate, we are so poor (God knows it and all the country) that what we have suffices not to our small sustenance, who must by day and night do the service of God, were it not for the aid of friends; nor can we be charged with seculars without reducing the number of us religious women, to the diminution of God's service and the perpetual prejudice of our poor house. And we have firm hope in God and in your great bounty that you will not take it ill that this thing be not done to the peril of our souls, for to entertain and to begin such a new charge in such a small place, a charge which would endure and would be demanded for ever afterwards, would be too great a danger to your soul, my Lady, in the sight of God, wherefrom God by His grace defend you ! Our most blessed Lady, may God give you a long and happy life, to His pleasure and to the aid and solace of ourselves and of other poor servants of God on earth; and we should have great joy to do your behests, if God had given us the power[1].

The nuns evidently asked the support of the Bishop (which accounts for the presence of their letter in his Register) for about the same time Grandisson also wrote an informal letter in French to the King, begging him to give up his design to place his cousin Johanete de Tourbevyle at Polsloe, on the ground that the nuns held all that they possessed in frank almoign and were so poor that it would be unpardonable to

---

[1] *Reg of Bishop Grandisson*, ed Hingeston-Randolph, I, pp 213–4

entail upon them a charge, which would become a precedent for ever:

"Wherefore, dear Sire," he continued, "If it please you, hold us excused of this thing and put this thought from you And for love of you, to whom we are much beholden aforetime, and to show you that we make no feigned pretence, ordain, if it please you, elsewhere for her estate, and we will very willingly give somewhat reasonable out of our own goods towards it; for this we may safely do[1] "

It is not impossible that the disinclination of the nunneries to receive royal and episcopal nominees was in part due to dislike of taking an entirely unknown person into the close life of the community, in which so much depended upon the character and disposition of the individual. The right seems nearly always to have been exercised in favour of well-born girls, but though the bishops endeavoured to send only suitable novices, their knowledge of the character of their protégées would sometimes appear to have rested upon hearsay rather than upon personal acquaintance—"*ut credimus*," "*come nous sumez enformez* " On at least one occasion the nuns who resisted a bishop's nominee were to our knowledge justified by later events. In 1329 Ralph of Shrewsbury, the new Bishop of Bath and Wells, wrote to the Prioress and Convent of Cannington, desiring them to receive Alice, daughter of John de Northlode, to whom he had granted the right, "par resoun de nostre premiere creacion," on the request of Sir John Mautravers; four years later he was obliged to repeat the order, because the convent "had not yet been willing to receive the said Alice." The end of the story is to be found in the visitation report of 1351[2]. It is impossible to say whether the convent corrupted Alice or Alice the convent; but it is unfortunate that the Bishop's nominee should have been implicated

The obligation to receive a nun on the nomination of the king or the bishop was not the only burden upon the finances of the nunneries. Abbeys in the patronage of the Crown were upon occasion obliged also to find maintenance for other persons, men as well as women, who never became members of their community The right to demand a pension for one of the royal

---

[1] *Op. cit.* I, pp 222–3 Does the Bishop mean that he will help to provide a dowry for Johánete out of his private purse, in another religious house?

[2] See below, p 452

clerks was sometimes exercised on the occasion of a voidance, and the money had in most cases to be paid until such time as the young man was provided with a suitable benefice by the Abbey. The Abbess of Romsey was ordered to give a pension to William de Dereham in 1315 by reason of her new election[1]; John de St Paul was sent to the same house in 1333[2], William de Tydeswell in 1349[3]. The right is also found in exercise at Wherwell[4], St Mary's, Winchester[5], Shaftesbury[6], Wilton[7], Delapré (Northampton)[8], Barking[9] and Elstow[10]. In certain cases the Bishop possessed a similar right on the occasion of his own consecration; for instance John of Pontoise, Bishop of Winchester, wrote to the Abbess of St Mary's, Winchester, in 1283, complaining

that whereas his predecessors had by a laudable custom presented their own clerks to the first benefice in the patronage of a religious house vacant after their establishment in the bishopric, they (the nuns) had recently presented a nominee of their own to a benefice then vacant.

Two years later the Abbess and Convent of Wherwell wrote to him, voluntarily offering him the next vacant benefice in their patronage for one of his clerks; and in 1293 he reminded the nuns of Romsey that they were bound by agreement to do likewise[11]. Similarly Simon of Ghent, Bishop of Salisbury, directed the Abbess of Shaftesbury to provide for Humphrey Wace in 1297[12]. The demand to pension a clerk, like the demand to receive a nun, was sometimes resisted by the convents. In the early part of his reign Edward II ordered the Sheriff of Bedford

to distrain the Abbess of Elstow by all her lands and chattels in his bailiwick and to answer to the King for the issues and to have her

---

[1] *Cal of Close Rolls* (1313–8), p 210 A few months later, however, Richard de Ayremnn was sent on the same pretext (p. 312)
[2] *Op. cit* (1333–7), p 175   [3] *Op. cit* (1349–54), p 82
[4] *Op cit* (1339–41), p 466   [5] *Op cit* (1337–9), p. 286.
[6] *Op cit* (1343–6), p 652
[7] *Op cit* (1318–23), p. 517; (1343–6), p. 475.
[8] *Op cit* (1327–30), p. 366.
[9] *Op. cit.* (1313–8), p 611; (1327–30), p 564; (1341–3), p. 133
[10] See below. For the prebendal stalls in the churches of five of these abbeys (Romsey, Wherwell, St Mary's Winchester, Shaftesbury and Wilton), see above, p 144
[11] *Reg. Johannis de Pontissara* (Cant. and York Soc), I, pp. 243–4, 300–1, 315–6
[12] *Reg. Simonis de Gandavo* (Cant. and York Soc), pp 2–3

body before the King at the octaves of Hilary next, to answer why, whereas she and her convent, by reason of the new creation of an Abbess, were bound to give a pension to a clerk, to be named by the King and he had transferred the option to his sister Elizabeth Countess of Hereford and had asked the Abbess to give it to her nominee they had neglected to do so[1].

The end of the story is contained in a petition printed in the *Rolls of Parliament*, wherein the Abbess and Convent of "Dunestowe" (Elstow) informed the King in 1320

que, come il les demaunde par son Brief devant Sire H le Scrop et ses compaignons une enpensione pur un de ses clercs par reson de la novele Creacion la dite Abbesse et tiel enpensione unqs devant ces temps ne fust demaunde ne donee de la dite meson, fors tant soulement que la dereyn predecessere dona a la requeste nostre Seigneur le Roy a la Dameysele la Countesse de Hereford, un enpension de c s Par qi eles prient que nostre Seigneur le Roy voet, si lui plest, comander de soursere de execucion faire de la dite demaunde, que la dite Abbay est foundee de Judit, jadis Countess de Huntingdon, et la dite enpension unques autrement done[2].

The reference to the Countess of Hereford's "dameysele" shows that the pension was not invariably given to a clerk, and it appears that the King tried to substitute corrodies, pensions and reception as a nun for each other according to the exigencies of the moment. In 1318 he sent Simon de Tyrelton to the Abbess and Convent of Barking,

they being bound to grant a pension to one of the King's clerks, by reason of the new creation of an abbess, and the King having requested them to grant in lieu of such pension the allowance of one of their nuns to Ellen, daughter of Alice de Leygrave, to be received by her for life, to which they replied that they could not do so, for certain reasons[3]

In 1313, in pursuance of his right to nominate a nun on the new creation of an abbess, he had sent Juliana de Leygrave "niece of the King's foster-mother, who suckled him in his youth," to St Mary's, Winchester, in order that she might be given a nun's corrody for life (the value of which was to be given her wherever she might be) and a suitable chamber within the nunnery for her residence, whenever she might wish to stay there[4]

---

[1] *Hist MSS Comm Report*, IV, p. 329.
[2] *Rot Parl* I, p 381 John de Houton, clerk, had been sent to Elstow in 1318 (*Cal of Close Rolls* (1318-23), p 119).
[3] *Cal of Close Rolls* (1313-8), p 611
[4] *Op cit.* (1307-13), pp 581-2.

The obligation to provide corrodies for royal nominees pressed more heavily than the duty of pensioning royal clerks. A corrody was originally a livery of food and drink given to monks and nuns, but the term was extended to denote a daily livery of food given to some person not of the community and frequently accompanied by suitable clothing and a room in which to live. Hence corrodians were often completely kept in board and lodging, having the right to everything that a nun of the house would have (a "nun's corrody") and sometimes allowed to keep a private servant, who had the right to the same provision as the regular domestics of the house (a "servant's corrody"). The King, indeed, looked upon the monastic houses of his realm as a sort of vast Chelsea Hospital, in which his broken-down servants, yeomen and officials and men-at-arms, might end their days. Thus he obtained their grateful prayers without putting his hand into his purse. There must have been hundreds of such old pensioners scattered up and down the country, and judging from the number of cases in which one man is sent to receive the maintenance lately given to another, deceased, some houses had at least one of them permanently on the premises. Many a hoary veteran found his way into the quiet precincts of a nunnery

> His helmet now shall make a hive for bees;
> And, lovers' sonnets turn'd to holy psalms,
> A man-at-arms must now serve on his knees,
> And feed on prayers, which are Age his alms

In the intervals between feeding on prayers he must have been vastly disturbing and enthralling to the minds of round-eyed novices, with his tales of court and camp, of life in London town or long campaigns in France, or of how John Copeland had the King of Scots prisoner and what profit he got thereby.

In the last three months of 1316 Edward II sent seventeen old servants to various religious houses, and among them Henry de Oldyngton of the avenary was sent to Barking, to receive such maintenance as William de Chygwell, deceased, had in that house[1]. In 1328 Roger atte Bedde, the King's yeoman, who served the King and his father, was sent to St Mary's, Winchester,

---

[1] *Cal of Close Rolls* (1313–8), p 437 The avenere was an officer of the household who had the charge of supplying provisions for the horses See *Promptorium Parvulorum* (Camden Soc), i, p 19, n 2.

instead of James le Porter, deceased[1]; and in 1329 the Abbess and Convent of Shaftesbury were requested to admit to their house Richard Knight, spigurnel of the King's chancery, who had long served the King and his father in that office, and to administer to him for his life such maintenance in all things as Robert le Poleter, deceased, had in their house[2]. The unlucky convent of Wilton apparently had to support two pensioners, for in 1328 Roger Liseway was sent there in place of Roger Danne and the next year John de Odiham, yeoman of the chamber of Queen Philippa, took the place of John de Asshe[3].

It was doubtless even more common for the widows of the King's dependents to be sent to nunneries, and he must often have received such a petition as was addressed by Agnes de Vylers to Edward III:

A nostre Seigneur le Roi et a son Conseil, prie vostre poure veve Agneys, qi fut la femme Fraunceys de Vylers, jaditz Bachiler vostre piere, qe vous pleise de vostre grace avoir regard du graunt service qe le dit Fraunceys ad fait a vostre dit piere et ed vostre ayel, en la Terre Seinte, Gascoigne, Gales, Escoce, Flaundres et en Engleterre, et graunter au dit Agneys une garisoun en l'Abbeye de Berkyng, c'est assaver une mesoun & la droite de une Noneyme pour la sustin-aunce de lui et de sa file a terme de lour vie, en allegaunce de l'alme vostre dit piere, qi promist al dit Fraunceys eide pour lui, sa femme et ses enfaunz.

"Il semble a conseil q'il est almoigne de lui mander la ou aillours, s'il plest a Roi," was the reply; so Agnes and her daughter might end their days in peace, and Barking be the poorer for their appetites[4]. At Barking the King had the right to claim a corrody at each new election of an abbess, as Agnes de Vylers doubtless knew, as early as 1253 its Abbess was exempted from being charged with *conversi* and others, because she had granted food and vesture for life to Philippa de Rading and her daughter[5]. Other nunneries in the royal patronage were under a similar obligation. In 1310 Juliana la Despenser was sent to Romsey, to be provided with fitting maintenance for herself and for her maid during her lifetime[6] and in 1319 Mary Ridel was sent to

---

[1] *Cal of Close Rolls* (1327-30), p 393.
[2] *Ib.* p 523   [3] *Ib* pp 396, 534
[4] *Rot Parl* ii, pp 381-2. Letters patent were duly sent to Barking bidding them admit Agnes, on Nov 6th, 1331 *Cal of Patent Rolls* (1330-3), p 407
[5] *V.C.H Essex*, ii, p 117   [6] *Cal of Close Rolls* (1307-13), p 267.

Stainfield to be maintained for life[1]. There were the usual attempts to escape from a costly and burdensome obligation, Romsey seems to have been successful in repelling Juliana la Despenser, for in the following month the King sent her to Shaftesbury, requesting the nuns to "find her for life the necessities of life according to the requirements of her estate, for herself and for the damsel serving her, and to assign her a chamber to dwell in, making letters patent of the grant"[2] Stainfield was less successful in the matter of Mary Ridel; the usual plea of poverty was considered insufficient and the convent was ordered to receive her, to supply her with food, clothing and other necessities and to make letters patent, specifying what was due to her[3].

Certain convents were in addition handicapped by the obligation to make certain grants or liveries, in kind or in money, to other monastic houses. The nunneries of St Clement's, York, and Moxby seem to have involved themselves—as a condition, perhaps, of some past benefaction—in a curious obligation to the friars of their districts. At a visitation of the former house in 1317, Archbishop Melton found that the Friars Minor of York, every alternate week of the year, and the Friars Preachers of York in the same manner, had for a long time been receiving fourteen conventual loaves; the nuns were ordered to show the friars the Archbishop's order and to cease from supplying the loaves as long as their own house was burdened with debt; and in no case was the grant to be made without special leave from the Archbishop[4]. The next year, on visiting Moxby, Melton was obliged to make an injunction as to the bread and ale called "levedemete," which the Friars Minor were accustomed to receive from the house, if it were owed to them it was to be given as due, if not it was not to be given without the will of the head[5] At Alnwick's first visitation in 1440 the Prioress of St Michael's, Stamford, declared that the house was burdened with the payment of an annual pension of 60s. to the monastery of St Mary's, York, "and that for tithes not worth more than forty pence annually; also it is in arrears for twenty years and

---

[1] *Op. cit.* (1318–23), p 117
[2] *Op. cit* (1307–13), p. 328. She was the niece of John de London, late the King's escheator south of Trent
[3] *Loc cit.*   [4] *V C.H Yorks.* III, p 129   [5] *Ib* p 237

more"[1]. The nuns also had to pay various small sums to Peter-borough Abbey, by which they had been founded and to which they always remained subordinated[2].

The support of resident corrodians and the payment of pensions and liveries were, however, less onerous than the duty of providing hospitality for visitors, which the nunneries per-formed as one of their religious obligations *Date* and *Dabitur* did not always accompany each other. The great folk who held the Pope's indult to enter the houses of Minoresses were probably generous donors; but the unenclosed orders had to lodge and feed less wealthy guests and often enough they found the obliga-tion a strain upon their finances. When the nuns of King's Mead, Derby, in 1326, petitioned the King to take the house into his special protection, they explained that great numbers of people came there to be entertained, but that owing to the reduction in their revenue they were unable to exercise their wonted hospitality[3]; and the number of guests was mentioned by the nuns of Heynings in 1401 as one reason for their im-poverishment[4]. At Nunappleton in 1315 the Archbishop of York had to forbid two sets of guests to be received at the same time, until the house should be relieved of debt, and at Moxby (which was also in debt) he ordained that relatives of the nuns were not to visit the house for a longer period than two days; Nunappleton was evidently a favourite resort, for in 1346 another archbishop speaks of guests flocking—*hospites confluentes*—to the priory and orders them to be admitted to a hostelry constructed for the

---

[1] *Alnwick's Visit.* MS f 83 The Taxation of Pope Nicholas mentions a pension due to the Abbot of York of £3 for the church of Corby, which was appropriated to the nuns, and for other tithes elsewhere The sum of £3 is occasionally mentioned in the account rolls of St Michael's, Stamford, as having been paid to "our Lady of York," or as being still due

[2] Dugdale, *Mon.* IV, pp 256 ff. Payments to the abbot and to other officiaries of Peterborough also occur very frequently in the conventual accounts

[3] See above, p 180 Compare the case of St Mary's, Winchester, where the nuns complained in 1468 that they were so burdened, that they could not fulfil the obligations of their order as to hospitality *V C H Hants* II, pp 123–4 The difficulty of keeping up the accustomed hospitality was one of the reasons for annexing Wothorpe to St Michael's, Stamford, after the Black Death Dugdale, *Mon* IV, p. 268

[4] *Cal of Papal Letters,* V, p. 347. Compare Gynewell's injunction in 1351: "E vous, Prioresse, chastiez les soers qils ne acuillent mie trop souent lour amys en la Priorie, a costage e damage de dit mesoun " *Linc Epis. Reg Memo Gynewell,* f 34d

purpose. At Marrick in 1252 it was ordered that guests were not to stay for more than one night, because the means of the house barely sufficed for the maintenance of the nuns, sisters and brethren[1].

Another charge which fell heavily upon the nunneries, sometimes not entirely by their own fault, was that of litigation. This was only an occasional expense, but when it occurred it was heavy, and a suit once begun might drag on for years Moreover the incidental expenses in journeys and bribes, which all had to be paid out of the current income of a house already (perhaps) charged with the payment of tithes and taxes and badly in need of repair, were often almost as heavy as the costs of the litigation. For instance an account of Christian Bassett, Prioress of St Mary de Pré (near St Albans), contains the following list of expenses incurred by her in the prosecution of a law suit in 1487, during the rule of her predecessor Alice Wafer:

Item when I ryde to London for the suyt that was taken ayenst dame Alice Wafer in the commen place, for myself and my preest and a woman and ij men, their hyre and hors hyre and mete and drynke, in the terme of Ester ye secunde yere of the regne of kyng Henry the vij[th] xx. s. Item paid aboute the same suyt at Mydsomer tyme, for iiij men, a woman and iiij horses xvi s. Item paid for the costs of a man to London at Mighelmas terme to Master Lathell, to have knowledge whethir I shuld have nede to come to London or not xij d[2]. Item for the same suyt of Dame Alice Wafer for herself and a suster wt her, ij men, ij horses, in costs at the same tyme xiij s. Item for the same suyt whan I cam from London to have councell of Master More and men of lawe for the same ple x s Item whan I went to Master Fforster to the Welde to speke wt him, to have councell for the wele of the place, for a kercher geven to hym, ij s Item on other tyme for a couple of capons geven to Master Fforster ij s Item for a man rydyng to London at Candilmas to speke wt Master Lathell and

---

[1] *V C H Yorks* III, pp 117, 171, 172, 239 On the subject of abuse of monastic hospitality, see Jusserand, *English Wayfaring Life*, p. 121 Edward I forbade anyone to eat or lodge in a religious house, unless the superior had invited him or that he were its founder, and even then his consumption was to be moderate

[2] Pope Boniface VIII's edict for the stricter enclosure of nuns contained a clause warning secular lords against summoning nuns to attend in person at the law courts, they were to act through their proctors (see version promulgated by Simon of Ghent, Bishop of Salisbury in 1299 *Reg. Simonis de Gandavo* [Cant. and York Soc.], p. 11). The heads of the larger houses often did act through proctors, but less wealthy convents usually sent the head or one of the other nuns in person See Eckenstein, *Woman under Monasticism*, pp 362–3

Master More and for iiij hennys geven to them and for the costs of
the same man and his hors uj s. iiij d. Item whan I went to London
to speke wt Master Lathell for to renewe our charter of the place
and other maters of our place xj s. Item in expenses made upon
Master Ffortescue atte dyvers tymes, whan I wente to hym to have
his councell for the same suyt in the common place xiij s. iiij d. Item
paid to a man to ryde to Hertford to speke wt. Norys, that he shuld
speke to Master Ffortescue for the same ple viij d. Item in costs for
a man to go to Barkhamsted to Thomas Cace viij d Item whan I
went to Master Ffortescue to his place, for mens hire and hors hire
for the same mater ij s Item whan I went to London at an other
tyme for the same plee, for iiij men and iiij hors hire xvj s [1]

After this one does not wonder that in 1517 the convent of
Goring pleaded that owing to lawsuits it was too poor to repair
its buildings[2].

The account rolls of the Priory of St Michael's, Stamford,
are full of references to expenses incurred in legal business. On
one occasion the nuns bought a "bill" in the Marshalsea "to
have a day of accord" and the roll for 1375-6 contains items
such as,

Paid for a purse to the wife of the Seneschal of the Marshalsea xx d
Paid for beer bought for the Marshalsea by the Prioress ij s ij d. Paid
for capons and chickens for the seneschal of the Marshalsea xxiij d. ob.[3]

Poor Dames Margaret Redynges and Joan Ffychmere "del office
del tresorie," ending the year £16. 8s 8½d in debt, must often
have sighed with Langland

> Lawe is so lordeliche. and loth to make ende,
> Withoute presentz or pens she pleseth wel fewe.

Nor was it only the expenses of great lawsuits which bore heavily
upon the nunneries, a great deal of lesser legal business had to
be transacted from year to year. The treasuresses' accounts of
St Michael's, Stamford, contain many notices of such business;
the expenses of Raulyn at the sessions, expenses of the clerks
at the Bishop's court or at the last session at Stamford, a suit

---

[1] Dugdale, *Mon* III, p 360.

[2] *V C H Oxon* II, p 104 Compare a long lawsuit waged by Carrow
Priory Rye, *Carrow Abbey*, App p xxi.

[3] *P R O Mins Accts* 1260/4 Compare the amusing account of how the
Prior of Barnwell secured a favourable judgment from the itinerant justices
"Ipsis eciam justiciariis dedit herbagium alicui tres acras et alicui quatuor,
et exennia panis, ceruisie et vini frequenter, in tantum quod in recessu suo
omnes tam justiciarii quam clerici, seruientes et precones, gracias uberes
referebant, et ipsi Priori (et) canonicis se et sua obligabant" *Liber Memo-
randorum Ecclesie de Bernewelle*, ed J. Willis Clark (1907), p 171

against a neighbouring parson over tithes, four shillings to Henry Oundyl for suing out writs; and innumerable entries concerning the inevitable "presentz or pens," a douceur to the Bishop's clerk, a courtesy to the king's escheator, a present to the clerks at the sessions, a gift "to divers men of law for their help on divers occasions " All nunneries had constantly to meet such petty expenses as these; and if we add an occasional suit on a larger scale the total amount of money devoured by the Law is considerable.

So far mention has been made only of such reasons for their poverty as cannot be considered the fault of the nuns. The inclemency of nature, the rapacity of lay and ecclesiastical authorities and the law's delays could not be escaped, however wisely a Prioress husbanded her resources. Nevertheless it cannot be doubted that the nuns themselves, by bad management, contributed largely to their own misfortunes. Bad administration, sometimes wilful, but far more often due to sheer incompetence, was constantly given as a reason for undue poverty. It was "negligence and bad administration" which nearly caused the dispersion of the nuns of Wintney during the famine year of 1316[1]; and those of Hampole in 1353[2] At Davington in 1511 one of the nuns deposed that "the rents and revenues of the house decrease owing to the guilt of the officers"[3]. The fault was often with the head of the house, who loved to keep in her own hands the disposal of the convent's income, omitted to consult the chapter in her negotiations, retained the common seal and did not render accounts. An illustration of the straits to which a house might be reduced by the bad management of its superior is provided by the history of Malling Abbey in the early part of the fourteenth century, as told by William de Dene in his *Historia Roffensis* In 1321 an abbess had been deposed, ostensibly on the complaint of her nuns and because the place had been ruined by her; but too much importance must not be assigned to the charge, for she was a sister of Bartholomew de Badlesmere, at that time a leader of the baronial party against

---

[1] *V.C.H Hants* II, p. 150.
[2] *V.C.H. Yorks* III, p. 164 The "misrule of past presidents" is mentioned as a contributory cause of distress at Lilleshall (1351), St Mary's Winchester (1364) and Tarrant (1366) *Cal. Pat Rolls*, 1351, p 177, 1364, p 485; 1366, p 239   [3] *E H R.* VI, p. 28.

Edward II, and it was by the King's command that Hamo of Hythe, Bishop of Rochester, visited Malling and deprived her[1]; her deposition was probably a political move. The same cannot however be said of Lora de Retlyng, who became abbess in 1324.

"The Bishop," says William de Dene, "although unwilling, knowing her to be insufficient and ignorant, set Lora de Retlyng in command as abbess, a woman who lacked all the capacity and wisdom of a leader and ruler, the nuns enthusiastically applauding; and the next day he blessed her, which benediction was rather a malediction for the convent. Then the Bishop forbade the Abbess to give a corrody to her maid-servant, as it had been the ill custom to do, and he sequestrated the common seal, forbidding it to be used, save when his licence had been asked and obtained[2]

Twenty-five years passed and in 1349 the chronicler writes

The Bishop of Rochester visited the abbeys of Lesnes and Malling, and he found them so ruined by longstanding mismanagement, that it is thought they never can recover so long as this world lasts, even to the day of judgment[3].

Malling had suffered severely from the Black Death in the previous year, but our knowledge of the character of Lora de Retlyng and the plain statement of William de Dene ("destructa per malam diutinam custodiam"), make it clear that bad management and not the pestilence was to blame for its poverty[4]

Financial mismanagement was, indeed, the most frequent of all charges brought against superiors at the episcopal visitations. When Alnwick visited his diocese of Lincoln several cases of such incompetence came to light At St Michael's, Stamford (1440), it was found that the Prioress had never rendered an account during the whole of her term of office, and one of the nuns declared that she did not rule and supervise temporal affairs to the benefit of the house; two years later the Bishop visited the convent again and the Prioress herself pleaded bodily weakness, adding

that since she was impotent to rule the temporalities, nor had they any industrious man to supervise these and to raise and receive the produce of the house, and since the rents of the house remained unpaid in the hands of the tenants, she begged that two nuns might be deputed to rule the temporalities, and to be responsible for receipts and payments.

---

[1] Wharton, *Anglia Sacra*, 1, p 362.   [2] *Ib* 1, p 364   [3] *Ib* 1, p 377
[4] Gasquet, however, mistakenly attributes its state entirely to the plague. *The Great Pestilence*, p 106.

In 1445, however, one of the appointed treasuresses, Alice de Wyteryng, admitted that she neither wrote down nor accounted for anything concerning her administration, and another nun complained that, if Wyteryng were to die, it would be impossible for any of them to say in what state their finances stood[1] At the poor and heavily indebted house of Legbourne (1440) the Prioress, unknown to the Bishop, but with the consent of the Convent, had sold a corrody to the bailiff of the house, Robert Warde, who was nevertheless not considered useful to the house in this post; the tenements and leasehold houses belonging to the house were ruinous and like to fall through the carelessness of the Prioress and bailiff, and one aggrieved nun stated that "the prioress is not circumspect in ruling the temporalities and cares not whether they prosper, but applies all the common goods of the house to her own uses, as though they were her own[2]." At Godstow also it was complained that the steward had an annual fee of ten marks from the house and was useless[3]. At Heynings (1440) the Prioress was charged with never rendering accounts and with cutting down timber unnecessarily, but she denied the last charge and said she had done so only for necessary reasons and with the express consent of the convent[4]. At Nuncoton corrodies had been sold and bondmen alienated without the knowledge of the nuns[5]. At Harrold it was found that no accounts were rendered, that a corrody had been sold for twenty marks, and that when the Prioress bought anything for the convent, no tallies or indentures were made between the contracting parties, so that after a time the sellers came and demanded double the price agreed upon; one nun also asked that the Bishop should prevent the selling or alienation of woods[6]. At Langley (which was miserably poor) there was a similar complaint of the sale of timber[7]. These are the less serious cases of financial mismanagement; the cases of Gracedieu, Ankerwyke and Catesby have already been considered. Sometimes the extravagance or incompetence of a Prioress became so notorious as to necessitate her suspension or removal, as at Basedale in 1307[8], Rosedale in 1310[9], Hampole in 1353[10], Easebourne in

[1] *Alnwick's Visit.* MS. ff. 39d, 83, 96　　　[2] *Linc Visit* II, p. 185.
[3] *Ib* II, p. 114　　　[4] *Ib.* II, p 133　　　[5] *Alnwick's Visit* MS. f 72.
[6] *Linc. Visit* II, pp 130, 131　　　[7] *Ib* II, p 175
[8] *V.C H. Yorks* III, p. 159　　　[9] *Ib* p. 174.　　　[10] *Ib* p 164.

1441[1] and St Mary de Pré at the end of the fifteenth century[2]. But more frequently the bishops endeavoured to hem in expenditure by elaborate safeguards, which will be described below.

Besides cases of incompetence and cases of misappropriation of revenues by an unscrupulous prioress, the mismanagement of the nuns may usually be traced to a desperate desire to obtain ready money. One means by which they sought to augment their income was by the sale of corrodies in return for a lump sum[3]. A man (or woman) would pay down a certain sum of money, and in return the convent would engage to keep him in board and lodging for the rest of his natural life, at Arden for instance, in 1524, Alice widow of William Berre paid twelve

[1] *Sussex Archaeol Coll* IX, p 7.

[2] Dugdale, *Mon* III, p 353

[3] It must be understood that the judicious sale of corrodies was not necessarily harmful to a house Sometimes it might lead to the acquisition of land or rents at comparatively little expense to the convent, as a glance at some of the charters in the English Register of Godstow Abbey will show See *Eng Reg of Godstow Abbey* (E E T S), pp xxvii–xxviii The convent probably drove a good bargain when in 1230 the harassed Stephen, son of Waryn the miller of Oxford, conveyed all his Oxford property to Godstow "and for this graunte, & cetera, the forsaid mynchons yaf to ther grete nede, that is to sey, to aquyte hym of the jewry and otherwise where he was endited, X markes of siluer in warison And furthermore they graunted to hym and to hys wyf molde, with ther seruant to serve them while they liued, two corrodies of ij mynchons and a corrodye of one seruant to their systeynynge" (*op. cit* p 392) Nor was there much harm in grants for a term of years, such as the grant of board and lodging made by the convent of Nunappleton in 1301 to Richard de Fauconberg, in return for certain lands bringing in an annual rent of two marks of silver, both the corrody and the tenure of these lands being for a term of twelve years Dugdale, *Mon* v, p 653 Sometimes, again, corrodies were granted in return for specified services, in 1270 Richard Grene of Cassington surrendered 5½ acres of arable and 2 roods of meadow land to Godstow in return for "the seruyce under the porter for ever at the yate of Godestowe and j half mark in the name of his wagis yerely." *Eng. Reg. of Godstow*, p 305 At Yedingham in 1352 an interesting grant of a *corrodium moniale* was made to one Emma Hart, who, in return for a sum of money, was given the position of deye or dairy woman, she was to have the same food-allowance as a nun and a share in all their small pittances, and a building called "le chesehouse" with a solar and cellar to inhabit and was allowed to keep ten sheep and ten ewes at the convent's charge In return she was to do the dairy-work and when too old to work any longer the convent engaged to grant her a place in "le sisterhouse" *V C H. Yorks* III, p. 128 Sometimes also corrodies were granted by way of pensioning off old servants, as when, in 1529, the nuns of Arden granted one to their chaplain "for the gud and diligent seruice yt oure wellbeloued sir Thomas parkynson, preste, hav done to vs in tyme paste " *V C H Yorks* III, p 115 To corrodies such as these there was little objection (though the last might lead to financial loss) The danger came from life-grants in return for an inadequate sum of ready money

pounds and was granted "mett and drynke as their convent hath" at their common table, or when sick in her own room, and "on honest chamber with sufficient fyer att all tyme, with sufficient apperell as shalbe nedful"[1]. Obviously, however, such an arrangement could only be profitable to the nuns, if the grantee died before the original sum had been expended in boarding her. The convent, in fact, acted as a kind of insurance agency and the whole arrangement was simply a gamble in the life of the corrodian The temptation to extricate themselves from present difficulties by means of such gambles, was one which the nuns could never resist They would lightly make their grant of board and lodging for life and take the badly needed money; but it would be swallowed up only too soon by their creditors and often vanish like fairy gold in a year. Not so the corrodian. Long-lived as Methusaleh and lusty of appetite, she appeared year after year at their common table, year after year consumed their food, wore their apparel, warmed herself with their firewood. Alice Berre was still hale and hearty after twelve years, when the commissioners came to Arden and would doubtless have lasted for several more to come, if his Majesty's quarrel with Rome had not swept her and her harassed hostesses alike out of their ancient home; but she must long before have eaten through her original twelve pounds[2] There is an amusing complaint in the Register of Crabhouse; early in the fourteenth century Aleyn Brid and his wife persuaded the nuns to buy their lands for a sum down and a corrody for their joint and separate lands. But the lands turned out barren and the corrodians went on living and doubtless chuckling over their bargain, and "si cher terre de cy petit value unkes ne fut achate," wrote the exasperated chronicler of the house[3]. Bishop Alnwick found two striking instances of a bad gamble during his visitations in 1440-1; at Langley the late Prioress had sold a corrody to a certain John Fraunceys and his wife for the paltry sum of twenty marks, and they had already held it for six years[4]; worse still, at Nuncoton there were two corrodians, each of whom had originally paid

---

[1] *V C.H. Yorks* III, p 115
[2] She received 68s 4d in part payment for the commutation of the corrody
[3] Jessopp, *Frivola*, pp 55-6.
[4] *Linc. Visit.* II, p 175

twenty marks, and they had been there for twelve and for twenty years respectively[1].

In the face of cases like these it is difficult not to suspect that unscrupulous persons took advantage of the temporary difficulties of the nuns and of their lack of business acumen. There is comedy, though not for the unhappy Convent, in the history of a corrody which, in 1526, was said to have been granted by Thetford to "a certain Foster." Six years later there was a great to-do at the visitation. The nuns declared that John Bixley of Thetford, "bocher," had sold his corrody in the house to Thomas Foster, gentleman, who was nourishing a large household on that pretext, to wit six persons, himself, his wife, three children and a maid, but Bixley said that he had never sold his corrody and there in public displayed his indenture. What happened we do not know; Thomas Foster, gentleman, must be the same man who had a corrody in 1526, and how John Bixley came into it is not clear. It looks as though the Convent (which was so poor that the Bishop had dissolved his visitation there some years previously) was trying by fair means or foul to get rid of Thomas Foster and his family; doubtless they had not bargained for a wife, three children and a maid when they rashly granted him one poor corrody[2]. It is easy to understand why medieval bishops, at nearly every visitation, forbade the granting of fees, corrodies or pensions for life or without episcopal consent; "forasmoche as the graunting of corrodyes and lyveryes hath bene chargious, bardynouse and greuouse unto your monastery" wrote Longland to Studley in 1531·

As itt apperithe by the graunte made to Agnes Mosse, Janet bynbrok, Elizabeth todde and other whiche has right soore hyndrede your place, In consideracon therof I charge you lady priores upon payne of contempte and of the lawe, that ye give noo moo like graunts, and that ye joutt away Elizabeth Todde her seruant.. and that

---

[1] *Alnwick's Visit* MS f 71d

[2] *Visit of the Diocese of Norwich* (Camden Soc), pp 243, 303-4 There is in the Record Office a petition to the Chancellor from Richard Englyssh and Marjorie his wife, setting out that the Bishop of Rochester had granted Marjorie for life a corrody in Malling Abbey of seven loaves and four gallons of convent ale and three pence for cooked food weekly, which corrody she and her husband had held for some time, but that now the abbess and convent withheld it Evidently it was a burden to the house, but it is not clear whether the bishop had forced a corrodian on the nuns, or had merely confirmed a grant by them *P R O Early Chanc Proc* 4/196.

Elizabeth Todde haue noo kowe going nor other bestes within eny of your grounds[1];

and Dean Kentwood, visiting St Helen's Bishopsgate in 1432 found that "diverce fees perpetuelle, corrodies and lyuers have been grauntyd befor this tyme to diverce officers of your house and other persones, which have hurt the house and be cause of delapidacyone of the godys of youre seyde house"[2] Even the nuns themselves sometimes realised that the sale of corrodies had brought them no good; they often complained at visitations that the Prioress had made such grants without consulting them; and the convent of Heynings gave "the multiplication of divers men who have acquired corrodies in their house," as one reason for their extreme poverty, when they petitioned for the appropriation of the church of Womersley[3].

The nuns were wont to have recourse to other equally im-provident expedients for obtaining money without regard to future embarrassment. They farmed their churches and alienated their lands and granges or let them out on long leases. These practices were constantly forbidden in episcopal injunctions[4]; at the visitation of Easebourne in 1524 the Prioress, Dame Margaret Sackfelde, being questioned as to what grants they had made under their convent seal, said that they had made four, to wit, one to William Salter to farm the rectory there, another of the proceeds of the chapel of Farnhurst, another of the proceeds of the chapel of Midhurst and another to William Toty for his corrody; this was corroborated by the subprioress, who also mentioned a grant of the proceeds of the church of Easebourne to a rather disreputable person called Ralph Pratt; and this is only a typical case[5]. The nunnery of Wix was reduced to such penury in 1283 on account of various alienations that Pope Martin IV granted the nuns a bull declaring all such grants void:

It has come to our ears that our beloved daughters in Christ, the Prioress and convent of the monastery of Wix (who are under the

---

[1] *Archaeologia*, XLVII, p. 58

[2] Dugdale, *Mon.* IV, p. 554 He had once before ordered the holders of corrodies there to display their grants, that it might be known whether they had fulfilled the services due from them *V.C.H. London*, I, p 459

[3] The appropriation was confirmed by the Pope in 1401 *Cal of Papal Letters*, V, p. 347 In 1440 Bishop Alnwick made an injunction at Heynings against the granting of corrodies. *Linc. Visit.* II, p. 135.

[4] See below, pp. 225–6. [5] *Sussex Archaeol. Coll.* IX, p. 25.

rule of a prioress), of the order of St Benedict, in the diocese of London, as well as their predecessors, have conceded tithes, rents, lands, houses, vineyards, meadows, pastures, woods, mills, rights, jurisdictions and certain other goods belonging to the said monastery to several clerks and laymen, to some of them for life, to some for no short time, to others in perpetuity at farm or under an annual payment, and have to this effect given letters, taken oaths, made renunciations, and drawn up public instruments, to the grave harm of the said monastery; and some of the grantees are said to have sought confirmatory letters in common form, concerning these grants, from the apostolic see[1].

This comprehensive catalogue gives some indication of the losses which a house would suffer from reckless grants. The sale of timber and the alienation or pawning of plate were other expedients to which the nuns constantly resorted and which were as constantly prohibited by the bishops[2] The Prioress of Nunmonkton in 1397, "alienated timber in large quantities to the value of a hundred marks"[3]; the cutting down of woods was charged against the Prioresses of Heynings, Harrold, Langley, Gracedieu, Catesby and Ankerwyke at Alnwick's visitations; at Langley it was moreover found that the woods were not properly fenced in after the trees were felled and so the tree-stumps were damaged[4]; the necessity for raising the money was sometimes specifically pleaded, as at Markyate, where a small wood had been sold "to satisfy the creditors of the house"[5]. These sales of timber were a favourite means of obtaining ready money; but too often the loss to the house by the destruction of its woods far outweighed the temporary gain and the Abbeys of St Mary's Winchester and Romsey made special mention of this cause of impoverishment in the middle of the fourteenth century[6] The alienation or pawning of plate and *jocalia* was often resorted to in an extremity. At Gracedieu in 1441 the jewels of the house had been pawned without the knowledge of the convent, so that the nuns (as one of them complained) had not one bowl from which to drink[7]; the next year it was asserted that

---

[1] Dugdale, *Mon.* IV, p. 516.
[2] See below, pp. 225–6   [3] Dugdale, *Mon* IV, p 194
[4] *Linc. Visit.* II, p. 175.   [5] *Alnwick's Visit* MS f. 6.
[6] Liveing. *op cit.* p 146, *Cal of Papal Petitions*, I, p. 122. At Studley in 1530 it was found that the woods of the priory had been much diminished by the late prioress and by "Thomas Cardinal of York for the construction of his college in the university of Oxford " *V.C H. Oxon* II, p 78
[7] *Linc. Visit.* II, p. 120.

the Prioress of Catesby "pawned the jewels of the house for ten years, to wit one cup for the sacrament, which still remained in pawn, and also other pieces of silver"[1]. When Bishop Longland visited Nuncoton in 1531 he found that the Prioress had in times past sold various goods belonging to her house, "viz. a bolle ungilte playn with a couer, oon nutt gilte with a couer, ij bolles white without couers, oon Agnus of gold, oon bocle of gold, oon chalice, oon maser and many other things"[2], and in 1436 it was ordered that the chalices, jewels and ornaments of St Mary's Neasham, which were then in the hands of sundry creditors, were to be redeemed[3]. In the case of Sinningthwaite in 1534 the convent was in such a reduced state that Archbishop Lee was actually obliged to give the nuns licence to pledge jewels to the value of £15[4]. The charge of pawning or selling jewels for their own purposes was often made against prioresses whose conduct in other ways was bad, for instance against Eleanor of Arden in 1396[5], Juliana of Bromhale in 1404[6], Agnes Tawke of Easebourne in 1478[7] and Katherine Wells of Littlemore in 1517[8].

To financial incompetence and to the employment of improvident methods of raising money, the nuns occasionally added extravagance. The bishops forbade them to wear gay clothes for reasons unconnected with finance; nevertheless their silks and furs must have cost money which could ill be spared, and it is amusing to notice that even at Studley, Rothwell and Langley, which were among the smallest and poorest houses in the diocese of Lincoln and in debt, the nuns had to confess to silken veils. The maintenance of a greater number of servants than the revenues of the house could support was another not uncommon form of extravagance[9]. Instances of luxurious living on the part of the heads of various houses have been given elsewhere[10]; it need only be remarked that a self-indulgent prioress might cripple the resources of a house for many years to come, whether by spending its revenues too lavishly, or by raising money by the alienation of its goods.

[1] *Linc. Visit.* II, p 147.
[2] *Archaeologia*, XLVII, pp 58–9
[3] *V.C.H Durham*, II, p 107
[4] *V.C H Yorks* III, p 177
[5] *Test. Ebor.* I, pp 283–4
[6] Dugdale, *Mon* IV, p 506, note *b*
[7] *Sussex Arch Coll* IX, p 19.
[8] *V C H. Oxon* II, p 76
[9] See above, p 153.
[10] See Ch IV.

One other cause of the poverty of nunneries must be noticed, before turning to the attempts of bishops and other visitors to find a remedy. Overcrowding was, throughout the earlier period under consideration, a common cause of financial distress; and the admission of a greater number of nuns than the revenues of the convent were able to support was constantly forbidden in episcopal injunctions. Certainly this was not invariably the fault of the nuns. They suffered (as we have seen) from the formal right of bishop or of patron to place a nun in their house on special occasions, and they suffered still more from the constant pressure to which they were subjected by private persons, anxious to obtain comfortable provision for daughters and nieces. It was sometimes impossible and always difficult to resist the importunity of influential gentlemen in the neighbourhood, whose ill-will might be a serious thing, whether it showed itself in open violence or in closed purses. The authorities of the church had sometimes to step in and rescue houses which had thus been persuaded to burden themselves beyond their means. In 1273 Gregory X issued a bull to the Priory of Carrow, with the intention of putting a stop to the practice.

Your petition having been expounded to us, containing a complaint that you have, at the instant requests of certain lords of England, whom you are unable to resist on account of their power, received so many nuns already into your monastery, that you may scarce be fitly sustained by its rents, we therefore, by the authority of these present letters, forbid you henceforth to receive any nun or sister to the burden of your house[1].

Some nine years later Archbishop Wickwane wrote in the same strain to the nuns of Nunkeeling and Wilberfoss:

Because we have learned from public rumour that your monastery is sometimes burdened by the reception of nuns and by the visits of secular women and girls, at the instance of great persons, to whom you foolishly and unlawfully grant easy permission, we order you.. henceforward, to receive no one as nun or sister of your house, or to lodge for a time in your monastery, without our special licence[2].

Bishop Stratford, in his visitation of Romsey in 1311, forbade additions to the nuns, the proper number having been exceeded, and again in 1327 he wrote:

[1] Dugdale, *Mon* IV, p 71.
[2] *Reg of Archbishop William Wickwane* (Surtees Soc), p 113

It is notorious that your house is burdened with ladies beyond the established number which used to be kept; and I have heard that you are being pressed to receive more young ladies (*damoyseles*) as nuns, wherefore I order you strictly that no young lady received by you be veiled, nor any other received, until the Bishop's visitation, or until they have special orders from him[1]

The situation at the great Abbey of Shaftesbury was the same. As early as 1218 the Pope had forbidden the community to admit nuns beyond the number of a hundred because they were unable to support more or to give alms to the poor, in 1322 Bishop Mortival wrote remonstrating with them for their neglect of the Pope's order and repeating the prohibition to admit more nuns until the state of the Abbey was relieved, on the ground that the inmates of the house were far too many for its goods to support; and in 1326 (in response to a petition from the Abbess asking him to fix the statutory number) the Bishop issued an order stating that the house was capable of maintaining a hundred and twenty nuns and no more and that no novices were to be received until the community was reduced to that number[2].

Episcopal prohibitions to receive new inmates without special licence were very common, especially in the late thirteenth and early fourteenth centuries. Bishops realised that overcrowding only increased the growing poverty of the nunneries. In the poor diocese of York, between 1250 and 1320, the nuns were over and over again forbidden to receive nuns, lay sisters or lay brothers without the licence of the Archbishop. Injunctions to this effect were issued to Marrick (1252), Swine (1268), Wilberfoss (1282), Nunappleton (1282, 1290, 1346), Hampole (1267, 1308, 1312), Arden (1306), Thicket (1309, 1314), Nunkeeling (1282, 1314), Nunburnholme (1318), Esholt (1318), Arthington

---

[1] Liveing, *Records of Romsey Abbey*, p 98 Similarly Bishop Edyndon wrote in 1346 and again in 1363 to St Mary's Winchester, Wherwell and Romsey, forbidding them to take a greater number of nuns than was anciently accustomed or than could be sustained by them without penury *Ib.* p. 165.

[2] *V.C.H Dorset*, ii, p 77 Nevertheless at Romsey and at Shaftesbury the King and the Bishop himself continued to "dump" nuns, in accordance with their prerogative right, throughout the career of both houses In the six years following this prohibition of 1326 Bishop Stratford not only gave permission for a novice to be received at the nuns' own request, but deposited no less than three there himself The words and the actions of bishops sometimes tallied ill.

(1318) and Sinningthwaite (1319)[1]. At Swine, after the visitation by Archbishop Walter Giffard in 1267-8, it was noted among the *comperta*

that the house of Swine cannot sustain more nuns or sisters than now are there, inasmuch as those at present there are ill provided with food, as is said above, and that the house nevertheless remains at least a hundred and forty marks in debt, wherefore the lord Archbishop decreed that no nun or sister should thenceforward be received there, save with his consent[2].

A very severe punishment was decreed at Marrick, where the Archbishop announced that any man or woman admitted without his licence would be expelled without hope of mercy, the Prioress would be deposed and any other nuns who agreed condemned to fast on bread and water for two months (except on Sundays and festivals)[3]. In other dioceses the bishops pursued a similar policy. But it was not easy to enforce these prohibitions. Four years after Archbishop Greenfield's injunction to Hampole (1308) he was obliged to address another letter to the convent, having heard that the prioress had received

a little girl (*puellulam*), by name Maud de Dreffield, niece of the Abbot of Roche, and another named Jonetta, her own niece, at the instance of Sir Hugh de Cressy, her brother, that after a time they might be admitted to the habit and profession of nuns[4]

The predicament of the Prioress is easily understood; how was she to refuse her noble brother and the Abbot of Roche? They could bring to bear far more pressure than a distant archbishop, who came upon his visitations at long intervals. Moreover the ever present need of ready money made the resistance of nuns less determined than it might otherwise have been, for a dowry in hand they were, as usual, willing to encumber themselves with a new mouth to feed throughout long years to come.

Prohibitions from increasing the number of nuns become more rare in the second half of the fourteenth and during the fifteenth century. Even when the population recovered from the havoc

---

[1] See *V C H Yorks* III, pp. 113, 117, 119, 120, 124, 161, 163, 171-2, 188; *Reg. of Archbishop Giffard* (Surtees Soc), p 148, *Reg. of Archbishop Wichwane* (Surtees Soc), pp 112, 113, 140-1

[2] *Reg Giffard, loc cit* [3] *V C H Yorks* III, p 117

[4] *Ib.* III, p. 163 The house was heavily in debt at the time and though the Bishop had forbidden the granting of corrodies and liveries without leave, the Prioress was also charged with having "sold or granted corrodies very burdensome to the house "

wrought by the Black Death, the numbers in the nunneries continued steadily to decline. Perhaps fashion had veered, conscious that the golden days of monasticism were over; more likely the growing poverty of the houses rendered them a less tempting retreat. A need for restricting the number of nuns still continued, because the decline in the revenues of the nunneries was swifter than the decline in the number of the nuns. Thus in 1440–1 Alnwick included in his injunctions to seven houses a prohibition to receive more nuns than could competently be sustained by their revenues[1], and the evidence given at his visitations shows the necessity for such a restriction. The injunction to Heynings is particularly interesting:

For as mykelle as we fonde that agayn the entente and the forbedyng of the commune lawe there are in your saide pryorye meo nunnes and susters professed then may be competently susteyned of the revenews of your sayde pryorye, the exilitee of the saide revenews and charitees duly considered, we commaunde, ordeyn, charge and enioyne yowe vnder payne etc. etc that fro this day forthe ye receyve no mo in to nunnes ne sustres in your saide pryory wyth owte the advyse and assent of hus (and) of our successours bysshope of Lincolne, so that we or thai, wele informed of the yerely valwe of your saide revenews may ordeyn for the nombre competente of nunnes and susters[2].

Nevertheless even at Nuncoton, one of the houses to which a similar injunction was sent, a nun gave evidence "that in her oun time there were in the habit eighteen or twenty nuns and now there are only fourteen," and the Bishop himself remarked that "ther be but fewe in couent in regarde of tymes here to fore"[3] Everywhere this decline in the number of nuns went steadily on during the fourteenth and fifteenth centuries[4]. And from the beginning of the fifteenth century there appear, here and there among visitatorial injunctions, commands of a

---

[1]. Heynings, Ankerwyke, Legbourne, Nuncoton, St Michael's Stamford, Gracedieu, Langley

[2] Linc Visit II, p 134   [3] Alnwick's Visit MS ff 71d., 77d.

[4] It would be interesting to collect statistics as to the relative size of different nunneries at different periods. It is here possible to give only a few examples of the decline in the number of inmates. The numbers at Nuneaton varied as follows· 93 (1234), 80 (1328), 46 (1370), 40 (1459), 23 (1539). (V C H Warwick II, pp. 66–9) At Romsey (where the statutory number was supposed to be 100) as follows: 91 (1333) and 26 (from 1478 to the Dissolution). (Liveing, Records of Romsey Abbey, passim) At Shaftesbury as follows: forbidden to receive more than 100 in 1218 and in 1322; number fixed at 120 in 1326, between 50–57 (from 1441 to the Dissolution) V C H Dorset, II, p 77

very different nature; here and there a Bishop is found trying, not to keep down, but to keep up the number of nuns. Instead of the repeated prohibitions addressed to Romsey at the beginning of the fourteenth century, there is an injunction from William of Wykeham in 1387, ordering the Abbess to augment the number of nuns, which had fallen far below the statutory number[1] Similarly in 1432 Bishop Gray wrote to Elstow,

since the accustomed number of nuns of the said monastery has so lessened, that those who are now received scarcely suffice for the chanting of divine service by night and day according to the requirement of the rule, we will and enjoin upon you the abbess, in virtue of obedience and under the penalties written above and beneath, that, with what speed you can, you cause the number of nuns in the said monastery to be increased in proportion to its resources[2]

At Studley in 1531, although the house was badly in debt, the nuns were ordered to live less luxuriously and "to augment your nombre of ladyes within the yere"[3]. In this connection Archbishop Warham's visitation of Sheppey in 1511 is significant. The Prioress, when questioned as to the number of nuns in the house, said that "she had heard there were seventeen; she knew of fourteen; she herself wished to increase the number to fourteen if she could find any who wished to enter into religion "[4]. It is an interesting reflection that Henry VIII may simply have accelerated, by his violent measure, a gradual dissolution of the nunneries through poverty and through change of fashion.

This account of the attempts of medieval bishops to prevent the nunneries from burdening themselves with inmates, beyond the number which could be supported by their revenues, leads to a consideration of the other methods employed by them to remedy the financial distress in which the nuns so often found themselves. These methods may be divided into three classes; (1) arrangements to safeguard expenditure by the head of the house and to impose a check upon autocracy, (2) arrangements to prevent rash expenditure or improvident means of raising money, by requiring episcopal consent before certain steps could be

---

[1] *New Coll* MS. f 55d.　　　　　[2] *Linc Visit* I, p 53.
[3] *Archaeologia*, XLVII, p 55
[4] *E.H R.* VI, pp 33-4 From the fact that the Prioress was ordered to make up the number again to fourteen, as soon as she conveniently could, it appears that the ten nuns who gave evidence before the Archbishop represented the full strength of the house

taken, and (3) if the incompetence of the nuns were such that even these restrictions were insufficient, the appointment of a male *custos*, master or guardian, to manage the finances of the house.

Arrangements for safeguarding expenditure by the head of the house were of four kinds· (1) provision for the consultation of the whole convent in important negotiations, (2) provision for the safe custody of the common seal, (3) provision for the regular presentation of accounts, and (4) the appointment of co-adjutresses to the Prioress, or of two or three treasuresses, to be jointly responsible for receipts and expenditure. It was a common injunction that the whole convent, or at least "the more and sounder part of it," should be consulted in all important negotiations, such as the alienation of property, the leasing of land and farms, the cutting down of woods, the incurring of debts and the reception of novices[1]. It has already been shown that Prioresses acted autocratically in performing such business on their own initiative, and the injunction sent by Peckham to the Abbess of Romsey shows the lengths to which this independence might lead them[2]. Flemyng's injunction to Elstow in 1421–2 is typical:

That the Abbess deliver not nor demise to farm appropriated churches, pensions, portions, manors or granges belonging to the monastery, nor do any other such weighty business, without the express consent of the greater and sounder part of the convent[3].

At Arthington in 1318 the Prioress was specially ordered to consult the convent in sales of wool and other business matters[4]; the Prioress of Sinningthwaite the next year was told to take counsel with the older nuns and in all writings under the common seal to employ a faithful clerk and to have the deed read, discussed and sealed in the presence of the whole convent, those who spoke against it on reasonable grounds being heard and the deed if necessary corrected[5]. Provision for the safe custody

---

[1] A few out of many specific instances may be given: Wroxall 1323 (*V C H Warwick.* II, p 71); Polesworth 1456 (*ib.* p 63); Fairwell 1367 (*Reg. of Bishop Stretton.* p 119), Romsey 1302 (*Reg Johannis de Pontissara* (Cant and York. Soc. p 127), Moxby 1318 (*V C H. Yorks.* III, p 239), Nuncoton 1531 (*Arch* XLVII, p 58); Sinningthwaite 1534 (*Yorks. Arch. Journ* XVI, p 441)

[2] See above, pp 64–5.   [3] *Linc. Visit.* I, p 50
[4] *V C H Yorks* III, p. 188   [5] *Ib.* III, p. 177.

of the common seal, and for the assent of the whole convent
to all writings which received its imprint, was a necessary
corollary to the demand that the Prioress should consult her
nuns in matters of business. Medieval superiors were constantly
charged with keeping the common seal in their own custody[1]
and nuns and bishops alike objected to a custom which rendered
the convent responsible for any rash agreement into which the
Prioress might enter. Elaborate arrangements for the custody
of the seal are therefore common in visitatorial injunctions. In
1302 Bishop John of Pontoise wrote to Romsey that

whereas from the bad keeping of the common seal many evils to the
house have hitherto happened (as the Bishop has now learned from
the experience of fact), and also may happen unless wholesome remedy
be applied, three at least of the discreeter ladies shall be appointed
by the Abbess and by the larger and wiser part of the convent to keep
the seal; and when any letter shall be sealed with the common seal
in the chapter before the whole convent, it shall be read and explained
in an intelligible tongue to all the ladies, publicly, distinctly and
openly and afterwards sealed in the same chapter, (not in corners or
secretly, as has hitherto been the custom,) and signed as it is read, so
that what concerns all may be approved by all Which done the
seal shall be replaced in the same place under the said custody[2]

These injunctions were repeated by Bishop Woodlock nine years
later, but in 1387 William of Wykeham laid down much more
stringent rules. The seal was to be kept securely under seven,
or at least five locks and keys, of which one key was to be in
the custody of the abbess and the others to remain with some
of the more prudent and mature nuns, nominated by the convent, no letter was to be sealed without first being read before
the whole convent in the vulgar tongue and approved by all
or by the greater and wiser part of the nuns[3]. Seven locks
was an unusually large number, usually three, or even two, were
ordered At Malling, where, as we have seen, Bishop Hamo of
Hythe unwillingly confirmed an "insufficient and ignorant"
woman as Abbess, he took the extreme step of sequestrating
the common seal and forbidding it to be used without his permission[4].

---

[1] E g Clemence Medforde at Ankerwyke in 1441 and Eleanor of Arden
in 1396. See above, pp 81, 85

[2] Liveing, *op cit.* pp 100–101.

[3] *New Coll* MS. f 88d   [4] See above, p 204

Another method of keeping some control over the expenditure not only of the head or treasuress of the house, but also of the other obedientiaries, was by ordering the regular presentation of accounts before the whole convent; and in spite of the injunctions of councils and of bishops no regulation was more often broken. Bishop Stapeldon's rules, drawn up for the guidance of Polsloe and Canonsleigh, afford a good example of these injunctions, and deal with the presentation of accounts by the bailiffs and officers of the house, as well as by the Prioress.

Item, let the accounts of all your bailiffs, reeves and receivers, both foreign and denizen, be overlooked every year, between Easter and Whitsuntide, and between the Feast of St Michael and Christmas, after final account rendered in the Priory before the Prioress, or before those whom she is pleased to put in her place, and before two or three of the most ancient and wise ladies of the said religion and house, assigned by the Convent for this purpose, and let the rolls of the accounts thus rendered remain in the common treasury, so that they may be consulted, if need shall arise by reason of the death of a Prioress, or of the death or removal of bailiffs, receivers or reeves Item, let the Prioress each year, between Christmas and Easter, before the whole convent, or six ladies assigned by the convent for this purpose, show forth the state of the house, and its receipts and expenses, not in detail but in gross (*ne mie par menue parceles mes par grosses sommes*), and the debts and the names of the debtors and creditors for any sum above forty shillings And all these things are to be put into writing and placed in the common treasury, to the intent that it may be seen each year how your goods increase or decrease[1].

Bishop Pontoise ordered that at Romsey an account should be rendered twice a year and at the end thereof the state of the house should be declared by the auditors of the convent, or at least by the seniors of the convent, but finding the practice in abeyance in 1302 he ordered the account to be rendered once a year[2], his ordinance was repeated by Bishop Woodlock in 1311[3] and by William of Wykeham in 1387[4], both of whom specially refer to the rendering of accounts by officials and obedientiaries

---

[1] *Reg of Bishop Stapeldon*, ed. Hingeston-Randolph, p. 318
[2] Liveing, *Records of Romsey Abbey*, pp 99–100
[3] *Ib* pp 102–3
[4] *New Coll* MS f 87   In 1492, at the visitation by Archbishop Morton's commissioners, a nun prays that injunctions be made to the sisters and abbess that they choose no one as auditor without consulting the Archbishop of Canterbury. Liveing, *op cit* pp 218–9

as well as by the Abbess[1]. More frequently, especially in the smaller houses, the Bishops confined their efforts to extracting the main account from the Prioress, with the double object, so ungraciously expressed by Archbishop Lee, "that it may appere in whate state the housse standith in, and also that it may be knowen, whethur she be profitable to the house or not"[2]. How far it was a common practice that the accounts should be audited by some external person, it is impossible to say. Our only evidence lies in occasional injunctions such as those sent by Bishops Pontoise and Woodlock to Romsey, or by Bishop Buckingham to Heynings; or an occasional remark, such as the Prioress of Blackborough's excuse that she did not render account in order "to save the expenses of an auditor"[3]; or an occasional order addressed by a Bishop to some person bidding him go and examine the accounts of a house. In 1314 William, rector of Londesborough, was made *custos* of Nunburnholme on peculiar terms, being ordered to go there three times a year and hear the accounts of the ministers and *prepositi* of the house; his duties were thus, in effect, those of an unpaid auditor and no more[4]. It is probable that the accounts of bailiffs and other servants were audited by the *custos*, in those houses to which such an official was attached[5]; whether his own accounts were scrutinised is another matter. In 1309 Archbishop Greenfield wrote to his own receiver, William de Jafford, to audit the accounts of Nunappleton[6], and after the revelations of Margaret Wavere's maladministration at Oatesby in 1445, a commission for the inspection of the accounts was granted to the Abbot of St James, Northampton[7]. In some cases the annual statement

---

[1] For other mentions of the rendering of accounts by bailiffs, officiaries, etc see Arden 1306 and Arthington 1315 (*V C H Yorks* III, pp 113, 188), Fairwell 1367 (*Reg of Robert de Stretton*, p 119), Elstow 1422 (*Linc Visit.* I, p. 50).
[2] Writing to Sinningthwaite in 1534 *Yorks Archaeol Journ* XVI, pp. 442-3
[3] *Visit of the Dioc of Norwich* (Camden Soc), p 108
[4] *V.C H Yorks* III, p. 119
[5] Sometimes specific mention is made of this duty, e g in 1318 Thomas de Mydelsburg, rector of Loftus, was ordered to administer the temporal goods of the Cistercian house of Handale, to receive the accounts of the servants and to substitute more capable ones for those who were useless *Ib* III, p 166 Cf the commission to the rector of Aberford to be *custos* of Kirklees about the same time *Yorks Archaeol Journ* XVI, p 362
[6] *V C H. Yorks* III, p 171   [7] *Linc Visit.* II, pp. 52-3.

of accounts was ordered to be made before the Bishop of the diocese, as well as the nuns of the house, and in such cases he would act as auditor himself[1].

It was also a common practice for the Visitor to demand that the current balance sheet and inventory (the *status domus*) of a monastic house should be produced, together with its foundation charter and various other documents, before he took the evidence of the inmates at a visitation The register of Bishop Alnwick's visitations shows the procedure very clearly, usually there is simply a note to the effect that the Prioress handed in the *status domus*, but at some houses the Bishop encountered difficulties.   At St Michael's Stamford, in 1440, the old Prioress (who, it will be remembered, had rendered no account at all during her twelve years of office) was unable to produce a balance sheet, or one of the required certificates, and Alnwick was obliged to proceed with her examination "hiis exhibendis non exhibitis." He made shift however to extract some verbal information from her; she said that the house was in debt £20 at her installation and now only 20 marks, that it could expend £40, besides 10 marks appropriated to the office of pittancer and besides "the perquisites of the stewardship"; she said also "that they plough with two teams and they have eight oxen, seven horses, a bailiff, four serving-folk, a carter for the teams, and a man who is their baker and brewer, whose wife makes the malt"[2]. At Legbourne also the Prioress

showed the state of the house, as it now stands, as they say, but not annual charges, etc... She says that the house owed £43 at the time of her confirmation and installation and now only £14; nevertheless because the state of the house is not fully shown, she has the next day at Louth to show it more fully[3].

At Ankerwyke also Clemence Medforde gave in an incomplete balance sheet:

she shewed a roll containing the rents of the house, which, after deducting rent-charges, reach the total of £22 6. 7. Touching the

---

[1] In 1442, for instance, the Prioress of Rusper was ordered to render accounts yearly before the Bishop of Chichester and the nuns of the house (*Sussex Arch Coll.* v, p 255), and at Sheppey in 1511, two nuns having complained that the Prioress did not account, she was ordered to render accounts, with an inventory to the convent and to Archbishop Warham (*E.H.R.* vi, p. 34).

[2] *Alnwick Visit* MS. f. 83   [3] *Linc Visit.* II, p 184.

stewardship of the temporalities and touching the other receipts, as from alms and other like sources, she shews nothing, and says that at the time of her preferment the house was 300 marks in debt, and now is in debt only £40, and she declares some of the names of the creditors of this sum[1]

A special demand for a complete statement of accounts was sometimes made in cases where gross maladministration was charged against a prioress. Thus in 1310 Archbishop Greenfield ordered an investigation of certain charges (unspecified, but clearly of this nature) made against the Prioress of Rosedale, her accounts,

as well as those of all bailiffs and other officials and servants who were bound to render accounts, were to be examined and the prioress was ordered to render to the commissioners full and complete accounts from the time of her promotion, as well as a statement of the then position of the house,

and a further letter from the Archbishop to the Subprioress and nuns ordered them to display the *status domus* to the commissioners, as it was when the Prioress took office and as it was at the time he wrote She resigned shortly afterwards, *sentiens se impotentem*, but in 1315 her successor was enjoined to draw up a certified statement showing the credit and debit accounts of the house and to send it to the Archbishop before a certain date[2]. Usually the Bishop demanded not only the account roll of a house, but also an inventory, doubtless in order that he might see whether anything had been alienated, and these inventories sometimes remain attached to the account of the visitation preserved in the episcopal register[3].

[1] *Linc Visit* II, p I   [2] *V C H Yorks* III, p. 174

[3] An inventory of the goods of Easebourne Priory, drawn up for the Bishop of Chichester on May 27th, 1450, has survived It is very complete and comprises all departments of the house, together with a list of land, chapels and appropriated churches and a note that the house can expend in all £22 3s on repairs and other expenses and that the debts "for repairs and other necessary expenses this year" amount to £66 6s 8d *Sussex Arch. Coll.* IX, pp. 10–13. It may be of interest to quote the briefer inventory of the poor house of Ankerwyke, as presented to Bishop Atwater at his visitation in 1519 and copied by his clerk into the register. There were at the time five nuns in the house and one in apostasy "Redditus ibidem extendunt prima facie ad xxxiij li x s Inde resoluunt pro libris (*sic*) reddit bus v li. x s Et sic habent clare ad reparacionem & alia onera sustinenda ultra xl marcas *Jocalia in Ecclesia* Habent ibidem vestimenta sacerdotalia ad minus serica xiij Habent eciam vnicam capam de serica & auro. j calicem de argento deaurato j par Turribulorum j pixidem de argento pro sacramento ij libros missales impressos j magnum par candelabrorum ante

If a Prioress were found to be hopelessly incompetent or unscrupulous, but not bad enough to be deprived of her position, Bishops sometimes took the extreme measure of appointing one or more coadjutresses, to govern the house in conjunction with her; and often (even when there was no complaint against the Prioress) the nuns were ordered to elect treasuresses, to receive and disburse the income of the house from all sources. One of the *comperta* at the visitation of Swine in 1268 was to the effect that

the sums of money which are bestowed in charity upon the convent, for pittances and garments and other necessary uses, are received by the Prioress; which ought the rather to be in the custody of two honest nuns and distributed to those in need of them, and in no wise converted to other uses[1].

At Nunkeeling in 1314 it was ordained that all money due to the house should be received by two bursars, elected by the convent[2], and in 1323 Bishop Cobham of Worcester made a similar injunction at Wroxall, that two sisters were to be chosen by the chapter, to do the business of the convent in receiving rents, etc [3] Elaborate arrangements for the appointment of treasuresses were made by Bishop Bokyngham at Elstow and at Heynings, in 1388 and 1392 respectively, and by Bishop Flemyng at Elstow in 1421-2[4]. It will suffice here to quote the much earlier arrangement made by Archbishop Peckham at Usk in 1284:

"Since," he wrote, "lately visiting you by our metropolitan right, we found you in a most desolate state (*multipliciter desolatas*), desiring to avoid such desolation in future, we order, by the counsel of discreet men, that henceforth two provident and discreet nuns be elected by the consent of the prioress and community; into whose hands all the money of the house shall be brought, whether from granges, or

summum altare. j paruum par candelabrorum super summum altare. ij urciolos argenteos j paxbread de argento, una parua campana argentea *Catalla·* Habent vaccas duas, ij equas, boues senes iij, unus bouiculus (*sic*), j vaccam anne (*sic*) (*blank*), iij equas pro aratro *Vtensilia* vj plumalia, x paria linthiaminum, iiij superpellectilia, iiij paria de le blanketts, ij le white Testers. Habent Redditus Annuales preter terras ipsarum dominicalium (*sic*) in earundem manibus occupatas xlvj li xj s x d." *Linc. Epis. Reg Visit Atwater,* f 42. A fair number of inventories of convent property made for this or for other purposes is extant; notably those drawn up, for purposes of spoliation instead of preservation, at the Dissolution See *Bibliography*

[1] *Reg of Walter Giffard* (Surtees Soc), p. 147.
[2] *V C H Yorks.* iii, p. 120
[3] *V.C H. Warwick,* ii, p 71   [4] See below, p. 226

from appropriated churches, or coming from any other offerings, to be carefully looked after by their consent And as well the Prioress as the other nuns shall receive (money for) all necessary expenses from their hands and in no manner otherwise And we will that these nuns be called Treasuresses, which Treasuresses thrice in the year, to wit in Lent, Whitsuntide and on the Feast of St Michael, shall render account before the Prioress for the time being and before five or six elders of the chapter"

In addition they were to have a priest as *custos* or administrator, of their temporal and spiritual possessions[1].

The appointment of a coadjutress to the head of a house in the administration of its affairs is of the same nature The appointment of coadjutresses was a favourite device with Archbishop Peckham, to check an extravagant or incapable head. At the great abbey of Romsey three coadjutresses were appointed, without whose testimony and advice the Abbess was to undertake no important business[2]. At Wherwell one coadjutress only, a certain J. de Ver, was appointed in 1284, and the same year the Archbishop wrote to his commissary on the subject of the Priory of the Holy Sepulchre, Canterbury:

Since by the carelessness and neglect of the Prioress the goods of the house are said to be much wasted, we wish you to assign to her two coadjutresses, to wit Dame Sara and another of the more honest and wise ladies, but let neither be Benedicta, who is said to have greatly offended the whole community by her discords.

Here, as at Usk, Peckham appointed in addition a master to look after their affairs[3]. At the disorderly house of Arthington Isabella Couvel was in 1312 associated with the Prioress Isabella de Berghby, but the Prioress seems to have resented the appointment and promptly ran away[4]. In the Exeter diocese Bishop Stapeldon made Joan de Radyngton coadjutress to Petronilla, Abbess of Canonsleigh in 1320[5], and in the diocese of Bath and Wells Bishop Ralph of Shrewsbury in 1335 appointed two coadjutresses to Cecilia de Draycote, Prioress of White Hall, Ilchester, and in 1351, when his visitation had revealed many scandals at Cannington, including the simoniacal admission of nuns and unauthorised sale of corrodies by the Prioress, the

---

[1] *Reg Epis Johannis Peckham* (Rolls Ser), III, pp. 805–6
[2] See below, pp 337–8
[3] See *Reg Epis. Johannis Peckham* (Rolls. Ser.), II, pp 654–5, 659, 708.
[4] *V C H. Yorks* II, pp. 187–8
[5] *Reg. of Bishop Stapeldon*, ed. Hingeston-Randolph, p 96

Bishop, instead of depriving her "tempered the rigour of the law with clemency" and appointed two coadjutresses without whose consent she was to do nothing[1]. Bishop Alnwick made use of this method of controlling a superior in several cases where serious mismanagement had come to light at his visitation[2], and other instances of this method of controlling the administration of a superior might be multiplied from the episcopal registers

The appointment of treasuresses and of coadjutresses and the provision for due consultation of the chapter, custody of the common seal and presentment of accounts had the purpose of safeguarding the nuns against reckless expenditure or maladministration by the head of the house, and, where the injunctions of the Visitor were carried out, such precautions doubtless proved of use Some further check was, however, necessary, to safeguard the nuns against themselves, and to prevent the whole convent from rash sales of land, alienation of goods and from all those other improvident devices for obtaining ready money, to which they were so much addicted. The Bishop often attempted to impose such a check by forbidding certain steps to be taken without his own consent. The business for which an episcopal licence was necessary usually comprised the alienation of land or its lease for life or for a long term of years, the sale of any corrodies or payment of any fees or pensions, and (as has already been pointed out) the reception of new inmates, who might overcrowd the house and thus impose a strain upon its revenues[3]. Other business, such as the sale of woods, was sometimes included[4]. The prohibition of corrodies, fees and pensions was doubtless intended to protect the nuns against the exactions of patrons and other persons, who claimed the right to pension off relatives or old servants by this means, as well as against their own improvidence in selling such doles for

---

[1] *Reg of Ralph of Shrewsbury* (Somerset Rec. Soc.), pp. 240–1, 684.

[2] At Ankerwyke, Catesby, Gracedieu and St Michael's Stamford *Linc Visit* II, pp. 6, 9, 52, 125, *Alnwick's Visit.* MS f 39d

[3] To this reception of boarders was sometimes added, but with a different purpose, viz to protect the nuns from contact with the world.

[4] At Moxby in 1318 no fresh debts, especially large ones, were to be incurred without the convent's consent and the Archbishop's special licence *V.C.H Yorks* III, p 239 At Nuncoton in 1440 "ne that ye aleyne or selle any bondman" was added to the usual prohibition *Alnwick's Visit* MS f 77d.

inadequate sums of ready money. As typical of such prohibitions may be quoted Alnwick's 'injunction (given in two parts) to Harrold in 1442-3:

Also we enioyne yow, prioresse, and your sucessours vndere payne of pry[v]acyone and perpetuelle amocyone fro your and thaire astate and dygnyte that fro hense forthe ye ne thai selle, graunte ne gyfe to ony persone what euer thai be any corrody, lyverye, pensyone or anuyte to terme of lyve, certeyn tyme or perpetuelly, but if ye or thai fyrste declare the cause to vs or our successours bysshoppes of Lincolne, and in that case have our specyalle licence or of our saide successours and also the fulle assent of the more hole parte of your couent Also we enioyne yow prioresse and ,your successours vndere the payne of priuacyone afore saide that ye ne thai selle, gyfe, aleyne, ne felle no grete wode or tymbere, saue to necessary reparacyone of your place and your tenaundryes, but if ye and thai hafe specyalle licence ther to, of vs or our successours bysshoppes of Lincolne and the cause declared to vs or our successours[1].

An exceptionally conscientious Bishop would sometimes send even more full and elaborate instructions to a nunnery on the management of its property, and examples of such minute regulations are to be found in the injunctions sent to Elstow Abbey at different times by Bishop Bokyngham (1387)[2], Archbishop Courtenay (1389)[3] and Bishop Flemyng (1421-2)[4]. Bishop Bokyngham also sent very full injunctions to Heynings in 1392 and these may be quoted to illustrate the care which the Visitors sometimes took to set a house upon a firm financial footing, so far as it was possible to do so by the mere giving of good advice:

The Prioress, indeed, shall attempt to do nothing without the counsel of two nuns, elected by the convent to assist her in the government

[1] *Linc Visit.* II, p. 131 A few other instances of these injunctions may be given. Arden (1306), Marrick (1252), Nunburnholme (1318), Nunkeeling (1314), Thicket (1309), Yedingham (1314), Esholt (1318), Hampole (1308, 1312), Nunappleton (1489), Rosedale (1315), Sinningthwaite (1315), Arthington (1318), Moxby (1314, 1318, 1328), *V.C.H Yorks* III, pp. 113, 117, 119, 124, 128, 161, 163, 172, 174, 177, 188, 239-40; Sinningthwaite (1534), *Yorks. Arch Journ.* XVI, p 441; Arthington (1286), *Reg John le Romeyn* (Surtees Soc I, p 55), Ankerwyke, Godstow, Gracedieu, Heynings, Langley, Legbourne, Markyate, Nuncoton, Stixwould, St Michael's Stamford (all 1440-5), *Linc Visit* II, pp. 8, 115, 124, 134, 186 and *Alnwick's Visit.* MS ff 6d, 77d, 81d, 75d, Elstow (1359), *Linc Epis Reg Memo. Gynewell,* f 139d; Elstow (1421), Burnham (1434), *Linc Visit.* I, pp 24, 49; Studley, Nuncoton (1531), *Arch* XLVII, pp 54, 58, Polsloe and Canonsleigh (1319), *Reg Stapeldon of Exeter,* p 317, Romsey (1302), *Reg. J de Pontissara,* p 127

[2] *Linc Epis Reg Memo Bokyngham,* f 343
[3] *Lambeth Reg Courtenay I,* f 336   [4] *Linc Visit* II, pp. 49-50

of the aforesaid priory, both within and without; and when any important business has to be done concerning the state of the priory, the same Prioress shall expound it to the convent in common, and shall settle and accomplish it according to their counsel, to the advantage of the aforesaid house. And each year the receiver shall display fully in chapter to the convent in common the state of the house and an account of the administration of its goods, clearly and openly written.. .Item we command and ordain that the common seal and muniments of the house be faithfully kept under three locks, of which one key shall be in the custody of the prioress, another of the subprioress and the third of a nun elected for this purpose by the convent ...Item we enjoin and command that two receivers be each year elected by the chapter, who shall receive all money whatsoever, forthcoming from the churches, manors or rents of the said priory, the which two elected (receivers), together with the Prioress and with an auditor deputed in the name of the convent, shall hear and receive in writing the computation, account and reckoning of all bailiffs without the precincts of the house, who receive any moneys, or any other goods whatsoever in the name of the said convent, from churches, manors or rents And afterwards the same two elected receivers, before the Prioress and two other of the greater, elder and more prudent nuns, elected to this end by the convent, shall faithfully render at least twice every year the account and computation of all the receipts and expenses of the same (receivers) within the precincts of the aforesaid house, to the said Prioress and two sisters elected and deputed in the name of the convent And when this has been done, we will and enjoin that twice in every year the Prioress of the aforesaid house show the whole state of the aforesaid house in chapter, the whole convent being assembled on a certain day for this purpose. And we will that the roll of the aforesaid balance sheet, or paper of account or reckoning, remain altogether in the archives of the aforesaid house, that the prioress and the elder and more prudent (nuns) of the aforesaid house may be able easily to learn the state of the same in future years and whenever any difficulty may arise And let bailiffs be constituted of sufficient faculties and of commendable discretion and fidelity, the best that can be found, and let them similarly render due account every year before the same prioress and convent... Furthermore we will that the Prioress and convent of the aforesaid house do not sell or concede in perpetuity or grant for a term corrodies, stipends, liveries or pensions to clerics or to laymen, save with our licence first sought and obtained[1].

At Elstow Bokyngham gave a more detailed injunction about the appointment of bailiffs and other officers.

[1] *Linc Epis Reg Memo Bokyngham,* ff 397–397d These injunctions are scattered among the others, but have been placed together here for the sake of reference

Let the Abbess for the government of the aforesaid monastery have faithful servants, in especial for the government and supervision without waste of the husbandry and the manors and stock and woods of the aforesaid house; the which the Abbess herself is bound, if she can, to supervise each year in person, or else let her cause them to be industriously supervised by others; and to look after the external and internal business of the house and to prosecute it outside let her appoint also some man of proven experience and of mature age[1].

The purpose of those regulations and restrictions which have hitherto been described, was to assist the nuns in managing their own finances. But the nuns were never very good business women, and they were moreover in theory confined to the precincts of the cloister, so that it was difficult for them to manage their own business, unless they imperilled their souls by excursions into the world. During the thirteenth and early fourteenth centuries, therefore, a common method of extricating them from their difficulties was by appointing a male guardian, known in different places as Custos, Prior, Warden or Master, to supervise the temporal affairs of a house and to look after its finances. In the early history of Cistercian nunneries each house was governed jointly by a Prior and Prioress and in some cases a few canons are found holding the temporalities jointly with the nuns. Of these Cistercian houses Mr Hamilton Thompson says:

As in the case of the Gilbertine priories, such nunneries are rarely found outside Lincolnshire and Yorkshire. they were under the bishop's supervision and their connexion with the order of Citeaux was nominal. Their geographical distribution, as well as the fact that St Gilbert attempted to affiliate his nunneries to the Cistercian order and modelled them upon its rule, provokes the suspicion that such houses were a result of the growth of the Gilbertine order, and, if not intended to become double houses, were at any rate imitations of the corporations of nuns at Sempringham and elsewhere[2].

References to canons occur in connection with the houses of Stixwould, Heynings and Legbourne in Lincolnshire[3], Catesby in Northamptonshire[4] and Swine in Yorkshire[5]. The *comperta*

---

[1] *Linc. Epis. Reg. Memo Bokyngham*, f 343. Compare Flemyng's injunctions in 1422. *Linc. Visit* I, p. 49.

[2] *Linc Visit* I, p 151

[3] *V C H Lincs.* II, pp 148, 150, 154 (note I).

[4] *V C H Northants.* II, p 121

[5] *V.C.H. Yorks* III, pp 178–9, and *Reg of Archbishop Giffard* (Surtees Soc.), pp 147–8. The canons at these houses must be distinguished from the

of Archbishop Giffard's visitation of Swine in 1267–8 show that
the house at that time closely resembled the double houses
belonging to the Gilbertine order.

Item compertum est, that the two windows, by which the food and
drink of the canons and lay brothers are conveyed (to them), are not
at all well guarded by the two nuns who are called janitresses, inasmuch as suspicious conversations are frequently held there between
the canons and lay brothers on the one hand and the nuns and sisters
on the other. *Item compertum est* that the door which leads to the
church is not, at all carefully kept by a certain secular boy, who
permits the canons and lay brothers to enter indiscriminately in the
twilight, that they may talk with the nuns and sisters, the which
door was wont to be guarded diligently by a trusty and energetic
lay brother

It has already been described how the ill-management of the
canons and lay brothers ("who dissipate and consume, under
colour of guardianship, the goods outside, which were wont to
be committed to the guardianship of one of the nuns") caused
the nuns to go short in clothes and food and even to be reduced
to drinking water instead of beer twice a week, though the
canons and their friends "did themselves very well" (*satis
habundanter et laute procurantur*)[1]. In most cases this double
constitution of nuns and canons was in abeyance in Cistercian
houses before the fourteenth century, though a prior and canons
are mentioned at Stixwould in 1308[2] and Richard de Staunton,

canons who held prebendal stalls in the Abbeys of Romsey, St Mary's,
Winchester, Wherwell, Wilton and Shaftesbury, these were often bad
pluralists and could have been of little use to the abbeys, as chaplains or as
custodes. See *V.C H. Hants* II, pp. 122–3 and p. 144 above, note 1.

[1] *Loc. cit* Compare the complaint of the nuns of Brodholme in 1321–2.
"A nostre Seyngnur le Roy e a son Counsaill monstrent le Prioresse el
Covente de Brodholme, qe lour Gardayns de la dit meson par lour defaute
sount lour Rentes abatez, e lour meson a poy ennente e le dit Gardayns
ne vollent nulle entent mettre ne despender pur les ayder kaunt eles sount
employdie, mes come eles meymes defendent a graunt meschef   Pur qoi
eles prient pur l'amour de Dieu, trescher Seygnour, pur l'alme vostre Pier,
e ouir de charite, qe Vous vollez graunter vostre Charter qe l'avantdit
Prioresse el covent pouissent avoir lour rentes e lour enproumens, de ordiner
a lour voluntes, e al profist de la dit meson, si pleiser Vous soit, Kare autrement ne poivent eles viver" The reply was "Injusta est peticio, ideo non
potest fieri" *Rot Parl* I, pp 393–4. Brodholme was one of the only two
convents of Premonstratensian nuns in England; the guardians were probably the canons of the Premonstratensian Abbey of Newhouse; for an ordinance (1354, confirmed 1409) regulating the relations between the two houses,
see *Cal. of Papal Letters*, VI, pp. 159–60.

[2] *V.C H. Lincs.* II, p. 148 (from Pat. 2 Edw. II, pt II, m. 22*d.*).

"canon of Catesby," was made master of that house as late as 1316[1].

In other houses where no trace of canons has survived there are often references to the resident Prior, especially in the dioceses of York and Lincoln, and this official is sometimes found in Benedictine houses (e.g. Godstow[2], St Michael's Stamford[3], and King's Mead, Derby[4]). He seems to have acted as senior chaplain and confessor to the nuns as well as supervising their financial business. In cases where a nunnery was in some sort of dependence upon an abbey or priory of monks, it is usual to find a religious of that house acting as *custos* of the nuns. At St Michael's Stamford, for instance, the abbots of Peterborough had the right of nominating a resident prior, subject to the approval of the Bishop of Lincoln, and the office was often held by a monk of Peterborough[5]. Similarly a monk of St Albans acted as *custos* of Sopwell[6] and a canon of Newhouse dwelt at Brodholme "to say daily mass for the sisters and to overlook their temporalities"[7] The joint rule of Cistercian houses by a Prior and Prioress seems to have died out in most cases by the end of the thirteenth century, but it was customary for some secular or regular cleric to be appointed in most of the small and poor houses of York and Lincoln to look after their business[8].

[1] *Linc. Epis. Reg. Memo. Dalderby*, f. 330 Roger de Dauentry, canon of Catesby, had been made master in 1297 *Reg Memo Sutton.* f 175

[2] *Reg Epis Johannis Peckham*, III, pp 850–1.

[3] *V C H. Northants* II, p. 98   [4] *V.C H. Derby*, II, p 43

[5] *Loc. cit.* see also *Linc. Epis. Reg. Institution Roll (Northampton)* of Sutton for the presentation of William de Stok, monk of Peterborough as Prior of St Michael's Stamford, by the Abbot, and the Bishop's ratification.

[6] Walsingham, *Gesta Abbatum* (Rolls Ser), II, p 519, and *V C H. Herts.* IV, p. 429 On their misdeeds see Archbishop Morton's famous letter in 1490 Wilkins, *Concilia*, III, p 632

[7] See *Cal. of Papal Letters*, VI, pp 159–160

[8] Mention of *custodes* occurs at the following houses, in addition to those mentioned in the text: Studley (1290), Goring (1309), *V.C H. Oxon* II, pp 78, 104, Markyate (1323), Harrold (late thirteenth century), *V C.H.Beds* I, pp 359, 388, Flamstead (1337), Rowney (1302, 1328), *V C H Herts* IV, pp 432, 434; Arden (1302, 1324), Marrick (1252), Nunburnholme (1314), Yedingham (1280), Basedale (1304), Hampole (1268, 1280, 1308), Handale (1318), Nunappleton (1306), Swine (1267, 1291, 1298), *V C H Yorks* III, pp 113, 117, 119, 127, 159, 163, 166, 171, 180; all in Lincoln or York, For mention of *custodes* in other dioceses, see Cookhill (1285), *Reg of Godfrey Giffard* (Worc. Hist Soc.), II, p 267; St Sepulchre's Canterbury, Davington, Usk, Whitehall (Ilchester), Minchin Barrow, Easebourne, St Bartholomew's Newcastle, King's Mead, Derby, below, pp. 231–5 *passim* The frequency with which *custodes* occur in houses in the diocese of Lincoln and York and

Usually the *custos* appointed was the vicar or rector of some neighbouring parish. Archbishop Romeyn, for instance, placed Sinningthwaite, Wilberfoss and Arthington under the guardianship of the rectors of Kirk Deighton, Sutton-on-Derwent and Kippax respectively, and he made the vicars of Thirkleby and Bossall successively masters of Moxby[1]. Bishop Dalderby of Lincoln appointed neighbouring rectors and vicars to be masters of Legbourne, Godstow, Rowney, Sewardsley, Fosse, Delapré, St Leonard's Grimsby, and Nuncoton[2].

Sometimes, on the other hand, canons or monks of religious houses in the vicinity were charged with looking after the affairs of nunneries. Swine was managed by Robert de Spalding, a canon of the Premonstratensian house of Croxton, and in 1289–90 Archbishop Romeyn wrote remonstrating with the Abbot of Croxton for recalling him, and begging that he might be allowed to continue at Swine, "cum idem vester canonicus proficuos labores ibidem impenderit ad relevacionem probabilem depressionis notorie dicte domus"; but the capable Robert was not allowed to return and in 1290 John Bustard, canon of St Robert's Knaresborough, was appointed in his place. John was not a success and the next year the Abbot removed him; in 1295 Robert of Spalding became master again and in 1298 the rector of Londesborough was appointed[3] At Catesby in 1293 the office of master was held by a certain Robert de Wardon, a canon of Canons Ashby, who had apparently left the nuns and gone back to his own house, to the great detriment of the nunnery, for Bishop Sutton wrote in 1293 to the Prior of Canons Ashby, bidding him send back the truant[4]. Similarly a canon of Wellow is found as warden of St Leonard's Grimsby in 1232 and in

their rarity in other dioceses would seem to support the theory of Gilbertine influence Of the cases quoted from other dioceses all are either *custodes* appointed as a deliberate policy by Archbishop Peckham, or *custodes* appointed to meet some special moral or financial crisis, not regular officials. King's Mead, Derby, seems to be the only nunnery outside the two dioceses of York and Lincoln (with the exception of those in direct dependence on a house of monks) which started its career under the joint government of a *custos* and a Prioress. *V C H. Derby*, II, p. 43

[1] *Reg of John le Romeyn* (Surtees Soc), I, pp xii, xiii, 86, 125, 157, 180.
[2] *Linc. Epis. Reg Memo Dalderby*, ff 23d, 37, 44, 60d, 79d, 118d, 328d, 366, 373, 378, 382, 388. (These comprise two appointments to Rowney, Godstow and Nuncoton, the dates are between 1301 and 1318)
[3] *Reg of John le Romeyn*, I, pp 203–4, 209, 211, 217.
[4] *Linc. Epis Reg Memo Sutton*, ff. 82d–83

1303[1], a monk of Whitby as guardian of Handale and Basedale in 1268[2], a canon of Newburgh at Arden in 1302[3] and a canon of Lincoln at Heynings in 1291 concerning the latter Bishop Sutton wrote to the nuns that since, "because of private business and various other impediments he is prevented from looking after your business as much as it requires, the vicar of Upton your neighbour is to look after your affairs in his absence," and in 1294 he was definitely replaced by the rector of Blankney[4]. It is clear from this letter that the masters of nunneries could be non-resident and this was no doubt usually the case when the office was held by the rector of a neighbouring parish Indeed sometimes the same man would be master of more than one nunnery; as in the case of the monk of Whitby mentioned above. It was probably rare after the beginning of the fourteenth century for a *custos* to reside at a nunnery, as the early Cistercian priors had done[5]

The appointment of *custodes* to manage the finances of nunneries was a favourite policy with Archbishop Peckham, doubtless because it facilitated the enforcement of strict enclosure upon the nuns. At Godstow there was already at the time a master, but Peckham also gave the custody of Davington to the vicar of Faversham in 1279, and that of Holy Sepulchre, Canterbury, to the vicar of Wickham in 1284, while at Usk in 1284 he ordered the nuns to have "some senior priest circumspect in temporal and in spiritual affairs to be, with the consent of the diocesan, master of all your goods, internal and external, temporal and spiritual"[6]. At other times a *custos* would be appointed to meet a particular difficulty when the financial state of a house had become specially weak About 1303, for

[1] *V C H Lincs.* II, p 179 But in 1318 Dalderby appointed the vicar of Little Coates, *loc cit* f 373 Originally St Leonard's Grimsby, had been placed under the protection of the canons of Wellow.

[2] *Reg. of Archbishop Giffard* (Surtees Soc.), p. 54.

[3] *V C H Yorks* III p 113

[4] *Linc Epis Reg Memo. Sutton,* ff 25, 92d

[5] Sometimes the chaplain of the house must have acted as an unofficial *custos* and sometimes he held the position by special mandate, e g in 1285 Bishop Giffard ordered the nuns of Cookhill that "for the better conduct of temporal business and for the increase of divine praise," Thomas their chaplain was to have full charge of their temporal affairs *Reg. of Godfrey Giffard* (Worc. Hist Soc), II, p. 267.

[6] *Reg Epis Johannis Peckham* (Rolls Ser), I, pp 72-3, II, pp 708-9, III, p 806.

instance, a monk of Peterborough was made for a season special warden of St Michael's, Stamford, "with full powers over the temporalities and of adjudicating and ordering all temporal matters both within and without the convent as he should think profitable"; the appointment is specially interesting because there was at the time a resident prior at St Michael's and the "spiritual disposition of all things concerning the house" is reserved to this prior and to the prioress[1]. A more serious crisis occurred at the Priory of White Hall, Ilchester, which was evidently in a disorderly condition at the beginning of the fourteenth century In 1323 Bishop John of Drokensford wrote to Henry of Birlaunde, rector of Stoke and to John de Herminal, announcing that the Prioress, Alice de Chilterne, was defamed of incontinence with a chaplain and had so mismanaged and turned to her own nefarious uses the revenues of the house that her sisters were compelled to beg their bread; she had however submitted herself to the Bishop, but as public affairs called him to London and as he did not wish to leave the nunnery unprovided for, he committed the custody to these two men, ordering them to administer the necessities of life to the Prioress and sisters, according to the means of the house, until his return[2]. Some ten years later Bishop Ralph of Shrewsbury similarly gave the custody of White Hall, Ilchester, to the rectors of Limington and St John's Ilchester[3]. The nunnery of Barrow, near Bristol, was also in a disorderly condition, in 1315 John of Drokensford wrote to the Prioress ordering her to leave the management of secular matters to a *custos* appointed by him, and the same day appointed William de Sutton, and in 1324-5, when he had been obliged to remove the Prioress Joanna Gurney, he committed the custody of the house to William, rector of Backwell, ordering him to do the best he could with the advice of the subprioress and one of the nuns[4] More often sheer financial distress, rather than moral disorder, was the reason for which a *custos* was appointed to a house. At St Sepulchre's

---

[1] *V.C H. Northants.* II, p 99
[2] *V.C.H. Somerset,* II, p 157 Text in Hugo, *Medieval Nunneries of the County of Somerset · Whitehall in Ilchester,* App VII, pp 78-9
[3] *Reg. of Ralph of Shrewsbury* (Somerset Rec Soc), p 177
[4] Hugo, *op. cit. Minchin Barrow Priory,* App II, pp. 81-3 With these cases compare the appointment of *custodes* to the worldly Prioress of Easebourne in 1441 See above, p. 77.

Canterbury, the rector of Whitstable was made *custos*, "by reason of the miserable want and extreme poverty of the said house" (1359) and for the same reason another secular cleric received the "supervision, custody or administration" of the same house in 1365[1]. In 1366 Thomas Hatfield, Bishop of Durham, pitying the miserable state of St Bartholomew's at Newcastle-on-Tyne, both as to spirituals and temporals, and dreading the immediate ruin thereof, unless some speedy remedy should be applied, committed it to the care of Hugh de Arnecliffe, priest in the church of St Nicholas in Newcastle-upon-Tyne, strictly enjoining the prioress and nuns to be obedient to him in every particular and trusting to his prudence to find relief for the poor servants of Christ here, in their poverty and distress[2].

Sometimes the nuns themselves begged for a *custos* to assist them, in terms which show that they found the management of their own finances too much for them. At Godstow in 1316 the King was obliged, at the request of the Abbess and nuns, to take the Abbey into his special protection "on account of its miserable state," and he appointed the Abbot of Eynsham and the Prior of Bicester as keepers, ordering them to pay the nuns a certain allowance and to apply the residue to the discharging of their debts[3]. Similarly in 1327 the Prioress and nuns of King's Mead, Derby, represented themselves as much reduced, and begged the King to take the house into his special protection, granting the custody of it to Robert of Alsop and Simon of Little Chester, until it should be relieved. Three months later Edward III granted it protection for three years and appointed Robert of Alsop and Simon of Little Chester custodians, who, after due provision for the sustenance of the prioress and nuns, were to apply the issues and rents to the discharge of the liabilities of the house and to the improvement of its condition[4]. Some interesting evidence in this connection was given during Alnwick's visitations of the diocese of Lincoln. When Clemence Medforde, the Prioress of Ankerwyke, was asked whether she had observed the Bishop's injunctions, she answered

that such injunctions were, and are, well observed as regards both her and her sisters in effect and according to their power, except the

[1] Dugdale, *Mon* IV, p. 413
[2] *Ib* IV, p. 485   [3] *V C H Oxon* II, p 73
[4] *V C H Derby*, II, pp 43–4 (from *Ancient Petitions*, No 11730); cf. *Cal Pat Rolls*, 1327–30, p. 139 See above, p 180.

injunction whereby she is bound to supply to her sisters sufficient raiment for their habits, and as touching the non-observance of that injunction she answers that she cannot observe it, because of the poverty and insufficiency of the resources of the house, which have been much lessened by reason of the want of a surveyor or steward (*yconomus*)   Wherefore she besought my lord's good-will and assistance that he would deign with charitable consideration to make provision of such steward or director .. And when these nuns, all and several, had been so examined and were gathered together again in the chapter house, the said Depyng (the Visitor) gave consideration to two grievances, wherein the priory and nuns alike suffer no small damage, the which, as he affirmed, were worthy of reform above the rest of those that stood most in need of reform, to wit the lack of raiment for the habit, of bedclothes and of a steward or seneschal, but in these matters, as he averred, he could not apply a remedy for the nonce without riper deliberation and consultation with my lord[1].

Similarly the old Prioress of St Michael's Stamford, when asking for the appointment of two nuns as treasuresses, complained "that she herself is impotent to rule temporalities, nor have they an industrious man to supervise these and to raise and receive (external payments)"; another nun said that "they have not a discreet layman to rule their temporalities," and a third also complained of the lack of a "receiver"[2]. At Gokewell, on the other hand, the Prioress said "that the rector of Flixborough is their steward (*yconomus*) and he looks after the temporalities and not she"; he was evidently a true friend to the nuns, for she said "that the house does not exceed £10 in rents and is greatly in debt to the rector of Flixborough"[3]. The terms of appointment of *custodes* often specify the inexpertness of the nuns, or their need for someone to supervise the management of their estates[4]. Perhaps the fullest set of instructions to a *custos* which have survived are those given by Archbishop Melton to Roger de Saxton, rector of Aberford, in making him *custos* of Kirklees in 1317:

Trusting in your industry, we by tenour of the present (letters) give you power during our pleasure to look after, guard and administer the temporal possessions of our beloved religious ladies, the Prioress and convent of Kirklees in our diocese, throughout their manors and buildings (*loca*) wherever these be, and to receive and hear the account of all servants and ministers serving in the same, and to make those

[1] *Linc Visit.* II, p. 7   [2] *Alnwick's Visit.* MS. f 39 d.
[3] *Linc Visit* II, p 117
[4] See e g *V C H. Yorks* III, pp. 113, 117, 119.

payments (*allocandum*) which by reason ought to be made, as well
as to remove all useless ministers and servants and to appoint in their
place others of greater utility, and to do all other things which shall
seem to you to be to the advantage of the place, firmly enjoining the
said prioress and convent, as well as the sisters and lay brothers of
the house, in virtue of holy obedience, that they permit you freely
to administer in all and each of the aforesaid matters[1]

It must have been of great assistance to the worried and incompetent nuns to have a reliable guardian thus to look after
their temporal affairs, and it is difficult to understand why the
practice of having a resident prior died out at the Cistercian
houses and at Benedictine houses (e.g. St Michael's, Stamford)
which had such an official in the thirteenth and early fourteenth
centuries. Even the appointment of neighbouring rectors as
custodes of nunneries in the York and Lincoln dioceses ceased,
apparently, to be common by the middle of the fourteenth
century[2]. It is a curious anomaly that this remedy should have
been applied less and less often during the very centuries when
the nunneries were becoming increasingly poor, and stood daily
in greater need of external assistance in the management of
their temporal affairs.

[1] *Yorks. Arch Journal*, XVI, p 362.
[2] It will be noticed that all the references to *custodes* given on p 230,
note 8, belong to the thirteenth and early fourteenth centuries, appointments at a later date are generally made to meet some regular crisis There
are no references to the Prior of St Michael's Stamford in the later account
rolls of that house, though one or two rolls belonging to the beginning of
the century mention him One of the few references to the regular appointment of a master in a Cistercian house after the first quarter of the fourteenth century is at Legbourne, where "later Lincoln regulations record the
appointment of several masters from 1294–1343 and in 1366 the same official
is apparently called an *yconomus* of Legbourne" (*V C H Lincs* II, p 154,
note 1). The will of Adam, vicar of Hallington, "custos sive magister domus
monialium de Legbourne," dated 1345, has been preserved. Gibbons, *Early
Lincoln Wills*, p 17 The *yconomus* of Gokewell in 1440 is a very late instance. (Compare Bokyngham's advice to the Abbess of Elstow in 1387,
above, p 228) Much the same function as that of the *custos*, was, however,
probably performed by the steward (*senescallus*), an official often mentioned
during the fourteenth and fifteenth centuries.

CHAPTER VI

EDUCATION

Abstinence the abbesse myn a. b c. me tauȝte

Piers Plowman

THE Benedictine ideal set study together with prayer and labour as the three bases of monastic life and in the short golden age of English monasticism women as well as men loved books and learning. The tale of the Anglo-Saxon nuns who corresponded with St Boniface has often been told Eadburg, Abbess of Thanet, wrote the Epistles of St Peter for him in letters of gold and sent books to him in the wilds of Germany. Bugga, Abbess of a Kentish house, exchanged books with him. The charming Lioba, educated by the nuns of Wimborne, sent him verses which she had composed in Latin, which "divine art" the nun Eadburg had taught her, and begged him to correct the rusticity of her style Afterwards she came into Germany to help him and became Abbess of Bischofsheim and her biographer tells how she was so bent on reading that she never laid aside her book except to pray or to strengthen her slight frame with food and sleep. From childhood upwards she had studied grammar and the other liberal arts, and hoped by perseverance to attain a perfect knowledge of religion, for she was well aware that the gifts of nature are doubled by study. She zealously read the books of the Old and New Testaments and committed their divine precepts to memory, but she further added to the rich store of her knowledge by reading the writings of the holy Fathers, the canonical decrees and the laws of the Church

So also an anonymous Anglo-Saxon nun of Heidenheim wrote the lives of Willibald and Wunebald[1].

The Anglo-Saxon period seems, however, to have been the only one during which English nuns were at all conspicuous for learning. There is indeed very scant material for writing their history between the Norman Conquest and the last years of the thirteenth century, when Bishops' Registers begin. It is

---

[1] See account in L Eckenstein, *Woman under Monasticism*, ch. IV.

never safe to argue from silence and some nuns may still have busied themselves over books, but two facts are significant: we have no trace of women occupying themselves with the copying and illumination of manuscripts and no nunnery produced a chronicle The chronicles are the most notable contribution of the monastic houses to learning from the eleventh to the fourteenth centuries; and some of the larger nunneries, such as Romsey, Lacock, and Shaftesbury, received many visitors and must have heard much that was worth recording, besides the humbler annals of their own houses. But they recorded nothing. The whole trend of medieval thought was against learned women and even in Benedictine nunneries, for which a period of study was enjoined by the rule, it was evidently considered altogether outside the scope of women to concern themselves with writing. While the monks composed chronicles, the nuns embroidered copes; and those who sought the gift of a manuscript from the monasteries, sought only the gift of needlework from the nunneries.

It is not, perhaps, surprising that the nuns should have written no chronicles and copied few, if any, books. But it is surprising that England should after the eighth century be able to show so little record of gifted individuals. Even if the rule of a professedly learned order were unlikely to prevail against the general trend of civilisation and to produce learned women, still it might have been expected that here and there a genius, or a woman of some talent for authorship, might have flourished in that favourable soil; or even that a whole house might have enjoyed for a brief halcyon period the zest for learning, when "alle was buxomnesse there and bokes to rede and to lerne" In Germany, at various periods of the middle ages, this did happen. The Abbey of Gandersheim in Saxony was renowned for learning in the tenth century and here lived and flourished the nun Roswitha, who not only wrote religious legends in Latin verse, but even composed seven dramas in the style of Terence, a poem on the Emperor Otto the Great and a history of her own nunnery. From the internal evidence of her works it has been thought that this nun was directly familiar with the works of Virgil, Lucan, Horace, Ovid, Terence and perhaps Plautus, Prudentius, Sedulius, Fortunatus, Martianus Capella and Boethius; but apart from this evidence of learning, her plays show her to have been a woman of originality and some genius; they are strange productions to have emanated from a tenth century convent[1] It was in Germany again, at Hohenburg in Alsace, that the Abbess Herrad in the twelfth century compiled and decorated with exquisite illuminations the great encyclopedia known as the *Hortus Deliciarum*. This book, one of the finest manuscripts which had survived from the middle ages and a most invaluable source of information for the manners and appearance of the people of Herrad's day, was destroyed in the German bombardment of Strasburg in 1870[2]. The same century saw the lives of the two great nun-mystics, St Hildegard of Bingen and St Elisabeth of Schönau, who saw visions, dreamed dreams and wrote them down[3]. In the next century the convent of Helfta in Saxony was the home of several literary nuns and mystics and was distinguished for culture; its nuns collected books, copied them, illuminated them, learned and wrote Latin, and three of them, the béguine Mechthild, the nun Saint Mechthild von Hackeborn and the nun Gertrud the Great, have won considerable fame by their mystic writings[4] Even in the decadent fifteenth century examples are not wanting of German nuns who were keenly interested in learning; and in the early sixteenth century Charitas Pirckheimer, nun of St Clare at Nuremberg and sister of the humanist Wilibald Pirckheimer, was in close relations with her brother and with many of his friends and full of enthusiasm for the new learning[5]

It is strange that in England there is no record of any house which can compare with Gandersheim, Hohenburg or Helfta; no record of any nun to compare with the learned women and great mystics who have been mentioned. The air of the English nunneries would seem to have been unfavourable to learning. The sole works ascribed to monastic authoresses are a *Life of St Catherine*, written in Norman-French by Clemence, a nun of Barking, in the late twelfth century[6], and *The Boke of St Albans*,

---

[1] L Eckenstein, *Woman under Monasticism*, ch IV, pp 160 ff
[2] *Ib* pp. 238 ff   [3] *Ib*. pp. 256 ff   [4] *Ib* pp 328 ff
[5] *Ib* pp 416, 419, 428, 458 ff.
[6] See *Romania* XIII (1884), pp 400–3
"Je ke la vie ai translatee
Par nun sui Clımence numee,
De Berekinge sui nunain,
Par s'amur pris ceste oevre en main "

a treatise on hawking, hunting and coat armour, printed in 1486, by one Dame Juliana Berners, whom a vague and unsubstantiated tradition declares to have been Prioress of Sopwell. Nor do nuns seem to have been more active in copying manuscripts. Several beautiful books, which have come down to our own day, can be traced to nunneries, but there is no evidence that they were written there and all other evidence makes it highly improbable that they were. It is true that in 1335 we find this entry among the issues of the Exchequer:

To Isabella de Lancaster, a nun of Amesbury, in money paid to her by the hands of John de Gynewell for payment of 100 marks, which the lord the King commanded to be paid her for a book of romance purchased from her for the King's use, which remains in the chamber of the lord the King, 66 l 13 s. 4 d[1],

but it is unlikely that the book thus purchased by the King from his noble kinswoman was her own work.

This period of the later ages was, indeed, unfavourable to learning among monks as well as among nuns. As the universities grew, so the monasteries declined in lustre; learning had no longer need to seek refuge behind cloister walls, and the most promising monks now went to the universities, instead of studying at home in their own houses. The standard of the chronicles rapidly declined and the best chronicler of the fourteenth century was not a monk like Matthew Paris, but a secular, a wanderer, a hanger-on of princes, Froissart. As the fifteenth century passed learning declined still further; and it is evident from the visitations of the time that the monks, whatever else they might be, were not scholars. We should expect the decline in learning to be more marked still among the nuns, considering how little they had possessed in preceding centuries; and the matter is worth some study, because it concerns not only the education of the nuns themselves, but the education which they were qualified to give to the children who were sent to school with them.

A word may first be said on the subject of nunnery libraries. Concerning these we have very little information; and, such as it is, it does not leave the impression that nunneries were rich in books. No catalogue of a nunnery library[2] has come down to

---

[1] Devon, *Issues of the Exchequer*, p 144
[2] There does exist a catalogue of Syon library, but unluckily it is that of the brothers' library and the catalogue of the sisters' library is missing,

us and such references to libraries as occur in inventories show
great poverty in this respect, the books being few and chiefly
service-books   An inventory of the small and poor convent of
Easebourne, taken in 1450, shows what was doubtless quite a
large library for a house of its size. It contained two missals,
two *portiforia* (breviaries), four antiphoners, one large *Legenda*,
eight psalters, one book of collects, one tropary, one French
Bible, two *ordinalia* in French, one book of the Gospels and one
martyrology[1]. The inventories of Henry VIII's commissioners
give very little information as to books and seem to have found
few that were of any value. The books found at Sheppey are
thus described: "ij bokes with ij sylver clapses the pece, and vj
bokes with one sylver clasp a pec, l bokes good and bad" (in
the church), "vij bokes, whereof one goodly mase boke of parche-
ment and dyvers other good bokes" (in the vestry), and "an
olde presse full of old boks of no valew" (in a chapel in the
churchyard) and "a boke of Saynts lyfes" (in the parlour)[2]. At
Kilburn were found "two books of *Legenda Aurea*, one in print,
the other written, both English, 4*d.*"; the one in print must have
been Caxton's edition, thus valued, together with a manuscript,
at something like 6*s.* 8*d.* in present money for the pair Also
"two mass books, one old written, the other in print, 20*d.*, four
processions in parchment (3*s.*) and paper (10*d.*), two Legends
in parchment and paper, 8*d* , and two chests, with divers books
pertaining to the church, of no value"[3] It will be noted that
the books are almost always connected with the church services.
It is perhaps significant that in only one list of the inmates
of a house is a nun specifically described as librarian[4].

it was probably a good one since we have notice of several books written for
them See M Bateson, *Cat of the Lib. of Syon Mon.* (1898) Only three
continental library catalogues survive, of which two are printed and acces-
sible; one is the library of the Dominican nuns of Nuremberg, made
between 1456–69 and containing 350 books, the other belonged to the
Franciscan tertiaries of Delft in the second half of the fifteenth century
and contained 109 books, the third comes from the women's cloister at
Wonnenstein in 1498 See M. Deanesly, *The Lollard Bible*, pp. 110–5
    [1] *Sussex Arch. Coll* IX, p 12
    [2] Mackenzie, Walcott, *Inventories of...the Ben. Priory...of Shepey for
Nuns*, pp 21, 23, 28
    [3] Dugdale, *Mon.* III, p. 424.
    [4] At a visitation of St Mary's Winchester by Dr Hede in 1501, "Elia
Pitte, librarian, was also well satisfied with that which was in her charge."
V C H. Hants II, p 124.

Something may be gleaned also from the legacies of books left to nuns in medieval wills. These again are nearly always psalters or service books of one kind or another; and indeed the average layman was more likely to possess these than other books, for all alike attended the services of the church Thus Sir Robert de Roos in 1392 leaves his daughter, a nun, "a little psalter, that was her mother's"[1]; Sir William de Thorp in 1391 leaves his sister-in-law, a nun of Greenfield, a psalter[2]; William Stow of Ripon in 1430 leaves the Prioress of Nunmonkton a small psalter[3], William Overton of Helmsley in 1481 leaves his niece Elena, a nun of Arden, "one great Primer with a cover of red damask"[4], and so on. There may be some significance in the fact that John Burn, chaplain at York Cathedral, leaves the Prioress and Convent of Nunmonkton "an English book of Pater Noster"[5]. It strikes a strange and pleasant note when Thomas Reymound in 1418 leaves the Prioress and Convent of Polsloe 20s. and the *Liber Gestorum Karoli, Regis Francie*[6], and when Eleanor Roos of York in 1438 leaves Dame Joan Courtenay "unum librum vocatum Mauldebuke," whatever that mysterious tome may have contained[7].

Some light is also thrown backward upon their possessors by isolated books which have come down to our own day and are known to have belonged to nuns These come mostly, as might be expected, from the great abbeys of the south, where the nuns were rich and of good birth, from Syon and Barking, Amesbury, Wilton and Shaftesbury, St Mary's Winchester, and Wherwell[8] Sometimes the MS. records the name of the nun owner. Wright and Halliwell quote from a Latin breviary, in

---

[1] *Test Ebor* I, p 179   [2] Sharpe, *Cal of Wills*, II, p 327
[3] *Test Ebor* II, p 13   [4] *Ib.* III, p. 262.
[5] *Ib* III, p 199 See an interesting list of books left by Peter, vicar of Swine, to Swine Priory some time after 1380. *King's Descrip Cat MS* 18
[6] *Reg. Stafford of Exeter*, p 419   [7] *Test. Ebor* II, p 66
[8] For Barking books (including a book of English religious treatises) see M Deanesly, *The Lollard Bible*, pp 337-9 Besides the books mentioned in the text there are fine psalters written for nuns at St Mary's Winchester, Amesbury and Wilton in the libraries of Trinity College, Cambridge, All Souls College, Oxford, and the Royal College of Physicians respectively. There is an interesting book in the Fitzwilliam Museum, Cambridge (*McClean MS.* 123), which belonged to Nuneaton; it contains (1) the metrical Bestiary of William the Norman, (2) the *Chasteau d'Amours* of Robert Grosseteste, (3) exposition of the Paternoster, (4) the Gospel of Nicodemus, (5) Apocalypse with pictures, (6) *Poema Morale*, etc.

which is an inscription to the effect that it belonged to Alice Champnys, nun of Shaftesbury, who bought it for the sum of 10s. from Sir Richard Marshall, rector of the parish church of St Rumbold of Shaftesbury. There follows this prayer for the use of the nun

Trium puerorum cantemus himnum quem cantabant in camino ignis benedicentes dominum. O swete Jhesu, the sonne of God, the endles swetnesse of hevyn and of erthe and of all the worlde, be in my herte, in my mynde, in my wytt, in my wylle, now and ever more, Amen Jhesu mercy, Jhesu gramercy, Jhesu for thy mercy, Jhesu as I trust to thy mercy, Jhesu as thow art fulle of mercy, Jhesu have mercy on me and alle mankynde redemyd with thy precyouse blode. Jhesu, Amen[1].

A manuscript of Capgrave's *Life of St Katharine of Alexandria*, which belonged to Katherine Babyngton, subprioress of Campsey in Suffolk, has a very different inscription.

Iste liber est ex dono Kateryne Babyngton quondam subpriorisse de Campseye et si quis illum alienauerit sine licencia vna cum consensu dictarum [sanctimonialium] conuentus, malediccionem dei omnipotentis incurrat et anathema sit[2]

Sometimes the owner of a manuscript is known to us from other sources There is a splendid psalter, now in St John's College, Cambridge, which belonged to the saintly Euphemia, Abbess of Wherwell from 1226 to 1257, whose good deeds were celebrated in the chartulary of the house[3]. In the Hunterian Library at Glasgow there is a copy of the first English translation of Thomas à Kempis's *Imitatio Christi*, which belonged to Elizabeth Gibbs, Abbess of Syon from 1497 to 1518; it is inscribed

O vos omnes sorores et ffratres presentes et futuri, orate queso pro venerabili matre nostra Elizabeth Gibbis, huius almi Monasterii Abbessa [sic], necnon pro deuoto ac religioso viro Dompno Wilhelmo Darker, in artibus Magistro de domo Bethleem prope sheen ordinis Cartuciensis, qui pro eadem domina Abbessa hunc librum conscripsit,

the date 1502 is given[4].

---

[1] Wright and Halliwell, *Reliquiae Antiquae*, II, p 117.
[2] Capgrave, *Life of St Katharine of Alexandria*, ed Horstmann (E E.T.S. 1893), Introd p. xxix.
[3] *St John's Coll. MS.* 68 Other psalters from the aristocratic house of Wherwell are *MS add* 27866 at the British Museum and *MS. McClean* 45 at the Fitzwilliam Museum, Cambridge
[4] *MS.* 136 (T. 6. 18) See J. Young and P Henderson Aitkin, *Cat of MSS in the Lib of the Hunterian Museum in the Univ of Glasgow* (1908). p. 124. In the introduction the book is conjectured to have belonged to the

The books known to have been in the possession of nuns throw, as will be seen, but a dim light upon the educational attainments of their owners. More specific evidence must be sought in bishops' registers, and in such references to the state of learning in nunneries as occur in the works of contemporary writers. It is clear that nuns were expected to be "literate"; bishops sending new inmates to convents occasionally assure their prospective heads that the girls are able to undertake the duties of their new state[1]. What to be sufficiently lettered meant, from the convent point of view, appears in injunctions sent to the Premonstratensian house of Irford, forbidding the reception of any nun "save after such fashion as they are received at Irford and Brodholme, to wit that they be able to read and to sing, as is contained in the statute of the order"[2]; and again in injunctions sent by Bishop Gray to Elstow about 1432·

We enjoin and charge you the abbess and who so shall succeed you... that henceforward you admit no one to be a nun of the said monastery .. unless she be taught in song and reading and the other things requisite herein, or probably may be easily instructed within a short time[3].

Further light is thrown on the question by an episode in the life of Thomas de la Mare, Abbot of St Albans from 1349 to 1396. At that time the subordinate nunnery of St Mary de Pré consisted of two grades of inmates, nuns and sisters, who were never on good terms. The Abbot accordingly transformed the sisters into nuns and ordained that no more sisters should be received, but only "literate nuns." But hitherto the nuns also had been illiterate; "they said no service, but in the place of the Hours they said certain Lord's Prayers and Angelic Salutations." The Abbot therefore ordered that they should be

Carthusian monastery at Sheen, where it obviously was written; but the reference to "sorores et fratres" and the name of Elizabeth Gibbs (see Blunt, *Myroure of Oure Ladye* (E.E T S), p xxiii), show clearly that it belonged to Syon

[1] So John of Pontoise sends Juliana de Spina to Romsey on the occasion of his consecration (1282), with the recommendation "Ejusdem Juliane competenter ad hujusmodi officii debitum litterate laudabile propositum speciali gracia prosequentes, etc " *Reg. J. de Pontissara* (Cant and York Soc.), i, p 240 Cp *ib* p. 252

[2] *Collectanea Anglo-Praemonstratensia*, ii, p 267.

[3] *Linc Visit* i, p. 53.

taught the service and that in future they should observe the canonical hours, saying them without chanting, but singing the offices for the dead at certain times. Since they had apparently no books, from which to read the services, he gave them six or seven ordinals, belonging to the Abbey of St Albans, which caused not a little annoyance among the monks. In order that nuns should not be rashly and easily admitted, he ordered that henceforth all who entered the house were to profess the rule of St Benedict in writing[1].

The requirements seem to be that the nun should be able to take part in the daily offices in the quire, for which reading and singing were essential. It was not, it should be noted, essential to write, though Abbot Thomas de la Mare required the nuns of St Mary de Pré to profess the rule in writing and about 1330 the nuns of Sopwell (another dependency of St Albans) were enjoined by the commissary of a previous Abbot to give their votes for a new Prioress in writing[2]. Nevertheless, strange as this may appear to many who are wont to credit the nuns with teaching reading, writing, arithmetic and a number of other accomplishments to their pupils, it is probable that some of the nuns of the fourteenth and fifteenth centuries were unable to write. The form of profession of three novices at Rusper in 1484 has survived and ends with the note "Et quelibet earum fecit tale signum crucis manu sua propria ✠"[3] which might possibly imply that these nuns could not write their names. It is significant that the official business of convents, their annual accounts and any certificates which they might have to draw up, were done by professional clerks, or sometimes by their chaplains. Payment to the clerk who made the account occurs regularly in their account rolls; and the Visitations of Bishop Alnwick, to which reference will be made below, show that they

---

[1] *Gesta Abbatum* (Rolls Ser 1867), ii, pp. 410–2 But professions were often written by others, and the postulant only put his or her cross So also with the vote.

[2] *Ib.* ii, p. 213 This was a not uncommon method of voting It is clear, too, from prohibitions of letter-writing in various injunctions that nuns could sometimes write

[3] *Sussex Archaeol Coll.* v, p 256. Compare the editor's note on the education of Christina von Stommeln. "Simul cum psalterio videtur tantum didicisse linguae latinae, quantum satis erat non solum illi legendo, sed etiam epistolis ad se Latine scriptis pro parte intelligendis, ac vicissim dictandis: nam scribendi ignoram fuisse habeo" *Acta SS Junii*, t iv, p 279

were often completely at a loss, when writing had to be done and there was no clerk to do it

Again it would seem clear that the nun who was fully qualified to "bear the burden of the choir" ought to be able to understand what she read, as well as to read it, and this raises at once the study of Latin in nunneries. Here again the nuns do not emerge very well from inquiry. Some there were no doubt who knew a little Latin, even in the fourteenth, fifteenth and sixteenth centuries; but the more the inquirer studies contemporary records, the more he is driven to conclude that the majority of nuns during this period knew no Latin; they must have sung the offices by rote and though they may have understood, it is to be feared that the majority of them could not construe even a *Pater Noster*, an *Ave* or a *Credo*. Let us take the evidence for the different centuries in turn. The language of visitation injunctions affords some clue to the knowledge of the nuns. It must be remembered that throughout the whole period Latin was always the learned and ecclesiastical language; and the communications addressed by a bishop to the monastic houses of his district, notices of visitation, mandates and injunctions would normally be in Latin; and when he was addressing monks they were in fact almost always in this tongue. After Latin the language next in estimation was French. This had been the universal language of the upper class and up till the middle of the fourteenth century it was still *par excellence* the courtly tongue. But it was rapidly ceasing to be a language in general use and the turning-point is marked by a statute of 1362, which ordains that henceforth all pleas in the law courts shall be conducted in English, since the French language "is too unknown in the said realm." At the close of the century even the upper classes were ceasing to speak French and the English ambassadors to France in 1404 had to beseech the Grand Council of France to answer them in Latin, French being "like Hebrew" to them[1]. In the fifteenth century French was a mere educational adornment, which could be acquired by those who could get teachers.

The linguistic learning of English nuns at different periods was similar to that of the gentry outside the convent   It was not

[1] Jusserand, *A Literary History of the English People*, i, pp. 239–40.

possible after the beginning of the fourteenth century (perhaps even during the last half of the thirteenth century) to assume in them that acquaintance with Latin, the learned and ecclesiastical tongue, which was generally assumed in their brothers the monks. Their learning was similar to that of contemporary laymen of their class, rather than of contemporary monks; and it went through exactly the same phases as did the coronation oath. About 1311 the King's oath occurs in Latin among the State documents, with the note appended that "if the King were illiterate" he was to swear in French, as Edward II did in 1307, but in 1399 when Henry IV claimed the throne, he claimed it in English, "In the name of the Fadir, Son and Holy Gost, I Henry of Lancastre, chalenge þis Rewme of Yngland"[1] Similarly towards the close of the thirteenth century the English bishops begin to write to their nuns in French, because they are no longer "literate," in the sense of understanding Latin. Throughout this century the nuns are able to speak the courtly tongue; they use it for their petitions; and Chaucer's Prioress boasts it among her accomplishments at the close of the century,

> And Frensh she spak ful faire and fetisly
> After the scole of Stratford atte Bowe,
> For French of Paris was to her unknowe.

But French, like Latin, is beginning to die away. It hardly ever occurs in petitions after the end of the century; and in the fifteenth and sixteenth centuries the Bishops almost invariably send their injunctions to the nuns in English. The majority of nuns during these two centuries would seem to have understood neither French nor Latin[2].

The evidence of the bishops' registers is worth considering in more detail. The bishops were genuinely anxious that the reforms set forth in their injunctions should be carried out by the nuns, and they were therefore at considerable pains to send the injunctions in language which the nuns could understand. There are few surviving injunctions belonging to the thirteenth century, and their evidence is missed Archbishop Walter Giffard

---

[1] Jusserand, *op. cit.* I, p. 236.

[2] It is interesting to find the Master-General of the Dominicans in 1431 giving Jane Fisher, a nun of Dartford, leave to have a *master* to instruct her in grammar and the Latin tongue. Jarrett, *The English Dominicans*, p. 11

in 1268[1] and Archbishop Newark in 1298[2] write to the nuns of Swine in Latin, a language which they seem to have employed habitually when writing to nunneries. Archbishop Peckham sometimes writes to the Godstow nuns in Latin (1279) and sometimes in French (1284)[3]; it is to be noted that his French letter is of a more familiar type. Bishop Cantilupe of Hereford writes about 1277 to the nuns of Lymbrook in Latin, but his closing words raise considerable doubt as to whether an understanding of Latin can be generally assumed in nunneries at this period, for he says "you are to cause this our letter to be expounded to you several times in the year by your penancers, in the French or English tongue, whichever you know best"[4].

The evidence for the next century is even less ambiguous, for nearly all injunctions are in French and sometimes it is specifically mentioned that the nuns do not understand Latin. Bishop Norbury in 1331 translates his injunctions to Fairwell into French[5], because the nuns do not understand the original in Latin, and Bishop Robert de Stretton, writing to the same house in 1367, orders his decree to be "read and explained in the vulgar tongue by some literate ecclesiastical person on the day after its receipt"[6]. Bishop Stapeldon's interesting injunctions to Polsloe and Canonsleigh in 1319 are in French, but he seems to assume some knowledge of Latin in the nuns, for he orders that if it be necessary to break silence in places where silence is ordained, speech should be held in Latin, though not in grammatically constructed sentences, but in isolated words[7]. In 1311 Bishop Woodlock sending a set of Latin injunctions to the great Abbey of Romsey, announces that he has caused them to be translated into French, that the nuns may more

---

[1] *Reg. Walter Giffard* (Surtees Soc), pp 147–8
[2] *Reg John le Romeyn*, etc (Surtees Soc), II, pp 222–4.
[3] *Reg Epis. J. Peckham* (Rolls Ser), III, pp. 845–52
[4] *Reg. Thome de Cantilupo* (Cant. and York Soc. and Cantilupe Soc), p. 202
[5] *Reg R de Norbury* (Wm Salt Archaeol Soc Coll I), p 257
[6] *Reg R de Stretton* (ib. New Series, VIII), p 119
[7] *Reg. W. de Stapeldon*, p 316. See below, p 286 In the same year Archbishop Melton writes to the nuns of Sinningthwaite that in all writings under the common seal a faithful clerk is to be employed and the deed is to be sealed in the presence of the whole convent, the clerk reading the deed plainly in the mother tongue and explaining it. *V C H Yorks.* III, p 177.

easily understand them[1]; but Wykeham writes to them in Latin in 1387[2]. In the Lincoln diocese during this century the custom of the bishops varies Gynewell writes to Heynings and to Godstow in French, but to Elstow in Latin[3]; Bokyngham writes to both Heynings and Elstow in Latin, but in ordering the nuns of Elstow in 1387 to keep silence at due times, he adds "Et vulgare gallicum addiscentes inter se eo utantur colloquentes"[4], a significant contrast to Stapeldon's recommendation of Latin in similar circumstances some seventy years earlier

When we pass from the fourteenth to the fifteenth century it is clear that even French was becoming an unknown tongue to the nuns; nearly all injunctions are from this time forward written in English. At Redlingfield in 1427, the seven nuns and two novices were assembled in the chapter house, where the deputy visitor read his commission, first in Latin and then in the vulgar tongue, in order that the nuns might better understand it[5]. It is true that Bishops Flemyng and Gray send Latin injunctions to Elstow and Delapré Abbeys in 1422 and 1433 respectively, but Flemyng orders "that the premises, all and sundry, be published and read openly and in the vulgar mother tongue eight times a year"[6], and Gray writes that his injunctions are to be translated into the mother tongue and fastened in some conspicuous place[7]. The best evidence of all for the state of learning in nunneries during the first half of the fifteenth century is to be found in the invaluable records of Alnwick's visitations of the Lincoln diocese. Now it should be noted that when Alnwick visited houses of monks or canons, the sermon, which was generally preached on such occasions by one of the learned clerics who accompanied him, was invariably preached in Latin Moreover, all injunctions sent to male houses after visitation were sent in Latin also. The assumption still was that these monasteries were homes of learning and acquainted with the language of learning. With the nunneries it was otherwise. The sermons were always preached "in the vulgar tongue" and

---

[1] Liveing, *Records of Romsey Abbey*, p. 105   [2] *New Coll.* MS. f 84
[3] *Linc. Epis. Reg Memo. Gynewell*, ff 34, 139d, 100d
[4] *Ib. Reg. Memo Bokyngham*, ff 343 (Elstow), 397 (Heynings).
[5] *V.C.H. Suffolk*, II, p. 83.   [6] *Linc Visit* I, p 52
[7] *Ib* I, p 45 At Kyme and Wellow, houses of canons, however, the injunctions are also to be expounded in the mother tongue.

the injunctions were always sent in English. It was not even pretended that the nuns would understand Latin Moreover it is quite plain that when the preliminary notices of visitation had been sent in Latin, they had been very imperfectly understood; and that when it was necessary for a Prioress herself to draw up a certificate in writing, she was often quite unable to do so.

A few extracts from Alnwick's records will illustrate the complete ignorance of Latin and general illiteracy in these houses. At Ankerwyke (1441) it is noted:

And then when request had been made of the prioress by the reverend father for the certificate of his mandate conveyed to the said prioress for such visitation, the same prioress, instead of the certificate delivered the original mandate itself to the said reverend father, affirming that she did not understand the mandate itself, nor had she any man of skill or other lettered person to instruct what she should do in this behalf[1].

At Markyate (1442), when the same certificate was asked for, the Prioress

said that she had not a clerk who was equipped for writing such a certificate, on the which head she submitted herself to my lord's favour and then showed my lord in lieu of a certificate the original mandate itself and the names of the nuns who had been summoned[2]

Similarly the Prioress of Fosse showed the original mandate in place of the certificate, and the Prioresses of St Michael's Stamford and Rothwell had failed to draw up the certificate[3]. The Prioress of Gokewell (1440) was said to be "exceedingly simple," all the temporalities of the house being ruled by a steward; she also declared that "she knows not how to compose a formal certificate, in that she has no lettered persons of her counsel who are skilled in this case," and she had been unable to find the document reciting the confirmation of her election[4]. The poor convent of Langley seems to have been reduced to complete confusion by the episcopal mandate. The Prioress

says that she received my lord's mandate on the feast of St Denis last Interrogated whether she has a certificate touching execution thereof, she says no, because she did not understand it, nor did her chaplain also, to whom she showed it, concerning the which she surrendered herself to my lord's favour. Wherefore, when the original

---

[1] *Linc Visit* II, p 1.   [2] *Alnwick's Visit* MS f 6.
[3] *Linc Visit* II, p. 91; *Alnwick's Visit* MS ff 83, 38.
[4] *Linc. Visit* II, p. 117

mandate had been delivered to my lord and read through in the vulgar tongue, my lord asked her if she had executed it. She says yes, as regards the summons of herself and her sisters.. .Interrogated if she has the foundation charter of the house and who is the founder, she says that Sir William Pantolfe founded the house, but because they are unversed in letters they cannot understand the writings[1].

It is unnecessary to multiply the evidence of visitation records for the rest of the fifteenth and for the early sixteenth century: the general effect is to show us nuns who know only the English language[2]. Let us turn to the interesting corroborative evidence provided by those who were at pains to make translations for their use. It must be admitted that this evidence only confirms the suggestion made above that the nuns often did not understand the very services which they sang, let alone the Latin version of their rule, or the Latin charters by which they held their lands That they often sang the services uncomprehendingly like parrots is actually stated by Sir David Lyndesay, the Scottish poet, in his *Dialog concerning the Monarché* (1553) He apologises for writing in his native tongue, unlike those clerks, who wish to prohibit the people from reading even the scriptures for themselves, and adds

> Tharefore I thynk one gret dirisioun
> To heir thir Nunnis & Systeris nycht and day
> Syngand and sayand psalmes and orisoun,
> Nocht vnderstandyng quhat thay syng nor say,
> Bot lyke one stirlyng or ane Papingay
> Quhilk leirnit ar to speik be lang usage
> Thame I compair to byrdis in ane cage[3]

Several translations of the rule of St Benet were made for the special use of nuns, who knew no Latin. A northern metrical version of the early fifteenth century explains

> Monkes and als all leryd men
> In Latin may it lyghtly ken,
> And wytt tharby how they sall wyrk
> To sarue god and haly kyrk.

[1] *Linc Visit* II, p. 174

[2] Archbishop Lee's visitations of the York diocese on the eve of the Dissolution (1534–5) are typical The injunctions sent to the nunneries of Sinningthwaite, Nunappleton and Esholt (*Yorks. Archaeol Journ.* XVI, pp. 440, 443, 451) are in English, but those sent to the houses of monks and canons are all in Latin

[3] Sir David Lyndesay's *Poems*, ed. Small, Hall and Murray (E E T S 2nd ed 1883), p 21.

Bott tyll women to mak it couth,
That lens no latyn in thar youth,
In inglis is it ordand here,
So that thay may it lyghtly lere[1].

About a century later, in 1517, Richard Fox, the Bishop of
Winchester, published for the benefit of the nuns of his diocese
another English translation of the Rule of St Benedict. In the
preface he rehearses how nuns are professed under the Rule and
are bound to read, learn and understand it·

and also after their profession they should not onely in them selfe
kepe observe execute and practise the said rule but also teche other
and heir sisters the same, and so moche that for the same intent they
daily rede and cause to be rede some parte of the sayd rule by one of
the sayd sisters amonges them selfe as well in their Chapiter House
after the redinge of the Martyrologe as some tyme in their Fraitur
in tyme of refections and collacions, at the which reding is always don
in the latin tonge, whereof they have no knowledge nor understandinge
but be utterly ignorant of the same, whereby they do not only lose
their tyme but also renne into the evident danger and perill of the
perdicion of their soules.

He adds that in order to save the souls of his nuns, and in particular to ensure that novices understand the Rule before profession,

so that none of them shall nowe afterward probably say that she
wyste not what she professed, as we knowe by experience that some
of them have sayd in tyme passed, for these causes at thinstant
requeste of our ryght dere and well-beloved daughters in oure Lorde
Jhesu, the Abbasses of the Monasteries of Rumsay, Wharwel, Seynt
Maries within the Citie of Winchester and the Prioresses of Wintnay,
our right religious diocesans, we have translated the sayd rule unto
our moders tonge, comune, playne rounde Englishe, easy and redy
to be understande by the sayde devoute religiouse women[2].

The inconvenience of not being able to read the foundation
charter and other legal documents of the house, as confessed by
the Prioress of Langley at Alnwick's visitation, was very great;
and about 1460 Alice Henley, the Abbess of Godstow, caused

---

[1] *Three Middle Eng Versions of the Rule of St Benet* (E E T S 1902),
p 48
On the other hand the Caxton abstract at the end of the century is
translated "for men and wymmen, of the habyte therof, the whiche vnder-
stande lytyll laten or none" *Ib* p. 119
[2] The preface is quoted in *The Register of Richard Fox while Bishop of
Bath and Wells, with a Life of Bishop Fox*, ed. E C Batten (1889), pp 102–4

a translation to be made of the Latin register, in which were copied all the charters of her abbey. The translator's preface to the work is interesting:

The wyseman tawht hys chyld gladly to rede bokys and hem well vndurstonde for, in defaute of vndyrstondyng, is ofttymes caused neclygence, hurte, harme and hynderaunce, as experyence prevyth in many a place. And for as muche as women of relygyone in redynge bokys of latyn, byn excusyd of grete vndurstandyng, where it is not her modyr tonge; Therfore, how be hyt that they wolde rede her bokys of remembraunce of her munymentys wryte in latyn, for defaute of undurstondyng they toke ofte tymes grete hurt and hyndraunce, and, what for defaute of trewe lernyd men that all tymes be not redy hem to teche and counsayl, and feere also and drede to shewe her euydence opynly (that oftyntyme hath causyd repentaunce), Hyt wer ryht necessary, as hyt semyth to the undyrstondyng of suche relygyous women, that they myght haue, out of her latyn bokys, sum wrytynge in her modyr tonge, wher-by they might haue bettyr knowlyge of her munymentys and more clerely yeue infor-macyon to her serauntys, rent gedurarys, and receyuowrs, in the absent of her lernyd councell. Wher-fore, a poore brodur and wel-wyller...to the goode Abbas of Godstowe, Dame Alice henley, and to all her couent, the whych byn for the more party in Englyssh bokys well y-lernyd, hertyly desyryng the worship, profyt and welfare of that deuoute place, that, for lak of vndurstondyng her munymentys sholde in no damage of her lyflod huraftur fallyn, In the worship of our lady and seynt John Baptist patron of thys seyd monastery, the sentence for the more partyre of her munymentys conteynd in the boke of her regystr in latyn, aftyr the same forme and ordyr of the seyd boke, hath purposyd with goddys grace to make, aftur hys conceyt, fro latyn into Englyssh, sentencyosly, as foloweth thys symple translacion[1].

It will be noticed that the benevolent translator of this Godstow register says that the nuns are for the most part well learned in English books. The same impression is given by the translations which were made for the nuns of Syon. The most famous of these is the *Myroure of Oure Ladye*, written for the nuns by Thomas Gascoigne (1403–58) and first printed in 1530. This book contains a devotional treatise on divine service, with a translation and explanation of the "Hours" and "Masses" of our Lady, as they were used at Syon. The author explains his purpose thus:

Forasmoche as many of you, though ye can synge and rede, yet ye can not se what the meanynge therof ys; therefore to the onely worshyp

---

[1] *Eng. Reg. of Godstow Nunnery* (E.E.T.S.), pp. 25–6

and praysyng of oure lorde Jesu chryste and of hys moste mercyfull
mother oure lady and to the gostly comforte and profyte of youre
soules, I haue drawen youre legende and all youre seruyce in to Eng-
lyshe, that ye shulde se by the vnderstondyng therof, how worthy and
holy praysynge of oure gloryous Lady is contente them & the more
deuoutely and knowyngly synge yt & rede yt and say yt to her worshyp

He adds that he has explained the various parts of the divine
service for "symple soulles to vnderstonde," but that he has
translated few psalms, "for ye may haue them of Rycharde
hampoules drawynge, and out of Englysshe bibles, if ye haue
lysence therto"[1].

From a passage in the *Myroure* it appears that the sisters
were accustomed to spend some of their time in reading and
advice is given to them as to the sort of books to read and the
way in which to profit by them; from this it is quite clear that
secular learning had no place among them, their reading being
confined to works of ghostly edification[2]. It was their ignorance
of Latin which caused the insertion of English rubrics in the
Latin *Processionale* of the house and which inspired Richard
Whytford, one of the brothers, to translate the splendid *Marti-
logium*, which is now in the British Museum, "for the edificacyon
of certayn religyous persones vnlerned that dayly dyd rede the
same martiloge in Latyn, not understandynge what they redde";
his translation was printed by Wynkyn de Worde in 1526[3].
Gascoigne's 'mention of English bibles is interesting. Miss
Deanesly, in her study of *The Lollard Bible*, has shown that "it
is likely that English nuns were the most numerous orthodox
users of English bibles between 1408 and 1526," but that the
evidence for this use is slight and drawn almost entirely from
Syon and Barking, two large and important houses[4]. Her conclusion is that

it was not the case that the best instructed nuns used Latin Bibles
and the most ignorant English ones. but that the best instructed

---

[1] *The Myroure of Oure Ladye* (E E T S), pp 2–3   [2] *Ib* pp 63 ff
[3] *Ib*. pp xliv–xlvi, Eckenstein, *op cit* p 395 Wynkyn de Worde's
edition was reprinted for the Henry Bradshaw Society in 1893
[4] Deanesly, *The Lollard Bible*, pp 320, 336–7 It may be noted as of
some interest that when in 1528 a wealthy London merchant was imprisoned for distributing Tyndale's books and for similar practices, he
pleaded that the abbess of Denney, Elizabeth Throgmorton, had wished
to borrow Tyndale's *Enchiridion* and that he had lent it to her. Dugdale,
Mon vi, p 1549

nuns were allowed to use English translations, perhaps by themselves, perhaps to help in the understanding of the Vulgate, while the smaller nunneries and least instructed nuns almost certainly did not have them at all

This goes to confirm the conclusion that even in the greatest houses, where the nuns were drawn from the highest social classes and might be supposed to be best educated, the knowledge of Latin was dying out.

Other occupations besides reading filled the working hours of the nuns and of these spinning and needlework were the most important. Most women in the middle ages possessed the art of spinning and Aubrey's Old Jacques may have remembered aright how "he saw from his house the nuns of the priory (Kington St Michael) come forth into the nymph-hay with their rocks and wheels to spin," though his memory misled him sorely as to the number of these ladies. Sometimes a visitation report gives us a glimpse of the nuns at work: at Easebourne in 1441 the nuns say that the Prioress "compels her sisters to work continually like hired workwomen and they receive nothing whatever for their own use from their work, but the prioress takes the whole profit"[1] and at Catesby in the following year a young nun complains that the Prioress "setts her to make beds, to sewing and spinning and other tasks"[2] Nevertheless it does not seem that the nuns were in the habit of spinning the wool and flax for their own and their servants' clothes and account rolls often contain payments made to hired spinsters, as well as to fullers and weavers.

It is more probable that they busied themselves with needlework and embroidery, which were the usual occupations of ladies of gentle birth[3]. Very few traces have unfortunately survived of the work of English nuns. In earlier centuries English needlework had been famous and the nuns had been pre-eminent in the making of richly embroidered vestments. In the thirteenth

---

[1] *Sussex Arch. Coll* IX, p 7

[2] *Linc Visit* II, p 49 At Bondeville in 1251 Archbishop Eudes Rigaud has to forbid the nuns to sell their thread and their spindles to raise money, "quod moniales non vendant nec distrahant filum *et lor fusees*," *Reg Visit. Archiepiscopi Roth* ed Bonnin (1852), p 111.

[3] "Nuns with their needles wrote histories also," as Fuller prettily says, "that of Christ his passion for their altar clothes, as other Scripture (and moe legend) Stories to adorn their houses." Fuller, *Church Hist* (ed 1837), II, p. 190

century, too, English embroidery far surpassed that made in
other countries and it has been conjectured that "the most
famous embroidered vestments now preserved in various places
in Italy are the handiwork of English embroiderers between 1250
and 1300 though their authorship is not as a rule recognised by
their present possessors"[1] Some of these may have been made
by nuns, it is thought that the famous Syon cope, for long in
the possession of the nuns of Syon, may have been made in a
thirteenth century convent in the neighbourhood of Coventry;
but such examples of medieval embroidery as have survived
usually bear no trace of their origin, since a vestment
cannot be signed like a book and it must be remembered that
there was a large class of professional "embroideresses" in the
country.

Some, however, of the splendid vestments and altar cloths
possessed by the richer nunneries were probably the work of
the nuns   At Langley in 1485 there were, among other rich
pieces of embroidery

iiij fronteys (altar frontals) of grene damaske powdered with swanys
and egyls,...iiij fronteys of blake powdered with swanys and rosys, .
a vestment of blew silke brodyt complete with all yt longyth to hyt,
a vestment of grene velwett complete with a crucifixe of silver and
gylte apon ye amys, a complete vestiment of redvelwet, a vestiment
of swede (sewed) work complete, a vestiment of blake damaske brodyrt.
with rosys and sterys, a complete vestiment of white brodyrte with
rede trewlyps (*true-love knots*),. .j gret cloth (banner) of rede powderyd
with herts heds and boturfleys...a large coverlet of red and blew with
rosys and crossys, a tapett of ye same; j large coverlett of rede and
yowlowe with flowrs de luce, a tapett of ye same; a large coverlett
of blew and better blew with swanys and coks, a tapett of ye same,
a coverlett of grene and yowlowe with borys and draguyns, a tapett of
ye same,. .a coverlett of ostrych fydyrs and crounyd Emmys
(*monogram of the Blessed Virgin Mary*); a coverlet of grene and yowlowe with vynys and rosys, a coverlet of grene and yowlowe with
lylys and swannys, a coverlet of blew and white whyl knotts (*wheel,
knots*) and rosys, a coverlet of red and white with traylest (*trellis*)
and Bryds, a coverlet of red and blew with sterrys and white rosys
in mydste; a coverlet of yowlowe and grene with egyles and emmys;
v coveryngs of bedds, yat hys to sey A coveryng of red saye, a coveryng
of panes (*stripes*) of red and grene and white saye, a coveryng of red

---

[1] J H Middleton, *Illuminated MSS.* (1892), p. 112 On nunnery embroidery at different periods see *ib.* pp. 224–30; but the book must be read
with great caution

and blake saye, a coveryng of red and blew poudyrd with white esses and sterys, a blew saye with a red dragne[1].

Many of these embroideries and tapestries were doubtless legacies or gifts; but it is impossible not to picture the white fingers of the nuns at work on swans and roses, harts' heads and butterflies, stars and true-love knots   One may deduce that the nuns of Yorkshire, at least, busied themselves in these pursuits from an injunction sent to Nunkeeling, Yedingham and Wykeham in 1314 that no nun should absent herself from divine service "on account of being occupied with silk work" (*propter occupacionem operis de serico*)[2].

Reference to the sale of embroidery by nuns is surprisingly rare in account rolls. The household roll of the Countess of Leicester in 1265 contains an item, "Paid to the nuns of Wintney, for one cope to be made for the use of Brother J. Angelus by the gift of the Countess at Panham 10*d.*"[3], which small sum must have been a part payment in advance, perhaps towards the purchase of materials; the nuns of Gracedieu, too, sold a cope to a neighbouring rector for £10, early in the fifteenth century[4], and on one occasion the cellaress of Barking derived a part of her income for the year from the sale of a cope[5], but search has revealed no further instances   The nuns also probably made little presents for their friends, such as purses (though the Gracedieu nuns always bought the purses which they gave to their bailiff, to Lady Beaumont, or to other visitors) and the so-called "blood-bands." In an age when bleeding was the most

---

[1] Mackenzie Walcott, *Inventory of St Mary's Ben. Nunnery at Langley, Co Leic* 1485 (Leic Architec Soc 1872), pp. 3, 4
[2] *V C H Yorks* III, 120, 127, 183   Greenfield may have so enjoined other houses; the injunctions are not always fully summarised As to nuns' embroidery there is an interesting passage in the thirteenth century German poem *Helmbrecht* by Wernher "the Gardener"   "Old farmer Helm-brecht had a son   Young Helmbrecht's yellow locks fell down to his shoulders   He tucked them into a handsome silken cap, embroidered with doves and parrots and many a picture. This cap had been embroidered by a nun who had run away from her convent through a love adventure, as happens to so many   From her Helmbrecht's sister Gotelind had learned to embroider and to sew   The girl and her mother had well earned that from the nun, for they gave her in pay a calf, and many cheeses and eggs " J. Harvey Robinson, *Readings in Eur. Hist.* I, pp. 418–9, translated from Freytag, *Bilder aus der deutschen Vergangenheit* (1876, II, pp 52 ff)
[3] *Manners and Household Expenses* (Roxburghe Club 1841), p 18
[4] Gasquet, *Engl Monastic Life*, p 170
[5] *Trans. St Paul's Eccles. Soc* VII, pt II (1912), p. 54.

common treatment for almost every illness and when monks, in particular, were regularly bled several times a year, these little bandages were common presents, being sometimes made of silk. The author of the *Ancren Riwle* thus bade his anchoresses "make no purses to gain friends therewith, not blodbendes of silk, but shape and sew and mend church vestments and poor people's clothes"[1] The nuns of the diocese of Rouen in the mid-thirteenth century were accustomed to knit or embroider silken purses, tassels, cushions or needlecases for sale or as gifts, and Archbishop Eudes Rigaud was continually forbidding them to do any silk work except for church ornament[2] There is some reason to think that the nuns, then as now, sometimes eked out their income by doing fine needlework for ladies of the world, though there is no mention of it in nunnery accounts, or indeed in any English records. Among the correspondence of Lady Lisle in the first half of the sixteenth century, however, are several letters to and from a certain Antoinette de Favences at Dunkirk, who would appear to have been a nun, for she signs herself *sister* Antoinette de Favences and is addressed by Lady Lisle as *Madame* and *Dame*. This woman was employed to make caps and coifs for Lady Lisle's family and friends and there is much correspondence between them as to night-caps which are too wide, lozenge-work and such matters, in one letter Lady Lisle speaks of sending "16 rozimbos and 2 half angels of Flanders, a Carolus of gold," in payment for the caps[3]

What other accomplishments the nuns may have possessed we do not know. They were possibly skilled in herbs and in the more simple forms of home medicine and surgery, for it was the function of the lady of the manor to know something of these things, though doctors were available (for nuns as well as for lay folk) in more serious illnesses[4]. They doubtless bled each other as did the monks, else how was the wicked Prioress of Kirklees, who slew Robin Hood, so skilled?

[1] *Ancren Riwle*, ed. Gasquet, p. 318   [2] See below, p. 655
[3] Wood, *Letters of Royal and Illustrious Ladies*, II, pp. 229–31
[4] Peckham, forbidding the nuns of Barking (1279) to eat or sleep in private rooms or to receive mass there, makes an exception for those who are seriously ill, "in which case we permit the confessor and the doctor, also the father or brother, to have access to them " *Reg Epis. Johannis Peckham*, I, p. 84. Cf *ib* II, pp 652, 663   For nuns and medicine see S Luce, *La Jeunesse de Bertrand de Guesclin* (1882), p 10 .

Doun then came Dame Priorèss
Doun she came in that ilk,
With a pair of blood-irons in her hand,
Were wrappèd all in silk . ..
She laid the blood-irons to Robin's vein
Alack the more pitye !
And pierc'd the vein and let out the blood
That full red was to see

There is an occasional brief reference to the recreation of nuns in their "seynys" in visitations[1], but the precaution was less necessary and less frequent than it was in houses of monks[2] No doubt, also, the nuns sometimes nursed their boarders, some of whom must have been old and ailing, wills are occasionally dated from nunneries[3]. The nuns of Romsey had a hospital attached to the house, in which were received as sisters any parents and relatives of the nuns, who were poor and ill[4], but this does not prove that the nuns nursed them, and references in visitation reports show that even sick nuns were often looked after by lay servants in the infirmary, or if permanently disabled, occupied a separate room, with a separate maid to attend them. It is not likely that the nuns left their convents, save very

[1] At Romsey Abbey a pittance of sixpence was due to each nun "when blood is let" (see Bishop John de Pontoise's injunctions in 1302 and those of Bishop Woodlock in 1311, both of which refer to the payments not having been made). Bishop Woodlock enjoined that "Nuns who have been bled shall be allowed to enter the cloister if they wish " Liveing, *Records of Romsey Abbey*, pp 100, 103, 104 In 1338 Abbot Michael of St Albans orders all the nuns of Sopwell to attend the service of prime, "horspris les malades et les seynes " Dugdale, *Mon* III, p 366 At Nuncoton in 1440 the sub-prioress deposed that "the infirm, the weakminded and they that are in their seynies.. do eat in the convent cellar." *Alnwick's Visit* MS f. 71 d. Bishop Stapeldon forbids the nuns of Polsloe in 1319 to enter convent offices outside the cloistral precincts "pour estre seigne ou pur autre encheson feynte." *Reg. Stapeldon,* ed Hingeston-Randolph, p. 317

[2] On the custom of periodical bleeding in monasteries see J. W. Clark, *The Observances. at Barnwel*, Introd pp lxi, ff. It is interesting to note that medieval treatises on the diseases of women occasionally refer specifically to nuns, e g in a fourteenth century English MS a certain "worschipfull sirop " for use in cases of anaemia is said to be "for ladyes & for nunnes and other also þat ben delicate " Brit. Mus MS Sloane 2463, f. 198 v°

[3] E g Nicholaa de Fulham dates her will in 1327 from Clerkenwell and leaves certain rents for life to Joan her sister, a nun there Sharpe, *Cal of Wills enrolled in Court of Husting*, I, p. 324. The will of Elizabeth Medlay "of the house of St Clement's in Clementthorpe" directs her body to be buried in the conventual church, bequeathes legacies to the high altar, the Prioress and each nun there and appoints dame Margaret Delaryver, prioress, as executor (1470) *V C H Yorks* III, p 130

[4] *New Coll* MS ff. 88, 88d°.

occasionally, to undertake sick-nursing; this would have been against the spirit of their rule, for their main business was not (as was that of the sisters who looked after spitals) to care for the sick, but to live enclosed in their houses, following the prescribed round of church services. It is however of interest that the will of Sir Roger Salwayn, knight of York (1420) contains this legacy: "Also I will that the Nunne that kepid me in my seknes haue ij nobles, and that ther be gif into the hous that she wonnes in xxs, for to syng and pray for me"[1]. Nuns may have emerged sometimes to nurse friends and relatives, whose sick-beds they were always allowed to attend; but there is no documentary evidence for the belief of modern writers, who would fain turn the nun into a district visitor, smoothing the pillows of all who ailed in her native village.

These then were the educational attainments of the English nuns in the later middle ages: reading and singing the services of the church, sometimes but not always writing, Latin very rarely after the thirteenth century, French very rarely after the fourteenth century; needlework and embroidery; and perhaps that elementary knowledge of physic, which was the possession of most ladies of their class. It was, in fact, very little more than the education possessed by laywomen of the same social rank outside and there is little trace of anything approaching scholarship. The study of the education of the nuns during this period leads naturally to one of the most vexed questions in the field of monastic history, the extent to which the nunneries acted as girls' schools. There is no doubt that every nunnery was prepared to educate young girls who entered in order to take the veil; if the nunnery were fairly large these *scolae internae* probably included several novices at a time. At Ankerwyke in 1441 three young nuns complained that they had no governess to instruct them in "reading, song and religious observance," and mention is made of three other sisters "of tender age and slender discretion, seeing that the eldest of them is not more than thirteen years of age"; the Bishop appointed a nun to be their teacher, "enjoining her to perform the charge laid upon her and to instruct them in good manners"[2]. Similarly at Thetford, where

---

[1] *The Fifty Earliest Wills in the Court of Probate*, ed F J. Furnivall (E E T S), p 54 But she may have been a sister from a hospital

[2] *Linc Visit*. II, pp. 4, 5, 6

PLATE V

PAGE FROM *LA SAINTE ABBAYE*

(In the bottom left hand corner the mistress of the novices, with birch in hand, is instructing two young novices; in the bottom right hand corner the abbess and a nun are at prayer.)

there were three novices in 1526, the Bishop found "non habent eruditricem"[1]. At the larger houses, such as Romsey, the *magistra noviciarum* was a regular obedientiary[2]

The vexed question, however, does not concern these schools for novices. It has been the custom, not only of writers on monasticism but also of the man in the street, to assume that the nunneries were almost solely responsible for the education of girls in the middle ages There was little evidence for the assumption, but it was always made, and until the combined attack made upon it in 1910 by Mr Coulton and Mr Leach it was unchallenged[3]. With the publication of bishops' registers, however, we have something more definite to go upon and it is now possible to come to some sort of conclusion, based on the evidence of visitation injunctions, account rolls and other miscellaneous sources This conclusion may be summarised as follows. It was a fairly general custom among the English nuns, in the two and a half centuries before the Dissolution, to receive children for education. But there are four limitations, within which and only within which, this conclusion is true. *First*, that by no means all nunneries took children and those which did take them seldom had large schools; *secondly*, that the children

---

[1] *Visit. of Dioc Norwich* (Camden Soc), p 243

[2] Liveing, *Records of Romsey Abbey*, pp 226, 236 William of Wykeham in 1387 ordered that three or four at least of the more discreet nuns of this large abbey, "in regula sancti benedicti et obseruanciis regularibus sufficienter erudite" should be chosen to instruct the younger nuns in these matters *New Coll* MS f 86 At St Mary's, Winchester, in 1501, besides Margaret Legh, mistress of the novices, there was Agnes Cox, senior teacher (*dogmatista*). *V C H Hants* II, p 124 At Elstow in 1421–2 the bishop ordered "That a more suitable nun be deputed and ordained to be precentress, and that elder nuns, if they shall be capable and fit for such offices, be preferred to younger " *Linc Visit* I, p 50 Dean Kentwode's injunction to St Helen's Bishopsgate in 1432 runs "That ye ordeyne and chese on of yowre sustres, honest, abille and cunnyng of discretyone, the whiche can, may and schall have the charge of techyng and informacyone of yowre sustres that be uncunnyng, for to teche hem here service and the rule of here religione " Dugdale, *Mon.* IV, p. 554.

[3] The controversy was roused by an article by Mr J E G de Montmorency entitled "The Medieval Education of Women in England" in the *Journal of Education* (June, 1909), pp 427–31. This was challenged by Mr Coulton, *loc cit* (July, 1910), pp. 456–7, see the correspondence *passim*, especially the two articles by Mr A F. Leach, *loc. cit* (Oct. and Dec. 1910), pp 667–9, 838–41 The subject was afterwards treated with great erudition by Mr Coulton in a paper read before the International Congress of Historical Studies in 1913, reprinted with notes as *Monastic Schools in the Middle Ages* (*Medieval Studies*, x, 1913).

who thus received a convent education were drawn exclusively
from the upper and the wealthy middle classes, from people,
that is to say, of birth and wealth; *thirdly*, that the practice
was a purely financial expedient on the part of the nuns, at first
forbidden, afterwards restricted and always frowned upon by
the bishops, who regarded it as subversive of discipline, and
fourthly, that the education which the children received from
the nuns, so far as book-learning as distinct from nurture is
concerned, was extremely exiguous In fine, though nunneries
did act as girls' schools, they certainly did not educate more
than a small proportion even of the children of the upper classes,
and the education which they gave them was limited by their
own limitations[1].

That the custom of receiving schoolgirls was fairly general
appears from the wide area over which notices of such children
are spread. The references range in date from 1282 to 1537; they
give us, if a doubtful reference to King's Mead, Derby, be
accepted, the names of forty-nine convents, which at one time
or other had children in residence. These convents are situated
in twenty-one counties. The greater number of references
naturally occur in those dioceses for which the episcopal registers .
are most complete; Yorkshire affords fifteen names and two which
are doubtful; Lincolnshire, Northamptonshire, Buckinghamshire, Bedfordshire, Oxfordshire, Hertfordshire and Leicestershire, counties in the large Lincoln diocese, afford seventeen
between them, five from Lincolnshire and two from each of the
others. These references do not prove that the houses in question
had continuously throughout their career a school for girls;
sometimes only one or two children are mentioned and usually
the evidence concerns but a single year out of two and a half
centuries Sometimes, however, a happy chance has preserved
several references to the same house, spread over a longer period,
from which it is perhaps not too rash to conclude that it was the
regular practice of that house to receive children. For Elstow,
for instance, there is an early reference to a boy of five sent
there for education by St Hugh, Bishop of Lincoln, towards the
close of the twelfth century. In 1359 Bishop Gynewell prohibited

---

[1] For the rest of this chapter I shall not give full references in footnotes, because they can easily be traced in Note B, p 568 below.

all boarders there, except girls under ten and boys under six. In 1421 Bishop Flemyng prohibited all except children under twelve and in 1432 Bishop Gray altered this to girls under fourteen and boys under ten, and children are mentioned at Alnwick's visitation in 1442. Similarly at Godstow there are references to children in 1358, 1445 and 1538, at Esholt in Yorkshire in 1315, 1318 and 1537, at Sopwell in 1446 and 1537, at Heynings in 1347, 1387 and 1393, at Burnham in 1434 and 1519.

The mention of boys in these references needs perhaps some further emphasis, for it is not usually recognised that the nunneries occasionally acted as dame-schools for very young boys. "Abstinence the abbesse myn a b.c. me tauʒte," says Piers Plowman, "And conscience com aftur and kennide me betere." It is true that a Cistercian statute of 1256–7 forbade the education of boys in nunneries of that order[1], but the ordinance soon became a dead letter, and five of the convents at which Alnwick found schoolboys (c. 1445) were Cistercian houses. Boys were specifically forbidden at Wherwell in 1284, at Heynings in 1359 and at Nuncoton in 1531, which argues that they were then present, and they are mentioned at Romsey (1311), at five Yorkshire convents (1314–17), at Burnham (1434), at Lymbrook (1437), at Swaffham Bulbeck (1483) and at Redlingfield (1514), a chronologically and geographically wide range of houses. Occasionally some details as to a particular boy may be gleaned; the five year old Robert de Noyon, sent by Bishop Hugh to Elstow "to be taught his letters," the two Tudor boys commended to Katharine de la Pole, the noble Abbess of Barking; the little son and heir of Sir John Stanley, who made his will in 1527 and then became a monk, leaving the boy to be brought up until twelve years of age by another Abbess of Barking, after which he was to pass to the care of the Abbot of Westminster; and Cromwell's son Gregory and his little companion, sent to be supervised, though not taught by Margaret Vernon, Prioress of Little Marlow[2]. But as a rule the boys in nunneries were very young; it was not considered decorous for them to stay with the nuns later than their ninth or tenth year; the bishop forbade it and

---

[1] *Cistercian Statutes*, 1256–7, ed J T Fowler (reprinted from *Yorks. Archaeol Journ*), p 105 .

[2] Probably, however, after the dissolution of her house

besides, the education which the good sisters could give them
would not have been considered sufficient. The rule which gives
a man child to a man for education is of very old standing.

Such is the evidence for concluding that the custom of receiving children for education in nunneries was widespread. It
remains to consider carefully the limitations within which this
conclusion is true. In the first place, not all nunneries received
children It is obviously impossible, considering the gaps in our
evidence, to attempt an exact estimate of the proportion which
did so Some sort of clue may be obtained by an analysis of the
Yorkshire visitations of Archbishops Greenfield and Melton at
the beginning of the fourteenth century (1306–20) and of Alnwick's Lincoln visitations (1440–5). The Yorkshire evidence is
rather scanty, being based on the summaries of injunctions,
which are given in the *Victoria County Histories*, and any statistics
must needs be approximate only. The two archbishops between
them visited nineteen nunneries and mention of children is made
at twelve, i.e. about two-thirds. The information given by the
invaluable Alnwick is more exact. From the *detecta* of some of
the nuns and from the number of prohibitions of this practice,
it is obvious that Alnwick was accustomed to ask at his visitations whether children were sleeping in the nuns' dorter; he also
made careful inquiry as to the boarders. The probability, therefore, is that we have in his register an exact record of those
houses in which children were received. Analysis shows that of
the twenty houses which he visited he found children, often
boys as well as girls, at twelve, i e a little over two-thirds, which
is substantially the same result as was given by the Yorkshire
analysis a century earlier. The estimate is interesting, but it
cannot be considered conclusive without the corroborative
evidence from other dioceses, which is unfortunately lacking
It is a hint, a straw, which shows which way the wind of research
is blowing, for if it is unsafe to argue from silence that the nuns
of other convents did take pupils, it is equally unsafe to argue
that they did not.

The fact is, however, clearly established that all nunneries
did not take children; possibly about two-thirds of them did.
The further fact has then to be recognised that even those nunneries had not necessarily what we should regard as a school

for girls. Not only does it sometimes seem as though children
were taken occasionally and intermittently, rather than regularly,
but the numbers taken were rarely great. Sometimes we do
hear of a house with a large number of pupils. At St Mary's
Winchester in 1536 there were as many as twenty-six children,
to twenty-six nuns; and at Polesworth in 1537 Henry VIII's
commissioners state vaguely that "repayre and resort ys made
to the gentlemens childern and studiounts that ther doo lif,
to the nombre sometyme of xxx^{ti} and sometyme xj^{ti} and moo."
There were fifteen nuns in the house at the time and it is likely
that the number of children given is a pardonable exaggeration
by local gentlemen who were interested in preserving the nunnery, but it seems undoubted that there was a comparatively
large school there. At Stixwould, again, in 1440 there were
about eighteen children to an equal number of nuns. These,
however, are the largest schools of which we have record At
St Michael's Stamford in 1440 there were seven or eight
children to twelve nuns, at Catesby in 1442 six or seven children
to seven nuns. At Swaffham Bulbeck, where there were probably
eight or nine nuns, there were nine children in 1483 These also
are schools, though small schools But at other houses there were
only one or two children at a time. The accounts of the Prioress
of St Helen's Bishopsgate in 1298 mention only two children,
there were only two at Littlemore in 1445 and two at Sopwell
at the time of the Dissolution. It must be remembered that
many nunneries were themselves very small and their inmates
could not have looked after a large number of children. The
examples quoted above suggest that the number of children
hardly ever exceeded the number of nuns. To what conclusion are
we driven when we find that a possible two-thirds of the convents
of England received children and that the largest school of which
we have record numbered only twenty-six children (or thirty
if we take the higher and less probable figure for Polesworth),
while most had far fewer? Surely to represent a majority
of girls, or even a majority of girls of gentle birth, as having
received their nurture in convents, would be on the evidence
absurd

The second limitation of convent education in medieval
England is contained in the words "girls of gentle birth."

Tanner's statement that "the lower rank of people, who could not pay for their learning[1]," as well as noblemen's and gentlemen's daughters, were educated in nunneries has not a shred of evidence to support it, though it has been repeated *ad nauseam* ever since he wrote it. Every scrap of evidence which has come down to us goes to prove that the girls educated in nunneries were of gentle birth, daughters of great lords, or more often daughters of country gentlemen, or of those comfortable and substantial merchants and burgesses, who were usually themselves sprung from younger sons of the gentry. The implication is plain in Chaucer's description, in *The Reves Tale*, of the Miller's wife, who was "y-comen of noble kin" and daughter of the parson of the toun, and who "was y-fostred in a nonnerye":

> Ther dorste no wight clepen hir but "dame"...
> And eek, for she was somdel smoterlich
> She was as digne as water in a dich,
> And ful of hoker and of bisemare.
> Her thoughte that a lady sholde hir spare,
> What for hir kinrede and hir nortelrye
> That she had lerned in the nonnerye

An analysis of some of the schoolgirls whose names have come down to us confirms this impression. The commissioners who visited St Mary's, Winchester, in 1536 drew up a list of the twenty-six "chyldren of lordys, knyghttes and gentylmen brought up yn the saym monastery." They were

Bryget Plantagenet, dowghter unto the lord vycounte Lysley (i e. Lisle); Mary Pole, dowghter unto Sir Geffrey Pole knyght; Brygget Coppeley, dowghter unto Sir Roger Coppeley knyght; Elizabeth Phyllpot, dowghter unto Sir Peter Phyllpot, knyght; Margery Tyrell; Adrian Tyrell, Johanne Barnabe, Amy Dyngley, Elizabeth Dyngley; Jane Dyngley, Frances Dyngley, Susan Tycheborne; Elizabeth Tycheborne, Mary Justyce, Agnes Aylmer; Emma Bartue; Myldred Clerke; Anne Lacy, Isold Apulgate, Elizabeth Legh; Mary Legh, Alienor North; Johanne Sturgys; Johanne Ffyldes; Johanne Ffrances, Jane Raynysford

The house was evidently at this time a fashionable seminary for young ladies. It must be remembered that it was a general

---

[1] Tanner, *Notitia Monastica* (1744 edit.), p xxxii (basing his opinion on three secondary authorities and on a misunderstanding of two medieval entries, one of which refers to lay sisters and the other to an adult boarder).

custom among the English nobility and gentry to send their
children away to the household of a lord, or person of good
social standing, in order to learn breeding and it was not uncommon to send boys to the household of an abbot. In 1450
Thomas Bromele, Abbot of Hyde, thus entertained in his house
eight "gentiles pueri," there were many "pueri generosi" at
Westacre in 1494, and Richard Whiting, the last Abbot of
Glastonbury, is stated by Parsons to have had, among his 300
servants, "multos nobilium filios"[1]. It was doubtless much in
the same way that the children of lords, knights and gentlemen
were put in the charge of the Abbess of St Mary's Winchester,
a great lady, who had her own "gentlewoman" to attend upon
her and her own private household. It is probable that the nuns
taught these children, but the boys who went as wards to abbeys
seem often to have taken their tutors with them, or at least to
have been taught by special tutors. At Lilleshall, for instance,
the commissioners found four "gentylmens sons and their scole-
master"[2] and it is significant that when little Gregory Cromwell
was sent to be brought up by Margaret Vernon, Prioress of
Little Marlow, he was taught by a private tutor and not by the
nun.

Other references to the children received in nunneries confirms the impression that they were of gentle birth. At Polesworth, as at St Mary's, Winchester, the commissioners specified
"gentylmens childern and studiounts." At Thetford a daughter
of John Jerves, *generosus*, is mentioned in 1532 and two daughters
of Laurens Knight, *gentleman*, were at Cornworthy, c. 1470 The
accounts of Sopwell in 1446 mention the daughter of Lady Anne
Norbery, at Littlemore in 1445 the daughter of John FitzAleyn,
steward of the house, and the daughter of Ingelram Warland
are boarders Among the Carrow boarders, who may be set down
as children, are the son and two daughters of Sir Roger Wellisham,

---

[1] N. Sanderus, *de Schismate Anglicana*, ed. 1586, p. 176. The statement is not in the original Sanders A well-known passage in the
Paston Letters illustrates the practice as regards girls; Margaret Paston
writes to her son in 1469 " Also I would ye should purvey for your sister to
be with my Lady of Oxford, or with my Lady of Bedford, or in some other
worshipful place whereas ye think best, for we be either of us weary of other "
It is probable that this method of educating girls was more common than
nunnery education
[2] Quoted by Mr Leach, *Journ of Educ* (1910), p 668.

the daughter of Sir Robert de Wachesam, a niece of William Bateman, Bishop of Norwich, and girls with such well-known names as Fastolf, Clere, Baret, Blickling, Shelton and Ferrers, though the last two may be adult boarders The Gracedieu boarders nearly all bear the names of neighbouring gentry and one was the daughter of Lord Beaumont In the course of time, as the urban middle class grew and flourished, the daughters of the well-to-do *bourgeoisie* were sometimes sent to convents for their education. Thus among the Carrow boarders we find a daughter of John de Erlham, a merchant and citizen of Norwich, and Isabel Barber, daughter of Thomas Welan, barber, who afterwards, however, became a nun. It is plain from the wills which have been preserved that the wealthy Norwich burgesses were in the habit of sending their daughters as nuns to Carrow, and it is a natural supposition that they should have sent them sometimes as schoolgirls; but by birth and by wealth these city magnates were not far removed from the neighbouring gentry. The school at Swaffham Bulbeck in 1483 was less fashionable than that at Carrow and did not cater for the nobly born; it was a small house and the names of the children suggest a sound middle class establishment, perhaps the very one in which Chaucer's Miller's wife of Trumpington was educated, full of the sons and daughters of the burgesses of Cambridge, Richard Potecary of Cambridge, William Water, Thomas Roch, unnamed fathers "of Cambridge," "of Chesterton," Parker "of Walden," and "the merchant "

None of these examples can possibly be twisted into a case for the free, or even the cheap, education of the poor. Just as we never find low-born girls as nuns, so we never find them as schoolgirls and for the same reason; "dowerless maidens," as Mr Leach says, "were not sought as nuns." As will be seen hereafter, the reception of school children was essentially a financial expedient; one of the many methods by which the nuns sought to raise the wind[1]. The fees paid by these children

[1] Possibly, as Mr Coulton points out (*Med Studies*, x, p 26), this may account for the fact that evidence of girl pupils is wanting for some of the wealthier and more important nunneries, he instances Shaftesbury, Amesbury, Syon, Studley and Lacock For the life of the nuns at Lacock and Amesbury we have very little information of any kind, but our information is fairly full for Shaftesbury, and very full for Syon and for Studley.

are recorded here and there, in nunnery accounts; education
was apparently thrown in with board, and the usual rate for
board for children during the century and a half before the
Dissolution seems to have been about 6*d.* a week, though the
charge at Cornworthy c. 1470 was 10*d.* a week and at Littlemore
in 1445 only 4*d.* a week[1]. Occasionally the good nuns suffered,
like so many schoolmistresses since their day, from the difficulty
of extracting fees. Among the debts owing to the nuns of Esholt
at the Dissolution was one of 33*s.* from Walter Wood of Timble
in the parish of Otley for his child's board for a year and a half;
and at Thetford in 1532 the poor nuns complained that "John
Jerves, gentleman, has a daughter being nurtured in the priory
and pays nothing." The most melancholy case of all has been
preserved to us owing to the fact that the nuns, goaded to
desperation, sought help from the Chancellor   About 1470
Thomasyn Dynham, Prioress of Cornworthy, made petition to
the effect that Laurens' Knyghte, gentleman, had agreed with
Margaret Wortham the late Prioress, that she should take his
two daughters "to teche them to scole," viz. Elizabeth, aged
seven years, and "Jahne," aged ten years, at the costs and
charges of Laurens, who was to pay 20*d.* a week for them. So
at Cornworthy they remained during the life of Margaret, to
the great costs and charges and impoverishing of the said poor
place, by the space of five years and more, until the money due
amounted to £21 13*s.* 4*d.*, "the which sum is not contented ne
paid, nor noo peny thereof " Laurense meanwhile departed this
life, leaving his wife "Jahne" executrix, and Jahne, unnatural
mother that she was, married again a certain John Barnehous
and utterly refused to pay for her unhappy daughters   One is
uncertain which to pity most, Thomasyn Dynham, a new Prioress
left with this incubus on her hands, or Elizabeth and Jane
Knyghte, trying hard to restrain their appetites and not to
grow out of their clothes under her justly incensed regard   Jane
was by now grown up and marriageable according to the
standards of the time and it is tantalising not to know the end
of the dilemma. A proneness to forget fees seems to have been

---

[1] For a discussion of these charges and of other prices and payments,
with which they may be compared, see J E G. de Montmorency in *Journ of
Educ.* (1909), pp 429–30 and Coulton, *op cit.* app iv. (School Children in
Nunnery Accounts), pp. 38–40

shared by greater folk than Mistress Knyghte, as the petition
of Katherine de la Pole, Abbess of Barking, concerning Edmond
and Jasper Tudor, whose "charges, costs and expenses" she
had taken upon herself, will show.

Both this matter of fees and the names of schoolgirls which
have survived are against any suggestion that the nuns gave
schooling to poor girls. There is not the slightest evidence for
anything like a day school, and the only hint for any care for
village girls on the part of the nuns is contained in a letter from
Cranmer, when fellow of Jesus College, to the Abbess of Godstow·

Stephen Whyte hath told me that you lately gathered round you a
number of wild peasant maids and did make them a most goodly
discourse on the health of their souls; and you showeth them how
goodly a thing it be for them to go oftentimes to confession. I am
mighty glad of your discourse[1].

But this is obviously an isolated discourse and in any case it
has nothing to do with education. So far as it is possible to be
certain of anything for which evidence is scanty, we may be
certain that poor or lower-class girls were no more received in
nunneries for education, than they were received there as nuns
No single instance has ever been brought of a lowborn nun or
a lowborn schoolgirl, in any English nunnery, for the three
centuries before the nunneries were dissolved

The third limitation to which convent education was subjected is an important one; the reception of children by the nuns
was never approved and always restricted by their ecclesiastical
superiors. The greater number of references to schoolchildren
which have come down to us are these restrictive references. The
attitude of monastic visitors towards children was in essence
the same as their attitude towards boarders The nuns received
both, because they were nearly always in low water financially
and wished to add to their scanty finances by the familiar expedient of taking paying guests. But the bishops saw in all
boarders, whether adults or schoolchildren, a hindrance to discipline, they objected to them for the same reason that they

---

[1] Quoted in S H Burke, *The Monastic Houses of England, their Accusers
and Defenders* (1869), p 32   Compare the words of a Venetian traveller,
Paolo Casenigo "The English nuns gave instructions to the poorer virgins
as to their duties when they became wives, to be obedient to their husbands
and to give good example," a curious note. *Ib.* p 31.

objected to pet dogs and silver girdles and with just as little success.

The ecclesiastical case against schoolchildren may be found delightfully set forth in the words addressed, it is true, to anchoresses, but expressing the same spirit as was afterwards shown by Eudes Rigaud, Johann Busch and other great medieval visitors towards nuns. Aelred, the great twelfth century Abbot of Rievaulx, writes thus:

Allow no boys or girls to have access to you. There are certain anchoresses, who are busied in teaching pupils and turn their chambers into a school. The mistress sits at the window, the child in the cloister. She looks at each of them; and, during their puerile actions, now is angry, now laughs, now threatens, now soothes, now spares, now kisses, now calls the weeping child to be beaten, then strokes her face, bids her hold up her head, and eagerly embracing her, calls her her child, her love[1].

Similarly the author of the *Ancren Riwle* warns his three anchoresses:

An anchoress must not become a schoolmistress, nor turn her anchoress-house into a school for children. Her maiden may, however, teach any little girl, concerning whom it might be doubtful whether she should learn among boys, but an anchoress ought to give her thoughts to God only[2]

The gist of the matter was that the children constituted a hindrance to claustral discipline and devotion. It is plain, however, that in this, as in so many other matters, the reformers were only "beating the air" in vain with their restrictions. Sympathy must be with the needy nuns, for even if discipline were weakened thereby, the reception of children was in itself a very harmless, not to say laudable expedient, and so the neighbouring gentry as well as the nuns considered it

An analysis of the attitude of medieval visitors to schoolchildren shows us the usual attempt to limit what it was beyond their power to prohibit. Eudes Rigaud, the great Archbishop of Rouen, habitually removed all the girls and boys whom he found in the houses of his diocese, when he visited them during the years 1249 to 1269. But in England, at least, the nuns very soon became too strong for the bishops, who gradually adopted the policy of fixing an age limit beyond which no children might

---

[1] Quoted in Fosbroke, *British Monachism* (1802), ii, p. 35
[2] *Ancren Riwle*, ed Gasquet, p 319

remain in a nunnery and sometimes of requiring their own licence to be given before the boys and girls were admitted. Since the danger of secularisation could not be removed, it was at least reduced to a minimum, by ensuring that only very young boys and only girls, who had not yet attained a marriageable age, should be received The age limit varied a little with different visitors and different houses. In the Yorkshire diocese early in the fourteenth century the age limit was twelve for girls, boys are rarely mentioned, but at Hampole in 1314 the nuns were forbidden to permit male children over five to be in the house, as the bishop finds has been the practice. Bishop Gynewell in 1359 allowed girls up to ten and boys up to six at Elstow, but forbade boys altogether at Heynings. Bishop Gray allowed girls under fourteen and boys under eight at Burnham in 1434 and Bishop Stretton in 1367 allowed boys up to seven at Fairwell. The age limit tended, it will be seen, to become higher in the course of time; Alnwick writing to Gracedieu in 1440, forbade all boarders "save childerne, males the ix and females the xiiij yere of age, whom we licencede you to hafe for your relefe"[1]; he allowed boys often at Heynings and Catesby and boys of eleven (an exceptionally high age) at Harrold

There was a special reason, besides the general interference with discipline, for which the bishops objected to children in nunneries. It seems very often to have been the custom for the nuns to take, as it were, private pupils, each child having its own particular mistress. This custom grew as the practice of keeping separate households grew Thus at Catesby the Prioress complained to Alnwick that sister Agnes Allesley had "six or seven young folk of both sexes, that do lie in the dorter"; at St Michael's Stamford, he found that the Prioress had seven or eight children, at Gracedieu the cellaress had a little boy and at Elstow, where there were five households of nuns, it was said that "certain nuns" brought children into the quire. In fact, the nuns would appear to have kept for their own personal use the money paid to them for the board of their private pupils. This was a sin against the monastic rule of personal poverty

---

[1] Notice the recognition of the financial reasons for taking school-children So also in 1489 the nuns of Nunappleton are to take no boarders "but if they be childern or ellis old persons by which availe by likelihod may grow to your place"—fees or legacies, in fact. Dugdale, *Mon.* IV, p 654

and the bishops took special measures against such manifestations of *proprietas*. William of Wykeham in 1387 forbids the
nuns of Romsey to make wills and to have private rooms or
private pupils, giving this specific reason, and at St Helen's
Bishopsgate in 1439 Dean Kentwode enjoined "that no nonne
have ne receyve noo schuldrin wyth hem...but yf that the
profite of the comonys turne to the vayle of the same howse."
Similarly the number of children who might be taken by a single
nun was sometimes limited; Gynewell wrote to Godstow in
1358 "that no lady of the said house is to have children, save
only two or three females sojourning with them" and at Fairwell
in 1367 no nun might keep with her for education more than
one child.

Another habit against which bishops constantly legislated
was that of having the children to sleep in the dorter with the
nuns. This practice was exceedingly common, for many of the
nunneries which took children were small and poor, they had
possibly no other room to set aside for them, and no person who
could suitably be placed in charge of them. Moreover in some
cases adult boarders and servants also slept in the dorter.
Alnwick was constantly having to bid his nuns "that ye suffre
ne seculere persones, wymmen ne childern lyg by nyghte in the
dormytory," but Atwater and Longland in the sixteenth century
still have to make the same injunction. Bokyngham in 1387
ordered that a seemly place outside the cloister should be set
apart for the children at Heynings; the reason was that (as Gynewell had expressly stated on visiting this house forty years before)
"the convent might not be disturbed" Indeed little attempt
was made by the nuns to keep the children out of their way.
They seem to have dined in the refectory, when not in the separate
rooms of their mistresses, for Greenfield forbids the Prioress
and Subprioress of Sinningthwaite (1315) to permit boys or girls
to eat flesh meat in Advent or Sexagesima, or during Lent eggs
or cheese, in the refectory, "contrary to the honesty of religion,"
but at those seasons when they ought to eat such things, they
were to be assigned other places in which to eat them. There
are references, too, to disturbances and diversions created by
the children in the quire. At Elstow in 1442 Dame Rose Waldegrave said that "certain nuns do sometimes have with them in

time of mass the boys whom they teach and these do make a noise in quire during divine service "[1]. To us the picture of these merry children breaking the monotony of convent routine is an attractive one; more attractive even than the pet dogs and the Vert-Verts. But to stern ecclesiastical disciplinarians it was not so attractive, and their constant restriction, though it never succeeded in turning out the children, must have kept down the number who were admitted.

The evidence which has so far been considered shows that, though the reception of children to be boarded and taught in nunneries was fairly common, it was subjected to well marked limitations. There remains to be considered one more question the answer to which is in some sort a limitation likewise. What exactly did the nuns teach these children? We are hampered in answering this question by the difficulty of obtaining exact contemporary evidence. Most modern English writers content themselves with a glib list of accomplishments, copied without verification from book to book, and all apparently traceable in the last resort to Fuller and John Aubrey, the one writing a century, the other almost a century and a half after the nunneries had been dissolved. Fuller (whom Tanner copies) says:

Nunneries also were good Shee-schools, wherein the girles and maids of the neighbourhood were taught to read and work; and sometimes a little Latine was taught them therein Yea, give me leave to say, if such Feminine Foundations had still continued...haply the weaker sex (besides the avoiding modern inconveniences) might be heightened to a higher perfection than hitherto hath been obtained[2].

[1] Caesarius of Heisterbach gives a picture of a less disturbing child in quire (though she was more probably a little girl who was intended for a nun). This is the English fifteenth century translation: "Caesarius tells how that in Essex" (really in Saxony, but the translator was anxious to introduce local colour for the sake of his audience), "in a monasterye of nonnys, ther was a litle damysell, and on a grete solempne nyght hur maistres lete hur com with hur to matyns So the damysell was bod a wayke thyng, and hur maistres was ferd at sho sulde take colde, and sho commaundid hur befor Te Deum to go vnto the dortur to her bed agayn And at hur commandment sho went furth of the where, thuff all it war with ill wyll, and abade withoute the where and thoght to here the residue of matyns"; whereat she saw a vision of the nuns caught up to heaven praising God among the angels, at the *Te Deum An Alphabet of Tales* (E E T S 1905), II, p 406
[2] Fuller, *Church Hist* See p. 255 above, note 3

Aubrey, speaking of Wiltshire convents says:

There the young maids were brought up...at the nunneries, where
they had examples of piety, and humility, and modesty, and obedience
to imitate, and to practise. Here they learned needle-work, the art
of confectionary, surgery (for anciently there were no apothecaries or
surgeons—the gentlewomen did cure their poor neighbours· their
hands are now too fine), physic, writing, drawing etc.[1]

One would have thought the familiar note of the *laudator
temporis acti* to be plainly audible in both these extracts. But
a host of modern writers have gravely transcribed their words
and even, taking advantage no doubt of Aubrey's "etc." (much
virtue in etc.), improved upon them In the work of one more
recent writer the list has become "reading, writing, some
knowledge of arithmetic, the art of embroidery, music and
French 'after the scole of Stratford atte Bowe,' were the recognised course of study, while the preparation of perfumes, balsams,
simples and confectionary was among the more ordinary departments of the education afforded"[2]. Another adds a few more
deft touches. "the treatment of various disorders, the com-
pounding of simples, the binding up of wounds,....fancy cookery,
such as the making of sweetmeats, writing, drawing, needlework
of all kinds and music, both vocal and instrumental"[3]. The most
recent writer of all gives the list as "English and French...
writing, drawing, confectionary, singing by notes, dancing, and
playing upon instruments of music, the study also of medicine
and surgery"[4]. Though the historian must groan, the student
of human nature cannot but smile to see music insinuate itself
into the list and then become "both instrumental and vocal";
confectionery extend itself to include perfumes, balsams, simples,
and the making of sweetmeats; arithmetic appear out of nowhere;
and (most magnificent feat of the imagination) dancing trip in
on light fantastic toe. From this compound of Aubrey, memories
of continental convents in the seventeenth and eighteenth

[1] Quoted in Gasquet, *Eng. Monastic Life*, p 177.
[2] Hugo, *Medieval Nunneries of Somerset* (*Minchin Buckland*), p. 107.
[3] G Hill, *Women in Eng. Life* (1896), p 79.
[4] *Times Educational Supplement* (Sept 4, 1919). This seems to be taken
from Fosbroke, *Brit Monachism*, ii, pp 6–7, who takes it from Sir H.
Chauncey's *Hist and Antiqs of Hertfordshire*, p. 423, it is the first appearance of dancing; as Fosbroke sapiently argued, "The dancing of nuns will
be hereafter spoken of and if they dance they must somewhere learn how."

centuries and familiarity with the convent schools of our own
day, let us turn to the considered opinion of a more sober
scholar, who bases it only upon contemporary evidence:

"No evidence whatever," says Mr Leach, "has been produced of what
was taught in nunneries. That...something must have been taught,
if only to keep the children employed, is highly probable That the
teaching included learning the Lord's Prayer, etc. by heart may be
conceded. Probably Fuller is right in guessing that it included reading;
but it is only a guess. One would guess that it included sewing and
spinning As for its including Latin, no evidence is forthcoming and
it is difficult to see how those who did not know Latin could teach it[1]."

Direct evidence is therefore absolutely lacking; all we can
do is to deduce probabilities from what we know of the education
of the nuns themselves, and it must be conceded that this was
not always of a very high order. It is quite certain, from the
wording of some of the visitation injunctions, that the quality
and extent of the teaching must have varied considerably from
house to house. It was probably good (as the education of
women then went) at the larger and more fashionable houses,
mediocre at those which were small and struggling Latin could
not have been taught, because, as has already been pointed out,
the nuns at this period did not know it themselves; but the
children were probably taught the *Credo*, the *Ave* and the
Pater Noster in Latin by rote. They may have been taught
French of the school of Stratford atte Bowe, as long as that
language was fashionable in the outside world and known to
the nuns, but it died out of the convents after the end of the
fourteenth century. It seems pretty certain that the children
must have been taught to read. "Abstinence the abbesse myn
a.b.c. me tauȝte," says Piers Plowman; the Abbess of St Mary's
Winchester buys the matins books for little Bridget Plantagenet;
and it will be remembered that the nuns of Godstow were said

---

[1] *Journ of Education*, 1910, p. 841 Mr Hamilton Thompson sends me
this note· "Probably, so far as any systematic teaching went, they were
taught 'grammar' and song, which would vary in quality according to the
teacher. These are the only two elements of which we regularly hear in the
ordinary schools of the day. I do not see any reason to suppose that they
were taught more or less Song (i e church song) takes such a very promi-
nent part in medieval education that I think it would not have been
neglected, it was also one of the things which nuns ought to have been able
to teach from their daily experience in quire Bridget Plantagenet's book
of matins (see below) would be an appropriate lesson book for both grammar
and song, as nuns would understand them "

about 1460 (fifteen years after Alnwick visited the house and gave permission for children to be boarded there) to be "for the more party in Englyssh bokys well y-lernyd." Caesarius of Heisterbach has a delightful story, repeated thus in a fifteenth century *Alphabet of Tales*:

Caesarius tellis how that in Freseland in a nonrie ther was ii little maydens that lernyd on the buke, and euer thai strafe whethur of thaim shulde lern mor than the toder So the tane of thaim happened to fall seke and sho garte call the Priores vnto hur & sayd. "Gude ladie! suffre nott my felow to lern vnto I cover of my sekenes, and I sall pray my moder to gif me vj d & that I sall giff you & ye do so, ffor I drede that whils I am seke, that sho sall pas me in lernyng, & that I wolde not at sho did." And at this wurde the priores smylid & hadd grete mervayle of the damysell conseyte[1].

Whether girls were taught to write, as well as to read, is far more doubtful It is probable that the nuns did not always possess this accomplishment themselves, nor did sober medieval opinion consider it wholly desirable that girls should know how to write, on account both of the general inferiority of their sex, and of a regrettable proclivity towards clandestine love letters[2]. Still, writing may sometimes have formed part of the curriculum; there is no evidence either way. For drawing (by which presumably the art of illumination must be meant) there is no warrant; a medieval nunnery was not a modern "finishing" school.

So much for what may be called book learning. Let us now examine for a moment the other accomplishments with which nunnery-bred young ladies have been credited We may, as Mr Leach suggests, make a guess at spinning and needlework, though here also there is no evidence for their being taught to

[1] *An Alphabet of Tales* (E E T.S 1905), p. 272, from Caesarius of Heisterbach, *Dialog Mirac* ed. Strange, I, p. 196.

[2] See e g the Knight of La Tour Landry, p. 178, "Et pour ce que aucuns gens dient que ilz ne voudroient pas que leurs femmes ne leurs filles sceussent rien de clergie ne d'escripture, je dy ainsi que, quant d'escryre, n'y a force que femme en saiche riens; mais quant a lire, tout femme en vault mieulx de le scavoir et cognoist mieulx la foy et les perils de l'ame et son saulvement, et n'en est pas de cent une qui n'en vaille mieulx, car c'est chose esprouvee" Quoted in A A. Hentsch, *De la littérature didactique du moyen âge s'addressant spécialement aux femmes* (Cahors, 1903), p 133 So Philippe de Novare († 1270) refuses to allow women to learn reading or writing, because they expose her to evil, and Francesco da Barberino († 1348) refuses to allow reading and writing except to girls of the highest rank (not including the daughters of esquires, judges and gentlefolk of their class); both, however, make exception for nuns *Ib.* pp 84, 106–7.

schoolgirls   Jane Scroupe, into whose mouth Skelton puts his
"Phyllyp Sparowe," was apparently being brought up at Carrow,
and describes how she sewed the dead bird's likeness on her
sampler,

> I toke my sampler ones,
> Of purpose, for the nones,
> To sowe with stytchis of sylke
> My sparow whyte as mylke.

Confectionery does not seem very probable, for at this period
the cooking for the convent was nearly always done by a hired
male cook and not (as laid down in the Benedictine rule) by
the nuns themselves, who were apt to complain if they had to
prepare the meals. For "home medicine" there is absolutely
no evidence, though all ladies of the day possessed some knowledge of simples and herb-medicines and the girls may equally
well have learned it at home as among the nuns. It is probable
that the children learned to sing, if the nuns took them into the
quire, but for this there is no definite evidence, nor has any document been quoted to prove that they learned to play upon instruments of music. It is true that the flighty Dame Isabel Benet
"did dance and play the lute" with the friars of Northampton[1]
and that "a pair of organs" occurs twice in Dissolution inventories
of nunneries[2], but an organ is hardly an instrument of secular
music to be played by the daughter of the house in a manorial
solar; and Dame Benet's escapade with the lute was a lapse from
the strict path of virtue. Finally to suggest that the nuns taught
dances verges upon absurdity That they did sometimes dance
is true, and grieved their visitors were to hear it[3]; but what
Alnwick would have said to the suggestion that they solemnly
engaged themselves to teach dancing to their young pupils is
an amusing subject for contemplation Evidence for everything
except the prayers of the church and the art of reading is non-
existent; we can but base our opinion upon conjecture and
probability; and the probability for instrumental music is so
slight as to be non-existent. If it be argued that gentlewomen
were expected to possess these arts, it may be replied that the
children whom we find at nunneries probably had opportunity

---

[1] See below, p 388.
[2] *Archaeologia*, XLIII (1871), p. 245 (Redlingfield and Bruisyard).
[3] See below, p. 309.

to learn them at home, for they seem sometimes to have spent
only a part of the year with the nuns. It is true that board is
sometimes paid for the whole year, and that little Bridget
Plantagenet stayed at St Mary's Winchester for two or three
years, while her parents were absent in France; moreover we
have already heard of poor Elizabeth and Jane Knyghte, left
for over five years at Cornworthy But an analysis of the
Swaffham Bulbeck accounts shows that the children (if indeed
they are children) stayed for the following periods during the
year 1483, viz., two for forty weeks, one for thirty weeks, one
for twenty-six weeks, two for twenty-two weeks, one for sixteen
weeks, one for twelve weeks and one for six weeks. It is much
more likely that girls were sent to the nuns for elementary
schooling than for the acquirement of worldly accomplishments.

As has already been pointed out, it is difficult to get any
specific information as to the life led by the schoolchildren in
nunneries. But by good fortune some letters written by an
abbess shortly before the Dissolution have been preserved and
give a pleasant picture of a little girl boarding in a nunnery.
The correspondence in question took place between Elizabeth
Shelley, Abbess of St Mary's Winchester, and Honor, Vis-
countess Lisle, concerning the latter's stepdaughter, the lady
Bridget Plantagenet, who was one of the twenty-six aristocratic
young ladies then at school in the nunnery[1]. Lord Lisle was
an illegitimate son of Edward IV, and had been appointed Lord
Deputy of Calais in 1533; and when he and his wife departed
to take up the new office, they were at pains to find suitable
homes for their younger children in England. A stepson of Lord
Lisle's was boarded with the Abbot of Reading and his two
younger daughters, the ladies Elizabeth and Bridget Plantagenet,
were left, the one in charge of her half-brother, Sir John Dudley,
and the other in that of the energetic Abbess of St Mary's
Winchester. It must be admitted that the correspondence
between the abbess and Lady Lisle shows a greater preoccupa-
tion with dress than with learning. The Lady Bridget grew like
the grass in springtime; there was no keeping her in clothes

"After due recommendation," writes the abbess, "Pleaseth it your
good ladyship to know that I have received your letter, dated the

---

[1] Wood, *Letters of Royal and Illustrious Ladies*, II, pp 213–7.

4th day of February last past, by the which I do perceive your pleasure is to know how mistress Bridget your daughter doth, and what things she lacketh. Madam, thanks be to God, she is in good health, but I assure your ladyship she lacketh convenient apparel, for she hath neither whole gown nor kirtle, but the gown and kirtle that you sent her last. And also she hath not one good partlet to put upon her neck, nor but one good coif to put upon her head. Wherefore, I beseech your ladyship to send to her such apparel as she lacketh, as shortly as you may conveniently. Also the bringer of your letter shewed to me that your pleasure is to know how much money I received for mistress Bridget's board, and how long she hath been with me. Madam, she hath been with me a whole year ended the 8th day of July last past, and as many weeks as is between that day and the day of making this bill, which is thirty three weeks; and so she hath been with me a whole year and thirty three weeks, which is in all four score and five weeks And I have received of mistress Katherine Mutton, 10s , and of Stephen Bedham, 20s ; and I received the day of making this bill, of John Harrison, your servant, 40s.; and so I have received in all, since she came to me, toward the payment for her board, 70s Also, madam, I have laid out for her, for mending of her gowns and for two matins books, four pair of hosen, and four pairs of shoes, and other small things, 3s 5d And, good madam, any pleasure that I may do your ladyship and also my prayer, you shall be assured of, with the grace of Jesus, who preserve you and all yours in honour and health. Amen."

But for the matins books, sandwiched uncomfortably between gowns and hosen, there is no clue here as to what the Lady Bridget was learning.

The tenor of the next letter, written about seven months later, is the same, for still the noble little lady grew:

"Mine singular and special good lady," writes the Abbess, " I heartily recommend me to your good ladyship, ascertaining you that I have received from your servant this summer a side of venison and two dozen and a half of pee-wits."

(What flesh-days there must have been in the refectory!)

"And whereas your ladyship do write that you sent me an ermine cape for your daughter, surely I see none, but the tawny velvet gown that you write of, I have received it I have sent unto you, by the bringer of your letter, your daughter's black velvet gown; also I have caused kirtles to be made of her old gowns, according unto your writing; and the 10s you sent is bestowed for her, and more, as it shall appear by a bill of reckoning which I have made of the same. And I trust she shall lack nothing that is necessary for her "

Another letter shows that the wardrobe difficulty was no whit abated, but the Abbess dealt with it by the rather hard-hearted expedient of sending poor Bridget away on a visit to her father's steward at Soberton in Hampshire, in her outgrown clothes, in order that he might be moved to amend her state. Clearly it was not always easy to get what was requisite for a schoolgirl from a gay and busy mother, disporting herself across the sea·

"This is to advertise your ladyship," says the Abbess, "Upon a fourteen or fifteen days before Michaelmas, mistress Waynam and mistress Fawkenor came to Winchester to see mistress Bridget Lisle, with whom came two of my lord's servants, and desired to have mistress Bridget to sir Anthony Windsor's to sport her for a week. And because she was out of apparel, that master Windsor might see her, I was the better content to let her go; and since that time she came no more at Winchester· Wherein I beseech your ladyship think no unkindness in me for my light sending of her for if I had not esteemed her to have come again, she should not have come there at that time "

The reason why lucky little Bridget was enjoying a holiday appears in a letter from the steward, Sir Anthony Windsor, to Lord Lisle, in which he not only takes a firm line over the dress problem (as the Abbess foresaw), but seems also to cast some aspersion upon the nunnery, the nuns, he evidently thought, had no idea how to feed a growing girl, or how to spoil her, as she ought to be spoiled:

Also mistress Bridget recommendeth her to your good lordship, and also to my lady, beseeching you of your blessing. She is now at home with me, because I will provide for her apparel such things as shall be necessary, for she hath overgrown all that she ever hath, except such as she hath had of late: and I will keep her here still if it be your lordship's and my lady's pleasure that I shall so do, and she shall fare no worse that I do, for she is very spare and hath need of cherishing, and she shall lack nothing in learning, nor otherwise that my wife can do for her

Apparently she never went back to the nunnery, and a few years later it was dissolved:

And when (s)he came to Saynte Marie's aisle
   Where nonnes were wont to praie,
The vespers were songe, the shryne was gone,
   And the nonnes had·passyd awaie.

A word should perhaps be added as to the "piety and breeding," which Lady Bridget and other little schoolgirls learned from the nuns, for good sentimentalists of later days often looked back and regretted the loss of a training, presumably instinct with religion and morality It is well nigh impossible to generalise in this matter, so greatly did convents differ from each other. St Mary's Winchester was of very good repute, and for this we have not only the testimony of the local gentlemen, who were commissioned to visit it by Henry VIII in 1536, but also of the visitation which was held by Dr Hede in 1501. Undoubtedly the aristocratic young ladies who went there did not lack the precept and example of pious and well bred mistresses. The statement of the commissioners at Polesworth that the children there were "right virtuously brought up" has often been quoted. So also has the plea of Robert Aske, who led the ill-fated Pilgrimage of Grace, by which the people of Yorkshire sought to bring back the old religion, and in particular the monastic houses; in the abbeys, he said, "all gentlemen (were) much succoured in their needs, with many their young sons there assisted and in nunneries their daughters brought up in virtue"[1]. Less well-known is the tribute of the reformer Thomas Becon (1512-67), the more striking in that he was a staunch Protestant, who had suffered for his faith. Although he refers in disparagement to the nunneries of his own day, his description of the relations between nuns and their pupils cannot be founded solely upon an imaginary golden age

"The young maids," he writes, "were not enforced to wear this or that apparel, to abstain from this or that kind of meats; to sing this or that service, to say so many prayers, to shave their heads; to vow chastity; and for ever to abide in their cloister unto their dying day. But contrariwise, they might wear what apparel they would, so that it were honest and seemly and such as becometh maidens that profess godliness. They might freely eat all kinds of meats according to the rule of the gospel, avoiding all excess and superfluity, yea, and that at all times. Their prayers were free and without compulsion, everyone praying when the Holy Ghost moved their hearts to pray; yea, and that such prayers as present necessity required, and that also not in a strange tongue, but in such language as they did right well understand To shave their heads and to keep such-like superstitious observances as our nuns did in times past and yet do in the kingdom of the pope, they were not compelled For all that they were commanded to do of their schoolmistresses and governesses was nothing else than the doctrine of the gospel and matters appertaining unto honest and civil manners; whom they most willingly obeyed Moreover, it was lawful for them to go out of the cloister when they

---

[1] Quoted Gasquet, *Hen. VIII and the Eng Monasteries* (1899), p 227.

would, or when they were required of their friends; and also to marry
when and with whom they would, so that it were in the Lord. And
would God there were some consideration of this matter had among
the rulers of the christian commonwealth, that young maids might
be godly brought up, and learn from their cradles 'to be sober-minded,
to love their husbands, to love their children, to be discreet, chaste,
housewifely, good, obedient to their husbands'''[1].

These eulogies are all necessarily tinged by the knowledge
that the nunneries either were about to disappear, or had disappeared, from England. They had filled a useful function and
men were willing to be to their faults a little blind. It cannot
be doubted that the gentry and the substantial middle class
appreciated them; up to the very eve of the Dissolution legacies
to monastic houses are a common feature in wills. Only an
inadequate conclusion, however, is to be reached from a study
of tributes such as those of the commissioners at St Mary's
Winchester and Polesworth and of Robert Aske. If we turn
to pre-Reformation visitation reports, which are free from the
desire to state a case, the evidence is more mixed. It is only
reasonable to conclude that many nunneries did indeed bring
children up, with the example of virtue before their eyes, and
the *omnia bene* of many reports reinforces such a conclusion.
But it is impossible also to avoid the conviction that other
houses were not always desirable homes for the young, nor nuns
their best example When Alnwick visited his diocese in the first
half of the fifteenth century there were children at Godstow,
where at least one nun was frankly immoral and where all
received visits freely from the scholars of Oxford, nor was the
general reputation of the house good at other periods. There were
children also at Catesby and at St Michael's Stamford, which
were in a thoroughly bad state, under bad prioresses. At Catesby
the poor innocents lay in the dorter, where lay also sister Isabel
Benet, far gone with child; and they must have heard the
Prioress screaming "Beggars!" and "Whores!" at the nuns and
dragging them round the cloister by their hair[2]. At St Michael's
Stamford, all was in disorder and no less than three of the nuns
were unchaste, one having twice run away, each time with a
different partner The visitation of Gracedieu on the same

---

[1] *The Catechism of Thomas Bacon, S.T P*, ed. John Ayre (Parker Soc
1894), p. 377.   See above, p. 82.

occasion shows too much quarrelling and misrule to make possible a very high opinion of its piety or of its breeding. If we turn to another set of injunctions, the great series for the diocese of York, it must be conceded that though the gentry of the county doubtless found the convents useful as schools and lodging houses, it is difficult to see how Aske's plea that "their daughters (were) brought up in virtue" could possibly have been true of the fourteenth century, when the morals and manners of the nuns were extremely bad There is not much evidence for the period of which Aske could speak from his own knowledge, but at Esholt, where two children were at school in 1537, one of the nuns was found to have "lyved incontinenthe and vnchast and .... broght forth a child of her bodie begotten" and an alehouse had been set up within the convent gates, in 1535[1]. The only safe generalisation to make about this, as about so many other problems of medieval social history, is that there can be no generalisation. The standard of piety and breeding likely to be acquired by children in medieval nunneries must have differed considerably from time to time and from house to house

[1] *Yorks Archaeol Journ.* XVI, pp. 452–3 Unluckily among Archbishop Lee's injunctions there remain only three sets addressed to nunneries; there are also two letters concerning an immoral and apostate ex-Prioress of Basedale. At the other two nunneries addressed, Nunappleton and Sinning-thwaite, no specific accusations are made, but the Archbishop enjoins that the nuns shall "observe chastity" (§ IX, p 440) and avoid the suspicious company of men (§ V, p 441)

CHAPTER VII

ROUTINE AND REACTION

Where is the pain that does not become deadened after a thousand years? or what is the nature of that pleasure or happiness which never wearies by monotony? Earthly pleasures and pains are short in proportion as they are keen, of any others, which are both intense and lasting, we can form no idea ...To beings constituted as we are, the monotony of singing Psalms would be as great an affliction as the pains of hell and might even be pleasantly interrupted by them.

JOWETT, Introduction to Plato's *Phaedo*.

ST BENEDICT'S common sense is nowhere more strikingly shown than in his division of the routine of monastic life between the three occupations of divine service, manual labour and reading. Not only has this arrangement the merit of developing the different sides of men's natures, spirit, body and brain, but it fulfils a deep psychological necessity. The essence of communal life is regularity, but no human being can subsist without a further ingredient of variety. St Benedict knew well enough that unless he provided the stimulus of change within the Rule, outraged nature would seek for it outside. Hence the careful adjustment of occupations to combine variety with regularity. The services were the supreme joy and duty of the monk and nun and the life of the convent was centred in its church. But these services were not excessively long and were divided from each other by periods of sleep by night and of work, or study, or meditation by day, after the manner which Crashaw inimitably set forth in his *Description of a Religious House and Condition of Life*:

> A hasty portion of prescribèd sleep;
> Obedient slumbers, that can wake and weep,
> And sing, and sigh, and work, and sleep again,
> Still rolling a round sphere of still-returning pain.
> Hands full of hearty labours; pains that pay
> And prize themselves, do much, that more they may,
> And work for work, not wages; let tomorrow's
> New drops wash off the sweat of this day's sorrows.
> A long and daily-dying life, which breathes
> A respiration of reviving deaths.

The monastic day was divided into seven offices and the time at which these were said varied slightly according to the season of the year. The night office began about 2 a m., when the nuns rose from their beds and entered their choir, where Matins were said, followed immediately by Lauds. The next service was Prime, said at 6 or 7 a m., and then throughout the day came Tierce, Sext, None, Vespers, and Compline, with an interval of about three hours between them. The time of these monastic Hours (as they were called) changed gradually after the time of St Benedict, and later None, which should have been at 3 p m., was said at noon, leaving the nuns from about 12 midday to 5 p.m. in the winter and 1 p.m. to 8 p.m in the summer for work. Compline, the last service of all, was said at 7 p.m. in winter and at 8 p.m. in summer, after which the nuns were supposed to retire immediately to bed in their dorter, where (in the words of the Syon *Rule*) "none shal jutte up on other wylfully, nor spyt up on the stayres, goyng up or down, nor in none other place repreuably, but yf they trede it out forthwyth"![1] They had in all about eight hours sleep, broken in the middle by the night service; and they had three meals, a light repast of bread and beer after Prime in the morning, a solid dinner to the accompaniment of reading aloud, and a short supper immediately after vespers at 5 or 6 p.m.[2]

Except for certain specified periods of relaxation, strict silence was supposed to be observed for a large part of the day, and if it were necessary for the nuns to communicate with each other, they were urged to do so in an abbreviated form, or by signs. Thus in 1319 Bishop Stapeldon of Exeter wrote to the nuns of Polsloe

that silence be kept in due places, according to the Rule and observances of St Benedict; and, if it be desirable that any word be spoken in the aforesaid places, for any reasonable occasion, then let it be gently and so low that it be scarce heard of the other nuns, and in as few words as may be needed for the comprehension of those who hear; and better in Latin than in any other tongue, yet the Latin need not be well-ordered by way of grammar, but thus, *candela, liber, missale, gradale, panis, vinum, cervisia, est, non, sic* and so forth[3].

[1] Aungier, *Hist. of Syon Mon.* p 385 Compare also the regulations for behaviour in choir, "There also none shal use to spytte ouer the stalles, nor in any other place wher any suster is wonte to pray, but yf it anone be done oute, for defoylyng of ther clothes " *Ib* p. 320
[2] The hours seem to have varied in length according to the season; see Butler, *Benedictine Monachism*, ch. xvii.   [3] *Reg. W de Stapeldon*, p 316

PLATE VI

DOMINICAN NUNS IN QUIRE

The nuns of Syon had a table of signs drawn up for them by Thomas Betsone, one of the brethren of the house, a person of extraordinary ingenuity and no sense of humour[1] The sort of dumb pandemonium which went on at the Syon dinner table must have been more mirth provoking than speech The sister who desired fish would "wagge her hande displaied sidelynges in manere of a fissh taill," she who wanted milk would "draw her left little fynger in maner of mylkyng"; for mustard one would "hold her nose in the uppere part of her righte fiste and rubbe it," and another for salt would "philippe with her right thombe and his forefynger ouere the left thombe", another, desirous of wine, would "meue her fore fynger vp and downe vpon the ende of her thombe afore her eghe"; and the guilty sacristan, struck by the thought that she had not provided incense for the mass, would "put her two fyngers vnto her nose thirles (nostrils)." There are no less than 106 signs in the table and on the whole it is not surprising that the Rule enjoins that "it is never leful to use them witheoute some reson and profitable nede, ffor ofte tyme more hurt ethe an euel sygne than an euel worde, and more offence it may be to God"[2].

The time set apart in the monastic day for work was divided between brain work and manual labour In the golden days of monasticism the time devoted to reading enabled the monasteries to become homes of learning; splendid libraries were collected for the use of the monks and in the scriptorium men skilled in writing and in illumination copied books and maintained the great series of chronicles, in which the middle ages live again. The nuns of certain Anglo-Saxon houses, and of certain continental houses at a later date, had some reputation for learning In early days, too, the hours devoted to labour were spent in the fields, or more often in the workshops of the house; and those who had been skilled in crafts in the world continued to exercise them. The nuns of Anglo-Saxon England were famed for the needlework executed during the hours of work., Besides this labour the Rule ordained that the monks and nuns should take it in turns to serve their brethren in the kitchen every week and an eleventh century chronicler records "in the monasteries

---

[1] Aungier, op cit pp 405–9 It is unlikely, however, that Betsone actually invented any of the signs, for similar lists are to be found in the early consuetudinaries of Cluniac houses and other sources The signs were probably to a great extent "common form." [2] Ib p 298

I saw counts cooking in the kitchens and margraves leading the pigs out to feed"[1]. It was by reason of this intellectual and manual labour that the early monks rendered, as it were incidentally, an immense service to civilisation. Their aim and purpose was the salvation of their souls, but because the Rule under which they lived declared that labour was one of the means to that salvation, they added many of the merits of the active to those of the contemplative life. The early Benedictines were great missionaries, ardent scholars, enlightened landowners and even energetic statesmen. The early Cistercians made the woods and wildernesses, in which they settled, blossom like a rose. But apart from the social services thus rendered to civilisation, the threefold division of monastic life into prayer, study and labour was vital to monasticism itself, since it afforded the essential element of variety in routine.

The benefits of routine are obvious: any life which exists for the regular performance of specific duties, above all any life which is carried on in a community, must depend very largely upon fixed hours and carefully organised occupations. The Rule of St Benedict made a serious attempt to render monastic life possible and beneficial to the average human being, by the combination of regularity and variety which has been described above. There was constant change of occupation, but there was no waste and no muddle. It is extremely significant that monasticism broke down directly St Benedict's careful adjustment of occupations became upset With the growing wealth of the monasteries manual labour became undignified; some orders relied on lay brethren, the majority on servants. Gone was the day when counts cooked in the kitchens; in the fourteenth century monks and nuns paid large wages to their cooks and even in a small nunnery it was regarded as legitimate cause for complaint not to have a convent servant. Learning also fell away after the growth of the universities in the twelfth century; the poverty of the monastic chronicles of the fourteenth and fifteenth centuries is one witness to the fact; the necessity to send injunctions to nunneries first in French and then in English, as the knowledge of Latin and then of French died out in them, is another. Of the three occupations, learning, manual labour

[1] Bernold, *Chron* (1083) in *Mon Germ Hist* v, p 439, quoted in Workman, *The Evolution of the Monastic Ideal*, p 157.

and divine service, only the last was left. Is it surprising that
that also began to be looked upon as a weary and monotonous
routine, when the monks and nuns came to it, not fresh from the
stimulus of study or of labour, but from indolence, or from the
worldly pleasures of the tavern, the hunt, the gambling board,
the flirtation, the gossip, wherewith they often filled the spare
time, which the wise Benedictine Rule would have filled with
a change of occupation?

All safeguards against a petrifying routine were now broken
down. We are wont to-day to look with disquiet upon the life
of a clerk in an office, endlessly adding up rows of figures, with
an interval for luncheon, but the clerk has his evenings, his
Sundays, his annual holiday, his life as son, or husband, or father.
For the medieval monk there was no such relaxation When the
salutary labour of hand and brain ordained by St Benedict no
longer found a place in his life, he was delivered over bound
to an endless routine of dorter, church, frater and cloister,
which stretched from day to night and from night to day again.
For nuns the monotony was even greater, for they had lost
more completely than monks their early tradition of learning
and they could not pass happy years in study at a university
(as a few monks from great abbeys were able to do), nor find
some solace in exercising the functions of a priest, moreover
women were more apt even than men to enter the religious life
without any real vocation for it, since there was hardly any
other career for unmarried ladies of gentle birth. It would be
an exaggeration to say that this uneventful life was necessarily
distasteful. To the majority it was doubtless a happy existence;
monotony appears peace to those who love it.

> No cruel guard of diligent cares, that keep
> Crown'd woes awake, as things too wise for sleep:
> But reverent discipline and religious fear,
> And soft obedience, find sweet biding here,
> Silence and sacred rest; peace and pure joys,
> Kind loves keep house, lie close and make no noise

Here behind the walls of the convent "a common grayness
silvered everything" and all care was remote, save that, never
to be escaped by womankind, of making two ends meet.

Nevertheless the danger was there. Only a minority, one
may be sure, revolted actively against the duties which are

sometimes, most significantly, called "the burthen of religion"[1].
That minority is known to us, for the sinner and the apostate,
whether inspired by lust or by levity, mere victims to their own
weakness, or active rebels against an intolerable dulness, have
left their mark in official documents. But the number can only
be guessed at of those others, who carried in their hearts for all
their staid lives the complaint of the Latin song·

> Sono tintinnabulum
> Repeto psalterium,
> Gratum linquo somnium
> Cum dormire cuperem,
>   Heu misella!
> Nichil est deterius tali vita
> Cum enim sim petulans et lasciva[2].

> The bell I am ringing,
> The psalter am singing,
> And from my bed creeping
> Who fain would be sleeping,
>   Misery me!
> O what can be worse than this life that I dree,
> When naughty and lovelorn and wanton I be?

"Nuns fret not at their convent's narrow room" is a charming
justification of the sonnet, but it is neither good psychology nor
good history

It can never be too often repeated that many monks and
nuns entered religion as a career while still children, with no
particular vocation for the religious life. To such, even though
they might experience no longing for the forbidden pleasures of
the world, the monotony of the cloister would often be hard to
bear. Their young limbs would kick against its restrictions and
the changing moods of adolescence would turn and twist in vain
within the iron bars of its unadaptable routine. Even to those
no longer young happiness would depend at the best upon the
fostering of a quick spiritual life, at the worst upon lack of
imagination and of vitality. The undaunted daughter of desires,
the man in whom religion burned as a strong fire, could find

---

[1] E g a nun asks that sufficient clothes and food be ministered to her
"ut fortis sit ad subeundum pondus religionis et diuini seruicii" *Linc
Visit* II, p 5 A bishop orders no nun to be admitted unless she be "talem
que onera chori. ceteris religionem concernentibus poterit supportare"
Ib. I, p 53

[2] Vattasso, *Studi Medievali* (1904), I, p 124 Quoted in *Mod Philology*
(1908), v, pp 10–11. I have ventured to combine parts of two verses

happiness in the life. But lesser brethren could not.' Ennui,
more deadly even than sensual temptation, was the devil who
tormented them. So in the convents of the fourteenth and
fifteenth centuries, a sympathetic eye and an understanding
mind will diagnose the fundamental disease as reaction against
routine by men and women in whom Nature, expelled by a
pitchfork, had returned a thousand times more strong.

This reaction from routine took several forms. It is somewhere at the bottom of all the more serious sins, which the pitchfork method of attaining salvation brought upon human creatures
with bodies as well as souls In this chapter, however, we are
concerned not with these graver faults of immorality, but with
things less gross, and yet in their cumulative effect no less fatal
to monastic life. Such was the neglect of that praise of God,
which was the primary *raison d'être* of the monk and nun, so
that services sometimes became empty forms, to be hurried
through with scant devotion, occasionally with scandalous ir-
reverence. Such was the deadly sin of *accidie*, the name of
which is forgotten today, though the thing itself is with us still.
Such were the nerves on edge, the small quarrels, the wear and
tear of communal life; such also the gay clothes, the pet animals
and the worldly amusements, with which nuns sought to enliven
their existence. For all these things were in some sense a reaction
from routine.

Carelessness in the performance of the monastic hours was
an exceedingly common fault during the later middle ages and
often finds a place in episcopal injunctions. Sometimes monks
and nuns "cut" the services, as at Peterborough in 1437, when
only ten or twelve of the 44 monks came on ordinary days to
church[1], or at Nuncoton in 1440, where many of the nuns failed
to come to compline, but busied themselves instead in various
domestic offices, or wandered idly in the garden[2]. Often they

---

[1] *Alnwick's Visit* MS f. 1d; but some of these would be absent from the
monastery.

[2] *Ib.* ff 71d, 72 For other injunctions against "cutting" services, see
Heynings, 1351 and 1392 (*Linc Epis Reg Memo Gynewell*, f. 34d, and *Bokyngham*, f 397), Elstow 1387 and 1421 (*ib. Bokyngham*, f. 343 and *Linc Visit* I,
p. 51), Godstow 1279 and 1434 (*Reg. J Peckham*, III, p. 846, *Linc Visit* I,
p 66), Romsey 1387 (*New Coll* MS f 84), Cannington 1351 (*Reg R of Shrewsbury*, p. 684), Nunkeeling 1314, Thicket 1309, Yedingham 1314, Swine 1318,
Wykeham 1314, Arthington 1318 (*V.C.H. Yorks* III, pp 120, 124, 127, 181,
183, 188), Sinningthwaite 1534 (*Yorks. Arch. Journ.* XVI, p 443), etc

came late to matins, a fault which was common in nunneries,
for the nuns were prone to sit up drinking and gossiping after
compline, instead of going straight to bed[1], and these nocturnal
carousals, however harmless in themselves, did not conduce to
wakefulness at one a.m. Consequently they were somewhat
sleepy, *quodammodo sompnolentes,* at matins and found an almost
Johnsonian difficulty in getting up early. At Stainfield in 1519
Atwater found that half an hour sometimes elapsed between
the last stroke of the bell and the beginning of the office and
that some of the nuns did not sing but dozed, partly because
they had not enough candles, partly because they went to bed
late; they also performed the offices very negligently[2]. But most
often of all the fault of monks and nuns lay in gabbling through
the services as quickly as possible in order to get them over.
They left out syllables at the beginning and end of words, they
omitted the *dipsalma* or *pausacio* between two verses, so that
one side of the choir was beginning the second half, before the
other side had finished the first, they skipped sentences, they
mumbled and slurred over what should have been "entuned in
their nose ful semely."

Episcopal injunctions not infrequently animadvert against
this irreverent treatment of the offices. At Catesby in 1442
Isabel Benet asserted that "divine service is chanted at so great
speed that no pauses are made," and at Carrow in 1526 several
of the older nuns complained that the sisters sang and said the
service more quickly than they ought, without due pauses.
A strong injunction sent to Nuncoton in 1531 declares that the
hours have been "doon with grete festinacon, haste and without
deuocon, contrarye to the good manner and ordre of religion"[3].

---

[1] See e g. *Linc Visit* II, pp 1, 8, 67, 131, 133, 134-5, *Linc. Epis Reg.
Memo Gynewell,* f 34d, *Sede Vacante Reg* (Worc Hist Soc), p. 276,
Reg Epis. J Peckham, II, pp 651-2, etc

[2] *V.C H. Lincs* II, p 131 For other instances of lateness at matins, see
Heynings 1442 (*Linc Visit* II, p 133), Godstow 1432 (*Linc Visit* I, p 66),
Flixton 1514 (Jessopp, *Visit of Dioc of Norwich,* p 143), Romsey 1302
(Liveing, *Records of Romsey Abbey,* p 100), Easebourne 1478, 1524 (*Sussex
Arch Coll* IX, pp. 17, 26-7), St Radegund's, Cambridge (Gray, *Priory of
St Radegund, Cambridge,* p 36)

[3] *Linc Visit* II, p. 48, Jessopp, *Visit. of Dioc of Norwich,* p. 209,
Arch XLVII, p 55; compare Romsey 1387, 1507 (*New Coll. MS* f. 84;
Liveing, *op cit.* p 231), St Helen's Bishopsgate, c 1432 (*Hist MS Com
Rep* IX, App. p. 57)

Indeed so common was the fault that the Father of Evil was obliged to employ a special devil called Tittivillus, whose sole business it was to collect the dropped syllables and gabbled verses and carry them back to his master in a sack. One rhyme distinguishes carefully between the contents of his sack:

> Hii sunt qui psalmos corrumpunt nequiter almos,
> Dangler, cum jasper, lepar, galper quoque draggar,
> Momeler, forskypper, forereynner, sic et overleper,
> Fragmina verborum Tutivillus colligit horum[1]

A holy Cistercian abbot once interviewed Tittivillus; this is the tale as the nuns of Syon read it in their *Myroure of Oure Ladye*.

We rede of an holy Abbot of the order of Cystreus that whyle he stode in the quyer at mattyns, he sawe a fende that had a longe and a greate poke hangynge about hys necke, and wente aboute the quyer from one to an other, and wayted bysely after all letters, and syllables, and wordes, and faylynges, that eny made, and them he gathered dylygently and putte them in hys poke. And when he came before the Abbot, waytynge yf oughte had escaped hym, that he myghte have gotten and put in hys bagge; the Abbot was astoned and aferde of the foulenes and mysshape of hym, and sayde vnto hym. What art thow; And he answered and sayd I am a poure dyuel, and my name ys Tytyuyllus, and I do myne offyce that is commytted vnto me. And what is thyne offyce sayd the Abbot, he answeryd I muste eche day he sayde brynge my master a thousande pokes full of faylynges, and of neglygences in syllables and wordes, that ar done in youre order in redynge and in syngynge. And else I must be sore beten[2]

Carelessness in the singing of the services was not, however, the most serious result of reaction against routine. If the men and women of sensibility failed to keep intelligence active in the pursuit of spiritual or temporal duties, if they cared no longer to use brain and spirit as they performed the daily round, *accidia*[3], that dread disease, half ennui and half melancholia, which, though common to all men, was recognised as the peculiar

---

[1] "These are they who wickedly corrupt the holy psalms · the dangler, the gasper, the leaper, the galloper, the dragger, the mumbler, the foreskipper, the forerunner and the over leaper: Tittivillus collecteth the fragments of these men's words" G G. Coulton, *Med Garn* p 423 He also collected the gossip of women in church On Tittivillus see my article in the *Cambridge Magazine*, 1917, pp 158–60

[2] *Myroure of Oure Ladye*, ed. Blunt (E E T S), p. 54.

[3] Greek ἀκηδία, whence *acedia* or *accidia* in Latin, English *accidie* It is a pity that the word has fallen out of use. The disease has not.

menace of the cloister, lay ever in wait for them   Against this
sin of intellectual and spiritual sloth all the great churchmen
of the middle ages inveigh, recognising in it the greatest menace
of religious life, from which all other sins may follow[1]. If *accidia*
once laid hold upon a monk he was lost; ceasing to perform
with active mind his religious duties, he would find them a
meaningless, endless routine, filling him with irritation, with
boredom and with a melancholy against which he might struggle
in vain The fourth century cenobite Cassian has left a detailed
description of the effects of *accidia* in the cloister, declaring
that it was specially disturbing to a monk about the sixth hour
"like some fever which seizes him at stated times," so that many
declared that this was "the sickness that destroyeth in the noon
day," spoken of in the ninetieth psalm[2]. Many centuries later
Dante crystallised it in four unsurpassable lines. As he passed
through the fifth circle of hell he saw a black and filthy marsh, in
which struggled the souls of those who had been overcome by
anger, but deeper than the angry were submerged other souls,
whose sobs rose in bubbles through the muddy water and who
could only gurgle their confession in their throats. These were the

[1] An interesting modern study of this moral disease is to be found in
a book of sermons by the late Bishop of Oxford, Dr Paget, *The Spirit of
Discipline* (1891), which contains an introductory essay "concerning
Accidie," in which the subject is treated historically, with illustrations from
the writings of Cassian, St John of the Ladder, Dante and St Thomas
Aquinas, in the middle ages, Marchantius and Francis Neumayer in the
seventeenth century, and Wordsworth, Keble, Trench, Matthew Arnold,
Tennyson and Stevenson in the nineteenth century. See also Dr Paget's
first sermon "The Sorrow of the World," which deals with the same subject
He diagnoses the main elements of *Accidia* very ably: "As one compares the
various estimates of the sin one can mark three main elements which help
to make it what it is—elements which can be distinguished, though in
experience, I think, they almost always tend to meet and mingle, they are
gloom and *sloth* and *irritation* " *Op cit* p 54 On *Accidia*, see also H B
Workman, *The Evolution of the Monastic Ideal* (1913), pp. 326–31 During
the great war the disease of *accidie* was prevalent in prison camps, as any
account of Ruhleben shows very clearly   For a short psychological
study of this manifestation of it, see Vischer, A L , *Barbed Wire Disease*
(1919)

[2] See book X of Cassian's *De Coenobiorum Institutis*, which is entitled
"De Spiritu Acediae" (Wace and Schaff, *Select Library of Nicene and Post-
Nicene Fathers of the Christian Church*, 2nd ser , vol XI, Sulpitius Severus,
Vincent of Lerins and John Cassian, pp 266 ff , chapters I and II are para-
phrased by Dr Paget, *op cit.* pp 8–10), Book IX, on the kindred sin of
Tristitia is also worthy of study, the two are always closely connected, as
is shown by the anecdotes quoted below

souls of men who had fallen victims to the sin of *accidia* in their lives

> Fitti nel limo dicon Tristi fummo
> Nel' aer dolce che dal sol s' allegra,
> Portando dentro accidioso fummo:
> Or ci attristiam nella belletta negra.

Fixed in the slime, they say, "Sullen were we in the sweet air, that is gladdened by the sun, carrying lazy smoke in our hearts, now lie we sullen here in the black mire"[1].

But the working of the poison is most brilliantly described by Chaucer, in his *Persones Tale*:

"After the sinnes of Envie and of Ire, now wol I speken of the sinne of Accidie. For Envye blindeth the herte of a man, and Ire troubleth a man, and Accidie maketh him hevy, thoghtful and wrawe Envye and Ire maken bitternesse in herte; which bitternesse is moder of Accidie and binimeth him the love of alle goodnesse. Thanne is Accidie the anguissh of a trouble herte .'.He dooth alle thing with anoy and with wrawnesse, slaknesse and excusacioun, and with ydelnesse and unlust....Now comth Slouthe, that wol nat suffre noon hardnesse ne no penaunce ..Thanne comth drede to biginne to werke any gode werkes; for certes he that is enclyned to sinne, him thinketh it is so greet an empryse for to undertake to doon werkes of goodnesse ... Now comth wanhope, that is despeir of the mercy of God, that comth somtyme of to muche outrageous sorwe, and somtyme of to muche drede, imagininge that he hath doon so much sinne, that it wol nat availlen him, though he wolde repenten him and forsake sinne: thurgh which despeir or drede he abaundoneth al his herte to every maner sinne, as seith seint Augustin Which dampnable sinne, if that it continue unto his ende, it is cleped sinning in the holy gost . . Soothly he that despeireth him is lyk the coward champioun recreant, that seith creant withoute nede. Allas! alias! nedeles is he recreant and nedeles despeired Certes the mercy of God is euere redy to every penitent and is aboven alle hise werkes .Thanne cometh sompnolence, that is sluggy slombringe, which maketh a man be hevy and dul in body and in soule; and this sinne comth of Slouthe "

He proceeds to describe further symptoms,

"Necligence or recchelesnesse...ydelnesse..'.the sinne that man clepen *Tarditas*" and "Lachesse,"

and concludes thus,

"Thanne comth a manere coldnesse, that freseth al the herte of man. Thanne comth undevocioun, thurgh which a man is so blent, as seith seint Bernard, and hath swiche langour in soule, that he may neither rede ne singe in holy chirche, ne here ne thinke of no devocioun, ne travaille with his handes in no good werk, that it nis him unsavory and al apalled Thanne wexeth he slow and slombry, and sone wol

---

[1] Dante, *Inferno*, VII, l 121 ff Translation by J. A Carlyle.

be wrooth, and sone is enclyned to hate and to envye. Thanne comth
the sinne of worldly sorwe, swich as is cleped *tristicia*, that sleeth man,
as seint Paul seith. For certes swich sorwe werketh to the deeth of the
soule and of the body also, for therof comth, that a man is anoyed of
his owene lyf. Wherfore swich sorwe shorteth ful ofte the lyf of a man,
er that his tyme be come by wey of kinde"[1]

This masterly diagnosis of the sin of spiritual sloth and its
branches is illustrated by several stories which bear unmistak-
ably the impress of a dreadful truth. Johann Busch's account
of his early temptations and doubts has often been quoted.
A strong character, he overcame the temptation and emerged
stronger[2]. But Caesarius of Heisterbach has two anecdotes of
weaker brethren which show how exactly Chaucer described the
anguish of a troubled heart. The first is of particular interest
to us because it concerns a woman:

"A certain nun, a woman of advanced age, and, as was supposed,
of great holiness, was so overcome by the vice of melancholy (*tristitiae*)
and so vexed with a spirit of blasphemy, doubt and distrust, that
she fell into despair And she began altogether to doubt those
things which she had believed from infancy and which it behoved
her to believe, nor could she be induced by anyone to take the holy
sacraments, and when her sisters and also her nieces in the flesh
besought her why she was thus hardened, she answered "I am of the
lost, of those who shall be damned " One day the Prior, growing angry,
said to her, "Sister, unless you recover from your unbelief, when you
die I will have you buried in a field." And she, hearing him, was silent
but kept his words in her heart. One day, when certain of the sisters
were to go on a journey I know not whither, she secretly followed them
to the banks of the river Moselle, whereon the monastery is situated,
and when the ship, which was carrying the sisters, put off, she threw
herself from the shore into the river Those who were in the ship
heard the sound of a splash, and looking out thought her body to be
a dog, but one of them, desiring (by God's will) to know more certainly
what it was, ran quickly to the place and seeing a human being,
entered the river and drew her out Then when they perceived that
it was the aforesaid nun, already wellnigh drowned, they were all
frightened, and when they had cared for her and she had coughed up
the water and could speak, they asked her, "Why, sister, didst thou
act thus cruelly?" and she replied, pointing to the Prior, "My lord
there threatened that I should be buried when dead in a field, wherefore I preferred to be drowned in the flood rather than to be buried

[1] Chaucer, *The Persones Tale*, §§ 53–9
[2] See the translation of the episode (from Busch, *Chronicon Windeshemense*, ed K Grube, p 395) in Coulton, *Med Garner*, pp 641–4 On the
subject of medieval doubt and despair see Coulton in the *Hibbert Journal*,
XIV (1916), pp 598–9 and *From St Francis to Dante*, pp 313–4

like a beast in the field " Then they led her back to the monastery and guarded her more carefully. Behold what great evil is born of melancholy (*tristitia*). That woman was brought up from infancy in the monastery She was a chaste, devout, stern and religious virgin, and, as the mistress [of the novices] of a neighbouring monastery told me, all the maidens educated by her were of better discipline and more devout than others[1].

The other anecdote tells of an old lay brother, who at the end of a long life fell into despair:

"I know not," says Caesarius, "by what judgment of God he was made thus sad and fearful, that he was so greatly afraid for his sins and despaired altogether of the life eternal He did not indeed doubt in his faith, but rather despaired of salvation He could be cheered by no scriptural authorities and brought back to the hope of forgiveness by no examples Yet he is believed to have sinned but little. When the brothers asked him, 'What makes you fear, why do you despair?' he answered, 'I cannot pray as I was used to do, and so I fear hell.' Because he laboured with the vice of *tristitia*, therefore he was filled with *accidia*, and from each of these was despair born in his heart. He was placed in the infirmary and on a certain morning he prepared him for death, and came to his master, saying, 'I can no longer fight against God ' And when his master paid but little attention to his words, he went forth to the fish pond of the monastery near by and threw himself into it and was drowned[2] "

Only a small minority, it is needless to say, was driven to this anguish of despair. For the majority the strain of conventual life found outlet, not in these black moods, but in a tendency to bicker one with another, to get excitement by exaggerating the small events of daily existence into matter for jealousies and disputes. For the strain was a double one; to monotony was added the complete lack of privacy, the wear and tear of communal life, not only always doing the same thing at the same time, but always doing it in company with a number of other people. The beauty of human fellowship, the happy friendliness of life in a close society are too obvious to need description.

> For if heuene be on this erthe · and ese to any soule,
> It is in cloistere or in scole · by many skilles I fynde;
> For in cloistre cometh no man · to chide ne to fiʒte,
> But alle is buxomnesse there and bokes · to rede and to lerne,
> In scole there is scorne · but if a clerke wil lerne,
> And grete loue and lykynge · for eche of hem loueth other[3].

[1] Caes. of Heist. *Dial Mirac* ed Strange, I, pp 209–10

[2] *Ib* I pp 210–11. For a case of doubt in an anchoress, which, however ended well, see *ib* I, pp. 206–8.

[3] Langland, *Piers Plowman*, ed Skeat, B, passus X, 300–5

But it is necessary also to remember the other side of the picture Personal idiosyncrasies were no less apt to jar in the middle ages than they are today; there are unfortunates who are born to be unpopular; there are tempers which will lose themselves; and in conventual life there is no balm of solitude for frayed nerves These nuns were very human people; a mere accident of birth had probably sent them to a convent rather than to the care of husband and children in a manor-hall, just as in the eighteenth and nineteenth centuries a mere accident of birth made one son the squire, another the soldier and a third the parson No special saintliness of disposition was theirs and no miracle intervened to render them immune from tantrums when they crossed the convent threshold. Nothing is at once more striking and more natural than the prevalence of little quarrels, sometimes growing into serious disputes, among the inmates of monasteries Browning's Spanish Cloister was no mere figment of his inventive brain; indeed it is, if anything, less startling than the medieval Langland's description of the convent, where Wrath was cook and where all was far from "buxomnesse." Certainly Langland's indictment is a violent one, the satirist must darken his colours to catch the eye; and, had Chaucer been the painter, we might have had a dispute couched in more courteous terms and more "estatlich of manere." But the satirist's account is significant, because his very office demands that he shall exaggerate only what exists; his words are a smoke which cannot rise without fire. So Langland may speak through the lips of Wrath, with two white eyes·

> I have an aunte to nonne · and an abbesse bothe,
> Hir were leuere swowe or swelte · þan suffre any peyne.
> I haue be cook in hir kichyne · and þe couent serued
> Many monthes with hem · and with monkes bothe.
> I was þe priouresses potagere · and other poure ladyes
> And made hem ioutes of iangelynge · þat dame Iohanne was a
>   bastard,
> And dame Clarice a kniȝtes douȝter · ac a kokewolde was hire
>   syre,
> And dame Peronelle a prestes file · Priouresse worth she neuere
> For she had childe in chirityme · all owre chapitere it wiste ·
> Of wycked wordes I, Wrath · here wortes imade,
> Til "thow lixte" and "thow lixte" lopen oute at ones,

And eyther hitte other · vnder the cheke;
Hadde thei had knyves, by Cryst · her eyther had killed other[1].

From "thow lixte" to "Gr-r-r you swine" how little change!

Sober records bear out Langland's contention that Wrath was at home in nunneries Some of the worst cases have already been described; election disputes, disputes arising from a prioress's favouritism, Margaret Wavere dragging her nuns about the choir by their hair, and screaming insults at them, Katherine Wells hitting them on the head with fists and feet[2]. Doubtless quarrels seldom got as far as blows; but bad temper and wordy warfare were common. Insubordination was sometimes at the root of the discord, nuns refused to submit meekly to correction after the proclamation of their faults in chapter, or to obey their superiors. The words of another satirist show that the monastic vow of obedience sometimes sat lightly upon their shoulders.

> Also another lady there was
> That hy3t dame dysobedyent
> And sche set now3t by her priores.
> Ans than me thow3t alle was schent,
> For sugettys schulde euyr be dylygent
> Bothe in worde, in wylle and dede,
> To plese her souerynes wyth gode entent,
> And hem obey, ellys god forbede.
> And of alle the defawtes that I cowde se
> Thorow3 schewyng of experience,
> Hyt was one of the most that grevyd me,
> The wantyng of obedyence
> For hyt schulde be chese in consciens
> Alle relygius rule wytnesseth the same
> And when I saw her in no reverence,
> I my3t no lenger abyde for schame,
> For they setten not by obedyence.
> And than for wo myne hert gan blede
> Ne they hadden her in no reuerence,
> But few or none to her toke hede[3]

---

[1] Langland, *Piers Plowman*, ed. Skeat, B, passus v, ll. 153–65 The C text has a variant for the last four lines

> Thus thei sitte the sustres · somtyme, and disputen,
> Til "thow lixt" and "thow lixt" · be lady over hem alle;
> And then awake ich, Wratthe · and wold be auenged.
> Thanne ich crie and cracche · with my kene nailes,
> Bothe byte and bete and brynge forthe suche thewes,
> That alle ladies me lothen · that louen eny worschep.

It is strange that the same hand which wrote these lines should have written the beautiful description of convent life quoted on p 297.

[2] See above, p. 82 and below, Note F

[3] From "Why can't I be a nun," *Trans. of Philol Soc* 1858, Pt ii, p 268.

Again the colours are darkened, but the eyes of the satirist had seen.

At St Mary's, Winchester, insubordination was evidently the chief fault. William of Wykeham writes to the Abbess:

By public rumour it has come to our ears that some of the nuns of the aforesaid house…care not to submit to or even to obey you and the deans and other obedientiaries lawfully constituted by you in those things which concern regular observances nor to show them due reverence, and that they will not bear or undergo the reproofs and corrections inflicted upon them by their superiors for their faults, but break out into vituperation and altercation with each other and in no way submit to these corrections, meanwhile other nuns of your house by detractions, conspiracies, confederacies, leagues, obloquies, contradictions and other breaches of discipline (*insolencus*) and laxities (concerning which we speak not at present)

neglect the rule of St Benedict and other due observances. The Abbess is warned to punish the nuns and to enforce the rule more firmly than heretofore and to furnish the Bishop with the names of rebels. At the same time he addresses a letter to the nuns bidding them show obedience to their superiors and receive correction humbly "henceforth blaming no one therefore nor altercating one with another, saying that these or those were badly or excessively punished"[1]. It would seem that discipline had become lax in the convent and that the Bishop's attempt to introduce reform by the agency of the abbess was meeting with opposition from unruly nuns. Visitors were forced constantly to make the double injunction that nuns should show obedience to their superiors and that those superiors should be equable and not harsh in correction

Also we enioyne you, pryoresse,…that oftentymes ye come to the chapitere for to correcte the defautes of your susters, and that as wele then as att other tymes and places ye treyte your said susters moderlie wyth all resonable fauour; and that ye rebuke ne repreue thaym cruelly ne feruently at no tyme, specyally in audience of seculeres, and that ye kepe pryvye fro seculeres your correccyons and actes of your chapitere . Also we enioyne yowe of the couent and eueryche oon of yowe vndere peyn of imprisonyng, that mekely and buxumly ye obeye the prioresse procedyng discretely in hire correccyone, and also that in euery place ye do hire dewe reuerence, absteynyng yowe fro all elacyone of pryde and wordes of disobeysaunce or debate[2].

[1] *Wykeham's Reg* II, pp 361–2 (1384) Compare case at Shaftesbury (1298) where the nuns had incurred excommunication. *Reg Sim de Gandavo*, p 14
[2] *Linc Visit* II, p. 8. Compare Winchelsey's injunctions to Sheppey in 1296. *Reg Roberti Winchelsey*, pp. 99–100.

Sometimes it was one unruly member who set the convent by the ears. There is an amusing case at Romsey, which is reminiscent of David Copperfield:

On 16 January 1527 in the chapter house of the monastery of Romsey, before the vicar general, sitting judicially, Lady Alice Gorsyn appeared and confessed that she had used bad language with her sisters [her greatest oath evidently transcended "by seynt Loy"] and spread abroad reproachful and defamatory words of them. He absolved her from the sentence of excommunication and enjoined on her in penance that if she used bad language in future and spread about defamatory words of them, a red tongue made of cloth should be used on the barbe under the chin (*in sua barba alba*) and remain there for a month[1].

a kinder punishment than the scold's bridle or the ducking stool of common folk. Occasionally an inveterate scold would be removed altogether by the Bishop and sent to some convent where she was not known; two nuns were transferred from Burnham to Goring in 1339 "for the peace and quiet of the house" and in 1298 a quarrelsome nun of Nuncoton was sent to Greenfield to be kept in solitary confinement as long as she remained incorrigible, "until according to the discipline of her order she shall know how to live in a community"[2]. It was more difficult to restore peace when a whole nunnery was seething with dispute and heart-burnings General injunctions to cease quarrelling would seem to show that this was sometimes the case, and, without having recourse to such an extreme instance as that of Littlemore in the sixteenth century, it is possible to quote from bishops' registers documents which go far to bear out even Langland's picture. One such document may be quoted in

---

[1] Liveing, *op cit* pp 245–6 The "bad language" may be scolding or defamation rather than swearing It is rare to find a nun accused of using oaths But see the list of faults drawn up for the nuns of Syon Abbey, among "greuous defautes" is "if any .be take withe.. any foule worde, or else brekethe her sylence, or swerethe horribly be Criste, or be any parte of hys blyssed body, or unreuerently speketh of God, or of any saynte, and namely of our blessyd lady", among "more greuous defautes" is "yf they swere be the sacramente, or be the body of Cryste, or be hys passion, or be hys crosse, or be any boke, or be any other thynge lyke", and among "most greuous defautes" is "yf any in her madness or drunkenesse blaspheme horrybly God, or our Lady, or any of hys sayntes" (Aungier, *Hist of Syon Mon* pp. 256, 259, 262) In 1331, on readmitting Isabella de Studley (who had been guilty of incontinence and apostasy) to St Clement's York, Archbishop Melton announced that if she were disobedient to the Prioress or quarrelsome with her sisters or *indulged in blasphemy* he would transfer her to another house. *V C H. Yorks* iii, p 130

[2] *V C H Bucks.* i, p. 383 and *V C H Lincs* ii, p 155.

illustration, the *comperta* of Archbishop Giffard's visitation of
Swine in 1268:

It is discovered that Amice de Rue is a slanderer and a liar and impatient and odious to the convent and a rebel, and so are almost all
the convent when the misdeeds of delinquents are proclaimed in
chapter; wherefore the prioress or whoever is acting for her is not
sufficient, without the help of the lord archbishop, to make corrections
according to the requirements of the rule....Item, it is discovered that
three sisters in the flesh and spirit, to wit, Sibyl, Bella and Amy,
frequently rebel against the corrections of the Prioress, and having
leagued together with them several other sisters, they conspire against
their sisters, to the great harm of the regular discipline, and Alice.
de Scrutevil, Beatrice de St Quintin and Maud Constable cleave to
them... Item, it is discovered that the Prioress is a suspicious woman
and too credulous and breaks out at a mere word into correction, and
frequently punishes unequally for the same fault and pursues with
long rancour those whom she dislikes, until the time of their vindica-
tion cometh, whence it befals that the nuns, when they suspect that
they are going to be burdened with too heavy a correction, procure
the mitigation of her severity by means of the threats of their relatives.
Item, it is discovered that the nuns and the sisters are at discord
in many things, because the sisters contend that they are equal to
the nuns and use black veils even as the nuns[1], which is said not to be
the custom in other houses of the same order[2].

Apostasy, *accidia*, quarrels, all rose in part from monotony.
The majority of nuns were probably content with their life, but
they strove to bring some excitement and variety into it, not
only unconsciously by cliques and contentions, but also by a
conscious aping of the worldly amusements which enlivened
their mothers and sisters outside the convent walls. The châtelaine or mistress of a manor, when not busied with the care of
an estate, amused herself in the pursuit of fashion, even the
business-like Margaret Paston hankered after a scarlet robe.
She amused herself with keeping pets, those little dogs which
scamper so gaily round the borders of manuscripts, or play so

---

[1] In 1311 Archbishop Greenfield issued a general order that nuns only
and not sisters were to use the black veil, sisters wore a white veil (*V C H
Yorks* III, p 188 note, and *Journ of Education*, 1910, p. 841) This order
was repeated at various houses, which shows that there must have been
a widespread attempt to usurp the black veil (*V C H Yorks* III, pp 124,
127, 175, 177, 188) At Sinningthwaite the Prioress was also ordered not to
place the sisters above the nuns A common punishment in this district
was to remove the black veil from a nun and this was reserved for the more
serious misdeeds

[2] *York Reg Giffard*, pp 147–8 For further instances, see Note C below.

gallant a part in romances like the Châtelaine of Vergi She
hawked and she hunted, she danced and she played at tables[1].
All these occupations served to break the monotony of daily
life The nuns, always in touch with the world owing to the
influx of visitors and to the neglect of enclosure, remembered
these forbidden pleasures. And they sought to spice their
monotonous life, as they spiced their monotonous dishes. Gay
clothes, pet animals, a dance, a game, a gossip, were to them
"a ferthyngworth of fenel-seed for fastyngdayes." So we find
all these worldly amusements in the convent

Dear to the soul of men and women alike, dear to monks
and nuns as well as to the children of the world, were the gay
colours and extravagant modes of contemporary dress. Popular
preachers inveighed against the devils' trappings of their flocks,
but when those trappings flaunted themselves in the cloister
there was matter for more than words. As early as the end of
the seventh century St Aldhelm penned a severe indictment of
the fashionable nuns of his day

A vest of fine linen of a violet colour is worn, above it a scarlet tunic
with a hood, sleeves striped with silk and trimmed with red fur;
the locks on the forehead and the temples are curled with a crisping
iron, the dark head-veil is given up for white and coloured head-dresses,
which, with bows of ribbon sewn on, reach down to the ground; the
nails, like those of a falcon or sparrow-hawk, are pared to resemble
talons[2].

Synods sat solemnly over silken veils and pleated robes with
long trains; they shook their heads over golden pins and silver
belts, jewelled rings, laced shoes, cloth of burnet and of Rennes,
dresses open at the sides, gay colours (especially red) and fur of
gris[3]. High brows were fashionable in the world and the nuns
could not resist lifting and spreading out their veils to expose

[1] Injunctions against dicing and other games of chance are common in
the case of monks (see e g *Linc Visit* i, pp 30, 46, 77, 89) I have found
none in nunneries, but a more stately game of skill, the fashionable tables,
was played by Margaret Fairfax with John Munkton Above, p 77
[2] Quoted from St Aldhelm's *De Laudibus Virginitatis* in Eckenstein,
Woman under Mon. p 115 Compare Bede's account of the nuns of Coldingham some years before "The virgins who are vowed to God, laying aside
all respect for their profession, whenever they have leisure spend all their
time in weaving fine garments with which they adorn themselves like brides,
to the detriment of their condition and to secure the friendship of men
outside " *Ib* pp 102-3
[3] For detailed examples, see Note D below.

those fair foreheads ("almost a spanne brood, I trowe"); when Alnwick visited Goring in 1445 he

saw with the evidence of his own eyes that the nuns do wear their veils spread out on either side and above their foreheads, (and) he enjoined upon the prioress...that she should wear and cause her sisters to wear their veils spread down to their eyes[1]

The words of Beatrix's maid in *Much Ado About Nothing* spring to the mind: "But methinks you look with your eyes as other women do." For three weary centuries the bishops waged a holy war against fashion in the cloister and waged it in vain, for as long as the nuns mingled freely with secular women it was impossible to prevent them from adopting secular modes. Occasionally a conscientious visitor found himself floundering unhandily through something very like a complete catalogue of contemporary fashions. So Bishop Longland at Elstow in 1531.

We ordeyne and by way of Iniuncon commande undre payne of disobedyence from hensforth that no ladye ne any religious suster within the said monasterye presume to were ther apparells upon ther hedes undre suche lay fashion as they have now of late doon with cornered crests, nether undre suche manour of light shewing ther forhedes moore like lay people than religious, butt that they use them without suche crestes or secular fashions and off a lower sort and that ther vayle come as lowe as ther yye ledes and soo contynually to use the same, unles itt be at suche tymes as they shalbe occupied in eny handy-crafte labour, att whiche tymes itt shalbe lefull for them to turne upp the said vayle for the tyme of suche occupacon. And undre like payne inoyne that noon of the said religious susters doo use or were here-after eny such voyded shoys, nether crested as they have of late ther used, butt that they be of suche honeste fashion as other religious places both use and that ther gownes and kyrtells be closse afore and nott so depe voyded at the breste and noo more to use rede stomachers but other sadder colers in the same[2]

It is interesting to conjecture how the nuns obtained these gay garments and ornaments. The growing custom of giving them a money allowance out of which to dress themselves instead of providing them with clothes in kind out of the common purse, certainly must have given opportunity for buying the

---

[1] *Linc Visit* II, p 118 Similar *detecta* and injunctions at Catesby, Rothwell and Studley (*ib.* pp. 47, 52, *Alnwick's Visit*. MS. ff 38, 26d) and at Ankerwyke (quoted above, p 76) Also at Studley (1531), *Archaeol* XLVII, p 55, and Romsey (1523), Liveing, *op. cit.* p 244

[2] *Archaeol* XLVII, p 52 For an equally detailed account see the case of the Prioress of Ankerwyke, quoted above p. 76.

gilt pins, barred belts and slashed shoes which so horrified their visitors. We know from Gilles li Muisis that Flemish nuns at least went shopping[1]. But an even more likely source of supply lies, as we shall see, in the legacies of clothes and ornaments, which were often left to nuns by their relatives[2]

Not only in their clothes did medieval nuns seek to enliven existence after the manner of their lay sisters. The bishops struggled long and unsuccessfully against another custom of worldly women, the keeping of pet animals[3]. Dogs were certainly the favourite pets Cats are seldom mentioned, though the three anchoresses of the *Ancren Riwle* were specially permitted to keep one[4], and Gyb, that "cat of carlyshe kynde," which slew Philip Sparrow, apparently belonged to Carrow; perhaps there was spread among the nunneries of England the grisly tradition of the Prioress of Newington, who was smothered in bed by her cat[5]. Birds, from the larks of the Abbaye-aux-Dames at Caen, to the parrot Vert-Vert at Nevers, are often mentioned[6]. Monkeys, squirrels and rabbits were also kept But dogs and puppies abounded. Partly because the usages of society inevitably found their way into the aristocratic convents, partly

---

[1] See below, p 543.

[2] See below, pp 325-30

[3] For nunnery pets as a literary theme, see Note E and for pet animals in the nunneries of Eudes Rigaud's diocese see below, p. 662.

[4] "Ye shall not possess any beasts, my dear sisters, except only a cat " *Ancren Riwle*, p 316 At the nunnery of Langendorf in Saxony, however, a set of reformed rules drawn up in the early fifteenth century contains the proviso "Cats, dogs and other animals are not to be kept by the nuns, as they detract from seriousness " Eckenstein, *op cit* p 415

[5] "Mem quod apud manerium de Newenton fuerunt quedam moniales.... Et postea contingit [*sic*] quod priorissa eiusdem manerii strangulata fuit de cato suo in lecto suo noctu et postea tractata ad puteum quod vocatur Nunnepet " Quoted from Sprott's Chronicle in *The Black Book of St Augustine's Abbey, Canterbury* (British Acad 1915), I, p 283 In Thorn's Chronicle, however, the crime is attributed to the prioress' *cook* See Dugdale, *Mon* VI, p 1620 The nuns were afterwards removed to Sheppey

[6] There really seems to have been a parrot at Fontevrault in 1477, to judge from an item in the inventory of goods left on her death by the Abbess Marie de Bretagne, "Item xviij serviecttes en une aultre piece, led linge estant en ung coffre de cuir boully, en la chambre ou est la papegault (perroquet) " Alfred Jubien, *L'Abbesse Marie de Bretagne* (Angers and Paris 1872), p 156. It is interesting to note that J B Thiers, writing on enclosure in 1681, mentions "de belles volieres à petits oiseaux" as one of those unnecessary works for which artisans may not be introduced into the cloister Thiers, *De la Clôture*, p. 412.

because human affections will find an outlet under the most severe of rules:

> (Objet permis à leur oisif amour,
> Vert-Vert était l'âme de ce séjour),

the nuns clung to their "smale houndes." Archbishop Peckham had to forbid the Abbess of Romsey to keep monkeys or "a number of dogs" in her own chamber and she was charged at the same time with stinting her nuns in food; one can guess what became of the "rosted flesh or milk and wastel-breed"[1]. At Chatteris and at Ickleton in 1345 the nuns were forbidden to keep fowls, dogs or small birds within the precincts of the convent or to bring them into church during divine service[2]. This bringing of animals into church was a common custom in the middle ages, when ladies often attended service with dog in lap and men with hawk on wrist[3], Lady Audley's twelve dogs, which so disturbed the nuns of Langley, will be remembered[4]. Injunctions against the bringing of dogs or puppies into choir by the nuns are also found at Keldholme and Rosedale early in the fourteenth century[5]. But the most flagrant case of all is Romsey, to which in 1387 William of Wykeham wrote as follows:

[1] *Reg Epis Peckham* (R S), II, p 660

[2] Dugdale, *Mon* II, p 619 (Chatteris) and *Camb Antiq Soc Proc.* XLV (1905), p 190 (Ickleton).

[3] A decree of the Council of Vienne (1311) complains that many church ministers come into choir "bringing hawks with them or causing them to be brought and leading hunting dogs" Coulton, *Med Garn* p 588 Similarly Geiler on the eve of the Reformation complains, in his *Navicula Fatuorum*, that "some men, when they are about to enter a church, equip themselves like hunters, bearing hawks and bells on their wrists and followed by a pack of baying hounds, that trouble God's service Here the bells jangle, there the barking of dogs echoes in our ears, to the hindrance of preachers and hearers" He goes on to say that the habit is particularly reprehensible in clergy The privilege of behaving thus was an adjunct of noble birth and in the cathedrals of Auxerre and Nevers the treasurers had the legal right of coming to service with hawk on wrist, because these canonries were hereditary in noble families *Ib.* pp 684–5 Medieval writers on hawking actually advise that hawks should be taken into church to accustom them to crowds "Mais en cest endroit d'espreveterie, le convient plus que devant tenir sur le poing et le porter aux plais et entre les gens aux églises et ès autres assamblées, et emmy les rues, et le tenir jour et nuit le plus continuelment que l'en pourra, et aucune fois le perchier emmi les rues pour veoir gens, chevaulx, charettes, chiens, et toutes choses congnoistre" Gaces de la Bugne gives the same advice *Le Ménagier de Paris* (Paris, 1846), II, p 296

[4] Below, p 412.

[5] *V.C H. Yorks* III, pp. 168, 175.

Item, because we have convinced ourselves by clear proofs that some
of the nuns of your house bring with them to church birds, rabbits,
hounds and such like frivolous things, whereunto they give more heed
than to the offices of the church, with frequent hindrance to their
own psalmody and that of their fellow nuns and to the grievous peril
of their souls, therefore we strictly forbid you, all and several, in
virtue of the obedience due unto us, that you presume henceforward
to bring to church no birds, hounds, rabbits or other frivolous things
that promote indiscipline, and any nun who does to the contrary,
after three warnings shall fast on bread and water on one Saturday
for each offence, notwithstanding one discipline to be received publicly
in chapter on the same day....Item, whereas through the hunting-
dogs and other hounds abiding within your monastic precincts, the
alms that should be given to the poor are devoured and the church and
cloister and other places set apart for divine and secular services are
foully defiled, contrary to all honesty, and whereas, through their
inordinate noise, divine service is frequently troubled, therefore we
strictly command and enjoin you, Lady Abbess, in virtue of obedience,
that you remove these dogs altogether and that you suffer them never
henceforth, nor any other such hounds, to abide within the precincts
of your nunnery[1]

But the crusade against pets was not more successful than the
crusade against fashions. The feminine fondness for something
small and alive to pet was not easily eradicated and it seems
that visitors were sometimes obliged to indulge it. The wording
of Peckham's decree leaves an opening for the retention of one
humble and very self-effacing little dog, not prone to unseemly
yelps and capers before the stony eye of my lord the Archbishop
on his rounds; Dean Kentwode in the fifteenth century ordered
the Prioress of St Helen's Bishopsgate, to remove dogs "and
content herself with one or two"[2], and in 1520 the Prioress of
Flixton was bidden to send all dogs away from the convent
"except one which she prefers"[3] Perhaps the welcome of a
thumping tail and damp, insinuating nose occasionally overcame
the scruples even of a Bishop, who probably kept dogs himself
and mourned
>   if oon of hem were deed,
>   Or if men smoot it with a yerde smerte.

Dogs kept for hunting purposes come into rather a different
category. It is well known that medieval monks were mighty

[1] *New Coll* MS ff. 88–88d, translated in Coulton, *Soc Life in Britain
from the Conquest to the Reformation*, p 397
[2] *Hist MSS Com. Rep.* IX, app pt. I, p 57
[3] Jessopp, *Visit. of Dioc of Norwich*, p 191

hunters before the Lord[1], and the mention of sporting dogs at Romsey and at Brewood (where Bishop Norbury found *canes venatici*[2]) encourages speculation as to whether the nuns also were not "pricasours aright" and

> yaf not of that text a pulled hen
> That seith that hunters been nat holy men

It is significant that Dame Juliana Berners is supposed by tradition (unsupported, however, by any other evidence) to have been a prioress of Sopwell. The gift of hunting rights to a nunnery is a common one; for instance, Henry II granted to Wix the right of having two greyhounds and four braches to take hares through the whole forest of Essex[3]. Doubtless these rights were usually exercised by proxy[4]; but considering the popularity of hunting and hawking as sports for women, a popularity so great that no lady's education was complete if she knew not how to manage a hawk and bear herself courteously in the field, it is

---

[1] Chaucer's description of the monk is well known,

> Therfore he was a pricasour aright;
> Grehoundes he hadde, as swiftc as fowel in flight;
> Of priking and of hunting for the hare
> Was al his lust, for no cost wolde he spare

Compare Langland's picture of the monk, riding out on his palfrey from manor to manor, "an hepe of houndes at hus ers as he a lord were" (*Piers Plowman*, C Text VI, 11, 157-61) Visitation documents amply bear out these accounts, in a single set of visitations (those by Bishops Flemyng and Gray of Lincoln during the years 1420-36) we have "Furthermore we enjoin and command you all and several. that no canon apply himself in any wise to hunting, hawking or other lawless wanderings abroad" (Dunstable Priory 1432), "further we enjoin upon you, the prior and all and several the canons of the convent aforesaid...that you utterly remove and drive away all hounds for hunting from the said priory and its limits, and that neither you nor any one of you keep, rear, or maintain such hounds by himself or by another's means, directly or indirectly, in the priory or without the priory, under colour of any pretext whatsoever" (Huntingdon Priory 1432), "also that hounds for hunting be not nourished within the precinct of your monastery" (St Frideswide's Oxford, 1422-3) and a similar injunction to Caldwell Priory *Linc Visit* I, pp 27, 47, 78, 97

[2] Wm Salt Arch Soc Coll I, p 261 Compare also the provision in one of Charlemagne's capitularies "Ut episcopi et abbates *et abbatissae* cupplas canum non habeant nec falcones nec accipitres," Baretius, *Capit. Reg. Franc* (1853), p 64 Some of the birds at Romsey may have been hawks, though it is more likely that they were larks and other small pets, such as Eudes Rigaud found in his nunneries

[3] *V C H Essex*, II, p 123, and see above, p. 105.

[4] The nuns of St Mary de Pré, St Albans, kept a huntsman. *V C H. Herts.* IV, p. 430 (note)

surprising that there is not actual mention of these pastimes among nuns as well as among monks.

Besides gay clothes and pets other frivolous amusements broke at times the monotony of convent life   Dancing and mumming and minstrelsy were not unknown and the nuns shared in the merrymaking on feasts sacred and profane, as is witnessed by the account rolls of St Mary de Pré (1461–90), with their list of payments for wassail at New Year and Twelfth Night, for May games, for bread and ale on bonfire nights and for harpers and players at Christmas[1]. In 1435 the nuns of Lymbrook were forbidden "all maner of mynstrelseys, enterludes, daunsyng or reuelyng with in your sayde holy place"[2], and about the same time Dean Kentwode wrote to St Helen's Bishopsgate: "Also we enioyne you that all daunsyng and reuelyng be utterly forborne among yow, except Christmasse and other honest tymys of recreacyone among yowre self usyd in absence of seculars in all wyse"[3]. The condemnation of dancing in nunneries is not surprising, for the attitude of medieval moralists generally to this pastime is summed up in Etienne de Bourbon's aphorism, "The Devil is the inventor and governor and disposer of dances and dancers"[4]. Minstrels were similarly under the ban of the church, and clerks were forbidden by canon law and by numerous papal, conciliar and episcopal injunctions to listen to their "ignominious art"[5], a regulation which, needless to say, went unobeyed in an age when many a bishop had his private *histrio*[6], and when the same stern reformer Grosseteste, who warned his clergy "ne mimis, ioculatoribus aut histrionibus intendant," loved so much to hear the harp that he kept his harper's chamber "next hys chaumbre besyde hys stody"[7]. Langland asserts that churchmen and laymen alike spent on

---

[1] *V C.H. Herts* IV, p. 431 (note); Dugdale, *Mon.* III, pp 359–60

[2] *Hereford Reg Thome Spofford*, p 82   (This was combined with an injunction against going to "comyn wakes and festes, spectacles and other worldly vanytees" outside the convent. Below, p 377.)

[3] Dugdale, *Mon* IV, p 554

[4] Quoted in Coulton, *Med Garn* p 304.

[5] See Chambers, *op. cit.* I, pp 38–41.

[6] *Ib* I, p 56 (note)   "The bishops of Durham in 1355, Norwich in 1362, and Winchester in 1374, 1422, and 1481 had 'minstrels of honour' like any secular noble "

[7] *Ib.* I, pp 39, 56 (notes)

mınstrels money wıth which they well mıght have succoured
the poor.

> Clerkus and kny3tes · welcometh kynges mynstrales,
> And for loue of here lordes · lıthen hem at festes,
> Muche more, me thenketh · rıche men auhte
> Haue beggars by-fore hem · whıch beth godes mynstrales[1].

Even in monasterıes they found a ready welcome[2] and the reforming councıl of Oxford passed an ıneffectual decree forbıddıng
theır performances to be seen or heard or allowed before the
abbot or monks, if they came to a house for alms[3] Indeed there
was sometimes need for care. Where but at one of those mınstrelsıes or interludes forbidden at Lymbrook dıd sıster Agnes
of St Mıchael's Prıory, Stamford, meet a jongleur, who sang
softly ın her ear that Lenten was come wıth love to town? The
Devıl (alas) had all the good tunes, even in the fifteenth century.
"One Agnes, a nun of that place," reported the Prıoress, "has
gone away into apostasy cleavıng to a harp-player, and they
dwell together, as ıt ıs saıd, ın Newcastle-on-Tyne"[4]. For her
no longer the straıt dıscıplıne of her rule, the black-robed nuns

---

[1] Langland, *Pıers the Plowman*, C, Text VIII, I, 97

[2] "Payments for performances are frequent ın the accounts of the
Augustınıan prıorıes at Canterbury, Bıcester and Maxstoke and the great
Benedıctıne houses of Durham, Norwıch, Thetford and St Swıthın's, Wın-
chester, and doubtless ın those of many another cloıstered retreat. The
Mınorıte chronıclers relate how, at the comıng of the frıars in 1224, two of
them were mıstaken for mınstrels by the porter of a Benedıctıne grange near
Abıngdon, receıved by the brethren wıth unbecomıng glee, and when the error
was dıscovered, turned out wıth contumely," Chambers, *op cıt.* I, pp 56–7
In the Regıster of St Swıthın's ıt ıs recorded under the year 1374 that "on
the feast of Bıshop Alwyn...sıx mınstrels wıth four harpers performed theır
mınstrelsıes And after dınner ın the great arched chamber of the lord Prıor,
they sang the same *geste*....And the saıd jongleurs came from the household
of the bıshop," *ıb* I, p. 56 (note) See extracts from the account books of
Durham, Fınchale, Maxstoke and Thetford Prıorıes relatıng to the vısıts
of mınstrels, *ıb* II, pp 240–6 At Fınchale there was even a room called
"le Playerchambre," *ıb* II, p 244 In 1258 Eudes Rıgaud had to order the
Abbot of Jumıèges "that he should send strollıng players away from hıs
premıses" *Reg Vısıt Arch Roth* p 607 At a later date, in 1549, a councıl
at Cologne dırected a canon agaınst comedıans who were ın the habıt of
vısıtıng the German nunnerıes and by theır profane plays and amatory
actıng excıted to unholy desıres the vırgıns dedıcated to God. Lea, *Hıst.
of Sacerdotal Celıbacy*, II, p 189

[3] "Hıstrıonıbus potest darı cıbus, quıa pauperes sunt, non quıa hıs-
trıones; et eorum ludı non vıdeantur, vel audıantur vel permıttantur fıerı
coram abbate vel monachıs" *Annales de Burton* (*Ann Monast. R S* I,
p 485), quoted Chambers, *op cıt.* I, p 39 (note)

[4] *Alnwıck's Vısıt* I. 83.

and heaven at the end. For her the life of the roads, the sore
foot and the light heart; for her the company of ribalds with
their wenches, and all the thriftless, shiftless player-folk, for
her, at the last, hell, with "the gold and the silver and the vair
and the gray,...harpers and minstrels and kings of the world"[1],
or a desperate hope that the Virgin's notorious kindness for
minstrels might snatch her soul from perdition[2].

But the merrymakers in nunneries were not necessarily
strange jongleurs or secular folk. The dancing and revelry, which
were forbidden at Lymbrook and allowed in Christmastime at
St Helen's, were probably connected with the children's feast of
St Nicholas. As early as the twelfth century the days immediately
before and after Christmas had become, in ecclesiastical circles,
the occasion for uproarious festivities[3]. The three days after
Christmas were appropriated by the three orders of the Church.
On St Stephen's Day (Dec. 26) the deacons performed the service,
elected their Abbot of Fools and paraded the streets, levying
contributions from the householders and passers-by; on St John
the Evangelist's Day (Dec. 27) the deacons gave way to the
priests, who "gave a mock blessing and proclaimed a ribald
form of indulgence", and on Innocents' Day it was the turn
of the choir or schoolboys to hold their feast. In cathedral and
monastic churches the Boy Bishop (who had been elected on
December 5th, the Eve of St Nicholas, patron saint of schoolboys)
attended service on the eve of Innocents' Day, and at the words
of the Magnificat "He hath put down the mighty from their
seat" changed places with the Bishop or Dean or Abbot, and
similarly the canons and other dignitaries of the church changed
places with the boys. On Innocents' Day all services, except
the essential portions of the mass, were performed by the Boy
Bishop, he and his staff processed through the streets, levying
large contributions of food and money and for about a fortnight

[1] *Aucassin and Nicolete*, ed Bourdillon (1897), p 22
[2] See the well-known story of "Le Tombeor de Notre Dame" (*Romania*,
II, p 315), and "Du Cierge qui descendi sus la viele au vieleeux devant
l'ymage Nostre Dame," Gautier de Coincy, *Miracles de Nostre Dame*, ed.
Poquet (1859), p 310 Both are translated in *Of The Tumbler of Our Lady
and Other Miracles* by A Kemp-Welch (King's Classics 1909)
[3] For the following account, see A. F Leach's article on "The Schoolboy's
Feast," *Fortnightly Review*, N S LIX (1896), p. 128, and Chambers, *op cit.*
I, ch. xv.

his rule continued, accompanied by feasting and merrymaking, plays, disguisings and dances. These Childermas festivities took place in monastic as well as in secular churches, but they seem to have been more common in nunneries than in male communities. Our chief information about the revelries comes from Archbishop Eudes Rigaud's province of Rouen[1]; but English records also contain scattered references to the custom. Evidently a Girl Abbess or Abbess of Fools was elected from among the novices, and at the *Deposuit* she and her fellow novices, or the little schoolgirls, took the place of the Abbess and nuns, just as the Boy Bishop held sway in cathedral churches, and feasting, dancing and disguising brought a welcome diversion into the lives of both nuns and children. Even the strict Peckham was obliged to extend a grudging consent to the *puerilia solemnia* held on Innocents' Day at Barking and at Godstow (1279), insisting only that they should not be continued during the whole octave of Childermas-tide and should be conducted with decency and in private:

The celebration of the Feast of Innocents by children, which we do not approve, but rather suffer with disapproval, is on no account to be undertaken by those children, nor are they to take any part in it, until after the end of the vespers of St John the Evangelist's Day; and the nuns are not to retire from the office, but having excluded from the choir all men and women. .they are themselves to supply the absence of the little ones lest (which God forbid) the divine praise should become a mockery[2].

A more specific reference still is found at Carrow in 1526; Dame Joan Botulphe deposed at a visitation that it was customary at Christmas for the youngest nun to hold sway for the day as abbess and on that day (added the soured ancient) was consumed and dissipated everything that the house had acquired by alms or by the gift of friends[3]. The connection between these revels and the Feast of Fools appears clearly in the injunction sent by Bishop Longland to Nuncoton about the same time:

---

[1] See below, p 662
[2] *Reg Epis J. Peckham*, I, pp 82–3. For a similar injunction to Godstow, see *ib* III, p 846   At Romsey the Archbishop forbade the festivities altogether "Superstitionem vero quae in Natali Domini et Ascensione Ejusdem fieri consuevit, perpetuo condemnamus," *ib* II, p 664   The superstition was probably the election of the youngest nun as abbess
[3] *Norwich Visit* pp 209–10.

We chardge you, lady priores, that ye suffre nomore hereafter eny lorde of mysrule to be within your house, nouther to suffre hereafter eny suche disgysinge as in tymes past haue bene used in your monastery in nunnes apparell ne otherwise[1]

The admission of seculars dressed up as nuns, and of boys dressed up as women, the performance of interludes and the wild dancing were reason enough for the distaste with which ecclesiastical authorities regarded these festivities. For the nuns clearly did not exclude strangers as Peckham had bidden. Indeed it seems probable that where they did not elect a Girl Abbess, they admitted a Boy Bishop, either from some neighbouring church, or just possibly one of their own little schoolboys. Among the accounts of St Swithun's monastery at Winchester for 1441 there is a payment

for the boys of the Almonry together with the boys of the chapel of St Elizabeth, dressed up after the manner of girls, dancing, singing and performing plays before the Abbess and nuns of St Mary's Abbey in their hall on the Feast of Innocents[2],

and the account of Christian Bassett, Prioress of St Mary de Pré, contains an item "paid for makyng of the dyner to the susters upon Childermasday iij s iiij d, item paid for brede and ale for seint Nicholas clerks iij d"[3]. The inventories of Cheshunt and Sheppey at the time of the Dissolution contain further references to the custom and seem to show that nunneries occasionally "ran" a St Nicholas Bishop of their own: at Cheshunt there was found in the dorter "a chisell (chasuble) of white ffustyan and a myter for a child bysshoppe at xx d"[4], and at Sheppey, in a chapel, "ij olde myters for S. Nicholas of fustyan brodered"[5].

These childish festivities sound harmless and attractive enough, and modern writers are sometimes apt to sentimentalise over their abolition by Henry VIII[6]. But in this, as in his

[1] *Archaeol* XLVII, p 56 On the Lord of Misrule, see Chambers *op. cit.* I, ch. XVII There is a vivid account (from the Puritan point of view) in Philip Stubbes, *The Anatomie of Abuses* (1583) quoted in *Life in Shakespeare's England*, ed. J D Wilson (1915), pp 25-7.

[2] Chambers, *op cit* I, p 361 (note 1).   [3] Dugdale, *Mon* III, p 360

[4] Cussans, *Hist of Herts*, Hertford Hundred, app II, p 268

[5] Walcott, *Inventory of Shepey*, p. 23 There is perhaps another reference in the inventory of Langley in 1485· "iij quesyns (cushions) of olde red saye, ij smale quechyns embrodred and ij qwechyns namyde Seynt Nicolas qwechyns," Walcott, *Inventory of Langley*, p 6.

[6] E g (besides the well-known case of Dr Rock in *The Church of Our Fathers*), Gayley, *Plays of our Forefathers*, pp 67-8

injunction of enclosure, Henry was fully in accordance with the best ecclesiastical precedent. For the Boy Bishop was originally a part of the Feast of Fools and the Feast of Fools had an ancient and disreputable ancestry in the Roman Saturnalia. At a very early date a regulation made to curtail such performances at St Paul's declared that "what had been invented for the praise of sucklings had been converted into a disgrace"[1] In 1445, at Paris, it was stated by the Faculty of Theology at the University that the performers

appeared in masks with the faces of monsters or in the dresses of women, sang improper songs in the choir, ate fat pork on the horns of the altar, close by the priest celebrating mass, played dice on the altar, used stinking incense made of old shoes, and ran about the choir leaping and shouting[2],

and about the same time the Synod of Basle had specifically denounced the children's festival in hardly less violent terms as

that disgraceful, bad custom practised in some churches, by which on certain high days during the year some with mitre, staff and pontifical vestments like Bishops and others dressed as kings and princes bless the people; the which festival in some places is called the Feast of Fools or Innocents or Boys, and some making games with masks and mummeries, others dances and breakdowns of males and females, move people to look on with guffaws, while others make drinkings and feasts there[3].

It is only necessary to compare these denunciations with such accounts of the festivities in nunneries as have survived, to understand that the revelling and disguising were less harmless than modern writers are apt to represent them. Mr Leach attributes the schoolboys' feast to the fact that regular holidays were unknown in the medieval curriculum and that the boys found in the ribaldries of Childermastide some outlet for their long suppressed spirits. Similarly the cramped and solemn existence led by the nuns for the rest of the year probably made their one outbreak the more violent. Nevertheless one cannot avoid feeling somewhat out of sympathy with the bishops. "Dost thou think because thou art virtuous there shall be no more cakes and ale?" Nuns were ever fond of ginger "hot i' the mouth."

[1] Leach, *op. cit.* p. 137   [2] *Ib.* p 131
[3] Leach, *op cit.* p. 137 (from *Martène*, III, p 39). I have slightly altered the translation

CHAPTER VIII

PRIVATE LIFE AND PRIVATE PROPERTY

All things are to be common to all.
Rule of St Benedict, ch xxxiii.

The Rule of seint Maure or of seint Beneit,
Because that it was old and somdel streit
This ilke monk leet olde thinges pace
And held after the newe world the space.
CHAUCER, Prologue, ll 173-6

THE reaction from a strict routine of life led monks and nuns to a more serious modification of the Rule under which they lived than that represented by pet dogs and pretty clothes, which were after all only superficial frivolities. They sought also to modify two rules which were fundamental to the Benedictine ideal. One was the rigidly communal life, the obligation to do everything in company with everyone else The other was the obligation of strict personal poverty A monastery was in its essence a place where a number of persons lived a communal life, owning no private property, but holding everything in the name of the community. The normal routine of conventual life, as laid down in the Benedictine Rule, secured this end. The inmates of a house spent almost the whole of their time together. They prayed together in the choir, worked together in the cloister, ate together in the frater, and slept together in the dorter. Moreover the strictest regulations were made to prevent the vice of private property, one of the most serious sins in the monastic calendar, from making its appearance All food was to be cooked in a common kitchen and served in the common frater, in which no meat was allowed All clothes were to be provided out of the common goods of the house, and it was the business of the chamberer or chambress to see to the buying of material, the making of the clothes and their distribution to the religious; so carefully was *proprietas* guarded against, that all old clothes had to be given back to the chambress, when the new ones were distributed. Above all it was forbidden to monks and nuns to possess and spend money, save what was delivered to them by the superior for their necessary expenses upon a journey[1].

But this combination of rigid communism with rigid personal poverty was early discovered to be irksome. It seems as though the craving for a certain privacy of life, a certain minimum of private property, is a deeply rooted instinct in human nature. Certainly the attempt of monasticism to expel it with a pitchfork failed. Step by step the rule was broken down, more especially by a series of modifications in the prescribed method of feeding and clothing the community. Here, as in the enclosure question, the monks and nuns came into conflict with their bishops, though the conflict was never so severe. Here also, the result of the struggle was the same. A steady attempt by the bishops to enforce the rule was countered by a steady resistance on the part of the religious and the end was usually compromise.

The most marked breakdown of the communal way of life in the monasteries of the later middle ages is to be seen in the gradual neglect of the frater, in favour of a system of private messes, and in the increasing allocation of private rooms to individuals. The strict obligation upon all to keep frater daily was at first only modified in favour of the head of the house, who usually had her own lodgings, including a dining hall, in which the rule permitted her to entertain the guests who claimed her hospitality and such nuns as she chose to invite for their recreation. From quite early times, however, there existed in many houses a room known as the *misericord* (or indulgence), where the strict diet of the frater was relaxed. Here the occupants of the infirmary, those in their seynies and all who needed flesh meat and more delicate dishes to support them, were served. From the fourteenth century onwards, however, the rules of diet became considerably relaxed and flesh was allowed to everyone on three days a week[2]. This meant that the *misericord* was in constant use and in many monasteries the frater was divided into two stories, the upper of which was used as the frater proper, where no meat might be eaten, and the lower as a *miseri-*

---

[1] On Benedictine poverty, see Dom Butler, *Benedictine Monachism*, ch. x

[2] The alteration was made even by the Cistercians in 1335 See *Linc Visit.* I, p 238 (under *Misericord*). Among Black Monks it began much earlier.

cord[1]. According to this arrangement a nun might sometimes be dining in the upper frater, sometimes in the *misericord* and sometimes in the abbess' or prioress' lodgings; and, of these places, there was a distinct tendency for the upper frater to fall into disuse, since it could in any case only be used on fish (or, according to later custom, white meat) days.

But a habit even more subversive of strictly communal life and more liable to lead to disuse of the frater was rapidly spreading at this period. This was the division of a nunnery into *familiae*, or households, which messed together, each *familia* taking its meals separately from the rest. The common frater was sometimes kept only thrice a week on fish days, sometimes only in Advent and Lent, sometimes (it would seem) never. This meant the separate preparation of meals for each household, a practice which, though uneconomical, was possible, because each nun's food allowance was fixed and could be drawn separately. Moreover, as we shall see hereafter, the growing practice of granting an annual money allowance to each individual, though used for clothes more often than for food, enabled the nuns to buy meat and other delicacies (if not provided by the convent) for themselves. The aristocratic ladies of Polsloe even had their private maids to prepare their meals[2].

This system was evidently well established at a comparatively early date. It is mentioned in Peckham's injunctions in 1279 and in Exeter and York injunctions belonging to the early years of the fourteenth century. To illustrate how it worked, we may analyse the references to *familiae* in Alnwick's visitations of the diocese of Lincoln (1440–5)[3]. The number of households in a

---

[1] *Linc. Visit.* i, p. 238 Alnwick's visitations sometimes mention this division of the frater "Also she prays that frater may be kept every day, since there is one upper frater wherein they feed on fish and food made with milk, and another downstairs, wherein they feed of grace on flesh" (Nuncoton 1440). "Also she says that they feed on fish and milk foods in the upper frater and on flesh in the lower" (Stixwould 1440) *Alnwick's Visit* MS ff. 71 d, 76.

[2] "Et qe nule Dame de Religion ne mange hors du Refreytour en chambre severale si ceo ne soit en compaignie la Priouresse, ou par maladie ou autre renable encheson .Item, purceo qe ascune foitz ascunes Dames de vostre Religion orent lur damoiseles severales por faire severalement lur viaunde, si ordinoms, voloms et establioms qe totes celles damoiseles soyent de tut oste de la cusine, et qe un keu covenable, qi eit un page desoutz lui soit mys por servir a tut le Covent" (1319) *Exeter Reg Stapeldon*, pp 317–8. Compare *V C H Yorks* iii, p 165 (Hampole 1411).

[3] For the following references, see *Linc. Visit.* ii, pp 46, 89, 114, 117, 119, 121, 175, *Alnwick's Visit* MS ff. 71 d, 76, 77, 83.

nunnery necessarily differed with the size of the house and it is not always easy to determine the proportion of households to nuns, because internal evidence sometimes shows that all the inmates were not present and enumerated at the visitation. Thus at Elstow the abbess "says that there are five households of nuns kept in the monastery, whereof the first is that of the abbess, who has five nuns with her, the second of the prioress, who has two; the third of the subprioress, who has two; the fourth of the sacrist, who has three, and the fifth of Dame Margaret Aylesbury, who has two"; but only thirteen nuns gave evidence[1]. In this house the frater was kept on certain days of the week, one nun deposing "that on the days whereon they eat together in frater, they eat larded food in the morning and sup on flesh, and they eat capons and other two-footed creatures in frater." At Catesby the prioress deposed that she had four nuns in her *familia* and that there were three other households in the cloister At Stixwould there were "five separate and distinct households", at Nuncoton there were three; at St Michael's Stamford, the prioress and subprioress each had one, but all ate together in the frater on fish-days; at Stainfield the prioress, the cellaress and the nun-sisters each kept a household. At Gokewell and Langley the nuns were said to keep divers households "by two and two" and at Langley the prioress added, "but they do eat in the frater every day; also she says that she herself has three women who board with her and the subprioress one; also she says that the nuns receive naught from the house but their meat and drink and she herself keeps one household on her own account. At Gracedieu the prioress deposed

that frater is not kept nor has it been kept for seven years and that the nuns sit in company with secular folk at table in her hall every day and that they have reading during meals, also she says there are two households only in the house, to wit in her hall and the infirmary, where there are three at table together;

here the prioress' hall simply took the place of the frater There were four households at Godstow and apparently several at Legbourne.

This division into households which messed separately went

---

[1] Pupils or boarders may account for these discrepancies.

hand in hand with another practice, which also softened the
rigours of a strictly communal life, to wit the allocation of
separate rooms to certain nuns. The obedientiaries of a house
often had private offices, or *checkers*, in which to transact their
business, and the custom grew by which the head of each *familia*
had her own room, in which her household dined. The visitation
reports continually refer to these private cells and to their use
as dining rooms and places of reception for visitors. Sometimes
the nuns even slept in them, though the dorter was always much
more strictly kept than the frater; at Godstow in 1432 for
instance, Bishop Gray enjoins "that the beds in the nuns'
lodgings (*domicilia*) be altogether removed from their chambers,
save those for small children" (apparently their pupils) "and
that no nun receive any secular person for any recreation in the
nuns' chambers under pain of excommunication"[1]. Some light
is thrown upon these *camerae* by the inventories of medieval
nunneries Thus the inventory of the Benedictine Priory of
Sheppey made at the Dissolution describes the contents of "the
greate chamber in the Dorter," which was used as a treasury
in which to keep the linen, vestments and plate of the house,
and in which one of the nuns Dame Agnes Davye seems to have
slept; there follows a description of the chambers of eight nuns,
with the furniture in each, from which it is clear that they had
brought their own furniture with them to the monastery. These
"chambers" may have been separate rooms or may have been
partitions of the dorter, but if the latter they were evidently
so large as to be to all intents and purposes separate rooms, for
the furniture commonly includes painted cloth or paper hangings
for the room, a chest and a cupboard, besides the bed; in three
there is mention of windows and in two of fire irons The most
likely conjecture is that the dorter was used as a treasury and
bedroom for one nun and the other chambers are separate
rooms[2]. At some other houses the dorter is mentioned but was
clearly divided into separate cells by wainscot partitions, and
the wainscotting was sometimes sold at the Dissolution[3].

---

[1] *Linc. Visit* I, p 67 (and note 3), compare *V C H Yorks.* III, p. 181
[2] Walcott, M E C , *Inventories of ..the Ben. Priory of...Shepey for Nuns*
(*Arch Cant.* 1869), pp 23 ff.
[3] E g at Gracedieu "*The dorter,* item ther three nunnes selles whyche as
sould for 30 s " Nichols, *Hist and Antiq. of Leic.* (1804), III, p 653; at

The attitude of ecclesiastical authorities to the modification of the communal rule involved in *familiae* and *camerae* was, for various reasons, one of strict disapproval The custom of providing separate messes was extremely uneconomical; the passing of much time in private rooms was open to suspicion, especially when male visitors were received there, communal life was an essential part of the monastic idea, finally the amenities of private life were apt (as we shall see) to bring in their train the amenities of private property. The policy of the bishops was, for all these reasons, to restore communal life They made general injunctions that frater and dorter should duly be kept by all the nuns, they made special injunctions for the abolition of separate households, and above all they condemned private rooms.

"Also we enioyne yow, pryoresse," writes Alnwick to Catesby in 1442, "that ye dispose so for your susters that the morne next aftere, Myghelmasse day next commyng wythe owten any lengare delaye, ye and thai aftere yowre rewle lyfe in commune, etyng and drynkyng in oon house, slepyng in oon house, prayng and sarufyng [serving] God in oon oratorye, levyng vtterly all pryuate hydles [hiding-places], chaumbres and syngulere housholdes, by the whiche hafe comen and growen grete hurte and peryle of sowles and noyesfulle sklaundere of your pryorye[1]

Catesby where the "sells in the dorter were sold at 6s 8d, apiece," *Archaeologia*, XLIII, p 241 In theory the nuns were supposed to get up and lie down in full view of each other and curtains were forbidden by Woodlock at Romsey in 1311 Liveing, *op cit* p 104 On the other hand at Redlingfield in 1514 a nun complained that "sorores non habent curricula inter cubilia, sed una potest aliam videre quando surgit vel aliquid aliud facit" and the Bishop ordered the Prioress to provide curtains between the cubicles in the dorter Jessopp, *Visit of Dioc of Norwich* (Camden Soc), pp 139–40 Dom Butler thus traces the transition from the open dorter to private cells: open dorter, side partitions between the beds, curtains in front, a latticed door in front, making a cubicle, a solid door with a large window, the window grew smaller and smaller until it became a peephole; the dorter became a gallery of private rooms *Downside Review* (1899), pp 119–21

[1] *Linc Visit* II, pp. 51–2 See also among many other injunctions and references to the custom the following. Gracedieu (1440–1), *ib*. II, p. 125; Godstow (1432), *ib* I, pp 67–8, Barking (1279), Wherwell (1284), *Reg Epis. Johannis Peckham*, I, p 84, II, p 653, Hampole (1311), *V C H Yorks.* III, p 181, Swine (1318), *ib* p 163; Nunappleton (1346 and 1489), *ib.* pp 171–2, Fairwell (1367), *Reg Stretton of Lichfield*, p 119, Romsey (1387 and 1492), *New Coll* MS ff. 85, 85*d*, 86, Liveing, *Records of Romsey Abbey*, p. 218, Aconbury (1438), *Reg Spofford of Hereford*, p 224; Stixwould (1519), *V C H. Lincs* II, p 148; Sinningthwaite (1534), *Yorks Arch Journ* XVI, p 441 Sometimes the system can be traced in one house over a long period of years At Elstow, for instance, in 1387, *Linc Epis Reg. Memo Bokyngham,*

But such injunctions were not easily enforced, and the politic
bishops sometimes tried to reduce rather than to abolish the
households and private rooms. It was often necessary—and
indeed reasonable—to recognise the three *familiae* of the abbess'
or prioress' lodgings, the *misericord* or infirmary and the frater[1].
Sometimes the bishops tried to enforce the rule, laid down by
the legate Ottobon (1268), to limit the number who dined at
the superior's table, viz. that at least two-thirds of the convent
were to eat each day in the frater[2]. At Godstow Bishop Gray, in
1432, allowed three households besides that of the frater[3] The
condemnation of private rooms, and more especially of the
reception of visitors therein, was more severe; but here too, it

f 343; in 1421-2, *Linc Visit.* I, pp 50, 51; in 1432, *ib* I, p 53; in
1442-3, *ib* II, p 89, and in 1531, *Archaeologia*, XLVII, p 51 For an admonition
to a nun by name see "Moneatis insuper dominam Johannam de Wakefelde
commonialem quod illam cameram quam modo inhabitat contra debitam
honestatem religionis predicte solitarie commorando omnino dimittat et
sequatur conventum assidue tam in choro, claustro, refectorio et dormitorio
quam in ceteris locis et temporibus opportunis, prout religionis convenit
honestati" (Kirklees 1315), *Yorks Arch Journ* XVI, p 359

[1] See, for instance, Longland's careful injunction to Elstow in 1531:
"Foras moche as the very ordre off sainct benedicte his rulen ar nott ther
obserued in keping the ffratrye att meale tymes .butt customably they
resorte to certayn places within the monasterye called the housholdes,
where moche insolency is use contrarye to the good rules of the said religion,
by reason of resorte of seculars both men women and children and many
other inconvenyents hath thereby ensewed.. we imoyne . that ye lady abbesse and your successours see that noo suche householdes be then kepte
frome hensforth, butt oonly oon place which shalbe called the mysericorde,
where shalbe oon sadde lady of the eldest sorte oversear and maistres to
all the residue that thidre shall resorte, whiche in nombre shall nott passe
fyve att the uttermoost, besides ther saide ladye oversear or maistres and
those fyve wekely to chaunge and soo. .all the covent have kepte the same,
and they agen to begynne and the said gouernour and oversear of them
contynally to contynue in thatt roome by the space of oon quarter of a
yere, and soo quarterly to chaunge att the nominacon and plesure of the
ladye abbesse for the tyme being. Over this it is ordered undre the said payne
and Iniunction that the ladye abbesse haue no moo susters from hensforth
in hir householde butt oonly foure with hir chapleyne and likewise wekely
to chaunge till they have goon by course thrugh the hole nomber off susters,
and soo agen to begynne and contynue *Archaeologia*, XLVII, p 51

[2] Wilkins, *Conc* II, p. 16 See also "Et fetez qe lez deuz parties du covent
a meyns mangent checun jour en le refreytour" (Wroxall 1338), *Sede
Vacante Reg* (Worc), p 276, cf Elstow (c 1432), *Linc Visit* I, p 53 It is
often accepted that the nuns shall keep frater only on the three fish days,
but see Gray's injunction to Delapré Abbey (c 1432-3) enjoining its observance on the three accustomed days (Sunday, Wednesday and Friday)
and on Monday as well *Linc. Visit* I, p 45.

[3] *Ib* I, p. 68

was necessary in large convents for the obedientiaries to have their offices, and other individuals were sometimes given special permission to use separate *camerae*. Some bishops allowed them to sick nuns, but others enforced the use of the common infirmary[1].

It has already been said that this approximation to private life was bound to bring with it an approximation to private property and it remains now to analyse the process by which these new methods of providing food, and even more effectively, new methods of providing clothes, resulted in a spread of *proprietas*, which was considered perfectly legitimate by the nuns and within limits condoned by the bishops. The impression left upon the mind by a study of monastic records during the last two centuries of the middle ages is that in many houses the rule of strict personal poverty was in practice almost completely abrogated, for it is quite obvious that the nuns had the private and individual disposal of money and goods. Indeed some convents seem almost like the inmates of a boarding house, each of whom receives lodging and a certain minimum of food from the house, but otherwise caters for herself out of her private income. This is a considerable departure from the rule of St Benedict, and it is worth while to analyse the sources from which the nuns drew the money and goods of which they disposed. These sources may be classified under five headings: (1) the annual allowance of pocket money (called *peculium*) which was allowed to each nun from the funds of the house and out of which she had to provide herself with clothes and other

---

[1] See, for instance, Bokyngham's injunction to Heynings in 1392: "Item that no nun there shall keep a private chamber, but that all the nuns, who are in good health, shall lie and sleep in the dorter and those who are ill in the infirmary, saving dame Margaret Darcy, nun of the aforesaid house, to whom on account of her noble birth we wish for the time being to allow that room which she now occupies, but without any service of bread and beer, save in case of manifest illness," *Linc. Epis. Reg. Memo. Bokyngham,* f 397*d* But see Gynewell's injunctions to the convent in 1351. *Linc Epis Reg Memo Gynewell,* f 34*d* For the use of separate rooms allowed to ill nuns, see Nunappleton (1489), *V C H. Yorks* III, p 172. At Romsey in 1507 the nuns, under the eye of the visitor, "concluded and provided that Joan Patent, nun, who had hurt her leg, by her consent shall in future have meals in her own chamber and shall daily have in her chamber the right of one nun " Liveing, *Records of Romsey Abbey,* p 230 But usually the use of the common infirmary is enjoined Separate lodgings were also allowed to ex-superiors after resignation. See above, p 57

necessities; (2) pittances in money, (3) gifts in money and kind from friends; (4) legacies; (5) the proceeds of their own labour.

(1) The practice of giving a *peculium* in money out of the common funds of the house to monks and nuns began at quite an early date (it is mentioned at the Council of Oxford in 1222) and was so much an established custom in the fourteenth and fifteenth centuries that to withhold it was considered by bishops a legitimate cause of complaint against superiors. The amount of the *peculium* varied at different houses. In the majority of cases it was intended to be used for clothes and its payment is sometimes entered in account rolls. At Gracedieu the nuns had "salaries" of 6s 8d a year each for their vesture and the careful treasuress enters all their names[1]. At St Michael's, Stamford, a chambress' account, which has been preserved among the treasuress' accounts, shows that in 1408-9 the prioress was paid 5s. for her "camise" and all the other eleven nuns 4s. each, while the two lay sisters had 3s. each[2]. Similarly at St Radegund's, Cambridge, a certain pension from St Clement's Church was ear-marked for the clothing of the nuns and was paid over directly to them[3]; and the Prioress of Catesby in 1414-5 includes under "customary payments" money paid "to the lady Prioress and her six nuns and to one sister and her three brethren by the year for clothing"[4]. The fact that the *peculium* was a payment made from the common funds and not the privately owned income of an individual allowed it to escape the charge of *proprietas*, but it was nevertheless an obvious departure from the Benedictine rule, which forbade the individual disposal of property and made quite different arrangements for the provision of clothing.

(2) Another class of payments made to individuals from the convent funds was that of pittances. A pittance was originally an extra allowance of food and it was quite common for a benefactor to leave money to a convent for a pittance on the anniversary of his death. These pittances were, however, sometimes paid in money and most account rolls will provide examples of both. The nuns of Barking receive "Ruscheaw silver" as well

[1] *P R O. Mins. Accts* 1257/10, ff. 46, 119, 170, 214
[2] *P R O Mins. Accts* 1260/14
[3] Gray, *Priory of St Radegund, Cambridge*, pp. 27, 147, 155, 163, 171
[4] Baker, *Hist. of Northants.* 1, p 280.

as the little pies called "risshowes" in Lent, the nuns of St
Mary de Pré (St Albans) had "Maundy silver" as well as ale
and wine on Maundy Thursday, the nuns of St Michael's
Stamford receive their pittances sometimes in money, sometimes
in spices or pancakes, wine or beer. The nuns of Romsey had
a pittance of 6d. each on the feast of St Martin and another of
6d. each "when blood is let"[1].

(3) The third source from which nuns obtained private possessions lay in the gifts, both in money and in kind bestowed
upon them by their friends It has already been shown, in
Chapter I, that there was a growing tendency in the later
middle ages for a nun to be supported by means of an annuity,
paid by her relatives and often ending with her life. The
fact that these annuities were ear-marked for the support of
individuals must have increased the temptation to regard
them as the property of those individuals, a temptation which
was not present in the old days when an aristocratic nun brought
with her a grant of land to the house One is tempted to conjecture that individuals occasionally retained in their own hands
the expenditure of part at least of their annuities. Specific
information from English sources is unfortunately rare, but in
the diocese of Rouen in the middle of the thirteenth century
Archbishop Eudes Rigaud sometimes found it necessary to
enjoin that certain nuns who possessed rents which were reserved
for their own use, should either transfer them to the common
funds, or else dispose of them only with the consent of the
prioress, a significant modification, which suggests that he was
unable to eradicate a deeply rooted custom, although it was
strictly against the rule[2]. It was some twenty years later
(c. 1277) that Bishop Thomas of Cantilupe, writing to the nuns
of Lymbrook, enjoined:

Let none of you keep in her own hand any possession or rent for
clothing and shoeing herself, even with the consent of the prioress,
albeit such possession or rent may be given to her by parents or
friends, because the goods of your community suffice not thereto;
but let it be given up wholly to your prioress, that out of it she may

---

[1] *Reg J de Pontissara*, I, p. 126 William of Wykeham writes to
Wherwell in 1387 concerning the abbess' illicit detention of "certain
distributions and pittances as well in money as in spices," which divers
benefactors had endowed *New Coll.* MS f 89 v⁰

[2] See below, p 653..

minister to those to whom the gift was made, according to their needs, otherwise they may easily fall into the sin of property and a secular craving for gifts, thus rashly violating their vow[1]

There are also occasional references to "poor" nuns, without such annuities or dress-allowances, which suggest that the annuitants had personal disposal of their own money. Thus John Heyden, esq., in 1480, bequeaths "to every nun in Norfolk not having an annuity 40d"[2], and Bishop Gray in 1432 refers to "a certain chest within the monastery [of Godstow] for the relief of needy nuns," to which the sum of a hundred shillings was to be restored[3].

But whether or not nuns were in the habit of retaining in their own possession regular annuities, it is plain that they did so retain the various gifts in kind and in money, brought to them from time to time by their friends; and, judging from the constant references in the visitation reports, these presents must have been fairly numerous They varied from the gifts, rewards, letters, tokens and skins of wine, which the gatekeeper of Godstow smuggled in to the nuns from the scholars of Oxford, to the more sober presents of money, clothes and food given to them by fond relatives for their relief "as in hire habyte and sustenaunce."

(4) One kind of gift deserves, however, a more careful consideration, for the preservation of many thousands of medieval wills allows us to speak in detail of legacies to individual nuns, which occur sometimes in company with legacies to the whole community, sometimes alone. These bequests took many different forms. Sometimes a father leaves an annuity for the support of his daughter in her convent[4]. More frequently a nun becomes the recipient of a lump sum of money and from the wording of the legacies it is perfectly clear that these sums are to be delivered into her own hands for her own use. Let us, for instance, analyse the legacies left by Sir John Depeden, a northern knight who was a good friend to poor nuns. He first of all leaves twenty shillings each to the following twelve

---

[1] *Reg Thome de Cantilupo*, p. 202   Compare Archbishop Winchelsey's injunction to Sheppey (1296) "ne qua monialis pecuniam vel aliam rem sibi donatam aut aliqualiter adquisitam sibi retineat sine expressa licencia priorisse" (a loophole). *Reg. Roberti Winchelsey*, p. 100

[2] W. Rye, *Carrow Abbey*, app IX, p. xix.

[3] *Linc. Visit* I, p. 68.   [4] See above, pp. 15, 17, 18.

nunneries, that they may pray for his soul and his wife's: Esholt Arthington, Wilberfoss, Thicket, Moxby, Kirklees, Yedingham, Clementhorpe, Hampole, Keldholme, Marrick (all in Yorkshire) and Burnham (in Buckinghamshire). He then continues:

And I give and bequeath to dame Joan Waleys, nun of Watton, to her own use (*ad usum suum proprium*), 40s. And I give and bequeath to dame Margaret Depeden, nun of Barking, to her own use, 5 marks and one salt cellar of silver. And I give and bequeath to Elizabeth, daughter of John FitzRichard, nun of Appleton, to her own use, 40s.;

moreover he leaves to the Prioress of the last mentioned house 6s. 8d and to each nun there 2s.[1] There is an obvious distinction here between the lump sums left to the common funds of the twelve nunneries grouped together and the gifts to individuals which follow. It is moreover quite common for a testator, who wishes to give money in charity to a whole house (as distinct from one who makes a bequest to a relative or friend therein), to distinguish the amounts to be paid to the prioress and to each of the nuns. Thus John Brompton, merchant of Beverley (n.d., c. 1441–4) while leaving a lump sum of 20s. to the nuns of Watton "for a pittance," 10s. to the nuns of Nunkeeling and 5s. to the nuns of Burnham, thus provides for all the inmates of Swine:

Item I bequeath to the Prioress of Swine, 3s 4d., and to each nun of the said house 2s., and to the vicar there 3s 4d. and to each chaplain there celebrating divine service in the churches of the said town 12d, item to Hamond, servant there 12d, and to each woman serving the aforesaid nuns within the aforesaid abbey, 6d.[2]

Thus also James Myssenden of Great Limber (1529) distinguishes between the convent and the individual nuns of Nuncoton: "To the monastery of Cotton, 3l 6s 8d, to Dame Johan Thomson, prioress of the same 40s, to Dame Margaret Johnson 6s 8d, to Dame Elynor Hylyarde 6s 8d, to every other nun of the convent 12d"; and Dame Jane Armstrong, vowess, of Corby, in the same year leaves the nuns of Sempringham 6s. 8d, "of which Dame Agnes Rudd is to have 40d"[3]. Similar instances may be multiplied from any collection of wills[4].

---

[1] *Test Ebor* I, pp. 296–7.   [2] *Ib* II, p 97
[3] *Lincolnshire Wills*, ed. A. R. Maddison (1880), pp 4, 6.
[4] See, for example, *Test. Ebor*. I, pp. 6, 9, 11, 12, 14, 15, 16, 18, 19, 31, 43, 54, 62, 90, 98, 109, 143, 166, 179, 216, 292, 337, 345, 349, 363, 376, 382

Moreover it seems plain that the money thus willed was actually paid over to individuals by their convent. The account roll of the treasuress of St Radegund's Cambridge, in 1449–50, contains an item:

And to Dame Alice Patryk lately dead in full payment of all debts 3s. 4d. from the legacy of Peter Erle, chaplain, lately deceased   And to Dame Joan Lancaster in part payment of 6s. 8d. bequeathed to her by the aforesaid Peter 3s 4d., and to Dame Agnes Swaffham, subprioress, in part payment of 6s 8d., 20d [1]

But it was not only money which was bequeathed to nuns. They often received quite considerable legacies of jewels and plate, robes and furniture What would we not give today to look for a moment at the beautiful things which Walter Skirlaw, Bishop of Durham, left to his sister Joan, the Prioress of Swine, in 1404?

Item, one large gilded cup, with a cover and a round foot, and in the bottom a chaplet of white and red roses and a hind carven in the midst and all round the outside carven with eagles, lions, crowns and other ingenious devices (babonibus), and in the pommel a nest and three men standing and taking the chicks from the nest, of the weight of 18 marks....Item a robe of murrey cloth of Ypres (? yp'n) containing a mantle and hood furred with budge (? purg'), another hood furred with ermine, a cloak furred with half vair, a long robe (garnach') furred with vair....Item one bed of tapestry work of a white field, with a stag standing under a great tree and on either side lilies and a red border, with the complete tester and three curtains of white boulter [2].

In the same year Anne St Quintin left the same noble lady " one silken quilt and one pair of sheets of cloth of Rennes "[3]. Eleven years earlier Sir John Fairfax, rector of Prescot, had left his sister Margaret Fairfax, Prioress of Nunmonkton (of whom we have already heard much that was not to her good):

one silver gilt cup with a cover, and one silver cup with a cover, one mazer with a cover of silver gilt, one pix of silver for spices, six silver

(chiefly wills of clergy and country gentry); Nicolas, *Test. Vetusta*, I, pp. 52, 70, 76, 79, 85, 115, 116, 120, 121, 123, 137, 155, 170, 196, 300, 377 (chiefly wills of the aristocracy), Gibbons, *Early Lincoln Wills*, pp 18, 21, 25, 26, 40, 41, 56, 60, 67, 71, 76, 80, 87, 97, 125, 138, 139, 150, 160 (chiefly wills of clergy and country gentry) The wills of the citizens of London preserved in the court of Husting contain many legacies to nuns, chiefly annual rents.

[1] Gray, *Priory of St Radegund, Cambridge*, p. 156.

[2] *Test. Ebor.* I, pp. 317, 322, 324 The items occur in the inventory of the Bishop's goods and against each is written "Detur Priorissae de Swyna sorori meae "

[3] *Ib* I, p 332

spoons, one cloak of black cloth furred with gray, one round silver basin and ten marks of silver[1]

Master John de Wodhouse in 1345 leaves Dame Alice Conyers, nun of Nunappleton, "fifteen marks [and] a long chest standing against my bed at York, one maser cup with an image of St Michael in the bottom and one cup of silver, which I had of her gift, with a hand in the bottom holding a falcon"[2], and Isabella, widow of Thomas Corp, a London pepperer, in 1356, leaves

to Margaret, sister of William Heyroun, vintner, nun at Barking, a silver plated cup with covercle, twelve silver spoons, two cups of mazer and a silver enamelled pix, together with three gold rings, with emerald, sapphire and diamond respectively and divers household goods[3]

Possibly some of these splendid pieces of plate found their way to the altar, and the cups and spoons to the frater of the house, but the nuns undoubtedly sometimes kept them for private use in their own *camerae*. Here also were kept the beds, such as that splendid one left by Bishop Skirlaw to his sister, the "bed of Norfolk" which Sir Robert de Roos left to his daughter Joan (1392)[4], the "bed of worstede with sheets, which she kindly gave me," left by William Felawe, clerk, to Katherine Slo, Prioress of Shaftesbury (1411)[5]. Doubtless Juliana de

---

[1] *Test Ebor* I, pp 187–9 He also left the Prioress 13s 4d and each nun 6s. 8d. and each sister 3s 4d To certain nuns he left special bequests, to Margaret de Pykering, "one piece of silver, with the head of a stag in the bottom and 2s ," to Elizabeth Fairfax 26s 8d and to Margaret de Cotam 13s. 4d.; also to the Prioress and convent "my white vestment with the gold stars and all the appurtenances thereof and my cross with Mary and John in silver and one gilt chalice " Nor were his legacies confined to Nunmonkton, he left his two sisters at Sempringham 100s and two nuns of Nunappleton and Marrick respectively, a cow each

[2] *Ib* I, pp 14–15 He also leaves 40s to the Prioress and convent "for a pittance," 20s to another nun there and 6s 8d to a nun of Watton He evidently had great confidence in Alice Conyers, for the injunctions of his will are to be carried out "according to the counsel and help of the said Alice Conyers and of my executors " For other gifts of plate to individuals, see *Test Ebor.* I, p 216, *Somerset Med. Wills*, I, pp 18, 144, *Reg Stafford of Exeter*, pp 392, 415, 416, *Testamenta Leodiensia* (Thoresby Soc. Pub II, 1890), p 108

[3] Sharpe, *Cal. of Wills ..in the Court of Husting*, I, p 688. She also leaves Margaret and two other nuns a piece of blanket to be divided between them

[4] *Test. Ebor.* I, p. 179 He also leaves her 40s and a silver cup

[5] *Somerset Medieval Wills*, I, p 47. Eleanor, Duchess of Gloucester, left a bed among other things to her daughter, a nun of the house of Minoresses without Aldgate (1399) Nicolas, *Test. Vetusta*, I, p. 148.

Crofton, nun of Hampole, knew what use to make of "six shillings and eightpence and a cloak lined with blue and two tablets and one saddle with a bridle and two leather bowls"[1], here at one gift was the wherewithal for writing a letter to announce a visit and for paying that visit on horseback, in gay and unconventual attire. Indeed the constant legacies of clothes to nuns go far to explain where it was that they obtained those cheerful secular garments, against which their bishops waged war in vain   In days when clothes were made of heavy and valuable stuffs and richly adorned, it was a very common custom for a woman to divide up her wardrobe between different legatees, and men also handed on their best garments. When in 1397 Margaret Fairfax is found using "divers furs and even gray fur (gris)"[2], one remembers, with a sudden flash of comprehension, the "cloak of black cloth furred with gray" which her brother left her four years earlier. What did Elizabeth de Newemarche, nun, do with the mantle of brounemelly left her by Lady Isabel Fitzwilliam?[3] What did Sir William Bonevyll's sister at Wherwell do with "his best hoppelond with the fur"?[4] What above all did the Prioress of Swine do with all those costly fur trimmings left her by the Bishop of Durham? Yorkshire nunneries were apt to be undisciplined and worldly; great ladies there, if Archbishop Melton is to be believed, sometimes considered that they might dress according to their rank[5]. We may safely guess that the Prioress of Swine, like her contemporary at Nunmonkton, wore the furs; and visitation records do not lead us to suppose that other nuns sold their blue-lined cloaks and houppelonds for the sake of their convents, or bestowed them on the poor

It is a common injunction that nuns are to wear no other ring than that which, at their consecration, made them brides

---

[1] *Test. Ebor* I, p 382
[2] Dugdale, *Mon* IV, p 194   [3] *Test Ebor* I, p 51.
[4] *Reg Stafford of Exeter*, p 392 For other gifts of clothes see Rye, *Carrow Abbey*, app p xix (a habit cloth), *Lincoln Wills*, ed Foster, p 84 ("a fyne mantyll of ix yerds off narow cloth"), *Test. Ebor.* I, p. 59 (my two robes with mantles), *ib* II, p 255 (my best harnassed belt)
[5] At Hampole in 1320 he warned the prioress to correct those nuns who used new-fangled clothes, contrary to the accustomed use of the order, "whatever might be their condition or state of dignity," *V.C H. Yorks.* III, p. 164 (where the date is wrongly given as 1314).

of Christ[1]; but the rule was often disobeyed and Dame Clemence Medforde's "golden rings exceeding costly with divers precious stones[2]" are explained when we remember the "three gold rings, one having a sapphire, another an emerald and the third a diamond" which the rich pepperer's widow left to Dame Margaret Heyroun[3] Madame Eglentyne herself may have owed to one of the many friends, who held her digne of reverence, her "peire of bedes, gauded al with grene," of small coral. When Sir Thomas Cumberworth died in 1451 he ordered that "the priors of Coton, of Irford, of Legburn and of Grenefeld have Ilkon of yam a pare bedys of corall, as far as that I have may laste, and after yiff yam gette [give them jet] bedes"[4], and so also Matilda Latymer left her daughter at Buckland a set of "Bedys de corall"[5] and Margerie de Crioll left a nun of Shaftesbury "my paternoster of coral and white pearls, which the Countess of Pembroke gave me"[6].

(5) The fifth and last source from which nuns could derive a private income was by the work of their own hands and brains. It has been stated above that very little is known about the sale of fine needlework by nuns, but a very interesting case at Easebourne seems to show that they sometimes considered themselves entitled to retain for their own private use the sums which they earned. In 1441 one of the complaints against the gay prioress was that she "compels her sisters to work continually like hired workwomen, and they receive nothing whatever for their own use from their work, but the prioress

[1] See e g. Wilkins, *Conc.* I, p 591, *V C H Bucks* I, p 383, *Linc Visit* I, p. 52; ib II, pp 3, 8

[2] See above, p 76

[3] See above, p. 328 For other bequests of rings, see the wills of Sir Guy de Beauchamp, 1359 (his fourth best gold ring to his daughter Katherine at Shouldham), Robert de Ufford, Earl of Suffolk, 1368 ("to the Lady of Ulster, a Minoress . a ring of gold, which was the duke's, her brother's"), Thomas Beauchamp, Earl of Warwick, 1369 (rings to his daughter and granddaughter at Shouldham) Nicolas, *Test Vetusta,* I, pp. 63, 74, 79 But rings might be put to pious uses The inventory of *jocalia* in the custody of the sacrist of Wherwell (c. 1333–40) contains the item, "a small silver croun, with eleven gold rings fixed in it, for the high altar, another better croun of silver, with nineteen gold rings." *V C H Hants.* II, p 135.

[4] *Linc Dioc. Doc* ed A Clark (E E T S), p 50

[5] *Reg Stafford of Exeter,* p. 415

[6] Gibbons, *Early Linc. Wills* p 5 In the Prioress' room at Sheppey at the Dissolution were found "iiij payre of corall beds, contaynyng in all lviij past gawdy (ed)." Walcott, *Invent. of ..Shepey,* p. 29.

takes the whole profit." The bishop's injunction is extremely significant:

the prioress shall by no means compel her sisters to continual work of their hands and if they should wish of their own accord to work, they shall be free to do so, but yet so that they may reserve for themselves the half part of what they gain by their hands, the other part shall be converted to the advantage of the house and unburdening it from debt[1].

In fine, the Bishop is obliged to acquiesce in a serious breach of the Benedictine rule. the plea of the nuns to commit the sin of *proprietas* is considered as a reasonable demand; and the compromise that half their earnings should go to the common fund is intended rather to check the prioress than the nuns. From the injunctions of other bishops it would appear that the private boarders and private pupils taken by individual nuns sometimes paid their fees to those individuals and not to the house[2]; the "household" system made the reception of such boarders easy.

From whatever source nuns obtained control of money and goods, whether from the *peculium*, from gifts, from legacies, or from the proceeds of their own labour, one thing is clear in a fourteenth or fifteenth century house, where the system of the *peculium* and the *familia* obtained, there was a considerable approximation to private life and to private property. The control of money and goods and the division into households, catering separately for themselves, worked in together. The responsibility of the convent towards its members was sometimes limited to a bare minimum of food, such as the staple bread and beer, and perhaps a small dress allowance. All the rest was provided by the nuns themselves In strict theory annuities, gifts and legacies, were put into common stock and administered by the convent. In practice they were obviously retained in individual possession and administered as private property by the nuns. Even legacies of lump sums to a whole convent were probably divided up between the nuns, an equal sum being paid to each and perhaps double to the prioress.

An analysis of the conditions revealed at Alnwick's visitation of the Lincoln diocese in 1440–5 throws an exceedingly

---

[1] *Sussex Arch. Coll.* IX, p. 8.   [2] See pp. 272–3.

interesting side-light, not only on the vow of monastic poverty, as understood in the fifteenth century, but also on the domestic economy of the houses, the majority of which were small and poor. It may also conveniently be compared with the evidence given by the same visitations as to the system of *familiae* in these houses. At some the house supplied all food and clothes or a *peculium* for clothes, at some it provided only a bare minimum of food, at some neither dress nor dress allowance was provided. At Legbourne

> every nun has one loaf, one half gallon of beer a day, one pig a year, 18d. for beef, every day in Advent and Lent two herrings, and a little butter in summer and sometimes two stone of cheese a year and 8d. a year for raiment and no more,

the sum of 2s. 2d. a year for beef and clothes was certainly not excessive[1]. At Stixwould

> every nun receives in the year one pig, one sheep, a quarter of beef, two stones of butter, three stones of cheese, every day in Advent and Lent three herrings, six salt fish and twelve doughcakes a year; and they were wont to have 6s. 8d. for their raiment, but for several years back (one nun said for twenty years) as regards raiment they have received nothing.

At St Michael's Stamford, the house provided only "bread and beer and a mark for fish and flesh and other things and as to their raiment they receive naught of the house"; out of the mark the nuns catered for themselves. Other houses provided still less out of the common funds: at Gokewell the nuns received nothing from the house but bread and beer and at Markyate (a poor house, of not unblemished reputation and badly in debt) "they receive of the house only bread, beer and two marks for their raiment and what else is necessary for their living, which are less than enough for their sundry needful wants"; Alnwick ordered all victuals to be given them "of the commune stores of the house owte of one selare and one kytchyne" and fixed the dress allowance at a noble yearly, but he did not say how the house was to raise funds. At Nuncoton the allowance was

---

[1] Another nun says that she has nothing at all for raiment and another deposes, "seeing that the revenues of the house are not above forty pounds and the nuns are thirteen in number with one novice, so many out of rents so slender cannot have sufficient food and clothing, unless some help be given them from other sources by their secular friends" *Linc Visit.* II, pp. 184, 186

8s. a year, but when Alnwick came the nuns had received only
1s each   At Fosse, Langley and Ankerwyke the houses provided
meat and drink, but no dress or dress allowance, and at Catesby
it was complained that "the prioress does not give the nuns
satisfaction in the matter of their raiment and money for victuals
and touching the premises is in the nuns' debt for
three-quarters of the year"[1]. From these references it is plain
that the nuns usually bought their own clothes and often catered
for themselves in flesh food; also that the poverty of many
houses was so great that the nuns could not have lived decently
without the help of friends, whether because their dress allowances were always in arrears, or because the house recognised
no responsibility to clothe them from its exiguous funds. Yet
as regards food at least, the habit of catering separately for
separate messes was undoubtedly less economical than the
regular maintenance of a common table would have been.

A highly interesting light on the control of money allowances
for the purchase of food by the individual nuns of a convent
is thrown by convent account rolls. These accounts show two
different methods of catering in force. In one all the housekeeping was done by the cellaress, who bought such stores as
were needed to supplement the produce of the home farm and
provided the nuns with the whole of their food. This is the
normal method, which accords with the Rule; it is to be found
in the Syon cellaresses' rolls and in the roll of Elizabeth Swynford,
Prioress of Catesby (1414–15)   The latter sets forth: (1) the
produce of the home farm, how many animals were delivered
to the larder, how many to the kitchen, how much grain was
malted, etc.; (2) the payments for food bought to supplement
this home produce:

in flesh and eggs bought from the feast of St Michael until Lent
33/0½, and in expenses of the house from Easter unto the feast of
St Michael in beef and eggs bought, £7 1. 9.,...in 2 barrels 4 kemps
of oil and salt fish bought in time of Lent £3 0. 6,

besides sundry odd purchases of red herrings, pepper, saffron,
salt, garlic and fat[2].

---

[1] For these references, see *Linc. Visit* II, pp 7, 47, 92, 117, 184, 186;
Alnwick's Visit. MS ff 6, 71d, 76, 83   Also injunctions as to food at Elstow
ib II, p. 39 (and note)
[2] Baker, *Hist. and Antiq. of Northants.* I, pp. 280, 282-3.

But some account rolls show an entirely different method of housekeeping. By this the convent provided the nuns with their daily ration of bread and beer and perhaps with a certain amount of green food and dairy produce, but paid them an allowance of money with which to buy their meat and fish food for themselves On this system the convent still had to provide the nuns with their pittances, though often enough these too were paid in money, and usually also with the bulk of their Lenten fare of salt fish and spices, which was bought in large quantities at a time and stored. An extreme example of this system is found in the account of Christian Bassett, Prioress of St Mary de Pré (St Albans) in 1486–8 Under the heading *Comyns, Pytances and Partycions* she pays to herself as prioress:

for her comyns for xxj monethes...vj l viij s iiij d ..Item paid to dame Alice Wafyr for her comyns for xxj monethes. .vj l viij s iiij d ...Item paid to vij susters of the same place for their comons for xxj monethis...xxj li. vj s viij d. Item paid to dame Johan Knollys for her comyns for v monethis xvj s viij d....Item paid for brede and ale and fewell departyd amongs the susters by a yere and a half lij s Item paid for ij bushell of pesyn departyd amongs the susters in Lente xvj d.

The rest of the section contains notices of special pittances, paid sometimes in money and sometimes in kind, for instance 10s. 6d. is paid for "Maundy Ale" and 10d. for wine on two Maundy Thursdays, but the sisters also get "Maundy money" amounting to 21d. One interesting item runs: "delyvered of the rente in Cambrigge amongs the susters for the tyme of this accompte xlviij s"; these rents, which are entered among the receipts, were no doubt ear-marked for the nuns, possibly as *peculia* for the purchase of clothes, possibly as a pittance[1]. The same system of housekeeping was obviously also in vogue at St Michael's, Stamford, at the time of Alnwick's visitation; but the account rolls of this house are not easy to interpret, because although they contain no reference to catering, other than certain pittances and feasts on Maundy Thursday and other festal occasions, neither do they contain any reference to commons money. No separate cellaress' accounts have survived to throw any further

[1] Dugdale, *Mon* III, p 359

light upon the subject. At Elstow Abbey some years later the practice of paying "commons" money was well established[1].

It is tempting to conjecture what considerations may have prevailed to make some houses substitute money grants for the provision of food in kind. The tendency certainly grew with the custom of forming *familiae* which messed separately and it certainly increased with time. Even at Catesby, which we saw to be a typical example of communal housekeeping in 1414-5, it seems to have become customary to give money for some at least of the victuals in 1442. The tendency also grew with poverty, as appears from Alnwick's visitations, though it is not clear whence the nuns obtained the wherewithal to feed themselves adequately, unless they had the use of extra funds of their own. It may also be conjectured that the system would be easier to work in a town than in the depths of the country. In a town the nuns could buy in the open market, and it was as easy for individuals to buy in small quantities as for the cellaress to buy wholesale. In the country, however, the convent would not only be more dependent on the home farm, but such purchases as had to be made at occasional fairs and weekly markets could more easily be made in bulk, a consideration which also accounts for the fact that the barrels and cades of salt fish for Lent were usually laid in wholesale by the cellaress. Moreover it would often be convenient for a town house to lease out the greater number of its demesnes and to depend upon what it could purchase for its daily fare. St Mary de Pré is particularly interesting in this respect, the 1486-8 account shows no sign of any home farm; the income of the house is derived almost entirely from "rents of assise and rents farm" within the town of St Albans and in other places and from tithes, and the proportion of farms or leases is noticeably large. Even the bread and beer distributed among the sisters did not come from a home farm; it was bought with 52s received from the Abbot of St Albans for that purpose; the kitchener of the parent abbey

---

[1] Temp Henry VII the Abbess of Elstow's account records the payment of double commons of 1s. a week to the Prioress and 6d a week single commons to each of the nuns Pittances (double to the prioress) are paid on days of profession and on the greater feast The nuns also had dress allowances in money. C T Flower, *Obedientiars' Accounts of Glastonbury and other Relig Houses* (St Paul's Ecclesiol Soc vii, pt ii, 1912), pp 52, 55

similarly provided the nuns with 12s., "for potage money departyd amongs the susters for a yere," and at the forester's
office they received 8s for their fuel

Occasional references show what a variety of household
charges the nuns sometimes had to bear out of their *peculia*, and
the other sources of their private income. At Campsey in 1532,
for instance,

the subprioress says that the prioress will not allow her servants to
go out upon the necessary errands of the nuns, but they hire outsiders
at their own cost and Dame Isabella Norwiche says that sick nuns in
the time of their sickness bear the cost of what is needful to them and
it is not provided at the charge of the house[1]

At Sheppey also, in 1511, there was no infirmary and when ill
the nuns had to hire women for themselves and pay for them
out of their own money[2]. At Langley in 1440 Alnwick ordered
that each nun should have yearly a cartload of fuel, cut at the
cost of the house, but carried at the cost of the nuns[3]. At
Wherwell there was a custom by which, on the first occasion
that a nun took her turn in reading from the pulpit, a certain
sum of money or a pittance was exacted from her for the benefit
of the convent, a custom forbidden by Bishop John of Pontoise
in 1302[4]; and there is mention of another pittance in 1311, when
Bishop Woodlock ordered that for digging the grave and preparing the coffin of a nun who had died and for pittances to
the sisters on the day of her burial, the goods of the deceased
nun should not be expended, because she ought not to have
private property, but the common goods of the church were
to be spent, which seems like locking the stable door after the
horse has gone[5].

It is interesting to trace the attitude of ecclesiastic authorities
to these various manifestations of *proprietas*. The bishops found
some difficulty in persuading nuns, accustomed to expend money
for themselves and to dine in *familiae* in separate rooms, accustomed also to receive gifts and legacies in money and kind,
that they must hold all things in common. At Arthington, in
1307, two nuns, Agnes de Screvyn, (who had resigned the post

---

[1] *Visit of Dioc of Norwich*, ed Jessopp, p. 290.
[2] *Eng Hist Rev* VI, p 34.   [3] *Linc Visit* II, pp 176, 177.
[4] *Reg. J de Pontissara*, I, p 125
[5] Liveing, *Records of Romsey Abbey*, p 103

of Prioress in 1303) and Isabella Couvel, asserted that certain animals and goods belonging to the priory were their private property and Archbishop Greenfield bids the Prioress admonish them to resign these within three days "to lawful and honest uses," according to her judgment[1]. Similarly Bishop Bokyngham writes to Heynings in 1392:

We order that cows, sows, capons, hens and all animals of any kind soever, together with wild or tame birds, which are held by certain of the nuns (whether with or without licence)...shall be delivered up to the common use of the convent within three days, without the alienation or subtraction of any of them[2].

In the light of these passages it is interesting to find that cows and pigs are among the legacies sometimes left to nuns[3]. At Nuncoton, in 1440, where certain nuns were in the habit of wandering in their gardens and gathering herbs, instead of attending Compline,

Dame Alice Aunselle prays that they may all live in common and that no nun may have anything, such as cups and the like, as her own, but that if any such there be, they be kept in common by their common servant and that they may not have houses or separate gardens appointed, as it were, to them[4],

which illustrates how easily the household system slid into *proprietas*. It was sometimes even necessary to forbid nuns to make wills and bequeath their property. This was forbidden by the Council of Oxford in 1222[5] and in 1387 William of Wykeham sent a stern injunction to the nuns of Romsey, pointing out that by making wills they were falling into the sin of property[6].

---

[1] *V C.H. Yorks.* III, p. 164.

[2] *Linc Epis Reg Memo Bokyngham*, f 397d Compare Eudes Rigaud's difficulties with the hens at Saint-Aubin, below, p. 653

[3] E g in the will of Agnes de Denton, 1356 (Item to dame Cecilie de Hmythwayt two cows), *Testamenta Karleolensia*, p 12, Sir John Fairfax, 1393 (Item I bequeath to dame Katherine de Barlay, nun of Appleton, one cow Item to dame Custance Colvyll, nun of Marrick, one cow), Sir William Dronsfeld, 1406 (Item I bequeath to dame Alice de Totehill, nun, one cow. Item I bequeath to dame Margaret de Barneby, one cow); Sir Thomas Rednes 1407 (Item to Alice Redness nun [of Hampole] one cow and one fat pig) *Test Ebor* I, pp 189, 345, 349

[4] *Alnwick's Visit* MS. f. 72.

[5] Wilkins, *Conc* I, p 593

[6] *New Coll.* MS. ff. 85d, 86. The sin of *proprietas* seems to have been serious in this house, for the Bishop couples his prohibition of wills with a prohibition of private rooms and pupils, and later (f 86d) makes a general injunction against private property.

In ·1394, on the death of Joan Furmage, Abbess of Shaftes-
·bury,

the bishop ordered the Abbey to be sequestrated and annulled the
will by which she had alienated the goods of the house in bequests
to friends, declaring such a disposition to be injurious to the community and contrary to the usage of religious women[1].

The history of the attitude of ecclesiastical authorities to
two sources of private income, the *peculium* and the gifts from
friends to individuals, is of even greater significance than these
attempts to cope with private goods, for it shows how powerless
the bishops were against the steady weakening of discipline in
monastic houses. Here, as in the enclosure struggle and the
struggle against *familiae*, they were forced into compromise at
best and at worst into acquiescence   At its first appearance
the custom of giving a *peculium* to individuals was severely condemned as a manifest breach of the rule:

"Moneys shall not be assigned to each separately for clothes," says
the Council of Oxford in 1222, "But such shall be diligently attended
to by certain persons deputed to this purpose, chamberers or chambresses, who according to the need of each and the resources of the
house, shall minister garments to them ·...Also it shall not be lawful
for the chamberer or chambress to give to any monk, canon or nun,
monies or anything else for clothes, nor shall it be lawful for monk,
canon or nun to receive anything, otherwise let the chamberer be
deposed from office and the monk, canon or nun' go without new
clothes for that year"[2].

Similarly, in the Constitutions of the legate Ottobon in 1268,
the *peculium* is grouped with other forms of property; ch. XL
enacts that no religious is to possess property and that the head
of the house is to make diligent search for such property twice
a year[3], and ch. XLI enacts that no money is to be given to a
religious for clothes, shoes and other necessities, but he is to be

---

[1] *V C H. Dorset*, II, p 78   [2] Wilkins, *Conc* I, p. 592.
[3] In connection with this, see Wickwane's injunction to Nunappleton
in 1281, "We also forbid locked boxes and chests, save if the prioress shall
have ordained some seemly arrangement of the kind and shall often see
and inspect the contents " *Reg Wickwane* (Surtees Soc), p 141. Also Newark's
injunction to Swine in 1298 that the Prioress and two senior nuns should
cause the boxes of any nuns of whom suspicion [of property] should arise
to be opened in her presence and the contents seen And if anyone will not
open her box...then let the prioress break it open." *Reg. of John le Romayn
and Hen. of Newark* (Surtees Soc.), II, p 223; compare Eudes Rigaud's
struggle against locked boxes, below, p. 652

given the article itself[1] In 1438 a severe injunction from Bishop Spofford of Hereford to the nuns of Aconbury shows the close connection between the *peculium* and the private *camera* of the nuns[2]. Yet in 1380 we find a bishop of Salisbury assigning a weekly allowance of 2*d*. to each nun of Shaftesbury from the issues of the house[3]; and in the fifteenth and sixteenth centuries nuns regularly complain to their visitors when their allowances are in arrears and the bishops regularly ordain that the money is to be paid[4]. In the thirteenth century it is a fault in the Prioress to give the nuns a *peculium*; in the fifteenth century it is a fault to withhold it

The custom as to presents from friends was that the nuns might receive gifts, only by the permission of their superior, to whom everything must be shown[5]. Thus Archbishop Wickwane writes to Nunappleton in 1281: "that no nun shall appropriate to herself any gift, garment or shoes of the gift of anyone, without the consent and assignment of the prioress"[6]; Archbishop Greenfield in 1315 forbids the nuns of Rosedale to accept or give any presents without the consent of the Prioress[7]; and Archbishop Bowet in 1411 enacts that any nun of Hampole receiving gifts or *legacies* from friends is at once on returning to reveal them to the Prioress[8]. Occasionally a Prioress, whether out of zeal for the Rule or for some other reason, showed herself unwilling to allow the nuns to receive presents The nuns of

---

[1] Wilkins, *Conc* ɪɪ, p. 16.

[2] "Where the lawe and the professyon of yche religyouse person that thei have shuld have one fraitoure and house to ete in in commyn and not in private chaumbers, and so to lygg and slepe in one house, in youre said covent sustren reteynen money and proveis thame selfe privatly ayensthe ordir of religion, etc " The injunction is coupled with a strong injunction against downes *Hereford Reg T Spofford*, p 224 Compare the injunction to Lymbrook, p 324 above

[3] *V.C.H. Dorset*, ɪɪ, p 77

[4] For other references to the *peculium* for clothing, see *Visit of Dioc of Norwich*, ed Jessopp, p 274; *Sussex Arch Coll* ɪx, p 23, Liveing, *Records of Romsey Abbey*, p 130

[5] Thus William of Wykeham, in the course of his severe injunction against *proprietas* at Romsey (1387), thus defines it "Vt autem quid sit proprium vobis plenius innotescat, nos sancti Benedicti regulam imitantes, id totum proprium siue proprietatem fore dicimus et eciam declaramus, quicquid videlicet dederitis vel receperitis sine iussu vestre Abbatisse aut retinueritis sine permissione illius " *New Coll* MS. f. 86*d*

[6] *Reg. Wickwane* (Surtees Soc), p 140.

[7] *V C.H. Yorks* ɪɪɪ, p 174   [8] *Ib* ɪɪɪ, p. 164

Flixton in 1514 complained: "that they receive no annual pensions and that the prioress is angry when anything is given to them by their friends"[1] and Alnwick in 1441 wrote to the Prioress of Ankerwyke, whose nuns complained both of insufficient clothes and of her bad temper when their friends came to see them,

And what euer thise saide frendes wyll gyfe your sustres in relefe of thaym as in hire habyte and sustenaunce, ye suffre your sustres to take hit, so that no abuse of euel come therbye noyther to the place ne to the persones therof[2]

It was indeed almost a necessity to encourage the reception of presents, when (as so often happened towards the close of the middle ages) nuns were dependent for clothes upon their friends. But with Bishop Praty ordering that the nuns of Easebourne shall receive half the sums paid them for their work, and with Bishop Alnwick encouraging presents and enforcing the payment of *peculia*, it is plain that the Lady Poverty had fallen upon evil days.

[1] Jessopp, *Visit of Dioc. of Norwich*, p. 143.
[2] *Linc Visit.* II, p 8.

CHAPTER IX

FISH OUT OF WATER

De sorte qu'une Religieuse hors de sa clôture est comme une pierre
hors de son centre; comme un arbre hors de terre, comme Adam et
Eve hors du Paradis terrestre; comme le corbeau hors de l'arche qui
ne s'arreste qu'à des charognes, comme un poisson hors de l'eau,
selon le grand Saint Antoine et Saint Bernard; comme une brebis
hors de sa bergerie et en danger d'estre devorée des loups, selon Saint
Theodore Studite; comme un oiseau hors de son nid et une grenouille
hors de son marais, selon le même Saint Bernard; comme un mort
hors de son tombeau, qui infecte les personnes qui s'en approchent,
selon Pierre le Vénérable et la Règle attribuée à Saint Jérôme, et
par consequent dans un état tout à fait opposé à la vie Régulière
qu'elle a embrassée.

J. B. THIERS (1681)

THE famous chapter LXVI of the Benedictine Rule enunciated
the principle that the professed monk should remain within the
precincts of his cloister and eschew all wandering in the world[1].
It is clear, however, that the Rule allowed a certain latitude and
that monks and nuns were to be allowed to leave their houses
under certain conditions and for necessary causes. Brethren
working at a distance or going on a journey may be excused
attendance at the divine office, if they cannot reach the church
in time[2]. Brethren sent upon an errand are forbidden to accept
invitations to eat outside the house without the consent of their
superior[3]. Moreover longer journeys are plainly contemplated,
in which they might have to spend a night or more outside their
monastery[4]. But no one might ever leave the cloister bounds

---

[1] "The monastery, however, itself ought if possible to be so constructed
as to contain within it all necessaries, that is, water, mill, garden and [places
for] the various crafts which are exercised within a monastery, so that there
be no occasion for monks to wander abroad, since this is in no wise expedient
for their souls" *Rule of St Benedict*, tr Gasquet, pp 117–8

[2] Chap. L, *ib* p 88   [3] Chap. LI, *ib*. p. 89.

[4] Chap. LXVII, *ib* p 118 This, however, is clearly exceptional, the
regulation comes in a later chapter and not in the first edition of the rule
The translations of the rule made at a later date for nuns, sometimes specify
visits "to fadir or moder or oþer frend" not mentioned in the original.

without the permission of the superior; and it was the obvious intention of St Benedict to reduce to a minimum all wandering in the world. Strictly speaking this system of enclosure applied equally to monks and to nuns; but from the earliest times it was considered to be a more vital necessity for the well being of the latter; and the history of the enclosure movement is in effect the history of an effort to add a fourth vow of claustration to the three cardinal vows of the nun[1]. The reasons for this severity are sufficiently obvious, and show that curious contradiction of ideas which is so common in all general theories about women. On the one hand the immense importance attached by the medieval Church to the state of virginity, exemplified in St John Chrysostom's remarks that Christian virgins are as far above the rest of mankind as are the angels, made it all important that this priceless jewel should not be exposed to danger in a wicked world[2]. On the other hand the medieval contempt for the fragility of women led to a cynical conviction that only when they were shut up behind the high walls of the cloister was it possible to guarantee their virtue, *aut virum aut murum oportet mulierem habere*[3]. Both views received support from the deep-

[1] In some reformed orders founded at a later date the formula of profession actually contained a vow of perpetual enclosure, e g the Poor Clares, whose vow, under the second rule given to them by Urban IV in 1263, comprised obedience, poverty, chastity and enclosure Thiers, *De la Clôture* (1681), pp 41-2 Compare the formula given in the rule of the Order of the Annunciation, founded at the close of the fifteenth century by Jeanne de France, daughter of Louis XI *Ib.* p 55 The nuns of the older orders did not make any specific vow of enclosure, and it was enforced upon them only as an indispensable condition for the fulfilment of their other vows, which accounts for the obstinacy of their opposition; some jurisconsults, indeed, were of the opinion that the Pope could not oblige a nun to be enclosed against her will. *Ib.* p 50

[2] The passage is quoted in the preface to Thiers, *op cit* For the Church's view of virginity, see especially St Jerome's famous *Epistola* (22) *ad Eustochium*

[3] Thiers, *op. cit* p 245 Quoting the jurisconsult Philippus Probus For a good example of the mixture of ideas, see Mr Coulton's account of the arguments used by the monk Idung of St Emmeram in favour of enclosure: "He begins with the usual medieval emphasis on feminine frailty, of which (as he points out) the Church reminds us in her collect for every Virgin Martyr's feast 'Victory ..even in the weaker sex ' Then comes the usual quotation from St Jerome, with its reference to Dinah, which Idung is bold enough to clinch by a detailed allusion to Danae This, of course, is little more than the usual clerkly ungallantry, but it is followed by a passage of more cruel courtesy The monk must needs go abroad sometimes on business, as for instance, to buy and sell in markets; 'but such occupations

rooted idea as old as the Greeks and an unconscionable time in dying, that "a free woman should be bounded by the street door"[1]. Medieval moralists were generally agreed that intercourse with the world was at the root of all those evils which dimmed the fair fame of the conventual system, by affording a constant temptation to frivolity and to grosser misconduct. Moreover the tongue of scandal was always busy and the nun's reputation was safe only if she could be placed beyond reproach. Hence those regulations which Mr Coulton compares to "the minutely ingenious and degrading precautions of an oriental harem"[2].

Based upon such considerations as these, the movement for the enclosure of nuns began very early in their history and continued with unabated vigour long after the Reformation[3]. Some years before the compilation of the Benedictine Rule St Caesarius of Arles, in his Rule for nuns, had forbidden them ever to leave their monastery, and from the sixth to the eleventh century decrees were passed from time to time by various provincial councils, advocating a stricter enclosure of monks and nuns, but especially of the latter. Already by the twelfth century monasticism had declined from its first fervour, and it is significant that the reformed orders which sprang up during the great renaissance of that century all made a special effort to enforce enclosure upon their nuns. The nuns of Prémontré and Fontevrault were strictly enclosed and in the middle of the following

as these would be most indecent for even an earthly queen, and far below the dignity of a bride of the King of Heaven '" Coulton, *Med Studies*, No 10, "Monastic Schools in Middle Ages" (1913), pp 21–2

[1] Words which Menander puts in the mouth of one of his characters Compare the famous Periclean definition of womanly virtue, which is "not to be talked about for good or for evil among men "

[2] Coulton, *Chaucer and his England*, p. 111

[3] The following references will be found conveniently collected in Part I chs 1–16 of a very interesting little book, the *Traité de la Clôture des Religieuses*, published in Paris in 1681 by Jean-Baptiste Thiers, "Prestre, Bachelier en Theologie de la Faculté de Paris et Curé de Chambrond " The treatise is divided into two parts, one of which shows "that it is not permitted to nuns to leave their enclosure without necessity," the other "that it is not permitted to strangers to enter the enclosure of nuns without necessity." The author contends that enclosure was the immemorial practice of the Church, though the first general decree on the subject was the Bull *Periculoso*, but what he proves is really that the demand grew up gradually and naturally out of the effort to reform the growing abuses in conventual life, which sprang from too free an intercourse with the world.

century the statutes promulgated by the Chapter-General of the Cistercian Order (1256–7) contain a clause ordering nuns to remain in their convents, except under certain specified conditions, while the rule given by Urban IV to the Franciscan nuns (1263) went further than any previous enactments in binding them by a vow of perpetual enclosure, against which no plea of necessity might avail Various synods and councils continued to repeat the order that nuns were not to leave their houses, except for a reasonable cause, but it is plain from the evidence of ecclesiastics, moralists and episcopal visitations that the nuns all over Europe paid small heed to their words. Finally, at the beginning of the new century, came the first general regulation on the subject which was binding as a law upon the whole church, the famous Bull *Periculoso*, promulgated by Boniface VIII about the year 1299.

This decree, often afterwards confirmed by Popes and Councils, remained the standard regulation upon the subject and in view of its cardinal importance its terms are worthy of notice·

Desiring to provide for the perilous and detestable state of certain nuns, who, having slackened the reins of decency and having shamelessly cast aside the modesty of their order and of their sex, sometimes gad about outside their monasteries in the dwellings of secular persons, and frequently admit suspected persons within the same monasteries, to the grave offence of Him to Whom they have, of their own will, vowed their innocence, to the opprobrium of religion and to the scandal of very many persons; we by the present constitution, which shall be irrefragably valid, decree with healthful intent that all and sundry nuns, present and future, to whatever order they belong and in whatever part of the world, shall henceforth remain perpetually enclosed within their monasteries, so that no nun tacitly or expressly professed in religion shall henceforth have or be able to have the power of going out of those monasteries for whatsoever reason or cause, unless perchance any be found manifestly suffering from a disease so great and of such a nature that she cannot, without grave danger or scandal, live together with others; and to no dishonest or even honest person shall entry or access be given by them, unless for a reasonable and manifest cause and by a special licence from the person to whom [the granting of such a licence] pertains; that so, altogether withdrawn from public and mundane sights, they may serve God more freely and, all opportunity for wantonness being removed, they may more diligently preserve for Him in all holiness their souls and their bodies.

The Bull further, in order to avoid any excuse for wandering abroad in search of alms, forbids the reception into any non-mendicant order of more sisters than can be supported without penury by the goods of the house; and, in order to prevent nuns being forced to attend lawcourts in person, requires all secular and ecclesiastical authorities to allow them to plead by proctors in their courts; but if an Abbess or Prioress has to do personal homage to a secular lord for any fief and it cannot be done by a proctor, she may leave her house with honest and fit companions and do the homage, returning home immediately. Finally Ordinaries are enjoined to take order as soon as may be for proper enclosure where there is none to provide that it is strictly kept according to the terms of the decree, and to see that all is completed by Ash Wednesday, notifying any reasonable impediment within eight days of Candlemas[1].

For the next three centuries Councils and Bishops struggled manfully to put into force the Bull *Periculoso*, but without success; the constant repetition of the order that nuns should not leave their convents is the measure of its failure. In the various reformed orders, which were founded in the fifteenth and sixteenth centuries, the insistence upon enclosure bears witness to the importance which was attached to it as a vital condition of reform: Boniface IX's ordinances for the Dominicans (1402), St Francis of Paula's rule for his order in Calabria (1435), the rule of the Order of the Annunciation, founded by Jeanne, daughter of Louis XI, at the close of the fifteenth century, Johann Busch's reforms in Saxony, the reformed rules given by Étienne Poncher, Bishop of Paris, to the nuns of Chelles, Montmartre and Malnoüe (1506) and by Geoffrey de Saint Belin, Bishop of Poitiers, to the nuns of the Holy Cross, Poitiers (1511), all insist upon strict enclosure[2]. Similarly a long list might be drawn up of general and provincial councils and synods which repeated the ordinance, culminating in the great general Council of Trent, which renewed the decree *Periculoso* and was itself

[1] *Sext Decret* lib. iii, tit xvi Quoted in *Reg. Simonis de Gandavo*, pp 10 ff., from which I quote. See also Thiers, *op. cit.* pp. 45–9

[2] See Thiers, *op cit* pp 53–60 for these, except the reforms of Busch, for which see below, App iii. Three papal bulls were published in the sixteenth century reinforcing *Periculoso*, viz. the Bull *Circa pastoralis* (1566) and *Decori et honestati* (1570) of Pius V and the Bull *Deo sacris* of Gregory XIII (1572)

followed by another long series of provincial councils, which endeavoured to put its decree into force. But these efforts were still attended by very imperfect success, for the worldly nuns of the sixteenth and seventeenth centuries chafed at the irksome restriction no less than did their predecessors of the middle ages. When, in 1681, Jean-Baptiste Thiers published his treatise on the enclosure of nuns he announced his reason to be that no point of ecclesiastical discipline was in his day more completely neglected and ignored[1].

This brief sketch of the enclosure movement in the Western Church is necessary to a right understanding of the special attempts which were made in England to keep the nuns in their cloisters by means of an absolute enforcement of the Benedictine Rule Visitatorial injunctions on this subject during the fourteenth and fifteenth centuries and up to the Reformation were based upon three enactments the constitutions of the legate Ottobon in 1268, the vigorous reforms of Archbishop Peckham (1279–92) and the Bull *Periculoso*. The Cardinal Legate Ottobon had come to England in 1265, on the restoration of Henry III after Evesham, with the purpose of punishing bishops and clergy who had supported the party of Simon de Montfort and the barons. When peace was finally signed in 1267, largely by his intervention, he was able to turn his attention to general abuses prevalent in the English church and one of the reforms which he attempted to enforce was the stricter enclosure of nuns. Chapter LII of his *Constitutions* [*Quod moniales a certis locis non exeant*] is an amplification of the Benedictine rule of enclosure, made far more rigid and severe. "Lest by repeated intercourse with secular folk the quiet and contemplation of the nuns should be troubled," minute regulations were laid down as to their movements. They were allowed to enter their chapel, chapter,

---

[1] "Cependant il n'y a gueres aujourd'hui de point de Discipline Ecclesiastique qui soit ou plus negligé, ou plus ignoré que celui de la clôture des Religieuses; et quoique les Conciles, les Saints Docteurs et les Pères des Monasteres, ayent en divers temps et en divers rencontres, employé leur zèle et leur authorité pour en établir la pratique; nous ne laissons pas neanmoins de voir souvent avec douleur qu'on le viole empunément, sans scrupule, sans réflexion et sans necessité L'Eglise gemit tous les jours en veuë de ce desordre qui la deshonore notablement, et c'est pour compatir en quelque façon à ses gemissemens, que j'entreprens de le combattre dans ce Traité." *Op cit* Preface

dorter and frater at due and fixed times; otherwise they were
to remain in the cloister; and none of these places were to be
entered by seculars, save very seldom and for some sufficient
reason. No nun was to converse with any man, except seriously
and in a public place, and at least one other nun was always to
be present at such conversations. No nun was to have a meal
outside the house except with the permission of the superior
and then only with a relative, or some person from whose
company no suspicion could arise. All other places, beyond those
specified, were entirely forbidden to the nuns, with the exception,
in certain circumstances, of the infirmary. No nun was to go
to the different offices, except the obedientiaries, whose duties
rendered it necessary and they were never to go without a
companion. The Abbess or head of the house was never to leave
it, except for its evident advantage or for urgent necessity, and
she was always to have an honest companion, while the lesser
nuns were never to be given licence to go out, except for some
fit cause and in company with another nun. Finally nuns were
not to leave their convents for public processions, but were to
hold their processions within the precincts of their own houses.
The legate strictly enjoined that "the prelates to whose jurisdiction belonged the visitation of each nunnery should cause
these statutes to be observed"[1].

It will be realised that these injunctions were exceedingly
severe and that the visitors were not likely to find their task
a sinecure. There is little evidence for determining how far any
serious attempt was made to enforce the legate's Constitutions[2],
but if we may judge from the language of Peckham, some ten
years later, any attempts which may have been made had not
been strikingly successful. One of the first actions of this
energetic archbishop on his elevation to the see of Canterbury
was to carry out a visitation of the nunneries of Barking and

---

[1] Wilkins, *Concilia*, II p 18
[2] See, however, the injunctions of Thomas of Cantilupe, Bishop of
Hereford, to Lymbrook in 1277, which are in part a recital of Ottobon's
Constitutions *Reg Thome de Cantilupo*, p 201 Peckham, in the injunctions which he sent to Barking and Godstow in 1279, states that they are
based respectively upon those issued by John de Chishull, Bishop of London,
and by Robert de Kilwardby, his predecessor as Archbishop of Canterbury,
and it is probable that both of these prelates had attempted to enforce
Ottobon's Constitutions *Reg Epis J. Peckham*, I, p 81, II, p 846

Godstow and to send to both houses injunctions laying great stress on strict enclosure (1279). In 1281 he followed up these injunctions by two general decrees for the enclosure of nuns; and in 1284 he visited the three nunneries of Romsey, Holy Sepulchre (Canterbury) and Usk and sent injunctions enforcing the Constitutions of 1281[1]. In these injunctions he laid down with great exactness the conditions to be observed in granting nuns permission to leave their convents. The Godstow injunction runs thus:

For the purpose of obtaining a surer witness to chastity, we ordain that nuns shall not leave the precincts of the monastery, save for necessary business which cannot be performed by any other persons. Hence we condemn for ever, by these present [letters] those sojourns which were wont to be made in the houses of friends, for the sake of pleasure and of escaping from discipline [*ad solatium et ad subterfugium disciplinae*] And when it shall befall any [nuns] to go out for any necessity, we strictly order these four [conditions] to be observed First, that they be permitted to go out only in safe and mature company, as well of nuns as of secular persons helping them. Secondly that having at once performed their business, so far as it can be by them performed, they return to their house; and if the performance of the business demand a delay of several days, after the first or second day it shall be left to proctors to finish it Thirdly that they never lodge in the precincts of men of religion or in the houses of clergy, or in other suspected habitations. Fourthly that no one absent herself from the sight of her companion or companions, in any place where human conversation might be held, nor listen to any secret whispering, except in the presence of the nuns her companions, unless perchance father or mother, brother or sister have something private to say to her[2].

The Barking injunctions are slightly different and the first condition imposed therein is interesting: "That they be sent forth only for a necessary and inevitable cause, that is in particular the imminent death of a parent, beyond which cause we can hardly imagine any other which would be sufficient"[3]. These injunctions are very severe, since they limit the occasions upon which a nun might leave her convent to the performance of some negotiation connected with the business of the house and

---

[1] He visited Wherwell in the same year, but his injunctions to that house dealt with the entrance of seculars into the nunnery, not with the exit of nuns

[2] *Reg. Epis J. Peckham*, II, p 247.   [3] *Ib* I, pp 85–6.

to attendance at the deathbeds of relatives and entirely forbid all visits for pleasure to the houses of friends.

In 1281 Peckham published a mandate directed against the seducers of nuns; after excommunicating all who committed or attempted to commit this crime and declaring that absolution for the sentence could be given only by a Bishop or by the Pope (except on the point of death), he proceeded to deal with the question of the enclosure of nuns, on the ground that their wandering in the world gave opportunity for such crimes, and sternly forbade them to pay visits for the sake of recreation, even to the closest relatives, or to remain out of their houses for more than two days on business[1]. The same year he also dealt with the subject in the course of a set of constitutions, concerning various abuses, which he considered to be in need of reform. The language of the chapter in which he treats of the claustration of nuns is in parts the same as that of the ordinance against seducers, but it is less severe, for it enacts only that nuns shall not stay "more than three natural days for the sake of recreation, or more than six days for any necessary reason, save in case of illness." Moreover the Archbishop adds: "we do not extend this ordinance to those who are obliged to beg necessities of life, while they are begging"[2]. It was this modified version of his ordinance which he tried to impose in his visitation of 1284, for at Romsey he recognised that the nuns might be leaving the house for recreation and not merely upon

---

[1] *Reg. Epis. J. Peckham*, I, pp. 265–6, and in Wilkins, *op cit* II, p. 61.

[2] Wilkins, *op cit* II, pp 53–9. Thiers' remarks on the practice of begging by nuns are interesting in this connection. He contends that only sheer famine justifies the breach of enclosure and adds: "C'est pourquoy je ne comprends pas d'où vient que nous voyons à Paris et ailleurs, tant de Religieuses, quelquefois assez jeunes et assez bien faites qui sous pretexte que leurs Monasteres sont dans le besoin, demandent l'aumône aux portes des Eglises, qui courent par les maisons des seculiers et qui demeurent un temps considerable hors de leurs Monasteres, le plus souvent sans sçavoir ne la vie ni les moeurs des personnes qui exercent l'hospitalité envers elles. On rendroit, ce me semble, un grand service à l'Eglise si on les reduisoit aux termes de la Bulle de Gregoire XIII *Deo sacris*, qui leur procure les moyens de subsister honnestement dans leurs Monasteres, sans rompre leur clôture Car ainsi les gens de bien ne seroient point scandalisez de leurs sorties ne de leurs courses, et elles feroient incomparablement mieux leur salut dans leurs Couvents que dans le Monde, où je n'estime pas qu'elles puissent rester en seureté de conscience" He quotes an ordinance of the General of the Franciscan Order in 1609, forbidding even the sisters of the Tertiary Order to beg. Thiers, *op. cit.* pp. 167–9.

the business of the convent; the Abbess, for instance, is to take her three coadjutresses with her when she goes out on business, and two of them if she go *causa solatii*. At this house he forbade nuns to go out without a companion, or to stay for more than three days with seculars and condemned their practice of eating and drinking in the town; no nun, either on leaving or returning to the convent, was to enter any house in the town of Romsey, or to eat or drink there, and no cleric or secular man or woman was to give them any food outside the precincts[1]. At St Sepulchre (Canterbury) Peckham regulated the visits of nuns to confessors outside the house, and at Usk he ordered that no nun was to go out without suitable companions, or to stay more than three or four days in the houses of secular persons[2].

The next effort made in England to enforce enclosure upon nuns was the result of Boniface VIII's Bull *Periculoso*. Bishops' registers about the year 1300 sometimes contain copies of this severe enactment. One of the earliest efforts to carry it out was made by Simon of Ghent, Bishop of Salisbury, who on November 28th, 1299, issued a long letter to the Abbess of Wilton (obviously inserted in the register as a specimen of a circular sent to each nunnery in the diocese), embodying the text of the bull and ordering her to put it into force, and in 1303 he issued a mandate for the enclosure of the nuns of Shaftesbury, Wilton, Amesbury, Lacock, Tarrant Keynes and Kington[3] The Register of Godfrey Giffard, Bishop of Worcester, contains a note in the year 1300:

As to the shutting up of nuns It is expedient that a letter of warning be sent according to the form of the constitution and directed to every house of nuns, that they do what is necessary for their inclusion and cause themselves to be enclosed this side the Gule of August.

The Bishop seems however from the beginning to have doubted his capacity to carry out the decree, for further on the register contains another note, "As to whether it is expedient to enclose the nuns of the diocese of Worcester"[4] An undated note of *Inhibiciones facte monialibus de Werewell* in the Register of John of Pontoise, Bishop of Winchester, among other documents belonging to 1299–1300, is probably in part a result of *Periculoso*:

[1] *Reg Epis. J. Peckham*, II, pp 659, 664–5.
[2] *Ib* II, pp 707, 806   [3] *Reg Simonis de Gandavo*, pp 10 ff , 109
[4] *Reg Godfrey Giffard*, II, pp. 515, 517.

We forbid on pain of excommunication any nun or sister to go outside the bounds of the monastery until we have made some ordinance concerning enclosure Item let no one be received as nun or sister until we have enquired more fully into the resources of the house Item we order the abbess to remove all secular women and to receive none henceforth as boarders in their house. Item let her permit no secular clerk or layman to enter the cloister to speak with the nuns[1].

But the most detailed information as to the efforts of a conscientious bishop to enforce Boniface VIII's decree in England is contained in the Register of Bishop Dalderby of Lincoln. Dalderby was a new broom in the diocese and he determined to sweep clean. On June 17th, 1300, he directed a mandate to the archdeacons of his diocese ordering each to associate with himself some other mature and honest man and to visit the religious houses in his own archdeaconry, explaining the terms of the new bull intelligibly to the nuns and ordering them to remain within their nunneries and to permit no one to enter the precincts contrary to the tenour of the decree, until the Bishop should be able to visit them in person; the heads of the houses were to be specially warned to carry out the decree and for better security a sealed copy of it was to be deposited in each house by the commissioners[2].

In the course of the next two months Dalderby visited, either in person or by commissioners, Marlow, Burnham, Flamstead, Markyate, Elstow, Goring, Studley, Godstow, Delapré (Northampton) and Sewardsley[3] At each house the bull was carefully explained to the nuns in the vulgar tongue, they were ordered to obey it and a copy was left with them. But this campaign was not unattended with difficulties. The nuns were bitterly opposed to the restriction of a freedom to which they were accustomed and which they heartily enjoyed, and an entry in Dalderby's Register, describing his visitation of Markyate, shows that even in the middle ages a bishop's lot was not a happy one:

On July 3rd, in the first year [of his consecration], the Bishop visited the house of nuns of Markyate and on the following day he caused to be recited before the nuns of the same [house] in chapter the statute put forth by the lord Pope Boniface VIII concerning the enclosure

---

[1] *Reg J. de Pontissara,* p. 546
[2] *Linc. Epis. Reg Memo Dalderby,* f. 9.
[3] *Ib.* ff 9d, 10d, 11, 12d, 15d.

of nuns, explained it in the vulgar tongue and giving them a copy of
the same statute under his seal, ordered them in virtue of obedience
henceforth to observe it in the matter of enclosure and of all things
contained in it, and especially to close all doors by which entrance is
had into the inner places of their house and to permit no person,
whether dishonest or honest, to enter in to them, without reasonable
and manifest cause and licence from the person to whom [the granting
of such a licence] pertains. Furthermore he specially enjoined the
Prioress to observe the said statute in all its articles and to cause it
to be observed by the others　But when the Bishop was going away,
certain of the nuns, disobedient to these injunctions, hurled the said
statute at his back and over his head, and as well the Prioress as the
convent appeared to consent to those who threw it, following the
bishop to the outer gate of the house and declaring unanimously that
they were not content in any way to observe such a statute. On
account of which, the Bishop, who was then directing his steps to
Dunstable, returned the next day and having made inquisition as to
the matters concerned in the said statute, imposed a penance on four
nuns, whom he found guilty and on the whole convent for their consent, as is more fully contained in his letters of correction sent to the
aforesaid house

Afterwards he sent letters to the recalcitrant convent warning
them for the third time (they had already been warned once by
the Official of the Archdeacon of Bedford and a second time at
the visitation which has just been described) to keep the new
decree, on pain of the major excommunication, from which only
the Pope could absolve them[1].

There was opposition at other convents, too, though we hear
of no more attacks on the episcopal shoulders. On August 19th
Dalderby wrote as follows to Master Benedict de Feriby, rector
of Broughton, Northants (a church in the presentation of the
Abbess and Convent of Delapré):

It has come to our ears, by clamorous rumour, that some of the nuns
of our diocese, spurning good obedience, slackening the reins of
honesty and shamelessly casting aside the modesty of their sex,
despise the papal statute concerning enclosure directed to them, as
well as our injunctions made to them upon the subject, and frequent
cities and other public places outside their monasteries, and mingle
in the haunts of men;

he proceeded to order Feriby to visit nunneries wherever he
considered it expedient to do so, and to punish those who were
guilty of breaking the statute, signifying to the Bishop, by a

---

[1] *Linc. Epis. Reg Memo. Dalderby*, f. 10d.

certain date, the names of all who had been accused of doing so, whether they had been found guilty or not[1]. This mandate is no doubt in part explained by two other letters which he dispatched on the same day; one of them was directed to the Archdeacon of Northampton and set forth (in language which often repeats *verbatim* the phrases of the papal bull) that at the Bishop's recent visitation of Delapré (Northampton) he had found three nuns in apostasy, having cast off their habits after being a long time professed, and left their house to live a secular life in the world[2]. The other letter contains a sentence of the greater excommunication against a nun of Sewardsley, for similar conduct[3]. These cases of apostasy were less rare than might be imagined; Dalderby had to deal with two others during his episcopate, one at St Michael's, Stamford[4], and the other at Goring[5], and during the rule of his predecessor Sutton three nuns had escaped from Godstow and one from Wothorpe[6]. They illustrate the undoubted truth that it was only the existence (already in the thirteenth century) of very grave disorders, which led reformers like Ottobon, Peckham and Boniface VIII to "beat the air" with such severe restrictions.

These three documents, the Constitutions of Ottobon and of Peckham and the Bull *Periculoso*, were the standard decrees on the subject of the claustration of nuns in England and were used as a model by visitors in the thirteenth and fourteenth centuries. William of Wykeham, for example, in the exceptionally full and formal injunctions which he sent to Romsey and to Wherwell in 1387 continually refers by name to Ottobon and to Peckham, and the wording of the Bull *Periculoso* is followed *verbatim* in the mandate directed by Bishop Grandisson of Exeter to Canonsleigh in 1329 and in the commission sent by his successor Bishop Brantyngham to two canons of Exeter in 1376, concerning the wanderings of the nuns of Polsloe. But a study of the visitation documents of the thirteenth and fourteenth centuries makes it clear that the nuns never really made any attempt to obey the regulations which imposed a strict enclosure upon them; and that the bishops upon whom fell the brunt of

---

[1] *Linc. Epis. Reg. Memo. Dalderby*, f. 35d.   [2] *Ib.* f. 16. See below, p 441.
[3] *Ib.*   [4] Agnes Flixthorpe See below, p. 443.   [5] *Ib.* f. 152.
[6] *Linc. Epis. Reg. Memo. Sutton*, ff. 5d, 32d, 154 For these and other cases of apostasy see Chap. xi, *passim.*

administering *Periculoso* themselves allowed a considerable latitude, directing their efforts towards regulating the conditions
under which nuns left their convents, rather than to keeping
them within the precincts *Le mieux est l'ennemi du bien* and
the steady opposition of the nuns forced a compromise upon
their visitors. The canonist John of Ayton, reciting the decrees
of Ottobon and of Boniface, with their injunction that bishops
shall "cause them to be observed," exclaims

Cause to be observed! But surely there is scarce any mortal man who
could do this: we must therefore here understand "so far as lieth in
the prelate's power." For the nuns answer roundly to these statutes
or to any others promulgated against their wantonness, saying "In
truth the men who made these laws sat well at their ease, while they
laid such burdens upon us by these hard and intolerable restrictions!"
Wherefore we see in fact that these statutes are a dead letter or are
ill-kept at the best. Why, then, did the holy fathers thus labour to
beat the air? Yet indeed their toil is none the less to their own merit,
for we look not to that which is but to that which of justice should be[1].

Dalderby's experience at Markyate shows that John of Ayton's
picture was not too highly coloured, and since it was impossible
to enforce "hard and intolerable restrictions" without at least
a measure of co-operation from the nuns themselves, the bishops
took the only course open to them in trying to minimise the
evil. Their expedients deserve some study, and as a typical
set of episcopal injunctions dealing with journeys by nuns outside their cloisters it will suffice to quote those sent by Walter
Stapeldon, Bishop of Exeter, to the nunneries of Polsloe and
Canonsleigh. These rules were drawn up in 1319, only twenty
years after the publication of the Bull *Periculoso*, but they are
already far removed from the strict ideal of Boniface VIII.
Stapeldon was a practical statesman and he evidently realised
that the enforcement of strict enclosure was impossible in a
diocese where the nuns had been used to considerable freedom
and where all the counties of the West saw them upon their
holidays

The clauses dealing with the subject run as follows:

De visitacione amicorum. No lady of religion is to go and visit her
friends outside the priory, but if it be once a year at the most and then
for reasonable cause and by permission; and then let her have a

[1] Lyndwood, *Provinciale* (1679), Pt II, p 155 Quoted by Mr Coulton
in *Med Studies,* No. 10, "Monastic Schools in the Middle Ages," p 21

companion professed in the same religion, not of her own choice, but whomsoever the Prioress will assign to her and she who is once assigned to her for companion shall not be assigned the next time, so that each time a lady goes to visit her friends her companion is changed, and if she have permission to go to certain places to visit her friends, let her not go to other places without new permission *De absencia Dominarum et regressu earum* Item, when any lady of religion eats at Exeter, or in another place near by, for reasonable cause and by permission, whenever she can she ought to return the same or the following day and each time let her have a companion and a chaplain, clerk or serving-man of good repute assigned by the prioress, who shall go, remain and return with them and otherwise they shall not go, and then let them return speedily to the house, as they be commanded, and let them not go again to Exeter, wandering from house to house, as they have oftentimes done, to the dishonour of their state and of religion *De Dominabus "Wakerauntes"* [i e. *vagantibus*] Item, a lady who goes a long distance to visit her friends, in the aforesaid form, should return to the house within a month at the latest, or within a shorter space if it be assigned her by the Prioress, having regard to the distance or proximity of the place, where dwell the friends whom she is going to visit, but a longer term ought the Prioress never to give her, save in the case of death, or of the known illness of herself or of her near friends. *Pena Dominarum Vagancium.* And if a lady remain without for a long time or in any other manner than in the form aforesaid, let her never set foot outside the outer gate of the Priory for the next two years; and nevertheless let her be punished otherwise for disobedience, in such manner as is laid down by the rule and observances of the order of St Benet for the fault; and leave procured by the prayer of her friends ought not to excuse her from this penance[1]. No lady of your religion, professed or unprofessed, shall come to the external offices outside the door of the cloister to be bled or for any other feigned excuse, save it be by leave of the Prioress or of the Subprioress, and then for a fit reason and let her have with her another professed lady of your religion, to the end that each of them may see and hear that which the other shall say and do[2]

[1] Apparently friends and relatives in the world outside sometimes intervened, by threats or prayers, to save a nun from punishment. A *compertum* of Archbishop Giffard's visitation of Swine in 1267–8 runs "*Item compertum est* that the Prioress is a suspicious woman and far too credulous, and easily breaks out into correction, and often punishes some unequally for equal faults, and follows with long dislike those whom she dislikes until occasion arise to punish them; hence it is that the nuns, when they suspect that they are going to be troubled with excessive correction, procure the mitigation of her severity by means of the threats of their kinsfolk " *Reg. Walter Giffard*, p 147

[2] *Reg. Walter de Stapeldon*, p. 317. Cf. p. 95. When the London mob had beheaded Stapeldon in Cheapside, his place was filled (after the short rule of Berkeley) by an even greater bishop, John Grandisson, who, in the

The main lines along which the bishops attempted to regulate the movements of the nuns outside their houses appear clearly in these injunctions. It was their invariable practice to forbid unlicensed visits, in accordance with the Benedictine rule; no nun might leave her house without a licence from her superior and such licences were not to be granted too easily[1] or with any show of favouritism[2]; sometimes the licence of the Bishop was required as well[3]. Such licences were not to be granted often (once a year is usually the specified rule)[4] and the bishops sometimes tried to confine the visits of nuns to parents or to near relatives[5]. An attempt was also made to regulate the length of

year of his consecration, directed a mandate to the nuns of Canonsleigh in which he attempted to carry out more closely than his predecessor, though still not exactly, the terms of *Periculoso* He forbade the abbess to allow any nuns to leave the precincts before his visitation "that is to such a distance that it is not possible for them to return the same day " This was on June 23rd 1329; a month later he was obliged to compromise, for on July 18th he sent a licence to Canonsleigh, recapitulating his former mandate but adding a special indulgence, permitting ("for certain legitimate reasons") the nuns to absent themselves from the monastery "with honest and senior ladies to visit near relatives and friends of themselves and of the house, who are free from all suspicion," and fixing the limit of their visit at fifteen days, an improvement on Stapeldon's month, but still far removed from the spirit of Boniface VIII's bull *Reg John de Grandisson*, I, pp 508, 511

[1] See e g Wroxall 1338, "Et vous emouvums [? emoiniums], dame prioresse, qe vous ne seyez mes si legere de doner licence a vos soers de isser de le encloystre et nomement la priourie cume vous avez este en ces houres saunz verreye et resonable enchesun et cause " *Worc Reg Sede Vacante*, p 276, and St Radegund's, Cambridge, 1373: "Item, the Prioress is too easily induced to give permission to the nuns to go outside the cloister " Gray, *Priory of St Radegund's, Cambridge*, p 36

[2] See e g Fairwell, 1367 *Reg Robert de Stretton*, p 118 The necessity for an injunction against favouritism is shown by the *comperta* of Archbishop Langham's visitation of St Sepulchre, Canterbury, in 1367–8 "Prioressa non permittit moniales ire in villam ad visitandum amicos suos nisi Margeriam Child et Julianam Aldelesse que illuc vadunt quociens eis placet " *Lambeth Reg. Langham*, f 76d She was also charged with allowing them to receive suspected visitors See below, p 399

[3] An example of such a licence for a particular nun to leave her house is printed in Fosbroke, *British Monachism* (1817), p. 361 (note g) and also in Taunton, *Engl Black Monks of St Benedict*, I, p. 108, note 2 It is said to be granted on the prayer of " Lady J. wife of Sir W. knight, of our diocese," whom the nun is to be allowed to visit, with a companion from the same priory and to go thither on horseback "notwithstanding your customs to the contrary "

[4] But Archbishop Melton said twice a year at Arthington in 1315. *V C.H Yorks* III, p 188

[5] See e g Bishop Spofford's regulation at Lymbrook in 1437. "nor to be absent lyggyng oute by nyght out of their monastery, but with fader and moder, excepte causes of necessytee " *Hereford Epis Reg Spofford,*

the visits. A maximum number of days was fixed and the nun
was to be punished if she outstayed her leave[1], except when she
was detained by illness This maximum differed from time to
time and from place to place. Bishop Stapeldon, it will be recalled, allowed the nuns in his diocese to remain away for a
month and longer; how he reconciled such laxity with his
conscience and the Bull *Periculoso* is not plain. Archbishop
Greenfield, at the same date, permitted his Yorkshire nuns a
maximum visit of fifteen days[2], and in 1358 Bishop Gynewell of
Lincoln forbade the nuns of Godstow to remain away for longer
than three weeks[3]. When Alnwick visited the diocese of Lincoln

1, f 77, and Archbishop Lee's injunction to Sinningthwaite in 1534: "that
she from henceforth licence none of her susters to go fourth of the housse,
onles it be for the profitt of the house, or visite their fathers and modres,
or odre nere kynsfolkes, if the prioresse shall think it conuenient " *Yorks
Arch Journ* xvi, p 442. Compare Bishop Gynewell's injunction to Godstow (1358), "par necessarie et resonable cause ouesque lour parents,
honestement au profit de vostre mesoun " *Linc Epis Reg Memo Gynewell*,
f 100d Sometimes, however, friends were mentioned, e g. at Nunkeeling
(1314) none was to go out "except on the business of the house or to visit
friends and relations." *V C H Yorks* iii, p 120. Sometimes the sickness
of friends was specified At Marrick (1252) none was to go out unless "the
sickness of friends or some other worthy reason" demanded it, *ib* p 117;
and at Studley in 1530-1 Bishop Longland ordained "that ye lycence not
eny of your ladyes to passe out of the precincte of our monastery to visite
their kynsfolks or frendes, onles it be for ther comforte in tyme of ther
sikenes, and yett not than onles it shall seme to you, ladye priores, to be
behouefull and necessarye, seing that undre suche pretence moche insolency
have been used in religion," *Archaeologia*, xlvii, p 54 One of the nuns of
Legbourne in 1440 complained bitterly that the Prioress will not suffer this
deponent to visit her parent who is sick [even] when it was thought that
he would die " *Linc Visit* ii, p 186

¹ As, needless to say, she sometimes did. In 1351 Bishop Gynewell was
obliged to write to Heynings rebuking such disobedience. "encement si
auoms entenduz que les dames de dit mesoun sount acustumez demurrer
od lour amys outre le terme par vous, Prioresse, assigne, nous commandoms
a vous, Prioress auant dit, qe taunt soulement une foith en 1 an donez
conge a les dames de visiter lour amys, et certeyn terme resonable pur
reuenir, outre qeule terme sils facent demoer, saunz cause resonable par
vous accepte, les chastes pur le trespasse solonc les obseruances de vostres
ordre saunz delay " *Linc. Epis Reg. Memo Gynewell*, f. 34d At Ivinghoe
in 1530 it was discovered that one of the nuns had gone on a visit to her
friends without permission and had stayed away from the Feast of St Michael
to Passion Sunday in the following year (i e. over six months), which came
perilously near to apostasy, *V C H Bucks* i, p 355 In the *Vitae Patrum*,
xc, 206, however, there is a tale of a nun who was lent by her Abbess to
a certain religious matron and lived with her for a year See the version in
Exempla e sermonibus, etc ed T F Crane, pp 26–7

² *V C H Yorks* iii, pp 120, 128, 175, 177, 178
³ *Linc Epis Reg Memo Gynewell*, f 100d

in 1440–5, he made careful inquiry into the length of the visits paid by the nuns and at Goring, Gracedieu, Markyate, Nuncoton and St Michael's, Stamford, he found that the superior usually gave the nuns licence to remain away a week, though the Prioress of Studley gave exeats for three or four days only[1]. A week does not seem a very lengthy absence, but Alnwick would have lifted horrified eyebrows at the action of his predecessor Gynewell, for he ordered the superiors "that ye gyfe no sustere of yowres leue to byde wythe thaire frendes whan thai visite thaym, overe thre dayes in helthe, and if thai falle seke, that he do fecche thaym home wythe yn sex dayes"[2]. He shared the views of an even stricter reformer, Peckham[3]. It was often stipulated that the nuns, whether they went on long or on short journeys, were to go only to the place which they had received permission to visit[4]; and sometimes they were specially told that if they were obliged to spend the night away from their friends they were to do so, whenever possible, in another nunnery[5].

[1] *Linc Visit* II, pp 118, 122, ff 6–7, 25, 72, 83, 109 At Godstow the prioress said "that the nuns have often access to Oxford under colour of visiting their friends," p. 114; and at Heynings a discontented nun said "that sisters Ellen Bryg and Agnes Bokke have often recourse to Lincoln and there make long tarrying" They denied the charge, but a note in the register states, "The nuns have access too often to the house of the treasurer of Lincoln, abiding there sometimes for a week" The Bishop forbade "accesse suspecte to Lincolne," pp 132, 133, 135.

[2] Ff. 28d, 77d, 95d. To Catesby, *op. cit.* p. 51. Compare injunctions to Godstow, Gracedieu, Nuncoton and St Michael's, Stamford, pp 116, 125

[3] Above, p 348 And compare William of Wykeham's injunction to Romsey, which repeats Peckham's constitution on this point word for word *New Coll* MS f 85

[4] See e g Drokensford's injunction to Minchin Barrow [i e Barrow Gurney] in 1315: "quod tunc bene incedant et in habitu moniali et non ad alia loca quam se extendit licencia se diuertant quoque modo, et ultra tempus licencie sue se voluntarie non absentent" Hugo, *Med Nunneries of Somerset, Barrow,* App II, p 81

[5] See e g the synodal Constitutions of c 1237, Wilkins, *Concilia,* I, p 650 Archbishop Courtenay in 1389 sent an interesting injunction to Elstow Abbey, which had evidently been remiss in offering hospitality to travelling nuns: "Inasmuch as it has happened that nuns coming to the monastery on their return from a visit to their friends, have been refused necessities for themselves and for their horses, inhumanly and contrary to the good repute of religion, which we wish to remedy, we order that for each nun thus tarrying provision be made according to the resources of the house, for four horses at least if by day for a whole day, and if [she come] by night or after the hour of nones for the rest of the day and for the night following" *Lambeth Reg Courtenay,* I, f 336 Injunction repeated by Bishop Flemyng of Lincoln in 1421–2 *Visit of Relig Houses in Dioc. Linc* I, pp 50–1

But they were strictly forbidden to harbour in the houses of monks, friars, or canons[1]. On short journeys, or on errands which could be speedily accomplished, they were forbidden to eat or drink out of their monasteries or to make unnecessary delay, but were to return at once and in no case to be out after nightfall[2]. Moreover it was invariably ordered that a nun was on no account to leave her house, without another nun of mature age and good reputation who would be a constant witness to her behaviour[3]; and both were to wear monastic dress[4].

The chief aim of the ecclesiastical authorities was, however, to secure that leave of absence should be granted only for a reasonable cause   All conciliar and other injunctions for enclosure added a saving clause of "manifest necessity" and this gave an opening for an infinite variety of interpretation. The nuns, indeed, could fall back upon a threefold line of defence against the intolerable restrictions. They could appeal to the undoubted fact that strict and perpetual enclosure went beyond the requirements of their rule. They could adduce the custom by which, as long as their memory ran, nuns had been allowed to leave their convents under conditions. Finally they could with a little skill, stretch the "manifest necessity" clause to cover almost all their wanderings. Thus it happened that in

---

[1] See e.g. Peckham's injunctions to Barking and Godstow. Above, p. 348. Religious houses of men were sometimes specially ordered not to receive them, e.g Bridlington in 1287 *Reg John le Romeyn*, I, p. 200 The necessity for such an order appears below, pp 446 ff

[2] E g. Peckham to St Sepulchre, Canterbury (1284). "Nullum quoque potum aut cibum ibidem sumat, moram non protrahat, sed statim expedita causa accessus hujusmodi redeat indilate " *Reg Epis J. Peckham*, II, p. 707; and Bokyngham to Elstow (1387) "Cum vero recreacionis causa, obtenta superioris licencia, moniales antedicte egrediuntur monasterii sui septa, incedant cum familiarium honesta comitiua et sufficiente, ad idem monasterium, redeuntes de eodem citra solis occasum " *Linc Epis Reg Memo. Bokyngham*, f 343

[3] At Wroxall in 1338 it was specially ordered " qe deux jeunes ne issent poynt ensemble pur male suspecioun qe de ceo purra legerement sourdre, ke Dieuz defent " *Worc. Reg Sede Vacante*, p 276 At Lymbrook in 1437 Bishop Spofford ordered that no nun was to go out without a companion, and "in case they lygge owte be nyght, two sustres to lye togeder in on bed," a practice which (according to the usual custom) he forbids in the dorter. *Hereford Epis. Reg. Spofford*, f 77

[4] See Thiers, *op cit* Pt I, chs XVIII, XXII, XXIII, XXIV, XXXI He quotes the stories of the nuns of Arles in the fifth century and of Marcigny in the eleventh century, who refused to break their enclosures even for fire and were miraculously preserved, pp. 12–13, 32–5.

enforcing the Bull *Periculoso* the visitors of the later middle ages found themselves obliged to define, more or less widely according to local conditions, what was and what was not a reasonable cause, and to combat one after another certain specific excuses put forward by the nuns. The sternest reformers were agreed that enclosure might be broken, when the lives of the nuns were endangered Fire, flood, famine, war and the ruin of their buildings were universally accepted as reasonable excuses[1] A nun could leave her house to be superior of another nunnery (a not infrequent practice), or to found new houses or to establish reform elsewhere[2]. Moreover when a culprit stood in need of

[1] The rhymed Northern Rule of St Benedict for nuns (l. 2094) says that when they go away into the country they should wear "more honest" clothes "In habitu moniali" is one of the conditions imposed on the nuns of Barrow Gurney in 1315 See above, p. 358, note 4 The necessity for such a regulation appears in the decree made by Henry Archbishop of Cologne, executing an enactment of the Provincial Council of Cologne (1310), promulgating *Periculoso*. "Nevertheless we often see that having come out of their monasteries they [the nuns] wander about the roads and public places and frequent the houses of secular persons And, what is more deplorable, having put off their religious habit, they appear in secular dress and bear themselves in public with so much vanity that their conduct may justly be considered suspicious, although their conscience be really pure and without sin And although hitherto they have been menaced with divers penalties, nevertheless the more strictly they are forbidden to live after this fashion, the more eagerly they disobey, so strongly do they hanker after forbidden things " The whole injunction is worthy of study Thiers, *op cit* pp 491–3. Discipline was laxer in German convents than in those of England In England, however, there are sometimes complaints that male religious leave their convents in secular attire, see a case at Huntingdon Priory in 1439, *Linc Visit* II, pp 154–5.

[2] See *ib.* XXV, XXVI, XXVII. A few examples may be given of nuns leaving their houses to become superiors elsewhere Basedale got prioresses from Rosedale in 1524 and 1527 (*Yorks Arch. Soc* XVI, p 431 note); Rosedale from Clementhorpe in 1525 (Dugdale, *Mon* IV, pp. 317, 385), Kington from Bromhale in 1326 (*ib* IV, p 398) and Ankerwyke from Bromhale in 1421 (*Visit of Relig Houses in Dioc Linc* I, p 156) Sometimes the prioress of one house left it to rule another, e g Elizabeth Davell, Prioress of Basedale, became Prioress of Keldholme in 1467 (*V C H Yorks* III, p 169) Alice Davy, who occurs as Prioress of Castle Hedingham in 1472 and was afterwards Prioress of Wix (*V.C H Essex*, II, p 123), and Eleanor Bernard, Prioress of Little Marlow (c 1516) became Abbess of Delapré (Dugdale, *Mon* IV, p 149). For a form of licence from a prioress, permitting a nun to accept the office of prioress elsewhere, see *MS Harl* 862, f 94 ("Literae Priorissae de Bromhale quibus licenciam impertit Clementiae Medforde ejusdem Domus, consorori et commoniali, ut Prioratui de Ankerwyke sicut Priorissa praeesse valeat"), and compare the reply of the Prioress of St Bartholomew's, Newcastle, to the Bishop of Durham about the election of Dame Margaret Danby, a nun of her house, to be Prioress of St Mary's,

condign punishment, she might be and often was sent to another house to do penance among strangers, who would neither sympathise with her nor run the risk of being contaminated by her[1].

At this point, however, agreement ceased. The question of illness was beset with difficulties. It was agreed that a nun might leave her house, if she suffered from some contagious disease which threatened the health of her sisters[2], but opinions

Neasham, "Whilk Postulacion I graunt fully with assent of my chapiter atte Reverence of God and in plesing of yor gracious lordship; not wythstondyng yat she is ful necessarye and profitable to us both in spirituall governance and temporall" (1428) (V.C H. Durham, II, p. 107) Sometimes a mother house from over the sea tried to assert its right to nominate the head of one of its daughter houses, but Cluniacs, Cistercians, Premonstratensians and houses affiliated to Fontevrault were all extremely jealous of French interference. See the letter written by Mary, daughter of Edward I, a nun of Amesbury, to her brother the King in 1316 protesting against the action of the Abbess of Fontevrault, who was reputed to be sending "a prioress from beyond the sea," instead of acceding to the convent's request that one of their own number might succeed to the office Wood, Letters of Royal and Illustrious Ladies, I, pp 60–63 It was always held desirable if possible to take a superior from among the nuns of the house in which the vacancy occurred, but sometimes no suitable person could be found

[1] See Thiers, I, ch XXII, who mentions the corollary that the superior of another house may be called in to correct rebellious nuns if their own head is unable to do so See below, p 466. In 1501 Emma Powes, then at Romsey, is said to have been professed at King's Mead near Derby "and from that place had been removed to another priory in the Hereford diocese, where she had been prioress, and thence had come to this house" A charge of incontinence was made against her, and we know from another source that she had been prioress of Lymbrook (she was deprived on or about 24 Nov 1488, Hereford Reg. Myllyng, p 112). It is interesting that in 1492 one of the nuns had asked that "a nun who has been brought in, be restored to the place to which she is professed" Liveing, Records of Romsey Abbey, pp. 219, 225 One of Alnwick's injunctions to Clemence Medforde, Prioress of Ankerwyke in 1441, was "that henceforth she should not admit that nun of Hinchinbrooke either into the house or to dwell among them, and also that she should not deliver to her that bond which she has from the house of Hinchinbrooke, or any other goods which she has of the same house" Linc Visit II, p 6 In a list of the nuns of Thetford in 1526 occurs the name of "Domina Elianora Hanam, professa in Wyke (Wix)" Jessopp, Visit in Dioc. Norwich, p 243.

[2] Such, for instance, as leprosy In 1287 Archbishop John le Romeyn sent a request to the master of Sherburn Hospital, Durham, to receive Basilia de Cotum, a nun of Handale, "quia,...lepre deformitate aspersa, propter suspectam morbi contagionem, morari non poterit inter sanos, devocionem vestram rogamus quatinus ipsam in hospitali vestro velitis recipere et seorsum in necessariis exhibere, ita, tamen, quod sub religioso habitu quem gerit Deo serviat dum subsistit" Reg John le Romeyn, I, p 163 Richard de Wallingford, the great abbot of St Albans, was a leper, but remained in his house.

differed as to whether any relaxation was to be allowed in less
severe cases, when only her own health was in question. The
visitors sometimes issued licences for nuns to leave their houses
in order to recruit their health, thus in 1303 Josiana de Anelaby,
Prioress of Swine, had licence to absent herself from her house
on account of ill-health[1], in 1314 Archbishop Greenfield licenced
a nun of Yedingham, who was suffering from dropsy, to visit
friends and relatives with honest company, for the sake of im-
proving her health[2] and in 1368 Joan Furmage, Abbess of
Shaftesbury, actually received a dispensation to leave the abbey
for a year and reside in her manors, for the sake of air and
recreation[3]. It is significant that the *Novellae Definitiones* of the
Cistercian Order in 1350 strictly forbade nuns to go to the
public baths outside their houses, which shows that they had
been in the habit of doing so[4]. But strict reformers were always
opposed to such licences, and the specific prohibition of exeats
for purposes of cures and convalescences was common in the

---

[1] Dugdale, *Mon* v, p 493 Dugdale remarks that "a little scandal also
appears to have been attached to her character" She finally resigned on
account of old age in 1320, and perhaps the leave of absence referred to
accounts for the appearance of another Prioress in 1308 who resigned in
1309 *V C H Yorks* III, pp 180-1
[2] *V C H Yorks.* III, p. 127, note 13
[3] *V C H Dorset*, II, p 78 In 1427 the papal licence was granted to one
Isabel Falowfeld, nun of St Bartholomew's, Newcastle on Tyne, to transfer
herself to another monastery of the same order, on account of her weak
constitution and the inclemency of the air near St Bartholomew's *Cal of
Papal Letters*, VII, p 516. See Thiers on the subject, *op. cit* pp 140-2, 213-5
He quotes the decision of the University of Salamanca on the question as
to whether the General or any minor official of the Minorites had the power
to give permission to a nun of the order who was dangerously ill, to leave
her house and enter another of the same order, so as to recover her health.
"Exactissima discussione facta circa praesentem difficultatem, omnes una-
nimiter atque uno ore responderunt atque dixerunt, non posse id fieri stando
in jure communi, quod et multis juribus atque rationibus comprobarunt"
(p 214). He also quotes the case of a nun of the Annunciation of Agen, of
whom the doctors said that if she stayed in her house she would infallibly
die, but if she went out for a change of air and medicinal baths she would
infallibly be cured To which alternative the General of the Order, on being
asked to give her a dispensation to go out, replied in one word "*Moriatur*"
(p 217) But these were both strictly enclosed orders.
[4] "Si quae vero moniales ad balnea qualitercumque processerint extra
monasteria, irremissibiliter priventur habitu regulari, et licentiantes easdem
ut praedicta petant balnea, sententiam excommunicationis incurrant"
Nomasticon Cisterciense, p 533, also in Thiers *op cit* p 220; cf pp 216 ff
But the public baths were of notoriously bad reputation

sixteenth and seventeenth centuries, when the practice had become almost universal in France[1].

Again there was some difference of opinion as to whether a nun might leave her house, in order to enter one professing a stricter rule. Such a desire was in theory laudable and by Innocent III's decretal *Licet* the principle was laid down that a bishop was bound *de jure* to grant leave for migration "sub praetextu majoris religionis et ut vitam ducant arctiorem," as long as the motive of the petitioner was love of God and not merely *temeritas*[2]. But *temeritas* was often to be suspected; women, as St Francis de Sales complained, were full of whimsies[3]; ennui, fancy, a craving for change, a friend in another house, might masquerade as a desire to lead a stricter life elsewhere Moreover a nun who desired to remove herself was not unlikely to encounter opposition from her own convent. An interesting case of such opposition occurred at Gracedieu in 1447-8. Margaret Crosse, a nun of that house, desired to be transferred to the Benedictine Priory of Ivinghoe "of a straiter order of religion and observance, not for a frivolous or empty reason, but that she may lead a life altogether and entirely harder." She obtained letters of admission from the Prioress of Ivinghoe, but when she came to ask for leave to migrate, the Prioress and Convent of Gracedieu refused to release her from her obedience and confiscated the letters. Bishop Alnwick then wrote to Gracedieu, requiring the Prioress either to let her go, or to furnish

---

[1] See Thiers, *op cit* Pt I, ch XLII–XLVII From the fact that he thinks it necessary to devote five chapters to the subject and from the evidence which he adduces and the language which he uses, it is clear that the practice was very prevalent

[2] *Decret* III, tit XXXI, c 18 See Thiers, *op. cit.* pp 161-2. Licences to migrate to a convent professing a stricter rule are sometimes found in episcopal registers See e.g *Hereford Reg Caroli Bothe*, p. 241.

[3] See his letter to a superior, quoted by Thiers. "Je suis tout-à-fait d'avis que l'on n'ouvre point la porte au changement des Maisons pour le souhait des filles· car ce changement est tout-à-fait contraire au bien des Monasteres qui ont la clôture perpetuelle pour article essentiel. Les filles comme foibles, sont sujettes aux ennuis et les ennuis leur font trouver des expediens et importuns et indiscrets Que les changemens doncques procedent des jugemens des superieurs et non du désir des filles, qui ne sçauroient mieux declarer qu'elles ne doivent point estre gratifiées, que quand elles se laissent emporter a des desirs si peu justes. Il faut donc demeurer là, et laisser chaque rossignol dans son nid, car autrement le moindre deplaisir qui arriveroit à une fille, seroit capable de l'inquieter et luy faire prendre le change· Et au lieu de se changer elle-même, elle penseroit d'avoir suffisament remedié à son mal, quand elle changeroit de Monastere " Thiers, *op. cit.* pp 160-1.

him with a reason for their refusal. The Prioress and Convent replied with some acerbity. Margaret, they said, desired to lead a life of less and not of more restraint and her real object was to join her sister, who was at that time Prioress of Ivinghoe, if indeed her request were not a mere pretext for apostasy; for

the said Margaret Crosse has caused and commanded certain goods, property and jewels belonging to our priory to be stealthily conveyed by certain of the said Margaret's friends in the flesh from our priory to foreign and privy places, and to such conveyance done in her name has lent her authority, with the purpose, as is strongly suspected, of taking advantage of the darkness one night.. and transferring herself utterly and entirely of her own motion to places wholly strange, without having or asking and against our will[1].

Moreover had the holy father considered the merits of their house and the loss to it, if Margaret seceded?

Inasmuch as in our priory according to the observances of the rule God is served and quire is ruled both in reading and singing and chanting the psalms and toiling in the vineyard of the Lord of Sabaoth at the canonical hours by day and night, while we also patiently endure grievous cares, fastings and watchings and further are instant together in contemplation, even as the holy Spirit designs to give us His inspiration. And the said Margaret Crosse, who is sufficiently trained in such regular observances and is very needful for the service of God in our priory aforesaid, wherein such regular observances and contemplations are not so fully kept as in our aforesaid priory...would give herself to secular business in all matters, rather than to such contemplation or observance of the rule; and thereout shall arise to us and our priory not only grievous ill repute, but also no small loss, especially in that such chantings and regular observances would in likelihood suffer damage by reason of the said Margaret's absence[2].

There is an air of verisimilitude about the injured convent's argument, though the visitation report of 1440–1 does not show them as the strict and pious community which they claim to be; but what came of the affair we do not know.

One plea to lead a stricter life was, however, less open to suspicion, that was the request to be enclosed as an anchoress

---

[1] Plainly she regarded the things as her own private property and was thus guilty of the sin of *proprietas* as well Compare the evidence of the Abbot of Bardney concerning one of his monks in 1439–40 "Also he deposes that brother John Hale sent out privily all his private goods, with the mind and intent, as it appeared, to leave the house in apostasy and especially a silver spoon and a mazer garnished with silver, and yet he has not yet gone, nor will he disclose to the abbot where such goods are." *Linc. Visit.* II, p. 26

[2] *Linc. Visit.* II, pp. 127–9

Sometimes an anchoress had a companion, sometimes a servant[1], but in any case her life was stricter than that of a nun, for she devoted herself to constant prayer and was bound to remain always in her little cell, which was usually attached to a church. There are several instances of nuns who left their communities to lead a solitary life in some anchorage   On one occasion when the nuns of Coldingham had been dispersed by the Scots, Beatrice de Hodesak left her convent and with the permission of the Archbishop and of her Prioress retired to an anchorage at St Edmund's Chapel, near the bridge of Doncaster; another anchoress Sibil de Lisle was already living there (c. 1300)[2]. Twenty years later Archbishop Melton gave Margaret de Punchardon, nun of Arden, permission to be enclosed, as an anchoress, in the cell attached to St Nicholas' Hospital at Beverley, in company with Agnes Migregose [? Mucegrose, i.e. Musgrave] already a recluse there[3]. The register of Bishop Gray of Lincoln contains an interesting commission (1435–6) addressed to the Abbot of Thornton, bidding him enclose Beatrice Franke, a nun of Stainfield, in the parish church of Winterton, together with the Abbot's certificate that he has examined her and found her steadfast in her purpose and therefore

shutting up the aforesaid sister Beatrice in a building and enclosure constructed on the north side of the church and making fast the door thereof with bolts, bars and keys, we left her in peace and calm of spirit, as it is believed by the more part, in the joy of her Saviour[4]

[1] The three anchoresses of *The Ancren Riwle* and their maids will be remembered

[2] Raine, *Letters from Northern Registers* (Rolls Ser), pp. 196–8. See also Rotha Clay, *Hermits and Anchorites of England*, pp 93–4

[3] *V C H. Yorks* iii, p 113 (cf. *Test Ebor.* ii, p 98) Two other Yorkshire nuns are found as anchoresses in the first part of the fourteenth century. Joan Sperry, nun of Clementhorpe, was anchoress at Beeston near Leeds in 1322, and in 1348 Margaret la Boteler, nun of Hampole, was anchoress at the chapel of East Layton, Yorks Clay, *op. cit* pp. 254–5, 256 See also the curious case of Avice of Beverley, a nun of Nunburnholme, concerning whom "the Prioress and nuns say that Avice of Beverley, sometime professed nun of Nunburnholme, thrice left the house to the intent that she might lead a stricter life elsewhere. They say that fourteen years at least have passed since she last went away; howbeit they believe her to have lived in chastity They say that she was disobedient every year and very often while she was with them They say that she dwelt with them for thirty years before she left the monastery for the first time." The inquiry which elicited this information was made because she wanted to return (1280). *Reg Wm. Wickwane*, p. 92 She had probably tried being an anchoress.

[4] *Visit of Relig Houses in Dioc Linc* i, pp 113–15 The prioress' licence addressed to Beatrice is also printed. It may be well here to repeat

Some nunneries themselves had anchorages attached, for instance Davington[1], Polesworth[2] and Carrow, and Julian of Norwich, anchoress at the parish church of Carrow in the fourteenth century, was one of the most famous mystical writers of the middle ages[3]. Anchoresses do not seem always to have been content with their life and the strict preliminary examination of Beatrice Franke "concerning her withdrawal from the life of a community to the solitary life, concerning the length of time wherein she had continued in this purpose, concerning the perils of them that choose such a life and afterwards repent thereof" was probably a necessary precaution. The register of Bishop Dalderby of Lincoln contains a mandate to the nuns of Marlow, to readmit one such faint-heart, Agnes de Littlemore, a lay sister of the house, who had left it to become an anchoress and had repented of her decision[4].

Illness and the desire to embrace a stricter rule were exceptional

the editor's warning that "acts of this description probably form the foundation for the ridiculous superstition, made famous by a striking passage of Scott's *Marmion*, that nuns and others who had broken the laws of the church were commonly walled up and left to perish " Another and perhaps more probable explanation of the superstition is that Scott probably, and certainly others after him, misinterpreted the words *immuratio, emmurer*, which are constantly used of strict imprisonment by inquisition officials and others See on the subject, H Thurston, S.J , *The Immuring of Nuns* (Catholic Truth Soc. Historical Papers, No v)

[1] Celestria (? Celestina), nun, and Adilda, nun, are mentioned as anchoresses there Clay, *op cit* pp 222–3

[2] *Ib* p 184 An "ancress" was found at this house at the time of the Dissolution.

[3] For her works see *Revelations of Divine Love, recorded by Julian, Anchoress at Norwich*, ed Grace Warrack (1901) She is apparently not to be confused with another famous anchoress, Julian Lampet, bequests to whom are often recorded in Norwich wills between 1426 and 1478 The priory seems to have had a succession of two or even three anchoresses named Julian See Rye, *Carrow Abbey*, pp. 7–8 and App ix, *passim* For anchoresses enclosed at conventual houses of men, see Clay, *op cit* pp 77–8, anchoresses are sometimes described as "nun," *ib.* pp 224, 232, 238, 244 Matilda Newton, a nun of Barking, who had been appointed to rule the new Abbey of Syon, but for some reason did not become abbess, returned to her own house as a recluse in 1417. *Ib* p 144

[4] *Linc Epis Reg Memo Dalderby*, f 10 (date 1300). The author of *Dives and Pauper* declares that such secessions were rare among women. "We se that whanne men take the to be ankeris and reclusys withinne fewe yerys comonly eyther they falle in reūsys or eresyes or they breke out for womãs loue or for inkyede of ther lufe or by some gile of þe fend But of wimē ancres so inclusid is seldome herde any of these defautys, but holely they begīne and holely they ende " *Dives and Pauper*, com vi, ch. B.

causes for a temporary breach of enclosure. The great difficulty
in administering *Periculoso* arose over more usual pretexts. The
least objectionable occasion for leaving cloistral precincts was
when convent business demanded it and this happened frequently
to the superior and the treasuress or cellaress. The journeys
which were frequently taken by the head of a house have already
been considered[1]; but the obedientiaries also found much scope
for wandering in the duties of their offices The treasuress and
cellaress might be obliged day by day to visit, in the course
of their duties, offices and buildings which lay outside the walls,
and if they were not sober minded women there were ample
opportunities for lingering and gossiping with secular persons
and with servants. The Constitutions of the Legate Ottobon in
1268 attempted to minimise this danger by enacting that no
nun was to go into the different *officinae*, except those whose
offices rendered it necessary to do so, and they were never to go
unaccompanied[2]. The complaints brought by the nuns of Gracedieu in 1440–1 against their self-confident cellaress Margaret
Belers show that some such regulation was necessary; it was
said that she was accustomed to visit all the offices by herself,
even the granges and other places where menfolk were working,
and that she went there (good zealous housewife!) "over early
in the morning before daybreak"; whereupon Bishop Alnwick
ordered the Prioress to "suffre none of thaym, officiere ne other,
to go to any house of office wythe owte the cloystere, but if
ther be an other nunne approveded in religyone assigned to go
wythe hire, eyther to be wytnesse of others conversatyon"[3].
Convent business, however, frequently took the officials further
afield than outlying granges and they undertook journeys hardly
less often than did the head of the house. The Cistercian statutes

---

[1] See above, pp 69–71

[2] Wilkins, *Concilia*, II, p 18 Compare William of Wykeham's injunctions
to Romsey in 1387· "Constitutiones bone memorie domini Othoboni
quondam sedis apostolice in Anglia legati in hoc casu editas ut conuenit
imitantes, vobis sub penis infrascriptis districcius inhibemus, ne ad officinas
aliquas aut alias cameras quascumque forinsecas extra septa claustri, vel
ad alia loca in villam vel alibi extra vestrum monasterium, illis quibus hoc
ex officio competit dumtaxat exceptis…exeatis " *New Coll MS* f 84
Compare also the injunctions (likewise modelled on Ottobon's constitution)
sent by Thomas of Cantilupe, Bishop of Hereford, to Lymbrook about 1277.
Reg. Thome de Cantilupo, p 201

[3] *Linc Visit* II, pp 122, 125

of 1256–7, in forbidding nuns to leave their convents, make exception "for the Abbess with two or at most three nuns and for the cellaress with one, who are permitted to go forth to look after the business of the house or for other inevitable causes"[1]. The evidence of account rolls is invaluable in this connection and shows us the nuns going marketing or seeking tithes from recalcitrant farmers, or interviewing tenants about rent. The Chambress of Syon went to London three times in 1536, doubtless to buy the russets, white cloth, kerseys, friezes and hollands which figure so largely in her account and to take the spectacles to be mended, she was a thrifty lady and her expenses were only 6d., 2d. and 2od. respectively. Her sister the cellaress also went to London that year and spent 6d. on the jaunt[2] The nuns of St Michael's, Stamford, sometimes took long journeys on convent business; in 1372–3 Dame Katherine Fitzaleyn went "to London and other places about our tithes," at the heavy cost of 15s 8d[3] From Stamford to London was a considerable journey, but the convent could not afford to lose its tithes The same business took Dame Katherine to the capital another year; she hired three horses for six days and a serving man to go with them and she took with her Dame Ida, in accordance with the regulations, the whole cost of the expedition was £2. 11s., a very large sum, and we will hope that the tithes brought in more than enough to cover it[4]

Sometimes, again, nuns left their houses to take part in ecclesiastical ceremonies, such as processions. There does not

---

[1] Cistercian Stat A D 1257–88, ed J T Fowler, 1890, p. 106.

[2] Blunt, Myroure of Oure Ladye (E E T S), Introd pp xxviii, xxxii

[3] P R O Mins Accts 1260/3.

[4] "Paid for the hire of three horses for six days going to London for our tithes..., paid for the hire of a serving-man and for his expenses going with the said horses 2/3, item sent to Dame Katherine Fitzaleyn at the same time 6/8" (Prioress' Account), ib. 1260/4 The treasuress' account for the same year throws further light upon her movements "Paid for the expenses of Dame Katherine Fitzaleyn and Dame Ida going to London and for the hire of their horses going and returning, for our tithes £2 11 0 ... In the expenses of the sub-Prioress and Dame Katherine Fitzaleyn and two men and three horses going to Fleet for rent and for salt 3/8 In the expenses of Dame Katherine Fitzaleyn and dame Joan Fishmere [the treasures] for hire of horses 8d" Ib 1260/5 Dame Katherine also went to the Bishop to get a certificate and in 1377–8 she went with the treasuress Dame Margaret Redinges to Corby and to Sempringham (perhaps to visit the Gilbertine nuns there) and Dames Margaret Redinges and Joan Fishmere went with Robert Clark to Clapton Ib 1260/7

seem much harm in the whole convent sallying forth on these
solemn occasions and indeed bishops sometimes gave orders that
they were to do so. In 1321 Rigaud de Asserio, Bishop of
Winchester, sent a letter to the Prior of St Swithun's monastery
"to pray for peace, with solemn processions"; he was to cause
the Abbot and Convent of Hyde, the Abbess and Convent of
St Mary's, Winchester, and all the other religious houses and
parish priests of Winchester to come together in the Cathedral
and then to proceed in solemn procession through the town[1].
The strictest disciplinarians, however, looked with suspicion even
upon religious processions and sought to keep nuns within the
precincts of their cloister. Ottobon's Constitutions contain a
proviso that nuns are not to go out for public processions, but
are to hold their processions within the bounds of their own
house[2] and the prohibition was repeated by Thomas of Cantilupe,
Bishop of Hereford, writing to Lymbrook in 1277[3], and by
William of Wykeham (who specifically based his words upon
Ottobon), writing to Romsey in 1387[4]. A century later the
custom was forbidden in France at the provincial Council of
Sens, in 1460 and again in 1485, where it was referred to as
"a dangerous and evil abuse"[5]. Some explanation of this severity,
which seems excessive, may perhaps be gleaned from an injunction sent by Bishop Longland to Elstow in 1531:

Moreover forasmoche as the ladye abbesse and covent of that house
be all oon religious bodye unite by the profession and rules of holy
sainct benedicte, and is nott conuenyent ne religious to be disseuerd
or separate, we will and inioyne that frome hensforth noon of the
said abbesse seruauntes nor no ther secular person or persones, what-
soeuer he or they be, goo in eny procession before the said abbesse
betwene hir and hir said covent, undre payne of exccommunycacon,
and that the ladye abbesse ne noon of hir successours hereafter be
ladde by the arme or otherwise in eny procession ther as in tymes paste
hath been used, undre the same payne[6].

Other religious ceremonies of a less formal nature occasionally
called nuns, in a body or individually, out of their cloister. For

---

[1] *Reg of John de Sandale and Rigaud de Asserio*, p 418. Similar letter
to Prior and Convent of the Cathedral Church, p 576
[2] Wilkins, *Concilia*, II, p. 18.
[3] *Reg. Thome de Cantilupo*, p 201   [4] *New Coll.* MS. f. 85d.
[5] Quoted in Thiers, *op cit* p 133, who considers the question in his
ch XIX
[6] *Archaeologia*, XLVII, pp. 52–3.

instance some of the greater abbeys were accustomed to receive into their fraternity benefactors and persons of distinction, both men and women, whom they wished to honour, nor were kings too proud to call themselves the *confratres* of Bury St Edmunds or St Albans and to receive from the monks the kiss of peace[1]. The ceremony took place with great solemnity in the chapter-house and it is recorded that on one occasion (in 1428), when the Earl of Warwick and the Duke of Gloucester and their house-holds were received into the Fraternity of St Albans, Cecilia Paynel and Margaret Ewer, nuns of Sopwell, were also admitted. At another time the Prioress of Sopwell, together with a certain John Crofton and his wife, were received and gave the abbey a pittance and wine and a sum of money; while on another occasion still the Prioress and another nun of St Mary de Pré were similarly made *consorores* of the abbey, and marked their appreciation by the gift of a frontal for the high altar in the lady chapel[2]. Sopwell and St Mary de Pré were dependents of St Albans and it is not improbable that their superiors and seniors often visited it on great occasions such as this; certainly the great magnates of the realm often called at Sopwell on their way from St Albans, and nuns of the house figure in its book of benefactors as donors of embroidery to the church[3], while in matters of government the Abbot always kept a tight hand upon both houses Again nuns sometimes attended the funerals of great folk; not only priors and prioresses, but also canons and nuns were expected to be present at Sir Thomas Cumber-worth's funeral and "month's-mind"[4] and in an account roll of St Michael's, Stamford, there is an entry "paye a nos com-paygnounes alaunt a Leycestre al enterment la Duchesse ij s"[5].

[1] See illustration of Henry VI being received as a Confrater at Bury St Edmunds, reproduced in Gasquet, *Engl Mon Life*, facing p. 126, from *Harl MS* 2278, f 6

[2] Amundesham, *Annales* (Rolls Ser), i, pp. 65–9, *passim*.

[3] *V C H. Herts* IV, p 424.

[4] "I will that Ilke prior and priores that comes to my beryall at y^t day hafe iii s iiij d and Ilke chanon and Nune xij d...and Ilke prior and priores that comes to the xxx day [i e. the so-called "month's-mind"] hafe vj s viij d and Ilke chanon or none that comes to the said xxx day haf xx d " *Lincoln Diocese Documents*, ed A Clark (E E T S), pp 50, 53

[5] *P R.O. Mins Accts* 1260/20 This was probably Constance of Castile, second wife of John of Gaunt, Duke of Lancaster, who died on March 24, 1394, and was buried with great magnificence at The Newarke, Leicester. *S Armitage Smith*, John of Gaunt (1904), pp 357–8 The date of the account

Attendance at religious processions and ceremonies might be, and attendance at funerals undoubtedly was, regarded by the more moderate and reasonable visitors as a legitimate reason for going outside the precincts of the cloister. One other excuse of the same nature, however, sometimes took a nun away from her convent for a considerable length of time and was never looked upon with any favour by the authorities of the church. Yet it is an excuse which we have the best of reasons for recognising, which is, indeed, bound up with all that most people know of the medieval nun—for Chaucer has taught us that nuns were wont to go upon pilgrimages. All pilgrimages did not, indeed, involve as long a journey as that taken by Madame Eglentyne. The ladies of Nuncoton could make a pilgrimage to St Hugh of Lincoln, without being away for more than a night and the ladies of Blackborough would not have to follow for a long distance the milky way to Walsingham[1]. Nevertheless it is unnecessary to go further than Chaucer to understand why it was that medieval bishops offered a strenuous opposition to the practice; one has only to remember some of the folk in whose company the Prioress travelled and some of the tales they told. If one could be certain that she rode with her nun and her priests, or at least between the Knight and the poor Parson! But there were also the Miller and the Summoner and, worst of all, that cheerful and engaging sinner the Wife of Bath. If one could be certain that she listened only to the tale of Griselda, or of Palamon and Arcite, or yawned over Melibeus, and that she fell discreetly to the rear when the company laughed over the "nyce cas of Absalon and hende Nicholas"! If one could be certain that it was to the Wife of Bath alone that the Merchant made his apology

> Ladies, I prey yow that ye be nat wrooth;
> I can nat glose, I am a rude man

Certainly the Wife of Bath was a host in herself, but the plural is ominous and the two nuns were the only other ladies in the

---

roll is unfortunately illegible, but from this internal evidence it should probably be dated 1393-4. There is another entry "paye a couent pur lalme le Duk de Lancastre vij s iij d," in which "Duk" is possibly a slip for "Duchesse."

[1] There were over seventy places of pilgrimage in Norfolk alone. Cutts, *Scenes and Characters of the Middle Ages* (3rd ed. 1911), p. 162.

company. The sterner moralists of the middle ages bear out
Chaucer's picture of a typical pilgrimage with most unchaucerian
denunciation[1]. Pilgrims got drunk at times, as drunk as the
Miller, "so that vnnethe up-on his hors he sat," on the very first
day of the journey, as drunk as the "sory palled gost" of a
cook, when the cavalcade reached that

> litel toun
> Which that y-cleped is Bob-up-&-doun
> Under the Blee in Canterbury weye.

Again, there are pilgrims, says Etienne de Bourbon, "who when
they visit holy places sing lecherous lays, whereby they inflame
the hearts of such as hear them and kindle the fire of lechery";
and like an echo rise the well-known words:

> Ful loude he song "Come hider, love, to me,"
> This somnour bar to him a stif burdoun
> Was never trompe of half so greet a soun,

and shrill and clear sound the miller's bagpipes, bringing the
pilgrims out of town[2]. No place for a cloistered nun was the inn
though one feels that mine host's wife, "big in arme," would
have kept the Tabard respectable, whatever might be said of the
Chequer-on-the-Hoop. No place for her the road to Canterbury,

---

[1] Jacques de Vitry does not mince his words "I have seen many pilgrims who, weary of wayfaring, used to drink themselves tipsy ...You will find many harlots and evil women in the inns, who lie in wait for the incautious and reward their guests with evil, even as a mouse in a wallet, a serpent in the bosom." Etienne de Bourbon has the same tale to tell: "A pilgrimage should be sober, lest the pilgrims be despoiled and slain and turned to scorn, both materially and spiritually For I have seen a person who had laboured greatly making a pilgrimage overseas lose both his virtue and his money, when drunk and lying with a chambermaid in an inn." *Anecdotes Historiques etc*, *d'Etienne de Bourbon*, ed Lecoy de la Marche (1877), pp. 167-8 Mine Host's words to the drunken cook (*Manciple's Prol.* II, pp. 15-19) are significant in the light of these quotations So also are the adventures of "that loose fish the Pardoner" with the tapster Kit at the Chequer Inn. *Tale of Beryn*, ed Furnivall and Stone (Chaucer Soc 1887). See also *An Alphabet of Tales* (E.E T S), p 258, No cccLxxvi

[2] Compare the words of the Lollard William Thorpe in 1407: "Such fond people waste blamefullie Gods goodes in their vaine pilgrimages, spending their goods upon vitious hostelars, which are oft uncleane women of their bodies .. Also, sir, I knowe well that when divers men and women will goe thus after their oun willes and finding, out on pilgrimage, they will ordaine with them before to have with them some men and women that can well sing wanton songes; and some other pilgrimages will have them with bagge-pipes," etc This and other information about pilgrimages may be found in Coulton, *Chaucer and his England*, pp 138-43 See also *The Book of the Knight of La Tour-Landry* (E E T S), pp 47 ff

nor yet Canterbury itself, where the monk with the holy-water sprinkler was so anxious for a peep at her face and where she hobnobbed over wine in the parlour, with the hostess and the Wife of Bath[1].

Madame Eglentyne, for all her simplicity, must have circumvented her Bishop before she got there. For the Bishops were quite clear in their minds that pilgrimages for nuns were to·be discouraged. They were of Langland's way of thinking:

Right so, if thow be religious, renne thow neuere ferther,
To Rome ne to Rochemadore, but as thi reule techeth,
And holde the vnder obedyence, that heigh wey is to heuene[2].

As early as 791 the Council of Fréjus had forbidden the practice[3] and in 1195 the Council of York decreed "In order that the opportunity of wandering about may be taken from them [the nuns], we forbid them to take the road of pilgrimage."[4] In 1318 Archbishop Melton strictly forbade the nuns of Nunappleton to leave their house "by reason of any vow of pilgrimage, which they might have taken; if any had taken such vows she was to say as many psalters as it would have taken days to perform

[1]   The wyff of bath was so wery, she had no will to walk;
She toke the Priores by the hond; "madam, wol ye stalk
Pryuely in-to þe garden, to se the herbis growe?
And aftir, with our hostis wyff, in hir parlour rowe,
I wol gyve jewe the wine, and yee shull me also:
ffor tyll wee go to soper, wee have nau3t ellis to do
The Priores, as womman tau3t of gentil blood and hend,
Assentid to hir counsell, and forthe (tho) gon they wend
Passyng forth (ful) softly in-to the herbery:
ffor many a herbe grewe, for sewe and surgery;
And al the Aleyis fair I-parid, I-rahd and I-makid·
The sauge and the Isope, I-frethid and I-stakid.
Tale of Beryn, p. 10. Cf p 6 for the scene with the holy water sprinkler
[2] Langland, *Piers Plowman*, B Text, Passus XII, 36–38.
[3] "Let it never be permitted to any abbess or any other nun, whosoever she may be, to undertake the journey to Rome or to any other holy places, for it is the Devil, taking the form of an angel of light, who inspires such pilgrimages under a false pretext of piety· and there is no one so foolish and so devoid of reason as not to know how irreligious and blameworthy a thing it is for Virgins vowed to God to hold converse with men, through the necessity of a journey If after the prohibition of this venerable Council, there be found anyone so bold as to disobey this ordinance, which has been promulgated by unanimous consent, let him be punished according to the rigour of the canons, to wit let him be excommunicated." Thiers, *op cit.* p. 135
[4] Wilkins, *Concilia*, I, p 502.

the pilgrimage so rashly vowed"[1]. One has a melancholy vision of Madame Eglentyne saying psalters interminably through her "tretys" nose, instead of jogging along so gaily with her motley companions and telling so prettily her tale of little St Hugh. But the nuns of Nunappleton retained their taste for pilgrimages and nearly two centuries later (in 1489) we find Archbishop Rotherham admonishing their successors

yat ye prioresse lycence none of your susters to goe pilgremage or visit yer frendes w'oute a grete cause, and yen such a sister lycencyate by you to have w' her oon of ye most sadd and well disposid sistirs to she come home agayne[2]

At Wix, twenty years later, the nuns were forbidden to undertake pilgrimages without the consent of the diocesan[3], and in 1531 Bishop Longland wrote to the Prioress of Nuncoton:

Forasmoche as by your negligent sufferaunce dyuers of your susters hath wandred a brode in the world, some under the pretence of pylgrymage, some to see ther frends, and otherwise whereby hath growen many Inconuenyences insolent behauiours and moche slaunder, as well to your house as to those susters, as by the texts of my said visitation doth euydently appere, I chardge you lady priores that from hensforthe ye neyther licence ne suffre eny your susters to goo out of your monastery,

without good cause and company of a "wise sobre and discrete suster," and an injunction not to "tary out of the monastery in the nighte tyme"[4]. But most significant of all is a case which occurred at the little Cistercian priory of Wykeham in Yorkshire in the fifteenth century. In 1450 Archbishop Kemp wrote to the Prioress, bidding her readmit an apostate nun Katherine Thornyf:

who, seduced by the Angel of Darkness, under the colour of a pilgrimage in the time of the Jubilee, without leave of the archbishop,

[1] V C H. Yorks. III, p 172 Compare Bishop Gynewell's injunction to Heynings in 1351 "Item pur ceo que ascun de les dames de dit mesoun sount trop acustumez de faire auowes de pilgrimage et dautres abstinences, saunz conge de lour souerayn, par quar ils ount souent occasion de les retrer de lour religion, si vous comandoms sur peyn descomengement que nul de vous face tiel maner auowe en destourbance de vostre religion, saunz especial conge de vostre souereyn Et que nul tiel auowe soit fait par ascun de vous, pur faire paregrinage ou autre abstinence a quel il nest pas tenuz par sa religion, nous lui relessoms tut maner de tel auowe, issint qil se poet doner entirement a sa religion parfaire " Linc Epis Reg Memo Gynewell, f 34d.
[2] V C H Yorks III, p. 172, and Dugdale, Mon v, p. 654
[3] V C H Essex, II, p. 124   [4] Archaeologia, XLVII, pp 56–7

or officials or even of the prioress, set out on a journey to the court
of Rome, in the company of another nun of the house, who, as it was
reported, had gone the way of all flesh and on whose soul the Archbishop prayed for mercy. After the death of this nun, Katherine
Thornyf had lived in sin with a married man in London.

Then she had been moved to penitence, after who knows what
agony of soul, and had gone to the Archbishop seeking absolution; and so the prodigal, weary of her husks, came back to the
nunnery she had left[1]. The melancholy tale is borne out by all
we know about medieval pilgrimages. Centuries before—in 774
—an Archbishop of Milan had written to an Archbishop of
Canterbury, advising that the Synod should prohibit women and
nuns from travelling to Rome, on account of the dangers and
temptations of the journey, "for very few are the cities in
Lombardy...France...Gaul, wherein there is not to be found
a prostitute of English race"[2]; and the trouvère Rutebeuf, in
the thirteenth century, spoke with less pity and a more biting
satire of the pilgrimages of French nuns to Paris and Montmartre[3].

Excursions on convent business or for attendance at ecclesiastical ceremonies (other than pilgrimages) were regarded as

---

[1] *V.C.H. Yorks.* III, p. 183. This episode is a striking illustration of the
complaint made about those Jubilee pilgrimages by the abbots of Fountains,
St Mary Graces and Stratford, who had been appointed by the Abbot and
Chapter-General of Cîteaux to report on the condition of English monasteries
of that order Writing to the Abbot of Cîteaux in 1500, they beg that several
bulls of Jubilee indulgence should be sent to England, adding, "for many
lesser religious of the order, under pretext of obtaining the grace of this
indulgence, led by a spirit less of devotion than of levity and curiosity, are
begging their superiors for licence to go to the Roman curia, and we have
besought them to remain at home in the hope of obtaining this jubilee
[indulgence] For we rarely see, in this country of ours, any good and devout
secular or religious man visiting the Mother City (most justly though it
be accounted holy), who returns home again in better holiness and devotion "
Mélanges d'Histoire offerts à M. Charles Bémont (Paris, 1913), p. 429.

[2] Quoted in Gregorovius, *Hist of Rome in the Middle Ages*, III, p. 78 note.
See the fifteenth century Florentine carnival song, quoted below, pp 617–8

[3]
    Les blanches et les grises et les noires nonains
    Sont sovent pelerines aus saintes et aus sainz,
    Les Diex lor en set gre, je n'en suis pas certains,
    S'eles fussent bien sages eles alassent mains

    Quant ces nonains s'en vont par le pays esbatre
    Les unes a Paris, les autres a Montmartre,
    Tels foiz enmaine deus qu'on en ramaine quatre,
    Quar s'on en perdroit une il les covenroit batre.

From "De la vie dou Monde," *Rustebeufs Gedichte hg. v Adolf Krefaner*
(1885), p 185.

legitimate, though strict disciplinarians sought to restrict them to occasions of real urgency. But for the most part we hear about journeys undertaken for pleasure and not for business, or at any rate the elastic term business is stretched to cover some very pleasant wandering in the world and much hob-nobbing with friends. In spite of the Bull *Periculoso*[1] bishops were never able to prevent nuns from going to stay with their friends, and sometimes the ladies made very long journeys for this purpose. Bishop Stapeldon, for instance, ordained that when the nuns of Canonsleigh in Devon went to visit their friends "in Somerset, Dorset, Devonshire or in Cornwall" they might not stay for longer than a month; but if they went outside these four counties the Abbess might allow them to stay longer still, having regard to the distance of their destination and to the time which would be spent in travelling[2]. The bishops indeed were forced to regard such visits as "reasonable occasions" for a breach of enclosure, and their efforts, as has already been shown, were confined to regulating rather than to stopping the practice; for the relatives of the nuns, as well as the ladies themselves, would have been the first to resent any interference with their visits. Whatever might be the theory of the Church on the subject, blood was thicker than holy water; family affections and family interests persisted in the cloister and the nun was welcomed at many a hospitable board for her family's sake as well as for her own. All this seems natural and obvious today and few would think the worse of the nuns for their opposition to the stricter form of enclosure Nevertheless the authorities of the Church had reason for their distrust of these absences from the convent. Once away from the cloister and staying in a private house there was nothing to keep a nun from joining in the secular revelries of friends, and though her behaviour might be exemplary the convent rule aimed at keeping her un-spotted even by temptation An anecdote related by Erasmus in his dialogue "Ichthyophagia" shows that the danger of allowing

---

[1] And of such specific decrees as that of the Council of Oxford (1222) which forbade them to go merely to visit relatives or for recreation except (there was always a saving clause under which nuns and bishops alike could shelter) in such case as might arouse no suspicion Wilkins, *Concilia*, I, p 592.

[2] *Reg Walter de Stapeldon*, p 95 Cf injunctions to Polsloe, above, p 355.

nuns to visit their friends might be a real one. Two nuns had
gone to stay with their kinsfolk, and at supper

they began to grow merry with wine, they laughed and joked and
kissed and not over-modestly neither, till you could hardly hear what
was said for the noise they made ...After supper there was dancing
and singing of lascivious songs and such doings I am ashamed to
speak of, inasmuch as I am much afraid the night hardly passed very
honestly[1]

Moreover even if nuns visited their friends for a very short
time, staying only one night, or even returning before nightfall
to the convent, there was danger that they might join in the
various revelries practised among secular folk, and reprobated
by the Church as occasions for unseemly and licentious behaviour.
Bishop Spofford of Hereford, indeed, found it necessary in 1437
to send a special warning against doing so to the nuns of Lymbrook; the Prioress was to "yife no lycence too noon of hur
sustres her after to go to no port townes, no to noon othir townes
to comyn wakes or festes, spectacles and othir worldly vanytees,
and specially on holy-dayes, nor to be absent lyggyng oute by
nyght out of thair monastery, but with fader and moder, except
causes of necessytee"[2]. The words which the Good Wife spoke
to her daughter come to mind.

> Go not to þe wrastelings ne schotynge at cok
> As it were a strumpet or a giggelot,
> Wone at hom, douȝter, and love þi work myche[3].

Clemence Medforde, Prioress of Ankerwyke, went to a wedding
at Bromhale[4]; yet weddings were of all those "comyn wakes
and festes" most condemned by the Church for the unseemly

---

[1] *All the Familiar Colloquies of Erasmus,* ed N. Bailey, 2nd ed 1733,
p. 379
[2] *Hereford Epis Reg Spofford,* p 81 Compare the charge made against
the clergy of Ripon Minster in 1312· "Vicarii capellani, et caeteri ministri
. spectaculis publicis, ludibriis et coreis, immo teatricalibus ludis inter
laicos frequentius se immiscent." J. T. Fowler, *Memorials of Ripon Minster*
(Surtees Soc), ii, p 68 Also one of the *comperta* at Alnwick's visitation
of Humberstone Abbey in 1440, "He says that Wrauby answered the abbot
saucily and rebelliously when [the abbot] took him to task for climbing up
a gate to behold the pipe-players and dancers in the churchyard of the
parish church" *Linc Visit* ii, p 140
[3] *Manners and Meals in Olden Time,* ed Furnivall (E E T S), p. 40.
[4] See above, p 81, and compare the injunctions sent by Cardinal Nicholas of Cues to the Abbess of Sonnenburg, c. 1454, forbidding her to go on
pilgrimages or to visit health resorts or to attend weddings Eckenstein,
Woman under Monasticism, p 425.

revelries which followed them. *The Christen State of Matrimony,* written in 1543, throws a flood of light upon the subject:

> When they come home from the Church, then beginneth excesse of eatyng and dryncking—and as much is waisted in one daye, as were sufficient for the two newe maried Folkes halfe a yere to lyve upon ... After the Bancket and Feast, there begynnethe a vayne, madde and unmanerlye fashion, for the Bryde must be brought into an open dauncynge place Then is there such a rennynge, leapynge, and flyng-ynge among them, then is there suche a lyftynge up and discoverynge of the Damselles clothes and other Womennes apparell, that a Man might thynke they were sworne to the Devels Daunce. Then muste the poore Bryde kepe foote with al Dauncers and refuse none, how scabbed, foule, droncken, rude and shameles soever he be Then must she oft tymes heare and se much wyckednesse and many an uncomely word; and that noyse and romblyng endureth even tyll supper[1].

It may be urged that the Brides of Heaven need not necessarily have attended these merry-makings after the ceremony; but the example of Isabel Benet, nun of Catesby, and the tenour of certain episcopal injunctions, show that nuns by no means despised dancing[2]. The strict disciplinarian's view of weddings is shown in the fact that members of the Tertiary Order of St Francis were forbidden to attend them; and even the civic authorities of London found it necessary to regulate the disorders which were prevalent on such occasions[3].

---

[1] Quoted in Brand's *Observations on Popular Antiquities* (ed. 1877), pp 382, 394 Compare the almost precisely similar account given by Erasmus in his *Guide to Christian Matrimony* (1526), quoted in Coulton, *Social Life in Britain from the Conquest to the Reformation,* pp 439–40.

[2] See above, p 309 and below, p. 388

[3] Coulton, *Chaucer and his England,* pp. 108–9 Weddings were, however, occasionally celebrated in convent churches, e g on Jan 3rd, 1465–6 the Bishop of Ely addressed a licence to Thomas Trumpington, "President of religion of the Minoresses of the convent of Denny," authorising him to celebrate matrimony in the convent church between William Ketterich junior and Marion Hall, domestic servants in the monastery, the bans to be put up in the parish church of Waterbeach. *Ely Epis Records,* ed. Gibbons, p 145. Compare case at Crabhouse in 1476, *V C H. Norfolk,* II, p 409. Dugdale notes that Henry VIII is said to have married one of his wives in the Chapel at Sopwell Dugdale, *Mon* III, p 364 Such weddings would necessarily have taken place in convent churches where the nave was also used as a parish church, but this was not so at Denny Wriothesley's *Chronicle* contains an account of a triple wedding held at Haliwell in 1536 "This yeare, the 3 daye of July, beinge Mondaye, was a greate solempnytie of marriage kept at the nonnerye of Halywell, besyde London, in the Erle of Ruttlandes place, where the Erle of Oxfordes sonne and heyer, called Lord Bulbeke maryed the Erle of Westmorelandes eldest daughter named

Again not only weddings, but also christenings, often involved unseemly revels and this could not fail to affect nuns
who, despite canonical prohibition, were somewhat in demand
as godmothers. Christening parties were gay affairs; the gossips
would return to the house of the child's parents to eat, drink
and make merry: "adtunc et ibidem immediate venerunt in
domam suam ad comedendum et bibendum et adtunc sibi revelaverunt de baptismo"[1]. If Antoine de la Sale's witty account of
the "third joy of marriage" has any truth[2], and it is upheld by
more sober documents, bishops did well to mislike the christening
parties for nuns; Mrs Gamp was quite at home in the middle
ages; she was probably a crony of the Wife of Bath. It was in
fact forbidden for monks and nuns to become godparents, not
only, as Mr Coulton has pointed out, "because this involved
them in a fresh spiritual relationship incompatible with their

Ladye Dorytye and the Erle of Westmorelandes sonne and heyre, called
Lord Nevell, maryed the Erle of Ruttlandes eldyste daughter, named Ladye
Anne, and the Erle of Rutlandes sonne and heire called Lord Roosse maryed
the Erle of Westmorelandes daughter, named Ladye Margaret; and all
these three lordes were maryed at one masse, goinge to churche all 3 together on by another and the laydes, there wyfes, followinge, one after
another, everye one of the younge ladyes havinge 2 younge lordes goinge
one everye syde of them when they went to church and a younge ladye
bearinge up everye of their gowne traynes; at wh. maryage was present all
the greate estates of the realme, both lordes and ladyes " Afterwards they
all went home and had a great feast, followed by a dance, to which the
King came dressed as a Turk. *Wriothesley's Chronicle*, ed. W. D. Hamilton
(Camden Soc 1875), I, pp 50–1. A reference may also be made to No XLVI
of *Les Cent Nouvelles Nouvelles*, ed Th Wright, t I, p 284: "Or advint
toutesfoiz ung jour que une des niepces de madame l'abbesse se marioit
et faisoit sa feste en l'abbaye; et y avoit grosse assemblée des gens du païs,
et estoit madame l'abbesse fort empeschée de festoyer les gens de bien qui
estoyent venuz à la feste faire honneur à sa niepce."

[1] From "Proofs of Age, temp. Henry IV," quoted in *Trans R Hist. Soc*
N S XVI (1902), p 163.

[2] "Or viennent commeres de toutes pars; or convient que le pauvre
homme [i e. the husband] face tant que elles soient bien aises La dame et
les commeres parlent et raudent, et dient de bonnes chouses et se tiennent
bien aises, quiconques ait la peine de le querir, quelque temps qu'il face...
et tousjours boyvent comme bottes ...Lors les commeres entrent, elles
desjunent, elles disnent, elles menjent a raassie, maintenant boivent au lit
de la commere, maintenant à la cuve, et confondent des biens et du vin plus
qu'il n'en entreroit en une bote, et à l'aventure il vient à barrilz ou n'en y
a que une pipe. Et le pauvre homme, qui a tout le soussy de la despense, va
souvent veoir comment le vin se porte, quant il voit terriblement boire ...
Briefment tout se despend; les commeres s'en vont bien coiffées, parlant
et janglant, et ne se esmoient point dont il vient " *Les Quinzes Joyes de
Mariage* (Bib. Elzevirienne, 1855), pp. 27–8, 30, 37–8

ideal, but because it entangled them with worldly folk and worldly affairs"[1]. Thus in 1387 William of Wykeham wrote to the nuns of Romsey "We forbid you all and singly to presume to become godmothers to any child, without obtaining our licence to do so, since from such relationships expense is often entailed upon religious houses"[2]. At Nuncoton in 1440 two nuns asked that their sisters might be forbidden the practice and Alnwick enjoined "that none of yowe have no children at the fount ne confirmyng"[3] and nearly a century later a similar injunction was sent by Bishop Longland to Studley[4].

There does indeed seem a certain incongruity in the presence of one who had renounced the world at a wedding or a christening, even had such ceremonies not been accompanied by very worldly revels. But they were less incongruous than was the attendance of Mary, daughter of Edward I, the nun-princess of Amesbury,

[1] G. G. Coulton, *French Monasticism in 1503* (Medieval Studies No XI. 1915), p 22 note 2

[2] *New Coll.* MS f 87 On the other hand such connections with rich families might be a source of wealth to a house Mr Coulton draws attention to "the letter of an abbot at Bordeaux in Father Denifle's *Désolation des Eglises, etc* I, p 583 (A D 1419) The abbey had been so impoverished by war that the Abbot begged for a papal indult permitting him to stand god-father to forty children of noble or wealthy families " Coulton, *loc cit*

[3] *Alnwick's Visit* MS. f. 77d

[4] "That frome hensforthe ye give noo more licence ne suffre eny of your susters to be godmother to eny child, nither at the christening nother at the confirmacon, and undre like payne chardge you nott to be godmother to eny child in christening nor confirmacon " *Archaeologia*, XLVII, p 54 Compare similar prohibitions by Eudes Rigaud, Archbishop of Rouen, addressed to the nuns of Montivilliers in 1257 and 1265. *Reg Visit Archiepis Rothomag* ed Bonnin (1852), pp 293, 517 The prohibition was frequently broken by monks as well as by nuns See e g the *comperta* at Alnwick's visitation of Higham Ferrers College in 1442: "Also Sir William Calverstone haunts suspect places and especially the house of Margery Chaumberleyn, for whose son he stood sponsor at his confirmation, and, though warned by the master, he does not desist The same does also haunt the house of one Plays, for whose son he likewise stood sponsor." *Linc Visit* II, p. 138 Also the complaint of Guy Jouenneaux, Abbot of St Sulpice de Bourges in his *Defence of Monastic Reform* (1503): "Sometimes they eat in the houses of their gossips, though the law forbids them such relationships, or again among citizens, at whose houses they are as frequent guests, or more frequent, than even worldly-minded folk " Coulton, *loc. cit.* It is interesting that Barbara Mason, ex-Prioress of Marham, who died shortly after the dissolution in 1538, mentions two god-daughters "I wyll Barbara Barcom my goddowter and servant, shall haue my wosted kyrtyll and clothe kyrtell and my frok in Hayll. Itm I bequeth to Elyn Mason's chyld, my goddowter xij d." *Bury Wills and Inventories*, ed S Tymms (Camden Soc), p 134 Henry VIII's visitors gave her a bad character.

upon her step-mother Queen Margaret and later upon her niece
Elizabeth de Burgh, during their confinements. A king's daughter,
however, could not be subjected to ordinary restraints; Mary led
a particularly free life, constantly visiting court and going on
pilgrimages, and there is no reason to suppose that ordinary
nuns shared her privileges[1].

Naturally occasions when a nun was away from her convent
for the night, whether on business or on pleasure, were com
paratively rare. For the most part the bishops had to deal with
casual absences during the day and it was found extraordinarily
difficult to confine such excursions to the "convent business"
and "necessary reasons" laid down by the various enactments
on enclosure. There seems to have been a great deal of wandering
about without any specific purpose. Short errands perhaps took
the nuns out for a few hours, or they went simply for air and
exercise Their rule and their bishops would have had them hear
the "smale fowles maken melodye" and tread "the smalle,
softe, sweete grass" within the narrow cloister court, or at least
in the privacy of their own gardens[2]. But the nuns liked highways and hedges, and often in springtime it was farewell their
books and their devotion. Certainly the convent often did come
out to take the air in its own meadows; John Aubrey (in a
much-quoted passage) tells of the nuns of Kington in Wiltshire,
and how "Old Jacques" could see them from his house

come forth into the nymph-hay with their rocks and wheels to spin·
and with their sewing work. He would say that he had told three-
score and ten, but of nuns there were not so many, but in all, with
lay sisters and widows, old maids and young girls, there might be
such a number[3].

[1] For her life see M. A E. Green, *Lives of the Princesses of England*, II,
pp. 404–42.

[2] Their gardens are often mentioned, e g at Nuncoton in 1440 it was
complained that the nuns had private gardens and that some of them did
not come to Compline, but wandered about in the gardens, gathering herbs
Alnwick's Visit. f. 72. At Stainfield in 1519 a similar complaint was made
that on feast days they did not stay in the church and occupy themselves in
devotion, between the Hours of Our Lady and High Mass, but came out
and walked about the garden and cloisters. *V C H Lincs* II, p 131. The
nuns of Sinningthwaite (1319) were ordered to provide themselves with
a competent gardener for their curtilage, so that they might always have
an abundance of vegetables *V C H Yorks* III, p. 177 Christine de Pisan's
description of the great gardens of the convent of Poissy is most attractive.
See below, p. 560

[3] Quoted in Gasquet, *English Monastic Life*, p. 177.

Sometimes, indeed, at the busy harvest-time, when every pair of hands was needed on the manor farm, the nuns even went hay-making in the meadows. The visitations of Bishop Alnwick provide two instances of this and show also the abuses to which it might give rise, since the fields were full of secular workers. At Nuncoton in 1440 the subprioress deposed that

in the autumn season the nuns go out to their autumn tasks, whereby the quire is not kept regularly[1], and...in seed time the nuns clear the crops of weeds in the barns, and there secular folks do come in and unbecoming words are uttered between them and the nuns, wherefrom, as is feared, there are evil consequences[2].

At Gracedieu the subprioress mentioned that "sometimes the nuns do help secular folk in garnering their grain during the autumn season," but the most amusing revelations concern the conduct of the haughty cellaress Margaret Belers, who, whether on account of her autocratic government or because she was of better birth than they, was regarded by her sisters with the utmost jealousy. Belers, ran one of the *detecta* to the Bishop,

goes out to work in autumn alone with Sir Henry [the chaplain], he reaping the harvest and she binding the sheaves, and at evening she comes riding behind him on the same horse. She is over friendly with him and has been since the doings aforesaid.

Here was a pretty scandal; the Bishop (hiding, we will hope, a smile) made inquiries; Sir Henry was charged with the heinous crime of going hay-making with Dame Belers. But Sir Henry specifically denied his solitary roaming in the fields with the cellaress; he said however "that he has been in the fields with the others and Belers, carting hay and helping to pile the sheaves in stacks in the barns"; and Alnwick contented himself with enjoining the Prioress "that ye suffre none of your susters to go to any felde werkes but alle onely in your presence"[3].

Such field work, when it was undertaken, must have afforded not only wholesome exercise, but a very pleasant relaxation

[1] One of the charges against Eleanor Prioress of Arden in 1396 was that "she compelled three young nuns to go out haymaking very early in the morning and they did not come back before nightfall and so divine service was not yet said." *Test Ebor* (Surtees Soc.), p 283

[2] *Alnwick's Visit* f 71d

[3] *Ib.* pp 120, 121, 123, 125. At Bishop Atwater's visitation of Legbourne in 1519 it was stated that the nuns often worked at haymaking, but only in the presence of the Prioress. *V C.H. Lincs.* II, p. 154.

from the cramping life of the cloister; and the necessities of harvest overrode all rules. Whether the nuns took part in farm work at other seasons of the year is more difficult to discover; one is tempted to think that they must sometimes have given a helping hand with their own cattle and poultry, especially at very poor houses. The private cocks and hens which occasioned such rivalry at Saint-Aubin[1], the never-to-be-forgotten donkey of Alfråd[2], bear witness not only to the sin of *proprietas*, but also to the personal care of the nuns for such livestock. But authority discouraged the practice at a later date, partly because it encouraged private property, partly because it brought the nuns into too close contact with the world[3]. Nowhere has the attitude been better stated than in the amusing description given in the *Ancren Riwle* of the anchoress' cow:

An anchoress that hath cattle appears as Martha was, a better house-wife than anchoress. nor can she in any wise be Mary, with peaceful-ness of heart. For then she must think of the cow's fodder and of the herdsman's hire, flatter the heyward, defend herself when her cattle is shut up in the pinfold and moreover pay the damage. Christ knoweth it is an odious thing when people in the town complain of the anchoresses' cattle If, however, any one must needs have a cow, let her take care that she neither annoy, nor harm any one, and that her own thoughts be not fixed thereon[4]

The more human bishops made allowance for a natural in-stinct by giving the convent permission to go for walks, though as a rule the grounds of the nunnery were specified:

"Let the door be closed at the right time," wrote Archbishop Courte-nay to Elstow in 1390, "And let no nun go out without licence of

[1] See below, p. 653.
[2] See below, p 589
[3] See Thiers on the subject "Si les Religieuses estoient aussi soigneuses de leur honneur et de leur reputation comme elles devroient, si elles vouloient asseurer la grace de leur vocation et de leur election...elles ne nourriroient point de vaches dans leur clôture, estant indecent que les Religieuses s'occu-pent à les mener paistre, à les retirer des pasturages, et à faire tout ce qui est necessaire pour en recevoir quelque profit. Je dis la même choses des asnesses, qu'elles y retiennient pour en prendre le lait dans leurs infirmitez. Car elles peuvent les avoir au dehors et en tirer à peu près les mêmes avantages, que si elles les renoient au dedans. Aussi est-il dit dans les Statuts du Couvent de Saint Estienne de Reims, de l'ordre des Chanoinesses regu-lieres de Saint Augustin Il ne sera loisible de recevoir dans le Monastere aucun gros bestail. ce qui est parfaitement conforme à cette défense du 1 Concile Provincial de Milan en 1565 *Moniales ne intus in septis Monasterii boves, equos et jumenta cujusvis generis alant* " *Op cit* p 415.
[4] *Ancren Riwle* (King's Classics). pp 316–7.

the abbess or other president, yet so that leave of walking for recreation in the orchard or in any other seemly and close place at suitable times be not out of malice denied to the nuns provided that the younger do not go without the society of the elder[1].

Bishop Spofford of Hereford went even further; after forbidding any revelries to be held in the nunnery of Lymbrook, he added:

and what dysport of walkyng forward in dewe tyme and place, so that yee kepe the dewe houres and tymes of dyuyne seruyce with inforth, and with honest company, and with lycence specyally asked and obteyned [from] the pryoresse or suppryoresse in her absence, and at yee be two to geder at the leest, we holde us content" (1437)[2]

So in 1367 Robert de Stretton, Bishop of Coventry and Lichfield, forbade any nun of Fairwell to go into Lichfield without the Prioress' leave, ordering that she should be accompanied by two sisters and should "make no vain and wanton delays," but added that "this is not intended to interfere with the laudable custom of the whole or greater part of the convent walking out together on certain days to take the air"[3]. This forerunner of the schoolgirls' "crocodile" was not, however, what the nuns desired. It was wandering about the roads in twos and threes (sometimes, alas, in ones also) that they really enjoyed, and against this freedom the bishops continually fulminated. It must be remembered that walking in the public streets in the middle ages was very different from what it is today, it is impossible otherwise, as Mr Coulton has pointed out, to explain the extraordinary severity of all rules for the deportment of girls[4]. The streets

---

[1] *Lambeth Reg Courtenay*, I, f 336 The injunction was repeated by Bishop Flemyng in 1421–2 *Visit of Relig. Houses in Dioc. Lincoln*, I, p 52 At Godstow Peckham made the following order concerning the conversations of nuns with seculars: "Cum insuper talia sunt colloquia terminata, inhibemus decetero ne moniales hujusmodi pro colloquentium conductu, locutorii januam exeant ullo modo, nec etiam stent exterius in atrio, ubi saecularium est concursus, *sed interius tantum in hortis et pomeriis* quatenus requirit necessitas et honestas patitur, si non desit omnimoda securitas, consolentur." *Reg Epis J Peckham*, III, p 848 At Romsey in 1311 Bishop Woodlock ordered that "there shall be an entrance into the garden by a gate or postern for the sick *in loco non suspecto* for their recreation and solace " Liveing, *Records of Romsey Abbey*, p. 104 At Clementhorpe in 1310 a nun confined to the cloister for penance might "for recreation and solace go into the orchard and gardens of the nunnery accompanied by nuns " *V C H. Yorks* III, p 129
[2] *Hereford Epis Reg. Spofford*, p 82.
[3] William Salt Archaeol Soc Coll New Series, VIII, pp. 118–9.
[4] Coulton, *Chaucer and his England*, p 109 He quotes one such rule from the "Ménagier de Paris " "When thou goest into town or to church,

were full of rough pastimes, hocking and hoodsnatching, football
and the games of noisy prentices in the town, and in the country
villages they resounded with the still more boorish sports of
country folk and with the shrill quarrels of alewives and regrateresses and all the good-natured but short-tempered people,
whom court rolls show us raising the hue and cry upon each
other and drawing blood from each other's noses There is
perhaps solicitude for the nuns in the injunction which Bishop
Fitzjames sent in 1509 to the convent of Wix in Essex, forbidding
them to permit "any public spectacles of seculars, javelin-play,
dances or trading in streets or open places"[1]. Manners were free
in that age and the nuns would see and hear much that were
best hidden from their cloistered innocence. Moreover if once
they began to stop and pass the time of day with their neighbours, religious and secular, or to go into houses for some more
private gossip, there was no knowing where such perilous
familiarity would end; and the outspokenness with which bishops
condemned such conduct by references to Dinah, the daughter
of Jacob, leaves no doubt as to what they feared[2].

But nothing availed to keep the nuns within their cloisters;
and hardly a set of episcopal injunctions but bears witness to
the freedom with which they wandered about the streets and
fields. The nuns of Moxby are not to go out of the precincts
of their monastery often, nor at any time to wander about the
woods[3]. Alas, poor ladies:

> In somer when the shawes be sheyne,
>   And leves be large and long,
> Hit is full mery in feyre foreste
>   To here the foulys song.

The nuns of Cookhill are more urban; they are not to wander
about in the town (1285)[4] and the nuns of Wroxall are not to
go on foot to Coventry or to Warwick "cum eles ount fet desorde-

walk with thine head high, thine eyelids lowered and fixed on the ground at
four fathoms distance straight in front of thee, without looking or glancing
sideways at either man or woman to the right hand or the left, nor looking
upward."

[1] V C H Essex, II, p 124

[2] Cf Coulton, *Medieval Studies* (first series, 2nd ed , p. 61) and Bishop
Hallam's admonition to Shaftesbury in 1410 V C H Dorset, II, p 78. Also
Peckham's Constitution in 1281. Wilkins, *Concilia*, II, p 58.

[3] V C H Yorks. III, p. 239

[4] *Reg Godfrey Giffard*, p. 267.

ment en ces houres" (1338)[1]. The nuns of White Hall, Ilchester, "walk through the strets and places of the vill of Ilchester and elsewhere, the modesty of their sex being altogether cast off and they do not fear to enter the houses of secular men and suspected persons" (1335)[2] The nuns of Polsloe are not to go without permission into Exeter and are to return at once when their errand is accomplished, instead of "wascrauntes de hostel en hostel, si come eles unt maynte foiz fait, en deshonestete de lur estat et de la Religioun" (1319)[3]—an echo here of the Good Wife's advice, "and run thou not from house to house, like a St Anthony's pig"[4], or of the reminiscences of that other Wife of Bath:

> For ever yet I lovede to be gay,
> And for to walke, in March, Averille and May,
> Fro hous to hous, to here sondry talis[5]

The nuns of Romsey "enter houses of laymen and even of clerics in the town, eating and drinking with them" (1284)[6]. The nuns of Godstow "have often access to Oxford under colour of visiting their friends" (1445)[7] The nuns of Elstow are a great trial to their diocesan; Bishop Gynewell finds that "there is excessive and frequent wandering of nuns to places outside the same monastery, whereby gossip and laxity are brought about" (1359)[8]; Bishop Bokyngham boldly particularises:

We order the nuns on pain of excommunication, to abstain from any dishonest and suspicious conversation with secular or religious men and especially the access and frequent confabulations and colloquies of the canons of the Priory of Caldwell or of mendicant friars, in the monastery or about the public highways and fields adjoining (1387)[9]

But the sisters of Elstow remain on good terms with their neighbours, Bishop Flemyng forbids the nuns "to have access to the town of Bedford or to the town of Elstow or to other towns or

---

[1] *Reg Sede Vacante* (Worc Hist Soc), p 276
[2] *Reg Ralph of Shrewsbury*, p 241
[3] *Reg Walter de Stapeldon*, p 317.
[4] *A Boke of Precedence*, ed F J Furnivall (E.E.T.S Extra Ser. VIII), p 39.
[5] *The Wife of Bath's Prologue*, ll 545-7
[6] *Reg Epis Peckham* (Rolls Ser.), II, p 664
[7] *Linc. Visit* II, p 114. Cf Gray's injunction in 1432 *Visit of Relig Houses in Dioc. of Linc.* I, p 67
[8] *Linc. Epis. Reg Memo Gynewell*, f 139d
[9] *Linc Epis Reg Memo Bokyngham*, f 343

neighbouring places" and straitly enjoins the canons "that no
canon of the said priory, under what colour of excuse soever,
have access to the monastery of the nuns of Elstow; nor shall
the same nuns for any reason whatever be allowed to enter the
said priory, save for a manifest cause, from which reproach or
suspicion of evil could in no way arise; nor even shall the same
canons and nuns meet in any wise one with another, in any
separate or private places; nor shall they talk together anywhere
one with another, save in the presence and hearing of more than
one trustworthy, who shall bear faithful witness of what they
say or do" (1421–2)[1] The nuns of Nuncoton in the sixteenth
century are even more addicted to the society of canons and
Bishop Longland writes to them in stern language:

And that ye, lady prioresse, cause and compell all your susters (those
oonly excepte that be seke) to kepe the quere and nomore to be
absent as in tymes past they haue been wont to use, being content
yf vj haue been present, the residue to goo att lybertie where they
wold, some att thornton [Augustinian house at Thornton-upon-
Humber], some at Newsom [or Newhouse, a Premonstratensian
house close to Nuncoton, in the same parish of Brocklesby], some at
hull, some att other places att their pleasures, which is in the sight
of good men abhomynable, high displeasur to God, rebuke shame and
reproache to religion and due correction to be doon according unto
your religion frome tyme to tyme[2].

Indeed these colloquies with monks and canons in their own
monastery were nothing unusual. Bishops and Councils constantly forbade nuns to frequent houses of monks, or to be
received there as guests, but the practice continued. Sometimes
they had an excuse; the nuns of St Mary's, Winchester, were in
the habit of going to St Swithun's monastery to confess to one
of the brothers, who was their confessor and in ill-health, and
Bishop Pontoise appointed another monk in his place, who
should come to the nuns when summoned, thus avoiding the
risk of scandal[3]. Similarly Peckham forbade the nuns of Holy
Sepulchre, Canterbury, to enter "any place of religious men or
elsewhere, under colour of confessing," unless they had no other
confessor, in which case they were to return directly their business

---

[1] *Visit. of Relig Houses in Dioc Linc.* I, pp. 25, 51.
[2] *Archaeologia*, XLVII, p 57
[3] *Reg. Johannis de Pontissara.* pp. 251–2

was accomplished and not to stay eating and drinking there[1]. But sometimes the nuns had less good reason At Elstow, as we know, they gossiped in the fields and highways; and if nuns were sometimes frivolous, so were monks. What are we to think of that nun of Catesby (gone to rack and ruin under the evil rule of Margaret Wavere), who

on Monday last did pass the night with the Austin friars at Northampton and did dance and play the lute with them in the same place until midnight (saltauit et citherauit usque ad mediam noctem) and on the night following she passed the night with the Friars preachers at Northampton, luting and dancing in like manner[2]

There rises to the memory an irresistibly comic sonnet of Wordsworth:

Yet more—round many a convent's blazing fire
Unhallowed threads of revelry are spun;
There Venus sits disguised like a nun,—
While Bacchus, clothed in semblance of a friar
Pours out his choicest beverage high and higher
Sparkling, until it cannot choose but run
Over the bowl, whose silver lip hath won
An instant kiss of masterful desire—
To stay the precious waste Through every brain
The domination of the sprightly juice
Spreads high conceits to madding Fancy dear,
Till the arched roof, with resolute abuse
Of its grave echoes, swells a choral strain,
Whose votive burthen is "Our kingdom's here."

Alack, had the nun of Catesby forgotten that "even as the cow which goeth before the herd hath a bell at her neck, so likewise the woman who leadeth the song and dance hath, as it were, the devil's bell bound to hers, and when the devil heareth the tinkle thereof he feeleth safe, and saith he: 'I have not lost my cow yet'"?[3] Had she forgotten the awful vision of that holy

---

[1] *Reg Epis Peckham* (Rolls Ser), II, p 707

[2] *Linc Visit* II, p 50 With this account of the entertainment provided by the Friars of Northampton for their visitors, compare the evidence given at Bishop Nykke's visitation of the Cathedral priory of Norwich in 1514. "Item, the Brethren are wont to dance in the guesten-house, by favour of the guest-master, by night (and) up to noon " *Visit of the Dioc. of Norwich* (Camden Soc), p 75 One of the Bishop's *comperta* was that suspicious women had access to the house of the guest-master, which throws further light on the Catesby case Incidentally the latter bears out Chaucer's description of the Friar, who was so fond of harping

[3] *Exempla e sermonibus vulgaribus Jacobi Vitriacensis*, ed T F Crane, p 131

PLATE VII

"Isabel Benet did pass the night with the Austin friars at Northampton and did dance and play the lute with them." (See page 388.)

The Legend of Beatrice the Sacristan. (See page 511.)

THE NUN WHO LOVED THE WORLD

man, to whom the devil appeared in the form of a tiny blacka-
moor, standing above a woman who was leading a dance, guiding
her about as he wished and dancing on her head?[1] But indeed
Isabel (or Venus) Benet was not the woman to care for so slight
a matter as the rule of her order or the dreams of holy men[2].
Her case provides an admirable illustration of the motives which
prompted the extreme severity of episcopal attempts to enforce
enclosure and to cut nuns off from the society of neighbouring
monasteries[3].

Even if they did not often go to such extremes as to spend
a night dancing with friars, the nuns foregathered sometimes in
the most strange places. The complaint that priests and monks
and canons were tavern-haunters occurs with wearisome iteration
in medieval visitation documents, but surely a tavern was the
last place where one would expect to find a nun; "Deus sit
propitius isti potatori," were a strange invocation on lips that
prayed to "Our blisful lady, Cristes moder dere." Yet nuns
sometimes abused their liberty to frequent such places. Archbishop Rotherham wrote to the Prioress of Nunappleton in
1489 "yat noon of your sistirs use ye alehouse nor ye watirside,
wher concurse of straungers dayly resortes"[4], and at Romsey
in 1492 Abbess Elizabeth Broke deposed that she suspected the
nuns of slipping into town by the church door and prayed that
they might not frequent taverns and other suspected places,
while her Prioress also said that they frequented taverns and
continually went to town without leave[5]. Bald statements, but
it is easy to call up a picture of what lies behind them, for of
medieval taverns we have many a description touched by master
hands So we shall see nuns at the tunning of Elynour Rummynge,
edging in by the back way "over the hedge and pale," to drink
her noppy ale[6] Or again we shall see Beton the Brewster standing
in her doorway beneath the ivy bush, hailing Dame Isabel and
Dame Matilda, as they patter along upon their "fete ful tendre";
and we shall hear her seductive cry "I have good ale, gossip"
(no nun ever despised good ale—only when it was *valde tenuis* did

[1] *Anecdotes Historiques, etc. d'Etienne de Bourbon,* ed. Lecoy de La
Marche, p. 229   [2] See below, p. 460
   [3] See also below, pp 448–50.   [4] Dugdale, *Mon* v, p. 654.
   [5] Liveing, *Records of Romsey Abbey,* p 218
   [6] *Poetical Works of John Skelton,* ed. Dyce, ı, p 95

she object) "I have peper and piones and a pounde of garlike,
A ferthyngworth of fenel-seed for fasting days." We shall never
—thanks to Langland—have any difficulty in seeing that interior, when the nuns have scuttled through the door, the heat,
the smell of ale and perspiring humanity, the babel of voices as
all the riff-raff of the village greets the nuns and gives them
"with glad chere good ale to hansel"; and the scene that follows,
"the laughyng and lowryng and 'let go the cuppe,'" the
singing, the gambling, the drinking, the invincible good humour
and the complete lack of all decency. We can only hope that
Dame Isabel and Dame Matilda left before Glutton got drunk[1].
But it is consoling to reflect that the alehouses frequented by
the nuns of Nunappleton and of Romsey were probably less low
places, for it is not easy to picture Chaucer's Prioress on a bench
between Clarice of Cokkeslane and Peronelle of Flanders.
Probably their taverns at the waterside were more like the
Chequer-on-the-Hoop, where Madame Eglentyne and the Wife
of Bath pledged each other in the hostess' parlour[2]; or like the
tavern where the good gossips

>   Elynore, Jone and Margery
>   Margaret, Alis and Cecely

met and feasted, all unknown to their husbands and cherished
the heart with muscadel[3]; or liker still, perhaps, to that lordly
tavern kept by Trick, where the city dames come tripping in
the morning, as readily as to minster or to market and where
he draws them ten sorts of wine, all out of a single cask, crying:
"dear ladies, Mesdames, make good cheer, drink freely your
good pleasure, for we have leisure enough"[4] But however select
the house, whether they met there buxom city dames drinking
away their husbands' credit, or merely Tim the tinker and twain
of his prentices, whether they were quizzed by "those idle
gallants who haunt taverns, gay and handsome," or hobnobbed
with "travellers and tinkers, sweaters and swinkers," the alehouse was assuredly no place for nuns[5].

[1] Langland, *Piers Plowman*, ed Skeat, Text B, Passus v, ll 304 ff
[2] See above, p 373
[3] *Songs and Carols*, ed Th Wright (Percy Soc), pp 91-5
[4] Gower, *Mirour de l'Omne*, ed G C Macaulay, p 289 Translated in
Coulton, *Med. Garn* pp 577-8
[5] At Esholt in 1535 Archbishop Lee even had to enjoin "that the
prioress suffer no ale house to be kept within the precinct of the gates of

Enough has been said to show why the authorities of the Church tried so hard to force enclosure upon nuns, and why they strove at least to limit excursions to "necessary occasions" and "convent business," to prevent unlicensed wandering and to provide that no nun went out without a companion. And enough has perhaps also been said to show how completely they failed The modern student of monasticism, bred in an age which regards freedom as its *summum bonum* and holds discipline at a discount, cannot but feel sympathy with the nuns. The enclosure movement did go beyond the restriction imposed upon them by their rule; they were themselves so often unsuited to the life into which circumstances, rather than a vocation, had forced them; and they would have been something less than human if they had not answered—as John of Ayton made them answer—"In truth the men who made these laws sat well at their ease while they laid such burdens upon us " It was the bishops, not the popes and the councils, who knew where the shoe pinched Dalderby, rubbing his insulted shoulders, Alnwick, laboriously framing his minute injunctions, Rigaud, going away from Saint-Saens "quasi impaciens et tristis," these had little time to sit well at their ease; and the compromises which were forced upon them are the best proof that the ideal of *Periculoso* was too high. Nevertheless sympathy with the nuns must not blind us to the fact that hardly a moralist of the middle ages but inveighs against the wandering of nuns in the world and adds his testimony to the fact (already clear from the visitation

the saide monasterie " *Yorks Arch Journ.* XVI, p 452. An explanation of this may be found by comparing the evidence at Archbishop Warham's visitation of the Hospital of St James outside Canterbury in 1511 "The Prioress complains that Richard Welles stays and talks in the precincts of the house and his wife sells beer in the precincts They are very quarrelsome people, brawlers and sowers of discord There is always a crowd of people at the house of Richard." *E H.R* VI, p 22 At both these houses the nuns probably employed a secular alewife to make their beer and she sold also to other customers within their precincts Compare Peckham's injunction to Wherwell in 1284: "Iterum ob Dei reverentiam et ecclesiae honestatem perpetuo inhibemus ne mercatores sedere in ecclesia cum suis mercibus permittantur " *Reg Epis Johannis Peckham* (Rolls Ser.), II, p. 654. Also Bishop Bokyngham's letter forbidding merchants to sell their wares in the conventual church or churchyard of Stainfield under pain of excommunication (1392) *V C H. Lincs* II, p. 131. Medieval churches were put to strange uses They served sometimes as a market-place, sometimes as a granary, sometimes as a playground, sometimes as a stage

comperta) that all the graver abuses which discredited monasticism rose in the first instance from the too great ease with which monks and nuns could leave their convents "De la clôture," as St François de Sales wrote long afterwards, "dépend le bon ordre de tout le reste" It is significant that on the very eve of the Reformation in England a last attempt was made to enforce a strict and literal enclosure. That ardent reformer of nunneries, Bishop Fox, frankly pursued the policy in his diocese of Winchester and was apparently accused of undue severity, for in 1528 he wrote to Wolsey in defence of his action:

Truth it is, my lord, that the religious women of my diocese be restrained of their going out of their monasteries. And yet so much liberty appeareth some time too much; and if I had the authority and power that your grace hath, I would endeavour me to mure and enclose their monasteries according to the observance of good religion And in all other matters, concerning their living or observance of their religion, I assure your grace they be as liberally and favourably dealt with as be any religious women within this realm[1].

Wolsey himself was driven to the same conclusion as to the necessity of enclosure, and tried to enforce it at Wilton, after the scandals which came to light there before the election of Isabel Jordan as Abbess. His chaplain, Dr Benet, who had been sent to reform the nunnery, wrote to him on July 18th and described his difficulty in "causing to be observed" the unpopular decree

Please it your grace to be advertised, that immediately after my return from your grace I repaired to the monastery of Wilton, where I have continually made mine abode hitherto and with all diligence endeavoured myself to the uttermost of my power to persuade and train the nuns there to the accomplishment of your grace's pleasure for enclosing of the same; whom I find so untoward and refusal (*sic*) as I never saw persons, insomuch that in nowise any of them, neither by gentle means nor by rigorous,—and I have put three or four of the captains of them in ward,—will agree and consent to the same, but only the new elect and her sisters that were with your grace, which notwithstanding, I have closed up certain doors and ways and taken such an order there that none access, course or recourse of any person shall be made there[2].

About the same time the Abbess-Elect herself wrote to Wolsey, telling him that:

[1] Wood, *Letters of Royal and Illustrious Ladies*, II, p. 35, note *b*
[2] Wood, *op. cit.* pp 35–6

since my coming home I have ordered me in all things to the best of my power, according to your gracious advertisement by the advice of your chancellors and have ofttime motioned my sisters to be re-clused within our monastery; wherein they do find many difficulties and show divers considerations to the contrary;

she besought him to have patience and promised to "order my sisters in such religious wise and our monastery according to the rule of religion, without any such resort as hath been of late accustomed"[1]. Evidently nuns had not changed since the day when the sisters of Markyate threw the Bull *Periculoso* at Bishop Dalderby's retreating back.

But their struggles were in vain and a worse fate awaited them The Dissolution of the monasteries by Henry VIII was preceded by an order to his commissioners, that they should enforce enclosure upon the nuns. The injunction met with the usual resistance at the time and later apologists of the monastic houses have blamed the King for undue and unreasonable harshness. But if Henry VIII was too strict, so also was Ottobon, so Peckham, so Boniface VIII, so almost every bishop and council of the past three hundred years. In this at least, low as his motives may have been, the man who was to claim the headship of the English Church was the lineal descendant of the most masterful of medieval popes. The instructions given to the commissioners were the last of a long series of injunctions, in which it was attempted to reform the nunneries by shutting them off from the world. It is plain that even in the thirteenth century some such reform was necessary, and the history of the fourteenth, fifteenth and sixteenth centuries only shows the necessity becoming more urgent. Whatever may have been Henry VIII's motives, how-ever greedy, however licentious, however unspiritual, it would be impossible to contend that his decree of enclosure was not in accordance with the best ecclesiastical tradition and amply justified by the condition of the monastic houses

[1] Wood, *op. cit.* pp 36–37 (No xv).

CHAPTER X

THE WORLD IN THE CLOISTER

Ès maisons de nonnains aucun sont bien venut,
Et as gens festyer n'a nul règne tenut,
On y va volentiers et souvent et menut
Mais mieuls sont festyet jovène que li kenut
                                 GILLES LI MUISIS († 1352).

In the last chapter the question of enclosure was considered only
from one point of view, that of keeping the nuns within the
precincts of their cloister. But there was another side to the
problem In order to preserve them unspotted from the world
it was necessary not only that the nuns should keep within their
cloisters, but that secular persons should keep outside. It was
useless to pass regulations forbidding nuns to leave their houses,
if visitors from the world had easy access to them and could
move freely about within the precincts Ottobon, Peckham,
Boniface VIII, Henry VIII, and all who legislated on the subject
from the earliest years to the Council of Trent, combined a
prohibition against the entrance of seculars, with their prohibition against the exit of nuns[1]. Some intercourse with seculars was
bound to occur, even in the best regulated nunnery. The nuns
·were often served by layfolk and it was a recognised obligation
that they should show hospitality to guests In both cases they
were of necessity brought in contact with worldly folk, and as
usual they made the most of their opportunity.

Even more disturbing to monastic discipline were the casual
visits of friends in the neighbourhood, coming to see and talk
with the nuns for a few hours. Visitation documents show that
there was a steady intercourse between the convent and the
world. Letters and messages passed between the nuns and their
friends outside, and a great many of the private affairs of the
convent found their way to the ears of seculars. "From miln and

---

[1] On this subject see Part II of Thiers' treatise *De la Clôture*, pp 265-497.

from market, from smithy and from nunnery, men bring tidings"
ran the proverb[1], and complaints were common that the secrets
of the chapter were spread abroad in the country side. At the
ill-conducted house of Catesby in 1442 the Prioress (herself the
blackest sheep in all the flock) complained that

secular folk have often recourse to the nuns' chambers within the
cloister, and talkings and junketings take place there without the
knowledge of the Prioress,....also the nuns do send out letters and
receive letters sent to them without the advice of the prioress Also...
that the secrets of the house are disclosed in the neighbourhood by
such seculars when they come there. Also the nuns do send out the
serving-folk of the priory on their businesses and do also receive the
persons for whom they send and with whom they hold parleyings and
conversations, whereof the Prioress is ignorant[2].

At Goring in 1530 the Prioress complained that one of the nuns
persisted in sending messages to her friends[3], and at Romsey
in 1509 Alice, wife of William Coke, the cook of the nunnery,
was enjoined "that she shall not be a messenger or bearer of
messages or troths or tokens between any nun and any lay person
on pain of excommunication and as much as in her lies shall
hinder communications of lay persons with nuns at the kitchen
window"[4]. At St Helen's, Bishopsgate, it was even necessary to
order the nuns to refrain from kissing secular persons[5].

Sometimes the visitation *detecta* or *comperta* or injunctions
give specific details as to the visitors who were most assiduous
in haunting a nunnery. It is amusing to follow the reference
to scholars of Oxford in the records of those houses which were
in the neighbourhood of the University. Godstow was the nearest
and the students seem to have regarded it as a happy hunting
ground constituted specially for their recreation Peckham, in
his set of Latin injunctions to the Abbey, wrote after giving
minute regulations as to the terms upon which nuns might
converse with visitors:

When the scholars of Oxford come to talk with you, we wish no nun
to join in such conversations, save with the licence of the Abbess

---

[1] *Ancren Riwle* (King's Classics), p 67.
[2] *Linc. Visit.* II, pp 46–7 The Benedictine rule runs. "It is by no
means lawful, without the abbot's permission, for any monk to receive or
give letters, presents and gifts of any kind to anyone, whether parent or
other." Cap. LIV.
[3] *V C H. Oxon.* II, p. 104   [4] Liveing, *op. cit.* p. 232.
[5] *Hist MSS Com Report*, IX, App p. 57 (early fifteenth century).

and unless they be notoriously of kin to her, in the third grade of consanguinity at least, we order the nuns to refuse to converse with all scholars so coming, nor shall you desire to be united in any special tie of familiarity with them, for such affection often excites unclean thoughts[1].

The most detailed information, however, is to be found in the injunctions sent by Bishop Gray to Godstow in 1432:

That no nun receive any secular person for any recreation in the nuns' chambers under pain of excommunication. For the scholars of Oxford say they can have all manner of recreation with the nuns, even as they will desire ..Also that the recourse of scholars of Oxford to the monastery be altogether checked and restrained ...Also that (neither) the gatekeeper of the monastery, nor any other secular person convey any gifts, rewards, letters or tokens from the nuns to any scholars of Oxford or other secular person whomsoever, or bring back any such scholars or persons to the same nuns, nay, not even skins containing wine, without the view and knowledge of the abbess and with her special licence asked and had, under pain of expulsion from his office (and) from the said monastery for ever; and if any nun shall do the contrary she shall undergo imprisonment for a year[2]

In a commission addressed two years later to the Abbot of Oseney and to Master Robert Thornton the Bishop spoke in very severe terms of the bad behaviour of the nuns, and ordered the commissioners to proceed to Godstow and to inquire whether a nun, who had been with child at the time of his visitation, had been preferred to any office or had gone outside the precincts and whether his other injunctions had been obeyed, especially "if any scholars of the university of Oxford, graduate or non-graduate, have had access to the same monastery or lodging in the same, contrary to the form of our injunctions aforesaid"[3]. But the situation was unchanged when, thirteen years later,

---

[1] *Reg Epis J Peckham*, III, p 847 From a letter which he wrote to the Abbess on Nov 12, 1284, it appears that the Prioress had been defamed of incontinence, for, while professing his belief in her innocence, he repeated his prohibition of casual conversation between nuns and seculars, adding "Oveke ceo nous defendons de part Deu ke nule nonein ne parle a escoler de Oxeneford, se il nest sun parent prechein, e ovekes ceo saunz le conge la abbesse especial E ceo meismes entendons nous de touj prestres foreins, le queus font mout de maus en mout de lus, e aussi de touj religieus ki ne venent pur precher u pur confesser oue lautorite le apostoile e le eveske de Nichole" *Ib* III, p 851 Compare an injunction to Nunmonkton in 1397 "Item non permittatis clericos prioratum vestrum frequentare absque causa rationabili" Dugdale, *Mon.* IV, p 194
[2] *Linc. Visit* I, pp 67-8.
[3] *Ib* p. 65

Alnwick came to Godstow. Elizabeth Felmersham, the Abbess, deposed

that secular folk have often access to the nuns during the divine office in quire, and to the frater at meal-time ..She cannot restrain students from Oxford from having common access in her despite to the monastery and the claustral precincts The nuns hold converse with the secular folk that come to visit the monastery, without asking any leave of the abbess.

Other nuns deposed that sister Alice Longspey[1] often conversed in the convent church with Hugh Sadler, a priest from Oxford, who obtained access to her on the plea that she was his kinswoman and that Dame Katherine Okeley:

holds too much talk with the strangers that come to the monastery in the church, in the chapter-house, at the church-door, the hall door and divers other places; nor is she obedient to the orders and commands of the abbess according to the rule[2].

Other houses also found the clerks of Oxford too attractive. At Alnwick's visitation of Littlemore Dame Agnes Marcham (a lady with a tongue) spoke of "the ill-fame which is current thereabouts concerning the place," and said

that a certain monk of Rievaulx, who is a student at Oxford and is of the Cistercian order, has common and often access to the priory, eating and drinking with the prioress and spending the night therein, sometimes for three, sometimes for four days on end Also she says that master John Herars, master in arts, a scholar of Oxford and a kinsman of the prioress, has access in like manner to the priory, breakfasting, supping and spending the night in the same[3].

The state of the house in the sixteenth century was infinitely worse and it well merited its early suppression in 1526[4]. At another house, Studley, visited by Alnwick in 1445, the significant request was made

that the vicar of Bicester, who is reckoned to be of ripe judgment and age and sufficient knowledge, may be appointed as confessor to the

---

[1] See below, p. 449

[2] *Linc. Visit.* II, p 114   Alnwick made a very strong injunction· "For as mykelle as your saide monastery and diuerse singulere persones ther of are greuously noysed and sclaundred for the grete and contynuelle accesse and recourse of seculere and regulere persones, and in specyalle of scolers of Oxenford to your said monastery and seculere persones ther of, that fro hense forthe ye suffre no seculere persones scolers no othere.. to hafe any accesse or recourse to your said monastery ne to any singulere persone ther of, ne there to abyde nyght ne daye, etc" *Ib* pp. 115–6

[3] *Ib* II, p 218   [4] See *V C.H Oxon* II, pp. 76–7.

convent and in no wise an Oxford scholar, since it is not healthy that scholars of Oxford should have a reason for coming to the priory[1].

Nor does the proximity of Cambridge appear to have had a less disturbing effect upon morals and discipline. In 1373 it was found that the Prioress of St Radegund's

did not correct Dame Elizabeth de Cambridge for withdrawing herself from divine service and allowing friars of different orders, as well as scholars, to visit her at inopportune times and to converse with her, to the scandal of religion[2],

and in 1496, when John Alcock, Bishop of Ely, converted the nunnery into the college afterwards known as Jesus College, its dilapidation was ascribed to "the negligence and improvidence and dissolute disposition and incontinence of the religious women of the same house, by reason of the vicinity of Cambridge University"[3]. Plainly the scholars who hung about the portals and tethered their horses in the paddocks of Godstow, and who gossiped with the sisters of Studley and Littlemore and St Radegund's, were not of the type of that clerk of Oxenford, who loved his twenty red and black-clad books better than "robes riche or fithele or gay sautrye"; and it is to be feared that their speech was not "souninge in moral vertu." Rather they belonged to the tribe of Absolon, who could trip and dance in twenty manners:

> After the scole of Oxenforde tho,
> And with his legges casten to and fro,
> And pleyen songes on a small rubible,

or of hende Nicholas ("of derne love he coude and of solas"), or of those two clerks of Cambridge, Aleyn and John, who harboured with the Miller of Trumpington, or of "joly Jankin," the Wife of Bath's first husband. The nuns certainly got no good from these young men of light heart and slippery tongue.

Sometimes, as it appears from the cases of Alice Longspey, Katherine Okeley and Elizabeth de Cambridge, certain nuns rendered themselves particularly conspicuous for intercourse with seculars, or certain men were assiduous nunnery-haunters and forbidden by name to frequent the precincts. At a visita-

---

[1] *Op. cit.* f 26d.
[2] Gray, *Priory of St Radegund, Cambridge*, p 35
[3] Dugdale, *Mon* IV, p. 190 See below p 602.

tion of St Sepulchre's, Canterbury, in 1367-8, it was found that

Dame Johanna Chivynton, prioress there, does not govern well the rule nor the religion of the house, because she permits the rector of Dover Castle and other suspect persons to have too much access to sisters Margery Chyld and Juliana Aldelesse, who have a room contrary to the injunction made there on another occasion by the Lord [Archbishop], and these suspect persons often spend the night there[1].

At Nuncoton in 1531 Longland writes:

We chardge you, lady prioresse, undere payne of excommunicacon that ye from hensforth nomore suffre Sir John Warde, Sir Richard Caluerley, Sir William Johnson, nor parson..., ne the parson of Skotton, ne Sir William Sele to come within the precincts of your monasterye, that if they by chance do unwares to you that ye streight banish them and suffre not theme ther to tary, nor noone of your sustres to commune with them or eny of them   And that ye voyde out of your house Robert lawrence and he nomore resorte to the same[2].

Incidents such as these can be multiplied from the records of episcopal visitations[3] and general complaints are even more common. It appears that secular persons set at naught the rule

---

[1] *Lambeth Reg. Langham*, f 76d Compare the note in Alnwick's visitation of Studley (1445) "Sister Isabel Bartone It is said that there is great recourse of seculare guests to the aforesaid Isabel and to her chamber " *Alnwick's Visit* MS f 26d

[2] *Archaeologia*, XLVII, p 57

[3] A few more examples may be quoted At Swine one of the *comperta* of Giffard's visitation in 1267-8 runs. "The household of Sir Robert de Hilton, knight, wanders about far too freely (*nimis dissolute*) in the cloister and parlour, and often holds very suspicious conversations with the nuns and sisters, whence it is feared that harm may come And this same Robert is very injurious and dangerous to them, wherefore, for fear of his oppression, the canons of the house lately, without the consent of the convent, gave him a barn full of corn, with which the convent should have been maintained " *Reg Walter Giffard*, p 148 At Nunmonkton in 1397 the Prioress, Margaret Fairfax, was ordered to see that John Munkton (the same who scandalised the convent by feasting and playing tables with her in her room), Sir William Aschby, chaplain, William Snowe and Thomas Pape held no conversation nor kept company with her, nor with any nun of her house, except in the presence of two of the elder nuns, and she was warned not to allow clerks to frequent the priory without reasonable cause Dugdale, *Mon* IV, p 194. At Rusper in 1524 "a certain William Tychenor has frequent access to the said priory and there sows discord between the prioress and sisters and others living there " *Sussex Arch Coll* v, p 257 It will be noticed how often these suspected visitors are clerics, the prefix "sir" in the Nuncoton extract quoted in the text almost certainly denotes a churchman and the persons mentioned are probably secular clergy or canons from neighbouring houses such as Newhouse, probably chantry-priests and parish chaplains See below, p 416

which confined them to the prioress' hall, the parlour and the guest-house, and penetrated at will into the private parts of the monastery, haunting now the cloister, now the infirmary, now the frater, now the choir[1] Bishop Gynewell's injunction to Heynings in 1351 called attention to a state of affairs which was common enough in the century which opened with *Periculoso*:

"Because," he wrote, "we have heard that great disturbance of your religion hath been made by seculars, who enter into your cloister and choir, we charge you that henceforth ye suffer no secular man, save your patron or other great lord[2] to enter your cloister, nor to hold therein parley or other dalliance with any sister of your house, whereby your silence or religion may suffer blame"[3].

Moreover it is clear that the nuns sometimes escaped to the guest-house to enjoy a gossip with their visitors; at Alnwick's visitation of Heynings in 1440 a lay sister deposed "that the nuns do hold drinkings of evenings in the guest-chamber even after compline, especially when their friends come to visit them" and the Bishop enjoined

for as muche as we founde that there are vsede late drynkynges and talkyng by nunnes as wele wythe yn as wythe owte the cloystere wythe seculeres, where thurgh some late ryse to matynes and some come not at thayme, expressly agayns the rule of your ordere, we

---

[1] The following examples are typical of a host of others At Nunapple-ton (1281) external visitors come into frater and cloister *Reg William Wickwane*, p 141 At Rosedale (1306) the infirmary is to be kept from the passing to and fro of seculars, at Arthington (1318) they are not to frequent cloister, infirmary or other private places, at Nunburnholme (1318) there is scandal from the frequent access and gossiping of seculars with certain of the nuns *V.C H Yorks.* III, pp 119, 174. At Ickleton (1345) the pre-cincts are not to be made the resort of any secular woman, nor is any such person to come into the choir during the hours of service Goddard, *Ickleton Church and Priory (Cambridge Antiq Soc Proc* XLV, p 190) At Gracedieu (1440–1) seculars and nuns eat together *commixtim* in the Prioress' hall *Linc Visit* II, p 122. At Heynings (1440) the infirmary was occupied by secular folk, "to the great disturbance of the sisters" *Ib.* p 133 At Romsey (1492) people stand about chatting in the middle of the choir Liveing, *op cit* p 220.

[2] On the right of the patron or founder of a monastery, or of persons of noble birth, to enter the cloistral precincts, see Thiers, *op. cit* pp 296–309 He quotes the rule of Fontevrault (cap VII) "If the most Christian King, the Queen, the Dauphin and other princes of the blood-royal, the founders and foundresses, being instantly besought, refuse nevertheless to desist from entering the precincts, let them enter with as small a suite of attendants as you can arrange, in long and decent garments and not otherwise; but let them not seek to pass the night on pain of excommunication" *Ib* p 297. It was never possible in practice to keep out great lords and ladies

[3] *Linc Epis Reg Memo Gynewell,* f 34d

charge yow and yche oon singulere that fro this day forthe ye neyther vse spekyng ne drynkyng in no place aftere complyne, but that after collacyone and complyne sayde ych oon of yow go wythe owte lengere tarying to the dormytorye to your reste[1].

In the course of time a series of regulations was devised to govern the entrance of seculars into the nunneries, hardly less detailed· than those which governed the visits of nuns to the world. An attempt was made to prevent certain classes of persons from being allowed to sleep in a house; also to keep all visitors out of certain places and during certain hours, and elaborate rules were made fixing the conditions under which nuns might hold conversations or exchange letters with seculars. The rule which forbade nuns to harbour in houses of religious men was often supplemented by a regulation forbidding friars, or other men belonging to religious orders, from being received as guests by nuns. At Godstow in 1284 Peckham forbade the reception of religious men for the night[2] and in 1358 Bishop Gynewell enjoined the same convent "for certain reasons, that no friars of any order whatever be harboured by night within the doors of your house, nor by day save it be for great necessity and reasonable cause, and not habitually"[3]. William of Wykeham directed a special mandate on the subject to Wherwell in 1368·

"Lately," he says, "it has come to our ears by popular report of trusty men, that contrary to the honesty of religion you admit various religious men, especially of the mendicant orders, lightly and promiscuously to pass the night in your habitations, from which grows much matter for laxity and scandal, since the cohabitation of religious clerks and nuns is altogether forbidden by the constitutions of the holy fathers."

[1] *Linc Visit* II, pp 133–5, *passim* Compare the injunctions to some Yorkshire houses at Marrick (1252) the nuns were forbidden to sit with guests or anyone else outside the cloister after curfew, or for a long time unless the guests arrived so late that it was impossible to serve them sooner, nor was a nun to remain alone with a guest. At Hampole (1302) no nun except the *hostillaria* was to eat or drink in the guest-house, save with worthy people, and at Wilberfoss (1302) they were forbidden to linger in the guest-house or elsewhere, for amusement with seculars *V.C H Yorks* III, pp 117, 126, 163 At Elstow in 1432, however, Bishop Gray enjoined "that when parents or friends or kinsfolk of nuns, or other persons of note and honesty, shall journey to the same monastery to visit any nuns of the said monastery, the same nuns be nowise bound for that day to observance of frater, but be excused to this end by grace of the abbess or president." *Visit of Relig Houses in Dioc Linc* I, p 54.
[2] *Reg Epis J Peckham*, III, pp 851–2.
[3] *Linc Epis Reg Memo, Gynewell*, f. 100d

He proceeds to forbid the reception of friars or other religious men to lodge in the abbey, though food might be given them in alms[1] As in the rules regulating visits paid by nuns, attempts were sometimes made though not insisted upon with any severity, to restrict the visitors who might spend the night to near relatives. At Godstow, for instance, Bishop Gray ordered in 1432 that strangers "in no wise pass the night there, unless they be father and mother, brother and sister of that nun for whose sake they have so come to the monastery"[2]; and Archbishop Lee wrote to Sinningthwaite in 1534 forbidding any visitor to have recourse to the Prioress or nuns "onles it be their fathers or moders or other ther nere kynesfolkes, in whom no suspicion of any yll can be thought"[3].

The chief efforts of the authorities were, however, directed not towards keeping certain persons altogether out of the nunneries, but towards keeping all visitors out of certain parts of the house and during certain hours. The general rule was that no secular was to enter after sunset or curfew, and elaborate arrangements were made for locking and unlocking the doors at certain times. At Esholt and Sinningthwaite Archbishop Lee enjoined

that the prioress provide sufficient lockes and keys to be sett upon the cloyster doores, incontinent after recept of thies injunctions and that the same doores surely be lockid every nyght incontinent as complane is doone, and not to be unlocked in wynter season to vij of the clock in the mornyng and in sommer vnto vj of the clock in the mornyng, and that the prioresse kepe the keyes of the same doores, or committ the custodie of them to such a discrete and religious suster, that no fault nor negligence may be imputed to the prioresse, as she will avoyde punyshment due for the same[4]

[1] *Wykeham's Reg* II, pp 73-4   The special prohibition of friars is significant, for their reputation was growing worse and worse throughout the fourteenth and fifteenth centuries   See also *V C H Yorks* III, pp 164, 171, 181 and *Arch.* XLVII, p 57 On the other hand it should be noted that "during the later thirteenth and earlier fourteenth centuries the bishops in many dioceses made a point of insisting that the confessors to the nuns should be chosen, not from the secular clergy, but from the Mendicant Orders, especially from the Minorites." A G Little, *Studies in English Franciscan Hist* (1917), p 119 (and the references which he gives).

[2] *Visit of Relig Houses in Dioc Linc* I, p 66

[3] *Yorks Arch Journ* XVI, p 441 Compare Alnwick's injunctions to Catesby (1442), Langley (1440-1) and St Michael's, Stamford (1440). *Linc Visit* II, pp 51, 117, *Alnwick's* MS f. 83*d*

[4] *Yorks Arch Journ* XVI, p. 452 (cf p 440) These injunctions were

PLATE VIII

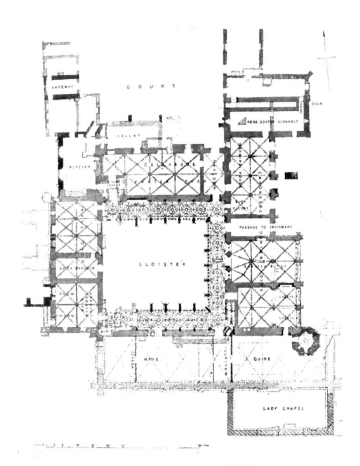

PLAN OF LACOCK ABBEY

At the same time, for better security, he ordered the nuns to be locked into their dorter every night until service time. Sometimes the nuns objected to being shut in the house so early in the summer time, when the days were long and the trees in the convent garden green The nuns of Sheppey were plaintive on the subject in 1511. Amicia Tanfeld said

that the gate of the cloister is closed immediately after the bell rings for vespers and remains shut until it rings for prime[1], this, in the opinion of the convent is too strict, especially in summer time, because it might remain open until after supper, as she says.

Elizabeth Chatok, *cantarista*[2], said the same "clauditur nimis tempestive tempore presertim estiuali"; perhaps she was thinking of better singers than herself, who piped their vespers outside that closed door,

> And songen, everich in his wyse
> The most solempne servyse
> By note, that ever man, I trowe,
> Had herd, for som of hem song lowe
> Some hye and al of oon accord[3].

Her sisters agreed with her, but the stern archbishop took no notice of their plaints[4].

Strict regulations were also made for keeping secular visitors out of certain parts of the convent The dorter, frater, fermery, chapter and cloister and the internal offices of the house were supposed to be entered only by the nuns[5]:

very common, for the rule was often broken. Peckham's regulation for Wherwell (1284) was that no man was to enter after sunset at night, or before the end of chapter (which followed directly after Prime) in the morning. *Reg. Epis. J. Peckham*, II, p. 653. For other examples see Romsey (1302–11), Liveing, *op cit* pp. 102, 103, Moxby (1318), *V.C H. Yorks.* III, p 239, Sopwell (1338), Dugdale, *Mon* III, p. 366; Wroxall (1338), *Worc Reg. Sede Vacante*, p. 275; Heynings (1351), *Linc Epis Reg. Memo. Gynewell*, f 34d; Elstow (1387), *ib*, *Reg Memo. Bokyngham*, f. 343; St Mary's Neasham (1436), *V C H Durham*, II, p 107; St Helen's, Bishopsgate (1439), Dugdale, *Mon.* IV, p. 552, Nunappleton (1489), *V C H. Yorks* III, p 172; Studley (1530–1), *Archaeologia*, XLVII, p. 59, Nuncoton (1531), *ib.* pp. 56, 59.

[1] This certainly seems very strict, for (as appears from the injunctions quoted) it was customary to order the doors to be shut when the bell rang for Compline, the last office of the day Vespers was the service immediately before supper.

[2] *Cantarista* usually means a chantry-priest. The more usual word is *Precentrix*

[3] Chaucer, *Boke of the Duchesse*, ll 300–4   [4] *E H R* VI, pp. 33–4.

[5] This was reiterated in Ottobon's Constitutions and in the Bull *Periculoso*. See also Thomas of Cantilupe's letter to Lymbrook in 1277 (*Reg.*

"And in order that the quiet of your cloister be in future observed better than has been customary," wrote Peckham to the nuns of Wherwell in 1284, "we order...that no secular or religious person be permitted to enter the cloister, nor the interior offices, save for a manifest and inevitable reason, that is bodily infirmity, for which a confessor or doctor or near relative may be allowed to enter, but always in safe and praiseworthy company So that no one shall hear the confession of a healthy nun or woman in cloister or chapter or in the interior offices... And we consider healthy anyone who is able, conveniently and without danger to life, to enter the church or the parlour[1] "

At Romsey he further ordered four nuns to be made scrutineers: "Who shall expel from the cloister as suspect all persons of whatsoever condition wishing to stare at the nuns or to chatter with them"[2]. But the rule was constantly broken and it has been shown that seculars penetrated to all parts of the convents. Injunctions order them to be excluded now from dorter, now from frater, now from fermery, according as visitation showed them to be in the habit of entering one part of a house or another. Sometimes special orders were given for the making and locking of doors separating the cloister from the outside court, or the nuns' choir from the rest of the church, a necessary precaution when the nave of a conventual church was used as a parish church. Bishop Longland wrote to Elstow (1531):

Forasmoche as the more secrete religious persones be kepte from the sight and visage of the world and straungers, the more close and entyer ther mynd and devoc[i]on shalbe unto god, we ordeyn and Inioyne to the lady abbesse that before the natiuyte of our lorde next ensewing she cause a doore with two leves to be made and sett upp att the lower ende of the quere and that doore to be fyve foote in hight att the leaste and contynually to stand shitt the tymes of dyvyne seruice excepte it be att comming in or out of eny off the ladyes and mynystres off the said churche And under like payne as is afore we chardge the said ladye abbesse that she cause the doore betwene the convent and the parishe churche contynually to be shitt, unless itt be oonly the tymes of dyvyne service, and likewise she cause the cloistre door

Thome de Cantilupo, p 201) and Archbishop Peckham's injunction to Godstow, both based upon Ottobon. Reg. Epis. J Peckham, III, p. 848. Also Bishop Brantyngham's commission concerning the nuns of Polsloe in 1376, which is based upon Periculoso Reg of Bishop Brantyngham, pt II, pp 152-3

[1] Reg. Epis Johannis Peckham, II, pp. 652-3. Compare injunctions to Barking, ib I, p. 84, and to St Sepulchre's, Canterbury, ib II, p 706

[2] Ib II, p 663 "volentes ibi moniales curiose respicere vel cum eis garrulas attemptare."

towardes the outward court to be continually shitt, unles itt be att suche tymes as eny necessaryes for the convent shall be brought in or borne out att the same, and thatt she suffre noo other back doures to be opened butt upon necessarye, grett and urgent causes by her approved[1]

Special attempts were made to prevent secret communications between nuns and secular persons in corners and passages or through windows, and to block up unnecessary doors by which persons might enter:

"We ordeyn and injoyne yow, prioresse and convent," writes Dean Kentwode to St Helens, "That ye, ne noone of yowre sustres use nor haunte any place withinne the priory, thoroghe the wiche evel suspeccyone or sclaundere mythe aryse, weche places for certeyne causes that move us, we wryte here inne owre present iniunccyone, but wole notyfie to yow, prioresse nor have no lokyng nor spectacles owtewarde, thorght the wiche ye mythe fall into worldly dilectacyone[2]."

Archbishop Lee showed no such desire to spare the feelings of the nuns of Esholt by not openly specifying the places where they were wont to whisper with their friends:

Item where there is on the backside of certen chambres, on the south side of the church where the sustres worke, an open way goyng to the watirside, and to the brige goyng over the water, without wall or

---

[1] *Archaeologia*, XLVII, p. 52. Compare Bishop Gray's injunction to Godstow in 1432-4 "Also that all the doors of the nuns' lodgings towards the outer court, through which it is possible to enter into the cloister precinct, even if the other doors of the cloister be shut for the time being, be altogether blocked up, or that such means of barring or shutting be placed upon them that approach or entrance through the same doors may not be given to secular folk" *Linc Visit* I, p 68 Compare also Dean Kentwode's injunction to St Helen's, Bishopsgate, in 1432: "Also we injoyn yow, Prioresse, that there may be a doore at the Nonnes quere, that noo straungers may loke on them, nor they on the straungers, wanne thei bene at dyvyne service Also we ordene and injoyne yow, prioresse, that there be made a hache of conabyll heythe, crestyd with pykys of herne to fore the entre of yowre kechyne, that noo straunge pepille may entre with certeyne cleketts avysed be yow and be yowre steward to suche personys as yow and hem thynk onest and conabell Also we injoyne yow, prioresse, that non nonnes have noo keyes of the posterne doore that gothe owte of the cloystere into the churche yerd but the prioresse, for there is moche comyng in and owte unlefulle tymys." Dugdale, *Mon.* IV, p 554.

[2] *Loc cit* With this compare Alnwick's visitation of Ankerwyke in 1441, at which one of Margery Kyrkeby's charges against the Prioress Clemence Medeforde was "Also she has ..blocked up the view Thamesward, which was a great diversion to the nuns. She confesses blocking up the view, because she saw that men stood in the narrow space close to the window and talked with the nuns" *Linc. Visit* II, p 3.

doore, so that many ylles may be committed by reason hereof; wherfore in avoyding such inconveniences that myght folow yf it shuld so remayne, by thies presentes we inioyne the prioresse, that she, incontinent withoutzt delay aftre the recept herof cause a strong and heigh wall to be made in the said voyde place[1].

Above all it was reiterated at visitation after visitation that no nun was to receive a man in her private chamber or to hold conversations with any stranger there and that certain conditions were to be observed in all conversations between the nuns and their visitors. Archbishop Rotherham's injunction to Nun-appleton in 1489 is typical:

Item yat none of your sustirs bring in, receyve or take any laie man, religiose or secular into yer chambre or any secret place, daye or knyght, not w[t] yaim in such private places to commyne ete or drynke w[t]out lycence of you, Prioresse[2].

At Sopwell in 1338 an interesting addition was made to the ordinary rule·

And because it is seemly that ladies of religion in the presence of seculars should bear themselves according to rule in dress and in deportment, we will and ordain that none of you henceforward come to the parlour to talk with seculars if she have not her cowl and her headdress of kerchiefs and veil, according to the rule (*son cool et son covert de cuverchiefs et de veil ordine*), as beseemeth your religion   And none save honest persons shall be suffered to enter, and if such person wish to remain for a meal, let him eat in the parlour, by permission of the confessor, and on no account in the chambers without our express permission, or that of our own prior, if we be absent   Concerning the workmen, whom you need for your necessities, to wit tailors and furriers, we will for that such workmen a place be ordained near the cloister, where such workmen may do their works, and that they be by no means called into the chambers, nor into any private place. And let the workmen be such that no suspicion of evil may be roused by them[3].

<hr/>

[1] *Yorks Arch Journ* xvi, pp. 452-3. Compare Bishop Stapeldon's injunction to Canonsleigh in 1320: "Et pur ceo que nous avoms oyi et entendu par ascune gent qe par my deus us dedenȝ vostre abbeye ileoqes plusours mals esclandres et deshonestetes sunt avenues avant cest hure, et purront ensement avenir apres, si remedie ne soit mys, ceo est asavoir, un us qe est en lencloistre au celer desouz la Sale la Abbesse devers la court voloms, ordinoms et comaundoms qe meisme ceux deus us soyent bien estupees par mur de pere, entre cy et la Paske procheyn avenir." *Reg. W. de Stapeldon*, p. 96

[2] *V C.H Yorks* iii, p 172 He also said that "No man loge undir the dortir nor oon the baksede, but if hit be such sad persones by whome your house may be holpyne and socured w[t]out slaundir or suspicion "

[3] Dugdale, *Mon.* iii, p 366 But at Barking Peckham ordered in 1279 "In officiis, autem, quae per foeminas fieri nequeunt, operariorum cum

At Barking Peckham ordered in 1279 that no secular man or woman was to enter the nuns' chambers, unless a nun were so ill that it was necessary to speak to her there, in which case a confessor, doctor, father or brother might have access to her[1].

The rules laid down for the holding of conversations between nuns and visitors required that the permission of the head of the house should first be obtained, and that the meeting should take place in the *locutorium* or parlour, or occasionally in the abbess's hall[2], and in the hearing of "at least one other nun of sound character," or more frequently two other nuns. Sometimes it was added that conversations were not to be too lengthy:

"Let it not be permitted to any nun," wrote Peckham to Romsey, "to hold converse with any man save either in the parlour or in the side of the church next the cloister   And in order that all suspicion may henceforth be removed, we order that any nun about to speak

eisdem cautelis introitus admittatur " *Reg Epis J. Peckham*, 1, p 84   On the entrance of carpenters, masons and other workmen into convents see Thiers, *op. cit* 11, ch xxvi   He insists that the work must be a necessity and something which could not be done by the nuns themselves   "Ainsi les artisans sont coupables du violement de la clôture, lorsqu'ils entrent pour des ouvrages de bienseance ou de commodité, pour des decorations ou des embelissemens; en un mot, pour des ouvrages dont les Religieuses se peuvent passer, et je ne vois pas en quelle seureté de conscience les abbesses, les Prieures et les autres superieures des Religieuses, les y laissent entrer, soit pour polir des grilles, pour tendre et pour detendre des chambres et des lits, pour faire et pour peindre des plat-fonds et des alcoves, pour boiser des chambres, des galleries et des cabinets, pour faire de beaux vitrages, de belle volieres à petits oiseaux et d'autres choses semblables   Car outre que tout cela est directement opposé à la modestie et à la pauvreté, dont elles font profession, quel pretexte peuvent-elles alleguer pour se mettre à couvert de l'excommunication que les Conciles, les Papes et les Eveques ont fulminée contre les Religieuses, qui laissent entrer les personnes étrangeres dans leur clôture sans necessité " *Op cit.* pp 412–3. He is particularly urgent that nuns should cultivate their own gardens and should have their vegetable gardens outside the precincts: "par ce moyen elles ne seroient point obligées d'ouvrer et fermer si souvent les portes de leur clôture, à des jardiniers qui ne sont pas toûjours exempts de scandale" (*ib* p 414), which recalls a famous story of Boccaccio's *Decameron*, 3rd day, novel I

[1] *Loc cit.* and compare his injunction to Wherwell, *ib.* p. 268. Bishop Flemyng's introduction to Elstow is rather contradictory: "Also that no nun admit secretly to her chamber any seculars or other men of religion and that if they be admitted she do not keep them there too long " *Visit of Relig Houses in Dioc Lincoln*, 1, p. 51   At Godstow (1432) the injunction ran: "Also that the beds in the nuns' lodgings be altogether removed from their chambers, save those for small children and that no nun receive any secular people for any recreation in the nuns' chambers under pain of excommunication " *Ib* 1, p 67

[2] As at Godstow in 1432 *Linc Visit* 1, p 67, or Romsey in 1523, Liveing, *Records of Romsey Abbey*, p. 244

with any man, save in the matter of confession, have with her two companions to hear her conversation, in order that they may either be edified by useful words, if these are forthcoming, or hinder evil words, lest evil communications corrupt good manners"[1]

Alnwick's injunction to Godstow in 1445 was couched in very similar terms

That ye suffre none of your susters to speke wythe any seculere persone ne religiouse, but all onely in your halle in your presence and audience, or, by your specyalle licence asked and had, in the presence of two auncyent nunnes approved in the religyon so that ye or the said two nunnes here and see what that say and do, and so that thaire spekyng to gedre be not longe but in shorte and few wordes[2]

It was also attempted to exercise control over communication between the nuns and the world by means of messages and letters. Alnwick sent injunctions on this point to Langley, Markyate and St Michael's, Stamford ("ne that ye suffre none of youre sustres to receyve ne sende owte noyre gyfte ne lettre, but ye see the gyftes and wyte what is contyened in the lettres")[3], and in 1432 Dean Kentwode wrote to St Helen's, Bishopsgate·

Also we ordeyne and injoyne yow, that noone of yow speke, ne comone with no seculere persone, ne sende ne receyve letteres myssyves or gyftes of any seculere persone, withowte lycence of the prioresse. .. and such letters or gyftes sent or receyved, may turne into honeste and wurchepe and none into velanye or disclaundered of yowre honeste and religione[4].

It is common to find among episcopal injunctions to nunneries one to the effect that no secular woman is to sleep in the dorter with the nuns. The fact that this injunction had constantly to be repeated shows that it was as constantly broken Servants, boarders and school children seem in many houses to have shared the dorter with the nuns, an arrangement which must have been exceedingly disturbing to all parties Alnwick found the practice at eleven out of the twenty houses which he visited in

---

[1] *Reg Epis J. Peckham*, II, p 664 Cf his injunctions to other nunneries.
[2] *Linc Visit* II, p 116 Compare injunctions to Catesby, Langley. Markyate and St Michael's, Stamford *Ib* pp 51, 177, and *Alnwick's Visit* MS. ff 6, 83*d*. For other examples see Lymbrook (1277), *Reg. Thome de Cantilupo*, p 201; Polsloe (1319), *Reg. W de Stapeldon*, p 317, Studley (1530), *Archaeologia*, XLVII, p. 54
[3] *Alnwick's Visit* MS f 83*d*, cf f 6, and *Linc Visit* II, p 177
[4] Dugdale, *Mon* IV, p 554 Compare Romsey (1387), *New Coll* MS f 86; Nuncoton (1531), *Archaeologia*, XLVII, p 60 St Benedict's Rule forbids all letters (cap LIV)

1440–5. At Catesby, Langley, Stixwould and St Michael's, Stamford, little girls, between the ages of five and ten, used to sleep with the nuns; there were six or seven of them at that ill-conducted house, Catesby, in the charge of Agnes Allesley, who was so disobedient to the bishop[1]. At Gracedieu the cellaress had a boy of seven with her in the dorter[2]. At Legbourne a nun complained that "the Prioress suffers secular women, both boarders and servants, to lie by night in the dorter among the nuns, against the rule"[3] and at Heynings (which was much haunted by visitors) a lay sister deposed that "the infirmary is occupied by secular folk, to the great disturbance of the sisters; …also that secular serving women do lie among the sisters in the dorter, and especially one who did buy a corrody there"[4] At the other houses (Godstow, Nuncoton and Stainfield) it was simply mentioned that secular persons lay in the dorter, without details as to whether they were servants, boarders or children[5] In all cases Alnwick strictly forbade the practice, and a prohibition to this effect is common in episcopal injunctions[6].

These injunctions against the use of the dorter by seculars illustrate another aspect of the movement for enclosure. The majority of the other injunctions which have been quoted were attempts to regulate the intercourse of nuns with casual visitors, strangers who came for a day, or perhaps for two or three days. But a far more dangerous menace to the quiet of the cloister lay in the constant presence of secular boarders and corrodians, who made their home in a nunnery. Ladies who wished to end their days in peace sometimes went there as boarders or as corrodians; it is, no doubt, decent sober women such as these,

[1] *Linc. Visit* II, pp 46, 177, *Alnwick's Visit.* MS. ff. 39*d*. 76, 95*d*.
[2] *Ib* p 119   [3] *Linc Visit* II, p 185.
[4] *Ib* p 133.   [5] *Ib.* pp 113, MS ff 71*d*, 72, 77
[6] For other examples see Romsey (1311), Liveing, *op cit.* p 104, Clementhorpe (1317), Hampole (1308, 1314), Nunappleton (1346), Rosedale (1315), Arthington (1315, 1318); *V.C H. Yorks* III, pp. 129, 163–4, 172, 174, 188 Sopwell (1338), Dugdale, *Mon* III, p 366, Heynings (1392), *Linc. Epis Reg Memo Bokyngham,* f. 397*d*, Lymbrook (1437), *Hereford Epis Reg Spofford,* p 81, Burnham (1432–6), *Visit. of Relig. Houses in Dioc. Lincoln,* I, p. 24; Redlingfield (1514), *Visit of Dioc of Norwich,* pp. 139–40, Flamstead (1530), *V C H Herts* IV, p 433; Nuncoton (1531), *Archaeologia,* XLVII, p 58, Sinningthwaite (1534), *Yorks Arch. Journ* XVI, pp 440–1 The injunction to St Helen's, Bishopsgate, in 1432 has an odd variation: "withowte specialle graunte hadde in the chapetter house, among yow alle" Dugdale, *Mon.* IV, pp 553–4

who are sometimes exempted by name in episcopal injunctions ordering the exclusion of boarders from a house. But more often women would seek the temporary hospitality of a nunnery when, for some reason, they wished to leave their homes. A monastic house was, on the whole, a safe refuge, and many a knight going to the wars went with a lighter heart when he knew that his wife or daughter was sleeping within convent walls In 1314 John of Drokensford, Bishop of Bath and Wells, licensed the Prioress of Cannington to lodge and board the wife and two daughters of John Fychet during his absence abroad[1], and in 1372 William of Wykeham sent letters to the Abbesses of Romsey and Wherwell on behalf of another wife left alone in England·

"The noble Earl of Pembroke," wrote the Bishop, "has begged us by his letters to direct our special letters to you on behalf of the noble and gently-born lady, Lady Elizabeth de Berkele, a kinswoman of the aforesaid Earl, that she may lodge within your house...while Sir Maurice Wytht [sic ? knyght] the same lady's husband, remains in the company of the aforesaid Earl in parts beyond the sea";

and so, in spite of a recent prohibition to these houses to receive boarders, they are to take in Lady Berkeley[2]. Sometimes the wording of these licences shows that the ladies required only a temporary shelter and had by no means retired from the world. Bishop Ralph of Shrewsbury gave leave to Joan Wason and Maude Poer to stay at Cannington from December 1336 till the following Easter, and Isabel Fychet received a similar licence; in 1354 Isolda wife of John Bycombe was licensed to stay there from March till August[3] Sometimes these ladies brought their servants or gentlewomen with them; Joan Wason and Maude Poer had permission to take two "dammoiselles" and Isabel

---

[1] *Reg. of John of Drokensford*, p 81 The Isabel Fychet mentioned in 1336 was probably one of these ladies

[2] *Wykeham's Reg* II, pp 162–3. On this couple, see Smyth, *Lives of the Berkeleys*, pp 364 ff.

[3] *Reg. Ralph of Shrewsbury*, pp. 277, 278, 744–5 A few out of many other examples may be quoted Alice, wife of John D'Aumarle, *domicellus*, may stay at Cornworthy from January till September (1333), *Reg. of J. de Grandisson*, pt II, p. 724, Beatrix Paynell, sister of Sir John Foxley, may stay at Wintney from December to the Feast of St John the Baptist (1367), *Wykeham's Reg* II, p 7, Avice de Lyncolnia, niece of William de Jafford, may stay for four years in Nunappleton (1309), he was the Archbishop's receiver. *V.C H Yorks* III, 171, Alice, wife of Alan of Ayste, may spend two years in Godstow (1363), *V C H Oxon* II, p 73 It will be noted that nearly all these are great folk, who cannot lightly be refused.

Fychet one maid to Cannington, when Lady Margery Treverbyn,
a widow, went with every profession of piety to Canonsleigh in
1328, she was accompanied by "a certain priest, a squire (*domicellus*) and a damsel (*domicella*)"[1]; the widow of Sir John Pateshull
was licensed to dwell in Elstow with her daughter and maids
in 1350[2]; the *familia* of Elizabeth Berkeley is mentioned in
William of Wykeham's licence and in 1291 John le Romeyn,
Archbishop of York, gave the convent of Nunappleton permission
to receive Lady Margaret Percy as a boarder for a year, "provided
that her household during that time shall not be other than
respectable (*honesta*)"[3]. In the list (compiled by Mr Rye) of
boarders in Carrow Priory during the thirteenth and fourteenth
centuries, several ladies are mentioned as being accompanied
by servants; Lady Maloysel and servant, Isabell Argentoin and
servant, the Lady Margaret Kerdeston and woman, Margaret
Wryght and servant, Lady Margaret Wetherby, her servant
Matilda and her chaplain William The same list shows that not
only women but men were received as boarders, sometimes alone
and sometimes accompanied by their wives, and though some
of the names given are doubtless those of little boys, who were
receiving their education in the nunnery, others can be clearly
identified as adults[4] The Paston Letters afford a famous case in
which both a girl and her betrothed, who had quarrelled with
her parents, were lodged for a time in a nunnery. Margery
Paston had fallen in love with her brother's bailiff, Richard Calle,
to the fury of her family, who swore that "he should never have
their good will for to make her to sell candle and mustard in
Framlingham." The two lovers plighted their troth, a ceremony
as binding in the eyes of the Church as marriage itself, and
Richard Calle appealed to the Bishop of Norwich to set the
matter beyond doubt by an inquiry. The spirited Margery "re-
hearsed what she had said, and said, if those words made it
not sure, she said boldly that she would make that surer or
than she went thence, for she said she thought in her conscience

---

[1] *Reg. J de Grandisson*, pt. 1, p. 190
[2] *V.C.H Beds.* 1, p 355.   [3] *Reg. John le Romeyn*, 1, p. 114
[4] See the list in Rye, *Carrow Abbey*, pp 48–52, *passim* Some of the men
also brought servants or chaplains with them, e g William Wryght and
servants, William Wade and William his chaplain, John Bernard and John
his chaplain. The men must have been lodged outside the cloister precincts

she was bound, whatsoever the words were," whereupon her
mother refused to receive her back into her house, and the
Bishop himself was obliged to find a lodging for her This he
did at first with some friends and afterwards at a nunnery,
where Richard Calle also was lodged, for John Paston mentions
him shortly afterwards in a letter to his brother, "As to his
abiding it is in Blakborow nunnery a little fro Lynn and our
unhappy sister's also "[1].

It is plain from visitation records that the boarders who
flocked to the nunneries were exceedingly disturbing to conventual life and sometimes even brought disrepute upon their
hostesses by behaviour more suited to the world than to the
cloister. Alnwick's register contains some amusing and instructive evidence on this point. At Langley, a very worldly and
aristocratic person, Lady Audley, was occupying a house or set
of rooms (*domum*) within the Priory, paying 40s. yearly and
keeping the house in repair; but she had no intention of giving
up the ways of the world, pet dogs were her hobby, and the
helpless Prioress complained to Alnwick (a Bishop must sometimes have had much ado to keep a straight face at these
revelations):

Lady Audley, who boards in the house, has a great abundance of
dogs, insomuch that whenever she comes to church there follow her
twelve dogs, who make a great uproar in church, hindering them in
their psalmody and the nuns hereby are made terrified [2]

"Let a warning be directed to Lady Audley to remove her dogs
from the church and the choir," says a note in the Register,
and Lady Audley, followed by her twelve dogs, recedes for ever
from our view, unless reincarnated four centuries later in the
person of Hawker of Morwenstow. A boarder at Legbourne had
a different taste in pets Dame Joan Pavy informed the Bishop·
"That Margaret Ingoldesby, a secular woman, lies of a night

[1] *Paston Letters*, ed Gairdner (1900 ed), II, p 390 (no 633) See also
no 617 and Introd pp ccxc–ccxcii
[2] *Linc Visit* II, p 175 (at this house there were also three women
boarding with the Prioress and one with the Subprioress) Compare the
case of Agnes de Vescy at Watton in 1272. The King wrote to the sheriff
of Yorkshire that "Agnes de Vescy has been to the house of Watton with
a great number of women and dogs and other things, which have interfered
with the devotions of the nuns and sisters." Graham, *St Gilbert of Sempringham and the Gilbertines*, p. 83. The fact was that no one had any real control
over these great ladies, least of all their hostesses

in the dorter among the nuns, bringing with her birds, by whose
jargoning silence is broken and the rest of the nuns is disturbed"[1].
Exasperated Dame Joan, trying to steal some sleep before groping
her way down to matins! She had never heard of Vert-Vert,
nor even of Philip Sparrow and she would not have been of the
young and pretty novices, whose toilet the immortal parrot
superintended with a connoisseur's eye. The Bishop cut the
Gordian knot for her by ordering all seculars to be turned out
of the dorter. At Stixwould there were two widows, Elizabeth
Dymmok and Margaret Tylney, with their maidservants, staying
with the Prioress, and two other adult women staying with the
cellaress; and

there is in the same place a certain woman suspect [she was probably
a servant] who dwells within the cloister precincts, Joan Bartone by
name, to whom one William Traherne had had suspicious access,
bringing her therafter before the ecclesiastical judge in a matrimonial
suit, and she is very troublesome to the nuns[2].

At Gracedieu it was found that the Prioress divulged the secrets
of the house to her secular boarders[3]. At other houses also it
was complained that the boarders not only disturbed convent
life, but attracted many visitors. At Nuncoton the Subprioress
"prays that the lodgers be removed from the house, so that
they mingle not among the nuns, for if there were none the
Prioress might be able to come constantly to frater; and because
there is great recourse of strangers to the lodgers, to the sore
burthen of the house"; another nun also deposed "that there is
great recourse of guests on account of the lodgers" and a third
asked that boarders of marriageable age should be altogether
removed from the house, frater and dorter, "by reason of the
divers disadvantages which arise to the house out of their stay"[4].
At Godstow in 1432 Bishop Gray enjoined:

[1] *Linc Visit* II. p 185
[2] *Alnwick's Visit.* MS f 76 Compare a *compertum* at St 'Sepulchre,
Canterbury, in 1367–8. "Perhendinantes male fame steterunt cum priorissa,
ad quas habebatur eciam accessus nimium suspectus," *Lambeth Reg. Langham,* f. 76d.
[3] *Linc Visit* II, pp. 120, 122
[4] *Alnwick's Visit* MS ff 71d, 72 Compare the state of affairs at Hampole in 1411, when the Archbishop ordered the removal of "secular servants
and *corrodiarii* who attracted to themselves other secular persons from the
country, by whom the house was burdened " *V C H Yorks.* III, p. 165. When
Bishop Grandisson of Exeter licensed the reception of Alice D'Aumarle at

that Felmersham's wife with her whole household, and other women of mature age be utterly removed from the monastery within one year next to come, seeing that they are a cause of disturbance to the nuns and an occasion of bad example by reason of their attire and those who come to visit them[1].

It is indeed easy to understand why bishops objected so much to the reception of these worldly women as boarders. If instead of Felmersham's wife we read "the wife of Bath" all is explained That lady was not a person whom a Prioress would lightly refuse; the list of her pilgrimages alone would give her the *entrée* into any nunnery. Smiling her gat-toothed smile and riding easily upon her ambler, she would enter the gates and alight in the court, and what a month of excitement would pass before she rode away again. It is hard not to suspect that it was she who introduced "caps of estate" (were they "as broad as is a buckler or a targe"?) to the Prioress of Ankerwyke and crested shoes to the nuns of Elstow, and it may have been she (alas) who taught some of them to step "the olde daunce"[2]. Bad enough for their peace of mind to meet her at a pilgrimage, but much worse to have her settled in their midst, gossiping as endlessly as she gossiped in her prologue, and amplifying her reminiscences for a less sophisticated audience. This was one reason why the bishops made a special injunction against the reception of married women. The presence of men was open to even more serious objections. At Hampole in 1411 the Archbishop of York made the significant injunction that the Prioress was not to allow any *corrodiarii* or others to retain suspected women with them in the house[3]. At St Michael's, Stamford, in 1442 Alnwick discovered

that Richard Gray lately boarding in the priory together with his legitimate wife, *procreavit prolem de domina Elizabetha Wylugby moniali*

Cornworthy (1333) he added "proviso quod ad vos, per moram hujusmodi, secularium personarum non pateat suspectis horis liberior frequencia vel accessus." *Reg Grandisson*, pt. II, p 724.

[1] *Visit. of Relig Houses in Dioc. of Lincoln*, I, p 87

[2] Note for instance the Archbishop of York's injunction when mitigating a severe penance on a nun of St Clement's, York, which is clearly for immorality "That twice a year if necessary she might receive friends . but she was to have nothing to do with Lady de Walleys and if Lady de Walleys was then in their house, she was to be sent away before Pentecost (1310)," *V C.H Yorks* III, p 129

[3] *V C H. Yorks*. II, p. 165.

ibidem, and boarded there until last Easter against the injunction of the lord (bishop)[1]

So also at Easebourne in 1478 it was deposed that "a certain Sir John Senoke[2] much frequented the priory or house, so that during some weeks he passed the night and lay within the priory or monastery every night, and was the cause. .of the ruin" of two nuns who had gone into apostasy at the instigation of various men[3].

The reception of secular women as boarders without the consent of the diocesan was forbidden as early as 1222 by the Council of Oxford[4] and the bishops henceforth pursued a steady policy of ejection:

"Since," wrote Bishop Flemyng to Elstow, "from the manifest conjectures and assurances of our eyes we have learned that by reason of the stay of lodgers, especially of married persons, in the said monastery, the purity of religion (and) pleasantness of honest conversation and character, (which) in their fragrance in our judgment far surpass temporal goods, and the destruction of which far exceeds the waste of temporal wealth, have suffered grave shipwreck, and may suffer, as is likely, more heavily in future, we ordain, enjoin and charge you who are now abbess and the other several persons who shall be abbesses in the said monastery, under pain of deprivation, beside the other penalties written beneath, which likewise, if you do contrary to that which we command, it is our will that you incur thereupon, that henceforward you admit or allow to be admitted or received to lodge or stay within the limits of the cloister, no persons male or female, how honest soever they be, who are beyond the twelfth year of their age, nor any other persons soever, and married persons in special, without the site of the same monastery, unless you have procured express and special licence in the cases premised from ourselves or from our successors, who for the time being shall be bishops of Lincoln"[5].

Always the reason given is that these boarders are a disturbance to conventual discipline

"Item because religion has been much disturbed among you by reason of secular women lodging in your house," wrote Bishop Gynewell to Heynings in 1351, "we forbid on pain of excommunication that after the feast of St Michael next to come any secular woman be allowed to remain in your Priory, save your servants who be necessary for your service"[6]

---

[1] *Alnwick's Visit.* MS. f. 39d.   [2] Possibly a priest.
[3] *Sussex Arch. Coll.* ix, p 18   [4] Wilkins, *Concilia,* I, p. 592.
[5] *Visit of Relig Houses in Dioc Lincoln,* I, pp 48–9 Compare Gray's injunction, laying more stress on married boarders *Ib* p 53
[6] *Linc Epis. Reg. Memo. Gynewell,* f. 34d.

"Also for as myche as we fynde detecte," Alnwick wrote nearly a century later to the same house, "that for the multitude of sujournauntes wythe [yow] as wele wedded as other ofte tymes the qwyere and the rest of yowe in your obseruances is troubled, we charge [yow] pryoresse vnder payne of the sentence of cursyng that fro this day forthe ye receyve no sodeiyouraunutes that pas[se a man] x yere, a woman xiii yere of age, wytheowten specyalle leve of hus or our successours bushops of Lincolne asked [and had]"[1].

But the attempt to clear the convents of secular boarders was entirely unsuccessful. The bishops had two powerful forces against them, the desire of the impoverished nuns to make money and the desire of seculars for a quiet and inexpensive hostel; and the nuns continued to take boarders, in spite of a series of prohibitions. At Romsey, for instance, Peckham forbids boarders, c. 1284; in 1311 Bishop Woodlock has to repeat the prohibition "because of the continual sojourn of seculars we find the tranquillity of the nuns to be much disturbed and scandals to arise in your monastery", in 1346 Edynton orders the removal of all secular persons within a month; in 1363 he has to write again, complaining that he has heard by public report that they have not obeyed his former letter and ordering them to remove all *perhendinatrices* within fifteen days[2] At Godstow injunctions to this effect are made in succession by Gynewell (1358), Gray (1432-4) and Alnwick (1445)[3]; at Elstow by Gynewell (1359), Bokyngham (1387), Flemyng (1421-2) and Gray (c 1432)[4]. Moreover the bishops themselves were sometimes obliged to leave the nuns a loophole of escape, by excepting certain women from the general prohibition, thus Alnwick excepted the two widows

[1] *Visit Linc* II, p 135 For other injunctions against boarders see Godstow, Gracedieu, Harrold, Langley, Nuncoton, Stixwould, *ib* pp 115, 124-5, 131, 177, *Alnwick's Visit.* MS. ff 77d, 75d, Wherwell, Romsey (1284), Sheppey (1286), *Reg Epis Peckham*, II, pp 653-4, III, p 924; Wilberfoss, Nunkeeling and Nunappleton (1281-2), *Reg. William Wickwane*, pp 112-3, 140-1, Polsloe (1319), *Reg W de Stapeldon*, p. 317, Canonsleigh (1391), *Reg of Brantyngham*, pt II, p 724, Farwell (1367), *Reg. R. de Stretton*, p. 119, Polesworth (1352, 1456), *V C H Warwick*, II, p 63 These are only a few examples taken at random; the registers of the Archbishops of York and of the Bishops of Lincoln alone record many more. (See the *V.C H.* for the counties in these dioceses, *passim*.)
[2] *Reg. Epis J Peckham*, II, p 664, Liveing, *op. cit* pp 102, 165
[3] *Linc. Epis. Reg Memo. Gynewell*, f 100d, *Linc Visit. I*, p. 67; II, p 115
[4] *Gynewell*, f 139d, *V C H Beds I*, p. 355, *Linc Visit. I*, pp. 48-9, 53.

Elizabeth Dymmok and Margaret Tylney at Stixwould[1]; Brantyngham excepted "the noble woman Lady Elizabeth Courtenay, wife of the noble man Sir Hugh de Courtenay, Knight" at Canonsleigh (1391)[2]; and Archbishop Rotherham at Nunappleton (1489) excepted children "or ellis old persones, by which availe bihklyhood may growe to your place"[3]. Often too they were persuaded to grant licences to boarders, at the prayer of influential persons who must not be offended[4]. The largest loophole which they were obliged by the pressure of circumstances to leave open was, however, the permission to receive small children for education[5].

It is clear from the evidence of visitation documents that nuns often took boarders of their own free will, for the sake of the money which thus accrued to their impecunious houses; certainly no episcopal injunction was more consistently disobeyed On the other hand great ladies often thrust themselves upon a convent, which dared not say them nay, and it is not at all unusual to find the nuns complaining of the disturbance caused to their daily life by visitors. The matter was complicated by the fact that the exercise of hospitality was one of the chief functions of monastic houses in the middle ages, and was so far regarded as a right by their neighbours that remonstrances were actually made if the quality of the entertainment offered was not considered sufficiently good. At Campsey in 1532 one of the nuns declared that "well-born guests (*hospites generosae*) coming to the priory complained of the excessive parsimony of the Prioress"[6]. Complaints by the nuns of the spiritual disturbance caused by this influx of visitors, show that the right was vigorously exercised. In 1364 the Pope granted permission to Margaret de Lancaster, an Augustinian Canoness of the same nunnery of Campsey, to transfer herself to the Order of St Clare,

---

[1] "That ye receyve ne holde no suiournauntes, men, women ne childerne, wyth ynne your place, and thoe that nowe are there, ye voyde thaym wythe yn a quartere of a yere after the receyvyng of thise our lettres, but if ye here yn hafe specyalle licence of hus or our successours, bysshops of Lincolne, except our wele belufede doghters, dame Elizabeth Dymmok and dame Margaret Tylney, by whose abydyng, as we truste, no greve but rathere avayle is procured to your place " *Alnwick's Visit* MS f. 75 d.

[2] *Reg. of Brantyngham*, pt II, p. 724
[3] *V C H. Yorks* III, p 173
[4] See examples above, p. 410   [5] See Ch. VI, *passim.*
[6] *Visit. of Dioc. of Norwich* (Camden Soc), p 290

she having already caused herself to be enclosed at Campsey in order to avoid the number of nobles coming to the house[1], and in 1375 he commanded the Bishop of St Andrews to make order concerning the Prioress and nuns of the Benedictine convent of North Berwick, "who have petitioned for perpetual enclosure, they being much molested by the neighbourhood and visits of nobles and other secular persons"[2]. Even enclosure was not always a protection against visitors; for the Popes constantly granted indults to great persons, allowing them to enter, with a retinue, the houses of monks and nuns belonging to enclosed orders. A few instances may be taken at random John of Gaunt in 1371 received an indult to enter any monasteries of religious men and women once a year, with thirty persons of good repute[3]; Joan Princess of Wales in 1372 was given permission to enter monasteries of enclosed nuns with six honest and aged men and fourteen women and to eat and drink, but not to pass the night therein[4], Thomas of Gloucester and his wife, the notorious Eleanor de Cobham, had an indult to enter monasteries of enclosed monks and nuns six times a year, with twenty persons of either sex[5]. Sometimes, it is true, the visitors were forbidden to eat, drink or spend the night in the house[6], but often they received special permission to do so, thus in 1408 Philippa, Duchess of York, was given an indult allowing her to take five or six matrons and to stay in monasteries of enclosed nuns for three days and nights at a time[7] and in 1422 Joan Countess of Westmoreland received one to enter any nunnery with eight honest women, and to stay there with the nuns, eating, drinking and talking with them and spending the night[8]. An indult granted in 1398 to Margery and Grace de Tylney "noblewomen," to enter "as often as they please with six honest matrons, the monastery of enclosed nuns of the Order of St Clare, Denney"[9], and a faculty granted in 1371 to "John, Cardinal of Sancti Quatuor Coronati"[10], empowering him to give leave to a hundred women of high birth of France and England, to enter nunneries once a year, accom-

---

[1] *Cal of Papal Letters*, IV, pp. 37–8   [2] *Ib.* IV, p 212
[3] *Ib.* IV, p 167.   [4] *Ib* IV, p 182   [5] *Ib* IV, p 394
[6] For example, *ib.* I. pp 522, 526; IV, p. 38, VII, pp. 70, 440, 617 Sometimes, too, they were ordered to pay their own expenses, e g *ib* VI, p 293
[7] *Ib.* VI, p 132.   [8] *Ib* VII, p 220   [9] *Ib* V, p 91
[10] I e Jean de Dormans, bishop of Beauvais 1360–8, cardinal 1368, d 1373

panied each by four matrons[1], give some idea of the extent to which it was usual for guests to visit even houses belonging to enclosed orders.

Nuns do not seem to have concerned themselves with political movements, unlike the monks, who in great abbeys were sometimes keen politicians   But it sometimes happened that the strife and intrigue and tragedy of the outside world entered into quiet convents, through this custom of using them as boarding houses   Not otherwise can we account for a curious case in which the nuns of Sewardsley were involved in 1470, when a certain Thomas Wake accused Jacquetta, Duchess of Bedford, of making an image of lead to be used in witchcraft against the King and Queen, which image he said had been shown to various persons and exhibited in the nunnery of Sewardsley[2]. Moreover echoes of great doings came to nuns when the hapless wives and daughters of the King's enemies were placed in their custody, a kindlier fate than imprisonment in a fortress or in charge of some loyal noble's sharp-tongued wife   The course of Edward II's troubled reign may be traced in the story of the women who were successively sent as prisoners, or (worse still) as nuns, to various priories   The first to suffer was the King's niece Margaret; she had been married by him to Piers Gaveston and had seen her husband miserably slain at Thomas of Lancaster's behest; she was married again to Sir Hugh Audley and ten years later, poor pawn in the game of politics, she suffered for her second husband's share in Lancaster's rebellion, when the crime of Blacklow Hill was expiated on the hill of Pontefract

"Margarete countesse de Cornewaille," says the chronicle of Sempringham, "La femme Sire Hugh Daudelee, e la niece le roi, fu ordinee a demorer en guarde a Sempringham entre les nonaignes, a quel lieu ele vint le xvi jour de Mai (1322) e la demorra"[3].

[1] Cal. of Papal Letters, iv, p 170

[2] V C H Northants ii, p. 126 Sewardsley was near Grafton Regis, where Jacquetta, then widow of Richard Wydville, earl Rivers, lived. This recalls the more famous case of Eleanor de Cobham, Duchess of Gloucester   It is worth noticing also that on the eve of the Reformation the famous Elizabeth Barton, called "the Holy Maid of Kent," found refuge for a part of her short career in the nunnery of St Sepulchre's, Canterbury.   Archbishop Warham secured her admission there in 1526, and she became a nun and remained there for seven years, until the fame of her outspoken condemnations of the royal divorce finally brought about her execution in 1533   See Gasquet, Hen VIII and the English Monasteries (Pop Edit 1899), ch iii, passim

[3] Le Livere de Engletere (Rolls Series), p. 344

In the same year the Abbess of Barkıng was ordered "to cause the body of Elizabeth de Burgo, late wıfe of Roger Damory, wıthin her abbey, to be kept safely and not to permıt her to go outside the abbey gates ın any wıse until further orders"[1]. In 1324 another rebel, Roger Mortimer, broke hıs prıson in the Tower and escaped across the sea to France But three poor children, his daughters, could not escape, and on April 7th of the same year the sherıff of Southampton received an order to cause Margaret, daughter of Roger Mortımer of Wygmore, to be conducted to the Priory of Shouldham, Joan, hıs second daughter, to the Priory of Sempringham, and Isabella, hıs thırd daughter, to the Prıory of Chicksand, "to be delıvered to the prıors of those places (all were Gılbertıne houses) to stay amongst the nuns ın the same priories." The Prior of Shouldham had 15d. weekly for Margaret's expenses and a mark yearly for her robe, and each of the other two little girls received 12d. weekly for expenses and a mark for her robe[2]. The she-wolf of France bided her tıme, and when the game was hers she was no less swıft to avenge her wrongs; to Sempringham (where her lover's daughter had gone two years before) now went the two daughters of the elder Hugh Despenser, to pray for the souls of a father and brother done most dreadfully to death[3]. The perennıal wars wıth Scotland also found theır echo in the nunnerıes. In 1306 the Abbess of Barkıng was ordered "to delıver Elızabeth, sıster of William Olifard [? Olifaunt] Knight, who is in their custody by the Kıng's permıssıon to Henry de Lacy, Earl of Lincoln, the King havıng granted her to the saıd Henry"[4]; she was doubtless a relative of that "Hugh Olyfard, a Scot, the King's enemy and rebel," who together wıth one "Wıllıam Sauvage the Kıng's approver" had broken hıs prıson at Colchester some three years before, and fled ınto sanctuary ın the convent church[5] Barkıng was a favourite prıson, doubtless on account of its sıtuation, and in 1314 the sherıffs of London were ordered "to receıve Elızabeth, wife of Robert de Brus, from the Abbess of Berkyngg, wıth whom she had been staying by the King's order and to take her

[1] *Cal. of Close Rolls* (1318–23), p 428
[2] *Ib* (1323–7), pp 88–9, cf. *Le Lıvere de Engletere*, p 350
[3] *V C H. Lıncs.* ıı, p 184.   [4] *Cal of Close Rolls* (1307–13), p 114
[5] *Ib.* (1302–7), p 419

under safe custody to Rochester and there deliver her to Henry
de Cobham, constable of the castle"[1].

The mention of the Scot Hugh Olyfard, who took sanctuary
in the church of Barking, recalls another reason for which the
world might break into the cloister. The terrified fugitive from
justice would take sanctuary in a convent church if it lay nearest
to him, and the peace of chanting nuns would be rudely broken,
when that unkempt and desperate figure sprang up the choir
between them and flung itself upon their altar steps. The hand
of a master has drawn for us what the trembling novices saw,
peeping from their stalls:

> ...the breathless fellow at the altar foot,
> Fresh from his murder, safe and sitting there
> With the little children round him in a row
> Of admiration, half for his beard and half
> For that white anger of his victim's son
> Shaking a fist at him with one fierce arm,
> Signing himself with the other because of Christ
> (Whose sad face on the cross sees only this
> After the passion of a thousand years),
> Till some poor girl, her apron o'er her head
> Which the intense eyes looked through, came at eve
> On tiptoe, said a word, dropped in a loaf,
> Her pair of ear-rings and a bunch of flowers
> The brute took growling, prayed and then was gone[2].

[1] *Cal of Close Rolls* (1313–18), p 43 Sometimes the King sent his
friends as well as his enemies to board in a convent and occasionally he
endeavoured to do so without paying for them   In 1339 he sent first to
Wilton and then to Shaftesbury "Sibyl Libaud of Scotland who lately
came to England to the king's faith and besought that he would provide
for her maintenance, requesting them to provide her and her son Thomas,
who is of tender age, with maintenance from that house, in food and clothing,
until Whitsuntide next, knowing that what they do at this request shall
not be to the prejudice of their house in the future" *Cal of Close Rolls*
(1339–41), pp 261, 335. John of Gaunt made use of the convent of Nuneaton
to provide a home for five Spanish ladies, who had doubtless come to England
with his duchess Constance of Castile, early in 1373 he wrote to his receiver
at Leicester bidding him pay the prioress for their expenses 13s 4d each
week, but evidently they found the convent too dull for their tastes, for
in August one of them was "demourrant a Leycestre ovesque Johan
Elmeshalle," and in December the Duke wrote to his receiver again to
say that he had heard "que noz damoisels d'Espaigne demurrantz a
Nouneton ne voullont pas illoeques pluis longement demurrer"; so it was
"Farewell and adieu to you, Spanish ladies" at Nuneaton. It is probable
that these "damoisels" were quite young girls, and had been placed at
the convent to learn "nortelry" *John of Gaunt's Reg.* (R Hist Soc.), ii,
pp 128, 231, 276–7. See, for more about these ladies, pp. 320–1, 328, 338.
[2] Browning, *Fra Lippo Lippi*

But sometimes more than a momentary disturbance was occasioned to the nunnery; in 1416, for instance, Edith Wilton, Prioress of Carrow, was attached, together with one of her nuns, on the charge of harbouring in sanctuary the murderers of William Koc of Trowse, at the appeal of his widow Margaret. She was arrested, imprisoned and called to answer at Westminster, but after the court had adjourned many times she was acquitted[1]. An abbess of Wherwell was involved in a lawsuit over a case of sanctuary for somewhat different reasons; she claimed the right of seizing chattels of fugitives in the hundred of Mestowe[2], a right which was disputed by the crown officials. One Henry Harold of Wherwell had killed his wife Isabel and fled to the church of Wherwell and the Abbess had promptly seized his chattels to the value of over £35, by the hands of her reeve[3]

These cases of violence will lead us to the consideration of breaches of enclosure which were in no sense the fault of the unhappy nuns. Visits from their peaceful friends they welcomed, the sojourn of great folk they bore; but they would fain have passed their days undisturbed by war's alarms and by the assault and battery of private feuds. But it was not to be. Alarums and excursions sometimes shattered their peace and, especially in the Northern counties, violent attacks at the hands of robbers, lawless neighbours, or enemies of the realm were only too common.

---

[1] *V.C.H Norfolk*, II, p 352 This case is particularly interesting, because it would seem to show that "benefit of clergy" was not claimed by nuns. On this point see Pollock and Maitland, *Hist of Engl Law*, 2nd ed I, p 445. "There seems no reason for doubting that nuns were entitled to the same privilege, though, to their credit be it said, we have in our period, found no cases which prove this " Maitland cites Hale, *Pleas of the Crown*, II, p. 328, as saying "Nuns had the exemption from temporal jurisdiction but the privilege of clergy was never granted them by our law", but elsewhere (*Pleas of the Crown*, II, p 371) "Anciently nuns professed were admitted to privilege of clergy", he cites a case from 1348 (Fitzherbert's *Abridgment Corone*, pl 461) which speaks of a woman, not expressly called a nun, being claimed by and delivered to the ordinary Stephen, *Hist of Crim. Law of England*, II, p 461, thinks that "all women (except, till the Reformation, professed nuns) were for centuries excluded from benefit of clergy, because they were incapable of being ordained "

[2] Mr Hamilton Thompson thinks that "Mestowe" is probably the hundred of Meon-Stoke (Hants), in a distant part of the county; it is difficult to see why the Abbess made a general claim there and in any case Wherwell, where Henry Harold lived, is in Wherwell Hundred.

[3] *V.C.H. Hants.* II, p. 135.

Disorder was general and grew worse in the course of the four-teenth and fifteenth centuries. The nunnery of Markyate was once assaulted in the night by fifty robbers and the nuns pillaged and robbed of everything valuable[1], and in 1408 the Bishop of Ely gave an indulgence for the relief of the nuns of Rowney, "whose chalices, books, ornaments and other goods have been stolen by evil men, so that they have not the wherewithal to perform the divine office"[2].

Neighbourly disagreements sometimes developed into petty warfare, as the Paston Letters show, and an almost exact parallel to the dispute between John Paston and Lord Molynes over the manor of Gresham is to be found in a complaint made in 1383 by the Prioress of Brodholme, who asserted that a gang of men (whom she named)

had broken her close at Brodholme felled her trees and underwood, dug in her soil, carried off earth, trees, underwood and other goods, depastured her corn and grass, assaulted her servants and besieged her and her nuns in the Priory and threatened them with death"[3].

Such instances might be multiplied[4] Sometimes the presence of secular boarders led to unpleasant experiences for the nuns. The Lincoln registers record two such cases, which incidentally furnish an additional reason why the reception of boarders was frowned upon by the Church. In 1304 certain

"satellites of Satan whose names we know not" (Bishop Dalderby informs his official), "lately came in great numbers to the monastery of the nuns of Goring, where they boldly laid violent hands upon Henry, chaplain of the parish church and brother John le Walleys, lay brother of the same place (from whom they drew blood) and upon certain nuns of the house who struggled to guard their monastery, and then they entered and rode their horses up to the high altar of the church, polluting that holy place shamefully with the footprints and dung of their horses "

Their object was apparently to seize a certain Isabella de Kent, a married woman then dwelling in the nunnery, and they pursued her to the belfry, where she had taken refuge and dragged her

---

[1] Dugdale, *Mon.* III. p 369.
[2] Gibbons, *Ely Epis. Records*, p. 406
[3] *Cal. of Pat Rolls* (1381–5), p 355.
[4] On the other hand for a case of spoliation in which Juliana Yong, a nun, was involved as one of the aggressors see *Cal. of Pap Petit.* I, pp. 333–4

away with them[1]. An even worse disturbance took place at Rothwell in 1421-2. A gang of ruffians broke open the cloister and doors, seized one Joan (a boarder) and carried her away to a lonely house, where their leader forcibly violated her, with every circumstance of brutality. She escaped back to the priory, whereupon the leader

entering the same priory a second time, like a tyrant and pirate with a far greater multitude of like henchmen and people untamed and savage in his company, with naked swords and other sorts of divers weapons of offence, fell ..upon the same woman, who was then in the presence of the prioress and the nuns in the hall of the said priory and . daringly laid wicked, sacrilegious and violent hands, notwithstanding the worship both of their persons and of the place, upon the prioress and nuns of the said place, honourable members of the church and persons hallowed to God accordingly—who endeavoured gently to appease their baseness and savagery, so far as their sex as women allowed—and cudgelled them with cruel strokes, threw them down on the ground and, trampling on them with their feet, mercilessly kicked them and violently dragged off their garments of their habits over their heads, and even as robbers, having caught their prey, carried off the said woman, dragging her with them out of the priory[2].

Even more significant is the licence granted to the Abbess and Convent of Tarrant Keynes in 1343 to cut down two hundred acres of under-wood in their demesne land, "on their petition setting forth that their house and possessions in the county of Dorset had been burned and destroyed by an invasion of the king's enemies in those parts"[3]; or the permission given to the Abbess of Shaftesbury in 1367 to crenellate her Abbey, presumably for purposes of defence[4]. The south coast was a constant

[1] *Linc. Reg. Dalderby*, f 16.

[2] *Linc. Visit* I, pp 108-9 Compare a case in 1375 at Romsey when certain persons broke into the houses of the Abbess within the Abbey and carried off Joan, late the wife of Peter Brugge, and her property, consisting of her gold rings, gold brooches or bracelets with precious stones, linen and woollen clothes and furs, her chaplain aiding. Liveing, *op. cit* p 166

[3] *Cal of Pat. Rolls* (1340-3), p 127

[4] *Ib* (1367-70), p 10. The Abbess was the worldly Joan Formage Licences for crenellating monasteries are rather unusual, but cathedral closes were very generally crenellated at the end of the thirteenth and beginning of the fourteenth centuries, e g Lincoln, York, Lichfield, Wells and Exeter There is a good example of a crenellated monastery at the Benedictine Priory of Ewenny near Bridgend, Glamorgan, a cell of Gloucester This is near the south coast of Wales, where, as along the Welsh border, towers either crenellated or with certain defensive features are common Cf the numerous fortified churches in the south of France, e g Albi Cathedral (Tarn) and Les Saintes-

prey to pirates, and it was still within the memory of man that, at the beginning of the French war

the Normayns Pycardes and Spanyerdes entred into the toune (of Southampton) and robbed and pilled the toune, and slewe dyvers and defowled maydens, and enforced wyves, and charged their vessels with the pyllage and so entred agayne into their shyppes[1]

The sanctity which attached to the person of a nun was apt to be forgotten in the brutal warfare of the day and the Abbess might well fear for her flock The English nunneries did not, indeed, experience anything to compare with the unimaginable sufferings endured by French convents during the hundred years' war[2]. But they were by no means immune from the effects of civil war; Wilton, Wherwell and St Mary's, Winchester, were all burned during the struggle between Stephen and Matilda[3], and during the Wars of the Roses the nuns of Delapré were unwilling witnesses of the Battle of Northampton (1460), which was held "in the medowys beside the Nonry"; after the fight was over the King, the Archbishop of Canterbury and the Bishop of London rested at the nunnery and many of the slain were buried in its churchyard[4].

The most striking example of the effect of warfare upon monastic houses in England is, however, provided by the history of the northern monasteries, which were throughout their history (but especially during the first part of the fourteenth century) in danger from the inroads of the Scots So great was the destruction wrought in 1318 that it was necessary to make a new assessment of church property for purposes of taxation, in part of the province of York[5]. Nor was the trouble purely material, though

Maries (Bouches-du-Rhône), the latter close to the shore of the Mediterranean. (For this note I am indebted to Mr A Hamilton Thompson)

[1] Froissart, tr Berners, I, ch xxxviii. For the sufferings of other monasteries on the south coast see P G Mode, *The Influence of the Black Death on the English Monasteries*, p 31

[2] See Denifle, *La Désolation des Eglises...pendant la Guerre de Cent Ans* (1899). In t. I is a long list of monasteries which had been ruined during the fourteenth century. The following (no 176) is typical "Monasterium monialium B Mariae de Bricourt O S B Trecen. dioec , causantibus a 40 annis guerris desolatum et destructum, libris aliisque destitutum et ab omnibus monialibus derelictum 1442 " (pp. 55–6).

[3] Dugdale, *Mon* II, pp 316, 452, 636.

[4] Serjeantson, *Delapré Abbey* (1909), pp 21–3

[5] Graham, *Essay on Engl. Monasteries* (Hist. Ass 1913), p 29. The text of the assessment is given in the notes to the *Taxatio Ecclesiastica Pape Nicholai* (Record Com 1802)

the poverty of the nunneries (in particular) was sometimes abject and the harrying of their lands must have made prosperity at all times a vain hope. The moral results of such disorder were even more serious. It was almost impossible to maintain an ordinary communal life, when at any moment it might be necessary to disperse the nuns and quarter them in other houses out of the line of the marauders' march. Even in houses which were never actually attacked, the prevalent unrest, the lawlessness which is naturally engendered by border warfare, must have been disorganising and demoralising It is easy to understand why cases of immorality and grave disorder are more prevalent in the convents of the north of England than in those of any other district

In 1296 the chronicler of Lanercost describes thus the first great raid of the Scots:

In this raid they surpassed in cruelty all the fury of the heathen, when they could not catch the strong and young people, who took flight, they imbrued their arms, hitherto unfleshed, with the blood of infirm people, old women, women in childbed and even children two or three years old, proving themselves apt scholars in atrocity, insomuch that they raised little span-long children pierced on pikes, to expire thus and fly away to the heavens. They burnt consecrated churches; both in the sanctuary and elsewhere they violated women dedicated to God [i e nuns] as well as married women and girls, either murdering them or robbing them, after gratifying their lust Also they herded together a crowd of little scholars in the schools of Hexham and having blocked the doors set fire to that pile [so] fair [in the sight of God]. Three monasteries of holy collegiates were destroyed by them, Lanercost, of the Canons Regular, and Hexham of the same order and [that] of the nuns of Lambley, of all of these the devastation can by no means be attributed to the valour of warriors, but to the dastardly conduct of thieves, who attacked a weaker community, where they would not be likely to meet with any resistance[1]

Some allowance must be made for the indignation of a canon of Lanercost, whose own house had been burnt; but even so it is plain that the religious houses must have endured terrible things at the hands of the Scots; and the peril of the nuns was to honour as well as to life and home

In several cases record of the actual dispersal of the nuns has

[1] *The Chronicle of Lanercost*, translated by Sir Herbert Maxwell [1913], p. 136

been preserved, though such dispersal lasted only for a short time. The priory of Holystone, which lay right upon the border, was in a particularly exposed position and in 1313, when Bruce was devastating the northern counties, a letter from the Bishop of Durham bears vivid testimony to its miserable plight.

"The house of the said nuns," he says, "situated in the March of England and Scotland, by reason of the hostile incursions which daily and continually increase in the March, is frequently despoiled of its goods and the nuns themselves are often attacked by the marauders, harmed and pursued and, put to flight and driven from their home, are constrained miserably to experience bitter suffering. Wherefore we make these things known to you, that you may compassionate their poverty, which is increased by the memory of happier things, and that your pity and benevolence may be shown them, lest (to the disgrace of their estate) they be forced publicly to beg"[1].

The expiration of the truce with Scotland in 1322 was followed by another raid and by Edward II's unsuccessful campaign, in the course of which the Scots overran Yorkshire and very nearly captured the King at Byland Abbey. The canons of Bridlington (whither he fled) departed with all their valuables to Lincolnshire, sending an envoy to purchase immunity from Bruce at Melton. The poor nuns of Moxby and Rosedale did not escape so easily. In November Archbishop Melton wrote to the Prioress of Nunmonkton, ordering her to receive two nuns of the house of Moxby, which had been "destroyed and devastated by the Scots"; the Prioress tried to excuse herself, on the plea that it was unseemly for Austin nuns to be received in a Benedictine convent and that her house barely sufficed to support herself and her sisters, but the Archbishop sternly replied that he was sending the nuns for a time only and that it behoved the convent of Nunmonkton to receive them, in order to avoid their being dispersed in the world   He added that he had placed a like burden upon other nunneries in his diocese which had escaped the horrors of the invasion, and a note in his Register shows that two nuns were sent to Nunappleton, two to Nunkeeling and two to Hampole, while the Prioress went to Swine. Three days later he boarded out the nuns of Rosedale, who had received

---

[1] *Reg Palat. Dunelm.* I, p 353   In 1291 the number of nuns was twenty-seven, together with four lay brothers, three chaplains and a master. Dugdale, *Mon.* IV, p 197.

similar injuries at the hands of the Scots, sending one to each
of the houses of Nunburnholme, Sinningthwaite, Thicket, Wykeham and Hampole[1]. The dispersal of the nuns of Rosedale did
not extend beyond six months and the nuns of Moxby probably
returned about the same time, for they were back in their
own house in 1325, when their Prioress resigned "super lapsu
carnis"[2]. The moral record of both houses—and indeed of the
majority of Yorkshire nunneries—is bad at this period, and at
least part of the responsibility must be laid at the door of the
Scottish invasions.

Yorkshire also suffered in the invasion which ended with the
Battle of Neville's Cross (1346), when the Scots

went forth brenning and destroying the county of Northumberland,
and their currours ran to York and brent as much as was without
the walls and returned again to their host within a days journey,
of Newcastle-upon-Tyne[3].

One of these marauding bands ("the most outrageoust people
in all the country," Froissart calls them) came galloping into
that lonely and beautiful dale, where the nunnery of Ellerton
stands beside the brown torrent of Swale They entered the
house and carried away seven charters and writings, so the nuns
complained later[4], what else they did in that quiet spot and
whether the nunnery of Marrick on the hill above escaped them
history will not tell us. Such disasters were common enough in
the north. The records of Armathwaite in Cumberland show that
an unlucky proximity to the border might hamper a convent

[1] *Hist Letters from the Northern Reg* ed Raine, pp 319–23
[2] *V C H Yorks* III, pp 175, 240
[3] Froissart, tr Berners, I, ch cxxxvii. The English army on its way to
Neville's Cross was also a sore burden to the religious houses of the neighbourhood. See the very interesting document about Egglestone Abbey quoted
from Archbishop Zouche's Register (under the date 1348) by A Hamilton
Thompson, *The Pestilences of the Fourteenth Century in the Diocese of York*
(*Archaeol Journ* vol LXXI, New Series, vol. XXI, p 120, n 4) It is probable
that this campaign, together with the Black Death which followed hard upon
it, brought about the final ruin of the little nunnery of St Stephen's near
Northallerton, which is not heard of after 1350 See *ib* p 121, n 12, and
V.C H Yorks III, p 116
[4] *V C H Yorks* III, p 160, cp the case of Armathwaite below The muniments of Carrow were burnt during the Peasants' Revolt of 1381 Hoare, C M ,
Hist of an East Anglian Soke (Bedford 1918), p 112. "The destruction of
charters, privileges and muniments was a severe loss, evidence for the holding
of each strip of land and in support of every custom was of the utmost importance " Graham, *St Gilb of Semp and the Gilbertines*, p 138

throughout the whole of its career. In 1318 pasture for cattle in Inglewood Forest was granted to "the poor nuns of Armathwaite, who had been totally ruined by the Scots"; in 1331 they were excused a payment of ten pounds for the same reason; and in 1474 they were obliged to apply for a ratification of their possessions, because their house had been almost destroyed by the Scots, who had not only spoiled them of their church ornaments, books, relics and jewels, but also of all their charters and evidences[1]. The obscure little nunnery of Lambley on Tyne suffered in the same way, for in the Receiver's Account made at its dissolution in 1536 there occurs, under the heading *Decasus Redditus*, the entry of a tenement in Haltwhistle called Redepath, "eo quod comburatum (*sic*) per Scottos"[2].

But the most horrible story of outrage suffered by a nunnery in time of war is that strange tale reported by the anonymous monk of St Albans, who wrote a *Chronicon Angliae* between the years 1376 and 1379[3]. The suffering of French nunneries at the hand of Free Companies and English was not more terrible than the fate of these English nuns at the hand of their own countrymen. In 1379 an army was mustered in England to replace Duke John of Brittany upon his throne, which had been annexed by Charles V of France. The main army, under John FitzAlan of Arundel, Marshal of England (the same who had "two and fiftie new sutes of apparell of cloth of gold or tissue") was delayed in England for some months, first by a difficulty in raising the money to equip it, and then by contrary winds, and it was December before Sir John was ready to sail. Complaints came from all hands of the depredations committed along the coast by the lawless soldiers, but their other misdeeds were insignificant compared with the crime recorded in the St Albans Chronicle:

"When," says the chronicler, "Sir John Arundel and his companions were come to the sea and no breeze favoured them, he ordered that a more favourable wind should be awaited. Meanwhile he proceeded to a certain monastery of virgin nuns, which stood not far away, and entering with his men, he asked the mother of the monastery

---

[1] *V C H Cumberland*, II, p 190, and Dugdale, *Mon* III, pp. 271–2
[2] *Aug Off Misc Books*, 281, f. 11 [*P R O*] For the sufferings of Northern monasteries from the Scots 1330–50 see references collected from the patent rolls in P G. Mode, *op cit* p 32.
[3] *Chronicon Angliae*, ed E. M. Thompson (R S. 1874), pp. 247–53.

to permit his fellow soldiers, engaged on the king's service, to lodge there. But the nun, considering in her mind that danger might arise from such guests and that his request was absolutely contrary to religion, pointed out to him with due reverence and humility that many of his followers were young and might easily be moved to commit an inexpiable crime, which would not only bring ill fame upon the place but would also be a danger and an evil to himself and his men, who should shun not only an offence against chastity but all manner of crimes, if they acted as befitted men about to go to the wars. But he began to insist with great fervour, declaring that her suspicions were false and her imaginings without truth, whereupon she prostrated herself on the ground before him, and answered, 'My lord, I know that your men are unbridled and fear not even God It is expedient neither for us nor for you that they should enter our cloister Wherefore I beseech and counsel you with clasped hands, that you give up this intention and seek other hosts (who abound in the neighbourhood) for yourself and for your men.' But he persisted and, contemptuously bidding her arise, swore that he would in no wise give up his determination to have hospitality for his people there. Wherefore he straightway ordered his men to enter the building and to occupy the public and private rooms until the time came for setting sail And they, inspired (it is thought) by a devil, burst into the cloister of the monastery, and as is the wont of such an un-disciplined mob, broke the one into this, the other into that room, wherein the maidens, daughters of the neighbouring gentry, were lodged to be taught; and many of these were already prepared to take upon them the habit of holy religion and had set their mind on the purpose of virginity These, scorning reverence for the place and casting aside the fear of God, the men oppressed and violated by force. Nor did their lust rage against these alone, for they feared not to pollute the widow's continence and the conjugal tie For many widows had gathered there to receive hospitality, as is customary in such abbeys, either for lack of property or in order the more perfectly and safely to preserve their chastity They forced into public adultery the married women who had gathered there for the same reasons, and not content (it is said) with these misdeeds they sub-jected the nuns themselves to their lust Whereupon at first those who suffered the injury, and soon all who dwelt in the neighbourhood and who heard the news of so great a crime, heaped very horrible curses upon their heads and called down upon them whatever mis-fortune and whatever adversity God might be able to raise against them "

The chronicler goes on to relate how, undeterred and indeed encouraged by Sir John Arundel, the men spread over the country-side and pillaged it, carrying off a bride and stealing plate from the altar of a church, for which sacrilege they were solemnly excommunicated. At last, however, Sir John (in spite of the protests of the shipman who was to carry him) decided to set sail. His men carried off with them the stolen bride and a number of wives, widows and virgins from the abbey, forced the wretched women on board and put to sea. But a storm came on and the ships were driven out into the Atlantic. In the midst of the roaring tempest the guilty soldiers seemed to see a spectre, more awful than death itself, which stalked among them on the deck and foretold the loss of all who sailed upon Sir John Arundel's ship. Even more pitiable was the condition of the women:

"Hard it is to relate," says the chronicler, "what clamour, what lamentation, what groans, what tears, arose among the women, who by force or of their own will had boarded the ship, when buffeted by the winds and waves they rose to the skies and descended to the depths, for now they saw not the spectre of death, but death itself among them, and could not doubt that they must die   What mental anguish, what bodily fear, what remorse and anxiety assailed the conscience of the men, who to satisfy their lust had dragged these women into the peril of the seas, they were best able to describe who, although sharers in so great a crime, were nevertheless permitted by God's mercy to reach a port of safety. Wherefore the men were doubtful what to do in the midst of the clamour, for on the one hand the wind and storm, on the other the tears and cries of the women, urged them to action   First, therefore, they tried to lighten the vessel, throwing overboard first the worthless baggage, then precious things, that perchance a hope of safety might arise. But when they perceived their desperate plight to be rather increased than diminished, they cast the blame of their misfortune upon the women, and in a spirit of madness they seized hold of them (with the same hands wherewith before they had sweetly caressed them, the same arms wherewith they had lustfully embraced them) and threw them into the sea, to be devoured by fishes and sea beasts, to the number (it is said) of sixty women   But not even thus was the tempest stayed, but rather it grew greater so that it deprived them of all hope of escaping the danger of death."

The story is soon ended   The ships were driven onto the coast of Ireland, Sir John Arundel's vessel ran upon a rock, and he was drowned, with all his suits of apparel, his goods and his horses; and twenty-five other vessels of the ill-fated expedition, laden with soldiers and horses and baggage, also went down in the storm. Public opinion did not fail to attribute these disasters to the crimes of which Sir John and his troops had been guilty; and so, with dramatic fitness, ends this tale of the golden days of chivalry[1]. Side by side with it must be set another episode, drawn from an earlier age and from an epic instead of a chronicle. It was part of the chivalrous convention to show a special respect to nunneries, in their double character of religious and aristocratic institutions. Yet the most striking account of a nunnery in the twelfth century, when this convention was at its height, has for subject a brutal sacrilege committed by a great baron upon a church of nuns This is the famous episode of the burning of Origny in the *chanson de geste* "Raoul de Cambrai. ' The writer of the poem makes Raoul's knights recoil in shame from a crime in which their allegiance has made them unwilling partners, and manifests the utmost horror and pity at this action so opposed to all the ideals of chivalry, but it is only one of the many proofs that the golden idol had feet of clay. Whether or not the account was founded upon an actual incident is unknown; but it deserves quotation because it illus-

---

[1] It is extremely difficult to identify the nunnery spoken of in the story. According to Froissart the expedition sailed from Southampton (Froissart, *Chron* I, ch ccclvi), according to another account the port of departure was Plymouth (see J H Ramsay, *The Genesis of Lancaster*, II, p 131). If Southampton be correct, Romsey Abbey would be the nearest nunnery answering to the description in the text, though it stands some miles from the coast If Sir John sailed from Plymouth the only nunnery in the vicinity would be the little priory of Cornworthy, which certainly never contained a large number of nuns and boarders (though as to this the chronicler may be exaggerating) It is strange that no record of the crime appears to have survived in episcopal registers or in any official document, but it seems unlikely that the story is pure invention, since we know from other sources that the troops were notorious for general depredations along the coast A petition presented to the King in Parliament (1379/80) runs "Item, beseech the commons and the good folk who dwell near the coasts of the sea, to wit, of Norfolk, Suffolk, Kent, Surrey, Hampshire, Dorset and Cornwall: That whereas they and their chattels have oftentimes been robbed, and are destroyed and spoiled by men-at-arms, archers and others coming and going by the said ports to the service of our Lord the king at the war and by their long sojourn, and chiefly the people of Hampshire during the last expedition which was ruled and ordered, for by the sojourn and destruction made by men ordered upon the said expedition, the goods and chattels of the good people of Hampshire are destroyed, spoiled and annihilated, to the very great abashment and destruction of all the Commons of those parts, as well folk of Holy Church as others, and they willl odge themselves of their own authority, having no regard to the billets (herbegage) assigned to them by our lord [the king], to the destruction of the common people, if it be not remedied as soon as may be " (*Rot Parl* III, p 80) The other nunneries in Hampshire were St Mary's Winchester, Wherwell, and Whitney

trates all too clearly the fate of nuns when their quiet houses
stood in the way of warring knights It represents one side of
chivalry as truly as "Queen Guenever in Almesbury, a nun in
white clothes and black" represents another. In the same century that produced "Raoul de Cambrai" a chronicler, writing
of the wars of Stephen and Matilda in England, records, "Burnt
also was the abbey of nuns of Wherwell by a certain William
of Ypres, an evil man, who respected neither God nor man,
because certain supporters of the Empress had taken refuge
therein"; and another:

The famous town [of Winchester] was given to the flames, wherein
a convent of nuns with its offices, and more than twenty churches,
with the greater part of the town and the monastery of St Grimbald's
and the dwellings attached to it, were reduced to ashes[1]

What these bald statements mean the *chanson de geste* can tell
us better.

Raoul de Cambrai, the greatest villain who ever led knights
to war, had in his train a young knight Bernier. One day he
set out to pillage Origny, in which town was a famous convent,
where Bernier's fair mother Marcens had retired to end her days
in peace. But as he hurled himself, with four thousand men,
upon the town, the gates of the convent opened

and the nuns came forth from the church, gentle ladies, each with
her psalter, for there they did the service of God Marcens was there,
who was Bernier's mother. "Mercy, Raoul, in the just God's name!
You do great sin if you allow harm to come to us, for easily can we
be driven forth " In her hand she held a book of the time of Solomon
and she was saying an orison to God.

After a tender inquiry for her son, Marcens proceeded to plead
with Raoul to raise the siege; clearly the burgesses regarded the
abbess of the great convent as their leader and a fit person to
negotiate with their enemy

"Sir Raoul," she said, "shall I beseech you in vain to withdraw you?
We be nuns, by all the saints of Bavaria, we shall never hold lance
nor banner, nor by our hand shall any man be brought to his grave."

But Raoul answered her with a stream of coarse abuse, showing
even less respect for her sex and calling than Sir John Arundel

---

[1] Dugdale, *Mon.* II, pp. 452, 636.

showed to the abbess who refused him lodging[1]. Marcens put aside his charges with a word of dignified denial and proffered him terms of truce:

"Sir Raoul, we know not how to wield arms, easily can you destroy us and put us to flight We have neither shield nor lance for our defence All our livelihood we have from this altar and within this town; noble men hold this place dear and send us silver and pure gold Therefore do you grant us a truce for hearth and church and go you and take your ease in our meadows; of our own substance we will feed you and your knights and your squires shall have corn and oats and plenty to eat for your steeds " "By the body of St Richier," answered Raoul, "For love of you and since you ask it, I will grant you the truce, whoever may dislike it."

But Raoul de Cambrai had no regard for his knightly word; he quarrelled with the townsfolk and swore to burn Origny about their ears.

"The rooms burn," the *chanson* continues, "The ceilings crumble, the barrels catch fire and their hoops burst. Woe and sin it is, for the children burn too Evil has Count Raoul done, for the day before he gave his faith to Marcens that they should not lose so much as a fold of silk; and on the morrow he burned them in his wrath In Origny, that great and rich town, the sons of Herbert, who love the place had put Marcens, Bernier's mother, and a hundred nuns to pray to God Count Raoul, the hot-heart, sets fire to the streets; the houses burn, the ceilings melt, the wine spills and the cellars flow with it; the bacon burns, the larders fall, the fat makes the great fire burn more fiercely It strikes up to the tower and to the high belfry and the roofs fall in, so great is the blaze between the two walls The nuns are burnt, all hundred of them are burnt (woe it is to tell), burnt is Marcens that was Bernier's mother, and Clamados the daughter of Duke Renier. The smell of burning flesh rises from the flames and the brave knights weep for pity When Bernier sees the fire grow worse, he is near mad with grief Could ye but have seen him sling on his shield! With drawn sword he comes to the church and sees the flames pouring from the doors, no man can come within

---

[1] To show how a twelfth century baron might speak to a cloistered nun, the mother of one of his knights, his words deserve quotation

Voir, dist R vos estes losengiere
Je ne sai rien de putain, chanberiere,
Qi est este corsaus ne maaillere,
A toute gent communax garsoniere
Au conte Y vos vi je soldoiere,
La vostre chars ne fu onques trop chiere;
Se nus en vost, par le baron S. Piere!
Por poi d'avoir en fustes traite ariere.
Raoul de Cambrai, ll 1328–1335.

a shaft's throw of the fire. Bernier sees a rich marble pavement, and upon it lies his mother, with her tender face laid on the ground and her psalter burning upon her breast Then says the boy, 'I am on a foolish errand. Never will any succour avail her now. Ha! sweet mother, yesterday you kissed me, you have but a poor heir in me, for I can neither aid nor help you God, who will judge the world, keep your soul!'"[1]

So ends this terrible episode; but that chivalry in this matter at least suffered no change from the twelfth to the fourteenth century Froissart's account of the burning of this same Origny-Saint-Benoit by the peerless John of Hainault and his troops in 1339 will show[2]. If the code of knighthood and the fear of God could not save the nuns from mischances such as these, it is plain that no injunctions against the breach of their enclosure could have done so. These were the risks of war, which nuns shared in common with all unhappy women. But the siege of Origny and even the outrage at Goring were still exceptional events; and the Church found its chief problem not in these unwelcome incursions, but in the number of welcome visitors who hung about the nunneries "The Lord deliver them from their friends" was in effect the bishop's prayer. The expulsion of these friends was a necessary corollary to the enclosure movement; and, like the injunctions to nuns to keep within their cloister, the injunctions to lay folk to keep outside remained a dead letter. John of Ayton's conclusion is true here also:

Why, then, did the holy fathers thus labour to beat the air? Yet indeed their toil is none the less to their own merit; for we look not to that which is, but to that which of justice should be.

[1] *Raoul de Cambrai*, pub P. Meyer et A Longnon, *Soc des Anc Textes Fr* 1882, stanzas LXIII–LXXI, *passim* (pp 42–50)
[2] "Incontynent it was taken by assaut and robbed and an abbey of ladyes vyolated and the town brent" Froissart, *Chronicles*, tr Berners

CHAPTER XI

THE OLDE DAUNCE

A child of our grandmother Eve, a female; or, for
thy more sweet understanding, a woman
Love's Labour's Lost, I, 1, 266–8.

IT is difficult to form any exact impression of the moral state
of the English nunneries during the later middle ages Certainly
there is widespread evidence of frailty on the part of individuals,
and there are one or two serious cases in which a whole house
was obviously in a bad condition. It is certain also that we
retain the record of only a portion of the cases of immorality
which existed; some never came to light at all, some were hushed
up and the records of others are buried in Bishops' Registers,
which are either unpublished or lost. On the other hand it is
necessary to guard against exaggeration The majority of nuns
certainly kept their lifelong vow of chastity. Moreover when the
conditions of medieval life are taken into account, the lapses
of the nuns must, to anyone who considers them with sympathy
and common sense, appear comprehensible. The routine of the
convent was not always satisfying to the heart, and the temptations to which nuns were submitted were certainly grosser and
more frequent than they are in similar institutions today.

Several considerations may fairly be urged in mitigation of
the nuns. The initial difficulty of the celibate ideal need not be
laboured. For many saints it was the first and necessary condition of their salvation; but for the average man it has always
been an unnatural state and the monastic orders and the priest-
hood were full of average men. It is not surprising, therefore,
that the history of ecclesiastical celibacy is one of the tragedies
of religious life The vow was constantly being broken The
focaria or priest's mistress is a well-known figure in medieval
history and fiction; and the priest who lived thus with an unofficial wife was probably less dangerous to his female parishioners
than was he who lived ostensibly alone. A crowd of clerks and

chaplains, sometimes attached to some church, chantry or great man's chapel, sometimes unattached, filled the country with an "ecclesiastical proletariat," all vowed to chastity; and any student of the criminal records of the middle ages knows how often these men were concerned in cases of rape and other crime. A survey of the monastic visitations of a careful visitor such as Alnwick shows that consorting with women was a common charge against the monks and there is some evidence which points to a suspicion of grosser forms of vice It would be strange indeed if the nuns were an exception to the rule. Even if they kept their vow, they kept it sometimes at a cost which psychologists have only recently begun to understand. The visions which were at once the torture and the joy of so many mystic women, were sexual as well as religious in their origin, as in their imagery[1]. The terrible lassitude and despair of *accidia* grew in part at least from the repression of the most powerful of natural instincts, accentuated by the absence of sufficient counter interests and employments.

The whole monastic ideal is, however, bound up with the vow of chastity and, had only women with a vocation entered nunneries, the danger of the situation would have been small. Unfortunately a large number of the girls who became nuns had no vocation at all. They were given over to the life by their families, sometimes from childhood, because it was a reputable career for daughters who could not be dowered for marriage in a manner befitting their estate[2]. They were often totally unsuited for it, by the weakness of their religious as well as by the strength of their sexual impulses. The lighthearted *Chansons de Nonnes*[3], whose theme is the nun unwillingly professed, had a real basis in fact. If cases of immorality in convents seem all too frequent, it should be remembered how young and often how unwilling were those who took the vows·

> Je sent les douls mals   leis ma senturete
> Malois soit de deu   ki me fist nonnete.

---

[1] See M K Brady, *Psycho-Analysis and its Place in Life* [1919], p. 117, H. O Taylor, *The Medieval Mind* [2nd ed , 1914], I, ch xx
[2] See above, p 29 For the effects of this at a later period in Italy see J. A. Symonds, *The Renaissance in Italy. VI. The Catholic Reaction*, pt I (1886), pp. 339 ff.
[3] See below, p 502.

The blame is justly placed and the wonder is not how many but how few nuns went astray.

Again the nunneries of the middle ages were subjected to temptations which rarely occur in our own time The chief of these was the ease with which· the nuns moved about outside their houses in a world where sex was displayed good-humouredly, openly, grossly, by the populace, and with all the subtle charm of chivalry by the upper classes The struggle to enforce enclosure had its root in the recognition of this danger, as episcopal references to the story of Dinah show; and it has already been seen how unsuccessful that struggle was Nuns left their precincts, visited their friends, attended feasts, listened to wandering minstrels, with hardly any restraint upon their movements. It is true that in church and cloister the praise of virginity was forever dinned into their ears; but outside in the world it was not virginity that was praised Were it a miller's tale or a wife of Bath's prologue, overheard on a pilgrimage, were it only the lilt of a passing clerk at a street corner,

> Western wind, when wilt thou blow,
> The small rain down can rain?
> Christ, if my love were in my arms
> And I in my bed again,

the nun's mind must often have been troubled, as she turned her steps back to her cloister. Moreover their guest rooms were full of visitors, men as well as women, if they copied so eagerly the fine dresses and the pet dogs of worldly ladies, is it strange that they sometimes copied their lovers too? Other conditions besides the imperfect enforcement of enclosure increased the danger. The disorders of the times, ranging from the armed forays of the Scots in the north to the lawlessness of everyday life in all parts of the country, were not conducive to a fugitive and cloistered virtue[1]. Nor was the constant struggle against financial need, leading as it did to many undesirable expedients for raising money, really compatible with either dignity or unworldliness There is a poverty which breeds plain living and high thinking, a fair Lady Poverty whom St Francis wedded. But there is also an unworthy, grinding poverty, which occupies the mind with a struggle to make two ends meet and dulls it

---

[1] See above, pp. 422 ff.

to finer issues. Too often the poverty of the nunneries was of the last type.

Let it be conceded, therefore, that the celibate ideal was a hard one, that the nuns were often recruited without any regard for their fitness to follow it, and that some of the conditions of convent life, insufficiently withdrawn from the temptations and disorders of the outside world, served to promote rather than to restrain a breach of it With these preliminary warnings, an attempt may be made to estimate the moral state of the English nunneries. The evidence for such a study falls into three classes, the purely literary evidence of moralist and story-teller, the general statements of ecclesiastical councils and the exact and specific evidence of the Bishops' Registers The literary evidence will be treated more fully in a further chapter and need not detain us here. Langland's nun, who had a child in cherry time, Gower's voice crying against the frailty of woman kind, the "Dame Lust, Dame Wanton and Dame Nice," who haunted the imaginary convent of the poem *Why I can't be a Nun*, are all well known, as are the serious *exempla*, the pretty Mary-miracles, and the ribald tales, which have for their subject an erring nun. They are useful as corroborative evidence, but without more exact information they would tell us little that is of specific value Similarly the enactments of church councils and general chapters are quite general By far the most valuable evidence as to monastic morals is contained in the Bishops' Registers, whether in the accounts of visitations and the injunctions which followed them, or in the special mandates ordering inquiry into a scandal, search after an apostate, or penance upon a sinner The visitation documents are particularly useful. Where full *detecta* are preserved, the moral state of a house is vividly pictured; there you may see the unworthy Prioress, whose bad example or weak rule has led her flock astray; there the nuns conniving at a love affair and assisting an elopement, or complaining bitterly of the dishonour wrought upon their house. If the register of visitations be a full one, it is possible to form an approximately exact estimate of the moral condition of all the nunneries in a particular diocese at a particular time, in so far as it was known to the Bishop If a diocese possess a long and fairly unbroken series of registers, as at York and

Lincoln, the moral history of the house may be traced over a long period of years. Supplementary evidence is sometimes also to be found in the Papal Registers, when the Pope had been petitioned in favour of some nun, or had heard rumours of the evil state of some nunnery; but Papal letters on the subject are comparatively rare. The mass of the information which follows is therefore derived from the invaluable records of the bishops.

It seems quite clear that the nuns who broke their vows were always willing parties to the breach Few men would have been bold enough to ravish a *Sponsa Dei*. Sometimes a bishop was led to suppose that a nun had been carried away against her will, but he always found out in the end that she had been in the plot, all abductions were in reality elopements In the Register of Bishop Sutton of Lincoln there is notice of an ex-communication pronounced in 1290 against the persons who abducted Agnes of Sheen, a nun of Godstow. The Bishop an-nounces that she and another nun were journeying peacefully towards Godstow in a carriage belonging to their house, when suddenly, in the very middle of the King's highway at Wycombe, certain sons of perdition laid violent hands upon them and dragged the unwilling Agnes out of her carriage and carried her off. But he seems to have received a different account of the affair later, for in the following year he announces that Agnes of Sheen, Joan of Carru and "a certain kinswoman of the Lady Ela, Countess of Warwick," professed nuns of Godstow, have fled from their house and, casting off their habit, are living a worldly and dissolute life, to the scandal of the neighbourhood; and he pro-nounces excommunication against the nuns and all their helpers[1].

Some nuns contrived to meet their lovers secretly, within the precincts of their own convents, or outside during the visits which they paid so freely despite the Bull *Periculoso*; they made no effort to leave their order, and were only discovered if their behaviour were such as to create a public scandal among the other nuns, or in the neighbouring villages. Others, smitten deeply by "amor che a nullo amato amar perdona," hailed insistently by the call of life outside, cast off their habits and left their convents They risked their immortal souls by doing so, for the Church condemned the crime of apostasy far more

---

[1] *Linc. Epis. Reg Memo Sutton*, ff 5d, 32d

severely than that of unchastity, since it involved the breach
of all the monastic vows, instead of only one, and brought
religion into dishonour in the eyes of laymen. The nun who
sinned was given a penance; the nun who apostatised was excommunicated; and there were few who could withstand for long
the sense of utter isolation, even from a God whose love they
had scorned. The bride of Christ who could live happily under the
shadow of the ban, who could marry knowing her union to be
unrecognised and even cursed by the Church[1], must have been
of a most unmedieval scepticism, a most unfeminine indifference
to the scorn of her fellows, or drowned so deep in love that she
counted Heaven well lost. There were not many such; and the
majority of apostates returned to their order, worn out by
remorse or by persecution, or convinced at last that mortal
love was but what the author of *Hali Meidenhad* named it,
"a licking of honey off thorns"

It is no wonder that the majority of these apostates returned
What were they but individuals? Against them was arrayed the
might of two great institutions, the Church and the State Sometimes the might of the Church alone availed to retrieve them,
terror brought them of their own free will, or they found themselves caught in a net of threats and excommunications, in-
volving not only themselves, but all who helped them. When
Isabel Clouvill, Maud Titchmarsh and Ermentrude Newark, for
some time nuns professed in the house of St Mary in the Meadows
(Delapré), Northampton, left their convent and went to live
in sin in the world, they were excommunicated. Moreover their
Bishop ordered the Archdeacon of Northampton to summon

---

[1] The unions were sometimes referred to as "marriages" and a priest
unaware of the facts of the case may have been got to celebrate them For
instance Bishop Gynewell recites how Joan Bruys, nun of Nuneaton, was
abducted by Nicholas Green of Isham and "postmodum se in nostram
diocesim divertentes matrimonium de facto in eadem nostra diocesi scienter
inuicem contraxerunt et incestum ibidem commiserunt et in ea cohabitant
indies vir et vxor." *Linc. Epis Reg. Memo Gynewell*, f 102 Marriage is
also referred to in the case of Joyce, an apostate from St Helen's, Bishopsgate, in 1388 *Hist MSS Com Rep* ix, App pt i, p 28 At Atwater's
visitation of Ankerwyke in 1519 it was stated "Domina Alicia Hubbart
stetit ibidem in habitu per quatuor annos et tunc in apostasiam recessit
et cuidam...Sutton consanguineo Magistri Ricardi Sutton Senescalli de
Syon fuit nupta et cum eo in patria ipsius Sutton remanet in adulterio"
Linc Epis. Reg Visit. Atwater, f 42

them to return within a week, and all who received them in
their houses or gave them any help and counsel, were to be
warned to desist within three days and to be given a penance.
The names of the villages where they were received were to be
notified to the Bishop and their aiders and abettors were to
appear before him[1]. How many people would suffer for long
the displeasure of the Church for the sake of three runaway
nuns? Lovers might be faithful, but even lovers must eat and
drink and sleep beneath a roof: a nun was no nut-brown maid
to live content in greenwood, "when the shawes be shene." If
the pair could escape to a town where their story was not known,
there was some chance for them, but sooner or later the Church
found them out

Suppose they scorned the Church, suppose powerful friends
protected them, or careless folk who snapped their fingers at
the priest and knew too much about begging friars to hold one
amorous nun a monstrous, unexampled scandal. Then the Church
could call in the majesty of the State to help, and what was a
girl to do? Can one defy the King as well as the Bishop? To a
soul in hell must there be added a body in prison? Elizabeth
Arundell runs away from Haliwell in 1382, nor will she return.
The Prioress thereupon petitions the King; let His Highness
stretch forth the secular arm and bring back this lamb which
wanders from the fold. His Highness complies; and his commission goes forth to Thomas Sayvill, sergeant-at-arms, John
Olyver, John York, chaplain, Richard Clerk and John Clerk to
arrest and deliver to the Prioress of Haliwell in the diocese of
London, Elizabeth Arundell, apostate nun of that house[2] The

---

[1] *Linc Epis Reg Memo Dalderby*, f. 16 Translated in R M Serjeantson, *Hist of Delapré Abbey, Northampton*, pp 7–8

[2] *P.R.O Chancery Warrants*, Series I, File 1759, *Cal of Patent Rolls*
(1381–5), p 235 This file of Chancery Warrants contains a large number of
petitions for the arrest of vagabond monks and nuns. These petitions
usually emanate from the head of the apostate's house, but occasionally
from the Bishop of the diocese, as in another warrant in the same file in
which the Bishop of Norwich petitions for the arrest of Katherine Montagu,
Benedictine nun of Bungay (1376). Other petitions besides those quoted
in the text concern Alice Romayn, Austin nun of Haliwell (1314, *ib*),
Matilda Hunter, Austin nun of Burnham (1392), (File 1762), Alice de
Everyngham, Gilbertine nun of Haverholm (1366), (File 1764); and the
following sisters of Hospitals, Agnes Stanley of St Bartholomew's, Bristol
(1389), Johanna atte Watre of St Thomas the Martyr at Southwark (1324)
and Elizabeth Holewaye of the same house (File 1769, nos 1, 15, 18) On

sheriffs of London and Middlesex and Essex and Hertford, as
well as a sergeant-at-arms and three other men, are all set
hunting for Joan Adeleshey, nun of Rowney, who is wandering
about in secular dress to the great scandal of her order[1]. The
net is wide; in the end the nun nearly always comes back She
comes to the Bishop for absolution. He sends a letter on her
behalf to her convent, bidding them receive her in sisterly wise,
but abate no jot of the penance imposed on her. The prodigal
returns kneeling at the convent gate and begging admission,
for it is an age of ceremony and in these dramatic moments
onlookers learn their lesson[2]. The gates swing open and close
again · Sister Joan is back.

The most interesting of all the stories of apostasy which have
been preserved is the romantic affair of Agnes de Flixthorpe
(alias de Wissenden), nun of St Michael's, Stamford, which for
ten years continually occupied the attention of Bishop Dalderby
of Lincoln[3]. The story of this poor woman is a tragic witness to
the desperation into which convent life could throw one who
was not suited for it, as well as to the implacable pursuit of her
by the Church; for indeed the Hound of Heaven appears in it

receipt of these petitions the writ *De apostata capiendo* would be issued
and the royal commissions for the arrest of the delinquents are sometimes
found enrolled on the patent rolls, as in the cases quoted in the text Alice
Everyngham was excommunicated by the master of Sempringham, but
on her case being brought to the papal court and committed by the Pope
to the dean and two canons of Lincoln, she was absolved by them. The
master appealed to the Pope against her absolution, and the case was
committed for trial to the Archbishop of York *Cal of Papal Letters,*
IV, pp. 69–70. For a royal commission to arrest Mary de Felton of the
House of Minoresses at Aldgate, see *Cal. Pat. Rolls,* 1385–9, p. 86.
  [1] *P R O Chancery Warrants,* Series I, File 1759, *Cal. of Pat Rolls,*
1401–5, pp. 418, 472.
  [2] There are several references to this ceremony "Dictam igitur commonialem vestram, iniuncta ei penitencia seculari pro suis reatibus atque
culpis, ad vos et domum vestram, a qua exiit, remittimus absolutam,
deuocionem vestram firmiter in Domino exhortantes quatinus...dictam
penitentem si in humilitatis spiritu, reclinato corpore more penitencium,
pulset ad portam, misericordiam deuote postulans et implorans, si suum
confiteatur reatum, si signa contricionis ac correccionis appareant in eadem,
secundum disciplinam vestri ordinis, filiali promptitudine admittatis"
(Maud of Terrington at Keldholme, 1321), *Yorks Arch Journ.* XVI, pp 456–7.
Compare *ib.* XVI, p. 363 (Margaret of Burton at Kirklees, 1337); Wm. Salt
Archaeol. Soc. Coll I, p 256 (case against Elizabeth la Zouche who, with
another nun, had escaped from Brewood in 1326, she was not recovered
until 1331)
  [3] *V C.H. Lincs* II, pp. 99–100.

in the aspect of a bloodhound. In 1309 Dalderby excommunicated Agnes for apostasy and warned all persons against receiving her into their houses or giving her any help. The next year he was obliged to call in the secular arm against her. She was then living at Nottingham and the Archdeacon of Nottingham was instructed to warn her to return. Shortly afterwards the Bishop wrote to the Abbot of Peterborough, asking him to see to her being taken back to her house and there imprisoned and guarded. The combined efforts of the Sheriff, the Archdeacon of Nottingham and the Abbot of Peterborough would appear to have succeeded. The hapless woman was taken back to her house by force and still obdurate; and the Bishop ordered her to be confined in a chamber with stone walls, each of her legs shackled with fetters until she consented to resume her habit. Her perseverance seems, however, to have worn out the nuns, and in 1311 the Bishop wrote to one Ada, sister of William de Helewell, instructing her to take custody of Agnes. The reason for thus placing her in secular charge was that her case was now *sub judice*, for two months later the Bishop sent two commissioners to inquire into the whole question of the apostasy. Agnes had declared that she was never professed at all, because she had been married to one whose name she refused to give, before she entered religion; and she still, said the bishop, continued in obstinacy.

But the Church did not easily relax its clutch. After three months the Bishop wrote to his colleague the Bishop of Exeter, stating that Agnes de Flixthorpe, after having been professed for twenty years, left her house and was found wearing a man's gilt embroidered gown, that she was brought back to her house, excommunicated and kept in solitude, and that she remained obstinate and would not put on the religious habit The Bishop, thinking it desirable that she should be removed from the diocese for a time, prayed his brother of Exeter that she might be received into the house of Cornworthy, there to undergo penance and to be kept in safe custody away from all the sisters A clerk, Peter de Helewell (the Helewells seem to have had some special interest in her), duly conveyed Agnes far away from the level fields of the Midlands and the friends who had hidden her from her persecutors, to the little Devonshire priory. Solitude and despair for the moment broke her spirit and the next year, in 1312, she declared her penitence and the Bishop of Exeter was commissioned to absolve her; but she was kept in solitary confinement at Cornworthy until 1314, when Peter de Helewell once more journeyed across to Devonshire and brought her back to Stamford. Her native air blew hope and rebellion once more into that wild heart. Four years later Dalderby addressed a letter to the Prioress stating that Agnes de Flixthorpe had three times left her order and resumed a secular habit and was now in the world again and had been for two years past; reiterating once more the futile injunction that the Prioress "under pain of excommunication and without any dissimulation" was to bring her back and to keep her in safe custody and solitude; the unfortunate Prioress had doubtless had more than enough of Agnes de Flixthorpe and wished for nothing better than to leave her in the world. The story ends abruptly here and it will never be known whether Agnes de Flixthorpe was caught again.

It was perhaps merciful to receive again apostates whose hearts failed them and who besought with tears to be reconciled to the Church. But the forcible return of a hardened sinner cannot have raised the moral tone of a house. Sometimes these nuns had lived for two or three years in the world before they were brought back Sometimes they broke out again, yielded their easy virtue to a new lover, or fled once more into the world. At Basedale (1308) Agnes de Thormondby had three times fallen thus and left her order[1]; and cases of more than one lover are not rare Sometimes the prioress of a house struggled to preserve her flock from contagion by refusing to admit the returned sinner; thus the Prioress of Rothwell in 1414 declined to comply with the Bishop's mandate to receive back a certain Joan, saying that by her own confession the girl had lived for three years with one William Suffewyk; whereupon the Bishop cited her for disobedience and repeated his order[2]. The only recorded case of a woman being refused admission concerns a sister and not a professed nun, in 1346 the Archbishop of York warned the Prioress of Nunappleton on no account to receive back Margaret,

---

[1] V C H Yorks III, p 159
[2] V.C.H. Lincs. II, p 138. The surname "Suffewyk" should probably read Luffewyk, i.e. Lowick.

a sister of the house, who had left it pregnant, as he found that in the past she had on successive occasions relapsed and been in a similar condition[1]. It is significant that the same Archbishop wrote to the Convent of Sinningthwaite (where they opportunely preserved "the arm of St Margaret and the tunic of St Bernard, believed to be good for women lying in") concerning one of their nuns Margaret de Fonten, who had left the house pregnant, that "as she had only done so once" her penance was to be mitigated[2]. There can be no plainer commentary on the literary theme of the nun unwillingly professed than these cases of recurring frailty and apostasy. In the world these girls might have been happy wives, each with a lover or two beside their lords, like the ladies admired by Aucassin, for convents they were totally unsuited and obeyed their natures only with woe and disgrace to themselves and to their orders.

The pages of the Registers throw some light upon the partners of their misdemeanours In the sixteenth, seventeenth and eighteenth centuries the convents of France and Italy were the haunts of young gallants, *monachini*, who specialised in intrigues with nuns[3]. But the seduction of a *Sponsa Dei* was not a fashionable pursuit in medieval England, and it was not as a rule lords and gentlemen who hung about the precincts. Now we hear of a married man boarding in the house[4], now of the steward of the convent[5], now of the bailiff of a manor[6], now of a wandering harp-player[7], now of a smith's son[8], now of this or that layman, married or unmarried. But far more often the theme is *Clericus et Nonna*. Nuns' lovers were drawn from that great host of vicars, chaplains and chantry priests, themselves the children of the Church and under the vow of chastity, whose needs were greatest and whose very familiarity with the bonds of religion possibly bred contempt. As visitors in their convents, or as acquaintances outside, the

---

[1] *V C H Yorks* III, p 171. [2] *Ib* III, p 177
[3] See for Renaissance Italy, J A Symonds, *The Renaissance in Italy* (1886), VI, p. 340, A Gagnière, *Les Confessions d'une Abbesse du xvie siècle* (Paris, 1888), pp. 128 ff (Felice Rasponi), G. Marcotti, *Donne e Monache* (Firenze, 1884), but ecclesiastics were found among these *monachini* In France the same pursuit became fashionable under the League. For a later date the *Memoirs* of Casanova provide the most striking illustrations
[4] *Alnwick's Visit* MS f 39d. [5] *Linc. Visit* I, p 84.
[6] *V.C H. Yorks.* III, p 113 [7] *Alnwick's Visit* MS. ff 83, 83d
[8] *V.C.H Yorks* III, p 181

nuns were constantly meeting members of this band of celibates, who roamed about "as thick as motes in the sunbeam." They knew well how to sing, with Chaucer's Pardoner, "Come hider, love, to me," and little enough like priests they looked with their short tunics, peaked shoes and silvered girdles,

> Bucklers brode and swerdes long,
> Baudrike with baselardes kene,
> Sech toles about her necke they hong,
> With Antichrist seche prestes been

Love would light on Alison, even were the lover a clerk and she a nun, and sometimes where the priest had tempted he could absolve. What the young man of fashion was to the Italian convent of the sixteenth century, the chaplain was to the English convent of the fourteenth and fifteenth. Sometimes the seducer was attached to the convent as chaplain and even dwelt within the precincts. Bishop Sutton had to write to the Prioress of Studley bidding her send away from the house John de Sevek-wurth, clerk, who had borne himself in such unseemly wise while he dwelt there, that he had seduced two of the nuns[1]. The chaplain of the house was involved in cases at White Hall, Ilchester (1323)[2], Moxby (1325)[3] and Catesby (1442)[4], which may lend some support to the complaints of Gower[5] and other medieval moralists and an additional sting to the good humoured chaff addressed by Chaucer's host to the nun's priest, Sir John. That the spiritual father of the nuns could thus abuse his position would seem almost incredible to anyone unfamiliar with medieval sources; yet Gower goes further still, suggesting that even the visitors of the convents were not always beyond suspicion[6].

[1] "En visitaunt vostre mesun por plusure fiez truuames nus ke Johan de Seuekwurth, clerk, se auoit si mauuesement porte en demurant en la mesun ke il esteit atteint de folie de cors od vne de vos nuneins e vne autre esteit de ly atteinte, par defaute de purgaciun ke ele ne se poeit de li purger. Par quei nus defendimes a vus ke vus ne le suffrissez en vostre mesun demurer, e a li ke la euene demurast" *Linc Epis. Reg. Memo. Sutton,* f 129d.

[2] *V C.H Somerset,* II, p 157   [3] *V C.H. Yorks* III, p 240.
[4] *Linc. Visit.* II, p 47   [5] See below, p. 545

[6] Gascoigne accuses John Stafford, Archbishop of Canterbury, of having had sons and daughters by a nun at a time when he was Bishop of Bath and Wells "In diebus meis, anno Domini 1443, electus fuit, vel verius intrusus, unus archiepiscopus qui fuit genitus ex manifesto adulterio, et existens genuit filios et filias ex una moniali, in episcopali gradu existens

More often the lover had no connection with the nunnery, but had some post as chaplain or vicar in the neighbourhood[1] Opportunities for a meeting were not hard to obtain in the houses and gardens of the town[2], even in the church and precincts of the priory itself[3], as visitation *comperta* show. Nor were cloistered monks proof against temptation They knew only too well what passionate hearts could beat beneath a monastic habit and they knew the merry rhyme of Cockaygne land, where every monk had his nun. It has already been shown that nuns and monks

antequam fuit archiepiscopus." *Loci e Libro Veritatum*, ed J. E Thorold Rogers (1881), p 231   Gascoigne was a learned Doctor of Theology and Chancellor of the University of Oxford   His theological dictionary gives an extraordinarily vivid and gloomy picture of the corruptions of the church in his day.   It must be noted however that Stafford's support of the heretical Bishop Reginald Pecok (author of the *Repressor of Overmuch Blaming of the Clergy*) made Gascoigne his implacable enemy, while there is no foundation for his statement that Stafford was of illegitimate birth His charge is therefore unworthy of belief   The scandal which later connected the name of John Stokesley, Bishop of London, with Anne Colte, Abbess of Wherwell, seems likely to be equally devoid of foundation, though she was several times summoned before the Council in 1534; the King and Cromwell evidently resented her refusal to give a farm to one of their protégés   *L. and P Hen VIII*, VI, 1361, VII, 527–9, 907; *V.C.H Hants* II, p 136

[1] See, besides the references given above, cases in which a priest or chaplain was implicated at St Stephen's Foukeholm (abduction of Cecilia by William, Chaplain of Yarm, 1293), *V.C.H. Yorks.* III, p 113; Nunkeeling (Avice de Lelle had confessed to incontinence, ordered not to talk to Robert de Eton, chaplain, or any other person, 1318), *ib.* p 121, Keldholme, 1318 (Mary de Holm and Sir William Lely, chaplain, 1318), *ib* p 169, Kirklees (Joan de Heton and Sir Michael, called the Scot, priest, 1315), *Yorks. Arch Journ* XVI, p 361; Godstow (Sir Hugh Sadylere of Oxford, chaplain, and Alice Longspee, 1445), *Linc Visit* II, p 114, Littlemore (Prioress Katherine Wells and Richard Hewes, priest of Kent, 1517), *V.C.H. Oxon* II, p. 76, Wintney (Prioress and Thomas Ferring, a secular priest, 1405), *Cal. Papal Letters*, VI, p 55, Romsey (charge against Emma Powes and the vicar of the parish church, 1502), *V.C.H Hants* II, p 130, Easebourne (Sir John Smyth, chaplain, concerned in abduction of two nuns, 1478), *Sussex Arch Coll* IX, p 17, and various other instances of suspicious behaviour or of chaplains and priests warned off the premises   Some of these cases are described in detail below, *passim*

[2] E g "Fatebatur se carnaliter cognitam a D B apud S in domo habitacionis sue ibidem situata," *Linc. Visit* I, p 71   "Item dicit quod priorissa consuevit sola accedere ad villam de Catesby ad gardinas cum vno solo presbytero " *Ib* II, p 47.

[3] E g "Domina Agnes Smyth inquisita dicit quod Simon Prentes cognovit eam et suscitavit prolem ex ea infra prioratum, extra tamen claustrum " Jessopp, *Visit of Dioc. Norwich*, p 109   There are many references to and injunctions against suspicious confabulations with men in the nave and other parts of the priory church

met freely and that Bishops were constantly sending injunctions against the admission of monks and friars to convents and the visits paid by nuns to monasteries[1] Yet we hear of a nun of St Sepulchre's, Canterbury, whose name scandal connected with the cellarer of the Cathedral (1284)[2], of a nun of Lymbrook, who was the mistress of William de Winton, Subprior of Leominster Priory, and not his only mistress (1282)[3]; of a nun of Swine, who had had two monks of the Abbey of Meaux for her lovers (1310)[4]. Bishop Alnwick's visitation of the Lincoln diocese brought to light two such cases and in both the monk was not the nun's sole lover. Agnes Butler (*alias* Pery *alias* Northampton) ran away from St Michael's, Stamford, for a day and a night with Brother John Harreyes, an Austin friar; her secret was kept, but when Alnwick visited her house in 1440 she had run away again, this time with a harp-player, and had been living with him a year and a half at Newcastle-on-Tyne, a far enough cry from Stamford[5] In 1445, when the Bishop went to Godstow, he found Dame Alice Longspey grievously suspected, by reason of her confabulations alone in the convent church with an Oxford chaplain, who gave himself out to be her kinsman. A week later, while visiting Eynsham Abbey, he received a further sidelight on her character from the evidence of the abbot that

one brother John Bengeworthe, a monk, who had been imprisoned for his ill desert, brake prison and went into apostasy, taking with him a nun of Godstow, but he has now been brought back to the monastery and is still doing penance.

The nun was Alice Longspey and it is significant that this particular escapade had been concealed from the Bishop at his recent visitation of Godstow[6]. The most spirited enterprise of all, however, was the combined effort of William Fox, parson of Lea (near Gainsborough) and John Fox and Thomas de Lingiston, Friars Minor of Lincoln, who were indicted before the Kings Justices at Caistor, because they came to Brodholme Nunnery (one of the only two Premonstratensian houses in the

---

[1] See above, pp. 386–9, 401.   [2] *Reg Epis. J. Peckham*, II, p 708.
[3] *Reg. Thome de Cantilupo, Epis Herefordensis* (Canterbury and York Society), p 265.
[4] *V.C.H. Yorks* III, p 181
[5] *Alnwick's Visit* MS. f. 83. See above, p. 310
[6] *Linc. Visit.* II, pp. 91, 116.

kingdom) on January 15th, 1350, and then and there "violently took and carried away, against the peace of their lord the King, a certain nun, by name Margaret Everingham, a sister of the said house, stripping her of her religious habit and clothing her in a green gown of secular habit, taking also divers goods to the value of 40 shillings"[1].

Much as the church hated sin, it hated scandal even more and a nun might often hope to have her frailty concealed by her fellows. Sometimes they may have condoned it, for they are occasionally found assisting an elopement[2], sometimes they feared episcopal interference and an evil reputation for their house. But it was not always possible to conceal these unhallowed unions and when a child was born the wretched nun could not hope to escape disgrace and punishment[3].

> And dame Peronelle a prestes file—Priouresse worth she neuere
> For she had childe in chirityme—all owre chapitere it wiste

Usually Dame Pernell fled in despair to any friendly asylum which she could find and only returned to her house after the birth and disposal of her child Sometimes she remained there in what privacy she might; and the affair was managed with as little scandal as possible. The nuns of St Michael's, Stamford, knew that their sister Margaret Mortimer had had a child on

---

[1] R. E. G. Cole, *The Priory of Brodholme* (*Assoc. Architec. Soc. Reports and Papers*, xxviii), p. 66

[2] At Markyate in 1336 "an apostate nun was received back again and absolved by Bishop Burghersh and three others sought absolution at the same time for having aided and abetted her in her escape" *V C H Beds* I, p. 360

[3] It must be conceded that the Church gave the nuns every inducement to take measures to prevent such disasters; for instance in the *Liber Poenitentialis* of Theodore the Anglo-Saxon nun guilty of immorality is given eight years of penance and ten if there be a child, a married layman and a nun who are lovers have six years of penance and seven if there be a child. Here, as ever, the Church went on the principle that sin was bad but scandal worse, *si non caste tamen caute* Of the practice of abortion I find no record in English pre-Reformation documents, though Henry VIII's disreputable commissioner, Dr Layton, accused the Yorkshire nuns of taking potations "ad prolem conceptum opprimendum." *Letters Relating to the Suppression of the Monasteries* (Camden Soc. 1843), p. 97. There is a proved case of it in Eudes Rigand's visitation of St-Aubin (1256), and a suspicion at St Saëns (1264), *Reg. Visit Rigaud*, ed. Bonnin, pp. 255, 491. See below, p 668. One of Caesarius of Heisterbach's *exempla* hangs upon it Caes. Heist *Dial Mirac* ed Strange, ii, p 331 In seventeenth and eighteenth century Italy the practice seems to have been common, witness Casanova

this side of Easter; but even the Subprioress did not know (or said she did not know) "of whom she conceived or whether she bare male or female; howbeit she was absent from quire for a fortnight"[1], Once we hear of an apostate, deserted and pregnant, coming back to St Mary's, Winchester, and the wise and humane William of Wykeham writes to the Abbess bidding her receive the girl gently and kindly, and keep her in safety until the birth of her child, after which he will himself make ordinance concerning her[2]. It is hard to discover what became of these most unwelcome children. It is not surprising that they sometimes died[3] But if they lived their origin probably weighed but lightly on them in those days, when it was regarded as no dishonour to have bastards, who were often acknowledged by their fathers and provided for in their wills side by side with true born sons and daughters. It is true that, like other illegitimates, they could not be ordained or hold ecclesiastical preferment, without a special dispensation. But even the son of a nun could obtain such dispensation[4] and even the daughter of a nun did not always go undowered. There were not many monastic parents like that seventeenth century abbess of Maubuisson who was rumoured to have twelve children, who were brought up diversely, each according to the rank of the father[5], or like the Prior of Maiden Bradley, as described by Henry VIII's commissioner, "an holy father prior and hath but vj children and but one dowghter mariede, yet of the goods of the monasteries trysting shortly to mary the rest, [and] his sones be tale men waytting upon him"[6]. Yet we hear of at least one Prioress who sold the goods of her house to make a dowry for her daughter[7].

---

[1] *Alnwick's Visit.* MS f 96
[2] *Wykeham's Reg.* II, pp. 114-5.
[3] "Et proles obiit immediate post" Jessopp, *op cit* p 109
[4] See e g faculty given "to dispense twenty persons of illegitimate birth of the realms of France and England, whether sons of priests or married persons, or monks, *or nuns,* to be ordained and to hold two benefices apiece." *Cal of Papal Letters,* IV, p 170
[5] M. E Lowndes, *The Nuns of Port Royal* (1909), p. 13. The Abbess in question was Angélique d'Estrées, sister of Gabrielle, Henry IV's mistress, and famous for her scandalous life and her struggle with her successor, the famous Mère Angélique (Jacqueline Arnauld) of Port Royal.
[6] *Letters Relating to the Suppression of the Monasteries* (Camden Soc. 1843), p. 58. But it must be remembered that we cannot believe uncorroborated a single word that Layton says
[7] See below, Note F.

If it be sought to know whether any houses were particularly liable to scandals and enjoyed a bad name, it must be answered that it is almost impossible to say. But isolated cases of immorality and apostasy come from nunneries so widely distributed in different dioceses, that one must conclude that most of them had at one time or another a sinner in their midst Often enough the case was isolated; occasionally there was scandal about the general condition of a house in its neighbourhood. The discipline and morals of convents were apt to vary with that of their heads. It is significant that when a house is in a bad moral state the fault may nearly always be traced to a weak or immoral prioress. So it was at Wintney in 1405, at Redlingfield in 1427, at Markyate in 1433, at Catesby in 1442, at St Michael's, Stamford, in 1445, at Littlemore in 1517, and at several Yorkshire nunneries. It is plain also that when a convent was very small and poor, it was apt to become lax and disorderly. The small Yorkshire houses bear witness to this and if further proof be required the state of Cannington in 1351 and Easebourne in 1478 may be quoted from among several other instances.

Cannington in Somerset was a small and poor house, but its nuns were drawn from some of the best county families In 1351 it was visited by commissioners of Ralph of Shrewsbury, Bishop of Bath and Wells, and they found something more like a brothel than a priory Maud Pelham and Alice Northlode (a young lady whom the Bishop had forced on the unwilling convent, on his elevation to the See some twenty years before) were in the habit of frequently admitting and holding discourse with suspected persons. The inevitable chaplain was again the occasion for a fall. On dark nights they held long and suspicious confabulations with Richard Sompnour and Hugh Willynge, chaplains, in the nave of the convent church. Hugh was apparently only too willing and Richard was even as Chaucer's summoner, "as hot he was and lecherous as a sparrow," for (say the commissioners) "it is suspected by many that as a result of these conversations they fall into yet worse sin" Moreover

"the said sisters, and in particular the said Maud, not content with this evil behaviour, are wont *per insolencias, minas et tactus indecentes* to provoke many of the serving men of the place to sin," and, "to make use of her own words she says that she will never once say *Mea culpa* for these great misdeeds, but turning like a virago upon the prioress and the other sisters who abhor the aforesaid things, when they reproach her, she threatens to do manly execution upon them with knives and other weapons "

Nor was this all.

In the said visitation the charge was made, dreadful to say, horrible to hear, and was proven by much evidence as to notoriety and by confession, that a certain nun of the said house, Joan Trimelet, having cast away the reins of modesty...was found with child, but not indeed by the Holy Ghost, and afterwards gave birth to offspring, to the grave disgrace and confusion of her religion and to the scandal of many

These were the most serious charges; but the same visitation revealed that the Prioress was weak and had been guilty of the simoniacal reception of four nuns, for the sake of scraping together some money, while the subprioress was incurably lazy, refused to attend matins and other canonical hours, and neglected to correct her delinquent sisters[1] It is plain that the whole house was utterly demoralised and the demoralisation was possibly of long standing, for there had been one of the usual election quarrels in the early part of the century, and in 1328 the then Bishop had issued a commission to inquire into the illicit wanderings of certain nuns[2]. Yet the priory was a favourite resort of boarders

Easebourne, again, was a poor but very aristocratic house, containing towards the close of the fifteenth century from six to ten nuns In 1478 Bishop Story of Chichester visited it and found grave need for his interference One of the nuns, Matilda Astom, deposed

that John Smyth, chaplain, and N. Style, a married man in the service of Lord Arundel, had and were accustomed to have great familiarity within the said priory, as well as elsewhere, with Dame Joan Portsmouth and Dame Philippa King, nuns of the said priory, but whether the said Sir John Smyth and N. Style abducted, or caused to be abducted, the said Joan Portsmouth and Philippa King she knows not, as she says

(Another nun deposed that they did.)

---

[1] *Reg Ralph of Shrewsbury* (Som Rec. Soc.), pp 683–4, the charge is not given in full in this edition of the Register and must be eked out from the extract in Dugdale, *Mon.* iv, p. 416 (note)

[2] *Reg. John of Drokensford*, pp. 60, 126, 167, 287.

And moreover she says that a certain William Gosden and John Capron of Easebourne aforesaid, guarded and kept in their own houses the said Joan and Philippa for some time before their withdrawal from the said priory and took their departure with them and so were great encouragers to them in that particular.

Another nun, Joan Stevyn, deposed that the two nuns had each had, long before their withdrawal, "children or a child." Another said that Sir John Senoke (i.e. Sevenoaks, clearly the same as John Smyth)

much frequented the priory, so that during some weeks he passed the night and lay within the priory every night, and was cause, as she believes, of the ruin of the said Sir John Smyth (*sic*, MS ? Joan Portsmouth). Also she says Sir John Smyth gave many gifts to Philippa King

All the nuns agreed in blaming the Prioress for not having properly punished the two sinners and one raked up a vague story that "she had had one or two children several years ago"; but as she admitted that this was hearsay and as the Prioress was then at least fifty years old, too much credit must not be given to it. On the same day a certain "Brother William Cotnall," evidently attached in some capacity, perhaps as *custos*, to the house, appeared before the Bishop and confessed that he had sealed a licence to Joan Portsmouth to go out of the Priory and had himself sinned with Philippa King. The two priests, Smyth and Cotnall, had not only debauched the convent, but had done their best to ruin it financially; for they had persuaded the Prioress to pawn the jewels of the house for fifteen pounds, in order to purchase a Bull of Capacity for Cotnall, who had then sealed with the common seal of the convent, against the wish of the Prioress, a quittance for John Smyth concerning all and every sort of actions and suits which the convent might have against him, and especially the matter of the jewels[1]

But if small houses fell easily into disorder, great abbeys were not exempt from contagion. Cases of immorality are found at Wilton, Shaftesbury, Romsey, St Mary's Winchester, Wherwell and Elstow, all of them abbeys and among them the oldest and richest in the land. It is the same with two other houses, famous in legend, Amesbury, where Guinevere "let make herself a nun and wore white clothes and black," and Godstow, where

[1] *Sussex Arch. Coll.* IX, pp. 17–19.

Fair Rosamond lay buried in the chapter house. Here, where deathless romance had its dwelling place, it is not strange that the winged god ever and again took his toll of the nuns But what sorry substitutes for Guinevere and Rosamond were the trembling apostates, who fled into hiding to bear their miserable infants and were haled back by bishops to do penance in the cloister.

> Thou hast conquered, O pale Galilean, the world has grown grey from thy breath.

The ancient house of Amesbury fell into evil ways in the twelfth century In 1177 its abbess was said to have borne three children and its nuns were notorious for their evil lives, where-upon the convent was dissolved, most of the nuns being placed in other houses, and Amesbury was then reconstituted as a cell of Fontevrault and peopled with a prioress and twenty-four nuns, brought over from that house[1] Queen Eleanor, widow of Henry III, took the veil there and by her influence Edward I allowed his daughter Mary to become a nun there, together with twelve noble maidens[2]. But the sin of Guinevere haunted it. About Mary herself there is an ancient unexplained scandal, for in a papal mandate she is declared to have been seduced by John de Warenne, the rather disreputable Earl of Surrey[3]; and she seems to have been as much out of her house as in it, for she constantly visited court and went on pilgrim-ages Later still the papal benevolence was exerted on behalf of Margaret Greenfield, nun of Amesbury, who had borne a child after her profession (1398)[4], and Cecily Marmyll, who "after having lived laudably for some time in the said monastery, allowed herself to be carnally known by two secular priests and had offspring by each of them" (1424)[5]. These ladies were doubtless well born, with wealthy friends, who could afford to petition the Pope and buy restoration to the monastic dignities and offices, which they had lost by their fault. The story of

---

[1] *Gesta Regis Henrici Secundi Benedicti Abbatis*, ed. Stubbs, Rolls Ser , I, pp 135–6.

[2] Dugdale, *Mon* II, p. 334.

[3] *Cal of Pap Letters*, III, p. 169. She was born 11 March 1278 and took the veil at the age of seven years Some annalists put the date of her pro-fession at 1285 and some at 1289; in any case the Warenne charge was not made until 1345. See above, p. 381, note 1.

[4] *Cal. of Papal Letters*, v, p 161.   [5] *Ib.* VII, p. 373.

Godstow is very similar. There seems to have been some scandal about the morals of the subprioress in 1284, but Peckham announced that he did not believe a word of it[1]. In 1290, however, a nun of noble birth was (as we saw) carried off from her carriage, and she and two others were apostate in the following year. Another apostate repented and was absolved in 1339. In 1432 a nun was found by the bishop with child and in 1445 Dame Alice Longspey indulged in the escapades already described with an Oxford priest and a monk of Eynsham. All through the career of the convent, it was continually being warned against the recourse of scholars from Oxford. Both Amesbury and Godstow enjoyed fame and good repute and at the latter children were received for education. Their history shows that even the most aristocratic and popular houses fell sometimes on evil days and sometimes sheltered unworthy inmates.

It is of considerable interest to study the condition of all the nunneries in a particular part of the country at a particular date. An analysis of the references to the Yorkshire houses has been made elsewhere[2]; here we may study a diocese in which the conditions of daily life were less abnormal than they were on the Scottish border. A rather imperfect view of the state of the diocese of Lincoln between the years 1290 and 1360 may be gleaned from the registers of Bishops Sutton, Dalderby, Burghersh and Gynewell, it is imperfect because there are not many visitation records, and information has chiefly to be derived from episcopal mandates for the return of apostates[3], which leave us with little knowledge of the internal discipline of houses from which nuns did not happen to run away. The names of eleven out of the four and thirty[4] nunneries of the diocese occur in connection with apostates during these years, six Benedictine, four Augustinian and one Cluniac. The apostasy of three

---

[1] *Reg Epis J. Peckham*, III, p 851.

[2] See Note G, p 597, below

[3] In general an apostate may be said to mean a lover, but there must also have been cases of nuns apostatising out of general discontent with the convent or Prioress

[4] Two of these, St Mary de Pré (St Albans) and Sopwell ought not, however, to be counted, being entirely under the control of the Abbey of St Albans and exempt from episcopal visitation. It was concerning St Mary de Pré that Archbishop Morton made the charges against St Albans, rendered famous by Froude

Godstow nuns in 1290 has already been described[1]. There was an
apostate at Wothorpe in 1296[2] and two years later a nun of
Harrold was found guilty of unchastity[3]. Apostates are also
mentioned from Sewardsley in 1300[4], from Goring in 1309 and
again in 1358[5], from Markyate in 1336[6] and from St Leonard's,
Grimsby, in 1337[7]. At Burnham there is the case of Margery
Hedsor, who was excommunicated at intervals for apostasy
between 1311 and 1317[8]. St Mary in the Meadows (Delapré),
Northampton, seems to have been in a bad state, for in
1300 three nuns, said to have been professed for some years,
were excommunicated for leaving their convent and living in
carnal sin in the world, and in 1311 there was another apostate
from the house[9] St Michael's, Stamford, provides the curious
story of Agnes de Flixthorpe, and the almost equally tragic case
of Agnes Bowes, ex-Prioress of Wothorpe, all of whose fellows
had died in the Black Death and whose house had therefore been
annexed to St Michael's, Stamford, in 1354. She was evidently
unable to settle down in her new home and she ran away from
it five years later[10]. In the plague year 1349, Ella de Mounceaux,
a nun of Nuncoton, who had obtained leave of absence and
instead of returning had become the mistress of John Haunsard,
appeared with tears before the Bishop and begged to be sent
back to her house[11].

This list of apostates is, as has been said, necessarily incomplete and gives no details as to the state of the nunneries
absolved. A much more exact impression can be gained of the
diocese a century later, during the twenty years between 1430
and 1450, when Bishops Gray and Alnwick were visiting the
religious houses under their control; Alnwick's Register is particularly valuable, since the verbal evidence of the nuns is preserved. If we take Gray's Register first, we find serious charges
of general misconduct made against three houses, Markyate and

[1] Above, p 440
[2] V C H. Northants. II, p. 101 (note), from Linc. Epis Reg. Memo.
Sutton, f 154
[3] V C.H. Beds. I, p 389   [4] V C H. Northants. II, p 126
[5] V.C.H. Oxon. II, p. 103.   [6] V C H. Beds I, p. 360.
[7] V C H Lincs. II, p. 179   [8] V.C.H. Bucks. I, p. 383.
[9] V.C H. Northants. II, p 114   [10] V C.H. Northants. II, p 101
[11] See A H. Thompson, "Registers of John Gynewell, Bishop of Lincoln,
for the Years 1347–1350." Archaeol Journ, 2nd ser , vol XVIII, p. 331.

Flamstead in 1431 and Sewardsley in 1432 The Bishop wrote to a canon of Lincoln that

abundant rumour and loud whisperings have brought to our hearing that in the priories of the Holy Trinity of the Wood by Markyate and of St Giles by Flamstead...certain things forbidden, hateful, guilty and contrary to holy religion and regular discipline are daily done and brought to pass in damnable wise by the said prioresses, nuns and other, servingmen and agents of the said places; by reason whereof the good report of the same places is set in jeopardy, the brightness and comeliness of religion in the same persons are grievously spotted, inasmuch as the whole neighbourhood is in commotion herefrom.

The canon is accordingly told to inquire into the scandals and punish delinquents[1]. Unfortunately the result of the inquiry has not been preserved; three years later the Bishop deputed another commissioner to inquire into the condition of Markyate and from his letters of commission it is plain that he had himself visited the house, but that the Prioress and sisters had managed to conceal their misdeeds from him. Since then he had learnt that one of the nuns, Katherine Tyttesbury, had been guilty of immorality and apostasy and that the Prioress herself had failed to obey his injunctions. The commissioner was therefore ordered to go to Markyate, absolve the apostate if she made submission and, if necessary, depose the Prioress The result of the inquiry was that the Prioress, Denise Loweliche, was charged with having consorted with Richard, the steward of the Priory, for five years and more, up to the time of his death, so that "public talk and rumour during the said time were busy touching the premises in the town of Markyate and other places, neighbouring and distant, in the diocese of Lincoln and elsewhere." The Prioress denied the charge and begged to be allowed to clear herself, so the commissioner ordered her, in addition to her own oath, to find five out of her ten nuns as compurgatresses, i.e. to swear to her innocence. She sought in vain for help among her sisters; at the appointed hour she begged for an extension of time and the commissioner granted her this boon, "so that she might be able meanwhile to communicate and take counsel with her sisters," and also "of a more liberal grace," declared himself ready to take the word of four nuns on her behalf. The picture

[1] *Linc. Visit.* I, pp. 81–2

of the wretched Prioress going from nun to nun, imploring each to forswear herself, with heaven knows what threats and entreaties, is a melancholy one. Not even four nuns could be found to swear to her innocence, so clear and notorious was her guilt, and she laid her formal resignation in the hands of the bishop[1].

The other nunnery against which a general charge of immorality was made by the Bishop in 1434 was the Cistercian house of Sewardsley, of which he said that the Prioress and nuns,

following the enticements of the flesh and abandoning the path of religion and casting aside the restraint of all modesty and chastity, are giving their minds to debauchery, committing in damnable wise in public and as it were, in the sight of all the people, acts of adultery, incest, sacrilege and fornication[2].

The report of the inquiry held has not been preserved, but there was obviously something seriously amiss. Gray had also to deal with individual cases of immorality at three other houses Already at Elstow in 1390 Archbishop Courtenay on his metropolitan visitation had made a general injunction that

no nun convicted or publicly defamed of the crime of incontinency, be deputed to any office within the monastery and especially to that of gatekeeper, until it be sufficiently established that she has made purgation of her innocence[3],

an injunction repeated *verbatim* by Bishop Flemyng of Lincoln in 1421[4]. Now in 1432 Gray found that a nun named Pernell had been "several times guilty of fleshly lapse" and was leading an apostate life in secular dress outside the house; which speaks but ill for the moral state of an important abbey[5]. In the same year he found one of the nuns of Godstow *enceinte*[6], and in 1433 inquiry showed that Ellen Cotton, nun of Heynings, had recently had a child[7].

The worst cases found by Alnwick when he visited the religious houses of the diocese ten years later have already been

---

[1] *Linc Visit* I, pp 82–6
[2] *Ib* pp. 111–2. It should be noted that the word "incest" is used in its religious sense; it was properly used of intercourse between persons who were both under ecclesiastical vows and thus in the relation of spiritual father and daughter, or brother and sister, but it soon came to be used loosely to denote a breach of chastity in which one party was professed.
[3] Lambeth, *Reg Courtenay*, I, f. 336
[4] *Linc. Visit.* I, p 50 Flemyng adds "or manifestly suspect."
[5] *Ib* p 54   [6] *Ib.* p. 65.   [7] *Ib.* pp. 69–71.

described and the evidence of his register can be summarised briefly. All was well at Elstow, Heynings and Markyate; Dame Pernell [Gauthorpe], Dame Ellen Cotton and Dame Katherine Tyttesbury were all dwelling peaceably among their sisters, even the disreputable Denise Loweliche was still, in spite of her resignation, ruling as Prioress of Markyate An echo of old difficulties remained, however, at this last house and one nun begged the Bishop to speak to the Prioress, "to the end that she take better heed to the nuns who have previously erred, so that they be kept more strictly from erring again than is wont"[1], evidently discipline was not strict. At Godstow disorders had not yet ceased. The nuns received visitors and paid visits freely and scholars of Oxford still haunted the house; moreover one of the nuns, Dame Alice Longspey (of whom we have heard before), was of very easy virtue[2]. In two other houses Alnwick found great disorder prevailing· the *régime* of Margaret Wavere, Prioress of Catesby, has already been described, her bad language, her temper, her dishonesty and her priestly lover; and her chief accuser Isabel Benet had borne a child to the chaplain of the house[3]. Similarly we have seen into what a disreputable state St Michael's, Stamford, fell under an aged and impotent Prioress, how one nun ran away with an Austin friar and then with a wandering harp-player, and how two others had borne children or were notoriously held to be unchaste, this is one of the worst houses which the records of medieval nunneries have brought to light[4]. Finally there is the doubtful case of Ankerwyke, where the Prioress is said through negligence to have allowed no less than six nuns to go into apostasy, a fact which she freely admitted; but whether they had merely removed themselves through discontent with an unpopular prioress, or whether they had eloped it is impossible to say. At any rate they had not returned[5].

It is interesting to attempt a statistical estimate of the moral condition of the Lincoln nunneries during the twenty years from 1430 to 1450. It is possible to do so with some accuracy because the nuns giving evidence in each convent are

[1] *Alnwick's Visit.* MS f 6   [2] See above, p. 449
[3] See above, pp. 82–4, 388   [4] See above, pp 80, 310, 449
[5] *Linc Visit* II, p 3. The form of her admission is curious "Fatetur totidem moniales recessisse, absque tamen sciencia sua "

enumerated in Alnwick's reports. If we omit the general charges against Sewardsley and Flamstead and the ambiguous apostasy of the six nuns of Ankerwyke, we have twelve out of 220 nuns guilty of immoral behaviour, or a little over five per cent.; but this is certainly an understatement, having regard to the loss of the Sewardsley and Flamstead inquiries and of other visitations by the two bishops, to say nothing of possible concealment by the nuns. Between them Gray and Alnwick have left on record visitations or inquiries relating to twenty-four houses and cases of immorality came to light at eight, that is to say at one-third of the number visited. All except two of these, Elstow and Heynings, were very seriously affected, more than one nun having succumbed to sin; and the Prioress was found guilty in two and probably suspected in two others. The situation seems a serious one and Alnwick's visitations of the houses of monks and canons which were in his diocese show that the men were more lax in their behaviour than the women.

A similar statistical estimate can be made of the condition of convents in the diocese of Norwich during the visitation by Bishop Nykke or his commissary in 1514[1]. Eight convents, containing between them seventy-two nuns, were visited and only one case of immorality was found, at Crabhouse[2]. This is a far more favourable picture than that presented by the diocese of Lincoln in the previous century. Again in 1501 Dr Hede visited the nunneries of the diocese of Winchester as commissary of the Prior of Canterbury, during the vacancy of the sees of Canterbury and Winchester[3]. The diocese contained only four houses, but three of them were important abbeys, St Mary's, Winchester, with fourteen nuns, Wherwell with twenty-two and Romsey with forty; the fourth was Wintney Priory, with ten nuns. All seem to have been in perfect order except Romsey, which had fallen into decay under the *régime* of an abbess who had herself been guilty of adultery, and where one of the nuns was charged

---

[1] Jessopp, *Visit. of Dioc. Norwich* (Camden Soc) gives also Bishop Goldwell's visitations some ten years before, which brought to light no cases of immorality among nuns.

[2] *Ib* p. 109.

[3] See *V.C.H Hants.* II, pp. 129–31 (Romsey, where the date is wrongly given as 1312 by a slip), 124, 135, 151. Unfortunately all but the Romsey visitation are given in the barest summary.

with incontinence with the vicar of the parish church. Unfortunately the record of the visitation is left incomplete and there are no injunctions, hence it is impossible to say whether the last charge was true, but the abbey had been in a disordered state for some years past[1]. Another diocese for which an estimate can be made is Chichester, but it contained only two nunneries, Rusper and Easebourne. At Bishop Story's visitation in 1478 all was well at Rusper, a poor and ruinous little house containing seven nuns, but all was very far from well at Easebourne, where six nuns remained and two had gone into apostasy after conducting themselves in the thoroughly dissolute manner described above[2] At Bishop Sherborne's visitation in 1524 the number of nuns at Rusper had fallen to four, but there was no complaint except that a certain William Tychenor had frequent access to the priory and sowed discord between the Prioress and her three sisters. At Easebourne there were eight nuns, but the house seems not to have recovered its tone after the scandals of 1524 The subprioress deposed that some twelve years before a certain Ralph Pratt had seduced a sister; yet the convent had granted him the proceeds of the church of Easebourne and he still had much access to the priory[3]. It is a pity that more of these statistical estimates, imperfect as they are, cannot be made

It remains to consider what steps were taken to punish offenders and to reform evils The crime of seducing a nun was always considered an extremely serious one; she was *Sponsa Dei*, inviolable, sacrosanct. Anglo-Saxon law fined the ravisher heavily, and a law of Edward I declared him liable to three years imprisonment, besides satisfaction made to the convent. There is, however, no evidence that the State imprisoned or otherwise punished persons guilty of this crime, though it was always ready to issue the writ *De apostata capiendo*, for the recovery of a monk or nun who had fled. Whenever the lover of a nun is found undergoing punishment, it is always a punishment inflicted by the Church. If a man had abducted a nun, or were accused of seducing her, he was summoned before the Bishop or Archdeacon and required to purge himself of the charge. If

---

[1] *V C H Hants* II, p. 130.
[2] Above, pp. 453–4
[3] *Sussex Arch. Coll* IX, pp. 25–6

he pleaded "Not guilty" a day was appointed, on which he had to clear himself by the oath of a number of compurgators. Thus the Prioress of Catesby's lover, the priest William Taylour, was summoned before Bishop Alnwick in the church of Brampton; there he denied the crime and was told to bring five chaplains, of good report, who had knowledge of his behaviour, in a few days' time to the parish church of Rothwell[1]. The result of his attempt to find compurgators is not known, but the Prioress had already failed to get four of her nuns to support her and had been pronounced guilty. One wonders what happened when the man produced compurgators and the lady failed to do so: for these misdemeanours *à deux* the compurgatorial system would seem a little uncertain.

If a man's guilt were proven by his failure to provide compurgators or to come before the Bishop, it remained to decree his punishment. The obdurate were excommunicated until such time as they submitted The penitent were adjudged a penance. There is abundant evidence that the penance given by the Church was always a severe one. The classical instance is that of Sir Osbert Giffard in 1286 The Giffards were a large and influential West country family and in the last quarter of the thirteenth century several of the children of Hugh Giffard of Boyton rose to high positions in the Church. His eldest son, Walter, became in turn Bishop of Bath and Wells and Archbishop of York, dying in 1279, and his second son Godfrey became Bishop of Worcester. Of his daughters one, Juliana, is found as Abbess of Wilton in 1275, another, Mabel, as Abbess of Shaftesbury in 1291, and a third, Agatha, would seem to have held a position of some importance at Elstow, though she was never Abbess there[2]. These great ladies do not seem to have had a very good influence in their nunneries, in spite of the exalted position of their brothers. In 1270 the Bishop of Lincoln writes apologetically to Walter Giffard, Archbishop of York, concerning scandals

[1] *Linc Visit.* II, p 48
[2] In Archbishop Walter Giffard's York Register occurs the following entry of payments for Agatha "Item A Giffard xxs. Item Thomae de Habinton ad Expensas versus Elnestowe" (1271), *Reg W Giffard* (Surtees Soc.), p 115. This seems sufficient reason for identifying the Elstow sister as Agatha, though the editor identifies her with Mabel "afterwards abbess of Shaftesbury," *ib.* p 164

which have arisen in Elstow, "whence more frequently than in any other house beneath our rule scandals of wicked deeds arise," and it is clear from his letter that the Abbess and the Bishop's sister were implicated[1]. In 1298 also the Abbess and nuns of Shaftesbury had incurred excommunication "for their offences against God and by the creation of scandal"[2]. But the most serious mishap occurred at Wilton in 1286. Here Juliana Giffard[3] had under her rule a young relative named Alice Giffard, and in this year Sir Osbert Giffard, knight (whose exact relationship to the Abbess and the Bishop and to Alice is not clear), "with sacrilegious hand ravished and abducted in the silence of the night sisters Alice Russel and Alice Gyffard, professed according to the rule of St Benedict in the monastery of Wylton " Archbishop Peckham and the Bishop of Salisbury forthwith excommunicated Sir Osbert, who eventually made his submission. It was indeed an unfortunate scandal to occur in a Bishop's family and created a great stir in the country round   Godfrey's concern is shown by the appearance in his Worcester Register of the Bishop of Salisbury's letter to the Sub-dean of Salisbury and others announcing the penance to be imposed upon the abductor[4].

This penance was as follows:

The bishop enjoined upon him that he should restore the aforesaid sisters and all goods of the monastery withdrawn and should make all the satisfaction that he possibly could to the abbess and convent And that on Ash Wednesday in the church of Salisbury, the said crime being solemnly published before the clergy and people, he should humbly permit himself to be taken to the door of the church, with bare feet, in mourning raiment and uncovered head, with other penitents and should be beaten with sticks about the church on three holy days and on three Tuesdays through the market of Salisbury and so often and in like manner about the church of Wylton and through the market there, and he should be likewise beaten about the church of Amesbury and the market there and about the church of Shaftesbury and the market there. In his clothing from henceforth

---

[1] *Reg. W. Giffard* (Surtees Soc) p. 164 and *Hist Letters and Papers from the Northern Regs* ed J Raine (Rolls Ser), pp. 33–4

[2] *V.C.H. Dorset*, II, p 78

[3] She was in trouble in 1287 for refusing to pay certain moneys left for an obit and had to be threatened with excommunication, see *Worc. Reg. Godfrey Giffard*, Introd. pp. cxxxvi–vii

[4] *Worc. Reg. Godfrey Giffard*, II, pp 278–80. It is followed by a letter enjoining the Abbess and convent of Wilton to receive back the two nuns.

there shall not appear any cloaks of lamb's wool, gilt spurs or horse trappings, or girdle of a knight, unless in the meantime he should obtain special grace of the king, but he shall take journey to the Holy Land and there serve for three years[1]

The penance was thus severe, but it is another matter to say that it was always duly performed. A man who had already risked his immortal soul once, by the seduction of a nun, might well choose to undergo excommunication and risk it a second time, by refusing to do penance. The lover of a nun of Harrold in 1298 was thus excommunicated for refusing to be beaten through the market-place[2]. Moreover there were endless ways of delaying the humiliating ceremony Take the case of Richard Gray, the married boarder to whom Elizabeth Willoughby bore a child at St Michael's, Stamford. On July 3rd, 1442, in the parish church of Wellingborough, the Bishop caused him to swear upon the Holy Book that he would abjure the priory and all communication with Elizabeth. He then sentenced him to four floggings round one of the churches of Stamford on four Sundays or feast days,

carrying in his hand before the procession of the same church a taper of one pound's worth of wax, being clothed in his doublet and linen garments only, and on the last of the said four days, after the procession is finished, he has to offer the said taper to the high altar of the said Church

Moreover he was to perform a like penance on four Fridays, going round the market-place of Stamford, and within a month he was also to make pilgrimage on horseback to Lincoln Cathedral and when he came within five miles of Lincoln, to dismount and go barefoot to the cathedral and there offer to the high altar a taper of one pound's weight. The very evening, however, that this severe penance was imposed, Richard Gray came before the Bishop again and made lowly supplication that he would deign to temper the penance; whereupon Alnwick, "moved with compassion on him," commuted the penance round the market-place to a payment of twenty shillings to the nuns of St Michael's, to be paid within a month, and another twenty shillings to the

---

[1] For another version of the penance see *Reg Epis. J. Peckham,* III, pp 916–7. This forbids him to enter any nunnery or speak with any nuns without special licence from their metropolitan.

[2] *V.C.H. Beds* I, p. 389.

fabric of the cathedral church, to be paid within six weeks. Gray was to bring the Bishop letters testimonial as to the payment of the forty shillings and the performance of the penance at Lincoln, also within six weeks. But Richard had no intention of buying expensive wax candles, paying forty shilling fines, catching cold in his shirt at Stamford or humiliating himself at Lincoln. When summoned to do his penance he appealed to the court of Canterbury The Bishop then got licence from the commissary of the official in that court to proceed against the delinquent and summoned him to show cause why he had not done penance. On November 15th, 1442, the slippery Richard appeared by proxy before the Bishop's commissioner and said that he was "withheld by so many and so sore infirmities of fevers and other kinds, lying in his bed every other day, that he could not without grievous bodily harm appear in person in or on the same day and place " The commissioner postponed his appearance until December 11th and eventually he appeared on that day, but showing no cause why he had not performed his penance, and was excommunicated again by the Bishop, at which point he drops out of history, with his penance still unperformed[1]

It was no doubt an easier matter to exact penance from a nun. The apostate was excommunicated until she made submission and returned to her convent Sometimes a very obdurate sinner was transferred to do penance at another nunnery; the punishment was a common one in the diocese of York[2] and a

---

[1] *Alnwick's Visit.* MS f 39d Compare the case of Thomas de Raynevill who in 1324 was ordered, as penance for seducing a nun of Hampole, to stand on a Sunday, while high mass was being celebrated, in the conventual church of Hampole, bareheaded, wearing only his tunic and holding a lighted taper of one pound weight of wax in his hand, which he was to offer, after the offertory had been said, to the celebrant, who was to explain to the congregation the cause of the oblation. Also on feast days he was to be beaten round the parish church of Campsall. But two years later the Archbishop was still repeating directions for the performance of the penance *V C.H Yorks* III, p 164

[2] From Nunkeeling to Yedingham (1444), from Arthington to Yedingham (1310), from St Clement's, York, to Yedingham (1331), from Basedale to Sinningthwaite (1308), from Hampole to Swine (1313); four disobedient nuns of Keldholme to Handale, Swine, Nunappleton and Wallingwells respectively (1308), and two others to Esholt and Nunkeeling (1309); from Nunappleton to Basedale (1308); from Rosedale to Handale (1321); from Swine to Wykeham (1291), from Wykeham to Nunappleton (1444);

wicked Prioress of Redlingfield was sent to Wix in 1427[1], but nunneries not unnaturally sometimes objected to having to support at their cost an evilly disposed woman from another house[2]. More commonly the sinner did penance in her own house. If particularly obdurate, she was imprisoned for a time and even, if need be, shackled, in some secure place in the convent[3]. A severe penance was imposed in 1321 by Archbishop Melton upon Maud of Terrington, an apostate nun of Keldholme, who had for long lived in sin in the world. She was to be last in choir at all the canonical hours, and when not in choir to be confined in solitude. She was never to go out of the precincts of the cloister and was to be forever debarred from speaking with lay folk and from sending or receiving letters. She was not to be allowed to wear the black Benedictine veil, which marked her as a nun, until such time as the Archbishop should mitigate her penance, and should fast with bread and vegetables on Wednesdays and bread and water on Fridays. For the rest of her life she was never to wear a shift next her skin. On Wednesdays and Fridays she was to go barefoot in the presence of the convent round the cloister, all secular persons having been excluded, and there receive two beatings by the hand of the Prioress and on each other day of the week she was to receive one such discipline. Every week she was to say two psalters, besides *Placebo* and *Dirige* and the commendation for the dead, which she was to say each day for the remission of her sins. She was never to be present at the daily consultations of the chapter,

from Arthington to Nunkeeling (1219) *V C H Yorks.* III, pp 121, 127, 130, 159, 163–4, 168, 171, 175, 180, 183, 189. Also from Kirklees to Hampole (1323) and from Basedale to Rosedale (1534). *Yorks. Arch. Journ.* XVI, pp. 362, 431–3

[1] *V C.H. Suffolk,* II, p. 84.

[2] See for instance the insistence on costs and charges in Archbishop Lee's letter transferring Joan Fletcher, ex-Prioress of Basedale, from Rosedale where she was doing (or not doing) her penance, back to Basedale again *Loc. cit* pp 431–3

[3] Joan Trimelet of Cannington was to be shut up for a year, fasting thrice a week on bread and water, *suos calores macerans juveniles* Dugdale, *Mon.* IV, p. 416. Margaret de Tang of Arthington was "if need be to be bound by the foot with a shackle, but without hurting her limbs or body" *V.C H. Yorks* III, p 189. The runaway Agnes de Flixthorpe was similarly to be bound, see above, p 444, Anne Talke was imprisoned for a month. Liveing, *Records of Romsey Abbey,* p. 244 Joan Hutton of Esholt, who had had a child (1535), for two years unless the Archbishop relaxed her penance *Yorks. Arch Journ* XVI. p 433.

or at any other convent business, but "let her lie prone before the convent at the entrance of the choir, to be spurned by their feet, if they will"[1].

This was a particularly severe, not to say inhuman, penance and it is unlikely that such was the rule even in the case of obdurate offenders. A guilty nun at Crabhouse in 1514 is told to sit last among her sisters for a month and to say seven psalters during that period[2] and a novice at Redlingfield in 1427 is to go in front of the solemn procession of the convent on Sunday, wearing no veil and clad in white flannel[3]. The former was not an apostate, though she had had a child, and the latter was not yet professed and had been led away by the bad example of her Prioress; nevertheless these penances seem sufficiently mild, in comparison with the orthodox view of their offence. Fasting and penitential psalms and some outward mark of degradation, such as the loss of the veil and of the place in choir and chapter, to which the nun's standing in the convent entitled her, were common penances. A guilty nun was also debarred from holding any conventual office; but it must be admitted that this salutary precaution was not always strictly carried out. Occasionally a visitor is obliged to make a general injunction against the holding of office by nuns convicted or suspected of incontinence; Archbishop Courtenay mentions specifically the office of portress[4], a necessary precaution when one remembers how often the French and Italian *tourière* of a later

---

[1] *Yorks Arch. Journ.* XVI, pp. 456–7. The recorded penances given by Archbishop Melton are all very severe, though it must be admitted that the state of the nunneries in his diocese gave him cause for severity and that the penitents were all hardened sinners. Compare penances given by him in *V C H Yorks* III, pp. 175, 189. There is an extremely severe penance imposed by Archbishop Zouche on a nun who had several times run away from Thicket, *ib* p. 124, and another by Archbishop Lee in 1535 cited in the last note.

[2] Jessopp, *Visit in Dioc Norwich*, p. 110

[3] *V C H Suffolk*, II, p. 84.

[4] "Expresse inhibentes, ne infuturum aliqua monialis de crimine incontinencie conuicta vel publice diffamata, antequam de innocencia sic diffamate constiterit, ad aliquod officium domus predicte et precipue ad ostiorum custodiam admittatur" Lambeth, *Reg Courtenay*, I, f 336. Injunction to Elstow in 1390 and repeated by Bishop Flemyng in 1421. See above, p 396. Compare the charge against Margaret Fairfax, Prioress of Nunmonkton, in 1397 "*Item*, moniales quae lapsae fuerint in fornicatione faciliter restituit." Dugdale, *Mon* IV, p. 194.

date was little better than a procuress Frequently notorious
evil-doers retained their position, and it is surprising to notice
how often persons who were obviously unsuitable and immoral
were elected to the headship of a house, or continued to hold
that position after conviction. Sabina de Apelgarth, who had
been in apostasy when a simple nun of Moxby in 1310, is found
holding office in 1318, for Archbishop Melton orders her to be
removed from all offices and not to go outside the convent and
couples his injunction with a general prohibition against any
office being held by a nun convicted *de lapsu carnis.* Yet she
apparently became Prioress of the house, for her removal on
account of further misconduct is noted in 1328[1]. Isabel de
Berghby, Prioress of Arthington, apostatised in 1312, but returned eighteen months later and was re-elected Prioress in 1349[2].
In 1310 Isabella de St Quintin was ordered to be removed from
the office of cellaress in the presence of the whole convent of
Nunkeeling, and the nuns were ordered not to appoint her to
any other office nor allow her to leave the house; but in 1316
Isabella de St Quintin was elected Prioress[3]. Denise Loweliche,
the Prioress of Markyate, who had been so ready to add perjury
to incontinence in 1433 and had resigned only because she could
not find four nuns to swear to her innocence, was still, despite
her resignation, Prioress when Alnwick visited the house in 1442.
Abbess Elizabeth Broke of Romsey was similarly re-elected, after
having been found guilty of perjury and adultery[4]. Even the
wicked Prioress of Littlemore (1517) was deprived but "allowed
to perform the functions of her office for the present, provided
she did nothing without the advice of the Bishop's commissary"
and she was still acting-Prioress and behaving as badly as ever
when the house was visited again some nine months later[5].
Moreover it was possible for an influential sinner to obtain a
dispensation reinstating her to her position and allowing her
to hold office. Some curious papal mandates to this effect are
extant. Joan Goldesburgh, a nun of Nunmonkton, is so dispensed in 1450 " to receive and hold any dignities, even of Abbess
and Prioress, even conventual, of her order, even if they be

---

[1] *V.C H Yorks.* ɪɪɪ, p 239   ·   [2] *Ib* p 183.
[3] *Ib* p. 120 For these Yorkshire cases see below, Note G, *passim*
[4] Liveing, *op. cit* pp. 213–6.   [5] See below, Note F.

elective and have cure of souls"[1], and two nuns of Amesbury were restored to their voice and place in stall and chapter, and rendered eligible for all offices even that of Abbess in 1398 and 1424[2]. On the other hand such a dispensation shows that the penance had been rigorously enforced; one of the nuns (a serious offender who had had children by two priests) is said to have lived laudably in the nunnery for six years since her condemnation. Occasionally, moreover, the office of head of the house is specifically excepted in the dispensation[3].

Besides punishing offenders, the Bishops took steps to effect a general reform of convents which they found in an unsatisfactory moral state, by removing as far as possible the conditions which facilitated immorality. Such steps usually consisted in forbidding the nuns to wander about freely outside their houses and in prohibiting the visits of men, except under safeguards. Sometimes a careful Bishop issues a special injunction against a particular visitor, sometimes he enumerates painfully a list of chaplains and others whose access to the precincts of a nunnery is forbidden. These attempts to enforce enclosure have been dealt with elsewhere[4], and a study of convent morals shows how necessary a principle of monastic life it was and how closely the breach of it was connected with moral decay. The attempt at reform by stricter enclosure was, as we know, not a success The Bishops "beat the air" in vain with their restrictions. In the nature of the case the control exercised by any Bishop over the monastic houses of his diocese varied according to his own energy or leisure. If visitation were made only at rare intervals, abuses persisted and became public scandals before they were reformed, and even after visitation it by no means followed that abuses would be corrected[5]. The fact is that the medieval bishops were too badly overworked to be able to keep any systematic control over the monastic houses in their dioceses, in spite of the energy

---

[1] *Cal of Papal Letters*, x, p 471. The dispensation mentions that she "has secretly lost her virginity and has not yet been publicly defamed."

[2] *Ib.* v, p. 161 and vii, p. 373

[3] The Pope writes to Mitford, Bishop of Salisbury, desiring him to restore Alice Wilton, nun of Shaftesbury, to the position which she had forfeited by the sin of incontinence. The Bishop reinstates the nun and declares her eligible for all offices except that of Abbess *V C H Dorset*, ii, p. 78, note 93.

[4] See Chs. ix, x, above   [5] See below, p. 491.

which some of them gave to the task and in spite of a liberal use of commissioners.

To pass a final judgment on the moral state of English nunneries, as revealed by the bishops' registers during the later middle ages, is, as has already been suggested, a difficult task. From the monastic standard it cannot be said to have been high, but from the human standard it is not difficult to excuse these women, professed so young and with so little regard for vocation, *suos calores macerantes juveniles* The nun was not a saint; she was "a child of our grandmother Eve, a female, or for thy more sweet understanding, a woman"; and only a habit of making allowances for human nature can give a right understanding of her. The explanation of the matter seems to be that monasticism as a career is not for *l'homme moyen sensuel,* or even for *la femme moyenne sensuelle*; and in the later middle ages many folk of average, or more than average, passions entered it. Indeed its whole career is from the beginning a magnificent series of recoveries from a melancholy series of relapses. Even in the Anglo-Saxon period, the golden age of the English nunneries, the scandal of Coldingham has to be set against the glory of Whitby[1]. In the height of the twelfth century the misdeeds of Amesbury provoke episcopal, royal, and papal interference and nuns from the new order of Fontevrault are brought in to reform the house[2]. In the middle of the splendid thirteenth century that hammer of the monks, Bishop Grosseteste, who *in religiosos terribiliter et in religiosas terribilius consuevit fulgurare,* conceived himself justified in employing measures of incredible brutality for assuring himself of the virtue of his nuns[3], and the

[1] Bede, *Eccles Hist* Book ɪv, ch 25

[2] Benedict of Peterborough, *Gesta Regis Henrici Secundi,* ed. Stubbs (Rolls Series, 1867), ɪ, pp. 135–6. Ralph Niger describes the transaction thus: "Juratus se tria monasteria constructurum, duos ordines transvertit, personas de loco ad locum transferens, meretrices alias aliis, cenomannicas Anglicis substituens " *Ib.* ɪɪ, p. xxx.

[3] "Et quod indignum scribi, ad domos religiosarum veniens, fecit exprimi mammillas earundem, ut sic physice si esset inter eas corruptela experiretur" [1251] Matt Paris, *Chron Majora,* ed H R Luard (Rolls Series, 1880), v, p 227 In 1248 he had deposed an abbess of Godstow, Flandrina de Bowes, and Adam Marsh writes to him "Plurimum credo fore salutiferam visitationem quam in domo Godestowe fieri fecistis Paternitatis vestrae sollicitudinem largitio divina remuneret." *Monumenta Franciscana,* ed J S Brewer (Rolls Series, 1858), p 117 If Matthew Paris'

evidence of bishops' registers for the second half of the century does not give an impression of much greater strictness of life than is found in the nunneries of the fourteenth and fifteenth centuries, when monasticism had, by the admission of its apologists, passed its prime[1]

Nevertheless there was a steady movement downhill in the history of the monasteries during the last two centuries and a half before the dissolution[2]. They shared in the growing degradation of the Church in its head and members. The "mighty lord who broke the bonds of Rome" may have been actuated merely by a desire to break the bonds of matrimony, but there was some need for reform among the monastic houses It is true that the so-called scandalous *comperta* of Henry VIII's visitors cannot be taken at their face value; these men had been sent to make a black case and they made it, nor was their own character such as to encourage the slightest belief in their words. Yet in those *comperta* themselves there is nothing which is unfamiliar to the student of episcopal registers for two centuries before, and charges which a Layton made with levity, an Alnwick was forced sometimes to make with despair[3]. Yet this may be

account of his procedure be true it would seem almost to rival the behaviour of Layton and Legh, however different the character and motive which inspired it

[1] The earliest list of *comperta* which we possess is the result of Archbishop Walter Giffard's visitation of Swine in 1268 Though there is no charge of actual immorality the house was in a thoroughly unsatisfactory state The Archbishop's two sisters, the one Prioress of Elstow and the other Abbess of Shaftesbury, were both in serious trouble in 1270 and 1298 respectively, their nuns being also involved, and in 1296 there occurred the famous Giffard abduction from Wilton Peckham's injunctions to nunneries show widespread breach of enclosure and some suspicious conduct during the '8os, a nun of Lymbrook is guilty with a monk of Leominster in 1282, and besides Matthew Paris' account of Grosseteste's proceedings in the diocese of Lincoln in 1251, we have notice of apostates there in 1295, 1296 and 1298 and in the York diocese in 1286, 1287, 1293 and 1299 See this chapter and notes, *passim*.

[2] For the disappearance or suppression of eight small nunneries prior to 1535 see Note H below

[3] At Chicksand, for instance, Layton "fownde two of the nunnes not baron," and at Harrold "one of them hade two faire chyldren, another one and no mo", but is this so much worse than what Alnwick found at Catesby and St Michael's, Stamford, in the same diocese a century before? Or take Layton's description of the Prior of Maiden Bradley, quoted above, is it not much less serious than the description of Alexander Black of Selby in one of Archbishop Giffard's visitation *detecta* in 1275? "Alexander Niger, monachus, tenet Cristinam Bouere et Agnetem filiam Stephani, de qua

said for the nunneries of the age, over and above the allowance
for human frailty· not all, nor even the majority, were tainted
with serious sin, though all were worldly. We think a house
particularly disordered, only because we have record of its
failings; of its virtues we have no record in inquisitions which
were directed towards the discovery of abuses. It is true that
this cuts both ways, and that in dioceses where few or no registers
and reports remain the fair fame of the nuns remains unblemished, whatever their lives may have been. Happy the
nunnery that has no history Nevertheless in this as in so many
other tales of human endeavour

> The evil that men do lives after them—
> The good is oft interred with their bones,

and it will never be known what lives of self-sacrifice and devotion may be hidden behind the *Omnia bene* of an obscure visitation record. The words of the sixteenth century poem are the
wisest judgment on medieval nuns:

> For sum bene devowte, holy and towarde,
> And holden the right way to blysse,
> And sum bene feble, lewde and frowarde,
> Now god amend that ys amys.

The dissolution of the monasteries amputated in England a
limb of the Church, which though diseased was yet far from
putrid. We have no means of guessing what the later history
of the nunneries might have been. The English nunneries compare on the whole favourably with contemporary French and
German houses, as revealed by the visitations of Rigaud and
Busch, and they certainly never reached such a laxity of morals
and such a complete absence of any spirituality as was reached
by the convents of the Latin countries at a later date It was
never, in the middle ages, the mode to be a *monachino* as it was

---

suscitavit prolem, et quamdam mulierem nomine Anekous, de qua suscitavit
vivam prolem apud Crol, et aliam apud Sneyth quae vocatur Nalle, et
alias infinitas apud Eboracum et Akastre et alibi, et quasi in qualibet villa
unam, et fetidissimus est, et recte modo captus fuit cum quadam muliere
in campis, sicut audivit " *Reg Walter Giffard*, p. 326 Or than what Alnwick
discovered at the New Collegiate Church at Leicester in 1440⸴ Layton's
general charges against the monks and nuns of Yorkshire are pure gossip
or invention; but we should not have been deeply surprised to find them
in a York archiepiscopal register of the early fourteenth century

later in France and Italy[1]. The life of a nun had not yet lost
all of its original purpose and meaning and the careers of a
Virginia Maria de Leyva, of a Lucrezia Buonvisi, of an Angélique
d'Estrées, even of such a virtuous flirt as Felice Rasponi, would
not have been possible then[2]. No Casanova could have found
in medieval England opportunity for those astounding intrigues
with the M.M. of Venice and the M.M. of Chambéry, which fill
so large a place in his *Memoirs* and are so significant a commentary upon monastic life in the eighteenth century[3]. The
reason lies perhaps in the less inflammable temperament of the
North, but still more in the different standards of the time. The
middle ages expressed and satisfied their passions freely, but
debauchery was then less all-pervading and less elegant. Passion
was not yet degraded to fashion and the lover had not yet
become the gallant. The sins of these fifteenth century nuns are
a matter of rude nature and not of "all the adulteries of art."
That which was expelled with a pitchfork had not yet returned
with a fan The distinction is a relevant one A vow broken for
love may yet have force and reality, a vow broken for amusement has none The medieval nunneries never sank to the moral
degradation of a more refined and artificial age.

---

[1] Of some of the Anglo-Saxon kings it was said, and said with horror,
that they most willingly chose their mistresses from convents. See a letter
from St Boniface to Ethelbald King of Mercia on this point, instancing the
similar habits and evil fates of Ceolred of Mercia and Osred of Northumbria
(*Bon. Epis* XIX)
[2] For these ladies, see references in p 451, note 5, and below, p 501,
note 3
[3] *Mémoires de J. Casanova de Seingalt* (edition Garnier, 1910), tt II, III, IV

CHAPTER XII

THE MACHINERY OF REFORM

And whan they had resceyuede [t]her charge
They spared nether mud ne myer,
But roden over Inglonde brode and large,
To seke owte nunryes in every schyre.
Why I can't be a Nun (15th century)

A COMMUNITY, living together under a somewhat rigid rule and obliged to concern itself with a large measure of temporal business, has to face many difficulties and abuses The strictness of its discipline and the prosperity of its affairs will necessarily depend very largely upon the character and intelligence of the individuals who compose it. A diseased limb may corrupt the whole body politic; or on the other hand a low state of vitality in the body politic may render the limb liable to corruption. Again rule and routine inevitably tend in the course of time to become slackened, as human nature wins its way against the austerity of a primitive ideal. Every community, therefore, needs some sort of machinery on the one hand for keeping itself up to the mark and on the other for the external inspection and regulation of its affairs. The monastic houses of the middle ages were provided with internal machinery for self-reform in the daily meeting of the whole convent in the chapter house, to transact business and to denounce and punish faults. The external machinery was provided by an elaborate system of visitation by ecclesiastical authorities, sometimes by a parent house, sometimes by the chapter-general of the order, sometimes by the bishop of the diocese, by means of such visitation breaches of discipline and morality could be rectified and the temporal business of the house could be scrutinised for evidence of mismanagement

The daily routine of the chapter house is too well known to need a detailed description here. The whole monastic community was bound by the rule to meet every day, usually after Prime, in the chapter house on the east side of the cloister, with the head of the house (to use modern terminology) in the chair At this meeting a chapter of the Rule was solemnly read, after which the corporate business of the house was discussed. Leases, sales, and corrodies were approved or disapproved, and the common seal of the convent was affixed to letters and grants, in the presence of all the monks or nuns The neglect to transact common business by common advice in chapter was not infrequently a legitimate source of complaint by a convent against its superior. Besides temporal business of this kind, the moral and spiritual welfare of the convent was considered. Wrongdoers publicly accused themselves of fault, or were publicly accused by their fellows, and correction was administered by a "discipline," or by some other penance. By means of the chapter, a convent of reasonable seriousness and goodwill could keep up its own standard of life and control its own backsliders.

Undoubtedly the chapter was a useful instrument of self-reform, but its efficacy obviously depended entirely on whether the convent as a whole were desirous of keeping the Rule and punishing black sheep. If the number of sheep who were black, or even grey, preponderated and if laxity were general in the community, the chapter would not concern itself to raise its own standard. From the frequent injunctions of medieval bishops that the daily meeting in the chapter should not be omitted, it would appear that not only the public transaction of business, but also the public confession and punishment of faults was sometimes neglected. Moreover, unless entered into with modesty and a sense of responsibility, the right of every member to charge another with fault was a sure source of discord, for it certainly provided ample opportunity for frail human nature to exhibit malice. The younger nuns were apt to indulge in what their elders regarded as impudent criticism; private grudges found an opportunity to vent themselves; and rival cliques sometimes turned the meeting into an unseemly hubbub. It was perhaps for this reason that the Abbot of St Albans, visiting Sopwell in 1338, decreed that

for the avoidance of evils and for the promotion and maintenance of peace and charity, but three voices shall henceforth be heard in chapter, to wit those of the president, of the subprioress or of another official of the order, and of her who shall be challenged or accused of a fault[1]

Another common abuse was the gossip to which such revelations in chapter sometimes gave rise, gossip which was not confined to the ears of the nuns. Bishop Flemyng's injunction to Elstow in 1421–2 "that the Abbess shall narrowly espy what secrets of chapter be in any way disclosed, punishing severely also those who trangress in this matter"[2] is only one of many similar injunctions; and visitation reports sometimes show considerable interference by lay folk in cloister disputes. During the election quarrel which raged at Nunkeeling from 1316 to 1319 Archbishop Melton accused certain nuns of revealing the secrets of the chapter to seculars and adversaries outside, and during a similar quarrel at Keldholme a number of laymen were cited, together with certain nuns, for obstructing the appointment of a new prioress in 1308[3]. One is left with the impression that the nuns called in the support of their friends and kinsfolk in the world, if they found themselves at odds with their Prioress. In the feud between the wicked Prioress of Littlemore and her nuns (1518) both parties had adherents in Oxford. the Prioress brought in her friends to subdue the nuns and the nuns fled to theirs, when they could no longer bear the Prioress[4]. At Hampole, where Archbishop Bowet found the Prioress and nuns out of all charity with each other in 1411, he even had to ordain that no nun, having any complaint against the Prioress, was to ignore the Archbishop's authority and call in the aid of any secular or regular person If any sister wished to complain and could find another to join with her, she was to have access to the Archbishop, the necessary expenses being given her by the Prioress If the Prioress refused leave or delayed it beyond three days, the two nuns were to have access to the Archbishop, without

[1] Dugdale, *Mon.* iii, pp 365–6 Compare a *detectum* at Crabhouse (1514): "Item, the younger nuns are disobedient and when the seniors charge them with their faults the prioress punishes alike the reformers and the sinners." *Visit of Dioc. of Norwich*, ed Jessopp, p. 109

[2] *Linc Visit.* i, p 50. Compare *Reg Walter Giffard*, p 249; *Visit of Dioc. of Norwich*, ed Jessopp ("Item Dna. A.D. et Dna G. S revelant secreta religionis et correctionis factae in conventu ") *Linc. Epis. Reg. Memo. Bokyngham*, ff. 397, 397d ("Et quod nullum decetero capitulum in domo capitulari in presencia secularis seu extranee persone quoquomodo teneatur sub pena iniunccionis nostre infrascripta").

[3] *V.C H Yorks* iii, 120, 167–8 , .[4] See below, Note F.

incurring the charge of apostasy[1]. Sometimes the revelation of convent *secreta* was made in a spirit of pure gossip, rather than with the object of obtaining external aid; the complaint of the nuns of Catesby in 1442 that the Prioress' mother "knows well the secrets of the chapter and publishes them in the town; so also does the Prioress publish them," and that of the nuns of Gracedieu in 1440-1 that "the Prioress makes the secrets of their religious life common among the secular folk that sit at table with her" are typical of many others[2].

The meeting of the chapter, therefore, though a useful instrument of self-reform, when the necessary goodwill was present, was liable to abuses. It was apt to be neglected; it gave rise to ill-feeling; and it sometimes led to undesirable gossip, both inside and outside the house. It is obvious, moreover, that a measure of external control was necessary to keep up the standard of life in the many monastic houses of Europe and to reform common breaches of discipline This external control was exercised in the middle ages by three distinct authorities (1) a parent house, (2) the chapter general of the Order and (3) the diocesan of the see.

Certain houses, which had founded other houses as offshoots or colonies, retained the right to visit and reform their daughter-houses. Some monasteries had small outlying priories, known as "cells," founded originally to look after distant estates of the house; sometimes such cells contained only one or two monks, living in an ordinary dwelling house, and had no real existence apart from the parent house. Sometimes, however, the cells grew and achieved an independent existence, though still maintaining their connection with their founders. This frequently happened to the English cells of foreign houses, and certain cells of English houses also grew into independent priories Among nunneries, originally founded as cells of foreign houses, may be mentioned Lyminster in Sussex. Few English nunneries had cells; but Seton in Coupland was a cell of Nunburnholme. The connection between mother house and cell is illustrated by a licence granted by Archbishop Greenfield to the Prioress of Nunburnholme in 1313 to visit, "your cell of Seton in Coupland, which is subject to your monastery," taking with her two honest

[1] *V C.H. Yorks.* III, p. 164.   [2] *Linc Visit* II, pp. 47, 120

nuns of the house, in order to visit the nuns of Seton, and
returning without delay[1]. The visitation of the cell was usually
included in that of the mother house and the larger independent
cells were often subject to episcopal visitation.

Rather different in origin from a cell was a house founded
by a monastery, less as a colony than as a distinct but dependent
institution. The most interesting example of this is provided by
the great Abbey of St Albans, which founded two nunneries,
St Mary de Pré and Sopwell. Both the nunneries were always
very dependent on St Albans and are often mentioned in the
chronicles of that house. St Mary de Pré, having been founded
in the twelfth century as a hospital for leprous women living
under a rule, became later an ordinary nunnery, containing nuns,
and both lay sisters and lay brothers, in the time of Abbot
Thomas de la Mare (1349–96) the rank of sister was abolished
and a higher standard of education was insisted upon for the
nuns, who were to profess the rule of St Benedict[2]. Sopwell was
also founded in the twelfth century as a Benedictine nunnery[3].
In both houses nuns were admitted only by consent of the Abbot
of St Albans, who also claimed the right to appoint their prioress.
In both the temporal affairs of the convent were administered
by wardens, appointed by the Abbot from among the monks of
the abbey[4] The close connection was not always maintained
without friction At Sopwell the nuns more than once tried to
elect their own prioress and seem to have found the Abbot
somewhat high-handed[5]. In 1481 Abbot Wallingford sent the
archdeacon and subprior of the house to remove the prioress
from office on account of her age and infirmities and to put

[1] *V.C.H. Yorks.* iii, p. 118.

[2] For an account of the house, see *V C H. Herts* iv, pp 428–32. The
regulations made by Abbot Richard de Wallingford (1328–36) are given
in *Gesta Abbat* ii, pp. 213–4 and those by Abbot Michael or his successor
Thomas de la Mare in Cott. MS Nero D 1 ff 173–4d; regulations by
Thomas de la Mare (1349–96) occur in *Gesta Abbat* ii, p 402 See also
W. Page, "Hist of the Monastery of St Mary de Pré" (*St Albans and Herts.
Arch Soc Trans* (New Series) i).

[3] For an account of the house, see *V C H Herts.* iv, pp 422–6.

[4] The accounts of the warden of St Mary de Pré for 1341–57 are preserved
in the Public Record Office (*Mins Accts* , bundle 867, Nos 21–6) and are
described in *V C H. Herts* iv, p 430 (notes) In the second half of the
fifteenth century the accounts seem to have been kept by the Prioress,
those for 1461–93 have survived. *Ib* p 431 (note)

[5] See *Gesta Abbat* ii, p 212.

Elizabeth Webbe in her place, but some years later the archdeacon deposed Elizabeth, whereupon she brought an action against him in the Court of Arches and was reinstated. Thereupon "two monks of St Albans, sent by the archdeacon, came to the nunnery, broke down Elizabeth's door with an iron bar, beat her and put her in prison," after which she appealed to Archbishop Morton as Chancellor[1]. She may have been at the bottom of the famous letter written by Morton to the Abbot of St Albans in 1490, accusing him of changing prioresses at Pré and at Sopwell as he pleased and deposing good and religious persons for the benefit of the evil and vicious, and stating that the Prioress of St Mary de Pré, Helen Germyn, was a married woman who had left her husband for a lover and that she and some of her nuns were leading immoral lives with monks of St Albans[2]. The same letter accused the monks put in as wardens of using their opportunities to dissipate the goods of the house, and the turbulent Prioress of Sopwell, Elizabeth, is found complaining to the Chancellor that a deed of lease by the convent had been secretly altered to their disadvantage by their "keeper" and his clerk, who had been bribed by a tenant[3].

It is difficult to say how much truth there was in these charges and they certainly do not seem to show overmuch care for the reform of the daughter houses by their august parent. But it would not be fair to judge St Albans by this quarrel at the end of its career, and there is evidence to show that past abbots tried conscientiously to maintain good order in the dependent nunneries. Among other rights the abbot possessed that of visitation, and chance has fortunately preserved an interesting set of injunctions sent by Abbot Michael to Sopwell, after a visitation held in 1338[4]. The orders given to the Warden of Sopwell by Abbot Thomas (1349–96) have also been preserved in the *Gesta Abbatum*[5].

Another nunnery founded by a famous abbey of monks was St Michael's, Stamford, founded by William of Waterville, Abbot

---

[1] Quoted from *P R O Early Chancery Proceedings*, 181/4 in *V C H Herts* IV, pp 424–5.
[2] Wilkins, *Concilia*, III, p 632.   [3] *V C H Herts* IV, p 425.
[4] Printed in Dugdale, *Mon* III, pp 365–6 and *Gesta Abbat* ed Riley, II, App. D pp 511–19.
[5] *Gesta Abbat* III, p 519

of Peterborough in 1155; and this house remained for long
dependent upon its parent abbey[1]. In its early years it was
customary for the prioress in the name of the chapter to pay
an annual pension of a mark of silver to the Abbot and to make
formal recognition of subjection, once every year, on the morrow
of the Feast of St Michael. The Abbot had the right of receiving
the profession of the sisters and his consent was necessary to
the election of the prioress. He also had the appointment of
the warden or prior, who looked after the temporalities of the
house. In 1270 Bishop Gravesend sanctioned the personal visitation of the house once a year by the abbot and two or three
monks, with power to correct and reform, and the Register of
the Abbey records such visitations in 1297, 1300, 1303 and 1323.
The tendency was, however, for the diocesan to oust the abbey
from the control of the house; from time to time he claimed and
exercised the right of instituting the warden, and from the end
of the thirteenth century he regularly instituted the prioress.
From this time the bishops' registers show that the regulation
and reform of the house were in the hands of the bishop and it
was duly visited by Alnwick in the fifteenth century. The accounts of St Michael's, Stamford, show that the nuns still had
dealings with the Abbey; but Peterborough did not retain over
this nunnery the exclusive rights of appointment and visitation,
which St Albans, owing to its exemption from diocesan control,
exercised to the end over Sopwell and St Mary de Pré. There is no
mention of either of these houses in the episcopal registers.

Nunneries subject to visitation by a parent abbey were highly
exceptional. Another exceptional method of external control
was visitation by the chapter-general of the order, to which the
nunnery belonged Nuns as well as monks were constantly legislated for by these chapters-general, but they were very rarely
visited, because (as we shall see) they were almost all subject
to visitation by the bishop of their diocese. A trace of visitation
by order of the chapter-general seems to survive in a letter
from the Abbot of Stratford (4 December, 1491), preserved
among the Cistercian documents in the archives at Dijon[2] The
Abbot relates that he had visited Cokehill, found it in a very

---

[1] See *V C.H Northants* II, pp. 98–101.
[2] *E H R* 1914, p 38 (note 60)

unsatisfactory condition and tried in vain to depose the prioress; at other times, however, Cokehill was visited by the Bishops of Worcester. The Cistercian order claimed exemption from episcopal visitation for male houses and we shall see that it made occasional attempts to exert its right over nunneries too

By far the most common method of reforming nunneries from outside was by means of the control of the bishop of the diocese[1]. It is an interesting fact that not even the greatest and most important Benedictine abbeys of women, such as Shaftesbury, Amesbury and Romsey, succeeded in obtaining an exemption from episcopal jurisdiction such as was enjoyed by St Albans and some other houses; and nunneries belonging to "exempt" orders were invariably under episcopal control   Bishops, who would never have dreamed of interfering with houses of Cistercian or Cluniac monks, visited the nuns of those orders as a matter of course and no objection was as a rule raised by the houses or by the orders. There is, it is true, one extremely interesting case in which this right of visitation was contested. In 1276 the nuns of Sinningthwaite contested the right of Archbishop Giffard of York to visit them and appealed against him to the Pope. Unfortunately the papal decision is not recorded, but as they were regularly visited until their dissolution, it was evidently against them. They possibly acted in collusion with the Cistercian abbots of their diocese, for in the same year Archbishop Giffard ordered them to have Friars Minor as their confessors, in spite of the inhibition of Cistercian abbots, who had no jurisdiction over them[2]. The Cokehill case quoted above may

---

[1] The religious houses were also subject to metropolitan visitation by the Archbishop   Among important records of visitations of nunneries by the Archbishop of Canterbury or by his commissioners are Peckham's visitations (*Reg Epis Johannis Peckham, passim*) in the last quarter of the thirteenth century, Courtenay's visitations in the last quarter of the fourteenth century (see Lambeth, *Reg Courtenay*, i, f 335d, for his injunctions to Elstow in 1389, used by Flemyng as a model for his own injunctions in 1421-2, *Linc Visit* i, p 48) and Archbishop Morton's visitations in the last quarter of the fifteenth century (see Liveing, *Records of Romsey Abbey*, pp 217-22 for the visitation of Romsey in 1492)   The visitations of the Winchester diocese by Dr Hede, commissary of the Prior of Canterbury, during the vacancy of the sees of Canterbury and Winchester in 1501-2 were made in the same right (see *V C H. Hants* ii, pp 124, 129, 135, 151).

[2] *V.C H. Yorks.* iii, p 176 (quoting Dugdale, *Mon* v, pp. 464-5 and *Reg Giffard* (Surtees Soc), p. 295)

represent a similar attempt of the Cistercian chapter-general to control a nunnery belonging to the order For the historian of the English nunneries it is an exceedingly fortunate thing that the diocesans enjoyed this unchallenged right of visitation over almost all the nunneries in the kingdom; for the episcopal registers are the best source of monastic history and an exempt house (save when it was a famous abbey with a chronicle) is not infrequently a house without history, because without visitation records.

Since the periodical visitation by the diocesan was not only the main method of external control and reformation, but also incidentally gave rise to the records on which so much of this history of nunneries is based, it is worth while to study what exactly happened when a bishop, or his commissioners, came to inspect a nunnery. A regular routine was followed, which can easily be reconstructed from such full records as those kept by Bishop Alnwick of Lincoln[1]. A formal summons was sent by the bishop to the house to be visited, warning the convent to hold itself in readiness for visitation by himself, or by one or more commissioners (named). On the appointed day he rode up to the house, accompanied by his clerks, and was met at the door of the church by the convent and conducted to the high altar. Here high mass was celebrated and the bishop, his clerks and the convent then adjourned to the chapter house for the business of visitation. The proceedings began with the preaching of a sermon by one of the bishop's clerks; in houses of monks this was given in Latin, until the end of our period, but knowledge of Latin had died out in nunneries before the fifteenth century and at Alnwick's visitation the sermon was always preached in the vulgar tongue, on some such text as "*Go forth, O ye daughters of Zion and behold king Solomon*" (Cant. iii. 11), "*Present your bodies a living sacrifice. . unto God*" (Rom xii 1), or others less specifically appropriate to nuns. When this had been finished, the head of the house was required to present a certificate of receipt of the summons to visitation, which had to be drawn up according to a common form, and this not infrequently caused some delay in nunneries, where the inmates were often too ignorant of Latin

---

[1] See *Linc Visit.* ii, *passim,* and also the Editor's admirable introduction to *Linc Visit.* i, pp ix-xiii.

to draw up the document correctly, unless they could call in the help of a clerk[1]. The head of the house then produced the certificate of her election, confirmation by the diocesan and installation. Here again there was sometimes a delay, for prioresses were occasionally all at sea over documents and the necessary certificates were apt to be lacking at the last minute. Thus Dame Alice Dunwyche, the incompetent old Prioress of Gracedieu, was unable to produce any evidence of her confirmation in 1440 and the bishop had to appoint a special commissary to inquire into the matter, three months later the commissary examined two laymen brought by her as witnesses to her confirmation and installation[2]. Meanwhile the visitation would continue; and the last formality to be observed was the production by the prioress of the foundation charter of the house, and the financial balance sheet (or *status domus*) for the year, this last an important item, since it enabled the bishop to see at a glance whether the financial affairs of the convent were in a satisfactory condition[3]. This completed the preliminary business.

There now followed the main business of the visitation, the verbal examination of the nuns, in order to detect what abuses might stand in need of reform. Some abuses were patent to the eyes of the bishop, he could see garments in holes, and veils spread wide to show fair foreheads; he might have caught the scuttle of little dogs round corners as he rode in at the gates, or the whisk of a boarder's murrey-coloured skirts behind a pillar. But the bulk of his information had to be obtained by careful cross-examination. The chapter house was cleared and he proceeded to question the nuns separately and in private, beginning with the prioress. Experience would teach him what were the most common breaches of discipline about which to make specific inquiry, but the nuns were encouraged to complain freely and the bishop's clerks were kept busy scribbling notes of what each shrill tale-bearer told, to be written out afterwards under her name as *detecta*, or things discovered to the bishop.

---

[1] See above, p 250   [2] *Linc Visit* II, pp. 119, 126–7.

[3] Sometimes the bishop's clerk summarises the information given as to the financial state of the house, which would seem to indicate that the prioress gave and the bishop accepted merely a verbal account. See *Alnwick's Visit* MS f 38. In *Linc. Epis. Reg. Atwater*, f. 42, is a brief account of a visitation of Ankerwyke in 1519, to which is added the *status domus* as submitted by the nuns, comprising an inventory

These *detecta* are an amusing commentary on life in a community and grist (it must be admitted) to the cynic's mill. Serious charges of immorality are mingled with trivialities, much as the chroniclers of the period mingle battles, monastic gossip and sea monsters cast upon the shore. The beer is too light, swine do come into the churchyard and root up the earth and befoul the churchyard; all corrections are made with so great harshness and so much ado that charity and loving-kindness are banished from the house, the nuns do hold drinkings of evenings in the guestchamber, even after Compline, the prioress has pawned the jewels of the house, sister so-and-so is defamed with sir so-and-so, sometime chaplain in that place and did conceive of him and bear a child; the buildings and tenements of the priory are dilapidated and many have fallen to the ground because of default in repairs; secular persons do lie in the dorter near the nuns; the nuns wear silken veils and robes; in the prioress' default six nuns have now left the house in apostasy, the nuns frequent taverns and continually go into town without leave; silence is not observed in due places; the nuns do help secular folk in garnering their grain during the autumn season; the nuns are somewhat sleepy and come late to matins, the prioress does not render an account. Besides this infinite variety of complaint, the *detecta* exhibit also an infinite variety of motive, ranging from the disciplinarian's zeal for reform to the private grudge of one individual against another. Sometimes the prioress and the nuns engage in mutual recriminations: she is harsh, or autocratic, or incompetent, they are lax or disobedient. Sometimes, on the other hand, a whole convent declares *omnia bene*. About some houses there still hangs a gentle atmosphere of peace and goodwill, others are rent with feud and petty bickering, others are in a condition of very lax morality. Human nature is truly unchanging, for all the types to be met with in a modern community, be it school or college, ship or government office, have their prototypes among these medieval monks and nuns. The amateur in human nature and the social historian alike may find in these little studied monastic *detecta* material of more absorbing interest and entertainment than is to be found in any other class of medieval documents

After the bishop had heard the evidence of the nuns, given

thus chaotically, the next business was to summarise, in some
sort of order, the result of the inquiry. Such complaints of the
nuns as the bishop considered worthy of notice were therefore
classified as *comperta*, or things discovered by the bishop If any
member of the convent had been accused of serious breaches
of the rule, she was summoned and the articles of accusation
were read to her, and one by one she was invited to admit or
to deny them If she pleaded guilty, a penance was enjoined
upon her. If she denied the charge, she was ordered to find a
certain number of compurgators, who would swear to her innocence, and to produce them by a certain hour. The number
of cases in which misconduct was sufficiently serious to make
this necessary was not great. During Alnwick's visitation it
happened at Catesby, where the prioress and Isabel Benet were
charged with immorality; the prioress denied the charge, but
was unable to find four sisters to vouch for her and was adjudged
guilty; Isabel Benet admitted misconduct, but not with the
man whose name was coupled with hers, and she seems to have
cleared herself of intercourse with him by the oath of four of
the nuns[1] Usually the bishop showed himself lenient and allowed the agitated sinner an extension of time, if she could not
find her compurgators within the period allotted to her[2]. Whether
this leniency is to be attributed to Christian charity, or to a
desire to avoid scandal, is not clear; but if a prioress could not
in two hours find four nuns to swear that she was not guilty,
the value of their oaths, when they appeared after four hours'
canvassing, would not appear to be very great. Yet it is impossible
not to understand the bishop's desire to give a sinner the benefit
of the doubt; fright and admonition alone might reform her,
and it was exceedingly difficult to deal with a really bad prioress,
when she could not be ejected from her order.

The bishop having dealt with individual offenders, the whole
convent was summoned once more to the chapter house. The
detecta and *comperta* were read aloud to the nuns and the bishop
made verbal injunctions upon points which stood in special need
of reform. He then dissolved the visitation; or, if any further

---

[1] *Linc Visit* II, pp. 49–50
[2] See e.g the case of Denise Lovelich at Markyate in 1433, *Linc Visit.*
I, pp. 83–5.

business remained to be dealt with, prorogued it until a later date. Then he rode away again, and the fluttered convent settled down again to gossip and to await further injunctions. For the admonitions of the bishop at the visitation were only *interim* injunctions; his business was not finished until he had sent to the nunnery a set of written injunctions, embodying the reforms shown to be necessary by the *comperta*. These written injunctions were sent to the convent shortly after the visitation Sometimes the clerk who brought them was ordered to expound them, or some reverend commissioner was sent to complete at the same time any special business arising out of the visitation For instance, when Peckham sent a set of injunctions on April 20th, 1284, to the Priory of the Holy Sepulchre, Canterbury, which had been visited by commissioners on his behalf, he also addressed a letter to his commissary Martin, bidding him go in person to the house and expound the injunctions to the nuns. At the same time he was ordered (1) to appoint two coadjutresses to the prioress, who had been wasting the goods of the house; one of these was named and Martin was particularly warned against appointing another nun, who was said to be contumelious; (2) to beseech the Vicar of Wickham on behalf of the Archbishop to undertake the office of master of the house, so as to order its temporal affairs; (3) to receive the compurgation of Isabella de Scorue, who was defamed with the cellarer of the cathedral church and to forbid all the nuns access to the cathedral and the cellarer access to the priory[1]. These pieces of specific and administrative business were not mentioned in Peckham's more general injunctions. The injunctions were left in the hands of the convent and from that moment became as canonically binding upon the nuns, as was their original rule; any breach of them was liable to punishment by excommunication. The prioress was usually ordered to display them in a place where they could be easily read by the sisters, or to have them solemnly read aloud in chapter a certain number of times each year.

It was by this machinery of visitation and injunction that the diocesans endeavoured to control and reform the nunneries.

---

[1] *Reg Epis Johannis Peckham*, II, pp. 706–8 (injunctions), 708–9 (mandate to commissary). Compare the proceedings at Ankerwyke six months after Alnwick's visitation. *Linc. Visit* II, p. 7.

But how far was the control adequate and the reform successful? It is obvious that the efficacy of the visitation system depended on three things· (1) the success of the cross-examination in drawing the real state of the convent from the nuns, (2) the regularity with which visitation was repeated, (3) the ability of the bishop to enforce his injunctions As to the first of these conditions, the extent to which breaches of discipline came to light depended on the skill of the bishop in cross-examination on the one hand, and on the other the honesty of the nun's desire to assist him. If a convent were seriously discontented the chances were that charges would be freely made : thus Alnwick experienced no difficulty in extracting an almost unanimous testimony against the Prioress of Catesby. But this did not always happen; as is shown by Gray's letter bidding his commissary visit Markyate in 1433:

When we some time ago made actual visitation...of the priory of the Holy Trinity of the Wood by Markyate......, we, making anxious inquiry touching the state of the same priory and the concerns of religion in the same, found that in such our visitation certain crimes, transgressions and offences worthy of reformation were discovered to us, by occasion whereof...we enjoined upon the prioress and convent of the same place certain injunctions ...But...it has lately come to our hearing, as loud whispering abounds and the notoriousness of the fact has made public, that more grievous offences than were discovered to us in the same our visitation were before the beginning of the same unhappily brought to pass and done in the same priory, the which the said prioress and her sisters of their design aforethought concealed from us undiscovered at the time of such our visitation[1]

One of the matters thus concealed was the immorality of the prioress with the steward of the house, a fact which seems to have been notorious throughout the neighbourhood.

When such a grave defect could be successfully hidden from the bishop at his visitation, it is obvious that he could do little against a unanimous determination on the part of a convent to keep him in the dark. He was really dependent upon disagreement within the house, a conscientious nun or a nun with a grudge served him equally well But it seems likely that concealment was not seldom practised, for, as Mr Coulton points out, "among the earliest and most frequently-repeated

---

[1] *Linc. Visit.* I, pp. 82–3.

general chapter statutes are those providing against (a)' conspiracy of the Religious against reformation, or (b) vengeance wreaked afterwards upon brethren who have dared to reveal the truth"[1]. Some of the *detecta* at Alnwick's visitation throw light on the efforts made (usually by the prioress) by conspiracy and by vengeance to prevent the nuns from testifying. At Catesby the evil prioress, Margaret Wavere, had excellent reasons for fearing a disclosure of her way of life Sister Juliane Wolfe deposed "that the prioress did threaten that, if the nuns disclosed aught in the visitation, they should pay for it in prison." Dame Isabel Benet (by no means a paragon of virtue herself) deposed that "in the last visitation which was made by the Lord William Graye, the prioress said that for a purse and certain moneys a clerk of the said bishop made known what every nun disclosed in that visitation" Sister Alice Kempe said that "because the nuns at the last visitation disclosed what should be disclosed, the prioress whipped some of them." All of these articles the prioress denied, but she was undoubtedly guilty and was unable to find compurgators[2]. At Legbourne the prioress took a course with which one cannot avoid a certain sympathy. Dame Joan Gyney deposed that

the prioress, after she received my lord's mandate for the visitation, called together the chapter and said, if there were aught in need of correction among them, they should tell it her, because she said it

---

[1] G G. Coulton in *Eng Hist Review* (1914), p 37 "The *locus classicus* here is the Evesham Chronicle, in which one of the most admirable abbots of the thirteenth century tells us how solemnly he and his brethren had promised to conceal all their former abbot's blackest crimes from the visiting bishop, and how they would never have complained even to the legate (whose jurisdiction they did recognize) if only the sinner had kept his pact with them in money matters."

[2] *Linc Visit.* ii, pp 47, 48, 49, 52 At Heynings (where nothing seriously amiss transpired) one nun said that "the prioress reproaches her sisters, saying that if they say aught to the bishop, she will lay on them such penalties that they shall not easily bear them." *Ib.* p. 133. The wicked Prioress of Littlemore was found in 1517 to have ordered her nuns on virtue of their obedience to reveal nothing to the commissioners and in 1518 : was stated that she had punished them for speaking the truth at the visitation. *V C H Lincs.* ii, p. 75. At Flixton in 1514 it was said "The sisters scarce dare to depose the truth on account of the fierceness of the prioress" *Visit of the Dioc of Norwich*, ed Jessopp (Camden Soc), p. 143. For episcopal injunctions against revealing or quarrelling over *detecta* made at the visitation, see *Linc. Visit.* ii, pp. 51, 124, etc., *Yorks. Arch. Journ* xvi, p 442, *Reg. Epis Johannis Peckham*, ii, p. 661.

was more suitable that they should correct themselves than that others should correct them[1]

At Ankerwyke Prioress Clemence Medforde, conscious of many misdeeds and of the cordial dislike of her nuns, "did invite several outside folk from the neighbourhood to this visitation at great cost to the house, saying to them, 'Stand on my side in this time of visitation, for I do not want to resign'" She admitted the entertainment of her friends, "but it was not to this end"[2]. Recriminations after the visitation are even commoner than preliminary attempts to circumvent it. At Gracedieu the ill-tempered old prioress confessed, on being confronted with the *detectum* of one of her nuns to that effect, that she

since and after the visitation last held therein by his [Alnwick's] predecessor, did reproach her sisters, because of the disclosures at the same visitation and did blame them therefore and has held and holds them in hatred, by reason whereof charity and loving-kindness were utterly banished and strivings, hatreds, back-bitings and quarrellings have ever flourished[3].

The second condition for the efficacy of episcopal visitation as a method of reform is the regularity of such visitation. Obviously if visitations are very rare the hold of the diocesan on a house will be weak; for much water may flow under the bridge between one visitation and the next The general rule in vogue in the middle ages was that each house should be visited once in every three years, which was in theory a very adequate arrangement. It seems clear, however, that it was not always carried out. The work was done by one overworked bishop in person or by commissioners specially appointed by him for the visitation of each house. In a big diocese, such as Lincoln or York, which abounded in monastic houses, the work of visitation was a really considerable labour, for it was only one part of the bishop's multifarious duties; and it is impossible not to conclude that the regularity of visitation differed very much from diocese to diocese and from time to time. The bishops themselves varied very much in energy and conscientiousness, but on the whole it is evident that they took their duties seriously and honestly endeavoured to keep up the standard of life in their dioceses No one can put down the record of Rigaud's visitations of the

---

[1] *Linc. Visit.* II, pp. 184–5   [2] *Ib* p 4
[3] *Ib* pp 120, 122, 123–4.

diocese of Rouen, Greenfield's visitations of the diocese of York, and Alnwick's visitations of the diocese of Lincoln, without a profound respect for those prelates. But though they did much, they could not do enough.

There is a good deal of incidental evidence in the visitation reports, which shows that visitations were held too seldom to be really effectual. Gracedieu, for instance, had not been visited between 1433, when Gray came, and 1440–1, and by this last date it had fallen into such laxity that reform must have been difficult. Markyate was unvisited between 1433 and 1442, in spite of the deprivation of the prioress for immorality and the apostasy of one of the nuns in 1433. There are few houses in the annals of English nunneries in so bad a state as Littlemore was in 1517; yet the Prioress, forced at last to confess her misdeeds, which comprised not only habitual incontinence but the persecution of her nuns, stated that though these things had been going on for eight years, yet no inquiry had been made and, as it seems, no visitation of the house had been held; only on one occasion certain injunctions of a general kind had been sent her[1]. On the other hand the registers show that a real attempt was often made to grapple with a really serious case St Michael's, Stamford, for instance, was visited by Alnwick in 1440 and found to be in a disorderly state; he gave careful *interim* injunctions on the spot and sent written injunctions afterwards. The house, however, was ruled by a thoroughly incompetent prioress, and the bishop seems to have made inquiries and found that his reforms had not been carried out, for in 1442 he came again,

and then after the cause of such his visitation had been set forth and explained to the said prioress and nuns by the same reverend father, to wit because his injunctions at his first visitation...were not duly kept, he proceeded to his preparatory inquiry.

This inquiry showed that matters were if anything worse than before; and in 1445 the bishop visited the house again[2]. Similarly, when once Bishop Atwater had awakened to the moral condition

[1] *V.C.H. Lincs.* II, p. 76

[2] *Alnwick's Visit* MS ff 83, 39d, 96. Similarly at Ankerwyke, where there was great discord between Prioress and nuns, he prorogued his visitation for six months and then sent down commissioners to expound his injunctions, inquire how they were followed and deal with further grievances. *Linc Visit* II, pp 6–8.

of Littlemore in the next century, he took pains to reform it.
The scandals were brought to light at the visitation by his
commissary Dr Horde in 1517, a few months later the bishop
summoned the prioress before him to answer the charges made
against her and after a lapse of nine months the house was
visited again in 1518[1]

But if visitations were sometimes not held regularly enough
to be really effective, a still greater cause of weakness was the
great difficulty experienced by the bishops in controlling the
religious houses in the period between one visitation and the next
and in enforcing their injunctions. A bishop might send a set of
the most salutary injunctions to an undisciplined house; but how
was he to secure that the nuns followed them, save by the most
solemn threats of excommunication, which they seem often
enough to have disregarded. Markyate, St Michael's, Stamford,
and Littlemore went steadily from bad to worse between each of
the visitations made by Gray, Alnwick and Atwater respectively.
In 1442

Dame Elizabeth the prioress [of St Michael's], being asked whether
she has observed and caused to be observed by the others my lord's
injunctions made to them at another time, says that, so far as she
has been able she has kept them and caused them to be kept by
the others· howbeit she says that she does not lie in the dorter, or
keep frater, or even keep cloister or church according to my lord's
injunction and this because of her bodily incapacity. And she avers
that my lord granted her a dispensation touching these things, the
which my lord utterly disavows[2]

These were comparatively trivial faults; since the last visitation
one of the nuns had had a child; and at the next visitation, three
years later, the same fate was found to have overtaken another,
which is a significant commentary on the effectuality of episcopal
control

The fundamental difficulty was that the bishop was obliged
in the nature of things to trust largely to the prioress and to
the nuns themselves to enforce his decrees. *Quis custodiet ipsos
custodes?* Sometimes the very women whom he singled out for
special trust were subsequently found to be worse than their
sisters. Indeed it is sometimes difficult to account for the
principle on which coadjutresses were appointed. It surely seems

---

[1] *V.C.H Lincs* II, pp 76–7　　　　[2] *Alnwick's Visit* MS f 39d.

somewhat like tempting providence that Alnwick should have
selected Isabel Benet, the only other nun in the house who was
defamed of incontinence, to be administrator in place of the
suspended Prioress of Catesby, and it is not surprising to read
of the later escapade of that lady at a dance with the friars of
Northampton and of their refusal to obey his ordinance against
private rooms[1]. The only intelligible principle of the bishop
would appear to have been that applied by Henry VII to the
Earl of Kildare, "All Ireland cannot rule this man; then he
shall rule all Ireland." It is moreover significant (as has already
been pointed out)[2] that in the majority of cases a prioress, however wicked, was suspended rather than deprived; even Denise
Lowelıche and Katherine Wells remained in office after their
resignation. It was indeed too embarrassing to know what to
do with a sinner. She could not be expelled from her order;
if she were kept in the same house in a subordinate position
she would probably make her successor's life a burden; if she
were transferred to another house she would probably corrupt
a hitherto unblemished flock. The bishops did their best in the
face of great difficulties, but it is plain that the prioresses sometimes thought little enough of their authority. The rather disreputable old Abbess of Romsey, Joyce Rowse, said openly
to her nuns that when the inquiry (held in 1492) was finished
she would do as she had done before; and she kept her word[3].
At Ankerwyke in 1441 one little nun of tender age explained
to the bishop "that the prioress doth not provide this deponent
with bed-clothes, insomuch that she lies in the straw, and when
my lord had commanded this deponent to lie in the dorter, and
this deponent asked bed-clothes of the prioress, she said chidingly
to her, 'Let him who gave you leave to lie in the dorter supply
you with raiment'"[4].

Though the bishops for the most part did their work conscientiously it is difficult, in the light of the considerations which
have been urged above, to conclude that their visitations had
a lasting effect. But if the visitations and the injunctions based
on them were sometimes of small value for their purpose, they
have an incidental value to historians which cannot be over-

[1] See above, pp. 388–9, 460
[2] See above, p 469.
[3] Liveing, *Records of Romsey Abbey*, p. 220.
[4] *Linc. Visit.* II, p. 5.

estimated. There have come down to us in the bishops' registers a comparatively small number of complete visitation reports, comprising *detecta* and *comperta* (or sometimes *comperta* only) and injunctions[1], and a much larger number of injunctions, without the *comperta* on which they were based. The similarity in wording of episcopal injunctions, combined with the fact that the most important collection of complete reports (Alnwick's visitations) was until recently unknown, has led many writers to argue that injunctions were mere general "common form," without any relation to specific abuses found at the house to which they were sent, "left," as Mr Hamilton Thompson says, "like portentous visiting cards upon a convent, to show that the diocesan had duly called"[2] The point is of great importance,

[1] As full reports containing *detecta* or *comperta* are specially valuable, it may be useful to indicate those concerning nunneries, which have been published· (1) The earliest *comperta* extant are those of Archbishop Giffard's visitation of Swine in Yorkshire in 1267–8; the individual *detecta* are absent, but there is a fine set of injunctions, issued two months later, the earliest English nunnery injunctions which we possess, *Reg Walter Giffard* (Surtees Soc), pp 147–8, 248–9 (2) The *comperta* of Archbishop Wittlesey's metropolitan visitation of St Radegund's, Cambridge (including only *interim* injunctions) have been published in Gray, *Priory of St Radegund, Cambridge*, pp 35–6 (3) The *Sede Vacante* visitation of Arden in 1396 includes *detecta* but no injunctions, *Test Ebor* I, pp 283–5 (note) and that of Nunmonkton in the same year includes *comperta* and injunctions, Dugdale, *Mon.* IV, p. 194, both of these are concerned almost entirely with charges against the respective prioresses (4) The finest collection in existence is Alnwick's book of Lincoln visitations, which is in the course of publication, *Linc. Visit* II and III (in the press) (5) Records of visitations of Rusper and Easebourne from the Chichester registers of the fifteenth and sixteenth centuries contain *detecta* and some injunctions, *Sussex Arch Coll* V and IX, *passim* (6) Records of the visitations of monastic houses in the diocese of Norwich by Bishops Goldwell (1492–3) and Nykke (1514–32) include *detecta* and *injunctions* (sometimes only *interim*), *Visit of Dioc of Norwich*, ed. Jessopp, *passim* (7) Dr Hede's *Sede Vacante* visitations of the four houses in the diocese of Winchester in 1501–2, summarised in *V C H Hants* II, *passim*, include *detecta*, but not injunctions (8) Archbishop Warham's visitations of houses in the diocese of Canterbury (Holy Sepulchre, Canterbury, the hospital of St James, Canterbury, Sheppey and Davington) in 1511 include *detecta* and sometimes injunctions, *Eng Hist Review*, VI. When more registers are published other *detecta* and *comperta* will doubtless appear, there are some valuable sets, still in manuscript, in *Linc Epis Reg Visit Atwater* and *ib. Reg Visit Longland*

[2] *Linc Visit* II, p. xlviii, for an admirable and detailed discussion of the whole question, in the light of Alnwick's records, Mr Hamilton Thompson's introduction to this volume (especially pp. xlv–li) should be studied See also the learned article by Mr Coulton on "The Interpretation of Visitation Documents," *E H.R.* 1914, pp 16–40

for it involves the reliability of injunctions as evidence of the state of a particular convent at a particular time.

The answer to this view of "common form" is easily found if we study the process by which injunctions were composed, as revealed in the great series of visitations by Bishop Alnwick They were drawn up with great care by the bishop's registrar and he based them upon two sources, the *detecta* and *comperta* of each visitation, which had been noted down on the spot by clerks, and the sets of injunctions sent to other religious houses, which were regularly copied into the episcopal register as models for future use It is inherent in the nature of the case that monasteries subject to the same original rule and statutory regulations and living under almost identical conditions, should be subject to similar breaches of discipline. It is only necessary to study those *detecta* which have been preserved to perceive how universal, in all dioceses and among both sexes, were (for instance) the customs of drinking after Compline, forming separate "households," taking unlicensed boarders, making unwise grants of corrodies and long leases, wandering abroad in the world, and wearing worldly garments The registrar did not wish to invent new wording every time these offences occurred; he used a common form for them But "common form" has here a different sense from that in which it is used by those who question the value of injunctions as evidence The registrar never made an injunction which was not based upon a *detectum* made at the house to which the injunction was directed. Injunctions are common form only because they deal with common errors. If an almost similar set be sent to two houses, it is because the houses have displayed (as is indeed only natural) almost similar faults; and where the two sets differ, they differ not accidentally, but of careful purpose. It was the business of the registrar to express the injunctions in general terms, even though a fault may have been that of a single individual, because they were intended to be canonically binding upon the whole convent. The reason why injunctions have survived in much greater numbers than the *detecta* upon which they were based, is that the clerks copied into the bishop's register only common forms, which would be likely to be useful. The record of individual evidence would not help them; but a carefully worded injunction might be used over and over again, whenever the fault with which it dealt recurred at the same or another house. No one who has studied the relation of *detecta* and injunctions in Alnwick's book of visitations can doubt the value of the latter as evidence, when they appear alone; the very process by which "Dame Alice Decun says that only two little girls, of six or seven years, do lie in the dorter" is transmuted into the common injunction "that ye suffre ne seculere persones wymmen ne childern lyg by nyghte in the dormytory" is patent in the register.

If the reliability of the injunctions be thus accepted, it is almost unnecessary to point out what an invaluable source of evidence is to be found in the bishops' registers. Controversialists have fought *ad nauseam* over the truth or falsehood of the "scandalous *comperta*" of Henry VIII's commissioners, without understanding that for nearly three hundred years before the Dissolution the *comperta* and injunctions in the registers give a picture of English monasticism coloured by no ulterior motive. Even after a large number of the registers have been published, historians are still content to paint monastic life in the later middle ages from the monastic rule, ignoring the evidence of practice which is always necessary to supplement the evidence of theory. Not even the chronicles of an earlier age are more interesting; the record of Alnwick is as valuable as that of Jocelin of Brakelonde. In dioceses where registers were regularly kept and have survived uninjured and where injunctions were punctiliously copied, the history of a house may be traced throughout the whole period covered by this book. The dioceses of Winchester, Lincoln and York are most fortunate in this respect. To select a few examples at random, there are extant records of the visitation of Romsey Abbey by Archbishop Peckham in 1284, by Bishop John of Pontoise in 1302, by Bishop Henry Woodlock in 1311, by Bishop William of Wykeham in 1387, by Archbishop Morton (through his vicar-general, Robert Shirbourne) in 1492, by Dr Hede, commissary of the Prior of Canterbury, during the vacancies of the sees of Canterbury and Winchester in 1502, by Bishop Fox (through his vicar-general, John Dowman) in 1507, again (through Master John Incent) in 1523 and again (through the vicar-general) in 1527[1]. It is thus

---

[1] Liveing, *op. cit.*, pp. 99, etc.

possible to describe with approximate accuracy the life of this great convent during the whole period from 1284 to the Dissolution. Similarly records have survived of visitations of Elstow Abbey by Bishop Gynewell in 1359, Bishop Buckingham in 1387, Archbishop Courtenay in 1389, Bishop Flemyng in 1421–2, Bishop Gray in 1434, Bishop Alnwick in 1442–3, and Bishop Longland in 1530 and 1531 Of Nunappleton Priory there are recorded visitations by Archbishop Wickwane in 1281, Archbishop Melton in 1318, Archbishop Zouche in 1346, Archbishop Rotherham in 1489 and Archbishop Lee in 1534. Moreover mandates concerning isolated pieces of business, elections, permits to receive boarders, orders to reform specific abuses, are scattered through the registers and provide useful supplementary information

All houses are not as well represented In some dioceses injunctions are rarely recorded: the fine series of registers for Hereford yield surprisingly few. Some houses emerge only rarely into the light with a single set of injunctions, others (and among them important houses such as Lacock and Amesbury) lack even a single visitation report to rescue their inmates from oblivion. But the geographical range of the surviving reports is sufficiently great to enable the formation of an accurate general account of English nunneries during the later middle ages One warning only must be borne in mind by the reader If it is unhistorical to write an account of monastic houses based solely upon the rule, it is also unhistorical to write one based solely on visitation documents. The *detecta* made to a bishop were, and were intended to be, revelations of faults, it was not the function of the bishop's clerk to catalogue virtues, though sometimes a string of "*omnia bene*," or a curt note to the effect that my lord, finding little in need of reformation, passed on, bears positive witness to a convent's good life. It must always be remembered, in estimating the state of a house from a set of *detecta* and injunctions, that though they are indubitably the truth, they are not the whole truth Goodness is after all largely a matter of proportion; and though convents are to be found which were positively bad, in others there were probably virtues of kindness, piety and a brave struggle against poverty, which would counterbalance (if we knew them), the unfavourable impression left by a string of accusations   Moreover by far the larger number of the *detecta* witnesses to a growing worldliness and to minor breaches of the rule, rather than to serious moral defects. If the community concerned were other than a nunnery ostensibly following a strict rule, we should hardly consider the faults to be faults at all. The immorality, bad temper and financial mismanagement revealed at some houses would be reprehensible in all communities at all ages; but in themselves boarders, pretty clothes, pet dogs and attendance at christenings are not heinous crimes   It is necessary, in dealing with medieval nuns as with all other subjects, to preserve a sense of proportion and a firm hold upon human nature.

CHAPTER XIII

THE NUN IN MEDIEVAL LITERATURE

"Or dient et content et fablent."
Aucassin et Nicolette

"LA SCIENCE," said a wise Frenchman, "atteint l'exactitude; il appartient à l'art seul de saisir la vérité." And another, "L'histoire vit de documents, mais les documents sont pareils aux lettres écrites avec les encres chimiques; ils veulent, pour livrer leur secret, qu'on les réchauffe, et les éclaire par transparence, à la flamme de la vie." The quotations are complementary, for what, after all, is literature but a form of life; the quintessence of many moods and experiences, the diffused flame concentrated and burning clearly in a polished lamp. The historian who wishes to reach beyond accuracy to truth must warm those invisible writings of his at the flame of literature, as well as at his own life. He must vitalise the visitation reports for himself (it is not difficult, they move and live almost without him), but he must make use also of the life of writers long since dead. There is hardly a branch of literature which has not its contribution for him. The story-teller has his tale, which holdeth children from play and old men from the chimney corner The ballad-man has his own pithy judgment in the guise of an artless rhyme. The teacher has his admonitions, whence may be learnt what men conceived to be the nun's ideal and purpose in this cloistered life The moralist has his satire, to show wherein she fell short of such lofty heights And the poet himself will hold his mirror up to nature, that we may see after five hundred years what he saw with his searching eyes, when Madame Eglentyne rode to Canterbury, or when the nuns of Poissy feasted a cavalcade from court. The world was subject matter for all these, whether they wrote with a purpose or without one, there is life even in the crabbed elegiacs of Gower, grumbling his way through the *Vox Clamantis*, there is much life in the kindly counsels of the *Ancren Riwle*, there is God's plenty indeed in the stories and songs which the people told. It is the historian's business to call in these literary witnesses to supplement his documents. To the account-roll and the bishop's register must be added the song, the satire and the sermon Alnwick's visitations, with the story of "Beatrix the Sacristan" behind them, have twice as much significance, Madame Eglentyne and Margaret Fairfax lend to each other a mutual illumination; little captured Clarice Stil needs Deschamps' Novice of Avernay by her side before her case can be well understood. It is of these composite portraits that truth is put together and history made.

An analysis of the classes of medieval literature in which there is mention of nuns shows from how wide a field the historian can draw. The most obvious of these classes is that which contains biographies and autobiographies of saints and famous women who were nuns. Such are the writings of the great trio who made famous the nunnery of Helfta in the thirteenth century, the béguine Mechthild of Magdeburg and the nuns Mechthild of Hackeborn and Gertrud the Great[1], the lives and writings of Luitgard of Tongres[2], of St Clare[3] and of St Agnes of Bohemia[4]; the memoir and letters of Charitas Pirckheimer, Abbess of a Franciscan convent at Nuremberg, who was a sister of the

[1] *Revelationes Gertrudianae ac Mechthildianae*, ed Oudin (Paris, 1875) See also Preger, *Geschichte der deutschen Mystik im Mittelalter* (1874), 1, pp. 70–132, Eckenstein, *Woman under Mon* pp. 328–53, Taylor, *The Medieval Mind*, 1, pp 481–6; A M F Robinson (Mme Darmesteter), *The End of the Middle Ages* (1889), pp. 45–72 (the Convent of Helfta); A Kemp-Welch, *Of Six Medieval Women* (1913), pp. 57–82 (Mechthild of Magdeburg), G. Ledos, *Ste Gertrude* (Paris, 1901) The name of the Abbess Gertrude of Hackeborn, who ruled the house during the greater part of the time that these three mystics lived there, deserves to be added to theirs For her life see *Revelationes, etc*, 1, pp 497 ff.

[2] See her life by Thomas of Chantimpré, *Acta SS Jun*, t III, pp. 234 ff. See also Taylor, *op. cit.* 1, pp 479–81

[3] See E. Gilliat Smith, *St Clare of Assisi, her Life and Legislation* (1914), Mrs Balfour, *Life and Legend of the Lady St Clare*, with introd by Father Cuthbert (1910), Fr. Marianus Fiege, *The Princess of Poverty* (Evansville, Ind 1900) which contains a translation of Thomas of Celano's *Life of St Clare* (*Acta SS. Aug* t II, pp 754–67), Paschal Robinson, *Life of St Clare* (1910), Locatelli, *Ste Claire d'Assise* (Rome, 1899–1900) Also *La Vie et Légende de Madame Sainte Claire* par le Frère François Ms. 13121 ed Arnauld Goffin (Paris, 1907)

[4] *Acta SS Mar* 1, pp 501–31 See also Jentsch, *Die Selige Agnes von Böhmen*. She is always regarded as a saint but was never officially canonised

humanist Wilibald Pirckheimer and herself a scholar of repute[1]. The autobiographies of one or two nuns in the later sixteenth century (for instance St Theresa[2] and Felice Rasponi[3]) have a certain retrospective value; and the lives of the three béguine mystics, St Douceline[4], St Lydwine of Schiedam[5] and St Christina of Stommeln[6] afford supplementary evidence, which is interesting as showing the similarities and dissimilarities between regular and secular orders For present purposes, however, these works may be neglected Their interest is always rather particular than general, since they deal with great individuals, and the information which they give as to the life of the average nun is conditioned always by the fact that a woman of genius will mould her surroundings to her own form, even in a convent. This is true of the medieval saints; while the careers of women such as Charitas Pirckheimer, Felice Rasponi and St Theresa owe much of their significance to the special circumstances of the time. An additional reason for neglecting biographies and autobiographies lies in the fact that the class is unrepresented in English literature belonging to this period. The short panegyric of Euphemia of Wherwell is the sole approach to a biography of an English nun which has survived, unless we are to count the

---

[1] Pirckheimer, *B Opera*, ed Goldast (1610) See also, T Binder, *Charitas Pirkheimer* (1878), and Eckenstein, *op. cit* pp 458–76.

[2] *The Life of St Theresa of Jesus, written by Herself*, tr. D Lewis, ed Zimmerman (1904). *The Letters of St Theresa*, tr. J. Dalton (1902) See also G Cunningham Grahame, *Santa Teresa*, 2 vols (1894)

[3] See A Gagnière, *Les Confessions d'une Abbesse du xvie siècle* (Paris, 1888), based on a manuscript at Ravenna ("Vita della Madre Donna Felice Rasponi, Badessa di S Andrea, scritta da una Monaca") which the author considers to be an autobiography Some interesting details as to the scandalous condition of Italian convents at the end of the century are to be found in J A Symonds' *Renaissance in Italy The Catholic Reaction*, pt. 1 (1886), pp. 341–70, dealing with the careers of Virginia Maria de Leyva, in the convent of S Margherita at Monza and Lucrezia Buonvisi (sister Umilia) in the convent of S. Chiara at Lucca

[4] *La Vie de Ste Douceline, fondatrice des béguines de Marseille*, ed J H. Albanès (Marseille, 1879) See also A Macdonell, *Saint Douceline* (1905)

[5] *Acta SS. Aprilis*, t ii, pp 266–365. See also Huysmans, *Ste. Lydwine de Schiedam* (3rd ed Paris, 1901)

[6] *Acta SS. Jun t iv*, pp. 270 ff. See also Th. Wollersheim, *Das Leben der ekstatischen Jungfrau Christina von Stommeln* (Cologne, 1859), and Renan, *Nouvelles Études d'Histoire Religieuse* (1884) (*Une Idylle Monacale au xiiie siècle· Christine de Stommeln*), pp. 353–96 Extracts from Christina's correspondence and life by Peter of Sweden are translated in Coulton, *Med. Garn* pp 402–21.

description of Joan Wiggenhall's building activities. For some
reason which it is impossible to explain, monasticism did not
produce in England during the later middle ages any women
of sanctity or genius who can compare with the great Anglo-
Saxon abbesses[1].

Outside the personal records of great individuals, our in-
formants fall (as has already been suggested) into four classes:
the people, with their songs and stories, the teachers, with their
didactic works, the moralists, with their satires and complaints,
and finally the men of letters, poets and "makers," for whom
the nun is sometimes subject-matter. First, and perhaps most
interesting of all, must come the people and the people's songs,
for in the literature of the continent there exists a class of lyrics
("Klosterlieder," "Nonnenklagen," "Chansons de Nonnes")
which is specially concerned with nuns[2]. There is much to be
learned about all manner of things from such popular poetry.
So the people feel about life, and so (reacting upon them) it
makes them feel. Songs crooned over the housework or shouted
at the plough steal back into the singer's brain and subtly
direct his conscious outlook; this was the wise man's meaning,
who said that he cared not who made the laws of a nation if
he might make its ballads. Now it is extremely significant that
almost all the popular songs about nuns, the songs which

> The spinsters and the knitters in the sun,
> And the free maids that weave their thread with bones
> Do use to chant,

are upon one theme. They deal always with the nun unwillingly
professed. It was the complaint of the cloistered love-birds which
these knitters sang.

> How can a bird that is born for joy
> Sit in a cage and sing?

[1] On these saintly and learned women see Eckenstein, *op cit* cc. III
and IV, and Montalembert, *The Monks of the West* (introd Gasquet), vol IV,
Book xv. The great fourteenth century mystic Julian of Norwich (1343–
c. 1413) was, it is true, connected with Carrow Priory, but she was an
anchoress and never a nun there, see above, p 366

[2] On these songs see A Jeanroy, *Les Origines de la Poésie Lyrique en
France au moyen âge* (2nd ed 1904), pp 189–92; and P. S. Allen in *Modern
Philology*, v (1908), pp. 432–5 The songs themselves have to be collected
from various sources, see below, Note I.

What, one may ask, is the reason for this unanimity of outlook?
Why do the people see a nun only as a love-bird shut within a
cage and beating its wings against the bars? Partly, no doubt,
because such songs always "dally with the innocence of love";
the folk are capable of a deep melancholy, as of a gaiety which is
light as thistledown; but Love is and was their lord and king,
and so even the nun must be in love when they sing her. It
may be, however, that there is a deeper meaning in the *chansons
de nonnes*. The nunneries were aristocratic; the ideal of the
religious life was out of the reach of women who lived among
fields and beasts of the field. These spinsters and these knitters
in the sun, who seem so gay and peaceful, we know what their
lives were like:

> Poure folke in cotes,
> Charged with children, and chef lordes rente,
> That thei with spynnynge may spare spenen hit in hous-hyre,
> Bothe in mylk and in mele to make with papelotes[1],

carding and combing, clouting and washing, suffering much
hunger and woe in winter time, no time to think, and hardly
time to pray, but always time to sing. "The wo of those women
that wonyeth in cotes" solaced itself in song; but when the echo
of the convent bell came to the singer at her clouting, or to her
husband, as he drove his plough over the convent acres, they
recognised a peace which was founded upon their labours and
which, though it could not exist without them, they could never
share[2] If the songs which the slaves of Athens sang among

---

[1] Langland, *Piers Plowman*, ed Skeat. C text, Passus **x**, 72–5.

[2] There was (as usual) however, more chance for a man than for a
woman of villein status to enter a monastery and even to rise to the highest
ecclesiastical dignities. A villein who could save enough to pay a fine to
his lord might put his son to school and might buy that son's enfranchise-
ment, so that he would be eligible for a place in a monastery. And though
it was forbidden by canon and by temporal law to ordain a serf, once
ordained he was free. Pollock and Maitland, *Hist of Engl Law* (1911),
I, p. 429; the lower ranks of the clergy probably contained many men of
low or villein birth (see e g Chaucer's Poor Parson, whose brother was a
ploughman and the complaint in "Pierce the Plouman's Crede" that
beggars' brats become bishops) Sometimes, though very rarely, a villein
rose high, for once he was a churchman, it was *la carrière ouverte aux talents*;
Bishop Grosseteste was of very humble, probably of servile, origin; and
Sancho Panza's motto will be remembered. "I am a man and I may be
Pope." For a woman, however, the Church offered no such chance of advancement through the religious orders; the nunneries were essentially upper
and middle class institutions

themselves in the slave quarter at night had come down to us, they would surely have thrown a new light upon those grave philosophers, artists and statesmen, to whom the world owes almost all that it cherishes of wisdom and of beauty. Nor would the Athenians be less great because we knew the slaves. Even so it is no derogation to the monastic ideal to say that the common people, shut out of it, looked at it differently from the great churchmen, who praised it; and, unlike those of the Athenian slaves, their songs'still live The popular mind (these songs would seem to say) had little sympathy for that career in which the daughters of the people had no share. It is immaterial whether they looked upon it with the eye of the fox in the fable, declaring that the grapes were sour, or whether the lusty common sense of those living close to nature gave them a contempt for the bloodless ecstasies they could not understand. At all events the cloister mirrored in their songs is a prison and a grave

> Mariez-vous, les filles,
> Avec ces bons drilles,
> Et n'allez jà, les filles,
> Pourrir derrièr' les grilles[1].

That was how the people and the nightingale envisaged it; and no mystic will be the less wise for pondering that brutal last line, the eternal revolt of common sense against asceticism.

All over western and southern Europe this theme was set to music, now with gaiety and insouciance, now with bitterness. The wandering clerk goes singing on his way:

Plangit nonna fletibus	The nun is complaining,
Inenarrabilibus,	Her tears are down raining,
Condolens gemitibus	She sobbeth and sigheth,
Dicens consocialibus	To her sisters she crieth·
Heu misella!	Misery me!

---

[1] From a charming round, sung in Saintonge, Aunis and Bas-Poitou.

> "Dans l'jardin de ma tante
> Plantons le romarin!
> Y'a-t-un oiseau qui chante,
> Plantons le romarin,
> Ma mie,
> Au milieu du jardin, etc"

Bujeaud, J , *Chants et chansons populaires des provinces de l'ouest* (1866), I, pp. 136–7.

Nichil est deterius	O what can be worse than this
Tali vita,	life that I dree,
Cum enim sim petulans	When naughty and lovelorn,
Et lasciva.	and wanton I be.

And he can tell the nun's desire

Pernoctando vigilo	All the night long I unwillingly
Cum non vellem	wake,
Iuvenem amplecterer	How gladly a lad in mine arms would
Quam libenter![1]	I take.

For those who know no Latin it is the same "In this year," [1359] says a Limburg chronicle, "Men sang and piped this song":

Gott geb im ein verdorben jar	God send to him a lean twelve
der mich macht zu einer nunnen	Who in mine own despite, [months
und mir den schwarzen mantel gab	A sooty mantle put on me,
der weissen rock darunten!	All and a cassock white!
Soll ich ein nunn gewerden	And if I must become a nun,
dann wider meinen willen	Let me but find a page,
so will ich auch einem knaben jung	And if he is fain to cure my pain
seinen kummer stillen,	His pain I will assuage
Und stillt he mir den meinen nit	His be the loss, then, if he fail
daran mag he verliesen[2].	To still my amorous rage

In Italy at Carnival time in the fifteenth century the favourite songs tell of nuns who leave their convents for a lover[3]. But above all the theme is found over and over again in French folk songs: "the note, I trowe, y maked was in Fraunce." Two little thirteenth century poems have survived to show how piquant an expression the French singers gave to it   In one of these the singer wanders out in the merry month of May, that time in which the "chanson populaire" is always set, in deep and unconscious memory of the old spring festivals, celebrated by women in the dawn of European civilisation. He goes

---

[1] M Vattasso, *Studi Medievali*, I (1904), p 124. A long poem of seven verses, much mutilated in parts.

[2] Uhland, *Alte hoch- und niederdeutsche Volkslieder* (1844–5), t II, p 854 (No. 328) A slightly modernised version Also printed in *Des Knaben Wunderhorn*, ed von Arnim and Brentano (Reclam ed), p. 25, and in *Deutsches Leben im Volkslied um* 1530, ed Liliencron (1884), p 226 Translation by Bithell, *The Minnesingers*, I (1909), p 200, except the last two lines, which are by Mr Coulton, there is another in Coulton, *Med. Garn* p 476

[3] Ferrari, *Canzone per andare in maschera per carnesciale*, pp. 31–2. Referred to in Jeanroy, *op. cit.* I have been unable to consult the book

plucking flowers, and out of a garden he hears a nun singing
to herself:

ki nonne me fist   Jesus lou maldie.
je di trop envie   vespres ne complies.
j'amaisce trop muels   moneir bone vie
ke fust deduissans   et amerousete
    Je sant les douls mals   leis ma senturete
    malois soit de deu   ki me fist nonnete
Elle s'escriait   comceux esbaihie !
e deus, ki m'ait mis   en cest abaie !
maix ieu en istrai   per sainte Marie,
ke ne vestirai   cotte ne gonnette.
    Je sant les douls mals   leis ma senturete.
    malois soit de deu   ki me fist nonnete.
Celui manderai   a cui seux amie,
k'il me vaigne querre   en ceste abaie;
s'irons a Parix   moneir bone vie,
car il est jolis   et je seux jonete
    Je sant les douls mals   leis ma senturete
    malois soit de deu   ki me fist nonnete.
quant ces amis ot   la parolle oie,
de joie tressaut,   li cuers li fremie,
et vint a la porte   de celle abaie:
si en getait fors .   sa douce amiete.
    Je sant les douls mals   leis ma senturete.
    malois soit de deu   ki me fist nonnete[1]

"The curse of Jesus on him who made me a nun ! All unwillingly
say I vespers and compline, more fain were I to lead a happy life
of gaiety and love *I feel the delicious pangs beneath my bosom. The
curse of God on him who made me be a nun!* She cried, God's curse
on him who put me in this abbey. But by our Lady I will flee away
from it and never will I wear this gown and habit. *I feel, etc.* I will
send for him whose love I am and bid him come seek me in this
abbey We will go to Paris and lead a gay life, for he is fair and I
am young *I feel, etc* When her lover heard her words, he leapt for
joy and his heart beat fast. He came to the gate of that abbey, and
stole away his darling love. *I feel, etc.*"

In the other song the setting is the same·

L'autrier un lundi matin
m'an aloie ambaniant;
s'antrai an un biau jardin,
trovai nonette seant

---

[1] Bartsch, *Altfranzösische Romanzen und Pastourellen* (1870), pp 28–9
(No. 33).

> ceste chansonette
> dixoit la nonette
> "longue demoree
> faites, frans moinnes loialz
>> Se plus suis nonette,
>> ains ke soit li vespres,
>> je morai des jolis malz"[1].

"Lately on a Monday morn as I went wandering, I entered into a fair garden and there I found a nun sitting This was the song that the nun sang: 'Long dost thou tarry, frank, faithful monk If I have to be a nun longer I shall die of the pains of love before vespers '"

The end hardly ever varies. The nun is either taken away by a lover (as in the first of these songs), or finds occasion to meet one without leaving her house (as in the second), or else she runs away in the hope of finding one like the novice of Avernay in Deschamps' poem, who had learned nothing during her sojourn "fors un mot d'amourette," and who wanted to have a husband "si comme a Sebilette "

> Adieu le moniage.
> Jamaiz n'y entreray.
> Adieu tout le mainage
> Et adieu Avernay!
> Bien voy l'aumosne est faitte:
> Trop tart me suy retraitte,
> Certes, ce poise my,
> Plus ne seray nonnette
>> (Oez de la nonnette
>> Comme a le cuer joly
>> S'ordre ne ly puet plere)[2].

"Farewell nunhood, never shall I enter thy state Farewell all the household and farewell Avernay! The alms are given, too late have I left the world Of a truth this wearies me; I will be a nun no more (Hear this tale of the nun, whose heart was gay and whose order could not please her)."

It is but rarely that the singer's sympathy is against the prisoned nun, and although one or two charming songs may be found which convey a warning, the moral sits all awry. A Gascon air (intended, like so many, to accompany a dance and having the favourite refrain " Va léger, légère, va légèrement ") threatens an altogether inadequate punishment for a nun who enjoys the sweets of this world.

---

[1] Bartsch, *op. cit* pp. 29–30 (No. 34).
[2] *Oeuvres Complètes d'Eustache Deschamps* (Soc des Anc. Textes Fr.), IV, pp 235–6. (Virelay, DCCLII, sur une novice d'Avernay)

"Down in the meadow, there is a convent. In it a nun lies ill " "Tell me, little nun, for what do you hunger?" "For white apples and for a young lad." "Do not eat, little nun, they will bury you not in the church, nor even in the convent, but out in the graveyard with the poor people"[1].

A Provençal song with a haunting air tells how the Devil carried off a nun who rebelled against her imprisonment·

> Dedins Aix l'y a'no moungeto,
> Tant pourideto,
> Di que s'avie soun bel amic
> Sera la reino dou pays....

"In Aix there is a little nun, a wicked little nun, she says that with her handsome lover she will be queen of all the land She weeps and weeps, that wicked little nun, and every day she grows thinner and thinner, because she may not put off her habit. But her father has sent her a message, a solemn message, that she cannot do as she would, that in the convent she must stay The little nun has cursed her father, who made her leave her handsome lover and take the veil and habit. The little nun has cursed the trowel that made the church and the mason who built it and the men who worked for him The little nun has cursed the priest who said mass and the acolytes who served him and the congregation who listened to him The little nun has cursed the cloth which made the veil and the cord of St Francis and the vow of poverty. One day when she was all alone in her room, the devil appeared to her. 'Welcome, my love!' 'I am not your love whom you desire, my pretty I am the devil, don't you see? I am come to rescue you from the convent.' 'You must first ask my father and also my mother and my friends and my kinsmen, to see if they will consent.' 'No, I will not ask your father, nor yet your mother, nor your friends nor your kinsmen. Now and at once we will go.' 'Farewell, my sister nuns, so little and young, do not do as I did, but praise God well in the convent.' The devil has taken the little nun, the wicked little nun; he has carried her high up into the sky and then he has hurled her down into hell, down, down into hell"[2].

There is a moral here to be sure, but it is the moral of a fairy tale, not of a sermon. As to the many variants of the "Clericus et Nonna" theme in which sometimes the nun makes love to a clerk and is repulsed and sometimes the clerk makes love to a nun and is repulsed[3] it is possible that the Church had a hand in them all. Wandering clerks and cloistered monks were capable of the most unabashed love-poetry, but sometimes they chose to set themselves right with heaven.

---

[1] Bladé, J F , *Poésies populaires de la Gascogne* (1882), III, pp 372–4. Also in Lénac-Moncaut, *Littérature populaire de la Gascogne* (1868), pp 291–2.

[2] Damase Arbaud, *Chants Populaires de la Provence* (1862–4), II, pp. 118–22.   [3] See below, p 611.

' In England the theme of the nun unwillingly professed is
not found in popular songs, such as abound in France, Italy and
Germany It received, however, a literary expression towards
the close of the fourteenth century. In the pseudo-Chaucerian
Court of Love the lover sees among those who do sacrifice to
the King and Queen of Love a wailing group of priests and
hermits, friars and nuns:

> This is the courte of lusty folke and gladde,
> And wel becometh hire abite and arraye;
> O why be som so sory and so sadde,
> Complaynyng thus in blak and white and graye?
> Freres they ben, and monkes, in gode faye:
> Alas for rewth! grete dole it is to sene,
> To se hem thus bewaile and sory bene.
>
> Se howe thei crye and wryng here handes white,
> For thei so sone wente to religion!
> And eke the nonnes with vaile and wymple plight,
> Here thought is, thei ben in confusion.
> "Alas," thay sayn, "we fayne perfeccion,
> In clothes wide and lake oure libertie
> But all the synne mote on oure frendes be
>
> For, Venus wote, we wold as fayne do ye,
> That ben attired here and wel besene,
> Desiren man and love in oure degree
> Ferme and feithfull right as wolde the quene.
> Oure frendes wikke in tender youth and grene,
> Ayenst oure wille made us religious;
> That is the cause we morne and waylen thus "
>
>   .   .   .   .   .
>
> And yet agaynewarde shryked every nonne,
> The pange of love so strayneth hem to cry.
> "Now woo the tyme" quod thay "that we be boune!
> This hatefull order nyse will done us dye!
> We sigh and sobbe and bleden inwardly
> Fretyng oure self with thought and hard complaynt,
> That ney for love we waxen wode and faynt "[1].

A kindred poem, *The Temple of Glas*, by Lydgate (who seems
himself to have become a monk of Bury at the age of fifteen)
contains the same idea. Among the lovers in the Temple are
some who make bitter complaint, youth wedded to age, or
wedded without free choice, or shut in a convent.

[1] *The Court of Love*, in *Chaucer's Poetical Works*, ed. R. Morris (1891),
iv, pp 38–40.

And riȝt anon I herd oþer crie
With sobbing teris and with ful pitous soune,
To fore þe goddes, bi lamentacioun,
That were constrayned in hir tender youþe
And in childhode, as it is ofte couþe,
Y-entred were into religioun,
Or þei hade yeris of discresioun,
That al her life cannot but complein,
In wide copis perfeccion to feine,
Ful couertli to curen al hir smert,
And shew þe contrarie outward of her hert.
Thus saugh I wepen many a faire maide,
That on hir freendis al þi wite þei liede[1]

The same idea is also repeated in King James I of Scotland's poem, *The King's Quair*[2], and later (with more resemblance to the continental songs) in the complaint of the wicked Prioress in Sir David Lyndesay's morality play, *Ane Satyre of the Thrie Estatis* [c. 1535]:

I gif my freinds my malisoun
That me compellit to be ane Nun,
   And wald nocht let me marie.

It was my freinds greadines
That gart me be ane Priores
   Now harthe them I warie.

Howbeit that Nunnis sing nichts and dayis
Thair hart waitis nocht quhat thair mouth sayis,
   The suith I ȝow declair.

Makand ȝow intimatioun,
To Christis Congregatioun
   Nunnis ar nocht necessair.

Bot I sall do the best I can,
And marie sum gude honest man,
   And brew gude aill and tun

Mariage, be my opinioun,
It is better Religioun
   As to be freir or Nun[3]

---

[1] Lydgate's *Temple of Glas*, ed J Schick (E E T S 1891), p 8
[2] *The Kingis Quair* in *Medieval Scottish Poetry*, ed G. Eyre-Todd (1892), p.47.
[3] *Ane Satyre of the Thrie Estatis*, by Sir David Lyndesay, ed. Small, Hall and Murray (E E.T S , 2nd ed , 1883), p 514
   "And seis thou now yone multitude, on rawe
      Standing behynd yon trauerse of delyte?
   Sum bene of thayme that haldin were full lawe
      And take by frendis, nothing thay to wyte,
      In youth from bye into the cloistre quite,
   And for that cause are cummyn, recounsilit,
   On thame to pleyne that so thame had begilit."

The concentrated bitterness of *The Court of Love* and the
social satire of Lindesay are only a literary expression of the theme
treated more lightheartedly in the popular *chansons de nonnes*.
The songs are one side of the popular view of asceticism, the
gay side The serious side may be found in the famous story of
The Nun who Loved the World:

Some time there was a nun that hight Beatrice, a passing fair woman,
and she was sacristan of the kirk, and she had great devotion unto
our Lady; and ofttimes men desired her to sin So at last she consented unto a clerk to go away with him when compline was done,
and ere she departed she went unto an altar of our Lady and said unto
her; "Lady, as I have been devout unto thee, now I resign unto thee
these keys, for I may no longer sustain the temptation of my flesh."
And she laid the keys on the altar and went her ways unto the clerk
And when he had defouled her, within a few days he left her and went
away; and she had nothing to live on and thought shame to gang
home again unto her cloister and she fell to be a common woman.
And when she had lived in that vice fifteen years, on a day she came
unto the nunnery gate, and asked the porter if he knew ever a nun
in that place that hight Beatrice, that was sacristan and keeper of the
kirk. And he said he knew her on the best wise and said she was a
worthy woman and a holy from when she was a little bairn, "and ever
has kept her clean and in good name " And she understood not the
words of this man and went her ways. And our Lady appeared unto
her and said: "Behold, I have fulfilled thine office these fifteen years
and therefore turn again now into thy place and be again in thine office
as thou wast, and shrive thee and do thy penance, for there is no
creature here that knows thy trespass, for I have ever been for thee in
thy clothing and in thine habit." And anon she was in her habit and
went in and shrove her and did her penance and told all that was
happened unto her[1]

[1] *An Alphabet of Tales*, ed M M. Banks (E E.T S), No CCCCLXVIII,
pp. 319–20. (In this and the following quotations from this work in this
chapter I have modernised the spelling.) This version is translated from
Caesarius of Heisterbach, *Dial. Mirac* , ed Strange, II, pp 42–3, which is
the original version of all the widespread legends on this theme. From
Caesarius it found its way into many other collections of miracles, in prose
and in verse, in Latin, French, Spanish, German, Icelandic, Dutch and
English Perhaps the most beautiful is the Dutch poem (c. 1320) published by
W. J. A Jenckbloet, *Beatrijs* (Amsterdam, 1846–59) and re-edited with a
grammatical introduction and notes in English by A. J. Barnouw (*Pub of
Philol Soc*. III, 1914). An edition with illustrations by Ch. Doudelet
accompanied by a translation into French by H de Marez was published
in Antwerp (1901) and was also issued with an English translation by
A W. Sanders vaz Loo The best English translations are those in prose
by L Simons and L Housman in *The Pageant*, ed. C H. Shannon and
J. W Gleeson White (1896) pp. 95–116 and in verse by H. de Wolf Fuller

This tale is interesting, because it is much more than a piece of naïve piety. The story of Beatrice is intimately connected with the *chansons de nonnes*, it is the serious, as they are the gay, expression of a whole philosophy of life. The songs are, indeed, purely materialistic and do not attempt (how should the spinsters and the knitters in the sun attempt it?) to give a philosophical justification for their attitude. The miracle is simple and seems on the surface to draw no moral, save that devotion to the Virgin will be rewarded. Nevertheless the philosophy and the moral are there; they are those of the most famous of all medieval songs, *Gaudeamus igitur, juvenes dum sumus*. The theme of the miracle and of the songs alike is the revolt against asceticism, the revolt of the body, which knows how short its beauty and its life, against the spirit which lives forever, and yet will not allow its poor yokefellow one little hour. The fact that the story of Beatrice takes the form of a Mary-miracle is itself significant. For the "Nos habebit humus" argument can be interpreted in two ways. On the one hand stands the human multitude, gathering rosebuds while it may, crying up and down the roads of the world to all who pass to rejoice today, for "ubi sunt qui ante nos in mundo fuere?" On the other hand stands the moralist, singing the same song.

> Were beth they biforen us weren,
> Houndes ladden and haukes beren,
> And hadden feld and wode,
> That riche *levedies* in *hoere* bour,   [ladies, their
> That wereden gold in hoere tressour,
> With hoere *brighte* rode?—   [complexion

(*Harvard Coop Soc.*, Cambridge, U S A 1910) Modern writers have retold the tale almost as often as their medieval forebears; see for example Maeterlinck's play, *Sœur Béatrice*, John Davidson's poem, *The Ballad of a Nun*, one of Villier de l'Isle-Adam's *Contes Cruels* (*Sœur Natalia*), one of Charles Nodier's *Contes de la Veillée* (*La Légende de Sœur Béatrice*), and one of Gottfried Keller's *Sieben Legenden* (*Die Jungfrau und die Nonne*). For a study of the Beatrice story see Heinrich Watenphul, *Die Geschichte der Marienlegende von Beatrix der Küsterin* (Neuwied, 1904); also P Toldo, *Die Sakristanin* (with bibliography by J Bolte) in *Zeitschrift des Vereins für Volkskunde* (1905), J. van der Elst, *Bijdrage tot de Geschiedenis der Legende van Beatrijs* in *Tijdschrift voor Nederlandsche Taal- en Letterkunde*, XXXII, pp 51 ff , and Mussafia, *Studien zu den Mittelalterlichen Marienlegenden*

—but drawing how different a moral,

> *Dreghy* here man, thenne, if thou wilt   [endure
> A luitel *pine*, that me the *bit*   [pain, bid
> Withdrau thine *eyses* ofte[1]   [ease

Often for long stretches at a time the wandering clerks and the singers were willing to leave to the moralist this heaven which was to be won by despising earthly beauty; they were content to go to hell singing with Aucassin and Nicolete and all the kings of the world. But at other times they ached for heaven too and would not believe that they might win there only by the narrow path of righteousness. So they invented a philosophical justification for their way of life. The Church had forgotten the love which sat with publicans and sinners; the people rediscovered it, and attributed it not to the Son but to the Mother. At one blow they outwitted the moralist by inventing the cult of the Virgin Mary[2]. In their hands this Mary worship became more than the worship of Christ's mother; it became almost a separate religion, a religion under which jongleurs and thieves, fighters and tournament-haunters and the great host of those who loved unwisely found a mercy often denied to them by the ecclesiastical hierarchy. The people created a Virgin to whom justice was nothing and law less than nothing, but to whom love of herself was all. "Imperatrix supernorum, super-

---

[1] Chambers and Sidgwick, *Early English Lyrics* (1907), No xc, p. 163. But perhaps the most beautiful of medieval English poems which moralise on this theme is the *Luue Ron* which Thomas of Hales wrote in the thirteenth century for a nun:

> "Hwer is Paris and Heleyne
>   That weren so bryght and feyre on bleo?
> Amadas, Tristram and Dideyne,
>   Yseude and alle theo,
> Ector with his scharpe meyne,
>   And Cesar riche of worldes feo?
> Heo beoth iglyden ut of the reyne,
>   So the scheft is of the cleo,"

—they have passed away as a shaft from the bowstring It is as if they had never lived All their heat is turned to cold (*An Old English Miscellany*, ed R Morris (E.E.T.S. 1872), p. 95.) This catalogue of the lovely dead was a favourite device, immortalised later by "ung povre petit escollier, qui fust nommé Francoys Villon" (who certainly was not a moralist) in his *Ballade des Dames du Temps jadis*.

[2] For an entertaining and stimulating account of the popular cult of the Virgin see Henry Adams, *Mont St Michel and Chartres* (1913), especially chs vi and XIII

natrix infernorum," hell was emptied under her rule and heaven
became a new place, filled with her disreputable, faulty, human
lovers. She was not only the familiar friend of the poor and
humble, she was also the confidante of the lover, of all the
Aucassins and Nicoletes of the world. It is not without significance that so great a stress was always laid upon her personal
loveliness. Her cult became the expression of mankind's deep
unconscious revolt against asceticism, their love of life, their
passionate sense of "beauty that must die" The story of Beatrice
has kept its undiminished attraction for the modern world largely
because in it, more than in all the other Mary-miracles, life has
triumphed and has been justified of heaven[1]. Even the cold garb
given to it by ecclesiastics such as Caesarius of Heisterbach cannot
conceal its underlying idea that all love is akin, the most earthy
to the most divine; the idea which Malory expressed many years
later, when he wrote of Queen Guinevere "that while she lived
she was a true lover and therefore she had a good end." The
theme most familiar to us in the didactic literature of the middle
ages is the theme of the soul "here in the body pent", for the
moralist has his deliberate purpose and sets down his idea more
directly and with more point than do the story-teller and the
singer, who have no aim but to say and speak and tell the tale.
But when we have been moved by the theme of the soul, let us
not fail also to recognise when we meet it—whether in the
wandering scholar's *Gaudeamus* or in the miracle of the nun who

[1] Modern poets who have written upon the same theme have drawn
this moral more overtly than the medieval authors. Maeterlinck's Virgin
in *Sœur Béatrice* sings

Il n'est péché qui vive
Quand l'amour a prié,
Il n'est âme qui meure
Quand l'amour a pleuré

Davidson's sacristan (in *A Ballad of a Nun*) cries.

"I care not for my broken vow,
  Though God should come in thunder soon,
I am sister to the mountains now
  And sister to the sun and moon,"

and the Virgin, welcoming her back on her return, tells her.

"You are sister to the mountains now,
  And sister to the day and night;
Sister to God" And on her brow
  She kissed her thrice, and left her sight

loved the world—the theme of the body, despised and maimed and always beautiful, crying out for its birthright. Even in the middle ages the Greeks had not lived in vain.

The miracle of Sister Beatrice leads to the consideration of another type of popular literature, which throws much light on convent life. Sometimes the people grow tired of singing to themselves; they want to be told stories, which they can repeat in the long evenings, when the sun goes down and the rushlight sends its wan uneven flicker over the floor. Even in the households of rich men story-telling round the fire is the favourite after-dinner occupation[1]. These stories come from every conceivable source, from the East, from the Classics, from the Lives of the Fathers, from the Legends of the Saints, from the Miracles of the Virgin, from the accumulated experience of generations of story-tellers. At first their purpose is simply to amuse, and the jongleur can always get a hearing for his *fabliau*; from village green to town market, from the ale house to the manor and the castle hall he passes with his repertoire of grave, gay, edifying, ribald, coarse or delightful tales and when he has gone his enchanted audience repeats and passes on all that he has said[2]. Then another professional story-teller begins to compete with the jongleur, a story-teller whose object is to point a moral rather than to adorn a tale. The Church, observing that attentive audience, adopts the practice. Preachers vie with jongleurs in illustrating their sermons by stories, "examples" they call them. Often they use the same tales; anything so that the congregation keep awake; and though the examples are sometimes very edifying, they are sometimes but ill-disguised buffoonery, and moralists cry out against the preacher, who instead of the Gospel passes off his own inventions, jests and gibes, so that the poor sheep return from pasture wind-fed[3].

---

[1] "Cum in hyemis intemperie post cenam noctu familia divitis ad focum, ut potentibus moris est, recensendis antiquis gestis operam daret" *Gesta Romanorum*, ed Oesterley (1872), ch clv. Quoted in Jusserand, *Lit. Hist of the Eng People*, i, p 182.

[2] One particular kind of story, the *fabliau* (defined by Bédier as "un conte à rire en vers") was brought to great perfection by French jongleurs See Montaiglon and Raynaud, *Recueil général et complet des Fabliaux* (Paris, 1872–90), 6 vols ; and Bédier, *Les Fabliaux* (Paris, 1873)

[3] See Dante, *Paradiso*, xxix, 11, for a violent attack on the practice. Compare the decree of the Council of Paris in 1528: "Quodsi secus fecerint, aut si populum more scurrarum vilissimorum, dum ridiculas et aniles

But the greatest preachers win many souls by a judicious use of stories[1], and diligent clerks make huge collections of such *exempla*, wherein the least skilled sermon-maker may find an illustration apt to any text[2]. Didactic writers and theologians also adopt the practice; they trust to example rather than to precept; their ponderous tomes are alive with anecdotes, but one half-pennyworth of bread to this intolerable deal of sack[3]. Then the literary men begin to seize upon the *fabliaux* and *exempla* for the purpose of their art; they borrow plots from this bottomless treasure-house; and so come the days of Boccaccio and *Les Cent Nouvelles Nouvelles* and the short story is made at last[4].

fabulas recitant, ad risus cachinnationesque excitaverint,. nos volumus tales tam ineptos et perniciosos concionatores ab officio praedicationis suspendi," etc., quoted in *Exempla of Jacques de Vitry*, ed T. F. Crane (1890), Introd p lxix The great preacher Jacques de Vitry himself, while advocating the use of *exempla*, adds "infructuosas enim fabulas et curiosa poetarum carmina a sermonis nostris debemus relegare...scurrilia tamen aut obscena verba vel turpis sermo ex ore predicatoris non procedant" *Ib* Introd., pp. xlii, xliii

[1] For instance *exempla* were much used by Jacques de Vitry (see *op. cit*) Etienne de Bourbon (see *Anecdotes Historiques, etc, d'Etienne de Bourbon*, ed. A. Lecoy de la Marche (Soc. de l'Hist de France), and John Herolt. On the whole subject of *exempla* see the Introduction to T. F. Crane's edition of the *Exempla of Jacques de Vitry*, and the references given there.

[2] The most famous is the *Gesta Romanorum   Gesta Romanorum*, ed. Oesterley (Berlin, 1872); and see *The Early English Version of the Gesta Romanorum*, ed. S. J. H. Herrtage (E.E.T.S. 1879). The largest is the *Summa Praedicantium* of John Bromyard, a fourteenth century English Dominican   See also an interesting fifteenth century English translation of a similar collection, the *Alphabetum Narrationum* (which used to be attributed to Etienne de Besançon), *An Alphabet of Tales*, ed. M M. Banks (E.E.T.S 1904–5); many of the *exempla* in this come from Caesarius of Heisterbach   Specimens of *exempla* from these and other sources are collected in Wright's *Latin Stories* (Percy Soc 1842), and many tales from Caesarius of Heisterbach, Jacques de Vitry, Etienne de Bourbon, Thomas of Chantimpré, etc, are translated in Coulton, *Med Garn*

[3] For instance Caesarius of Heisterbach, *Dialogus Miraculorum*, ed. Strange (1851), Thomas of Chantimpré (Cantimpratanus), *Bonum Universale de Apibus* (Douay, 1597); and the knight of la Tour Landry, who wrote a book of deportment for his daughters, copiously illustrated with stories *The Book of the Knight of la Tour Landry*, ed. T Wright (E.E.T.S. revised ed 1906)   For some account of Caesarius of Heisterbach's stories, other than those quoted in the text, see below Note K.

[4] Collections of stories, such as those of the *Decameron*, the *Cent Nouvelles Nouvelles*, the *Il Pecorone* of Ser Giovanni, the *Novelle* of Bandello, the *Heptameron* of Margaret of Navarre, became very popular. But individual stories have also given plots to many great writers from the middle ages to the present day, it is only necessary to mention Chaucer, Shakespeare, Molière and La Fontaine, to illustrate the use which has been made of them.

They all, jongleurs, preachers, theologians and men of letters repeat each other, for a tale once told is everyone's property; the people repeat them; and so the stories circulate from lip to lip through the wide lands of Europe and down the echoing centuries. And since these tales deal with every subject under the sun (and with many marvels which the sun never looked upon), it is not surprising that several of them deal with nuns.

Across six centuries we can, with the aid of a sympathetic imagination, slip into the skins of these inquisitive and child-like folk, and hear some of the stories to which they lent such an absorbed attention. Let us

> Forget six counties overhung with smoke,
> Forget the snorting steam and piston stroke,
> Forget the spreading of the hideous town,
> Think rather of the pack-horse on the down,
> And dream of London, small and white and clean,
> The clear Thames bordered by its gardens green.

Or rather, let us imagine not London but some other little English town, on just such an April morning as moved Chaucer and his fellow-voyagers to seek the holy blissful martyr by way of the Tabard Inn. Having sloughed the film of those six hundred years from off our eyes, we can see more clearly the shadowy forms of our fathers that begat us. We can see a motley crowd gathered in the market place, chiefly made up of women. There are girls, demure or wistful or laughing, fresh from their spinning wheels or from church; there are also bustling wives, in fine well-woven wimples and moist new shoes, arm in arm with their gossips. By craning a neck we may see that flighty minx Alison, the carpenter's wife, "long as a mast and upright as a bolt," casting about her with her bold black eyes and looking jealously at the miller's wife from across the brook, who is as pert as a pye and considers herself a lady. There is a good wife of beside Bath, with a red face and ten pounds' weight of kerchiefs on her head; a great traveller and a great talker she is—we can hear her chattering right across the square; it is a pity she is so deaf. There, under her own sign-board, is the inn-keeper's ill-tempered dame, who bullies her husband and ramps in his face if her neighbours do not bow low to her in church; and there is the new-made bride of yonder merchant with the forked beard—they say she is a shrew too There is Rose the

Regrater, who also weaves woollen cloth and cheats her spinsters. There is Dame Emma, who keeps the tavern by the river—our neighbour Glutton's wife would like to scratch out her eyes, for Glutton always has to be carried home from that inn. There also are Elinor, Joan and Margery, Margaret, Alice and Cecily, merry gossips, their hearts well cherished with muscadel Mingled with these good wives of the town we see, as we look about us, other folk; portly burgesses, returning from a meeting of the borough court, full of wine and merchant law; a couple of friars, their tippets stuffed with knives and pins, and a fat monk, with a greyhound slinking at his heel, an ale-taster, reeling home from duties performed too well; a Fleming or two, ever on the look-out for snarls and sharp elbows from the true-born native craftsmen, several pretty supercilious ladies " with browen blissful under hood," squired by a gay young gentleman, embroidered all over with flowers, two giggling curly-haired clerks (Absolon and Nicholas must be their names) ogling the carpenter's wife and sniggering at their solemn faced companion—that youth there, with the threadbare courtepy and a book of Aristotle under his arm, a bailiff buying tar and salt for the home farm and selling his butter and eggs to the townsmen; numbers of beggars and idlers and children; and on the outskirts of the crowd little sister Joan from St Mary's Convent, who ought not to be out alone, but who cannot resist stopping to hear the sermon.

For we have all come running together in this year of our Lord 1380 to hear a sermon[1]. We look upon sermons as an excellent opportunity "for to see and eek for to be seen", in the same spirit, compact one-third of sociability, one-third of curiosity and one-third of piety, we always crowd

> To vigilies and to processiouns,
> To preaching eek and to thise pilgrimages,
> To pleyes of miracles and mariages[2]

---

[1] For examples of medieval mission sermons, with their colloquialisms, interruptions from the audience and strings of stories, the reader cannot do better than turn to the sermons of Berthold of Regensburg (1220–72) and of St Bernardino of Siena (1380–1444). Specimens of these are translated in Coulton, *Med Garn* pp 348–64, 604–19 See also for Berthold, Coulton, *Medieval Studies*, 1st series, No 11 ("A Revivalist of Six Centuries Ago ") and for St Bernardino, *Paul Thureau-Dangin, St Bernardine of Siena*, trans Baroness von Hügel (1906), and A G Ferrers Howell, *St Bernardino of Siena* (1913)

[2] Chaucer, *Cant Tales, Wife of Bath's Prol.* ll. 556–8.

There is the preacher under the stone market cross   He is bidding us shun the snares of the world; if we cannot shut ourselves up in a cloister (which is best), he says, we must make our hearts a cloister, where no wickedness will come. He will have to tell us a story soon, for we are restless folk and do not love to sit still on the cobbles at his feet, but with a story he can always hold us   Sure enough he has left his theme now and is giving us an example:

Jacobus de Vetriaco tells how some time there was a mighty prince that was founder of a nunnery that stood near hand him; and he coveted greatly a fair nun of the place to have her unto his leman. And not withstanding neither by prayer nor by gift he could overcome her; and at the last he took her away by strong force   And when men came to take her away, she was passing feared and asked them why they took her out of her abbey, more than her other sisters. And they answered her again and said, because she had so fair een   And anon as she heard this she was fain and she gart put out her een anon and laid them in a dish and brought them unto them and said · "Lo, here is the een that your master desires and bid him let me alone and lose neither his soul nor mine " And they went unto him therewith and told him and he let her alone, and by this mean she kept her chastity. And within three years after she had her een again, as well as ever had she, through grace of God[1]

A shudder of horror and admiration runs through us, but the preacher continues with a second example ·

"How different," he says, "Was this most chaste and wise virgin from that wretched nun who was sought by a noble knight, that he might seduce her, and her abbess hid her in a certain very secret place in the monastery. And when that knight had sought her in all the offices and corners of the monastery and could in no wise find her he grew at length weary and tired of the quest and turned to depart. But she, seeing that he had stopped looking for her, because he had been unable to find her, began to call 'Cuckoo!', as children are wont to cry when they are hidden and do not wish to be found. Whereupon the knight, hearing her, ran to the place, and having accomplished his will departed therefrom, deriding the miserable girl[2].

[1] Translated from Jacques de Vitry (*Exempla...*, ed T F Crane, p 22) in *An Alphabet of Tales* (E.E.T.S.), p. 95 (No. CXXXVI). The story is a very old one, first found in the *Vitae Patrum*, x, cap. 60. It is sometimes attributed to St Bridget of Ireland, but Etienne de Bourbon, who repeats the story twice, tells it of Richard King of England and "a certain nun" (*Anec Hist*, etc., d'Etienne de Bourbon, ed. Lecoy de la Marche, Nos. 248 and 500), and other medieval versions make the persecuting lover "a king of England." (See T. F Crane, *op cit* p 158.)

[2] *Exempla of Jacques de Vitry*, No LVIII, pp. 22-3 For other versions of this story, see *ib* p 159

"See how evil are the ways of the world," says our preacher; "how much better to be simple and unworldly, like that nun of whom you may read in the book of the wise Caesarius which he wrote to instruct novices. I will tell you of her,"

In the diocese of Trèves is a certain convent of nuns named Lutze-rath, wherein by ancient custom no girl is received, but at the age of seven years or less, which constitution hath grown up for the preser-vation of that simplicity of mind, which maketh the whole body to shine. There was lately in that monastery a maiden full-grown in body, but such a child in worldly matters that she scarce knew the difference twixt a secular person and a brute beast, since she had had no knowledge of secular folk before her conversion. One day a goat climbed upon the orchard wall, which when she saw, knowing not what it might be, she said to a sister that stood by her· "What is that?" The other, knowing her simplicity, answered in jest to her wondering question, "That is a woman of the world," adding, "when secular women grow old they sprout to horns and beards" She, believing it to be the truth, was glad to have learned something new[1].

All this time the preacher has been illustrating his sermon with any story that came into his head. But he has been doing more, he has been describing for the information of posterity the raw material (so utterly different in different individuals), out of which the unchanging pattern of the nun had to be moulded. However we are not (for the moment) posterity; and we grow weary of this praise of austerity and simplicity. But, brother John, we say (interrupting) here are we, living in the world; you would not have us tear out our eyes when our husbands would be fondling us? You would not have us take our good Dame Alison for a goat, which is (heaven save us) but a brute beast and no Christian? and what if we cry cuckoo sometimes, we girls, for a lover? there are some we know that have married five husbands at the church door, and still think themselves right holy women, and make pilgrimages to St James beyond the sea, and will ever go first to the offering on Sunday. What have your nuns to do with us? Tell us rather what we young fresh folk may do to be saved; or how we good housewives should bear ourselves day by day. And that I will (says the

[1] Caesarius of Heisterbach, *Dial Mirac* ed Strange, I, p. 389 I have used the translation by Mr Coulton, *Med Garn* p. 124 The story is a variant of the theme of "the novice and the geese," one of the most popular of medieval stories (see Coulton, *ib* p. 426), for analogues, see A C Lee, *The Decameron, its Sources and Analogues*, pp 110–16

preacher with some acerbity). Shame upon you, with your chattering tongues You cannot even keep quiet at mass; and at home it is well known to me how ye pester your husbands, with your screeching and scolding, and how ye chatter all day to your gossips, not minding what lewd words ye speak. Remember therefore holy St Gregory's example of the nun who spake naughty words, which brother Robert of Brunne of the order of Sempringham found in the French book and set into fair English rhymes:

> Seynt Gregori of a nunne tellys
> Þat ȝede to helle for no þyng ellys
> But for she spake ever vyleyny
> Among her felaws al ahy.
> Þys nunne was of dedys chaste,
> But þat she spake wurdys waste
> She made many of here felawys
> Þenke on synne for here sawys

And then she died, and she was buried at the steps of the altar; and in the night the sacristan of the place was awakened by a great crying and weeping, and beheld fiends around that wretched nun, who burnt half her body and left the other half unscathed:

> Seynt Gregorye seyþ þat hyt was synge
> Þat half here lyfë was nat dygne;
> for þoghe here dedys werè chaste,
> Here wurdys were al vyle and waste.
>
> . . . . . .
>
> See how her tungge madë here slayn
> and foulé wurdes broghte here to payn[1].

Mind therefore your tongues, and do not whisper so lightly among yourselves when you sit in the tavern (unknown to your husbands, fie upon you!), and stuff yourselves with capons and Spanish wine. Nay more, have a care that greed does not destroy you Gula, he is one of the seven sins that be most deadly. Look to it lest you one day receive the devil into your bodies, with a mouthful of hot spices:

For the same blessed Gregory "telleth of a certain nun who omitted to make the sign of the cross when she was eating a lettuce, and the devil entered into her, and when he was ordered by a holy man to

---

[1] Robert of Brunne's *Handlyng Synne*, ed. F. J Furnivall (Roxburghe Club, 1862), pp. 50–52. (This is an amplified translation of William of Wadington's *Le Manuel des Pechiez*) See also *Exempla of Jacques de Vitry*, No. CCLXXII, p. 113, which is translated in *An Alphabet of Tales* (E.E T S.).

come forth he replied: 'What fault is it of mine and why do you rebuke me? I was sitting upon the lettuce and she did not cross herself and so ate me with it'"[1]. How different, now, was the reward of that saintly nun of whom Caesarius telleth For when "a pittance, to wit fried eggs, was being distributed by the cellaress to the whole convent, she was by some chance neglected. But indeed I deem not that it befel by chance, but rather by divine ordering, that the glory of God might be manifest in her For she bore the deprivation most patiently, rejoicing in the neglect, and therefore, when she was returning thanks to God, that great Father-Abbot set before her an invisible pittance, whereof the unspeakable sweetness so filled her mouth, her throat and all her body, that never in her life had she felt aught like to it This was bodily sweetness, but next God visited her mind and soul so copiously with spiritual sweetness ..that she desired to go without pittances for all the days of her life"[2]

Thus our preacher might be supposed to speak, but all nun tales are not so edifying; the ribald jongleur was fond of them too. A good example of the nun theme used as a *conte gras* is Boccaccio's famous tale of the abbess, who went in the dark to surprise one of her nuns with a lover; but having, when aroused, had with her in her own cell a priest (brought thither in a chest) she inadvertently put upon her head instead of her veil the priest's breeches. She called all her nuns, seized the guilty girl and came to the chapter house to reprimand her; and

the girl happened to raise her eyes, when she saw what the abbess bore upon her head, and the laces of the breeches hanging down on each side of her neck, and being a little comforted with that, as she conjectured the fact, she said "Please, madam, to button your coif, and then tell me what you would have " "What coif is it that you mean," replied she, "you wicked woman, you? Have you the assurance to laugh at me? Do you think jests will serve your turn in such an affair as this?" The lady said once more, "I beg, madam, that you would first button your coif and then speak as you please " Whereupon most of the sisterhood raised up their eyes to look at the abbess, and she herself put up her hand. The truth being thus made evident, the accused nun said, "The abbess is in fault likewise," which obliged the mother to change her manner of speech from that which she had begun, saying that it was impossible to resist the temptations that assail the flesh Therefore she bade them, as heretofore, secretly to make the best possible use of their time"[3].

---

[1] *Exempla of Jacques de Vitry*, No cxxx, p. 59. For other versions, see *ib.* p. 189. There is an English version in *An Alphabet of Tales* (E.E T S), p. 78 (No cviii).

[2] Caesarius of Heisterbach, II, pp 160–1. Compare the tale of Abbess Sophia whose small beer was miraculously turned into wine *Ib* p 229.

[3] Boccaccio, *Decameron*, 9th day, novel 2 But the story is older than Boccaccio, who constantly uses old tales There is a French version by

Another famous tale of Boccaccio's concerns the young man who pretended to be dumb and was made gardener at a nunnery[1].

In a different category from these stories sacred and profane are the didactic works, wherein churchmen set down the reasons for which a conventual life was to be preferred to all others, or the spirit in which such a life was to be lived. In this class fall poems and treatises in praise of virginity and books of devotion or admonition addressed to nuns. The former are fairly common in the middle ages[2] and, since they throw little light on the actual life of a professed nun, need not be considered at great length. Among the most graceful are a series of little German songs, probably composed by clerks and generally classed with folk-songs, though they are as different as possible from the popular *Nonnenklagen*. The longest of these poems tells of a fair and noble lady who walked in a garden and cried out at the beauty of the flowers, vowing that could she but see the

Jean de Condé: "Le Dit de la Nonnete" (Montaiglon et Raynaud, *op cit* t. VI, pp. 263–9) It was often afterwards copied in various forms in French, German and Italian jest- and story-books and there is an extremely gross dramatic version entitled "Farce Nouvelle a cinq personnages, c'est a sçavoir l'Abesse, sœur de Bon Cœur, seur Esplourée, seur Safrete et seur Fesne" in a collection of sixteenth century French farces (*Rec de farces, moralités et sermons joyeux*, ed. Le Roux de Lincy et Francisque Michel, Paris, 1837, vol II) It is also referred to in *Albion's England*

> It was at midnight when a Nonne, in trauell of a childe,
> Was checked of her fellow Nonnes, for being so defilde,
> The Lady Prioresse heard a stirre, and starting out of bed,
> Did taunt the Nouasse bitterly, who, lifting up her head,
> Said "Madame, mend your hood" (for why, so hastely she rose,
> That on her head, mistooke for hood, she donde a Channon's hose)

For these and references to other analogues see A. C. Lee, *The Decameron, its Sources and Analogues* (1909), pp 274–7. See also a curious folk-song version, below, p 611 La Fontaine founded his fable of *Le Psautier* on Boccaccio's version.

[1] Boccaccio, *Decameron* (3rd day, novel 1). For analogues and imitations, see A C. Lee, *op cit* pp 59–62. The story is the source of La Fontaine's *Mazet de Lamporechio* For other ribald stories about nuns see Note J , below, p. 624.

[2] I have made no attempt to describe the many treatises in praise of virginity composed by the fathers of the church These include works by Evagrius Ponticus, St Athanasius, Sulpicius Severus, St Jerome, St Augustine, St Caesarius of Arles and others Among the most interesting is one of English origin, the *De Laudibus Virginitatis* of Aldhelm († 709). For short analyses of these works, see A. A. Hentsch, *De la Littérature Didactique du Moyen Age, s'adressant spécialement aux Femmes* (Cahors, 1903), *passim*. From the eleventh century onwards several imitations of these treatises occur A few of the more interesting will be noted later.

artist who created so much loveliness, she would thank him as
he deserved At that moment a youth entered the garden and
greeted her courteously, answering her cry of surprise by saying
that neither stone walls nor doors could withstand him, and that
all the lovely flowers in the garden were his and he made them,
for "I am called Jesus the flower-maker " Then the lady was
stirred to the heart and cried "O my dearest lord, with all my
faith I love thee and I will ever be true to thee till my life ends."
But "the youth withdrew himself and went his way to a convent
which lay close by, and by reason of his great power he entered
speedily into it." The lady did not linger, but fled after him to
the convent and in great woe knocked upon the gates, crying,
"Ye have shut him in who is mine only joy." Then the nuns in
the convent bespake her wrathfully saying:

"Why dost thou lament so loudly? thou speakest foolishness Our
convent is locked and no man entered therein. If thou hast lost him,
the loss is thine and thou must bear it " "Ye have let in the man to
whom I am vowed With mine own eyes I saw him pass through the
gate Ye have let in mine own dear lord. Were the whole world
mine I would give it up ere I gave up him Ye have let in the man to
whom I am vowed and truly I say to you that I will have him again.
I will keep the vow which I sware to him and never shall my deathless
loyalty fail."

Then the maidens in the convent became wroth and they said:

"Thou spakest foolish things and against our honour. Our convent
is shut and no man is allowed therein and the dear Lord Jesus
knoweth well that this is true." "How little ye know him," said the
lovely lady, "Ye have spoken the name of mine own dear lord Ye
have named him and well is he known to me; he is also called Jesus
the flower-maker "

The maidens in the convent deemed then that her words were
of God and marvelled thereat:

"Let Jesus our beloved lord stay with us for ever, for all who are in
this convent have vowed themselves to him." "If all ye who are in
the convent have vowed yourselves to him, then will I stay with you
all my days and I will keep the troth I plighted with him and never
will I waver in my firm faith in him"[1].

[1] Uhland, *Alte hoch und niederdeutsche Volkslieder* (1845), II, pp. 857-62
(No. 331). The first verse may be quoted to give the style·
        Es war ein jungfrau edel
        Si war gar wol getan,
        in ainen schonen paungarten
        wolt si spacieren gan,

Another song contrasts the love of the lord of many lands with that of the lord of life, to the disparagement of the former[1]. A similar contrast between earthly and heavenly love is the *motif* of the beautiful English poem called *A Luue Ron*, made by the Franciscan Thomas of Hales at the request of a nun[2]; of a somewhat similar (though poetically inferior) poem entitled *Clene Maydenhod*[3]; and of a coarse and brutal treatise in praise of virginity known as *Hali Meidenhad*[4]. This alliterative homily of the thirteenth century is startlingly different from the two other contemporary works in middle English, with which its subject would cause it to be compared. It has none of the delicate purity of the *Luue Ron*, nor even of the mystical, ascetic visions of Mary of Oignies, Luitgard of Tongres, Mechthild of Magdeburg, and the many saints and song writers who realised the marriage of the soul with Christ in the concrete terms of human passion[5]. Neither, on the other hand, has it the moderation and urbanity of the *Ancren Riwle*, though the same hand was once supposed to have written both treatises The author of *Hali Meidenhad* persuades his spiritual daughter to vow her virginity to God by no better means than a savage and entirely materialistic attack upon the estate of matrimony. He admits that wedlock is lawful for the weak, for

this the wedded sing, that through God's goodness and mercy of his grace, though they have driven downwards, they halt in wedlock and softly alight in the bed of its law, for whosoever falleth out of the grace of maidenhood, so that the curtained bed of wedlock hold them not, drive down to the earth so terribly that they are dashed limb from limb, both joint and muscle[6]

And again:

of the three sorts, maidenhood and widowhood and thirdly wedlockhood, thou mayst know by the degrees of their bliss, which and by

---

in ainen schonen paungarten
durnach stuont ir gedank,
nach pluomen mangerlaie,
nach vogelein suessem gesank

[1] Uhland, *op. cit* ii, p 852 (No 326) See also Nos 332 and 334.
[2] *An Old English Miscellany*, ed. R Morris [E E T S 1872], pp. 93–99.
[3] Printed in *The Stacions of Rome*, etc., ed. F. J. Furnivall (E.E.T.S. 1867), and again in *Minor Poems of the Vernon MS.*, Part ii, ed. F. J. Furnivall (E.E.T S 1901), No. XLII, pp 464–8.
[4] *Hali Meidenhad*, ed. O. Cockayne (E.E.T.S. 1866).
[5] See on this point Taylor, *The Medieval Mind* (2nd ed 1914), I, pp 475 ff.
[6] *Hali Meidenhad*, ed O. Cockayne (E.E.T.S. 1866), p. 20

how much it [maidenhood] surpasses the others For wedlock has its fruit thirtyfold in heaven, widowhood sixtyfold; maidenhood with a hundredfold overpasses both. Consider then, hereby, whosoever from her maidenhood descended into wedlock, by how many degrees she falleth downward[1].

This comparative moderation of tone does not, however, last long and the author proceeds to draw a picture of the discomforts of wifehood and of motherhood so gross and so entirely one-sided that it is difficult to imagine any sensible girl being con-'verted by it:

Ask these queens, these rich countesses, these saucy ladies, about their mode of life. Truly, truly, if they rightly bethink themselves and acknowledge the truth, I shall have them for witnesses that they are licking honey off thorns. They buy all the sweetness with two proportions of bitter. ..And what if it happen, as the wont is, that thou have neither thy will with him [thy husband] nor weal either and must groan without goods within waste walls and in want of bread must breed thy row of bairns?...or suppose now that power and plenty were rife with thee and thy wide walls were proud and well supplied and suppose that thou hadst many under thee, herdsmen in hall, and thy husband were wroth with thee, and should become hateful, so that each of you two shall be exasperated against the other, what worldly good can be acceptable to thee? When he is out thou shalt have against his return sorrow, care and dread. While he is at home, thy wide walls seem too narrow for thee, his looking on thee makes thee aghast; his loathsome voice and his rude grumbling fill thee with horror. He chideth and revileth thee and he insults thee shamefully, he beateth thee and mawleth thee as his bought thrall and patrimonial slave Thy bones ache and thy flesh smarteth, thy heart within thee swelleth of sore rage, and thy face outwardly burneth with vexation[2].

Then, after an unquotable passage, the author considers the supposed joys of maternity and gives a brutal and painfully vivid account of the troubles of gestation and childbirth and of the anxieties of the mother, who has a young child to rear. He seems to feel that some apology is needed for his brutality, for he adds:

Let it not seem amiss to thee that we so speak for we reproach not women with their sufferings, which the mothers of us all endured at our own births, but we exhibit them to warn maidens, that they be the less inclined to such things and guard themselves by a better consideration of what is to be done[3]

---

[1] *Hali Meidenhad*, ed O Cockayne (E.E T S 1866), p 22
[2] *Ib*. pp 8, 30.   [3] *Ib* p. 36.

The point of view is a strange one   No girl of moderate strength of character, good sense and idealism would shirk marriage solely for the purely material reasons set down by the author   One cannot but wonder at the lack of spiritual imagination which can display convent life as the easy, comfortable, leisured existence, the primrose path which a harassed wife and mother cannot hope to follow[1], thus inevitably securing for the brides of Christ all who are too lazy and too cowardly to undertake an earthly marriage. Self-sacrifice and high endeavour alike are outside the range of the narrow materialist who wrote *Hali Meidenhad*. His treatment represents the ugly, just as *A Luue Ron* represents the beautiful side of medieval praise of virginity and of monastic life.

Of all treatises for the use of nuns the most personal and the most interesting is the thirteenth century *Ancren Riwle* (Anchoresses' Rule). The book was originally written for the use of three anchoresses, but the language of the original version (the English version is by most scholars considered to be a translation from a French original), the author and the anchoresses for whom it was written are alike uncertain[2]. The conjecture that it was written by Richard Poore, Bishop of Salisbury from 1217 to 1229, is discredited by recent research. It is usually said that the book was compiled for the anchoresses of Tarrant Keynes

[1] See e g. p. 28. "Under a man's protection thou shalt be sore vexed for his and the world's love, which are both deceptive and must lie awake in many a care not only for thyself as God's spouse must, but for many others and often as well for the detested as the dear, and be more worried than any drudge in the house, or any hired hind and take thine own share often with misery and bitterly purchase it. Little do blessed spouses of God know of thee here, that in so sweet ease without such trouble in spiritual grace and in rest of heart love the true love and in his only service lead their life.

[2] The *Ancren Riwle* was translated and edited by J Morton for the Camden Soc (1853) I quote from the cheap and convenient reprint of the translation, with introduction by Gasquet, in The King's Classics, 1907 For the most recent research as to the different versions, authorship, etc., see article by G. C Macaulay, "The *Ancren Riwle*" in *Modern Language Review*, IX (1914), pp. 63–78, 145–60, 324–31, 464–74, Father MacNabb's article *ib* XI (1916), and Miss Hope Emily Allen's thesis, *The Origin of the Ancren Riwle* (Publications of the Mod Lang Assoc. of Amer XXXIII, 3, Sept 1918), see also her note in *Mod Lang Review* (April 1919), XIV, pp 209–10, and Mr Coulton's review of her thesis, *ib* (Jan 1920), XV, p 99; also Father MacNabb's attack on her theory, *ib*. (Oct. 1920) XV and her reply, *ib*. Research is gradually pushing the date of the first English translation (if indeed it be not after all the original) further and further back.

in Dorsetshire, but this view rests upon the evidence of a rubric
attached to a Latin version of the rule, which states that it was
written by Simon of Ghent Bishop of Salisbury (who died in
1313) for his sisters, anchoresses at Tarrant; but though the
Latin translation was doubtless due to Simon of Ghent, there is
no evidence that the original anchoresses lived at Tarrant; and
the most recent research seeks to identify them with Emma,
Gunilda and Cristina, who were anchoresses at Kilburn about
1130 and whose settlement developed into Kilburn Priory. The
book is certainly of English origin, though the original seems
to have been written in French   It must be noticed that
the women for whom the *Ancren Riwle* was intended were
anchoresses and not professed nuns, the essence of their life was
solitude, whereas nuns were essentially members of a community.
But the moment an anchoress ceased to live alone and took to
herself companions the distinction between anchorage and convent tended to disappear; several English nunneries originated
in voluntary settlements of two or three women, who desired
to lead a solitary life withdrawn from the world. Nine-tenths
of the *Ancren Riwle* is equally applicable to a community of
recluses and to a community of nuns and may therefore with
advantage be used to illustrate convent life. The treatise has a
dual character. It is partly a theological work, telling the three
sisters how to think and feel and believe. It is partly a practical
guide to the ordering of their external lives. The author cares
for the stalling and feeding of Brother Ass the Body, as well as
of his rider the Soul. His book is divided into eight parts, of
which the first seven are concerned with the religious and spiritual
welfare of the anchoress and the eighth part is (in his own words)
"entirely of the external rule; first of meat and drink and of other
things relating thereto; thereafter of the things that ye may
receive and what things ye may keep and possess; then of your
clothes and of such things as relate thereto; next of your tonsure
and of your works and of your bloodlettings; lastly the rule
concerning your maids, and how you ought kindly to instruct
them "[1] This mixture of soul and body, of spiritual and practical,
is amusingly illustrated in the chapter on confession, when he
gives the following summary of all mentioned and known sins,

---

[1] *Ancren Riwle* (King's Classics), p. 12.

as of pride, of ambition or of presumption, of envy, of wrath, of
sloth, of carelessness, of idle words, of immoral thoughts, of any idle
hearing, of any false joy, or of heavy mourning, of hypocrisy, of
meat and of drink, too much or too little, of grumbling, of morose
countenance, of silence broken, of sitting too long at the parlour
window, of hours ill said, or without attention of heart, or at a wrong
time, of any false word, or oath; of play, of scornful laughter, of
dropping crumbs, or spilling ale, or letting a thing grow mouldy, or
rusty, or rotten, clothes not sewed, wet with rain, or unwashen; a
cup or a dish broken, or anything carelessly looked after which we
are using, or which we ought to take care of; or of cutting or of
damaging, through heedlessness[1].

The author of the *Ancren Riwle* shows throughout true
religious feeling, compact of imagination and passion, but (as
the above passage shows) he never loses hold on reality. He
is sober and full of common sense, almost one had said a man
of the world   He brings to his assistance (what writers on holy
maidenhood so often lack) a sound knowledge of human nature,
a sense of humour and a most observant eye. His psychological
power appears in his account of some of the sins to which the
nun is exposed, in his picture of the backbiter, for instance, or
in the passage in which he explains that the worst temptations
of the nun come not (as she expects) during the first two years
of her profession, when "it is nothing but ball-play," but after
she has followed the life for several years; for Jesus Christ is
like the mortal lover, gentle when he is wooing his bride, who
begins to correct her faults as soon as he is sure of her love, till
in the end she is as he would have her be and there is peace and
great joy[2] Not only is the *Ancren Riwle* full of flashes of wisdom
such as these. It is illustrated throughout by a profusion of
metaphors and homely illustrations drawn from the author's
own observation of the busy world outside the anchorage. Moreover it contains passages of a high and sustained eloquence
almost unmatched in contemporary literature, such as the famous
allegory of the wooing of the soul by Christ, under the guise
of a king relieving a lady who loved and scorned him from the
castle where she was besieged[3].

Even more interesting than the spiritual counsels of the
Ancren Riwle are its practical counsels. The moderation and
humanity of this most unfanatical author are never more striking

[1] *Ancren Riwle*, p. 259   [2] Pp. 164–5.   [3] Pp 294–6.

than when he is dealing with the domestic life of the anchoresses. When laying down the general rule that no flesh nor lard should be eaten, except in great sickness, and that they should accustom themselves to little drink, he adds "nevertheless, dear sisters, your meat and drink have seemed to me less than I would have it. Fast no day upon bread and water, except ye have leave"[1], and again:

Wear no iron, nor haircloth nor hedgehog skins and do not beat yourselves therewith, nor with a scourge of leather thongs nor leaded; and do not with holly nor with briars cause yourselves to bleed without leave of your confessor and do not, at one time, use too many flagellations[2]

When he describes the sin of idle gossip, he breaks off with "Would to God, dear sisters, that all the others were as free as ye are of such folly"[3]. Nothing could be more sensible than his regulations for their behaviour after the quarterly blood-letting:

When ye are let blood ye ought to do nothing that may be irksome to you for three days; but talk with your maidens and divert yourselves together with instructive tales. Ye may often do so when ye feel dispirited, or are grieved about some worldly matter, or sick. Thus wisely take care of yourselves when you are let blood and keep yourselves in such rest that long thereafter ye may labour the more vigorously in God's service and also when ye feel any sickness, for it is great folly, for the sake of one day, to lose ten or twelve

He clearly has no belief in the theory of the medieval ascetic that filthiness is next to godliness, for he bids his dear sisters "wash yourselves wheresoever it is necessary, as often as ye please"[4]. Some of the precepts in this section of the *Riwle* are obviously more closely applicable to anchoresses than to nuns; for instance the instructions against hospitality and almsgiving. Others are equally suitable for both:

Of a man whom ye distrust, receive ye neither less nor more—not so much as a race of ginger . Carry ye on no traffic An anchoress that is a buyer and a seller selleth her soul to the chapman of hell. Do not take charge of other men's property in your house, nor of their cattle, nor their clothes, neither receive under your care the church vestments, nor the chalice, unless force compel you, or great fear, for oftentimes much harm has come from such caretaking. Let no man sleep within your walls ...Because no man seeth you, nor do ye see any man, ye may be well content with your clothes, be they

[1] Pp 313-4.   [2] Pp 317-8.   [3] P. 68.   [4] Pp 319-20

white, be they black; only see they be plain and warm and well made—skins well tawed; and have as many do you need, for bed and also for back. ..Have neither ring nor brooch, nor ornamented girdle, nor gloves, nor any such thing that is not proper for you to have. I am always the more gratified, the coarser the works are that ye do Make no purses to gain friends therewith, nor blodbendes of silk; but shape and sew and mend church vestments and poor people's clothes ...Ye shall not send, nor receive, nor write letters without leave. Ye shall have your hair cut four times a year to disburden your head, and be let blood as oft and oftener if it is necessary; but if anyone can dispense with this, I may well suffer it[1].

There follows a short account of the kind of servants who should attend upon the anchoresses and the way in which these must behave and be ruled; and then the author ends characteristically:

In this book read every day, when ye are at leisure—every day, less or more, for I hope that, if ye read it often, it will be very beneficial to you, through the grace of God, or else I shall have ill employed much of my time. God knows, it would be more agreeable to me to set out on a journey to Rome, than to begin to do it again ..As often as ye read anything in this book, greet the Lady with an Ave Mary for him who made this rule, and for him who wrote it and took pains about it. Moderate enough I am, who ask so little[2].

And six centuries later, as we lay down this delightful little book, we cannot but agree that the claim is "moderate enough "

Other didactic works addressed to nuns may be considered more briefly, for the majority are purely devotional and throw little light upon the daily life of the nun. The largest and most important book in English is the *Myroure of Oure Ladye*, written for the Brigittine sisters of Syon Monastery at Isleworth by the famous theologian and chancellor of Oxford, Thomas Gascoigne (1403–58)[3]. It consists of a devotional treatise on the divine service, followed by a translation and explanation of the *Hours and Masses of Our Lady* as used by the sisters. The first treatise is profusely illustrated throughout by *exempla* taken from Caesarius of Heisterbach and similar sources and makes lively reading. Speaking of attendance at divine service Gascoigne remarks:

They that have helthe and strengthe and ar nor lettyd by obedience, they ought to be full hasty and redy to come to this holy seruyce and lothe to be thense They ought not to spare for eny slowth or dulnes of the body, ne yet though they fele some tyme a maner of

[1] Pp. 316–19, *passim*.   [2] P 325–6
[3] *The Myroure of Oure Ladye*, ed. J. H. Blunt (E.E T S 1873, 1898)

payne in the stomacke or in the hed, for lacke of sleape or indyges-
tyon ...For lyke as they that styrre up themselfe with a quycke and a
feruent wyll thyderwarde ar holpe fourth and comforted by oure
lordes good aungels, right so fendes take power ouer them that of
slowthe kepe them thense, as ye may se by the example of a monke
that was suffycyently stronge in body but he was slepy, and dul to
ryse to mattyns. Often he was spoken to for to amende, and on a
nyght he was callyd sharpely to aryse and come to the quyer Then
he was wrothe and rose up hastly and wente towarde the pryue
dortour. And whan he came to the dore, there was redy a company
of fendes comynge to hym warde, that cryed agenst hym wyth
ferefull noyse and hasty, often saynge and cryyng: Take hym, take
hym, gette hym, holde hym; And with thys the man was sodenly
afrayde and turned agayne and ran to chyrche as fast as he myght,
lyke a man halfe mad and out of hys wytte for dreade. And when he
was come in to hys stalle, he stode a whyle trembelyng and pantyng,
and sone after he fel doune to the grounde, and lay styll as dede a
longe tyme without felyng or sturyng. Then he was borne to the
farmery and after he was come agayne to hym selfe he tolde his
bretherne what him eyled and from thense fourth he wolde be in
the quyer wyth the fyrste. And so I trowe wolde other that ar now
slowthefull, yf they were hastyd on the same wyse

The prevalence of such stories shows how common was the mis-
demeanour against which they are directed. It may be noted
that as preface to the second part of the *Myroure* there stands
an excellent little dissertation on the value and method of
reading[1]. It is unnecessary to deal further with the other didactic
works in English intended for the use of nuns, since their interest
is purely religious[2].

Before leaving the subject of didactic treatises it is however
necessary to mention one little English prose work, for though
not addressed to nuns, it throws some light upon the organisa-

[1] *Op. cit.* pp 65–9, *passim.*
[2] As for instance the various other books written or translated for the
nuns of Syon (on which see Eckenstein, *op. cit.* pp 394–5) and the mystical
treatise "Ego dormio et cor meum vigilat," which was written by Richard
Rolle of Hampole for a nun of Yedingham. Rolle was kindly cherished by
the nuns of Hampole, where he settled, they often sought his advice during
his lifetime and after his death they tried to obtain his canonisation, an
office for his festival was composed and a collection of his miracles made
(See *Cambridge Hist of Engl. Lit.* ii, pp. 45, 48) For similar treatises of
foreign origin, see the *Opusculum* of Hermann der Lahme (1013–54),
Francesco da Barbarino's *Del Reggimento e Costumi di Donne* (which contains a section dealing with nuns), (c. 1307–15), Francisco Ximenes'
Libre de les dones († 1409) and John Gerson's († 1429) letter to his sister.
See Hentsch, *op cit* pp. 39, 114, 151, 152.

tion of a convent and in particular provides a' very complete list of obedientiaries. This is the *Abbey of the Holy Ghost*, which was printed by Wynkyn de Worde in 1500 and has been erroneously attributed to various authors, including Richard Rolle of Hampole and John Alcock, Bishop of Ely († 1480)[1]. The allegory of a ghostly abbey seems to have been popular in the middle ages. It had already been used by the béguine Mechthild in the thirteenth century and it would be interesting to determine whether there is any direct connection between her treatise *Von einem geistlichen closter* and the *Abbey of the Holy Ghost*. In her convent Charity is abbess, Meekness her chaplain, Peace prioress, Kindliness subprioress, Hope chantress, Wisdom schoolmistress, Bounty cellaress, Mercy chambress, Pity infirmaress, Dread portress and Obedience provost or priest[2]. The English book is addressed to men and women who are unable to take regular vows in some monastic order, and the allegory is carried out in great detail.

The study of didactic literature addressed to nuns, in order to assist them in a godly way of life, leads to the consideration of another type of didactic literature, didactic however with an *arrière-pensée*, being concerned to point out and to condemn evils which had crept into monasteries. This is the work of the satirists and moralists, who castigated by scorn or by condemnation the irregularities of the different orders. Like didactic writers they describe an ideal, but an ideal which emerges only from their attack on the dark reality, like sparks of light which the blacksmith's hammer beats from iron Occasionally they

---

[1] Printed from the Thornton MS in *Religious Pieces in Prose and Verse*, ed. G. G Perry (E E.T.S 1867, 1914), No III, pp. 51–62. Compare *Brit. Mus. MS*. Add 39843 (La Sainte Abbaye), some pictures from which are reproduced in this book.

[2] Mechthild von Magdeburg, *Offenbarungen, oder Das fliessende Licht der Gottheit*, ed. Gall Morel (1869), pp 249 ff ; see Eckenstein, *op. cit.* p 339 The same idea is found in a little German Volkslied:

> Wir wellen uns pawen ein heuselein
> Und unser sel ain klosterlein,
> Jesus Crist sol der maister sein,
> Maria jungfraw die schaffnerein.
> Götliche Forcht die pfortnerein,
> Götliche Lieb die kelnerein,
> Diemuetikait wont wol do pei
> Weisheit besleust daz laid all ein

—Uhland, *Alte hoch- und niederdeutsche Volkslieder*, II, pp. 864–5

use the gay satire of the writer of fabliaux; their condemnation
is an undercurrent beneath a lightly flowing stream, their moral
is implicit, they poke fun at the erring monk or nun, rather than
chastise them. It is so in that delicious poem, *The Land of
Cokaygne*[1], which French wit begat in the thirteenth century
upon English seriousness[2]. *The Land of Cokaygne* is partly an
attack on the luxury of monastic houses, and partly an ebullition
of irresponsible gaiety and humour, which might just as well
(one feels) have taken another form. The author has perhaps in
his mind the idea of the imaginary abbey of the Virtues, which
was so popular among serious writers, but he puts it to a very
different use. Far in the sea by West Spain, he says, there is a
land which is called Cokaygne [*coquina*, kitchen]. No land under
heaven is like it for goodness. Paradise may be merry and
bright, but Cokaygne is fairer; for what is there in Paradise
but grass and flower and green branches? though there be joy
and great delight there, there is no meat but fruit, no hall
or bower or bench, nothing but water to drink But in Cokaygne
there is plenty of meat and drink of the best, with no need to
labour for it; in Cokaygne there is muckle joy and bliss and
many a sweet sight, for it is always day there and always life;
there is no anger, no animals, no insects

> (N'is there fly, flea no louse,
> In cloth in town, bed, no house),

[1] English text in Furnivall, *Early English Poems* (Berlin, 1862), printed
in *Trans of Philological Soc.* 1858, pt II, pp 156–61; and in Goldbeck and
Matzner, *Altenglische Sprachproben* (Berlin, 1867), pt. I, p 147, W. Heuser,
Die Kildare-Gedichte (Bonn, 1904), p. 145; and in a slightly modernised
form in Ellis, *Specimens of Early English Poets*, 1801, I, pp 83 ff., who took
it from Hickes' *Thesaurus*, pt I, p. 231. I have here used the modernised
version for the sake of convenience. An attempt has been made to identify
the religious houses mentioned in the poem with real monasteries in Kildare;
the poem is certainly of Anglo-Irish origin and occurs in the famous "Kildare
Manuscript" (MS Harl 913) See W Heuser, *op cit.* pp 141–5. There is
a French version in Barbazon et Méon, *Fabliaux* III, p. 175

[2] "It is not until French wit flashes across English seriousness that we
travel to the Land of Cokaygne," G. Hadow, *Chaucer and His Times*, p 35
Stories of a food country are, however, common in medieval literature, being
sometimes legends of a vanished golden age, as in the Irish "Vision of Mac-
Conglinne" (late twelfth century), and sometimes ideal pictures of a life
of lazy luxury, as in the French and English Lands of Cokaygne and the
German Schlaraffenland On the whole subject, see Fr Joh. Poeschel, *Das
Märchen vom Schlaraffenland* (Halle, 1878), and the introduction by
W. Wollner to *The Vision of MacConglinne*, ed. Kuno Meyer (1892).

no vile worm or snail, no thunder, sleet, hail, rain or wind, no
blindness. All is game and joy and glee there. There are great
rivers of oil and milk and honey and wine—but as for water,
it is used only for washing.

Then the satire becomes slightly more pointed·

> There is a well-fair abbey,
> Of white monkes and of grey,
> There beth bowers, and halls:
> All of pasties beth the walls,
> Of flesh, of fish, and a rich meat,
> The likefullest that man may eat.
> Flouren cakes beth the *shingles* all   [tiles
> Of church, cloister, bowers and hall,
> The pinnes beth fat *puddings*   [sausages
> Rich meat to princes and kings.

All may have as much as they·will of the food. There is also in
the abbey a fair cloister, with crystal pillars, adorned with green
jasper and red coral. In the meadow near by is a tree, most
"likeful for to see."

> The root is ginger and galingale,
> The scions beth all *sedwale*.   [zedoary
> *Trie* maces beth the flower,   [choice
> The rind, *canel* of sweet odour,   [cinnamon
> The fruit *gilofre* of good smack,   [cloves
> Of *cucubes* there is no lack.   [cubebs (a spice)

There are also red roses and lilies that never fade. There are
in the abbey four springs of *treacle* (i.e. any rich electuary),
halwei (healing water), balsam and spiced wine, ever running in
full stream, and the bed of the stream is all made of precious
stones, sapphire, pearl, carbuncle, emerald, beryl, onyx, topaz,
amethyst, chrysolite, chalcedony and others. There also are many
birds, throstle, thrush and nightingale, goldfinch and woodlark,
which sing merrily day and night. Better still

> ...I do you mo to wit,
> The geese y-roasted on the spit,
> Flee to that abbey, God it wot,
> And *gredith* "Geese all hot! all hot!"   [cry
> Hi bringeth garlek, great plentee,
> The best y-dight that man may see.
> The *leverokes* that beth *couth*   [larks, well-known
> Lieth adown to manis mouth;
> Y-dight in stew full *swithe* well,   [quickly
> Powder'd with gingelofre and canell

The writer, having set his monks in the midst of this abundance of good things, proceeds to describe their daily life. When they go to mass, he says, the glass windows turn into bright crystal to give them more light, and when the mass is ended and the books are laid away again, the crystal turns back again into glass:

> The young monkes each day
> After meat goeth to play;
> N'is there hawk, no fowl so swift,
> Better fleeing by the lift,
> Than the monkes, high of mood,
> With their sleeves and their hood.
> When the abbot seeth them flee,
> That he holds for much glee.
> Ac natheless, all there among,
> He biddeth them light to evesong.

And if the monks pursue for too long their airy gambols, he recalls them by means of an improvised drum, the nature of which is best not indicated to a more squeamish generation. Then the monks alight in a flock and so "wend meekly home to drink," in a fair procession.

So far the Paradise has been without an Eve. But the author will provide these jolly monks with companions worthy of their humour:

> Another abbey is thereby,
> Forsooth a great fair nunnery:
> Up a river of sweet milk,
> Where is plenty great of silk.
> When the summer's day is hot,
> The young nunnes taketh a boat,
> And doth them forth in that river,
> Both with oarés and with steer.
> When they beth far from the abbey
> They maketh them naked for to play,
> And lieth down into the brim,
> And doth them slily for to swim.
> The young monks that *hi* seeeth,   [them
> They doth them up and forth they fleeeth,
> And cometh to the nuns anon.
> And each monke him taketh one,
> And *snellich* beareth forth their prey   [quickly
> To the mochil grey abbey,
> And teacheth the nuns an orison
> With *jambleue* up and down.   [gambols

The monk that acquits him best among the ladies may have twelve wives in a year, if he will, and if he can outdo all his companions

Of him is hope, God is wot,
To be soon father abbot!

But whoever will come to this delectable country must first serve a hard penance, seven years must he wade in swines' muck up to the chin ere he win there Fair and courteous lordings, good luck to you in the test!

More of a fairy tale than a satire, this jovial and good humoured poem was immensely popular in the middle ages. Another thirteenth century lampoon on the monastic orders, written in French in the reign of Edward I, is less well known, possibly because its satire, while still essentially gay, is more obvious than that of *The Land of Cokaygne*. The poem is known as *L'Ordre de Bel-Eyse*[1]. The author has had the happy idea (not however a new one)[2] of combining all the characteristic vices of the different orders into one glorious Order of Fair Ease, to which belong many a gentleman and many a fair lady, but no ribald nor peasant. From the Order of Sempringham it borrows one custom, that of having brothers and sisters together, but while at Sempringham there must be between them ("a thing which displeases many") ditches and high walls, in the Order of Fair Ease there must be no wall and no watchword to prevent

---

[1] *Polit. Songs of England*, ed. T. Wright (Camden Soc 1839), pp. 137–48.
[2] The idea of the *Ordre de Bel-Eyse* is probably taken from the twelfth century Anglo-Latin poem by Nigel Wireker entitled *Speculum Stultorum*, which tells the story of the ass Burnellus, who goes out into the world to seek his fortune. At one point Burnellus decides to retire to a convent and passes the different orders under review, to see which will suit him. This gives the author an opportunity for some pointed satire, including a reference to nuns; "they never quarrel save for due cause, in due place, nor do they come to blows save for grave reasons", their morals are very questionable, "Harum sunt quaedam steriles et quaedam parturientes, virgineoque tamen nomine cuncta tegunt. Quae pastoralis baculi dotatur honore, illa quidem melius fertiliusque parit Vix etiam quaevis sterilis reperitur in illis, donec eis aetas talia posse negat." Finally Burnellus decides to found a new order, from the Templars he will borrow their smoothly pacing horses, from the Cluniacs and the black Canons their custom of eating meat, from the order of Grandmont their gossip, from the Carthusians the habit of saying mass only once a month, from the Premonstratensians their warm and comfortable clothes, from the nuns their custom of going ungirdled; and in this order every brother shall have a female companion, as in the first order which was instituted in Paradise. *Anglo-Latin Satirical Poets of the Twelfth Century*, ed T Wright (Rolls Series, 1872), I, pp. 94–6.

the brethren from visiting the sisters at their pleasure; their
intimacy must be separated by nothing, says this precursor of
Rabelais, not by linen nor wool, nor even by their skins! And
all who enter the order must feast well and in company, thrice
a day and oftener From the canons of Beverley they have taken
the custom of drinking well at their meat and long afterwards
(the pun is on *bever*, to drink), from the Hospitallers that of
going clad in long robes and elegant shoes, riding upon great
palfreys that amble well. From the Canons they borrow the
habit of eating meat, but whereas the canons eat it thrice a
week these brethren are bound to eat it daily. From the Black
Monks (as from the canons of Beverley) they take their heavy
drinking, and if a brother be visited by a friend who shall know
how to carouse in the evening, he shall sleep late in the morning
(for the sake of his eyesight), till the evil fumes have issued from
his head. From the secular Canons ("who willingly serve the
ladies") they have taken a rule which is more needful than any
other to solace the brethren—that each brother must make love
to a sister before and after matins, a point which is elaborated
with cheerful indecency, under the guise of borrowing from the
Grey Monks their manner of saying prayers. From the Carthusians they take the custom of shutting each monk up in his cell
to repose himself, with fair plants on his window-ledge for his
solace, and his sister between his arms. The Friars Minor are
founded in poverty, which they seek by lodging ever with the
chief baron, or knight, or churchman of the countryside, where
they can have their full; and so must the brethren of Fair Ease
do likewise. The Preachers go preaching in shoes and if they are
footsore they ride at ease on horseback; but the brethren of Fair
Ease are vowed always to ride, and always they must preach
within doors and after they have dined. This is our Order of
Fair Ease; he who breaks it shall be chastised and he who makes
good use of it shall be raised to the dignity of abbot or prior
to hold it in honour, for thus do the Augustine canons, who
know so many devices. Now ends our Order, which agrees with
all good orders, and may it please many all too well![1]

---

[1] With these two highly successful *jeux d'esprit* at the expense of
monastic luxury may be compared a passage in the curious thirteenth
century poem entitled "A Disputison bytwene a cristene mon and a Jew,"

The inventors of these two imaginary orders were not serious or embittered moralists   Cokaygne lies upon the bonny road to Elfland; and Bel Eyse is a coarser, stupider Abbey of Theleme[1], whose inmates lack that instinct for honour and noble liberty which makes Gargantua's "Fais ce que vouldras" an ideal as well as a satire. As a rule the medieval satirists of monasticism deal in grave admonitions, or in violent reproaches. But one contemporary poem, hailing this time from France, may be added to the two English works in which the frailties of nuns are treated in a jesting spirit. This is a piece by the famous trouvère-Jean de Condé entitled *La messe des oisiaus et li plais des chanonesses et des grises nonains*[2]. The poem begins with an account of a mass sung in due form by all the birds and followed by a feast presided over by the goddess Venus   After this unwieldy introduction comes the main theme, which consists of a lawsuit brought by the nobly born canonesses against the grey Cistercian nuns, for the judgment of Venus. A canoness speaks first on behalf of her order, attended by several gentlemen and knights, who are proud to claim her acquaintance:

"Queen," she says, "Deign to hear us and to receive us favourably, for we have ever been thy faithful subjects and we shall continue ever to serve thee with ardour. For long noblemen held it glorious to have our love; the honour cost them nothing and was celebrated by round-tables, feasts and tourneys   But now the grey nuns are stealing our lovers from us   They are easy mistresses, exacting neither many attentions nor long service and sometimes men are base enough to prefer them to us. We demand justice. Punish their insolence, that henceforward they may not raise their eyes to those who were created for us and for whom we alone are made "

Venus then bids a grey nun speak and the grey nun's words are dry and to the point:

Has not nature made us too for love? are not there among us many who are as fair, as young, as attractive and as loving as they   Do not

in which an incidental shaft is perhaps aimed at nunneries, which affected the habits of Cokaygne and Fair Ease   *The Minor Poems of the Vernon MS*, pt II, ed F. J. Furnivall (E E.T S. 1901), No XLVI, p 490

[1] See e g Rabelais, *Gargantua*, cap. LII (Comment Gargantua fit bastir pour le moine l'abbaye de Theleme)

[2] Text in *Dits et Contes de Badouin de Condé et de son fils Jean de Condé*, pub par Aug Scheler, Ac Roy de Belgique, Brussels, 1866–7, III, No XXXVII, pp. 1–48 The portion of the poem containing the lawsuit is translated in part into modern French by Le Grand d'Aussy, in *Fabliaux et Contes*, ed Le Grand d'Aussy et Renouard, 1829, I, pp. 326–36.

doubt it. True their dress is finer than ours, but in affairs of the heart we serve as well as they. They say we steal their lovers. In truth it is they who by their pride and haughtiness drive those lovers away, we do but reconquer them by courtesy and gentleness. We do not seek them in love; but we have pleased them and they return to us. And, if they are to be believed, that studied elegance, which must be costly, has sometimes offered them a love less pure and disinterested than that which they find with us.

This last charge pricks the canonesses and their faces grow scarlet with rage:

What? do these serving girls add insult to injury? Do they dare to claim to be as good lovers as we, who have ever had the usage and maintenance of love? Their bodies, clad in wool, are not of such lordship as to be compared to ours and grave shame were it if a man knew not how to choose the highest. Bold and foolish grey-robes, great ill have you done Without your importunities and officious advances no great lord or knight or man of honour would think of you This is your secret and to the shame of love it is spoken, for you degrade thus the joys which he would have true lovers long desire in vain You have your monks and lay brothers; love them, give them heavy alms and share your pittances with them: you are welcome to them for our part But as to gentlemen, leave them to us, who are gentlewomen.

The grey nun replies quietly that her cause is too good to be weakened by insults, which can only offend the assembly and the respect due to the goddess, and that love considers neither birth nor wealth

Our grey robes of Cîteaux are not as fine as your vair-lined mantles and rich adornments; but in such things we do not wish to compare ourselves with you. It is in the heart and in love that we claim to be as good as you

There follows a hum of discussion in the assembly, some taking one side and some the other, but most favouring the grey nuns Then Venus rises to give judgment and makes a long speech on the theme that all are equal in her eyes·

"White-robed canonesses," she concludes, "I have always held your services dear Your grace, your elegance, your fine manners will always bring you lovers, keep them, but do not drive from my court these modest nuns, who serve me with so much constancy and whose hearts burn for me the more ardently, owing to the constraint under which they live You are finer and know better, perhaps, how to entertain, but sometimes the labourer's humble hackney goes further than the palfrey of the knight. It lies with yourselves alone to keep your lovers Imitate your rivals and be gentle and gracious as they are and you will not have to fear for the fidelity of a single lord "

Obviously hitherto the poem has had none of the characteristics of a moral piece. The *débat* was a common literary device, the law court presided over by Venus a favourite literary theme Jean de Condé is merely concerned to amuse the court of Hainault with a polished poem cast in this familiar mould, just as at other times he might regale it with the *fabliau* of *Les Braies au Prestre* or the *dit* of *La Nonnette*. Any satirical value which the poem has is due simply to the implication in his choice of parties to the suit; that is to say it is no more a satire than are the numerous *fabliaux*, which have for their subject the peccadillos of the Church. But the trouvère, even an aristocrat of the confraternity, such as Jean, who would have held in utter scorn the mere buffoon at the street corner, was never able to forget that he plied a dangerous trade, a "trop perilous mester." He was continually aware of the necessity to put himself right with Heaven, lest haply Aucassin spoke truth and to hell went the harpers and singers, for the Church's condemnation of his tribe was unequivocal. Therefore at the end of Venus' speech Jean de Condé abruptly tacks on a most untimely moral, which gives a sudden seriousness to his poem. He will sit in the seat of the moralists. So he interprets the whole debate according to a theological and moral allegory, even going so far as to compare the strife between the canonesses and the grey nuns with the resentment of the first workers against those who came last, in the parable of the Vineyard! He concludes with a bitter reproach against moral disorders among the nuns, accusing them of paying service to Venus to their damnation, and bidding "canonesses, canons, priests, monks, nuns and all folk of their sort" to give up the evil love of the world, which passes away like a dream, and to cling to the love of God which endureth for ever. A strange point of view; but one which would strike no sense of incongruity in an audience accustomed to the moralisation of the *Gesta Romanorum* and of many another profane story, forced to do pious service as an *exemplum* It is the spirit which built cathedrals and filled them with grotesques.

Jean de Condé was not really a moralist, even in the sense in which the authors of *The Land of Cokaygne* and *The Order of Fair Ease* deserve the name. But there were a number of genuine moralists in the last three centuries of the middle ages, who shook sober heads over the misdeeds of nuns[1]. In two thirteenth century French "Bibles," by Guiot de Provins and the Seigneur de Berzé respectively[2], their chastity is impugned and the author of *Les Lamentations de Matheolus* (c. 1290) goes to the root of the matter and attributes their immorality to the ease with which they are able to wander about outside their convents. They are continually inventing stories, he says, in order to escape for a moment from the cloister; their father, mother, cousin, sister, brother is ill; so they receive *congé* to wander about where they will—"par le pais s'en vont esbattre." Moreover he has hard words for the rapacity of nuns in love; distrust them, he warns, for they pluck and shear their lovers worse than thieves or than Breton pirates; you must be always giving, giving, giving with those ladies—it is the usage of their convent; you have to reward the messenger and the mistress, the chambermaid, the matron and the companion[3]. The mention of the companion shows that the precaution of sending the nuns out in twos was not always successful, and Gui de Mori (writing about the same time) has the same tale to tell; the nun's lover has to give to two at least, to her and to her companion; and since nuns have plenty of spare time, they are fond of feeding love by the exchange of messages, which mean more *douceurs* from the purse of the luckless gallant[4].

The most interesting of all French moralists who deal with nuns is, however, Gilles li Muisis, Abbot of the Benedictine monastery of St Martin of Tournai, who began about 1350 to write a "Register" of his thoughts upon contemporary life and

[1] A convenient collection of these is summarised in an excellent little book by Ch.-V. Langlois, entitled *La Vie en France au Moyen Age d'après quelques Moralistes du Temps* (2me éd. 1911).

[2] The text of both *La Bible Guiot* and *La Bible au Seigneur de Berzé* is printed in *Fabliaux et Contes*, ed. Barbazon-Méon, t. II (Paris, 1808), and both are fully analysed, with extracts in Langlois, *op. cit.* pp. 30–88. The text of *La Bible Guiot* is also printed in San Marte, *Parcival Studien* (Halle, 1861), with a translation into German verse.

[3] *Les Lamentations de Matheolus*, pub. A. G. Van Hamel (*Bib. de l'Ecole des Chartes*, 1892, t. I, pp. 89–90). See also the analysis in Langlois, *op. cit.* pp. 223–75, especially p. 248.

[4] Langlois, *op. cit.* pp. 248–9, Note 2.

morality, one section of which concerns "Les maintiens des nonnains"[1]. Like Matheolus, Gilles li Muisis considers that the root of all evils is the ease with which nuns are able to leave their convents·

"Of old," he says, "the nun was approved by God and man, when she kept her cloister and wandered little in the world; but now I see them go out often, whereat I am greatly displeased, for if this thing were stopped many scandals would cease and it were greatly to the profit of their souls."

He represents the "très doulces nonnains" as behaving "like ladies"; they keep open house for visitors, and the young men go in more easily than the old and guilty love is born. They exchange messages and letters with their lovers; moreover they very often take *congé* without any other reason than the desire to meet these young men, and the sight of nuns upon every road sets men's tongues chattering They ought to sit at home, spinning and sewing and mending their wimples. instead they hurry from stall to stall, spending their money on fine cloths and collars. The Pope would do well if he enclosed them. The young nuns are the worst of all; they are forever pestering their abbesses for leave to go out, they will have all their elders at their will, cellaress, treasuress, subprioress. Everything is topsy-turvy now and all are in the same rank, those who are lettered and those who are not; the young desire to have a finger in every pie. Even their vow of poverty these nuns will not keep They will have incomes of their own and if they have none they grumble until they obtain one somehow: "It is for this reason," they say, "that we desire the money—our houses are growing poor and everywhere we grow weak." But it is not so, for they want it in order to be able to go out more often. "I recognise," says Gilles, "and it is true, that nuns have many duties to fulfil, for there is great resort of guests to their houses, and if it were possible without harm to diminish these expenses, one might do something to help them " But it is necessary to remember that the ownership of private property is a sin; canon law condemns it, and if there is a rule permitting these private incomes I have never met it. Moreover one sees every day the evil results of such possessions.

[1] *Poésies de Gilles li Muisis*, pub Kervyn de Lettenhove (Louvain, 1882), t. 1, pp. 209–36. The whole register is analysed in Langlois, *op cit* pp 305–53.

What is the result of this laxity of morals, of this continual wandering of nuns in the world? Secular folk everywhere talk about them and miscall them ·

"Religious ladies," says Gilles, "if you often heard what people say about many of you, the hearts of good nuns would be dismayed, for the world has but a poor opinion of you And why? because men see the nuns wandering so often, see them packing up all these goods in their carts and going up and down the hills and dales. It is not you alone who are slandered, everywhere it is the same, the folk of holy church are held in little respect and men complain because they have so many possessions and such fat endowments But be assured, all of you, when you go along the highways, that people look and see how well you are shod and how daintily you are clad; and they hurl evil words against you. 'Look at those nuns, who are more. ike fairies. They are attired even better than other women. They go about the roads, so that men may gaze upon them; what they covet is to be well stared at. God! well they know how to entertain men. They have left their cloisters and are going to enjoy themselves. Better were it for them if they prayed for people, instead of going to chatter with their friends '"

Even those who keep company with these nuns are at the same time disturbed and a little dismayed by their behaviour. "Such men go about with them and have their will of them; but pay them behind their backs with fierce slanders ..." So the worthy abbot continues, and every word that he says is borne out by the unimpeachable evidence of the visitation reports. His long lament is the most interesting of all moral works which have the behaviour of nuns as their subject and it would be possible to annotate almost every verse with a visitation *compertum* or injunction.

Serious writers in condemnation of nuns were not lacking in England as well as in France in the fourteenth and fifteenth centuries, when, as Gilles li Muisis complained, "les gens de Saint-Eglise petits sont déportées " Langland's pungent satire on the convent where Wrath was Potager has already been quoted[1]. Gower, for whom the world was still more out of joint, has a long passage concerning nuns in that portentous monument of dulness, the *Vox Clamantis*, and draws a pessimistic picture of their weakness and the readiness with which they yield to temptation[2].

---

[1] See above, p. 298

[2] See *Vox Clamantis*, Lib. iv, ll. 578–676 in *The Complete Works of John Gower*, ed. G. C. Macaulay, *Latin Works* (1902), pp 181–5 The same subject is treated more shortly by Gower in his *Mirour de l'Omne*, ll 9157–68. (*Ib. French Works*, p. 106.)

Like monks, he says, the nuns are bound to chastity, but since
they are by nature more frail than man, they must not be
punished as severely as men if they break their vows; for the
foot of woman cannot stand or step firmly like the foot of man
and she has none of those virtues of learning, understanding,
constancy and moral excellence, with which the more admirable
sex is endowed:

> Nec scola, nec sensus, constancia nullaque virtus
> Sicut habent homines, in muliere vigent!

He proceeds to illustrate the moral superiority of the male by
the statement that nuns are often led astray by priests, who enter
their convents as confessors or visitors, and under guise of a
reforming visitation make the frail women worse than they were
before. "I should hold this a most damnable crime," says Gower,
"were it not that—really, woman falls so easily!"

> Hoc genus incesti dampnabile grande putarem
> Sit nisi quod mulier de leuitate cadit[1].

After further reflections in this strain, he bursts into a long
panegyric of virginity and then passes on to attack the manners
of the friars.

Far more interesting than Gower's conventional moralising
is a poem entitled *Why I can't be a Nun*, and written early in
the fifteenth century[2]. The favourite device of a ghostly abbey,
peopled by personified qualities, is here employed, but the inmates of the convent are chiefly vices and such virtues as have
a place among the nuns are treated with scant respect by their
companions. The poem is unfortunately incomplete and begins
abruptly in the middle of a sentence, but the gist of the missing
introduction is clear enough. The author represents herself as
a young girl named Katherine, whose desire to become a professed nun has been opposed by her father. The father charges
a number of messengers to visit all the nunneries of England

---

[1] Compare the priestly logic of Alvar Pelayo who enumerates the abuse
of the confessional among the habitual sins of *women*! *De Planctu Ecclesiae,*
Lib. II, Art. 45, n. 84. (See Lea, *Hist. of Sacerdotal Celibacy,* I, 435–6 for
this and other medieval complaints of the corruption of nuns by their
confessors.)

[2] Text in Furnivall, *Early Engl. Poems* (Berlin, 1862), printed in *Trans.
of Philological Soc.* 1858, pt. II, pp. 138–48 (from Cotton MS. Vesp. D, IX,
f. 179).

and the poem opens with the departure of these messengers, full of zeal to accomplish their task, and their return with the news that the nuns were ready to do his will. Whereupon her father told Katherine that she could not be a nun, and merely laughing at her protests, went his way. Then she mourned and was sad and thought that fortune was against her; and one May morning, when her sorrow was more than she could bear, she walked in a fair garden, where she was wont to go daily to watch the flowers and the birds with their bright feathers, singing and making merry on the green bough; and going into an arbour, she set herself upon her knees and prayed to God to help her in her distress.

At last she fell asleep in the garden and in her sleep a fair lady came to her and called her by her name and bade her awake and be comforted. This lady was called Experience and told Katherine that she had come to take pity on her and teach her, saying·

> Kateryne, thys day schalt thow see
> An howse of wommen reguler,
> And diligent loke that thow be,
> And note ryȝt welle what þou seest there.

Then they went through a green meadow till they came to a beautiful building and entered boldly by the gates; and it was a house of nuns, "of dyuers orderys bothe old and yong," but not well governed, after the rule of sober living, for self-will reigned there and caused discord and debate:

> And what in that place I saw
> That to religion schulde not long,
> Peradventure ȝe wolde desyre to know,
> And who was dwellyng hem among
> Sum what counseyle kepe I schalle,
> And so I was tawȝt whan I was yong,
> To here and se, and sey not all

Then follows an enumeration of the inmates of the convent:

> But there was a lady, that hyȝt dame pride,
> In grete reputacion they her toke
> And pore dame mekenes sate be syde
> To her vnnethys ony wolde loke,
> But alle as who sethe I her forsoke,
> And set not by her nether most ne lest;

Dame ypocryte loke vpon a boke
And bete her selfe vpon the brest.
On every syde than lokede vp I
And fast I cast myne ye abowte;
Yf I cowde se, beholde or aspy,
I wolde have sene dame deuowte
And sche was but wyth few of that rowʒt;
For dame slowthe and dame veyne glory
By vyolens had put her owte;
And than in my hert I was fulle sory.
But dame envy was there dwellyng
The whyche can sethe stryfe in every state
And a nother lady was there wonnyng
That hyʒt dame love vnordynate,
In that place bothe erly and late
Dame lust, dame wantowne, and dame nyce,
They ware so there enhabyted, I wate,
That few token hede to goddys servyse.
Dame chastyte, I dare welle say,
In that couent had lytylle chere,
But oft in poynt to go her way,
Sche was so lytelle beloved there;
But sum her loved in hert fulle dere,
And there weren that dyd not so,
And sum set no thyng by her,
But ʒafe her gode leue for to go....
And in that place fulle besyly
I walked whyle I myʒt enduer,
And saw how dame enevy
In every corner had grete cure;
Sche bare the keyes of many a dore.
And than experience to me came,
And seyde, kateryne, I the ensuer,
Thys lady ys but seldom fro home.
Than dame pacience and dame charyte
In that nunry fulle fore I sowʒt;
I wolde fayne have wyst where they had be,
For in that couent were they nowʒt;
But an owte chamber for hem was wrowʒt,
And there they dweldyn wyth-owtyn stryfe,
And many gode women to them sowʒt
And were fulle wylfulle of her lyfe

There was also another lady, Dame Disobedience, and says
Katherine:

Of all the faults that Experience showed me, this lack of obedience
grieved me most, so that I might no longer abide for shame, for I
saw that they had obedience in no reverence and that few or none

took heed of her; and I sped at great speed out of the gates, to escape from that convent so full of sin.

Then Katherine and the Lady Experience sat down upon the grass, where they could behold the place, and they began to talk:

And than I prayed experience for to have wyst
Why sche schewed me thys nunery,
Sche seyde "now we bene here in rest,
I thenk for to tellen the why,
Thy furst desyre and thyne entent
Was to bene a nune professede,
And for they fader wolde not consent,
Thyne hert wyth mornyng was sore oppressede,
And thow wyst not what to do was best;
And I seyde, I wolde cese thy grevaunce,
And now for the most part in every cost
I have schewed the nunnes gouernawnce.
For as thou seest wythin yonder walle
Suche bene the nunnes in euery warde,   -
As for the most part, I say not alle,
God forbede, for than hyt were harde,
For sum bene devowte, holy and towarde,
And holden the ryȝt way to blysse;
And sum bene feble, lewde and frowarde,
Now god amend what ys amys!
And now keteryne, I have alle do
For thy comfort that longeth to me,
And now let vs aryse and go
Vn-to the herber there I come to the

There Experience departed and Katherine awakened from her dream, determined never to be a nun, unless the faults that she had seen were amended.

Then follows a long exhortation to the nuns. They are adjured (by the well-worn example of Dinah) not to wander from their convents, and are reminded that the habit does not make the nun:

Yowre barbe, your wympplle and your vayle,
Yowre mantelle and yowre devowte clothyng,
Maketh men wythowten fayle
To wene ȝe be holy in levyng.
And so hyt ys an holy thyng
To bene in habyte reguler;
Than, as by owtewarde array in semyng,
Beth so wythin, my ladyes dere
A fayre garland of yve grene
Whyche hangeth at a tavern dore,

> Hyt ys a false token as I wene,
> But yf there by wyne gode and sewer;
> Ryȝt so but ȝe your vyes forbere,
> And alle lewde custom be broken,
> So god me spede, I yow ensewer
> Ellys yowre habyte ys no trew token.

The poem ends as abruptly as it began with a catalogue of holy women, whose lives are worthy of imitation, St Clare, St Edith, St Scolastica and St Bridget, "that weren professed in nunnes habyte," and a bevy of English saints, St Audrey, St Frideswide, St Withburg, St Mildred, St Sexburg and St Ermenild. Whether or not the author really was a woman, the poem seems to show some knowledge of monastic life, and a certain sincerity and rugged directness render it more impressive than Gower's long-winded accusations.

There remain to be considered two satires which were written on the very eve of the Reformation and perhaps have a particular significance by reason of the cataclysm, which was so soon to effect what all the denunciations of the moralists had failed to do. These are the dialogues on "The Virgin averse to Matrimony" and "The Penitent Virgin" in Erasmus' *Colloquies* (c. 1526) and a morality (which has already been mentioned) by the Scottish poet Sir David Lyndesay, entitled *Ane Pleasant Satyre of the Thrie Estaits, in commendatioun of vertew and vituperatioun of vyce* (c. 1535) Erasmus' dialogues are (as might be expected) strongly anti-monastic and the two which concern nuns are intended to attack those "kidnappers" as he calls them:

> that by their allurements draw young men and maids into monasteries, contrary to the minds of their parents, making a handle either of their simplicity or superstition, persuading them there is no hope of salvation out of a monastery.

The dialogue entitled "The Virgin averse to Matrimony"[1] takes place between Eubulus and a seventeen-year old girl, Katherine, who like that other Katherine, the heroine of *Why I can't be a Nun*, has set her heart upon entering a convent, but has encountered the opposition of her parents:

> "What was it," asks Eubulus, "that gave the first rise to this fatal resolution?" "Formerly," replies Katherine, "when I was a little

---

[1] *All the Familiar Colloquies of Desiderius Erasmus of Rotterdam*, trans N. Bailey (2nd ed 1733), pp 147-55.

girl, they carried me into one of these cloisters of virgins, carried me all about it and shewed me the whole college I was mightily taken with the virgins, they looked so charmingly pretty, just like angels; the chapels were so neat and smelt so sweet, the gardens looked so delicately well-ordered, that, in short, which way soever I turned my eye everything seemed delightful. And then I had the prettiest discourse with the nuns, and I found two or three that had been my play-fellows when I was a child and I have a strange passion for that sort of life ever since

Eubulus argues with the girl. She can live as purely in her father's house as in a nunnery; more purely indeed—and he makes a grave indictment against the morality of nuns[1]. Moreover she has no right to run contrary to the wishes of her parents and to exchange their authority for that of a fictitious father and a strange mother.

"The matter in question here," he says, "is only the changing of a habit or of such a course of life, which in itself is neither good nor evil And now consider but this one thing, how many valuable privileges you lose together with your liberty. Now, if you have a mind to read, pray or sing, you may go into your own chamber as much and as often as you please When you have enough of retirement you may go to church, hear anthems, prayers and sermons and if you see any matron or virgin remarkable for piety, in whose company you may get good, if you see any man that is endowed with singular probity from whom you may learn what will make for your bettering, you may have their conversation; and you may choose that preacher that preaches Christ most purely. When once you come into a cloister all these things, which are the greatest assistance in the promotion of true piety, you lose at once." "But," says Katherine, "in the meantime I shall not be a nun." "What signifies the name?" replies Eubulus "Consider the thing itself. They make their boast of obedience and will you not be praiseworthy in being obedient to your parents, your bishop and your pastor, whom God has commanded you to obey? Do you profess poverty? And may not you too, when all is in your parents' hands? Although the virgins of former times were in an especial manner commended by holy men for their liberality towards the poor; but they could never have given anything if they had possessed nothing Nor will your charity be ever the less for living with your parents. And what is there more in a convent than these? A veil, a linen shift turned into a stole, and certain ceremonies,

[1] Nec omnes virgines sunt, mihi crede, quae velum habent.. Nisi fortasse elogium, quod nos hactenus judicavimus esse Virgini matri proprium, ad plures transit,,ut dicantur et a partu virgines .quin insuper, nec alioqui inter illas virgines sunt omnia virginea...quia plures inveniuntur, quae mores aemulentur Sapphus, quam quae referant ingenium " Erasmus, *Colloquia, accur Corn. Schrevelio* (Amsterdam, 1693), p 196

which of themselves signify nothing to the advancement of piety and make nobody more acceptable in the eyes of Christ, who only regards the purity of the mind." "Are you then against the main institution of a monastic life?" asks Katherine "By no means," answers Eubulus. "But as I will not persuade anybody against it that is already engaged in this sort of life to endeavour to get out of it, so I would most undoubtedly caution all young women, especially those of generous tempers, not to precipitate themselves unadvisedly into that state from whence there is no getting out afterwards And the rather because their charity is more in danger in a cloister than out of it; and beside that, you may do whatever is done there as well at home "

But Katherine remains unpersuaded.

In the next dialogue, called "The Penitent Virgin"[1] Eubulus and Katherine meet again, and Katherine informs her friend how she has entered the nunnery, but has repented and gone home to her parents before being fully professed:

"How did you get your parents' consent at last?" asks Eubulus. "First by the restless solicitations of the monks and nuns and then by my own importunities and tears, my mother was at length brought over, but my father stood out stiffly still But at last being plyed by several engines, he was prevailed upon to yield; but yet, rather like one that was forced than that consented. The matter was concluded in their cups, and they preached damnation to him, if he refused to let Christ have his spouse... I was kept close at home for three days, but in the mean time there were always with me some women of the college that they call *convertites*, mightily encouraging me to persist in my holy resolution and watching me narrowly, lest any of my friends or kindred should come at me and make me alter my mind. In the meanwhile my habit was making ready, and the provision for the feast." "Did not your mind misgive you yet?" asks Eubulus. "No, not at all, and yet I was so horridly frightened that I had rather die ten times over than suffer the same again...I had a most dreadful apparition." "Perhaps," remarks Eubulus slyly, "it was your evil genius that pushed you on to this " "I am fully persuaded it was an evil spirit," replies Katherine "Tell me what shape it was in? Was it such as we use to paint with a crooked beak, long horns, harpies claws and swinging tail?" "You can make game of it," says poor Katherine, "but I had rather sink into the earth than see such another." "And were your women solicitresses with you then?" "No, nor I would not so much as open my lips of it to them, though they sifted me most particularly about it, when they found me almost dead with the surprise." "Shall I tell you what it was?" says Eubulus. "These women had certainly bewitched you,

[1] *Op. cit* pp. 155-7.

or conjured your brain out of your head rather[1]. But did you persist
in your resolution for all this?" "Yes, for they told me that many
were thus troubled upon their first consecrating themselves to Christ;
but if they got the better of the Devil that bout, he'd let them alone
for ever after" "Well, what pomp were you carried out with?"
"They put on all my finery, let down my hair and dressed me just
as if it had been for my wedding.. .I was carried from my father's
house to the college by broad daylight and a world of people staring
at me" "O these Scaramouches," interrupts Eubulus, "how they
know how to wheedle the poor people!"

Katherine then tells him that she remained only twelve days
in the nunnery, and after six changed her mind and besought
her father and mother to take her away, which they eventually
did. But what she saw that made her recant she refuses to tell
Eubulus, though he announces himself well able to guess what
it was. The dialogue ends on a significant note, "In the meanwhile you have been at a great charge." "Above four hundred
crowns." "O these guttling nuptials!"[2]

The racy dialogues of Erasmus illustrate the characteristic
hostility of the new learning towards contemporary monastic
orders, and embody the main charges which were customarily
made against them, viz the undue pressure brought to bear
upon young people to take vows for which they were not necessarily suited, the avarice of the convents and the immorality of
their inmates. Sir David Lyndesay's *Satyre of the Thrie Estaits*
dwells more specifically upon the latter accusation. In this lively
castigation of the vices of the day, which was acted for nine
hours before the court of King James V of Scotland at Cupar in
1535, Chastity comes upon the stage, lamenting that she has
long been banished, unheeded and unfriended and that neither
the temporal estate, nor the spiritual estate nor the Princes will
befriend her. Diligence bids her seek refuge among the nuns,
who are sworn to observe chastity, pointing to a Prioress of

---

[1] This account of Katherine's experiences, whether they were due (as
the translator suggests) to "the crafty tricks of the monks, who terrify
and frighten unexperienced minds into their cloysters by feigned apparitions
and visions," or (as was more probably Erasmus' meaning) to the mere
power of suggestion upon a hysterical girl, should be compared with the
numerous accounts of such apparitions seen by novices or intending novices,
which are to be found in lives of saints and in edifying *exempla*. See the
examples quoted from Caesarius of Heisterbach, below, pp. 628 *sqq.*

[2] For the expenses incidental to taking the veil, see above, pp. 19–20.

renown, sitting among the other spiritual lords. "I grant," says
Chastity,

> ʒon Ladie hes vowit Chastitie
> For hir professioun; thairto sould accord.
> Scho maid that vow for ane Abesie,
> Bot nocht for Christ Jesus our Lord.
> Fra tyme that thay get thair vows, I stand for'd,
> Thay banische hir out of thair cumpanie.
> With Chastitie thay can mak na concord,
> Bot leids thair lyfis in Sensualitie.
> I sall obserue our counsall, gif I may.
> Cum on, and heir quhat ʒon Ladie will say,
> My prudent, lustie, Ladie Priores,
> Remember how ʒe did vow Chastitie.
> Madame, I pray ʒow, of your gentilnes,
> That ʒe wald pleis to haif of me pitie,
> And this ane nicht to gif me harberie.
> For this I mak ʒow supplicacioun
> Do ʒe nocht sa, Madame, I dreid, perdie!
> It will be caus of depravatioun.

But the Prioress has given her allegiance to the notorious Lady
Sensuality, who, serving Queen Venus, has corrupted the court
of King Humanity and especially his clergy. "Pass hynd,
Madame," she says,

> Be Christ I ʒe cum nocht heir:
> ʒe are contrair to my cumplexioun...
> Dame Sensuall hes geuin directioun
> ʒow till exclude out of my cumpany.

Chastity then applies in vain to the Lords of Spirituality for
shelter; an abbot jeers at her and a parson bids her

> Pas hame amang the Nunnis and dwell,
> Quhilks ar of Chastitie the well.
> I traist thay will, with Buik and bell
>   Ressaue ʒow in thair Closter,

to which Chastity replies:

> Sir, quhen I was the Nunnis amang,
> Out of thair dortour thay mee dang,
> And wold nocht let me bide se lang
>   To say my Pater noster[1].

At the end of the play the evil counsellors of King Humanity
and corruptors of his Estates are punished by Sir Commonweal,

---

[1] *Ane Satyre of the Thrie Estaits*, in Sir David Lyndesay's *Poems*, ed
Small, Hall and Murray (E E.T S 2nd ed , 1883), pp. 421–3

with the assistance of Good Counsel and Correction. Correction,
with his Scribe, examines the spiritual lords as to how they keep
their vows, and thus interrogates the Prioress:

> Quhat say ʒe now, my Ladie Priores?
> How have ʒe vsit ʒour office, can ʒe ges?
> Quhat was the caus ʒe refusit harbrie
> To this young lustie Ladie Chastitie?

and the Prioress replies:

> I wald have harborit hir, with gude intent,
> Bot my complexioun therto wald not assent
> I do my office efter auld vse and wount:
> To ʒour Parliament I will mak na mair count[1]

The punishment of Flattery the Friar, the Prioress and the other
prelates follows; and the Sergeants proceed to divest her of her
habit, gaily adjuring her:

> Cum on, my Ladie Priores
>   We sall leir ʒow to dance—
> And that within ane lytill space—
>   Ane new pavin of France
>
> (*Heir sall thay spuilʒe the Priores; and scho sall haue
> ane kirtill of silk vnder hir habite*)
>
> Now, brother, be the Masse!
>   Be my iudgement, I think
> This halie Priores
>   Is turnit in ane *cowclink*[2].   [courtesan

The Prioress then makes a lament, which has already been quoted,
blaming her friends for making her a nun, and declaring that nuns
are not necessary to Christ's congregation and would be better
advised to marry Finally the Acts of Parliament of King Correction and King Humanity, for the better regulation of the realm,
are proclaimed; and these include a condemnation of nunneries:

> Because men seis, plainlie,
> This wantoun Nunnis ar na way necessair
> Till Common-weill, not ʒit to the glorie
> Of Christ's kirk, thocht thay be fat and fair.
> And als, that fragill ordour feminine
> Will nocht be missit in Christ's Religioun;
> Thair rents vsit till ane better fyne
> For Common-weill of all this Regioun[3].

---

[1] *Ane Satyre of the Thrie Estaits,* in Sir David Lyndesay's *Poems,* ed.
Small, Hall and Murray (E E T.S 2nd ed , 1883), p. 506.
[2] *Ib.* p 514.   [3] *Ib* p 521.

The date when these words were first proclaimed from a stage is
significant, it was 1535, the year of the visitation of the monasteries in England The confiscation of those rents was soon to
be an accomplished fact; but it was a king rather than a commonweal that reaped the benefit.

There remains for consideration only one other class of literature which speaks of the nun. It is interesting to see the part
which she plays in literature proper, outside popular songs and
stories, or popular and didactic works written for purposes of
edification. Considering the important part played by monastic
institutions in the life of the upper classes it is perhaps surprising
that the part played by the nun in secular literature is so small.
But the explanation lies in the definitely romantic basis of the
greater part of such literature, combined with the fact that it
was aristocratic in origin and therefore inherited a respect for
the nunneries, which prevented a romantic treatment of the nun,
such as is found in the *chansons de nonnes*. Even so it is to be
remarked that the treatment is romantic with a difference, the
nun is willingly professed, pious, aloof, but it is because death
or misfortune has put an end to lovers' joys; the type of nun
who appears in this literature has retreated to a convent at the
close of a life spent in the world. If the nun unwillingly professed
has always been a favourite theme, so also has the broken-
hearted wife or lover, hiding her sorrows in the silent cloister;
from the twelfth to the nineteenth century she remains
unchanging, from Belle Doette and Guinevere to the Lady
Kirkpatrick:

> To sweet Lincluden's holy cells
>   Fu' dowie I'll repair:
> There peace wi' gentle patience dwells—
>   Nae deadly feuds are there.
> In tears I'll wither ilka charm,
> Like draps o' balefu' dew,
> And wail a beauty that could harm
>   A knight sae brave and true[1]

The anonymous twelfth century romance of Belle Doette
contains some charming verses, describing her grief at her
husband's death and her determination to enter a cloister:

---

[1] Quoted from the ballad by Charles Kirkpatrick Sharpe ("The Murder
of Caerlaverock") in McDowall, W., *Chronicles of Lincluden*, p. 28.

Bèle Doette a pris son duel a faire·
"Tant mari fustes, cuens Do, frans de bon aire!
Por vostre amor vestirai je la haire,
Ne sor mon cors n'avra pelice vaire.
　　E or en ai dol
Por vos devenrai nonne en l'eglyse Saint Pol

Por vos ferai une abbaie téle
Quant iért li jors que la feste iért nomée
Se nus i vient qui ait s'amor fausee
Ja del mostier ne savera l'entree.
　　E or en ai dol.
Por vos devenrai nonne en l'eglyse Saint Pol.

Bèle Doette prist s'abaise a faire,
Qui mout est grande et ades sera maire·
Toz cels et celes vodra dedans atraire
Qui por amor sévent peine et mal traire.
　　E or en ai dol.
Por vos devenrai nonne en l'eglyse Saint Pol[1]

Lovely Doette, she weeps a husband fair.
"O count, my lord, frank wast thou, debonair!
For thy dear love I'll wear a shirt of hair,
Never again be clad in robe of vair
　　Great grief have I.
Now in St Paul's a nun I'll live and die

For thy dear love an abbey I will raise.
And when therein first sounds the song of praise
If one shall come who falsely love betrays
Ne'er shall she find an entrance all her days
　　Great grief have I.
Now in St Paul's a nun I'll live and die.

Lovely Doette, she makes her abbey so
Great now it is and greater still shall grow.
And lovers all into that church shall go
Who for love's sake know pain and bitter woe.
　　Great grief have I
Now in St Paul's a nun I'll live and die"

To English readers the supreme representative of this type
must always be Malory's Guinevere:

And when queen Guenever understood that king Arthur was slain,
and all the noble knights, Sir Mordred and all the remnant, then the
queen stole away and five ladies with her, and so she went to Almesbury, and there she let make herself a nun, and wore white clothes
and black, and great penance she took, as ever did sinful lady in
this land, and never creature could make her merry, but lived in
fasting, prayers and alms-deeds, that all manner of people marvelled

[1] Constans, *Chrestomathie de l'Ancien Français* (1890), pp 178–9.

how virtuously she was changed. Now leave we queen Guenever in Almesbury a nun in white clothes and black, and there she was abbess and ruler as reason would.

There follows that incomparable chapter of parting, when Launcelot seeks his queen in her nunnery:

and then was queen Guenever ware of Sir Launcelot as he walked in the cloister, and when she saw him there she swooned thrice, that all the ladies and gentlewomen had work enough to hold the queen up. So when she might speak, she called ladies and gentlewomen to her, and said, Ye marvel, fair ladies, why I make this fare. Truly, she said, it is for the sight of yonder knight that yonder standeth: wherefore, I pray you all, call him to me. When Sir Launcelot was brought to her, then she said to all the ladies, Through this man and me hath all this war been wrought, and the death of the most noblest knights of the world; for through our love that we have loved together is my noble lord slain. Therefore, Sir Launcelot, wit thou well I am set in such a plight to get my soul's health; and yet I trust, through God's grace, that after my death to have a sight of the blessed face of Christ and at doomsday to sit at his right side, for as sinful as ever I was are saints in heaven. Therefore, Sir Launcelot, I require thee and beseech thee heartily, for all the love that ever was betwixt us, that thou never see me more in the visage; and I command thee on God's behalf that thou forsake my company and to thy kingdom thou turn again and keep well thy realm from war and wrack. For as well as I have loved thee, mine heart will not serve me to see thee; for through thee and me is the flower of kings and knights destroyed.

And so on, through the last parting, and the last kiss refused, and the lamentation "as they had been stung with spears," through the six long years of fasting and penance, till the day when Guinevere died and a vision bade Launcelot seek her corpse.

And when Sir Launcelot was come to Almesbury, within the nunnery, queen Guenever died but half an hour before. And the ladies told Sir Launcelot that queen Guenever told them all, or she passed, that Sir Launcelot had been priest near a twelvemonth—And hither he cometh as fast as he may to fetch my corpse; and beside my lord king Arthur he shall bury me. Wherefore the queen said in hearing of them all, I beseech Almighty God that I may never have power to see Sir Launcelot with my worldly eyes. And thus, said all the ladies, was ever her prayer these two days, till she was dead[1].

This is a different romance from that of the gay *chansons de nonnes*, but it is romance all the same. There is little in common between Queen Guinevere and the lady who was loved and rescued by a king in the *Ancren Riwle*[2].

[1] Malory, *Morte Darthur*, ed. Strachey (Globe ed., 1893), pp. 481–5.
[2] See above, p. 529.

One of the last—as it is one of the most graceful—pieces of courtly literature concerned with a convent is the delightful *Livre du dit de Poissy*, in which the French poetess Christine de Pisan tells of a journey, which she took in 1400, to visit her daughter, a nun at the famous convent of Poissy This Dominican abbey, founded in 1304, was exceedingly rich and the special favourite of the kings of France, for it had been put under the protection of St Louis. The number of nuns, originally fixed at a hundred and twenty, soon rose to two hundred, and the aristocratic character of the house was very marked, for its inmates had to be of noble birth and to receive a special authorisation from the king before they could be admitted. At the time of Christine de Pisan's visit Marie de Bourbon, aunt of Charles VI, was prioress, and the convent also contained the nine year old Marie de France, his daughter (who took the veil at the age of five) and her cousin Catherine d'Harcourt. There were no nunneries so large and so rich in England at this late date, but Christine's description may serve to suggest what great houses like Shaftesbury and Romsey must have been like in the earlier days of their prime. Her account of the convent, with its fine buildings and gardens, its church, its rich lands and its gracious and dignified way of life forms a useful counterpoise to the bald and unidealised picture presented by the *comperta* of visitations; for assuredly truth lies somewhere between the *comperta*, which deal solely with faults, and the poem, which deals solely with virtues.

. Christine describes the brilliant cavalcade of lords and ladies riding in the spring morning through beautiful scenery, enlivening their journey with laughter and song and talk of love, until they came to the great abbey of Poissy. She describes their reception by the Prioress Marie de Bourbon and by the king's little daughter "joenne et tendre"·

> Par les degrez de pierre, que moult pris,
>   En hault montames
> Ou bel hostel royal, que nous trouvames
> Moult bien pare, et en sa chambre entrames
>   De grant beaulty

The Prioress' lodging was evidently such as befitted a royal princess, even though she were a humble nun. Christine describes the manner of life of the nuns, how no man might enter the precincts to serve or see them, save a relative, and how they never left the convent and seldom saw strangers from the world:

> Et de belles plusiers y a comme angelz
> Si ne vestent chemises, et sus langes
> Gisent de nuis; n'ont pas coultes a franges
>   Mais materas
> Qui sont couvers de biaulx tapis d'Arras
> Bien ordenées, mais ce n'est que baras,
> Car ils sont durs et emplis de bourras,
>   Et la vestues
> Gisent de nuis celles dames rendues,
> Qui se lievent ou elles sont batues
> A matines; la leurs chambres tendues
>   En dortouer
> Ont près a près, et en refectouer
> Disnent tout temps, ou a beau lavourer.
> Et en la court y a le parlouer
>   Ou a trellices
> De fer doubles a fenestres coulices,
> Et la en droit les dames des offices
> A ceulz de hors parlent pour les complices
>   Et necessaires
> Qu'il leur convient et fault en leurs affaires
> Si ont prevosts, seigneuries et maires,
> Villes, Chastiaulx, rentes de plusieurs paires
>   Moult bien assises;
> Et riches sont, ne nulles n'y sont mises
> Fors par congié de roy qui leurs franchises
> Leur doit garder et maintes autres guises
>   A la en droit.

Christine then tells how the Prioress invited the party to "desjuner" and how in a fair room they were served with rich wines and meats, in vessels of gold, and were waited upon by the nuns. Then the nuns led them through the buildings and grounds of the convent, showing them all the beauties of this "paradise terestre." She gives an extremely minute and interesting picture of Poissy as it was in 1400, the vaulted cloister with its carven pillars, surrounding a square lawn with a tall pine in the middle; the spacious frater, with glass windows; the fine chapter house; the stream of fresh water carried in pipes through all the different buildings; the great storehouses, cellars, ovens and other offices; the large, airy dorter; and finally the magnificent church, with its tall pillars and vaulted roof, its hangings, images, paintings and ornaments of glittering gold. She tells of the services held there, when the nuns knelt within a screen in the nave and the townsfolk and visitors and priests outside it. She gives a detailed account of the clothes worn by the nuns; a woman she, and not to be content with Malory's simple "white clothes and black." Finally she describes the wide gardens and woods of the convent, surrounded by a high wall and full of fruit-trees and birds and deer and coneys, with two fishponds, well-stocked with fish. In the exploration of these delights the day passed quickly. The gay party retired at night-fall to a neighbouring inn and early the next day paid a farewell visit to the hospitable nuns, who gave them gifts of belts and purses embroidered by themselves

> Et reprendre
> De leurs joyaulx
> Il nous covint, non fermillez n'amaulx
> Mais boursetes ouvrees a oysiaulx
> D'or et soies, ceintures et laz biaulx,
> Moult bien ouvrez,
> Qui autre part ne sont telz recouvrez

Then lords and ladies took horse again and, debating of love, rode back to Paris[1].

---

[1] See *Le Livre du Dit de Poissy*, ll 220–698, *passim*, in *Oeuvres Poétiques de Christine de Pisan*, ed. Maurice Roy (Soc. des Anc. Textes Fr. 1891), t II, pp 160–80 With this may be compared another, but much slighter "courtly" description of a nunnery, contained in the *roman d'aventure*, *L'Escoufle*, written at the close of the twelfth century. At the beginning of the poem the author describes the service of the mass in the Abbey of Montivilliers (see below, p. 637), on the occasion of the departure of the Count of Montivilliers on a crusade; the Archbishop of Rouen and the Bishop of Lisieux took part in the service and a large concourse of lords and ladies was present. The author describes the singing of the service,

> Li couvens avoit ja la messe
> Commencie et l'abbesse
> Commanda a ij damoiseles
> Des mix cantans et des plus beles
> Les cuer a tenir, por mix plaire
> Et por la feste grignor faire

He describes the rich offerings made at the altar by the Count and the rest of the congregation, and the stately visit of farewell paid by them afterwards to the nuns in the chapter house, when the Count asked for their prayers and in return gave them an annual rent of 20 or 30 silver marks. *L'Escoufle*, ed. H. Michelant and P Meyer (Soc. des Anc. Textes Fr. 1894), pp 7–9, *passim*. The other notable twelfth century description of a nunnery (in Raoul de Cambrai) is very different. See above, pp 433–5

Against this courtly idyll of monastic life one more picture of a nun must be set as complement and as contrast It is deservedly well known, but no study of the nun in medieval literature would be complete without quoting in full Chaucer's description of Madame Eglentyne, a masterpiece of humorous observation, sympathetic without being idealised, gently sarcastic without being bitter. It is a fitting note on which to close this book.

> Ther was also a Nonne, a Prioresse,
> That of her smyling was ful simple and coy;
> Hir grettest ooth was but by seynt loy,
> And she was cleped madame Eglentyne
> Ful wel she song the service divyne,
> Entuned in hir nose ful semely;
> And Frensh she spak ful faire and fetisly,
> After the scole of Stratford atte Bowe,
> For Frensh of Paris was to hir unknowe
> At mete wel y-taught was she with-alle,
> She leet no morsel from hir lippes falle,
> Ne wette hir fingres in hir sauce depe.
> Wel coude she carie a morsel and wel kepe,
> That no drope ne fille up-on hir brest.
> In curteisye was set ful muche hir lest.
> Hir over lippe wyped she so clene,
> That in hir coppe was no ferthing sene
> Of grece, whan she dronken hadde hir draughte.
> Ful semely after hir mete she raughte,
> And sikerly she was of greet disport,
> And ful plesaunt and amiable of port,
> And peyned hir to countrefete chere
> Of court, and been estatlich of manere,
> And to be holden digne of reverence.
> But, for to speken of hir conscience,
> She was so charitable and so pitous,
> She wolde wepe, if that she sawe a mous
> Caught in a trap, if it were deed or bledde.
> Of smale houndes had she, that she fedde
> With rosted flesh, or milk and wastel-breed
> But sore weep she if oon of hem were deed,
> Or if men smoot it with a yerde smerte:
> And al was conscience and tendre herte.
> Ful semely hir wimpel pinched was,
> Hir nose tretys, hir eyen greye as glas;
> Hir mouth ful smal, and ther-to softe and reed;
> But sikerly she hadde a fair forheed,
> It was almost a spanne brood, I trowe,

For, hardily, she was nat undergrowe.
Ful fetis was hir cloke, as I was war
Of smal coral aboute hir arm she bar
A peire of bedes, gauded al with grene;
And ther-on heng a broche of gold ful shene,
On which ther was first write a crouned A,
And after, *Amor vincit omnia*[1].

[1] Chaucer, Prologue to *The Canterbury Tales*, ed. Skeat, ll. 118–64.

APPENDIX I

ADDITIONAL NOTES TO THE TEXT

NOTE A.

THE DAILY FARE OF BARKING ABBEY.

THE *Charthe* [charter] *longynge to the office of the Celeresse of the Monasterye of Barkinge*[1] is one of the most interesting domestic documents which has survived from the middle ages. The *Ménagier de Paris* gives a first rate account of the work of a housewife who has to provide for a private household. The *Charthe* sets forth the duties of a housewife who has to feed a large institution. No bursar of a college or housekeeper of a school can fail to read it with a sympathetic smile. Like a good business woman the nameless cellaress, who drew it up for the guidance of her successors, sets out first of all the sources of revenue by which the charges of her office were supported. These are of three sorts: (1) the rents from thirteen rural manors, together with certain annual rents from the canons of St Paul's, the priory of St Bartholomew's and the lessees of various tenements in London, which were supposed to yield her a little over £95 per annum; (2) "the issues of the Larder," to wit all the ox skins, "inwards" of oxen, tallow coming from oxen and messes of beef, which she sells; and (3) "the foreyn receyte," to wit the money received for the sale of hay at any farm belonging to her office. These represent only her money revenues; but she also received the greater part of meat and dairy produce consumed by the convent from the home farm and from the demesnes of the manors appropriated to her. The *Charthe* warns her to be certain of hiring pasture for her oxen at such times as it is needful, to see that her hay is duly mown and made and to keep all the buildings belonging to her office in repair, both those within the monastery and those at the outlying manors and farms.

The *Charthe* throws some light upon the domestic staff employed in working the department. An important gentleman called the steward of the household had the general supervision of its business affairs; he kept an eye on the bailiffs and rent collectors of the cellaress's manors and presided at their courts. The cellaress solemnly presented him with a "reward" of 20d. every time that he returned with the pecuniary proceeds of justice, and on Christmas day. The management of the department was done by the head cellaress herself, with an under-cellaress to assist her and a clerk to keep her

---

[1] See Dugdale, *Mon.* I, pp. 442–5.

accounts and write her business letters, at a wage of 13s 4d The kitchen was in the special charge of a nun kitchener and the actual cooking was done by a "yeoman cook," a "groom cook" and a "pudding wife[1]", she paid her yeoman cook a wage of 26s 8d, her pudding wife, 2s a year and bought her groom cook a gown at Christmas She wisely gave a Christmas box to each of the underlings, great and small, with whom she had to do, 20d. to the Abbess' gentlewoman, 16d to every gentleman, "and to every yoman as it pleaseth her for to doo, and gromes in like case"; moreover it was her pleasant duty to hand to herself as cellaress and to her under-cellaress 20d. apiece

The *Charthe* gives exceedingly minute directions as to the conventual housekeeping Barking Abbey was a large house, consisting at the time this document was drawn up of thirty-seven ladies. The Abbess dwelt in state in her own apartments, with a gentlewoman to wait upon her and a private kitchen, with its own staff, which was not under the control of the cellaress The cellaress, however, sent in to the Abbess 4 lbs of almonds and eight cakes called "russheaulx" in Lent, eight chickens at Shrovetide, one pottle of wine called Tyre[2] on Maundy Thursday and a sugar loaf on Christmas Day, while the Abbess' kitchen had to provide the convent with "pittances" and "liveries" of pork, bacon, mutton or eggs on certain days of the year, as will appear hereafter From the convent kitchen the cellaress had to purvey for· (1) the ladies of the convent, (2) the prioress, two cellaresses and kitchener, who receive a double allowance of almost all food given out, and (3) the priory.

The *Charthe* sets forth exactly how much is to be delivered to each person, the separate allowances of meat being called "messes." It will be convenient to consider the stores to be provided under the five headings of (1) meat, (2) grain, (3) butter and eggs, (4) fish and condiments for Advent and Lenten fare, and (5) pittances, or extra delicacies provided on certain days of the year It is to be noted that the *Charthe* deals for the most part with the special fare appropriate to special occasions. There is no mention of the daily allowance of bread and beer made on the premises, the only fish mentioned is salt fish for Lent; the only vegetables are dried peas and beans; the only fowls are for a special pittance on St Alburgh's day

(1) *Meat* The chief meat food of the convent, eaten three times a week (on Sunday, Tuesday and Thursday), except in Advent and Lent and on vigils, was beef. The cellaress had to purvey 22 "gud oxen" by the year for the convent These oxen were fed on her own pastures, and, says the cellaress, "she shall slay but every fortnyght and yf sche be a good huswyff"; accordingly at the end of the first week, she must look and see if she has enough beef to last out the

---

[1] 'Pudding' was a sausage

[2] Tyre was a favourite sweet wine in the middle ages, "if not of Syrian growth [it] was probably a Calabrian or Sicilian wine, manufactured from the species of grape called *tirio*" *Early Eng Meals and Manners*, ed. Furnivall (E E T.S 1868), p 90

fortnight and if not she must buy what she needs in the market
It would seem that besides the beef provided by the cellaress from
the convent kitchen the convent had an extra allowance of beef
provided from some source not mentioned in the *Charthe*, or else
that they did not always eat each week what was delivered to them
For the cellaress sets down as follows the entry which her clerk is
to make in her book each week on Saturday 20 Sept (doubtless the
day on which she was writing) she answers for four or five messes
remaining in store of the week before, and of 63 messes of beef from
an ox slain the same week, also of 80 messes of beef bought by her
of the convent " of that they lefte behynd of ther lyvere, paying for
every mess 1½d.," total 147 messes, whereof she delivers to each lady for
the three meat days three messes and to the priory six messes After
beef the meat food most commonly eaten consisted in various forms
of pig's flesh. At Martinmas the cellaress had to ask at the abbess'
kitchen for a pittance of pork for each lady and also a livery of
"sowsse"[1], thus defined "every lady to have three thynges, that is
to sey, the cheke, the ere and the fote is a livery, the groyne and two
fete ys anodyer leveray, soe a hoole hoggs sowsse shall serve three
ladyes " At the same time she had to give them "of sowce of hyre
owne provisione two thynges to every lady, so that a hoole hog
sowce do serve four ladyes." She also had to provide pork from her
own kitchin for two anniversary pittances (of which more anon) and
she notes that every hog yields 20 messes. Moreover on Christmas
Day she had to ask at the abbess' kitchen for "livery bacon" for the
convent, four messes for each lady, a flitch was reckoned to provide
ten messes. Of mutton the convent ate very little Three times a
year, between the feasts of the Assumption (Aug 15) and of St
Michael (Sept 29), the abbess' kitchen had to provide "pittance
mutton" for the ladies, a mess to each, "and every mutton yields
twelve messes", and twice a year on certain anniversaries the cellaress
had to provide a similar allowance out of her own kitchen.

  (2) *Grain.* Under this heading comes three quarters of malt, to
be brewed into ale for the festal seasons of St Alburgh's[2] (or Foundress')
Day (Oct 11) and Christmas; one quarter and seven bushels of wheat to
be baked into bread or cakes for various pittances, two bushels of

─────────────

[1] Sowce (Lat *salsagium*, verjuice) was a sort of pickle for hog's flesh
Promptorium Parvulorum, ed A L Mayhew (E E.T.S 1908), notes, p 701
See the rather ominous verse in Tusser·
>   Thy measeled bacon, hog, sow, or thy bore,
>   Shut up for to heale, for infecting thy store.
>   Or kill it for bacon, or sowce it to sell,
>   For Flemming, that loues it so deintily well

Tusser, *Five Hundred Pointes of Good Husbandrie* (Eng Dialect Soc 1878),
p 52 The word is still in use in the north of England for a concoction of
mincemeat, vegetables, cloves and vinegar and in 'soused herrings' i e.
herrings cooked in vinegar

[2] I e St Ethelburga, for whom the Abbey was founded by her brother
Erconwald, Bishop of London, in 666.

dried peas to be eaten in Lent and one bushel of dried beans "against Midsummer." The brewer and baker were paid a tip of 20d and 6d respectively, when they had to make the extra pittance beer and bread The convent also had a livery of oatmeal from the cellaress, four dishes delivered once a month.

(3) *Butter and Eggs*. The cellaress had to provide the convent with butter at certain times, to every lady and double one "cobet," every dish containing three cobets What was called "feast butter" was payable on St Alburgh's Day, Easter, Whitsunday and Trinity Sunday What was called "storing butter" was payable five times a year, "to wit Advent and four times after Christmas " What was called "fortnight butter " was payable once for every fortnight lying between Trinity Sunday and Holy Rood Day (Sept 14). The cellaress was also responsible for providing the convent with money to buy eggs ("ey silver"); each lady had weekly from Michaelmas (Sept 29) to All Hallows' Day (Nov 1), $1\frac{1}{2}d$, from All Hallows' Day to Advent, $1\frac{3}{4}d$, from Advent to Childermas Day (Dec 28), $1\frac{1}{4}d$., from Childermas Day to Ash Wednesday, $1\frac{3}{4}d$., and from Easter to Michaelmas, $1\frac{1}{2}d$.; also an extra allowance of $\frac{1}{2}d$. on each vigil of the year, when no meat was eaten Out of this "ey silver" the nuns had to purvey eggs for themselves as best they might; but the cellaress had to give the priory each week in the year 32 eggs or else $2\frac{3}{4}d$. in money, except in the four Advent weeks when she provided only 16 and in Lent, when none were due; for every vigil she gave them eight eggs, "or else $1\frac{3}{4}d$ and the fourth part of $\frac{1}{2}d$ " in money At the five principal feasts of the year the abbess left her hall and dined in state in the frater, to wit on Easter Day, Whit Sunday, Assumption Day, St Alburgh's Day and Christmas Day; and on these occasions the cellaress had to ask the clerk of the abbess' kitchen for "supper eggs" for the convent, two for each lady

(4) *Lenten Fare* For Lent and Advent the cellaress had to provide the convent with their diet of fish, enlivened for their comfort with dried fruits and rice. She laid in two cades of red herring for Advent, a cade being 600 (counting six score to the 100)

For Lent she purveyed seven cades of red herring and three barrels (containing 1000 at six score to the hundred) of white herring To every lady she gave four a day (i e. in all 28 a week), and to the priory she gave four on every day except Sunday, when she gave them fish, and Friday, when they had figs and raisins She also had to lay in 18 salt fish (nature unspecified), out of which she provided each lady with a mess and the priory with two messes every other week in Lent, each fish producing seven messes; in the alternate weeks they received salt salmon, of which she laid in fourteen or fifteen, each salmon yielding nine messes To spice this Lenten fare she bought 1200 lbs of almonds, three "peces" and 24 lbs of figs, one "pece" of raisins, 28 lbs of rice and 12 gallons of mustard Each lady received 2 lbs of almonds and $\frac{1}{2}$ lb of rice to last for the whole of Lent, and every week 1 lb of figs and raisins

(5) *Pittances*, or extra allowances of more delicate food, were due to the nuns on certain feasts of the Church and on the anniversaries of five benefactors, viz Sir William Vicar, Dame Alys Merton "dame Mawte the kynges daughter," dame Maud Loveland and William Dun. The pittances on the anniversaries of William Vicar and William Dun were of mutton; on each occasion the cellaress had to lay in three "carse" of mutton, and for William Dun's pittance she had to make sure also of 12 gallons of good ale For the pittances of Dame Alice Merton and Maud the king's daughter (which fell in the winter) she had to purvey four bacon hogs, each hog producing 20 messes, also six *grecys*[1], six *sowcys* and six *inwardys*; also 100 eggs for "white puddings," together with bread, pepper and saffron for the same, and "marrow bones for white wortys"[2], also three gallons of good ale Evidently the convent had a royal feast on those days and had good cause to remember their former abbesses There are no details as to Dame Maud Loveland's pittance Another red letter day was Foundress' Day (Oct 11) On this occasion the abbess' kitchen had to provide each lady of the convent with half a goose, the two chantresses, as well as the four usual recipients, receiving doubles, and with a hen or a cock, the fratresses and the subprioress also receiving doubles Moreover the cellaress had to give the ladies "frumenty"[3], for which she laid in wheat and three gallons of milk

On the feast of the Assumption of the Virgin (Aug. 15) each received half a goose. At Shrovetide the cellaress gave each lady "for their

---

[1] Probably *gris*, i e a little pig Compare *Piers Plowman*, Prol l 226·
Cokes and here knaues crieden, ʻhote pies, hote !
Gode gris and gees gowe dyne, gowe !ʼ

[2] "White worts," was a kind of *potage* ("potage is not so moche used in all Chrystendome as it is used in Englande Potage is made of the licour in the whiche flesshe is sod in, with puttynge to, chopped herbes and Otmell and salte," *Early Eng Meals and Manners*, p 97) This is a recipe for *White Worts*, written down, c 1420 "Take of the erbys as thou dede for *jouutes* and sethe hem in water tyl they ben neyshe; thanne take hem up, an bryse hem fayre on a potte an ley hem with flowre of Rys, take mylke of almaundys and cast therto and hony, nowt to moche, that it be nowt to swete, an safron and salt; an serve it forth ynne, rygth for a good potage." The herbs used for *jouutes* are "borage, violet, mallows, parsley, young worts, beet, avens, buglos and orach"; and it is recommended to use two or three marrow bones in making the broth. *Two Fifteenth Century Cookery Books*, ed T Austen (E E T S 1888), pp. 5, 6.

[3] Frumenty or Furmety (Lat. *frumentum*, wheat) is wheat husked and boiled soft in water, then boiled in milk, sweetened and spiced. Here is a recipe for it from the same book as that for white worts: "Take whete and pyke it clene and do it in a morter, an caste a lytel water theron, an stampe with a pestel tyl it hole [hull, lose husks]; than fan owt the holys [hulls, husks], an put it in a potte, an let sethe tyl it breke; than set yt doun, an sone after set it ouer the fyre an stere it wyl; an whan thow hast sothyn it wyl, put therinne swete mylke, an sethe it yfere, an stere it wyl; and whan it is ynow, coloure it wyth safron, an salt it euene, and dresse it forth " *Op. cit* pp 6—7 See the rhymed recipe in the *Liber cure cocorum* (c 1460), ed Morris (Phil. Soc. 1862), p. 7.

cripcis[1] and for their crumkakers 2*d*."; she had also to purvey eight chickens for the abbess and "bonnes"[2] for the convent and also four gallons of milk. On Shere or Maundy Thursday she had 12 "stub" eels and 60 "shaft" eels baked with wheat and 8 lbs of rice, and she sent the abbess a bottle of Tyre and the convent two gallons of red wine; unglorified by a name On Palm Sunday they had "russheaulx"[3], for which she provided 21 lbs of figs These were little highly spiced pies (rather like mince pies), of which the chief ingredients were figs and flour, and besides providing them in kind on Palm Sunday the cellaress had to pay the ladies "Ruscheaw silver, by xvj times payable in the yere to every lady and doubill at eche time ½*d*., but it is paid nowe but at two times, that is to say at Ester and Michelmes " On Easter Eve they had three gallons of ale and one gallon of red wine On St Andrew's Day and on every Sunday in Lent they had fish (doubtless fresh fish, as a welcome change from salted herrings).

NOTE B.

SCHOOL CHILDREN IN NUNNERIES

The subject is of such interest from the point of view of educational as well as of monastic history, that I have thought it worth while to print in full all the references to convent education in England (c 1250–1537), which I have been able to find For the convenience of the reader I have translated references in Latin and Old French and have arranged the houses under counties Doubtful references are marked with an asterisk

---

[1] Crisps (Mod Fr *crêpe*) were fritters. Here is a recipe for them in a cookery book written c 1450 "Take white of eyren [eggs], Milke, and fyne flowre, and bete hit togidre and drawe hit thorgh a streynour, so that hit be rennyng, and noght to stiff, and caste thereto sugar and salt And then take a chaffur ful of fressh grece boyling; and then put thi honde in the batur and lete the bater ren thorgh thi fingers into the chaffur, And whan it is ren togidre in the chaffre, and is ynowe, take a skymour and take hit oute of the chaffur, and putte oute al the grece, And lete ren, and putte hit in a faire dissh and cast sugur thereon ynow and serue it forth." *Op cit.* p. 93.

[2] Buns Compare the instructions to the cellaress of Syon· "On water days [i.e days when the sisters drank water instead of beer] sche schal ordeyne for bonnes or newe brede " Aungier, *Hist. and Antiq of Syon Mon.* p 393

[3] Here is a recipe. "*Risshewes* Take figges and grinde hem all rawe in a morter and cast a litull fraied oyle there-to; and then take hem vppe yn a versell, and caste thereto pynes, reysyns of corance, myced dates, sugur, Saffron, pouder ginger, and salt: And then make Cakes of floure, Sugur, salt and rolle the stuff in thi honde and couche it in the cakes, and folde hem togidur as risshewes, and fry hem in oyle, and serue hem forth." *Op cit* p 93 There are other recipes, *ib.* pp 43, 45, 97. The word survives in *rissole*

BEDFORDSHIRE.

1. *Elstow.*

Late 12th century. Bishop Hugh of Lincoln sent a little boy, Robert of Noyon, here. "He seemed to be about five years old, or a little older; and after a short space of time (the Bishop) sent him to Elstow to be taught his letters (*literis informandum*)." *Magna Vita S. Hugonis Episcopi Lincolniensis* (Rolls Ser.), p. 146.

1359. Gynewell enjoins boarders to be sent away on pain of excommunication. "But boys up to the completion of their sixth year and girls up to the completion of their tenth year,...we do not wish to be understood or included in the above (prohibition)." *Linc. Epis. Reg. Memo. Gynewell*, f. 139d.

1421–2. Flemyng enjoins "that henceforward you admit or allow to be admitted or received to lodge or stay within the limits of the cloister, no persons male or female,...who are beyond the twelfth year of their age." *Linc. Visit.* I, p. 49.

c. 1432. Gray enjoins that all secular persons shall be removed from the cloister precincts, "...males to wit, who have passed their tenth year, or females who have passed their fourteenth." *Linc. Visit.* I, p. 53.

1442–3. "Dame Rose Waldegrave says that...certain nuns do sometimes have with them in the quire in time of mass the boys whom they teach, and these do make a noise in quire during divine service." *Linc. Visit.* II, p. 90.

2. *Harrold.*

1442–3. At Bishop Alnwick's visitation "Dame Alice Decun says that only two little girls of six or seven years do lie in the dorter." Another nun says the same. The Bishop forbids adult boarders, "ne childere ouere xj yere olde men and xij yere olde wymmen wythe owten specyalle leue of us or our successours bysshops of Lincolne fyest asked and had; ne that ye suffre ne seculere persones, wymmen ne childern, lyg by nyght in the dormytory." *Linc. Visit.* II, pp. 130–1.

BUCKINGHAMSHIRE.

3. *Burnham.*

c. 1431–6. Gray enjoins "that henceforward no secular women who are past the fourteenth year of their age, and no males at all, be admitted in any wise to lie by night in the dorter or be suffered so to lie....That you henceforth admit or suffer to be admitted and received to lodge in the said monastery no women after they have completed the fourteenth year of their age and no males after the eighth year of their age....That you remove wholly from the said monastery all...secular folk, male and female, who, being lodgers in the said monastery, have passed the ages aforesaid." *Linc. Visit.* I, p. 24.

1519. Atwater enjoins "that infants and small children be not admitted into the dorter of the nuns." *Linc. Epis. Reg. Visit. Atwater*, f. 42d.

* 4. *Little Marlow.*

c. 1530? Margaret Vernon, Prioress of Little Marlow and friend of Cromwell, was entrusted by him with the care of his little son Gregory. Several of her letters are preserved, but they are undated and it is difficult to gather from those which refer to Gregory Cromwell whether they were written before or after the dissolution of Little Marlow. There was in any case no question of her teaching the boy herself. He had with him a tutor, Mr Copland, and the Prioress writes to tell Cromwell that Mr Copland every morning gives Gregory and Nicholas Sadler, his schoolfellow, their Latin lesson, "which Nicholas doth bear away as well Gregory's lesson as his own, and maketh him perfect against his time of rendering, at which their Master is greatly comforted." Master Sadler also had with him a "little gentlewoman," whom Margaret wished permission to educate herself. In another letter she speaks of a proposed new tutor for Gregory and expresses anxiety that he should be one who would not object to her supervision. "Good master Cromwell, if it like you to call unto your remembrance, you have promised me that I should have the governance of your child till he be twelve years of age, and at that time I doubt not with God's grace but he shall speak for himself if any wrong be offered unto him, whereas yet he cannot but by my maintenance; and if he should have such a master which would disdain if I meddled, then it would be to me great unquietness, for I assure you if you sent hither a doctor of divinity yet will I play the smatterer, but always in his well doing to him he shall have his pleasure, and otherwise not." Wood, *Letters of Royal and Illustrious Ladies*, II, 57–9.

CAMBRIDGESHIRE.

5. *Swaffham Bulbeck.*

1483. The following references to boarders in the account roll of the Prioress Margaret Ratclyff for 22 Edw. IV almost certainly indicate children. "By Richard Potecary of Cambridge 11s. for board for 22 weeks, at 6d. per week. By 11s. received from John Kele of Cambridge for 22 weeks, viz. 6d. per week. By £1 received from William Water of...his son for 40 weeks, viz. 6d. per week. By 13s. received from Thomas Roch...his son for 26 weeks, viz. 6d. per week. By 15s. received from Manfeld for the board of his son for 30 weeks, viz. 6d. per week. By £1 received from...of Cambridge for the board of his daughter for 40 weeks, viz. 6d. per week. By 8s. from...of Chesterton for the board of his son for 16 weeks, viz. 6d. per week. From... Parker of Walden for the board of his son for 12 weeks. By

3s received from...the merchant for the board of his daughter for 6 weeks, viz 6d per week " Dugdale, *Mon.* IV, pp. 459–60.

*6 *St Radegund's, Cambridge.*

1481–2 The account roll for 1481–2 contains the item "And she answers for 20s received from Richard Woodcock for the commons of 2 daughters of the said Richard, as for [*blank*] weeks, at [*blank*] per week." Gray, *Priory of St Radegund's, Cambridge,* p 176. This is probably a child, because I am inclined to think that payments so worded, as from a father for a son or daughter, usually refer to children. Unfortunately the nuns of this priory kept the details of their receipts from boarders on a separate sheet, and entered only the total, thus "And by £1. 12 1 received for the board or repast of divers gentlefolk, particulars of whose names are noted in the paper book of accounts displayed above this account." *Ib* p. 163 (see also, p. 147) These separate papers are unluckily lost, so no details are available.

DERBYSHIRE.

*7. *King's Mead, Derby.*

Dr J C. Cox says "Evidence of this priory being used as a boarding school occurs in the private muniments of the Curzon, Fitzherbert and Gresley families " *V C.H. Derby*, II, p. 44 (note 14) Without more exact reference it is impossible to say whether this is correct, because adult boarders are so often confused with schoolchildren.

DEVON

8 *Cornworthy*

c 1470 Petition from Thomasyn Dynham, Prioress of Cornworthy concerning two children at school in her house, whose fees have not been paid for five years See description in text (above, p. 269).

ESSEX

9 *Barking.*

1433. Katherine de la Pole, Abbess of Barking, petitions Henry V, "for as much as she, afore this tyme hath bene demened and reuled, by th'advis of youre full discrete counsail, to take upon hir the charge, costes and expenses of Edmond ap Meredith ap Tydier and Jasper ap Meredith ap Tydier, being yit in her kepyng, for the which cause she was payed, fro the xxvii day of Juyll, the yere of youre full noble regne xv, unto the Satterday the last day of Feverer, the yere of your saide regne xvii, 1 livres and after the saide last day of Feverer, youre saide bedewoman hath borne the charges as aboven unto this day and is behynde of the payement for the same charge . the somme of lii livres xii sols," she asks for payment.

Dugdale, *Mon* I, 437 (note *m*), (quoted from Rymer, *Foedera*, x, p. 828)

1527. Sir John Stanley made his will on June 20, 1527, and in 1528, after a solemn act of separation with his wife, entered a monastery. The will is largely concerned with provisions for the education of his son and heir, who was at that time three years old. He set aside the proceeds of a certain manor "whych is estemed to be of the yerly valewe of xl li , to the onely use and fyndynge of my said sonne and heyre apparaunte, tyll he comme and be of the full ayge of xxj¹¹ yeres; and I woll that my sayd sonne and heyr shalbe in the custodye and kepynge of the saide Abbes of Barckynge, tyll he accomplyshe and be of thayge of xij yeres and after the sayd ayge of xij yeres I woll that he shalbe in the custodye and guydynge of the sayd Abbot of Westmynster, tyll he come and be of hys full ayge of xxi¹¹ yeres." The Abbess and Abbot were to have £15 yearly for the use of their houses in return for their pains and £20 yearly was to be paid them "to fynde my sayd sonne and heyre and hys servauntes, mete, drynke and wayges convenyent and all other thynges necessare un to theym, durynge and by all the tyme that he shalbe in the rule and guydynge of the sayd Abbesse and of the sayd Abbot." *Archaeol. Journ* xxv (1868), pp 81–2

It should be noted that there is nothing to suggest that these boys were being taught by the nuns; they were young noblemen attached to a noblewoman's household to learn breeding

HAMPSHIRE.

10. *St Mary's, Winchester.*

1536. Henry VIII's commissioners, who visited the house 15th May, found here twenty-six "chyldren of lordys, knyghttes and gentylmen brought up yn the saym monastery " For the list of names (given in Dugdale, *Mon* II p. 457), see above p 266

11. *Romsey*

1311 Bishop Woodlock decreed "There shall not be in the dormitory with the nuns any children, either boys or girls, nor shall they be led by the nuns into the choir, while the divine office is celebrated." Liveing, *Records of Romsey Abbey*, p. 104

*1387. William of Wykeham enjoins (in an injunction dealing with various manifestations of the *vitium proprietatis*) "Moreover let not the nuns henceforth presume to call their own rooms or pupils (*discipulas*), hitherto assigned to them or so assigned in future, on pretext of such assignation, which is rather to be deemed a matter of will than of necessity; nathless it is lawful for the abbess to assign such rooms and pupils according to merit as she thinks fit, etc., etc." But this more probably refers to young nuns or novices The word *discipula* is used in this sense in Alnwick's visitation of Gracedieu (See above, p. 80)

12 *Wherwell.*

1284 Archbishop Peckham forbids boarders, adding "Let not virgins be admitted to the habit and veil (*induendae virgines et velandae*) before the completion of their fifteenth year and let not any boy be permitted to be educated with the nuns " *Reg. Epis. J. Peckham*, II, p. 653.

HEREFORDSHIRE

13 *Lymbrook.*

1422. Bishop Spofford writes "Wee ordayne and charge you under payne of unobedyence that no suster hald nor receyfe ony surgyner, man or woman weddyd, other maydens of lawful age to be wedded, knave chyldren aboven eght yeer of age " *Reg. Thome Spofford* (Cant. and York. Soc.), p. 82.

HERTFORDSHIRE.

14 *Flamstead.*

1530 At the visitation of Longland one nun "reported that young girls were allowed to sleep in the dormitory .. The Prioress was enjoined . to exclude children of both sexes from the dormitory." *V C H. Herts.* IV, p 433

15 *Sopwell*

*1446 In the Warden's Accounts of 1446 there is entered payment of 22/6 for Lady Anne Norbery, for the commons of her daughter, apparently a boarder here. (*Rentals and Surveys*, R. 294.) *V C H Herts* IV, p 425 (note 41).

1537 At the time of the Dissolution two children were living in the priory *Ib.* p. 425

KENT

16 *Dartford*

In 1527 was confirmed the concession made to sister Elizabeth Cresner by F Antoninus de Ferraria, formerly vicar of Garsias de Lora, Master General of the Dominican order (1518-24), that she might receive any well born matrons, widows of good repute, to dwell perpetually in the monastery, with or without the habit, according to the custom of the monastery; and also that she might receive young ladies and give them a suitable training, according to the mode heretofore pursued. *Archaeol Journ* (1882) XXXIX, p 178

LEICESTERSHIRE.

17. *Gracedieu*

The following references to boarders occur in the Gracedieu accounts (*P R.O Minister's Accounts*, 1257/10)

1413-14. "Item received from William Roby for the board of his daughter on the Feast of the Holy Trinity vj s viij d. Item received from Robert Penell for the board of his daughter on the same day v s Item received for the board of Cecily Nevell on St James' Day in part payment vj s viij d " (p. 7).

1414-15. "Item received from Giles Jurdon for the board of his daughter in Whitsun week vij s. Item received from Thomas Hinte for the food of a certain daughter of his, in part payment of liij s iiij d,—xl s Item received for the board of Isabel Jurdon xj s, Alice Strelley xxij s, Alice Grey xiij s iiij d, Robert Drewe xxvj s iiij d, Philip Scargell xxxiij s vj d, Alice Smyth, iij s iiij d and Dame Joan Scargell iiij s—cxiij s ix d " (p. 79). There is a supplementary list for this year written on a loose sheet: "Item, first, received for the board of Isabel Jurdon for the half year, in part payment ix s. Item received for the board of Alice Strelley from the feast of the Finding of the Holy Cross to the feast of [St Peter] in Chains in the following year, vj s viij d Item received for the board of Alice Gray from the feast of the Holy Trinity to the feast of the Purification of the blessed Virgin Mary xiij s iiij d Item received for the board of Alice Strelley for ij quarters of the year and v weeks, at the Feast of St Gregory xv s iiij d Item received for the board of the daughter of Robert Drowe for half a year, xxvj s viij d. Item received for the board of Philip Scargell, in part payment, from the feast of St John etc., paid for the quarter xxij s iiij d, whence at the Feast of Corpus Christi xxij s iiij d Item received for the board of Isabel Jurdon at the feast of the Translation of St Thomas of Canterbury, in part payment—ij s Item received for the board of Alice Smyth in part payment at vj s viij d for the quarter, iij s iiij d Item received for the board of Dame Skargeyle for two weeks, ij s per week, iiij s Item received for the board of Philyppe Skergell from the feast of St Laurence to the feast of St Michael, for the half quarter xj s ij d Total, cxiij s x d "

1416-17 "Item received for the board of the daughter of William Rowby, as for the purchase of one ox—xiij s iiij d "

1417-18. "Item received for the board of Mary de Ecton on the feast of All Saints, in part payment of a larger sum, xxxiij s iiij d Item received for the board of Joan Vilers on the Feast of St Andrew the Apostle vj s viij d Item received for the board of Katerine Standych on the morrow of the Epiphany vj s viij d Item received for the board of the daughters of Robert Nevell, knight, on the feast of St Hilary x s. Item received for the board of Joan Villars on the feast of St Hilary xx d. Item received for the board of Mary de Ecton on the Sunday next before the feast of St Valentine xx s Item received from Joan Villers for her board on the second sunday of Lent vj s viij d. Item received from Katerine Standych in full payment of her board on Whitsunday x s Item received for the board of the daughters of Robert Neuel on Good Friday x s. Item received from Mary Ecton for her board on the feast of the Purification of the B.V. then owing vj s. Item received from Joan Colyar in part payment of xx s owing for J. Dalby xij s" (p. 179).

These accounts obviously contain ordinary adult boarders as well as children Moreover in some cases the visitors seem merely to have come for the great feasts and not to have stayed for any length of time, a practice which does not suggest schooling. Mr Coulton has analysed the accounts closely. He writes. "The records of four years give us, at the most liberal interpretation, only nineteen children, whose total sojourn amounted to 648 weeks; that is an average of three pupils all the year round and one extra for two or three months of the time." He adds "I have, of course ruled out 'Dame Joan Scargill,' who paid 2s a week, or four times the sum paid by a child, and Philip Scargill, who paid eighteen pence and was pretty evidently the Dame's husband; but I have included five others on p. 89, though they are distinctly labelled as *perhendinantes*, and the sums they pay would in any case have suggested boarders rather than schoolgirls. If these were omitted (and I note that Abbot Gasquet also interprets them as merely boarders), this would bring down the average of actual children to about two at any given time." (*Monastic Schools in the Middle Ages*, p 27.) He infers the weekly rate of pay (where it can be inferred with any certainty) to be 6*d* a week for children and 1s or more for their elders. (*Ib* p. 39)

1440–1 At Bishop Alnwick's visitation the prioress deposed "that a male child of seven years sleeps in the dorter with the celleress" Alnwick makes an injunction forbidding boarders, "save childerne, males the ix and females the xiij yere of age, whome we licencede yow to hafe for your relefe." *Linc. Visit* II, pp 119, 125

18. *Langley.*

1440 At Bishop Alnwick's visitation Dame Margaret Mountgomerey "says that secular children, female only, do lie of a night in the dorter." The Bishop forbids boarders "men, women ne childerne" without licence *Linc. Visit* II, pp. 175–6.

LINCOLNSHIRE.

19 *Heynings.*

1347 Bishop Gynewell writes to Heynings. "Item we command you on your obedience that henceforth no secular female child who has passed the tenth year of her age and no male child, of whatever age he may be, be received to dwell among you; and that no child lie in your dorter with the ladies, nor anywhere else whereby the convent might be disturbed " (*Linc Epis. Reg. Memo Gynewell,* f. 34*d.*)

1387. Bishop Bokyngham writes "Item, for the removal of all fleshly wantonness (*carnis pruritus quoscumque*), we will and ordain that secular children and especially males shall henceforth in no wise be permitted to sleep with the nuns, but let an honest place be set aside for them outside the cloister, if by our recent and special grace they should chance to be staying there." (*Linc. Epis. Reg. Memo. Bokyngham*, f. 397*d*.)

1442 Alnwick enjoins at his visitation and afterwards in his written injunctions "that fro this day forthe ye receyve no sudeiour-nauntes that passe a man x yere, a woman xiiij yere of age, wythowten specyalle leve of hus or our successours bysshops of Lincolne asked and had." (*Linc. Visit* II, pp 134–5.)

20 *Gokewell.*

1440. At Alnwick's visitation the Prioress "says that they have no boarders above ten years of age of female and eight years of male sex" (*Linc. Visit.* II, p 117)

21. *Legbourne.*

1440 Alnwick ordains "that fro hense forthe ye suffre no seculere persone, woman ne childe, lyg be night in the dormytorye." (*Alnwick's Visit* MS. f. 68.)

22 *Nuncoton*

1531 Bishop Longland enjoins. "and that ye suffre nott eny men children to be brought upp, nor taught within your monastery, nor to resorte to eny of your susters, nouther to lye within your monastery, nor eny person young ne old to lye within your dorter, but oonly religious women" (*Archaeologia*, XLVII. p 58)

23 *Stixwould.*

1440 At Alnwick's visitation· "Dame Alice Thornton says that young secular folk female, of eight or ten years old, do lie in the dorter, but in separate beds....Also she says that, as she believes, there are males and females, about eighteen in number, who board with divers nuns, not passing fourteen or sixteen years in age . Dame Maud Shirwode speaks of the children that lie in the dorter" Alnwick in his injunctions forbids seculars ("women ne childern") to lie in the dorter or to be received as boarders without licence (*Alnwick's Visit.* MS 75*d*, 76)

MIDDLESEX

24. *St Helen's, Bishopsgate (London).*

1298 The Prioress' account for 25–6 Edward I, contains the following items which probably refer to child boarders. "And by xx s received from Dionisia Miles for her daughter [*gap*]...after the Nativity of St John the Baptist And by one mark received for the niece of Robert Morton [?]." *P.R.O. Ministers' Accounts,* 1258/2

1432. The injunctions sent by the Dean and Chapter of St Paul's to St Helen's contain the item· "Also we ordeyne and injoyne yow, prioresse and convent, that noo seculere be lokkyd with inne the boundes of the cloystere, ne no seculere persones come within aftyr the belle of complyne, except wymment servaunts and mayde childeryne lerners .. Also we ordeyne and injoine that nonne have ne receyve noo schuldrin wyth hem into the house forseyde, but yif that the profite of the comonys turne to the vayle of the same howse " (Dugdale, *Mon.* iv, pp. 553–4, wrongly dated 1439.)

*25. *Stratford "atte Bowe."*

1346. In the will of John Hamond, pepperer, occurs the legacy· "To his niece the daughter of Thomas Hamond, residing with the nuns of Stratford, he leaves a sum of money for her maintenance." (Sharpe, *Cal of Wills...in the Court of Hustings,* London, 1, p 516.) The girl *may* have been a nun, but if so the legacy is curiously worded.

NORFOLK.

26. *Carrow.*

In Rye, W., *Carrow Abbey* (1889), pp. 49–52, is a list of boarders at Carrow, compiled by Norris from account rolls now lost. Some of these were almost certainly children; I should suggest that those described as "son of" or "daughter of" N. or M. are children. On these lists, see G G Coulton, *Mon. Schools in the Mid. Ages* (Med. Studies, No. 10), p 7.

27. *Thetford.*

1532. At Nykke's visitation it was discovered that "John Jerves, gentleman, has a daughter being brought up (*nutritam*) in the priory and he pays nothing." (*Visit. of Dioc of Norwich,* ed. Jessopp (Camden Soc), p 304)

NORTHAMPTONSHIRE.

28. *Catesby.*

1442. At Alnwick's visitation the Prioress, Margaret Wavere, deposed that "sister Agnes Allesley has six or seven young folk of both sexes that do lie in the dorter." Alnwick makes the usual injunction against boarders, "ouer thage of x yeere, if thei be men, wommene ouer thage of a xj yere " *Linc. Visit.* II, pp. 46, 51

29. *St Michael's, Stamford.*

1440. At Alnwick's first visitation the sacrist "says that the prioress has seven or eight children, some male, some female, of twelve years of age and less, to her board and to teach them." Alnwick forbids secular persons ("women ne childrene") to lie in the dorter and boarders ("yong ne olde") to be received without licence. (*Alnwick's Visit.* MS. ff. 83–83d.)

1442. At Alnwick's second visitation: "Dame Maud Multone says that little girls of seven or five years of age do lie in the dorter, contrary to my lord's injunction." (*Ib.* f. 39*d.*)

OXFORDSHIRE.

30. *Godstow.*

1358. Bishop Gynewell writes: "Item we ordain that no lady of your said house shall have children, save only one or two females sojourning with them." *Linc. Epis. Reg. Memo. Gynewell,* f. 100.)

1445. Bishop Alnwick forbids boarders to be received "but if ye hafe lefe of hus or our successours, bysshope of Lincolne, but if it be yong childerne, a man not ouere ix yere of age and a woman of xii yere of age." (*Linc. Visit.* II, p. 115.)

31. *Littlemore.*

1445. The Prioress says that "the daughter of John fitz Aleyn, steward of the house, and Ingram Warland's daughter are boarders in the house and each of them pays fourpence a week." These are clearly children, for another boarder "sometime the serving woman of Robert fitz Elys" is mentioned and she pays eightpence a week. Alnwick makes the usual injunction forbidding boarders "ouere the age of a man of nyne yere ne woman of xij yere, ne noght thaym wythe owten specyalle lefe of vs or our successours." (*Linc. Visit.* II, pp. 217–8.)

STAFFORDSHIRE.

32. *Fairwell.*

1367. Bishop Robert Stretton of Lichfield enjoined that "no nun was to keep with her for education more than one child, nor any male child over seven years of age and even that may not be done without the Bishop's leave. If any have more they are to be removed before the Feast of Purification next." (*Reg. Robert de Stretton,* II, p. 119.)

SOMERSET.

33. *Cannington.*

1407. The will of Thomas Woth contains the following legacy: "To the Prioress of Canyngton 40 marks to provide (*inveniendum*) Elizabeth my daughter, if she shall happen to live to the age of ten years." He also leaves Elizabeth 11 marks as a marriage dowry. (*Somerset Medieval Wills,* ed. F. W. Weaver (Somerset Rec. Soc.), I, p. 28.)

SUFFOLK

34. *Redlingfield.*

1514. At Bishop Nykke's visitation Dame Grace Sampson deposed that "boys (*pueri*) sleep in the dorter and are harmful to the convent," and another nun said the same. The Bishop ordained "that boys shall not lie in the dorter." (*Visit. of Dioc. of Norwich*, ed Jessopp (Camden Soc.), pp. 139–40.)

WARWICKSHIRE.

35. *Polesworth.*

1537. Henry VIII's commissioners addressed a letter to Cromwell on behalf of this house, representing among other things "the repayre and resort that ys made to the gentylmens childern and studiounts that ther doo lif, to the nombre sometyme of xxx^ti and sometyme xl^ti and moo, that their be right vertuously brought upp." (Dugdale, *Mon* II, p. 363.) The house at this time contained an abbess and twelve nuns.

YORKSHIRE.

36. *Arden.*

1306. Archbishop Greenfield decreed that no girls or boarders were to be taken without special licence of the Archbishop 'All girls staying in the house without authority were to be removed within eight days (*V C H. Yorks.* III, p 113.)

37. *Arthington.*

1315. Archbishop Greenfield decreed that no boys or secular persons were to sleep in the dorter with the nuns

1318. Archbishop Melton repeated the decree (*V C.H Yorks.* III, p. 188.)

38. *Esholt.*

1315. Archbishop Greenfield decreed that all women boarders over the age of twelve were to be removed within six days and no more taken without special licence

1318. Archbishop Melton repeated the decree. (*V.C H. Yorks.* III, p 161)

1537. Among the debts owing to the Priory at the Dissolution was one of 33s. from Walter Wood of Timble, in the parish of Otley, for his child's board for a year and a half, ended at Lent, 28 Hen. VIII. (*Yorks. Archaeol. Journ.* IX, p. 321, note 23.)

39. *Hampole.*

1313. Archbishop Greenfield granted the convent licence to receive a young girl Agnes de Langthwayt as a boarder, at the instance "nobilis viri Ade de Everyngham"

1314 He issued a decree that no male children over five years of age should be permitted in the house, "as the Archbishop finds has been the practice." (*V C.H. Yorks* III, pp 163–4.)

40 *Marrick.*

1252. Archbishop Gray forbade any girl or woman to be taken as boarder or to be taught without special licence. (*V.C.H. Yorks* III, p. 117.)

41. *Moxby.*

1314   Archbishop Greenfield forbade boarders or girls over twelve
to be taken without licence. (*V.C H Yorks.* III, p. 239.)

42   *Nunappleton.*

1489.   Archbishop Rotheram enjoined "Item þat yee take noe per-
hendinauntes or sogerners into your place from hensforward,
but if þei be children or ellis old persones, by which availe
by liklyhod may growe to your place" (*V C.H Yorks* III,
173, and Dugdale, *Mon.* v, p 654)

43. *Nunburnholme.*

1318   Archbishop Melton forbade persons of either sex over twelve
years of age to be maintained as boarders (*V C H. Yorks* III,
p 119.)

44. *Nunkeeling.*

1314.   Archbishop Greenfield forbade boarders to be taken, or girls
to be kept in the house after the age of twelve years (*V C H.
Yorks.* III, p. 120.)

*45. *Nunmonkton*

1429.   Isabel Salvayn leaves "xiij s iiij d to be paid for Alice Thorp
at Nunmunkton for her board " (*Test Ebor.* I, p. 419.)

46. *Rosedale.*

1315   Archbishop Greenfield decreed, under pain of the greater excommunication, that no nun was to cause a girl or boy to
sleep under any consideration in the dorter, and if any, nun
broke this command, the Prioress, under pain of deposition,
was to signify her name without delay to the Archbishop.
(*V C.H. Yorks.* III, p 174)

47   *St Clement's, York.*

1310   Archbishop Greenfield forbade girls over twelve as boarders.

1317   Archbishop Melton forbade little girls, or males of any age,
or secular women to sleep in the dorter with the nuns. (*V.C.H.
Yorks.* III, p 129)

48. *Sinningthwaite.*

1315.   Archbishop Greenfield enjoined the Prioress and Subprioress
not to permit boys or girls to eat flesh meat in Advent or
Sexagesima, or during Lent eggs or cheese, in the refectory,
contrary to the honesty of religion, but at those seasons when
they ought to eat such things, they were to be assigned other
places in which to eat them

1319   Archbishop Melton forbade girls over twelve to be retained
without special licence. (*V.C H. Yorks.* III, p 177.)

*49 *Swine*

1345   Peter del Hay of Spaldynton leaves in his will "to Joan my
daughter residing (*manenti*) in Swyn vj s viij d " (*Test Ebor* I,

p 12) This is probably a boarder in the convent, perhaps a child.

15th century Thorold Rogers (*Six Centuries of Work and Wages* (1909), p. 166), says· "During the course of the [fifteenth] century I find it was the practice of country gentlefolks to send their daughters for education to the nunneries, and to pay a certain sum for their board A number of such persons are enumerated as living *en pension* at the small nunnery of Swyn in Yorkshire Only one roll of expenditure for this religious house survives in the Record Office, but it is quite sufficient to prove and illustrate the custom " I have been unable to trace this roll in the Record Office.

NOTE C.

NUNNERY DISPUTES.

OTHER instances of nunnery disputes may be quoted, among which Peckham's letter to the Holy Sepulchre, Canterbury, is a good example. "If there be any nun above you who is quarrelsome and sharp and is of custom unbearable towards her sisters, we order her to be separated from the communion of the convent according to the form of the rule, and to be kept in some solitary place (so that meanwhile no man or woman have conversation with or access to her) until she shall be brought back to humility of spirit and show herself amiable and devout to all Therefore let there cease among you quarrels, altercations and sharp words, which stain and deform the splendours of monastic honour. And for such contumelious members who have to be separated as aforesaid we assign that dark room under the dorter, if you have none other more suitable "[1]. The nuns of Wroxall in 1338 were warned to "cease from scoldings, reproofs and other evil words" and were particularly told not to speak "en reproce ne en vilenie" of a certain Dame Margaret de Acton, who had evidently been guilty of some serious fault, but had been duly corrected by the Visitor[2], and in the same year it was ordained at Sopwell that "if it happen that any one scold ..let her be placed in silence by all and do penance for three days"[3] At Heynings in 1392 Bokyngham ordered "that all the nuns treat their sisters affably, not with an austere but with a benignant countenance and with sisterly affection, nor visit them with railing and hurtful words in public, especially in the presence of laymen, nor threaten or scold them, on pain, etc"[4]. At Elstow in 1421–2 there was an injunction against the formation of cliques, upon the need for which light is

[1] *Reg. Epis. Peckham*, II, p 706
[2] *Worc. Sede Vac Reg p 276*
[3] Dugdale, *Mon.* III, p. 366.
[4] *Linc MS. Reg. Bokyngham Mem* f. 397d.

thrown by the *detecta* at Alnwick's visitation of Gracedieu[1], "That no nun make any secret cabals or say or imagine anything by way of insinuation or disparagement, whereby charity, unity or the comeliness of religion may be hindered or troubled in the convent"[2].

The *detecta* at visitations often give details as to the ill-temper or insubordination of individuals. At Wothorpe in 1323 Bishop Burghersh "ordered inquiry into certain irregularities within the priory, caused by the discords raised among the nuns by sister Joan de Bonnwyche"[3]. At Littlemore one of the nuns deposed that Dame Agnes Marcham "is very quarrelsome and rebellious and will not do her work like the others", it appears that the convent resented the fact that although she had worn the habit of profession for twelve years she was not expressly professed and refused to make public profession; she on her part asserted that "she does not mean to make express profession while she stays in that place, because of the ill-fame which is current thereabouts concerning that place and also because of the barrenness and poverty which in likelihood will betake the place on account of the slenderness of the place's revenues," and she proceeded to give details of the access to the priory of two scholars of Oxford and a parish chaplain[4] It is difficult to tell who was in the right, Littlemore certainly was a place of ill-repute and went from bad to worse, but Agnes Marcham had stayed there for half her lifetime (she had entered at the age of thirteen and was twenty-six or twenty-eight at the time of the visitation) and it looks as though she had really no intention of departing, but found the threat to do so useful[5] At Godstow in the same year it was sister Maud, a laywoman, who caused trouble, she was very rebellious against the abbess and rumour ran high in the convent that she had "obtained a bull from the apostolic see to the prejudice of the monastery and without the abbess's knowledge"[6] At Easebourne (1524) the subprioress Alice Hill said that three of the younger nuns were disobedient to her in the absence of the Prioress, but the three delinquents and another nun deposed that "Lady Alice Hill is too haughty and rigorous and cannot bear patiently with her sisters" and the Visitor apparently considered that the complaint was justified, for afterwards Lady Alice Hill, subprioress, appeared and humbly submitted herself to correction, in the presence of the said prioress and co-sisters, upon what has been discovered against her in the visitation. Afterwards my lord enjoined her that from henceforth she should conduct herself well and religiously in all things towards the said prioress and nuns, and as to the other portion of her penance he adjourned it for a time After doing which (he) enjoined all to be obedient to the Lady Prioress and in her absence to the said subprioress[7]

The difficulty was perhaps the old one, that crabbed age and youth cannot live together. At Rusper, when the same Visitor came there,

---

[1] *Linc Visit.* II, pp. 120-1. [2] *Ib* I, p. 51
[3] *V C.H Northants.* II, p 101 [4] See above, p. 397
[5] *Linc. Visit* II, p 115 [6] *Ib.* p 115.
[7] Sussex Arch. Soc. Coll IX, pp. 25-7.

it was found that the four sisters were disturbed by the intrigues of an external visitor, for the nuns deposed "that a certain William Tychenor hath frequent access to the said priory and there sows discord between the prioress, sisters and other persons living there"[1]; sometimes the lay servants of a house seem to have stirred up quarrels among their mistresses and in 1302 John of Pontoise ordered the nuns of Wherwell "to punish well secular persons, both sisters and others, whoever they may be, who reply improperly and impudently to the religious ladies, and especially those who sow quarrels and disputes among the ladies"[2]

Injunctions as to the making of corrections usually had in view the prevention of ill feeling, by ensuring that such corrections should not be made in a harsh or unfair manner and should take place only in the chapter-house and not in the presence of strangers. It will be remembered that the wicked prioress of Catesby, Margaret Wavere, used to rebuke and reproach her nuns before secular folk, and treat them with great cruelty, her the Bishop charged

vnder payne of cursyng that moderly and benygnely ye trete your susters, specyally in correctyng thaire defautes, so that ye make your correcyones oonly in the chaptre hous of suche defautz and excesse as be open and in presence of your sustres[3].

Bokyngham sent a long and detailed injunction on the subject to Elstow in 1387:

In making corrections the abbess, prioress, and others of superior rank shall so observe a moderate and modest temperance and an equitable reasonable-ness, that having laid aside all hatred and malice and excessive rigour, they shall in charitable zeal proceed to (deal with) the complaints, offences and faults reported to them and shall hear the accused parties, silencing or repelling their excuses, punishing, correcting and reforming their offences and excesses, grave and venial, without harshness or railing words and quarrels or abuse, according as the quality of the fault, the compunction of the delinquents and the repetition or frequency of the offence demand it And when faults and offences have been punished and excesses corrected let them not reiterate fresh reproaches, but treat their fellow-nuns affably, not with an austere but with a benignant countenance, nor visit them with railing and insulting words in public, especially in the presence of laymen, nor scold them when they have committed excesses, but only in the chapter deal with all that concerns the discipline of regular observance[4].

For an injunction to the nuns on obedience see Woodlock's injunction to Romsey in 1311:

Item, because they are unaware that amongst the vows of religion the vow of obedience is the greater, it is ordered that the younger ladies

---

[1] Sussex Arch. Soc. Coll v, p 257.   [2] *Reg. J de Pontissara*, 1, p. 125
[3] *Linc. Visit* 11, p. 51.
[4] *Linc. Reg. Memo. Bokyngham*, f. 343 Compare Buckingham's similar injunction to Heynings, ib. f 397, Gynewell's injunction to Elstow in 1359, ib *Reg. Gynewell*, ff. 139d–140, Pontoise's injunction to Wherwell in 1302, *Reg J de Pontissara*, 1, p. 125, and Peckham's injunction to the Holy Sepulchre, Canterbury, in 1284, *Reg. Ep Peckham*, 11, p. 706.

reverently obey the seniors and especially their presidents and if any rebels are found they shall be sharply rebuked in chapter before all and, the fault growing, the penalty of disobedience shall be increased[1]

At Rosedale, where in 1306 the nuns had been warned not to quarrel, it was enacted nine years later that

any nun disobedient or rebellious in receiving correction was for each offence to receive a discipline from the president in chapter and say the seven penitential psalms with the litany, and if still rebellious the archbishop would impose a still more severe penance[2].

It is to be feared that these quarrels sometimes got to blows Besides the notorious instances of Margaret Wavere and Katherine Wells, the excommunication of three nuns of St Michael's, Stamford, for laying violent hands upon a novice may be quoted[3] Of another kind were the assaults of a certain nun of Romsey, who was excommunicated for attacking a vicar in church[4], and of a Prioress of Rowney It appears from the court rolls of Munden Furnivall (1370) that the latter "had been guilty of a hand to hand scuffle with a chaplain, called Alexander of Great Munden; each was fined for drawing blood from the other and the lady also for raising the hue and cry unjustly"[5]. In both cases the nun was blamed, but it is perhaps permissible to quote in this connection an anecdote told by Thomas of Chantimpré

When I was in Brussels, the great city of Brabant, there came to me a maiden of lowly birth, but comely, who besought me with many tears to have mercy upon her When therefore I had bidden her tell me what ailed her, then she cried out amidst her sobs "Alas, wretched that I am! for a certain priest would fain have ravished me by force, and he began to kiss me against my will, wherefore I smote him with the back of my hand, so that his nose bled; and for this, as the clergy now tell me, I must needs go to Rome " Then I, scarce withholding my laughter, yet speaking as in all seriousness, affrighted her as though she had committed a grievous sin, and at length, having made her swear that she would fulfil my bidding, I said, "I command thee, in virtue of thy solemn oath, that if this priest or any other shall attempt to do thee violence with kisses or embraces, then thou shalt smite him sore with thy clenched fist, even to the striking out, if possible, of his eye, and in this matter thou shalt spare no order of men, for it is as lawful for thee to strike in defence of thy chastity, as to fight for thy life " With which words I moved all that stood by, and the maiden herself, to vehement laughter and gladness[6].

The list of faults given in the "Additions to the Rules" of Syon Abbey, contains several references to ill temper, though such references are, to be sure, no more proof that the faults were committed than are the model forms of self-examination ("Have I committed murder? ") sometimes given to-day to children in preparation

[1] Liveing, op cit. p 104   [2] V C H Yorks. III, p 174
[3] V.C H. Northants II, p 99.   [4] Liveing, op cit p. 168.
[5] V C.H Herts. IV, p. 434
[6] Translated from his Bonum Universale de Apibus, Lib II, c. 30, written about 1260, in Coulton, Med Garn pp 372–3

for the Communion service. Among "greuous defautes" are mentioned, "if any suster say any wordes of despyte, reprefe, schame or vylony to any suster or brother," "if any sowe dyscorde amonge the sustres and brethren," "if any be founde a preuy rouner or bakbyter." Among "more greuous defautes" are·

if any whan thei fal chydyng or stryuyng togyder, if the souereyne or priores, or any serche say thus—"*Sit nomen domini benedictum*" wyl not cese, knokkyng themselfe upon their brestes, answerynge and saynge mekely, and withe a softe spyryte "*Mea culpa*"...and so utterly cese, if any manesche by chere or wordes to smyte another at any tyme, or for to auenge her own injurye, or els by ungodly wordes repreve another of her contre, or kynrede, or any other sclaunderous fortune, or chaunse fallen at any tyme

Among "most greuous defautes" are·

If any ley vyolente hande upon her souereyne or spituosly smyte or wounde her or elles make any profer to smyte be sygne or token leftying up her fest, stykke, staffe, stone, or any other wepen what ever it be, or else schofte, pusche, or sperne any suster from her withe armes or scholders, handes or fete, violently, in wrekyng of her own wrethe[1].

NOTE D.

GAY CLOTHES.

A COUNCIL at London in 1200 had restrained the black nuns from wearing coloured headdresses[2] but the standard English decree on the subject was that issued by the council of Oxford in 1222

Since it is necessary that the female sex, so weak against the wiles of the ancient enemy, should be fortified by many remedies, we decree that nuns and other women dedicated to divine worship shall not wear a silken wimple, nor dare to carry silver or golden tiring-pins in their veil Neither shall they, nor monks nor regular canons, wear belts of silk, or adorned with gold or silver, nor henceforth use burnet or any other unlawful cloth. Also let them measure their gown according to the dimension of their body, so that it does not exceed the length of the body, but let it suffice them to be clad, as beseems them, in a robe reaching to the ankles; and let none but a consecrated nun wear a ring and let her be content with one alone[3].

Fifteen years later a synod declared·

Item, we forbid to monks, regular canons and nuns coloured garments or bed clothes, save those dyed black. And when they ride, let them use decent saddles and bridles and saddle-cloths[4]. And nuns are not to use

[1] Aungier, *Hist and Antiq. of Syon Mon* pp 256, 257, 259, 261–2 For further instances of quarrels in the province of Rouen, see below, pp. 664–6.
[2] Wilkins, *Conc.* I, p 508
[3] *Ib.* pp 590–1. Compare a decree of the contemporary Council of Trier (1227) for German nuns, Harzheim, *Conc Germ.* III, p 534
[4]
      And, whan he rood, men might his brydel here
      Ginglen in a whistling wind as clere,
      And eke as loude as dooth the chapel-belle
      Ther as this lord was keper of the celle

trained and pleated dresses, or any exceeding the length of the body, nor delicate or coloured furs, nor shall they presume to wear silver tiring-pins in their veil[1].

These regulations were repeated almost word for word by William of Wykeham in his injunctions to Romsey and Wherwell in 1387[2]. With them may be compared the rule as to dress in force at Syon Abbey in the fifteenth century:

whiche (clothes) in nowyse schal be ouer curyous, but playne and homly, witheoute weuynge of any straunge colours of silke, golde or syluer, hauynge al thynge of honeste and profyte, and nothyng of vanyte, after the rewle; ther knyves vnpoynted and purses beyng double of lynnen clothe and not of sylke[3]

The unsuccessful efforts of monastic Visitors to enforce these rules have been described, a few instances may be added here to show the directions in which the nuns erred. Peckham wrote to Godstow:

Concerning the garments of the nuns let the rule of St Benedict be carefully observed For which reason we forbid them ever in future to wear cloth of burnet, nor gathered tunics nor to make themselves garments of an immoderate width with excessive pleats (*nec etiam birrorum immoderantia vestes sibi faciant latitudine fluctuantes*); with this nevertheless carefully observing what was aforetime ordained in such matters by the Council of Oxford[4]

Buckingham's injunction to Elstow in 1387 gives some interesting details; he forbade the nuns to wear any other veil than that of profession, or to "adorn their countenances" by arranging it in a becoming fashion, spreading out the white veil, which was meant to be worn underneath

> (Ainsi qu'il est pour le monde et les cours
> Un art, un goût de modes et d'atours,
> Il est aussi des modes pour le voile,
> Il est un art de donner d'heureux tours[5]
> À l'étamine, à la plus simple toile)[6]

They were not to wear gowns of black wide at the bottom, or turned back with fur at the wrists[7], and they were in no wise to use "wide girdles or belts plaited (*spiratis*) or adorned with silver, nor wear these above their tunics open to the gaze of man"[8] Curious details are also given by Bishop Spofford, writing to the nuns of Lymbrook in 1437, their habit was to "be formed after relygyon in sydnesse and wydnesse, forbedyng long traynes in mantellys and kyrtellys and almaner of spaires and open semes in the same kyrtellys"[9]. "Large collars, barred girdles and laced shoes" were forbidden at Swine in

---

[1] Wilkins, *Conc* I, p. 660.   [2] *New Coll* MS f. 86.
[3] Aungier, *op. cit.* p. 392.   [4] *Reg Ep Peckham*, III, p. 849.
[5] Ful semely hir wimpel pinched was!
[6] Gresset, *Vert Vert*, ll 142–6 See below, p 593.
[7]   I seigh his sleves purfiled at the hond
     With grys, and that the fyneste of a lond.
          Chaucer, *Prologue*, ll 193–4.
[8] *Linc Reg Memo. Bokyngham*, f 343*d*.
[9] *Hereford Reg. Spofford*, I, f. 77*d*.

1298[1], red dresses and long supertunics "like secular women" at Wilberfoss in 1308[2], at Nunmonkton in 1397 (after Margaret Fairfax's fashionable clothes had been discovered) a general injunction was made to the nuns "not to use henceforth silken clothes, and especially silken veils, nor precious furs, nor rings on their fingers, nor tunics laced-up or fastened with brooches nor any robes, called in English 'gownes,' after the fashion of secular women"[3]. These Northern houses were continually in need of admonition, sometimes their slashed tunics, sometimes their barred girdles, sometimes their shoes being condemned[4] Bishop Alnwick found silken veils at Langley, Studley and Rothwell[5], Bishop Fitzjames forbade silver and gilt pins and kirtles of fustian or worsted at Wix in 1509[6], and at Carrow in 1532 the subprioress complained that some of the nuns not only wore silk girdles, but had the impudence to commend the use thereof[7]

Nor could nuns always resist the temptation to let their shorn hair grow again, e g at the visitation of Romsey by the commissary of the Prior of Canterbury in 1502, the cellaress deposed "that Mary Tystede and Agnes Harvey wore their hair long"[8] Eudes Rigaud had some difficulty in this matter with the frivolous nuns of his diocese of Rouen; at Villarceaux in 1249 he recorded "They all wear their hair long to their chins," and at Montivilliers he had to condemn ringlets[9] One is reminded of the scene in *Jane Eyre*, where Mr Brocklehurst visits Lowood:

Suddenly his eye gave a blink, as if he had met something that either dazzled or shocked its pupil; turning, he said in more rapid accents than he had hitherto used: "Miss Temple, Miss Temple, what—*what* is that girl with curled hair? Red hair, ma'am, curled—curled all over?" and extending his cane he pointed to the awful object, his hand shaking as he did so "It is Julia Severn," replied Miss Temple, very quietly "Julia Severn, ma'am! And why has she, or any other, curled hair? Why, in defiance of every precept and principle of this house, does she conform to the world so openly—here in an evangelical, charitable establishment—as to wear her hair a mass of curls?. .Tell all the first form to rise up and direct their faces to the wall ". .He scrutinised the reverse of these living medals some five minutes, then pronounced sentence. These words fell like the knell of doom. "All those top-knots must be cut off "

Or, as Eudes Rigaud expressed it some seven centuries earlier. "Quod comam non nutriatis ultra aures."

[1] *V C H. Yorks.* III, p. 181.
[2] *Ib.* p. 126.   [3] Dugdale, *Mon* IV, p. 194
[4] *V C H. Yorks* III, pp. 119, 120, 127, 164, 168, 174-5, 181, 183, 240
[5] *Linc. Visit.* II, p. 176; *Alnwick's Visit* MS ff 26d, 38
[6] *V C H. Essex*, II, 124   [7] *Norwich Visit.* p 274.
[8] *V C H. Hants* II, p 130, where the date is wrongly given as 1512.
[9] See below, p 663

NOTE E.

CONVENT PETS IN LITERATURE.

It would be possible to compile a pretty anthology of convent pets, which have played a not undistinguished part in literature. The best known of all, perhaps, are Madame Eglentyne's little dogs, upon which Chaucer looked with a kindly unepiscopal eye:

> Of smale houndes had she, that she fedde
> With rosted flesh, or milk and wastel-breed,
> But sore weep she if oon of hem were deed,
> Or if men smoot it with a yerde smerte:
> And al was conscience and tendre herte[1].

The tender-hearted Prioress risked a terrible fate by so pampering her dogs, if we are to believe the awful warning related by the knight of La Tour-Landry, to wean his daughters from similar habits:

Ther was a lady that had two litell doggis, and she loued hem so that she toke gret plesaunce in the sight and feding of hem. And she made euery day dresse and make for her disshes with soppes of mylke, and after gaue hem flesshe. But there was ones a frere that saide to her that it was not wel done that the dogges were fedde and made so fatte, and the pore pepill so lene and famished for hunger. And so the lady, for his saieing, was wrothe with hym, but she wolde not amende it. And after she happed she deied, and there fell a wonder meruailous sight, for there was seyn euer on her bedde ij litell blake dogges, and in her deyeng thei were about her mouthe and liked it, and whanne she was dede, there the dogges had lyked it was al blacke as cole, as a gentillwoman tolde me that sawe it and named me the lady[2].

Poor Madame Eglentyne!

The anthologist would, however, have to go further back than Chaucer, into the eleventh century, and begin with that ill-fated donkey, which belonged to sister Alfrâd of Homburg, and which the

---

[1] *Prologue*, ll. 146–9. Chaucer was certainly a dog-lover: a passage in the *Book of the Duchess* (ll. 387 ff.) puts it beyond doubt:

> I was go walked fro my tree,
> And as I wente ther cam by me
> A whelp, that fauned me as I stood
> That hadde y-folowed, and coude no good.
> Hit com and creep to me as lowe,
> Right as hit hadde me y-knowe,
> Hild doun his heed and joyned his eres,
> And leyde al smothe doun his heres.
> I wolde han caught hit, and anoon
> Hit fledde, and was fro me goon.

[2] *The Book of the Knight of La Tour-Landry*, ed. T. Wright (E.E.T.S. revised ed. 1906), pp. 28–9.

wit of a nameless goliard and the devotion of the monks of St Augustine's, Canterbury, have preserved for undying fame[1]:

Est unus locus	There is a township
Hómburh dictus,	(Men call it Homburg)
in quo pascebat	There 'twas that Alfråd
asinam Alfråd	Pastured her she-ass,
viribus fortem	Strong was the donkey,
atque fidelem.	Mighty and faithful.
Que dum in amplum	And as it wandered
exiret campum,	Out to the meadow,
vidit currentem	It spied a greedy
lupum voracem,	Wolf that came running,
caput abscondit,	Head down and tail turned,
caudam ostendit	Off the ass scampered
Lupus occurrit:	Up the wolf hurried,
caudam momordit,	Seized tail and bit it
asina bina	Quickly the donkey
levavit crura	Lifted its hind legs,
fecitque longum	With the wolf bravely,
cum lupo bellum.	Long did it battle
Cum defecisse	Then when at last it
vires sensisset,	Felt its strength failing,
protulit magnam	Raised it a mighty
plangendo vocem	Noise of lamenting,
vocansque suam	Calling its mistress,
moritur domnam	So died the donkey.
Audiens grandem	Hearing the mighty
asine vocem	Voice of her donkey
Alfråd cucurrit,	Alfråd came running
"sorores," dixit,	"Come, sisters" cried she
"cito venite,	"Sisters, come quickly,
me adiuvate!	Come now and help me!
Asinam caram	My darling donkey
misi ad erbam.	Out to grass put I.
illius magnum	I hear a mighty
audio planctum,	Sound of complaining.
spero cum sevo	Sure with a cruel
ut pugnet lupo "	Wolf is it fighting!"
Clamor sororum	Heard is her crying
venit in claustrum,	In the nuns' cloister,
turbe virorum	Men come and women,
ac mulierum	Crowding together,
assunt, cruentum	All that the bloody
ut captent lupum	Wolf may be taken.
Adela namque	Adela also,
soror Alfråde,	sister of Alfråd,
Rikilam querit,	Rikila seeketh,
Agatham invenit,	Agatha findeth,
ibant ut fortem	All go to vanquish
sternerent hostem.	The mighty foeman

[1] Printed in *The Cambridge Songs*, ed Karl Breul (1915), No. 29, p. 62; and in *Denkmäler*, ed Mullenhoff und Scherer, *Deutscher Poesie und Prosa aus dem* VIII–XII *Jahrhundert* (Berlin, 1892), I, pp. 51–3 (No XXIV). I have ventured to attempt a translation.

At ille ruptis	But he tore open
asine costis	Sides of the donkey,
sanguinis undam	Flesh and blood gobbled
carnemque totam	All up together,
simul voravit,	Then helter-skeltered
silvam intravit.	Back to the forest.
Illud videntes	And when they saw him
cuncte sorores	Wept all the sisters,
crines scindebant,	Tearing their tresses,
pectus tundebant,	Beating their bosoms,
flentes insontem	Weeping the guiltless
asine mortem.	Death of their donkey.
Denique parvum	Long time a tiny
portabat pullum;	Foal it had carried.
illum plorabat	Sadly wept Alfrâd
maxime Alfrâd,	Thinking upon it,
sperans exinde	All her hopes ended
prolem crevisse.	Of rearing the offspring.
Adela mitis	Adela gentle,
Fritherûnque dulcis	Fritherûn charming,
venerunt ambe,	Both came together,
ut Alverâde	That they might strengthen
cor confirmarent	Sad heart of Alfrâd,
atque sanarent.	Strengthen and heal it.
"Delinque mestas,	"Leave now thy gloomy
soror, querelas!	Wailing, O sister!
lupus amarum	Wolf never heedeth
non curat fletum:	Thy bitter weeping.
dominus aliam,	The Lord will give thee
dabit tibi asinam."	Another donkey."

Exquisite ending! "The Lord will give thee another donkey." With
what delighted applause must the unknown jongleur have been
greeted by the monks or nobles, who first listened after dinner to this
little masterpiece of humour.

All the convent pets who are famed in literature came by a
coincidence to a bad end. Our anthologist would seize on two other
hapless creatures, both of them birds, Philip Sparrow and the never-
to-be-forgotten Vert-Vert. Philip Sparrow needs no introduction to
English readers; Skelton was never in happier vein than when he
sang the dirge of that pet of Joanna Scrope, boarder at Carrow
Priory, dead at the claws of a "vylanous false cat." Space allows
only a few lines of the long poem to be quoted here. It begins with
the office for the dead, sung by the mourning mistress over her bird:

> *Pla ce bo,*
> Who is there, who?
> *Di le xi,*
> Dame Margery;
> *Fa, re, my, my,*
> Wherefore and why, why?
> For the sowle of Philip Sparowe,
> That was late slayn at Carowe,
> Among the Nones Blake,
> For that swete soules sake,

And for all sparowes soules,
Set in our bederolles
Pater noster qui,
With an *Ave Mari,*
And with the corner of a Crede
The more shalbe your mede.

Whan I remembre agayn
How mi Philyp was slayn,
Neuer halfe the payne
Was betwene you twayne,
Pyramus and Thesbe,
As than befell to me.
I wept and I wayled,
The tearys doune hayled,
But nothynge it auayled
To call Phylyp agayne,
Whom Gyb our cat hath slayne.

It was so prety a fole,
It wold syt on a stole,
And lerned after my scole
For to kepe his cut,
With, Phyllyp, kepe your cut!
It had a veluet cap,
And wold syt vpon my lap,
And seke after small wormes,
And somtyme white bred crommes,
And many tymes and ofte
Betwene my brestes softe
It wolde lye and rest,
It was propre and prest.
Somtyme he wolde gaspe
Whan he sawe a waspe,
A fly or a gnat,
He wolde flye at that,
And prytely he wold pant
Whan he saw an ant,
Lord, how he wolde pry
After the butterfly!
Lorde, how he wolde hop
After the grassop!
And whan I sayd, Phyp, Phyp,
Than he wold lepe and skyp,
And take me by the lyp
Alas, it wyll me slo,
That Phillyp is gone me fro!
Si in i qui ta tes,
Al as, I was euyll at ease!
De pro fun dis cla ma vi,
Whan I sawe my sparowe dye!

That vengeaunce I aske and crye,
By way of exclamacyon,
On all the hole nacyon

> Of cattes wyld and tame,
> God send them sorowe and shame!
> That cat specyally
> That slew so cruelly
> My lytell prety sparowe
> That I brought vp at Carowe. .[1].

It is impossible for a cat-lover to leave the whole nation of cats under this terrific curse Yet literature will supply no nunnery cat beside the unhappy Gyb and the uncharacterised cat of the *Ancren Riwle* We must needs turn to the monks, and borrow the truer estimate of feline qualities made in the eighth century by an exiled Irish student, who sat over his books in a distant monastery of Carinthia, and wrote upon the margin of his copy of St Paul's Epistles this little poem on his white cat ·

> I and Pangur Bán, my cat,
> 'Tis a like task we are at;
> Hunting mice is his delight,
> Hunting words I sit all night.
>
> Better far than praise of men
> 'Tis to sit with book and pen;
> Pangur bears me no ill-will,
> He, too, plies his simple skill
>
> 'Tis a merry thing to see
> At our tasks how glad are we,
> When at home we sit and find
> Entertainment to our mind.
>
> Oftentimes a mouse will stray
> In the hero Pangur's way,
> Oftentimes my keen thought set
> Takes a meaning in its net
>
> 'Gainst the wall he sets his eye
> Full and fierce and sharp and sly;
> 'Gainst the wall of knowledge I
> All my little wisdom try
>
> When a mouse darts from its den,
> O! how glad is Pangur then,
> O! what gladness do I prove
> When I solve the doubts I love
>
> So in peace our task we ply,
> Pangur Bán, my cat, and I,
> In our arts we find our bliss,
> I have mine and he has his.
>
> Practice every day has made
> Pangur perfect in his trade,
> I get wisdom day and night,
> Turning darkness into light[2].

O cat! even at the cost of relevancy we have done thee honour.

[1] Skelton, *Selected Poems*, ed W. H. Williams (1902), pp 57 ff.
[2] Translation by Robin Flower in *The Poem Book of the Gael*, ed. Eleanor Hull (1913), p 132. The poem has also been translated by Kuno Meyer and by Alfred Perceval Graves

Two little tragedies of the cloister are concerned with parrots—
yet with what different birds and what different mistresses! In the
twelfth century Nigel Wireker tells of an ill-bred and ill-fated parrot,
kept in a nunnery, who told tales about the nuns and was poisoned
by them for his pains

> Saepe mala
> Psittacus in thalamum domina redeunte puellas
> Prodit et illorum verba tacenda refert;
> Nescius ille loqui; sed nescius immo tacere
> Profert plus aequo Psittacus oris habens.
> Hinc avibus crebro miscente aconita puella
> Discat ut ante mori quam didicisse loqui;
> Sunt et aves aliae quae toto tempore vitae
> Religiosorum claustra beata colunt[1].

Quite other was the fate of Vert-Vert, whose tragedy told with exquisite irony by Gresset in the eighteenth century deserves a place
on every shelf and in every heart which holds *The Rape of the Lock*.
Vert-Vert was a parrot who belonged to the nuns of Nevers,
the most beautiful, most amiable, the most devout parrot in the
world The convent of Nevers spoiled Vert-Vert as no bird has
ever been spoiled:

> Pas n'est besoin, je pense, de décrire
> Les soins des sœurs, des nonnes, c'est tout dire,
> Et chaque mère, après son directeur,
> N'aimait rien tant Même dans plus d'un cœur,
> Ainsi l'écrit un chroniqueur sincère,
> Souvent l'oiseau l'emporta sur le père.
> Il partageait, dans ce paisible lieu,
> Tous les sirops dont le cher père en Dieu,
> Grâce aux bienfaits des nonnettes sucrées,
> Réconfortait ses entrailles sacrées
> Objet permis à leur oisif amour,
> Vert-Vert était l'âme de ce séjour . .
> Des bonnes sœurs égayant les travaux,
> Il béquetait et guimpes et bandeaux,
> Il n'était point d'agréable partie
> S'il n'y venait briller, caracoler,
> Papillonner, siffler, rossignoler;
> Il badinait, mais avec modestie,
> Avec cet air timide et tout prudent
> Qu'une novice a même en badinant.

He fed in the frater, and between meals the nuns' pockets were always
full of bon-bons for his delectation He slept in the dorter, and happy
the nun whose cell he honoured with his presence; Vert-Vert always
chose the young and pretty novices Above all he was learned, he
talked like a book, and all the nuns had taught him their chants and
their prayers·

> Il disait bien son *Benedicite,*
> Et *notre mère,* et *votre charité,* ..

---

[1] Quoted in Fosbroke, *Brit Monachism,* II, p. 34.

> Il était là maintes filles savantes
> Qui mot pour mot portaient dans leurs cerveaux
> Tous les noëls anciens et nouveaux.
> Instruit, formé par leurs leçons fréquentes,
> Bientôt l'élève égala ses régentes,
> De leur ton même, adroit imitateur
> Il exprimait la pieuse lenteur,
> Les saints soupirs, les notes languissantes
> Du chant des sœurs, colombes gémissantes.
> Finalement Vert-Vert savait par cœur
> Tout ce que sait une mère de chœur

Small wonder that the fame of this pious bird spread far and wide; small wonder that pilgrims came from all directions to the abbey parlour to hear him talk. But alas, it was this very fame which led to his undoing. The physical tragedy of Philip Sparrow, an unlearned bird of frivolous tastes, pales before the moral tragedy of Vert-Vert. One day his renown reached the ears of a distant convent of nuns at Nantes, many miles further down the river Loire, and they conceived a violent desire to see him.

> Désir de fille est un feu qui dévore,
> Désir de nonne est cent fois pire encore.

They wrote to their fortunate sisters of Nevers, begging that Vert-Vert might be sent in a ship to visit them Consternation at Nevers The grand chapter was held; the younger nuns would have preferred death to parting with the darling parrot, but their elders judged it impolitic to refuse and to Nantes must Vert-Vert go for a fortnight The parrot was placed on board a ship, but the ship

> Portait aussi deux nymphes, trois dragons,
> Une nourrice, un moine, deux Gascons:
> Pour un enfant qui sort du monastère,
> C'était échoir en dignes compagnons.

At first Vert-Vert was confused and silent among the unseemly jests of the women and the Gascons and the oaths of the boatmen But too soon his innocent heart was acquainted with evil; desiring always to please he repeated all that he heard; no evil word escaped him, by the end of his journey he had forgotten all that he had learned in the nunnery, but he had become a pretty companion for a boatload of sinners. Nantes was reached; Vert-Vert (all unwilling) was carried off to the convent, and the nuns came running to the parlour to hear the saintly bird But horror upon horrors, nothing but oaths and blasphemies fell from Vert-Vert's beak. He apostrophised sister Saint-Augustin with "la peste te crève," and

> Jurant, sacrant d'une voix dissolue,
> Faisant passer tout l'enfer en revue,
> Les B, les F, voltigeaient sur son bec
> Les jeunes sœurs crurent qu'il parlait grec

The scandalised nuns dispatched Vert-Vert home again without delay. His own convent received him in tears. Nine of the most venerable sisters debated his punishment; two were for his death, two for sending him back to the heathen land of his birth, but the votes of the other five decided his punishment:

> On le condamne à deux mois d'abstinence,
> Trois de retraite et quatre de silence;
> Jardins, toilette, alcôve et biscuits,
> Pendant ce temps, lui seront interdits.

Moreover the ughest lay sister, a veiled ape, an octogenarian skeleton, was made the guardian of poor Vert-Vert, who had always preferred the youngest and coyest of the novices. Little remains to be told. Vert-Vert, covered with shame and taught by misfortune, became penitent, forgot the dragoons and the monk, and showed himself once more "plus dévot qu'un chanoine." The happy nuns cut short his penance, the convent kept fête, the dorters were decked with flowers, all was song and tumult. But alas, Vert-Vert, passing too soon from a fasting diet to the sweets that were pressed upon him.

> Bourré de sucre, et brûlé de liqueurs
> Vert-Vert, tombant sur un tas de dragées,
> En noir cyprès vit ses roses changées[1].

Doubtless so godly an end consoled the nuns for his untimely death. Yet one hardly knows which to prefer, the regenerate or the unregenerate Vert-Vert. The appreciative reader, remembering the inspired volubility with which (after such short practice) he greeted the nuns of Nantes, is almost moved to regret the destruction of what one of Kipling's soldiers would call "a wonderful gift of language." There is an apposite passage in Jasper Mayne's comedy of *The City Match* (1639), in which a lady describes the missionary efforts of her Puritan waiting-woman

> Yesterday I went
> To see a lady that has a parrot. my woman
> While I was in discourse converted the fowl,
> And now it can speak nought but Knox's works;
> *So there's a parrot lost*

NOTE F.

THE MORAL STATE OF LITTLEMORE PRIORY IN THE SIXTEENTH CENTURY

LITTLEMORE PRIORY, near Oxford, in the early sixteenth century, was in such grave disorder that it may justly be described as one of the worst nunneries of which record has survived. Its state was, as usual, largely due to a particularly bad prioress, Katherine Wells.

---

[1] *Oeuvres Choisies de Gresset* (Coll. Bibliothèque Nationale), pp. 3 ff. There is an eighteenth century English translation (1759) by J. G. Cooper in Chalmers, *English Poets*, xv, pp. 528-36.

The following account of it is taken from the record of Bishop Atwater's visitations in 1517 and 1518, the first held by his commissary Edmund Horde, the second by the bishop in person[1].

The *comperta* are that the prioress had ordered the five nuns under her to say that all was well; she herself had an illegitimate daughter, and was still visited by the father of the child, Richard Hewes, a priest in Kent[2]; that she took the "pannes, pottes, candilsticks, basynes, shetts, pelous, federe bedds etc." the property of the monastery, to provide a dowry for this daughter; that another of the nuns had, within the last year, an illegitimate child by a married man of Oxford; that the prioress was excessive in punishments and put the nuns in stocks when they rebuked her evil life; that almost all the jewels were pawned, and that there was neither food, clothing nor pay for the nuns; that one who thought of becoming a nun at Littlemore was so shocked by the evil life of the prioress that she went elsewhere. A few months afterwards the bishop summoned the prioress to appear before him, and after denying the charges brought against her, she finally admitted them; her daughter, she said, had died four years before, but she owned that she had granted some of the plate of the monastery to Richard Hewes. In her evidence she stated that though these things had been going on for eight years, no inquiry had been made, and, as it seems, no visitation of the house had been held; only, on one occasion, certain injunctions of a general kind had been sent her. As a punishment she was deposed from the post of prioress, but was allowed to perform the functions of the office for the present, provided that she did nothing without the advice of Mr Edmund Horde.

But some months later when the bishop himself made a visitation "to bring about some reformation," things were as scandalous as ever. The prioress complained that one of the nuns "played and romped (*luctando*)" with boys in the cloister and refused to be corrected. When she was put in the stocks, three other nuns broke the door and rescued her, and burnt the stocks; and when the prioress summoned aid from the neighbourhood, the four broke a window and escaped to friends, where they remained two or three weeks; that they laughed and played in church during mass, even at the elevation. The nuns complained that the prioress had punished them for speaking the truth at the last visitation; that she had put one in the stocks without any cause; that she had hit another "on the head with fists and feet, correcting her in an immoderate way," and that Richard Hewes had visited the priory within the last four months. From the evidence it is clear that the state of things was well known in Oxford, where each party seems to have had its adherents.

Several morals may be drawn from this lurid story. It shows how inadequate, in some cases, was the episcopal machinery for control and reform of religious houses. It shows that the "scandalous *comperta*" of Henry VIII's commissioners some sixteen years later were in no way untrue to type. It shows also that Wolsey was not entirely unjustified in his desire to dissolve the house and to use its revenues for educational purposes; he may have been no more disinterested than was his master later, but in the case of Littlemore at least it is difficult not to approve him.

[1] Summarised in *V.C.H. Oxon.* II, pp. 76–7.

[2] When the nuns exhorted her to abstain from his company, she replied "quod ipsum amavit et amare volet." *Linc. Epis. Reg. Visit. Atwater*, f. 87.

NOTE G.

THE MORAL STATE OF THE YORKSHIRE NUNNERIES IN THE FIRST HALF OF THE FOURTEENTH CENTURY.

It is possible to study in some detail the nunneries in the diocese of York during the first half of the fourteenth century, or roughly between the years 1280 and 1360. The Archbishops' Registers for most of the period have survived, and have either been printed or drawn upon very fully in the admirable accounts of monastic houses given in the *Victoria County History* of Yorkshire. As these accounts are not very widely known and as Yorkshire contained an unusual number of nunneries (twenty-seven) it is worth while to give some description of the state of these houses during a troubled period in their career

Reasons have been suggested elsewhere for some of the disorder which prevailed among the monastic houses of the North They were most of them both small and poor and, what is of greater significance, they lay in the border country, exposed to the forays of the Scots, and continually disturbed by English armies or raiders, riding north to take revenge. Life was not easy for nuns who might at any moment have to flee before a raid and whose lands were constantly being ravaged; they grew more and more miserably poor and as usual poverty seemed to go hand in hand with laxity Moreover the conditions of life set its stamp upon the character of the ladies from whom convents were recruited These Percies and Fairfaxes and Mowbrays and St Quintins schooled their hot blood with difficulty to obedience and chastity and the Yorkshire nunneries were apt to reflect the fierce passions of the Border, quick to love and quick to fight. There were no more quarrelsome nunneries in the kingdom, witness their election fights[1], and none in which discipline was more lax. During these sixty years nineteen out of the twenty-seven houses came before the Archbishop of York's notice, at one time or another, in connection with cases of immorality and apostasy.

It is evident at once, from a study of the registers, that seven houses, i.e , Basedale, Keldholme, Kirklees and Swine of the Cistercian order, Arthington and Moxby of the Cluniac order and St Clement, York, of the Benedictine order were in a serious condition[2]. At Basedale in 1307 the Prioress Joan de Percy was deprived for dilapidation of the goods of the house and perpetual and notorious misdeeds; whereupon she promptly left the nunnery, taking some of her partisans among the nuns with her. The Archbishop wrote to his official, bidding him warn them to return and not to go outside the cloister precincts and "in humility to take heed to the salutary monitions of their prioress", but humility dwelt not in the breast of a Percy and in

---

[1] See above, p. 58
[2] So also was Nunkeeling, where there was a particularly violent election struggle, but no mention of immorality.

1308 Joan was packed off to Sinningthwaite, "as she had been disobedient at Basedale." The troubles of the house were not ended; for
the same year Agnes de Thormond by a nun, confessed that she had on
three separate occasions allowed herself to be "deceived by the temptations of the flesh," a vivid commentary on the *régime* of Joan Percy.
In 1343 another well-born Prioress is in trouble at the house and
the Archbishop issues a commission "to inquire into the truth of the
articles urged against Katherine Mowbray and if her demerits required
it to depose her, and the commission was repeated two years later,
nothing apparently having been done[1]."

The state of Keldholme was even worse. In 1287 Archbishop
Romanus ordered the nuns to receive back an apostate, Maud de
Tiverington. In 1299 a similar order was issued on behalf of Christiania
de Styvelington. In 1308 began the violent election struggle over
Emma of York and Joan of Pickering, which has already been
described. In the course of the struggle four nuns were sent as rebels
to other convents in 1308 and two in 1309, and from the nature of
the penance imposed on the last two it would seem that they had
been guilty of immorality. In 1318 Mary de Holm, who was one of the
ejected rebels of 1308 and had been censured for disobedience to the
new prioress in 1315, was sentenced to do penance "for the vice of
incontinence committed by her with Sir William Lyly, chaplain"[2];
and in 1321, Maud of Terrington (who may be the Maud of Tiverington who apostatised in 1287), was given a heavy penance for incontinence and apostasy[3]. The history of the house during the stormy
years from 1308 to 1321 shows how far from being a home of peace
and good living a nunnery might be; and illustrates well the difficulty
of reforming it while even one incorrigible rebel and sinner such as
Mary de Holm dwelt there.

The state of Arthington was very similar. Here in 1303 Custance
de Daneport of Pontefract had apostatised and was to be received
back; trouble seems to have begun in that year, for the Prioress
Agnes de Screvyn resigned. In 1307 a visitation revealed considerable
disorder and Dionisia de Hevensdale and Ellen de Castleford were
forbidden to go outside the convent precincts. In 1312 the subprioress and convent were ordered to render due obedience to the
Prioress Isabella de Berghby, who was given Isabella Couvel as a
coadjutress. Evidently she resented having to share her authority
in temporal matters with another nun, for soon afterwards Isabella
de Berghby and Margaret de Tang are said to have cast off their
habits and left the convent. Eighteen months later a new prioress
was appointed and the two runaways returned and did penance.
In 1315 there is mention of quarrels among the nuns and in 1319
Margaret de Tang once more engaged the attention of the Archbishop
and was sent to Nunkeeling and prescribed the usual penalty for
immorality. In 1321 she was again in trouble; she had apostatised

[1] *V.C.H. Yorks.* III, p. 159.   [2] *Ib.* pp. 167–9.
[3] *Yorks. Arch. Journ.* XVI, pp. 456–7.

and committed grave misdemeanours, and was again sent back to her convent, to be imprisoned and if necessary chained there, until she showed signs of repentance In 1349 Isabella de Berghby, in spite of her past apostasy, was once more elected Prioress[1].

At Moxby, the other Cluniac house in the diocese, Archbishop Greenfield ordered the Prioress to receive back Sabina de Apelgarth, who had apostatised, but was returning in a state of penitence Her penitence was of the usual type of these Yorkshire ladies and her reputation did not prevent her from rising to the high rank in the convent, for in 1318 Archbishop Melton ordered her to be removed from office and ordained that henceforward no one convicted of incontinence was to hold any office[2]. In 1321 a penance was pronounced on Joan de Brotherton for having been twice in apostasy; but a note in the margin of the register where the penance is entered takes her history a stage further· "Memorandum quod dominus Walterus de Penbrige, stans cum domina regina, postea impregnavit eandem"[3] The next year a Scottish raid dispersed the nuns; Sabina de Apelgarth and Margaret de Neusom were sent to Nunmonkton; Alice de Barton, the Prioress, to Swine; Joan de Barton and Joan de Toucotes to Nunappleton; Agnes Ampleford and Agnes Jarkesmill to Nunkeeling, Joan de Brotherton and Joan Blaunkfront to Hampole[4] This disturbance did not improve their morals. In 1325 the Prioress Joan de Barton resigned, having been found guilty of incontinence with the inevitable chaplain The nuns could find no better successor for her than Sabina de Apelgarth and in 1328 that lady was once more in difficulties; the Archbishop removed her "for certain reasons" and imposed the usual penance for immorality and Joan de Toucotes became Prioress in her stead At the same time Joan Blaunkfront's penance was relaxed, so she too had apparently fallen; lovely and white-browed she must have been, from her name ("But sikerly she hadde a fair foreheed"), nor could she bear to hide her beauties beneath the hideous garb of a nun. Seventeen long years afterwards, when the forehead was growing wrinkled and the beauty fading, she wished to reconcile herself with the God whom she had flouted She had powerful friends and could afford to petition the Pope himself, and in 1345 Clement VI gave orders for Joan Blankefrontes, nun of Moxby, who had left her order, to be reconciled to it[5].

Kirklees, known to romance as the house where a wicked prioress bled Robin Hood to death, was in a deplorable state about the same time. In 1306 Archbishop Greenfield wrote to the house bidding them take back Alice Raggid, who, several times led astray by the temptations of the flesh, had left her convent for the world; in 1313

---

[1] *V C H Yorks.* III, pp. 187–9 A Prioress was deposed here for incontinence in 1494.

[2] *V.C.H. Yorks* III, pp 239–40

[3] *Yorks Arch Journ* XVI, pp. 457–8. Queen Isabella, wife of Edward II, is referred to.

[4] See above, p 427   [5] *Cal. of Papal Letters*, III, p. 1345.

a similar order was made for Elizabeth de Hopton. The two nuns seem, however, to have been incorrigible, for in 1315 the Archbishop wrote to the Prioress saying that public rumour had reached his ears that some of the nuns of the house, and especially Elizabeth de Hopton, Alice "le Raggede" and Joan de Heton, were wont to admit both secular and religious men into the private parts of the house and to hold many suspicious conversations with them. He forbids these or any other nuns to admit or talk with any cleric or layman save in a public place and in the presence of the Prioress, subprioress or two other nuns; and he specially warns a certain Joan de Wakefield to give up the private room, which she persists in inhabiting by herself. He refers also to the fact that these and other nuns were disobedient to the Prioress, "like rebels refusing to accept her discipline and punishment." On the same day he imposed a special penance on Joan de Heton for incontinence with Richard del Lathe and Sir Michael, "called Scot," a priest, and on the unhappy Alice Raggid for the same sin with William de Heton of Mirfield, possibly a relative of her fellow nun[1]. Here again we have an incorrigible offender, guilty of apostasy and immorality off and on during ten years. Swine was not much better. In 1289 a nun of the great St Quintin family was in disgrace, probably (though not certainly) for immorality. In 1290 there was the usual trouble over a new Prioress and Elizabeth de Rue was sent to Nunburnholme under the charge of a brother of the house and a horseman, apparently for immorality as well as contumacy. At the same time another nun, Elizabeth Darrains, had part of her penance lightened; but in 1291 she was sent away to Wykeham Priory. In 1306 John, son of Thomas the Smith, of Swine, was charged with having seduced Alice Martel, a nun of the house, and in 1310 Elizabeth de Rue (whom we have seen was in trouble twenty years before) was said to have sinned with two monks from the Abbey of Meaux. The house had evidently not improved very much at a later date, for in 1358 Alice de Cawode had twice been out in apostasy[2].

Even close to the city of York itself, the Benedictine house of St Clement's or Clementhorpe did not escape the prevalent decay of morals. In 1300 the Archbishop rehearses unsympathetically a romantic tale of how "late one evening certain men came to the priory gate, leading a saddled horse; here Cecily a nun, met them and, throwing off her nun's habit, put on another robe and rode off with them to Darlington, where Gregory de Thornton was waiting for her; and with him she lived for three years and more." In 1310 Greenfield mitigated a penance, of the kind usually imposed for immorality, upon another nun Joan de Saxton. In 1318 there is mention of Joan of Leeds, another apostate, and in 1324 the Prioress resigned after

---

[1] *Yorks. Arch. Journ.* XVI, pp. 355, 358–62. Another nun apostatised and lived a dissolute life for some time in the world, returning in 1337. *Ib.* p. 363.

[2] *V.C.H. Yorks.* III, pp. 179–81. The house was in an unsatisfactory condition as early as 1268. *Reg. Walter Giffard*, pp. 147–8.

serious trouble in the house, details of which have not been preserved.
In 1331 Isabella de Studley (who had been made a nun there by express
permission of the primate in 1315) was found guilty of apostasy and
fleshly sin, besides blasphemy and other misdeeds, she had apparently
been sent to Yedingham for a penance some time before and was
now allowed to return, with the warning that if she disobeyed, quarrelled or blasphemed any more she would be transferred permanently
to another house[1].

These houses were all clearly extremely immoral, but there is
evidence of less extreme trouble in other houses in the same diocese
At Arden Joan de Punchardon had become a mother in 1306 and
Clarice de Speton confessed herself guilty with the bailiff of Bulmer-
shire in 1311[2]. At Thicket Alice Darel of Wheldrake was an apostate
in 1303 and in 1334 Joan de Crackenholme was said to have left her
house several times[3] At Wilberfoss Agnes de Lutton was in trouble
in 1312[4] At Esholt Beatrice de Haukesward left the house pregnant
in 1303[5]. At Hampole Isabella Folifayt was guilty in 1324, and Alice
de Reygate in 1358[6]. At Nunappleton Maud of Ripon apostatised
in 1309 and in 1346 Katherine de Hugate, a nun, went away pregnant
and a lay sister was said to have been several times in the same
condition[7]. At St Stephen's, Foukeholm, a nun Cecilia, who had run
away with a chaplain, returned of her own accord in 1293 and another
apostate, Elena de Angrom, returned in 1349[8] Agnes de Bedale, an
apostate, was sent back in 1286, and in 1343 Margaret de Fenton,
who left the house pregnant, had her penance mitigated "because
she had only done so once," a startling commentary on the state of
the Yorkshire houses[9] At Rosedale an apostate Isabella Dayvill was
sent back to do penance in 1321[10]. Of Nunmonkton there is little
record during the first half of the century, but it was in a bad state
at the end[11]; at Wykeham also there seems to have been no case of
apostasy in the fourteenth century, but in the fifteenth century the
Prioress Isabella Wykeham was removed for serious immorality in
1444 and in 1450 two nuns had gone on an unlicensed pilgrimage
to Rome, which had led to one of them living with a married man
in London[12].

---

[1] V.C H. Yorks. III, pp. 129–30.
[2] Ib III, p. 113. The house seems to have been in much the same
condition later. A nun had run away in 1372 and the misdeeds of the
bad prioress Eleanor came to light in 1396 Ib 114–5
[3] Ib. p 124.   [4] Ib p. 126.
[5] Ib. p 161. In 1535 Archbishop Lee found that a nun here, Joan
Hutton, "hath lyved incontinentlie and unchast and hath broght forth a
child of her bodie begotten." Yorks Arch Journ xvi, p 453
[6] V C H Yorks III, p. 164.   [7] Ib p 164
[8] Ib p 116 and Yorks. Arch Journ IX, p. 334
[9] Ib. pp. 176–7.   [10] Ib. p. 175.
[11] Dugdale, Mon. IV, p 194; see also Cal of Pap Letters, x, p. 471.
[12] Ib. p. 183

NOTE H.

THE DISAPPEARANCE OR SUPPRESSION OF EIGHT
NUNNERIES PRIOR TO 1535.

It seems clear that even before the Dissolution proper decay was manifest in some of the smaller nunneries; numbers were dwindling and morals were not always beyond suspicion. At all events in the forty years before Henry VIII's first act of dissolution, no less than eight nunneries[1], all of which had at one time been reasonably flourishing, faded away or were dissolved. Something may, and indeed must, be allowed for the ulterior motives of those who desired the revenue of these houses; but it is impossible to suspect men like John Alcock, Bishop of Ely, John Fisher, Bishop of Rochester, even Cardinal Wolsey, of being willing without any excuse to suppress helpless nunneries in order to endow their new collegiate foundations with the spoils. Some truth there must be in the allegations of ill behaviour brought against certain of these houses; and the reduction in numbers seems to point to a decay, more spontaneous than forced.

The first of the houses thus to be dissolved was St Radegund's, Cambridge, the accounts of which we have so often quoted. In 1496 John Alcock, Bishop of Ely, visited the house and found but two sisters left there; and he thereupon obtained letters patent from Henry VII to convert the nunnery into a college, founded (like the nunnery) in honour of the Virgin, St John the Evangelist and St Radegund, but called henceforward Jesus College. Some light is thrown by these letters patent on the condition of the convent in 1496. It is therein stated that the king,

as well by the report of the Bishop as by public fame, that the priory... together with all its lands, tenements, rents, possessions and buildings, and moreover the properties, goods, jewels and other ecclesiastical ornaments anciently of piety and charity given and granted to the same house or priory, by the neglect, improvidence, extravagance and incontinence of the prioresses and women of the said house, *by reason of their proximity to the university of Cambridge*, have been dilapidated, destroyed, wasted, alienated, diminished, and subtracted; in consequence of which the nuns are reduced to such want and poverty that they are unable to maintain and support divine services, hospitality and other such works of mercy and piety, as by the primary foundation and ordinance of their founders are required; that they are reduced in number to two only, of whom one is elsewhere professed, the other is of ill-fame, and that they can in no way provide for their own sustenance and relief, insomuch as they are fain to abandon their house and leave it in a manner desolate[2].

---

[1] It may be noted that five nunneries had already disappeared between 1300 and 1500, viz. Waterbeach (transferred to Denny, 1348), Wothorpe (annexed to St Michael's, Stamford, 1354) and St Stephen's, Foukeholme, all of which owed their end to the Black Death; Lyminster (dissolved as an alien priory, 1414); and Rowney (suppressed on account of poverty, 1459).

[2] Gray, *Priory of St Radegund*, pp. 44–5. For evidence of the decay of the nunnery during the last half of the fifteenth century, see *ib*. pp. 39–44.

The next nunneries to disappear were Bromhale in Windsor Forest and Lillechurch or Higham in Kent. Their dissolution was begun in 1521 and completed in 1524, when their possessions were granted to St John's College, Cambridge, the foundation of which was then being carried out by John Fisher, Bishop of Rochester, as executor of the Lady Margaret. Only three nuns were left in Bromhale and Wolsey directed the Bishop of Salisbury to "proceed against enormities, misgovernance and slanderous living, long time heretofore had, used and continued by the prioress and nuns"[1]; but there is no further evidence as to the moral condition of the convent. The moral as well as the financial decay of Lillechurch is more certain, for the resignations of the three nuns who remained, together with the depositions of those who accused them of want of discipline, have survived. Their revenues were stated to be in great decay and divine service, hospitality and almsgiving had almost ceased. Moreover it was said that "the same priory was situated in a corner out of sight of the public and was much frequented by lewd persons, especially clerks, whereby the nuns there were notorious for the incontinence of their life," two of them having borne children to one Edward Sterope, vicar of Higham. Some witnesses were heard as to one of them, including a nurse who had taken charge of her baby and a former servant of the nunnery, who had been sent by the bishop to investigate the matter. "He entered the cloister of the aforesaid priory, where he saw the lady sitting and weeping and said to her 'Alas madam, howe happened this with you?' and she answered him, 'And [if] I had been happey [i e lucky] I myght a caused this thinge to have ben unknowen and hydden'"[2]

The next nunneries to be suppressed were a group which went to enrich Cardinal Wolsey's foundations. The Cardinal's policy of dissolving small decayed houses in order to devote their revenues to collegiate foundations, especially to his new college at Oxford, was by no means generally approved and a passage in Skelton's bitterly hostile *Colin Clout* refers particularly to the case of the nunneries

> And the selfe same game
> Begone ys nowe with shame
> Amongest the sely nonnes
> My lady nowe she ronnes,
> Dame Sybly our abbesse,
> Dame Dorothe and lady Besse,
> Dame Sare our pryoresse,
> Out of theyr cloyster and quere
> With an heuy chere,
> Must cast vp theyr blacke vayles[3]

[1] Eckenstein, *Woman under Mon.* p. 436.
[2] Dugdale, *Mon.* IV, p. 378.
[3] *Selected Poems of John Skelton*, ed W. H Williams (1902), p. 113. There is an interesting *compertum* at Dr Rayne's visitation of Studley in 1530 to the effect that "the woods of the priory had been much diminished by the late prioress and also by Thomas Cardinal of York for the construction of his College in the University of Oxford" *V C H. Oxon* II, p. 78.

The nunneries dissolved were Littlemore (1525), Wix (1525), Fairwell (1527), and St Mary de Pré, St Albans, of which all went to Cardinal College, except Fairwell, which went to Lichfield Cathedral. Of these Littlemore, under the evil prioress Katherine Wells, had been in a state of great disorder since 1517[1], while Cardinal Morton's famous letter of 1490 showed that there was at least suspicion of immoral relations between the nuns of St Mary de Pré and the monks of St Albans[2] Of the other two nunneries little is known at this time, save that they were very small; there were four nuns at Wix Another house, Davington in Kent, vanished only a few months before the act which would have dissolved it; in 1535 it was found before the escheator of the county that no nuns were left in it[3].

NOTE I.

CHANSONS DE NONNES.

THE theme of the nun in popular poetry deserves a more detailed study than it has yet received, both on account of the innate grace of the *chansons de nonnes* and on account of their persistence into modern times The earliest examples (with the exception of the two old French poems quoted in the text) occur in German literature, always rich in folk song With the song from the *Limburg Chronicle* and the Latin *Plangit nonna fletibus* should be compared the following amusing little poem

> Ich solt ein nonne werden
> ich hatt kein lust dazu
> ich ess nicht gerne gerste
> wach auch nicht gerne fru;
> gott geb dem klaffer ungluck vil
> der mich armes mägdlein
> ins kloster haben wil!
>
> Ins kloster, ins kloster
> da kom ich nicht hinein,
> da schneidt man mir die har ab,
> das bringt mir schware pein,
> gott geb dem kläffer ungluck vil
> der mich armes mägdlein
> ins kloster haben wil!
>
> Und wenn es komt um mitternacht
> das glocklein das schlecht an,
> so hab ich armes magdlein
> noch keinen schlaf getan;
> gott geb dem klaffer ungluck vil
> der mich armes magdlein
> ins kloster haben wil!

[1] See above, Note F   [2] See above, p 480.
[3] Dugdale, *Mon.* IV, p 288

Und wenn ich vor die alten kom
so sehn sie mich sauer an,
so denk ich armes magdlein
hett ich ein jungen man
und der mein stater bule sei
so war ich armes magdlein
des fasten und betens frei

Ade, ade feins klösterlein,
Ade, nu halt dich wol!
ich weiss ein herz allerliebsten mein
mein herz ist freuden vol,
nach im stet all mein zuversicht,
ins kloster kom ich nimmer nicht,
ade, feins klösterlein[11]

From the time of the Minnesingers comes a charming, plaintive
little song, which rings its double refrain on the words "Lonely"
and "O Love, what have I done?" It tells how the nun, behind a
cold grating, thinks of her lover as she chants her psalter, and how
her father and mother visit her and pray together, clad like gay
peacocks, while she is shrouded in cord and cowl; and how

At even to my bed I go—
The bed in my cell is lonely.
And then I think (God, where's the harm?)
Would my true love were in my arm!
O Love—what have I done?[2]

A thirteenth century poem, hailing from Bavaria or Austria, strikes
a more tragic note:

Alas for my young days, alas for my plaint. They would force me into a
convent Nevermore then shall I see the grass grow green and the green
clover flowers, nevermore hear the little birds sing. Woe it is, and dead is
my joy, for they would part me from my true love, and I die of sorrow.
Alas, alas for my grief, which I must bear in secret! Sisters, dear sisters,
must we be parted from the world? Deepest woe it is, since I may never
wear the bridal wreath and must make moan for my sins, when I would
fain be in the world and would fain wear a bright wreath upon my hair,
instead of the veil that the nuns wear. *Alas, alas for my grief, which I must
bear in secret!* I must take leave of the world, since the day of parting is
come I must look sourly upon all joy, upon dancing and leaping and
good courage, birds singing and hawthorn blooming. If the little birds
had my sorrow well might they sit silent in the woods and upon the green
branches. *Alas, alas for my grief, which I must bear in silence[3].*

[1] Uhland, *Alte hoch- und niederdeutsche Volkslieder* (1844–5), II, p. 854
(No. 329), also in R. v. Liliencron, *Deutsches Leben im Volkslied um* 1530
(1884), p. 226, and (in a slightly different and modernised version) in
L A v Arnim and Clemens Brentano, *Des Knaben Wunderhorn* (Reclam
edit), p 24
[2] Translated in Bithell, *The Minnesingers* (Halle, 1909), I, p. 200 I have
been unable to trace the original. I have slightly altered the wording of
the translation.
[3] Karl Bartsch, *Deutsche Liederdichter des zwölften bis vierzehnten Jahrhunderts* (4th ed Berlin, 1901), p 379 (No xcviii, ll. 581–616). Slightly
modernised version in Uhland, *op. cit.* II, p. 853 (No. 327)

A sixteenth century French song has something of the same
serious tone, though it is more sophisticated and less poignant than
the medieval German version

> Une jeune fillette
> de noble cœur
> gratieuse et honeste
> de grand valeur,
> contre son gré l'on a rendu nonette
> point ne le voloit estre
> par quoy vit en langueur

One day after Compline she was sitting alone and lamenting her fate
and she called on the Virgin to shorten her life, which she could
endure no longer·

If I were married to my love, who has so desired me, whom I have so desired,
all the night long he would hold me in his arms and would tell me all
his thought and I would tell him mine If I had believed my love and the
sweet words he said to me, alack, alack, I should be wedded now. But
since I must die in this place let me die soon O poor heart, that must die
a death so bitter! Fare you well, abbess of this convent, and all the nuns
therein Pray for me when I am dead, but never tell my thought to my
true love. Fare you well, father and mother and all my kinsfolk, you made
me a nun in this convent; in life I shall never have any joy, I live unhappy,
in torment and in pain[1].

Usually, however, the *chanson de nonne* is more frivolous than
this and all ends happily. A well defined group contains songs in
the form of a round with a refrain, meant to be sung during a dance[2].
One of the prettiest has a refrain rejecting the life of a nun for the
best of reasons·

> Derrière chez mon père
> Il est un bois taillis
> (Serai-je nonnette, oui ou non?
> Serai-je nonnette? je crois que non!)
>
> Le rossignol y chante
> Et le jour et la nuit.
> Il chante pour les filles
> Qui n'ont pas d'ami
> Il ne chante pas pour moi,
> J'en ai un, dieu mercy[3]

Another (first found in a version belonging to the year 1602) has
the dance-refrain·

---

[1] *Zeitschrift fur romanische Philologie,* v (1881), p 545 (No 28) A
slightly different version in Moriz Haupt, *Französische Volkslieder* (Leipzig,
1877), p 152.

[2] In a round the last two lines of each verse are repeated as the first
two lines of the following verse, and the refrain is repeated at the end of
each verse. The songs lose much of their charm by being quoted in com-
pressed form, for the cumulative effect of the repetition is exceedingly
graceful and spirited.

[3] Haupt, *op cit.* p 40

> Trépignez vous, trépignez,
> Trépignez vous comme moy,

and the words seem to trip of themselves:

> Mon père n'a fille que moy—
> Il a juré la sienne foy
> Que nonnette il fera de moy,
> Et non feray, pas ne voudray.
> J'amerois mieux mary avoir
> Qui me baisast la nuit trois fois.
> L'un au matin et l'autre au soir,
> L'autre a minuit, ce sont les trois[1].

Another song of the same date has the refrain:

> Je le diray,
> Je le diray, diray, ma mère,
> Ma Mère, je le diray,

and tells the same tale:

> Mon père aussi ma mère
> Ont juré par leur foy
> Qu'ils me rendront nonnette
> Tout en despit de moy.
> La partie est mal faite
> Elle est faite sans moy.
> J'ay un amy en France
> Qui n'est pas loin de moy,
> Je le tiens par le doigt
> La nuit quand je me couche
> Se met auprès de moy,
> M'apprend ma patenostre,
> Et aussi mon *ave*,
> Et encore autre chose
> Que je vous celeray.
> De peur que ne l'oublie
> Je le recorderay![2]

The passage of years never diminished the popularity of these gay little songs; age could not wither them, and when nineteenth century scholars began to collect the folk songs sung in the provinces of France, they found many *chansons de nonnes* still upon the lips of the people. In Poitou there is a round whose subject is still the old distaste of the girl for the convent:

> Dans Paris l'on a fait faire
> Deux ou trois petits couvents,
> Mon père ainsi que ma mère
> Veulent me mettre dedans.
> (Point de couvent, je ne veux, ma mère,
> C'est un amant qu'il me faut vraiment)

---

[1] Weckerlin, *L'Ancienne Chanson Populaire en France* (1887), p. 354,
[2] *Ib.* p. 319

She begs her parents to wait another year, perhaps at the end of a year she will find a lover, and she will take him quickly enough·

> Il vaut mieux conduire à vêpres
> Son mari et ses enfants,
> Que d'être dedans ces cloétres
> À faire les yeux dolents;
> À jeûner tout le carême,
> Les quatre-temps et l'avent;
> Et coucher dessus la dure
> Tout le restant de son temps.
> Serais-je plus heureuse
> Dans les bras de mon amant?
> Il me conterait ses peines,
> Ses peines et ses tourments.
> Je lui conterais les miennes,
> Ainsi passerait le temps[1]

Another round from the same district sings the plaint of a girl whose younger sister has married before her; "lads are as fickle as a leaf upon the wind, girls are as true as silver and gold, but my younger sister is being married. I am dying of jealousy, for they are sending me into a convent"

> Car moi, qui suis l'aînée
> On me met au couvent.
> Si ce malheur arrive
> J'mettrai feu dedans!
>
> (Vous qui menez la ronde,
> Menez-le rondement)[2]

Many folk-songs take the form of a dialogue between a mother and daughter, sometimes (as in two of the·rounds quoted above) preserved only in the refrain An old song taken down at Fontenay-le-Marmion contains a charmingly frivolous conversation "Mother," says the daughter of fifteen, "I want a lover." "No, no, no, my child, none of that," says her mother, "you shall go to town to a convent and learn to read " "But tell me, mother, is it gay in a convent?":

> "Dites-moi, ma mère, ah! dites-moi donc,
> Dedans ce couvent, comme s'y comporte-t-on?
> Porte-t-on des fontanges et des beaux habits,
> Va-t-on à la danse, prend-on ses plaisis?"
>
> "Non, non, non, ma fille, point de tout cela;
> Une robe noire et elle vous servira,
> Une robe noire et un voile blanc;
> Te voilà, ma fille, à l'état du couvent."

"No, mother, to a convent I will not go, never will I leave the lad I love"; as she speaks her lover enters, "Fair one, will you keep your promise?" "I will keep all the promises I ever made to you, in my youth I will keep them, it is only my mother who does not

---

[1] Bujeaud, J , *Chants et Chansons populaires des Provinces de l'ouest* (1866), I, p. 137. [2] *Ib.* I, p 132.

wish it—but all the same, do not trouble yourself, for it shall be so. My father is very gentle when he sees me cry; I shall speak to him of love and I shall soon make him see that without any more delay I must have a lover"[1]. In another of these dialogues the seventeen-year-old girl begs her mother to find her a husband. "You bold wicked girl," says the mother·

> Effrontée, hélas! que vous êtes!
> Si je prends le manche à balai,
> Au couvent de la sœur Babet
> Je te mets pour la vie entière,
> Et à grands coups de martinet
> On apaisera votre caquet!

But "Mother," says the girl, "When you were my age, weren't you just the same? When love stole away your strength and your courage, didn't you love your sweetheart so well that they wanted to put you into a convent? don't you remember, mother, that you once told me that it was high time my dear father came forward, for you had more than one gallant?" The horrified mother interrupts her, "I see very well that you have a lover"

> Mariez-vous, n'en parlons plus
> Je vais vous compter mille écus![2]

Another group of songs (in narrative form and more *banal* than the rounds and dialogues) deals with the escape from the convent. Among folk-songs collected in Velay and Forez there is one in which the girl is shut in a nunnery, whence her lover rescues her by the device of dressing himself as a gardener and getting employment in the abbess's garden[3]; and another in which a soldier returns from the Flemish wars to find his mistress in a convent and takes her away with him in spite of the remonstrances of the abbess[4]. In a version from Low Normandy (which probably goes back to the seventeenth century) the lover invokes the help of a chimney sweep, who goes to sweep the convent chimneys and pretends to be seized with a stomach-ache, so that the abbess hurries away for a medicine bottle and enables him to pass the young man's letter to his mistress; on a second visit the sweep carries the girl out in his sack, under the very nose of the reverend mother[5]. An Italian version is less artificial.

In this city there is a little maid, a little maid in love They wish to chastise her until she loves no more Says her father to her mother "In what manner shall we chastise her? Let us array her in grey linen and put her into a nunnery." In her chamber the fair maiden stood listening "Ah, woe is me,

---

[1] *Romania*, X, p. 391.   [2] *Ib.* X, p. 395 (No XLVIII).
[3] *Ib.* VII, p. 72 (No. XX). Another version in De Puymaigre, *Chants Populaires recueillis dans le Pays Messin* (1865), p. 39 (No X).
[4] *Ib* VII, p. 73 (No. XXI) Other versions in Jean Fleury, *Littérature Orale de la Basse-Normandie* (Paris, 1883), p. 311, and De Puymaigre, *op. cit.* p 35 (No. IX), and note on p 37 Compare Schiller's ballad *Der Ritter von Toggenburg.*
[5] Fleury, *op. cit* p 313.

for they would make me a nun!" Weeping she wrote a letter and when she
had sealed it well, she gave it to her serving man, and bade him bear it
to her lover. The gentle gallant read the letter and began to weep and sigh:
"I had but one little love and now they would make her a nun!" He goes
to the stable where his horses are and saddles the one he prizes most.
"Arise, black steed, for thou art the strongest and fairest of all; for one
short hour thou must fly like a swallow down by the sea." The gentle
gallant mounts his horse and spurs forward at a gallop. He arrives just
as his fair one is entering the nunnery. "Hearken to me, mother abbess,
I have one little word to say." As he spake the word to the maiden, he
slipped the ring on her finger. "Is there in this city no priest or no friar
who will marry a maiden without her banns being called?" "Goodbye to
you, Father, goodbye to you, Mother, goodbye to you all my kinsfolk.
They thought to make me a nun, but with joy I am become a bride"[1].

Another very ribald Italian folk-song of the fourteenth or fifteenth
century is specially interesting because it is founded upon Boccaccio's
famous tale of the Abbess and the breeches. It is somewhat different
from the usual nun-song; less plaintive and more indecent, as befits
its origin in a *conte gras*; it is a *fabliau* rather than a song, but it is
worth quoting:

> Kyrie, kyrie, pregne son le monache!
>   Io andai in un monastiero,
>   a non mentir ma dir el vero,
>   ov' eran done secrate:
>   diezi n' eran tute inpiate,
>   senza [dir de] la badesa,
>   che la tiritera spesa
>   faceva con un prete.
> > Kyrie, etc.
>
> Or udirete bel sermona:
>   ciascuna in chiesa andone,
>   lasciando il dileto
>   che si posava in sul leto;
>   per rifare la danza
>   ciascuno aspetta l' amanza
>   che diè retonare.
> > Kyrie, etc.
>
> Quando matutin sonava
>   in chiesa nesuna andava,
>   [poi] ch' eran acopiate
>   qual con prete e qual con frate:
>   con lui stava in oracione
>   e ciascuno era garzone
>   che le serviva bene.
> > Kyrie, etc.
>
> Sendo in chiesia tute andate,
>   e tute erano impregnate,
>   qual dal prete e qual dal frate,
>   l' una e l' altra guata;
>   ciascuna cred' esser velata
>   lo capo di benda usata;
>   avrino in capo brache.
> > Kyrie, etc.

[1] Nigra, *Canti Popolari del Piemonte* (1888), No. 80, pp. 409–14.

E l' una a l' altra guatando
si vengon maravigliando;
credean che fore celato,
alor fu manifestato
questo eale convenente:
a la badessa incontenente
ch' ognun godesse or dice.
                    Kyrie, etc.

Or ne va, balata mia,
va a quel monastiero,
che vi si gode in fede mia
e questo facto è vero,
ciascuna non li par vero,
e quale [è] la fanziulla
ciascuna si trastulla
col cul cantano kyrie
                    Kyrie, etc [1]

One characteristic form of the nun-theme has already been referred to in the text. the dialogue between the clerk and the nun, in which one prays the other for love and is refused. A terse version in which the nun is temptress exists in Latin and evidently enjoyed a certain popularity:

Nonna. Te mihi meque tibi genus, aetas et decor aequa[n]t:
        Cur non ergo sumus sic in amore pares?
Clericus. Non hac ueste places aliis nec uestis ametur:
        Quae nigra sunt, fugio, candida semper amo.
N.   Si sim ueste nigra, niueam tamen aspice carnem
        Quae nigra sunt, fugias, candida crura petas.
C.   Nupsisti Christo, quem non offendere fas est.
        Hoc uelum sponsam te notat esse Dei
N.   Deponam uelum, deponam cetera quaeque:
        Ibit et ad lectum nuda puella tuum.
C.   Si uelo careas, tamen altera non potes esse
        Vestibus ablatis non mea culpa minor.
N.   Culpa quidem, sed culpa leuis tamen ipsa fatetur
        Hoc fore peccatum, sed ueniale tamen
C.   Uxorem uiolare uiri graue crimen habetur,
        Sed grauius sponsam te uiolare Dei.
N.   Cum non sit rectum uicini frangere lectum
        Plus reor esse reum zelotypare Deum[2].

In the Cambridge Manuscript there is a famous dialogue, half-Latin and half-German, in which a clerk prays a nun to love him in springtime, while the birds sing in the trees, but she replies: "What care I for the nightingale? I am Christ's maid and his betrothed."

[1] T. Casini, *Studi di Poesia antica* (1913). There is a very racy French song called *Le Comte Orry* which deserves notice here. see H. C. Delloye, *Chants et Chansons Populaires de la France* (1re série), 1843
[2] Hagen, *Carmina Medii Aevi* (Berne, 1877), pp. 206-7. There is an exceedingly long and tedious sixteenth century French version, evidently founded on the Latin poem, in Montaiglon, *Rec. de Poésies Françoises des XVIe et XVIIe siècles*, t viii, pp. 170-5.

Almost the whole of the dialogue, in spite of the nun's irreproachable attitude, has been deleted with black ink by the monks of St Augustine's, Canterbury, who were accustomed thus to censor matter which they considered unedifying; but modern scholars have been at infinite pains to reconstruct it[1].

It is rare to find in popular songs the idea of the convent as a refuge for maidens crossed in love; but some pretty poems have this theme. In a sixteenth century song a girl prefers a convent, if she cannot have the man she loves best, but she wishes her lover could be with her there:

> Puis que l'on ne m'at donne
> A celuy que j'aymois tant,
> avant la fin de l'annee
> quoy que facent mes parens,
> je me rendray capucine
> capucine en un couvent.
>
> Si mon amis vient les feste
> a la grille regardant,
> je luy feray de la teste
> la reverence humblement
> come pauvre capucine;
> je n'oserois aultrement.
>
> S'il se pouvait par fortune
> se couler secretement
> dedans ma chambre sur la brune,
> je lui dirois mon tourment
> que la pauvre capucine
> pour luy souffre en ce couvent.
>
> Mon dieu, s'il se pouvoit faire
> que nous deux ensemblement
> fussions dans ung monastere
> pour y passer nostre temps,
> capucin et capucine
> nous vindrions tous deux content.
>
> L'on me vera attissee
> d'ung beau voille de lin blanc;
> mais je seray bien coiffee
> dans le cœur tout aultrement,
> puis que l'on m'a capucine
> mise dedans ce couvent.
>
> N'est ce pas une grand raige
> quand au gre de ses parens
> il faut prendre en mariaige
> ceulx qu'on n'ayme nullement?
> j'ameroy mieulx capucine
> estre mise en ce couvent[2].

---

[1] *The Cambridge Songs*, ed. Karl Breul (1915), No. 35, p. 16. See also Koegel, *Geschichte der Deutschen Litteratur* (1897), I, pp. 136–9.
[2] *Zeitschrift für romanische Philologie*, v (1881), p. 544, No. 27. Also in Weckerlin, *op. cit.* p. 405 (under date 1614).

Somewhat similar is the song (first printed in 1640) of the fifteen
year-old girl married to a husband of sixty·

> M'irai-je rendre nonette
> Dans quelque joly couvent,
> Priant le dieu d'amourette
> Qu'il me donne allegement
> Ou que j'aye en mariage
> Celuy là que j'aime tant?[1]

A round, with the refrain

> Ah, ah, vive l'amour!
> Cela ne durera pas toujours,

goes with a delightful swing:

> Ce matin je me suis levée
> Plus matin que ma tante;
> J'ai descendu dans mon jardin
> Cueillire la lavande.
> Je n'avais pas cueilli trois brins
> Que mon amant y rentre;
> Il m'a dit trois mots en latin:
> Marions nous ensemble
> —Si mes parents le veul' bien,
> Pour moi je suis contente.
> Si mes parents ne le veul' pas
> Dans un couvent j'y rentre.
> Tous mes parents le veul' bien,
> Il n'y a que ma tante.
> Et si ma tante ne veut pas
> Dans un couvent je rentre
> Je prierai Dieu pour mes parents
> Et le diable pour ma tante![2]

In another song, with the refrain

> Je ne m'y marieray jamais
> Je seray religieuse,

the girl laments her own coyness which has lost her her lover[3].
Sometimes, on the other hand, it is the lover's falseness which drives
her to enter a convent. In a song, which first occurs about 1555,
the maiden laments "qu'amours sont faulses".

> Je m'en iray rendre bigotte
> Avec les autres,
> Et porteray le noir aussi le gris
> (sont les couleurs de mon loyal amy)
> si porteray les blanches patenostres
> comme bigotte[4].

---

[1] Rolland, *Rec. de Chansons Populaires*, II, p 81.
[2] *Ib* I, pp 226–7.
[3] Weckerlin, *op cit* p 355
[4] Haupt, *Französische Volkslieder* (1877), p. 84 A slightly different
version in Weckerlin, *op. cit.* p. 297.

In another very graceful little ditty the lover goes through the world
in rain and wind, seeking his true love and finds her at last in a green
valley.

> Je luy ay dit "doucette,
> où vas tu maintenant?
> (m'amour)"
> "m'en vois rendre nonnette
> (helas)
> en un petit couvent.
>
> Puis que d'aultre que moy
> vous estes amoureux.
> (m'amour)
> qui faict qu'en grand esmoy
> (helas)
> mon cœur soit langoureux.
>
> Helas, toute vestue
> je seray de drap noir
> (m'amour)
> monstrant que despourveue
> (helas)
> je vis en desespoir"[1].

Moreover the convent also plays its part in that numerous class
of folk songs, which tells of the discomfiture of a too bold gallant
by the wits of a girl. An early example occurs in 1542:

> L'autrier, en revenant de tour
> Sus mon cheval qui va le trou,
>   Par dessoubs la couldrette
>   L'herbe y croit folyette.
>
> Je m'en entray en ung couvent
> Pour prendre mes esbatemens.
> Par ung petit guinchet d'argent
>   Je vis une nonnette,
>   Vray Dieu, tant jolyette
>
> Dessoubz les drabs quand je la vys
> Blanche comme la fleur du lys,
> Je masseitys aupres du lit
>   En lui disans nonnette
>   Serez vous ma miette?
>
> Chevallier, troup me detenez,
> D'en faire a vostre voulente
> Si m'en laissez ung peu aller,
>   Tant que je soye parée,
>   Tost seray retournée
>
> Sire chevallier, rassemblez
> A l'ésperirer vous resemblez,
> Qui tient la proye enmy ses pieds
>   Et puis la laisse enfuire
>   Ainsi faictes vous, sire.

---

[1] Haupt, op. cit. p. 63

La nonnette sı s'en alla
A son abbesse racompta
Là en ces boıs a ung musart
　　Qui d'amour m'a priée,
　　Je luy suıs eschappée

Le chevallıer ıl demeura
Soulz la branche d'ung olıvıer
　　Attendant la nonnette—
　　Encore y peust ıl estre !¹

Folk-songs, like flowers, spring up—or perhaps are transplanted—in the same form ın different lands and under different skies; they laugh at polıtıcal divisions and are a living monument to the solıdarıty of Europe Thus a song taken down from the lıps of a Pıedmontese *contadına* ın the nineteenth century is almost exactly the same as the sıxteenth century French poem just quoted, even to such details as the olıve and the fowler

Gentıl galant cassa'nt el bosc,
S'è rıscuntrà-se'nt una múnıa,
L'era tan bela, fresca e brunda.
Gentıl galant a ı'à ben dıt:
— Setè-ve sì cun mi a l'umbreta,
Maı pı vıu sarl mumıgheta.
　— Gentıl galant, spetei-me sì,
Che vada pozè la tunıcheta
Poı turnrò con vuı a l'umbreta —
A l'à spetà-la tre dì tre nóit
Sut a l'umbreta de l'olıva.
E maı pı la múnıa venıva
Gentıl galant va al munastè,
L'à pıca la porta grandeta;
J'e sortì la madre badessa.
　— Coza cerchei-vo, gentil galant?
　— Mı ma cerco na munıghcta,
Ch'a m'à promess d'avnì a l'umbreta.
　— J'avıe la quaja dnans aı pè,
V'la sì lassà-v-la vulè vıa.
Cozi l'à faìt la múnıa zolıa².

¹ Weckerlin, *op cıt* p 262; also ın E Rolland, *Rec. de Chansons Populaıres* (1883–90), t. ıı, p. 36
² "A gentle gallant went hunting in the wood and there he met a nun. She was so lovely, so fresh and so faır. Said the gentle gallant to her: 'Come, sıt with me ın the shade and never more shalt thou be a lıttle nun ' 'Gentle gallant, waıt here for me; I wıll go and put off my habıt and then I wıll come back to you ın the shade.' He waıted for her three days and three nıghts and never came the faır one. The gentle gallant goes to the monastery and knocks at the great door; out comes the mother abbess. 'What are you lookıng for, gentle gallant?' 'I am lookıng for a little nun, who promised to come ınto the shade.' 'You once had the quaıl at your feet and you let ıt fly away. Even so has flown the pretty nun '" Nıgra, *Cantı Popuları del Pıemonte* (1888), No 72, p 381 With these two songs should be compared the English poem ın Percy's *Relıques*, called *The*

Another version, still sung in many parts of France, is called *The Ferry Woman*. In this a girl ferrying a gentleman from court across a stream, promises him her love in return for two thousand pounds, but bids him wait till they land and can climb to the top room of a house. But when the gallant leaps ashore she pushes off her boat, taking the money with her and crying· "Galant, j't'ai passé la rivière:

> Avec ton or et ton argent
> Je vais entrer dans un couvent,
> Dans un couvent de filles vertueuses
> · Pour être un jour aussi religieuse!
>
> "Si je passe par le couvent,
> J'irai mettre le feu dedans,
> Je brûlerai la tour et la tournière
> Pour mieux brûler la belle batelière"[1]

Occasionally the references to nuns in folk-songs have even less significance. Thus one of the metamorphoses gone through by the girl, who (in a very common folk theme) assumes different shapes to elude her lover, is to become a nun

> "Si tu me suis encore
> Comme un amant
> Je me ferai nonne
> Dans un couvent,
> Et jamais tu n'auras
> Mon cœur content."
>
> "Si tu te fais nonne
> Dans un couvent
> Je me ferai
> Moine chantant
> Pour confesser la nonne
> Dans le couvent"[2]

Baffled Knight or Lady's Policy, and the Somerset folksong, *Blow away the morning dew*, with its *dénouement*:

> But when they came to her father's gate
> So nimble she popped in,
> And said "There is a fool without
> And here's the maid within.
>
> We have a flower in our garden
> We call it marygold—
> And if you will not when you may
> You shall not when you wolde."

Folk Songs from Somerset (1st Series, 1910), ed Cecil Sharp and Charles Marson, No. VIII, pp. 16–17.

[1] Fleury, *op. cit.* p 308   Other versions in De Puymaigre, *op cit* pp 145–8 (Nos XLV–XLVI)

[2] Rolland, *op cit* IV, p 31. Cf. versions on pp. 30, 32, 33. The theme recalls a pretty poem by Leigh Hunt:

> If you become a nun, dear,
> A friar I will be,

Again in *Le Canard Blanc* occur the question and answer:

> Que ferons nous de tant d'argent?
> Nous mettrons nos filles au couvent
> Et nos garçons au régiment.
> Si nos fill's ne veul' point d'couvent
> Nous les marierons richement[1]

One very curious song deserves quotation, a Florentine carnival song of the time of Lorenzo the Magnificent, written by one Guglielmo called *Il Giuggiola*. It retails the woes of some poor "Lacresine" or "Lanclesine" who have come to Rome on a pilgrimage and been robbed of all their money on the way, and the ingenious suggestion has been made that "Lacresine" is a corruption of "Anglesine" and that the song is supposed to be sung by English nuns; certainly it is in broken Italian, such as foreigners would use:

> Misericordia et caritate
> Alle pofer Lacresine
> Che l'argente pel chammine
> Tutt'a spese et consumate.
>
> Del paese basse Magne,
> Dove assai fatiche afute
> Tutte noi pofer compagne
> Per ir Rome sian fenute.
> Ma per tanto esser piofute,
> Non pofer Lanclesine.
>
> Nelle parte di Melane
> State noi mal governate,
> Che da ladri et gente strane
> Nostre robe star furate,
> Talche noi tutte bitate
> [Non mai più far tal chammine.]
> Pero pofer Lanclesine
> Buon messer dà caritate.

> In any cell you run, dear,
> Pray look behind for me
> The roses all turn pale, too;
> The doves all take the veil, too;
> The blind will see the show
> What! you become a nun, my dear?
> I'll not believe it, no!
>
> If you become a nun, dear,
> The bishop Love will be;
> The Cupids every one, dear,
> Will chant "We trust in thee."
> The incense will go sighing,
> The candles fall a-dying,
> The water turn to wine;
> What! you go take the vows, my dear?
> You may—but they'll be mine!

[1] Rolland, *op. cit.* 1, p. 253, cf. pp. 249–54

Queste pofer Nastasie
Le fu tutte rotte stiene
Talchè sue gran malattie
Per vergognia sotto tiene.
Cosl zoppe far conviene
Con fatiche suo chammine
Però pofer Lanclesine
Buon messer dà caritate.

Chi è dijote San Branchatie
Che star tant' in ciel potente,
Per afer sue sancte gratie
Voglia a noi donare argente,
Che le pofer malcontente
Pessin compier lor chammine,
Però pofer Lanclesine
Buon messer dà caritate[1].

"Pity and charity for poor English ladies, who have spent and used up all their money on the road. From the land of low Germany, where we have had great difficulties, all we poor sisters are on our way to Rome, but because it has rained so hard, we have not been able to continue our road. *Therefore, good sirs, give alms to us poor English ladies.* In the district of Milan ill-used were we, for thieves and strangers stole all our goods; so buffetted were we, never again will we go on such a journey. *Therefore, good sirs, give alms to us poor English ladies.* Poor Anastasia was so knocked about, that in shame she hides her ill and must needs continue her road limping. *Therefore, good sirs, give alms to us poor English ladies.* Whoever is a devotee of St Pancras, who is so powerful in heaven, whoever wishes to have his grace, let him give us money, so that we poor miserable creatures may get to our journey's end; *therefore, good sirs, give alms to us poor English ladies.*"

Sometimes the nun is found playing a part in the romantic ballad-literature of Europe. A Rhineland legend of the dance of death, interesting because it embodies the names and dates of the actors, has for its setting a convent; it is thus summarised by Countess Martinengo-Cesaresco[2]:

In the fourteenth century Freiherr von Metternich placed his daughter Ida in a convent on the island of Oberwörth, in order to separate her from her lover, one Gerbert, to whom she was secretly betrothed. A year later the maiden lay sick in the nunnery, attended by an aged lay sister. "Alas!" she said "I die unwed though a betrothed wife." "Heaven forfend!" cried her companion, "then you would be doomed to dance the death-dance." The old sister went on to explain that betrothed maidens who die without having either married or taken religious vows, are condemned to dance on a grassless spot in the middle of the island, there being but one chance of escape, the coming of a lover, no matter whether the original betrothed

---

[1] *Chants de Carnaval Florentins (Canti Carnascialeschi) de l'époque de Laurent le Magnifique.* Pub. par P. M. Masson (Paris, 1913). For a copy of the song and for the suggestion that it refers to English nuns I am indebted to Mr E. J. Dent of King's College, Cambridge. But the mention of Low Germany sounds more like German nuns.

[2] Countess Martinengo-Cesaresco, *Essays in the Study of Folksongs* (Everyman's Lib. Ed.), pp. 191–2.

or another, with whom the whole party dances round and round till he dies; then the youngest of the ghosts makes him her own and may henceforth rest in her grave The old nun's gossip does not delay the hapless Ida's departure, and Gerbert, who hears of her illness on the shores of the Boden See, arrives at Coblenz only to have tidings of her death He rows over to Oberwörth; it is midnight in midwinter. Under the moonlight dance the unwed brides, veiled and in flowing robes; Gerbert thinks he sees Ida among them He joins the dance; fast and furious it becomes, to the sound of a wild unearthly music. At last the clock strikes and the ghosts vanish—only one, as it goes, seems to stoop and kiss the youth, who sinks to the ground. There the gardener finds him on the morrow, and in spite of all the care bestowed upon him by the sisterhood, he dies before sundown.

Another German ballad, taken down from oral recitation, at the beginning of the nineteenth century, opens with a good swing·

> Stund ich auf hohen bergen
> Und sah ich uber den Rhein
> Ein Schifflein sah ich fahren,
> Drei Ritter waren drein.

"I stood upon a high mountain and looked out over the Rhine, and I saw three knights come sailing in a little boat. The youngest was a lord's son, and fain would have wed me, young as he was. He drew a little golden ring from off his finger, "Take this, my fair, my lovely one, but do not wear it till I am dead " "What shall I do with the little ring, if I may not wear it?" "O say you found it out in the green grass " "O that would be a lie and evil. Far sooner would I say that the young lord was my husband." "O maiden, were you but wealthy, came you but of noble kin, were we but equals, gladly would I wed you." "Though I may not be rich yet am I not without honour, and my honour I will keep, until one who is my equal comes for me." "But if your equal never comes, what then?" "Then I will go into a convent and become a nun." There had not gone by a quarter of a year when the lord had an evil dream; it seemed to him that the love of his heart was gone into a convent. "Rise up, rise up, my trusty man, saddle horses for thee and me. We will ride over mountains and through valleys—the maid is worth all the world." And when they came to the convent, they knocked at the door of the tall house, "Come forth, my fair, my lovely one, come forth for but a minute " "Wherefore should I come forth? Short hair have I, my locks they have cut off—for a long year has passed." Despair filled the lord's heart, he sank upon a stone and wept glittering tears and could never be glad again. With her snow-white little hands she dug the lord a grave and the tears fell for him out of her brown eyes And to all young men this happens who seek after great wealth They set their love upon beautiful women; but beauty and riches go not always hand in hand[1].

It is a strange thing that in all the ballad and folk-song literature of England and Scotland there should be one and only one reference to a nun. But that reference is a profoundly interesting one, for it is to be found in the fine ballad of the *Death of Robin Hood*, which

---

[1] L. A. v. Arnim und Clemens Brentano, *Des Knaben Wunderhorn* (Reclam ed.), p. 50.

tells how the great outlaw came to his end through the treachery
of the Prioress of Kirklees·

> When Robin Hood and Little John
> *Down a-down, a-down, a-down,*
> Went o'er yon bank of broom
> Said Robin Hood to Little John,
> "We have shot for many a pound.
> *Hey down, a-down, a-down.*
>
> "But I am not able to shoot one shot more,
> My broad arrows will not flee;
> But I have a cousin lives down below,
> Please God, she will bleed me."
>
> "I will never eat nor drink," he said,
> "Nor meat will do me good,
> Till I have been to merry Kirkleys
> My veins for to let blood.
>
> "The dame prior is my aunt's daughter,
> And nigh unto my kin;
> I know she wo'ld me no harm this day
> For all the world to win."
>
> "That I rede not," said Little John,
> "Master, by th' assent of me,
> Without half a hundred of your best bowmen
> You take to go with yee."
>
> "An thou be afear'd, thou Little John,
> At home I rede thee be "
> "An you be wrath, my deare master
> You shall never hear more of me."
>
> Now Robin is gone to merry Kirkleys
> And knocked upon the pin,
> Up then rose Dame Prioress
> And let good Robin in.
>
> Then Robin gave to Dame Prioress
> Twenty pounds in gold,
> And bade her spend while that did last,
> She sho'ld have more when she wo'ld
>
> "Will you please to sit down, cousin Robin;
> And drink some beer with me? "—
> "No, I will neither eat nor drink
> Till I am blooded by thee."
>
> Down then came Dame Prioress
> Down she came in that ilk,
> With a pair of blood-irons in her hand,
> Were wrappèd all in silk.
>
> "Set a chafing dish to the fire," she said,
> "And strip thou up thy sleeve "
> —I hold him but an unwise man
> That will no warning 'leeve

> She laid the blood-irons to Robin's vein,
>   Alack the more pitye!
> And pierc'd the vein, and let out the blood
>   That full red was to see.
>
> And first it bled the thick, thick blood,
>   And afterwards the thin,
> And well then wist good Robin Hood
>   Treason there was within.
>
> And there she blooded bold Robin Hood
>   While one drop of blood wou'd run,
> There did he bleed the livelong day,
>   Until the next of morn.

Then Robin, locked in the room and too weak to escape by the casement, blew three weak blasts upon his horn, and Little John came hurrying to Kirklees and burst open two or three locks and so found his dying master. "A boon, a boon!" cried Little John.

> "What is that boon," said Robin Hood
>   "Little John, thou begs of me?"—
> "It is to burn fair Kirkleys-hall
>   And all their nunnerye"
>
> "Now nay, now nay," quoth Robin Hood,
>   "That boon I'll not grant thee,
> I never hurt woman in all my life,
>   Nor men in their company."
>
> "I never hurt maid in all my time,
>   Nor at mine end shall it be;
> But give me my bent bow in my hand,
>   And a broad arrow I'll let flee;
> And where this arrow is taken up
>   There shall my grave digg'd be[1]"

So died bold Robin Hood. The English boy nurtured on his country's ballads, has little cause to love the memory of the nun

[1] *The Oxford Book of Ballads*, ed. Quiller-Couch (1910), p 635 (No 125) In the long collection of ballads narrating Robin Hood's career known as *A Little Geste of Robin Hood and his Meiny* (which was in print early in the sixteenth century) the Prioress is said to have conspired with her lover, one Sir Roger of Doncaster, to slay Robin   *Ib* p. 574   In the version in Bishop Percy's famous folio MS. "Red Roger" is described as stabbing the weakened outlaw, but losing his own life in the act   *Bishop Percy's Folio MS.* ed. Hales and Furnivall (1867), 1, pp 50–58 "In 'Le Morte de Robin Hode,' a quite modern piece printed in Hone's *Every-day Book* from an old collection of MS. songs in the Editor's possession, the prioress is represented as the outlaw's sister and as poisoning him " *Ib* p. 53.

NOTE J.

THE THEME OF THE NUN IN LOVE IN MEDIEVAL POPULAR LITERATURE

It may be of interest to note some further examples of the nun in love as a theme for medieval tales, and in particular (1) other versions of the eloping nun theme, (2) the story of the abbess who was with child and was delivered by the Virgin, and (3) some other *contes gras.*

(1) Various versions of the eloping nun tale enjoyed popularity, though never as great popularity as was enjoyed by the story of Beatrice the Sacristan An old French version in the form of a miracle play tells of a knight, who loved a nun and persuaded her to leave her convent with him; but she saluted the Virgin's image in passing and twice the image descended from its pedestal and barred her way when she tried to pass the door, until at last she ran by without saluting it and escaped with her lover They married and had two children and lived happily together for several years Then one day Our Lady came down from heaven to seek her faithless friend She bade the nun return and the husband, hearing this, was moved in his heart and said "since for love of me thou didst leave thy convent, for love of thee I will leave the world and become a monk." Thus they departed together and their babies were left to cry for mother and father in vain[1]

In another story the nun, trying to insert the key of the convent into the lock and make her escape, was prevented by some invisible object, which formed a barrier between her and the lock, she beat and pushed in vain and at last turned to go, and saw in her path, the Virgin with white hands bleeding "Behold," said the Virgin, "it was I who withstood thee and see what thou hast done to me"[2] In another a nun, the sacristan of a convent, was tempted by a clerk and agreed to meet him after Compline But when she was trying to pass through the door of the chapel, she saw Christ standing in the arch, with hands outspread, as though upon the cross She ran to another doorway and to another and to another, but in each she found the crucifix. Then, coming to herself, she recognised her sin and flung herself before an image of the Virgin to ask pardon. The image turned away its face; then, as the trembling nun redoubled her entreaties, stretched out its arm and dealt her a buffet saying. "Foolish one, whither wouldst thou go? return to thy dorter." And so powerful was the Virgin's blow that the nun was knocked down thereby and lay unconscious upon the floor of the chapel until

---

[1] *Miracles de Nostre Dame par Personnages*, pub. G Paris and U. Robert (Soc des Anc Textes Français, 1876), t I, pp 311–51.

[2] Translated in Evelyn Underhill, *The Miracles of Our Lady Saint Mary* (1905), pp 195–200

morning[1]. In another version the nun falls asleep on the night upon which the elopement is fixed and has a vivid dream of the pains of hell, from which she is rescued by the Virgin, who exhorts her to chastity, so that she awakes and sends away her lover's messenger[2] In another the Virgin's image prevents the nun from going through one door, but she escapes by another and is seduced[3]. A more rational version makes the nun strike her head so violently against the lintel of the door, by which she is trying to escape, that she is rendered unconscious and when she recovers her senses the temptation has gone from her and she returns to her bed[4]. In another the nun packs her clothes into two bundles and passes them out of the window to her lover, climbing out after them herself; but thieves intercept her and her bundles and carry them off into a wood The unhappy nun calls upon the Virgin for help and forthwith falls into a deep sleep, from which she awakes to find herself back in her dorter, with the bundles beside her[5]. A rather different tale of the nun turned courtesan makes her return after many years to her convent, where by meditating upon the childhood of Christ she is reconverted[6]

(2) Another theme, which is almost as widespread as that of the eloping nun, is that known as *l'abbesse grosse*. In this an abbess, who was famed for the strict discipline which she kept among her nuns, fell in love with her clerk and became his mistress, so that she soon knew herself to be with child

Then it happened that she waxed great and drew near her time and her sisters the nuns perceived, and were passing fain thereof, because she was so strait unto them, that they might have a cause to accuse her in. And her accusers gart write unto the bishop and let him wit thereof and desired him to come unto their place and see her. So he granted and the day of him coming drew near. And this abbess, that was great with child, made mickle sorrow and wist never what she might do; and she had a privy chapel within her chamber, where she was wont daily as devoutly as she couth [knew how] to say Our Lady's matins. And she went in there and sparred the door unto her and fell devoutly on knees before the image of Our Lady and made her prayer unto her and wept sore for her sin and besought Our Lady for to help her and save her, that she were not shamed when the bishop came. So in her prayers she happened to fall on sleep, and Our Lady, as her thought, appeared unto her with two angels, and comforted her and said unto her in this manner of wise. "I have heard thy prayer and I have gotten of my son forgiveness of thy sin and deliverance of thy

[1] Caesarius of Heisterbach, II, pp. 41–2. "Although the buffet was hard," says Caesarius, conscious perhaps that the Virgin had acted with less than her wonted gentleness, "she was utterly delivered from temptation by it. A grievous ill requires a grievous remedy."

[2] Gautier de Coincy, *Miracles de N.D*, ed. Poquet, p. 474.

[3] *Exempla of Jacques de Vitry*, ed Crane, p 24 See variant in *An Alphabet of Tales* (E E T S), p 321

[4] Caesarius of Heisterbach, *Dial Mirac*. ed. Strange, I, pp. 222–3.

[5] Wright, *Latin Stories*, p. 96.

[6] Etienne de Bourbon, *Anecdotes Historiques*, ed. Lecoy de la Marche, p. 83 (translated in Taylor, *The Medieval Mind*, I, pp. 508–9).

confusion." And anon she was delivered of her child and Our Lady charged these two angels to have it unto an hermit and charged him to bring it up unto it was seven years old; and they did as she commanded them, and anon Our Lady vanished away. And then this abbess wakened and felt herself delivered of her child and whole and sound.

In the sequel the bishop came to the house and could find no sign that the abbess was with child and was about to punish her accusers, when she told him the whole tale He sent messengers to the hermit and there the child was found; and (in fairy tale phrase, for what are these but religious fairy tales), they all lived happy ever afterwards[1].

(3) Ribald stories on the same theme are, naturally enough, common in medieval literature, which never spared the Church A few of the more interesting may here be added to those quoted or referred to in the text. The *Cento Novelle Antiche* contains a curious tale of a Countess and her maidens, who, having disgraced themselves with a porter, retired to hide their shame in a nunnery, the story continues thus.

They became nuns and built a convent that is called the Convent of Rimini. The fame of this convent spread and it became very wealthy And this story is narrated as true, viz they had a custom that when any cavaliers passed by that had rich armour the abbess and her attendants met them on the threshold and served them with all sorts of good fare and accompanied them to table and to bed In the morning they provided them with water for washing and then gave them a needle and thread of silk for them to thread and if they could not accomplish this in three tries, she took from them all their armour and accoutrement and sent them away empty, but if they succeeded she allowed them to retain their possessions and gave them presents of jewellery, etc.[2]

Francesco da Barberino in his book of deportment, *Del reggimento e costumi di donne*, has a tale of a convent in Spain, which Satan receives permission to tempt; accordingly his emissary Rasis sends into the house three young men, disguised as nuns, to whom all the

---

[1] I have used the version in *An Alphabet of Tales* (E.E T S), pp 11-12. For other versions, see *Miracles de Nostre Dame* (Soc. des Anc Textes) I, pp. 59-100 For other versions, see Etienne de Bourbon, *op cit.* p. 114, Wright, *op cit.* p 114, Barbazon et Méon, *Nouveau Recueil de Fabliaux*, II, p 314, *Dodici conti morali d'anonimo Senese Teste inedite del sec XIII* (Bologna, 1862), No 8, Small, *Eng Metrical Homilies*, p 164 There is a very interesting Ethiopian version (told of Sophia the abbess of Mount Carmel) in *Miracles of the B V M* (Lady Meux MSS), ed. E. A. Wallis Budge (1900), pp 68-71 Most versions preserve the interesting detail that the nuns dislike their abbess and are anxious to betray her on account of her strictness and particularly because she will not give them easy licence to see their friends. In the French dramatic version Sister Isabel stays away from a sermon and gives as her excuse that a cousin came to see her, with some cloth to make a veil and a "surplis," whereupon she is scolded and then pardoned by the Abbess

[2] *Le Cento Novelle Antiche*, ed. Gualteruzzi (Milan, 1825), No. 62 I quote the translation by A. C. Lee, *The Decameron, its Sources and Analogues*, p. 60.

nuns and the Abbess in turn succumb[1] In one Italian version of an extremely widespread theme, found among the *Novelle* of Masuccio Guardata da Salerno (1442–1501), a Dominican friar deceives a devout and high-born nun. The story is thus summarised by A C Lee

In one of her books of devotion were some pictures of saints, amongst others the third person of the Trinity, from the mouth of this figure he makes proceed the words in letters of gold, "Barbara, you will conceive of a holy man and give birth to the fifth evangelist" He acts as the holy man and on the lady becoming *enceinte* he deserts her[2].

Among medieval French stories may be mentioned those which occur in *Les Cent Nouvelles Nouvelles*, a fifteenth century collection of tales, probably written by Antoine de la Sale in imitation of the *Cento Novelle* No. XV, concerning the relations between two neighbouring houses of monks and nuns respectively, is too gross to be summarised, No XXI is the story of the sick abbess, who was recommended by her physician to take a lover and out of respect for her all her nuns did the same; No. XLVI is one of the many tales of a Jacobin friar, who haunted a convent and obtained the favours of a nun[3] These are really prose fabliaux, and verse fabliaux on this theme are not wanting, for example Watriquet Brassenal's story of *The Three Canonesses of Cologne*[4] and the most indecent fabliau of *The Three Ladies*[5] There is a rather delightful and merry little German poem called *Daz Maere von dem Sperwaere*, which is a version of the popular French fabliau of *The Crane*[6] In this thirteenth century poem a little nun, who has never seen the world, looks over her convent wall and sees a knight with a sparrow hawk, she begs for it and he says he will sell it her for "love," a thing of which she has never heard. He teaches her what it is and gives her the sparrow hawk. But the nun, her schoolmistress, is so angry with her, that she watches on the wall again and next time the knight passes, she makes him give her back her "love" and take the sparrow hawk again[7].

English versions of these tales are extremely rare; for the English were always less adroit than the French and the Italians in the matter of *contes gras*. The nun theme occasionally appears, however, in the sixteenth century, Boccaccio's "breeches" story is in Thomas Twyne's *The Schoolmaster* (1576)[8] and the behaviour of nuns and "friars" at

---

[1] Francesco da Barberino, *Del Reggimento e Costumi di Donne*, ed Carlo Baudi di Vesme (Bologna, 1875), p. 273. See A C Lee, *loc. cit.*

[2] A. C. Lee, *op. cit* p 125. The story is of Eastern origin and for its many analogues see *ib.* pp 123–35.

[3] *Les Cent Nouvelles Nouvelles*, ed Th. Wright (Bib Elzévirienne, 1858), t. I, pp. 81–4, 114–20, 283–7.

[4] Montaiglon et Raynaud, *Rec. Gén. des Fabliaux*, III, pp. 137–44.

[5] *Ib.* IV, pp. 128–32.

[6] Barbazon et Méon, *Nouv Rec de Fabliaux*, IV, p 250.

[7] *Erzählungen und Schwänke*, hrsg. von Hans Lambel (Leipzig, 1888), No. VIII, pp. 309–22.

[8] Koeppel, *Studien zur Geschichte der italienischen Novelle in der englischen Litteratur des XVI Jahrhunderts* (1892), p 183.

Swineshead Abbey forms a comic interlude in *The Troublesome Raigne
of King John* (1591), which was one of the sources used by Shakespeare
in his more famous play. In Scene x of the old play Philip Falcon-
bridge comes to Swineshead, with his soldiers, and bids a friar show
him where the abbot's treasure is hid They break open a chest and
a nun is discovered inside it The friar cries

> Oh, I am undone
> Fair Alice the nun
> Hath took up her rest
> In the Abbot's chest.
> *Sante benedicite,*
> Pardon my simplicity
> Fie, Alice, confession
> Will not salve this transgression.

Philip remarks

> What have we here? a holy nun? so keep me God in health,
> A smooth-faced nun, for aught I know, is all the abbot's wealth.

The nuns begs for the life of the first friar and offers in exchange to
show Philip a chest containing the hoard of an ancient nun They
pick the lock and discover a friar within The first friar cries·

> Friar Laurence, my lord;
> Now holy water help us:
> Some witch or some devil is sent to delude us:
> *Haud credo, Laurentius,*
> That thou shouldst be pen'd thus
> In the press of a nun:
> We are all undone,
> And brought to discredence,
> If thou be Friar Laurence.

Philip's comment is pertinent.

> How goes this gear? the friar's chest fill'd with a sausen nun.
> The nun again locks friar up to keep him from the sun.
> Belike the press is purgatory, or penance passing grievous·
> The friar's chest a hell for nuns! How do these dolts deceive us?
> Is this the labour of their lives, to feed and live at ease?
> To revel so lasciviously as often as they please?
> I'll mend the fault, or fault my aim, if I do miss amending,
> 'Tis better burn the cloisters down than leave them for offending

Eventually, Friar Laurence buys his freedom for a hundred pounds[1].

In conclusion may be mentioned the entertaining little English
fabliau, which was at one time attributed to Lydgate, called *The Tale
of the Lady Prioress and her three Suitors*, this is not a *conte gras*, but
recounts the adroit expedient, by which a prioress succeeded in ridding
herself of her three wooers, a knight, a parson and a merchant[2]

---

[1] *King John by William Shakespeare together with the Troublesome Reign
of King John*, ed. F G Fleay (1878), pp 158-62
[2] Printed in *A Selection from the Minor Poems of Dan John Lydgate*, ed.
J O Halliwell (Percy Soc 1840), pp 107-17 Professor MacCracken denies
the authorship to Lydgate, see *The Minor Poems of John Lydgate*, ed.
H N. MacCracken (E E T S 1911), I, p xlii (note)

NOTE K.

NUNS IN THE *DIALOGUS MIRACULORUM* OF CAESARIUS OF HEISTERBACH

THE *Dialogus Miraculorum*, written between 1220 and 1235 by Caesarius, Prior and Teacher of the Novices in the Cistercian Abbey of Heisterbach in the Siebengebirge, is one of the most entertaining books of the middle ages[1] Caesarius in a prologue describes how it came to be written and the plan upon which it is arranged, taking as his text a quotation from John vi. 12 "Gather up the fragments lest they perish".

Since I was wont to recite to the novices, as in duty bound, some of the miracles which have taken place in our time and daily are taking place in our order, several of them besought me most instantly to perpetuate the same in writing For they said that it would be an irreparable disaster if these things should perish from forgetfulness which might be an edification to posterity. And since I was all unready to do so, now for lack of the Latin tongue, now by reason of the detraction of envious men, there came at length the command of my own abbot, to say naught of the advice of the abbot of Marienstatt, which it is not lawful for me to disobey Mindful also of the aforesaid saying of the Saviour, while others break up whole loaves for the crowd (that is to say, expound difficult questions of the Scriptures or write the more signal deeds of modern days) I, collecting the falling crumbs, from lack not of good will but of scholarship, have filled with them twelve baskets. For I have divided the whole book into as many divisions The first division tells of conversion, the second of contrition, the third of confession, the fourth of temptation, the fifth of demons, the sixth of the power of simplicity, the seventh of the blessed Virgin Mary, the eighth of divers visions, the ninth of the sacrament of the body and blood of Christ, the tenth of miracles, the eleventh of the dying, the twelfth of the pains and glories of the dead Moreover in order that I might the more easily arrange the examples, I have introduced two persons in the manner of a dialogue, to wit a novice asking questions and a monk replying to them. I have also inserted many things which took place outside the [Cistercian] order, because they were edifying, and like the rest had been told to me by religious men God is my witness that I have not invented a single chapter in this dialogue If anything therein perchance fell about otherwise than I have written it, the fault should rather be imputed to those who told it to me[2].

It will be seen from this sketch that the book is really a collection of stories grouped round certain subjects which they are intended to illustrate and connected by a slender thread of dialogue. Such

---

[1] The edition used is that of Joseph Strange in two volumes (Cologne, Bonn and Brussels, 1851). For a study of the life and times of Caesarius, see A Kaufmann, *Caesarius von Heisterbach, Ein Beitrag zur Kulturgeschichte des zwölften und dreizehnten Jahrhunderts* (Cologne, 1850). For anecdotes from this source already quoted in the text, see pp 27–9, 296–7, 511, 520 ff , etc.

[2] *Op cit* I, pp. 1–2

collections of *exempla* are nearly always valuable, but the work of Caesarius is particularly so, because he does not confine himself to "stock" stories, but relates many with details of time and place, drawn from his own experience and from that of his friends The book is full of local colour and gives an exceedingly vivid picture of lay and ecclesiastical life in medieval Germany For our purpose it is interesting because it contains many *exempla* concerning nuns, and any reader attracted by this particular class of didactic literature may be glad to add some more stories to those quoted in the text.

Caesarius has much to say of the devil, a very visible and audible and tangible devil and one who can be smelt with the nose His tales of devil-haunted nuns display a side of convent life about which English records are in the main silent; but that they represent with fair accuracy the sufferings of some half-hysterical, half-mystical women cannot be doubted by anyone familiar with the lives of medieval saints and mystics, such as Mary of Oignies, Christina of Stommeln and Lydwine of Schiedam He tells in his section on "Confession" of a nun Alice or Aleidis, who had led an ill life in the world, but had repented her when her lover, a priest, hanged himself, and had taken the veil at Langwaden in the diocese of Cologne

Once when she was standing in the dorter and looking out of the window, she beheld a young man, nay rather a devil in the form of a young man, standing hard by a well, which was near the wall of the dorter, who in her sight set one foot upon the wooden frame which surrounded the well, and as it were flying with the other, conveyed himself to her in the window, and tried to seize her head with his extended hand; but she fell back stricken with terror and almost in a faint, and cried out and hearing her call, her sisters ran to her and placed her upon her bed And when they had gone away again and she had recovered her breath and lay alone, the demon was once more with her, and began to tempt her with words of love, but she denied him, understanding him to be an evil spirit. Then he answered "Good Aleidis, do not say so, but consent to me, and I will cause you to have a husband, honest, worthy, noble and rich. Why do you torture yourself with hunger in this poor place, killing yourself before your time by vigils and many other discomforts? Return to the world and use those delights which God created for man; you shall want for nothing under my guidance " Then said she, "I grieve that I followed thee for so long, begone for I will not yield to thee."

Then the foul fiend blew with his nostrils and spattered her with a foul black pitch and vanished. Neither the sign of the cross, nor sprinkling with holy water, nor censing with incense prevailed against this particular demon; he would retreat for a time and return again as soon as Aleidis ceased to employ these weapons against him She was in despair, when one day

One of the sisters, of maturer years and wisdom than the others, persuaded her when the demon tried to approach her to hurl the angelic salutation[1]

---

[1] I.e "*Ave Maria, gratia plena.*" The Virgin Mary was always the most potent help against the devil, as may be seen from any collection of her miracles (e.g. that made by Gautier de Coincy in French verse in the thirteenth century and edited by the Abbé Poquet)

in a loud voice in his face; and when she had done so the devil, as though struck by a dart or driven by a whirlwind, fled away and from that hour never dared to approach her.

Another time the same Aleidis went to confession, hoping thus to rid herself forever of her tormentor.

And behold as she was hastening along the road, the devil stood in her path and said "Aleidis, whither away so fast?" And she replied. "I go to confound myself and thee" Then said the devil: "Nay, Aleidis, do not so! Turn again!" And she replied· "Oft hast thou put me to confusion, now will I confound thee. I will not turn back" And when he could turn her back neither by blandishments nor by threats, he followed her to the place of confession flying in the air above her in the form of a kite, and as soon as she bent her knee before the Prior and opened her lips in confession, he vanished, crying and howling and was never seen or heard by her from that hour Behold here ye have a manifest example of what virtue lieth in a pure confession These things were told to me by the lord Hermann, Abbot of Marienstatt[1].

In his section "De Daemonibus" Caesarius has a yet more startling collection of stories about devils. The trials of sister Euphemia are described as having been related to him by the nun herself, at the instance of her abbess.

When the aforesaid nun was a little maid in her father's house, the devil ofttimes appeared to her visibly in divers shapes, and in divers ways affrighted and saddened her tender age And since she feared to be driven mad she expressed her wish to be converted[2] into our order One night the devil appeared to her in the form of a man and tried to dissuade her, saying: "Euphemia, do not be converted, but take a young and handsome husband and with him thou shalt taste the joys of the world Thou shalt not want for rich garments and delicate meats But if thou enter the order, thou wilt be forever poor and ragged, thou wilt suffer cold and thirst, nor will it ever be well with thee henceforth in this world" To which she replied: "How would it be with me if I should die amidst those delights, which thou dost promise me?" To these words the devil made no reply, but seizing the maid and carrying her to the window of the chamber wherein she was lying, he sought to throw her out And when she said the angelic salutation the enemy let her go, saying, "If thou goest to the cloister, I will ever oppose thee For hadst thou not in that hour called upon *that woman* I should have slain thee" And having spoken thus, squeezing her tightly, he sprang out of the window in the shape of a great dog and was seen no more Thus was the virgin delivered by invoking the Virgin Mother of God. How harassing the devil is to those who have been converted and in how many and divers ways he vexes and hinders them, the following account shall show When the aforesaid maiden had been made a nun, one night as she lay in her bed and was wakeful, she saw around her many demons in the form of men And one of them of aspect most foul was standing at her head, two at her feet and the fourth opposite her. And he cried in a loud voice to the others· "Why are you standing still? Take her wholly up as she lies and come" And they replied. "We cannot. She has called upon *that woman*." Now the same demon, after she had said the

---

[1] *Ib* I, pp 125–7. For an abbreviated version of this story, taken from Caesarius, see *An Alphabet of Tales* (E E T S), pp. 178–9 (No ccLv)

[2] Used in the common medieval sense of entering a religious order

angelic salutation, seized the maiden by her right arm, and squeezed her so tightly as he dragged at it, that his grasp was followed by a swelling and the swelling by a bruise Now when she had her left hand free, she in her great simplicity dared not make the sign of the cross therewith, deeming that a sign with the left hand would avail her nought. But now, driven by necessity, she signed herself with that hand, and put the demons to flight Delivered from them she ran half fainting to the bed of a certain sister, and, breaking silence, told her what she had seen and suffered Then, as I was informed by the lady Elizabeth of blessed memory, abbess of the same convent, the sisters laid her in her bed, and reading over her the beginning of the Gospel of St John, found her restored on the morrow Now in the following year, in the dead of night when the same nun was lying awake on her couch, she saw at a distance the demons in the shape of two of the sisters who were most dear to her, and they said to her "Sister Euphemia, arise, come with us to the cellar to draw beer for the convent " But she suspecting them, both on account of the lateness of the hour and of their breach of silence, began to tremble, and, burying her head in the bedclothes, replied nothing Straightway one of the malignant spirits drew near and laying hold of her breast with his hand, squeezed it until the blood burst forth from her mouth and nose Then the demons, taking the shape of dogs, leaped out of the window. When the sisters, rising for matins, beheld her worn out, as it were pale and bloodless, they inquired of her the reason by signs, and when they had learned it from her, they were much perturbed, both on account of the cruelty of the demons and of the distress of the virgin Two years before this, when a new dorter had been made for the convent and the beds had been placed therein, the same nun saw a demon in the shape of a deformed and very aged mannikin, going round the whole dorter and touching each of the beds, as though to say. "I will take careful note of each place, for they shall not be without a visit from me "[1]

The abbey of Hoven, which sheltered Euphemia, seems to have been subjected to a continual siege by devils, or perhaps, as the more maternally-minded might suggest, Euphemia's malady was contagious Sister Elizabeth of the same house had a short way with such gentry.

"In the same monastery," says Caesarius, "was a nun named Elizabeth, who was oftentimes haunted by the devil One day she saw him in the dorter, and since she knew him, she boxed his ears Then said he 'Wherefore dost thou strike me so hardly?' and she replied· 'Because thou dost often disturb me,' to which the devil replied 'Yesterday I disturbed thy sister the chantress far more, but she did not hit me.' Now she had been much agitated all day, from which it may be gathered that anger, rancour, impatience, and other vices of the sort are often sent by the devil On another

[1] *Ib* I, pp 328-30 At the end of this story the novice asks· "Why is it that the good Lord allows maidens so tender and so pure to be thus cruelly tormented by rough and foul spirits?" And the monk replies "Thou hast experienced how if a bitter drink be first swallowed a sweet one tastes the sweeter, and how if black be placed beneath it, white is all the more dazzling Read the Visions of Witinus, Godescalcus and others, to whom it was permitted to see the pains of the damned and the glory of the elect, and almost always it was the vision of punishment which came first The Lord, wishing to show his bride his secret joys, permitteth well that she should first be tempted by some dreadful visions, that afterwards she may the better deserve to be made glad, and may know the distance between sweet and bitter, light and darkness "

occasion when the same Elizabeth, very late for matins (owing, as afterwards appeared, to the machinations of the devil), was hurrying along to
the belfry, bearing a lighted candle in her hand, just as she was about to
enter the door of the chapel, she saw the devil in the shape of a man,
dressed in a hooded tunic, standing in front of her. Thinking that some man
had got in, she recoiled in alarm and fell down the dorter stairs, so that for
some days she lay ill of the sudden fright as well as of the fall . And when
she was asked the cause of her fall and her scream and had expounded
this vision, she added 'If I had known that it was the devil and not a
man, I would have given him a good cuff ' By that time, however, she had
girded her loins with strength and strengthened her arm against the devil "[1].

Not all the visions seen by these nuns of whom Caesarius writes
were evil visions He has several tales to tell of appearances of the
Virgin Mary and of the saints Besides the well-known story of
Sister Beatrice and of the nun whose ears were boxed by the Virgin,
the most charming Mary-miracle related by Caesarius tells of a nun
who genuflected with such fervour to the blessed Mother that she
strained her leg; and as she lay asleep in the infirmary, she saw before
her the Virgin, bearing a pyx of ointment in her hand; and the Virgin
anointed her knee with it, till the sweet odour brought the sisters
running to find out the cause; but the nun held her peace and bade
them leave her Sleeping again, she found herself once more in the
company of the Virgin, who led her into the orchard, and

placing her hand beneath the nun's chin, said to her, "Now do thou kneel
down upon thy knee"; and when she had done so our Lady added. "Henceforth do thou bow thy knee thus, modestly and in a disciplined manner,"
showing her how. And she added "Every day thou shouldst say to me
the sequence 'Ave Dei Genitrix,' and at each verse thou shouldst bow thy
knee. For I take great delight therein " And the nun, waking, looked upon
her knee, to see whether aught had been accomplished in the vision, and in
great surprise she saw that it was whole[2].

Another pretty story tells how, when a certain sister was reading
her psalter before a wooden statue of the Virgin and child, "the
little boy suddenly came to her and as though he would know what
she was reading, peeped into her book and went back again "[3]
Sometimes it is not the Virgin or her Son but a patron saint who

[1] *Ib* i, pp 330–31.
[2] *Ib*. ii, pp 68–9. "As I infer from this vision," says the Novice, "an
indiscreet fervour in prayers is not pleasing to the blessed Virgin, neither
an undisciplined movement in genuflections " On the other hand she did
not like her devotees to hurry over their prayers, for Gautier de Coincy has
a tale of a nun, Eulalie, who was accustomed to say at each office of the
Virgin the full rosary of a hundred and fifty *Aves*, but she had much work
to do and often hurried over her prayers, till one night she saw a vision of
the mother of God, who promised her salvation and told her that the *Ave
Maria* was a prayer which gave herself much joy, therefore she bade
Eulalie not to hurry over it, but of her bounty permitted her to say a
chaplet of fifty *Aves*, instead of the long rosary See Gautier de Coincy,
Les Miracles de la Sainte Vierge, ed Poquet (Paris, 1857)
[3] *Ib*. ii, p. 100

appears to a nun who holds him in veneration. Caesarius tells the
following tale of a nun who specially venerated St John the Baptist.
More than all the saints she took delight in him Nor did it suffice her to
think upon him, to honour him with prayers and devotions, to declare his
prerogatives to her sisters, but in order to perpetuate his memory she made
verses concerning his annunciation and nativity and the joy of his parents.
For she was learned and sought therefore to describe in verse anything
which she had read concerning his sanctity Moreover she exhorted and
besought all secular persons with whom she spoke to call their children
John or Zacharias, if they were boys, Elizabeth if they were girls. Now
when she was about to die John a monk of the Cloister came to visit her,
and knowing her affection towards St John, said. "My aunt, when you are
dead, which mass would you have me say first for your soul, the mass for
the dead or of St John the Baptist?" To which she without any hesitation
replied "Of St John, of St John!" And when she was at the point of
death, having compassion upon the sister who was tending her, she said
"Go upstairs, sister, and rest for a little " When the sister had done so
and was resting in a light sleep, she heard in her slumber a voice saying,
"Why liest thou here? St John the Baptist is below with Sister Hildegunde"—
for that was her name Roused by this voice the sister, not waiting to
put on her clothes, came down in her shift and found the nun already dead;
and round her was so sweet a perfume that the sister doubted not that St
John had been there, to accompany the soul of his beloved to the angelic
host[1].

Some of Caesarius' anecdotes show an amusing rivalry, if not
among the company of heaven, at least among their votaries on
earth. Two delightful stories may be quoted to show how deep-rooted
is the competitive instinct, which, baulked in one direction by the
prohibition of property, showed itself in hot disputes as to the rival
merits of patron saints

There were and I think still are, in Fraulautern in the diocese of Trèves,
two nuns, of whom one took special delight in St John the Baptist and the
other in St John the Evangelist. Whenever they met, they contended together concerning which was the greater, so that the mistress was scarce able
to restrain them The one declared the privileges of her beloved in the presence of all, the other set up against them the very real prerogatives of hers

One night, however, before matins St John the Baptist appeared to
his worshipper in her sleep and set forth a list of the virtues of the
other St John, declaring that the latter was far greater than he, and
bidding her the next morning call her sister before the mistress and
seek her pardon for having so often annoyed her because of him
That morning after matins, however, St John the Evangelist also
visited his champion in her sleep and after retailing all St John the
Baptist's claims to superiority, assured her that the latter was far
greater and gave her a similar order to ask pardon of her sister

"On the morrow," says Caesarius, "they came separately to the mistress
and revealed what they had seen Then together prostrating themselves
and asking pardon of each other as they had been bidden, they were
reconciled by the mediation of their spiritual mother, who warned them

1 *Ib.* II, pp 121-2

that henceforth they should not contend about the merits of the saints, which are known to God alone"[1]

In spite of this excellent moral, however, Caesarius has very clear ideas himself as to the respective merits of certain saints, and, if we are to believe him, even St John the Evangelist was sometimes guilty of a scandalous neglect of duty·

"It is not long ago," says he, "that a certain nun of the monastery of Rheindorf near Bonn, by name Elizabeth, went the way of all flesh. Now this monastery is of the rule of St Benedict the Abbot But the said Elizabeth delighted specially in St John the Evangelist, lavishing on him all the honour she could. She had a sister in the flesh in the same monastery, who was called Aleidis. One night when the latter was sitting upon her bed after matins and saying the office of the dead for the soul of her sister, she heard a voice near her And when she demanded who was there, the voice replied, 'I am Elizabeth, thy sister' Then said she, 'How is it with thee, sister, and whence comest thou?' and it answered, 'Ill indeed has it been with me, but now it is well' Aleidis asked, 'Did St John in whom thou didst so ardently delight avail thee aught?'—and it replied, 'Truly, naught It was our holy father Benedict who stood by me For he bent his knee on my behalf before God"[2].

St John the Evangelist, it will be perceived, suffered from the incalculable disadvantage of never having thought of founding a monastic order.

Caesarius narrates a great many other *exempla* concerning nuns, but I have quoted the most characteristic There never was a book so full of meat, and it is greatly to be regretted that no translation has as yet placed it within the reach of all who are interested, not only in medieval life but in the medieval point of view[3]

[1] *Ib* II, pp 122–3 For a variant in which the place of the two nuns is taken by two doctors of divinity, see *An Alphabet of Tales* (E E.T S), pp. 274–5

[2] *Ib* II, pp. 343–4. With these holy rivalries should be compared Caesarius' tales of the drawing of apostles by lot. "It is a very common custom among the matrons of our province to choose an Apostle for their very own by the following lottery: the names of the twelve Apostles are written each on twelve tapers, which are blessed by the priest and laid on the altar at the same moment Then the woman comes and draws a taper and whatsoever name that taper shall chance to bear, to that Apostle she renders special honour and service A certain matron, having thus drawn St Andrew, and being displeased to have drawn him, laid the taper back on the altar and would have drawn another; but the same came to her hand again Why should I make a long story? At length she drew one that pleased her, to whom she paid faithful devotion all the days of her life, nevertheless when she came to her last end and was at the point of death, she saw not him but the Blessed Andrew standing at her bedside 'Lo,' he said, 'I am that despised Andrew!' from which we can gather that sometimes saints thrust themselves even of their own accord into men's devotions." Another matron was so much annoyed at drawing St Jude the Obscure instead of a more famous Apostle that she threw him behind the altar chest, whereupon the outraged Apostle visited her in a dream and not only rated her soundly but afflicted her with a palsy. See *ib* II, pp 129, 133, translated in Coulton, *A Medieval Garner*, pp. 259–60

[3] Several of the stories have, however, been translated by Mr Coulton, *op. cit.* Nos. 102–32.

APPENDIX II

VISITATION OF NUNNERIES IN THE DIOCESE OF ROUEN BY ARCHBISHOP EUDES RIGAUD, 1248–1269

FOR twenty-seven years in the thirteenth century the Archbishopric of Rouen was held by a man who was at once a scholar and a man of action, a great saint and a great reformer Eudes Rigaud (Odo Rigaldi), "the Model of Good Life," as he was afterwards called, was among the most able and energetic churchmen produced by the middle ages Salimbene, that gossiping friar of Parma to whom we owe perhaps the most entertaining chronicle of all the middle ages, describes him thus·

> Now this Brother Rigaud was of our order [Franciscan] and one of the most learned men in the world He had been doctor of theology in the convent [at Paris]: being a most excellent disputator and a most gracious preacher. He wrote a work on the Sentences, he was a friend of St Louis, King of France, who indeed laboured that he might be made Archbishop of Rouen He loved well the Order of the Friars Preachers, as also his own of the Friars Minor and did them both much good, he was foul of face but gracious in mind and works, for he was holy and devout and ended his life well, may his soul, by God's mercy, rest in peace[1]

This great scholar, with an admirable devotion to duty, renounced for ever the leisure of a man of books, and spent his life, from the moment that he became Archbishop, in a ceaseless peregrination of his diocese, and by a dispensation of providence (so the historian must think) he kept a diary For twenty-one years (1248–1269) he moved about from parish to parish, from monastery to monastery, inquiring into the life and discipline of secular and of regular clergy alike, hearing complaints, giving injunctions, removing (though seldom) offenders, and making notes of the results of his visits, place by place and day by day, in his great *Regestrum Visitationum*[2]. His diocese was in a bad state; and his discouragement sometimes found its way into the official record of his inquisitions The few words which betray his feelings, together with the particularity and detail with which the visits are recorded, make the register of Eudes Rigaud a very human document.

---

[1] Translated in Coulton, *From St Francis to Dante* (1907), p 290, see *ib* pp. 289–91, for a short account of Eudes Rigaud, also references on p 395 (n 17)

[2] *Regestrum Visitationum Archiepiscopi Rothomagensis*, ed Bonnin (1852). See analysis by L Delisle in the *Bibliothèque de l'École des Chartes*, 1846

It would be beyond the scope of this book to enter into any discussion of the general picture of the medieval church which it leaves upon the mind But it is both useful and interesting to detach those parts of it which deal with the nunneries visited and reformed (with varying success) by the Archbishop In the first place the records of his visitations, though not as complete as those of the visitations of the Lincoln diocese by Bishop Alnwick in the early fifteenth century, or of the diocese of Norwich by Bishops Goldwell and Nykke, during the late fifteenth and early sixteenth centuries, or of the Sede Vacante visitations of the Winchester diocese by Dr Hede in 1502, are nevertheless a great deal more detailed than any series of English visitation records of an equally early date The report of Walter Giffard's visitation of Swine in 1267-8, which comprises both the *comperta* and the injunctions based upon them, is indeed fuller than any of Rigaud's notes, which contain only *comperta* and *ad interim* injunctions[1], but this is an isolated case. The only other thirteenth century documents at all comparable with those of Rigaud are Peckham's injunctions to Barking (1279), Godstow (1279 and 1284), Wherwell (1284) and Romsey (? 1284), and Wickwane's injunctions to Nunappleton (1281) and these are the final injunctions only, the *comperta* upon which they were based having disappeared There is, so far as it is possible to ascertain, no English register of the thirteenth century recording regular visitations of all the nunneries in a diocese over a period of years and the study of Rigaud's register is therefore of unique interest In the second place it is of special interest to English readers because of the close connection which at one time existed between the religious houses of England and Normandy. Most of the alien priories in England were cells of Norman houses and several of the nunneries visited by Rigaud had possessions in England Stour in Dorset was a cell of St Léger de Préaux, founded by Roger de Beaumont as early as William I's reign[2] Levenestre or Lyminster in Sussex was founded some time before 1178 as a cell of Almenêches probably by Roger de Montgomery Earl of Arundel, to whom the mother house owed its foundation and was apparently the only alien priory in England in which a community of nuns actually resided during the later middle ages

[1] There is however a copy of the Bishop's letter of injunctions, sent on later, appended to his report of the state of Villarceaux in 1249 (*Reg* pp. 44-5).

[2] Walcott, M. E C, *English Minsters. II (The English Student's Monasticon)*, pp 210 and *V C H Dorset*, II, p 48

[3] *V C H Sussex*, II, p 121 and Dugdale, *Mon* VI, pp 1032-3 The later history of this cell can be traced from occasional references It was a very small house and contained only a prioress and two nuns in 1380. Dugdale says that after the French wars Richard Earl of Arundel treated with the Abbess of Almenêches for the purchase of some lands belonging to Lyminster and in 1404 a papal brief enumerated the possessions of Almenêches in England and elsewhere, with a threat of penalties against all who should disturb them. Dugdale, *Mon.* VI, pp. 1032-3. Five years later a memorandum in the

In 1255 Almenèches possessed twenty-five marks of annual rent in England[1]. The great Abbaye aux Dames at Caen had two cells in England, Horstead in Norfolk (which afterwards became part of the endowment of King's College, Cambridge, and was founded in William II's reign[2]) and Minchinhampton in Gloucestershire (afterwards cell of Syon)[3] In Rigaud's day this house had rents to the value of £160 sterling in England[4] and at the visitation of 1256 the Abbess did not appear, because she was absent there[5]. French moreover was still the language of daily speech in thirteenth century England, and there was constant intercourse between the two countries. It is not unreasonable to expect that we may learn something to our purpose by a comparison of French and English nunneries

The Register includes visitations of fourteen religious houses of women[6]. Seven of these were visited with great regularity during the twenty-one years covered by the Register; the Priory of St Saens fourteen times, the abbey of Bival and the priory of St Aubin each thirteen times, the abbey of Montivilliers twelve times, the abbeys of Villarceaux and St Amand of Rouen each eleven times and the priory of Bondeville ten times. Of the others the abbeys of St Léger de Préaux and St Désir de Lisieux (both in the diocese of Lisieux) and St Sauveur of Evreux each received four visits and the abbeys of St Mary of Almenèches and the Holy Trinity of Caen three   Two other houses, St Paul by Rouen (a dependent cell of Montivilliers) and Ariete (a very poor and small Benedictine house), appear to have been visited only once. For the most part these nunneries were large houses, often having lay sisters and sometimes lay brothers attached to them. The Archbishop made very careful notes of the temporal affairs of each and generally entered in his Register the number of nuns and lay sisters and often also the number of secular maidservants in the employ of each house The largest of all was the Abbaye aux Dames or Holy Trinity at Caen, "one of the great nunneries of Christendom", in Rigaud's time its numbers ranged between sixty-

---

Register of Bishop Rede of Chichester notes the admission of a new Prioress, Nichola de Hereez, on the presentation of the Abbess and Convent of Almenèches, in place of Georgete la Cloutiere, deceased Reg Robert Rede (Sussex Rec Soc 1908), pp 38–9 Clearly French women were ruling over the house, though the nuns may possibly have been English Shortly afterwards Henry V finally dissolved the alien priories in England and the lands belonging to Lyminster were settled by Henry VI upon Eton College

[1] Reg p 236
[2] Walcott, op cit p 141 and V C H. Norfolk, II, p 463, and Dugdale, op. cit p 1057.
[3] Walcott, op. cit. p 173.   [4] Reg p 94
[5] Ib p 261 In 1314–5 the Abbess of the Holy Trinity petitioned the King of England, complaining that she had been distrained in aid of the marriage of his eldest daughter, whereas she held all her lands in frank almoin Rot Parl. I, p. 331.
[6] Irrespective of double houses such as the Magdalen of Rouen

five and eighty St Sauveur of Evreux and Montivilliers both contained at least sixty nuns and the other houses were all comparatively large, with the exception of St Saens, Villarceaux, St Aubin and Ariete Even these, however, were large compared with some of the small nunneries in England.

The financial condition of many of these houses was very bad, and there is evidence both of the poverty and of the bad management which seem to have been characteristic of nunneries everywhere The care with which Rigaud entered into his diary, at almost every visitation, the debts owed by a house and the condition of its stores, makes it possible to follow with some ease the financial progress of the nunneries from year to year. Some houses were evidently in a flourishing condition, the abbey at Caen' was very rich and never in difficulties (its debts were suddenly assessed at the huge sum of £1700 in 1267 but at the previous visitations it had been stated that more was owed to the nuns than they owed). Montivilliers was also well managed and in a good condition, here again the debts due to it were larger than those which it owed, and on several occasions the Archbishop found a good round sum in the treasury, a plentiful supply of stores and some valuable plate, which the nuns had been rich enough to purchase recently Similarly St Désir de Lisieux and St Léger de Préaux, though debts are mentioned, were evidently living well within their respective incomes of £500 and £700 (in rents) But the other houses display a lamentable list of debts growing heavier and heavier. In spite of St Amand's income of £1000 to £1200, its debts rose from £200 in 1248 to £900 in 1269. Almenèches, with an income of a little over £500, had debts to the amount of £500 in 1260. Bondeville obviously had a quite insufficient income (it was given as £93 in 1257), on three occasions its debts reached the sum of £140 and on two other occasions they were £200 and £250 St Saëns, St Aubin, Bival and Villarceaux (it is significant that these are the houses whose moral record was bad) were always in difficulties. Bival went steadily from bad to worse, its debts rose from £40 in 1251 to £60 in 1268 and in 1269 they had exactly doubled themselves (£120) since the previous visitation. The debts of St Saens rose from £60 in 1250 to £100 in 1269; and in 1260 they stood at £350 At Villarceaux (the income of which was placed at £100 in 1249) the debts ranged between £30 in 1251 and £100 in 1264 and 1265 At St Aubin the actual sums of money owed by the nuns were small, ranging between £5 and £40 (except in 1257 when their debts were assessed at £1000, which is probably a mistake), but the house was evidently in grave financial straits When even a wealthy house such as St Sauveur of Evreux could not keep out of debt (the amount owed by it varied from £200 to £600), one cannot wonder that smaller and poorer houses were deeply involved Occasionally the diary throws some light on special causes of impoverishment; thus the nuns of St Amand were in debt to the large sum of £400 in 1254 and the reason given was "on account of a conduit (*aqueductum*), which they had to make again, because it was needed"[1], St Sauveur of Evreux was burdened with the payment of about £40 in pensions[2], and in 1263 the nuns of St Aubin complained that they owed some £20 "for a certain ferm (or payment) by which they held themselves to be greatly burdened"[3]

Other evidence besides that of debts is not wanting to show that some of the houses were in great financial straits. The Archbishop constantly gave poverty as a reason for limiting the number of nuns, e g at St Aubin, Bival and Villarceaux[4] At Almenèches poverty was given as a reason for the imperfect observance of the rule[5] At St Saens (1262) and at Villarceaux (1264) the roofs of the monastic buildings were in need of repair[6], in the latter year the roofs of the buildings at St Aubin were *male cooperte* also and that of the nave of the church was so bad that the nuns could hardly stay there in rainy weather[7]. Bondeville was so badly in need of repairs in 1257 that it was said that £80 would not suffice for the work[8] Sometimes the devices by which the nuns strove to gain a little ready money are noted down in Rigaud's diary. At Villarceaux in 1254 a book of homilies and some silken copes were in pledge to the Prior of Serqueu[9], at Bival in 1269 the old abbess had pledged a chalice which the new abbess was ordered to redeem[10]; and at Bondeville in 1257 the nuns had pawned two chalices "for their needs"[11] When they tried to borrow money outright matters were even worse, at Villarceaux in 1266, Rigaud notes, "they owed £100, of which £20 was owed to the Jews and Caursini (*Caiturcensibus*) of Mantes at usury"[12]. Sometimes they were reduced to selling part of their property, as at St Saens, where they sold a wood at Esquequeville[13], and at Bondeville, where they parted with land to the value of £300[14]. But they were apparently bad women of business, for at the latter house in 1257 the Archbishop complained that they had pledged a certain tithe for £75 for three years, whereas its real value was £40 per annum[15]; and in 1256 it transpired that the nuns of Bival had given up the manor of Pierremains (without Rigaud's consent) to a certain Master William of the Fishponds (*de Vivariis*) for £50, while it was really worth £140[16] Perhaps the difficulty found by so many of the houses in collecting the debts due to them may be set down in part to the incompetence of the nuns At St Amand, for instance, in 1262, as much as £377 7s seems to have been owing to the nuns at a time when they themselves were £142 in debt, and at the next two visitations complaint was made of debts (described in 1264 as "bad" debts, *debitis male solubilibus*) owing to them[17] Other nunneries were from time to time owed large

[1] *Reg.* p 202   [2] p 73.
[3] p 471.   [4] E.g pp 43, 207, 323, 351.   [5] pp. 235, 374.
[6] pp 451, 490   [7] p 194   [8] p 299.
[9] p 194.   [10] pp. 636-7   [11] p 298.
[12] p 572.   [13] p. 419.   [14] p. 298.
[15] p. 298.   [16] p 268.
[17] pp 456, 486, 512

sums of money, religiously recorded by Rigaud in his diary. The case of St Saens illustrates this difficulty particularly well, in 1261 the nuns had sold part of their wood at Esquequeville for £350 and had received £240 of the total sum owing to them; the next year the £110 left owing had swelled with interest to £160; in 1264 £40 was said to be owing on the same sale and £55 on a sale of fallen trees and wood (*de caablo*), but in 1267 the Archbishop noted, "A great sum of money is to come to them from the sale of woods," and in 1269 the amount still owing on the sale had risen with interest to £100, while £80 was owing to the nuns from another source[1]

Another instance of the incompetence of the nuns was their laxity in the matter of keeping accounts, in which the Rouen nuns were in no way exceptional. At Caen, in 1250 Rigaud wrote·

They do not know how much they have in rents and they say that more is owed to them than they owe, neither do they know the state of the monastery; but the Abbess accounts in her chamber before several nuns annually elected for this purpose, and the account is announced in the chapter before them all, and they said that this was quite sufficient for them.

The Archbishop appears to have obtained a statement of their rents by some means and he contented himself with confirming the arrangement that the Abbess should account annually to certain nuns elected *ad hoc*[2] Certainly when the head of the house was competent there was no need for the convent to know the details of administration, but sometimes even the head was unable to inform Rigaud of those details At Villarceaux in 1258 he wrote: "They did not know how much they owed and they were somewhat ignorant of the state of the house"[3], and in the following year the Prioress of St Saens was found to be an incompetent administrator and was ordered to draw up an account, which two neighbouring priors were deputed to hear[4] At St Amand in 1262 the Abbess had not prepared a proper account, so that the Archbishop was unable to get full information as to the state of the house, he noted however that the nuns believed that more was owing to them than they owed, and he ordered the Abbess to inspect her papers and to certify him concerning the state of the house[5] On several other occasions he ordered her to account more often (on one of these it had transpired that she had not done so for three years) before the elder nuns, and to call in the Prioress, Subprioress or one of these *maiores* to help her[6]. At Villarceaux in 1253 the Prioress did not account and in 1254 a coadjutress was appointed to assist her[7]. Sometimes Rigaud ordered the income of a house to be written down in rolls, or in books[8] Sometimes he provided

[1] pp. 419, 451, 491, 598, 634   [2] p. 94.
[3] p 323   [4] p 338   [5] p 456.
[6] pp. 16, 121, 201, 326, 512, 588   [7] pp. 166, 194.
[8] E g at St Désir de Lisieux (1249), at Bondeville (1259), and at St Saens (1262) At Bival (1257 and 1259) such a roll was kept. See pp. 62, 299, 339, 348, 451

for the more frequent rendering of accounts; twice or thrice yearly was the usual injunction, sometimes simply "more often," the minimum being once a year[1], occasionally a small account of current expenses was to be read monthly[2]. Sometimes he ordered the accounts to be read before certain nuns elected *ad hoc* (with the addition of the priest at Villarceaux in 1249), the elder nuns being often specified[3] At the same time, although nothing was to be done without the knowledge and consent of the convent, the nuns were not to interfere unduly in the management of temporal affairs, for the prioress of Bondeville was sentenced to receive one discipline before the assembled chapter, as a punishment for giving up the common seal to them, without the Archbishop's knowledge, "because of their clamour"[4]. Nuns were notoriously bad financiers, but even where a male *custos* had charge of their business the arrangement was not invariably satisfactory, and at Bondeville in 1261 Rigaud noted, "We removed Melchior the priest, who had managed the business of the convent for some time, for the reason that the convent had not full confidence in him and that he was odious to them." The house was heavily in debt, so that the mistrust of the nuns, if not their dislike, was clearly justified, and the Archbishop evidently decided not to replace Melchior by another man, for he ordered the Abbess to make one of the nuns treasures to look after the expenditure of the house, receiving the income and administering it[5].

Another matter about which Rigaud inquired and entered particulars in his diary was the amount of provisions in the granaries and storehouses of the nuns Had they enough corn and oats to last till the next harvest? Had they a good supply of wine and cider to drink? The number of cases in which it is noted that the nuns had "*pauca estauramenta*," or not enough to last till the new year, points to a mixture of poverty and bad management[6] The nuns of Bival in 1263 had few stores and no corn for sowing[7]; those of St Saens in 1250 had no wine or cider to drink nor corn to last till Whitsuntide[8]; at St Aubin in 1259 the Archbishop noted comprehensively that they had no stores[9]. Oats seem to have run short in a number of cases[10], and sometimes wine[11].

But occasionally Rigaud's diary contains even fuller information about the temporal affairs of a nunnery It was his regular practice at Villarceaux (why at Villarceaux only it is impossible to say) to enumerate the live stock possessed by that impecunious house, horses, mares, foals, bullocks, cows, calves, sheep and pigs And on two occasions the happy accident of a Prioress' resignation (always an

---

[1] pp. 16, 60, 62, 73, 121, 197, 199, 201, 220, 266, 339, 348, 431, 512
[2] pp 43, 44, 220, 305, 326   [3] pp. 43, 44, 326, 431, 588, 602.
[4] p 348   [5] p. 410.
[6] See e g pp 100, 274, 299, 339, 361, 402, 407, 410, 451, 468, 471, 523, 602, 619.
[7] p. 468.   [8] p. 100.   [9] p 361.
[10] pp 487, 598, 615.   [11] pp. 100, 572, 592

occasion for the presentation of an account) has left us with complete inventories of the possessions and expenses of two houses, St Saens in 1257 and Bondeville in the same year The inventory of St Saens runs as follows:

They owe £212. The king gave them Esquequeville with its appurtenances, which is worth £230 and 4 carucates of land worth £40, and thus they have in all rents to the value of £290 (*sic*). To the house of nuns of St Saens there belong 245 acres of land in all and 7 acres of meadow, of which 115 acres in all are sown with wheat (*frumento*), corn (*blado*, probably rye), barley and other vegetables (*leguminibus*) They have in money rents £170 2s 8d.; in corn rents 8 *modii*, in rents of oats 66 *minae*[1], in rents of capons 220; item in egg rents 1100 eggs[2], item they have in money rents, paid with the capons and the eggs, 27s 6d Item they have a mill at Esquequeville and a wood of which they do not know the size[3] and the priest of the same place takes a tithe in the said mill Item they have rights of pannage and stubble and multure (i e payment by their tenants for grinding at their mill) of which they know not the value Item they have a mill at St Saens of small value Item they have 57 sheep, item 12 plough horses and one waggon (*quadrigam*); item they have 18 beasts, as well cows as oxen. Item they have only 2 *modii* of corn for their food until harvest. They have nothing to drink. There is owing to them £26. 5s 2d The debts which they owe amount in all to £234. 3s. 3d[4]

The inventory of Bondeville for the same year is equally interesting·
These are the goods and rents of the house of Bondeville: £93 *tournois*; of common corn 30 *modii*, in the grange of Heaus they believe that they have 7 *modii* of common corn, in the abbey grange about one *modium* of barley; in the other granges nothing In the abbey there are 2 waggons (*quadrige*), with 6 horses and one riding horse, 6 cows and 14 calves They have in the granges 264 sheep, item in the grange of Heaus 27 cows; item 30 little pigs, item three ploughs (*aratra*) in all, each for three beasts; item 4 little foals. These are the debts of the house, concerning which account has been rendered to the convent: £220 in money and 2 *modii* of barley, [wages] to the household for the harvesting Item they had no oats save for sowing time They expend each month at least 68 *minae* of corn; item they have in the cellar 6 barrels of wine and 2 of cider; item they do not think that the buildings can be repaired [at a less cost than] for £80 *tournois*, item after Easter they will be obliged to buy all the other foodstuffs for the house, save bread, peas and vegetables[5].

Mention is sometimes made in Rigaud's register of dependent cells attached to some of the houses St Paul by Rouen was thus attached to Montivilliers, Bourg-de-Saane to St Amand and Ste Austreberte to St Saens. These cells were doubtless used partly as centres of administration for the more distant estates of the convent, partly as places

---

[1] The exact definition of these measures is a thorny subject, but probably the *modius* was roughly a quarter and the *mina* a little more.
[2] The list of rents in kind is an interesting illustration of the monastic economy, such rents were probably retained, where estates belonged to large communities, for some time after they were commuted for money on secular lands.
[3] The same which they sold in 1261.
[4] pp. 273-4 Compare the inventory of Bondeville, *ib*. p. 299
[5] p 299

of recreation or convalescence, where sick nuns could be sent for a change For instance there were six nuns of Montivilliers at St Paul by Rouen in 1263 and it was noted that there ought to be four, but that two others were there because of illness, the nuns had a lay boarder staying with them and two servants, their income—as assessed for the tithe—was £140 and their debts amounted to £40; they complained that the king's foresters oppressed them by frequently dining at their expense and by unjustly molesting their servants in the forest, although they had usage (i.e rights of hunting, gathering wood, etc.) there, the Archbishop had no fault to find with them except that they did not sing the service *cum nota*, because there were so few of them, and that they had only a single mass, the parochial mass, daily[1] It is evident that a close connection was supposed to be kept up between the mother house and the cell, for in 1260 the Abbess of Montivilliers had been ordered to visit them diligently[2]; and in 1258 Rigaud noted, "Alice prioress of Saint Paul by Rouen was presented to us by the prioress of Montivilliers, she having been elected by the convent of the said place"[3] At his first visitation of St Amand in 1248 the Archbishop found that they had a single priory at Saane, where there are four nuns"[4] In 1261 he ordered the Abbess to visit these nuns at Saane more often than had been her custom and at subsequent visitations he noted the number of nuns (varying from four to five) in residence there[5]. Ste Austreberte, the daughter cell of St Saens, was hardly more than a grange with a chapel attached. In 1254 Rigaud found that one nun was living there alone and ordered that another should be sent to join her; in 1257 there was still a single inmate, but in 1258 and 1259 the number had been raised to two[6] In 1260 the Archbishop decided to recall the inmates to St Saens.

Because truly the place of St Austrebert is very slenderly endowed with rents, so that these two nuns cannot live there conveniently and decently, we ordered the prioress to call them back and forbade her henceforth to send any more thither, on account of the danger[7].

But now complications arose Evidently the dependent house had been used for the purpose of getting rid of a quarrelsome nun, for in 1261 Rigaud found that the Prioress had not obeyed his order to recall the two nuns, "because, as she says, Marie d'Eu (*de Augo*) one of these two, was a scold and she feared lest she should upset the whole convent if she returned"[8] The order was repeated and was apparently obeyed as far as the ill-tempered Marie was concerned (although there were still two nuns at Ste Austreberte in 1264[9]), for in 1265 the Archbishop found the whole convent "living in discord and in disorder, especially the prioress and Marie d'Eu"[10], he would perhaps have done better to leave her where she was An echo of her *régime* at

[1] p. 457.	[2] p. 384	
[3] p 316.	[4] p. 16	[5] pp 401, 456, 471, 512
[6] pp 187, 273, 310, 338		[7] p 380
[8] p 419	[9] p. 491	[10] p. 522.

Ste Austreberte was heard in 1265, when Marie d'Eu was ordered to return the chalice of the chapel of Ste Austreberte as quickly as possible and to restore to the Prioress any charter or letters concerning the manor of Ste Austreberte, which she had received from the convent At the same time the Prioress was ordered to provide the chapel there with a suitable server (*servitore*)[1] Mention of visits to the granges or farms of the convents sometimes occurs At Bondeville in 1251 it was found that "the sisters drank in the granges"[2] and in 1255 that a lay sister and a lay brother were living alone in a grange (perhaps in the grange of Heaus, mentioned in the inventory), whereupon the Archbishop ordered the sister to be withdrawn or else given a companion[3] In 1268 the Abbess of Bival was ordered to remove "a certain child," whom she was having brought up in the grange of Pierremans (which had been so improvidently let to William of the Fishponds twelve years before) and a penance was imposed upon her in 1269 because she had not obeyed the injunction[4]

So far only the temporal affairs of these Rouen nunneries have been considered; there remains the more important question of their social, moral and spiritual condition. A clearer idea will be formed of the results of Eudes Rigaud's investigations, if the chief sources of complaint be classified under the following heads:

(1) Complaints of incompetence and irregular behaviour against the head of a house,

(2) General laxity in keeping the rule,

(3) The sin of property and the failure to live a communal life,

(4) Various attempts to make money by illicit means,

(5) Leave of absence and intercourse with seculars, both within and without the cloister precincts,

(6) Frivolous clothes and amusements, and

(7) Serious moral faults, such as drunkenness, quarrelsomeness and incontinence

(1) Complaints of incompetence, laxity, self-indulgence or favouritism against the head of a house are common in visitation records The charge of failure to render accounts has already been dealt with, but hardly less usual was the charge of failure to live a communal life The abbess or prioress of a house had separate apartments and it was always a temptation to dine or to sleep alone, instead of keeping the frater and the dorter. Again the charges of favouritism on the one hand and of undue harshness on the other were very common Rigaud's register provides examples of all these faults. At two visitations (1254 and 1257) the Archbishop remarked that the Abbess of St Léger de Préaux did not live a communal life in dorter and frater nor attend the chapter[5]; the same charge was made against the Prioress of Villarceaux in 1253 and it was mentioned that she did not often get up to matins nor daily hear mass[6]; and the Abbess

---

[1] p 522· he probably means *vicar*.   [2] p 111   [3] p. 217.
[4] pp. 610, 636   [5] pp. 197, 295.   [6] p. 166.

41—2

of St Amand did not keep the frater, but ate in her own room and always had the same companions there, instead of calling the others for recreation[1]. Not all prioresses were, like Chaucer's, "ful plesaunt and amiable of port." The Abbess of Montivilliers seems to have been a forbidding lady, in 1260 the Archbishop ordered her to minister pilches, cloth and other necessary things more carefully than had been her custom to the nuns, not forgetting their ginger "hot i' the mouth"[2], and also to bear herself more courteously and affably towards their friends particularly in the matter of their admission (on visits), at the same time she was warned to be present in chapel more often and to live the communal life better[3] This warning apparently bore no fruit and in 1262 the Archbishop noted, "because she was slow to administer new pilches, headdresses and cloth and other things to the nuns for their needs, we ordered her to labour to minister better and more fitly to them in this matter and to be careful about it"; it was also remarked that she frequented the convent but little and was seldom present at chapter and frater; and she was ordered to render a general account once a year and to hear and receive the particular accounts of the obedientiaries The next year her failure to frequent chapter, dorter and choir was again noted and some of the nuns still complained of her harshness, whereupon the Archbishop (apparently despairing of inducing her to look after them properly herself), ordered her to depute two or three nuns, "with whom the others could talk more familiarly and more boldly, to minister to their sisters small things for their needs, ginger and other things of the kind"; the quality of the wine was also to be improved The difficulties, however, continued. In 1265 the Abbess was ordered to provide the nuns more carefully with pilches and in the following year she was again ordered

"prudently to cause the pilches and robes of the nuns to be repaired, so that she may provide them with such things more fitly than she is used and have more workpeople than she has been accustomed to do. For in this," adds the Archbishop, "we found a deficiency"[3].

Rigaud had a great deal of difficulty with the Prioress of Bonde-ville. In 1251 there were many complaints against her; she exercised favouritism in the distribution of clothes and in the provision of food in the infirmary and she did not look after the sick; when in the infirmary she ate at a table by herself and she did not live a communal life; she wandered about a great deal outside the convent, even without the excuse of convent business, and when she went to Rouen she stayed there for three or four days; moreover she was

---

[1] p 285.
[2] For other references to the fondness of nuns for ginger see the *Life of Christina von Stommeln*. "Item per annum cum dimidio non comedit aliud quam gingiber" (*Acta SS.* t IV, p 454 A). Also the *Ancren Riwle*, p 316: "Of a man whom ye distrust receive ye neither less nor more—not so much as a race of ginger." Cf *ib* p 279
[3] pp. 384, 431, 472, 517, 564.

quarrelsome and stirred up discord in the house "so that she could not have peace with the convent nor with anyone" The next year she resigned, probably as a result of these complaints and of the financial condition of the house, but in 1255 the register has an entry· "We found the Prioress quarrelsome and sharp of tongue, not knowing how to make corrections and also speaking ill of her sisters; we warned her to desist from these things", so that her resignation had evidently not been accepted In 1257 she made another attempt at resignation, and the occasion is interesting because it provides us not only with an inventory of Bondeville, but also with the sole complete list of inmates preserved among the Rouen nunneries[1] The Archbishop decided to take an inquisition in the convent as to whether the Prioress should or should not be removed; and the votes of the twenty-six nuns and three brothers of the house were taken upon oath. Of these nineteen were in favour of her removal and nine of her retention, while Brother Roger permitted himself to express the ambiguous opinion that "it would be evil for temporal affairs and good for spiritual affairs to remove the prioress" (quod dampnum esset temporale et utilitas spiritualis removere priorissam!)[2] It is not clear from the Register whether she was removed, Rigaud notes "Item we received the resignation of Marie, late the prioress," but in 1261 there occurs a further entry. "Item the Prioress offered us her seal, begging us to absolve her from her office, but we, being unwilling to condescend to her in this matter, ordered her to exercise her office with greater zeal" In particular she was ordered "to frequent the convent at least by day (viz chapter, frater and choir) better than she was wont and not to stand about talking in the cemetery or outside the house after Compline, as she had been in the habit of doing"[3] At Bival an abbess resigned in 1248, doubtless owing to the unsatisfactory moral conditions revealed at the visitation[4], there were no complaints against her successor until 1268 (though two cases of immorality occurred in the convent before that date); then, among minor injunctions concerning matters of administration, she was ordered to bear herself more kindly and courteously towards the nuns[5].

(2) Besides injunctions dealing specially with the behaviour of the head of a house, the Archbishop was obliged to deal with breaches of the rule by the convent generally Many of his regulations were concerned with the strictly religious duties of the nuns Sometimes the church services were not being properly performed, as at St Amand, St Aubin, Villarceaux, St Saëns and Montivilliers The most common defect was failure to sing these services with music (cum

---

[1] See pp. 793–4 for the inquisition. The name of the house is not given and the editor places the list in the appendix, but the date is 1257 and from internal evidence it is quite clear that it refers to the resignation of Marie, prioress of Bondeville.

[2] P. 793
[3] pp. 111, 133, 217, 298, 410
[4] p 6.
[5] p. 610.

nota or *ad notam*)[1], at St Saens (a constant offender—Rigaud notes the fault at eight visitations) the nuns did not do so even on Sundays[2] Occasionally a specific excuse was given; the nuns of Villarceaux omitted the music on the days upon which they received the periodical bleeding considered necessary to the health of those who embraced the monastic life[3]; at St Aubin in 1264 they complained that many of them were often ill[4] and at St Saens also (in 1257) they dwelt upon their infirmities[5] At St Paul's by Rouen they were too few in number to perform the service properly[6] The Archbishop contented himself at St Aubin (1251) with the injunction that they should sing at least in monotone—*saltem cum bassa nota*[7] Moreover even when the nuns did sing the services they occasionally did so carelessly. At St Amand the Archbishop made a significant injunction

They sometimes sing the hours of the Blessed Virgin and the psalms of suffrage with too great haste and precipitation of words. We ordered them to sing in such a way that the side [of the choir] singing the first half of the verse should hear the end of the preceding verse and the side singing the second half should hear the beginning of the next verse[8].

Evidently both sides of the choir came in too soon in their anxiety to hurry through the service—a clear case for Tuttivillus. At Montivilliers the fault lay in beginning too late and Rigaud ordered that better provision should be made for ringing a bell at the due hours, so that the service might be said without haste and finished while it was light (*de luce*)[9] At Villarceaux he ordered that all the nuns should at once assemble in the church when the bell rang, unless they were ill or had special leave of absence[10]. Even at the great abbey of Caen the service was being said "*confuse et male*, one part in the choir and one outside"[11]. At St Amand (1263), which evidently contained young and obstreperous—or perhaps only ignorant—members, it was ordered that the nuns should be equally divided in the choir, so that all the young ones might not be together[12]. At St Saens (1254) a nun served the mass with the priest; and at Bondeville (1263) the nuns had not the necessary priests and did not hear enough sermons[13]. St Aubin apparently shared the parish priest; there were only fifteen parishioners (most of them doubtless dependents of the nunnery) and the priest dwelt with the nuns and was maintained at their expense; in 1257 the Archbishop ordered them to find a clerk to assist him[14]. The nuns of St Paul's heard only one mass—that of the parish—daily[15] Sometimes deficiencies in the services may have been due to lack of books At St Sauveur d'Evreux, in 1258, it was found that the nuns did not possess adequate books and they were ordered to procure some[16]; at Villarceaux in 1257 they lacked two antiphonaries

---

[1] pp 44, 115, 166, 255, 273, 338, 419, 451, 457, 491, 500, 522, 550
[2] p 522, compare p. 550.   [3] pp 166, 194.
[4] p. 500   [5] p. 273.   [6] p 457.
[7] p 115   [8] p 15   [9] pp 384, 431, 472
[10] p. 44.   [11] p 575   [12] p 486
[13] p 487.   [14] pp 283, 319, 361   [15] p 457   [16] p. 305.

and in 1261 it was again noted that their books were insufficient and worn out[1]. At Montivilliers the Archbishop in 1260 ordered the chantress to have an ordinal of the hours made at the Abbess' cost; this had not yet been done in 1262 and from Rigaud's injunction on this occasion it appears that the nuns were expected to write the book themselves, for the ordinal was "to be made by the chantress and by the more discreet nuns, i e. by the older ones who knew and understood better the service of the order." At the same house reference was made three years later to a certain glossed psalter which had been bequeathed to it by a benefactor, and had been alienated without the knowledge of the convent, the Abbess was told to have it restored without delay and replied "that she could do so easily enough, because Master William de Beaumont had it"[2].

Another common fault was negligence in the matter of confession and communion. Sometimes a house had a fixed rule as to the number of times the nuns had to confess and communicate. At Bival, for example, the nuns seem to have attended communion seven times a year, though they confessed more often[3] At Villarceaux they confessed and communicated six times a year[4] At St Aubin the Archbishop noted that they were bound to confess and to communicate seven times a year, but that they had sometimes been negligent in the matter, they gave an inadequate excuse, and Rigaud ordered them on no account to be absent from communion and warned the Prioress to consider any such absence without due cause as a serious fault[5] At St Léger de Préaux in 1249 he found that the nuns confessed and communicated only four times a year and ordered them to do so monthly[6] At Montivilliers[7] and at Bondeville[8] they were supposed to confess and to communicate monthly, but at the latter house he found them negligent in 1261, and ordered that the nun who did not communicate with the others or within the next two or three days was to be punished by abstention from wine and pottage for three days[9]. The Archbishop's usual custom was to order monthly confession and communion[10] Sometimes there seems to have been some difficulty about getting a confessor; at Almenèches (where,

---

[1] pp. 281, 402   [2] pp 384, 431, 817.

[3] pp 268, 299, 339 On one occasion the number is given as 12. p. 207.

[4] pp 43, 534 However in 1268 Rigaud noted that they ought to do so monthly. p. 602

[5] p. 412.

[6] p 62, but in 1267 Rigaud noted that they were obliged to do so seven times a year. p. 600

[7] pp 293, 517, 564.

[8] pp 298, 487. In 1255 he noted that they did so seven times a year and ordered fortnightly confessions and communions instead (p. 217), but from the later visitations it appears that the seven times rule referred only to lay brothers and sisters

[9] p. 410

[10] (St Amand), pp. 121, 202, 326, 456, (St Désir de Lisieux), p. 199; (St Sauveur d'Evreux), pp 220, 305.

in 1250, the nuns had no rule or term for confession or communion[1]) it was found in 1260 that they were in the habit of confessing to passing friars when they wished to do so, and Rigaud ordered the Bishop to provide them with regular confessors, friars minor or others[2] At St Saens in 1261 they had not had a confessor for a long time and were ordered to procure the Prior of Crissy[3], but in 1265 the Archbishop still found that they did not go to confession as well as they should[4]. At Ariete the nuns did not all confess to their own priest[5].

Other minor faults were late rising[6], breach of silence[7] and laxity in causing novices to make their profession[8]. At Villarceaux in 1249 only four out of the twenty-three nuns had been properly professed[9] The Archbishop ordered the vows to be taken when the novices reached the age of fourteen years[10], this was not to be done before[11] and if any refused to do so at the appointed age they were to be sent back to the world[12], he also ordered in several cases that only the three vows of poverty, chastity and obedience should be taken[13].

Another set of injunctions is concerned with the conduct of the frater, the infirmary and the chapter house The Archbishop dealt with the observances of the frater from the point of view of the communal life, from that of the food eaten by the nuns and from that of almsgiving. The growing practice among the nuns of dining separately in their rooms or in little cliques, instead of keeping the frater, was a menace to a strictly communal life, and as such will be considered later, with other practices which tended in the same direction. Here it may be noted that already in the thirteenth century the regulations of the monastic rule as to diet were being contravened. Many convents were convicted of eating meat unnecessarily, *etiam sane*, "even when in good health"[14], and it was becoming the custom —in Rigaud's diocese as elsewhere—to use the infirmary as a *misericord*, in which meat was eaten on certain days of the week, generally thrice a week[15] Sometimes even fast days were not regularly kept[16] Another breach of the rule frequently encountered by the Archbishop was inadequate almsgiving The nuns were supposed to give alms regularly to the poor and in particular to give them the food which remained over from the convent meals; but in view of the poverty of some of the houses it is not surprising that the rule was sometimes unobserved Very often the nuns, instead of collecting the fragments

---

[1] p 82.   [2] p 374   [3] p. 419   [4] p 522.
[5] p. 245.   [6] p 517 (Montivilliers)
[7] pp 43, 44 (Villarceaux), 117, 146 (Bival), 170, 310 (St Saens), 261 (Caen); 285, 486 (St Amand), 305 (St Sauveur), 348 (Bondeville).
[8] pp 15 (St Amand); 60 (St Léger de Préaux).
[9] p. 43   [10] pp. 15, 121 (St Amand), 207 (St Aubin).
[11] p 207 (Bival)   [12] p 207 (St Aubin).
[13] pp 197, 295, 591 (St Léger-de-Préaux); 201 (St Amand); 261 (Caen).
[14] p 170 (St Saens)
[15] pp. 16 (St Amand), 62, 199 (St Désir de Lisieux), 60 (St Léger de Préaux), 170, 187 (St Saëns)
[16] pp 62 (St Désir de Lisieux); 884 (Montivilliers)

left over in frater and infirmary, each kept what remained of her own share and sold it or gave it away to people outside the convent. St Amand was a constant offender, in 1248 the Archbishop had occasion to forbid the unequal distribution of wine to the nuns "to one more and to another less," and he added that if any of them gave away any part of her measure of wine to anyone outside the house without licence she was to be punished by being deprived of wine the next day[1], in 1251 he enjoined that no nun was to put forth any of her food save in the way of alms[2]; but some thirteen years later St Amand (doubtless on account of its poverty) was still remiss in the matter of almsgiving and Rigaud warned the nuns separately that it must not be diminished and that everything left over from meals must be given to the poor[3] At St Saens it was discovered that the nuns had separate portions of bread allotted to them and that the fragments were never given in alms, because each either sold or gave away these fragments as she pleased[4] At Montivilliers almsgiving was diminished because the nuns gave away the remnants of the portions of bread, wine and other food to "serving maids and other acquaintances"[5], and at Villarceaux and Bival also it was necessary to warn the nuns not to give away or sell any of their clothes or food[6] The practice was the more reprehensible in the Archbishop's eyes in that it savoured of the private ownership of property Rigaud made general orders for the increase of almsgiving and for the more careful collection of food after meals in the frater and in the infirmary[7]. Sometimes the custom of a house prescribed special obligations, the Abbess of Montivilliers was required to give alms thrice a week and to entertain thirteen poor men daily[8] Sometimes the revenues of a special manor or rent were earmarked for the expenses of almsgiving; the recalcitrant St Amand was found to have abstracted the rents of a certain manor from the almoness and was ordered to restore them to their proper purpose[9]

Other departments of the convent of which mention is made in Rigaud's Register are the infirmary and the chapter house. At Montivilliers the Archbishop, in 1262, ordered the infirmary to be repaired and the convent to be provided with physic[10], and at Bondeville, St Sauveur and St Amand he was obliged to order that sick nuns should be better looked after[11]. There are some interesting notes about the meetings of the chapter in various houses At several (Bondeville, St Saens and Villarceaux) the Archbishop found that the chapter was seldom held[12] At others the duty incumbent upon the nuns to accuse or proclaim (*clamare*) each other's faults was imperfectly performed. There was a most natural reluctance on the part of the elder nuns to

[1] p. 16.   [2] p. 121   [3] p 512   [4] p. 338.
[5] p. 384.   [6] pp 44, 468
[7] pp 431, 451, 472, 517, 564, 600, 624 Cf also p 652, below.
[8] pp. 384, 431, 472, 517, 600. Cf. St Saëns, p. 451   [9] p 638.
[10] p. 431.   [11] pp 111, 285, 486, 625
[12] pp. 111, 166, 170, 194.

allow the indiscriminate criticism of their juniors and a tendency to keep the latter in their place by allowing them only to be accused and never to retaliate At Caen (1250) the Archbishop found that none made the statutory accusations save certain nuns who were deputed to reveal the faults of the younger ones[1] and at St Amand also only the elder nuns made accusations, and he ordered that all without exception should reveal what they saw amiss[2] At Montivilliers the same complaint that the nuns refrained from accusing each other was made[3]. From one point of view this imperfect performance of their duty in chapter meant that the nuns were winking at each other's peccadilloes, and it was for the sake of discipline that the Archbishop insisted upon a more strict obedience to the rule From another point of view the obligation certainly gave rise to much ill-feeling; the author of the *Ancren Riwle* placed "Exposing faults" and "Backbiting" among the brood of seven, offspring of "the venomous serpent of hell, Envy", for human nature would need to be very perfect if the accusations were always to be made in the spirit of sisterly admonition, "sweetly and affectionately," which the same treatise describes so eloquently a few pages later[4] It is significant that the Abbess of Montivilliers had to be warned in no way to molest one of her nuns, nor to conceive rancour against her on account of anything that she said in chapter[5]

[1] p 94. Cf p 261. "Una non clamat aliam" (1256)
[2] p 201.   [3] p 293.
[4] *Ancren Riwle*, tr Gasquet, pp 151, 192
[5] p 518. An amusing example of convent amenities on these occasions and particularly of the way in which the younger nuns seized a chance of "getting even" with their elders is to be found in Johann Busch's account of his visitation of Dorstadt (in the *Liber de Reformatione Monasteriorum* described below, App III) At this house it was the custom for the chapter disciplines to be administered to the whole convent by two of the youngest nuns, who then received discipline themselves "And," says Busch, "they had somewhat large rods and beat each other somewhat severely, because the younger nuns were ordained to give disciplines for this reason, that they were stronger than the others I asked one of them after confession whether she ever gave one more or sharper blows than another. She answered, 'Truly I do I hit more sharply and as much as I can her who in my judgment deserves more.' This girl was about eight or ten years old I asked one elderly sister, who was prioress in another monastery of her order, but because she was unwilling to reform was expelled from it, whether she received severe disciplines from them. She replied, 'I have counted ten or eight strokes, which she has often given me as hard as she could, within the space in which "Misereatur tui" is read ' Then I said to her, 'You ought to make her a sign, that she may understand that you have had enough ' She answered, 'When I do that, she hits me all the more. And I dare not say anything to her on account of the prioress's presence, but I think to myself I must bear these on account of my sins, because the prioress and all the seniors receive from them as much as they like to give, without contradiction.' And she added, 'before her profession I used to teach her and often beat her with a rod. now she pays me back as she likes '"
Busch, *Chron Wind et Liber de Ref Mon.*, ed Grube, pp 644-5

Finally the Archbishop sometimes found fault with the management of the secular servants and of the lay brothers and sisters attached to different houses. It was his custom to note the number of maidservants (*ancille, pedissece*) employed and to reprove the nuns if he thought that they were employing too many, or falling into the sin of property by keeping certain maids in the service of individual nuns, as they did at Almenèches in 1255[1], at St Léger de Préaux in 1267[2] and at St Sauveur in 1269, at the last house he noted

The convent had three common maids and several special maids were kept at the cost of the house; so we ordered that there were henceforth to be no special maids, but that if necessary the number of common maids might be increased[3]

At St Amand he twice ordered the removal of all superfluous servants, adding in 1267 that all were to be paid at a fixed rate out of the common funds[4] At St Aubin in 1265 he found two servants, one of whom was incontinent and of ill repute (little wonder, considering the evil morals of the nuns) and he ordered her instant expulsion[5] Of the lay sisters attached to some of the houses there is less mention, in 1259 Rigaud noted that two of those at Bondeville were of weak intellect (*fatue*)[6]. There was sometimes trouble with the lay brothers, at Bondeville (1251) he made a list of corrections for them[7] and in 1259 a certain brother Roger (doubtless the same whose dark saying about the Prioress has already been recorded) was announced to be disobedient and rebellious, and the injunction that he should obey the Prioress had to be repeated in 1268, nearly ten years later[8]. There was occasionally also need for correction in the behaviour of the convent priest, for it is clear that an unsuitable chaplain might give great cause for scandal The not very reputable houses of St Saens and Bival both suffered in this way, in 1254 the Archbishop found that the priest of the former house was incontinent and ordered the nuns to find another[9], and in 1256, at Bival, he noted "We removed the priest from this place on account of the scandal of the nuns and of the populace, though we found nothing which we could prove against him"[10] At St Aubin in 1261 the nuns were ordered not to drink with seculars in the priest's house[11]

(3) The most frequent fault which Eudes Rigaud found in the nunneries under his care was the persistent hankering of the nuns after private property and their failure to live a communal life according to the rule. The possession of private property was a very common charge. The nuns had chests in which to keep such possessions as they were allowed and there was a perpetual struggle over the

[1] p 235   [2] p. 591.   [3] pp 624–5.
[4] pp. 512, 588   [5] p. 550
[6] p 348 Perhaps one of these is referred to in 1251 when Rigaud noted "Ibi est quedam filia cuiusdam burgensis de Vallibus que stulta est" (p 111). It may however refer to a boarder
[7] p 111   [8] pp 348, 615   [9] p 187.
[10] p. 268   [11] p. 412

question as to whether or not they were to be allowed keys, with which to lock the boxes The nuns of Montivilliers begged for keys in 1257 and the stern Rigaud refused[1], of this refusal they took not the smallest notice, and in 1262 the Register contains the injunction that keys were to be given up and that those who were unwilling to obey were to be severely punished, "for," added the Archbishop,

We understood that when the abbess asked them for their keys certain of them would not give the keys up for two or three days, until they should have gone through their things and taken away those which they did not want the Abbess to see, and so we ordered these nuns to be punished for disobedience and for the ownership of property[2]

The injunction that the boxes should be inspected frequently was repeated at three subsequent visitations[3] It was the Archbishop's usual custom to order the Abbess or Prioress to look into the nuns' boxes often and unexpectedly in order to remove private property, and the injunction was repeated from year to year, which looks as though it were greatly honoured in the breach[4]. Besides the injunction against closed boxes there was an oft-repeated injunction to the effect that, in accordance with the rule[5], no nun was to have more than one set of garments, directly new clothes were given out the old ones were to be handed back (and given to the poor), so that no nun might rejoice in the semblance of a wardrobe[6] At St Amand in 1264 the Archbishop made the following note of his action

Item we ordered them that when they received new pilches, shifts and any sort of new garments or foot-wear (*calciamentorum*), they were to give the old in alms, whereat they murmured somewhat to our displeasure, and we forbade the abbess to give them any new clothes until they had rendered up the old[7].

It appears from an injunction given at St Sauveur in 1258[8] that the nuns sometimes sold or gave away their old clothes as they did with the remains of their portions of food and drink; in both cases the sin of property was encouraged and almsgiving diminished. Rigaud made the most comprehensive injunction on these points at Villarceaux in 1249·

We warn you, all and sundry, that ye observe the communism which ought to be observed in religion in the matter of clothes, food and other like

[1] p 293   [2] p 431   [3] pp 472, 517, 564
[4] pp. 170, 187, 522 (St Saëns), 201, 326, 401, 512 (St Amand); 298, 348, 455 (Bondeville), 73, 220, 305 (St Sauveur); 117, 146 (Bival); 199, 296 (St Désir de Lisieux), 295–6, 592 (St Léger de Préaux); 402 (Villarceaux), 412 (St Aubin).
[5] See *Rule of St Benedict*, tr Gasquet, pp. 95–6: "When receiving new clothes the monks shall always give back the old ones at the same time, to be put away in the clothes room for the poor For it is sufficient that a monk have two cowls, as well for night wear as for the convenience of washing Anything else is superfluous and must be cut off "
[6] pp. 384, 517, 564 (Montivilliers), 295 (St Léger de Préaux), 62 (St Désir de Lisieux), 220, 305 (St Sauveur).
[7] p 512   [8] p 305

things, neither sell nor give away at your own will any of those things which belong to the common food or dress, and if ye shall have received anything from your friends, ye shall apply it to the use of the community and not each to your own use[1].

In one case at least, that of Bival, the practice (which afterwards became common) of giving each of the nuns a separate allowance with which to buy her own clothes or food was already in force, the Abbess of Bival gave to each an annual sum of 12s out of which to buy her clothes[2] At Montivilliers Rigaud ordered the nuns to be clothed in common[3] and at St Aubin he made a special injunction that they were to use their scapularies in common[4].

But the sin of property crept into convents in every direction and was most difficult of all to eradicate. At Almenêches in 1250 Rigaud noted· "All are *proprietarie*, owning saucepans, copper kettles and necklaces of their own"[5] At St Aubin in 1265 there is the entry:

Because divers of the nuns have divers cocks and hens and often quarrel over them, we ordered that all cocks and hens were to be nourished alike and to be kept in common and the eggs ministered equally among the nuns and fowls sometimes given to the sick to eat in the infirmary[6]

But in vain; each nun clung to her own hen; still there continued the rivalry when eggs were counted, the jealousy over the possession of a good layer, the turmoil when some fickle fowl laid in the wrong nest. After all it was a *Nonnes Prest* who described that immortal farmyard lorded over by Chantecler and his seven wives Could the happy owner of "damoysele Pertelote," bearing herself so fair and companionable, be expected to give her up into cold communal ownership? Two years later the Archbishop remarked in his diary that nothing had been done about the poultry[7]. Some nuns even had rents of their own, which they kept for their private use instead of adding the money to the common income of the priory This was the case at Bondeville[8] and at St Désir de Lisieux[9] At the latter Rigaud began by ordering these rents to be held in common, but in later years contented himself with an injunction that they should be retained only at the discretion of the Abbess At St Saëns in 1250 it was noted. "They receive gifts and retain and expend them without licence"[10]. Usually the injunction was that the nuns were to receive nothing from their friends without licence from the head of the house[11], the poverty of some convents made it impossible altogether to prohibit such gifts.

Closely connected with this sin of property was the failure to live a communal life Already at this early date the practice of eating

[1] pp. 44–5.
[2] "Abbatissa dat cuilibet moniali per annum xii solidos pro vestibus tantummodo, et singule earum provident sibi de residuo " p 339; cf. p. 299 Cf. also Almenêches in 1250, p. 82.
[3] p. 384   [4] p. 207.   [5] p. 82   [6] p. 550.
[7] p. 587.   [8] p. 615   [9] pp 62, 199, 296   [10] p. 100
[11] pp. 115, 273, 285 Cf. injunctions to Villarceaux in 1249, quoted above.

in separate chambers and of receiving separate allowances of food was becoming common The most comprehensive indictment was made at Almenèches In 1250 (the same year that Rigaud found them to be *proprietarie*, owning pots and pans) he noted ·

They run up debts in the town and eat together and sit at table in cliques (*per societates*). To each money is given to provide herself with food. Many stay away from compline and from matins and they drink after compline[1]

On this occasion the moral record of the convent was found to be peculiarly bad In 1255 there was no further complaint of immorality but the nuns were as lax as ever in keeping the rule as to communal life:

They have chambers with partitions in the dorter They have separate maids of their own, who do not serve the community[2] They do not eat out of the same dish but have divers dishes Each had one loaf to herself and kept what was over, we ordered the abbess to give them bread without livery (i e in common) and to take back what was over. They do not live on the same pittance; in short they do not live in common[3].

In 1260 it was the same story

The frater was often left empty, to wit because they did not eat together therein, but they ate meat scattered in cliques by twos and by threes in their chambers (*due et due, tres et tres, sparsim et socialiter in cameris*) They had many chambers and five maid servants to boot... Each of them had one loaf daily and retained what remained over. We ordered that the remnant should be given in alms and counselled them to eat and to live in common and to remove the chambers[4]

At Montivilliers the order to dine together was repeated at almost every visitation; the nuns had separate dishes cooked for themselves in the kitchen and when they were in the infirmary "for recreation or for slight ailments" they used to eat separately in little companies (*per conventicula*)[5]. At St Saens[6] and at St Léger de Préaux[7] also the nuns had separate food allowances and ate in the infirmary, at Bival some of them had food prepared separately[8] and at Villarceaux in 1266 the Archbishop made the following injunction

We ordered her (the Abbess) to permit them to dine together twice a day according to their rule and to have a bell rung twice, to wit for dinner and for supper, so that they might come together at the sound into the frater, in a more seemly way than they have been wont. For they often ate separately in their chambers[9]

At St Sauveur also Rigaud ordered all to dine together in the frater, and in the infirmary all nuns, except those actually in bed, were to

---

[1] p. 82.
[2] Cf. the case of Johanna Martel at St Saens, p. 338, quoted below, p. 668
[3] p 235.   [4] p. 374
[5] pp 384, 431, 472, 517, 564. In 1260 the injunction was · "Item quod omnes sane insimul comederent, item inhibuimus ne in refectorio per conventicula et colligationes comederent sed sederent in mensis indifferenter et escis communibus vescerentur" (p. 384)
[6] pp 170, 380, 522.   [7] pp 60, 197, 295.   [8] p. 146.
[9] p. 572

use the same food at the same table[1] At Bondeville the nuns seem to have been in the habit of congregating, with the servants of the house, in a certain oven room, doubtless for the sake of the warmth, and the Archbishop several times forbade the practice on account of possible scandal[2]. Private drinking parties sometimes occurred, at St Sauveur the nuns occasionally drank outside the frater or infirmary in their own chambers[3] and at Almenèches they drank after Compline[4]

(4) It has already been said that the nunneries were often reduced to great straits by poverty. As a result they invented a number of devices for obtaining ready money. Some of these devices seem to modern eyes harmless enough; but they were opposed by medieval Visitors because they brought the nunneries into too close contact with the world and were subversive of discipline. One of their devices has already been described At St Saens, Villarceaux, Bival and St Sauveur it is evident that the nuns were in the habit not merely of giving away but actually of selling the food and drink left over from meals and their old clothes to people outside the convent At Bondeville Rigaud had, in 1251, to forbid them to sell their thread and their spindles[5] At many houses they were accustomed to knit or embroider silken purses, tassels, cushions or needle cases, either for sale or as gifts to their friends, and the Archbishop forbade them to do any silkwork except for church ornament[6] He was not remarkably successful, since he had to repeat the injunction eight times at St Amand, between 1254 and 1267 It is interesting to compare his attitude with the similar prohibition made to the anchoresses of the *Ancren Riwle* early in the same century: "Make no purses to gain friends therewith, nor blodbendes of silk, but shape and sew and mend church vestments and poor people's clothes"[7].

Another means of getting money was by taking school-children as boarders and the general attitude of the Church towards this custom is strikingly illustrated in Eudes Rigaud's Register. The provincial council of Rouen in 1231, attempting to deal with the bad discipline in Benedictine nunneries, had promulgated a statute forbidding the reception of children to be educated, and the context shows that the practice was regarded solely in the light of an interference with convent discipline, by bringing the nuns into contact with the world·

On account of the scandals which rise out of the conversation of nuns, we ordain for black nuns that they shall receive nothing to be deposited with

---

[1] p. 220

[2] pp III, 217, 571. The oven room of St Amand was looked after by a lay brother, p 588

[3] p 73   [4] p. 82

[5] p III. "Quod moniales non vendant nec distrahant filum et *lor fusees.*"

[6] pp. 202, 283, 326, 401, 456, 486, 512, 588 (St Amand), 73, 624 (St Sauveur), 518 (Montivilliers); 451 (St Saëns), 534 (Villarceaux).

[7] *Ancren Riwle*, tr. Gasquet, p. 318.

them in their houses by any persons, above all let them by no means permit the strong-boxes of clergy, or of the laity too, to be placed in their custody[1]. Boys and girls who are accustomed to be brought up and taught there are immediately to be put away[2].

In accordance with this statute and with the invariable custom of ecclesiastical authorities it was Eudes Rigaud's practice to order the expulsion of children wherever he found them, and the number of these prohibitions increased during the last years covered by his diary, which points to a firm determination to eradicate the fault, though it would also seem to imply a certain flouting of his authority by the nuns. In four cases (St Saens, St Aubin, Bival and Villarceaux) the moral record of the houses concerned was so disgraceful that the Archbishop might well be thought to have been actuated by concern for the children growing up under such evil influences[3], but the fact that he took the same course at Bondeville, St Sauveur, St Amand and St Léger de Préaux, against which none but minor breaches of the rule were charged, shows that his policy was dictated by care for the nuns and not for their pupils   Bondeville was an obstinate offender. There in 1255 the Archbishop ordered the Prioress and Subprioress to remove their little nieces[4] and a certain other girl[5]; in 1257 he noted the presence of five ladies (domicelle) who had not been received as novices[6]; and in 1261 he noted again that "Many secular girls were used to be placed there with their costs"[7]. In the two last cases the Register—probably, as Mr Coulton suggests, by a clerical oversight—contains no injunction to remove the children, and in 1266 only one boarder, "a lady of Rouen, Laurentia called *quatuor Homines*" was ordered to be sent away, though the Archbishop explicitly stated that "Certain girls (*iuvencule*), daughters of burgesses of Rouen, were there as it were in charge [of the nuns],

[1] The custom of depositing valuables in a monastery for safety was very general.   Caesarius of Heisterbach has an entertaining anecdote on the point "A certain usurer committed a large sum of his money to a certain cellarer of our order to be kept for him   The monk sealed it up and put it in a safe place together with the money belonging to the monastery. Afterwards the usurer came to ask for his deposit, but when the cellarer opened the chest, he found neither that nor his own money. And when he beheld that the locks of the chest were intact and the seals of the bags unbroken and that there was no suspicion of theft, he understood that the money of the usurer had eaten up the money of the monastery." Caes of Heist., *Dial. Mirac.* ed Strange (1851), I, p 108   For another example of goods being deposited for safety in a nunnery see *V C H Herts.* IV, p. 431 (note 40)   A certain Joan Sturmyn entrusted goods to the value of £50 to the keeping of Alice Wafer, Prioress of St Mary de Pré (near St Albans), which afterwards gave rise to a case in chancery, 1480–5
[2] Coulton, *Monastic Schools in the Middle Ages* (Medieval Studies, No. 10) quoting from Martène, *Thesaurus*, IV, col. 175, § IV.
[3] See references to convent schools by Gerson and by Erasmus quoted in Coulton, *op. cit* pp 22–3, note 17
[4] Or grandnieces (*nepotulas*)   [5] p. 217
[6] p. 298.   [7] p. 410.

which displeased us"[1]. There was, however, no ambiguity about his action in 1268 when he ordered a certain

> Basiria, daughter of Amelina of Aulnay, who was there as a boarder, to be sent away and forbade the Prioress henceforth to keep any girl or girls there, except such as had been received as novices[2].

But it was a difficult task to force the needy nuns, reduced already to pawning the very vessels of the altar, to give up this more certain and less sacrilegious method of adding to their income.

It is indeed a significant fact, as Mr Coulton has pointed out, that "the prohibitions are in inverse proportion to the temporal prosperity of the convent"[3]. The wealthy Abbaye-aux-Dames at Caen had no need to take in school children. But Villarceaux, £50 in debt in 1249 and going steadily downhill, vainly struggling in the toils of Jews and Caursini, was the most frequent offender of all and resisted the most stubbornly Rigaud's attempts at reform In 1257 he ordered the nuns to remove all the boys and girls who were in the house, except one girl who was going to be veiled[4] The next year they were threatened with severe punishment if they postponed any longer the ejection of the children "whom they are bringing up in their house against our inhibition"[5]. Follows silence for the next three visitations; then, eight years later, "There were several girls there, as it were in the charge of certain nuns, which displeased us exceedingly and shortly afterwards we ordered the Prioress by our letters to remove all secular girls" within a certain date[6], and in 1268

> We ordered, as we had done before, that the nuns should utterly put away all secular ladies or girls (domicellas seu puellulas), if any were there, and that they should suffer neither one nor more of such girls to remain there, except such as were to be made nuns[7]

What of St Saens, with bad morals, growing debts and a deficiency of cider? In 1260, "We ordered secular girls to be removed," with one favoured exception[8], in 1261, "They were keeping in the priory two ladies, to wit the daughter of the châtelain of Belencombre and the elder daughter of the lord of Mesnières (de Maneriis) whom we ordered to be sent away"[9]. It is the same with St Aubin, with its bad morals and its tumble-down buildings[10], with Bival, immoral also, overcome with debts even to its own servants for their wages, and always short of stores; in 1252 the nuns had ten children there to be brought up (pueros decem nutriendos) and Rigaud ordered their removal[11] It is the same, too, with St Amand, where the debts increased from year to year and the nuns could not even get in the money due to them, in 1263 a certain daughter of Lady Aeliz de Synoz was found there and removed[12] At St Léger de Preaux (1249)

---

[1] p. 571.   [2] p. 615
[3] Coulton, op cit p. 5.   [4] p. 282
[5] p. 324.   [6] p 572   [7] p 602   [8] p. 380   [9] p 419.
[10] p. 412. "Item ne pueros admitterent ad nutriendum."
[11] p. 146.   [12] p 486.

secular girls were all to be sent away[1], and at St Sauveur d'Evreux all unveiled children (*infantes non velatas*) were immediately to be removed[2], while some years later Rigaud made a general injunction there against receiving relatives of the nuns as boarders[3] A mysterious child was being brought up in a grange belonging to the Abbey of Bival at Pierremans, but why or whose we know not; was it a needy relative of the Abbess, or an indiscretion of sister Isabel or sister Florence, or merely an ordinary paying boarder? History is silent, but the Archbishop was sufficiently annoyed when his order to remove it in 1268 was still disregarded in the following year[4]

The constant attempts of the nuns to add to their numbers were actuated by the same desire to obtain ready money, in the shape of a dowry, the Archbishop was more far-seeing and recognised that the immediate good would be out-balanced by the strain on their scanty revenues in the future, nor was he unmindful of the fact that the demand for a dowry was contrary to the rule The heavy debts and the insufficiency of stores, which he found at convent after convent, certainly seem to indicate that their only hope lay in a rigid limitation of membership. Moreover overcrowding was certainly subversive of discipline and it looks as though Rigaud had, in some cases (e.g at Villarceaux in 1249)[5], been unwilling to permit new recruits to enter a house whose moral record was bad This may explain in part his long struggle with St Saens and with St Aubin, though here, as at Villarceaux, poverty was always the chief reason noted in his diary. At St Aubin the financial *arrière pensée* is very clear. In 1251 Rigaud noted that nuns were received simoniacally; on this and on the four subsequent visitations the Prioress was forbidden to receive any girl as a nun without special licence, and girls received in contravention of this rule were not to be considered veiled or recognised as nuns[6] (this was the usual form in which his prohibition was couched) Then in 1259 came another case of simony, in spite of the Archbishop's former inhibition the nuns had received and veiled a certain lady, the daughter of Sir Robert Mauvoisin (*Mali Vicini*), knight Asked why they had done this they said that urgent necessity and poverty had forced them to it and that the father of the girl had given them an annual rent of 10s with her, but they admitted that they had acted against the wish of the Prioress and without her consent. The Archbishop "seeing them to have acted with cupidity and with the vice of simony" soon afterwards ordered the girl to be removed, unveiled and sent back to her father's house and enjoined a penance upon the nuns[7]; the prohibition to receive nuns without licence was repeated at subsequent visitations[8] There were similarly protracted struggles between the Archbishop and the nuns at St Saens and at St Amand At St Saens,

[1] p. 60.
[2] p 220
[3] p 305.
[4] pp. 610, 636
[5] pp 43, 44
[6] pp. 115, 207, 255, 283, 319.
[7] p. 361.
[8] pp. 412, 471, 550, 587

when he came to visit it in 1258, he found two little girls in residence and in spite of the prayers of the Prioress and some of the nuns that he would allow the children (*puellule*) to be received and veiled, he ordered them to be removed within a week[1]. The next year, however he found that the obstinate nuns had promised four girls, nieces of certain of the nuns, that they should be received if his consent could be obtained, whereupon the Archbishop in great irritation tore up the letters before the assembled chapter and once more repeated his prohibition[2] In 1260 he made an exception in favour of one girl[3], and in 1261, when the nuns asked permission to veil five new inmates "in order that the divine service might be increased" (*ampliandum*), he ordered them to send the candidates or their relatives to him and promised to give the necessary licence if it seemed expedient[4]. In 1262 and 1264[5] the usual prohibition was repeated.

The nuns of St Amand persisted with equal obstinacy in admitting novices without licence In 1254 and again in 1257 the Archbishop noted the presence of four girls who had been promised admission as soon as there was a vacancy[6]. In 1263 he ordered one of them to be removed[7]. In the next year he found that four ladies (*domicelle*) in secular habit had been received, one of them in spite of his inhibition; the Abbess was punished for disobedience and the girl was sent home[8] In 1267 seven girls were waiting to be veiled, but he seems to have made no objection[9]. At Villarceaux in 1257 the niece of a neighbouring prior was found in the house, in secular dress; "and she in the chapter," says Rigaud, "throwing herself upon her knees, besought us to permit her to be received by them, because the Prioress and convent had promised to veil her"[10]. Whether he acceded to her request is not known, but in the following year there was serious trouble, because the Prioress had raised the number of nuns above the statutory number of twenty, by receiving two girls against the bishop's order and the convent's will, one to be a nun and the other to be a lay sister The Archbishop ordered their instant expulsion and specifically mentioned that his former prohibition had been dictated by a desire to do what was best for the convent, "since its resources hardly suffice for a small number of persons"[11] At Bondeville also a girl had been received without licence in 1266 and the Archbishop forbade her to be veiled[12]. Sometimes it is clear that he had to protect the nuns, less against their own improvidence than against the enforced reception of nuns "dumped" upon them by powerful people outside their own ranks. The nuns of Villarceaux were forbidden to receive any lay sister or novice "even if the abbess of St Cyr send her"[13]. At Bival, in 1254, where it is specifically stated that no more nuns are to be received without licence on account of the poverty of the house, he ordered no exception to be made even for two girls

---

[1] p 310. [2] p. 338 [3] p 380. [4] p 419.
[5] pp 451, 491. [6] pp 201, 285. [7] p. 486.
[8] p. 512. [9] p. 588. [10] p 281. [11] p. 323.
[12] p. 571 [13] pp. 44, 572.

sent by the bishop and one by Sir William of Poissy[1]; and at Monti-villiers in 1266 he noted that in spite of his prohibition a girl had been placed there by the Legate[2]

(5) A very common fault in these Rouen (and indeed in all) house was the imperfect claustration of the nuns, seculars entered the precincts, nuns left them There were constant injunctions that no secular or suspected persons were to enter the cloister precincts[3] or to talk with the nuns anywhere save in the parlour[4] At Bival, how-ever, a significant exception was made to the general prohibition; no one was to be introduced except those whom it would be a scandal to turn away[5]—potential benefactors and other powerful folk, no doubt It seems that the nuns were in the habit of dining and of eating meat with seculars (at Bival they absented themselves from Compline for this purpose)[6], and the Archbishop forbade, time after time, the eating together of nuns and seculars[7] No secular person was to sleep in the house[8]; and no nun was to converse with seculars, even in the parlour, without licence from the head of the house and without a suitable companion, such as the doorkeeper[9] These pre-cautions seem to have been necessary, for one is left with the impres-sion that secular visitors gained access without much difficulty to the cloister precincts, at Bival it was complained that brothers and relatives of the nuns and others, entered the house[10]; and at Bonde-ville friends and relatives used to come into the cloister at will and talk with the nuns in the meadows and guest rooms of the house[11], at a later visitation the archbishop remarked that the house where guests were received was too close to the cloister and to the conventual buildings[12] The abuses to which such freedom of access might give rise are obvious They appear in the case of St Aubin, morally the worst of all the houses, the state of that community at the visitations of 1254, 1256, 1257 and 1261 will be referred to later, in 1266 a certain miller was not to be allowed to frequent the house, as scandal had arisen through him, and the schoolmaster (*Rector scolarum*) of Beauvoir had "sometimes impudently frequented the said house or priory, from which evil rumours had arisen," and he was to be warned to desist[13], next year the same miller and two clerics (a rector and a clerk) were frequenting the house and causing scandal and the Archbishop forbade them to enter it[14].

The wandering of nuns outside the precincts was even more danger-ous, and it is significant that after the terrible revelations at Villar-ceaux in 1249 the Archbishop, in his injunctions, paid special atten-tion to the entrance of seculars into the convent and to the conditions under which the nuns were wont to leave it Rigaud strictly forbade

[1] p. 207. [2] p 564. [3] pp. 43, 82, 146, 348.
[4] pp 348, 410. [5] p. 117. [6] p 146
[7] pp 146, 207, 220, 235, 255, 283, 305, 319, 348, 419, 624, 636
[8] pp. 43, 207, 255, 283, 305.
[9] pp. 43, 326. [10] p 117 [11] p. 348. [12] p. 220.
[13] pp. 43, 117, 220, 235, 268, 486, 491, 534, 550. [14] p. 587.

any nun to go out without special licence from the head of the house and that licence was not to be given except for an adequate reason[1]; "not quickly and easily but with difficulty and for an appointed time only"[2], ran the injunction to the Abbess of St Amand. A term was always to be fixed by which the nun had to return and she was always to have a suitable companion allotted to her[3] This seems to have been a necessary precaution, for at St Saëns the nuns were found to stay away alone for fifteen days or more[4], it is perhaps not accidental that St Saëns was one of the immoral houses. At St Léger de Préaux, also, the nuns were in the habit of going out alone to the houses of relatives[5] "They go outside the abbey when they can and return when they will," says the Archbishop[6], in 1267 one of them was found to be alone with her mother at Argoulles, "which displeased us and we forbade the Abbess to give any nun permission to go out without company"[7]. At Bondeville they used often to go to Rouen[8]. Another precaution taken against the wandering of nuns in the world was the closing or careful guarding of the cloister doors; it was ordered at Bival in 1257 that a door opening on to the meadows, which was often unlocked, should be kept locked[9] The causes which took nuns outside the gates were many· sometimes they seem to have gone simply to take a walk; sometimes to visit relatives or to act as god-mothers to the children of friends (a practice which was specifically forbidden at Montivilliers in 1257 and again in 1265)[10]; sometimes on business to the granges of the convent; sometimes to work in the fields (three of the nuns of St Aubin were absent at the vintage (*in vindemiis*) when the Archbishop came in 1267[11], sometimes to beg (at St Aubin in 1261 it was ordered that the younger nuns were not to be sent out to beg (*pro questu*)[12] and two years later two nuns of this poverty-stricken house were absent in France, seeking alms)[13], sometimes for less reputable reasons There is no more striking commentary on the writings of contemporary moralists like Matheolus and Gilles li Muisis than the Register of Eudes Rigaud[14], and the stress laid upon the ill results of allowing seculars to enter and nuns to leave the cloister, shows that the attempts of the medieval Church to impose strict claustration upon nuns, harsh as they seem to modern minds, were dictated by a real social necessity.

(6) Modern minds would also be inclined to consider as trifling offences the various cases of frivolous behaviour—games, gay clothes, pet animals—which the Archbishop entered from time to time in his

---

[1] p 44   [2] p. 285.

[3] pp 43, 197, 296, 338, 348, 374, 380, 419, 451, 455, 486, 491, 534, 591, 624.

[4] p 187 (1254), in 1259 it is again complained that the nuns stay for a long time when they have licence to go outside and on three other occasions it is noted that the nuns go out alone, in 1262 a penance was enjoined on the Prioress for allowing one nun to do so. See pp 338, 380 419, 451, 491.

[5] p. 197.   [6] p 295   [7] p 591.   [8] p 298; cf p 455

[9] p 281, cf pp 146, 486, 588.   [10] pp 293, 517

[11] p. 587.   [12] p. 412.   [13] p. 471.   [14] See above, pp. 542 ff

diary The custom of indulging in games on Innocents' Day, which prevailed in certain English nunneries, was fairly common in Rigaud's diocese In 1249 he made the following injunction at Villarceaux

Item we forbid you in future to indulge in your accustomed gaieties (*ne ludibria exerceatis consueta*) to wit, dressing yourselves up in secular clothes or leading dance-songs (*choreas*) among yourselves or with seculars[1].

But the nuns clung to their rare amusements and in 1253 the Archbishop noted. "They sing ditties (*cantilenas*) on the Feast of Innocents"[2] At St Léger des Préaux in 1254 the diary has· "We forbade disorders (*inordinaciones*) on the Feast of Innocents"[3] and at the Holy Trinity of Caen two years later "The younger ones on the Feast of Innocents sing the scriptures with *farsa*; this we forbade"[4] Montivilliers was a serious offender and the Archbishop's note is learnedly technical over the different kinds of songs sung by the nuns:

Item on the Feasts of St John, St Stephen and the Innocents they use excessive frivolity (*nimia iocositate*) and scurrilous songs, to wit, farces (*farsis*), canticles (*conductis*) and motets (*motulis*), we ordered that they should bear themselves more fittingly and with greater devotion[5].

The order seems to have borne fruit, for in 1262 he noted "The frivolities which used to take place on Innocents' Day have been utterly given up, so they say", and then, and again in 1265, he simply repeated the injunction that such things should cease[6] At St Amand in 1263 he ordered:

That the younger nuns are not to remain behind in the choir on the Feast of Innocents, as they have done in the past, singing the office and proses which belong to the day, the seniors having gone away and left the juniors there[7].

But afterwards we hear no more of these sports among the nuns, so perhaps Rigaud succeeded in stamping them out They were perhaps (if one may judge from the usual character of the Feast of Fools) more scurrilous and less innocently pretty than they sound; but it is difficult not to feel a little out of sympathy with the conscientious Archbishop[8]

The keeping of pet animals here, as in England, was a common fault and one against which Rigaud's animadversions were singularly unsuccessful. The nuns of St Sauveur d'Evreux had small dogs, squirrels and birds, "and we ordered such things to be removed; they do not profit the rule"[9], but we had to repeat our injunction in 1258 and again in 1269[10] At St Léger des Préaux they had two small dogs and three squirrels[11], and at the Holy Trinity of Caen they kept larks and little birds in cages, which were to be removed[12], but the cage birds were still there six years later[13] The most amusing case was at Villarceaux in 1268, where for once one of the nuns gave the Archbishop a piece of her mind "Eustachia, late prioress" (we shall hear of her again), "had a certain bird, which she kept to the annoyance and displeasure of some of the more elderly nuns" (did it disturb

[1] p. 44.   [2] p. 166.   [3] p. 197.   [4] p 261
[5] p 384   [6] pp 431, 517   [7] p 486
[8] See above p 311 and E K Chambers, *The Medieval Stage*, I, ch xv, *passim*.   [9] p. 73   [10] pp 305, 624
[11] p. 295.   [12] p. 95.   [13] p. 201

their slumbers?) "For the which reason we ordered her to remove it, and she thereupon bespake us with little discretion or reverence, which greatly displeased us"[1] One may forgive the archbishop for this lapse in his sense of humour, he had had trouble with Eustachia before, it was just like her to keep a bird that squawked in the dorter.

Nor probably did Rigaud fare better than any other medieval visitor in his attempts to turn fashionable clothes out of the nunneries The disreputable ladies of Villarceaux (1249) curled their hair and scented their veils with saffron, they had pilches of rabbit and hare and fox fur, they wore belts adorned with silver-work and steel-work[2] Those of Montivilliers (1265 and 1266) were nearly as luxurious, though their morals were unimpeachable; they also wore their hair in ringlets, had pilches of squirrel fur and of the costly "griz," and used girdles curiously adorned with ironwork, they ornamented their collars and cuffs with expensive cloth trimmings and possessed "excessively curious and precious knives, with carved and silvered handles"[3] The nuns of St Amand also used not only shifts and pilches, but also pillows and bedclothes soft with the fur of rabbit, hare, fox and cat[4]; and the ornamented girdles of ironwork were found at St Aubin and at St Sauveur[5]. The Archbishop strenuously forbade long hair and curls, belts of ironwork, saffron, rich cloth and the more costly kinds of fur. It is unlikely that he was successful. The world never called more seductively to medieval nuns than in contemporary fashions The Church clung to the belief that the habit made the nun, but the souls of sister Jacqueline and sister Johanna, and sister Philippa and sister Marguerite expressed themselves appropriately in furs and saffron and, one fears, would not have been less frivolous in the regular garb of their order

> Il est bien vray que tourel, voille ou guymple
> Fort scapullaire ou autre habit de corps,
> Ne rend jamais homme ou femme plus simple,
> Mais rompt souvent l'union et accords
> Mectant divorce entre l'âme et le corps[6].

(7) It is now necessary to consider the more serious faults, such as quarrelling, drunkenness or immorality, detected by Eudes Rigaud in his visitations, and to give a fuller account of those nunneries which were in a particularly evil state. The quarrels which were inseparable from convent life continually occupied his attention; and nine out of the twelve houses which he visited more than once were at one time or another disturbed by petty squabblings among the nuns. It is clear—as might be expected—that the discord was worse in those convents where discipline was loose, and where the behaviour of the nuns in other directions was open to grave censure At the visitation

[1] p 602, compare a similar case at Legbourne, above, p. 412.
[2] p 43   [3] pp 518, 564   [4] p. 16.
[5] pp 73, 207, 220, 305, 624.
[6] Montaiglon, *Recueil de Poésies Françoises des XVIe et XVIIe siècles*, t. VIII, pp. 171, 173.

of Villarceaux in 1249, for instance, Ermengarde of Gisors and Johanna of Auvilliers beat one another and the Archbishop was obliged to order the punishment of quarrels passing from words to blows[1] (*de verbis ad verbera*—he was not above a mild ecclesiastical pun in the privacy of his diary)[2] At St Aubin (1254) Agnes of the Bridge (*de Ponte*) and Petronilla refused to speak to each other, and Agnes, "who is a fomenter of discord and a scold," was ordered to give up her rancour against Petronilla, on pain of being removed from the convent[3] At Bival in 1252 two sisters were described as rebellious[4] and two years later the Register contains the following entry·

There are two sets of couples who refuse to speak to one another and we caused them to make peace with each other and to kiss and be friends (*quantum ad os, et deosculari ad invicem*), and we forbade that any mention should henceforth be made of the bone of contention between them, on pain of excommunication, which we have called down upon her who shall be the first to mention it, and we ordered the Abbess to keep us informed[5].

At St Saens a certain Johanna Martel—evidently a lady of substance with relatives in the neighbourhood—was said in 1259 to be rebellious, disobedient and given to wrangling with the Prioress[6], and in 1265 the house was full of discord[7]. At Almenèches (1250) there was a good deal of quarrelling in cloister and choir[8]

Quarrels were common, however, in houses against which no grave moral disorders were ever charged   St Amand was perhaps the worst of these, there in 1258 the Archbishop ordered that each nun was to forget the injury and offence of the other, before she presumed to receive communion[9], but the discords continued and in 1262 he wrote.

Because we found there many heart-burnings and rancours among the nuns, we ordered the abbess and the confessor that they should reconcile those whom they knew to have fallen into this fault before, and that they should live in charity as far as they were able, punishing offenders by taking away their beer and pittances[10].

But it was in vain, and after seven years Rigaud was still commanding the Abbess to labour to the best of her ability that the nuns should live in peace and concord[11] At Bondeville (1251 and 1255) it will be remembered that one of the charges against the Prioress was her quarrelsomeness[12]; and in 1259 a certain Lucy was found to be a

---

[1] pp. 43–4.

[2] But a better example of his wit is shown in his repartee to another's pun, quoted in Coulton, *A Medieval Garner*, p. 289. "A clerical buffoon once ventured to ask him across the table, 'What is the difference, my lord, betwixt *Rigaud* and *Ribaud* [rascal]?' 'Only this board's breadth,' replied the Archbishop." The jest is however widespread, *mutatis mutandis*, in the east as well as in the west. It is told of one John Scot, 'What difference is there between sot and scot?' 'Just the breadth of the table' *Calendar of Jests, Epigrams, Epitaphs etc* (Edinburgh 1753); it also occurs in Gladwin's *Persian Moonshee* and in several Indian collections of *facetiae* W A. Clouston, *Popular Tales and Fictions* (1887) I, p 51

[3] p 207   [4] p 146   [5] p 207   [6] P 338.
[7] p 522   [8] p 82   [9] p 326   [10] p. 456
[11] p 638   [12] See pp 645–6, above

quarrelsome and ill-tempered person, disobedient to the Prioress and
given to wrangling with her in the frater, whereupon the Archbishop
enjoined a penance of silence upon her[1] At St Désir de Lisieux (1254)
there were two or three nuns who would not speak to the rest[2]; and
even at the great Abbaye aux Dames at Caen Rigaud noted in 1267,
"There was great contention among them and concerning this they
had a case in the law-courts"[3]

Quarrelsomeness was, however, a mild fault compared with the
really bad immorality which prevailed in some of the houses At
three of them, St Aubin, St Saëns and Bival, this state of affairs
continued from visitation to visitation, they were evidently hopelessly
corrupt. At the two others (Villarceaux and Almenèches) there is
mention of serious disorders only once and from the Archbishop's
silence on later occasions it may be hoped that he succeeded in
reforming the houses One of these isolated cases was in many ways
the most serious of all, Rigaud's note of his visitation of Villarceaux
in 1249 reads more like a description of La Maison Tellier than that
of a priory; except that the former was more discreet

We visited the priory of Villarceaux There are twenty-three nuns and three
lay sisters [Here follow several minor disorders.] Only four nuns there
are fully professed, to wit Eustachia, Comitissa, Ermengarde and Petronilla
Many of them have pilches made from the fur of rabbits, hares and foxes.
They eat flesh unnecessarily in the infirmary; they do not observe silence
anywhere and they do not keep within the cloister Johanna of "Aulular"
once went out of the cloister and lived with someone, by whom she had a
child; and she sometimes goes out of the cloister to see that child, item she
is ill-famed (infamata) with a certain man called Gaillard Isabella la Treiche
is a fault finder, murmuring against the Prioress and others The cellaress
is ill-famed with a man called Philip of Villarceaux. The Prioress is too
negligent and does not reprove, nor does she get up [for matins] Johanna
of Auvilliers goes outside the house alone with Gayllard and within the year
she had a child by him. The cellaress is ill-famed with Philip of Villarceaux
and with a certain priest of her own neighbourhood Item the subprioress
with Thomas the carter. Idonia her sister with Crispinatus Item the prior
of Gisors frequents the house for the sake of the said Idonia Philippa of
Rouen is ill-famed with the priest of Suentre, in the diocese of Chartres;
Marguerita the treasuress with Richard de Geneville, clerk. Agnes of Fonte-
noy is ill-famed with the priest of Guerreville, of the diocese of Chartres
La Toolière [? the chambress] is ill-famed with Sir Andrew de Monchy,
knight They all wear their hair long to their chins (nutriunt comam usque
ad mentum) and scent their veils with saffron Jacqueline came back
pregnant from a certain chaplain, who was expelled from the house for
this. Item Agnes de Montsec was ill-famed with the same. Ermengarde
of Gisors and Johanna of Auvilliers beat each other. The Prioress is drunk
almost any night ..she does not rise for matins nor eat in the frater nor
correct faults[4].

[1] Reg p. 348.   [2] p. 199
[3] p. 575 Cf the case of the Priory of Couz, when it was visited in
1283 by Simon of Beaulieu, Archbishop of Bourges Baluze, Miscellanea,
1, 281.
[4] pp. 43–4. Notice the disjointed character of the report and the repetition of charges, e g. against Johanna of Alto Villari (who is probably the

After these terrible revelations the Archbishop directed a letter of injunctions to the convent, which, contrary to his usual practice, was copied into his diary[1]. These injunctions deal only with general breaches of the rule, which by loosening discipline would tend to give opportunities for the behaviour described in the *comperta*, and they contain no reference to specific cases of immorality. Thus he provides for the proper performance of divine service, for the maintenance of silence; for the simultaneous entry of the nuns into their dorter, the keys of which and of the cloister were to be carefully kept and a "Visitor" appointed to see that the rule was kept in these matters, he forbids secular or suspected persons to be entertained or lodged within the cloister, and nuns to be given permission to go outside without good reason and a companion, or to speak with any external person unlicensed and unaccompanied; he deals also with the frivolous garments, the sports on Innocents' Day and the quarrels which he had found; he forbids the reception of any more nuns without licence, orders the frequent rendering of accounts, warns them to live in common, and ends with an order to recite his letter at least once a month in the chapter. These injunctions seem strangely superficial in comparison with the *comperta* which precede them; but a note entered in the Register, on the occasion of the next visitation of Villarceaux, would seem to suggest that the Archbishop had taken other steps to deal with the matter It is there written. "Here are twenty nuns, but six of them were not present, for one of them left the house and married in the world and two are without the house, according to a previous mandate and ordinance of ours"[2] It is possible that the Archbishop had sent separate letters (not copied into his Register) dealing with the worst cases of immorality, and that he had sent two of the erring nuns to do penance in another house. At any rate there are no further complaints of immorality against Villarceaux, and perhaps prompt measures at the beginning of his career as visitor had stayed the nuns on their downward course

It was on Rigaud's first visitation of Almenêches also that moral disorders were found. He went there in 1250 and found that the rule had been greatly relaxed The nuns (who were among the most inveterate property owners recorded in the Register) used to run up debts in the town, doubtless with the money given to them for the purchase of their food. They did not live a communal life, they admitted seculars to talk with them in the cloister, they remained away from Matins and Compline, they had drinking parties after Compline, and they were always quarrelling The result of this laxity showed in more serious faults Sister Tiphaine was a drunkard (*ebriosa*), three other nuns, Hola, Aaliz the chantress and the late prioress had each had a child, and a fourth, Dionisia Dehatim, was

same as Johanna of *Auluları*) the cellaress and the Prioress This probably indicates that it is a verbatim report of evidence taken down from the lips of the nuns, as they came before the Archbishop.

---

[1] pp. 44–5.　　　　　　　　　　[2] p. 117.

ill-famed with a certain Master Nicholas de Bleve In this case some of the disorder may have been due to the fact that the house was without an abbess, she having died shortly before[1] Here again it is impossible to tell what steps the Archbishop took to reform the house, but at his two subsequent visitations, although the nuns persisted in their refusal to live a communal life, there were no further notices of immorality.

One may hope that these were exceptional cases in the history of the houses concerned But there was nothing exceptional about the bad behaviour of St Aubin and St Saens and to a lesser degree of Bival The Archbishop first visited the latter house in 1248 and found there "several nuns ill-famed of the vice of incontinence"; the abbess resigned, probably as a result of this discovery[2] No complaint of immorality was made at the next two visitations; then in 1254 the Archbishop noted that sister Isabella had had a child at Whitsuntide by a priest[3] At the next visitation (1256) he found that Florence had had a child recently and that the whole house had fallen into ill-repute because of this; Rigaud on this occasion ordered the removal of the convent priest, "on account of the scandal of the nuns and populace, though we found nothing that could be proved against him"[4]. On the eight subsequent visitations there were no further charges of immorality.

St Aubin and St Saens must be charged with persistent immorality, continuing over a long period of years. They seem indeed to have been little better than brothels. At St Aubin in 1254 Aeliz of Rouen was incontinent and had lately had a child by a priest[5] In 1256 she was in trouble again:

We unveiled Aeliz of Rouen and Eustachia of Etrepagny for a time, on account of their fornication Item we sent Agnes of the Bridge (de Ponte) [the same whose quarrelsomeness had been reproved in 1254] to the lazar-house of Rouen, because she consented to Eustachia's sin and even procured it, as the rumour runs, *et quia dedit dicte Eustachie herbas bibere ut interficeretur puer conceptus in dicta Eustachia, secundum quod dicitur per famam*[6]. We removed the Prioress from office We postponed the infliction of a punishment upon Anastasia, the subprioress, for ill-fame of incontinence against her, until she should be made prioress there[7].

Here at last we have definite information of the steps taken by Rigaud to deal with a bad case, two nuns were unveiled and sent to do penance among lepers and the prioress was deposed; but what a confession of weakness that Rigaud should propose to fill the place of the latter with a woman herself ill-famed of sin The effect of his punishment upon the two nuns whom he had unveiled was, moreover, unfortunate, for they went from bad to worse. The next year Eustachia was in

[1] p 82   [2] p. 6   [3] p 207.   [4] p 268.   [5] p 207.
[6] A similar charge was made at the convent of St Saëns in 1264 where scandal imputed to Nicholaa, a notoriously immoral nun, "*quod ipsa nondum erat mensis elapsus fecerat abortivum*", but the Archbishop apparently disbelieved the charge p. 491 See p. 669, below.
[7] p. 255

apostasy (*vagabunda*) and had been pregnant when she left the convent and the blame for it was set down to John, the chaplain of Fry. Aeliz of Rouen also was "in grave sin"[1]. In 1261 the Archbishop came again. Aeliz had borne a child since his last visitation and she was said to have had three children in all; Beatrice of Beauvais had had a child at Blaacort and her lover was the Dean of St Quentin, of the Diocese of Beauvais. The Prioress informed Rigaud that these two had long been in serious fault and that they had undergone penance according to the rule[2] In 1263 Aeliz and Beatrice had run away ("led," Rigaud confided to his diary, "by the levity of their spirits and by the instigation of the devil") and he ordered them not to be readmitted without his special licence[3] The next year Beatrice was still wandering abroad and was said to have had several children[4] No more is heard of these erring sisters at the three subsequent visitations, but it is evident that the discipline of the house was still far from good, and the constant visits of a miller and of several other men (all clerics)[5] had caused scandals in 1265 and again in 1267[6]. In 1267 the Subprioress was punished for giving up her office at her own will[7], and in 1268 there is an ambiguous entry which leads one to suppose that Anastasia had never become prioress after all and that Eustachia (it may not be the same woman) was back again; on that occasion Anastasia "late subprioress" was punished because she gave up her office contrary to the will of the Prioress, while Eustachia and Margaret were punished because they would not undertake it, when commanded to do so[8].

The case of St Saens was hardly less serious; for the first six visitations there was no charge of immorality, though it is clear from the Archbishop's note in 1254 that the discipline of the house was lax and in particular that the nuns had leave of absence to stay away alone for as long as a fortnight at a time and that their priest was incontinent[9] In any case the visitation of 1259 showed a state of things so disgraceful, that it is difficult to believe that it could have arisen within the two years that had elapsed since the last visitation

Some of them stayed away unduly long when they happened to go out with the licence of the Prioress We ordered that such were to be given a shorter term by which to return. Johanna Martel was rebellious and disobedient and she wrangled with the Prioress and went out riding to see her relatives, wearing a mantle of burnet with sleeves; and she had a private messenger whom she used often to send to those relatives Nicholaa had had a child in the same house on Maundy Thursday and its father was said to be Master Simon, the parson of St Saens, the boy was baptized in the monastery and then sent to a certain sister of Nicholaa's She lay in the monastery and underwent her churching with them; she was attended in childbed by

---

[1] p. 283.   [2] p. 412.   [3] p 471.   [4] p 500
[5] It is noticeable how often in these visitations the nuns are reported to have been led astray by priests, but when one considers the character borne by many of the parochial and other clergy of the diocese, as it is recorded in the Register, this is hardly surprising.
[6] pp. 550, 587   [7] p. 587   [8] p 619   [9] p. 187.

two midwives from the village Item another of the nuns had a child by
the same Simon. The Prioress was held suspect with Richard of Maucomble,
it was also said that she managed the goods and business of the house
badly and that she concealed some of the rents and returns The same
Richard had lodged in the house together with the brother and parents
of the Prioress and had often dined there[1].

Five years later (in 1264) Petronilla of Dreux was ill-famed of
incontinence with Ralph, the hayward (*messerius*) of the Priory, and
also with a married man, and the Archbishop ordered the former to
be removed from his office and not to be permitted to frequent the
priory. The Prioress was ill-famed with a priest, and it was said that she
often went to the manor of Esquequeville and elsewhere, where she
entertained many guests and kept ill company (*ubi secum habebat
multos convivas et inhonestam societatem ducebat*), for which Rigaud
censured her and ordered her to improve There was more scandal about
Nicholaa (now called "of Rouen" and described as the chantress),
it was apparently common talk in the village that she used to dine
with her sister at Rouen, in the house of Master Simon, Rector of
St Saens, and rumour made a yet more serious charge against her[2]
"But," says the Archbishop, "we could find nothing to prove concerning this in our visitation and the nuns said that the last charge
was falsely and mendaciously imputed to her"[3] Nevertheless it is
significant that Nicholaa's name should still, after five years, be
connected with the Rector of St Saens and with her complacent sister
In 1265 there was no mention of immorality, but the nuns were
living together "in discord and disorder"·

"Because indeed," wrote Rigaud, "we perceived them to be in a bad state,
particularly as concerning certain observances of the rule, we sought eagerly
how we might labour to reform them to a more honest and salutary condition, according to God and to their rule";

and he returned the next day to complete his measures for this reform[4]. But in 1266-7 the cellaress Petronilla of Dreux was again very
gravely ill-famed (*plurimum diffamata*) with Ralph, "a certain yeoman
who served them in harvest time" and there can be no better proof
that the Archbishop's injunctions often went unfulfilled, for he had
ordered Ralph's expulsion in 1264[5]. Nevertheless the rest of the
house was in good order, so perhaps his eager labour had not been
altogether in vain. In 1267, however, things were as bad as ever
The Prioress, Johanna of Morcent, was ill-famed with the same priest
against whom she had been warned in 1264; Petronilla of Dreux was
still "very gravely ill-famed with Ralph de Maintru, as she was
before; and," says the Archbishop, with one of those personal touches
which make his Register a real human document, "Agnes of Equetot
and Johanna of Morainville we found to be liars and perjurers, when
we demanded certain things of them on oath, wherefore we came away
from the place, as it were impatient and sad...(*Quasi impacientes
et tristes*)"[6]; it was indeed no wonder.

<hr>

[1] p. 338.   [2] See above, p. 667, note 6.   [3] p. 491.   [4] p. 522.
[5] p. 566.   [6] p. 598.

APPENDIX III

FIFTEENTH CENTURY SAXON VISITATIONS
BY JOHANN BUSCH

THREE accounts of medieval visitations stand out in general interest above all others, the thirteenth century Norman visitations of Eudes Rigaud, Archbishop of Rouen, described in his diary, the fifteenth century English visitations of Alnwick, Bishop of Lincoln, described in his Register[1] and the almost contemporary German visitations of the Austin Canon and reformer Johann Busch, described in his *Liber de Reformatione Monasteriorum* Busch's account is less formal and more literary than those of Rigaud and Alnwick; he sets out not to keep a journal, like the former, nor to record official documents, like the latter, but to look back in retrospect upon his work and to make for posterity a chronicle of the reforms connected with the congregation of Windesheim For this reason, and because Busch was a remarkable man, his book will probably transcend the others in interest for the general reader; his account of the difficulties which he encountered is so vivid and at times so humourous, the sidelight thrown upon his own character shows him so admirable and yet so human

Johann Busch was born in 1399 and in 1419 became a canon in the Austin monastery of Windesheim, a new foundation, famed for the strictness of its rule and already the head of a congregation of daughter houses He has left an interesting account of the doubts and temptations which assailed him during his novitiate; they were the stormy dawn clouds of a day which was to become glorious in the annals of his order. During the next twenty years he held from time to time various posts in different houses of the reformed congregation, in 1431 he was attached to the nunnery of Bronopia, in 1436 he became Subprior of Wittenberg and in 1439 he went to Sulte, near Hildesheim, where he was made Prior in the following year He had therefore had considerable experience of monastic houses and it was when he became Prior of Sulte that his great work as a reformer of monasteries began He undertook it originally at the request of the Bishop and Chapter of Hildesheim, who were appalled at the decadence of monastic life in that diocese and anxious for the introduction of reforms on the model of Windesheim. His success in Hildesheim prompted Archbishop Günther of Magdeburg to invite him to carry the reforming movement into that diocese and in 1447 Busch became *praepositus*[2] of the Neuwerk in Halle. This brought him to the notice of the Papal Legate Nicholas of Cues, who came to hold

[1] Or rather on loose sheets, which were not intended for official preservation and have survived only by accident

[2] I e abbot These German Augustinians never used the term *abbas*, but used *praepositus* instead

a provincial council in Magdeburg in 1451, and Nicholas, himself an ardent reformer, issued a general mandate empowering him to enter and reform the Austin monasteries of the provinces of Magdeburg, Mainz, Saxony and Thuringia Unfortunately Busch now quarrelled with the Archbishop of Magdeburg and had to resign in 1454 He returned to Wittenberg and continued his campaign of reform, turning his attention specially to nunneries. Then, after a short sojourn at Windesheim he returned to Sulte in 1459, where he remained until his death in 1480. He left behind him two books, a *Chronicon Windeshemense*, and the *Liber de Reformatione Monasteriorum*, which between them give an invaluable account not only of the rise of Windesheim and of the reforming movement which emanated from it, but of the life and character of Busch himself[1].

Book II of the *Liber de Reformatione Monasteriorum* describes the reform of twenty-three nunneries and two houses of lay sisters, of which the great majority belonged to his own order of Austin Regular Canons[2] The work was not carried out without considerable opposition, not only from the nuns themselves, for the desire for reform seldom came from within the unreformed orders[3], but also from their friends and kinsmen in the world, to whom they frequently appealed for help Moreover certain ecclesiastical magnates, notably the Bishop of Minden, opposed and impeded reforms in their districts, and even when they submitted to such reforms lent them an indifferent and easily discouraged support On the other hand Busch received his

---

[1] *Des Augustinerpropstes Iohannes Busch Chronicon Windeshemense und Liber de Reformatione Monasteriorum* bearbeitet v Dr Karl Grube (*Hist Com der Provinz. Sachsen* Halle, 1886).

[2] The nunneries dealt with by Busch are the following (A = Austin, B. = Benedictine, C = Cistercian, M M = penitentiary order of St Mary Magdalen, following the Cistercian rule). (1) Wennigsen (S. of Hanover, dioc. Minden, A.), (2) Mariensee (N. of Hanover, dioc. Minden, C.), (3) Barsinghausen (S. of Hanover, dioc Minden, A); (4) Marienwerder (N of Hanover, dioc. Minden, A), (5) St George, or Marienkammer (in Glaucha, a suburb of Halle, dioc Magdeburg, C), (6) Magdalenenkloster, Hildesheim (dioc Hildesheim, M.M.), (7) Derneburg (W. of Hildesheim, dioc. Hildesheim, A), (8) Escherde (S W of Hildesheim, B); (9) Heiningen (in Hanover, between Wolfenbuttel and Goslar, dioc Hildesheim, A); (10) Stederburg (near Brunswick, dioc Hildesheim, A.); (11) Frankenburg (in Goslar, dioc. Hildesheim, M M), (12) Kloster zum hl. Kreuze (Holy Cross) or Neuwerk, Erfurt (dioc. Mainz, A), (13) St Cyriac's in Erfurt (dioc Mainz, B), (14) Weissfrauenkloster (White Ladies) in Erfurt (dioc Mainz, M M), (15) St Martin's in Erfurt (dioc Mainz, C), (16) Marienberg (near Helmstedt, dioc. Halberstadt, A.), (17) Marienborn (near Helmstedt, dioc. Halberstadt, A.), (18) Weinhausen (near Lüneburg, dioc. Hildesheim, C); (19) Weissfrauenkloster (White Ladies) in Magdeburg (dioc Magdeburg, M M), (20) Wulfinghausen (near Wittenberg, dioc Hildesheim, A); (21) Fischbeck (near Rinteln on the Weser, in Hessen-Nassau, dioc. Minden, A.); (22) Dorstadt (near Wolfenbuttel, dioc Hildesheim, A.), (23) Stendal (in the mark of Brandenburg A). Also (24) Bewerwijk in N. Holland (Franciscan tertiaries), and (25) Segeberghhus in Lübeck, both houses of lay sisters.

[3] But see *Liber*, pp. 600, 637, 640.

most powerful support from great ecclesiastics such as the Cardinal Legate Nicholas of Cues, the Archbishop of Magdeburg and the Bishops of Halberstadt and Hildesheim, and also from the superiors and chief inmates of houses belonging to the congregation of Windesheim, or already reformed under its influence Men such as Rutger, prior of Wittenberg, were of the greatest assistance to him, they accompanied him as co-visitors and promoted his work in every possible way, while the reformed nunneries often provided him with nuns to dwell for a time in the houses which he was reforming and to teach their inmates how to comport themselves Apart from such powerful ecclesiastical support Busch was particularly fortunate in the assistance which he received from the Dukes of Brunswick, Otto, William and Henry, who reigned during his lifetime These nobles, especially Duke William, had the greatest esteem for Busch and not infrequently accompanied him on his visitations, lending the temporal intimidation of their arguments and armed retainers to his more spiritual menaces The support of the secular arm was, indeed, necessary, in view of the opposition of lay kinsfolk to the reform of their daughters and sisters.

The monastic houses of Germany had by the fifteenth century fallen into great laxity of rule. The nuns seem to have lost all knowledge of how to perform the ordinary offices of convent life, in choir, chapter and frater, according to the rule, and Busch was often at pains to go carefully through the routine with them, teaching them what to do at each moment This occasionally gave rise to some amusing scenes At one of the first houses to be reformed, St Mary Magdalen near Hildesheim (1440), Busch and an elderly monk of Sulte were teaching the nuns by ocular demonstration how to comport themselves in frater. Having arranged the sisters in seemly order Busch and brother John Bodiker began to intone *Benedicite*, after the fashion of reformed religious, but the nuns, who had not been accustomed to singing the *Benedicite* at table, all burst out laughing, instead of following Busch and the brother, however, kept on until the nuns collected themselves and came in with bowed heads at the verse *Gloria patri* Similarly when Busch was showing them how to confess their own and proclaim others' faults in chapter (a custom which they had completely lost), brother John, acting the sinner, rose up among the sisters and cast himself flat upon the pavement, whereat "the astonished nuns fell to marvelling that such an old brother should seek thus to lie prone"[1]

The most serious fault found by Busch, serious not only because it was a breach of one of the three substantial vows of monasticism, but because it brought in its train other and worse evils, was the ownership of private property The nuns were almost universally *proprietarie*, owning money and annual rents, to say nothing of their own private cooking and dining utensils, for, as always, communal life had gone with individual poverty and the nuns provided their

[1] *Liber*, p. 580

own meals and dined in *familia*. At Derneburg Busch describes the
girls and women of the village coming up to the doors and windows
of the house with bread and meat and cheese in sacks and baskets
for the nuns to buy[1]. It was his custom on visiting a house to demand
that all the private possessions of the nuns should be brought and
heaped up before him. Unwillingly they came with the charters
reciting their private rents, the ready money from their purses and
chests, the gold and silver rings, the coral paternosters, and all the
pots and pans and basins, the cups and plates and spoons which they
used for their private meals. All these Busch carefully noted down.
"I marvelled," he says on one occasion, when he had collected a
particularly large heap from quite a small house, "how they could
have collected from their parents and predecessors and reserved for
themselves, as it were by right of inheritance, such a large number
of utensils"[2]. All the money, endowments and implements thus
brought together Busch then handed over to the common treasury
and store-room of the house.

This rooting out of private property gave rise to the bitterest
opposition. The nuns had been wont to evade the charge of *proprietas*
by the merest quibble, which Busch contemptuously swept away.
They had deposited all their money and charters with the abbess
and when they wanted any they had asked her for it, but she was
merely the guardian of their private incomes, which were never
merged in a common stock[3] When they found that this device was
rejected by Busch, they did all they could to preserve their hoards.
Sometimes they secretly sent their money out of the house before
his arrival[4], sometimes they locked it up and tried to conceal it[5]
The attitude of their kinsfolk also was a stumbling block. These
gentlemen were willing enough to endow their own daughters and
nieces, but not so willing to support the children of others by gifts
which were turned to the common use. Thus it was the nuns who
frequently protested that their house was too poor to permit of their
living in common, since it was only by these individual endowments
that they maintained their existence. It was therefore Busch's practice, before completing the reformation of a house, to make the nuns
obtain from their kinsfolk an undertaking to continue, and if possible
to augment, the rents which they had been wont to give their relatives,
on the threat of turning out the nuns and distributing them among
other houses[6] The nobles and burghers of the district naturally wished
to keep their kinswomen near them and the endowments were usually
forthcoming At St George (or Marienkammer) near Halle even this
device did not result in a large enough income for the nuns; so Busch
caused sermons to be preached in all the churches of the district,

---

[1] *Liber*, p. 591.
[2] *Ib.* p 610. For interesting lists of money and goods put into common
stock by Busch see also pp 614, 616, 617, 633
[3] *Ib.* pp 633–4   [4] *Ib* p. 633.
[5] *Ib* pp. 571–2,   [6] See *ib* pp. 572, 591.

saying that because of their poverty the fathers of their order wished to distribute the nuns in other houses in the dioceses of Hildesheim and Halberstadt, but that they would be able to remain if they were helped by alms Whereupon the townsfolk, out of pity for them, gave generously enough to support them for a whole year. Busch led the way himself, sending them openly two large cartloads of corn and a sack of cheeses, an example which was soon followed by the townsfolk, who had ample opportunity of observing the progress of the cart from Busch's door to the gates of the convent, "for" (says he), "I lived on the eastern, they on the western side of the town" Dr Paul, the *praepositus* of St Maurice, Halle, also helped with a cask of wine[1].

Closely connected with the question of private property was the dowry system, against which Busch also set his face, for it was not only in itself contrary to the rule, but it was one method by which the nuns received those private endowments which they afterwards turned to their own uses·

"All the nuns of Saxony," says Busch, "whatever their order, made a simoniacal entry into their monasteries before the new reform, giving a sum of money for their reception, and according to ancient custom the newcomers give a certain potation to all the *praepositi*, priests and chaplains and a great feast for their many friends and for all the nuns and inhabitants [of the house] This was the common custom in all the nunneries of Saxony and particularly in those which were rich"[2].

Busch forbade the custom everywhere.

The nuns thus lived like seculars, performing the minimum number of services and owning private property   Like seculars also they loved to give that "fetis" pinch to their wimples, that elegant turn to their mantles, which changed the sombre habit of their order into the dress of a lady of fashion. Busch, in common with all the reformers of the later middle ages, has a great deal to say about their clothes All the nuns of Saxony and Thuringia refused to crop their heads, and contented themselves with cutting their hair short at the neck[3]. The nuns of Wulfinghausen and Fischbeck wore long flowing white veils over their heads, so that it was hardly possible to recognise them as nuns[4] Those of St Cyriac's appeared very pompously arrayed in long tunics and mantles, with tall peaked caps and flowing veils, "que non monialium sed domicellarum castrantium apparatum habuerunt"[5] The nuns of Barsinghausen

were very slender, having underneath long tight tunics of white cloth, and above being clad in almost transparent robes of black linen, which they called *superpellicia*, not girdled but flowing, with long sleeves, which they turned back for capes, beneath which almost all their form, which was bare underneath, could be seen[6]

[1] *Liber*, pp 573-4 Compare the exertions of Berthold, Prior of Sulte, to provide the poor nuns of Heiningen with sufficient stores of food and to pay off their debts, *ib* pp. 601-2; see also, p. 599.
[2] *Ib* p 614.   [3] *Ib* p 582.   [4] *Ib*. p. 643
[5] *Ib* p. 614.   [6] *Ib* p 567

The nuns of the penitential order of St Mary Magdalen near Hildesheim wore

"a pleated veil, called in the vulgar tongue *Ranse*, such as they imagine
the blessed Mary Magdalen used to wear, and over tunics very straitly
girdled at the breast, so as to make them appear slender, and with very
loose pleated trains behind, from the girdle to the hem, after the fashion
of secular women I and my brother John Bodiker," adds Busch, "censured
their habit, for that it was not religious but rather ministered to worldly
vanity, and with many pious admonishments we led them all in turn to
put off those pleated veils and put over their heads plain white veils without
folds and to give up those gowns, which were tight in the upper part and
in the lower part wide and pleated, lest they should seem to be following
worldly vanity and the subtlety of their own hearts, rather than religion"[1].

As might be expected laxity of rule and widespread *proprietas*
brought immorality in their train and Busch in several cases mentions
that a convent was ill-famed for incontinence On the other hand
this was by no means invariably the case. At Wulfinghausen, for
instance, Busch told the nuns that he had never heard a word
breathed against their chastity[2] At Weinhausen, where the old abbess
withstood reform so strenuously that she had to be removed by force,
and where all the nuns possessed private incomes, he specially notes
"these nuns observed well the vow of chastity, for their lady the
old abbess ruled them very strictly, and they held her in great reverence
and fear and called her 'gracious lady,' because of her high birth"[3].
Moreover certain houses received reform so readily and became so
soon models of good behaviour, that there cannot have been any very
serious moral decay in them But a passage in the course of Busch's
account of the reform of the Magdalenenkloster at Halle, shows his
own opinion as to the relation between absolute immorality and lesser
breaches of the rule, and shows in particular the important part which
he held to be played by the vice of *proprietas* in the downward path
of a nun It is interesting also because in it he attributes a great
deal of the decadence of nunneries to insufficient control by their
pastors and above all to too infrequent visitation

"The feminine sex," he says, "cannot long persist in the due observance
of their rule without men, who are proven, and reformed and who often
call them by wise counsels to better things For our eyes saw no monastery
of nuns belonging to any order (and there is no small number of them in
Saxony, Misnia and Thuringia) who remained for long in their good intent,
holy life and due reform without reformed fathers. For wherever nuns and
holy sisters do not confess at set times, nor communicate, nor hold chapter
meeting concerning their faults at least once a week, nor are visited by
their [spiritual] fathers every year , such nuns and sisters we saw and
heard often to be fallen from the observance of their rule and from the
religious life to a dissolute life, odious in the sight of God and men, to the
grave peril and eternal damnation of their souls For first laying aside the
fear of God, they fall into the sin of property in small things, then in greater
things and then in the *peculium* of money and clothes, thence they break

---

[1] *Liber*, pp. 582–3; compare pp. 603, 638. [2] *Ib.* p. 639.
[3] *Ib.* p. 633.

out into the desires of the flesh and incontinence of the outward senses and so to the evil act, and thus they fear not to give themselves over bit by bit to all uncleanliness and foulness"[1].

He ends with an eloquent plea for a closer watch to be kept over nuns by those responsible for their spiritual welfare

Such were the main faults which Busch strove to abolish in bringing the nunneries under the reformed rule of Hildesheim. It remains to give some account of the difficulties which he encountered in the course of his work In some houses he was well received; at Erscherde he says of the nuns:

These virgins were well obedient, pious and tractable, dealing with us and with each other kindly and benignantly by word and deed, wherefore we were no little edified by them[2],

and at St Martin's, Erfurt, he says:

We found a prioress and nuns living in great poverty, very simple and humble, but of good will and ready for all good work, for they applied themselves promptly to obedience and to the observance of their rule, and very willingly brought to us all those things which they held in private possession[3].

In other houses reform was not so easy. Busch was frequently impeded by old and obstinate members of a convent, who refused to accept a change in the routine which they had followed for so long. Such was the nobly born abbess of Weinhausen, who was over seventy years of age and had to be removed by force from the house, before any reforms could be carried out· "I found this way of life kept in this monastery forty years ago; this way have I served during as many years and this way and not otherwise will I continue to serve " One cannot but pity the poor old lady, brought out of her house and forced to ascend the carriage which was to take her away, with Busch pulling her by one sleeve and the Abbot of St Michael by the other; and one is relieved to hear that she was allowed back again shortly afterwards, though forced to resign the position of Abbess[4] But Busch's experience in reforming monasteries caused him to dread the opposition of men and women who had been long in religion. In the course of his panegyric on Fischbeck, which had been reformed from within by a remarkable Abbess, he says·

This monastery hath this advantage over many other Saxon houses, as well of monks as of nuns, that it contains no old people, for these old folk do not fear God nor care they for conscience or for obedience, but when no one is looking, then they do all that they think or desire, chattering with one another and with anyone else, by day and by night, even in places where it is forbidden by the rule[5].

Besides the obstinacy of old members of the house Busch had also to contend with the occasional opposition of confessors or *praepositi*, who resented his interference in their domain At the Magdalenen-

[1] *Liber*, p 587   [2] *Ib* p 599.
[3] *Ib* p 617. Compare Marienwerder, *ib*. pp 567–8
[4] *Ib*. pp. 630–2.   [5] *Ib*. p. 642.

kloster at Hildesheim, their confessor, who had been with the nuns
for eight years, desired to be released after the reformation of the
house, saying to the *praepositus*: "I have been their confessor for so
many years, yet nought do I receive from them, save one or two
refections in three or four weeks I would fain be free of them and
let them get another confessor." Busch comments significantly "He
said this, because when they were property-owners, they gave him
many little gifts in money, and spices. Now, because they had no
private property, they gave him nothing"[1]. At the convent of White
Ladies and at Marienberg the *praepositus* of the house did everything
possible to hinder the reform[2] Moreover in several cases Busch had
also to deal with the opposition of laymen, objecting either to the
enclosure of their kinswomen, or to the abolition of private endowments, or merely supporting on general grounds the objections of
the nuns.

The difficulties encountered by a fifteenth century German reformer
are best estimated by giving an account of some of Busch's adventures
at recalcitrant houses. At his first attempt to reform Wennigsen
in Hanover (1455) he had against him the Bishop of Minden and all
the nobles of the neighbouring castles, but he was supported by
William Duke of Brunswick and by the authority of the Council
of Basel. Taking with him the Duke, his minister Ludolph von
Barum and Rutger, Prior of Wittenberg, Busch went to the house
and they all four entered the nuns' choir. The Duke addressed the
assembled sisters and bade them receive reformation, but they, crossing
their hands above their breasts, replied "We have all concluded
together and sworn that we will not reform nor observe our rule.
We beseech you not to make us perjured " Twice the Duke sent them
out to reconsider their decision and twice they made the same reply,
finally throwing themselves on their faces on the ground, spreading
out their arms in the form of a cross and intoning in a loud voice
the antiphon "Media vita in morte sumus " The visitors, however,
thought they were singing "Revelabunt celi iniquitatem Iude" (used
as a spell in the middle ages) and the Duke was terrified, lest he should
lose all his possessions But Busch said:

"If I were duke of this land I would rather have that song than a hundred
florins, for there is no curse over us and over your land, but a benediction
and heavenly dew, but over these nuns is a stern rebuke and the sign of
their reformation But we are few, being but our four selves, and the nuns
are many. If they were to attack us with their distaffs and with stones
hidden in their long sleeves, what should we do? Let us call in others to
help " Then the duke, going up alone to them said, "May what you sing
be upon you and your bodies"; and to his servants who were standing with
the nuns in the choir, he said, "come hither to us."

The nuns followed the Duke and the servants, thinking that their
chests and money boxes were going to be broken up, whereupon the

[1] *Liber*, p. 581.
[2] *Ib.* pp 615, 652–3 But the *praepositus* of Erfurt, when he saw the
result of the reforms, was delighted and thanked Busch.

Duke rebuked them, saying that if they and their noble friends and the Bishop of Minden opposed reform any longer, he would turn them off his lands The nuns then asked to be allowed to take counsel with their friends and relatives, to which the Duke, on Busch's intercession, unwillingly agreed The friends accordingly came to a conference, but all they did was to repeat the nuns' request in the same form, and they continued to do so after the Duke had given them two or three chances to reconsider the matter, whereupon he sent them away, and they rode off, followed by their shield-bearers The Duke then ordered the gates of the house to be opened to Busch, but the nuns returned a message that the keys were lost The Duke, on Busch's authority, sent for several rustics and villeins, who brought a long bench and broke open the door. The reformers went up into the choir and there found the nuns, flat on their faces with arms out like a cross, and round them a circle of little wooden and stone images of saints, with a burning candle between each Seeing that it was useless to resist, they approached the visitors, and the Duke addressed them, saying that if they would receive reform, he would keep them on his land, and if not carriages were ready to take them away for ever The nuns begged him to "remove those monks from their necks," when they would do his will, but the Duke replied that he did everything by the advice of Rutger and Busch.

The nuns then gave way and the reform was begun, after which the Duke and his followers rode away, leaving his councillor and notary with Busch But at nightfall the nuns sent their *praepositus* to Busch, with the message. "My ladies the prioress and nuns say that they are not willing to serve as they promised, but they wish to remain as they were and are " The Duke had to be sent for once more and eventually all the nuns submitted except one, who seems to have fallen into a fit, and the reform went on apace

"Because we instructed them kindly and not austerely," says Busch, "they said to us, 'At first we thought that you would be very austere and unkind, but now we see that you are gentle as the angels of heaven Now we have more faith in you than in the lord duke '"

Busch's troubles, however, were not over, for twice within the next few days he was attacked by armed men objecting to the new enclosure of the nuns, and only his native wit and conciliatory words saved him from a very dangerous situation[1]

Almost equally difficult was the reform of Mariensee, where again the Bishop of Minden did all in his power to oppose reform, having (according to Busch) been bribed by the nuns to defend them The Duke of Brunswick, however, forced the nuns to admit the reformers and forced the Bishop to send four emissaries to assist in carrying out the reform These four prelates entered the house first to ask the nuns if they would consent to receive reform, but they refused, and one young woman tore off her veil and crown and casting them at the feet of the Bishop's suffragan cried: "Always hitherto you have

[1] *Liber*, pp 555–62.

told me that I need not be reformed and now you want to compel me to be reformed Behold your crown and veil! I will no longer be a nun.'' The Bishop's emissaries after this gave up their half-hearted attempt to reform the house and retired, leaving the field to Busch and his companions The Duke then caused four carriages to be brought to the door, in which the rebellious nuns could be taken away, whereat the Abbess and the nuns climbed up into the vaults of the church and hid themselves there The Duke ordered his servants to fetch ladders and place them against the roof and then to climb up and fetch down the nuns, but the prudent Busch prevented this, saying that the nuns would push over and kill the first who went up the ladder Instead he went into the choir and, finding one nun still walking there, threatened her that unless the whole convent came down from the roof at once, they should be taken away in the carriages, "to-night you shall be in the Duke's castle of Nyerstadt, tomorrow in his castle of Calenberg, and after that outside his lands, perchance never to return " Whereupon the horrified nuns descended

Then followed an amusing scene. All the nuns agreed to accept the new reforms, except one young woman, who refused.

"Then," says Busch, "I said to the lord Duke, 'This sister scorns obedience and contradicts everything' Whereupon, finding how perverse she was, he seized her and tried to draw her to the carriage But when he had thrown his arms about her, she fell back flat on the ground, the Duke on the top of her, and the other nuns on the top of the Duke, each pushing the other on to him, so that the Duke could not raise himself from off her, especially as his arms were crushed beneath her scapular And we, who saw him lying thus, stood away, waiting for the end of the business. At length he got one arm away from her, and with it pushed off the nuns who were lying upon him, hitting them and drawing blood from their arms, for he was a man and the nuns were like children, without strength and resistance "

(This was the age of chivalry!) When he had got rid of these nuns he lifted the nun on whom he was lying, pulled his other arm free and sprang to his feet again, saying to the vassals and servants, who were standing round "Why do you allow your liege lord thus to be trampled under foot by nuns?" One of them replied for all, "Gracious lord! we have ever stood by thee where the war engines were hurling their stones and the bows their arrows; only tell us what we are to do and we will willingly do it " Then said he, "Whichever nun I seize, do you seize her too," and they replied, "Willingly, gracious lord " Whereupon the nuns gave in and professed themselves willing to be reformed. But they were still recalcitrant at heart, and when Busch, Rutger and the Duke were going away, they all began to sing the antiphon "Media vita" at the top of their voices and pursued the hapless reformers through the church, pelting them with burning candles One girl followed them outside to the cemetery, chanted "Sancte deus, sancte, fortis, sancte et immortalis" three times and falling on her knees, bit the ground thrice in sign of a curse, and threw stones and earth after them In the end, however, even this stormy convent was reduced to peace and reform, after three reformed nuns from Derneburg were brought in to teach them[1]

Busch had almost as much difficulty with the nuns of Derneburg, an Austin house near Hildesheim, in which, as he says "the nuns had long lived an irregular life, owning private property, and, according to public rumour, incontinent," paying long visits outside their house as often as they pleased and performing only the minimum routine of monastic life. On one occasion, Busch tells us,

When I was taking their private possessions away from the nuns and placing them in the common stock, it happened that I was going through their cupboards and cellars, for several of them had a small cellar encircling the monastery, which was entered by three or four steps and had covered vaults, in which they kept their beer and other private allowances They were showing me the cellars, and going down into them before me, and the last nun said to me "Do you go first now, father, for my cellar is the same as those of the other sisters," and without thinking I did so But when I went down into it, she suddenly clapped to the door or vault over my head and stood upon it. I was shut up alone in there, thinking what would have happened if the nuns had shut me up there secretly, and I shouted to my brother, who was standing outside with them, bidding him cause them to open the door and let me out. At length after some delay they opened the trap-door of the cellar and let me come out After that I was never willing to go first into any closed place in any nunnery, lest anything of the kind should happen, and lest I should be unable to get out easily But when two or three preceded me, then I followed them One only going in front did not suffice me, lest they should shut me up for some time alone with her and then spread tales about me. The sister who did this was good enough and very simple, whence I was astonished that she should think of such a thing

It was while he was reforming this house, too, that he was attacked by several armed laymen, who took the part of the nuns. The nuns of Derneburg were never effectually reformed, although Busch gave himself the greatest trouble over them At the end of three years they prevailed upon their friends and relatives in the neighbourhood to get rid of Busch and his brethren, and the nuns received Henry, Abbot of Marienrode, as their spiritual father and reformer instead. But they did not gain by the change, for he, being a Cistercian, introduced a nun of his own order as their prioress, and finally the Bishop of Hildesheim, the Abbot of Marienrode and other reformers came one morning to the house and, rebuking the nuns for their imperviousness to reform, made them come away in all their old clothes, leaving their books and possessions behind them, placed them in carriages and distributed them among other houses, where many were forced to become Cistercians. The house itself was turned into a Cistercian priory. "Thus," says Busch, not without some satisfaction, "they lost the holy father St Augustine with me!"[2]

The methods employed by Busch to carry out a reform were to undertake the initial stages himself and if necessary to obtain a few nuns from a previously reformed house to live in the convent and bring

[1] *Liber*, pp. 562-5.   [2] See *ib.* pp. 591-7.

it to right discipline He always began by hearing the confessions of the nuns, which often caused considerable fluttering in the convent. At St George, near Halle, he found that the convent was subordinated to the monastery of Zinna, and received its confessor from that house, which Busch decided to alter, for the Abbot of Zinna was impeding his reforms He therefore bade the Abbess send the sisters to confess to him, but she replied

"The sisters dare not confess to you by reason of the apostolic mandate and the abbot of Zinna and our own confessor, who comes from him."

Then Busch said.

"Because I have authority to do so, say to them. the confessor is sitting in the church, in front of the window, where you are wont to confess, so you may go there and confess " Then the prioress or eldest of the sisters came to the window and confessed fully to me ..and when she had finished I said, "Sister, have you more to say?" Whereat she cried in alarm, "Are you the provost of the Neuwerk?" I answered, "Even so " "Then have I confessed to the provost?" "Yea " "What now shall I do and say?" I replied, "Be silent and tell no one that I have heard your confession, so that the others may come to confess, otherwise you will be the only one to have confessed to me " She did so and receiving absolution left me, telling no one that she had confessed to me.

After that each nun who came received the same advice, until all had confessed[1].

At Derneburg the nuns were afraid to come and confess for another reason There was current in the taverns and dining halls of the whole country side a tale of the terrible penance imposed by Busch upon a brother of his monastery of Sülte, who took a larger draught of drink from the drinking cup than Busch thought seemly, whereupon he was said to have caused the unfortunate man to lie for three hours before the dining table in the frater, with his mouth stretched open by a large horse-bone, and when one of the brothers burst out laughing at the sight, Busch was said to have thrown the drinking cup in his face. The weeping nuns informed him between their sobs· "We are virgins and maids, we cannot do such a great penance for such a little fault." Busch was obliged to assure them that the whole tale was a fabrication[2] At Escherde he had the same difficulty.

The frightened nuns were afraid to confess to me, because they had heard that I was wont to inflict very severe penances, which was not true, as I afterwards told them Then their *praepositus* said to them "The bishop's mandate orders you to confess to him under pain of excommunication and if you refuse then you will be under an interdict My good ladies, I counsel you to confess to him. I will place beside him my servant with a drawn sword and if he says one bad or harsh word to you it shall cleave his head." When they saw and heard that they could not escape they consented to confess to me, but they sent before them first one bold nun in order to beard me. Seated in the confessional, she began, "Sir, what do you here?" I answered, "I lead you all to the kingdom of heaven." Half the nuns

---

[1] *Liber*, pp 575–6.   [2] *Ib.* p. 589.

confessed to me that day To the third of them I said, "Sister, am I as harsh as you said I was?" and she replied, "You are a man of gold, gentle and kind beyond all things " In the evening, when we were supping I said to the *praepositus·* "What are your nuns saying about me? Am I as severe as they thought?" He replied, "When it was their turn to go to confession, the hair of their heads stood on end, but when they came away from you, they returned in great consolation " The next day I finished the others before dinner, and towards the end I asked one of them, "Am I as hard and severe as you heard?" and she replied, "Now you are honey-tongued But when you have got our consent and have tied a rope to our horns to drag us along, then you will say to us You must and shall do all that I desire " I answered her, "Beloved sister, fear not, for I shall always remain kind and benign towards you "[1]

Besides confessing the nuns Busch and his fellow visitors went through the conventual routine with them, showing them how they ought to perform divine service, to behave in the frater and to hold chapters The most efficacious means of reform employed, however, was to send for some reformed nuns from another convent, to dwell in the newly reformed house. Nuns of the order of Mary Magdalen in Hildesheim went to Heiningen, Stederburg, Frankenburg, and the White Ladies of Magdeburg Fischbeck was reformed by nuns of the Windesheim order Marienberg was reformed by nuns of Bronopia and in its turn sent reformers to Marienborn and Stendal, where nuns of Dorstadt had already made reforms, from which the original members soon fell away Two nuns and a *conversa* were sent from Heiningen to the Holy Cross at Erfurt and the Abbess and four nuns of Derneburg went to Weinhausen[2] The newcomers were usually gladly lent and graciously received in their new homes; sometimes they remained and held office in the latter and sometimes they returned to their own houses, when the reform was firmly rooted The tale of the reform of Marienberg is charming[3] Busch, with the consent of the chapter-general of the congregation of Windesheim, took from Bronopia two nuns, Ida and Tecla and a lay sister Aleidis, who for his sake and for the sake of the good work left their own country and their noble friends and relatives, and made a long and sometimes dangerous journey with Busch across Westphalia and Saxony to Helmstedt Here they were joyfully received Ida was made subprioress to introduce reforms and to order all the internal discipline of the house, Tecla, who was a learned lady, was made governess of the novices, teaching them to sing and to read Latin and "to write letters and missives in a masterly manner, in good Latin, as I have seen and examined with my eyes." Aleidis was made mistress of the *conversi*

For three years these nuns dwelt at Helmstedt, beloved of all and bringing the place to excellent order. Then Tecla fell ill The Prioress sent for Busch·

[1] *Liber*, pp. 597–8
[2] *Ib.* pp. 580, 607, 612, 619, 628, 631, 635, 642 649, 651.
[3] *Ib.* pp 618–22.

and I came and found her sitting in the infirmary and ordered her to be bled and to receive suitable medicine And when I had remained there for two or three days I decided to go away without taking them and I bade them farewell at eventide,

for Busch had decided that it was time for the sisters to return to Bronopia

After this the proctress of the house came to me, saying "Beloved father! Sister Tecla is asking for you with tears, for she says she will never see you again I beseech you that you will go and speak to her once again tomorrow, before you leave" I answered, "Willingly, for she is my dear sister and for God's sake and mine she left all her rich friends and her own country and followed me to this strange and distant land" The next day, therefore, I visited her in her bed, in the presence of Ida and Aleidis Then she was better and was well content that I should go away and soon she recovered altogether from that illness

Shortly afterwards Busch took the three nuns with him and they set off to drive back to Bronopia, staying at various monastic houses on the way; and the nuns of Helmstedt all the time sent messengers after them, with letters assuring the three sisters of their love and sorrow The journey was at length completed without any accident, except that fat sister Ida tumbled into a cellar at Wittenberg and hurt her leg, so that Busch had to carry her into the carriage

To his account of this episode Busch subjoins four letters, one from himself, one from the prioress and stewardess of Helmstedt to the three sisters, one from the young scholars of the house to their mistress Tecla, and the reply of the three sisters to the convent and of Tecla to her scholars[1] In the Prioress' letter there is a vivid description of the sorrow of the nuns at the departure of their three visitors·

Our sister Geseke Zeelde wept most tearfully and could not go into the workroom, so grieved she after sister Aleydis Sister Mettike Guestyn was so miserable that she could not eat or drink. When I went into the kitchen sister Tryneke wept so much that all who were with her in the kitchen wept too and said "O wi, now has our leader gone away!" When sister Elyzabeth Cyriaci began the office of the mass, she sang it so dolefully through her tears, that she could hardly sing. When she had to begin the 'Benedictus' after the 'Sanctus' she burst out crying, so that she could not sing at all, but sister Elyzabeth Broysen had to go on with it and she could hardly finish it Geseke Obrecht and Heylewich the chantress are very sorrowful, because they did not say goodbye to you, for they did not know you were going so early. They now send you as many good wishes as there are sands in the sea. When the scholars come to school on Sunday, we cannot describe to you how many tears are shed there The stewardess and I have to console the other sisters, but we are the rather in need of someone to console us. When we look on your places in choir and frater and dorter, then we grow sad and weep, saying, "O God, if only Bronopia were where Heiningen is, five miles away from us, then we might often visit each other, which now we cannot do, for we are forty miles away. We are as it were dead to each other at the two ends of the earth." We have many other things to write to you, but because it is the middle of the night, we must separate and go to matins. Dearest sisters, we give you deepest thanks for all the good

[1] *Liber,* pp 622–7.

you have done for us, in spiritual and in temporal matters. God speed you a thousand times, in Jesus' name ...As many as there are pearls, as many as there are planets in the heaven, as many as there are ends to the earth, so many godspeeds send we to you[1].

The letter of the little novices to sister Tecla deserves quotation, to show their progress under her tuition.

Ihesum pium consolatorem merentium pro salute! Notum facimus charitati vestre, charissima soror Tecla magistra nostra, quod nos omnes scholares vestre in magna sumus tristitia et dolore de vestro a nobis recessu. Non enim possumus oblivisci presentiam vestram, sed cotidie querimus vos, et dum non invenimus, tunc contristamur et dolemus Vix potestis credere, quanta tristitia et quantus dolor est in claustro nostro de vestra absentia tam de senioribus quam de iunioribus Quapropter petimus cordintime, sicut amplius non sumus nos invicem visure in hac mortali vita, ut oretis pro nobis deum, ut taliter vivamus in hoc seculo, ut nos invicem videre valeamus in conspectu sancte Trinitatis Valete, soror dilectissima, cum charissimis sororibus vestris Ida et Aleide in domino semper! Et deus omnipotens omnem tribulationem et angustiam a vobis removeat et vestram sanctitatem conservet tempora per eterna, Amen[2].

It is a pretty picture of affection and concord, which is given by these letters, and may well be set against the pictures of conventual bickering, which are too often to be found in visitation reports.

Busch's reforms seem to have been very successful. He often mentions that such and such a house remained in a good state of reform for such and such a number of years, or up to the day on which he wrote Sometimes he describes reforming prioresses or other nuns, who did good work in their houses[3], sometimes also he mentions the assistance given by a wise confessor or *custos* His only real failure seems to have been Derneburg; this house withstood both his efforts (for three years he had acted as confessor, walking two miles before breakfast to confess the nuns before communion) and those of the Cistercian abbot of Marienrode, who had been their benefactor for over 300 florins; and Busch quotes rather bitterly the proverb current in Germany

> Gratia nulla perit, nisi gratia sola sororum
> Sic fuit, est et erit. 'ondanc' in fine laborum[4].

But he seldom got *ondanc* at the end of his work, and when his life drew to a close he could look back on hundreds of monks and nuns not only reformed by him, but also cherishing for him the greatest gratitude and affection. His was a large and humane spirit, and for all his zeal for reform and his reputation for sternness, it is plain that he had that greatest of gifts, the capacity to win the hearts of men

---

[1] *Liber*, pp. 624–5.
[2] *Ib.* p. 625. For the learning of reformed nuns, see pp. 576, 607, 642.
[3] See e g *ib* pp 585–6, 636, 640.   [4] *Ib.* p. 596.

APPENDIX IV

LIST OF ENGLISH NUNNERIES. c. 1275-1535

[In this list Ab = Abbey, Pr. = Priory, A. = Austin, B = Benedictine, C. = Cistercian, Cl = Cluniac, Dom = Dominican, Fr = Franciscan, Bng. = Brigittine. P. = Premonstratensian Gilbertine houses are not included]

House	Dedication	Order	County	Diocese	Founder and date
1 ACONBURY	Holy Cross	A Pr	Her	Her	Margery, wife of Walter de Lacy, temp John
2. AMESBURY	St Mary and St Melor	B Pr.	Wilts.	Salis.	Saxon Abbey. refounded as a priory for nuns of Fontevrault by King John, 1199
3. ANKERWYKE	St Mary Magd.	B Pr.	Bucks.	Linc.	Gilbert de Muntfichet, c 1160
4 ARDEN	St Andrew	B Pr	York, N.R	York	Peter de Hoton, temp. Henry II
5. ARMATHWAITE	St Mary	B Pr	Cumb	Carl	Unknown, before 1200
6. ARTHINGTON	St Mary	Cl.Pr.	York., W R	York	Peter, son of Serlo de Arthington, middle of twelfth century
7. BARKING	St Mary and St Ethelburga	B Ab	Essex	Lon	St Earconwald, Bishop of London 675-93, probably in 666
8. BARROW GURNEY (MINCHIN BARROW)	St Mary and St Edward	B Pr.	Som	B and W	Unknown. probably a Gurney, before 1212
9 BASEDALE	St Mary	C Pr	York, N R	York	Guy de Bovincurt, c 1190 (see V.C.H. Yorks. III, 158)
10 BLACKBOROUGH	St Mary and St Katherine	B Pr.	Norf	Norw	Roger de Scales and Muriel his wife, c 1150
11 BLITHBURY	St Giles	B Pr	Staffs.	C L	Hugh Malveysin, after 1129

House	Dedication	Order	County	Diocese	Founder and date
12 BREWOOD (Black Ladies)	St Mary	B Pr	Staffs	C L	Unknown, twelfth century
13 BREWOOD (White Ladies)	St Leonard	C Pr	Salop	C L	Unknown, twelfth century
14 BRISTOL	St Mary Magd	A Pr	Gloucs	Worc	Eva, widow of Robert Fitzhardinge, c. 1173
15 BRODHOLME	St Mary	P Pr	Notts	York	Agnes de Camville, wife of Peter de Gousla, temp Stephen
16 BROMHALE	St Margaret	B Pr	Berks	Salis	Unknown, before 1200
17 BRUISYARD	Ann of St Mary	Fr.Ab.	Suff.	Norw.	Edward III, 1366, at instigation of Lionel, Duke of Clarence
18 BUCKLAND (Minchin)	St John Bapt.	A Pr (nuns of St John of Jerusalem)	Som	B and W	Henry II, c 1186 (instead of House of Austin canons founded 1166 by Wilham de Erlegh)
19. BUNGAY	St Mary and Holy Cross	B Pr	Suff	Norw	Roger de Glanville and Gundred his wife, c 1160
20 BURNHAM	St Mary	A Ab.	Bucks	Linc	Richard, King of the Romans, 1266
21 CAMBRIDGE	St Radegund	B Pr	Cambs	Ely	c 1133–8, temp Nigel, Bishop of Ely
22 CAMPSEY	St Mary	A Pr	Suff.	Norw	Theobald de Valognes, c 1195
23 CANNINGTON	St Mary	B Pr.	Som.	B. and W.	Robert de Courcy, c 1138
24 CANONSLEIGH	St Mary, St John Evangelist and St Audrey	A Ab	Devon	Ex	Maud de Clare, Countess of Gloucester and Hertford, temp Edward I (previously a house of canons)
25 CANTERBURY	St Sepulchre	B Pr	Kent	Cant	St Anselm, 1100
26 CARROW	St Mary and St John	B Pr	Norf.	Norw.	King Stephen, 1146
27 CATESBY	St Mary, St Edmund and St Thomas the Martyr	C.Pr	Northants	Linc.	Robert de Esseby, c 1175
28 CHATTERIS	St Mary	B Ab	Cambs	Ely	Eadnoth, Abbot of Ramsey, c 1010
29 CHESHUNT	St Mary	B Pr	Herts.	Lon.	Unknown, twelfth century
30 CHESTER	St Mary	B Pr	Chester	C L	Ranulf, Earl of Chester, c 1140

No	Name	Dedication	Type	County	Diocese	Founder / date
31	CLEMENTHORPE	St Clement	B Pr	York, W R	York	Thurstan, Archbishop of York, c 1130
32.	CLERKENWELL	Assumption of St Mary	B Pr	Midd	Lon	Jordan Brisett, c 1100
33	COKEHILL	—	C Pr	Worc.	Worc	Isabel, Countess of Warwick, end of twelfth century
34	CORNWORTHY	St Mary	A.Pr.	Devon	Ex	Uncertain, fourteenth century
35	CRABHOUSE	St Mary Magd St John Evang. St Thomas and St Peter	A Pr	Norf	Norw.	Roger, prior, and canons of Rainham, c 1181
36	DARTFORD	St Mary and St Margaret	A.Pr (according to rule and in charge of Dom friars)	Kent	Roch	Edward III, 1355
37	DAVINGTON	St Mary Magd	B Pr	Kent	Cant	Fulk de Newenham, 1153
38	DELAPRÉ (de Pratis)	St Mary	Cl Ab	Northants	Linc	Simon of Saint-Liz, Earl of Northampton, temp Stephen (first at Fotheringay)
39	DELAPRÉ (de Prato)	St Mary	B Pr	Herts	Linc	Under abbey of St Albans
40	DENNY	St James and St Leonard	Fr Ab	Cambs	Ely	Mary de Valence, Countess of Pembroke, 1342
41	DERBY (Kingsmead or de Pratis)	St Mary	B Pr.	Derby	C L	Aubin, Abbot of Darley, c 1160
42	EASEBOURNE	Nativity of B V M	B Pr	Suss	Chich.	. de Bohun, before 1248
43	ELLERTON (in Swaledale)	St Mary	C.Pr.	York, N R	York	Uncertain, before 1227
44	ELSTOW	St Mary and St Helen	B.Ab	Beds	Linc	Judith, Countess of Huntingdon, late eleventh century
45	ESHOLT	St Mary, St Leonard and St James	C.Pr.	York, W R.	York	Uncertain, twelfth century
46	FAIRWELL	St Mary	B Pr	Staffs	C L	Roger, Bishop of Coventry and Lichfield, c 1140

House	Dedication	Order	County	Diocese	Founder and date
47. FLAMSTEAD	St Giles	B Pr.	Herts	Linc	Roger de Tony, temp Stephen
48. FLIXTON	St Mary and St Katherine	A Pr	Suff	Norw	Margery, widow of Geoffrey de Hanes and daughter of Bartholomew de Crek, 1258
49. FOSSE	St Nicholas	C Pr	Linc	Linc	The men of Torksey, before the reign of John
50. GODSTOW	St Mary and St John Baptist	B Ab	Oxon	Linc	Edith, widow of Sir William Launcelene, c 1133
51. GOKEWELL	St Mary	C Pr	Linc	Linc	William Dawtrey, before 1148 or 1185
52. GORING	St Mary	A Pr.	Oxon	Linc.	Thomas de Druval, temp Henry I
53. GRACEDIEU	Holy Trinity and St Mary	A.Pr.	Leices	Linc	Rohese de Verdon, c 1239
54. GREENFIELD	St Mary	C Pr	Linc.	Linc.	Eudes of Grainsby and Ralph his son, before 1153
55. GRIMSBY	St Leonard	A Pr.	Linc	Linc	Before 1184
56. HALIWELL (Shoreditch)	St John Baptist	B Pr	Midd	Lon.	Roger son of Gelren, before 1127
57. HAMPOLE	St Mary	C Pr.	York, W.R.	York	William de Clarefai and Avice de Tany his wife, c. 1170
58. HANDALE (or Grendale)	St Mary	C Pr.	York, N.R.	York	William Percy of Dunsley, 1133
59. HARROLD	St Peter	A.Pr.	Beds	Linc.	Sampson le Fort, before 1148 (as Arroasian house) Nunnery, 1181
60. HEDINGHAM, CASTLE	Holy Cross, St Mary and St James	B Pr	Ess	Lon	Aubrey de Vere, Earl of Oxford, and Lucy his wife, before 1191
61. HENWOOD	St Margaret	B Pr.	Warw	Worc	Ketelbern de Langdon, between 1149 and 1161
62. HEYNINGS	St Mary	C Pr	Linc.	Linc	Reyner d'Evermue, temp Stephen
63. HINCHINBROOKE	St James	B Pr.	Hunts.	Linc	Removed from Eltisley, Cambs, temp William I
64. HOLYSTONE	—	B Pr	Northumb.	Dur.	...Umfraville of Harbottle, before 1235
65. ICKLETON	St Mary Magd	B.Pr.	Cambs.	Ely	Uncertain, c 1190
66. ILCHESTER	Holy Trinity	A Pr	Som	B and W	William Dennis, c 1220 (as a hospital) A nunnery before 1281
67. IRFORD	St Mary	P.Pr.	Linc	Linc	Probably Ralph d'Albini, temp Henry II

No. & Name	Dedication	Order	County	Diocese	Founder
68. IVINGHOE	St Margaret	B.Pr	Bucks	Linc	[William Giffard?], Bishop of Winchester, twelfth century
69. KELDHOLME	St Mary	C.Pr.	York., N.R	York	Robert de Stuteville, temp Henry 1
70. KILBURN	St Mary and St John Baptist	B.Pr.	Midd	Lon	Herbert, Abbot of Westminster, 1139
71. KINGTON St Michael	St Mary	B.Pr	Wilts	Salis.	Before 1155
72. KIRKLEES	St Mary and St James	C.Pr.	York., W.R	York	Reiner le Fleming, temp Henry II
73. LACOCK	St Mary and St Bernard	A.Ab.	Wilts	Salis.	Ela, Countess of Salisbury, 1232
74. LAMBLEY	St Patrick	B.Pr	Northumb.	Durh	Adam de Tynedale, temp. John
75. LANGLEY	St Mary	B.Pr.	Leic.	Linc.	William Pantulf and Burga his wife, temp. Henry II
76. LEGBOURNE	St Mary	C.Pr	Linc.	Linc.	Robert, son of Gilbert of Tathwell, after 1150 (removed from earlier site)
77. LILLECHURCH (Higham)	St Mary	B.Pr	Kent	Roch.	King Stephen, before 1151
78. LITTLEMORE	St Mary, St Nicholas and St Edmund	B.Pr	Oxon	Linc	Robert de Sandford, temp Stephen
79. LONDON (Bishopsgate)	St Helen and Holy Cross	B.Pr	Midd.	Lon,	William, son of William, the goldsmith, before 1216
80. LONDON	St Mary and St Francis	Fr.Ab.	Midd.	Lon.	Edmund, Earl of Lancaster, 1293
81. LYMBROOK	St Mary	A.Pr	Her.	Her.	Uncertain
82. LYMINSTER	St Mary	B.Pr.	Suss,	Chich.	Roger de Montgomery, c 1082 (as cell of Almenêches)
83. MALLING	St Mary and St Andrew	B.Ab	Kent	Roch	Gundulf, Bishop of Rochester, 1090
84. MARHAM	St Mary, St Barbara and St Edmund	C.Ab.	Norf,	Norw.	Isabel, widow of Hugh de Albini, Earl of Arundel, 1249
85. MARKYATE	Holy Trinity	B.Pr.	Beds.-	Linc,	1145, under influence of Geoffrey, Abbot of St Albans

House	Dedication	Order	County	Diocese	Founder and date
86. MARLOW, LITTLE	St Mary	B Pr	Bucks	Linc.	Uncertain, twelfth century
87. MARRICK	St Andrew and St Mary	B Pr.	York., N.R	York	Roger de Aske, temp Henry II
88. MOXBY	St John Evangelist	A. Pr.	York, N R	York	Henry II, before 1167 (removed from double house at Marton)
89. NEASHAM	St Mary	B Pr	Durh	Durh	Probably the Lord of Greystoke, before 1157
90. NEWCASTLE-UPON-TYNE	St Bartholomew	B.Pr.	Northumb	Durh	Uncertain, twelfth century
91. NUNAPPLETON	St Mary and St John Evangelist	C Pr.	York, W.R.	York	Eustace de Merch and Alice St Quintin his wife, c 1150
92. NUNBURNHOLME	—	B Pr	York., E.R	York	Ancestors of Roger de Merlay, Lord of Morpeth, twelfth century
93. NUNCOTON	St Mary	C Pr	Linc.	Linc.	Alan de Mounceaux, before 1129
94. NUNEATON	St Mary	B Pr.	Warw	Worc.	Robert, Earl of Leicester, c 1155, for nuns of Fontevrault
95. NUNKEELING	St Mary and St Helen	B Pr	York, E R	York	Agnes de Arches, widow of Herbert St Quintin, 1152
96. NUNMONKTON	St Mary	B Pr.	York, W.R.	York	William de Arches and Ivetta his wife, temp. Stephen
97. PINLEY	St Mary	C.Pr	Warw	Worc	Robert de Pillarton, temp Henry I
98. POLESWORTH	St Edith	B Ab	Warw.	C L	Saxon foundation Refounded by Robert Marmion, temp Stephen
99. POLSLOE	St Katherine	B Pr.	Devon	Ex.	Traditional founder, William Bruere, before 1169
100. REDLINGFIELD	St Andrew and St Mary	B Pr	Suff.	Norw.	Manasses, Count of Gusnes, and Emma de Arras his wife, 1120
101. ROMSEY	St Mary and St Elfrida	B Ab.	Hants.	Win	Edward the Elder, c 907: refounded by King Edgar, 967
102. ROSEDALE	St Mary and St Lawrence	C Pr	York, N R.	York	Robert, son of Nicholas de Stuteville, temp. Richard I
103. ROTHWELL	St John Baptist	A Pr	Northants	Linc	. de Clare, thirteenth century

104	ROWNEY	St John Baptist	B.Pr	Herts	Linc	Conan, Duke of Britanny and Earl of Richmond, temp. Henry II, suppressed 1459
105	RUSPER	St Mary Magd	B Pr	Suss.	Chich.	Twelfth century, probably by one of the Braose family
106	St STEPHEN'S (Foukeholme)	St Stephen	B.Pr.	York., N R	York	Uncertain Disappeared after 1349
107	SETON (Lekeley)	St Mary	B Pr	Cumb.	York	Henry son of Arthur son of Godard, Lord of Millom, twelfth century
108	SEWARDSLEY	St Mary Magd	C Pr	Northants	Linc	Richard de Lestre, temp. Henry II
109	SHAFTESBURY	St Mary and St Edward	B.Ab	Dorset	Salis	King Alfred, c 888
110	SHEPPEY (Minster)	St Mary and St Sexburga	B Pr	Kent	Cant	St Sexburga, 675
111	SINNINGTHWAITE	St Mary	C Pr	York, W R.	York	Bertram Haget, c 1160
112	SOPWELL	St Mary	B Pr	Herts	Linc	Under abbey of St Albans
113	STAINFIELD	St Mary	B.Pr.	Linc	Linc.	William or Henry de Percy, temp. or before Henry II
114	STAMFORD	St Mary and St Michael	B.Pr	Northants	Linc.	William Waterville, Abbot of Peterborough, c 1155
115	STIXWOULD	St Mary	C.Pr.	Linc	Linc.	Lucy, Countess of Perche, temp Stephen
116	STRATFORD-BY-Bow	St Leonard	B.Pr	Midd.	Lon	William, Bishop of London, temp. Henry I
117	STUDLEY	St Mary	B.Pr	Oxon	Linc	Probably Bernard of St Valery, before 1176
118	SWAFFHAM BULBECK	—	B Pr.	Cambs.	Ely	Uncertain, before temp John
119	SWINE	St Mary	C Pr.	York., E R	York	Robert de Verli, temp Stephen
120	SYON	St Saviour, St Mary and St Bridget	Brig.Ab	Midd	Lon	King Henry V, 1414
121	TARRANT KEYNES	St Mary and All Saints	C.Ab.	Dorset	Salis.	Ralph de Keynes, before 1235
122	THETFORD	St George and St Gregory	B.Pr	Norf.	Norw	Hugh, Abbot of Bury St Edmunds, c. 1160 (removed from Lyng)
123.	THICKET	St Mary	B Pr.	York , E.R.	York	Roger FitzRoger, temp. Richard I

House	Dedication	Order	County	Diocese	Founder and date
124 Usk	St Mary	B Pr	Monm	Llan	Sir Richard de Clare, before 1236
125 Wallingwells	St Mary of Pitty	B.Pr.	Notts	York	Ralph de Chevrecourt, temp. Stephen
126. Waterbeach	and St Clare	Fr.Pr.	Cambs.	Ely	Denise de Mountchesney, 1294 Removed to Denny, 1348
127 Westwood	St Mary	B.Pr	Worc.	Worc.	Osbert son of Hugh and Eustacia de Saye, his mother, temp Henry II (for nuns of Fontevrault)
128 Wherwell	Holy Cross and St Peter	B.Ab	Hants	Win.	Queen Elfrida, c 986
129 Whiston	St Mary Magd.	C Pr	Worc	Worc.	Walter de Cantilupe, Bishop of Worcester, before 1255
130 Wilberfoss	St Mary	B Pr.	York, E.R	York	Uncertain, temp Stephen
131 Wilton	St Mary, St Bartholomew and St Edith	B Ab	Wilts	Salis	St Alburga, c 800 refounded by King Alfred, c 871
132 Winchester	St Mary and St Edburga	B Ab	Hants.	Win.	King Alfred and Queen Ealhswith, c 900 Refounded by St Ethelwold, 963
133 Wintney	St Mary, St Mary Magd and St John Baptist	C.Pr	Hants	Win	Richard Holte and Chrstine his wife, daughter of Thomas Cobreth, twelfth century
134 Wix	St Mary	B Pr.	Ess	Lon	Walter Mascherell, Alexander and Edith, children of Walter the Deacon, temp Henry I
135 Wothorpe	St Mary	B.Pr.	Northants.	Linc	Uncertain. united to St Michael's, Stamford, 1354
136. Wroxall	St Leonard	B Pr.	Warw.	Worc.	Hugh, Lord of Hatton and Wroxall, temp Henry I
137 Wykeham	St Mary and St Michael	C Pr	York, N R	York	Pain FitzOsbert, c 1153
138 Yedingham	St Mary	B Pr	York, E R	York	Helewise de Clere, before 1163

BIBLIOGRAPHY

A. MANUSCRIPT SOURCES

I. EPISCOPAL REGISTERS

(a) *Lincoln Episcopal Registers*

Register of Memoranda, Sutton (1280–99).
Register of Memoranda, Dalderby (1300–20).
Register of Memoranda, Gynewell (1347–62)
Register of Memoranda, Bokyngham (1363–98).
Register of Visitations, Alnwick[1] (1436–49)
Register of Visitations, Atwater (1514–21).
Register of Visitations, Longland (1521–47).

(b) *Lambeth Palace Registers*

Register of Langham (1366–8)
Register of Courtenay (1381–96).

(c) *New College Oxford*

Register of William of Wykeham Bishop of Winchester, for
1386–7, ff 84d–89d (Injunctions to Romsey and Wherwell)[2].

II. DOCUMENTS IN THE PUBLIC RECORD OFFICE

(a) *Account Rolls*

Ministers Accounts, 867/21–6, 30, 33–6   (Delapré, St Albans.
Between 16 Edw III and 2 Ric III)
Ib. 1257/1 (Catesby, 11–14 Hen VI).
Ib 1257/2 (Denny, 14 Hen IV–1 Hen. V).
Ib. 1257/10 (Gracedieu, 1–5 Hen. V)
Ib. 1260 (St Michael's, Stamford, 24 rolls between 32 Edw. I and
20 Hen VI).
Ib. 1261/4 (Syon, Cellaress' Account, 21–2 Edw. IV).
Ib 1307/22 (Syon, Cellaress' Account, 36 Hen VI).

---

[1] In course of publication, edited by Mr A Hamilton Thompson. The printed portion is cited in the text as *Linc Visit.* II, and the unprinted portion as *Alnwick's Visit MS*

[2] Bishop Lowth says "This MS. belonged to Wykeham himself, for the injunctions are the original drafts corrected. It came afterwards into the hands of Robert Shirborn, Master of St Cross Hospital, afterwards Bishop of Chichester" It contains a long series of documents relating to a controversy between the Bishop and the masters of St Cross Hospital and injunctions sent to the Cathedral Church of Winchester, the monasteries of Hyde, Merton, Romsey and Wherwell, and the Hospital of St Thomas the Martyr, Southwark, covering the years 1386 and 1387. It is of the highest interest and should certainly be published My thanks are due to Dr Moyle, Bursar of New College, for permission to transcribe the injunctions sent to the two nunneries

(b) *Petitions*

Early Chancery Proceedings, 181/4 (Petition from Elizabeth Webley, late Prioress of Sopwell, concerning her deposition and imprisonment by John Rothbury, Archdeacon of St Albans Abbey).

Ib 4/196 (Petition from Richard English and Margery his wife concerning a corrody withheld from them by the Abbess of Malling).

Ib. 7/70 (Petition from Richard Haldenby and Agnes his wife concerning the daughters of Agnes by a former marriage, one of whom has been made to take the veil by an uncle, for the sake of her inheritance).

Ib. 44/227 (Petition from Thomasyn Dynham, Prioress of Cornworthy, concerning two children at school in her house, whose fees have not been paid for five years).

Ancient Petitions 302/15063 (Petition from the Prioress and nuns of Rowney for leave to have a proctor to beg alms for them, as their buildings are ruinous).

Ancient Correspondence, 36/201 (Petition to Queen Isabel from the Prioress and Convent of Clerkenwell, asking her to obtain the King's leave for them to receive certain lands, by reason of their poverty).

Chancery Warrants, Series 1/1759, 1762, 1764, 1769 (Petitions for the arrest of apostate nuns, nine in all).

B. PRINTED SOURCES

I. Archiepiscopal and Episcopal Registers

(a) *Bath and Wells*

Registers of Walter Giffard (1265–6) and of Henry Bowet (1401 –7), ed T. S Holmes (Somerset Record Soc 1899)

Register of John of Drokensford (1309–29), ed. E. Hobhouse. (Somerset Record Soc 1887.)

Register of Ralph of Shrewsbury (1329–63), ed. T S Holmes (Somerset Record Soc. 1896) 2 vols

(b) *Canterbury*

Registrum Epistolarum Fratris Johannis Peckham Archiepiscopi Cantuariensis (1279–92), ed C. Trice Martin (Rolls Series, 1882–5) 3 vols

Visitations of Archbishop Warham in 1511, ed. Mary Bateson (English Historical Review, VI, 1891, pp 28 ff.) (Full abstracts) See also The British Magazine, vols. XXIX–XXXII, *passim* (abstracts).

(c) *Chichester*

Episcopal Register of Robert Rede, Bishop of Chichester (1397– 1415), ed. Cecil Deedes. (Sussex Rec. Soc. 1908.)

Blaauw, W. Episcopal Visitations of the Priory of Easebourne (1442–1527) (Sussex Archaeol. Collections, IX, 1857, pp. 1–32)

Way, A. Notices of the Benedictine Priory of St Mary Magdalen at Rusper (1442–1527). (Sussex Archaeol. Collections, v, 1852, pp 244–62)

Durham, York, Carlisle

Historical Papers and Letters from the Northern Registers, ed. James Raine (Rolls Series, 1873.)

Durham

Registrum Palatinum Dunelmense. Register of Richard de Kellawe, Lord Palatine and Bishop of Durham, 1311–16, ed Sir T. Duffus Hardy (Rolls Series, 1873–8.) 4 vols.

Exeter

Register of Walter de Stapeldon, Bishop of Exeter, 1308–26 ed. F. C. Hingeston-Randolph (1892).

Register of John de Grandisson, Bishop of Exeter, 1327–69, ed. F. C Hingeston-Randolph (1894–9)

Register of Thomas de Brantyngham, Bishop of Exeter, Part I; 1370–94, ed F C Hingeston-Randolph (1901).

Register of Edmund Stafford, Bishop of Exeter, 1395–1419, ed. F. C Hingeston-Randolph (1886).

Hereford

Registrum Thome de Cantilupo, Episcopi Herefordensis, 1275–82, transcribed by R. C. Griffiths, with an introduction by W. W. Capes (Canterbury and York Soc. and Cantilupe Soc. 1907.)

Registrum Ricardi de Swinfield, Episcopi Herefordensis, 1283–1317, ed. W.'W. Capes (Canterbury and York Soc and Cantilupe Soc 1909.)

Registrum Adae de Orleton, Episcopi Herefordensis, 1317–27, ed. A. T. Bannister (Canterbury and York Soc. and Cantilupe Soc 1908)

Registrum Roberti Mascall, Episcopi Herefordensis, 1404–16, transcribed by J. H Parry with introductory note by Charles Johnson (Canterbury and York Soc. and Cantilupe Soc. 1917)

Registrum Thome Spofford, Episcopi Herefordensis, 1422–48, ed. A. T. Bannister. (Canterbury and York Soc and Cantilupe Soc. 1919.)

Registrum Thome Myllyng, Episcopi Herefordensis, 1472–92, ed. A. T. Bannister (1920)

Coventry and Lichfield

Register of Roger de Norbury, Bishop of Coventry and Lichfield, 1322–59, ed. Edmund Hobhouse (William Salt Archaeol Soc. Collections, I, 1881) (Table of contents only.)

The Second Register of Bishop Robert de Stretton, 1360–85, abstracted into English by R A. Wilson. (William Salt Archaeol. Soc. Coll., New Series, vol. VIII, 1905) (Brief calendar.)

(*i*) *Lincoln*

Visitations of Religious Houses in the Diocese of Lincoln, ed. A Hamilton Thompson Vol. I Injunctions and other Documents from the Registers of Richard Flemyng and William Gray, 1420–36. (Lincoln Record Soc and Canterbury and York Soc. 1915)

Visitations of Religious Houses in the Diocese of Lincoln, ed. A Hamilton Thompson. Vol. II Alnwick's Visitations (1436–49) (Lincoln Record Soc. and Canterbury and York Soc)

Injunctions of John Longland, Bishop of Lincoln, to certain Monasteries in his Diocese, 1531, ed E. Peacock (Archaeologia, XLVII, pp. 49–64, 1883.)

(*j*) *London*

Registrum Radulphi Baldock, Gilberti Segrave, Ricardi Newport et Stephani Gravesend, Episcoporum Londoniensium, 1306–38, ed. R. C. Fowler. (Canterbury and York Soc. 1911.)

(*k*) *Norwich*

Visitations of the Diocese of Norwich, 1492–1532, ed. A. Jessopp. (Camden Soc. 1888.)

(*l*) *Rochester*

Registrum Hamonis Hethe Episcopi Roffensis(1319–52). (Canterbury and York Soc 1914 ff., in course of publication)

(*m*) *Salisbury*

Registrum Simonis de Gandavo Episcopi Saresbiriensis (1297–1315), ed. C T. Flower. (Canterbury and York Soc. 1914, in course of publication)

(*n*) *Winchester*

Registrum Johannis de Pontissara (1282–1304, ed C Deedes. (Canterbury and York Soc 1913–15)

Registers of John de Sandale and Rigaud de Asserio, Bishops of Winchester, 1316–23, ed. F. J Baigent (Hants. Rec. Soc. 1897)

Wykeham's Register, 1367–1404, ed. T F. Kirby. (Hants Rec Soc 1896–9) 2 vols

(*o*) *Worcester*

Register of Godfrey Giffard, 1268–1302, ed J W. Willis-Bund. (Worcester Hist. Soc. 1898–1902) 2 vols.

Register of the Diocese of Worcester during the vacancy of the see, usually called Registrum Sede Vacante, 1301–1435, ed J W Willis-Bund (Worcester Hist Soc 1893–7)

York

Register of Walter Gray, Archbishop of York, 1216–55, ed J. Raine (Surtees Soc. 1872.)

Register of Walter Giffard, Archbishop of York, 1266–79, ed W. Brown (Surtees Soc 1904.)

Register of William Wickwane, Archbishop of York, 1279–85, ed W. Brown (Surtees Soc 1907.)

Register of John le Romeyn, Archbishop of York, 1286–96, ed W. Brown. Vol. I (Surtees Soc 1913)

Registers of John le Romeyn Archbishop of York, 1286–96, Part II, and of Henry of Newark, Archbishop of York, 1298–99, ed W Brown Vol II. (Surtees Soc 1917)

Visitations in the Diocese of York, holden by Archbishop Edward Lee (1531–44), ed W Brown (Yorks Archaeol. Journal, XVI, 1901, pp. 319–68.)

Foreign Visitations

Des Augustinerpropstes Iohannes Busch Chronicon Windeshemense und Liber de Reformatione Monasteriorum, bearbeitet von Dr Karl Grube (Halle, 1886.)

Regestrum Visitationum Archiepiscopi Rothomagensis, Journal des Visites Pastorales d'Eude Rigaud Archevêque de Rouen, 1248–69, pub par Th Bonnin (Rouen, 1852.)

II. ACCOUNT ROLLS

Catesby (2–3 Hen. V)

Baker, History of Northampton (1822–30), vol. I, p 278.

Romsey (1412–13, summary)

Liveing, H G. D., Records of Romsey Abbey (1906), p. 194.

St Helen's, Bishopsgate (sixteenth century, extracts)

Victoria County History· London, I, p. 460.

St Radegund's, Cambridge (1449–51, 1481–2)

Gray, A , The Priory of St Radegund, Cambridge (1898), pp 145–179

St Mary de Pré, St Albans (1487–9)

Dugdale, Monasticon, III, p 358

Swaffham Bulbeck (1483–4)

Dugdale, Monasticon, IV, p. 458.

Syon (Cellaress' and Chambress' Accounts, 1536–7)

Myroure of Oure Ladye, ed. J H. Blunt (E.E.T.S. 1873.) Introduction, pp xxvi–xxxi.

(h) *Miscellaneous (Extracts)*

C T. Flower, Obedientiars' Accounts of Glastonbury and other Religious Houses Trans St Paul's Ecclesiological Soc. vol. VII, Pt. II (1912), pp 50–62.

III. INVENTORIES

(a) *Brewood* (1536)

Dugdale, Monasticon, IV, p 500.

(b) *Cheshunt* (1536)

Cussans, History of Hertfordshire, Hertford Hundred, App. II, pp 267–71.

(c) *Easebourne* (1450)

Sussex Archaeol Coll. IX, pp 10–13

(d) *Gracedieu* (1536)

Nichols, History and Antiquities of the County of Leicester (1804), III, pp. 653–4.

(e) *Hedingham, Castle* (1536)

Trans. Essex Archaeological Soc. IX, pp. 289–92.

(f) *Kilburn* (1536)

Dugdale, Monasticon, IV, p. 424.

(g) *Langley* (1485)

Walcott, Mackenzie E. C., Inventory of St Mary's Benedictine Nunnery at Langley, Co. Leicester, 1485. (Leicestershire Architec Soc. 1872.)

(h) *Lillechurch* (1525)

R. F. Scott, Notes from the Records of St John's College, Cambridge, 3rd series (privately printed, 1906–13), pp. 403–8

(i) *Sheppey* (1536)

Walcott, Mackenzie E. C., Inventories of St Mary's Hospital, Dover, St Martin New-Work, Dover, and the Benedictine Priory of SS. Mary and Sexburga in the Island of Shepey for Nuns (Reprinted from Archaeologia Cantiana, 1868, pp. 18–35)

(j) *Wherwell* (*Sacristy,* c. 1340)

Victoria County History, Hants. II, pp 134–5.

k) *Wintney* (*Frater,* 1420)

Victoria County History, Hants. II, pp. 150–1.

l) *Miscellaneous Fragments*

Fowler, R. C., Inventories of Essex Monasteries in 1536. (Trans. Essex Archaeol Soc. vol IX, Pt IV)

Walcott, Mackenzie E C , Inventories and Valuations of Religious Houses at the Time of the Dissolution. (Archaeologia, XLIII, 1871.)

IV. Cartularies

(a) *Buckland*

A Cartulary of Buckland Priory in the County of Somerset, ed. F. W Weaver (Somerset Rec Soc 1909)

(b) *Crabhouse*

The Register of Crabhouse Nunnery, ed. Mary Bateson (Norfolk and Norwich Arch. Soc Norfolk Archaeology, xi, 1892)

(c) *Godstow*

The English Register of Godstow Nunnery, ed Andrew Clark. (Early Eng Text Soc. 1905–11.)

V. Wills

Calendar of Wills proved and enrolled in the Court of Husting, London, ed R. R Sharpe (1889)

Early Lincoln Wills, ed. A Gibbons (1888)

The Fifty Earliest English Wills in the Court of Probate, London, ed F. J. Furnivall. (Early Eng. Text Soc. 1882)

Lincoln Diocese Documents, ed. A. Clark. (Early Eng. Text Soc. 1914.)

Lincoln Wills, ed C W. Foster Vol I. (Lincoln Record Soc. 1914.)

Testamenta Eboracensia, a Selection of Wills from the Registry at York, ed James Raine 6 vols (Surtees Soc 1836–1902)

Somerset Medieval Wills (1383–1558), ed. F. W Weaver 3 vols. (Somerset Record Soc 1901–5)

VI. Miscellaneous Records and Letters

Calendar of Close Rolls

Calendar of Patent Rolls.

Calendar of Papal Letters

Calendar of Papal Petitions.

Dugdale Monasticon Anglicanum, ed J. Caley, H Ellis and B. Bandinel. 6 vols in 8 (1817–30)

Ellis, H. Original Letters illustrative of English History, 1st series, vol. ii (1824).

Fowler, J T. Cistercian Statutes, A D. 1256–7, with supplementary statutes of the order, 1257–8 (Reprinted from Yorks. Archaeol. Journal, vols ix–xi, 1885–90.)

Gasquet, F A Collectanea Anglo-Premonstratensia, 3 vols. (Camden Soc 1906)

Gibbons, A. Ely Episcopal Records (1891).

Lyndwood. Provinciale (1679)

Madox Formulare Anglicanum (1702).

Paston Letters, ed. J. Gairdner. 4 vols. (1900).

Rotuli Parliamentorum. (Record Com 6 vols n d Index, 1832)

Valor Ecclesiasticus. (Record Com. 1810–34).

Wharton Anglia Sacra, 2 vols. (1691)

Wilkins. Concilia Magnae Britanniae et Hiberniae, 4 vols. (1737).

Wood, M A. E Letters of Royal and Illustrious Ladies of Great Britain. 3 vols. (1846).

VII. Contemporary Literature[1]

An Alphabet of Tales, An English 15th Century Translation of the Alphabetum Narrationum once attributed to Etienne de Besançon, ed. M M Banks (Early Eng. Text Soc. 1904–5)

Amundesham. Annales Monasterii S Albani (Rolls Series, 1870), I.

Ancren Riwle, ed. and trans. James Morton (Camden Soc 1853). Also trans (by Morton) with introd. by F. A. Gasquet in The King's Classics, 1907.

Caesarius of Heisterbach Dialogus Miraculorum, ed. Joseph Strange, 2 vols (Cologne, 1851.)

Chaucer, Complete Works, ed. Skeat (1906)

Chronicle of Lanercost, translated by Sir Herbert Maxwell (1913).

Clene Maydenhod, ed. F. J. Furnivall. (Early Eng Text Soc 1867.)

Court of Love, The, printed in Chaucer's Complete Works, ed. R. Morris (1891), vol IV.

Early English Lives of Saints, ed. F. J. Furnivall. (Trans of the Philological Soc. 1858.) For *The Land of Cokayne* and *Why I can't be a Nun*

Etienne de Bourbon Anecdotes Historiques, etc., ed. Lecoy de la Marche (Soc. de l'Hist. de France, 1877.)

Fifteenth Century Cookery Book, A, ed R. W. Chambers, and Two Fifteenth Century Franciscan Rules, ed W. W Seton (Early Eng. Text Soc. 1914)

Gower Vox Clamantis, ed G Macaulay (1902)

Hali Meidenhad, ed. O. Cockayne. (Early Eng. Text Soc 1866)

Jacobi Vitriacensis Exempla e Sermonibus Vulgaribus, ed. T. F. Crane (Folk Lore Soc 1890)

Langland Vision of William Concerning Piers the Plowman, ed. Skeat, 2 vols. (1886).

Medieval Garner, A, selected, translated and annotated by G. G. Coulton (1910)

Myroure of Oure Ladye, The, ed. J. J. Blunt. (Early Eng. Text Soc. 1873.)

Rule of St Benedict, ed. Gasquet (King's Classics, 1909)

Tale of Beryn, The, ed. Furnivall and Stone. (Chaucer Soc 1887)

Three Middle English Versions of the Rule of St Benet, ed. E A Kock (Early Eng. Text. Soc. 1902.)

Walsingham Gesta Abbatum Monasterii Sancti Albani, ed. H T. Riley (Rolls Series, 1867–9), 3 vols

—— Historia Anglicana, ed. H. T. Riley (Rolls Series, 1863), vol I.

VIII. Plans

Burnham Abbey, by H Brakspear, in Archaeol. Journal, LX (1903). (See Bucks. Archit. and Archaeol Soc. Records, XXXI)

Carrow Priory, by R. M Phipson, in Norf and Norw. Arch. Soc. Trans IX, and Rye, Carrow Abbey (1889).

[1] Foreign books mentioned only in ch XIII are not included here.

Kirklees Priory, by J. Bilson, in Yorks. Archaeol. Journ. xx (1908).
Lacock Abbey, by H. Brakspear, in Archaeologia, LVII (1900) (See
    also Wilts. Archaeol Journ xxxi.)
Marlow, Little, by C. R. Peers, in Archaeol Journ. LIX (1902).
Marrick Priory, facsimile of plan taken at time of Dissolution in
    Coll Topog et Gen v (1838).
St Radegund, Cambridge (now Jesus College) in Gray, The Priory
    of St Radegund, Cambridge (1898).

C. MODERN WORKS

I. On Particular Nunneries (including charters, etc.)

Aldgate (*Minoresses*). Fly, H. Some account of an Abbey of Nuns,
    formerly situated in the street now called the Minories Archaeo-
    logia, xv (1803).
Barrow Gurney Hugo, T Medieval Nunneries of the County of
    Somerset (1867).
Brodholme. Cole, R E. G. The Priory of St Mary of Brodholme.
    (Linc Archit. and Archaeol Soc) in Assoc. Archit Socs Reports
    and Papers, xxviii (1905–6).
Bromhale. Scott, R. F. Notes from the Records of St John's College,
    Cambridge (reprinted from The Eagle, 1890–1903, *passim*),
    Series I and III (Documents from Bromhale and Lille-
    church.)
Buckland Hugo, T. History of Minchin Buckland Priory and Pre-
    ceptory in Somerset (1861).
Cannington See Barrow Gurney
Carrow. Beecheno, F. R. Notes on Carrow Priory (1886).
        Rye, W. Carrow Abbey (1889).
        Rye and Tillett in Norfolk Antiq Misc II.
Crabhouse Jessopp, A. Frivola (1896) For 'Ups and Downs of an
    Old Nunnery' (Crabhouse).
Dartford. C. F. Palmer. Hist. of the Priory of Dartford in Kent.
    Archaeol. Journ. xxxvi (1879).
        Notes on the Priory of Dartford in Kent *Ib* xxxix (1882)
Delapré, Northampton. Serjeantson, R. M. A History of Delapré
    Abbey, Northampton (Northampton, 1909)
Delapré, St Albans. Page, W History of the Monastery of St Mary
    de Pré. St Albans and Herts. Archit. and Archaeol. Soc. Trans.,
    New Ser. x.
Easebourne. Hope, Sir W. H. St John. Cowdray and Easebourne
    Priory in the county of Sussex (1920).
Elstow. Wigram, S R. Chronicle of Elstow Abbey (1909)
Fosse Cole, R E G. The Royal Borough of Torksey, its Churches,
    Monasteries and Castle. Linc. Archit. and Archaeol. Soc. In
    Assoc. Archit. Soc. Reports and Papers, xxviii (1905–6)
Ickleton. Goddard, A. R Ickleton Church and Priory. Cambridge
    Antiq. Soc. Proc. and Commun. xLV (1905).

Ilchester, White Hall. See Barrow Gurney.

Kirklees. Armytage, Sir G. Kirklees Priory. Yorks. Archaeol Journ. XX (1908).

Chadwick, S. J. Kirklees Priory. Yorks. Archaeol. Journ. XVI (1901), XVII (1902), XX (1908).

Lacock. Bowles, W. L and Nichols, J. C. Annals of Lacock Abbey (1835).

Clark-Maxwell, W. G. Outfit for the Profession of an Austin Canoness at Lacock, etc. Archaeol. Journ. LXIX (1912).

Lillechurch. See Bromhale.

Marlow. Peers, C. R. The Benedictine Nunnery of Little Marlow. Archaeol Journ LIX (1902).

Nunburnholme. Morris, M C K. Nunburnholme and its Antiquities (1907).

Romsey. Liveing, H. G. D. Records of Romsey Abbey (1906).

St Helen's, Bishopsgate. Hugo, T. The Last Ten Years of the Priory of St Helen, Bishopsgate (1865)

St Radegund, Cambridge Gray, A. The Priory of St Radegund, Cambridge (1898)

Syon. Aungier, G. J. History and Antiquities of Syon (1840).

Swine. Duckett, Sir G. Charters of the Priory of Swine in Holderness Yorks. Archaeol Journ VI (1881)

Thompson, T. History of the Church and Priory of Swine in Holderness (1824)

II. GENERAL

BUTLER, C. Benedictine Monachism (1919).

CLAY, R. M Hermits and Anchorites of England (1914)

COULTON, G. G. The Interpretation of Visitation Documents. (Eng. Hist Review, 1914.)

—— Medieval Studies (First Series, 1915)

—— Monastic Schools in the Middle Ages (Medieval Studies, No. 10, 1913)

DEANESLY, M. The Lollard Bible (1920).

ECKENSTEIN, L. Woman under Monasticism (1896).

FOSBROKE, T. D. British Monachism (1802).

FOWLER, R C Episcopal Registers of England and Wales. (S P.C.K 1918.)

GASQUET, F. A. English Monastic Life (1904).

GRAHAM, R. An Essay on English Monasteries. (Hist. Assoc. 1913.)

—— St Gilbert of Sempringham and the Gilbertines (1901).

GREEN, M. A EVERETT Lives of the Princesses of England Vol. II (1849)

JACKA, H T The Dissolution of the English Nunneries. Thesis submitted for the degree of M.A in the University of London (Unpublished, deposited at the University)

JARRETT, B. The English Dominicans (1921).

Journal of Education, 1909 and 1910. (Articles and Correspondence by J. E. G. de Montmorency, G. G Coulton and A. F. Leach on "The Medieval Education of Women in England.")

Mode, P. G. The Influence of the Black Death on the English Monasteries (A Dissertation for the Degree of Ph D) (Privately printed, Univ of Chicago Libraries, 1916.)

Savine, A English Monasteries on the Eve of the Dissolution, in Oxford Studies in Social and Legal History, ed P. Vinogradoff (1909), 1.

Thiers, J. B. Traité de la Clôture des Religieuses. (Paris, 1681)

. Thompson, A Hamilton. English Monasteries (1913).

—— Double Monasteries and the Male Element in Nunneries (In The Ministry of Women, A Report by a Committee appointed by his Grace the Archbishop of Canterbury (1919), App, VIII.)

—— The Monasteries of Leicestershire in the Fifteenth Century. (Leicester. Archit and Archaeol. Soc. Trans 1913–14)

—— Registers of John Gynewell, Bishop of Lincoln, for the years 1347–50. (Archaeol. Journ vol. LXVIII (2nd Ser vol XXI), 1914)

—— Visitations of Religious Houses by William Alnwick, Bishop of Lincoln, 1436–49 (Proceedings of the Soc of Antiquaries, 2nd ser. XXVI, 1914.)

Victoria County Histories. Articles on Religious Houses, *passim.* (Cited as V.C.H)

Walcott, Mackenzie E C. English Minsters (1879), 2 vols. Vol II. The English Student's Monasticon.

Workman, H. B. The Evolution of the Monastic Ideal (1913).

INDEX

PRINTED IN ENGLAND BY J. B. PEACE, M.A., AT THE CAMBRIDGE UNIVERSITY PRESS

ENGLISH NUNNERIES

IN THE LATER MIDDLE AGES

(EXCLUDING DOUBLE GILBERTINE HOUSES)

County Boundaries . . ..
Diocesan Boundaries . . ..

SCOTLAND

NORTHUMBERLAND

Holystone

Lambley *Newcastle*
           (St Bartholomew's)
Armathwaite

CUMBERLAND CARLISLE DURHAM

WESTMORLAND

Neasham *Basedale* *Handale*
Marrick *St Stephens* *Rosedale*
           (Foukholme)
Ellerton *Arden* *Wykeham*
Keldholme *Yedingham*
Nunmonkton *Mosby* K
Sinningthwaite *Clementhorpe* *Nunkeeling*
Arthington *Wilberfosse* *Nunburnholme*
Nunappleton *Thicket* *Swine*
Kirklees *Hampole*
CHESHIRE *Nuncotton*
Chester *Grimsby*
St Mary's *(St Leonard's)*
COVENTRY *Gokewell* *Irford*
           Heynings
AND *Fosse* *Legbourne*
Wallingwells *Greenfield*
NOTTS *Broadholme* *Stainfield* *Sixwould*
DERBY LINCOLN
STAFFS *Derby* *Blackborough*
LICHFIELD *Kingsmead* *Marham*
Blithbury *Langley* *Crabhouse*
Brewood *Fairwell* *Grucedieu* *Shouldham*
White Ladies *Stamford* NORFOLK *Carrow*
SHROPSHIRE *Brewood* *St Michael's*
(Black Ladies) LEICESTER *Wothorpe*
Nuneaton HUNTS NORWICH
WARWICK *Rothwell* *Chatteris* *Thetford* *Bungay*
Henwood *Hinchinbrook* *Waterbeach* *Flixton*
Westwood *Redlingfield*
Whiston *Wroxall* *Pinley* *Cookhill* CAMBRIDGE *Bruisyard*
HEREFORD *Cookhill* *St Sepulchre's* SUFFOLK *Campsey*
Lymbrook BEDS *Cambridge*
Acornbury *Studley* *Elstow* *Castle*
Markyate *Hedingham*
Ivinghoe HERTFORD SEX
LLANDAFF OXFORD *Flamstead*
Godstow BUCKS *Sopwell* *Cheshunt*
Usk *Studley* *Little Marlow* *Cheshunt* *Wix*
Kington *Ankerwyke* *Barking*
Littlemore MIDDLESEX *Stratford*
BERKS LONDON *Dartford* *Blackburgh* *Sheppey*
Bristol *Bromhale* *Davington* *Canterbury*
(St Magd) WILTS *Wintney* SURREY ROCHESTER *(St Sepulchre's)*
Lacock *Wherwell* KENT CANTERBURY
BATH *Amesbury* *Winchester* *Rusper*
SOMERSET *Wilton* WINCHESTER
AND WELLS *Romsey* *Easebourne*
Buckland Minchin *St Mary's* SUSSEX
Canonsleigh *Ilchester* *Shaftesbury* HANTS CHICHESTER
DEVON *White Hall* *Tarrant* *Lyminster*
           Keynes
Polsloe DORSET

Cornworthy

LONDON *Clerkenwell*
        Cripplegate *Halliwell*
        Newgate *Bishopsgate*
        St Helens *Aldgate*

Cambridge Studies in Medieval Life and Thought

ERRATA FOR

THE PASTONS AND THEIR ENGLAND

Add to List of Authorities:

Berkeley *Extracts*. Abstracts and extracts of Smyth's *Lives of the Berkeleys*. Fosbroke, T D. London. 1821.

Libraries. Old English Libraries. Savage, E. A. London. 1911.

p. 9, l. 6. *For* " in the cathedral " *read* " at the door of the cathedral," and so on pp. 174, 184, and 221 *n.*

p 53, ll. 14 ff. I have somewhat exaggerated the amount of spinning and weaving done at home for purely domestic use in the fifteenth century. The industry in East Anglia was by then highly organised under capitalist clothiers, who employed workers to perform the various processes of the industry in their own homes, providing the raw materials and taking away the finished cloth. Spinning was thus essentially a bye industry as well as a purely domestic occupation. The Bury citizen was probably a clothier " putting out " work and following the quite common practice of having a number of webbers or websters under his eye in his own house See *The Paycockes of Coggeshall*, Power, Eileen, pp. 45–8.

p. 113, ll. 11 ff. *For* " *de Regimine Principum* of Hoccleve " *read* " *de Regimine Principum* of Lydgate " and so on p. 261.

p 154, l. 23. *For* " Brabraham " *read* " Babraham."

p. 168, l. 1. *For* " Paston's " *read* " Pastons' "

p. 193, l. 31. *For* " S Peter's Hungate " *read* " S. Peter, Hungate," and so on p. 285.

p. 198, l. 32. *For* " herse " *read* " hearse."

p. 208, n. 2. *For* " Oddy " *read* " Addy."

p 219, n. 1. *For* " Prothero " *read* " Ernle (Lord)."

p 240, n. 5. *For* " Jessop, J. J." *read* " Jessopp, A "

p. 280, Index, sub Cambridge, corporal punishment at. *For* 88 read 82.

p. 284, Index, sub Margaret of Anjou. *For* " (Queen of Edward IV) " *read* " (Queen of Henry VI) "

p 286, Index, sub Paston, Sir John II. *For* " make knight " *read* " made knight."

p. 288, Index. *For* " Straton Richard," *read* " Stratton, Richard."

ERRATA FOR

SOCIAL LIFE IN THE DAYS OF
PIERS PLOWMAN

The main errata are on matters of coinage (pp 69–70)

(a) There were no "copper" coins in England in the 14th (or 15th) centuries

(b) The designs of "noble" and "groat" were not so exactly similar as the text might imply. The noble bears a king with sword and shield on a ship; the groat has a king's head crowned.

(c) "Groats" were first struck in the reign of Ed III; it is therefore questionable whether they had become the "commonest" silver coins.

(d) "Pence" and "farthings" were of silver.

(e) There was no coined "shilling" until Henry VII's reign; until then, the "shilling" was only money of account.

p. 103. For "signing" of charters read "sealing." No signing was necessary until the Statute of Frauds See B. II. 112, "this dede I assele."

p. 100. A reviewer in *The Manchester Guardian* has expressed strong disagreement with these generalizations on the medieval woman; and we are loth to neglect such criticisms from a serious source, even when they cannot be called corrections of fact. Both author and editor, on careful reconsideration, are still convinced that these words represent the actual documentary evidence; but their epigrammatic conciseness, necessitated by the whole plan of the book, may well have misled some readers They would prefer now, therefore, to write thus:

"There was a very general tendency, *in ecclesiastical circles*, to a painful depreciation of women Marriage (in spite of frequent protests that no such blame was intended) was often regarded by the clergy as a practical confession of failure, since the titles of 'virgin' and 'martyr' were most desirable It will be remembered that Chaucer is even more explicit than Langland on the subject of clerical antifeminism; and if Chaucer, like Dante, gives us fine types of women, these owe far more to the troubadour tradition than to any ecclesiastical source."

CPSIA information can be obtained
at www.ICGtesting.com
Printed in the USA
LVHW082357150620
658199LV00017B/298